dBASE IV : The Complete Reference

Geoffrey T. LeBlond
William B. LeBlond
Brent Heslop
Suzanne Polenberry
Cheryl Post

Osborne **McGraw-Hill**

Berkeley New York St. Louis San Francisco
Auckland Bogatá Hamburg London Madrid
Mexico City Milan Montreal New Delhi Panama City
Paris São Paulo Singapore Sydney
Tokyo Toronto

Osborne **McGraw-Hill**
2600 Tenth Street
Berkeley, California 94710
U.S.A.

For information on translations and book distributors outside of the U.S.A., please write to Osborne **McGraw-Hill** at the above address.

A complete list of trademarks appears on page 1469.
Screens produced with Inset, from Inset Systems, Inc.

Pages were produced for this book by using Ventura Publisher

Acqusitions Editor: Elizabeth Fisher
Technical Reviewer: Ed Jones
Project Editor: Dusty Bernard
Production: Kevin Shafer
Cover supplier and color separation: Phoenix Color Corp.

dBASE IV™: The Complete Reference

1234567890 DOCDOC 898

ISBN 0-07-881503-7

This book is dedicated to the Sikes—Reid, Barb, Willie, Graydon, and Evan

—G.T.L.

CONTENTS

ACKNOWLEDGMENTS

The authors would like to thank the following people, without whom this book would not have been possible: Liz Fisher, for her constant support and gentle pressure relentlessly applied; Cindy Hudson, for setting up the deal and for her creative solutions; Jeff Pepper, for considering us for the project; Ilene Shapera, for her great humor and for her trip to Santa Cruz to pick up the final chapters; Karen Fredriksen of 3Com Corporation, for an amazing feat of network installation and support; Ed Jones, for the best technical edit imaginable; Laurie Beaulieu, for making sure things got from one place to another—on time; Deborah Craig, for editing everything; Kevin Shafer and Dusty Bernard, for shepherding the book through production; and Inset Systems, for InSet and HiJaak, which enabled us to generate all the screen shots.

INTRODUCTION

In its latest incarnation, dBASE IV is the most powerful database management system available for microcomputers. With that power comes a new level of complexity and detail that you may not have encountered in a software program before. It can be especially challenging to understand, let alone use, the many aspects of the program. This book is our effort to help you do just that—to understand and use nearly every important aspect of dBASE IV.

Any book identified as a "complete reference" makes a promise that is hard to fulfill. By its very nature, a complete reference on dBASE IV cannot cover every last detail of the program. For this reason, we have restricted ourselves to those topics that we believe are the most important in dBASE IV. Still, if you're looking for information on just about any significant subject in dBASE IV, you should find it here, with an easy-to-find, understandable explanation.

How This Book Is Organized

Whereas the original dBASE IV documentation is organized according to the program's structure, this book is organized according to how you might actually use dBASE IV to accomplish a task. For example, in the beginning chapters, you learn how to use the new Control Center to create and use a database. In the chapters that follow, you build on that knowledge as you perform more advanced tasks.

The book is divided into five parts. The first four are a "using" section, which describes the fundamental parts of the program—the Control Center, the dot prompt, and so on. The fifth is for reference purposes. It includes a complete list of dBASE IV commands and functions; you can refer to this section as you're working from the prompt and creating programs. You'll also find this section helpful when customizing dBASE IV.

We've organized the book so that you can read many of the early parts in one sitting, but you'll more likely want to keep this book near your computer and refer to it as you have questions and encounter problems. For example, if you are in the middle of building a network application, you can easily refer to the network programming section of the book to help you as you go.

In addition to covering the fundamentals, this book tries to fill in where the dBASE IV documentation is especially vague. For example, we've taken particular care to provide you with useful information on two important topics: networking and programming.

Who Should Buy This Book?

This book is for every dBASE IV user, novice, and expert alike. Because it covers nearly every important aspect of dBASE IV, you are sure to find helpful information for your particular situation. For example, if you are a beginner, you can start with the first section of the book and begin building your dBASE IV knowledge. If you are a more knowledgeable dBASE user, you can find information in sections that apply to the more advanced features.

Every topic in this book is accompanied by example files and blocks of code that you can copy and use in your own work. For example, if you are writing a dBASE IV program, you can turn to Part Three, "Programming in dBASE IV," to find examples of different coding techniques.

What's Covered in This Book

This book is organized into 5 parts with 35 chapters.

Part One, "Using dBASE IV," gives a complete description of the new dBASE IV Control Center, macros, the Forms Design screen, and more. It also shows you how to use the dBASE dot prompt. Read this part of the book to get a good grasp of the many new built-in data management tools that dBASE IV offers.

Part Two, "The Applications Generator," describes the important facets of dBASE IV's new facility for generating programs automatically. To help reinforce your understanding, this part shows you how to build a sample application.

Part Three, "Programming in dBASE IV," starts with an introduction to database programming and progresses all the way to advanced programming techniques. Here you'll find important information about writing your own dBASE IV programs.

Part Four, "Networking dBASE IV," is one of the most comprehensive descriptions of networking dBASE IV that you'll find anywhere. It takes you through the installation process and goes on to describe the various aspects of file- and record-locking and security, as well as offering a comprehensive listing of networking commands and functions. If you plan to use dBASE IV for networking, you'll find this part of the book invaluable.

Part Five, "Command Reference," lists all the dBASE IV commands, SET commands, functions, and system memory variables in alphabetical order. Each command description includes at least one example to help increase your understanding.

Conventions

Throughout this book, certain conventions are used to make the text easier to read and understand.

In general, user input appears as you would enter it from the keyboard. It is either displayed in boldface, as in "enter **USE Orders**," or set off from regular text, as shown here:

```
USE Orders
```

When a command is preceded by a period, don't type the period. It simply means that you enter the command at the dBASE IV dot prompt.

Command menu names and options are set off in boldface; for example, **Print database structure**. Occasionally, you'll find that command menu options are separated from their parent command by a slash (/), as in **Layout/Print database structure**.

Keys appear in small caps; for example, INS or ESC. When two or more keys must be pressed simultaneously, those keys are separated by hyphens; for example, SHIFT-F10.

File names, commands, and functions always appear in capital letters, as in "the ORDERS90.DBF file," "the BEGIN TRANSACTION command," and "the DATE( ) function."

There are also numerous tips in this book. Tips are set off from other text to make them easily identifiable, as shown here:

Tip: To print your labels in a particular order, you'll need to sort or index your database.

As you work with dBASE IV, you'll soon discover that there is a variety of ways to accomplish any given task. You may find yourself wondering which is the best one. Usually the answer isn't entirely clear. The way that is best for you depends on your work habits and your experience with dBASE IV. Therefore, as new topics are introduced in this book, you will find a discussion of the various ways you can perform a task so that you can choose the one that is right for you. It is unlikely that you'll find a better, more thorough explanation of *all* aspects of dBASE IV, or one that will better meet your needs as you build your knowledge of dBASE IV, than *dBASE IV: The Complete Reference.*

—Geoffrey T. LeBlond

Using dBASE IV

PART ONE

The chapters in this part give you the skills you need to get up and running with dBASE IV as quickly as possible. If you're new to dBASE, you'll find information to help you understand the various aspects of dBASE IV. If you're an experienced dBASE user, this part will bring you quickly up to speed with all the new enhancements to dBASE IV's interactive environment.

The part begins with how to install dBASE IV on your system. You then learn how to use the Control Center to work with databases. Next, you will see how to sort and index your databases, as well as how to query a database using query by example.

After laying the groundwork for the Control Center, this part introduces the dBASE IV dot prompt, an alternate way of controlling dBASE IV. From the dot prompt, you use the dBASE IV command language to manage your databases directly.

Topics common to both the Control Center and the dot prompt are then discussed—including macros, building custom input forms, creating reports and labels, and the various methods of printing. The part concludes with how to organize your files in catalogs and how to use dBASE IV's built-in tools to manage your files and alter many of dBASE IV's default settings.

Introduction

ONE

Definition of a Database
Database Structure
An Overview of dBASE IV
The dBASE IV Developers Edition

Since 1982, dBASE has sold over 2 million copies, making it the most popular database management system for microcomputers. dBASE IV is by far the most comprehensive version of dBASE yet. It is bigger, faster, and more powerful than before. At the same time, it should be easier to use than any of its predecessors.

This chapter describes dBASE IV's various features and how you can use them to meet your data management needs. First, however, it discusses the concept of databases.

Definition of a Database

The term *database* describes a collection of information organized in columns and rows. Each row is an entry, or *record*, in the database. Each column contains the items, or *fields*, that make up each record.

Your local phone directory is a familiar database application. Each listing in that directory is the equivalent of a record in a database. The items that make up a listing are the equivalent of fields. For example, Figure 1-1 displays ten rows (records). Each

Rec#	Lastname	Firstname	Address	Phone_no
1	Segal	James	2814 Winding Way	561-8111
2	Smith	Martha	221 Maple Street	874-2221
3	Snyder	John	682 Hardesty Dr.	963-7238
4	Williams	Sarah	3525 Sevilla St.	475-8854
5	Adams	Joan	633 Columbus Ave.	891-1976
6	Baker	Ginger	17 Howard Rd.	655-1383
7	Frank	Lisa	4975 Drake Rd.	871-1524
8	Lowell	Bob	3621 Aptos Station	682-5555
9	Ramsey	Alicia	9 Seaside Manor	221-9632
10	Grant	Bill	2741 Emerson St.	382-4231

Figure 1-1. Viewing a phone directory as a database

record is composed of four columns (fields) of information. The fields are Lastname, Firstname, Address, and Phone_no.

In Figure 1-1, each row is a data record because it holds all of the data items necessary for a single entry in the database. For example, row 1 contains all the pertinent data for James Segal including first name, last name, address, and phone number. However, each column is a data field because it holds a single item of data for a record. For example, the last name field holds all the last names for each record in the database.

As you add each record to a database, it is given a sequential number to signify the order in which it was added to the database. Furthermore, each field is given a field name. For example, the field names in Figure 1-1 are Firstname, Lastname, Address, and Phone_no. You use these record numbers and field names to identify individual data items in each record.

You can also use a field name to have a single dBASE IV command apply to all of the records in a database. For example, the information in Figure 1-1 appears in a random order, the order in which the data was entered. It would be impractical to search for anyone's phone number in a directory of this kind. On the other

Rec#	Lastname	Firstname	Address	Phone_no
5	Adams	Joan	633 Columbus Ave.	891-1976
6	Baker	Ginger	17 Howard Rd.	655-1383
7	Frank	Lisa	4975 Drake Rd.	871-1524
10	Grant	Bill	2741 Emerson St.	382-4231
8	Lowell	Bob	3621 Aptos Station	682-5555
9	Ramsey	Alicia	9 Seaside Manor	221-9632
1	Segal	James	2814 Winding Way	561-8111
2	Smith	Martha	221 Maple Street	874-2221
3	Snyder	John	682 Hardesty Dr.	963-7238
4	Williams	Sarah	3525 Sevilla St.	475-8854

Figure 1-2. Database records in order by last name

hand, you can order the records in a database based on the data in a given field. For example, in Figure 1-2, the records are ordered by last name. This type of data organization makes it easy to quickly find someone's phone number.

Database Structure

A database's structure is really a description of each field that makes up a data record. Each field description is composed of the following:

- **Field name** The name for the field (for example, Firstname, Lastname, Address).
- **Field type** Whether the field will contain numeric, character, date, logical (yes/no), or memo data.
- **Field width** The maximum width of an entry allowed for a field.

Giving each data field a field name enables you to refer to that field in a command. For example, the Lastname field was used to specify the order in which the records appeared in Figure 1-2.

Each data field must have a specified data type. You can choose from one of five data types: numeric, character, logical, date, or memo. Numeric fields contain numbers. You can use the information in these fields to perform calculations. Characters fields contain alphanumeric character strings, such as a last name like "Smith" or a part identifier like "RG241". Character fields have many uses. For example, you can use them to specify the order of the records in a database or to search the database for specific records.

Date fields contain dates, such as 12/31/90. You can use date fields in a numeric fashion. For example, you might need to see the information in all of the records entered between 1/1/90 and 3/31/90. You use logical fields to specify a true/false yes/no data type, for example, bonus=true or married=false. In memo fields, you can include a note about a record. For example, you might enter several sentences describing the record.

Each field must also have a defined field width—the maximum number of characters allowed in that field. For example, if the field you're defining is to contain company names, choose a field width that can safely contain the longest company name that you intend to enter in the database.

An Overview of dBASE IV

dBASE IV is a *database management system* (DBMS). This term describes an organized method of managing data in databases. The purpose of a DBMS, and of dBASE IV, is to provide a systematic method for organizing and managing a large collection of information in one or more databases. For example, you can use dBASE IV to store information in many different databases and to retrieve, sort, query, and report on that information in a variety of ways.

There are two main ways you can use dBASE IV: through the *Control Center* or through the dBASE IV *command language.* The Control Center is a task-oriented menu-driven system for managing your data. As you'll discover in a few pages, the Control Center is the the first thing you see when you load dBASE IV. If you're new to dBASE IV, the Control Center is an excellent place to start.

On the other hand, the dBASE IV command language is for more advanced users. It is composed of a series of English-like commands, each of which performs a very specific operation. You can type these commands at the dot prompt (dBASE's version of the DOS prompt), or you can place a series of commands in a program file and process them all at once.

The dBASE IV Control Center and command language actually compliment each other quite well. For example, in many instances, a single menu choice in the Control Center performs the same function as several dBASE IV commands. In these cases, you may find it easier and faster to use the Control Center, regardless of your level of expertise.

The dBASE IV Control Center and the command language work as a team. For example, you can use the Control Center to generate anything from a simple report to a full-blown multipurpose application. To perform these functions, the Control Center actually creates a variety of files. When you look behind the scenes, many of the files consist of the dBASE IV command language.

SQL is another new and much talked-about facet of dBASE IV. SQL, which stands for "Structured Query Language," is a separate command language for creating and managing tables of information. The SQL language is an emerging standard for database management. Its presence in dBASE IV is a recognition of that standard. Because SQL is a major topic and operates fairly independent of dBASE IV, it is not covered in this book. However, you will find occasional references to SQL-related topics.

You can also use dBASE IV on a local area network (LAN). In fact, dBASE IV is more "network-aware" than before, handling many file- and record-locking chores automatically. It is easier than ever for users to share the power of dBASE to add and edit information in common databases.

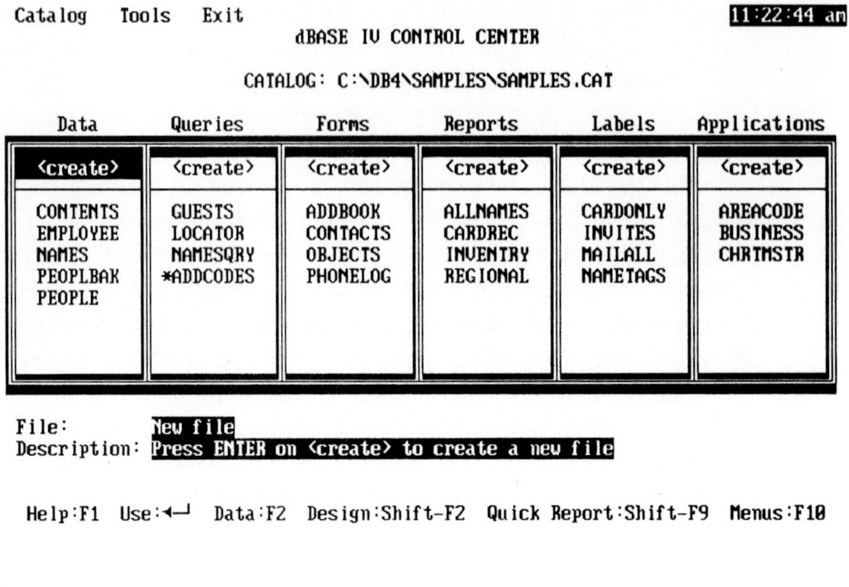

Figure 1-3. The Control Center

The Control Center

The Control Center gives you centralized access to various design screens. You can use each design screen to map a different element of your database management system. The Control Center itself is made up of different panels. These panels begin with the name of a particular design screen and show the names of files created by each design screen. Figure 1-3 shows an example of what the Control Center looks like. The design screens you can access from the Control Center are

- The Database Design screen
- The Queries Design screen
- The Forms Design screen

- The Reports Design screen
- The Labels Design screen
- The Applications Generator

The Control Center is the source of an extensive menu system—each design screen that you access has its own menu bar. The menu bar appears at the top of each screen.

The Control Center itself also features two powerful menus, **Catalogs** and **Tools**. You can use the **Catalog** menu to organize your files into meaningful groups. Catalogs and the **Catalog** menu are discussed in Chapter 13. You can use the **Tools** menu to perform DOS-like operations on your files as well as to import files from and export files to other programs. The **Tools** menu is discussed in Chapter 14. You can also use the **Tools** menu to create macros—recording keystrokes and assigning them to a key sequence (an ALT-key or a function key). You can later replay the same keystrokes by pressing the key sequence you assigned to the macro. Creating and using macros is discussed in Chapter 8.

The Database Design Screen

You use the Database Design screen to create databases. Figure 1-4 shows an example of this screen. Using this screen, you can define the structure of a database and determine the order in which information is displayed. Chapter 4 describes how to create and modify the structure of a database and how to enter, edit, and display data in a database. Defining the order of the information in a database is described in Chapter 5.

The Queries Design Screen

The Queries Design screen allows you to design powerful queries that select specific information from a database. You can also use the Queries Design screen to link two or more databases and use data from all of them. You can also sort the data in a database, group the data in a database based on common values, or update

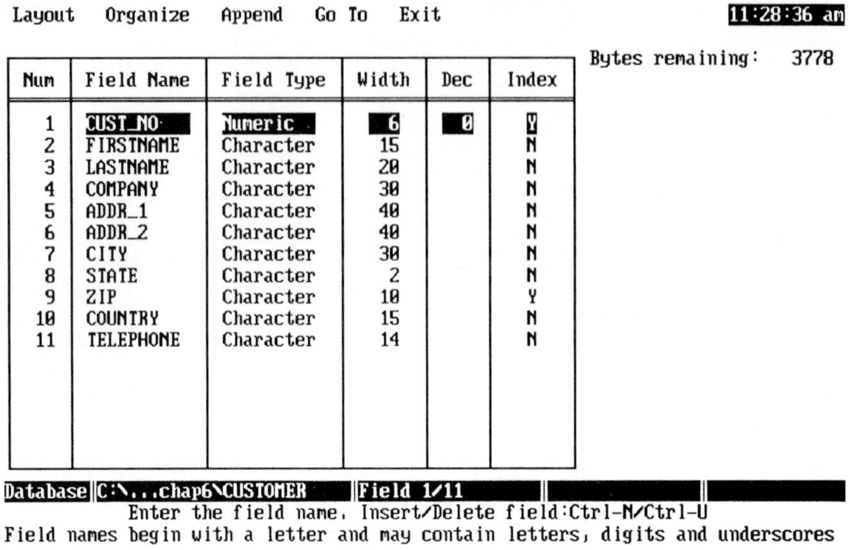

Layout Organize Append Go To Exit 11:28:36 am

Bytes remaining: 3778

Num	Field Name	Field Type	Width	Dec	Index
1	CUST_NO	Numeric	6	0	Y
2	FIRSTNAME	Character	15		N
3	LASTNAME	Character	20		N
4	COMPANY	Character	30		N
5	ADDR_1	Character	40		N
6	ADDR_2	Character	40		N
7	CITY	Character	30		N
8	STATE	Character	2		N
9	ZIP	Character	10		Y
10	COUNTRY	Character	15		N
11	TELEPHONE	Character	14		N

Database C:\...chap6\CUSTOMER Field 1/11

Enter the field name. Insert/Delete field:Ctrl-N/Ctrl-U

Field names begin with a letter and may contain letters, digits and underscores

Figure 1-4. The Database Design screen

one database from another. When you're finished designing a query, you can save it in a file and activate it later from either the Control Center or a program file. You can use query results either for display purposes or as the basis for a report.

The Queries Design screen uses a query by example (QBE) interface. This approach to queries design lets you display images of databases and select fields of information from them. You can also specify conditions for the data to be drawn from those fields. Figure 1-5 shows a sample Queries Design screen. For more on the Queries Design screen, see Chapter 6, "Querying the Database."

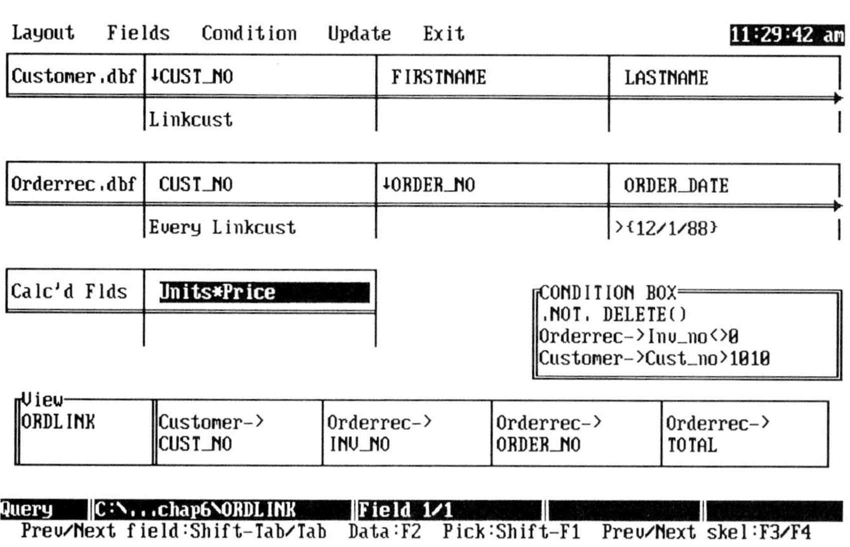

Figure 1-5. The Queries Design screen

The Forms Design Screen

You can use the Forms Design screen to create custom screens for displaying and entering data in a database. Figure 1-6 shows a sample Forms Design screen with a custom form in the making. This screen uses a bulletin-board-like approach to forms design. You can display your database fields surrounded by text, boxes, and lines and then move these different elements around as you like. You can also define calculated fields and memo windows and choose different colors for the display. The end result is a professional looking data entry and display form. For a complete discussion of the Forms Design screen, see Chapter 9, "Creating Input Forms."

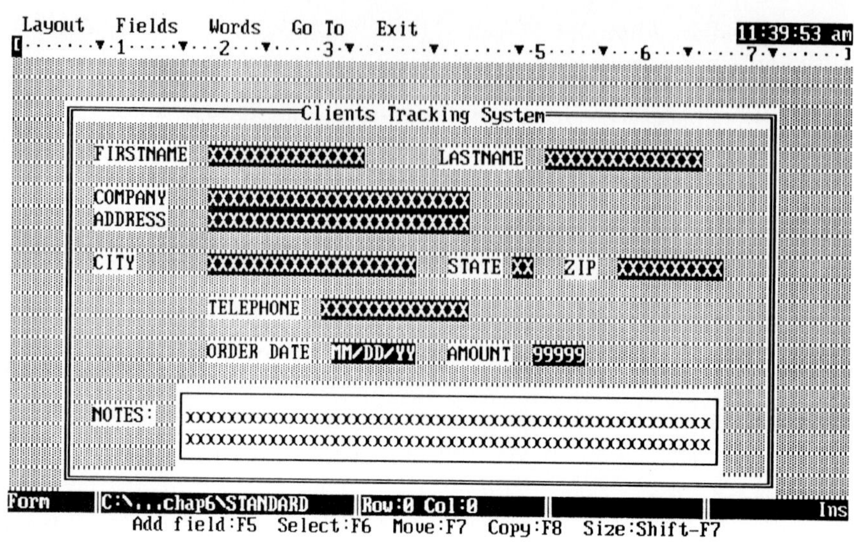

Figure 1-6. The Forms Design Screen

The Reports Design Screen

The Reports Design screen lets you design custom reports for printing the data stored in your databases. This screen lets you specify where fields from your databases should appear on the page. It also lets you surround those fields with text, boxes, and lines. You can use the Reports Design screen to generate custom reports and form letters.

The Reports Design screen also lets you group and summarize related data. You can, for example, create a report that summarizes company sales by region or by division. You can also specify an introduction or a summary for the report. Figure 1-7 shows the Reports Design screen with a custom report underway. When you've finished designing a report, you can save it to a file for later use. The Reports Design screen is discussed in detail in Chapter 10, "Creating Reports."

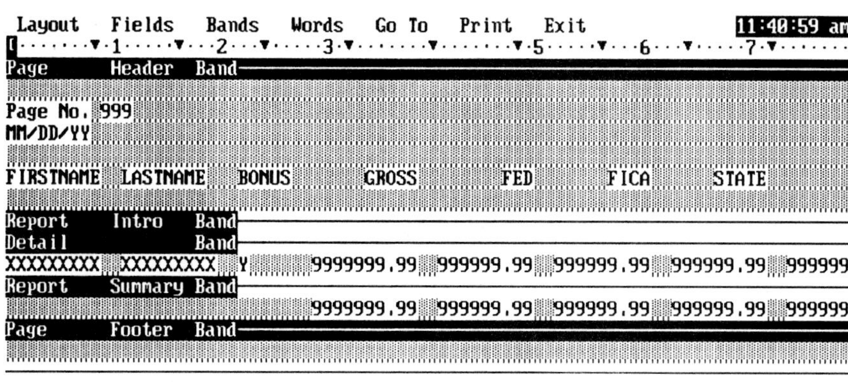

Figure 1-7. The Reports Design screen

The Labels Design Screen

The Labels Design screen, shown in Figure 1-8, lets you design custom labels of varying sizes and descriptions. Using this screen, you can create a customized form for mailing labels, shipping tags, employee identification badges, and much more. When you're finished designing your label, you can save it to a file for later use. Chapter 11 provides a complete description of how to use the Labels Design screen.

The Applications Generator

The Applications Generator lets you create a professional quality application without writing a single program. dBASE IV generates the code for you. Use the Applications Generator to tie together

```
Layout   Dimensions   Fields   Words   Go To   Print   Exit            12:17:14 pm

          [·······▼·1·····▼···2···▼·····3·▼········▼········▼]

                HELLO.

            My name is  XXXXXXXXXX XXXXXXXXXXXXXXX.

            I'm from XXXXXXXXXXXXXX.
```

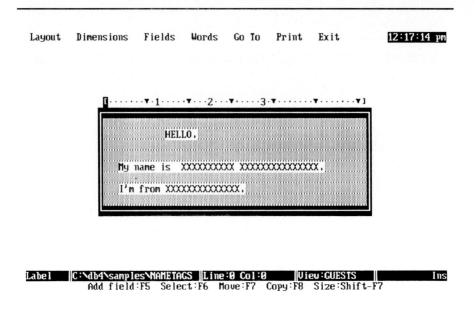

Figure 1-8. The Labels Design screen

into a cohesive unit your databases, custom forms, queries, labels, and reports. The Applications Generator also includes a sophisticated menu-driven system that allows you to incorporate pop-up and pull-down menus in your application. Whether you're new to applications programming or you're an experienced programmer, the Applications Generator can save you time by generating the code you'd ordinarily have to write. The Applications Generator is discussed in Chapters 15 and 16.

The dBASE IV Language Processor

Fundamental to dBASE IV is its command language and language processor. As mentioned, the dBASE IV command language is composed of a series of English-like commands. You can enter these commands at the dot prompt to perform routine data management tasks. You can also combine them in a program file and run them as a group.

Chapter 7 discusses how to enter commands at the dot prompt and includes some pointers about building dBASE IV expressions. You can also use the expression-building tips from Chapter 7 to further refine and customize the queries, forms, reports, labels, and applications you build using the Control Center's design screens.

By combining dBASE IV commands in a program, you can develop highly sophisticated applications that perform virtually any database management task. Chapters 17 through 25 describe everything from the fundamentals of command-file programming to advanced topics. For example, you'll learn how to use a program to enter information in databases as well as how to create and use memory variables, custom forms, user-defined functions, arrays, pop-up menus, and much more. Each programming chapter includes examples of programming code you can use in your own applications.

To give you easy access to the dBASE IV command language, there is a complete alphabetical command reference at the back of this book. It includes standard dBASE IV commands, SET commands, functions, and system memory variables. An example is provided with each command. Furthermore, for each command you're given references to related commands.

SQL

SQL (Structured Query Language) gives an added dimension to dBASE IV. SQL has for many years been a corporate standard that enabled nonprogrammers to make inquiries to databases stored on mainframes and minicomputers. Now dBASE IV brings SQL to the PC.

SQL is an advanced database management language with powerful selection capabilities. You can use it to define sets, or *tables,* of information and to study relationships found in and between them with queries. In dBASE IV, you sift through database records, picking out the ones you need. In SQL, you indicate what you want, and SQL scans the tables to meet your query.

SQL does not provide the same level of person-machine interaction as dBASE IV (that is, data entry forms, menus, printer manipulation, and so forth). However, you can use dBASE code with SQL code to provide these functions, deriving the benefits from both of these powerful command languages at the same time. For example, you can save the results of a SQL query in a dBASE IV compatible database file. You can then print that data by using a report form created with the Reports Design screen.

Networking

Networking is one of the most powerful features of dBASE IV. On a local area network (LAN), multiple users can edit, view, print, and query a single database, all at the same time. The multi-user version of dBASE IV offers file- and record-locking features that work with your networking software to allow file sharing among multiple network users.

An entire section of this book is devoted to running dBASE IV on a network. In Chapters 26 through 30, you'll learn how to install dBASE IV on your network, and also about network administration, security, file sharing, transaction processing, and programming considerations.

Chapter 30 provides an alphabetical command reference of network- related commands. You can refer to this chapter for specific information on a network-related command as well as for examples of how to use the command.

The dBASE IV Developer's Edition

This book is about the standard version of dBASE IV. However, dBASE IV has a special Developer's Edition with a few additional features. These features are primarily for building applications for distribution. Although this book does not cover the distribution-related features of the Developer's Edition, it covers most relevant topics, in particular programming and networking.

dBASE IV has more new features than any previous release of the program. With its new Control Center, design screens, Applications Generator, and SQL, you can create sophisticated applications without writing a single line of programming code. On the other hand, if you prefer to control the program yourself, there are many new additions to the dBASE IV command language that you can enter from the dot prompt or use in programs. Finally, with its powerful new networking features, dBASE IV is better suited than ever for a multi-user environment.

Getting Started

TWO

This chapter explains how to quickly install and set up dBASE IV on your system, including configuration details and helpful hardware information. dBASE IV uses the DBSETUP program to install dBASE IV on your system. However, it uses only a few of the DBSETUP options, those corresponding to the **Install** menu.

The second part of the chapter describes the range of menu options available in the DBSETUP program. If you want to change your dBASE IV configuration settings, run the DBSETUP program after you've installed dBASE IV.

If you have any questions as you read the quick installation guide at the start of the chapter, refer to "The **Install** Menu" section later in the chapter. There you'll find more detailed background information on the menu options that you'll encounter during the installation procedure.

Minimum Configuration

In order to install dBASE IV on your PC, you must have

- 640K of RAM (random access memory)
- An IBM PC, XT, AT, PS2, or IBM 100% compatible computer with PC DOS version 2.0 (or greater), Compaq DOS 3.31, or OS/2 version 1.0 (or greater)
- A monochrome or color monitor
- The fourteen 5.25-inch or the eight 3.5-inch dBASE IV system disks
- A 9-digit serial number from System Disk #1
- A hard disk with 3.7 megabytes of space (actually 3770K)

Some Helpful Hardware Information

Listed here is some helpful hardware information you should know before you install dBASE IV. Take a minute to review this information; it may save you some time.

- **Expanded and extended memory** Although the documentation for dBASE IV version 1.0 states that expanded memory boards meeting the LIM (Lotus-Intel-Microsoft) standards will work with dBASE IV, they don't. Version 1.1 of dBASE IV will address expanded and extended memory.
- **Mouse support** Version 1.0 of dBASE IV does not support a mouse driver. This option will probably be available in future versions of dBASE IV.

- **Hard Disk Space and dBASE IV** You must have 3.7 megabytes of hard disk space available in order to install dBASE IV. However, if you choose not to copy the Sample and Tutorial files, dBASE IV takes up only 3.1 megabytes (3105K).

Preparing to Install dBASE IV

What follows are some tips that will help guarantee your success in installing dBASE IV.

Make Backup Copies of Your Disks

It is a good idea to make backup copies of your original disks before installing dBASE IV on your hard disk. If you would like your copies to be registered with your company's name, copy them after installing dBASE IV.

Tip: You must remove any write-protection tabs from the Installation Disk, System Disk #1, and System Disk #2 in order to install them.

Installing dBASE IV with dBASE III PLUS

If you have a previous edition of dBASE on your computer and you want to save it, uninstall it before installing dBASE IV. If a copy-protected version of dBASE is found in the directory, you are prompted to uninstall it if you wish to save it. If you do not uninstall it, dBASE IV will write over the previous edition's files, making it unusable.

If you want to run both dBASE III PLUS and dBASE IV from the same hard disk, you will need to keep them in separate directories since similar file names are used for both versions.

Memory Resident Programs and dBASE IV

Before attempting to install dBASE IV, unload any memory-resident programs such as SideKick or SuperKey. You need to unload them before running the dBASE IV installation program. If you use a memory-resident program, it will adversely affect the performance of dBASE IV. Unloading any memory-resident programs will make dBASE IV run faster.

A Quick Installation Guide

Depending on your dexterity at disk switching and the speed of your computer, installation will take approximately 20 to 30 minutes. To get more background information on the different menu options that appear during the installation procedure, be sure to check the "The **Install** Menu" section.

1. If you have met all of the preceding minimum requirements, you can now begin by inserting the Installation Disk into drive A and typing **INSTALL** at the A:> DOS prompt.

2. After you enter the INSTALL command, the software license screen appears. You are prompted to accept the agreement by pressing ENTER to continue.

3. You are then instructed to "Please insert: System Disk #1 and press ENTER."

4. At this point, you are prompted to complete the software registration form. This form includes your name, your company name, and the serial number from System Disk

#1, which is currently in drive A. Press CTRL-END to save and continue.

5. The next screen explains that there are three phases to installing dBASE IV. Press ENTER or P to proceed.

6. Unless you would like to change the video display mode for extra lines, accept the default. Then use your cursor keys to go directly to **Optimize color display**, and press ENTER. This menu choice optimizes the display technique by checking for snow on the screen. Press ENTER or P to proceed, and answer the question with a Y for yes if you do or N for no if you do not see snow on your screen. Again, press ENTER or P to proceed.

7. Next, select the **Printers** menu choice. If you press SHIFT-F1, a box will appear with printer names. Select the printer you will be using. If your printer is not listed, choose **Generic Driver**. Press ENTER.

8. Two additional sidebar boxes will appear next to the printer box. Press SPACEBAR or ENTER to accept the highlighted printer and driver, or use the arrow keys to select another printer driver.

9. The cursor should now appear in the device column. Again, press SHIFT-F1. A menu box that lists optional output devices will appear. Choose the device that your printer is connected to (usually LPT1) and press ENTER. You will be asked to verify whether you would like to use the printer driver you have chosen or change to the default driver (GENERIC.PR2). Highlight your driver and press ENTER. To install more than one printer, use the DOWN ARROW to move to the second line and repeat steps 7 through 9. Press CTRL-END to save your selections.

10. A prompt box appears telling you that you are now ready to install dBASE IV. If you have made any mistakes, you

can return to the **Modify hardware** setup menu. Otherwise, press ENTER or P to proceed.

11. You are asked in which directory to install dBASE IV. If you would like to use the default directory, press ENTER or P to proceed. If you would like to change the directory name, enter the new directory. If the directory does not exist, a prompt will ask if you want dBASE IV to create the directory for you. Press ENTER or P to proceed.

12. Follow the procedure described in step 11 for the next two screens, which set up the SQL (Structured Query Language) subdirectory named C:\DBASE\SQLHOME.

13. After creating this directory, dBASE IV asks you to, once again, insert the Installation Disk and press ENTER.

14. You are then prompted to reinsert System Disk #1 and press ENTER.

15. From this point on, you are prompted to enter System Disks #2 through #9, which are followed by a verification screen prompt stating that Single-User dBASE IV has been installed successfully.

16. You are prompted to modify your AUTOEXEC.BAT and CONFIG.SYS files. If you don't want dBASE to change your AUTOEXEC.BAT and CONFIG.SYS files, press S to skip this procedure. Otherwise, press ENTER or P to proceed.

17. If you would like to append the dBASE IV directory to the path in your AUTOEXEC.BAT file, press ENTER or P to proceed. (Your previous AUTOEXEC.BAT file will be renamed with a .BAK extension.) If you do not have an AUTOEXEC.BAT file, dBASE IV creates one for you.

18. In order to run dBASE IV, you must set up DOS to contain the FILES=40 and BUFFERS=15 files. If you want dBASE IV to update your CONFIG.SYS file with this

information, press ENTER or P to proceed. (Your previous CONFIG.SYS file will be renamed with a .BAK extension.) If you do not have a CONFIG.SYS file, dBASE IV will create one for you.

19. The last part of installing dBASE IV involves transferring the sample and tutorial files that are used throughout the dBASE IV documentation. If you really can't wait to start using dBASE IV, or have a limited amount of space on your hard disk, press S to skip the copying of these files. If you would like these files, press ENTER or P to proceed. This will bring up a prompt explaining that you are about to copy the sample files. Press ENTER or P to proceed.

Tip: If you decide not to install the sample and tutorial files during the installation procedure, you can install them later using the DBSETUP program. See "The **Install/Transfer other files** Menu" section later in this chapter.

Also, you can save hard disk space by running the tutorial from drive A. To do so, place the Tutorial Disk in drive A and make drive A the default drive by typing **A:** at the DOS prompt. Next, type **INTRO** to start the tutorial.

20. You are offered a default directory of C:\DBASE\SAMPLES for the sample files to be copied to. Press ENTER or P to proceed.

21. This time you will see a smaller verification box asking if the drive is OK. Press ENTER, or O for OK. Press C to cancel the operation.

22. You are then instructed to insert Sample Disks #1 through #3.

23. Follow the same procedure as in steps 20 through 22 for the tutorial files. The default directory in this case is C:\DBASE\DBTUTOR.

24. The last step of installing dBASE IV is to, once again, insert the Installation Disk and press ENTER. This will

bring up a prompt to choose either "Exit to DOS" or "Transfer to dBSETUP." Press E for "Exit to DOS."

25. To start exploring dBASE IV, reboot your computer; type **DBASE** at the C:> prompt and press ENTER.

dBASE IV is now fully installed.

The DBSETUP Program

Once you've installed dBASE IV, you won't need to perform the installation procedure again unless you erase or uninstall dBASE IV. If you want to change the dBASE IV configuration settings, however, you can use the DBSETUP program in your dBASE directory.

To activate the DBSETUP program, you must run it from the DOS prompt. While in the C:\DBASE directory, or whichever drive and directory you've installed dBASE IV on, type **DBSETUP** and press ENTER. You are then presented with a series of menus that let you modify any of your dBASE IV configuration settings.

Figure 2-1 shows the main menu of the DBSETUP program. The sections that follow describe the different menu options available. If you want to abort the DBSETUP program at any time, select the **Exit** menu option.

The Install Menu

After you have successfully installed dBASE IV, you can use the **Install** menu to alter your dBASE IV setup. This menu includes the **Modify hardware setup**, **Install dBASE IV**, **Transfer other files**, and **Uninstall dBASE IV** options.

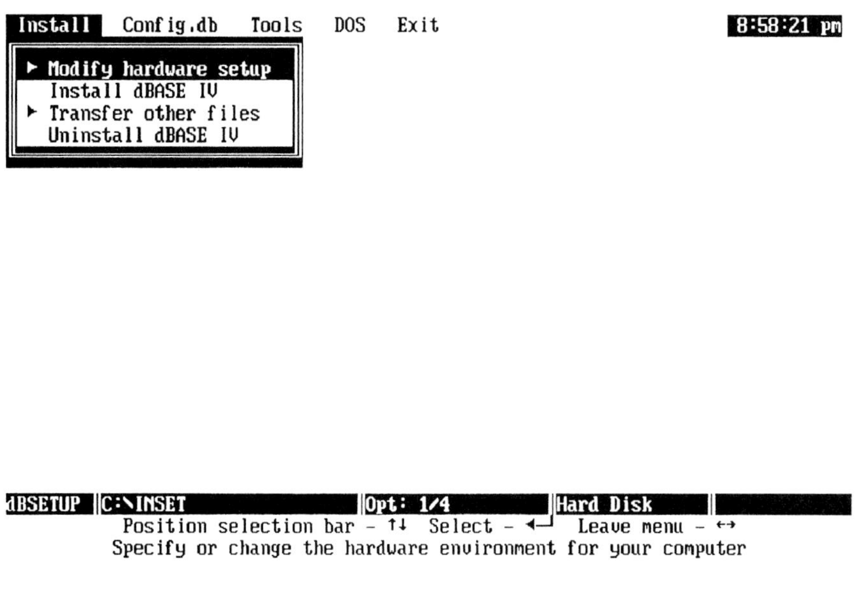

Figure 2-1. The **DBSETUP** main menu

The Modify hardware setup Menu

The first choice in the **Install** menu is the **Modify hardware setup** menu. This is the same menu that appears when you perform the initial installation procedure (that is, when you type **INSTALL** at the DOS prompt). The **Install** menu has four options: **Multi-user installation**, **Display mode**, **Optimize color display**, and **Printers**.

Hardware setup/Multi-user installation Option A **Multi-user installation** option is used to install dBASE IV on a network. Normally, you'll leave the **Multi-user installation** option set to No unless, of course, you are installing dBASE IV on a network. For more information on this option, see Chapter 26, "Installing dBASE IV on a Network."

The Hardware setup/Display mode Option When you install dBASE IV, your display mode will be automatically set to the screen type you are using. However, you can use the **Display mode** option if you want to change this setting. By pressing SPACEBAR, you can access any of the following five choices:

- **COLOR** The color graphics adapter using an RGB monitor
- **EGA25** An enhanced graphics adapter set up for a 25-line screen
- **MONO43** A monochrome monitor set up for a 43-line screen
- **EGA43** An enhanced graphics adapter set up for a 43-line screen
- **MONO** A monochrome screen

Hardware setup/Optimize color Display Option You use the **Optimize color display** option to eliminate the snow effect that exists with some graphics cards. After selecting this option, you're asked, "Do you see snow?" If you do, press Y for yes. Otherwise, press N for no.

Hardware setup/Printers Menu The **Printers** menu lets you install printers and printer drivers to dBASE IV. You can install up to four different printers.

When you select the **Printers** option, you see a box menu with options numbered 1 through 4. To select a printer driver from a list of those available, press SHIFT-F1. A list of printers will appear. When you select a printer, two adjacent frames appear, displaying the model and the file name of the model's printer driver. Use the arrow keys to highlight the printer and driver you want to install. If the printer you are using is not listed, try choosing the **Generic Driver** option; the GENERIC.PR2 printer driver supports bold and underlined type for most printers. If you have an unlisted printer, you can also check to see if your printer is compatible with a printer that is listed.

After you've highlighted a printer with the adjoining printer driver and pressed ENTER, a list of devices appears. These are the devices that your printer may be connected to. Your choices include

- **LPT1** The first parallel printer port. This is the most common type of printer port.
- **LPT2** The second parallel printer port.
- **LPT3** The third parallel printer port.
- **COM1** Stands for asynchronous communications port number 1. Use this if you have a serial printer attached to your first serial port.
- **COM2** Stands for asynchronous communications port number 2. Use this if you have a serial printer connected to your second serial port.

The following two commands, \\SPOOLER and \\CAPTURE, are used for networking and do not affect the single-user setup. Use \\SPOOLER to send your printing task to memory rather than tie up computer time. Use \\CAPTURE to capture data to another device rather than direct it to a printing device, modem, or disk. For more information on these options, see Chapter 26, "Installing dBASE IV on a Network."

After you have selected the correct printer and driver, press CTRL-END. The printer and driver files will be copied to your hard disk. As in the installation process, you will be asked to verify your printer driver or choose the default (GENERIC.PR2). Again, highlight your driver and press ENTER. Press CTRL-END to save these selections to your hard disk.

The Install/Install dBASE IV Option

If for any reason you would like to install dBASE IV again, you can do so using the **Install** option. This option is, for all intents and purposes, exactly the same program that you used to initially install dBASE IV on your hard disk.

The Install/Transfer other files Menu

You can use the **Transfer other files** menu to transfer files or to change your AUTOEXEC.BAT and CONFIG.SYS files. There are two groups of files that you can transfer from your master disks to your hard disk using this menu: sample and tutorial. The sample files are for use with the original dBASE IV documentation. The dBASE IV tutorial files are used in a stand-alone topical tutorial.

The Transfer other files/Sample files Option

After choosing the **Sample files** option from the **Transfer other files** menu, you are prompted for the drive and directory in which your dBASE IV files are located. You are then prompted for the drive and directory that contains your SQL files. Next, you are requested to enter the drive and directory for your sample files; the default directory is C:\DBASE\SAMPLES. You can change the drive and the main directory (C:\DBASE), but not the subdirectory name. The sample files must be copied to a subdirectory designated as \SAMPLES. If you do not have enough room for the sample directory files, you are asked to either change your drive or skip the sample file installation. If you choose to change your drive, you are prompted to enter the drive and directory. If dBASE IV successfully copies all the sample programs to your SAMPLES directory, the path to this sample database will also be inserted in your configuration file (CONFIG.DB).

The Transfer other files/Tutorial files Option

If you transfer the tutorial files, you will be able to use the on-disk tutorial to learn dBASE IV. Insert your Tutorial Disk into drive A and select the **Tutorial files** option. You are prompted to enter the directory for your dBASE IV files; the default is C:\DBASE. You are presented with a default directory of C:\DBASE\DBTUTOR for your tutorial files to be copied to. If you would like to change either the drive or the directory, you can do so now. To run the dBASE IV tutorial, change to the directory that you have copied the tutorial files to, type **INTRO** at the DOS prompt, and press ENTER.

The Transfer other files/Autoexec.bat Option

If you would like to have access to dBASE IV from any directory, choose the **Transfer other files** selection on the **Install** menu, highlight the **Autoexec.bat** menu choice, and press ENTER. The **Autoexec.bat** choice appends the path statement (a path opens a route to access files in different directories) in the AUTOEXEC.BAT file that is automatically executed when you boot up your computer. If you do not have a path command in your AUTOEXEC.BAT file, the one created is PATH=C:\DBASE. If you would like to have this path recognized immediately, end the install session and reboot the computer.

The Transfer other files/Config.sys Option

The next option in the **Install** menu is the **Config.sys** option. If you choose this option, you are notified that "Dbase IV will not run properly unless adequate file and buffer space is reserved." If you select this option, dBASE IV automatically updates your CONFIG.SYS file and renames your previous CONFIG.SYS file CONFIG.BAK. If you did not previously have a CONFIG.SYS file, dBASE IV creates one consisting of the following two commands, each on a different line: FILES=15 BUFFERS=40.

The Install/Uninstall Option

Choose the **Uninstall** option from the **Install** menu if you want to uninstall dBASE IV from your computer. You are asked from which directory you would like to uninstall dBASE IV. If the designated drive or directory does not exist, you are prompted to modify your entry. Unlike the dBASE III PLUS UNINSTALL command, which prompts you to insert the original disk to uninstall the program to, dBASE IV simply erases your system files but leaves data files unchanged. You are then prompted to make backup files of existing database files (.DBF files). After you uninstall dBASE IV, a prompt will substantiate that the uninstall procedure is complete.

The Config.db Menu

As you continue to use dBASE IV, its power and flexibility will become evident. There are several ways of achieving the same results with dBASE IV menus and commands. Whenever you start up dBASE IV, any commands in a configuration file—named CONFIG.DB— are performed. If a CONFIG.DB file exists, dBASE IV takes you to the Control Center. If a CONFIG.DB file does not exist, dBASE IV goes directly to the dBASE dot prompt, at which point you can enter dBASE IV commands. The CONFIG.DB file is one way to customize dBASE IV to suit your particular needs. The types of control that can be addressed from the **Config.db** menu are configuration commands, memory allocation, function key definitions, and most of the dBASE IV SET commands and color settings. The SET commands are covered extensively in the "Command Reference" part of this book; see also Chapter 32, "SET Commands."

To tailor the CONFIG.DB file to your needs, choose the **Config.db** menu. Figure 2-2 shows the **Config.db** menu with the **Display** submenu selected.

Since there are close to 100 menu options in the **Config.db** menu, there is a complete CONFIG.DB reference in Chapter 35, "Customizing dBASE IV." This section is only a general introduction to the types of menu selections and an explanation of some of the parameters already set in the default CONFIG.DB file. Don't worry if any of the information on these settings is difficult to understand because they will all be covered in detail in the ensuing chapters.

Remember, if you change any of the CONFIG.DB commands, you will have to save the changes you have made. To save your changes, highlight the **Exit** menu choice and choose the **Save and exit** selection.

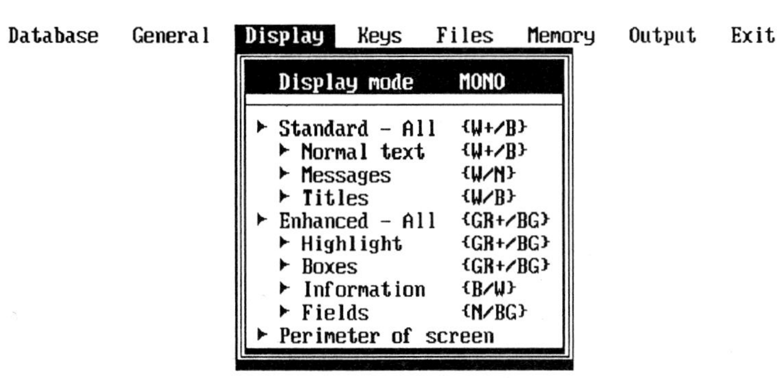

Figure 2-2. The **Config.db** menu

When you choose the **Config.db** menu, you are given the choice of seven submenus. They are described in the sections that follow.

The Config.db/Database Menu

The **Database** menu contains a diverse list of commands relating to how your databases will be handled. For instance, if you want to automatically save the database being worked on, you can turn **Autosave** on. If you want to carry information from the previous database entry onto the next record (so you can edit out the differences rather than reenter data), you should set the **Carry** selection to On.

The Config.db/General Menu

The **General** menu choice consists of information that is not database specific. This is the menu you use to let dBASE IV know your working preferences, for example, the type of clock time displayed on the screen (a 24-hour clock or 12-hour clock) or different currency types. You can also direct dBASE IV to use your own word processor instead of the default Text Editor.

The Config.db/Display Menu

Use the **Display** menu choice to change the colors found in any of dBASE IV's screens. If you encounter a blank screen when dBASE IV is running, your color setting may not correspond to your monitor. For example, if you are using a color graphics card with a single-color monitor, you can change the colors by choosing the **MONO** selection on the **Display** menu or by scrolling through the different color choices dBASE IV offers. Another possibility is to change the line "SET DISPLAY = COLOR" to "SET DISPLAY = MONO" in your CONFIG.DB file by using your ASCII-compatible word processor.

The Config.db/Keys Menu

When you first bring up dBASE IV, the function keys are already defined. For example, pressing the key marked F2 always enacts the dBASE IV ASSIST command. However, if you would like to give any of the function keys numbered F2 through F10 your own definition, you can do so using the **Keys** menu choice. Neither F1 nor SHIFT-F10 is programmable. F1 invokes dBASE IV's help system and SHIFT-F10 invokes the **Macro** menu. If you highlight F2 and press ENTER, you are prompted to enter a command to be performed each time the F2 key is pressed. The semicolon (;) immediately following the commands represents the ENTER key.

The Config.db/Files Menu

The **Files** menu allows you to tell dBASE IV where your files are located and how they are to be handled. If you are using more than one database at a time, you can enter the name of an alternate database. If you would like to change your path or default drive, you can do so from this menu.

The Config.db/Memory Menu

This **Memory** management menu covers commands that control memory blocks allocated to memory variables. For instance, you can increase the maximum number of memory variables by increasing the default number of the selection **Mvmaxblks** (move maximum blocks).

The Config.db/Output Menu

The **Output** menu selection deals with any output device that dBASE IV is connected to. If, for example, you would like to send information to the printer rather than the screen, you could change the device from the screen to the printer. You can also use this menu to set up your printer fonts.

Addressing Multiple CONFIG.DB Files

Before loading its program files, dBASE IV reads the CONFIG.DB file to get the program's configuration. You can have more than one CONFIG.DB file with different configuration settings. If you want to access a particular CONFIG.DB file, either it must be in dBASE IV's directory or you must start dBASE IV from the directory that contains it.

The following example shows how you might use more than one CONFIG.DB file. This is how you would leave the current DBASE directory's CONFIG.DB file set up for a 25-line screen while accessing a CONFIG.DB file set up to use an EGA 43-line screen:

1. Make a directory by typing, for example, **MD\DBSMALL** at the C:> prompt. (Unlike the INSTALL program, DBSETUP does not create a directory for you.)
2. Create a CONFIG.DB file using the DBSETUP submenu **Config.db**. Choose the **Display** selection and change the screen to EGA43 mode. Select the **Save and exit** option from the **Exit** menu. Save the new CONFIG.DB file in your new DBSMALL directory (C:\DBSMALL).
3. Create a batch file that changes to the directory that contains your new CONFIG.DB file. The batch file, called DBSMALL.BAT, will set up dBASE IV for a 43-line screen and reads as follows:

```
C:
CD\DBSMALL
DBASE
```

Provided you have included the directory of your dBASE IV program in your path statement, you can start this 43-line configuration of dBASE IV from any directory by typing **DBSMALL** at the DOS prompt.

The Tools Menu

Similar to several of the DOS shells and utility packages, dBASE IV now offers three menu choices that help illustrate the technical limitations and possibilities of your computer. If you are an average user, these menu choices offer interesting, but superfluous, information about your system.

The Tools/Display disk usage Option

The **Display disk usage** menu contains everything you wanted to know about your disk, but didn't think to ask, including data on the drives' sector sizes, number of tracks, the space used or unused by DOS, the amount of space on the disk, and the space allocated to bad sectors.

The Tools/Test disk performance Option

The dBASE IV manual says that the **Tools** menu provides "information you can use for optimizing your system to improve dBASE IV's performance." The operative word here is "optimizing." The **Test disk performance** menu tells you how fast dBASE IV is accessing the information from the disk. If you have several files that are scattered throughout your hard disk, this menu choice may help point out the problem. However, this menu does not let you optimize your disk. If you would like to do so, you'll need to purchase a third-party product, such as The Norton Utilities: Advanced Edition or Soft Logic's Disk Optimizer.

The Tools/Review system configuration Option

If you are unsure of what hardware is under your PC's hood, this menu choice will save you some trouble. You can ferret out the following hardware options by using **Review system configuration**: the chip or CPU (central processing unit), the ROM BIOS (read only memory basic input output system), number of floppy disk drives, memory available for use by DOS, serial and parallel ports, math coprocessor, DMA (direct memory access), game adaptor, and video modes.

The DOS Menu

The **DOS** menu has three choices: **Perform DOS command, Go to DOS**, and **Set default drive:directory**. The sections that follow describe these options.

The DOS/Perform DOS command Option

The **DOS/Perform DOS command** choice allows you to execute any single DOS command without leaving the DBSETUP program. After selecting this option, simply enter the desired DOS command at the prompt.

The DOS/Go to DOS Option

Using the **Go to DOS** command lets you temporarily go to the DOS prompt to perform multiple DOS operations. To return from DOS to the DBSETUP program, type **EXIT** at the DOS prompt.

The DOS/Set default drive:directory Option

The **Set default drive:directory** menu selection allows you to change the dBASE IV default drive and directory from inside the DBSETUP program.

The Exit Menu

The **Exit** menu is the simplest and most concise of the DBSETUP menus. Use this menu to leave the DBSETUP program and return to DOS.

In this chapter, you've learned how to install dBASE IV on your system. You've also learned how to access the DBSETUP program in case you want to change any of your dBASE IV configuration settings.

An Introduction to the Control Center

THREE

A significant improvement in dBASE IV is its innovative Control Center. This chapter takes you on a general tour of this powerful menu-driven system. The Control Center allows you to perform complex database management tasks with minimal effort.

The Control Center Screen

The Control Center's screen is divided into five sections—the menu bar, the current catalog, the current file, the work surface, and the navigation line—each of which is labeled in Figure 3-1. The sections that follow describe these components in the order in which they appear on the screen.

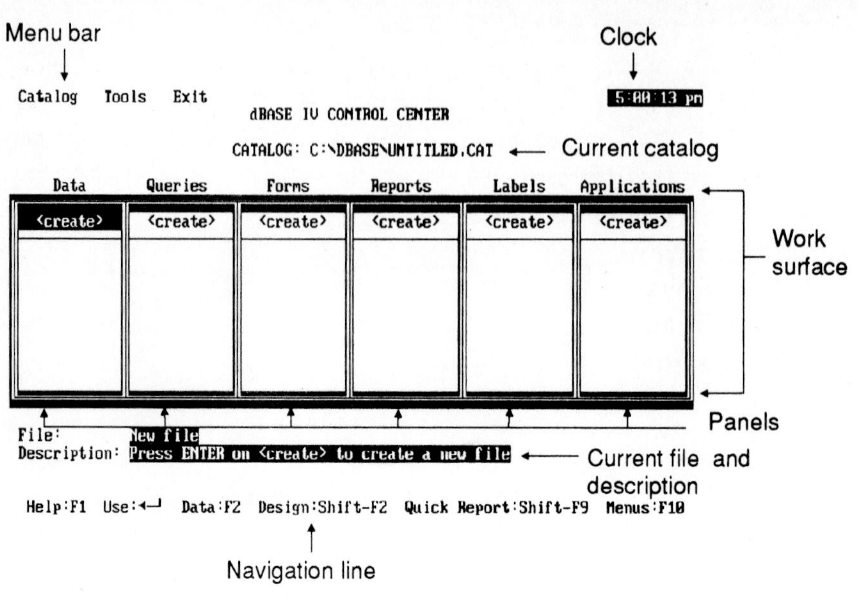

Figure 3-1. The Control Center screen

Invoking the Control Center

If you start dBASE IV and the Control Center screen (Figure 3-1) does not automatically appear, press F2 or type **ASSIST** at the dot prompt. (ASSIST is the default assignment for the F2 key.) Either of these methods invokes the Control Center.

The Control Center Menu Bar

In the Control Center, the *menu bar* consists of three options: **Catalog**, **Tools**, and **Exit**. Each of these options represents a pull-down menu and is described later in the chapter. A clock also appears in the upper-right corner of the Control Center screen.

The Catalog

The name of the current catalog appears centered below the menu bar. A *catalog* is a tool you use to organize information from a collection of any number of associated files assembled for easy access. In Figure 3-2, the current catalog begins with the name of the disk drive and the catalog's directory. The current catalog is the circled file name with the .CAT extension. Catalogs are discussed in detail in Chapter 13.

The Control Center Panels

Six panels—Data, Queries, Forms, Reports, Labels, and Applications panels—make up an area referred to as the *work surface*. The work surface is the area of your screen where you display, edit, and manage data. Each of the panels includes a **<create>** option.

- The Data Panel displays the names of the database files that store data.
- The Queries Panel enables you to extract information easily in customized formats. Queries are one of the Control Center's most useful features.
- The Forms Panel allows you to create customized screen displays. You can enter, edit, and view records using customized forms created from the Forms Panel.
- The Reports Panel enables you to create customized reports. Report files print information from your database in a designated format.

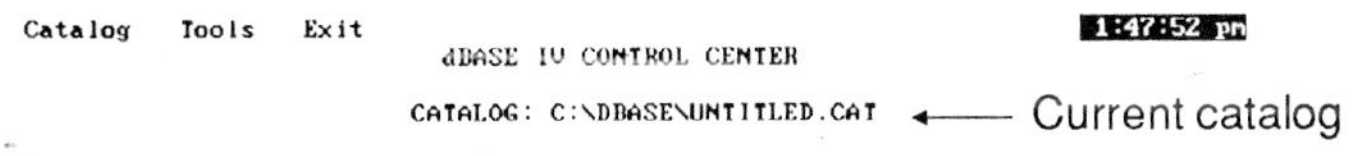

Figure 3-2. The current catalog

- The Labels Panel consists of the names of your customized layout formats for labels.
- The Applications Panel consists of programs that accomplish an assortment of database management tasks.

The Navigation Line

At the bottom of the screen is the *navigation line*, which contains a list of useful options that are currently available. For instance, **Menus:F10** indicates that you can activate the menu bar by pressing F10.

The Message Line

When you're using a menu, the *message line* below the nagivation line gives a concise definition of the highlighted menu option. When you're not using a menu, the message line displays instructions or information about the current screen. For example, opening the **Exit** menu by pressing ALT-E displays the following message on the message line:

```
 Position selection bar: ↑↓     Select: ◄┘     Leave menu: Esc
Leave the Control Center and return to the dBASE IV dot prompt
```

The Status Bar

The status bar is not on the Control Center screen but appears in several operations you start from the Control Center. For example, when you install dBASE IV, create a database, or issue a command from the dot prompt, the status bar appears at the bottom of your screen. The status bar provides information about the current file you are using, your location in the work surface, and your keyboard settings. Figure 3-3 labels each section of the status bar.

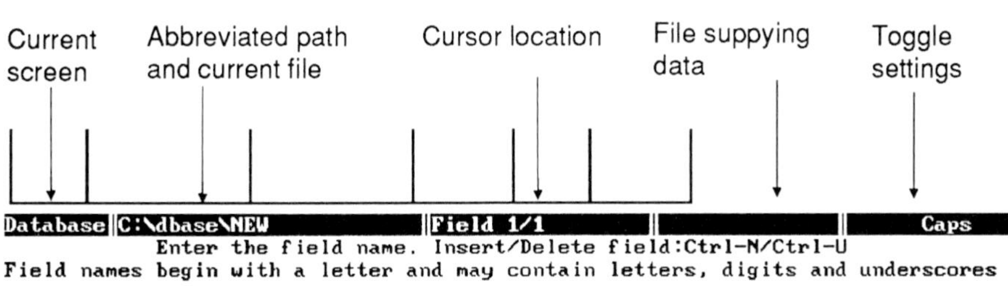

Figure 3-3. The status bar

The Control Center Menus

Figure 3-1 displays the Control Center's menu bar. The sections that follow explain how to access the options in the Control Center menu bar and give descriptions of their respective menus.

Activating the Control Center Menus

To activate the Control Center menu bar, press F10 or hold down the ALT key while pressing the first letter of a menu name. The menu bar will open the corresponding menu. For example, ALT-C opens the **Catalog** menu.

Once you have activated the menu bar, you can select a menu option by using the arrow keys to highlight the option and pressing ENTER. Alternatively, you can press the first letter of the menu option. To deactivate the menu bar or remove a menu from the screen, press ESC.

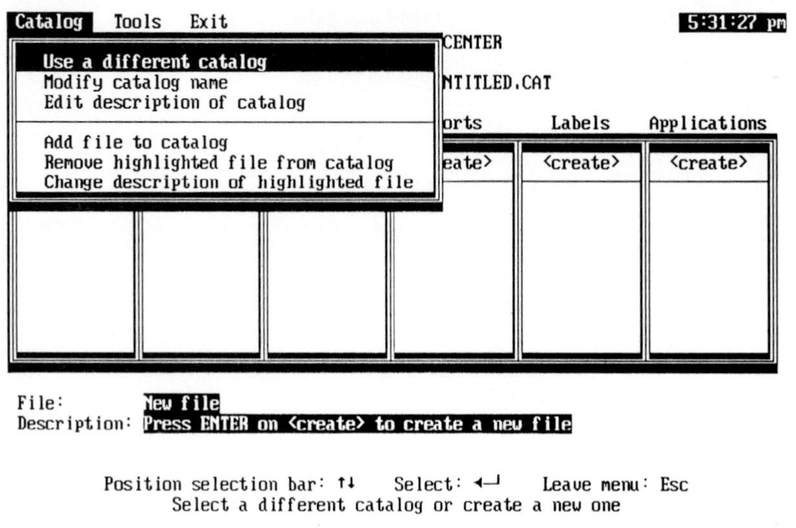

Figure 3-4. The **Catalog** menu

The Catalog Menu

The **Catalog** menu (Figure 3-4) contains options for controlling catalogs and their associated files. This menu consists of two sets of options. The first set allows you to use or modify a catalog name or description. The second set allows you to alter a catalog by adding or removing a file or changing the file description.

The catalog menu is covered in greater depth in Chapter 13.

The Tools Menu

The **Tools** menu (Figure 3-5) contains utility options that can increase your efficiency. Through this menu you can create and control macros, import and export data, invoke DOS utilities from within dBASE, set file protection, and customize dBASE IV settings. The **Macros** option of the **Tools** menu is discussed in detail

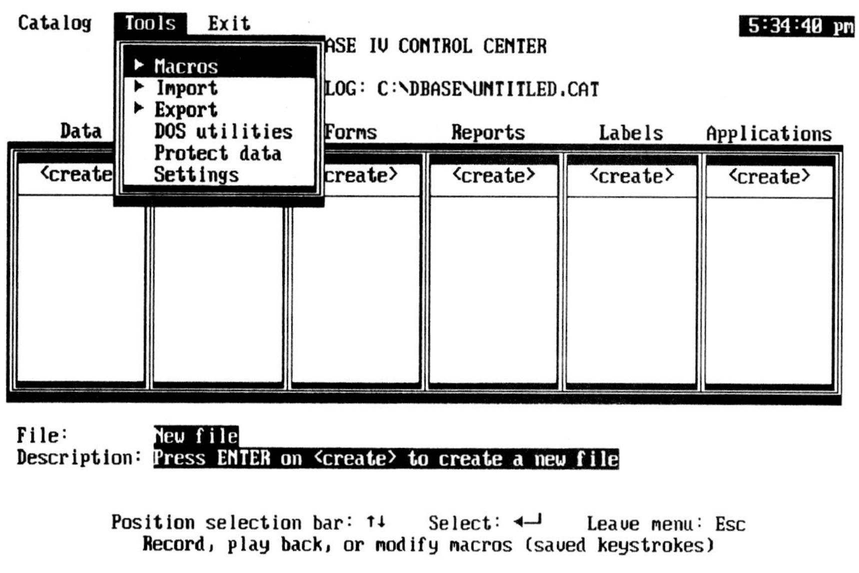

Figure 3-5. The **Tools** menu

in Chapter 8, and the other options of the **Tools** menu are covered in Chapter 14.

The Exit Menu

You can use the **Exit** menu to exit from the Control Center. You can choose **Quit to DOS**, which takes you to the DOS prompt, or **Exit to dot prompt**, which takes you to the dBASE IV dot prompt.

Navigation Keys

There are several different work surfaces available throughout dBASE IV, including browse, edit, layout, and word wrap. These are discussed in subsequent chapters. Table 3-1 lists the dBASE IV navigation and editing keys for these varied work surfaces, including CTRL-key equivalents.

Function Keys

The default settings for the function keys are listed in Table 3-2. The dBASE IV names for these keys are right next to the key. For example, the **F2** key is referred to as the Data key

Data and Design

The Control Center is built around the understanding that there are two fundamental domains in the database world—data and design.

- *Data* is the raw information that you enter, edit, and examine in a database. Fields and records contain the data in a database.
- *Design* is the finished format that displays your data in its various forms. Databases, queries, forms, labels, and reports are all part of design.

F2—the Data Key

If you highlight a file name in the Data Panel and press F2 (the Data key), dBASE presents your data in browse or edit mode. Browse shows several records at once, while edit displays one record at a time. You can switch between the browse and edit modes by pressing F2. If you are designing a report and want to see the database associated with the report, you can press F2 to see the data in the database.

Keys	Action	Work Surface
→ or CTRL-D	Moves cursor one character to the right	All
← or CTRL-S	Moves cursor one character to the left	All
↓ or CTRL-S	Moves cursor down one row	All
	Moves to next field	Edit
↑ or CTRL-E	Moves cursor up one row	All
	Moves to previous field	Edit
PGDN or CTRL-R	Displays next screen	Browse, edit, layout, word wrap
PGUP or CTRL-C	Displays previous screen	Browse, edit, layout, word wrap
END	Moves to end of the field	Edit
	Moves to last field in the record	Browse
	Moves to last portion of text	Word wrap
	Moves to last field on the line	Layout
	Moves to last column of the skeleton	Queries
HOME	Moves to beginning of the field	Edit
	Moves to beginning of the record	Browse
	Moves to left margin	Layout
	Moves to left margin or indentation	Word wrap
	Moves to first column of skeleton	Queries
BACKSPACE	Deletes one character to the left of cursor	All
CTRL-BACKSPACE	Deletes one word to the left of cursor	Layout, word wrap
TAB	Moves to next field	Edit, browse
	Moves to next tab stop	Layout, word wrap (if INS is off)
	Moves to next column	Queries, lists, tables

Table 3-1. The dBASE IV Navigation and Editing Keys

Keys	Action	Work Surface
	Inserts tab character	Word wrap (if INS is on)
	Moves margin to next tab stop	Word wrap (with Enable automatic indent)
SHIFT-TAB	Moves to previous field	Edit, browse
	Moves to previous tab stop	Layout, word wrap
	Moves margin to previous tab stop	Word wrap (with Enable automatic indent)
	Moves to previous column	Queries, lists, tables
ENTER	Moves to next field	Browse, edit
	Moves to next line	Layout, word wrap
	Breaks the line and moves to a new one	Layout (if INS is on), word wrap (if INS is on)
ESC or CTRL-Q	Aborts or cancels operation	All
DEL or CTRL-G	Deletes currently selected item	All
INS or CTRL-V	Toggles insert mode on or off	All
CTRL-→ or CTRL-F	Moves to end of a field or right one word	All
CTRL-← or CTRL-A	Moves to beginning of a field or left one word	All
CTRL-PGDN	Moves to end of text	Word wrap
	Moves to bottom of layout surface	Layout
	Moves to current field in last record	Browse, edit
CTRL-PGUP	Moves to beginning of text	Word wrap
	Moves to top of the layout surface	Layout

Table 3-1. The dBASE IV Navigation and Editing Keys (*continued*)

Keys	Action	Work Surface
	Moves to current field in the first record	Browse, edit
CTRL-HOME	Moves into a memo field	Memo field
CTRL-END	Saves your work and exits	All
	Moves out of the memo field	Memo field
CTRL-ENTER	Saves your work	Design screens
CTRL-Y	Delete line	Word wrap, layout
CTRL-T	Delete word right	Word wrap, layout
CTRL-KR	Read text file	Word wrap, layout
CTRL-KW	Write text file	Word wrap, layout

Table 3-1. The dBASE IV Navigation and Editing Keys (*continued*)

SHIFT-F2—the Design Key

Just as there are two ways to use the Data key, there are two ways to use the Design key, SHIFT-F2. Suppose, for example, that you want to modify the design of a label you have created. You can highlight the label file in the Labels Panel of the Control Center and press SHIFT-F2. dBASE takes you to the Labels Design screen, where you can modify the labels design. If, while you are working on the label design, you decide you want to limit the records for which you print labels, you can press SHIFT-F2 to create a *view query*. Using a view query, you can, for example, limit the data to only clients from California. You can easily flip back and forth from designing the view query to designing the label by pressing SHIFT-F2. You can apply this same method of design for forms and reports as well.

Keys	Action
F1 Help	Displays help system
F2 Data	Switches from Browse to Edit screens
F3 Previous	Moves to previous field in browse or edit modes, to previous object in Queries Design screen, or to previous page in help system
F4 Next	Moves to next field in the browse or edit modes, to next object in Queries Design screens, or to next page in help system
F5 Field	Adds field to layout the surface or the skeleton
F6 Extend Select	Selects adjoining text and fields
F7 Move	Moves selected text and fields
F8 Copy	Copies selected text and fields
F9 Zoom	Enlarges or shrinks memo fields, condition boxes, file skeletons, and shows or hides files in the utilities directory tree
F10 Menus	Activates menus for the current screen
SHIFT-F1 Pick	Displays list of items available for fill in
SHIFT-F2 Design	Displays design screens
SHIFT-F3 Find Previous	Locates previous occurrence of a search string
SHIFT-F4 Find Next	Locates next occurrence of a search string
SHIFT-F5 Find	Finds specified search string
SHIFT-F6 Replace	Replaces one search string with another string
SHIFT-F7 Size	Changes size of design elements and column widths in Browse
SHIFT-F8 Ditto	Copies data from the corresponding field of the previous record into the current field
SHIFT-F9 Quick Report	Prints quick report
SHIFT-F10 Macros	Accesses macros option

Table 3-2 The Default Function Key Settings

Selecting Files

When you first encounter the Control Center, the work surface panels contain only the **<create>** option at the top. In order to use the Control Center, you must select one or more files to work with. For example, to select a file from the SAMPLES subdirectory, press ALT-C to open the **Catalog** menu and then press A for the **Add file to catalog** option. A box will appear in the upper-right corner of your screen. Use the arrow keys to highlight your SAMPLES subdirectory and press ENTER. Next, select a database file in the same manner. A prompt appears, allowing you to change the description of the file you've selected. When you press ENTER, the file appears in the Data Panel of your work surface.

Tip: If you did not transfer the sample files to your hard disk and would like to access them, insert the backup copy of Samples Disk #3 into drive A. After pressing A for **Add a file to catalog**, select the C:> prompt. This produces a list of available drives directly to the left of the previous C:> prompt. Select drive A to see a list of the sample files, and choose a file from the list.

Tip: When you are adding files to the catalog, dBASE lists only the class of files marked by the cursor location. For example, if the cursor is in the Labels Panel, you can only choose label files.

Deleting Files

You can delete a file from your work surface by highlighting the file and pressing DEL. (If you're using the file, dBASE IV displays an error message stating that you cannot delete an open file. To close the file, highlight the filename, press ENTER, and then select the **Close file** option.) A prompt verifies that you want to remove the file from the current catalog. A second prompt asks if you would like to delete the file from disk. If you choose to delete the file from disk, dBASE erases the file permanently.

The Dot Prompt

To get to the dBASE IV dot prompt, select the **Exit** menu from the Control Center menu bar. Then select the **Exit to dot prompt** option. You're now at the dBASE IV command line, or *dot prompt.* The Control Center commands have dBASE IV dot prompt equivalents. For example, to select a file called CONTENTS.DBF using the dBASE IV dot prompt, enter the following command at the dot prompt:

```
.USE Contents
```

Every menu in the Control Center performs one or more dBASE IV commands to manage your data. To learn more about the dot prompt, see Chapter 7.

When You Need Help

When you need help, press the Help key, F1. The dBASE IV Help system is context-sensitive, which means that it attempts to find the Help screen appropriate to the subject suggested by your current location. The F1 key is available with any dBASE IV command or screen. If you know the command that you need help with, type **HELP** followed by that command. For example, if you want help with the USE command, type **HELP USE** at the dot prompt.

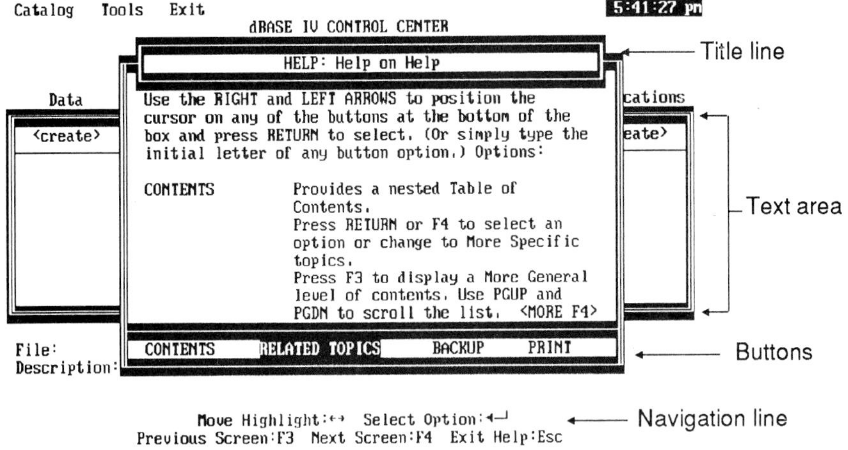

Figure 3-6. The Help screen

The Help Screen

The Help screen contains four sections: the title line, text area, buttons, and navigation line. Figure 3-6 identifies each of these sections. The *title line* identifies the topic covered by the Help passage. The *text area* is the explanation of the Help topic.

Help Buttons

There are four selections available from the **Help** menu: **CONTENTS**, **RELATED TOPICS**, **BACKUP**, and **PRINT**. You can select these *buttons* by highlighting them and pressing ENTER or by pressing the first initial of the button.

- CONTENTS displays a table of contents for the current area of Help.
- RELATED TOPICS lists topics associated with the screen currently displayed.
- BACKUP follows the exact sequence of Help boxes that you have stepped through, but in reverse order.
- PRINT sends the current Help box to your printer so you can refer to it at your convenience.

The Help Navigation Line

The following keys help you navigate through dBASE IV's Help system:

- **Move Highlight** Use the arrow keys to move between Help topics.
- **Select Option** Press ENTER to select a particular option.
- **F3 or Previous Screen** Displays a general list of topics associated with the highlighted subject.
- **F4 or Next Screen** Displays a specific list of subjects associated with the highlighted subject.
- **ESC** Exits the Help system.

In this chapter, you learned about the new dBASE IV Control Center. You're now familiar with the various aspects of the Control Center screen, and you know how to access the Control Center menu bar. You also know how to use the dBASE IV Help system.

Entering, Editing, and Displaying Data

UR

Data Types
Database Design Strategy
Creating a Database
Saving the Database File Structure
Adding a Database Description
Changing the File Structure
Printing the Database File Structure
Entering and Changing Data
Controlling Fields in Browse Mode
Controlling Records in Browse or Edit Mode
Moving Between Records—the Go To Menu
Appending Records from Other Files
Using Memo Fields
Entering Memo Text

Before you begin creating a database, you'll need to know the types of options with which you can design, create, enter, edit, and display information. Once you know these database management fundamentals, you can effectively manage any data with dBASE IV.

This chapter provides you with the information you need to begin creating a database with dBASE IV. It also explores the fundamentals of dBASE IV data management, including data types and various ways to enter, edit, and display your data from the Control Center. Whenever a new Control Center menu option is discussed, the dot prompt equivalent is also included as a tip. This will give you some general background if you decide to leave the Control Center and enter commands from the dot prompt.

Data Types

When you create a database, the first step is to decide on a field-by-field basis exactly what information you want to store and how you want to store it. Selecting the proper storage method for your fields is one of the more important decisions you'll make when you build a database. It affects the size of your database as well as how you'll need to lay out any custom reports and screens.

dBASE IV has four data types that you can use to store your data: character, numeric, date, and logical. dBASE IV also has a special storage mechanism—the memo field—that you can use to store large amounts of text.

Character Type

You use the character type to store character strings, which consist of letters, symbols, blank spaces, and uncalculated numbers (for example, phone numbers and ZIP codes). You can store a string of up to 254 characters with the character data type.

The Two Numeric Data Types

dBASE IV distinguishes between two numeric data types: *numeric* and *float*. These two types look the same when displayed, but they are stored differently. dBASE IV refers to the numeric type as *type N* and the float type as *type F.* If you have a very large or small number, dBASE IV displays both type F and type N numbers in scientific notation—the exponent is preceded by the letter "E," as in 123E+20.

Numeric Type

You use the numeric data type for binary coded decimal (BCD) numbers. dBASE IV stores any real number up to 20 digits long in this data type, which is accurate up to 15 digits. You can enter negative numbers by using the minus sign (-). Numeric data types include both integer and decimal numbers and are not subject to rounding errors. Numeric type numbers are useful in business and financial applications. Numbers that you input into dBASE IV are numeric by default, unless the field specifies a float type.

Float Type

You use the float data type for floating-point binary numbers. Like the numeric data type, the float data type is accurate to 15 digits and can also accept negative numbers. Type F numbers are useful when you're dealing with exceptionally large or small numbers. They may yield approximate results when rounded or truncated. Scientific applications frequently use floating-point numbers. If you use dBASE IV for business applications, you'll probably never use the float data type.

Date Type

dBASE IV stores dates in the following default American format: mm/dd/yy. You can alter the date format in any of the following ways:

- With the **Settings** option from the Control Center's **Tools** menu
- With the SET DATE command from the dot prompt
- By changing the DATE setting in the CONFIG.DB file (see Chapter 35).

When you use a date field in your database, dBASE IV automatically sets the width to eight spaces and inserts the forward slashes in the field. Using the date format allows you to perform calculations based on dates.

Logical Type

dBASE supports a Boolean logic data type that lets you store a true (.T.) or false (.F.) value. When you enter a true or false value in a logical field, dBASE IV accepts T, t, Y, or y for true, and F, f, N, or n for false. If you create a database with a logical field, dBASE IV automatically sets the field's value to false (.F.).

When you use a logical type in a dBASE statement, you must use the period (.) as a delimiter on both sides of the logical type value. That is, you must enter **.T.** for a value of true and **.F.** for a value of false. For example, the command

```
STORE .T. TO Mtrue
```

stores the value of true (.T.) to a variable named Mtrue. You can enter this command from the dot prompt or in a program.

Memo Field

dBASE IV automatically assigns a width of ten characters to a memo field. A memo field is actually a pointer to a separate text file. This file has the same name as the database file but with a .DBT extension. dBASE can manage memo field entries that contain up to 512K of text.

Database Design Strategy

Before creating a database, you need to consider how much data you want to manage and how much space you think it will require. Trying to keep track of too much data may be as confusing and time-consuming as not having enough data. Also, the more data you include, the more disk space you use and the longer it takes dBASE IV to answer your queries. Rather than using a single database to handle a large amount of diverse data, you may want to separate the data into related groups and use more than one database.

Try to keep your database fields as small as possible without sacrificing readability or relevant information. This saves you both time and disk space. For example, rather than entering the entire state name in your database, use the two-letter abbreviation.

Determining the Size of a Database

The following exercise should help you determine the eventual size of your database. Each character in your database occupies one byte of memory. When you create a database, dBASE IV represents your field width in bytes. The number of bytes is the same as the number of spaces required to put the field on a typewritten page.

By multiplying the number of characters and digits used to store a record, estimating the number of records that you're tracking in your database, and adding the bytes that dBASE IV uses to manipulate your file, you can determine the size of your database. For example, if you have 33 clients that you want on a mailing list, add the size of the fields and multiply the result by the total number of records (in this case 33).

First name	15 characters
Last name	15 characters
Company	25 characters
Address	25 characters
City	20 characters
State	02 characters
Zip	10 characters
Telephone	14 characters
	126 characters × 33 records = 4,158 bytes

Now you need to add the size of the file header that dBASE IV uses to maintain the database file. The following equation determines the size of your file header:

32 * # of fields + 35

For the current example, the equation would be

32 * 8 + 35 = 291 bytes

The total space taken up by your database is

4,158 + 291 = 4,449 bytes

A Simple Database Design

Suppose you've just purchased dBASE IV to help you manage a small list of clients for your company. Here is a list of some of the information that you may want to keep track of:

- First name
- Last name
- Company
- Address
- City
- State
- ZIP code
- Telephone number
- Date last contacted
- Notes about clients

You can easily create a CLIENTS database to manage this information. The examples in the remainder of this chapter will show you how.

Creating a Database

When you first start dBASE IV, the highlight is on **<create>** in the Data Panel of the Control Center. Press ENTER, and you will

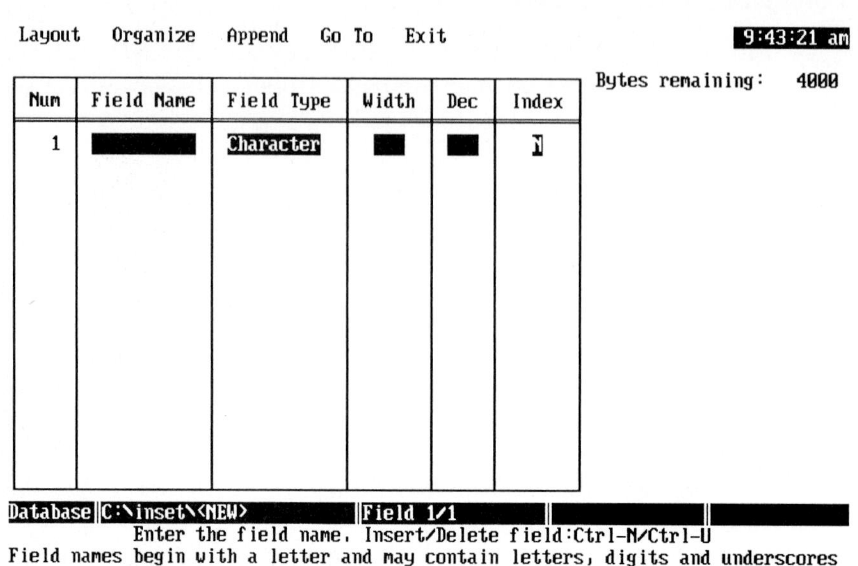

Figure 4-1. The Database Design screen

be on your way to creating your first dBASE IV database. The Database Design screen appears (Figure 4-1) with the cursor in the "Field Name" column.

Tip: Using the CREATE command from the dot prompt is the same as selecting the **<create>** option from the Data Panel of the Control Center. Both allow you to create a database.

Defining the Database Structure

Before you can store information in a database, you must define the database structure. You need to establish the field parameters—name, type, width, decimal points—and whether you want dBASE IV to create an index for that field. You use the Database

Design screen to set these parameters. The following sections show you how to use the Database Design screen to establish a database structure.

Tip: When you create a database structure, keep in mind that dBASE IV converts any lowercase entries to uppercase.

Entering a Field Name

To enter a field name, choose a name that best describes the information that that field contains. Field names can contain up to 10 letters. You can also use digits or underscores, but you must begin the field name with a letter. The field name cannot include spaces.

For example, type **LASTNAME** for the field name to contain the last name of a person on your CLIENTS database. Then press ENTER.

Changing a Field Type

After filling in the field name, you're automatically moved to the "Field Type" column. The default for the field type is character. To change the field type, press SPACEBAR; dBASE IV will cycle through the available field types. If you prefer, you can select the field type by pressing the first letter of the type. For example, press C to select character for the Lastname field. After you select the field type, press ENTER.

The "Width" Column

After you've selected your field type, you're taken to the "Width" column. This entry defines how many characters or digits to store in the field. Character fields can contain up to 254 characters. Numeric and floating fields can contain up to 20 digits. dBASE IV presets the widths for date, logical, and memo fields. Date fields are 8 digits, logical fields are 1 character, and memo fields are 10 characters wide.

The "Dec" Column

The "Dec," or decimal, column only works if the field type is one of the two numeric data types. Otherwise, the cursor skips this field. If the field type is a numeric or float data type, dBASE IV prompts you to enter the number of decimal places. Numeric and floating fields can have 0 to 18 decimal places.

The "Index" Column

The "Index" column lets you build an index on the field that you're creating. Because indexes provide a quick way to find information in a database, they can be extremely helpful for tracking database information. For now, press N for no to bypass creating an index. Chapter 5, "Sorting and Indexing," discusses indexes at length.

Try entering the field names for the CLIENTS database list, as pictured in Figure 4-2.

Tip: If you make any mistakes while creating the file structure for a database, you can easily correct them. For example, you can press TAB to move one column to the right and SHIFT- TAB to move one column to the left to change any problem entries. You can also delete an entire field by pressing CTRL-U.

Saving the Database File Structure

After creating a database file structure, you can save it in one of the following five ways:

- Press ENTER while the cursor is on an empty field.
- Access the **Exit** menu and select the **Save changes and exit** option.
- Access the **Layout** menu and select **Save this database file structure**.

```
Layout   Organize   Append   Go To   Exit                         10:02:16 am
                                                      Bytes remaining:   3851
 Num | Field Name | Field Type | Width | Dec | Index
  1  | FIRSTNAME  | Character  |  15   |     |   N
  2  | LASTNAME   | Character  |  15   |     |   N
  3  | COMPANY    | Character  |  25   |     |   N
  4  | ADDRESS    | Character  |  25   |     |   N
  5  | CITY       | Character  |  20   |     |   N
  6  | STATE      | Character  |   2   |     |   N
  7  | ZIP        | Character  |  10   |     |   N
  8  | TELEPHONE  | Character  |  14   |     |   N
  9  | AMOUNT     | Numeric    |   5   |  0  |   N
 10  | DATE       | Date       |   8   |     |   N
 11  | NOTES      | Memo       |  10   |     |   N

Database C:\dbase\CLIENTS        Field 1/11
        Enter the field name. Insert/Delete field:Ctrl-N/Ctrl-U
Field names begin with a letter and may contain letters, digits and underscores
```

Figure 4-2. The CLIENTS database structure

- Press CTRL-W.
- Press CTRL-END.

After you choose one of these options, the prompt to name your database appears. Enter the name that you would like your file saved as. File names cannot contain more than eight letters and must begin with a character. For example, to save the CLIENTS database, answer the dBASE prompt by entering the file name **clients**. dBASE IV will automatically give your database an extension of .DBF (database file).

If you use the **Save changes and exit** option from the **Exit** menu, dBASE brings you back to the Control Center. If you select **Save this database file structure**, dBASE leaves you in the Database Design screen and allows you to make further changes. If you save your database in any other way, you will see the prompt

"Input data records now? (Y/N)." If you select Y, dBASE IV takes you to edit mode where you can add records to your database. If you select N, dBASE takes you back to the Control Center. Press N to return to the Control Center.

Tip: If you try to save a database structure using the name of an existing database, dBASE IV displays the following options:

Overwrite	To overwrite the existing file
Cancel	To cancel the save operation and choose another file name

Be careful. If you choose **Overwrite**, you'll write over the existing database file and may lose some important data.

Adding a Database Description

From the Control Center, you can add a description to a database in either of two ways:

- By opening the **Catalog** menu and selecting the **Change description of highlighted file** option
- By pressing the Design key (SHIFT-F2) and opening the **Layout** menu

Whichever method you choose, you can then select the **Edit database description** option. This option allows you to add a string of up to 80 characters to describe your database. Once you've entered the description, press ENTER to save it.

Using the Design key, try entering the CLIENTS database description as illustrated in Figure 4-3. Then use the **Exit** menu to return to the Control Center.

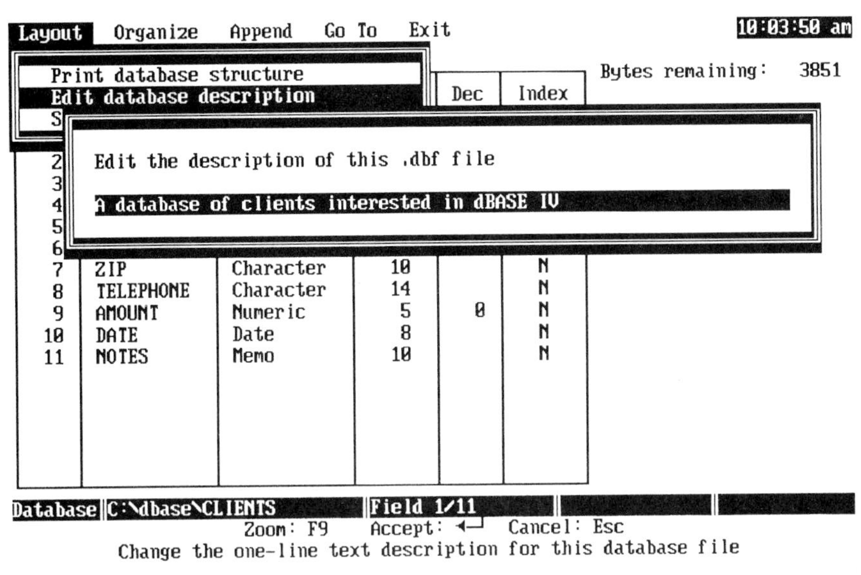

Figure 4-3. The CLIENTS database description

Changing the File Structure

Once you've created and saved the file structure for a database, you'll probably want to change it. Before you can change the structure, however, the database file must be listed in the Data Panel of the Control Center. If your file doesn't appear in this list, you can add it by selecting the **Catalog** menu and choosing the **Add a file** option.

To modify a database's file structure, you need to return to the Database Design screen. You can return to this screen in either of the following two ways.

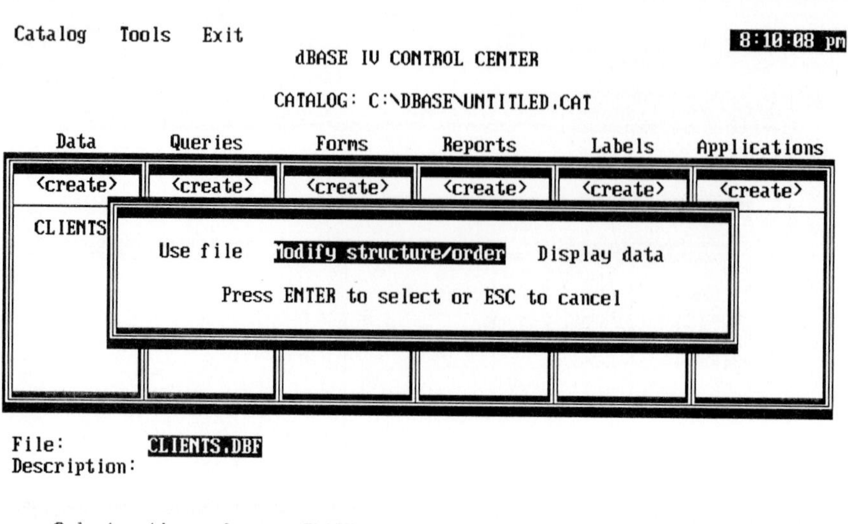

Figure 4-4. The **Modify structure/order** option

- In the Data panel, highlight the database file you want to change (for example, CLIENTS) and press SHIFT-F2.
- Highlight the database file you want to change and press ENTER. The box depicted in Figure 4-4 appears, listing the following three options: **Use file**, **Modify structure/order**, and **Display data**. To change the structure of your database, select the **Modify structure/order** option.

Whichever method you choose, dBASE takes you to the Database Design screen and opens the **Organize** menu. Press ESC to close the **Organize** menu. Does the screen look familiar? It is the screen pictured in Figure 4-1 that you used to create your database.

Tip: To modify the structure of a database from the dot prompt, use the MODIFY STRUCTURE command. If you're not currently using a database, dBASE IV prompts you for a database file name.

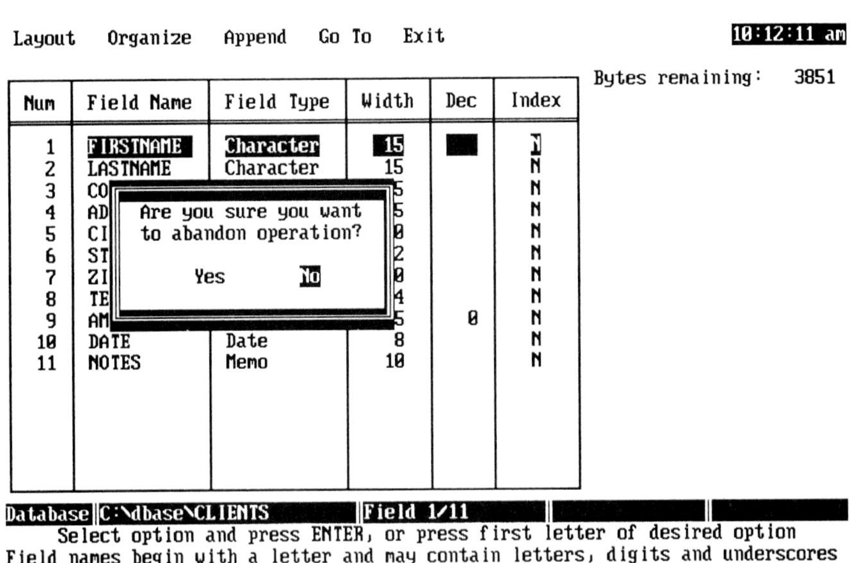

Figure 4-5. A dBASE IV confirmation prompt

Adding or Deleting a Field

To add a new field to a database, you must first place a blank field where you want the new field to reside. The **Go To** menu allows you to relocate your cursor to the first field with the **Top field** option, to the last field with **Last field** option, or to a particular field with the **Field number** option. Use the **Go To** menu to put the cursor where you want to add the blank field and press CTRL-N.

To delete a field, position the cursor on the field to be deleted and press CTRL-U. To save these changes, press CTRL-END. To quit without saving changes, press ESC or CTRL-Q.

Practice adding and deleting a field in the CLIENTS database. Use the ESC key to quit without saving any changes. A confirmation prompt will appear, as seen in Figure 4-5. Press Y to quit without saving your changes.

A Warning About Changing Your Database Structure

When you change the structure of a database file, dBASE IV creates a completely new database and copies the data from the old structure into the new structure. It then erases the old database. dBASE determines where to copy the data based on the names or positions of the fields in the previous database structure. If you change the field names, rearranging the field positions at the same time, dBASE IV can't find the correct fields in the new structure.

For example, suppose you want to move the Amount field from the ninth field in your CLIENTS database to the first field, and you want to rename it Total. If you make both these changes at once, the contents of your Amount field will be lost forever, since dBASE uses either the field's name or position to add your existing records to the new structure. In other words, you can't change both the position and the name of a field at the same time. You can, however, change the field name from Amount to Total, save your change by pressing CTRL-END, change the position of the Total field as outlined, and press CTRL-END to save your second change.

Printing the Database File Structure

To print the file structure of your database, select the **Layout** menu in the Database Design screen and then select the **Print database structure** option, shown in Figure 4-6. (To get to the Database Design screen from the Control Center, highlight your database in the Data Panel and press SHIFT-F2.)

Tip: To print your database's file structure from the dot prompt, use the LIST STRUCTURE TO PRINTER command.

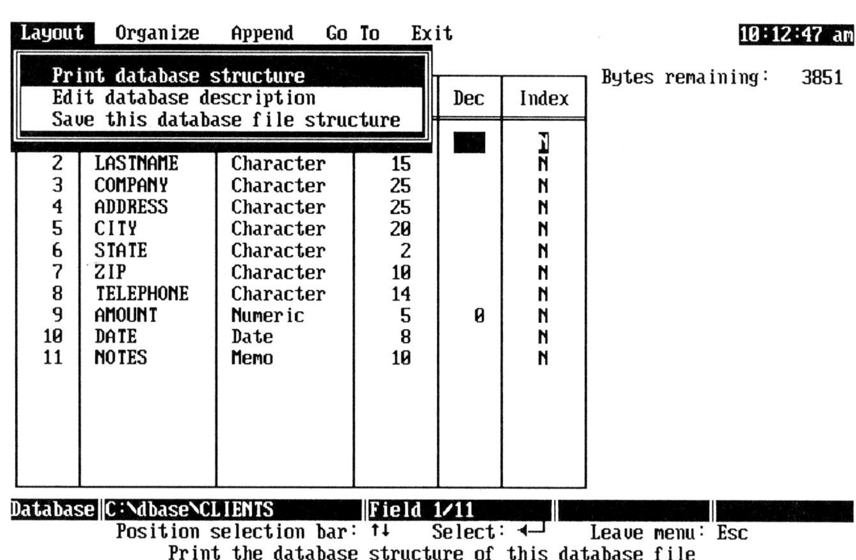

Figure 4-6. The **Print database structure** option

Entering and Changing Data

To enter or change records in a database, you need to be in edit or browse mode. There are several ways that you can get into these modes, depending on where you're starting from.

If you're starting from the Data Design screen (where you created or changed your database file structure), you can use either one of the following methods to get to edit or browse:

- After you finish creating or modifying your database file structure, press Y when dBASE IV asks you "Input data record now? (Y/N)."

- Choose the **Append** menu and then choose the **Enter records from keyboard** option.

To enter edit or browse mode from the Control Center, use either one of the following methods after highlighting a database in the Data Panel:

- Press the Data key (F2).
- Press ENTER and then select the **Display data** option.

Using Edit Mode

Edit mode allows you to add or edit one record at a time in your database. Edit mode uses the full screen and displays the database field names along the left-hand side. While in edit mode, you can display the next record by pressing PGDN and the previous record by pressing PGUP. Figure 4-7 shows a sample Edit screen.

Tip: To enter edit mode from the dot prompt, use the EDIT command.

Using the Edit screen, try entering a record in the CLIENTS database:

1. At the Firstname field, type the name **George** and press ENTER.
2. dBASE IV places you in the Lastname field. Type **Thomas** and press TAB.

Tip: The TAB key, like the ENTER key, moves you to the next field. If you prefer, use the TAB key rather than the ENTER key when you enter your data.

3. Enter George's company as **Texasville Pumps** and press ENTER.

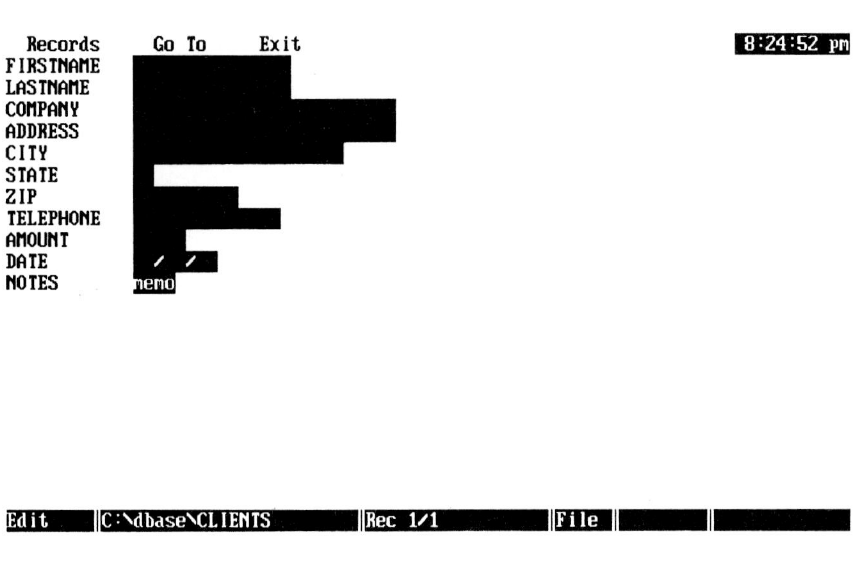

Figure 4-7. An example of the edit mode

4. Enter Texasville Pumps'address as **221 Texasville Way** and press ENTER.

5. Enter the city where George sells his pumps as **Dallas** and press ENTER.

6. Enter the abbreviation for Texas, **TX**, and press ENTER.

Notice that the bell sounded when you typed **X**. The bell sounds to let you know that you've reached the end of a field, as a typewriter bell sounds when you've reached the right margin.

Tip: To turn the bell off, so it doesn't beep every time you enter a state, return to the Control Center by pressing CTRL- END. (This saves your work.) Next, select the **Tools** menu and then the

Settings option. Then press ENTER to toggle the BELL setting to OFF. Press ESC to return to the Control Center and F2 to return to edit mode.

7. Enter George's ZIP code as **75690** and press ENTER.
8. Enter George's telephone number, **(214)453-9021** and press ENTER.
9. Enter **300** in the amount field and press ENTER.
10. Enter the date **07/16/90** in the date field and press ENTER.
11. For now, leave the Notes memo field blank and press ENTER.

When you enter the last field in the database, dBASE IV shows the prompt "===> Add new records? (Y/N)." To add new records to the database, press Y for yes. For the current example, press N for no. (You'll add more records later in browse mode. See the next section, "Using Browse Mode.")

Tip: If you move back to change a mistake you made while entering data, notice that dBASE IV overwrites your existing text as you type. This means that insert mode is off. To turn insert mode on, press the INS key. With insert mode on, characters move to the right as you enter new characters. If insert mode is on, the status bar displays "INS" in the bottom right corner of your screen.

Using Browse Mode

In browse mode, dBASE IV can display up to 17 records at a time in a tabular format. You can add and edit records in browse mode as you do in edit mode. Figure 4-8 shows an example of browse mode.

If you've entered the first record in the CLIENTS database from the edit mode, press F2 to switch to browse mode and continue the example. Press DOWN ARROW and type Y for yes at the

```
Records     Fields     Go To     Exit                                8:28:48 pm
| FIRSTNAME  | LASTNAME | COMPANY               | ADDRESS             |
| George     | Thomas   | Texasville Pumps      | 221 Texasville Way  |

Browse  |C:\dbase\CLIENTS          |Rec 1/1          |File  |      |
                          View and edit fields
```

Figure 4-8. An example of browse mode

"===>Add new records? (Y/N)" prompt. Try entering the following information:

FIRSTNAME	Paul
LASTNAME	Simon
COMPANY	dBASE Users Group
ADDRESS	1234 Primrose Lane
CITY	Sunnyvale
STATE	CA
ZIP	94086
TELEPHONE	(408)732-1637
AMOUNT	20
DATE	01/22/90

Key	Action
F1	Displays Help
F2 Data	Toggles between the browse and edit screens
F3 Previous	Moves to previous field Opens a memo field
F4 Next	Scrolls to the next field Opens a memo field
SHIFT-F8	Copies data from the previous field in current record to current field
F9 Zoom	Enlarges and shrinks memo fields
F10	Activates the menu bar
INS or CTRL-V	Turns insert mode on or off
DEL or CTRL-G	Deletes a character
BACKSPACE	Deletes character to the left of the cursor
↓ or CTRL-X	Moves cursor down one row (browse) Moves to the next field (edit)
↑ or CTRL-E	Moves cursor up one row (browse) Moves to the previous field (edit)
→ or CTRL-D	Moves cursor to the right one position
← or CTRL-S	Moves cursor to the left one position
PGUP	Displays previous screen (browse) Moves up one record (edit)
PGDN	Displays next screen (browse) Moves down one record (edit)
HOME	Moves to the first field of the current record (browse) Moves to the first character of the first field (edit)
END	Moves to the last field of the current record (browse) Moves to the end of the current field (edit)
TAB	Moves to the next field

Table 4-1. Edit and Browse Navigation Keys

Key	Action
SHIFT-TAB	Moves to the previous field
ENTER	Moves to the next field
ESC or CTRL-Q	Leave browse or edit screen withoutsaving changes
CTRL-→ or CTRL-F	Moves cursor to the beginning of the next word
CTRL-← or CTRL-A	Moves cursor to the beginning of the previous word
CTRL-PGUP	Moves to the same field in the first record
CTRL-PGDN	Moves to the same field in thelast record
CTRL-HOME	Moves into a memo field
CTRL-END or CTRL-W	Saves changes and leaves the browse or edit screen or a memo field
CTRL-T	Deletes from the cursor position to the beginning of the next word
CTRL-Y	Deletes from the right of the cursor position to the end of the current field

Table 4-1. Edit and Browse Navigation Keys (*continued*)

NOTES	Leave the Notes memo field blank for now. Memo fields are explained later in this chapter.

Tip: To enter browse mode from the dot prompt, use the BROWSE command.

Table 4-1 lists the navigation keys for the browse mode.

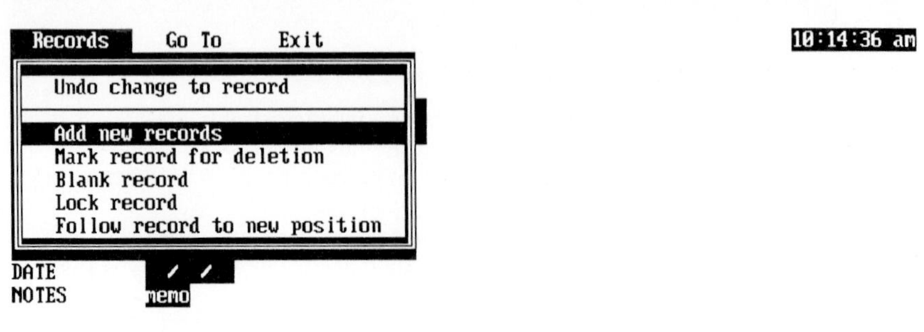

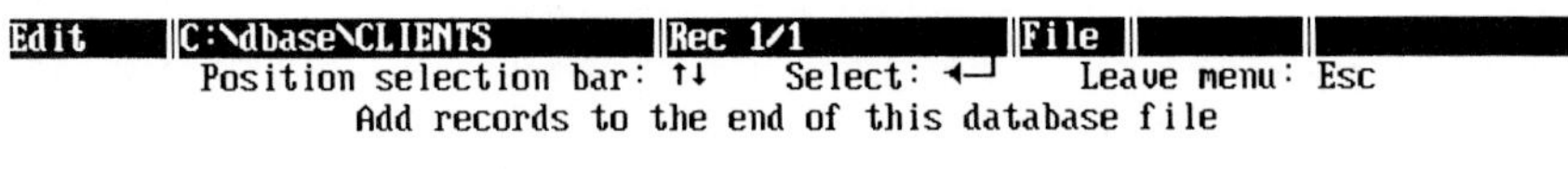

Figure 4-9. The **Records** menu in the edit mode

Adding Records in Edit or Browse Mode

You can add new records in either the edit or browse modes by highlighting the last field in the last record in the database and pressing DOWN ARROW. A prompt appears, "===>Add new records? (Y/N)." To add new records, press Y for yes.

You can also add records to a database by using the **Add new records** option from the **Records** menu while in edit or browse mode. For example, suppose you're working with the CLIENTS database in the browse mode and you want to add new records. If you open the **Records** menu and select the **Add new records** option, dBASE IV adds a blank record to the end of the database and places the cursor in the first field of that record. You can then input the data for that record. Figure 4-9 shows the options available from the **Records** menu.

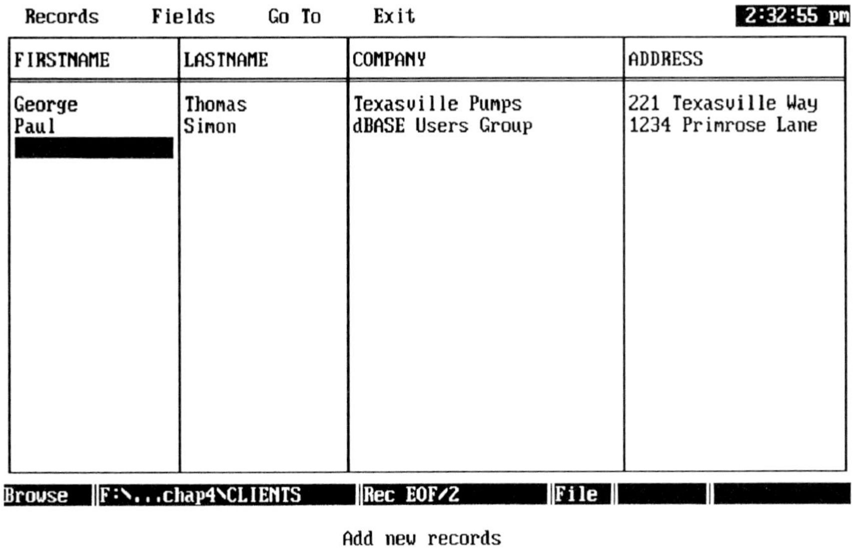

```
Records     Fields     Go To     Exit                                2:32:55 pm
┌──────────────┬──────────────┬───────────────────────┬───────────────────┐
│FIRSTNAME     │LASTNAME      │COMPANY                │ADDRESS            │
├──────────────┼──────────────┼───────────────────────┼───────────────────┤
│George        │Thomas        │Texasville Pumps       │221 Texasville Way │
│Paul          │Simon         │dBASE Users Group      │1234 Primrose Lane │
│              │              │                       │                   │
└──────────────┴──────────────┴───────────────────────┴───────────────────┘
Browse  ║F:\...chap4\CLIENTS   ║Rec EOF/2       ║File ║
                          Add new records
```

Figure 4-10. Adding a record to the CLIENTS database

Tip: You can use the APPEND command from the dot prompt to add records to the end of a database.

SHIFT-F8—The Ditto Key

Suppose the information that you're entering is the same from one record to the next. By pressing SHIFT-F8, the Ditto key, you can copy the information from a field in the previous record to the same field in the current record.

For example, suppose you've entered the first two records in the CLIENTS database and you're in browse mode. You've also added a new blank record to the end of the database by pressing Y at the "===>Add new records? (Y/N)" prompt. Your screen should look like Figure 4-10. To copy the value in the Firstname field of the second record to the third record, place the cursor in the

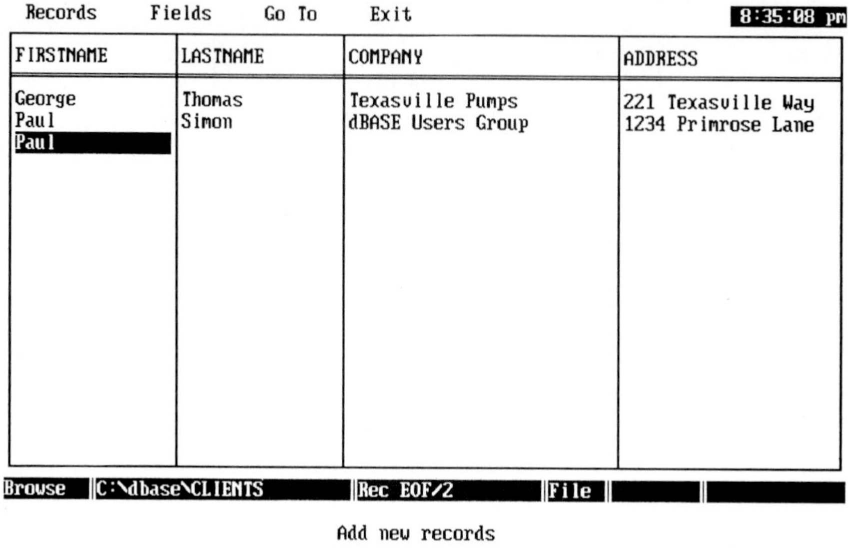

Records Fields Go To Exit 8:35:08 pm

FIRSTNAME	LASTNAME	COMPANY	ADDRESS
George	Thomas	Texasville Pumps	221 Texasville Way
Paul	Simon	dBASE Users Group	1234 Primrose Lane
Paul			

Browse | C:\dbase\CLIENTS | Rec EOF/2 | File

Add new records

Figure 4-11. The results of SHIFT-F8 (Ditto key)

Firstname field of the third record and press SHIFT-F8. The name Paul will appear in the third record. Figure 4-11 shows the results.

Try adding the information in Figures 4-12 and 4-13 to your CLIENTS database. If you enter this information, you can use the CLIENTS database to help you understand the examples in the remainder of the chapter.

Saving Your Data from Edit or Browse Mode

When you've finished entering data from edit or browse mode, you can save your work and return to the Control Center in any one of the following ways:

- Press CTRL-END.
- Press CTRL-W.
- Choose the **Exit** option from the **Exit** menu.

To leave edit or browse mode *without* saving your work, press ESC.

Using a Database

With several operations in the Control Center, you must explicitly open a database before you can perform an operation with it. For

Records Fields Go To Exit 4:30:56 pm

FIRSTNAME	LASTNAME	COMPANY	ADDRESS
George	Thomas	Texasville Pumps	221 Texasville Way
Paul	Simon	dBASE Users Group	1234 Primrose Lane
Paul	Shaffer	Texas Connections	890 Circle Street
Sherman	Mc Coy	Mc Coy Instruments	876 Bradford Street
Owen	Meany	Meany Intl Parcel Service	6711 Waites Street
John	McCrae	Rhode Island Research	9001 Frost Way
Zeb	Smith	Smith, Smith & Smith	512 Blackhawk Avenue
Kim	Smith	Smith, Smith & Smith	7950 Park Avenue
Diana	Jones	Rayman and Associates	1000 Frontage Road
Steven	Hill	Micro Processes Inc.	36800 Luau Lane
Adene	Smith	Smith, Smith & Smith	2948 El Camino Real
Kilgore	Trout	Ashton-Trout	9743 Pine Ave
Melissa	Williams	Lettuce Development Corp	640 Nashua Court
Jake	van de Kammps	Braland	1010 Main Street
Nathan	Zuckerman	Microshop	43000 Rainbow Drive

Browse C:\dbase\CLIENTS Rec 1/15 File Ins

View and edit fields

Figure 4-12. Part 1 of the CLIENTS database

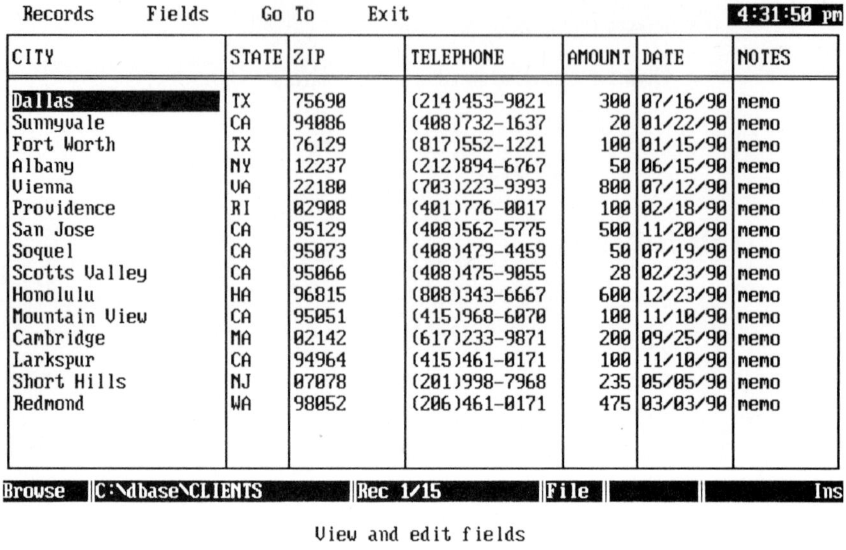

Records Fields Go To Exit 4:31:50 pm

CITY	STATE	ZIP	TELEPHONE	AMOUNT	DATE	NOTES
Dallas	TX	75690	(214)453-9021	300	07/16/90	memo
Sunnyvale	CA	94086	(408)732-1637	20	01/22/90	memo
Fort Worth	TX	76129	(817)552-1221	100	01/15/90	memo
Albany	NY	12237	(212)894-6767	50	06/15/90	memo
Vienna	VA	22180	(703)223-9393	800	07/12/90	memo
Providence	RI	02908	(401)776-0017	100	02/18/90	memo
San Jose	CA	95129	(408)562-5775	500	11/20/90	memo
Soquel	CA	95073	(408)479-4459	50	07/19/90	memo
Scotts Valley	CA	95066	(408)475-9055	20	02/23/90	memo
Honolulu	HA	96815	(808)343-6667	600	12/23/90	memo
Mountain View	CA	95051	(415)968-6070	100	11/10/90	memo
Cambridge	MA	02142	(617)233-9871	200	09/25/90	memo
Larkspur	CA	94964	(415)461-0171	100	11/10/90	memo
Short Hills	NJ	07078	(201)998-7968	235	05/05/90	memo
Redmond	WA	98052	(206)461-0171	475	03/03/90	memo

Browse C:\dbase\CLIENTS Rec 1/15 File Ins

View and edit fields

Figure 4-13. Part 2 of the CLIENTS database

example, before you can create a report (using the Reports Panel) or labels (using the Labels Panel), you must open a database.

To open a database, highlight the file you've loaded in the Data Panel and press ENTER. Then select the **Use file** option. Notice that the database now appears above the line next to the **<create>** option in the Data Panel.

In many operations from the Control Center, your database gets opened automatically. For example, to add or edit records, just highlight a file in the Data Panel and press F2. dBASE IV will open the file automatically and then enter edit or browse mode.

In general, the Control Center will tell you when you need to open a database before performing an operation. Use the **Use file** option in this situation.

Tip: To open a file from the dot prompt, enter the USE command.

Closing a Database

dBASE requires that you close your database before you can perform various operations. For example, you cannot delete an open database.

To close a database, highlight an open file in the Data Panel and press ENTER. Select the **Close file** option, and the database now appears below the line under the **<create>** option in the Data Panel.

In general, whenever you need to close a database to perform an operation, the Control Center will tell you. When it does, use the **Close file** option.

Tip: To close a file from the dot prompt, enter the CLOSE command. Enter the CLOSE DATABASES command to close several open database files at once.

Controlling Fields in Browse Mode

dBASE IV offers several ways for controlling fields while in browse mode. For example, you can lock fields on the left or "freeze" fields for editing. You can also blank and resize fields. All of these options are available from the **Fields** menu in browse mode. Figure 4-14 shows the **Fields** menu options, which are described in the sections that follow.

Locking Fields

If you select the **Lock fields on left** option from the **Fields** menu, you can "fix" a specified number of fields when you scroll to the right. When you select this option, dBASE IV prompts you to enter the number of fields on the left to lock. Using this option, you can view and edit two or more divergent fields on the same screen.

For example, suppose you are working with the CLIENTS database in browse mode and you want to view simultaneously the

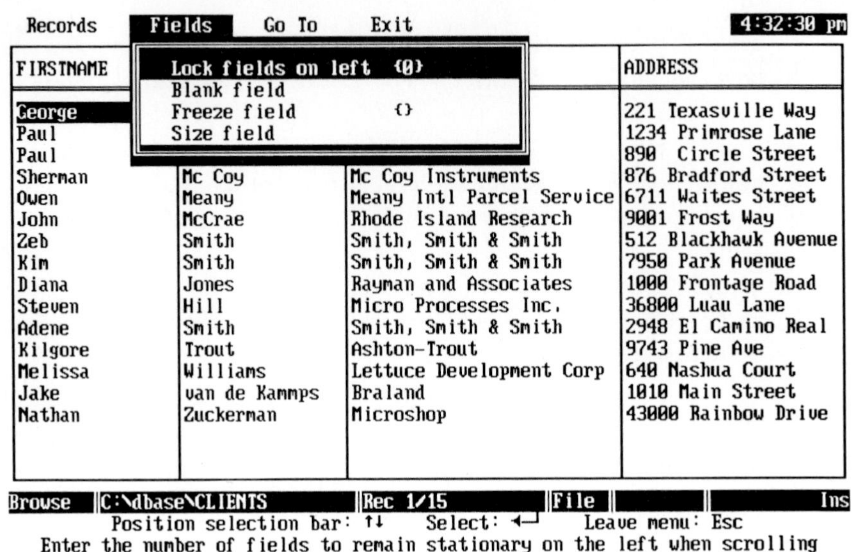

Figure 4-14. The **Fields** menu

Firstnames, Lastnames, and telephone numbers of your clients. To do so, select the **Lock fields on left** option from the **Fields** menu. When dBASE prompts you to "Enter the number of fields to remain stationary," enter **2**. When you use TAB to move to the Telephone field, notice that the first two fields remain fixed. Your screen now displays your your clients' names and telephone numbers, as illustrated in Figure 4-15.

To reset dBASE IV so that the fields are no longer locked on the left, select the **Lock fields on left** option from the **Fields** menu and enter **0** for the number of fields to lock.

Freezing a Field

At times you'll want to change one field in several records. You can edit the data in a single field by selecting the **Freeze field** option

```
Records     Fields     Go To     Exit                                      4:34:07 pm
```

FIRSTNAME	LASTNAME	STATE	ZIP	TELEPHONE	AMOUNT	DATE
George	Thomas	TX	75690	(214)453-9021	300	07/16/9
Paul	Simon	CA	94086	(408)732-1637	20	01/22/9
Paul	Shaffer	TX	76129	(817)552-1221	100	01/15/9
Sherman	Mc Coy	NY	12237	(212)894-6767	50	06/15/9
Owen	Meany	VA	22180	(703)223-9393	800	07/12/9
John	McCrae	RI	02908	(401)776-0017	100	02/18/9
Zeb	Smith	CA	95129	(408)562-5775	500	11/20/9
Kim	Smith	CA	95073	(408)479-4459	50	07/19/9
Diana	Jones	CA	95066	(408)475-9055	28	02/23/9
Steven	Hill	HA	96815	(808)343-6667	600	12/23/9
Adene	Smith	CA	95051	(415)968-6070	100	11/10/9
Kilgore	Trout	MA	02142	(617)233-9871	200	09/25/9
Melissa	Williams	CA	94964	(415)461-0171	100	11/10/9
Jake	van de Kammps	NJ	07078	(201)998-7968	235	05/05/9
Nathan	Zuckerman	WA	98052	(206)461-0171	475	03/03/9

```
Browse  C:\dbase\CLIENTS    Rec 1/15    File                Ins
                    View and edit fields
```

Figure 4-15. The CLIENTS database showing the Telephone field with the first two fields locked

from the **Fields** menu. When you select this option, dBASE prompts you for the name of the field to freeze. When you enter the name, the cursor jumps to that field (if it isn't there already), and you can move between entries in the field by using the TAB, ENTER, RIGHT ARROW, or LEFT ARROW keys.

For example, suppose you're updating the phone numbers in the CLIENTS database and you want to change several of the area codes in the Telephone field to 212. Begin by selecting the **Freeze field** option from the **Fields** menu. When dBASE IV prompts you for a field to freeze, enter **Telephone**. You can then move freely among the Telephone field entries. You cannot, however, move outside of the Telephone field.

To deactivate the **Freeze field** setting so you can edit other fields, unfreeze the field by selecting this option again and deleting the field name.

Sizing a Field

To temporarily change the size of a column on the Browse screen, use the **Size Field** option from the **Fields** menu. After choosing this option, you can use the RIGHT ARROW and LEFT ARROW keys to change the current field's width. Once you've expanded or contracted the field to the desired column size, press ENTER to lock in the size.

For example, to change the size of the Lastname field in the CLIENTS database, move the cursor to that field, select the **Size field** option, and use the RIGHT ARROW or LEFT ARROW to stretch or shrink the column size. When you've arrived at the desired size, press ENTER to lock it in.

Eliminating the Contents of a Field

If you've made a mistake while entering a field, you can start over by selecting the **Blank field** option from the **Fields** menu. Selecting this option deletes the entry in the current field. You can also blank part of a field by pressing CTRL-Y where you would like to begin correcting your entry. This deletes all the characters from the cursor position to the end of that field.

For example, try moving to the Firstname field in the third record of the CLIENTS database. When you select the **Blank field** option from the **Fields** menu, dBASE erases Paul.

Controlling Records in Browse or Edit Mode

dBASE IV gives you several tools for controlling records while in edit or browse mode. For example, you can undo a change to a record, mark a record for deletion, blank a record, or lock a record. All these options are available from the **Records** menu, shown in Figure 4-16.

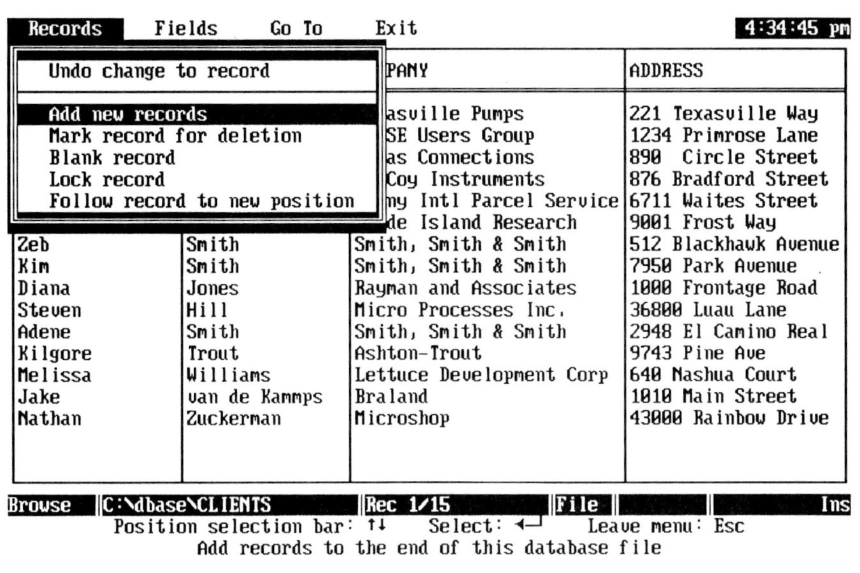

Figure 4-16. The **Records** menu in the browse mode

Undoing a Change to a Record

You can easily reverse a change you've made to a record. dBASE IV saves any changes you've made to the current record only after you leave the record or exit the browse or edit mode. To undo a change in the current record, leave the cursor in the record, select the **Records** menu, and then select the **Undo change to record** option. dBASE will abandon all the changes made to the current record, not just the current field. If you haven't made any changes to the current record, the **Undo change to record** option is shaded, indicating that there are no changes to undo. You can also abandon a record without recording changes by pressing CTRL-Q or ESC.

If you haven't left the third record in the CLIENTS database, try undoing the last change you made, which erased the name Paul.

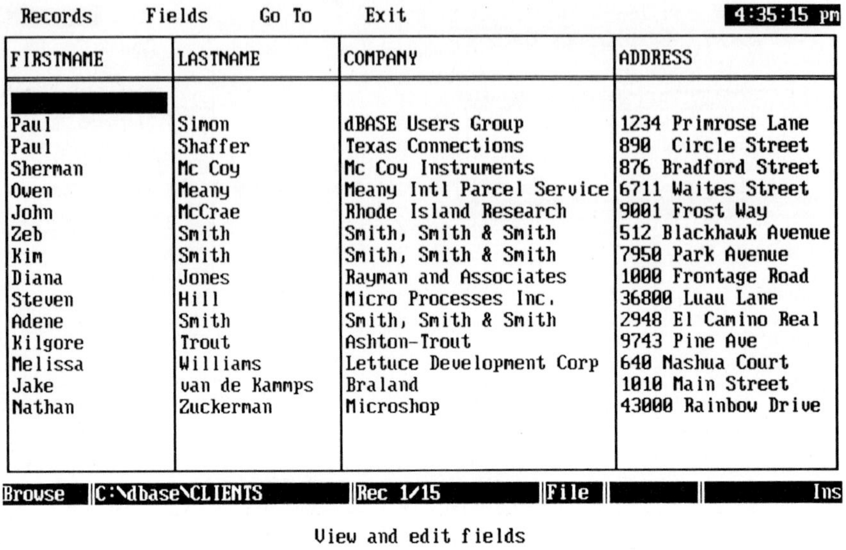

Records Fields Go To Exit 4:35:15 pm

FIRSTNAME	LASTNAME	COMPANY	ADDRESS
Paul	Simon	dBASE Users Group	1234 Primrose Lane
Paul	Shaffer	Texas Connections	890 Circle Street
Sherman	Mc Coy	Mc Coy Instruments	876 Bradford Street
Owen	Meany	Meany Intl Parcel Service	6711 Waites Street
John	McCrae	Rhode Island Research	9001 Frost Way
Zeb	Smith	Smith, Smith & Smith	512 Blackhawk Avenue
Kim	Smith	Smith, Smith & Smith	7950 Park Avenue
Diana	Jones	Rayman and Associates	1000 Frontage Road
Steven	Hill	Micro Processes Inc.	36800 Luau Lane
Adene	Smith	Smith, Smith & Smith	2948 El Camino Real
Kilgore	Trout	Ashton-Trout	9743 Pine Ave
Melissa	Williams	Lettuce Development Corp	640 Nashua Court
Jake	van de Kammps	Braland	1010 Main Street
Nathan	Zuckerman	Microshop	43000 Rainbow Drive

Browse C:\dbase\CLIENTS Rec 1/15 File Ins

View and edit fields

Figure 4-17. The first record blanked before selecting **Undo record change**

Eliminating the Contents of a Record

To delete data from every field in a record, open the **Records** menu and select the **Blank record** option. When you select this option, the entire record appears blank.

To test this option, try eliminating the first record in the CLIENTS database while in browse mode. If you want to restore the contents of the record before leaving browse, use the **Undo change record** option from the **Records** menu. See Figure 4-17.

Deleting Records

You delete records in two stages. First you mark the records you want to delete. Then you erase the marked records from the database.

To mark a record for deletion, select **Mark record for deletion** from the **Records** menu or press CTRL-U while highlighting the record to be deleted. After you've marked a record for deletion, the message "Del" appears on the right side of the status bar whenever you place the cursor in the record. What's more, once you've marked a record for deletion, the menu choice changes from **Mark record for deletion** to **Clear deletion mark** whenever the cursor is positioned in that record. If you select **Clear deletion mark**, dBASE unmarks the record. You can also use CTRL-U to unmark a record that is marked for deletion.

To erase the marked records, see the section, "Erasing Marked Records."

Try marking for deletion the third record in the CLIENTS database.

Tip: You can mark a record for deletion using the DELETE command at the dot prompt. This is the same as choosing the **Mark record for deletion** option from the **Records** menu.

Recalling or Unmarking All Records in a Database

You can unmark all records that are marked for deletion by pressing SHIFT-F2 (the Design key), opening the **Organize** menu, and selecting the **Unmark all records** option. dBASE will remove the "Del" messages from all the marked records.

Tip: The RECALL command is the dot prompt equivalent of selecting **Unmark all records** from the **Organize** menu.

Erasing Marked Records

To permanently erase marked records from your database, you need to pack your database. You can pack a database from the Database Design screen. To get to the Database Design screen, highlight your database from the Data Panel of the Control Center and press SHIFT-F2. To erase the marked records, select the **Orga-**

nize menu, if it isn't already open, and choose the **Erase marked records** option. Press Y when dBASE IV asks "Are your sure you want to erase all marked records?". A box appears with the word "PACK" in the upper left corner. The bottom of the box lists the total remaining records in the database.

Tip: You can enter the PACK command from the dot prompt to erase all marked records from a database file. You can also erase *all* the records in a database file by using the ZAP command from the dot prompt. When you use ZAP, only the file structure of the database remains intact. All the records are permanently lost.

Following a Record to a New Position

The **Follow a record to a new position** option in the **Records** menu is only available when you use an index. When you use an index and change a field that your database is currently indexed on, dBASE automatically changes the database order specified by the index. dBASE moves the record and the cursor to the new database position. If you want the cursor to stay at your current position rather than following the record to the new position, you can toggle the **Follow a record to a new position** off. This menu option is discussed in greater detail in Chapter 5, "Sorting and Indexing."

Locking a Record

The **Lock record** option allows you to lock records in a network environment. If you want to prevent others from changing data while you are using a record in a network environment, you can use this option to lock the record. This keeps the data from being changed as long as your cursor is in the record. For more information on the **Lock record** option, see Chapter 27.

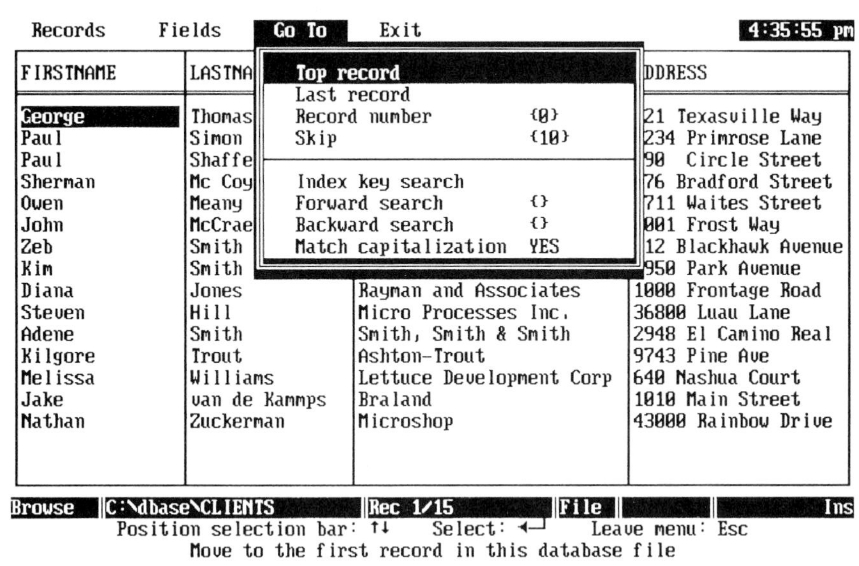

Figure 4-18. The **Go To** menu

Moving Between Records—The Go To Menu

Just as dBASE IV provides several ways to input records, it provides several ways to move between records and search for the information located within them. While in browse or edit mode, you can use the **Go To** menu to quickly move between records. For example, you can go directly to a specified record number, the top record, or the last record. You can also skip forward or backward a certain number of records in a database. In addition, the **Go To** menu has several options that help you search for information within your records. For example, you can search forward or backward in a database for a particular character string. You can also perform an index key search. Figure 4-18 shows the options available in the **Go To** menu.

Jumping to a Specific Record

Every record in a database file has a number that identifies its location in the file. Using the **Go To** menu, you can direct dBASE IV to go to any record number in your database.

The **Record number** option in the **Go To** menu lets you select a record number to go to. For example, if you enter **2** in response to this option, dBASE takes you directly to the second record of the current database. If you enter a number greater than the number of records in the database, you receive an "Illegal value" message. dBASE then returns you to the record number prompt to enter a new record number.

Tip: From the dot prompt, you can use the GO or GOTO command to move between records. For example, entering **GO 10** moves you to record number 10 in the current database.

Jumping to the First or Last Record

If you select the **Top record** option in the **Go To** menu, you can move to the first record of the current database. The **Last record** option positions you at the last record.

To test these options, try using the CLIENTS database in browse mode and moving the cursor to the Lastname field. Next, open the **Go To** menu and select the **Last record** option. dBASE stays in the same field and takes you directly to Zuckerman, the last record of your CLIENTS database. To move to the first record in the CLIENTS database, Thomas, use the **Top record** option.

Tip: You can use the GO TOP command at the dot prompt to move from any record to the first record of the database. The GO BOTTOM dot prompt command moves you to the last record in the database.

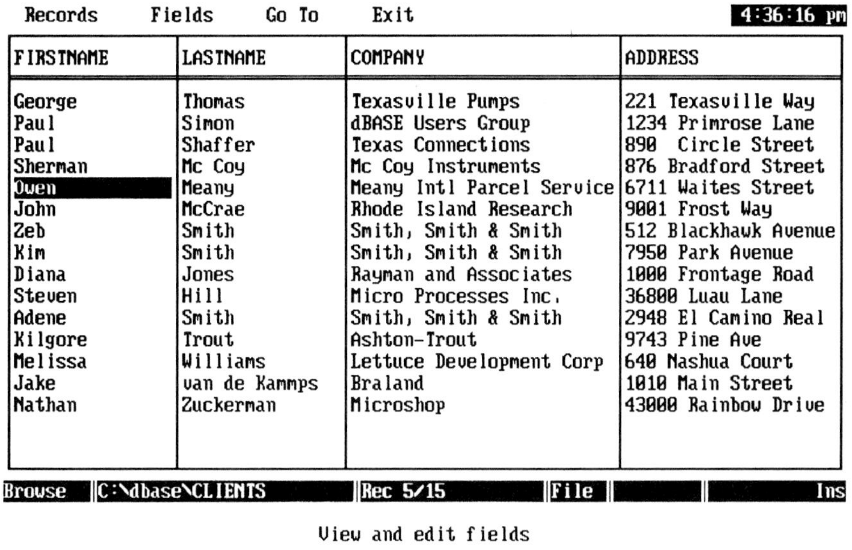

```
Records     Fields     Go To     Exit                                4:36:16 pm
```

FIRSTNAME	LASTNAME	COMPANY	ADDRESS
George	Thomas	Texasville Pumps	221 Texasville Way
Paul	Simon	dBASE Users Group	1234 Primrose Lane
Paul	Shaffer	Texas Connections	890 Circle Street
Sherman	Mc Coy	Mc Coy Instruments	876 Bradford Street
Owen	Meany	Meany Intl Parcel Service	6711 Waites Street
John	McCrae	Rhode Island Research	9001 Frost Way
Zeb	Smith	Smith, Smith & Smith	512 Blackhawk Avenue
Kim	Smith	Smith, Smith & Smith	7950 Park Avenue
Diana	Jones	Rayman and Associates	1000 Frontage Road
Steven	Hill	Micro Processes Inc.	36800 Luau Lane
Adene	Smith	Smith, Smith & Smith	2948 El Camino Real
Kilgore	Trout	Ashton-Trout	9743 Pine Ave
Melissa	Williams	Lettuce Development Corp	640 Nashua Court
Jake	van de Kammps	Braland	1010 Main Street
Nathan	Zuckerman	Microshop	43000 Rainbow Drive

```
Browse  C:\dbase\CLIENTS      Rec 5/15      File                 Ins
                        View and edit fields
```

Figure 4-19. The result of using the **Go To** menu to go to the fifth record

Skipping Between Records

You can use the **Skip** option from the **Go To** menu to move forward or backward in a database. When you use this option, you must enter a number corresponding to the number of records to move; you can use both positive or negative numbers. For example, suppose you're using the CLIENTS database and your cursor is located in the last record (record number 15). If you select the **Skip** option and enter **-10**, the record pointer moves 10 records up from your current position. In Figure 4-19, the status bar shows that the cursor is now located in the fifth record.

Tip: You can skip between records at the dot prompt using the SKIP command.

Performing an Index Key Search

If your database is indexed on a particular field, the **Index key search** option in the **Go to** menu will rapidly find matching data. This option is detailed in Chapter 5.

Searching Forward and Backward

To help you locate records in your database, dBASE IV lets you search for character strings. (One or more letters constitute a character string.) The **Forward search** and **Backward search** options in the **Go To** menu let you search for a given string. To use either of these options, you need to be in the field on which you want to perform the character string search.

For example, to test dBASE IV's searching capabilities, go to the first record in the CLIENTS database and move to the State field. Next, use the **Forward search** option from the **Go To** menu and enter the string **CA** (do not include quotes). The highlight moves to the first occurrence of the string "CA" in the State field. You can then use SHIFT-F4 (Find Next) to search forward for the next occurrence of the string, or SHIFT-F3 (Find Previous) to search backward for a previous occurrence. If dBASE can't find a match, it displays a "** Not Found **" message.

Note: When you specify a character string to search for, do not delimit the string in quotes.

Matching Capitalization

The **Go To** menu offers the **Match capitalization** option. This option lets you control whether the search string and the text that you find must have the same capitalization.

For example, suppose that you're looking for the string "dBASE Users Group" that you know resides somewhere in the Company field of the CLIENTS database. If the **Match capitalization** option is set to YES (the default) and you search for the string "Dbase Users Group" within the field, dBASE responds with the message "** Not Found **" because the capitalization doesn't match.

Access the **Match capitalization** option and toggle its value to NO by pressing either TAB or ENTER. If you repeat the search for the string "Dbase Users Group," the highlight moves directly to the record containing the "dBASE Users Group" string.

Using the ? and * Wildcards

dBASE IV lets you use the question mark (?) and the asterisk (*) as wildcards when searching for a string. The ? lets you search for a single unknown character; the * lets you search for a series of unknown characters.

For example, suppose the string "Simon" resides somewhere in the Lastname field of the CLIENTS database, but you are not sure whether the spelling is "Simon" or "Simen." To get around this problem, you can use the search string "Sim?n" to locate the string.

As another example, perhaps you don't know if the correct string is "dBASE User Group" or "Dbase Users Group" for a record in the Company field of the CLIENTS database. If you use the search string "*User*", dBASE IV will locate the record you're interested in.

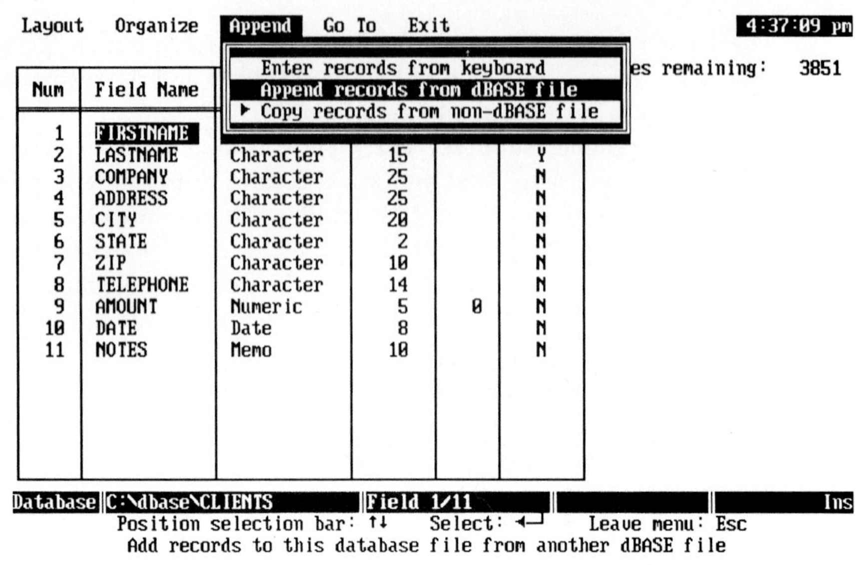

Figure 4-20. The **Append** menu

Tip: You can use the LOCATE command from the dot prompt to sequentially search a database file.

Appending Records from Other Files

At some point, you may want to add data from other files to the end of the active database file. For example, you may want to merge a mailing list on disk to the mailing list in the current database. dBASE IV lets you append records from existing dBASE IV database files as well as other types of files.

To add records from other files to the active database file, use the **Append** menu shown in Figure 4-20. As mentioned, to access the **Append** menu you must be in the Database Design screen. To

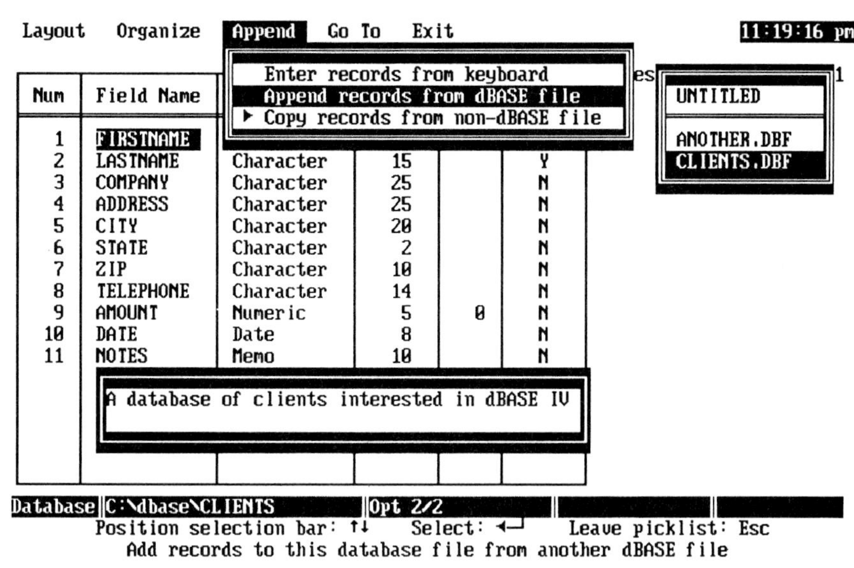

Figure 4-21. The **Append records from dBASE file** option

get to that screen, highlight a database in the Data Panel of the Control Center and press SHIFT-F2 (the Design key).

Appending Records from Other dBASE Files

You can add records from an existing dBASE IV file to the end of the active database file by using the **Append records from dBASE file** option in the **Append** menu. For this option to work, the file structures must be the same in both files. If the file structures are different, dBASE appends only those fields whose names are the same in both files. The fields do not have to be in the same order.

When you select the **Append records from dBASE file** option from the **Append** menu, a list of file names appears in a box in the upper right corner of the screen, as in Figure 4-21. Select

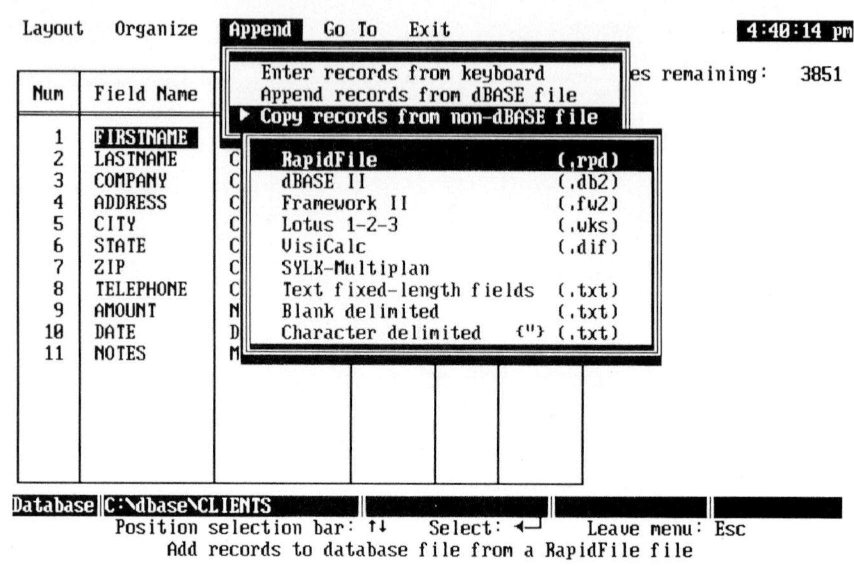

Figure 4-22. The **Copy records from non-dBASE file** menu

the database file that you want to append the records from, and dBASE appends the records to the bottom of the current database.

Tip: To append records from the dot prompt, use the APPEND FROM command.

Appending Data from External Sources

In dBASE IV, you can append data from a non-dBASE IV file by choosing the **Copy records from non-dBASE file** option from the **Append** menu. When you select this option, dBASE displays another menu showing the file types that you can use, as shown in Figure 4-22. When you select a menu item corresponding to the file type you want, dBASE IV displays a list of the available files. In order for a file name to appear in the list, it must have the proper extension corresponding to its type, as shown in Figure 4-22. If a file does not have the proper extension, you must change the extension before you can append records from it. For example, to append to the active file data from a Framework II file named FWLIST, you must save FWLIST in a Framework II format with a file extension of .FW2.

Tip: If you have a non-dBASE IV file without the proper extension, you can append the data without renaming the file. Exit from the Control Center to the dot prompt and use the APPEND FROM command. For more details on APPEND FROM, see Chapter 35.

The file structures must be the same in both files for dBASE to append records successfully. If the file structures are different, dBASE appends only those fields whose names are the same in both files. The fields do not have to be in the same order.

If a field in the non-dBASE IV file is larger than the same field in the active database, dBASE IV ignores any excess characters. Also, in numeric fields, numbers that are larger than the field width are converted to asterisks.

If you choose the **Text fixed-length fields**, **Blank delimited**, or **Character delimited** option from the **Copy records from non-dBASE file** menu, dBASE IV lists only the files with an extension of .TXT.

If you select the **Character delimited** option, dBASE prompts you to choose a delimiter. (A *delimiter* is a character used to separate one item or set of data from another.) Use the arrow keys to select a delimiter from the list of available characters.

Using Memo Fields

When you're working in browse or edit mode, you can easily add text to a memo field. As mentioned, a memo field is itself only ten characters long, but it contains a pointer to a separate text file. By storing your text in a separate file, you save memory. You can effectively store a large amount of information for one record, without reserving the same space for records that don't need it.

When you add a memo field to a database's file structure, dBASE IV automatically creates a separate memo file. That file bears the same name as the database but has a .DBT extension. If you move a database file to a new directory, you must also move its associated memo file. Otherwise, dBASE IV will not be able to find your memo field text.

If you try to use a database's memo field when the memo file is not present, dBASE IV asks if you want to create an empty memo file. If you already have a memo file for this database, press N for no and copy the memo file into the directory where your database resides. If you choose yes, you won't be able to use the old memo file with the database, even if you copy the old memo file over the new one.

Memo Markers

Every memo field contains a *memo marker*. If the memo field contains any data, the marker appears as the word **MEMO** in uppercase. If the memo field is empty, the memo marker appears in lowercase as **memo**. For example, the memo marker shown in Figure 4-23 shows that the current record contains some text in its memo field.

As you learn more dBASE IV, you'll discover that when you design customized forms you can display a memo field on the Edit screen as either a marker or an open window. Memo fields that appear as open windows are called *static memo windows*, since they can't be changed into memo markers. Use static memo windows when you want the information in memo fields to be displayed each time you move to a record. For more on creating and using memo windows, see Chapter 9, "Creating Input Forms."

Entering the Memo Field

To enter text in a memo from edit or browse mode, you must first place your cursor on the memo field. You can then open a memo

```
Records    Fields    Go To    Exit                                          8:05:44 pm
```

CITY	STATE	ZIP	TELEPHONE	AMOUNT	DATE	NOTES
Dallas	TX	75690	(214)453-9021	300	07/16/90	MEMO
Sunnyvale	CA	94086	(408)732-1637	20	01/22/90	memo
Fort Worth	TX	76129	(817)552-1221	100	01/15/90	memo
Albany	NY	12237	(212)894-6767	50	06/15/90	memo
Vienna	VA	22180	(703)223-9393	800	07/12/90	memo
Providence	RI	02908	(401)776-0017	100	02/18/90	memo
San Jose	CA	95129	(408)562-5775	500	11/20/90	memo
Soquel	CA	95073	(408)479-4459	50	07/19/90	memo
Scotts Valley	CA	95066	(408)475-9055	28	02/23/90	memo
Honolulu	HA	96815	(808)343-6667	600	12/23/90	memo
Mountain View	CA	95051	(415)968-6070	100	11/10/90	memo
Cambridge	MA	02142	(617)233-9871	200	09/25/90	memo
Larkspur	CA	94964	(415)461-0171	100	11/10/90	memo
Short Hills	NJ	07078	(201)998-7968	235	05/05/90	memo
Redmond	WA	98052	(206)461-0171	475	03/03/90	memo

```
Browse  C:\dbase\CLIENTS        Rec 1/15        File

                    View and edit fields
```

Figure 4-23. A memo field that contains memo text

window for that field. Once you open the memo window, your screen should look like the one in Figure 4-24. The text that you enter in the memo window is stored in the memo file for that record.

You can use any of the following methods to open a memo window:

- Position the cursor on a memo field and press CTRL-HOME.
- Position the cursor on a memo field and press F9 (the Zoom key).
- When you move to a memo field with F3 (Previous) or F4 (Next), dBASE IV automatically opens the memo window.

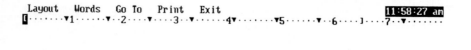

Figure 4-24. A blank memo window

Exiting the Memo Field and Saving Changes

You can save your changes with any one of the following options:

- Press CTRL-END.
- Press F9.
- Select the **Save changes and exit** option from the **Exit** menu.

You can also save the contents of a memo field without exiting the memo field window. To do this, select the **Save this memo field** option from the **Layout** menu.

Exiting the Memo Field and Abandoning Changes

You can leave the memo field window without saving changes you have made in any one of the following ways:

- Select the **Abandon changes and exit** option from the **Exit** menu.
- Press ESC.
- Press CTRL-Q.

dBASE IV confirms that you want to abandon any changes made to the memo text before exiting.

Entering Memo Text

When you open a dBASE memo field, you're brought to a 65-character-wide work surface. This work surface uses the dBASE IV Text Editor, the same editor that you use in a variety of situations in dBASE IV. The sections that follow give you some background on the Text Editor and then explain how to use its different options to enter and edit text.

Most of the examples in this section involve entering and editing memos. However, the same concepts apply whenever you enter text with the dBASE IV Text Editor. For example, if you are creating a program using MODIFY COMMAND from the dot prompt, you use the keys and menus you use when you enter memo text. As you use the Text Editor in later chapters, return to this chapter for more detailed information.

Tip: You can edit your memo fields with an external word processor by changing the WP setting in your CONFIG.DB file. If you use an external editor, be sure to save your files in an ASCII format. See Chapter 35 for more on this topic.

The dBASE IV Text Editor

The dBASE IV Text Editor provides two text editing modes: word wrap and layout.

dBASE IV uses the *word wrap mode* when you create programs, text files, macros, and memo fields. Word wrap wraps your text around to the next line when it extends over the right margin, just like a traditional word processor. When you remove or add a portion of text, the editor automatically rearranges the subsequent text.

dBASE IV uses the *layout mode* when you create custom input forms, reports, and labels. In layout mode, dBASE treats the screen like a designer's desk top or work surface. You build different objects in this mode and then rearrange them. For example, you design report bands that control where certain data appears on the printed page. In layout mode, text does not automatically wrap to the next line.

Actually, the term "word wrap mode" is a misnomer. When you're creating programs (with MODIFY COMMAND) or text files (with MODIFY FILE), text doesn't automatically wrap to the next line. Nor would you want it to. Therefore, you think of the two modes as a *writing* mode and a *drawing* mode. You use the writing mode to enter text and the drawing mode to place objects on the screen or printed page.

Using Word Wrap Mode

When you first enter word wrap mode, the cursor is in the upper left corner of the screen, and you can immediately begin entering text. Figure 4-25 shows some sample text.

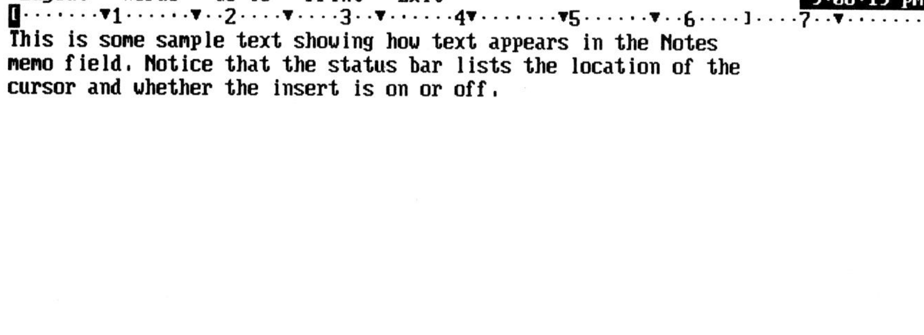

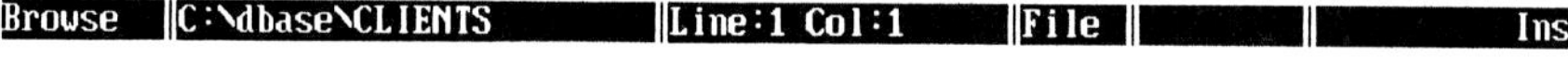

Figure 4-25. Sample text in a memo field

Tip: To turn insert mode off and on, use the INS key. When insert is on (the default), the cursor appears as a square block, and you can see an "INS" message at the right of the status bar. If insert mode is off, the cursor appears as a flat line.

When insert is on, words automatically reformat themselves in word wrap mode when you add or delete characters. If you turn

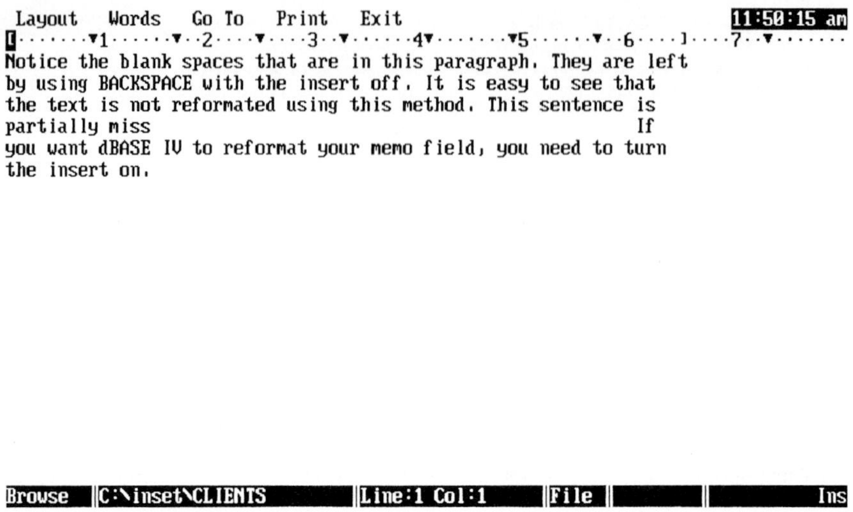

```
 Layout   Words   Go To   Print   Exit                                        11:50:15 am
[·······▼1······▼··2····▼····3··▼······4▼·······▼5······▼··6····]····7··▼·······
Notice the blank spaces that are in this paragraph. They are left
by using BACKSPACE with the insert off. It is easy to see that
the text is not reformated using this method. This sentence is
partially miss                                              If
you want dBASE IV to reformat your memo field, you need to turn
the insert on.









Browse  |C:\inset\CLIENTS          |Line:1 Col:1     |File |        |               Ins
```

Figure 4-26. The results of setting insert off and pressing BACKSPACE

insert off and press BACKSPACE, dBASE replaces the character to the left of the cursor with a blank space, and all the other text remains in its original position, as illustrated in Figure 4-26.

To get a feel for the word wrap mode works, enter the text in Figure 4-27 into George Thomas's memo field in the CLIENTS database. As you enter the text, experiment with insert on and off.

Tip: For a complete list of the keys available in word wrap mode, see Table 3-1 in Chapter 3.

Moving, Copying, and Deleting Text

Before you can move, copy, or delete text, you need to select it. To select text, press F6, the Extend Select key, and dBASE highlights the character your cursor is on. You can use the arrow keys to

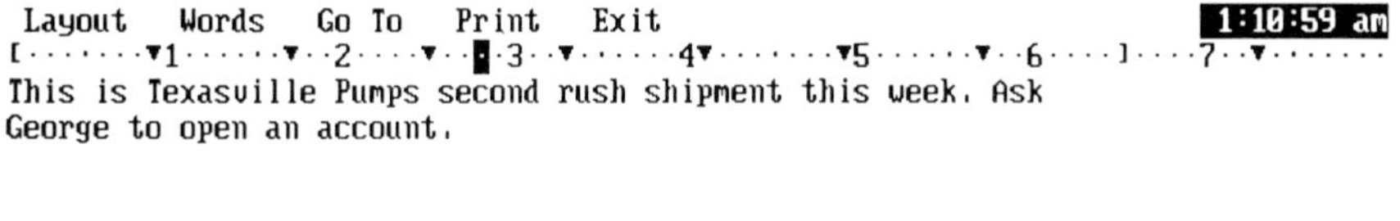

Figure 4-27. Text to add to George Thomas's memo field

extend the selection forward or backward. Press ENTER to complete your selection. You can then move the cursor to any other position in the text without losing the highlighted selection. You can cancel an extended selection by pressing ESC.

To practice moving a selection, move the cursor to the beginning of the first sentence in George Thomas's memo field. Press F6 (Extend Select) to select text, as shown in Figure 4-28. Use RIGHT ARROW to highlight the sentence "This is Texasville Pumps second rush shipment this week," and press ENTER to finish your extended selection. To move the highlighted text, position the cursor at the end of the last sentence, "Ask George to open an account," and press F7 (Move). dBASE moves the text to the new position.

To copy an extended selection, use F6 (Extend Select) to select a portion of text, position the cursor at the new location, and press

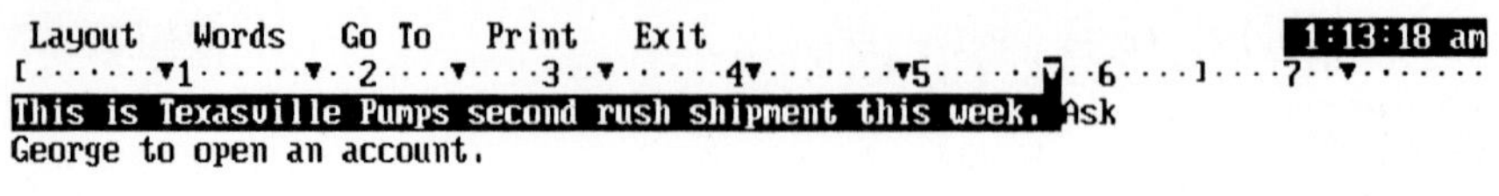

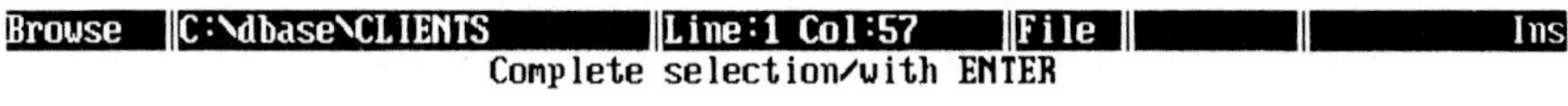

Figure 4-28. Text selected with F6 (Extend Select)

F8 (Copy). dBASE copies the highlighted section to the new position.

To delete a selection, use F6 (Extend Select) to select your text, and press DEL. dBASE responds with the prompt "Press y to perform the block deletion." When you press Y, dBASE deletes the highlighted selection from your text.

The Word Wrap Menu

When you use the Text Editor in word wrap mode, its menu bar consists of the **Layout**, **Words**, **Go To**, **Print**, and **Exit** menus. The sections that follow describe each of these menus.

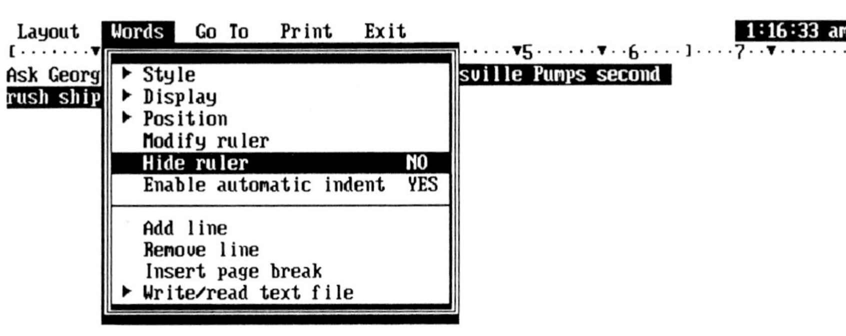

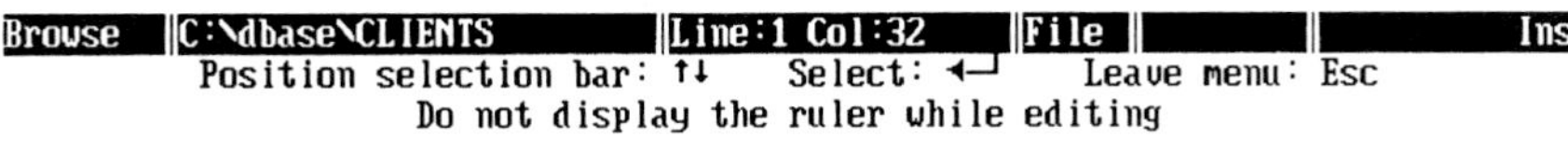

Figure 4-29. The **Words** menu

The Layout Menu

When you are editing a memo field, the **Layout** menu displays the single option **Save this memo field**. This option lets you save your memo text, but, unlike CTRL-END, F9, or the **Save changes and exit** option from the **Exit** menu, this selection allows you to continue editing the memo field.

The Words Menu

When you are editing a memo field, the **Words** menu displays the **Hide ruler**, **Enable automatic indent**, **Add line**, **Remove line**, **Insert page break**, and **Write/read text file** options, as shown in Figure 4-29. All of these options are available when you use the word wrap work surface and are discussed later in this chapter.

The **Words** menu has four other options—**Style**, **Display**, **Position**, and **Modify ruler**—that appear shadowed, indicating that they are not available while you are creating and editing memo fields.

- Use the **Style** option to select print styles, such as bold or underline, in reports and labels. You can read more about the **Style** option in Chapter 10.
- Use the **Display** option when you design forms on the display screen. You can use it to customize the color settings of dBASE. The **Display** option appears exactly like the **Display** option in the the **Tools/Settings** menu discussed in Chapter 14.
- You can use the **Position** option when creating or modifying forms reports and labels. This option allows you to align text either to the right, left, or center in the current margins. For more information on the **Position** option, see Chapter 9.
- The **Modify ruler** option allows you to modify margins, paragraph indentation, and tab stops. You can use this option when you are creating forms, reports, and labels. For more on the **Modify ruler** option, see Chapter 9.

Controlling the Ruler—the Hide ruler Option dBASE IV displays a ruler at the top of the memo screen directly below the menu bar, as shown in Figure 4-30. The ruler is divided into inch increments and displays tab positions with half-diamond arrow markers. The left bracket at the beginning of the ruler and the right bracket near the end of the ruler identify the margins.

When you're entering a memo field, the **Modify ruler** option is shaded because it is unavailable. However, you can choose to display or hide the ruler. To hide the ruler, highlight the **Hide ruler** option in the **Words** menu and press ENTER. The ruler disappears from the editing screen. **Hide ruler** is a toggle option. To redisplay the ruler, select **Hide ruler** again, and the ruler reappears on the screen.

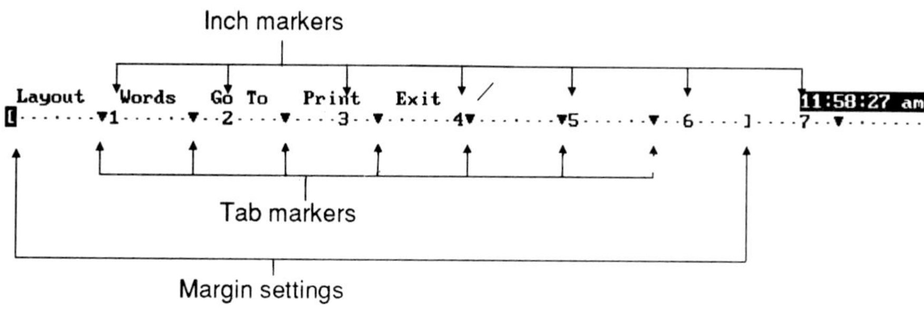

Figure 4-30. The parts of the memo screen ruler

Indenting Text — the Enable automatic indent Option

In word wrap mode, your text can be treated in two different ways when you press the TAB key to indent. When **Enable automatic indent** is set to Yes (the default), your text is automatically indented. When you begin a new paragraph, it begins where the previous paragraph began. For example, Figure 4-31 shows what happens if you use TAB to indent three paragraphs in the word wrap work surface with the **Enable automatic indent** set to Yes.

If you set the **Enable automatic indent** option to No, your text wraps around to the beginning of the line, as you can see in Figure 4-32.

Tip: Suppose you use the TAB key to indent a paragraph in the dBASE IV Text Editor and the **Enable automatic indent** option is set to Yes. It may seem impossible to move the next paragraph back to the previous tab position, but actually it's quite easy. Press SHIFT-TAB to move the text back to the previous tab position. You can use SHIFT-TAB to move to the previous tab stop whether the **Enable automatic indent** option is set to Yes or No.

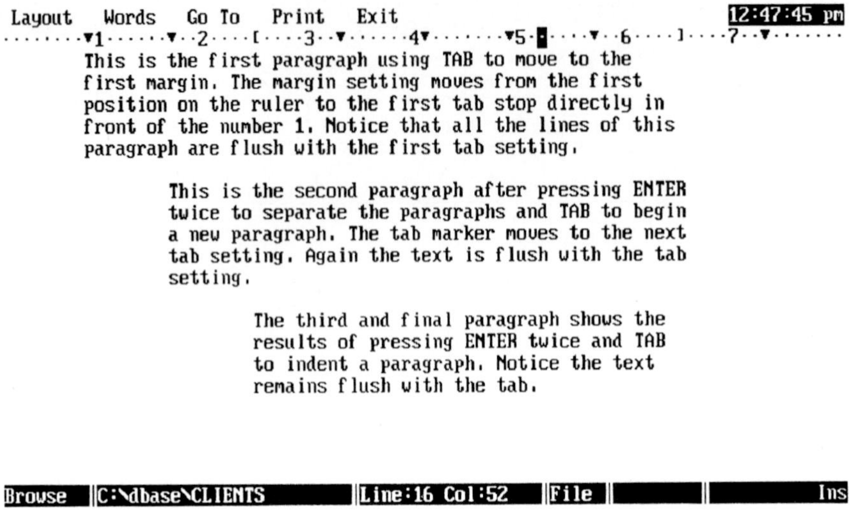

```
Layout   Words   Go To   Print   Exit                                    12:47:45 pm
········▼1······▼··2····[····3··▼······4▼·······▼5·█····▼··6····]····7··▼·······
         This is the first paragraph using TAB to move to the
         first margin. The margin setting moves from the first
         position on the ruler to the first tab stop directly in
         front of the number 1. Notice that all the lines of this
         paragraph are flush with the first tab setting.

                 This is the second paragraph after pressing ENTER
                 twice to separate the paragraphs and TAB to begin
                 a new paragraph. The tab marker moves to the next
                 tab setting. Again the text is flush with the tab
                 setting.

                         The third and final paragraph shows the
                         results of pressing ENTER twice and TAB
                         to indent a paragraph. Notice the text
                         remains flush with the tab.
```

Figure 4-31. The results of using TAB to indent three paragraphs with the **Enable automatic indent** set to Yes

The status of the insert mode affects how the TAB key works when **Enable automatic indent** is set to Yes. If insert is toggled off, pressing TAB moves the cursor to the next available tab stop. If insert is on, pressing TAB inserts a tab character in your text and moves your text to the next available tab stop. SHIFT-TAB moves to the previous tab stop, regardless of the insert setting.

The Add line, Remove line, and Insert page break Options

The **Add line** option simply adds a line below your cursor location in the memo field. The **Remove line** option erases the current line in the memo field. The **Insert page break** option inserts a page break just above the current line.

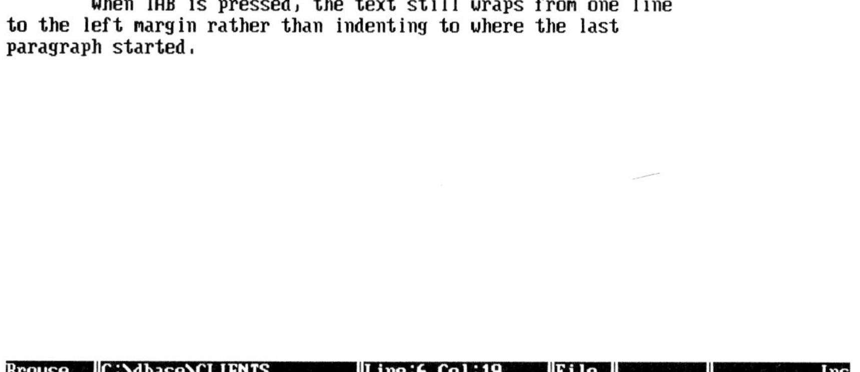
Layout Words Go To Print Exit 9:22:31 pm
This is an example of turning the Enable automatic indent to no.
This paragraph is treated like regular text in a traditional word
processor.
When TAB is pressed, the text still wraps from one line
to the left margin rather than indenting to where the last
paragraph started.
Browse C:\dbase\CLIENTS Line:6 Col:19 File Ins

Figure 4-32. The results of **Enable automatic indent** option set to No

Reading in a Text File — the Read text from file Option

Suppose you've written a letter that you want to include in your CLIENTS database. dBASE allows you to add an existing text file to a memo field.

Before you can add the letter, you must save it in an ASCII file from your word processor and give the file a .TXT extension. Next, enter the memo field that you want to have the text added to. Select the **Write/read text file** option from the **Words** menu and choose the **Read text from file** option. dBASE prompts you to enter the name of file to read. If you enter a file name that doesn't contain a .TXT extension, dBASE displays the error message "File does not exist." If you enter a file name and press ENTER, dBASE adds the contents of the file to the beginning of the current memo field.

Tip: You can use the APPEND MEMO command from the dot prompt to import an external data file into a named memo field.

Writing to a Text File — the Write selection to file Option

You may sometimes need the text in a memo field placed in another file. For example, suppose you want to copy some information in your database memo field to a letter. You can write a text file that contains the contents of your memo field by selecting the **Write/read text file** menu from the **Words** menu and choosing the **Write selection to file** option.

For example, while in George Thomas's memo field in the CLIENTS database, open the **Words** menu, select the **Write/read text file** menu, and then select the **Write selection to file** option. dBASE prompts you to enter the name of the file to write. Enter **GEORGE** as the file name and press ENTER. dBASE stores the memo field contents in a file named GEORGE.TXT. (dBASE automatically adds a .TXT extension to your file name.) If the file name already exists, dBASE displays the message "File already exists" along with the **Overwrite** and **Cancel** options.

Tip: While at the dot prompt, use the COPY MEMO command to copy the contents of a memo field to another file.

Jumping to a Line and Searching for Text—the Go To Menu

The **Go To** menu allows you to jump to a particular line number in your text or search your text for a character string. You can search for character strings as you did in the **Go To** menu in the browse and edit modes (see the earlier section, "Searching Forward and Backward"). Jumping to a line number is a little different, however.

To jump to a particular line in your text, open the **Go To** menu and select the **Go to line number** option. dBASE IV prompts you to enter a line number to move to. To track your cursor's movement, look in the status line and notice your location. For example, if you enter **15** as the number to jump to, the cursor moves to the same column location in line 15, if possible. If there aren't 15 lines available, dBASE places the cursor at the end of the file.

The Print Menu

The following is a brief description of the **Print** menu options that apply to memo fields. For more information on using the **Print** menu, see Chapter 12.

The **Begin printing** option tells dBASE to start printing. If you want dBASE to pause while printing, press CTRL-S. To cancel the printing process, press ESC.

To help you start and end pages at the proper locations, dBASE enables you to manually eject a single page with either the **Eject page now** option or the **Control of printer/New page** option.

You can print to the screen, a file, or to one of the printers you've installed by using the **Destination** option. If you choose to write to a DOS file, a file is created that contains the control codes of the printer selected in the **Printer model** option.

You can determine the quality and size of printed text and regulate form feed settings by using the **Control of printer settings** option. Among other things, you can choose to print in output quality or draft mode and you can control the number of characters printed per inch. dBASE supports four text pitches: pica, elite, condensed, and default. Default is the current printer pitch.

If you select the **Output** option, you can select portions of text or the number of copies to send to your printer.

The **Page dimensions** option helps you to define how your text is placed on a page. You can set the length of a page, line spacing, and print margins from this option.

In this chapter, you learned about dBASE IV's data types. You also learned how to create a database structure, add and edit records, and various ways to display data including locking, sizing, and freezing fields. You can now change a record and undo the change as well as mark and unmark records for deletion. You should also be familiar with all the different facets of working with memo fields.

Sorting and Indexing

FIVE

When you first enter data into your database, it may not be in an appropriate order. To rearrange your data in a more useful way, you can sort or index it. Sorting and indexing allow you to order your database according to a particular field or set of fields to more closely match your needs.

This chapter introduces sorting and indexing. It shows you how to rearrange your data in alphabetical, numerical, or chronological order using one or more fields. The main emphasis is on indexing—the most efficient and the fastest way to rearrange your data. This chapter also explains the differences between sorting and indexing and the options that each offers to help you organize your data.

Sorting a Database

When you sort a database, dBASE creates a new database file that contains the same field structure and data as your original database. However, in this new file, the records are in different positions. You can sort records in alphabetical, chronological, or

Records Fields Go To Exit 6:37:49 pm

FIRSTNAME	LASTNAME	COMPANY	ADDRESS
George	Thomas	Texasville Pumps	221 Texasville Way
Paul	Simon	dBASE Users Group	1234 Primrose Lane
Paul	Shaffer	Texas Connections	890 Circle Street
Sherman	Mc Coy	Mc Coy Instruments	876 Bradford Street
Owen	Meany	Meany Intl Parcel Service	6711 Waites Street
John	McCrae	Rhode Island Research	9001 Frost Way
Zeb	Smith	Smith, Smith & Smith	512 Blackhawk Avenue
Kim	Smith	Smith, Smith & Smith	7950 Park Avenue
Diana	Jones	Rayman and Associates	1000 Frontage Road
Steven	Hill	Micro Processes Inc.	36800 Luau Lane
Adene	Smith	Smith, Smith & Smith	2948 El Camino Real
Kilgore	Trout	Ashton-Trout	9743 Pine Ave
Melissa	Williams	Lettuce Development Corp	640 Nashua Court
Jake	van de Kammps	Braland	1010 Main Street
Nathan	Zuckerman	Microshop	43000 Rainbow Drive

Browse C:\dbase\CLIENTS Rec 1/15 File

View and edit fields

Figure 5-1. The CLIENTS database before sorting

numerical order. You determine the type and order of the sort by the fields you choose and by specifying an ascending or descending order.

For example, Figure 5-1 shows the CLIENTS database before it is sorted. Figure 5-2 shows a new database called SCLIENTS sorted on the Lastname character field. Note that the last names in SCLIENTS are all in alphabetical order.

Setting Up the Sort

Before you can sort a database, you need to be in the Database Design screen. Highlight the database's name in the Data Panel of the Control Center and press the Design key (SHIFT-F2). dBASE takes you to the Database Design screen and opens the **Organize** menu.

```
 Records     Fields     Go To     Exit                              6:40:54 pm

|FIRSTNAME  |LASTNAME     |COMPANY                   |ADDRESS              |
|Steven     |Hill         |Micro Processes Inc.      |36800 Luau Lane      |
|Diana      |Jones        |Rayman and Associates     |1000 Frontage Road   |
|Sherman    |Mc Coy       |Mc Coy Instruments        |876 Bradford Street  |
|John       |McCrae       |Rhode Island Research     |9001 Frost Way       |
|Owen       |Meany        |Meany Intl Parcel Service |6711 Waites Street   |
|Paul       |Shaffer      |Texas Connections         |890  Circle Street   |
|Paul       |Simon        |dBASE Users Group         |1234 Primrose Lane   |
|Zeb        |Smith        |Smith, Smith & Smith      |512 Blackhawk Avenue |
|Kim        |Smith        |Smith, Smith & Smith      |7950 Park Avenue     |
|Adene      |Smith        |Smith, Smith & Smith      |2948 El Camino Real  |
|George     |Thomas       |Texasville Pumps          |221 Texasville Way   |
|Kilgore    |Trout        |Ashton-Trout              |9743 Pine Ave        |
|Jake       |van de Kammps|Braland                   |1010 Main Street     |
|Melissa    |Williams     |Lettuce Development Corp  |640 Nashua Court     |
|Nathan     |Zuckerman    |Microshop                 |43000 Rainbow Drive  |

Browse  |C:\dbase\SCLIENTS   |Rec 1/15        |File |
                          View and edit fields
```

Figure 5-2. The sorted CLIENTS database named SCLIENTS

To set up the sort, select the **Sort database on field list** option from the **Organize** menu and press SHIFT-F1 to see the list of field names from which to choose. Follow these steps with the CLIENTS database; your screen should look like Figure 5-3.

Selecting a Field on Which to Sort

To select a field within the list of available fields, you can highlight the field name and press ENTER. An alternative is to type the first letter of the field name. For example, if you type **L** in the CLIENTS database, dBASE takes you to the first entry beginning with the letter "L," in this case Lastname. If more than one field begins with a particular letter, you can enter the field's second character to have dBASE search for a field name beginning with the two

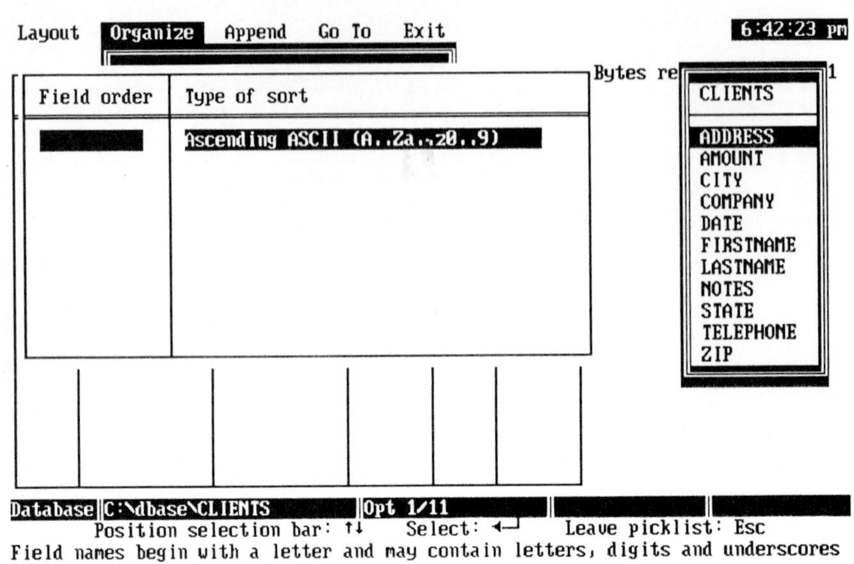

Figure 5-3. The field list displayed after SHIFT-F1

specified characters. Press ENTER and dBASE automatically adds the field to the "Field order" column.

Now that you've selected the field to sort on, you can decide how to sort your records. Move the cursor to the "Type of sort" column by pressing TAB or ENTER.

The Four Sorting Options

dBASE IV has four different sorting methods.

- **Ascending ASCII (A...Za...z0...9)** Sorts uppercase before lowercase, as in the ASCII table (see Appendix A). For example, dBASE places Williams before van de Kampps and McCrae before Meany.

- **Descending ASCII (z...aZ...A9...0)** Sorts lowercase before uppercase. For example, dBASE places van de Kampps before Williams and Meany before McCrae.
- **Ascending Dictionary (Aa...Zz0...9)** Sorts in ascending order and treats upper- and lowercase letters alike. For example, dBASE places van de Kampps before Williams and McCrae before Meany.
- **Descending Dictionary (zZ...aA9...0)** Sorts in descending order and treats upper- and lowercase letters alike. For example, dBASE places Williams before van de Kampps and Meany before McCrae.

To change the sorting method in the "Type of sort" column, press the SPACEBAR to cycle through the options. If you don't specify the type of sort, dBASE defaults to the first option, **Ascending ASCII**. If you're following the CLIENTS database example, select **Ascending Dictionary** and press CTRL-END.

Entering a Sort File Name

After you've selected a sort type, dBASE prompts you for a file name. In dBASE, you can't sort a file onto itself. Therefore, you must enter the name of a file other than the one you're currently using.

For example, to enter a new file name for the sorted version of the CLIENTS database, type **CLIENTSA** and press ENTER. dBASE IV creates a new sorted database called CLIENTSA.DBF. You now have two databases—CLIENTS and CLIENTSA—with the same information but organized differently.

To see the contents of the new CLIENTSA file, return to the Control Center and enter browse mode. First, select **Abandon changes and exit** from the **Exit** menu. This returns you to the main Control Center screen. Highlight CLIENTSA in the Data Panel and press F2 to enter browse mode. Your screen will look like Figure 5-4, with the records alphabetized by last name.

Records Fields Go To Exit 6:45:59 pm

FIRSTNAME	LASTNAME	COMPANY	ADDRESS
Steven	Hill	Micro Processes Inc.	36800 Luau Lane
Diana	Jones	Rayman and Associates	1000 Frontage Road
Sherman	Mc Coy	Mc Coy Instruments	876 Bradford Street
John	McCrae	Rhode Island Research	9001 Frost Way
Owen	Meany	Meany Intl Parcel Service	6711 Waites Street
Paul	Shaffer	Texas Connections	890 Circle Street
Paul	Simon	dBASE Users Group	1234 Primrose Lane
Zeb	Smith	Smith, Smith & Smith	512 Blackhawk Avenue
Kim	Smith	Smith, Smith & Smith	7950 Park Avenue
Adene	Smith	Smith, Smith & Smith	2948 El Camino Real
George	Thomas	Texasville Pumps	221 Texasville Way
Kilgore	Trout	Ashton-Trout	9743 Pine Ave
Jake	van de Kammps	Braland	1010 Main Street
Melissa	Williams	Lettuce Development Corp	640 Nashua Court
Nathan	Zuckerman	Microshop	43000 Rainbow Drive

Browse C:\dbase\CLIENTSA Rec 1/15 File

View and edit fields

Figure 5-4. The three Smith first name fields in unsorted order

Tip: You can sort from the dot prompt by using the SORT command. For example, the format for the SORT command you just performed to create the CLIENTSA database is

```
. SORT ON Lastname to Clientsa
```

dBASE uses an ascending dictionary order by default. You can perform a descending order sort by adding /D after the field name. You can also use the /C option to have dBASE treat both uppercase and lowercase letters alike.

Sorting on Multiple Fields

dBASE lets you sort up to ten different fields at once. To include additional fields, place them in the "Field order" column one after the other.

As you add fields to the column, remember that, dBASE IV sorts the database according to the first field, and, using those results, sorts according the second field, and so on. For example, in Figure 5-4 three people have the last name of Smith. To have Zeb Smith follow Adene Smith, sort on the Lastname and the Firstname fields. Return to the Database Design screen and enter the Lastname field and the **Ascending Dictionary** sort method,

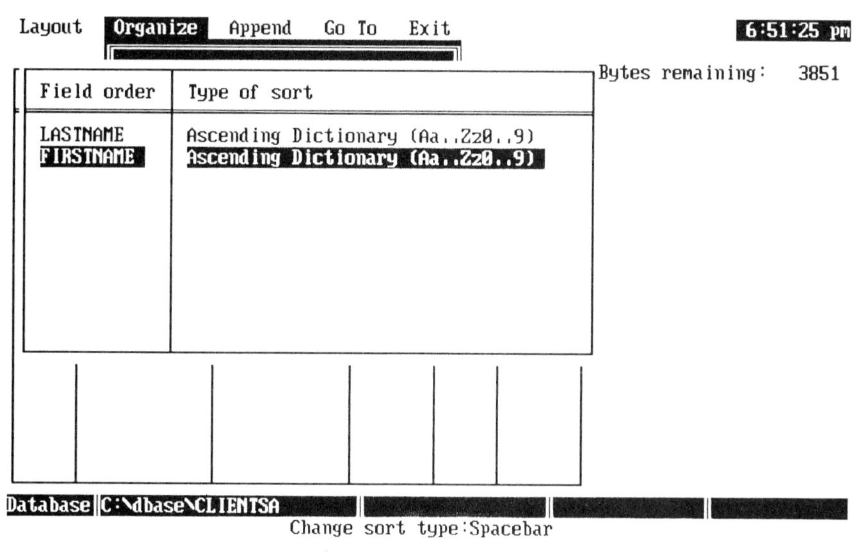

Figure 5-5. Selecting **Ascending Dictionary** as the Type of sort

Records Fields Go To Exit 6:52:33 pm

FIRSTNAME	LASTNAME	COMPANY	ADDRESS
Steven	Hill	Micro Processes Inc.	36800 Luau Lane
Diana	Jones	Rayman and Associates	1000 Frontage Road
Sherman	Mc Coy	Mc Coy Instruments	876 Bradford Street
John	McCrae	Rhode Island Research	9001 Frost Way
Owen	Meany	Meany Intl Parcel Service	6711 Waites Street
Paul	Shaffer	Texas Connections	890 Circle Street
Paul	Simon	dBASE Users Group	1234 Primrose Lane
Adene	Smith	Smith, Smith & Smith	2948 El Camino Real
Kim	Smith	Smith, Smith & Smith	7950 Park Avenue
Zeb	Smith	Smith, Smith & Smith	512 Blackhawk Avenue
George	Thomas	Texasville Pumps	221 Texasville Way
Kilgore	Trout	Ashton-Trout	9743 Pine Ave
Jake	van de Kammps	Braland	1010 Main Street
Melissa	Williams	Lettuce Development Corp	640 Nashua Court
Nathan	Zuckerman	Microshop	43000 Rainbow Drive

Browse C:\dbase\CLIENTSB Rec 1/15 File

View and edit fields

Figure 5-6. The **Ascending Dictionary** sort

as in the previous example. Next, press ENTER to move down one line, and enter the Firstname field *below* the Lastname field in the "Field order" column. To enter the sort method for the Firstname field, move to the "Type of sort" column and select **Ascending Dictionary**. Your screen should look like Figure 5-5. To enter a file name for the sorted database, press CTRL-END, type **CLIENTSB**, and press ENTER.

To view the results of the sort, return to the Control Center by selecting **Abandon changes and exit** from the **Exit** menu. Highlight CLIENTSB in the Data Panel and enter browse mode (press F2). Figure 5-6 shows the results of the sort.

Tip: You can also sort on more than one field by using the SORT command from the dot prompt. Use commas to separate the fields.

For example, to create the CLIENTSB database from the last example, enter

```
. SORT ON Lastname,Firstname/C to Clientsb
```

dBASE sorts by the Lastname field as well as by the Firstname field in ascending ASCII order. It also treats upper- and lowercase alike (the effect of the /C option). For more information on sorting from the dot prompt, see Chapter 7, "The Dot Prompt."

When you choose the fields on which to sort, you're not restricted to character fields alone. You can sort on any type of field and on any combination of different types.

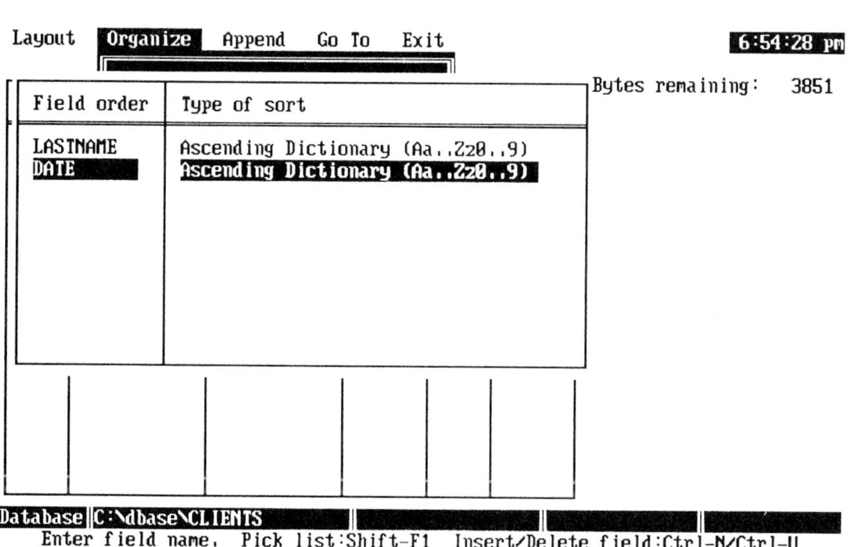

Figure 5-7. Sorting on two different field types

Records Fields Go To Exit 6:57:22 pm

FIRSTNAME	LASTNAME	ZIP	TELEPHONE	AMOUNT	DATE	NOTE
Steven	Hill	96815	(808)343-6667	600	12/23/90	memo
Diana	Jones	95066	(408)475-9055	28	02/23/90	memo
Sherman	Mc Coy	12237	(212)894-6767	50	06/15/90	memo
John	McCrae	02908	(401)776-0017	100	02/18/90	memo
Owen	Meany	22180	(703)223-9393	800	07/12/90	memo
Paul	Shaffer	76129	(916)552-1221	100	01/15/90	memo
Paul	Simon	94086	(408)732-1637	20	01/22/90	memo
Kim	Smith	95073	(408)479-4459	50	07/19/90	memo
Adene	Smith	95051	(415)968-6070	100	11/10/90	memo
Zeb	Smith	95129	(408)562-5775	500	11/20/90	memo
George	Thomas	56902	(916)453-9021	300	07/16/90	memo
Kilgore	Trout	02142	(617)233-9871	200	09/25/90	memo
Jake	van de Kammps	07078	(201)998-7968	235	05/05/90	memo
Melissa	Williams	94964	(415)461-0171	100	11/10/90	memo
Nathan	Zuckerman	98052	(206)461-0171	475	03/03/90	memo

Browse C:\dbase\CLIENTSC Rec 8/15 File

View and edit fields

Figure 5-8. Sort on the Lastname and Date fields

For example, you can sort the CLIENTS database by the Lastname field, a character type field, and by the Date field, a date type field. Try entering the Lastname field and the Date field as pictured in Figure 5-7. When you press CTRL-END to enter the new file name, type **CLIENTSC** and press ENTER.

To review the results, return to the Control Center (select **Abandon changes and exit** from the **Exit** menu). Next, highlight the CLIENTSC database and enter browse mode (press F2). Lock the first two fields including the Lastname field (select the **Lock fields on left** option from the **Fields** menu and enter **2** for the number of fields to lock). You can then use TAB to move to the Date field. Your screen should look like Figure 5-8. As you review the results, notice that the last names are all in alphabetical order, and, where the last names are the same, the dates are in chronological order.

If you've followed the examples, you now have three files that contain the same records in different order—CLIENTSA, CLIENTSB, and CLIENTSC. If you want to delete these files from your hard disk, return to the Control Center and make sure that the files are closed (they should appear below the line in the Data Panel). To close a file, highlight it in the Data Panel, press ENTER, and select the **Close file** option. To delete the CLIENTSA database, highlight it and press DEL. You will see the prompt "Are you sure you want to remove this file from the catalog?" Press Y for yes. dBASE then asks "Do you want to delete this file from disk?" Press Y again. Repeat these steps for CLIENTSB and CLIENTSC.

Indexing a Database

There are several advantages to indexing rather than sorting. To fully appreciate the benefits of indexing, you should know what an index file is.

What Is an Index File?

When you index a database, dBASE creates a separate index file. The original database is not affected. dBASE uses an index file as you use a book index. For instance, to look up the command for changing the position of the dBASE IV clock, you can look it up in the index rather than searching page-by-page through this book for the word "clock." The book's index helps you go directly to the page with the dBASE clock information.

You create an index file using one or more fields in the currently active database. Depending on the data type of fields that you choose, dBASE sorts the information in an index file in alphabetical, numerical, or chronological order.

You can use an index file to rapidly locate information in a database or display your records in a certain order. An index file maintains an internal table of record numbers and field pointers. The record numbers refer to the original position of each record in the currently active database. The field pointers refer to the fields on which you've created your index. dBASE uses the index file's record numbers and field pointers to point to the records in your database, enabling it to quickly jump to a particular record. It can also efficiently rearrange and display an indexed database.

The Advantages of Indexing

There are several advantages to indexing rather than sorting your database.

- dBASE can create an index much more quickly than it can sort a database.
- When a database is indexed, dBASE does not have to read sequentially through the records but can move directly to a particular record. Therefore, dBASE can find information much faster in an indexed database.
- dBASE can rearrange and display an indexed database quite rapidly.
- When you use an index and change a record, dBASE updates your index files automatically to reflect the change. You don't have to recreate an index file each time, as you would a sorted database.
- Indexing takes up less space than sorting. As mentioned, when you sort a database, you can't sort it onto itself. You must create an entirely new database. As a result, you use almost twice the disk space when you sort.
- You can create several different indexes, and index files, and activate them as needed.

The Two Types of Index Files

dBASE IV uses two types of index files: *.MDX (multiple index) files*, which can store up to 47 indexes per file, and *.NDX (single index) files,* which can store only one index per file. .MDX files are new to dBASE IV. .NDX files are a carry-over from previous dBASE releases.

When you first tell dBASE IV to create an index for a database, it automatically creates an .MDX file for that database file—the *production .MDX file*. This file has the same name as the database it corresponds to, but uses an .MDX extension. The production .MDX file manages the information for all the different indexes that you create for a database. When you alter your database or create a new index, dBASE automatically updates the production .MDX file.

dBASE identifies the individual indexes within an .MDX file with *tags*. For example, suppose you have a database named MAIL for which you have three different indexes, one on ZIP code, another on the fields Lastname+Firstname, and another on Date. The production .MDX file (MAIL.MDX) contains all three of these indexes. Since dBASE can only use one index at a time, each index has a separate tag name so dBASE can distinguish between them. Index tag names can be up to ten characters long. They must begin with a letter and may also contain numbers and underscores.

Previous versions of dBASE do not support .MDX files. However, dBASE IV allows you to create .NDX files that are compatible with dBASE III and III PLUS. These index files end with the extension .NDX. You might want to use an .NDX file, for example, when you don't want your production .MDX file updated with a certain index, or when you want to create an index that is compatible with a previous version of dBASE.

Creating an Index Tag

You create an .MDX index tag by using the menu in the Database Design screen menu. Press SHIFT-F2 from the Control Center to enter the Database Design screen. Next, select the **Create new index** option from the **Organize** menu (see Figure 5-9). dBASE prompts you for the four items that follow.

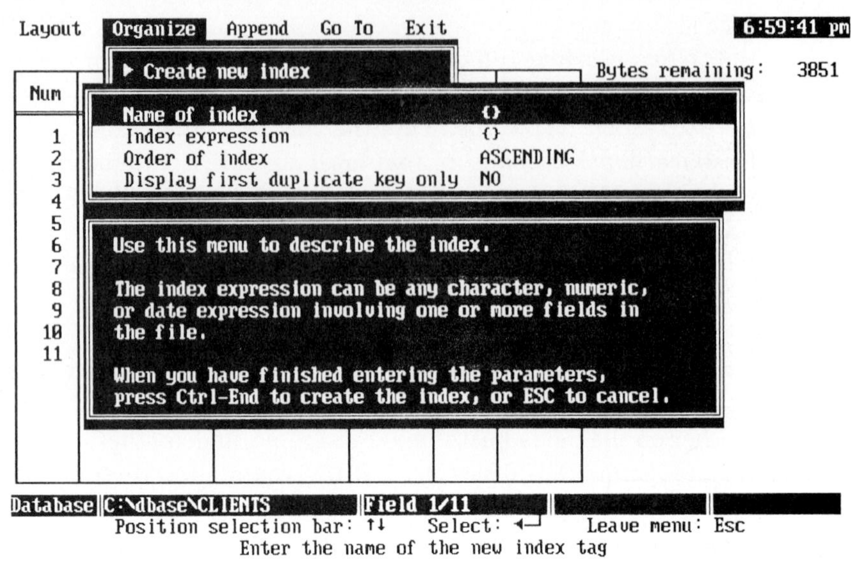

Figure 5-9. Using the **Organize** menu to create a new index

- **Name of index** You assign this tag to the index, and dBASE uses it to identify your index in the production .MDX file.
- **Index expression** An index expression is made up of one or more fields on which to index your database. For example, if you use the expression Lastname, dBASE indexes your database on the field Lastname.
- **Order of index** You can set the order of the index to ascending or descending. Ascending is regular alphabetical order; descending is the reverse. Ascending is the default.
- **Display first duplicate key only** This option lets you determine whether to display records that contain identical data for the key expression. The default is No. For example, suppose you index the CLIENTS database according to the State field, and choose Yes for this option.

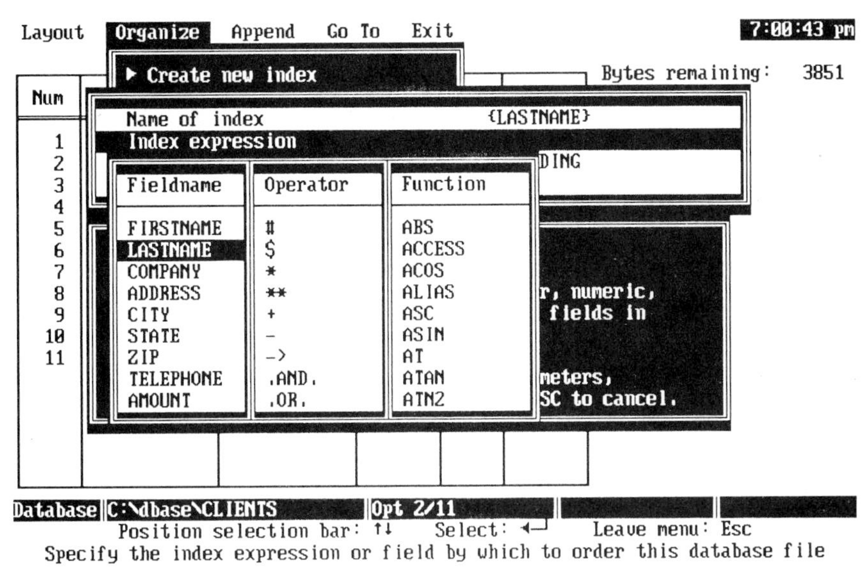

Figure 5-10. Creating an index expression with the Expression Builder

If you have more than one record with the same state, only the first record with that state will appear when you display the database in browse mode.

An Example

Suppose you want to index the CLIENTS database by last name. Highlight the CLIENTS database in the Data Panel of the Control Center and press SHIFT-F2. Next, select the **Create new index** option from the **Organize** menu. To create a new index for the Lastname field, select the **Name of index** option. You should use a tag name that identifies which fields are in the indexed expression. For the current example, type **LASTNAME** and press ENTER.

Select the **Index expression** option. You can press SHIFT-F1 to display the *Expression Builder*, which is a list of possible field names, dBASE operators, and functions from which to choose, as shown in Figure 5-10. You can't index on memo or logical fields, so

```
 Records    Fields    Go To    Exit                          7:02:38 pm
FIRSTNAME    LASTNAME        COMPANY                    ADDRESS
Steven       Hill            Micro Processes Inc.       36800 Luau Lane
Diana        Jones           Rayman and Associates      1000 Frontage Road
Sherman      Mc Coy          Mc Coy Instruments         876 Bradford Street
John         McCrae          Rhode Island Research      9001 Frost Way
Owen         Meany           Meany Intl Parcel Service  6711 Waites Street
Paul         Shaffer         Texas Connections          890  Circle Street
Paul         Simon           dBASE Users Group          1234 Primrose Lane
Zeb          Smith           Smith, Smith & Smith       512 Blackhawk Avenue
George       Thomas          Texasville Pumps           221 Texasville Way
Kilgore      Trout           Ashton-Trout               9743 Pine Ave
Melissa      Williams        Lettuce Development Corp   640 Nashua Court
Nathan       Zuckerman       Microshop                  43000 Rainbow Drive
Jake         van de Kammps   Braland                    1010 Main Street

Browse  C:\dbase\CLIENTS      Rec 7/15       File
                        View and edit fields
```

Figure 5-11. Setting the **Display first duplicate only** option to Yes

dBASE doesn't list them. You can move to any of the field name, operator, and function options by using the arrow keys. If you need more space for your expression, you can open an edit box by pressing F9. Select Lastname from the list of field names in the **Index expression** option.

Choose the **Order of index** option and accept the default, Ascending, to index alphabetically on the Lastname field. To change from ascending to descending, you can press SPACEBAR or ENTER.

Use the DOWN ARROW to move to **Display first duplicate key only**. As mentioned, when you set this option to Yes, dBASE IV displays only the first occurrence of any entries that satisfy the index expression selected in the **Index expression** option. If you select Yes for the current example, which uses the Lastname field as the index, the last name of Smith appears only once in your database, as in Figure 5-11. Leave this option set to No to create your new index on Lastname.

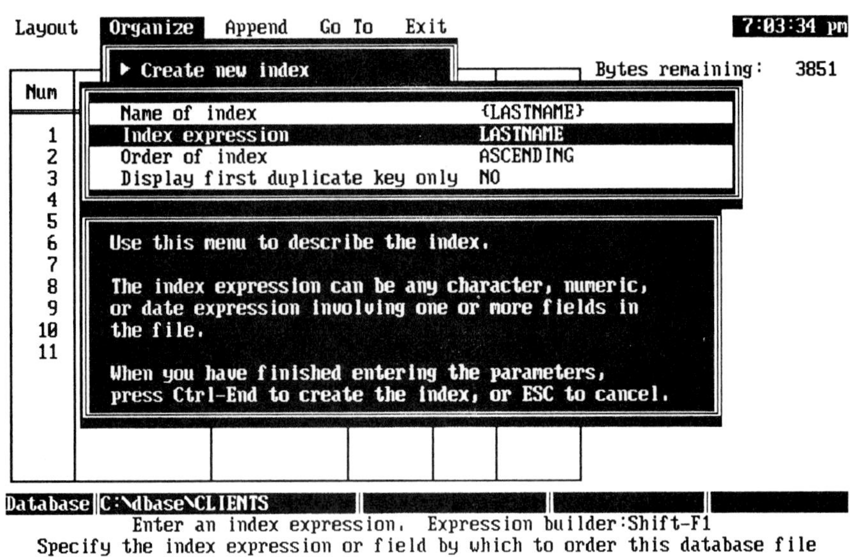

Figure 5-12. Creating an index on the Lastname field named Lastname

Now that you've entered the index information, check that your screen matches the screen in Figure 5-12. If it does, press CTRL-END to start the index. Otherwise, make the proper changes before pressing CTRL-END. You can view your newly indexed database by pressing F2.

Tip: You can create both .MDX and .NDX files by using the INDEX command from the dot prompt. See Chapter 7, "The Dot Prompt," and the INDEX command in Chapter 31 for more information.

Indexing on Multiple Fields

You can index on several fields at once if they are of the same field type. If the fields are of different field types, you must convert them to the same type by using dBASE IV functions before you can build an index. This section describes how to index on multiple fields in both situations.

Indexing on the Same Field Type

When you create an index for a single field, dBASE organizes only that field in alphabetical order. The other fields in the database appear in their *natural* order (the order you originally entered them in). For example, in the CLIENTS database, the Lastname index alphabetizes the database according to last name, but the order of the first names is not changed. For example, Zeb Smith appears before Adene and Kim Smith.

Suppose you want to arrange the records in the CLIENTS database alphabetically by first and last names, as in a telephone directory. To do so, you need to index the database on both the Lastname and Firstname fields, both character type fields.

To create an index for the Lastname and Firstname fields in the CLIENTS database,

1. Select the **Create new index** option from the **Organize** menu.

2. Select **Name of index** from the next menu.

3. Type **LFNAME** to name the index.

4. Next, select the **Index expression** option from the **Organize** menu.

5. Press SHIFT-F1 to open the Expression Builder, and choose the Lastname field.

6. Reactivate the Expression Builder with SHIFT-F1, and use the RIGHT ARROW to move to the Operators column. Select the + operator. (The + operator is a string operator that joins two or more character fields.)

7. Open the Expression Builder again, and select the Firstname field.

8. Press CTRL-END to build the index.

9. Press F2 to view your newly indexed database.

When you enter the expression "Lastname+Firstname," dBASE creates an index that displays the Lastname *and* the Firstname fields in alphabetical order. For example, Adene Smith now comes before Kim Smith and Kim Smith before Zeb Smith.

Indexing on Different Field Types

You can index on two different field types by creating an index expression that converts the two fields to the same data type and then combines them. In dBASE IV, you can easily build such an expression using the Function column in the Expression Builder.

There are several functions you can choose in the Function column of the Expression Builder. This chapter discusses only two of them—the STR( ) and DTOS( ) functions. The STR( ) function converts a numeric data type to a character data type. The DTOS() function converts a date data type to a character data type.

Suppose you want to create an index for the CLIENTS database that combines the Lastname field with the Amount field. To change a numeric field to a character data type, select the STR( ) function from the Expression Builder. To create an index using the numeric field Amount and the character field Lastname from your CLIENTS database, use SHIFT-F2 to access the **Organize** menu. Then follow these steps:

1. Select the **Create new index** option from the **Organize** menu.

2. Select the **Name of index** menu option and then enter **LNAME_AMT**.

3. To start your index expression, select the **Index expression** option, press SHIFT-F1 to activate the Expression Builder, and select the Lastname field.

4. Enter the + operator yourself or reopen the Expression Builder and select it from the Operator column.

5. Use SHIFT-F1 to select the STR( ) function from the Operator column in the Expression Builder.

Tip: Type **ST** (case doesn't matter) to quickly get to the STR( ) function within the Expression Builder.

6. The **Index expression** option now appears with the characters LASTNAME+STR( ).

7. Move the cursor between the parentheses after the letters "STR."

8. Reopen the Expression Builder, move to the Fieldname column, and select the Amount field. dBASE places this field between the parentheses, as shown in Figure 5-13.

9. Press CTRL-END and dBASE creates an index from the expression you've built.

10. Press F2 to view the data.

You can create an index on the Lastname field and the Date field by choosing a new name for your tag and following the previous procedure. This time, however, use the DTOS( ) function to convert the Date field to a character data type using the following index expression:

```
Lastname+DTOS(Date)
```

As you might expect, this expression organizes the CLIENTS database by last name and by date. For more information on functions, see Chapter 33.

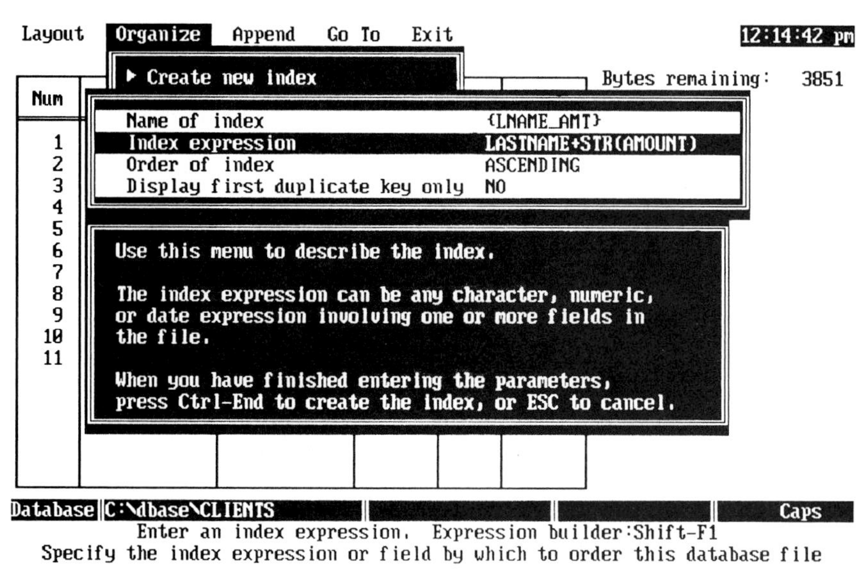

Figure 5-13. Using the STR( ) function in an index expression

Modifying an Existing Index

Modifying an existing index is much like creating a new one. When you select the **Modify existing index** option from the **Organize** menu, dBASE IV displays a window containing a list of available indexes for the current database. After you select an index name from the list, you see the screen you get when you create a new index with the **Create new index** option. However, all the options already contain information for the existing index.

You modify the existing index by changing the information for the various options, as you do with the **Create new index** option (see the preceding section). Press CTRL-END to save your modifications. For example, Figure 5-14 shows what your screen would look like if you were modifying the Lfname index in the CLIENTS database.

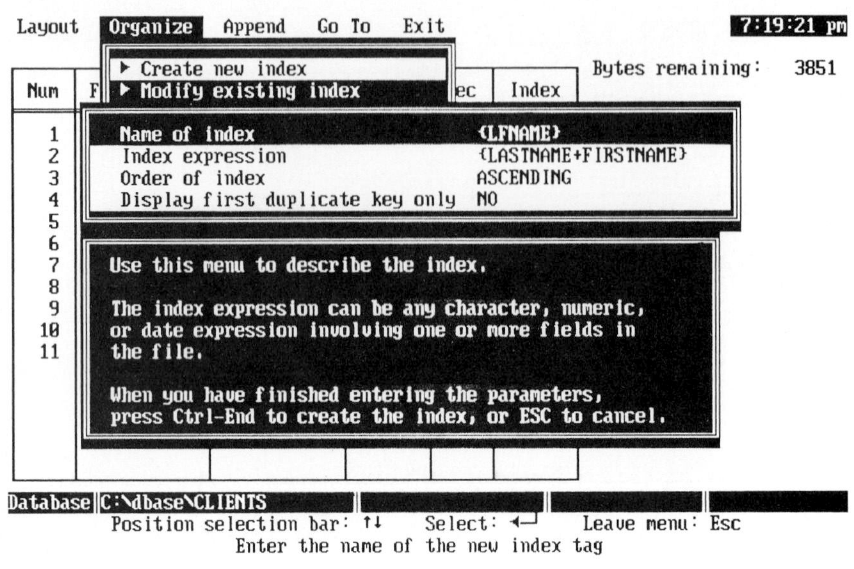

Figure 5-14. Modifying the CLIENTS Lfname index

Activating an Index

Although dBASE automatically opens the production .MDX file when you use a database, it does not automatically activate an index tag. Therefore, dBASE displays the records in the order in which you originally entered them into the database. To activate an index tag, use **Order records by index** from the **Organize** menu. When you select this option, two boxes appear on the upper-right corner of your screen, as shown in Figure 5-15. These boxes show you the production .MDX tags and the index expressions for the highlighted tag.

You can have up to ten open index files per active database, but only one *master* or controlling index manages your database

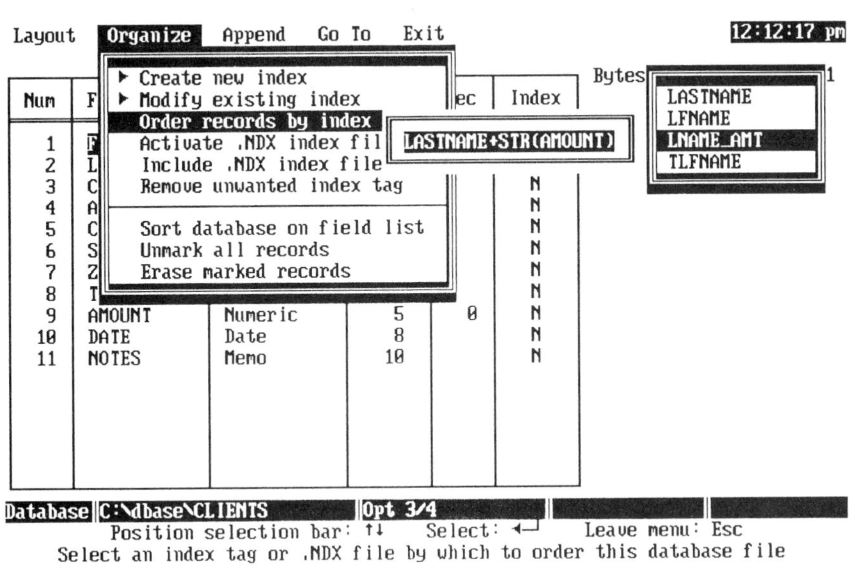

Figure 5-15. Selecting the **Order records by index** option from the **Organize** menu

at a time. The index you select from the **Order records by index** box becomes the master index.

To move from one index tag to another, use the UP ARROW and DOWN ARROW keys. When you've located the index you want as the master index, press ENTER.

For example, choose the Lfname tag as the master index in the CLIENTS database, and press F2 to view the newly indexed database. The records now appear in alphabetical order by the Lastname field.

Tip: If you expect to be changing index tags frequently, enter the Database Design screen rather than entering the edit or browse mode directly from the Control Center. This way, when you press F2 after creating, modifying, or choosing an index, you enter browse or edit mode directly. Then, when you press SHIFT-F2 from edit or browse, dBASE IV takes you back to the Database Design screen and you can change your indexes.

Tip: You can activate an existing index from the dot prompt by using the SET ORDER command. This command is similar to the **Order records by index** option in the **Organize** menu, but you must enter the tag name instead of selecting it from the box prompt. For example, the command to activate the master index Lastname is SET ORDER TO Lastname.

Including .NDX Files

If you select the **Include .NDX index file** option from the **Organize** menu, you can include an .NDX file in your current catalog so that you can use the .NDX file in conjunction with the index tags in your production .MDX file. When you select this option, dBASE displays a box in the upper-right corner of your screen, listing the available files, drives, and directories from which you can select the appropriate .NDX file.

For example, suppose you have an .NDX file named FNAME.NDX for the CLIENTS database. You can add it to the current catalog by selecting **Include .NDX file** from the **Organize** menu and choosing FNAME.NDX from the box listing the available files, as shown in Figure 5-16.

Editing When an Index Is Active

When you change the information in a database, dBASE IV automatically updates the indexes in your production .MDX file. Therefore, when an index is active, dBASE IV automatically updates the screen to reflect the changes made to the database. In other words, if you change an entry in a field while an index is active for that field, the position of that record changes as soon as you leave the record.

For example, try opening the CLIENTS database, activating the Lastname index tag, and entering edit mode. Next, change the name Zuckerman to Alther. After you leave the record, dBASE ac-

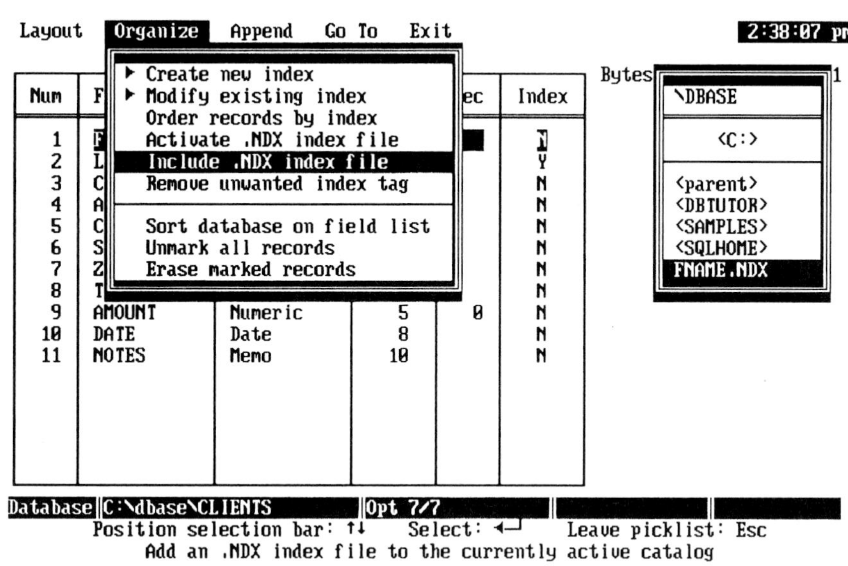

Figure 5-16. Selecting the FNAME.NDX file using the **Include .NDX file** option

cepts your changes to the record and updates the Lastname index tag. Alther now appears at the top of the Lastname field.

Although dBASE IV updates all index tags, it only shifts the positions of records in the database for changes to the master index. In the last example, the Lastname tag was the master index. If you make a change to the Company field, the order of the records in the database doesn't change because an index tag for the company field hasn't been activated as the master index.

Remaining at a Record Position with an Active Index

By setting the **Follow record to new position** option in the **Records** menu to No, you prevent dBASE from automatically moving your record position in a database every time you change an indexed field. Your database is still automatically sorted according to the expression for the active index; however, the cursor remains at the same record location rather than following each record to its new position.

For example, using the CLIENTS database with the Lastname index as the master index, set the **Follow record to new position** option to No and change the name Alther back to Zuckerman. Use the DOWN ARROW to leave the record. Once you move from the changed record, dBASE rearranges the order of the records, but leaves you where you changed the database, in this case the first record.

Searching an Indexed Database

In the last chapter, you explored several of the **Go To** menu options in browse and edit mode. One of the unavailable options was the **Index key search** option. After activating an index from the **Order records by index** option in the **Organize** menu, you can use the **Index key search** option from the **Go To** menu to search your database in either the browse mode or the edit mode. You can search your database much faster with an index.

When you select the **Index key search** option, dBASE displays a prompt box in which you enter the desired string. When you enter a string, dBASE uses the master index to find your string in the indexed field.

If you are following the CLIENTS database examples, select the Lastname index tag and choose the **Index key search** option from the **Go To** menu. Enter the name **Trout**. dBASE displays the record almost immediately.

Although index searches are very fast, they have some drawbacks. You can't use wildcard characters, and an index key search only works when the case matches, even after you set **Match capitalization** to No. For example, you can't look up McCrae by typing **MCCrae**, **M??rae**, or **M***.

When dBASE searches an index, however, it looks for a match beginning with the first characters in the database field. Therefore, you can enter the first few letters in a string and find a match. Entering **Mc**, for example, takes you to the first record in the Lastname field beginning with the letters "Mc." If there are several entries, as there are for Smith, you can type **Sm** and use the DOWN ARROW to select the correct one.

Tip: To repeat a search for the next matching record, press SHIFT-F4 (Find Next); for the previous matching record, press SHIFT-F3 (Find Previous).

Tip: You can also use the dot prompt commands FIND and SEEK to search an indexed database. FIND is similar to the **Index key search** option. However, FIND doesn't display the matching record; it only positions the record pointer to that record. Normally, you use the SEEK command with memory variables, but you can also search for data by delimiting the desired string with quotation marks. For example, you can search for the name Smith by typing either **FIND Smith** or **SEEK "Smith"** at the dot prompt. For more on the FIND and SEEK commands, see Chapter 31.

Removing .MDX Tags

If you no longer need an .MDX tag, you can eliminate it by selecting the **Remove unwanted index tag** option from the **Organize** menu. Removing a tag permanently deletes it from the production .MDX file. If you delete all of the tags in a production .MDX file, dBASE deletes the production .MDX file itself.

Tip: Using the DELETE TAG command from the dot prompt is the equivalent of using **Remove unwanted index tag** from the **Organize** menu. For example, you can delete the tag Lfname from the production .MDX file by typing

```
. DELETE TAG Lfname
```

at the dot prompt.

Tip: Two index-related dot prompt commands do not have equivalent options in the **Organize** menu. COPY TAG copies tags from a production .MDX file to an .NDX index file. COPY INDEXES copies a list of up to 47 index files to a production .MDX file. If the production .MDX file doesn't exist, dBASE creates one with the same name as the active database. For more on these commands, see Chapter 31.

In this chapter, you learned about the benefits and limitations of sorting and indexing. You can now sort or index your database according to a particular field (or set of fields) in alphabetical, numerical, or chronological order. You also know how to modify and use indexes to organize and search your database.

Querying the Database

SIX

This chapter explains how to query a database using the Queries Panel in the Control Center. The Queries Panel gives you access to the *Queries Design screen,* which you can use to design powerful queries to locate, organize, and edit data in databases.

Overview

The Queries Design screen, new to dBASE IV, is based on the premise of query by example. This concept involves placing on the screen a pictorial representation, or *file skeleton,* of the structure of one or more databases. You can then select fields from each database file skeleton and specify conditions for the data to be

Records Fields Go To Exit 12:05:32 pm

FIRSTNAME	LASTNAME	BONUS	GROSS	FED	FICA	STATE	NET
Mary	Jones	F	24000.00	6000.00	1802.40	720.00	15477.60
Drew	Gibson	T	22000.00	5500.00	1652.20	660.00	14187.80
Ralph	Moriarity	F	26000.00	6500.00	1952.60	780.00	16767.40
Clive	Bunker	F	23000.00	5750.00	1727.30	690.00	14832.70
John	Patrovich	F	32000.03	8000.01	2403.20	960.00	20636.82
Suzanne	Chambers	F	17000.00	4250.00	1276.70	510.00	10963.30
Keith	Campbell	T	52000.00	13000.0	3905.20	1560.00	33534.80
George	Haenszel	T	22000.00	5500.00	1652.20	660.00	14187.80
Jeff	Hill	T	25000.00	6250.00	1877.50	750.00	16122.50
Sam	Hammons	T	31000.00	7750.00	2328.10	930.00	19991.90
Kevin	Anderson	T	28000.00	7000.00	2102.80	840.00	18057.20

Browse C:\...chap6\SALARY Rec 1/11 File

View and edit fields

Figure 6-1. SALARY on the Browse screen

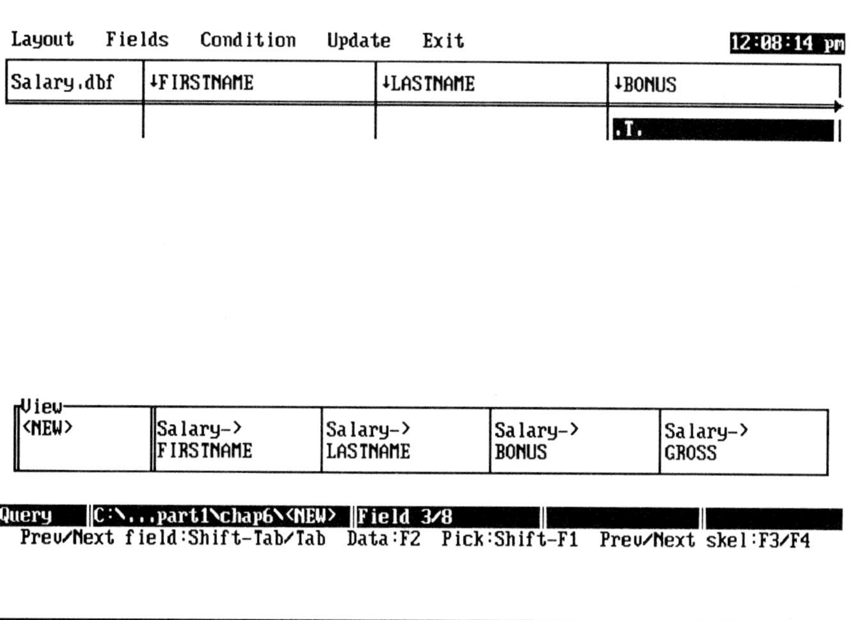

Figure 6-2. SALARY on the Queries Design screen

drawn from those fields. The fields you select are used to compose yet another pictorial representation, or skeleton, the *view skeleton.* The conditions you specify filter the data supplied to the fields that appear in the view skeleton. Putting it all together, dBASE IV uses the fields you select and the conditions you specify to compose a *view* of the database. This view is representative of your query. When you run the query, dBASE IV uses the view to draw specific information from selected fields in one or more databases.

The best way to show you what a query is, what it does, and how you might use one in your daily work, is to take you through a short example. Figure 6-1 shows on the Browse screen an example database called SALARY. Figure 6-2 shows a sample Queries Design screen, containing both a database skeleton (at the top) and a view skeleton (at the bottom) for the SALARY database.

Select the SALARY.DBF database by highlighting the SALARY database in the Data Panel of the Control Center, and pressing ENTER. This results in an option box from which you select the **USE file** option. Next, you access the Queries Design screen by moving the highlight to the **<create>** marker in the Queries Panel and pressing ENTER. dBASE IV will automatically enter the Queries Design screen and place the database file skeleton for the SALARY database on the work surface.

The SALARY database skeleton (top of Figure 6-2) actually contains eight columns, one for each field in the SALARY database. However, dBASE IV can only display three field columns at once. The view skeleton for this query (bottom of the screen) contains four field columns, representing four fields—Firstname, Lastname, Bonus, and Gross—selected from the SALARY database.

To select the fields on the view skeleton from the SALARY database file skeleton, press TAB to move the highlight to the desired field columns in the SALARY database file skeleton and press F5. Pressing F5 selects a field and appends it to the view skeleton.

The letter under the Bonus logical field of the SALARY database skeleton (located in the upper-right corner of the screen in Figure 6-2) represents a condition. The .T., or true, condition specifies that only records with a logical (.T.) true (true meaning that the employee is scheduled to receive a bonus) are to be included in this query. To enter this condition, press TAB to move the cursor to the Bonus field column of the SALARY file skeleton and type the condition.

Pressing F2 at this point takes you to the Browse screen, where the results of the query are displayed (Figure 6-3). The four fields—Firstname, Lastname, Bonus, and Gross—originally specified in the view skeleton at the bottom of the Queries Design screen in Figure 6-2 now appear as field heads on the Browse screen in Figure 6-3. The data for those fields comes from the SALARY database. However, only records that contain a logical true (.T.) in the Bonus field are included in the display. This is a query that your payroll clerk might use to determine the names and gross salaries of employees who are to receive bonuses.

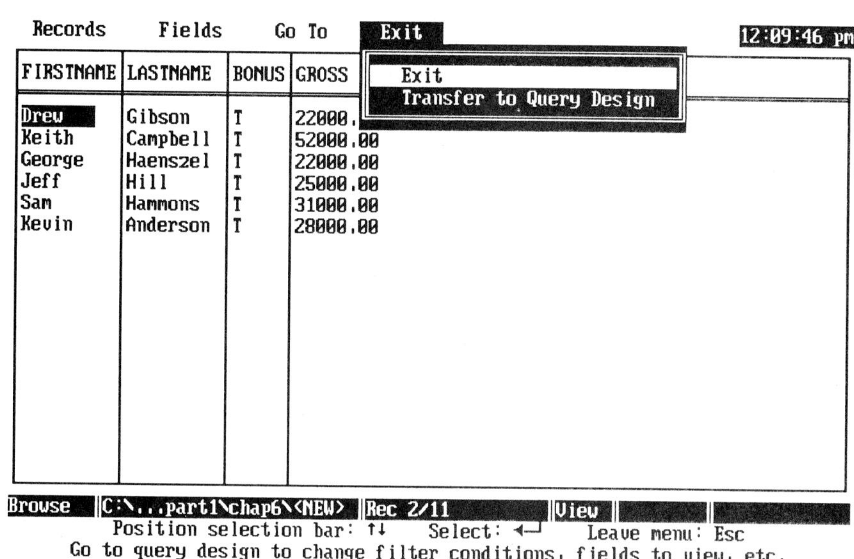

Figure 6-3. Query displayed on the Browse screen

To return from the Browse screen to the Queries Design screen, press F10 and select **Transfer to Query Design** from the **Exit** menu, shown in Figure 6-3. dBASE IV returns you to the Queries Design screen and you can refine or revise your query.

When you've finished your query, you can name it and save it in a file for later use. Query files are given a .QBE (query by example) file extension. Since the file name for the this query is BONUSPAY, dBASE IV creates BONUSPAY.QBE. You save this query by pressing F10, highlighting the **Save Changes and exit** option from the **Exit** menu, typing a file name at the prompt, and pressing ENTER. The name of that file is then displayed in the Queries Panel of the Control Center (Figure 6-4).

After you save a query to a .QBE file, you can activate that file at any time. To activate a query, highlight its name in the Queries Panel, and press ENTER. To see the results of the query,

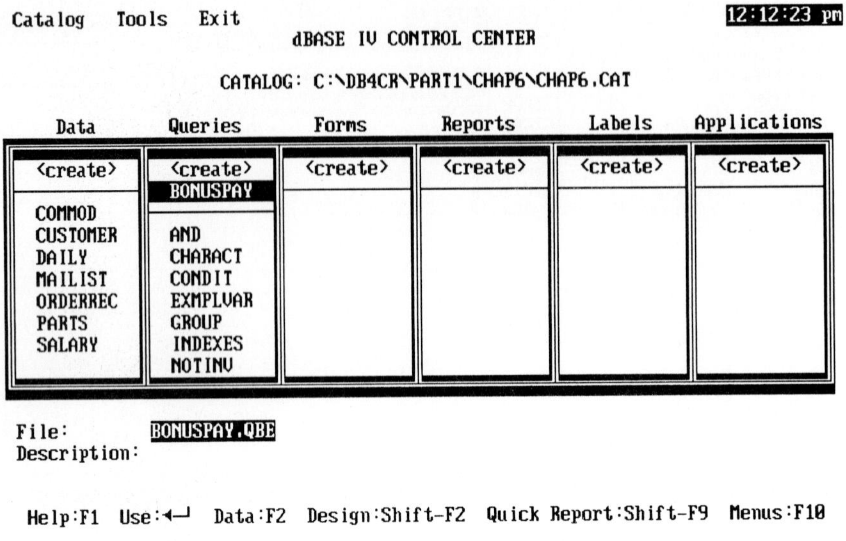

```
Catalog   Tools   Exit                                              12:12:23 pm
                         dBASE IV CONTROL CENTER

                   CATALOG: C:\DB4CR\PART1\CHAP6\CHAP6.CAT

   Data        Queries        Forms        Reports        Labels     Applications

 <create>     <create>      <create>      <create>      <create>      <create>
              BONUSPAY

 COMMOD       AND
 CUSTOMER     CHARACT
 DAILY        CONDIT
 MAILIST      EXMPLVAR
 ORDERREC     GROUP
 PARTS        INDEXES
 SALARY       NOTINV

File:          BONUSPAY.QBE
Description:

Help:F1  Use:◄┘  Data:F2  Design:Shift-F2  Quick Report:Shift-F9  Menus:F10
```

Figure 6-4. The BONUSPAY.QBE file in the Queries Panel

press F2. dBASE IV takes you to the Browse screen and displays query results.

When you activate a query file, dBASE IV opens the same databases, selects the same fields, and specifies the same conditions as when you originally designed and saved the query file. With a few simple keystrokes, you can activate and rerun even the most complex query.

As mentioned, when you save your query, dBASE IV creates a .QBE (query by example) file. This file actually contains a series of dBASE IV commands similar to those you might enter at the dot prompt or in a program file. Figure 6-5 shows an example of the BONUSPAY.QBE file created using the Queries Design screen. The commands in Figure 6-5 may seem complicated to you now. However, if you read Chapter 7, "The Dot Prompt," and Part Three of this book, "Programming dBASE IV," you'll learn that the

```
 Layout   Words   Go To   Print   Exit                                 12:14:56 pm
[·······▼1······▼··2····▼····3··▼·······4▼·······▼5······▼··6····▼····7··▼·······
* dBASE IV .QBE file •
SET FIELDS TO
SELECT 1
USE SALARY.DBF AGAIN
SET EXACT ON
SET FILTER TO ((A->BONUS=.T.))
GO TOP
SET FIELDS TO A->FIRSTNAME,A->LASTNAME,A->BONUS,A->GROSS
```

Figure 6-5. The commands of the BONUSPAY.QBE file

Queries Design screen is a convenient visual method for designing queries. You can achieve the same results yourself from the dot prompt or by using a command file.

Two Types of Queries

In dBASE IV, you can create two types of queries through the Queries Design screen: *view queries* and *update queries.* These two types of queries perform different tasks. View queries are designed to select certain records from a single database or to combine data from more than one database. Update queries are designed to change data in a database. When an update query is performed, dBASE IV modifies data in the database based on conditions you specified in the update query.

View Queries

As mentioned, you can use view queries to select from a database records that meet a given condition. You can also use a view query to select information from more than one database. With view queries, you can filter the information used by dBASE IV. This applies to Control Center menu selections as well as dot prompt and program file commands. Furthermore, you can use a view query to provide only selected information for custom reports, labels, forms, and applications created with the Applications Generator.

In addition, view queries, when activated, are stored in your computer's RAM, which runs much faster than its hard or floppy drive. Moreover, view queries save you disk space and the trouble of maintaining a duplicate set of data to match the special attributes of the data model defined in the query.

Update Queries

You use update queries to change data in a database. Update queries can append data, replace data, or mark and unmark records for deletion. These operations are analogous, respectively, to the APPEND, REPLACE, DELETE, and RECALL commands entered at the dot prompt (described in detail in Chapters 7 and 31).

There are a number of daily operations that you can perform quickly by using an update query. For example, you might append today's orders to the master orders database. Next, you could change the state payroll tax percentage withheld for each employee in the salary database. Or, you could mark for deletion those records in the accounts receivable database for which the balance due has been paid.

Getting to the Queries Design Screen

To create a query, you use the Queries Design screen. You can access the Queries Design screen from practically anywhere in dBASE IV. Here is a list of the various methods that you can use.

- From the Control Center, move the highlight to the **<create>** marker in the Queries Panel and press ENTER or SHIFT-F2 to create a new query.
- From the Control Center, move the highlight to the name of an existing query in the Queries Panel and press SHIFT-F2 to modify existing queries.
- From the Control Center, move the highlight to the name of an existing query in the Queries Panel and press ENTER. dBASE IV displays an option box (Figure 6-6). Highlight **Modify query** and press ENTER.
- From the Browse or Edit screen, press SHIFT-F2. Or, press F10 to access the menu and select **Transfer to Query Design** from the **Exit** menu. Use this method to create a new query or edit an existing query.
- Press SHIFT-F2 from either the Database, Forms, Reports, or Labels Design screens.
- From the dot prompt, enter the commands **CREATE VIEW <*filename*>** or **MODIFY VIEW <*filename*>**. For example, to create a query file called NOTINV.QBE, type **CREATE VIEW Notinv** at the dot prompt. You can also use this method to modify an existing view.
- From the dot prompt, enter **CREATE QUERY <*filename*>** or **MODIFY QUERY <*filename*>**. These commands perform the same function as CREATE/MODIFY VIEW.

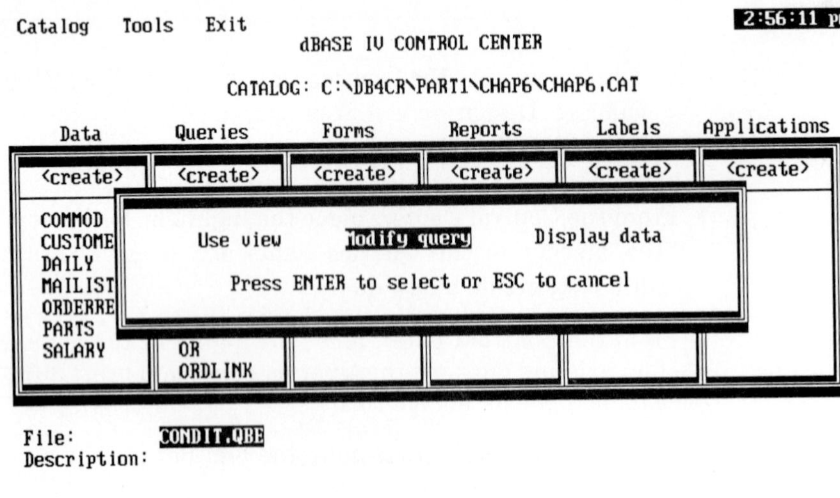

Figure 6-6. Modify query takes you to the Queries Design screen

The Queries Design Work Surface

The Queries Design screen consists of five components. They are listed here and shown in Figure 6-7.

- **Database file skeleton** Database file skeletons appear at the top of the Queries Design screen. As mentioned, this skeleton consists of columns that are a graphical illustration of a database. The first column shows the name of the database. The remaining columns represent the database fields. In the rows beneath the field names, you can enter commands that specify conditions for the data in each field. You can have as many as eight database file skeletons on the screen at any one time.

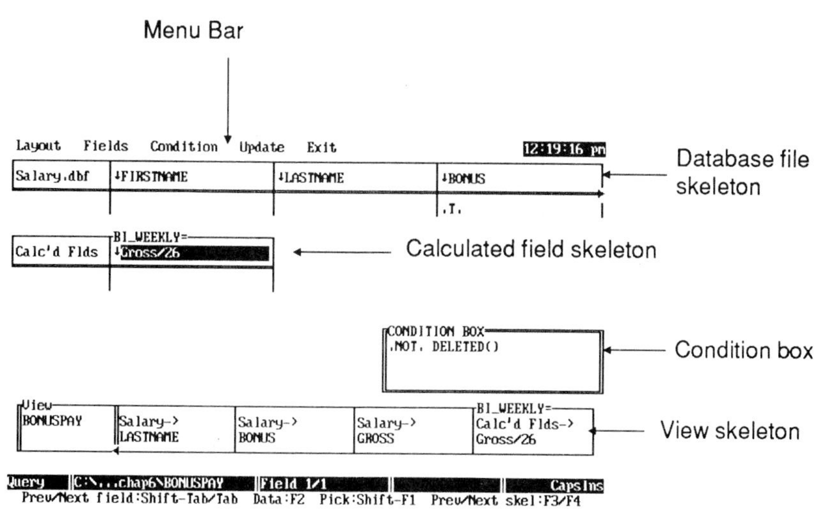

Figure 6-7. The components of the Queries Design screen

- **View skeleton** The view skeleton, which appears at the bottom of the screen, represents the database fields to be included in the view query you're designing. View skeletons may include fields from more than one database.
- **Calculated field skeleton** The Queries Design screen supports calculated fields. You can create calculated fields using the data from two or more fields in one or more of the database file skeletons. These calculated fields are not added to any database. They appear only in the query and in the Browse or Edit screens with which you view the query.
- **Condition box** You use the condition box to state conditions for data drawn from one or more fields in one or more of the current database file skeletons.

- **Menu system** You use the Queries Design screen menu system throughout the queries design process. Each element of the menu system is explained at some point in this chapter.

Navigating the Queries Design Screen

You can move back and forth between the database file, view, and calculated field skeletons, as well as the condition box, by using F3 for Previous and F4 for Next. For example, imagine there is a single database file skeleton, a single condition box, and a single view skeleton on the screen, as in Figure 6-8. The cursor is on the database file skeleton. Pressing F4 moves the cursor to the condi-

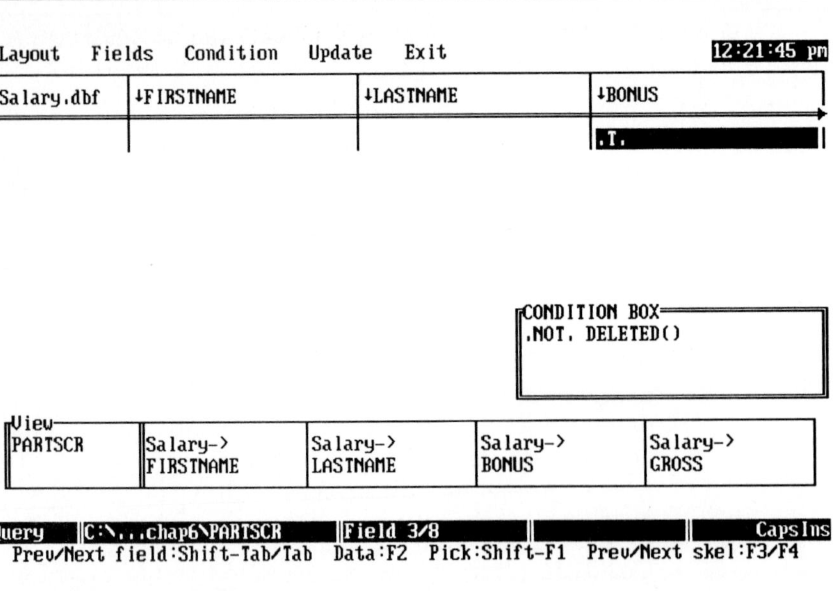

Figure 6-8. Use F3 or F4 to move within the Queries Design screen

tion box. Pressing F4 again moves the cursor to the view skeleton. Pressing F3 moves the cursor back to the condition box.

Tip: To cycle the cursor through the various components of the Queries Design screen, press F4 repeatedly.

To move back and forth between columns in database file, view, or calculated field skeletons, press TAB or SHIFT-TAB. TAB moves the cursor one column to the right. SHIFT-TAB moves the cursor one column to the left. Within a column, press RIGHT ARROW to move the cursor one space to the right and LEFT ARROW to move the cursor one space to the left. To quickly move between the first and last columns in a skeleton, press HOME or END.

You can have more than one row beneath a field column name. To move up and down between the rows in a column, press UP ARROW or DOWN ARROW. To move quickly to the top or bottom of the rows in a column, press CTRL-PGUP or CTRL-PGDN.

You can have up to eight database file skeletons on the Queries Design screen at once. When you have more database file skeletons than will fit on a single screen, press PGDN to move to the next page of database file skeletons and PGUP to return to the previous page. When there are database file skeletons below the ones currently displayed, dBASE IV places an arrow in the lower-left corner of your screen.

Adding a Database File to a Query

As mentioned, you can include up to eight database file skeletons in the current query. You can add database files to a query in one of two ways. You can open a database file and then enter the Queries Design screen. Whether you enter the Queries Design screen from the Control Center, the Browse or Edit screens, or one of the other design screens, the database file currently in use is displayed as the first file skeleton on the Queries Design screen. If no

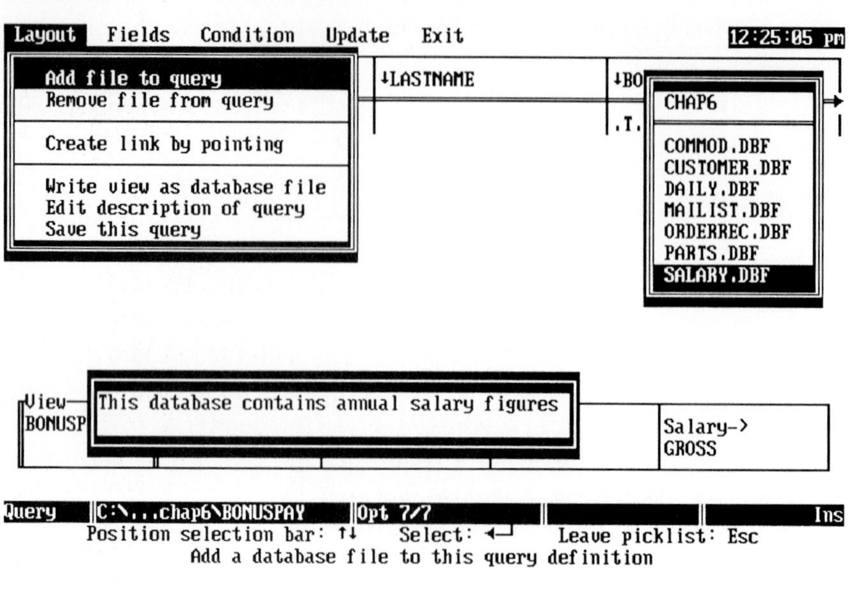

Figure 6-9. Adding a file to a query

database is in use when you enter the Queries Design screen, dBASE IV displays a blank work surface.

You can also add a database file to a query by pressing F10 and selecting **Add file to query** from the **Layout** menu. When you select this option, dBASE IV displays the database files in the current catalog or directory in the upper-right corner of your screen, as in Figure 6-9. Highlight the database file name of your choice and press ENTER. dBASE IV adds a database file skeleton to the current query. If database file skeletons already exist in the query, dBASE IV adds the new database file skeleton to the end of the list.

For example, Figure 6-10 shows the SALARY database file skeleton on the Queries Design screen. Note that the name "Salary.dbf" appears in the first column of the skeleton. The field names for the SALARY database appear in the other columns.

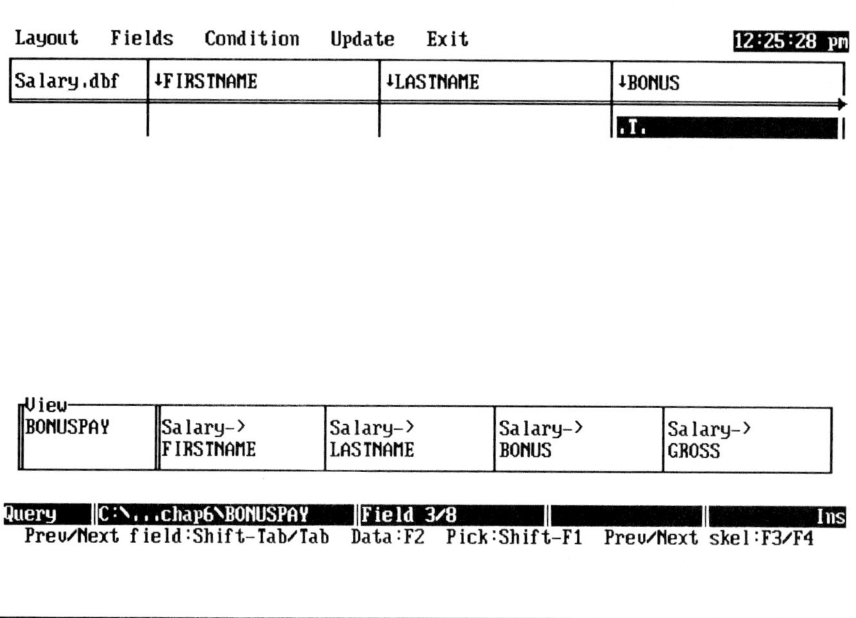

Figure 6-10. The first column shows the name of the database

Removing Database Files from a Query

To remove a database file skeleton from a query, use the F4 key to locate the cursor in the database file skeleton you want to remove. Next, press F10 and select the **Remove file from query** option from the **Layout** menu. Press ENTER and dBASE IV removes the database file skeleton from the Queries Design screen.

Adding Fields to the View Skeleton

As mentioned, a view skeleton represents the fields from various databases that are to be used in the current query. Since each

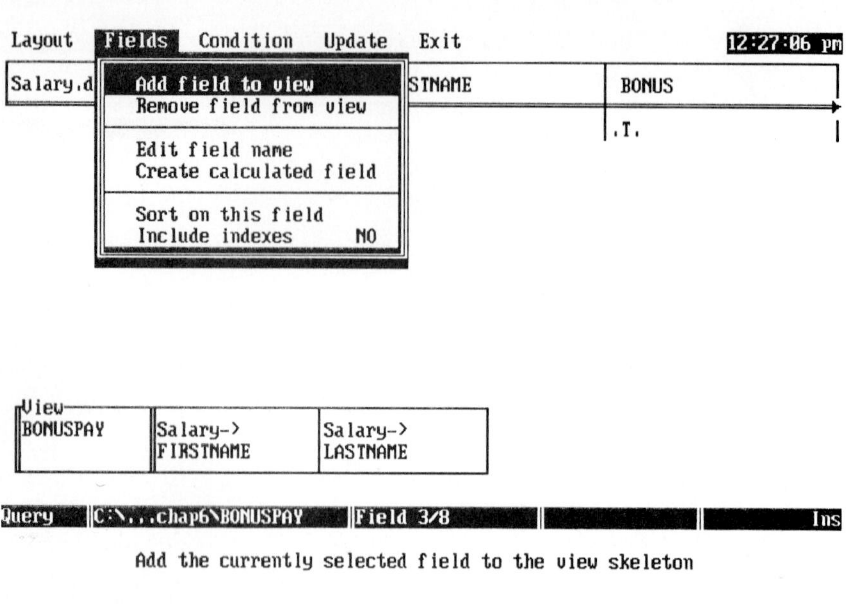

Figure 6-11. Adding a field to the view skeleton

query only generates one view, there is only one view skeleton per query. To add database fields to the current view, use the F4 key to locate the cursor on the database file skeleton that contains the field. Next, press TAB to move the cursor to the database field of your choice and press F5 to add that field name to the current view. Each field name you select with F5 is added to the end of the view skeleton. dBASE IV places a DOWNARROW next to these field names in the database file skeleton.

To add all of the fields in the current database file skeleton to the view skeleton, move the cursor into the first column (the name column) of a database file skeleton and press F5. dBASE IV adds all of the field names in the file skeleton to the current view.

You can also use the **Add field to view** option in the **Fields** menu to add database field names to the current view. Figure 6-11 shows what your screen will look like. To use this method, you must first move the cursor into the column containing the field name. When you execute this menu selection, dBASE IV adds the field name to the end of the current view.

You can also add a field from a calculated field skeleton to the current view. As with database file skeletons you move the cursor to the appropriate field name column and press F5.

All of the field names in the current view skeleton must be unique. If you try to add a field twice, dBASE IV refuses the command. However, you can add two fields with the same name from different database file skeletons; dBASE IV can differentiate between the two.

Update queries do not produce a view and therefore do not require a view skeleton. As you'll soon see, you use update queries to append or replace the data in a database, not to display the data. For this reason, a view skeleton is not required. When you create an update query and save it in a file, dBASE IV gives that file a .UPD file extension. dBASE IV also places an asterisk next to the file names of update queries when they appear in the Queries Panel of the Control Center.

Changing the Names of Fields in the View Skeleton

To change the name of a field in the view skeleton, use the **Edit field name** option from the **Fields** menu. You must first position the cursor on the view skeleton and place it on the field name you want to change. Next, enter the menu selection. dBASE IV prompts you for a new field name. Enter the field name of your choice and press ENTER. dBASE IV places the new field name in the upper-left corner of the box in the view skeleton that contains the old name.

Removing a Field from the View Skeleton

To remove a field from the current view skeleton, move the cursor to the column of the database file skeleton that contains the field name and press F5. dBASE IV removes the field name from the current view skeleton. To remove all of the fields in a particular database file skeleton from the current view skeleton, move the cursor to the first column of the database file skeleton that contains the field names and press F5. If all of the field names for that database are not already included in the view, dBASE IV adds them. To remove all of the fields, press F5 again.

You can also use the **Remove field from view** option in the **Fields** menu to remove fields from the current view skeleton. To use this method, move the cursor to the column of the database file skeleton that contains the field name and then use the **Remove field from view** option. dBASE IV removes the specified field from the current view skeleton.

Changing Field Position in a View Skeleton

As mentioned, dBASE IV adds fields to the current view skeleton in the order in which you add them with F5. To change the position of one or more fields in the current view skeleton, use the F4 key to move the cursor to the current view skeleton. Next, use TAB or SHIFT-TAB to locate the cursor on the field you want to move. Then, press the F6 key to select the field to move. If you want to move more than one field, you can include adjacent fields by pressing TAB or SHIFT-TAB. When you're ready, press ENTER to confirm the selection. Next, use RIGHT ARROW or LEFT ARROW to move the cursor to the new location of the field(s) and press F7 to complete the move.

Saving a Query

As mentioned, you can save your queries in a file and reuse them later. There are four ways you can save a query.

- Save the current query and continue editing it by using the menu system.
- Save the current query under a new name by using the menu system.
- Save your changes to a query and exit the Queries Design screen by using the menu system.
- Press CTRL-END to save the query and exit the Queries Design screen.

To save a query to a file without exiting the Queries Design screen, press F10 and select **Save this query** from the **Layout** menu. Your screen should look like Figure 6-12. This option places a prompt box on the screen. If the query is new, the prompt box is empty. Enter a file name of eight characters or less and press ENTER. The file name must begin with a letter but may contain letters, numbers, and underscores. If it is an existing query, or you are creating a new query from the dot prompt by using CREATE/MODIFY QUERY <*filename*>, the prompt box already contains a file name. To confirm the file name, press ENTER. dBASE IV saves the query as a file, using a .QBE extension.

When you save a query, dBASE IV checks that the conditions and calculated fields you've defined contain acceptable dBASE IV expressions. If not, dBASE IV stops the save, returns to the Queries Design screen, and displays a message that briefly describes the error.

To save an existing query under a new name, press F10 and select **Save this query** from the **Layout** menu. dBASE IV displays a prompt box showing the path and file name of the existing query file. Enter the new file name of your choice and press ENTER. dBASE IV saves the query under a new file name.

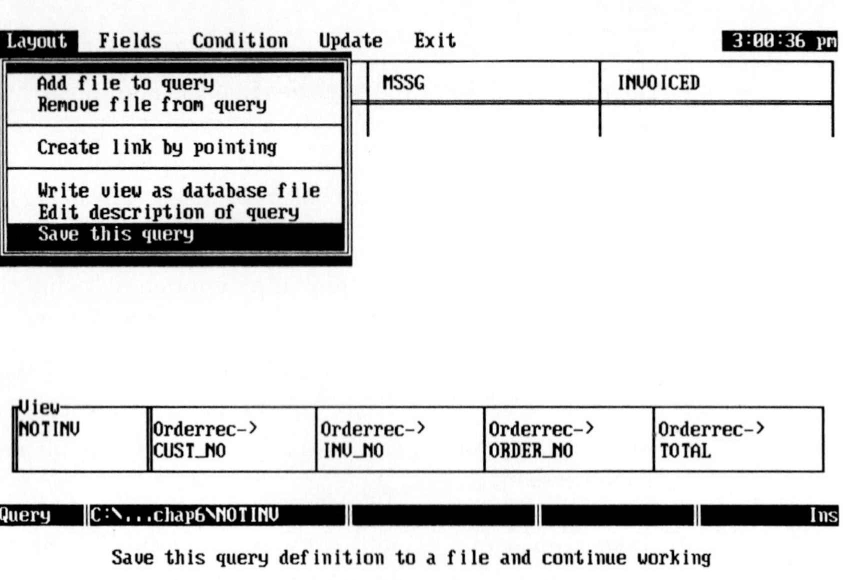

Figure 6-12. Saving or renaming a query file

To save the changes you've made and exit the Queries Design screen, press F10 and select **Save changes and exit** from the **Exit** menu. If the query is new, dBASE IV displays a prompt box that requests a file name, as in Figure 6-13. Enter the file name of your choice and press ENTER. dBASE IV saves the file with a .QBE extension and exits the Queries Design screen. If the file being saved is an existing file, or you entered the Queries Design screen from the dot prompt by using the CREATE QUERY *<filename>* command, dBASE IV already has a name for the file. Therefore, dBASE IV saves the file using that name and exits the Queries Design screen.

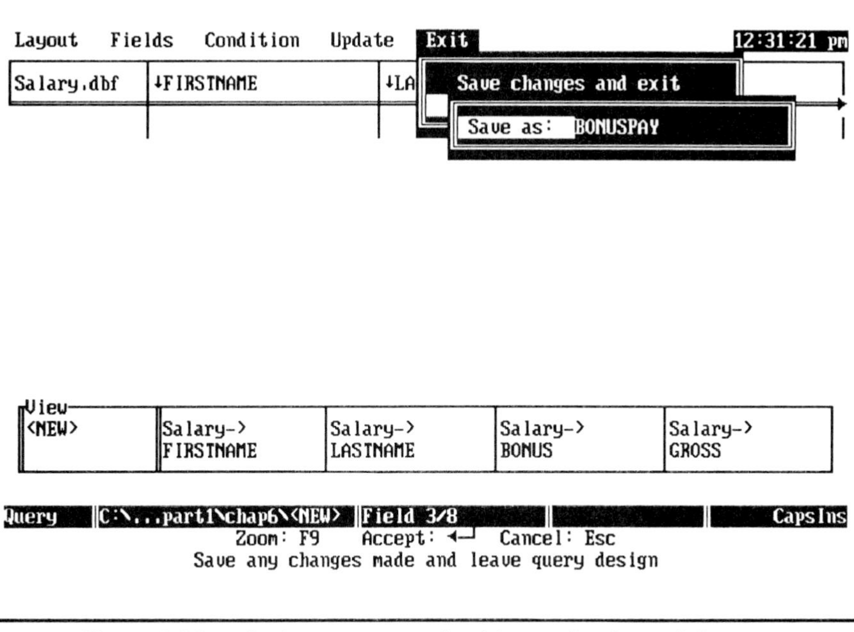

Figure 6-13. Saving a query and exiting to the Control Center

Tip: You should give your query files descriptive names. When you look at them in a directory listing or the Queries Panel, this will help you remember their functions.

When you save a view query file, dBASE IV actually creates two files, one with a .QBE extension and another with a .QBO extension. As mentioned, the .QBE file contains a series of dBASE IV commands, similar to those you might enter at the dot prompt. The .QBO file is a compiled file, which runs a great deal faster than does the .QBE file. dBASE IV actually uses this file when you press F2 on the file name in the Control Center or type **SET VIEW TO *<filename>*** from the dot prompt.

dBASE IV also creates two files when you save an update query file. The first file has a .UPD extension and the second has a .UPO extension. The .UPD file contains dBASE IV commands; the .UPO file is the compiled file.

Leaving the Queries Design Screen

You can exit the Queries Design screen either by pressing ESC or by using the menu system. When you press ESC, dBASE IV prompts you with an option box containing the message "Are you sure you want to abandon this operation?" Your screen should look like the one in Figure 6-14. If you select **No**, dBASE IV returns you

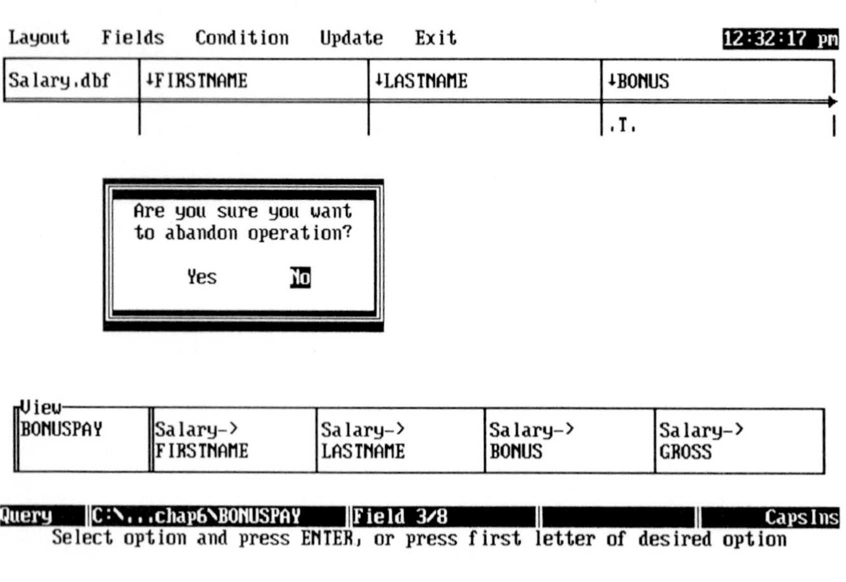

Figure 6-14. Pressing ESC abandons a query without saving changes

to the Queries Design screen. On the other hand, if you select **Yes**, dBASE IV exits the Queries Design screen without saving any changes you've made to the current query.

To use the menu system to exit the Queries Design screen, select either **Save changes and exit** or **Abandon changes and exit** from the **Exit** menu. When you select the **Save changes and exit** option, dBASE IV saves any changes you've made to the query. If a file name does not already exist for the query, dBASE IV prompts you for one. When you select the **Abandon changes and exit** option, dBASE IV exits the Queries Design screen without saving any changes.

Activating a Query

Once a query file is activated, dBASE IV uses the view from that query file to display data, perform your commands, and provide information to custom forms, reports, and labels. dBASE IV only allows one active query at a time.

You can use several methods to activate a query file.

- Create a query on the Queries Design screen and press F2. Whenever you create a new query and press F2, the query is activated.
- Press ENTER on an existing query file name in the Queries Panel of the Control Center. dBASE IV displays an option box. Select **Use view** from the option box and press ENTER. dBASE IV activates the specified query file.
- Press F2 on an existing query file name in the Queries Panel of the Control Center. dBASE IV activates and runs the query file, displaying the results on the Browse screen.
- Type **SET VIEW TO *<query filename>*** at the dot prompt, or include this command in a program file. dBASE IV activates the specified query file.

The query file name above the line in the Queries Panel of the Control Center is the currently active query.

Running View and Update Queries

You can use several methods to run view and update queries from both the Control Center and the dot prompt.

- From the Control Center, press F2 on the file name of an existing view query file name in the Queries Panel. dBASE IV activates and runs the query, displaying the results on the Browse screen.
- From the Control Center, press ENTER on the update query file name to run an update query. (Update query file names appear with an asterisk next to them in the Queries Panel). dBASE IV displays an option box on the screen. Select the **Run update** option and press enter. dBASE IV asks you if you really want to run the update query. Select **Yes** and dBASE IV will run the update query. To see the results, press F2 to display the database on the Browse screen.
- From the Queries Design screen, press F10 and select the **Perform the update** option from the **Update** menu to run an update query.
- From the dot prompt, type **SET VIEW TO *<query filename>***. Follow this with the BROWSE command to see the results. This applies to view queries only. If you type **DO *<query filename>*** and use the name of a view query, dBASE IV compiles your .QBE file into a .DBO compiled file. The view query is activated, but to no purpose. You now have a .QBO and a .DBO file that both perform the same function.
- From the dot prompt, use the DO command followed by the file name of an update query file. Make sure to include the .UPD file extension. Otherwise, dBASE IV assumes you are referring to a .PRG file and may give you the "File does not

exist" error message. dBASE IV runs the update query. To see the results, enter the BROWSE command.

At the dot prompt, when you type the DO command followed by the name of an update query file, dBASE IV compiles your .UPD update query file and creates a .DBO compiled file. It actually runs the .DBO file to perform your update query. To avoid confusion, dBASE IV allows you to rename the new .DBO file with a .UPO extension. From then on, you can type **DO *<update query filename>*.UPO** to run the file. To rename the file, use the **DOS Utilities** option from the **Tools** menu or, at the dot prompt, the RENAME command.

Closing a Query File

Closing a view query file releases dBASE IV from the conditions specified by the query files. dBASE IV returns to its normal operation. You can close a query file in two ways

- From the Control Center, press ENTER on the name of an existing view query file name in the Queries Panel. dBASE IV displays an option box on the screen. Select **Close view** and press ENTER.
- From the dot prompt, enter **CLOSE ALL**.

Update query files are closed automatically by dBASE IV immediately after you run them.

Defining Filter Conditions

dBASE IV also lets you define filter conditions for data used by a view query. Filter conditions limit the scope of the query to a

Operator	Description
ASC	Ascending ASCII sort
ASCDICT	Ascending dictionary sort
AVG	Average
CNT	Count the number of records
DSC	Descending ASCII sort
DSCDICT	Descending dictionary sort
EVERY	Specifies every record
FIND	Locates a record
FIRST	Specifies the first matching record
GROUP BY	Groups similar values
LIKE	Specifies an exact match
MIN	Minimum
MAX	Maximum
SOUNDS LIKE	Specifies a sound-alike match (SOUNDEX())
SUM	Sum
UNIQUE	Ignores duplicates

Table 6-1. Queries Design Screen Special Operators

specific set of records that meet the condition. To define a filter condition, you enter instructions underneath the field names in the database file skeleton. You can enter special operators specific to the Queries Design screen, or any acceptable dBASE IV expression. dBASE IV then uses these instructions to filter the data used by the query. You do not have to include a field in the view skeleton in order to use that field to state a condition for the current query. For example, imagine you are building the query in the overview to this chapter. In that query, the Bonus logical field is used to state a condition. You do not have to include the Bonus logical field within the query's view skeleton to use it to state a condition for the query.

The special operators specific to the Queries Design screen are shown in Table 6-1. The use of these operators is illustrated throughout the rest of this chapter.

Expression Type	Expression
Character	"Los Angeles"
Numeric	>5000
Logical	.T. or .F.
Date	>{12/15/90}

Table 6-2. Example dBASE IV Expressions

Table 6-2 shows some example dBASE IV expressions that you might use as filter conditions in a view query. Note that there are four types of dBASE IV expressions: character, numeric, logical, and date. Character expressions are enclosed in quotes and are used for character fields. Numeric expressions involve numbers and apply to numeric fields. Logical expressions state a yes/no (.T. or .F.) condition and apply to logical fields. Instead of using just .T. (true) or .F. (false), you may also use .t., .f., .Y., .N., .y. or .n.. Date expressions are enclosed by curly braces ({}) and apply to date fields. To apply a condition to a memo field, you must use a condition box. For more about condition boxes, see the section "Creating a Condition Box" later in this chapter.

Note that the numeric and date expressions in Table 6-2 include the > sign, a relational operator meaning greater than. You may also use mathematical, logical, and string operators. For more about both operators and building dBASE IV expressions, see Chapter 7.

You can also use dBASE IV functions to help form filter conditions in view queries. Table 6-3 shows some dBASE IV functions. Functions always return a result. For example, the DATE( ) function returns today's date. You can combine these functions with operators to specify a condition. For example, .NOT. DELETED( ) combines the logical operator .NOT. with the DELETED( ) function to exclude from the current view query records marked for deletion. For more information about available dBASE IV functions, see Chapter 33.

Function	Returns
DATE()	Today's date
RECNO()	The current record number
DELETED()	Deletion status
STR()	Converts number to character string

Table 6-3. Example dBASE IV Functions

Tip: Press SHIFT-F1 to see and select from a complete list of available fields in the currently active database as well as dBASE IV operators and functions. dBASE IV places the Expression Builder on your screen (see Figure 6-15). Highlight the field, operator, or function of your choice and press ENTER. dBASE IV will add it to the current expression.

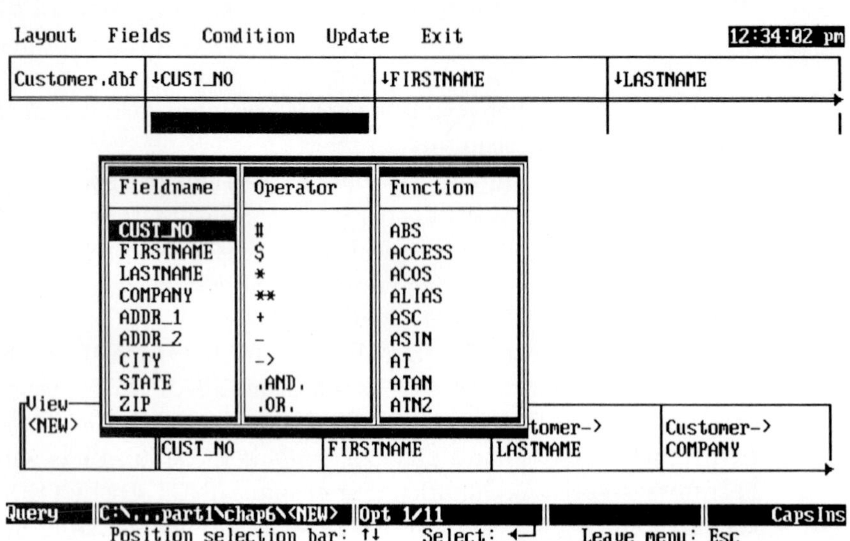

Figure 6-15. The Expression Builder builds expressions

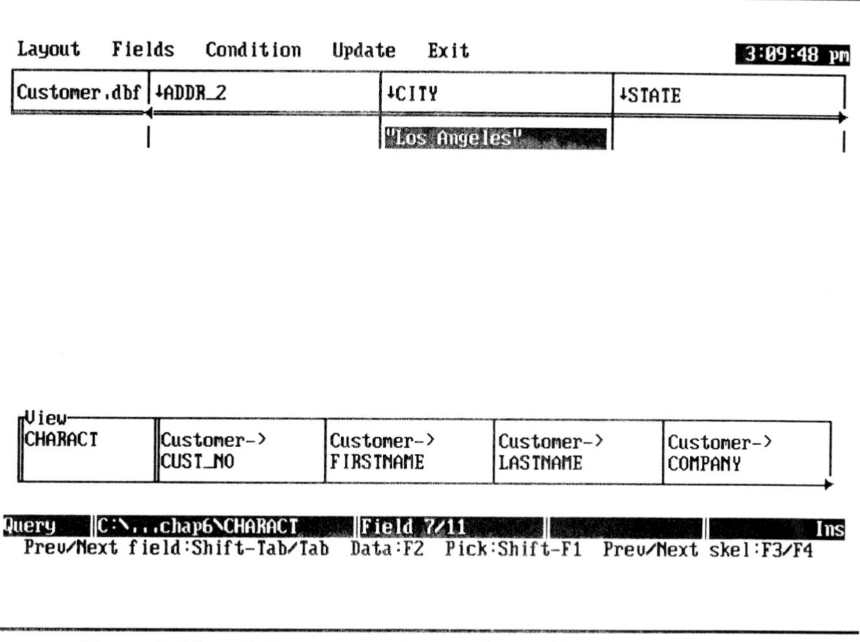

Figure 6-16. A character string used as a filter condition

Using Filter Conditions

As mentioned, you specify filter conditions for a view query by typing instructions underneath a field name in a file skeleton. For example, in Figure 6-16, a condition appears in the City field column of the CUSTOMER database. The condition is the character string "Los Angeles". Note that the character string is enclosed in quotes in order to make it an acceptable dBASE IV expression. This condition limits the data used by the view query to customers in Los Angeles.

You can precede this character string with the special LIKE operator. This operator lets you specify only part of a character string. For example, the condition LIKE "Los" will yield customers in Los Angeles, Los Gatos, Los Alamos, and Los Altos. The LIKE

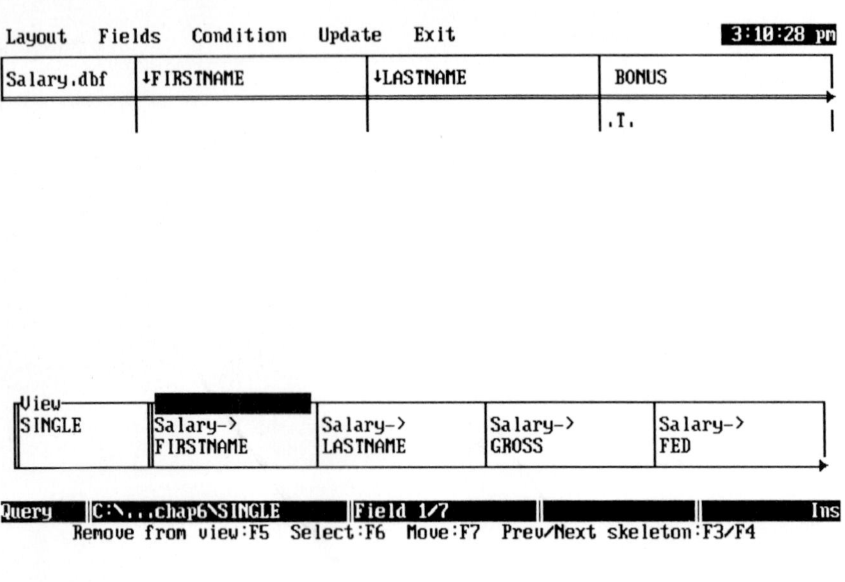

Figure 6-17. A logical expression used as a filter condition

operator is analogous to the LIKE( ) function covered in detail in Chapter 33.

You can also use the SOUNDS LIKE operator to locate character strings in quotes. However, this operator finds words that match the sound of the quoted character string. For example, to find the character string "Borrowes", enter **SOUNDS LIKE "borros"**. The SOUNDS LIKE operator is analogous to the SOUNDEX() function covered in detail in Chapter 33.

You can also use the $ operator to locate character strings. For example, to locate the character string "ACME Manufacturing", enter **$"ACME Manufacturing"** in the appropriate column. You can also use this operator to search memo fields; however you

Records Fields Go To Exit 3:11:19 pm

FIRSTNAME	LASTNAME	BONUS	GROSS	FED	FICA	STATE	NET
Mary	Jones	F	24000.00	6000.00	1802.40	720.00	15477.60
Drew	Gibson	T	22000.00	5500.00	1652.20	660.00	14187.80
Ralph	Moriarity	F	26000.00	6500.00	1952.60	780.00	16767.40
Clive	Bunker	F	23000.00	5750.00	1727.30	690.00	14832.70
John	Patrovich	F	32000.03	8000.01	2403.20	960.00	20636.82
Suzanne	Chambers	F	17000.00	4250.00	1276.70	510.00	10963.30
Keith	Campbell	T	52000.00	13000.0	3905.20	1560.00	33534.80
George	Haenszel	T	22000.00	5500.00	1652.20	660.00	14187.80
Jeff	Hill	T	25000.00	6250.00	1877.50	750.00	16122.50
Sam	Hammons	T	31000.00	7750.00	2328.10	930.00	19991.90
Kevin	Anderson	T	28000.00	7000.00	2102.80	840.00	18057.20

Browse C:\...chap6\SALARY Rec 1/11 File Ins

View and edit fields

Figure 6-18. SALARY before the query

must use it in an expression in the condition box. Furthermore, you must place the **$** operator after the character string, instead of before it, and follow it with the name of the memo field. For example, to find the character string "Stockout" in a memo field called Comments, enter in the condition box **"Stockout" $ Comments**. For more on using condition boxes, see the next section.

The query in Figure 6-17 uses a single logical condition, .T., under the Bonus field in the database file skeleton for the SALARY database. This field defines those employees who will receive a bonus this year. This single condition confines the current query to records in the SALARY that have a logical true (.T.) in the Bonus field. Figure 6-18 shows the SALARY database on the Browse

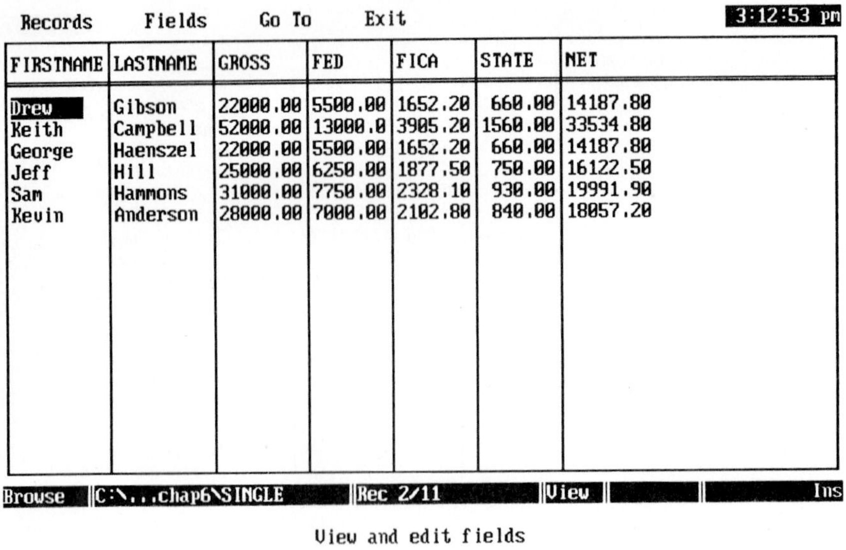

Records   Fields   Go To   Exit   3:12:53 pm

FIRSTNAME	LASTNAME	GROSS	FED	FICA	STATE	NET
Drew	Gibson	22000.00	5500.00	1652.20	660.00	14187.80
Keith	Campbell	52000.00	13000.0	3905.20	1560.00	33534.80
George	Haenszel	22000.00	5500.00	1652.20	660.00	14187.80
Jeff	Hill	25000.00	6250.00	1877.50	750.00	16122.50
Sam	Hammons	31000.00	7750.00	2328.10	930.00	19991.90
Kevin	Anderson	28000.00	7000.00	2102.80	840.00	18057.20

Browse | C:\...chap6\SINGLE | Rec 2/11 | View | | Ins

View and edit fields

Figure 6-19. SALARY after the query

screen before the query is activated. Figure 6-19 shows the same database after you activate the query by pressing F2.

You can also stipulate a condition for more than one field. For example, two conditions are present in Figure 6-20. The Bonus field keeps its logical true condition. However, the Gross field of the SALARY database also contains the numeric expression >25000. This combined condition limits the records used by the query to employees scheduled for a bonus *and* who make more than $25,000 per year. Figure 6-21 shows the results of this query when you press F2 to display the query on the Browse screen. Note the much smaller number of records selected.

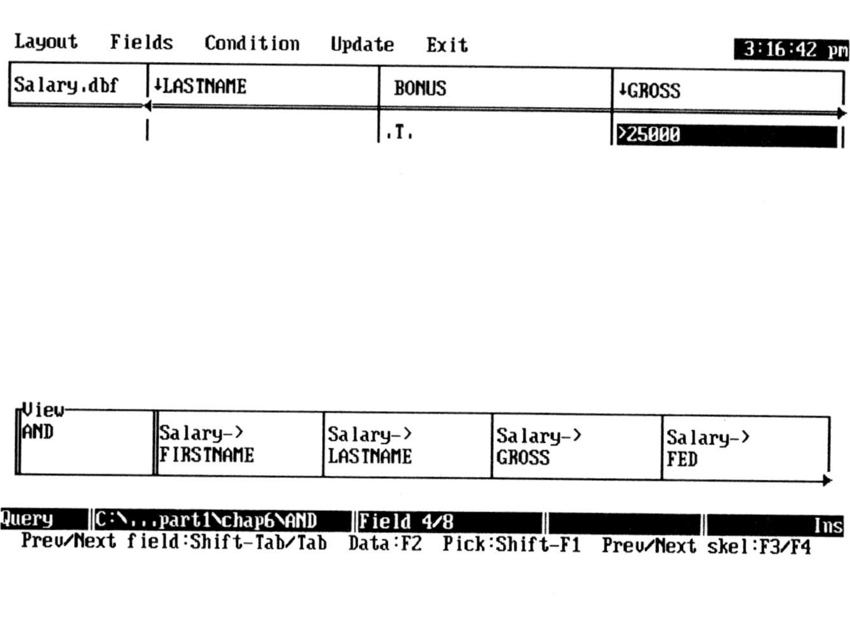

Figure 6-20. Combining conditions in the same row (.AND.)

You can also place conditions in more than one row beneath a field column in a database file skeleton. To expand and contract the length of the columns beneath a database file skeleton, press DOWN ARROW or UP ARROW. When you use this method to define combined conditions, the query uses records where either condition applies. For example, in Figure 6-22, the .T. value in the Bonus field appears in the second row. Additionally, the numeric expression >25000, under the Gross field is now placed in the first row. This query calls for records in the SALARY database where an employee is scheduled to receive a bonus, or makes more than $25,000 per year.

```
Records      Fields      Go To      Exit                              3:17:20 pm

FIRSTNAME LASTNAME  GROSS     FED      FICA     STATE    NET
Keith     Campbell  52000.00 13000.0  3905.20  1560.00  33534.80
Sam       Hammons   31000.00 7750.00  2328.10   930.00  19991.90
Kevin     Anderson  28000.00 7000.00  2102.80   840.00  18057.20

Browse  C:\...part1\chap6\AND   Rec 7/11        View               Ins
                        View and edit fields
```

Figure 6-21. The results of the combined condition query

If you run out of room while entering an expression in a field column, dBASE IV scrolls the entry from right to left as you add characters. However, you can see and edit the entire entry by pressing F9, Zoom. dBASE IV places a window on the screen that shows the entire entry, as in Figure 6-23. When the entry is the way you want it, press F9 again. dBASE IV returns you to the Queries Design screen.

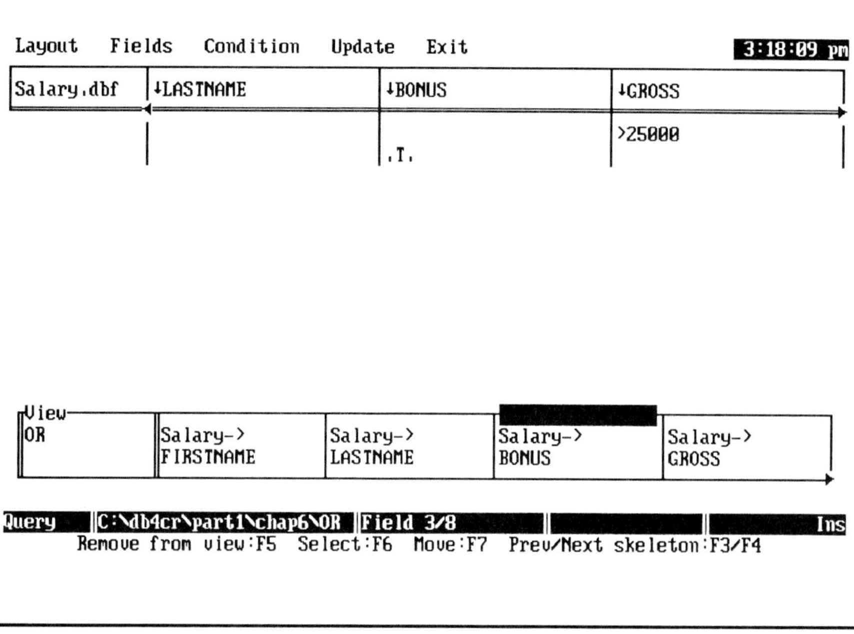

Figure 6-22. Combining conditions in two rows (.OR.)

Creating a Condition Box

You can use a condition box when you need to define conditions for more than one database file skeleton. The condition box is optional and is displayed on the lower-right portion of your screen, as in Figure 6-24. When you use a condition box, the condition you specify applies to the entire view query. Furthermore, there is only one condition box per query.

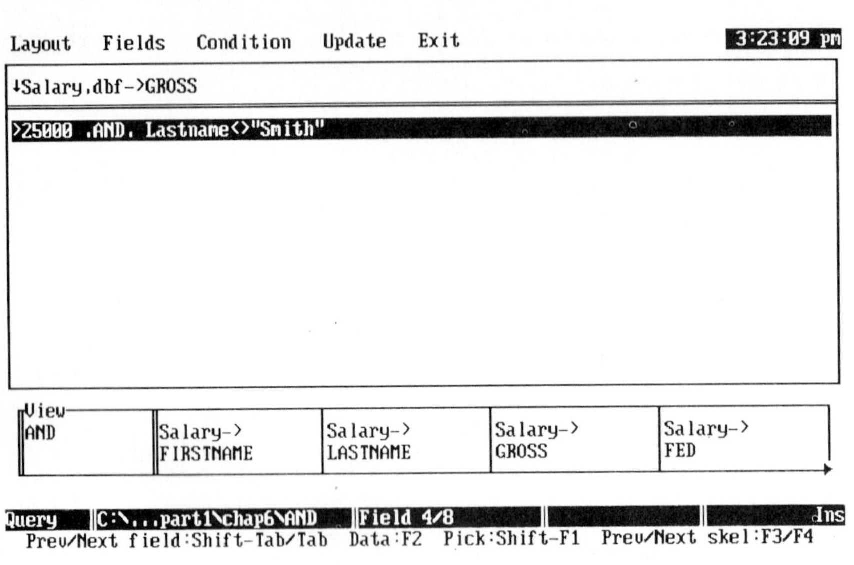

Figure 6-23. Press F9 to use a Zoom window

To have dBASE IV place a condition box on the Queries Design screen, press F10 and select **Add condition box** from the **Condition** menu. Your screen should look like Figure 6-25. To delete a condition box, use the **Delete condition box** option. To hide the condition box, use **Show condition box**. This option toggles the screen display of a condition box on and off. When the setting is off, dBASE IV displays the marker CONDITION BOX in place of the condition box. However, when you press F3 or F4 to move to the condition box, the condition box reappears.

When you create a condition box, dBASE IV places the cursor in the box and you can begin typing your condition. You can also press SHIFT-F1 to select field names, operators, and functions via the Expression Builder. As with database file skeleton columns, dBASE IV scrolls your entry from right to left when you reach the

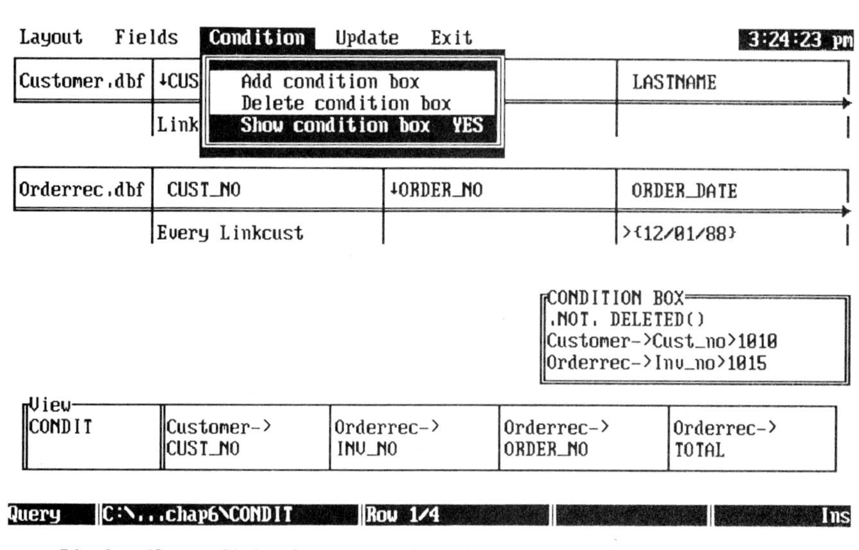

Figure 6-24. The condition box menu

right side of the condition box. To see the entire entry, press F9. dBASE IV will place your condition in a Zoom window.

You can place more than one condition in a condition box—dBASE IV supports up to 13 conditions per query. However, you must place each condition on a separate line. To get to the next line, press DOWN ARROW. For example, the condition box in Figure 6-25 contains three conditions, each on a separate line. The first condition, .NOT. DELETED( ), precludes the use of records marked for deletion. The next two conditions involve field pointers.

If more than one database file skeleton is present, you must point to the fields in each database using the -> field pointer. You create the -> pointer by pressing - followed by **>**, or by selecting the field pointer from the Expression Builder. For example, the expression Customer->Cust_no>1010 points to the Cust_no field in the

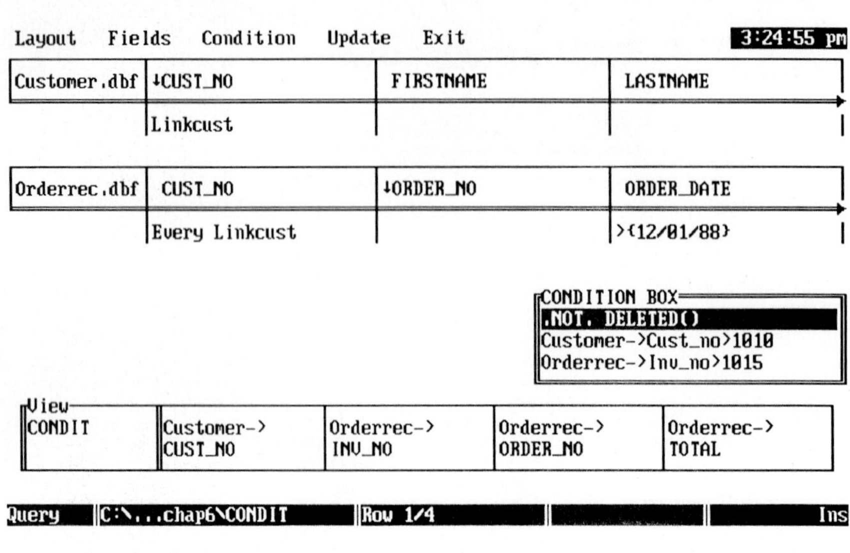

Figure 6-25. Use the condition box to specify conditions for more than one database

CUSTOMER database and limits the records used in the query to customer numbers greater than 1010.

To modify data in an existing condition box, press F3 or F4 to locate the cursor in the condition box. Press DOWN ARROW or UP ARROW to get to the expression you want to modify. Then modify the condition using the usual editing keys.

Creating Calculated Fields

The Queries Design screen also supports *calculated fields*. Calculated fields use data from one or more fields in one or more of the displayed database file skeletons. For example, suppose you are working with an orders database that contains the fields Units and Price. You can create a calculated field called Totl by multiplying the Units field by the Price field to create a numeric total for each

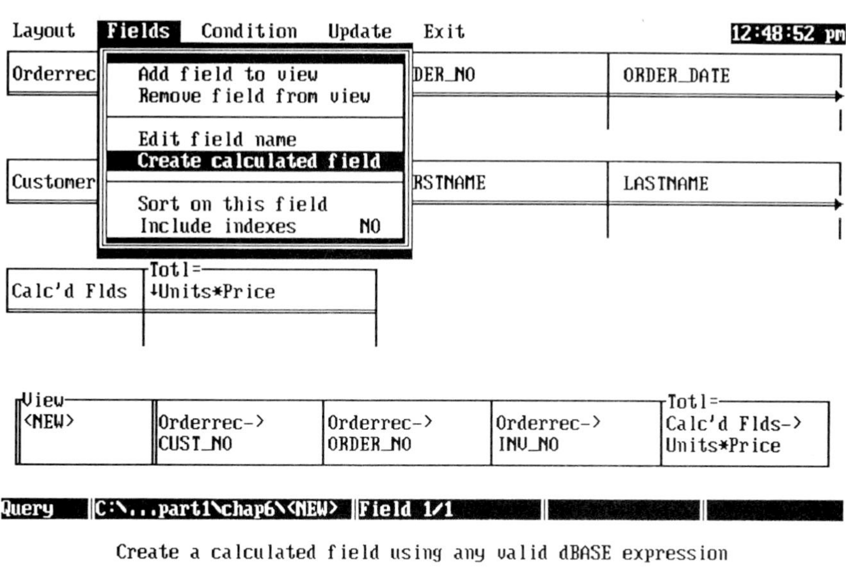

Figure 6-26. The **Create calculated field** menu

record in the view. Once you create a calculated field, its name is displayed on the Browse screen when you press F2 to display the view query.

To create a calculated field, press F10 and select the **Create calculated field** option from the **Fields** menu (Figure 6-26). dBASE IV places a new calculated field file skeleton with the name Calc'd Flds on the lower-left portion of your screen. The cursor is automatically located in the first column. You can then type your calculation, for example **Units*Price**. To add additional fields to the skeleton, repeat the **Create calculated field** menu selection. To remove the **Calc'd Flds** file skeleton, place the cursor on the calculated field, and use the **Remove file from query** option from the **Layout** menu.

To add a calculated field to the current view, press F5 on the calculated field. dBASE IV prompts you for a field name. Type the name of your choice and press ENTER. dBASE IV adds the new name to both the current view skeleton and the calculated field header. To change the name of the field, use the **Edit field name** option from the **Fields** menu.

When you create a calculated field expression that uses fields from more than one database, you must use field pointers (->) to point to the selected fields in each database. For example, to point to the Cust_no field in the CUSTOMER database, enter **Customer->Cust_no** in the Calculated field column.

Tip: When you create a calculated field, you can use the name of that field on the queries design work surface as well as in the condition box.

Searching the Database

You can use a view query to search a database for records that meet specific conditions by using the FIND operator. To use the FIND operator, first enter the search conditions in the appropriate field columns of a database file skeleton. For example, to find a record that contains a first name of John and a last name of Smith, enter **"John"** in the Firstname field column and **"Smith"** in the Lastname field column. Then, type the word **FIND** under the name of the database in the first column of the file skeleton. When you execute this query, dBASE IV locates the first record that meets your search conditions. Since the FIND operator does not filter data, all the records are displayed on the Browse screen. However, the cursor appears on the record that meets your conditions.

Sorting, Summarizing, and Grouping

The Queries Design screen offers ways to sort, summarize, and group data without creating a new database. Each of these topics is discussed in the sections that follow.

Sort Operator	Sort Description	Sort Order
ASC	Ascending ASCII	A..Z, a..z, 0..9
DSC	Descending ASCII	z..a, Z..A, 9..0
ASCDICT	Ascending Dictionary	Aa..Zz, 0..9
DSCDICT	Descending Dictionary	zZ..aA, 9..0

Table 6-4. Queries Design Screen Sort Operators

Sorting Records in a View

You can sort the data in a view in alphabetical or numeric order by using *sort operators*. Sort operators specify sort conditions for database fields. When dBASE IV sorts the data in a specific field, the records in the database are presented in that order as well.

Table 6-4 lists four types of sort operators. You place sort operators under the field names in a database file skeleton. You can enter the sort operators yourself or you can select **Sort on this field** from the **Fields** menu.

To enter sort operators yourself, press F3 or F4 to move the cursor into the file skeleton representing the database you want to sort. Next, press TAB to move to the field name on which you want to sort the database. Then, enter one of the four sort operators in that field's column. For example, if you want to sort the CUSTOMER database by company, move the cursor to the Company field and type in a sort operator. Finally, follow that sort operator with the number 1. The number 1 specifies that the Company field is to be given first priority when the database is sorted. For example, in Figure 6-27, the sort operator in the Company field is ASCDICT1. This sorts the CUSTOMER database by company in ascending dictionary order.

You can also use the menu system to enter sort operators. To do this, move the cursor to the field name on which you want to sort the database. Next, select **Sort on this field** from the **Fields** menu. dBASE IV displays an option box with the sort options

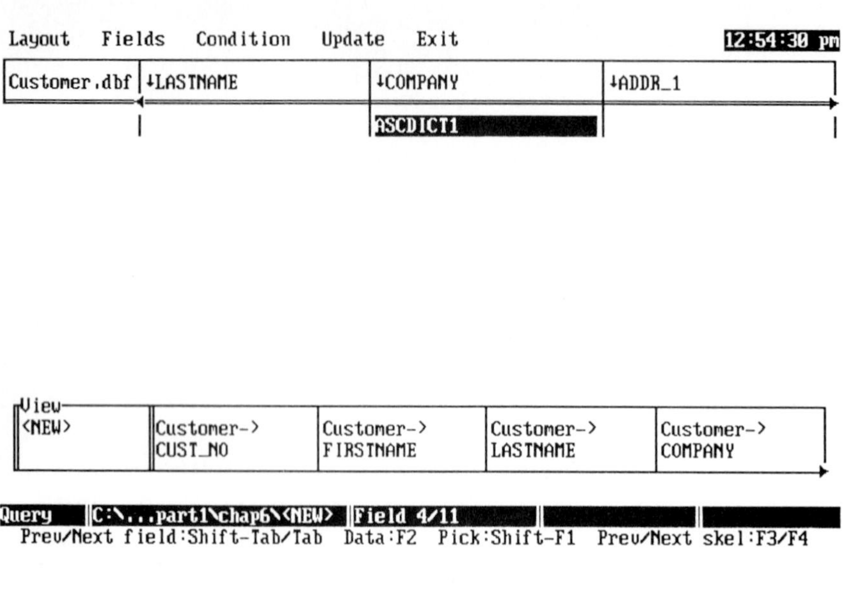

Figure 6-27. A single sort operator

shown in Table 6-4. Highlight the desired sort order and press ENTER. dBASE IV enters the specified sort operator in the current column of the current database file skeleton. The first sort operator is automatically followed with the number 1, and the second sort operator with a 2, and so on. These numbers indicate the order of precedence in the sort.

You can also sort on more than one field at a time. For example, you can sort a mailing database by last name first and first name second. (Jack Smith will appear before John Smith). To sort a database in this manner, enter two sort operators in different columns of the current file skeleton. For example, in Figure 6-28, the ASCDICT1 operator is in the Lastname field of the CUSTOMER database. The 1 following the sort operator gives this field first order of precedence when the sort is performed. The

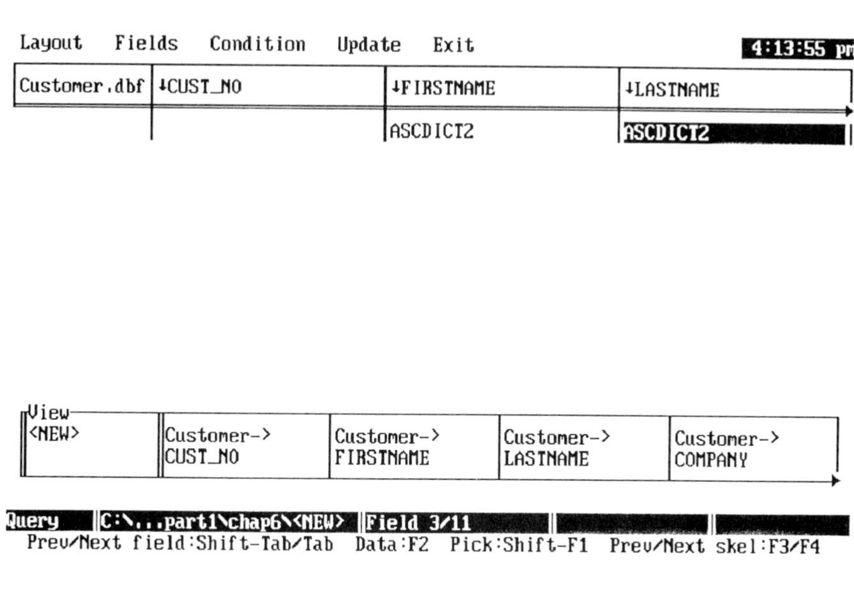

Figure 6-28. Combining sort operators

ASCDICT2 operator is in the Firstname field; the 2 gives this field the second order of precedence.

Summarizing Records in a View

To summarize the records in a view, you use *summary operators*. Summary operators allow you get the sum, average, minimum, maximum, and record count from a group of records—SUM, AVG, MIN, MAX, and CNT, respectively. You can only apply these operators to fields with certain data types (see Table 6-5).

To use a summary operator, place it in a column beneath the name of a specific field. For example, in Figure 6-29, the AVG operator is used to return the average quantity on hand per part number in the PARTS database. (The On_hand field defines the

Field Type	Summary Operators Supported
Numeric	AVG,SUM,MIN,MAX,CNT
Character	MIN,MAX,CNT
Date	MIN,MAX,CNT
Logical	CNT
Memo	Not supported

Table 6-5. Summary Operators Applicable to Various Field Types

total parts on hand for each part number.) The CNT operator is also placed in the Part_no field column, returning the total number of values in that field. When you press F2 to display the view, the AVG operator returns the sum for the On_hand field column

```
Layout   Fields   Condition   Update   Exit                        3:28:54 pm
Parts.dbf  |↓PART_NO        |↓DESCRIPT        |↓ON_HAND
           |CNT             |                 |AVG

View
SUMMARY  |Parts->   |Parts->   |Parts->   |Parts->
         |PART_NO   |DESCRIPT  |ON_HAND   |ON_ORDER

Query  C:\...chap6\SUMMARY    File 1/1                    CapsIns
 Next field:Tab  Add/Remove all fields:F5  Zoom:F9  Prev/Next skeleton:F3/F4
```

Figure 6-29. Using the CNT and AVG summary operators

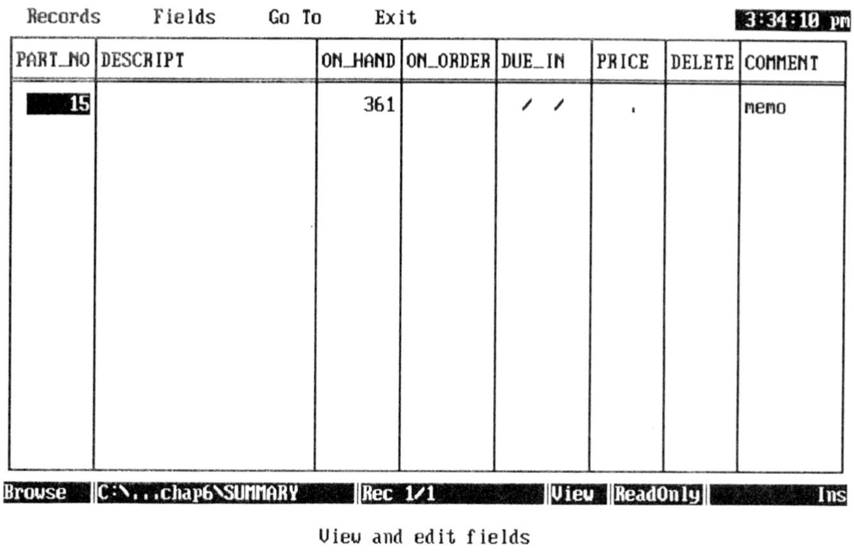

PART_NO	DESCRIPT	ON_HAND	ON_ORDER	DUE_IN	PRICE	DELETE	COMMENT
15		361		/ /	.		memo

Records Fields Go To Exit 3:34:10 pm

Browse C:\...chap6\SUMMARY Rec 1/1 View ReadOnly Ins

View and edit fields

Figure 6-30. The view from the CNT and AVG summary query

divided by the number of records in the database. The CNT operator returns the total count of all part numbers. The other fields are left blank. Figure 6-30 shows the displayed results of this view query.

Using summary operators in filter condition expressions can cause a conflict. When dBASE IV performs a query, it starts at the top of the database and reviews the records one by one. If you use a summary operator in a condition, the value of that operator is not known until all of the records in the database are reviewed. Thus, when you use a summary operator in a condition, the condition calls for a value that does not yet exist and dBASE IV issues an error message.

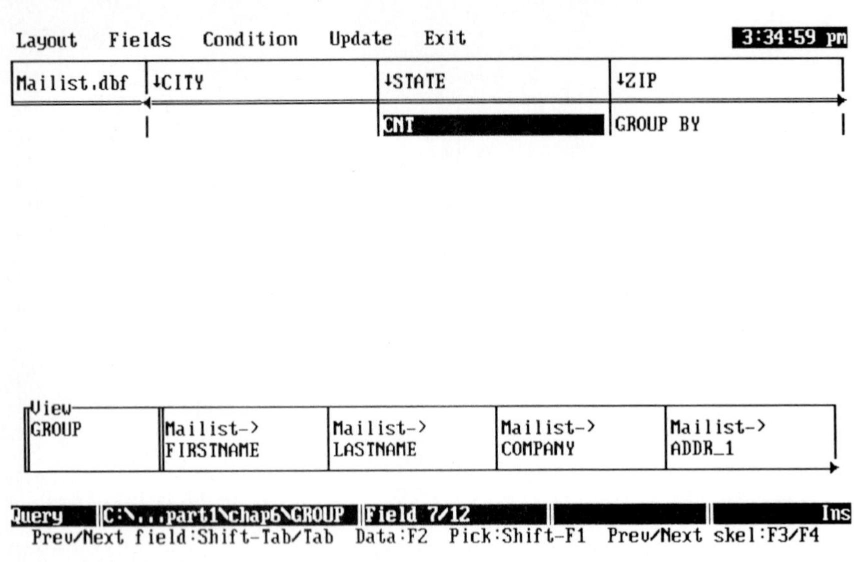

Figure 6-31. The GROUP BY operator groups records with similar values in a selected field column

Grouping Records in a View

You can use the GROUP BY operator to group records that have the same value in a given field. You can then use summary operators to return information about those individual groups. For example, if you're working with a mailing list database, you may need to know how many records there are for each ZIP code. To get this information, use the GROUP BY operator in conjunction with the CNT operator.

Figure 6-31 shows an example that uses a small sample from the MAILIST database. The GROUP BY operator is placed in the Zip field, which groups the records in the MAILIST database by ZIP code. The CNT operator appears in the State field. The placement of the CNT operator is appropriate here because there are no

Records Fields Go To Exit 4:02:00 pm

CITY	STATE	ZIP	COUNTRY	AREACODE	T
	4.00				
	1.00	01783			
	1.00	02158-163			
	1.00	06680			
	4.00	06880			
	3.00	07782			
	3.00	10020			
	1.00	11733			
	2.00	15321			
	1.00	18934			
	3.00	19317			
	5.00	20005			
	5.00	32303			
	3.00	45245			
	3.00	46240			
	1.00	48356			
	5.00	56902			

Browse | C:\...part1\chap6\GROUP | Rec 1/34 | View | ReadOnly

View and edit fields

Figure 6-32. The results of the GROUP BY query

empty records in this database. Thus, the CNT operator just returns the total number of records in each group. Figure 6-32 shows the results of this view query displayed on the Browse screen. Note that the individual ZIP codes that comprise each group appear in the Zip field. The count for each ZIP code group is shown in the State field.

When you perform a view query that contains a GROUP BY operator, dBASE IV automatically sorts the groups in ascending alphabetical or numeric order. However, you can sort the groups in a different order by following the GROUP BY operator with one of the sort operators. For example, the query in Figure 6-33 uses the ZIP code example from Figure 6-31; however, the DSC sort operator follows the GROUP BY operator. This returns the same information, but displays the ZIP code groups in descending order.

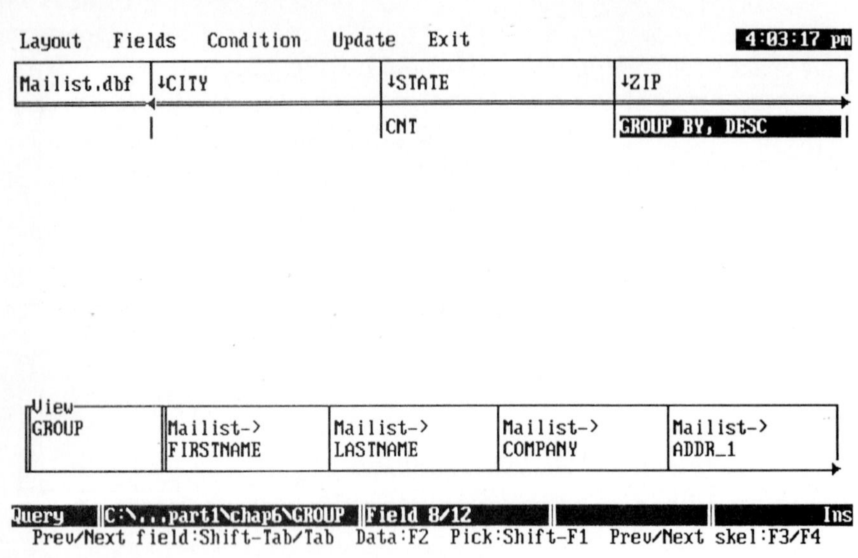

Figure 6-33. The DESC sort operator following the GROUP BY operator

Avoiding Duplicate Records and Values

You can eliminate duplicate records and values from a view by using the UNIQUE operator. For example, suppose you are composing a view query for a mailing. Furthermore, the view you're composing includes two databases, the CUSTOMER database and the VENDOR database. One of your vendors may also be one of your customers. To avoid printing duplicate information, you can place the UNIQUE operator under one of the database names in its file skeleton. Now when dBASE IV processes the view query, duplicate records are filtered out.

You can also use the UNIQUE operator in conjunction with a summary operator to avoid duplicate values. For example, say you need to know how many unique last names there are in the mailing list database. You can enter the expression **CNT UNIQUE** in the Lastname field of the mailing list database file skeleton. This returns the total number of unique last names in the database.

The power of the UNIQUE operator is somewhat limited. If the total size of the fields in a unique query exceeds 100, you will get the error message "Total size of fields in view too large for UNIQUE query."

Editing the Data from a View Query

When you display the results of a view query on the Browse or Edit screens, you can usually edit that data. However, there are several types of Browse or Edit displays that you cannot edit.

- You cannot edit a view display that involves two databases.
- You cannot edit the data displayed in a calculated field.
- You cannot edit data defined by one or more of the summary operators (CNT, AVG, MIN, MAX or SUM).
- You can edit views containing a single sort operator, but only if that operator is placed in an indexed field. For more about using indexed fields in your queries, see the section "Using Index Files" later in this chapter.

Although you cannot edit certain views on the Browse or Edit screen, you can still use that data to print reports. For example, you cannot edit calculated fields, but you can use them in reports.

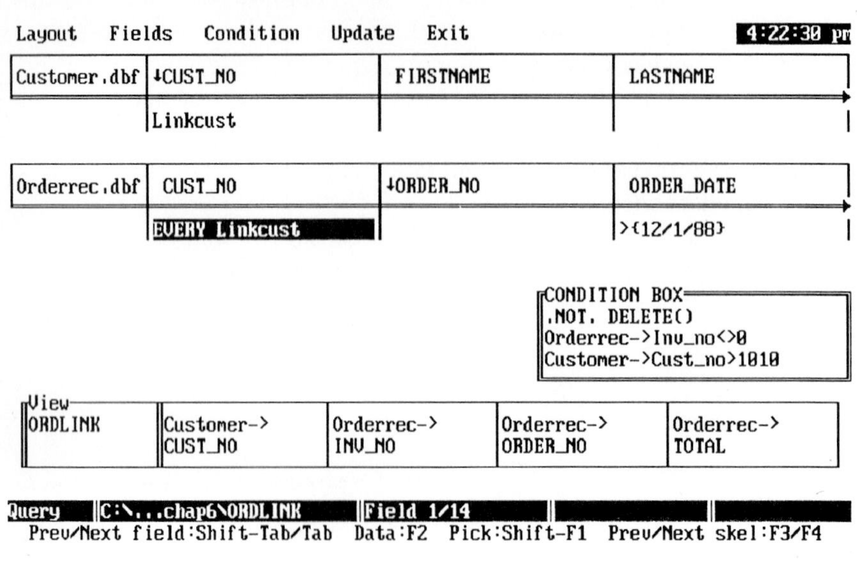

Figure 6-34. Linking databases using example variables

Linking Databases

You can also link databases by using a view query. Once the databases are linked, you can compose a view that includes data from both files. Suppose you have a two-database order-entry system. Customer names and addresses are stored in one database. Each customer in that database is identified by a unique customer number. The second database contains all of the orders placed by those customers. Each order placed by a customer includes his or her unique customer number. You can then link the two databases by using those unique customer numbers. This links a customer's name and address to all of his or her orders.

To link two or more databases by using a view query, you use *example variables*. Example variables are simply words that you make up. You place these variables in a field that both databases

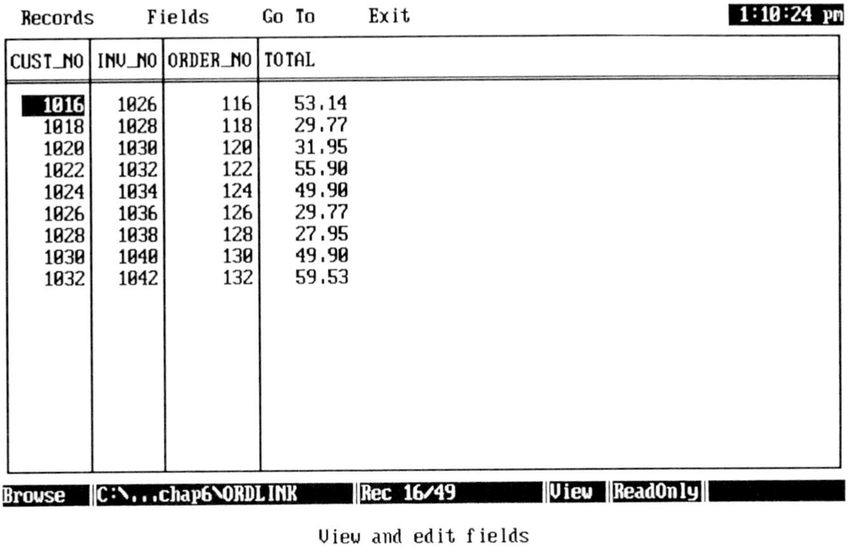

Records Fields Go To Exit 1:10:24 pm

CUST_NO	INV_NO	ORDER_NO	TOTAL
1016	1026	116	53.14
1018	1028	118	29.77
1020	1030	120	31.95
1022	1032	122	55.90
1024	1034	124	49.90
1026	1036	126	29.77
1028	1038	128	27.95
1030	1040	130	49.90
1032	1042	132	59.53

Browse C:\...chap6\ORDLINK Rec 16/49 View ReadOnly

View and edit fields

Figure 6-35. The view from link query in Figure 6-34

have in common. For example, using the customer and orders databases just described, you place matching example variables in the field columns that contain the unique customer numbers in each database. In Figure 6-34, that field is called Cust_no.

In Figure 6-34, the two databases to be linked are CUSTOMER and ORDERREC. The example variable Linkcust appears in the Cust_no field of each database. The EVERY operator also appears in front of the Linkcust example variable in the ORDERREC database. This operator (explained later in this section) selects every record in the ORDERREC database. When dBASE IV performs this query, it uses the value from the Cust_no field in the first database, CUSTOMER, and searches for a matching value in the Cust_no field of the second database, ORDERREC. When the view is displayed on the Browse screen, a customer's name and address are matched with an order placed by that customer. Figure 6-35 shows the results of this view.

The EVERY operator that appears in the Cust_no field of the ORDERREC database displays all of the records in that database. This operator catches blank records as well as records with bad customer numbers. Without EVERY, dBASE IV displays only records for which a matching customer number is found, ignoring blank records or records with invalid customer numbers.

dBASE IV will enter example variables for you if you select the **Create link by pointing** option from the **Layout** menu. First locate the cursor on the appropriate field column in the first database. Press F10, select the **Create link by pointing** option from the **Layout** menu, and press ENTER. dBASE IV places the example variable Link1 in the field column. Next, move the cursor to the appropriate field column in the second database and press ENTER. dBASE IV links the two databases using the specified fields. To link on more than one field, repeat the procedure. dBASE IV uses the example variable Link2 to identify the second link.

Comparing Fields Using Example Variables

You use example variables to compare the information in one field to the information in another field. Example variables can be any word or character, can be up to ten characters long, must begin with a letter, and may contain numbers and underscores. The same word or character appearing in two fields of the same database, or different databases, serves as a placeholder with which you can perform a comparison between the two fields.

For example, the view query in Figure 6-36 queries a commodities futures database, COMMOD. The fields in the database are Future (the name of the commodity), High, Low, Settle, Lifehigh, and Lifelow. The query evaluates the COMMOD database and returns futures whose Settle price is within 15 points of their lifetime high (the Lifehigh field). The two fields are compared by using the example variable Marker, which appears in the Lifehigh field as a placeholder. Marker also appears in the Settle field in

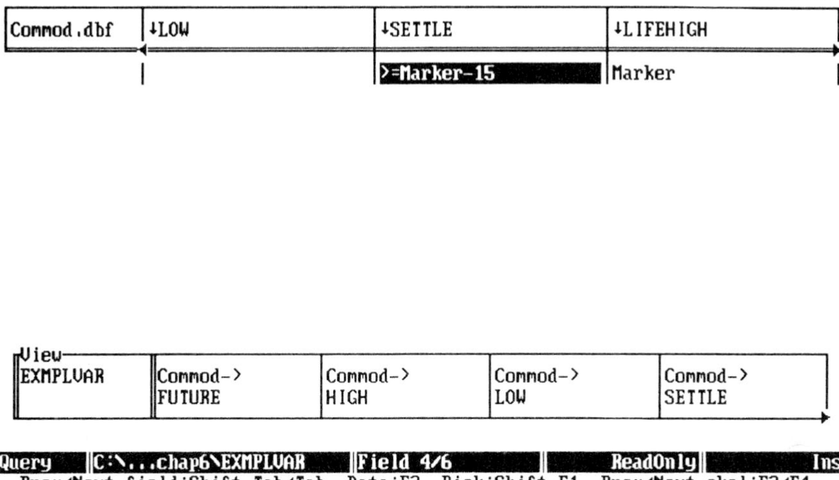

Figure 6-36. Using example variables to compare fields

the formula >=Marker-15. dBASE IV uses this formula to compare the current value in the Settle field to the value for the same record in the Lifehigh field, less 15 points. Records meeting the condition are returned, as shown in Figure 6-37.

You can also use a field name as an example variable. For example, the formula in the Settle column of Figure 6-36 could just as easily read >=Lifehigh-15.

Using Index Files

You can include your existing indexes in a view query. This can speed up queries that use sort operators. When you perform a

Records Fields Go To Exit 4:06:38 pm

FUTURE	HIGH	LOW	SETTLE	LIFEHIGH	LIFELOW
Hogs	46.65	46.20	46.65	47.25	44.20
Pork Bellies	45.80	44.75	44.77	58.25	44.52
Corn	285.75	284.75	284.75	289.50	280.50
Oats	237.50	236.00	236.75	243.00	200.00
Soybeans	762.50	758.00	758.00	770.00	700.00
Wheat	410.00	408.00	408.50	412.75	378.00
Barley	131.20	131.00	129.00	140.00	124.00
Rye	158.00	156.90	156.90	164.00	157.50
Cattle	81.30	81.00	81.30	81.30	77.40
Sugar	9.40	9.23	9.23	10.62	8.50
Cotton	58.00	57.70	57.70	65.50	57.50

Browse C:\...chap6\EXMPLVAR Rec 1/13 View Ins

View and edit fields

Figure 6-37. The view from the example variable query

query that uses a sort operator such as ASC, dBASE IV needs a certain amount of time to sort your data. However, if you've already created an index that specifies the same sort, the query is performed much more quickly.

To add an index to the current query, use the **Include indexes** option from the **Fields** menu. When you select this option, the NO is displayed next to the **Include indexes** choice. This means do not include indexes, and is the default. However, pressing ENTER on this option toggles the NO to a YES. dBASE IV will add your current indexes to the current file skeleton. This includes both single and complex indexes.

Single indexes involve a single field and *complex indexes* involve more than one field. A pound sign (#) is placed next to the field names that have a single index. Complex indexes are appended to the database file skeleton, as in Figure 6-38. You can

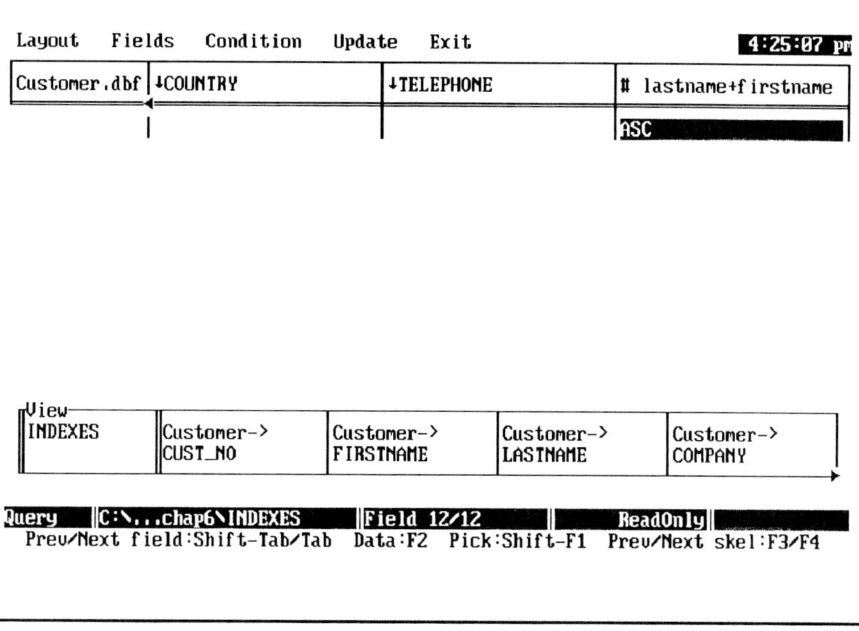

Figure 6-38. Appending complex indexes to the file skeleton

treat these complex indexes like any other database field in the file skeleton for both sorting and linking databases. However, you cannot add a complex index field to a view skeleton.

You can use sort operators with fields that have single as well as complex indexes. However, the sort operator must match the sort order of the index. For example, if your index orders a given field in ascending order, the sort operator must also specify an ascending order.

You can use the complex index field in Figure 6-38 as a substitute for a multiple sorting condition. For example, rather than place **ASC1** in the Lastname field of the current database, and **ASC2** in the Firstname field, you can include a single complex index field at the end of the file skeleton. In this field, you place a single **ASC** sort operator that specifies an ascending sort. This query will run significantly faster because the data is already organized by last and first names.

You can also link files using complex index fields. This method of linking is appropriate when you need to link two databases that do not have a unique key field in common. For example, imagine you have two databases that contain the exact same data in the Firstname and Lastname fields. To link the databases, place matching example variables in the complex index fields of each database file skeleton.

Creating a Database from a View

You can also use a view query to create an entirely new database. To do this, select **Write view as database file** from the **Layout** menu. (You cannot use this option to save a view with a total record length longer that 4000 characters.) dBASE IV will prompt you with a file name that matches the current query view name. You can accept this name or change it. Then press ENTER to have dBASE IV create a new database using the filter conditions and fields specified in the current view query.

Creating a database in this fashion tends to duplicate information. Also, it is no more efficient than leaving your information in separate databases and using queries to extract the needed data. However, it may be appropriate to create a database from a view when you need "snapshot" views of data from a specific point in time, or where you need to start an entirely new database that uses selected information from other databases.

Creating Update Queries

As mentioned, you can use an update query to have dBASE IV make changes to the data in a database. You can tailor an update query to change only specific records or fields in a database. You can also use an update query to update one database from another.

An update query uses four operators: REPLACE, APPEND, MARK, and UNMARK. You use the REPLACE operator to replace data in the database with some new value. You use the APPEND operator to append data from another database. You use the MARK and UNMARK operators to mark and unmark records for deletion.

To use one of these operators, type it under the database name column in the file skeleton. This defines that database as the *target* file—the file that will be updated. Although you can have more than one database field skeleton on the screen, only one of them can have an update operator and be the target file. When you place an update operator in a file skeleton, dBASE IV displays the word "Target" to identify that file as the target.

Rather than entering an update operator manually, you can locate the cursor in the appropriate field skeleton and select **Specify update operation** from the **Update** menu. dBASE IV presents you with the four update operator options. Make your selection and press ENTER. dBASE IV places the selected update operator in the name column of the file skeleton.

Entering an update operator in the name column of a database file skeleton defines the current query as an update query. Any view skeleton you may have already defined is deleted. This is because update queries are not used to define views, only to change data. dBASE IV does, however, ask you whether or not you want to delete the current view skeleton.

To perform an update query, use the **Perform the update** option from the **Update** menu. This option first checks your query for errors. If no errors exist, the update query is performed. To see the results of the update, press F2 to display the target database on the Browse screen.

The REPLACE Operator

Use the REPLACE operator to replace data in the target database when an update query is performed. To specify which fields are to be replaced, as well as what they are to be replaced with, use the

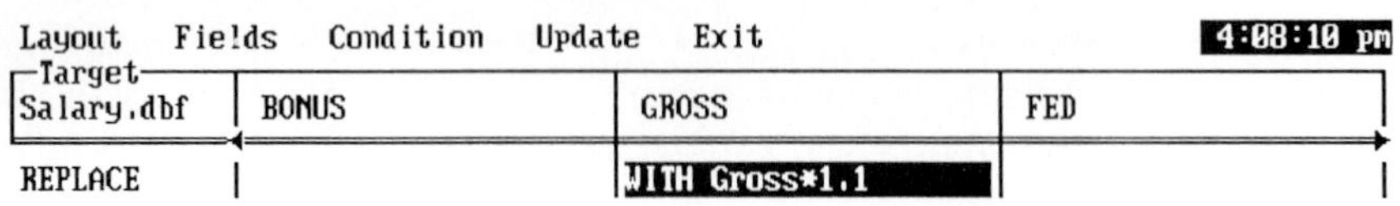

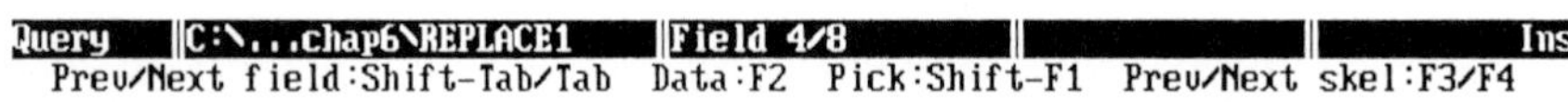

Figure 6-39. REPLACE Gross WITH Gross*1.1

WITH clause. Place the WITH clause in the field column of the field whose value is to be replaced. Follow the WITH clause by an expression that specifies the replacement value. For example, in Figure 6-39, the REPLACE operator appears in the file name column of the SALARY database. The WITH clause appears in the Gross field and is followed by the expression Gross*1.1. The Gross field contains the gross annual salaries for each employee. This update query gives all of the employees in the SALARY database a 10% raise.

The REPLACE operator is analogous to the REPLACE command entered at the dot prompt. For example, to perform the operation in Figure 6-39, you could enter **REPLACE Gross WITH Gross*1.1** at the dot prompt.

You can also use multiple WITH clauses with a single REPLACE operator. For example, in Figure 6-40, two WITH

```
Layout   Fields   Condition   Update   Exit                         4:08:42 pm
┌Target─────┬──────────────────────┬──────────────────────┬──────────────────────┐
│Salary.dbf │ GROSS                │ FED                  │ FICA                 │
REPLACE     │WITH Gross*1.1        │                      │WITH Gross*.0751      │
```

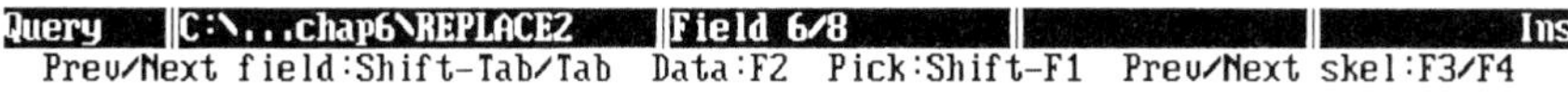


```
 Prev/Next field:Shift-Tab/Tab  Data:F2  Pick:Shift-F1  Prev/Next skel:F3/F4
```

Figure 6-40. REPLACE Gross WITH Gross*1.1, Fica WITH Gross*.0751

clauses appear in the SALARY file skeleton. The Gross field column includes the expression WITH Gross*1.1. However, the Fica field column contains the expression WITH Gross*.0751. The Fica column identifies the amount of social security tax to be withheld for each employee. This update query gives all employees a 10% raise and calculates the amount of social security tax withheld as 7.51% of their gross salary.

The REPLACE operator is not limited to numeric values. You can also use it to replace character strings. For example, suppose the SALARY database contains a Title column that identifies the title for each employee. You can change all titles of Secretary to Assistant by entering **"Secretary", WITH "Assistant"** in the Title column.

You can also replace a condition. For example, imagine the SALARY database contains a Class field in which a character identifies the allowable salary range of each employee. The A class is the highest paid, the B class the next highest paid, and so forth. The database also contains a Title field that identifies the title for each employee. You need to create a whole new class of employee in the B range, called B1, for the title Manager. To perform this update, enter **$"Manager"** in the Title field. This expression uses the $ (contains) operator to include all records that contain the character string "Manager". In the Class field, enter **"B" WITH "B1"**.

The APPEND Operator

You use the APPEND operator to add records from one database to another. The APPEND command is analogous to the APPEND FROM command entered at the dot prompt. To define which fields are added to the target database, use the field names of the database from which you're appending data.

For example, in Figure 6-41 the CUSTOMER and MAILIST databases appear in the Queries Design screen. This update query adds the names and addresses in the CUSTOMER database to the MAILIST database. The APPEND operator appears in the MAILIST database file skeleton, making it the target file. In the Firstname field column, the expression TRIM(Firstname) appends the contents of the Firstname field in the CUSTOMER database to the Firstname field in the MAILIST database. Similar expressions appear in the remaining MAILIST fields. The TRIM() function trims trailing blank spaces from the character fields being appended. Otherwise, this update query will not be accepted by dBASE IV.

You can also use filter expressions in the CUSTOMER database file skeleton to limit the records appended to the MAILIST database. For example, to limit records appended from the CUSTOMER database to customer numbers greater than 1010, enter **>1010** in the Cust_no field column of the CUSTOMER database file skeleton.

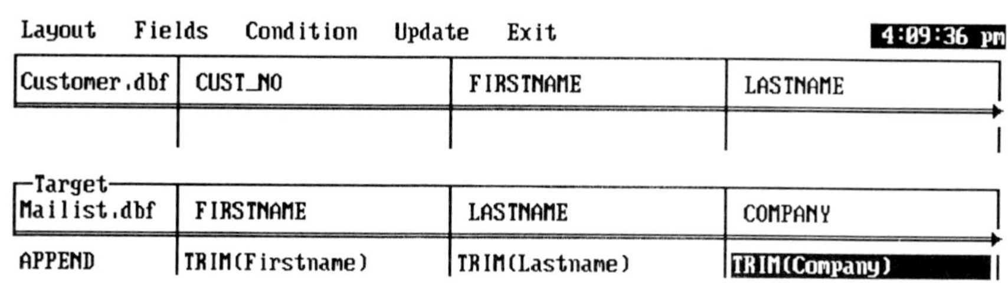

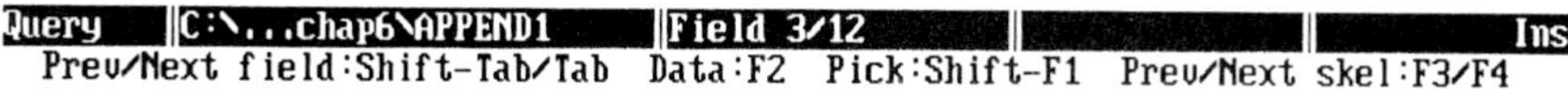

Figure 6-41. MAILIST is the target database for this APPEND update query

The MARK and UNMARK Operators

The MARK and UNMARK operators mark and unmark records for deletion. The MARK operator is analogous to the DELETE command entered at the dot prompt. The UNMARK operator is analogous to the RECALL command entered at the dot prompt. Once you mark records for deletion, you can delete them from the database by using either **Erase marked records** from the **Organize** menu on the Database Design Screen, or the PACK command from the dot prompt.

To use the MARK and UNMARK operators, place them in the file name column of the target database. To specify which records

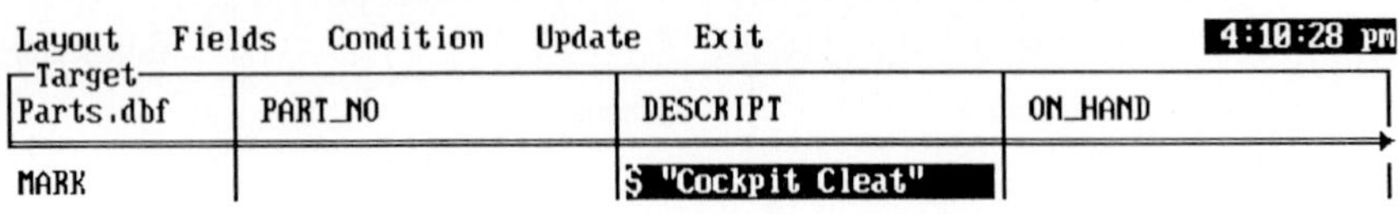

Figure 6-42. The MARK operator marks the records with Cockpit Cleat in the Descript field

to mark or unmark for deletion, enter a condition in the appropriate field. For example, in Figure 6-42, the MARK operator appears in the file skeleton for the PARTS database. Moreover, the expression, **$ "Cockpit Cleat"** appears in the Descript field column. This update query marks for deletion the record with a description of Cockpit Cleat. To reverse the effects of this update, use the same condition with the UNMARK operator.

In this chapter, you learned how to use the Queries Design screen to create view queries. You now know how to use a view query to create a view that specifies selected fields from a database. In addition, you know how to use conditions to specify only selected records from that view. You can also link files by using a view. Furthermore, you know how to sort, summarize, and group information in databases by using a view. You can now use this information to provide selected information to custom forms, reports, and labels as well as custom applications created with the Applications Generator.

This chapter, also explained update queries. You can now use an update query to quickly change the information in a database. You also know how to use an update query to replace data in a database and append records to a database. In addition, you can mark and unmark records for deletion by using an update query.

The Dot Prompt

SEVEN

Getting to and from the Dot Prompt
Some Basics
Creating a Database
Opening a Database
Modifying the Database Structure
Displaying the Database Structure
Adding Records
Carrying Information Forward
Editing Records
Viewing the Database
Inserting Records into a Database
Replacing Data in Records
Moving Around in a Database
Deleting Records
Deleting a Database
Displaying Data
Writing to a Text File
Reports and Labels
Copying a Database
Closing a Database
Memory Variables
Sorting a Database
Indexing a Database
Searching a Database
Summarizing a Database
Using Custom Forms
Querying the Database
Importing and Exporting Data to External Programs

The dot prompt allows you to enter dBASE IV commands without the use of the menus. In dBASE IV, the dot prompt is the next step up from the Control Center. Generally, experienced dBASE IV users almost immediately graduate from the Control Center to the dot prompt. You can do many things from the dot prompt that you cannot do from the Control Center. In addition, with a little practice, using dBASE IV at the dot prompt tends to be faster than using the Control Center. Moreover, once you've gained some proficiency with dot prompt commands, you can collect your commands in a file to create a program.

The dot prompt is in many ways an alternative to the Control Center. In the Control Center you work through menus; at the dot prompt you use the dBASE IV *command language*. The dBASE IV command language is composed of a series of English-like commands that perform specific tasks. From the dot prompt, you can enter commands and watch dBASE IV perform them on your screen.

This chapter introduces the dot prompt. Many of commands that are discussed here have been briefly covered in previous chapters as alternatives to Control Center menu options. This chapter delves into these and other commands in more detail.

Getting to and from the Dot Prompt

When you start your copy of dBASE IV for the first time, dBASE takes you directly to the Control Center. You can access the dot prompt from the Control Center by pressing ESC. dBASE IV displays an option box that asks "Are you sure you want to abandon operation?" Press Y for yes, or highlight the **Yes** option and press ENTER. dBASE IV displays the dot prompt in the lower left-hand corner of the screen. Your screen will look like Figure 7-1.

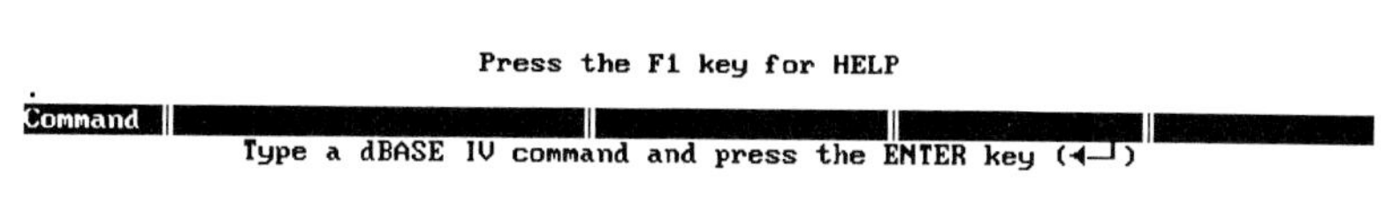
Press the F1 key for HELP
Command
Type a dBASE IV command and press the ENTER key (◄┘)

Figure 7-1. The dot prompt screen

Tip: If you place an asterisk (*) in front of the command line COMMAND = ASSIST in your CONFIG.DB file, dBASE IV takes you directly to the dot prompt on start-up. For more on this topic, see Chapter 35.

To get back to the Control Center from the dot prompt, type **ASSIST** or press F2. dBASE IV returns to the Control Center and waits for your next menu selections.

To quit dBASE IV and return to DOS from the dot prompt, type **QUIT**.

Some Basics

Before you enter commands at the dot prompt, you need to know a few basics. Type **? VERSION( )** at the dot prompt and press ENTER. dBASE IV returns the version number of dBASE you're currently using, as shown in Figure 7-2. This is a small example of the interactive power of the dot prompt. That is, when you enter a command, DBASE IV evaluates that command and returns a result. This example also demonstrates how you enter commands at the dot prompt: you type the command and then press ENTER to activate it.

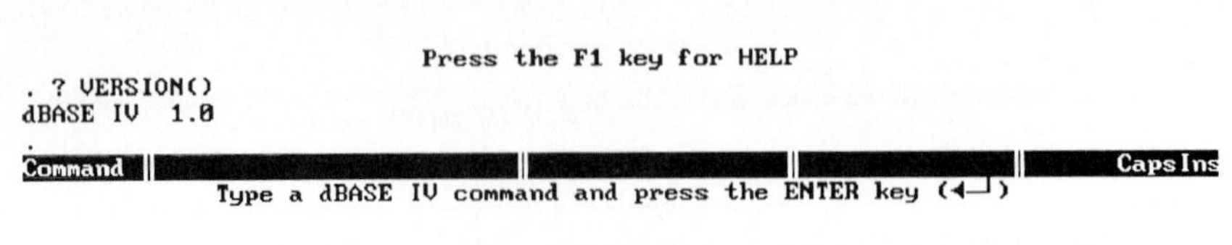
Press the F1 key for HELP
. ? VERSION()
dBASE IV 1.0
Command
Caps Ins
Type a dBASE IV command and press the ENTER key (◄┘)

Figure 7-2. The VERSION( ) function

Command Syntax

The format of dBASE IV commands conforms to a five-part structure. The format of a command is often referred to as its *syntax*. Not every command requires that you use all five parts. Furthermore, not all commands conform to this precise syntax. However, the general syntax of dBASE IV commands is as follows:

> *verb* [<*scope*>] [<*expression list*>] [FOR <*condition*>] [WHILE <*condition*>]

The brackets ([ ] and < >) that separate the command sections have a special meaning. Square brackets ([ ]) mean that the command section is optional. Angle brackets (< >) mean that you must use a specific data type. Do not include the brackets themselves in your commands.

dBASE IV commands always begin with a verb such as USE, GO, or LIST. Often these verbs are followed by nouns that refer to a database or a dBASE IV operation such as USE Customer, GO BOTTOM, or LIST STRUCTURE.

dBASE IV commands can also be followed by a clause. The *scope* clause lets you specify which records are affected by the current command. For example, imagine you have 100 records in a database. The command LIST NEXT 10 tells dBASE IV to list the next ten database records. The *scope* is NEXT 10, and it confines the LIST command to only the next ten records. Unlike the verb that begins a dBASE IV command, the *scope* is optional. Other *scope* options include

- RECORD <*n*>, where *n* is a specific record number
- ALL, for all the records in the database
- REST, which means, starting with the current record, include all the records to the end of the database

Expression list refers to a list of acceptable dBASE IV expressions separated by commas. For example, *expression list* might contain database field names, as in the command

```
LIST FIELDS Firstname,Lastname,Address
```

Expression lists can include database field names, memory variables, array elements, constants, functions, operators, and system memory variables. Functions, operators, constants, and memory variables are explained next. See Chapter 24 for an explanation of array elements. Chapter 34 explains system memory variables.

The FOR *condition* clause lets you establish a condition for a command. For example, the command

```
DISPLAY ALL FOR Lastname = "Smith"
```

tells dBASE IV to display all records that have the name Smith in the database field named Lastname in the currently active database. A FOR *condition* takes precedence over any *scope* condition included in a command.

The WHILE *condition* clause lets you further limit the scope of the current command. When you include a WHILE *condition* in a command, dBASE IV starts processing with the current record and continues processing until the WHILE *condition* becomes false. For example, the command

```
DISPLAY ALL FOR Lastname = "Smith" WHILE Zip < 59999
```

tells dBASE IV to display all database records with a last name of Smith until it reaches a record with a number greater than or equal to 59999 in the Zip database field.

Entering Commands

dBASE IV command lines can be up to 255 characters in length, including spaces. When your command exceeds the width of the screen, keep typing; dBASE IV will scroll the command across the screen from right to left. When you complete the command, press ENTER and dBASE IV executes the command.

You can enter your dBASE IV commands in either upper- or lowercase, or a combination of both. Additionally, dBASE IV is very forgiving as to spacing. As long as you leave at least one space between words, dBASE IV will accept a command. For example, the three following commands are all acceptable:

```
. USE Customer
. GO    BOTTOM
. STORE    RECNO()    TO    mrec
```

Editing Commands

If you make a mistake while entering a command at the dot prompt, you can edit the command before pressing ENTER. To edit a command, press BACKSPACE to delete characters immediately to the left of the cursor. Furthermore, since dBASE IV always comes up in overstrike mode you can use the cursor movement keys to move to the problem area and type over the errant characters. If dBASE IV is in insert mode (you pressed the INS key) you can use the cursor movement keys to move back to the error and press DEL to delete the problem characters and type in the correct ones. In either case, once the problem characters are deleted you can reenter the correct ones. If the error is not worth fixing, press ESC. dBASE IV will erase the entire command and you can start over.

If you enter an unacceptable command and press ENTER, dBASE IV beeps and places an option box on the screen. The op-

```
. DISPLAY HISTORY
USE Salary
DISPLAY ALL
GO TOP
BROWSE
EDIT
LOCATE FOR Lastname="Hill"
INDEX ON Lastname TAG Lastname
SEEK "Hill"
LIST
? Firstname,Lastname,Gross
SET ORDER TO GROSS
FIND 24000
CLEAR
DISPLAY HISTORY

.
Command ||C:\...chap7\SALARY     ||Rec 1/11       ||File ||
```

Figure 7-3. The history buffer

tion box contains an error message, such as "Unrecognized command verb," plus the options **Cancel**, **Edit**, and **Help**. If you choose **Cancel**, dBASE IV clears the command line and returns to the dot prompt. If you choose **Edit**, dBASE IV returns you to the dBASE IV command and displays the errant command line for editing. If you choose **Help**, dBASE IV takes you to its on-line Help facility.

The History Buffer

dBASE IV remembers your last 20 commands. It stores them in a section of memory called the *history buffer*. To reuse the commands in the history buffer, press UP ARROW until you reach the desired command and press ENTER to confirm it. dBASE IV executes the command.

You can manage the history buffer with various commands. For example, DISPLAY HISTORY displays the commands in the history buffer. Figure 7-3 shows an example. LIST HISTORY performs the same function but does not pause after displaying each screenful of commands. The SET HISTORY TO command allows

```
 Layout   Words   Go To   Print   Exit                                    2:07:46 pm
[·······▼1······▼··2····▼····3··▼······4▼····█··▼5······▼··6····▼····7··▼······]
REPLACE Gross WITH Gross*1.1,Fed WITH (Gross-40)*.15,Fica WITH Gross*.0751,State
WITH Gross*.035,Net WITH Gross-Fed-Fica-State
```

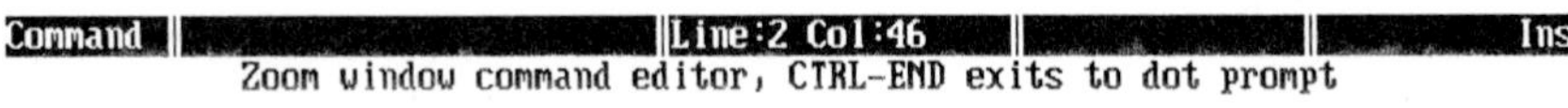

Figure 7-4. Using a Zoom window to enter a command

you to set the number of commands stored in the history buffer, ranging from 0 to 16,000. The LIST HISTORY TO PRINTER command prints the contents of the history buffer. For more on these commands, see Chapter 31.

The Zoom Window

You can also enter a command using a Zoom window, which enables you to increase the length of a command line to 1024 characters. To access a Zoom window, press CTRL-HOME. dBASE IV takes you to the dBASE IV Text Editor. Type your command as you would at the dot prompt. Figure 7-4 shows an example. When you complete the command, press CTRL-END. dBASE IV returns you to the dot prompt, places your command on the screen, and executes it.

There are two advantages to using a Zoom window for lengthy commands. First, you can see the entire command as you enter it;

dBASE IV will not scroll the left portion of it off the screen. Second, you have access to the word processing power of the dBASE IV Text Editor. For example, the Block (F6), Move (F7), and Copy (F8) keys are particularly useful as you enter and edit your command. Furthermore, if you press F10, dBASE IV displays the dBASE IV Text Editor menu.

You can also use a Zoom window to edit a previous command. To do so, press UP ARROW to have dBASE IV display a previous command from the history buffer. Next, press CTRL-HOME to place the command in a Zoom window. Then, edit the command to suit your needs. When you're finished, press CTRL-END. dBASE IV returns to the dot prompt, places the edited command on the screen, and executes it.

File Management

When you're working at the dot prompt, you can use a number of commands to manage your files. For example, if you need to know what database files are in the current directory, use the dBASE IV DIR command.

The DIR Command

The DIR command is dBASE IV's substitute for the DOS DIR command. For example, to see all the files with a .DBF extension in the current directory, type **DIR**. Your screen will look like Figure 7-5. To see all the files in the current directory, regardless of their extension, type **DIR *.*. This command is explained in more detail in Chapter 31.**

The SET Commands

You can also use the SET commands to help manage your files. For example, to set the default disk drive, use the SET DEFAULT command followed by the disk drive letter. For example, SET DEFAULT TO A: establishes drive A as the default drive.

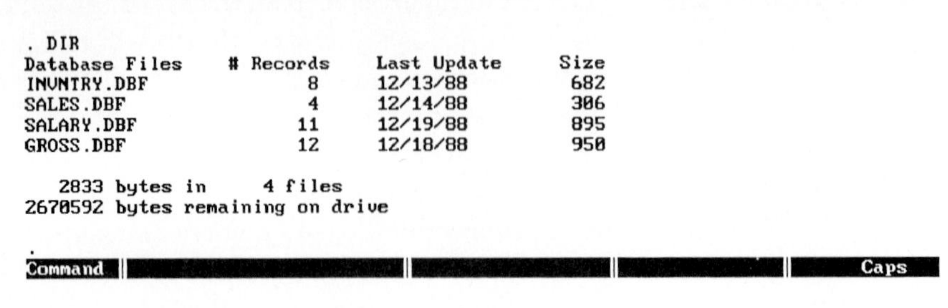

```
. DIR
Database Files     # Records     Last Update     Size
INVNTRY.DBF                8     12/13/88         682
SALES.DBF                  4     12/14/88         306
SALARY.DBF                11     12/19/88         895
GROSS.DBF                 12     12/18/88         950

   2833 bytes in     4 files
2670592 bytes remaining on drive

.
Command                                                Caps
```

Figure 7-5. The DIR command displays files

You can set dBASE IV's file search path using the SET PATH command. For example, SET PATH TO C: \MYFILES sets dBASE IV's search path to include the directory MYFILES on drive C. For a complete list of SET commands, see Chapter 32.

Accessing DOS with !/RUN

In dBASE IV, you can use ! or RUN followed by a DOS command to perform DOS operations from within dBASE IV. For example, the command !COPY THISFILE.DBF A: copies the file named THISFILE.DBF in the current directory to drive A. The command !CD C:\MYFILES changes the current directory to MYFILES on drive C. For other DOS commands, see your DOS user's manual.

The Function Keys

The function keys behave slightly differently at the dot prompt. For example, in the Control Center F2 takes you into browse or edit mode. However, from the dot prompt F2 places the ASSIST command on the screen and executes it. This command takes you back to the Control Center. Table 7-1 shows the default commands that dBASE IV enters and executes when you press the function keys.

Function Key	Command
F1	HELP
F2	ASSIST
F3	LIST
F4	DIR
F5	DISPLAY STRUCTURE
F6	DISPLAY STATUS
F7	DISPLAY MEMORY
F8	DISPLAY
F9	APPEND
F10	EDIT

Table 7-1. The Dot Prompt Function Keys

Operators

Operators are symbols that you can use in commands to compare data and perform calculations. For example, the command

```
LOCATE FOR Lastname = "Smith"
```

tells dBASE IV to find the first record in the database where the field Lastname contains the name Smith. The operator in this command is the equal symbol (=). dBASE IV supports four types of operators in commands.

- **Mathematical Operators** As you might imagine, these symbols perform numeric calculations. The mathematical operators include

+	Addition/unary positive
-	Subtraction/unary negative
*	Multiplication

/	Division
** or ^	Exponentiation
=	Equality
( )	Grouping

- **Relational Operators** The relational operators compare data and issue a logical result of either true (.T.) or false (.F.). You can use these operators with data of character, numeric, logical, or date data type. However, make sure that the data on either side of these operators is of the same data type. The relational operators include

<	Less than
	Greater than
=	Equal
< > or #	Not equal to
<=	Less than or equal to
=	Greater than or equal to
$	Equals any of the following characters

- **Logical Operators** The logical operators let you combine and exclude conditions. These operators can compare two expressions and return a logical true or false response. The logical operators include .AND., .OR., and .NOT. The first two operators (.AND. and .OR.) mean more or less what you would expect. For example,

```
DISPLAY ALL FOR Firstname = "John" .AND. Lastname
= "Smith"
```

displays records with both John in the Firstname field and Smith in the Lastname field. Substituting .OR. yields all records that include either the first name John or a last name of Smith. The .NOT. operator is a little trickier. For example, the command

```
DISPLAY ALL FOR .NOT. "Smith"
```

displays all records except those that have Smith in the Lastname field.

- **String Operators** The string operators combine one character string with another. This is called *concatenation*. The string operators include + and -. For example,

  DISPLAY ALL TRIM(Firstname)+" "+TRIM(Lastname)

  displays the character data in the Firstname and Lastname fields of the current database, with a blank space in between them. When you use + to combine character strings, dBASE IV leaves any trailing blanks attached to the end of the character strings. When you use - to combine character strings, dBASE moves trailing spaces to the end of the last string being combined. Trailing blanks occur often because a database field character is usually wider than the character string it contains.

Precedence

In dBASE IV, the rules that determine the order in which operators are evaluated are referred to as the *order of precedence*. That is, when two operators from a given category, such as + and *, appear together in a command line, dBASE IV evaluates one before it does the other. The operator that is evaluated first has a higher order of precedence than does the second.

The relational and string operators do not have an order of precedence. They are evaluated from left to right, as they occur. However, the mathematical and logical operators do have an order of precedence. Furthermore, one category of operator can take precedence over another.

The precedence of mathematical operators is

1. Unary + (positive) and unary - (negative)
2. ** and ^ (exponentiation)
3. * (multiplication) and / (division)
4. + (addition) and - (subtraction)

The precedence of logical operators is

1. .AND.
2. .NOT.
3. .OR.

The precedence of combined categories is

1. Mathematical or string
2. Relational
3. Logical

Operators at the same level of precedence are performed from left to right, as they occur. In addition, you can use parentheses to group expressions and thus have dBASE IV evaluate one expression before it does another. The operators inside the inner set of parentheses are evaluated first. For example, in the equation Units*(Price+Ship), dBASE IV adds Price and Ship before multiplying the result by Units.

Creating a Database

To create a database from the dot prompt, use the CREATE command. The syntax for this command is

CREATE *<database name>*

For example, to create a database called SALARY, type the following command at the dot prompt:

```
. CREATE Salary
```

```
Layout   Organize   Append   Go To   Exit                                4:33:33 pm

                                                          Bytes remaining:   3946
 Num   Field Name    Field Type   Width   Dec   Index

  1    FIRSTNAME     Character      7             N
  2    LASTNAME      Character      9             Y
  3    BONUS         Logical        1             N
  4    GROSS         Numeric        8      2      Y
  5    FED           Numeric        7      2      N
  6    FICA          Numeric        7      2      N
  7    STATE         Numeric        7      2      N
  8    NET           Numeric        8      2      N

Database C:\...chap7\SALARY      Field 1/8                             Caps
          Enter the field name. Insert/Delete field:Ctrl-N/Ctrl-U
Field names begin with a letter and may contain letters, digits and underscores
```

Figure 7-6. The Database Design screen

dBASE IV takes you to the same Database Design screen you use in the Control Center to create a database. Figure 7-6 shows an example. For a complete discussion of how to create and design a database, see Chapters 4 and 17.

When you have designed and saved your database, dBASE IV asks you if you want to add records to the database. If you do, press Y for yes. dBASE IV enters full-screen data entry mode and displays a data entry form like the one in Figure 7-7.

The data entry form represents the first record in the database and shows all the field names. Next to each field name is a data entry blank. Type the data for the record and then confirm each field entry by pressing ENTER. If your database contains a memo field, press CTRL-HOME to enter the memo and CTRL-END to save it. When you reach the last field in the database and press

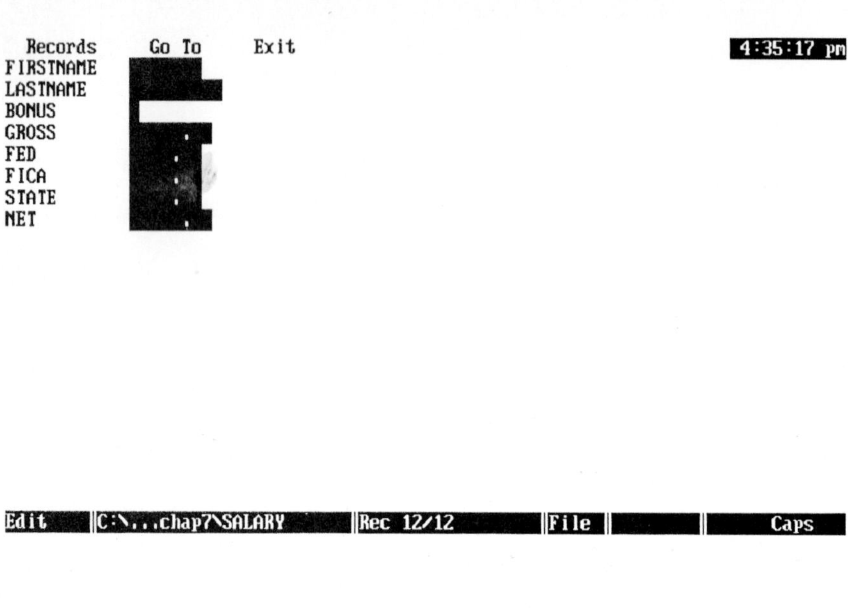

Figure 7-7. A sample blank data entry form

ENTER, dBASE IV adds another blank record to the database and displays the data entry form.

You can press PGUP to see the previous record and PGDN to see the next record. If you're on the last record in the database and press PGDN, dBASE IV asks you if you want to add an additional record. If you do, press Y. dBASE IV will add a blank record to the end of the database and display a blank data entry form. If you don't want to add an additional record, press N. dBASE IV will return you to the data entry form for the last record in the database.

To end the data entry process and save your changes, press ENTER on the first field of a new record, without entering any data. dBASE IV will return you to the dot prompt. You can also press CTRL-END on the current data entry form to end data entry and save your changes. If you move to the next record and press CTRL-END, dBASE IV adds a blank record to the database and exits to the dot prompt. To end the data entry process without saving the current record, press ESC.

Opening a Database

You open a database with the USE command. The syntax for this command is

USE <*database name*>

For example, to open the database named SALARY, type the following command at the dot prompt:

```
. USE Salary
```

You must activate a database with the USE command before you can enter commands that apply to it. If you enter a command that affects a non-activated database, dBASE IV issues the message "No database in use. Enter filename:." If you enter the name of an existing database, dBASE IV executes the command.

When you enter the USE command, dBASE IV activates the database you specify and closes the currently open database. This applies only to the current work area. In dBASE IV you can have up to ten active databases in ten different work areas. Using multiple databases in different work areas is discussed in Chapter 21.

Once you open a database with the USE command, it remains open until you either activate another database in the current work area, close the database, or quit dBASE IV. As long as a database remains open, you can enter an unlimited number of commands that apply to it.

You can only have one database at a time open in the current work area. If you try to reopen the same database in another work area without first closing it in the current work area, dBASE IV gives you the error message "File already open."

Modifying the Database Structure

To modify the structure of a database, use the MODIFY STRUCTURE command. Before you enter this command you must activate a database. For example, to modify the structure of a database named INVNTRY, type the following at the dot prompt:

```
. USE Invntry
. MODIFY STRUCTURE
```

dBASE IV will take you directly to the Database Design screen. The structure for the database you specified is placed on the screen and you can modify it to suit your needs. For a complete discussion of how to modify a database using the Database Design screen, see Chapter 4. When you complete your modifications, press CTRL-END or press F10 and select **Exit/Save changes and exit** to save the changes. dBASE IV returns you to the dot prompt.

Displaying the Database Structure

To display the structure of a database, use the DISPLAY STRUCTURE command. Before you enter this command you must activate a database. For example, to display the structure of a database called MAILIST, type the following at the dot prompt:

```
. USE Mailist
. DISPLAY STRUCTURE
```

dBASE IV will display the structure of the currently active database. Figure 7-8 shows an example. This list is for display purposes only; you cannot modify it.

The LIST STRUCTURE command also displays the structure of a database. LIST STRUCTURE is like DISPLAY STRUCTURE, but LIST STRUCTURE does not pause between each screenful of

```
. DISPLAY STRUCTURE
Structure for database: C:\DB4CR\PART1\CHAP7\SALARY.DBF
Number of data records:       11
Date of last update    : 12/19/88
Field  Field Name  Type       Width    Dec    Index
    1  FIRSTNAME   Character      7               N
    2  LASTNAME    Character      9               Y
    3  BONUS       Logical        1               N
    4  GROSS       Numeric        8      2        Y
    5  FED         Numeric        7      2        N
    6  FICA        Numeric        7      2        N
    7  STATE       Numeric        7      2        N
    8  NET         Numeric        8      2        N
** Total **                      55

.
Command ||C:\...chap7\SALARY    ||Rec 11/11    ||File ||    ||    CapsIns
```

Figure 7-8. The results of the DISPLAY STRUCTURE command

information. For example, to list the structure of a database called MAILIST, type the following at the dot prompt:

```
. USE Mailist
. LIST STRUCTURE
```

Tip: To get a printed copy of a database structure, use the TO PRINTER clause after the LIST STRUCTURE command. For example, to print the structure of the currently active database, type **LIST STRUCTURE TO PRINTER** at the dot prompt. dBASE IV will send a copy of the database structure to your printer.

Adding Records

You can add records to the end of a database with the APPEND command. Before you enter this command, however, you must activate a database. For example, to add records to the INVNTRY database, type the following at the dot prompt:

```
. USE Invntry
. APPEND
```

When you enter the APPEND command, dBASE IV adds a record to the end of the database specified in the USE command. It then places on the screen the blank data entry form you have already seen. To enter data into the form, use the procedures described earlier.

Carrying Information Forward

If you're entering repetitive data, you can save yourself some work with the SET CARRY command. This command lets you carry information forward from one record to the next. For example, if all your records have USA for the Country field, you can have dBASE IV carry that information forward for each record appended to the database.

The SET CARRY command sets a carry condition for the APPEND, BROWSE, and INSERT commands. When you enter the SET CARRY command before using one of these commands, dBASE IV carries forward either all the information from one record to the next, or just the fields you specify. The SET CARRY command has two formats.

- SET CARRY ON carries forward all information in all fields for the APPEND and INSERT commands.
- SET CARRY TO [<*field list*>] ADDITIVE lets you specify a list of fields to be brought forward from the previous record, and works with the APPEND, BROWSE, and INSERT commands. The ADDITIVE option lets you add to the field list in a previous SET CARRY command.

The following dot prompt commands activate a database and specify a list of fields to be carried forward. The APPEND command then appends records to the database. Each time a new record is added, dBASE IV carries forward the data in the Country and Zip fields of the MAILIST database.

```
. USE Mailist
. SET CARRY TO Country,Zip
. APPEND
```

Editing Records

You can edit the records in a database with the EDIT command. You must activate a database before using this command. When you enter the EDIT command at the dot prompt, dBASE IV displays the familiar edit screen, as in Figure 7-9. You can use this form to edit some, or all, of the records in the database. For example, to edit the records in the INVNTRY database, type the following at the dot prompt:

```
. USE Invntry
. EDIT
```

When you enter the EDIT command by itself, dBASE IV gives you access to all the records in the database. However, you can also limit the EDIT command to specific records, or to specific fields within those records. For example, to limit editing to the next five records in the INVNTRY database, enter the following at the dot prompt. dBASE IV allows you to edit only the next five records and then returns the dot prompt.

```
. USE Invntry
. EDIT NEXT 5
```

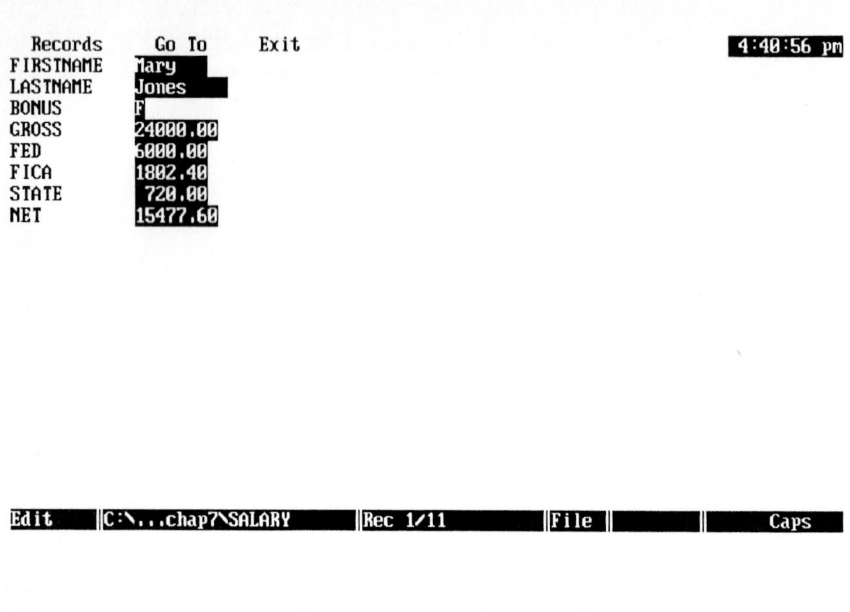

Figure 7-9. The EDIT command calls a data entry form

To start editing at record number 5, enter the following:

```
. USE Invntry
. EDIT 5
```

To edit just specific fields throughout the database, enter

```
. USE Invntry
. EDIT FIELDS Part_no,On_hand
```

You can stop the editing process when you reach a specific point in the database by including a WHILE condition with your EDIT command. The editing process will only continue while the condition remains true. For example, the following command starts editing at the current record and stops when a number greater than 12345 is encountered in the Part_no field:

```
. USE Invntry
. EDIT FIELDS Part_no,On_hand WHILE Part_no<=12345
```

You can also mark records for deletion while in edit mode. To do this, page up or down to the record you want to delete and press CTRL-U. dBASE IV marks the current record for deletion. You can then delete all the records marked for deletion by using the PACK command, explained later in the section "Deleting Records."

Tip: The CHANGE command is a direct substitute for the EDIT command. Their syntax and usage are the same in all respects.

Chapter 31 discusses more about the various options available with the EDIT command.

Viewing the Database

To view the database in tabular format, use the BROWSE command. Using the BROWSE command from the dot prompt is similar to using the F2 key from the Control Center. From the Control Center, the F2 key displays the currently active database, as in Figure 7-10.

When you enter the BROWSE command, dBASE IV takes you directly to the menu-assisted browse screen you access from the Control Center. For a complete description of how to use the menus in the browse screen, see Chapter 4.

If you do not open a database before using the BROWSE command, dBASE IV prompts you for a database name. Enter the database name of your choice and press ENTER. To avoid this prompt, open a database first and then use the BROWSE com-

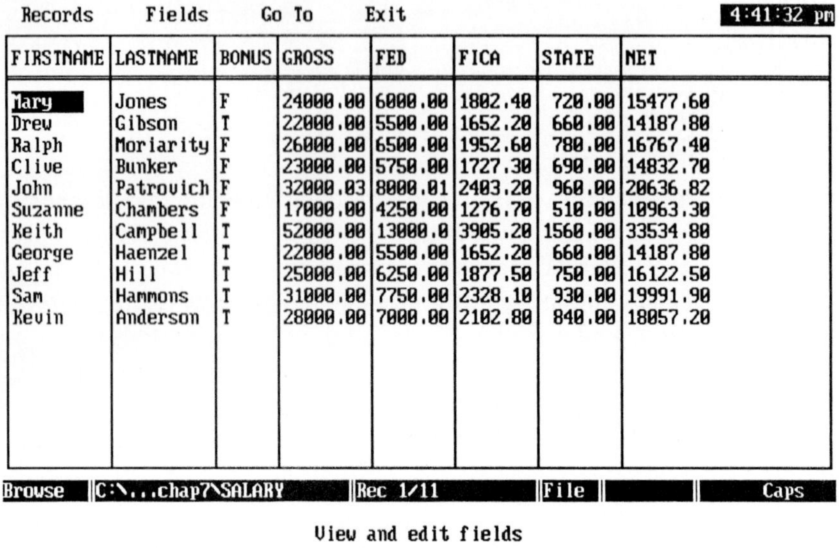

Records Fields Go To Exit 4:41:32 pm

FIRSTNAME	LASTNAME	BONUS	GROSS	FED	FICA	STATE	NET
Mary	Jones	F	24000.00	6000.00	1802.40	720.00	15477.60
Drew	Gibson	T	22000.00	5500.00	1652.20	660.00	14187.80
Ralph	Moriarity	F	26000.00	6500.00	1952.60	780.00	16767.40
Clive	Bunker	F	23000.00	5750.00	1727.30	690.00	14832.70
John	Patrovich	F	32000.03	8000.01	2403.20	960.00	20636.82
Suzanne	Chambers	F	17000.00	4250.00	1276.70	510.00	10963.30
Keith	Campbell	T	52000.00	13000.0	3905.20	1560.00	33534.80
George	Haenzel	T	22000.00	5500.00	1652.20	660.00	14187.80
Jeff	Hill	T	25000.00	6250.00	1877.50	750.00	16122.50
Sam	Hammons	T	31000.00	7750.00	2328.10	930.00	19991.90
Kevin	Anderson	T	28000.00	7000.00	2102.80	840.00	18057.20

Browse C:\...chap7\SALARY Rec 1/11 File Caps

View and edit fields

Figure 7-10. SALARY.DBF displayed on the browse screen

mand. For example, to view and edit the CUSTOMER database, enter the following at the dot prompt:

```
. USE Customer
. BROWSE
```

There are a number of options you can use with BROWSE. For example, you can use a FIELDS clause with the BROWSE command. The FIELDS clause lets you choose field names and the order in which they appear in the BROWSE table. For example, to specify and display three fields from a database called INVNTRY, enter the following at the dot prompt:

```
. USE Invntry
. BROWSE FIELDS Part_no,On_hand,On_Order
```

```
. USE SALES
. DISPLAY STRUCTURE
Structure for database: C:\DB4CR\PART1\CHAP7\SALES.DBF
Number of data records:        4
Date of last update    : 12/14/88
Field  Field Name  Type        Width    Dec    Index
    1  DISTRIB     Character      20               N
    2  REGION      Character       1               N
    3  TOTAL_SALE  Numeric        10               N
    4  RATE        Numeric         4      2        N
** Total **                       36

.
Command  ||C:\...part1\chap7\SALES  ||Rec 1/4          ||File ||
```

Figure 7-11. The SALES.DBF database structure

You can also specify calculated fields with BROWSE. For example, imagine you are working with a sales database whose structure is like that shown in Figure 7-11. The following command lines activate the SALES database, display all but one of its fields, and add a calculated field to the BROWSE table. The calculated field, called Commission, is a function of the Total_sales field multiplied by the Rate field. Figure 7-12 shows the results.

```
. USE Sales
. BROWSE FIELDS Distrib,Total_sale,Rate,Commission=Total_sale*Rate
```

Inserting Records into a Database

To insert a record into a database, use the INSERT command. This command inserts a blank record immediately after the current record. For example, if the record pointer is on record 8 and you

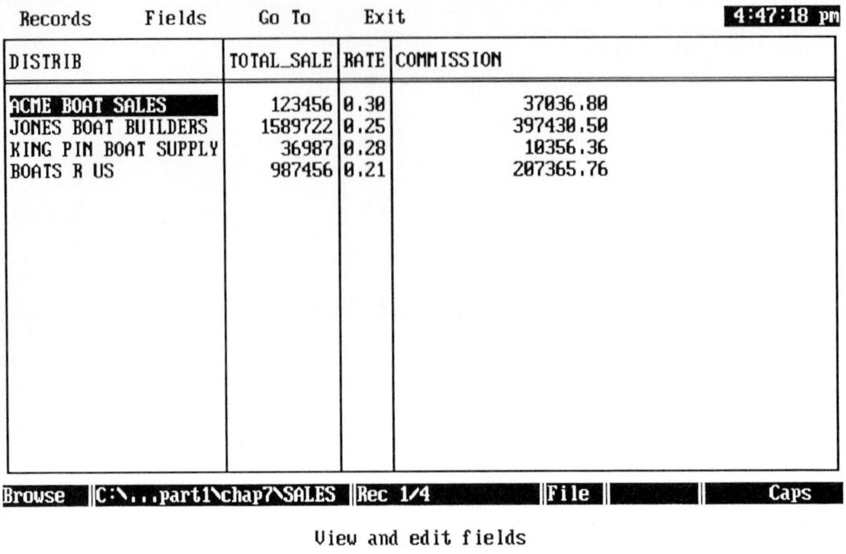

```
Records      Fields      Go To      Exit                                4:47:18 pm

DISTRIB              TOTAL_SALE RATE COMMISSION

ACME BOAT SALES          123456 0.30            37036.80
JONES BOAT BUILDERS     1589722 0.25           397430.50
KING PIN BOAT SUPPLY      36987 0.28            10356.36
BOATS R US               987456 0.21           207365.76

Browse  C:\...part1\chap7\SALES  Rec 1/4           File           Caps
                           View and edit fields
```

Figure 7-12. The BROWSE command shows a calculated field

enter the INSERT command, dBASE IV inserts a new blank record as record 9. The old record 9 becomes record 10, and so forth.

When you enter the INSERT command, dBASE IV takes you to the edit screen. However, you can edit only the newly inserted record. When you press ENTER to confirm the data in the last field, you return to the dot prompt. For example, the following command lines insert a new record number 7 in a database called INVNTRY:

```
. USE Invntry
. GO 6
. INSERT
```

You can also use the INSERT command with the BEFORE clause to insert a record before the current one. For example, the following command lines insert a record as record number 5 in the INVNTRY database:

```
. USE Invntry
. GO 6
. INSERT BEFORE
```

Tip: The INSERT command is very slow with large databases. As an alternative, you may want to use the APPEND command to append a record to the end of the database and later reindex the database to maintain the desired order. See "Indexing a Database" later in this chapter.

Replacing Data in Records

You can replace data in database fields by using the REPLACE command. This command allows you to replace the contents of a single record or to globally change the contents of a field throughout an entire database. You can also use the FOR and WHILE condition clauses with the REPLACE command to limit replacement to records that meet a specified condition.

The REPLACE command works with any data type. However, you must replace the data in a field with the same data type. For example, if you try to replace numeric data with character data, dBASE IV gives you an error message. The syntax for REPLACE is

REPLACE *<field>* [*<scope>*] WITH *<exp>* [FOR *<condition>*] [WHILE *<condition>*]

Normally, the REPLACE command replaces field contents for a single record. However, you can use the ALL clause with the REPLACE command to make global changes to a database field. For example, imagine you're working with a salary database similar to the one in Figure 7-13. To give everyone in your company a

Records Fields Go To Exit 5:58:15 pm

FIRSTNAME	LASTNAME	BONUS	GROSS	FED	FICA	STATE	NET
Mary	Jones	F	24000.00	6000.00	1802.40	720.00	15477.60
Drew	Gibson	T	22000.00	5500.00	1652.20	660.00	14187.80
Ralph	Moriarity	F	26000.00	6500.00	1952.60	780.00	16767.40
Clive	Bunker	F	23000.00	5750.00	1727.30	690.00	14832.70
John	Patrovich	F	32000.03	8000.01	2403.20	960.00	20636.82
Suzanne	Chambers	F	17000.00	4250.00	1276.70	510.00	10963.30
Keith	Campbell	T	52000.00	13000.0	3905.20	1560.00	33534.80
George	Haenzel	T	22000.00	5500.00	1652.20	660.00	14187.80
Jeff	Hill	T	25000.00	6250.00	1877.50	750.00	16122.50
Sam	Hammons	T	31000.00	7750.00	2328.10	930.00	19991.90
Kevin	Anderson	T	28000.00	7000.00	2102.80	840.00	18057.20

Browse C:\...chap7\SALARY Rec 1/11 File

View and edit fields

Figure 7-13. The SALARY database

10% raise, use the following commands with the SALARY database:

```
. USE Salary
. REPLACE ALL Gross WITH Gross*1.1
```

The REPLACE command in this instance is confined to the Gross database field. Every record in the SALARY database will have its Gross field overwritten with the value in the Gross field multiplied by 1.1.

You can also qualify the REPLACE command using the FOR clause. For example, to give the employee named Bunker a raise, enter the following at the dot prompt:

```
. USE SALARY
. REPLACE Gross WITH Gross*2 FOR Lastname="Bunker"
```

In this case, the REPLACE command is confined to those records with the name Bunker in the Lastname field. This employee's gross salary is doubled. Note that the name Bunker is enclosed in quotes to denote a character string. If the name Bunker were not enclosed in quotes, dBASE IV would issue the error message "Variable not found."

You can also replace the contents of multiple fields in a database by using the REPLACE command with a list of fields. For example, suppose you are notified by federal and state authorities of a change in tax rates. To deal with this situation, you might use the following command lines:

```
. USE Salary
. REPLACE ALL Fica WITH Gross*.0751,State WITH Gross*.035
```

In this instance, the REPLACE command replaces the contents of the Fica and State fields in each record of the database. The contents of these fields are replaced with the Gross salary field multiplied by the new tax rates at the federal and state levels.

If you remove the ALL clause after the REPLACE command in the previous command line, the REPLACE operation is performed only on the current record. For example, if the record pointer were on record number 5, the Fica and State fields would be replaced for that record only.

As with many dBASE IV commands, you can also specify a *scope* for the REPLACE command. For example, the following command line only affects the next ten records, starting with the current record:

```
. REPLACE NEXT 10 Gross WITH Gross*1.1
```

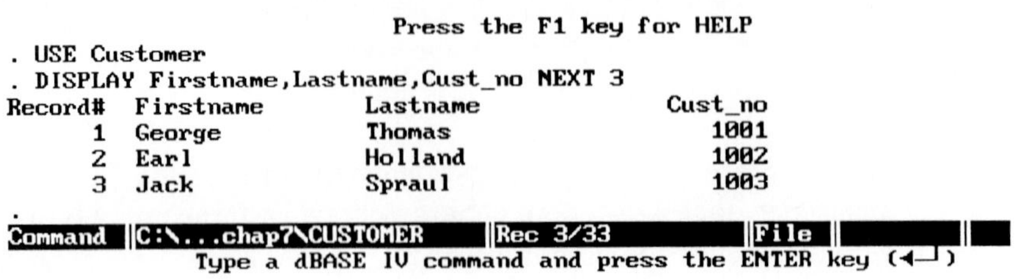

Press the F1 key for HELP
. USE Customer
. DISPLAY Firstname,Lastname,Cust_no NEXT 3
Record# Firstname Lastname Cust_no
1 George Thomas 1001
2 Earl Holland 1002
3 Jack Spraul 1003
Command C:\...chap7\CUSTOMER Rec 3/33 File
Type a dBASE IV command and press the ENTER key (◄┘)

Figure 7-14. The status bar shows the record pointer position

Moving Around in a Database

dBASE IV assigns a sequential number to each record in a database. You can use these record numbers to navigate to a specific record in a database. The current, or *active,* record number is shown in the status bar at the bottom of the dBASE IV screen. For example, Figure 7-14 shows a database with 33 records; the record pointer is on record number 3.

This chapter refers frequently to the *record pointer.* The record pointer identifies the active record in a database. When you move around in a database, you are actually making the record pointer point to the specific record you're working with. For example, imagine you are in browse mode. If you move the cursor down to record number 3 and press ESC to return to the dot prompt, the record pointer remains on record number 3.

You can change the position of the record pointer in various ways. The GOTO command, or GO, is a popular method.

The GO Command

The GO command, followed by a record number, repositions the record pointer to the specified record number. That record then becomes the active record to which you can then apply a command. For example, the following commands reposition the record pointer to record number 5 in the database SALARY. The contents of the Gross field are replaced.

```
. USE Salary
. GO 5
. REPLACE Gross WITH Gross*1.1
```

Tip: You can reposition the record pointer to a specific record in an active database by entering just the record number at the dot prompt.

You can also use the TOP and BOTTOM clauses with the GO command to move quickly to the first or last record in a database. For example, assuming that the SALARY database is already in use, the following command lines move the record pointer to the top of the database and replace the contents of the Lastname field in that record by using the REPLACE command:

```
. GO TOP
. REPLACE Lastname WITH "Bunker"
```

The GO BOTTOM command repositions the record pointer to the last record in the database. For example, the following command lines move the record pointer to the last record in the SALARY database before displaying the record with the ? command:

```
. USE SALARY
. GO BOTTOM
. ? Firstname,Lastname,Gross,Fed,Fica,State,Net
```

Tip: If an index is active, the GO TOP and GO BOTTOM commands reposition the record pointer to the top or the bottom of the database as defined by the index, not the natural order of the database. For more about indexing, see the section "Indexing a Database" later in this chapter.

The SKIP Command

You can advance the record pointer by a specified number of records with the SKIP command. When you use the SKIP command without a number, dBASE IV skips down one record in the database. For example, assuming that a database is in use, the following command lines send the record pointer to the top of the database and then have it skip down to the second record:

```
. GO TOP
. SKIP
```

To have dBASE IV skip more than one record at a time, follow the SKIP command with a number. For example, the following command lines reposition the record pointer to the top of the active database and have it skip down to record number 5:

```
. GO TOP
. SKIP 5
```

You can also use SKIP to move backwards in a database. To do this, follow the SKIP command with a negative number. For example, the following commands reposition the record pointer to the last record in the database and then skip backwards to the next-to-last record:

```
. GO BOTTOM
. SKIP -1
```

If the record pointer is on the last record in the database and you enter **SKIP**, dBASE IV trips the end-of-file marker. The end-of-file function, EOF( ), returns a logical true.

The end-of-file marker signifies that the last record in the database has been passed. If you enter **SKIP** again, dBASE IV gives you the error message "End of file encountered." Similarly, if the record pointer is on the first record in the database and you enter **SKIP -1**, dBASE IV trips the beginning-of-file marker. The beginning-of-file function, BOF( ), returns a logical true. If you enter **SKIP -1** again, dBASE IV gives you a beginning-of-file error message.

dBASE IV uses the beginning-of-file and end-of-file markers to mark the boundaries of a database. With these markers, dBASE IV controls commands that try to access nonexistant records.

Deleting Records

You can mark records for deletion with the DELETE command. Once a record is marked for deletion, you can delete it with the PACK command. The DELETE command applies only to the currently active database. For example, the following commands activate the SALARY database, position the record pointer on record 5, and erase it from the database:

```
. USE Salary
. GO 5
. DELETE
. PACK
```

The PACK command erases all records in the currently active database that are marked for deletion. As you might imagine, the results of the PACK command cannot be reversed.

If you change your mind before using the PACK command, you can use the RECALL command to unmark records marked for deletion. The RECALL command by itself applies to a single record. However, you can broaden its scope by including a qualifier. For example, the following command recalls all records marked for deletion in the currently active database:

```
. RECALL ALL
```

Tip: If the record pointer is past the last record in a database, which means EOF() equals .T., the RECALL command has no effect. In this situation, you can use the GO TOP command followed by the RECALL command.

You can use the DELETE command selectively. For example, the following command line marks for deletion records that have the name Smith in the Lastname field:

```
. DELETE FOR Lastname="Smith"
```

The DELETED( ) function can tell you whether a database contains records that are marked for deletion. It returns a logical true (.T.) if a record is marked for deletion and a logical false (.F.) if it is not. For example the following command displays all records that are marked for deletion:

```
. DISPLAY ALL FOR DELETED()
```

When you use the APPEND, EDIT, CHANGE, or BROWSE command, dBASE IV displays the message "Del" in the status bar to signify that a record is marked for deletion. When you display records marked for deletion by using the DISPLAY or LIST command, dBASE IV places an asterisk (*) next to them to signify that they are marked for deletion.

Other forms of the DELETE command you might use are shown here:

DELETE ALL	Marks all the records in a database for deletion
DELETE NEXT 20	Marks the next 20 records for deletion
DELETE REST	Marks all records for deletion, from the current one to the end of the database

The SET DELETED ON command hides records marked for deletion from many dBASE IV commands. For example, when you use the DISPLAY or LIST command to display the data in a database, dBASE IV ignores records marked for deletion. However, when SET DELETED is set to On, dBASE IV ignores marked records when you use the RECALL ALL command. To bring marked records out of hiding, use the command SET DELETED OFF.

Deleting a Database

To delete all the records in a database, use the ZAP command. This command erases an entire database and all of its records. The effects of this command are permanent. The syntax for ZAP is

USE <*database name*>
ZAP

Displaying Data

You can use a number of commands from the dot prompt to display the contents of a database on your screen. The three most common are the DISPLAY, LIST, and ? commands.

The DISPLAY and LIST Commands

The DISPLAY and LIST commands are interchangeable. Both commands display a list of the records in the database. However, the DISPLAY command stops after displaying each screenful of data; you press a key to continue. The LIST command, on the other hand, scrolls data down the screen until you press either CTRL-S or LEFT ARROW or the end of the database is reached. Since the DIS-

```
. USE SALARY
. DISPLAY ALL
Record#  FIRSTNAME LASTNAME  BONUS    GROSS      FED     FICA    STATE       NET
      1  Mary      Jones     .F.   24000.00 6000.00 1802.40   720.00 15477.60
      2  Drew      Gibson    .T.   22000.00 5500.00 1652.20   660.00 14187.80
      3  Ralph     Moriarity .F.   26000.00 6500.00 1952.60   780.00 16767.40
      4  Clive     Bunker    .F.   23000.00 5750.00 1727.30   690.00 14832.70
      5  John      Patrovich .F.   32000.03 8000.01 2403.20   960.00 20636.82
      6  Suzanne   Chambers  .F.   17000.00 4250.00 1276.70   510.00 10963.30
      7  Keith     Campbell  .T.   52000.00 13000.0 3905.20  1560.00 33534.80
      8  George    Haenzel   .T.   22000.00 5500.00 1652.20   660.00 14187.80
      9  Jeff      Hill      .T.   25000.00 6250.00 1877.50   750.00 16122.50
     10  Sam       Hammons   .T.   31000.00 7750.00 2328.10   930.00 19991.90
     11  Kevin     Anderson  .T.   28000.00 7000.00 2102.80   840.00 18057.20
.
Command  C:\...chap7\SALARY      Rec EOF/11        File                  CapsIns
```

Figure 7-15. The DISPLAY ALL command

PLAY and LIST commands are so similar, this section uses DISPLAY to illustrate the attributes of both commands.

You can use the DISPLAY command to display all of the records in the database or just selected records. You must open a database before using DISPLAY. The syntax for the DISPLAY command is

DISPLAY [[FIELDS] <*expression list*>] [<*scope*>] [FOR <*condition*>] [WHILE <*condition*>] [TO PRINTER/TO FILE <*filename*>]

To display all of the records in the current database, use the DISPLAY ALL command as follows:

```
. DISPLAY ALL
```

Figure 7-15 shows the results of the DISPLAY ALL command when you use it to display the contents of a database called SALARY.

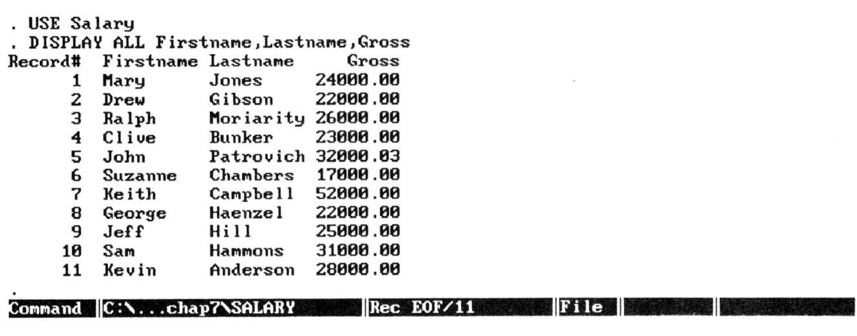

```
. USE Salary
. DISPLAY ALL Firstname,Lastname,Gross
Record#  Firstname Lastname      Gross
      1  Mary      Jones      24000.00
      2  Drew      Gibson     22000.00
      3  Ralph     Moriarity  26000.00
      4  Clive     Bunker     23000.00
      5  John      Patrovich  32000.03
      6  Suzanne   Chambers   17000.00
      7  Keith     Campbell   52000.00
      8  George    Haenzel    22000.00
      9  Jeff      Hill       25000.00
     10  Sam       Hammons    31000.00
     11  Kevin     Anderson   28000.00
.
Command  C:\...chap7\SALARY    Rec EOF/11    File
```

Figure 7-16. The DISPLAY ALL command with a fields list

When the combined width of the database fields exceeds the 80 characters allowed by a conventional monitor, DISPLAY ALL displays your data in wraparound fashion. Furthermore, if the number of records in the database exceeds the length of a conventional screen, dBASE IV displays your data one screen at a time. To see the next screenful of data, press any key. To halt the DISPLAY ALL command in mid-screen, press CTRL-S.

To display only selected fields with the DISPLAY ALL command, use a fields list separated by commas. For example, using the SALARY database, you can display just the Firstname, Lastname, and Gross fields using the following command. Figure 7-16 shows the results.

```
. DISPLAY ALL Firstname,Lastname,Gross
```

To display only selected records with the DISPLAY command, use the conditional FOR clause. The FOR clause allows you stipulate a condition for the DISPLAY command. The syntax for the DISPLAY command then becomes

DISPLAY FOR *<search field><operator><search object>*

The DISPLAY FOR command can search both character and numeric fields to find the search object. The data type of the search object must match the data type of the search field. For example, if you use a numeric search field to find a character search object, dBASE IV issues the error message "Data type mismatch." Logical fields do not require a search object. In order to use a date field as a search fields you must use a function to temporarily convert that date field to a character string for the life of the comparison. For example, you can use the DTOS( ) (date to string) function to convert a date field. You can then compare that field to a character string such as "11/31/90".

Using the SALARY database, the following command lines use the relational operator > to display all employees who earn in excess of $24,000. Figure 7-17 shows the results.

```
. DISPLAY FOR Gross>24000
```

In this command, the numeric field Gross is the search field, > is the operator, and 24000 is the search object. Together they form a condition that must be met before DISPLAY includes a given record in the final screen output.

```
. DISPLAY FOR Gross>24000
Record#  FIRSTNAME LASTNAME   BONUS     GROSS      FED     FICA    STATE       NET
      3  Ralph     Moriarity  .F.    26000.00  6500.00  1952.60   780.00  16767.40
      5  John      Patrovich  .F.    32000.03  8000.01  2403.20   960.00  20636.82
      7  Keith     Campbell   .T.    52000.00  13000.0  3905.20  1560.00  33534.80
      9  Jeff      Hill       .T.    25000.00  6250.00  1877.50   750.00  16122.50
     10  Sam       Hammons    .T.    31000.00  7750.00  2328.10   930.00  19991.90
     11  Kevin     Anderson   .T.    28000.00  7000.00  2102.80   840.00  18057.20
.
Command  C:\...chap7\SALARY      Rec EOF/11        File
```

Figure 7-17. The FOR clause displays selected records

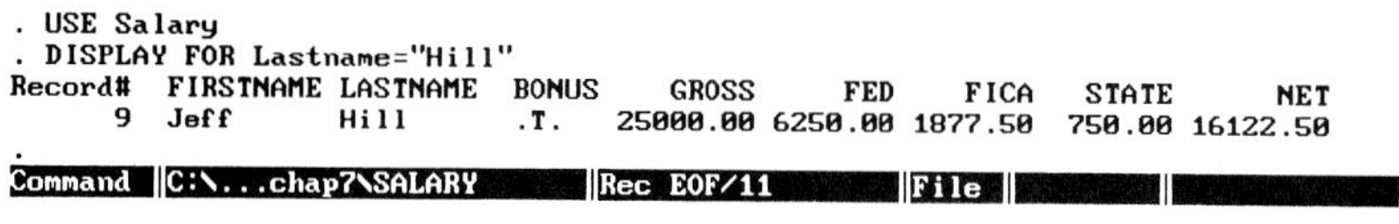

Figure 7-18. The DISPLAY command displays a specific record

The following command displays a single record. It uses a character field as the search field and the relational operator =. Figure 7-18 shows the output.

```
. DISPLAY FOR Lastname="Hill"
```

Note that the search object "Hill" is enclosed in quotes. This defines it as a character string. When you use the = operator with character strings, dBASE IV goes for an exact match. In this case it searches the Lastname field for the character string "Hill". It won't find and display records with "hill" or "HILL".

The following command line searches and displays data from the SALARY database using the logical field Bonus. This field designates those employees who qualify for a bonus this year. Since Bonus is a logical field, it contains a true or false value. Thus, you need only use the name of the logical field with the DISPLAY FOR command to display all records where Bonus is true. An operator and a search object are not required. Figure 7-19 shows the results of the command.

```
. DISPLAY FOR Bonus
```

The next command line uses a logical operator, .NOT., to display those employees who are not eligible for a bonus this year.

```
. USE Salary
. DISPLAY FOR Bonus
Record#  FIRSTNAME LASTNAME  BONUS     GROSS      FED     FICA    STATE       NET
      2  Drew      Gibson    .T.    22000.00 5500.00 1652.20   660.00  14187.80
      7  Keith     Campbell  .T.    52000.00 13000.0 3905.20  1560.00  33534.80
      8  George    Haenzel   .T.    22000.00 5500.00 1652.20   660.00  14187.80
      9  Jeff      Hill      .T.    25000.00 6250.00 1877.50   750.00  16122.50
     10  Sam       Hammons   .T.    31000.00 7750.00 2328.10   930.00  19991.90
     11  Kevin     Anderson  .T.    28000.00 7000.00 2102.80   840.00  18057.20
.
Command ||C:\...chap7\SALARY     ||Rec EOF/11       ||File ||
```

Figure 7-19. The DISPLAY command with a logical field

The .NOT. operator with a logical search field searches for those records that do *not* have a logical true (.T.) in the Bonus field. Instead, these records have a logical false (.F.). See Figure 7-20 for the results.

```
. DISPLAY FOR .NOT. Bonus
```

```
. USE Salary
. DISPLAY FOR .NOT. Bonus
Record#  FIRSTNAME LASTNAME   BONUS     GROSS      FED     FICA    STATE       NET
      1  Mary      Jones      .F.    24000.00 6000.00 1802.40   720.00  15477.60
      3  Ralph     Moriarity  .F.    26000.00 6500.00 1952.60   780.00  16767.40
      4  Clive     Bunker     .F.    23000.00 5750.00 1727.30   690.00  14832.70
      5  John      Patrovich  .F.    32000.03 8000.01 2403.20   960.00  20636.82
      6  Suzanne   Chambers   .F.    17000.00 4250.00 1276.70   510.00  10963.30
.
Command ||C:\...chap7\SALARY     ||Rec EOF/11       ||File ||
```

Figure 7-20. DISPLAY FOR .NOT. Bonus

```
. USE Salary
. DISPLAY FOR Bonus .AND. Gross>20000
Record#  FIRSTNAME LASTNAME  BONUS     GROSS       FED     FICA    STATE       NET
      2  Drew      Gibson    .T.    22000.00 5500.00 1652.20   660.00 14187.80
      7  Keith     Campbell  .T.    52000.00 13000.0 3905.20  1560.00 33534.80
      8  George    Haenzel   .T.    22000.00 5500.00 1652.20   660.00 14187.80
      9  Jeff      Hill      .T.    25000.00 6250.00 1877.50   750.00 16122.50
     10  Sam       Hammons   .T.    31000.00 7750.00 2328.10   930.00 19991.90
     11  Kevin     Anderson  .T.    28000.00 7000.00 2102.80   840.00 18057.20
.
Command  C:\...chap7\SALARY    Rec EOF/11    File
```

Figure 7-21. The DISPLAY command with the .AND. operator

The next command uses the .AND. logical operator to state a dual condition for the DISPLAY command. In order for a given record to be included in the display, there must be a logical true (.T.) in the Bonus field *and* the Gross field must contain a number in excess of 20,000. See Figure 7-21 for the output.

```
. DISPLAY FOR Bonus .AND. Gross>20000
```

Tip: To send data to your printer, follow the DISPLAY command with the TO PRINTER option. For example,

. DISPLAY FOR Gross>20000 TO PRINTER

prints all records with a number greater than 20,000 in the Gross field.

Other forms of the DISPLAY command are as follows:

DISPLAY RECORD 5	Displays the data in record number 5 only

DISPLAY NEXT 15	Displays only the next 15 records, starting with the current one
DISPLAY ALL FOR Lastname< >"Hill"	Displays all records except those with Hill in the Lastname field
DISPLAY ALL WHILE Lastname<>"Smith"	Displays all records until the name Smith is encountered in the Lastname field

The ? Command

The ? command is one of dBASE IV's more versatile display commands. Like the DISPLAY command, it can display raw data. However, you can also use it to return the value of one or more dBASE IV expressions. Use the ? command when you want to answer questions like "What is the value of *<expression>*?"

The ? command works somewhat like the DISPLAY command to display data. For example, it supports a fields list. However, it does not support the FOR or WHILE qualifiers. Thus, its primary function is to display raw or calculated data. The ? command does allows you to format the appearance of your data and to specify its location on the screen. The syntax for the ? command is

? [*<expression* 1>] [PICTURE *<character expression>*] [AT *<numeric expression>*], [*<expression* 2>]...[,]

When you use the ? command to display data, dBASE IV displays the data on the next line. That is, the ? command issues a carriage return line feed just before displaying results.

```
. USE Salary
. GO TOP
SALARY: Record No       1
.
. ? Lastname,Gross,Fed,Fica,State,Net
Jones      24000.00 6000.00 1802.40  720.00 15477.60
.
. ? Fed+Fica+State
     8522.40
.
. ? Firstname,Lastname+"Tax:"+STR(Fed+Fica+State)
Mary     Jones     Tax:       8522
.
. ? Firstname,Lastname,Gross PICTURE "$99999.99"
Mary     Jones      $24000.00
.
. ? Firstname AT 10,Lastname AT 20,Gross AT 40 PICTURE "$99999.99"
          Mary      Jones               $24000.00
.
Command ||C:\...chap7\SALARY        ||Rec 1/11          ||File ||
```

Figure 7-22. The ? command displays data

The following command line uses ? with a fields list to display the contents of a record in the SALARY database. Figure 7-22 shows the results.

```
. USE Salary
. GO TOP
. ? Lastname,Gross,Fed,Fica,State,Net
```

This next command line illustrates the calculative powers of the ? command. This time the ? command adds the contents of the Fed, Fica, and State fields in the SALARY database and displays them on the screen. Figure 7-22 shows the results.

```
. ? Fed+Fica+State
```

With the ? command you can build complex display expressions involving either character or numeric database fields. However, when you combine database fields for display with the ? command, the data types for the database fields must be the same throughout the expression. If you try to combine numeric and character data in an expression following the ? command, dBASE IV gives you an error message.

You can combine numeric and character data after the ? command by converting numeric expressions to character strings with the STR( ) function. For example, the following command line uses two character fields, a character string enclosed in quotes, and the STR( ) function to convert a numeric expression to a character string. The numeric expression in this case is Fed+Fica+State. Figure 7-22 shows the results.

```
. ? Firstname,Lastname+"Tax:"+STR(Fed+Fica+State)
```

You can also format the appearance of your display with the ? command. For example, you can include the optional PICTURE clause to show numeric output as currency. The following command line uses a PICTURE clause to display the Gross field in the SALARY database. For more on using the PICTURE clause in command lines, see Chapter 23.

```
. ? Firstname,Lastname,Gross PICTURE "$99999.99"
```

You can also use the optional AT clause with the ? command to position your data on the display line. A conventional monitor is 80 columns (characters) wide. The following command line displays the Firstname field starting at column 10, the Lastname field at column 20, and the Gross field starting at column 40.

```
. ? Firstname AT 10,Lastname AT 20,Gross AT 40 PICTURE "$99999.99"
```

For more about the many options available with the ? command, see Chapter 31.

Printing Data

There are a number of dot prompt commands for sending displayed output to your printer. This section discusses two of them: the SET PRINTER ON command and the TO PRINTER clause.

The SET PRINTER ON Command

The SET PRINTER ON command activates your printer. When you enter this command, dBASE IV sends its output to your printer as well as to your screen. To stop sending output to your printer, use the SET PRINTER OFF command. The next three command lines activate the printer, send output to it, and then deactivate the printer.

```
. SET PRINTER ON
. DISPLAY ALL FOR Gross>24000
. SET PRINTER OFF
```

The TO PRINTER Clause

You can also send output to your printer by including the optional TO PRINTER clause at the end of a DISPLAY or LIST command. For example, the following commands send various types of output to your printer:

```
. DISPLAY ALL FOR Gross>24000 TO PRINTER
. LIST STRUCTURE TO PRINTER
. DISPLAY FOR .NOT. Bonus TO PRINTER
. LIST All Firstname,Lastname,Gross TO PRINTER
```

Writing to a Text File

You can also send your displayed output to an ASCII text file using the optional TO FILE *<filename>* clause with the DISPLAY or LIST command. For example, the following command line sends all records with a number greater than 40,000 in the Gross field to a new file called BOSSFILE.ASC:

```
. LIST ALL FOR Gross>40000 TO FILE Bossfile.asc
```

To record the commands and output from the current dBASE IV session, use the SET ALTERNATE command. First you name and open a file to send the information to. Then you start sending information to that file. The syntax is as follows:

SET ALTERNATE TO *<filename>* [ADDITIVE]
SET ALTERNATE ON

The SET ALTERNATE TO *<filename>* command creates and opens an ASCII text file. The SET ALTERNATE ON command starts sending dBASE IV input and output to that file in the form of text. The optional ADDITIVE clause lets you append dBASE IV input and output to an existing alternate file. You can later view the results with the dBASE IV Text Editor or another word processor that works with ASCII files. You end the recording with the SET ALTERNATE OFF command. You then close an open alternate file with the CLOSE ALTERNATE command.

Reports and Labels

You can also enter commands at the dot prompt to print custom reports and labels you've created using the Reports and Labels Design screens. The Reports and Labels Design screens let you create custom reports and labels for displaying and printing data from your dBASE IV databases.

Custom Reports

You can access the Reports Design screen from the dot prompt by using the CREATE REPORT command. When you enter this command, dBASE IV takes you directly to the Reports Design screen. The syntax for the CREATE REPORT command is

CREATE REPORT *<report filename>*

As mentioned, you can use the Reports Design screen to build custom reports that attractively display the data in your database. For a complete description of how to create custom reports, see Chapter 10. The command for activating custom reports from the dot prompt is REPORT FORM. The syntax for this command is

REPORT FORM *<report filename>* [HEADING *<character expression>*] [FOR *<condition>*] [WHILE *<condition>*] [TO PRINTER/TO FILE *<filename>*]

When you enter the REPORT FORM command followed by a report file name, dBASE IV sends the report to your screen. However, you can also send a custom report to your printer by adding the optional TO PRINTER clause. For example, the following command line prints a custom report called SALRY. dBASE IV adds the proper file extension for you.

```
. REPORT FORM Salry TO PRINTER
```

Unless you specify otherwise, the REPORT FORM command uses all the records in the currently active database when it displays or prints your report. You can, however, qualify the data by including the optional FOR and WHILE clauses. For example, in the following command lines the SALRY.FRM report can only use those records that have a number in excess of 24,000 in the Gross field of the SALARY database.

```
. USE Salary
. REPORT FORM Salry TO PRINTER FOR Gross>24000
```

You can give your custom report a new heading by using the optional HEADING clause with the REPORT FORM command. For example, the following command line uses the HEADING clause to give the SALRY report the title "Upper Management." It also uses a select group of records with a Gross field that contains a number in excess of 45,000.

```
. REPORT FORM Salry HEADING "Upper Management" FOR Gross>45000
```

Custom Labels

You can create custom labels from the dot prompt by using the Labels Design screen. This screen lets you design custom labels for mailings and much more. For a complete discussion of how to use the Labels Design screen, see Chapter 11. You access the Labels Design screen from the dot prompt with the CREATE LABEL command. The syntax for the CREATE LABEL command is

CREATE LABEL *<label filename>*

The command for activating a custom label form is LABEL FORM. The syntax for this command is

LABEL FORM *<label filename>* [FOR *<condition>*] [WHILE *<condition>*] [TO PRINTER/TO FILE*<filename>*]

When you enter the LABEL FORM command followed by the file name of a custom label format, dBASE IV generates the labels using all the records in the currently active database. However, you can limit the scope of the LABEL FORM command by using the optional FOR and WHILE conditions. For example, the following command lines activate the MAILIST database and select specific records from it for use with the LABEL FORM command. For a record in MAILIST to be selected by the LABEL FORM command, the Oktomail logical field must contain a logical true (.T.). The name of the label file being activated is PROMO. dBASE IV includes the proper extension for you.

```
. USE Mailist
. LABEL FORM Promo FOR Oktomail
```

You can also include the optional TO PRINTER clause at the end of the LABEL FORM command to send the output to your printer. For example, the following command line uses the TO PRINTER clause with the LABEL FORM command:

```
. LABEL FORM Promo TO PRINTER FOR Oktomail
```

Copying a Database

You can copy the contents of a database from the dot prompt with several commands. A description of these commands follows.

The COPY FILE Command

You can copy the contents of a database file to a new database file with the COPY FILE command. This command duplicates any dBASE IV file. The syntax for the COPY FILE command is

COPY FILE *<filename>* TO *<new filename>*

When you use the COPY FILE command, you must specify the file extensions for both files. If the file you're writing to is an existing file, dBASE IV overwrites the contents of the existing file.

For example, the following command line copies the contents of the SALARY database to a new file called SALARY2:

```
. COPY FILE Salary.dbf TO Salary2.dbf
```

The COPY STRUCTURE and APPEND FROM Commands

You can copy the contents of one database to another with the two commands COPY STRUCTURE and APPEND FROM. The COPY STRUCTURE command creates a new database file on disk with the same structure as the currently active database. However, the new database contains no records. To load this new database, use the APPEND FROM command, which takes records from a database file on disk and appends them to the currently active database. For example, the following command lines create a new database called SALARY2 and then append to it records from the SALARY database file:

```
. USE Salary
. COPY STRUCTURE to Salary2
. USE Salary2
. APPEND FROM Salary
```

You can be selective with the APPEND FROM command. For example, the following command lines create a new database, but because of the optional FOR clause only selected records are appended to the new database. In this case, only those records with a number greater than or equal to 40,000 in the Gross field of the SALARY.DBF database are appended to the new MNGMT.DBF database.

```
. USE Salary
. COPY STRUCTURE TO Mngmt
. USE Mngmt
. APPEND FROM Salary FOR Gross>=40000
```

The COPY TO Command

The COPY TO command copies all or part of a database to a new database file on disk. The syntax for the COPY TO command is

> COPY TO <*filename*> [[TYPE] <*file type*>] [FIELDS <*fields list*>] [<*scope*>] [FOR <*condition*>] [WHILE <*condition*>]

You must activate a database before using the COPY TO command. Once a database is active, you can copy all of its fields and records to a new database file on disk. For example, the following command line copies all of the fields and records in the SALARY database to a new database called SALARY1:

```
= . USE SALARY
. COPY TO Salary1
```

You can also copy records that meet specified criteria by using FOR and WHILE clauses with the COPY TO command. For example, the following command line copies only those records in the SALARY database that have a number in excess of 24,000 in the Gross field:

```
. COPY TO Salary1 FOR Gross>24000
```

The TYPE clause for the COPY TO command allows you to specify the type of file you want to create. dBASE IV supports multiple file types, including file types compatible with previous versions of dBASE as well as programs other than dBASE IV.

For example, you can use the TYPE clause with the COPY TO command to make dBASE IV memo files (.DBT files) compatible with dBASE III PLUS. Whenever you enter data into memo fields, both dBASE III PLUS and dBASE IV create a separate file with a .DBT extension to hold those memos. dBASE IV can read dBASE III .DBT memo files. However, dBASE III PLUS cannot read dBASE IV .DBT memo files unless you copy them first using the TYPE clause with the COPY TO command. When you use the COPY TO command to copy a database, dBASE IV automatically copies an associated .DBT memo file along with it. To create a dBASE III PLUS compatible .DBT memo file, use the DBMEMO3 file type option with the TYPE clause of the COPY TO command. For example, the command

```
. COPY TO Salary1 TYPE DBMEMO3
```

copies the SALARY database, and an associated .DBT file, to a new database called SALARY1 where the associated .DBT file is compatible with dBASE III PLUS.

Closing a Database

You can close an open database with the CLOSE command. This command closes all open databases and their associated index files (.NDX and .MDX), .DBT memo files, and .FMT format files. The syntax for the CLOSE command for databases is

CLOSE DATABASES

The CLOSE DATABASES command is an important housekeeping tool. Foremost, it helps you to protect your files. For example, if you leave a database open, someone with a minimum of dBASE experience can easily alter the data in your database. Furthermore, the CLOSE DATABASES command lets you close a database in one work area and open that same database in another work area.

An alternative to the CLOSE DATABASES command is the USE command. The USE command closes the current database in the current work area and replaces it with a specified database.

Type	Store	=
Character	STORE "hello" TO Greet	Greet="hello"
Numeric	STORE 0 TO Findit	Findit=0
Date	STORE {12/31/89} TO Today	Today={12/31/89}
Logical	STORE .T. TO Verify	Verify=.T.

Table 7-2. Assigning Data Types to Memory Variables

Memory Variables

In dBASE IV, you can assign a name to a small section of your computer's RAM and store data in it. The term for a small section of named memory is a *memory variable*. You can create and name memory variables with either the STORE command or the = command. For example, the following command lines both create a memory variable called Number10 and store the number 10 in it:

```
. STORE 10 TO Number10
. Number10=10
```

Memory variable names must begin with a letter and can be up to ten characters in length, including letters, numbers, and underscores. Also, you must assign memory variables a character, numeric, date, or logical data type just as you do database fields. You designate a memory variable's data type when you create it. For example, Table 7-2 shows some commands you might use to create the various memory variable data types. Note the use of

```
. STORE 10 TO Units
         10
. STORE 24.95 TO Price
         24.95
. STORE .065 TO Tax
          0.07
. STORE 5 TO Ship
          5
. Totl=Units*Price
       249.50
. Gtotl=Totl+Totl*Tax+Ship
       270.72
. ? Gtotl
       270.72
.
Command
```

Figure 7-23. Memory variables forming an equation

curly braces ({ }) with date variables. You can also use memory variables with search commands, as explained later, or to perform calculations. Figure 7-23 shows some numeric variables and how you might use them to perform a calculation.

You cannot mix numeric, character, date, and logical variables in an expression. If you do, dBASE IV gives you the error message "Data type mismatch." For example, if you multiply a memory variable named Cost that contains the number 24.95 by another variable called Units that contains the character string "5", you will get an error message.

Sorting a Database

In dBASE IV, you cannot sort the current database to itself. However, you can create a new database with the data from the current database sorted to your specifications. The new database matches the structure of the old database. You may not sort a file

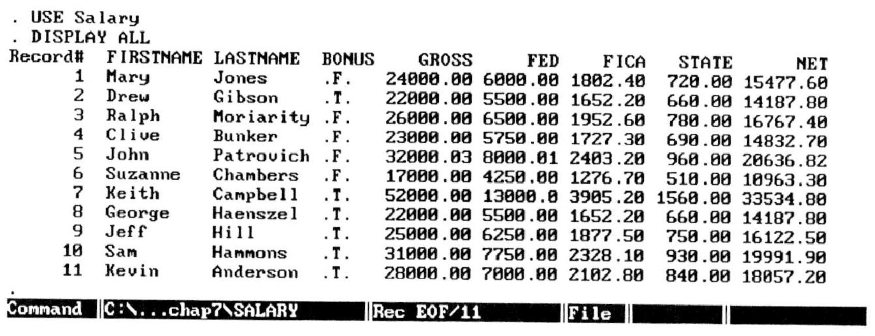

```
. USE Salary
. DISPLAY ALL
Record#  FIRSTNAME LASTNAME  BONUS    GROSS      FED     FICA   STATE      NET
      1  Mary      Jones      .F.  24000.00 6000.00 1802.40  720.00 15477.60
      2  Drew      Gibson     .T.  22000.00 5500.00 1652.20  660.00 14187.80
      3  Ralph     Moriarity  .F.  26000.00 6500.00 1952.60  780.00 16767.40
      4  Clive     Bunker     .F.  23000.00 5750.00 1727.30  690.00 14832.70
      5  John      Patrovich  .F.  32000.03 8000.01 2403.20  960.00 20636.82
      6  Suzanne   Chambers   .F.  17000.00 4250.00 1276.70  510.00 10963.30
      7  Keith     Campbell   .T.  52000.00 13000.0 3905.20 1560.00 33534.80
      8  George    Haenszel   .T.  22000.00 5500.00 1652.20  660.00 14187.80
      9  Jeff      Hill       .T.  25000.00 6250.00 1877.50  750.00 16122.50
     10  Sam       Hammons    .T.  31000.00 7750.00 2328.10  930.00 19991.90
     11  Kevin     Anderson   .T.  28000.00 7000.00 2102.80  840.00 18057.20
.
Command  C:\...chap7\SALARY   Rec EOF/11   File
```

Figure 7-24. The SALARY database before the SORT command

to another open file. However, you may overwrite a closed file. To create a new sorted database, use the SORT command. The syntax for the SORT command is

> SORT TO *<filename>* ON *<field 1>* [/A] [/C] [/D] [,*<field 2>*] [/A] [/C] [/D] ...] [ASCENDING]/[DESCENDING] [*<scope>*] [FOR *<condition>*] [WHILE *<condition>*]

You sort a database by using one or more specified fields. For example, if you specify the Lastname field of the current database as the sort field, dBASE IV creates a new database with the records sorted by Lastname. Unless you specify otherwise, dBASE IV copies all of the records in the old database to the new sorted database. For example, the following command uses the Lastname field of the SALARY database to specify the sort order for a new database called INORDER. Figures 7-24 and 7-25 show the SALARY and INORDER databases before and after the sort. Note that the records in INORDER are in ascending order by last name.

```
. SORT ON Lastname TO Inorder
```

```
. USE Salary
. SORT ON Lastname TO Inorder
  100% Sorted           11 Records sorted
. USE Inorder
. DISPLAY ALL
Record#  FIRSTNAME LASTNAME  BONUS    GROSS      FED    FICA   STATE      NET
      1  Kevin     Anderson  .T.   28000.00  7000.00 2102.80  840.00 18057.20
      2  Clive     Bunker    .F.   23000.00  5750.00 1727.30  690.00 14832.70
      3  Keith     Campbell  .T.   52000.00  13000.0 3905.20 1560.00 33534.80
      4  Suzanne   Chambers  .F.   17000.00  4250.00 1276.70  510.00 10963.30
      5  Drew      Gibson    .T.   22000.00  5500.00 1652.20  660.00 14187.80
      6  George    Haenzel   .T.   22000.00  5500.00 1652.20  660.00 14187.80
      7  Sam       Hammons   .T.   31000.00  7750.00 2328.10  930.00 19991.90
      8  Jeff      Hill      .T.   25000.00  6250.00 1877.50  750.00 16122.50
      9  Mary      Jones     .F.   24000.00  6000.00 1802.40  720.00 15477.60
     10  Ralph     Moriarity .F.   26000.00  6500.00 1952.60  780.00 16767.40
     11  John      Patrovich .F.   32000.03  8000.01 2403.20  960.00 20636.82
.
Command  C:\...chap7\INORDER    Rec EOF/11    File
```

Figure 7-25. INORDER.DBF holds the sorted data from SALARY

You can specify up to 16 sort fields with the SORT command. You specify multiple fields by including them in a fields list, separated by commas. The order of the field names in the list specifies their order of precedence in the sort. The following command illustrates a fields list with the SORT command:

```
. SORT ON Lastname,Gross TO Inorder
```

Normally, dBASE IV sorts in ascending order (/A). However, you can specify descending order by using the optional /D after a field name. You can also specify a case-sensitive sort by using the optional /C after the SORT command. For example, the following command line specifies a descending sort using the Gross field of the SALARY database:

```
. SORT ON Gross /D TO Inorder
```

You can also combine sort order conditions. For example, the following command line specifies a descending order case-sensitive sort using the Lastname field of the SALARY database:

```
. SORT ON Lastname /DC TO Inorder
```

The ASCENDING or DESCENDING clause after the SORT command applies only to the balance of the fields in the database that do not have /D or /A after them. When /D or /A appears after a database field, the ASCENDING or DESCENDING clause is ignored for that field.

You can have the SORT command select only certain records from the old database to create the new database. You do this by using the optional FOR and WHILE clauses with the SORT command. For example, in the following command line a FOR clause is used to include in the new database specific records from the old database:

```
. SORT ON Gross TO Inorder FOR Gross>24000
```

You can also use multiple fields with the SORT command. For example, the following command line combines two fields:

```
. SORT ON Lastname,Firstname TO Inorder FOR Gross>24000
```

Indexing a Database

Indexing a database is different from sorting it. When you index a database, you create a separate index file. This index file is used to specify the order of information in the database.

An index file for a database works much like a card catalog for a library. It contains the information from at least one field from all the records in a database; this information is sorted in alphabetical, chronological, or numeric order. Next to the field information in an index file is the record number for that database field. dBASE IV can very quickly search the field data in an index file and use the record numbers to point back to the correct record in the database.

Index files are always associated with a specific database. That is, you create them from specific database fields and they are only useful with the database from which you created them.

Index file names follow the same conventions as database file names. They must begin with a letter and can be up to eight characters long, including letters, numbers, and underscores.

There are two types of index files in dBASE IV: *single index files* and *multiple index files.* Single index files have an .NDX extension and contain a single index. Multiple index files have an .MDX extension and contain multiple indexes, each with a *tag name.* The tag name identifies a specific index within a multiple index file. You can have up to 47 tag names in an .MDX file. Tag names must start with a letter and can be up to ten characters long, including letters, numbers, and underscores.

When you create a database, dBASE IV automatically creates a *production index file* for that database. A production index file is a multiple (.MDX) index file linked to that specific database. A production .MDX file bears the same name as its host database but has an .MDX extension. Whenever you open a database, its production .MDX file is also opened.

If you're new to dBASE, you may never need single index (.NDX) files. However, this section covers .NDX files for those who own versions of dBASE prior to dBASE IV and wish to keep using their existing .NDX files.

Creating an Index

You can use the INDEX command to create an index file. Unless you specify otherwise with the UNIQUE clause, all of the records in the database are included when you create an index file. You can create both multiple index (.MDX) files and single index (.NDX) files with the INDEX command. The syntax for this command is

INDEX ON <*key expression*> TO <*.ndx file*>/TAG <*tag name*> [OF <*.mdx filename*>] [UNIQUE] [DESCENDING]

You can use any field from the current database, other than logical and memo fields, to create an index file. You can also use combinations of fields, but they must all be of the same data type. If you need to use fields of different data types, convert them to the same data type with a dBASE IV function. Some of these functions are explained in the next section.

The following command line creates an index tag called Lastname in the production .MDX file for the SALARY database. The INDEX command is followed by the field name (Lastname) and the command ends with the new tag name (also called Lastname) to be included in the production .MDX file. The TAG keyword tells dBASE IV that a multiple index file is involved.

```
. USE Salary
. INDEX ON Lastname TAG Lastname
```

Figure 7-26 shows the results of the previous command line after you use the DISPLAY ALL command. Note that the last

```
. INDEX ON Lastname TAG Lastname
  100% indexed         11 Records indexed
. DISPLAY ALL
Record# FIRSTNAME LASTNAME  BONUS    GROSS      FED     FICA   STATE      NET
     11 Kevin     Anderson  .T.   28000.00 7000.00 2102.80  840.00 18057.20
      4 Clive     Bunker    .F.   23000.00 5750.00 1727.30  690.00 14832.70
      7 Keith     Campbell  .T.   52000.00 13000.0 3905.20 1560.00 33534.80
      6 Suzanne   Chambers  .F.   17000.00 4250.00 1276.70  510.00 10963.30
      2 Drew      Gibson    .T.   22000.00 5500.00 1652.20  660.00 14187.80
      8 George    Haenszel  .T.   22000.00 5500.00 1652.20  660.00 14187.80
     10 Sam       Hammons   .T.   31000.00 7750.00 2328.10  930.00 19991.90
      9 Jeff      Hill      .T.   25000.00 6250.00 1877.50  750.00 16122.50
      1 Mary      Jones     .F.   24000.00 6000.00 1802.40  720.00 15477.60
      3 Ralph     Moriarity .F.   26000.00 6500.00 1952.60  780.00 16767.40
      5 John      Patrovich .F.   32000.03 8000.01 2403.20  960.00 20636.82
.
Command ||C:\...chap7\SALARY      ||Rec EOF/11       ||File ||    ||    Ins
```

Figure 7-26. SALARY indexed on the Lastname field

```
. INDEX ON Gross TO Gross
  100% indexed          11 Records indexed
. DISPLAY ALL
Record# FIRSTNAME LASTNAME  BONUS    GROSS      FED     FICA   STATE      NET
      6 Suzanne   Chambers  .F.   17000.00 4250.00 1276.70  510.00 10963.30
      2 Drew      Gibson    .T.   22000.00 5500.00 1652.20  660.00 14187.80
      8 George    Haenszel  .T.   22000.00 5500.00 1652.20  660.00 14187.80
      4 Clive     Bunker    .F.   23000.00 5750.00 1727.30  690.00 14832.70
      1 Mary      Jones     .F.   24000.00 6000.00 1802.40  720.00 15477.60
      9 Jeff      Hill      .T.   25000.00 6250.00 1877.50  750.00 16122.50
      3 Ralph     Moriarity .F.   26000.00 6500.00 1952.60  780.00 16767.40
     11 Kevin     Anderson  .T.   28000.00 7000.00 2102.80  840.00 18057.20
     10 Sam       Hammons   .T.   31000.00 7750.00 2328.10  930.00 19991.90
      5 John      Patrovich .F.   32000.03 8000.01 2403.20  960.00 20636.82
      7 Keith     Campbell  .T.   52000.00 13000.0 3905.20 1560.00 33534.80
.
Command  C:\...chap7\SALARY      Rec EOF/11       File                     Ins
```

Figure 7-27. SALARY indexed on the Gross field

names, not the record numbers, are in order. When you create an index with the TAG keyword, it is automatically added to the production .MDX file for the current database. Moreover, the tag is activated, and it controls the order of the records in the currently active database.

Tip: You should give your index tags names that match, or are derived from, the field name used to create them. This will help you remember the tag names.

The next command line creates a single index (.NDX) file called GROSS.NDX. (This type of index file is compatible with dBASE III). The INDEX command is followed by a field name (Gross) in the currently active database. The command ends with a file name for the new index file. The TO keyword tells dBASE IV that a single index (.NDX) file is to be created. Figure 7-27 shows the results after you use the LIST command.

```
. INDEX ON Gross TO Gross
```

The next command line creates an independent (non-production) multiple index (.MDX) file with a single tag name. The name of the field within the currently active database is Lastname. The name of the tag in the new index file is also Lastname. The name of the independent .MDX file created to hold the index tag is HOLDER.MDX. The OF part of the command tells dBASE IV to place the index tag in a file name other than the current production .MDX.

```
. INDEX ON Lastname TAG Lastname OF Holder
```

Indexing on Multiple Fields

You can use more than one field to create an index. For example, the following command line uses the fields Firstname and Lastname from the SALARY database. These fields are combined to create the index tag Bothname in the production .MDX file for the SALARY database. Plus signs (+) are used to combine the fields.

```
. INDEX ON Lastname+Firstname TAG Bothname
```

As mentioned, when you index on multiple fields, you must use the same data types. For example, in the previous command, both fields are character data types. If you try to combine a numeric and a character field with the INDEX command, dBASE IV issues an error message.

dBASE IV has several functions you can use to combine fields with different data types in an INDEX command. For example, the following command line uses the STR( ) function to convert a numeric field called Gross to a character data type. Ultimately, the command creates an index tag called Byname.

```
. INDEX ON Lastname+STR(Gross) TAG Byname
```

The next INDEX command line uses the DTOS( ) (date to string) function with a date field so that you can combine it with two other character fields. This way, all of the fields in the expression following the INDEX command are of the same data type. The DTOS( ) function does not affect the Next_pay field itself, other than making it compatible with the Firstname and Lastname fields in the INDEX expression. The command line creates an index tag called Payorder in the current production .MDX file.

```
. INDEX ON DTOS(Next_pay)+Lastname+Firstname TAG Payorder
```

Activating .MDX Files

As mentioned, once you create an index file it becomes the controlling index and you can use it immediately. dBASE IV only allows one controlling index at a time per database. The controlling index is referred to as the *master index.*

You can have more than one index file open at a time. In addition, you can switch from one index to another to establish the master index that controls the database. You can have up to ten open index files at once.

As mentioned, when you open a database, its production .MDX file is automatically opened. When you activate an index, it is automatically updated for any changes to the database. Thus, all tags within the production .MDX file are automatically updated. However, if you use an .NDX index file with a database, you should open it before making changes to the database. Otherwise, you must later update the .NDX file with the REINDEX command.

You can activate index tags within an .MDX file in the following three ways:

- The USE command with an ORDER clause
- The SET ORDER TO command
- The SET INDEX TO command

The USE command with an ORDER clause is appropriate when you first open a database and need to establish a master index. The SET ORDER TO and SET INDEX TO commands are appropriate after a database is already open. You use these commands to change to a new controlling index.

In the following command line, the USE command with an ORDER clause activates the Lastname tag in the production .MDX file for the SALARY database. When you use this command, the Lastname index tag must already exist or dBASE IV will give you an error message.

```
. USE Salary ORDER Lastname
```

The next command line uses the SET ORDER TO command to activate another index tag called Gross in the production .MDX file of the SALARY database. When you use the SET ORDER TO command, both the SALARY.DBF file and its associated production .MDX file, SALARY.MDX, must already be open.

```
. SET ORDER TO Gross
```

There are two advantages to using the SET ORDER TO command to establish the master index. First, the command syntax is simple. Second, the SET ORDER TO command shifts control to a new index without closing any other open independent .MDX or .NDX files. Thus, other open index files continue to be updated for changes to the database.

You can also use the SET INDEX TO command to establish a master index tag for a production .MDX file. However, the SET INDEX TO command first closes other independent .NDX and .MDX files in the current work area, except the current production .MDX. Furthermore, its syntax is slightly longer. For example, in the following command, the SET INDEX TO command opens the Lastname tag in the production .MDX for the SALARY database:

```
. SET INDEX TO Salary ORDER TAG Lastname
```

Activating .NDX Files

You can open and activate .NDX files with the USE command followed by the INDEX clause. For example, the following command line opens the SALARY database and activates the .NDX file called GROSS.NDX:

```
. USE Salary INDEX Gross
```

You can also open a series of .NDX files and choose the master index with the USE command. For example, the following command line opens the SALARY.DBF database. With the INDEX clause, it then opens two index files called LASTNAME.NDX and GROSS.NDX. Finally, with the ORDER clause, it specifies LASTNAME.NDX as the master index.

```
. USE Salary INDEX Lastname,Gross ORDER Lastname
```

You can use the SET ORDER TO command to establish a single .NDX file as the master index. However, you must first open the single .NDX file with the SET INDEX TO command before using the SET ORDER TO command. Recall that the SET INDEX TO command closes all other .NDX and .MDX files in the current work area, except for the current production .MDX file.

```
. SET INDEX TO Lastname,Gross
. SET ORDER TO Gross
```

When both a production .MDX and .NDX files are opened, you can use the SET ORDER TO command to establish a master index. To do this, follow the SET ORDER TO command with either a tag name in the .MDX file or the name of the .NDX file. For example, suppose you have a production .MDX file that contains a tag called Lastname. Furthermore, you have an .NDX file named GROSS.NDX. Once both files are open, you can use the SET ORDER TO command followed by the file names to switch back and forth between them. When you use the SET ORDER TO command in this instance, the .NDX file remains open and continues to be updated for changes to the database.

You can also use the SET INDEX TO command to open a series of .NDX files. For example, the following command line opens two .NDX files, LASTNAME.NDX and GROSS.NDX. Both .NDX files are opened but only the first one, LASTNAME.NDX, is activated.

```
. SET INDEX TO Lastname,Gross
```

To activate the GROSS.NDX file in the previous example, use the SET ORDER TO command as follows:

```
. SET ORDER TO Gross
```

As mentioned, when an .NDX file is not opened and you make changes to the database, the .NDX file is not updated. To update the .NDX file, activate it with SET INDEX TO and then use the REINDEX command.

```
. SET INDEX TO Gross
. REINDEX
```

Tip: The COPY INDEXES TO command copies .NDX files to .MDX files. If you give no file name after the TO in the command, dBASE IV assumes you are referring to the production .MDX. For example,

COPY INDEXES Lastname,Gross TO

copies the FIRSTNAME.NDX and GROSS.NDX index files to the current production .MDX file as the tag names Lastname and Gross.

Deleting Tags from .MDX Files

You can delete tags from an .MDX file with the DELETE TAG command. The effects of this command are permanent.

The following command line deletes two tags from the production .MDX file for the SALARY database. Note that the tag names are separated by commas.

```
. DELETE TAG Lastname,Gross
```

When you delete all the tags from a production .MDX file, dBASE IV also erases the file. When you later try to put another tag into the production .MDX file, dBASE IV gives you an error message. To solve this problem, use the OF clause after the INDEX command, without a file name. When no file name appears after the OF clause, dBASE IV assumes you are referring to a production .MDX file. If one doesn't exist, it sets one up.

```
. INDEX ON Lastname TAG Lastname OF
```

Closing Index Files

The more index files that you have open, the slower dBASE IV runs. This is because dBASE IV is constantly updating the index files. If you no longer need to have your .NDX files open, use the CLOSE INDEX command. For example, enter

```
. CLOSE INDEX
```

Searching a Database

You can search for data in a database by using the LOCATE, SEEK, and FIND commands. SEEK and FIND require that a database be indexed, but LOCATE does not.

The LOCATE and CONTINUE Commands

The LOCATE command searches an active database for a record that meets a specific condition. If the search is successful, you can use the CONTINUE command to search for another record that meets the condition. The syntax for the LOCATE command is

LOCATE [FOR] *<condition>* [*<scope>*] [WHILE *<condition>*]

The LOCATE command tells dBASE IV to search the database sequentially until it finds a record that matches the specified condition. When such a record is found, dBASE IV leaves the record pointer on that record and awaits further instructions. For example, the following command line uses an optional FOR clause to state a condition for the LOCATE command. This command tells dBASE IV to locate the first record in the currently active database that has the string "Smith" in the Lastname field.

```
. LOCATE FOR Lastname="Smith"
```

You can extend the condition following the LOCATE command by using a logical operator in a FOR clause. For example, the following command line uses the .AND. operator. This command tells dBASE IV to locate the first record in the currently active database that has the strings "Smith" in the Lastname field and "Harry" in the Firstname field.

```
. LOCATE FOR Lastname="Smith" .AND. Firstname="Harry"
```

The LOCATE command automatically begins a search at the first record in the database, unless you specify otherwise. It then positions the record pointer on the first record that meets the condition. If the LOCATE command is not successful (no records meet the condition), dBASE IV issues the "End of Locate Scope" error message. The FOUND( ) (data record found) function returns false (.F.), and the EOF( ) (end of file) function returns true (.T.).

To see if other records in the database meet the condition specified with the LOCATE command, use the CONTINUE command. The CONTINUE command continues the search started by the previously successful LOCATE command. The search is started at the record following the record found with the LOCATE command. If you use several LOCATE commands with a database, the CONTINUE command applies to the most recent one.

You can also limit the scope of the LOCATE command. When you use a *scope* condition with the LOCATE command, dBASE IV does not automatically position the record pointer at the beginning of the database. For example, the following command lines specify different scopes for the LOCATE command. The first command limits the scope of the LOCATE command to the next 20 records, starting with the current one. The second command starts the LOCATE process at the current record and includes the rest of the records in the database.

```
. LOCATE FOR Gross=24000 NEXT 20
. LOCATE FOR Lastname="Jones" REST
```

You can also use a memory variable with the LOCATE command. For example, the following command lines create the memory variable Lname and then use it to search the database:

```
. STORE "Smith" TO Lname
. LOCATE FOR Lastname=Lname
```

When specifying a search string for the LOCATE command, you need not be exact. As dBASE IV searches each record in the database for a character string, it compares your search string to the character strings in a database field, working from left to right. If the character-by-character comparison is successful, dBASE IV considers it a match. However, the character string in the database may in fact have trailing characters. For example, the command

LOCATE FOR Lastname="James"

may produce a record with Jameson in the Lastname field. If you need exact matches for character strings, use the SET EXACT ON command prior to a search. This command tells dBASE IV that two character strings in a comparison must both be of the same length.

The FIND Command

The FIND command conducts a very rapid search of an indexed database. FIND searches the currently active indexed database for a *literal* value. This means that you do not have to enclose character strings in quotes when you use them with the FIND command (for example, use Smith rather than "Smith"). Furthermore, the FIND command does not support functions or operators; thus,

FIND Lastname="Smith"

is an invalid command.

The FIND command positions the record pointer on the first record in an indexed database that matches the string or number following the FIND command. For example, the following command lines activate an index tag called Gross in the current production .MDX file. The FIND command then finds the first record with 24000 in the Gross database field.

```
. USE Salary ORDER Gross
. FIND 24000
```

You can also search a database for a character string by using the FIND command. For example, the following command lines activate the Lastname tag in the current production .MDX file and find the string "Sims". Note that Sims does not have to be enclosed in quotes.

```
. USE Salary ORDER Lastname
. FIND Sims
```

The SEEK Command

The SEEK command rapidly searches an indexed database using a specified expression. Since this command supports expressions, you must enclose character strings in quotes.

The SEEK command positions the record pointer on the first record in an indexed database that matches the expression following the SEEK command. However, the expression following the SEEK command must be of the same data type as the index in use. For example, the following command lines use the SEEK command to search a character field, a numeric field, and a date field. Note the use of the curly braces ({ }) to enclose a date.

```
. SET ORDER TO Lastname
. SEEK "Smith"
. SET Order TO Gross
. SEEK 24000
. SET ORDER TO Date
. SEEK {12/21/91}
```

The SET NEAR Command

The SET NEAR command positions the record pointer on the record immediately following the nearest match for a sought-after search string. When you use this command, the database must be indexed on the field you intend to search. In addition, you are limited to the FIND and SEEK commands to conduct the search.

When SET NEAR is ON, dBASE IV searches the indexed field to find a match for the specified search string. If an exact match is found, the record pointer is positioned on that record. If an exact match is not found, dBASE IV positions the record pointer on the record immediately following the closest match. To determine if an exact match has been found, enter **? FOUND()** at the dot prompt. If the FOUND( ) function returns true, the record has been found and you can display it. If FOUND( ) returns false, dBASE IV has positioned the record pointer on the record immediately following the closest match to the search string in that database field. To view the previous record, enter **SKIP-1** followed by **DISPLAY**.

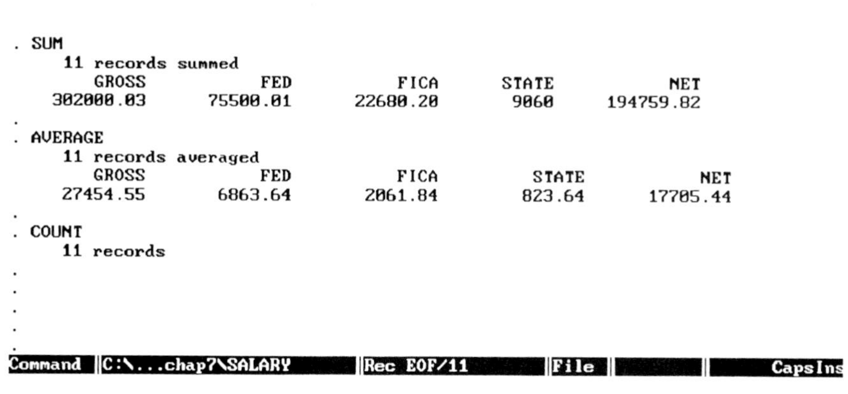

```
. SUM
    11 records summed
       GROSS              FED            FICA        STATE          NET
    302000.03        75500.01        22680.20         9060    194759.82
.
. AVERAGE
    11 records averaged
       GROSS              FED            FICA         STATE           NET
    27454.55          6863.64         2061.84        823.64      17705.44
.
. COUNT
    11 records
.
.
.
.
.
Command ||C:\...chap7\SALARY     ||Rec EOF/11      ||File ||     ||     CapsIns
```

Figure 7-28. The SUM, AVERAGE, and COUNT commands

Summarizing a Database

dBASE IV offers a number of commands with which you can summarize the numeric fields in a database. Five of these commands are SUM, AVERAGE, COUNT, CALCULATE, and TOTAL ON.

The SUM command, without a qualifier, sums the contents of all the numeric fields in a database. Figure 7-28 shows an example. However, you can follow the SUM command with the name of a database field to limit the scope of the command. For example, the following command line sums the fields Gross and Net for those records with a logical true in the Bonus field of the SALARY database:

```
. SUM Gross,Net FOR Bonus
```

The AVERAGE command takes an average of all numeric database fields. Figure 7-28 shows an example. You can also qualify the fields used by the AVERAGE command by following it with a fields list and a qualifier.

```
. CALCULATE MAX(Gross)
     11 records
MAX(Gross)
     52000
. CALCULATE MIN(Gross)
     11 records
MIN(Gross)
     17000
. CALCULATE AVG(Gross)
     11 records
   AVG(Gross)
     27454.55
. CALCULATE STD(Gross)
     11 records
   STD(Gross)
      8763.19
. CALCULATE SUM(Gross)
     11 records
   SUM(Gross)
    302000.03
.
Command ||C:\...chap7\SALARY      ||Rec EOF/11      ||File ||      ||
```

Figure 7-29. The CALCULATE command uses various functions

```
. Average Gross,Net FOR Bonus
```

The COUNT command counts the number of records in a database. Figure 7-28 shows an example. You can also qualify the COUNT command with a FOR clause.

```
. COUNT FOR Bonus
```

The CALCULATE command allows you to use various statistical functions to summarize numeric fields in the database. For example, the following two commands return the highest and lowest salary in the Gross field of the SALARY database. Figure 7-29 shows some other examples.

```
. CALCULATE MAX(Gross)
. CALCULATE MIN(Gross)
```

Unlike the previous commands in this section, the TOTAL ON command creates a new database. The TOTAL ON command sums the numeric fields in a database and creates a new database to hold the results. The syntax for the TOTAL ON command is

TOTAL ON *<key field>* TO *<new database name>* [FIELDS *<fields list>*] [FOR *<condition>*][WHILE *<condition>*

For the TOTAL ON command to work, the active database you intend to summarize must be indexed on a given field. The TOTAL ON command uses that field. For example, imagine you are working with a database called ORDERS that holds all of your customer orders for the last quarter. Furthermore, each record in the database contains a field called Cust_no. The Cust_no field in each record holds a customer number unique to each customer. This is how you identify each of the many different orders placed by a given customer during the quarter. The following command line creates a new database called QTRSALE that summarizes total sales by customer for the quarter:

```
. USE Orders ORDER Custno
. TOTAL ON Cust_no TO QTRSALE FIELDS Cust_no,Total_sale
```

Using Custom Forms

dBASE IV lets you design custom data entry forms with the Forms Design screen. This screen lets you design attractive forms that determine how database fields are displayed on the screen when you use full-screen editing commands such as EDIT or APPEND. Figure 7-30 shows an example. (For a complete description of how to use the Forms Design screen to create and save a custom form, see Chapter 9.)

You can access the Forms Design screen from the dot prompt by using the CREATE SCREEN command. When you enter this command, dBASE IV takes you directly to the Forms Design screen

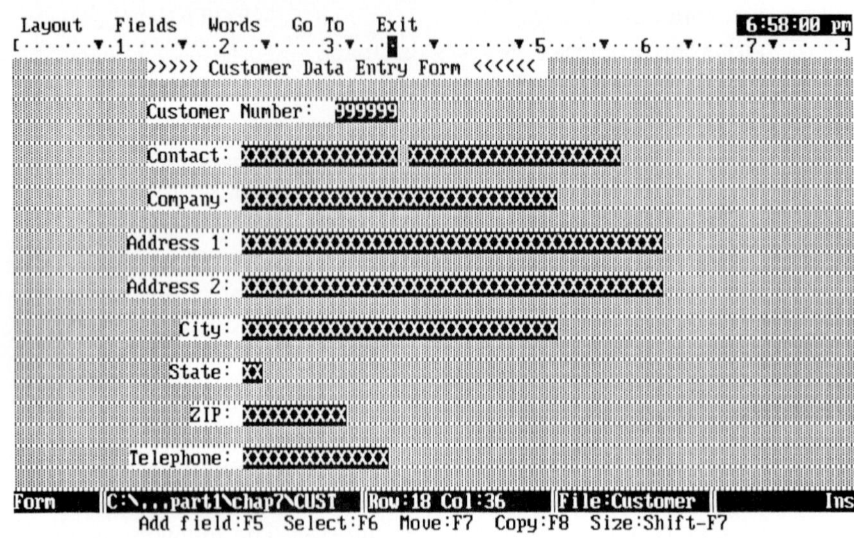

Figure 7-30. The Forms Design screen

and you can begin designing your custom form. The syntax for CREATE SCREEN is

CREATE SCREEN *<form filename>*

You can also modify an existing custom form with the MODIFY SCREEN command. This command takes you directly to the Forms Design screen and places the specified form on the screen. The syntax for the MODIFY SCREEN command is

MODIFY SCREEN *<form filename>*

You activate a format file using the SET FORMAT TO command. The syntax for this command is

SET FORMAT TO <*form filename*>

Once you activate a format file with the SET FORMAT TO command, dBASE IV uses that custom form to display database fields for full-screen editing commands such as APPEND or EDIT. For example, to activate the custom form SCREEN1, type the following at the dot prompt:

```
. SET FORMAT TO Screen1
```

Querying the Database

With the Queries Design screen, you can create powerful queries that display selected records in the database. Figure 7-31 shows a sample of the Queries Design screen. For a complete description of how to create a query using the Queries Design screen, see Chapter 6. You can access the Queries Design Screen from the dot prompt using the CREATE QUERY command. The syntax for this command is

CREATE QUERY <*query filename*>

To modify an existing query file, use the MODIFY QUERY command. When you enter this command, dBASE IV takes you directly to the Queries Design screen and displays the specified query file. The syntax for the MODIFY QUERY command is

MODIFY QUERY <*query filename*>

To activate a query file from the dot prompt, use the SET VIEW TO command. This command activates the specified query file. You can then see the results of the query by using the LIST command. For example, to activate the query file called ALLNAMES and see the results, type the following at the dot prompt:

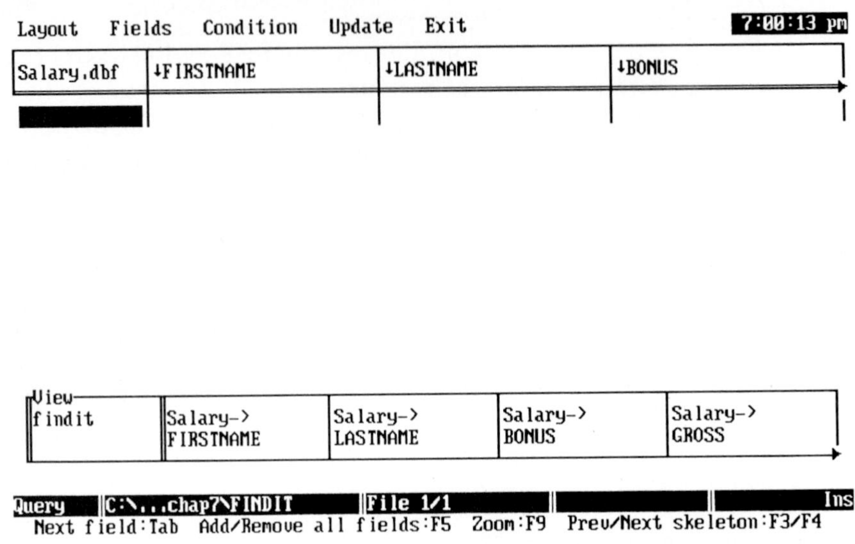

Figure 7-31. The Queries Design screen

```
. SET VIEW TO Allnames
. LIST
```

You can also use the SET FILTER command to specify a query condition. This command allows the display of only those records that meet a given condition. The condition applies to commands that require a database to be in use, like BROWSE, EDIT, or REPORT FORM. The syntax for the SET FILTER command is

SET FILTER TO <*condition*>

You can use more than one SET FILTER condition at a time. For example, using the SALARY database,

SET FILTER TO Gross>24000

allows the display of only those records that have a number in excess of 24,000 in the Gross field.

```
SET FILTER TO Bonus
```

allows the display of only those records with a logical true in the Bonus field. Both filter conditions can be present at the same time.

Whenever you use the SET FILTER command, immediately follow it with the GO TOP command to ensure accurate results. The GO TOP command activates the SET FILTER command by moving the record pointer to the first record that meets the specified filter condition.

Importing and Exporting Data to External Programs

You can import and export data to and from programs other than dBASE IV by using the COPY TO and APPEND FROM commands. The COPY TO command exports dBASE IV data to other programs. Use the TYPE clause after the COPY TO command to specify one of the following eight external program file types:

DBASEII	dBASE II database (.DB2) files
RPD	RapidFile data (.RPD) files
DELIMITED	ASCII files
SDF	System Data Format ASCII (.TXT) files
FW2	Framework II (.FW2) database files
SYLK	Multiplan spreadsheet files
DIF	VisiCalc version 1 (.DIF) files
WKS	Lotus 1-2-3 Release 1A (.WKS) spreadsheet files

A1: [W10] 'FIRSTNAME READY

	A	B	C	D	E	F	G	H
1	FIRSTNAME	LASTNAME	B	GROSS	FED	FICA	STATE	NET
2	Mary	Jones	F	24000.00	6000.00	1802.40	720.00	15477.60
3	Drew	Gibson	T	22000.00	5500.00	1652.20	660.00	14187.80
4	Ralph	Moriarity	F	26000.00	6500.00	1952.60	780.00	16767.40
5	Clive	Bunker	F	23000.00	5750.00	1727.30	690.00	14832.70
6	John	Patrovich	F	32000.03	8000.01	2403.20	960.00	20636.82
7	Suzanne	Chambers	F	17000.00	4250.00	1276.70	510.00	10963.30
8	Keith	Campbell	T	52000.00	13000.00	3905.20	1560.00	33534.80
9	George	Haenzel	T	22000.00	5500.00	1652.20	660.00	14187.80
10	Jeff	Hill	T	25000.00	6250.00	1877.50	750.00	16122.50
11	Sam	Hammons	T	31000.00	7750.00	2328.10	930.00	19991.90
12	Kevin	Anderson	T	28000.00	7000.00	2102.80	840.00	18057.20
13	Harry	Jones	T	20000.00	5000.00	1502.00	600.00	12898.00
14								
15								
16								
17								
18								
19								
20								

19-Dec-88 07:33 PM

Figure 7-32. SALARY copied to a 1-2-3 spreadsheet

For example, the following command line copies a dBASE IV database called SALARY to a Lotus 1-2-3 Release 1A spreadsheet file. Figure 7-32 shows the results.

```
. USE Salary
. COPY TO Salary.wks TYPE WKS
```

Tip: You can use Lotus 1-2-3 Release 1A files in 1-2-3 Release 2.01 without conversion.

To import data from an external program, use the APPEND FROM command. You must follow the APPEND FROM command with a TYPE clause to specify one of eight external program file types supported by dBASE IV. The syntax for importing from an external source is

APPEND FROM *<filename>* [[TYPE] *<filetype>*] [FOR *<condition>*]

For example, the following command line imports a Lotus 1-2-3 spreadsheet file:

```
. USE Mailist
. APPEND FROM Promo.wks TYPE WKS
```

If you import data from one of the supported spreadsheet programs, the incoming data must match the structure of the currently active database in terms of data type and number of fields. If the character strings in the spreadsheet are wider than the corresponding fields in the database, the excess characters are cut off and lost. In addition, leading blank columns and rows in a spreadsheet may cause problems when you are importing. Make sure the data in your spreadsheet is justified in the upper left-hand corner.

In this chapter, you learned some basic information about how to use the dot prompt. You now know how to create a database, add records, edit records, and display data at the dot prompt. You also know how to use the dot prompt to send data, reports, and labels to your printer. Furthermore, you're familiar with various dot prompt commands for sorting, indexing, searching, and summarizing information in a database.

Macros

EIGHT

The Macro Keys
Starting the Macro Recorder
Stopping the Macro Recorder
Playing Back a Macro
A Control Center Example
A Dot Prompt Example
Selecting from Menus and Lists in a Macro
Appending to a Macro
Saving a Macro Library to Disk
Loading a Macro Library into Memory
Naming a Macro
Modifying Macros
Nesting Macros
Getting User Input from a Macro
Deleting Macros
Copying Macros
Troubleshooting Your Macros

The more you use dBASE IV, the more you'll find certain sets of keystrokes that you repeatedly perform. Rather than reenter these keystrokes manually each time, you can save them in a *macro* and replay them automatically by pressing a single key, or set of keys, to activate the macro.

To create a macro in dBASE IV, you use the *macro recorder*. When you start the macro recorder, it saves your keystrokes as you type them. Then, when you've finished entering your keystrokes, you simply stop the recorder. If you like, you can start the recorder again to restart recording where you left off.

You can record and play back macros from anywhere in dBASE IV. For example, you can start and stop macros from the Control Center, the dot prompt, SQL, the dBASE IV Text Editor, or any combination thereof. Because you can use macros anywhere, they help automate many different kinds of tasks.

This chapter shows you how to create macros and store them in macro libraries. It also discusses how to execute macros from inside and outside the Control Center as well as how to modify macros as your needs change.

The Macro Keys

In dBASE IV, the macro keys are ALT-F1 through ALT-F9 and ALT-F10 followed by a single letter key (A through Z). You can't assign a macro to ALT-F10 because dBASE reserves that key combination for activating macros. You assign a macro to a key when you start the macro recorder.

Starting the Macro Recorder

There are two ways to start the macro recorder in dBASE IV. You can use the **Macros** menu of the Control Center. You can also press SHIFT-F10 from anywhere in dBASE IV. When you start using macros, you should use the **Macros** menu. As you get more experienced, you'll probably find it easier to use SHIFT-F10.

Starting from the Macros Menu

The easiest way to start the macro recorder when you're learning dBASE IV is to use the **Begin recording** option in the **Macros**

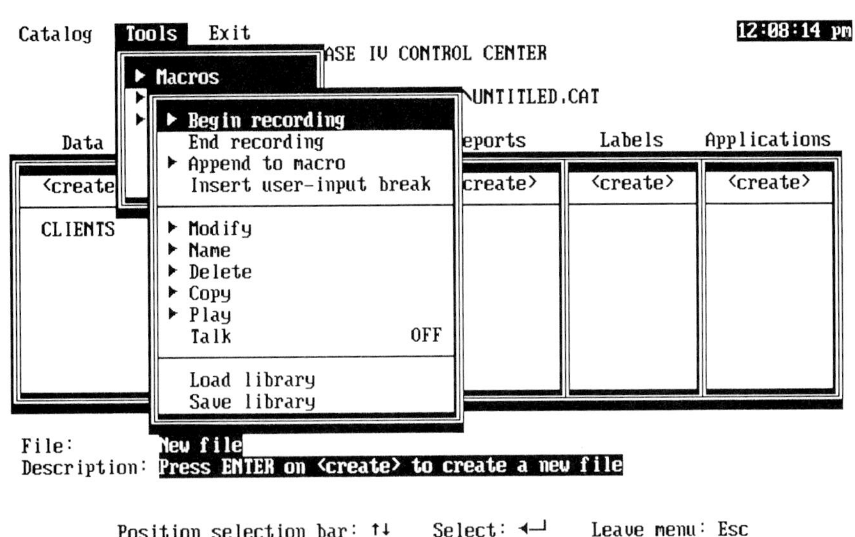

Figure 8-1. The **Begin Recording** option in the **Macros** menu option

menu of the Control Center. You access the **Macros** menu from the **Tools** menu. Figure 8-1 shows the options available in the **Macros** menu.

When you select the **Begin recording** option from the **Macros** menu, you see a table, and a prompt asks you to choose the key to which you want to assign the macro (see Figure 8-2). The table shows the contents of the current macro library. As the table indicates, you can use up to 35 different keys (A through Z and F1 through F9) and assign each one a unique macro.

To select a macro key, simply press the letter corresponding to the key you want assigned in the macro library. dBASE returns you to the Control Center and places the message "Recording Macro; Press Shift-F10 E to end" at the bottom of the screen. You can then type the keystrokes you want for your macro.

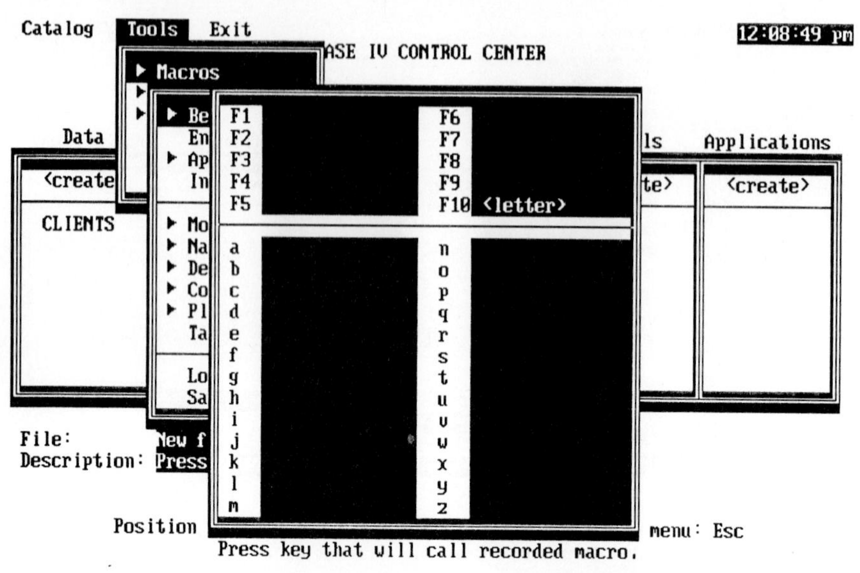

Figure 8-2. The **Begin recording** option produces a macro key assignment table

Starting the Recorder with SHIFT-F10

You can also start the macro recorder by pressing SHIFT- F10. The advantage of this method is that you can be anywhere in dBASE IV—the Control Center, the dot prompt, SQL, or the Text Editor.

When you press SHIFT-F10 the first time, dBASE displays two options: **Begin recording** and **Cancel**. If you select **Begin recording**, dBASE IV displays the message "Press the key that will call this macro." If you press a key that already belongs to a macro in the current library, dBASE displays the message "Do you really want to overwrite *x*?(Y/N)" (where *x* is the letter you chose). If you press Y and ENTER, dBASE will record your keystrokes and overwrite the macro. If you press N, dBASE will cancel the macro operation.

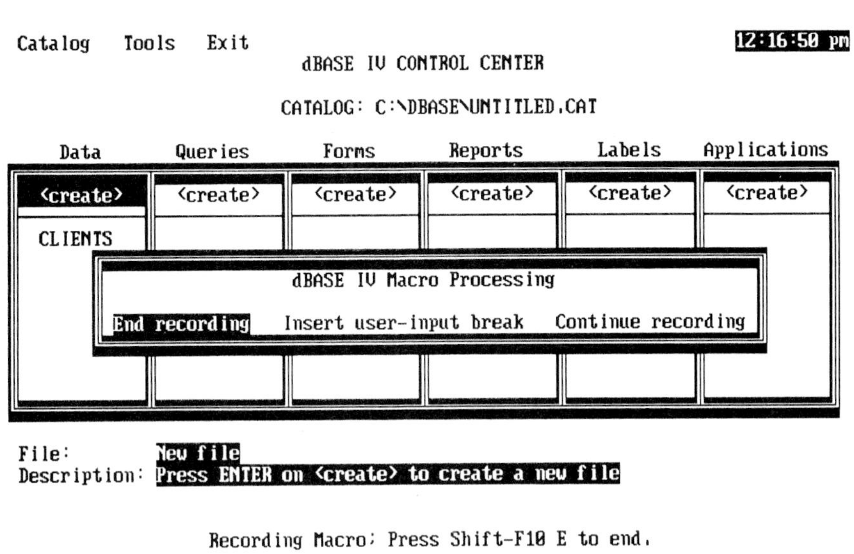

Figure 8-3. The **End recording** option of the Macro Processing screen

Stopping the Macro Recorder

You stop the macro recorder in the same way no matter where you are in dBASE IV and no matter how you started the recorder. Press SHIFT-F10, and dBASE displays the menu shown in Figure 8-3. Press the letter E to select the **End recording** option. dBASE stops the recording, displays the message "Macro recording has been finished," and stores the macro under your chosen key in the current macro library.

Playing Back a Macro

There are three ways to play back a macro, depending on whether you assigned the macro to a letter key or a function key and depending on where you want to start the macro from. To start a macro, you can

- Type the macro key from the keyboard. Press ALT-F1 through ALT-F9, or ALT-F10 followed by a letter key (A through Z).
- Choose the **Play** option from the **Macros** menu in the Control Center.
- Use the PLAY MACRO command from the dot prompt, from SQL, or inside an application program.

Whichever method you choose, your macro performs the same keystrokes no matter where you are in dBASE IV. Therefore, you need to start a macro where it can execute properly, usually where you began recording the macro.

Using the Macro Keys

If you assigned your macro to a letter key, you must first tell dBASE that you want to start the macro by pressing ALT-F10. dBASE prompts you to "Press an alphabetic key of the macro to playback." When you press a key that you've assigned to a macro, dBASE plays back that macro.

If you assigned your macro to a function rather than a letter key, you can activate it by holding down ALT and pressing the function key to which you assigned the macro. For example, if you assigned the macro to F1, you can execute it by pressing ALT-F1.

Using the Play Option from the Macros Menu

To execute a macro from the Control Center, select the **Play** option from the **Macros** menu. This opens the macros table, and you

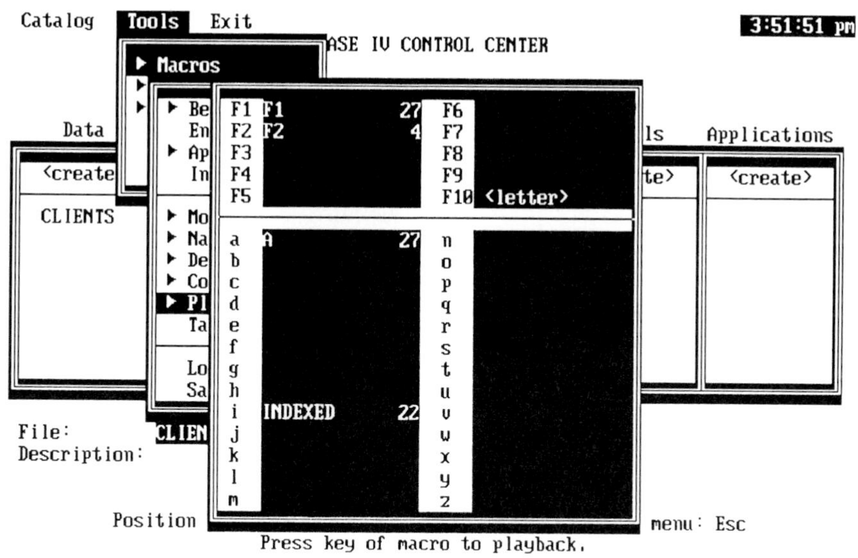

Figure 8-4. A macros table displayed by the **Play** option

can select the macro to play back by pressing the letter you assigned to the macro. Figure 8-4 shows four macros that you can play back from the macros table.

Using the PLAY MACRO Command

You can play back a macro from the dot prompt, from SQL, or from inside a program by using the PLAY MACRO command. For example, to play back from the dot prompt a macro that is assigned to F9, enter

```
.PLAY MACRO F9
```

Records Fields Go To Exit 12:20:35 pm

FIRSTNAME	LASTNAME	COMPANY	ADDRESS
George	Thomas	Texasville Pumps	221 Texasville Way
Paul	Simon	dBASE Users Group	1234 Primrose Lane
Paul	Shaffer	Texas Connections	890 Circle Street
Sherman	Mc Coy	Mc Coy Instruments	876 Bradford Street
Owen	Meany	Meany Intl Parcel Service	6711 Waites Street
John	McCrae	Rhode Island Research	9001 Frost Way
Zeb	Smith	Smith, Smith & Smith	512 Blackhawk Avenue
Kim	Smith	Smith, Smith & Smith	7950 Park Avenue
Diana	Jones	Rayman and Associates	1000 Frontage Road
Steven	Hill	Micro Processes Inc.	36800 Luau Lane
Adene	Smith	Smith, Smith & Smith	2948 El Camino Real
Kilgore	Trout	Ashton-Trout	9743 Pine Ave
Melissa	Williams	Lettuce Development Corp	640 Nashua Court
Jake	van de Kammps	Braland	1010 Main Street
Nathan	Zuckerman	Microshop	43000 Rainbow Drive

Browse | C:\dbase\CLIENTS | Rec 1/15 | File

View and edit fields

Figure 8-5. CLIENTS database

Similarly, to play back a macro that is assigned to the letter key I, enter

```
.PLAY MACRO I
```

Finally, to play back a macro that has been named "Indexed," enter

```
.PLAY MACRO Indexed
```

See the section "Naming a Macro" later in this chapter for information on assigning a name to a macro.

Records Fields Go To Exit 12:37:01 pm

CITY	STATE	ZIP	TELEPHONE	AMOUNT	DATE	NOTES
Dallas	TX	75690	(214)453-9021	300	07/16/90	memo
Sunnyvale	CA	94086	(408)732-1637	20	01/22/90	memo
Fort Worth	TX	76129	(817)552-1221	100	01/15/90	memo
Albany	NY	12237	(212)894-6767	50	06/15/90	memo
Vienna	VA	22180	(703)223-9393	800	07/12/90	memo
Providence	RI	02908	(401)776-0017	100	02/18/90	memo
San Jose	CA	95129	(408)562-5775	500	11/20/90	memo
Soquel	CA	95073	(408)479-4459	50	07/19/90	memo
Scotts Valley	CA	95066	(408)475-9055	28	02/23/90	memo
Honolulu	HA	96815	(808)343-6667	600	12/23/90	memo
Mountain View	CA	95051	(415)968-6070	100	11/10/90	memo
Cambridge	MA	02142	(617)233-9871	200	09/25/90	memo
Larkspur	CA	94964	(415)461-0171	100	11/10/90	memo
Short Hills	NJ	07078	(201)998-7968	235	05/05/90	memo
Redmond	WA	98052	(206)461-0171	475	03/03/90	memo

Browse C:\dbase\CLIENTS Rec 1/15 File

View and edit fields

Figure 8-6. CLIENTS database

A Control Center Example

The following example shows you how to record and execute a macro from the Control Center. It creates a macro that uses a database, organizes it by an existing index, and displays it in browse mode. This example uses the CLIENTS database in Figure 8-5 and Figure 8-6. It also assumes that you've set up an index for the CLIENTS database according to the Lastname field but that the index is not activated. To work through the example, use the CLIENTS database and Lastname index or substitute another database and index name.

Notice that the example emphasizes a particular way of selecting menu options and list items (for example, file names and index names) in the Control Center. To ensure that your macros work the same way each time, you should use the same selection techniques. See the section "Selecting from Menus and Lists in a Macro" in this chapter.

Before you record the example macro, you must set up the environment. You don't actually start the macro recorder until step 5 of the procedure.

Perform the following steps to create the example macro:

1. Move to the Data Panel of the Control Center if you're not already there.

2. If the CLIENTS database, or the database you want to use, is not in the Data Panel of the Control Center, press ALT-C followed by A to select the **Catalog** menu and the **Add a file** option. dBASE prompts you to "Edit the description of this .dbf file." If you don't want to add a description to your database, just press ENTER.

3. Choose the CLIENTS database, or the database you wish to substitute, from the box displaying the available databases. Select the database by typing the file name. For example, to choose the CLIENTS database file, type **CLIENTS** and press ENTER. dBASE adds the CLIENTS database file to the Control Center's Data Panel.

4. Press ALT-T followed by M to select the **Tools** menu and the **Macros** option.

5. Press B to select the **Begin recording** option from the **Macros** menu.

6. Press the letter I (case doesn't matter) to assign the macro you're about to enter to the I key in the macro library. dBASE returns you to the Control Center and places the message "Recording Macro; Press Shift-F10 E to end" at the bottom of the screen.

7. Type **CLIENTS**, or the file name you are using, to highlight the file in the Data Panel, and press SHIFT-F2 to enter the Database Design screen.

```
Records     Fields     Go To     Exit                          12:43:07 pm

FIRSTNAME    LASTNAME        COMPANY                     ADDRESS

Steven       Hill            Micro Processes Inc.        36800 Luau Lane
Diana        Jones           Rayman and Associates       1000 Frontage Road
Sherman      Mc Coy          Mc Coy Instruments          876 Bradford Street
John         McCrae          Rhode Island Research       9001 Frost Way
Owen         Meany           Meany Intl Parcel Service   6711 Waites Street
Paul         Shaffer         Texas Connections           890  Circle Street
Paul         Simon           dBASE Users Group           1234 Primrose Lane
Zeb          Smith           Smith, Smith & Smith        512 Blackhawk Avenue
Kim          Smith           Smith, Smith & Smith        7950 Park Avenue
Adene        Smith           Smith, Smith & Smith        2948 El Camino Real
George       Thomas          Texasville Pumps            221 Texasville Way
Kilgore      Trout           Ashton-Trout                9743 Pine Ave
Melissa      Williams        Lettuce Development Corp    640 Nashua Court
Nathan       Zuckerman       Microshop                   43000 Rainbow Drive
Jake         van de Kammps   Braland                     1010 Main Street

Browse  C:\dbase\CLIENTS        Rec 10/15        File              Caps
              Recording Macro: Press Shift-F10 E to end.
                         View and edit fields
```

Figure 8-7. CLIENTS database organized by last name

8. Press ALT-O and the letter O to select the **Organize** menu and the **Order records by index** option.

9. Enter the name of the index with which you want to organize your database. For example, type **LASTNAME** to specify the Lastname index tag for the CLIENTS database, and press ENTER.

10. Press F2 to enter browse mode.

11. Select ALT-G followed by T to select the **Go To** menu and the **Top record** option. The database now appears organized by last name (see Figure 8-7).

12. Press SHIFT-F10 followed by the letter E to select the **End recording** option. dBASE stops the recording, displays the message "Macro recording has been finished," and

stores your macro under the letter "I" in the current macro library.

To play back the macro you've just recorded, return to the Control Center (press ESC), and perform either of the following:

- Select the **Play** option from the **Macros** menu and press I (case doesn't matter).
- Press SHIFT-F10 followed by I (case doesn't matter).

A Dot Prompt Example

The following example shows you how to record and play back a macro from the dot prompt. It prints the contents of the current directory to the printer.

1. From the dot prompt, press SHIFT-F10 and B to select the **Begin recording** option.
2. Press F2 to assign your macro to the F2 function key. dBASE places the message "Recording Macro; Press Shift-F10 E to end" at the bottom of the screen.
3. Type the following instructions at the dot prompt, making sure to press ENTER after each line (you don't need to type the period at the start of each line):

```
.SET PRINTER ON
.DIR *.*
.SET PRINTER OFF
.EJECT PAGE
```

dBASE IV prints the current directory to your printer.

4. Press SHIFT-F10 and E to stop macro recording.

To start the macro you just created, press ALT-F2. dBASE IV will print the current directory to the printer.

If you want to save this macro to disk so you can use it later, see the section "Saving a Macro Library to Disk" later in this chapter.

Selecting from Menus and Lists in a Macro

When you create macros that operate in the Control Center, you should use a few techniques to ensure that your macros work properly every time. First, when you access a menu while recording a macro, always use the ALT-key method rather than pressing F10 and moving the highlight. For example, to properly select the **Organize** option from the Database Design screen, press ALT-O. If you use the F10 method, dBASE displays the previous menu selection and, when the macro moves the highlight, it may select the wrong menu item.

When you select an option from a pull-down menu, always use the option's first letter rather than moving the highlight to the option and pressing ENTER. Suppose certain menu options are not available when you first create your macro. As you move the highlight, it jumps over the inaccessible options. However, when you run your macro, the inaccessible options may have become available, in which case the highlight will not skip them. Once again, your macro may select the wrong menu option if your macro depends on the movement of the highlight.

When selecting a file name, field name, or any other item from a list, always type the name (or the first few letters of the name) of the item you're choosing. For example, to select the CLIENTS database from the Data Panel in the Control Center, type **CLIENTS**. If you instead rely on the movement of the highlight, your macro may select the wrong item if the content of the list has changed or shifted.

Appending to a Macro

If you would like to append new keystrokes to an existing macro, you can select the **Append to macro** option from the **Macros** menu in the Control Center. dBASE IV displays the macro table, and you can press a key corresponding to the macro you want to append to. After you press the key, dBASE IV reactivates the macro recorder, and you can enter keystrokes as you normally do when recording a macro.

Note: You can only append to a macro by using the **Macros** menu in the Control Center. You cannot append to a macro from outside of the Control Center.

Saving a Macro Library to Disk

When you first record a macro, dBASE stores it in your computer's memory, not on disk. If you quit dBASE IV without first saving the macro, you'll lose the contents of your macro. To save your macro to disk so you can use it again later, you must save the current macro library. You can save the current macro library from inside or outside the Control Center.

A macro library can contain up to 35 macros (A through Z and F1 through F9). dBASE stores each library in a separate file and gives the file a .KEY extension. If you use an extension other than .KEY, you'll need to specify that extension when loading your library. You can create as many macro libraries as you like in dBASE IV and load them as you need them.

To save the current macro library from the Control Center, use the **Save library** option from the **Macros** menu. You can use this option to create, accept, or change a macro library's name. When you select the **Save library** option, dBASE prompts you to enter a file name to use for the library. Enter a name of up to eight characters and press ENTER. For example, to save the current

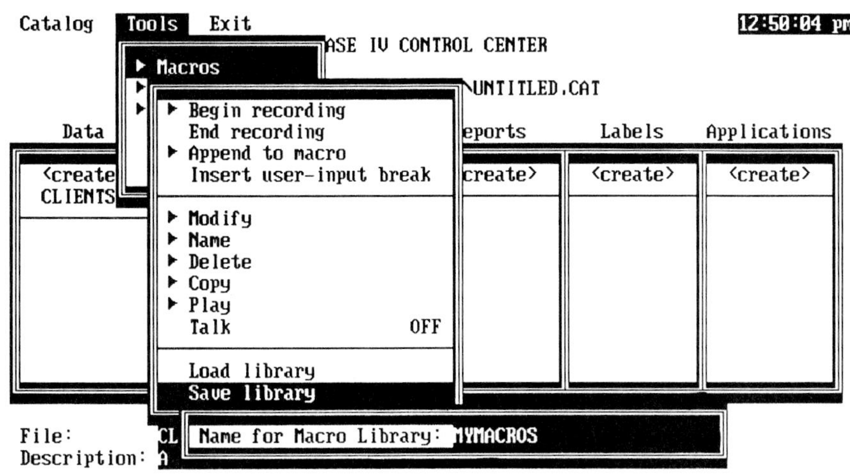

Figure 8-8. File name MYMACROS entered at the **Save library** option

macro library in a file called MYMACROS.KEY, at the prompt enter **MYMACROS**. Your screen should look like that shown in Figure 8-8.

You can save macros from the dot prompt, from SQL, or from a program by using the SAVE MACROS command. For example, to save a macro library file called MYMACROS from the dot prompt, type:

```
.SAVE MACROS TO Mymacros
```

dBASE will save all macros that are currently in memory to the MYMACROS.KEY file.

Loading a Macro Library into Memory

There are two ways to load a macro library from disk into memory, depending on whether you want to load from inside or outside of the Control Center.

You can load a macro library from the Control Center by selecting the **Load library** option from the **Macros** menu. If you've added or changed macros in the current library, you get the prompt "The current library hasn't been saved. Do you want to replace it (Y/N)." If you press Y, dBASE IV returns you to the **Macros** menu so you can save the current library before loading a new one. If you press N to load a new library without saving the current library, you may lose changes you've made to the current library.

You can load a macro library from outside the Control Center by using the RESTORE MACROS command. For example, to load a macro library called GO from the dot prompt, enter

```
.RESTORE MACROS FROM Go
```

dBASE IV loads the GO library, and you can immediately begin using the macros in that library.

Tip: In dBASE IV, there is no command for loading a macro library automatically on startup. You can, however, modify your CONFIG.DB file to assign the loading to a program that executes on startup. For example, to run a program named LOADMAC that loads a macro library called GO, place the following line in your CONFIG.DB file:

```
COMMAND = DO Loadmac
```

You can then create the LOADMAC program from the dot prompt by typing **MODIFY COMMAND LOADMAC** and entering the line

```
RESTORE MACROS FROM Go
```

Press CTRL-END to save your program. The next time you start dBASE, your macro library will load automatically. For more on modifying your CONFIG.DB file, see Chapter 35.

When dBASE loads a new macro library, it loads only existing macros in the new library. If a key has a macro in the old library but doesn't have one in the new library, the previous macro is retained. For example, suppose your macro library includes macros for the keys A, E, I, O, and U, and you overwrite it with a macro library that has macros assigned to A, B, and C. The macros assigned to E, I, O, and U are still available, since there are no macros assigned to those keys in the new library. You now have macros assigned to A, B, C, E, I, O, and U.

Naming a Macro

You can name any macro by selecting the **Name** option from the **Macros** menu in the Control Center. When you choose this option and select the key assigned to a macro, dBASE prompts you to enter a name of up to ten characters. For example, Figure 8-9 shows the macro table after you've given the name "Indexed" to the macro assigned to the I key.

You can't actually use the name to execute the macro from within the Control Center; it just serves as a reminder of what the macro does. However, you can use the name to execute the macro from outside the Control Center (see the "Using the PLAY MACRO Command" section earlier in this chapter).

Note: You can only name a macro by using the **Name** option from the **Macros** menu in the Control Center. You cannot name a macro from outside the Control Center.

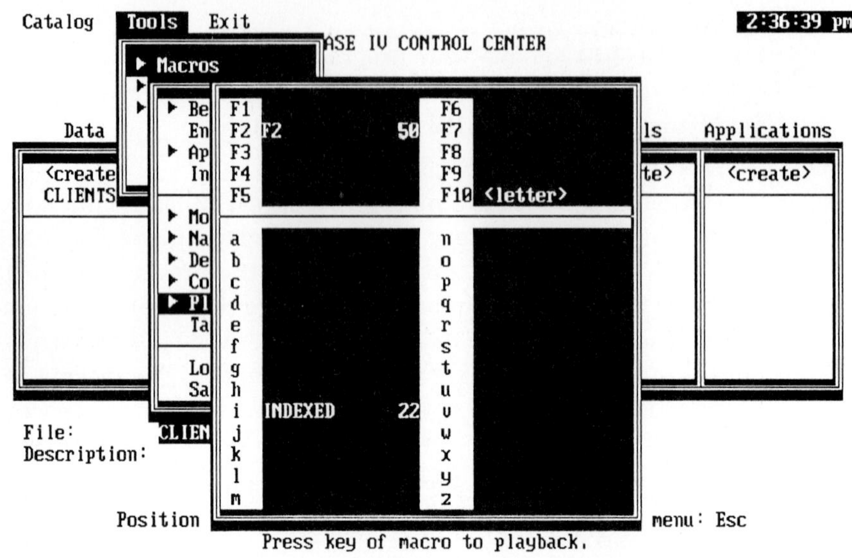

Figure 8-9. Macro table with "Indexed" assigned to the I key

Modifying Macros

You can easily modify the contents of a macro by using the **Modify** option from the **Macros** menu in the Control Center. dBASE presents the macro display table and prompts you to choose the macro you want to modify. After you choose a macro, dBASE takes you to a special version of the word wrap text editor and places the contents of your macro on the work surface. Figure 8-10 shows an example, using the I macro that you created earlier.

Note: You can only modify a macro from the Control Center by using the **Modify** option in the **Macros** menu. You cannot modify a macro from outside the Control Center.

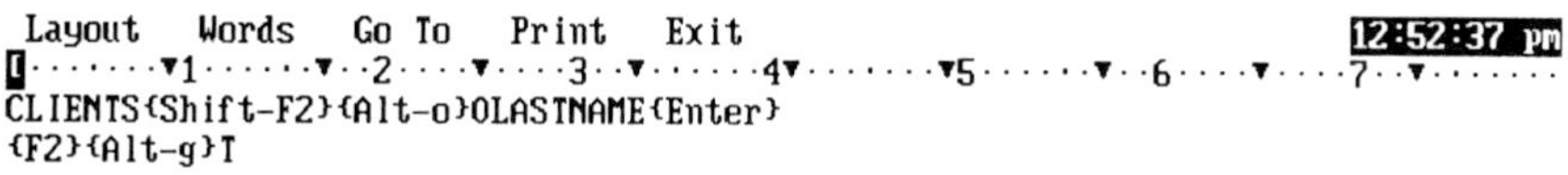

Figure 8-10. Displaying the contents of the macro with the **Modify** option from the **Macros** menu

Notice that most of the keys in Figure 8-10 appear in curly braces ({ }). dBASE uses curly braces to distinguish between any letters that you type from the keyboard and any nonalphabetical or nonnumeric keys you type. For example, suppose you type the letters **ESC** in the editor. When dBASE executes the assigned macro, it also types the letters "ESC" on your screen. If, however, you surround the letters "ESC" or "esc" with curly braces (for example, {ESC} or {esc}), dBASE interprets this as the ESC key. When you run the macro, dBASE acts as though the ESC key were pressed.

If you want your macro to display text in curly braces, you can do so by adding curly braces before and after the brace you want to use. For example, the following example places the word "text" inside curly braces in a macro:

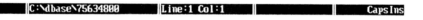

{{}text{}}

Table 8-1 shows the keywords for nonalphabetical and nonnumerical keys and acceptable key combinations.

Nesting Macros

In dBASE IV, a macro can perform any keystrokes that you normally enter from the keyboard, including activating another macro. In fact, you can *nest* or embed macros within other macros up to 16 levels deep. However, you can't nest a macro inside itself. As you can imagine, this would set up an endless loop, making your macro useless.

The following example shows you how to nest macros from the Control Center. It uses the CLIENTS database, but you can use any database with a memo field. This example creates two macros, one assigned to F1 and the other assigned to F2. The F1 macro types your company name and address in a memo field. The F2 macro closes the current memo field, moves to the next record's memo field, and activates the F1 macro to type your company name and address in that memo field.

1. If the CLIENTS database, or the database you are using, is not already in the Data Panel of the Control Center, add it now by pressing ALT-C and the letter A to open the **Add a database** option from the **Catalogs** menu. dBASE prompts you to enter a description for your database. If you don't want to add a description, just press ENTER. Select the database in the Data Panel (highlight it), and press F2 to enter the browse mode.

2. Move to the memo field of the first record and press CTRL-HOME to open it.

3. Press SHIFT-F10 and select **Begin recording** to begin creating your macro.

Keys	Keywords in Macro Editor
ENTER	{ENTER}
ESC	{ESC}
DEL	{DEL}
PRINT SCREEN	{PRTSC}
BACKSPACE	{BACKSPACE}
TAB	{TAB}
SHIFT-TAB	{SHIFT-TAB}
RIGHT ARROW	{RIGHTARROW}
LEFT ARROW	{LEFTARROW}
UP ARROW	{UPARROW}
DOWN ARROW	{DOWNARROW}
PGUP	{PGUP}
PGDN	{PGDN}
HOME	{HOME}
END	{END}
SHIFT	{SHIFT}
INS	{INS}
CTRL-	{CTRL-}
ALT-	{ALT-}
F1	{F1}
F2	{F2}
F3	{F3}
F4	{F4}
F5	{F5}
F6	{F6}
F7	{F7}
F8	{F8}
F9	{F9}
F10	{F10}
USER INPUT BREAK	{INPBREAK}

You can combine ALT with any number (0-9), character (A-Z), or function key (F1-F10) and the hyphen keyword.

You can combine CTRL with any character (A-Z) or function key (F1-F10) and the hyphen keyword. You can also use it with the navigation keys RIGHT ARROW, LEFT ARROW, UP ARROW, DOWN ARROW, HOME, END, PGUP, PGDN, and the ENTER, BACKSPACE, and PRTSC keys.

You can combine the SHIFT key with any function key (F1-F10) or with TAB.

Table 8-1. Key Equivalents to Modify Macros

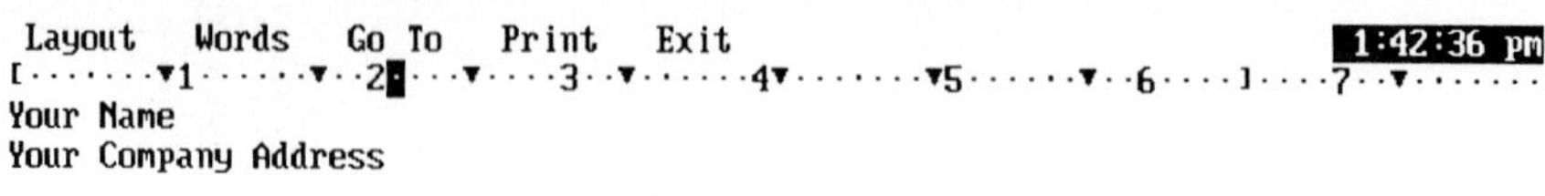

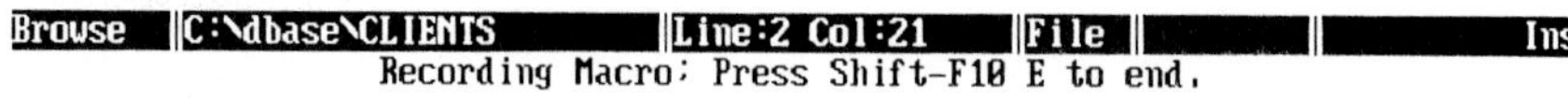

Figure 8-11. Entering name and company address assigned to the F1 macro

4. Press F1 to assign your macro to the F1 key.
5. Type your name and press ENTER to move down to the next line. Type your company address, as in Figure 8-11.
6. Press SHIFT-F10 and the letter E to stop recording your F1 macro.
7. Press SHIFT-F10 and the letter B to begin recording a new macro.
8. Press F2 to assign the macro to the F2 key.
9. Press CTRL-END, DOWN ARROW, and CTRL-HOME to close the current memo field, move down to the next record, and open the next memo field.

10. Now that you're in the new memo field, press ALT-F1 to activate your F1 macro.

11. Press SHIFT-F10 and the letter E to stop recording your F2 macro.

Since you're already in a memo field, press ALT-F2 to play back your new macros. If you want to save your macros, open the **Tools** menu and select the **Save library** option from the **Macros** menu.

Getting User Input from a Macro

In dBASE IV, you can create a macro that gets input from the user. To do this, you use a *user-input break.* A user-input break pauses a macro and waits for the user to enter keystrokes. It displays the message "Macro playback suspended, press Shift-F10 to resume macro playback" in a box at the top of the screen. If the user enters data, the prompt moves to the message line.

To add a user-input break to a macro, press SHIFT-F10 while recording a macro and select the **Insert user-input break** option. You can then continue with your macro in the normal fashion. When you play back the macro, it stops at the user-input break and lets you input data. You can add as many user-input breaks as you like in a macro. When the macro performs a user-input break, a message appears telling you that you must press SHIFT-F10 to resume the macro.

The following example macro performs a user-input break. The macro begins by freezing the first two fields of a database. Next, it locks a field to limit the user's movement to that field. It then performs a user-input break to allow the user to change the contents of one or more of the locked field's entries. When the user is finished changing the field, the macro unlocks and unfreezes the affected fields and saves the database.

This example uses the CLIENTS database, but you can easily adapt it to any database or field name. To create the macro, perform the following steps:

1. If the CLIENTS database, or the database you are using, is not already in the Data Panel of the Control Center, add it now by pressing ALT-C and the letter A to open the **Add a database** option from the **Catalogs** menu. Select the database in the Data panel (highlight it).

2. Press SHIFT-F10, and select the **Begin recording** option to begin creating your macro. Press the letter A to assign your macro to the A key.

3. Press F2 to enter browse mode.

4. Press ALT-F and the letter L to select the **Lock fields** option from the **Fields** menu. Enter 2 to lock the first two fields (Firstname and Lastname, if you are using the CLIENTS database) and press ENTER.

5. Press ALT-F and the letter F to select the **Freeze fields** option from the **Fields** menu. Type the field name you want to edit (Amount, if you're using the CLIENTS database) and press ENTER.

6. Press SHIFT-F10, and select the **Insert user-input break** option to allow the user to edit or input information in the locked field during macro execution.

7. Press ALT-F and the letter L to select the **Lock fields** option from the **Fields** menu. Enter 0 to unlock the first two fields (Firstname and Lastname) and press ENTER.

8. Press ALT-F and the letter F to select the **Freeze fields** option from the **Fields** menu. Press HOME to move the cursor to the beginning of the option's text. Press CTRL-Y to delete the previously selected field and then press ENTER.

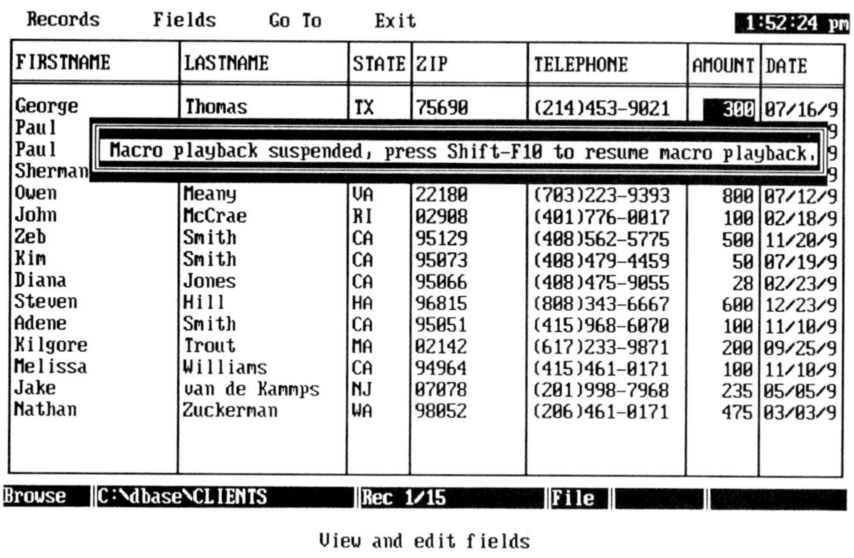

Records Fields Go To Exit 1:52:24 pm

FIRSTNAME	LASTNAME	STATE	ZIP	TELEPHONE	AMOUNT	DATE
George	Thomas	TX	75690	(214)453-9021	300	07/16/9
Paul						9
Paul						9
Sherman						9
Owen	Meany	VA	22180	(703)223-9393	800	07/12/9
John	McCrae	RI	02908	(401)776-0017	100	02/18/9
Zeb	Smith	CA	95129	(408)562-5775	500	11/20/9
Kim	Smith	CA	95073	(408)479-4459	50	07/19/9
Diana	Jones	CA	95066	(408)475-9055	28	02/23/9
Steven	Hill	HA	96815	(808)343-6667	600	12/23/9
Adene	Smith	CA	95051	(415)968-6070	100	11/10/9
Kilgore	Trout	MA	02142	(617)233-9871	200	09/25/9
Melissa	Williams	CA	94964	(415)461-0171	100	11/10/9
Jake	van de Kammps	NJ	07078	(201)998-7968	235	05/05/9
Nathan	Zuckerman	WA	98052	(206)461-0171	475	03/03/9

Macro playback suspended, press Shift-F10 to resume macro playback.

Browse C:\dbase\CLIENTS Rec 1/15 File

View and edit fields

Figure 8-12. User-input break in a macro

9. Press CTRL-END to save any changes made to the database.

10. Press SHIFT-F10 and select the **End recording** option to end your macro.

To activate the macro you've just created, start from the Control Center and select the **Play** option from the **Macros** menu (if you prefer, you can press ALT-F10) then press F2. When dBASE encounters the user-input break, your screen should look like Figure 8-12. You can then make any desired changes to the Amount field. To end the user-input break and continue replaying the macro, press SHIFT-F10. Remember, if you want to save this macro, select the **Save macro library** option from the **Macros** menu.

Deleting Macros

You can delete a macro from the current macro library by selecting the **Delete** option from the **Macros** menu. dBASE prompts you to "Press key of macro to delete." After you press the key to which the macro is assigned, dBASE asks "Do you really want to delete *x*? (Y/N)" (where *X* is the key you originally assigned to the macro). Press Y, and dBASE deletes the macro.

Note: You can only delete macros by using the **Delete** option in the **Macros** menu of the Control Center. You can't delete macros from outside the Control Center.

Copying Macros

You can copy a macro from one key to another by selecting the **Copy** option from the **Macros** menu. When you select this option, the macro display table for the current library appears on the screen. dBASE prompts you to press the key that plays back the macro followed by the new key you want to copy the macro to. After you press the appropriate keys, dBASE copies the macro to the new key.

Note: You can only copy macros by using the **Copy** option in the **Macros** menu of the Control Center. You can't copy macros from outside the Control Center.

Troubleshooting Your Macros

One of the best (and worst) features of macros is that they play back exactly what you've entered. Therefore, if you accidentally

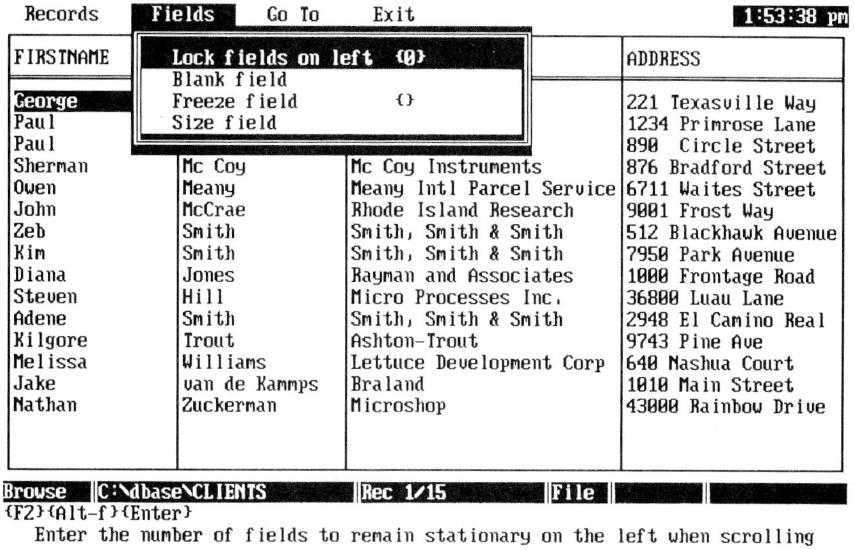

```
Records   Fields   Go To   Exit                                     1:53:38 pm

FIRSTNAME  | Lock fields on left  {0}                      | ADDRESS
           | Blank field                                   |
George     | Freeze field          {}                      | 221 Texasville Way
Paul       | Size field                                    | 1234 Primrose Lane
Paul       |                                               | 890  Circle Street
Sherman    | Mc Coy         | Mc Coy Instruments           | 876 Bradford Street
Owen       | Meany          | Meany Intl Parcel Service    | 6711 Waites Street
John       | McCrae         | Rhode Island Research        | 9001 Frost Way
Zeb        | Smith          | Smith, Smith & Smith         | 512 Blackhawk Avenue
Kim        | Smith          | Smith, Smith & Smith         | 7950 Park Avenue
Diana      | Jones          | Rayman and Associates        | 1000 Frontage Road
Steven     | Hill           | Micro Processes Inc.         | 36800 Luau Lane
Adene      | Smith          | Smith, Smith & Smith         | 2948 El Camino Real
Kilgore    | Trout          | Ashton-Trout                 | 9743 Pine Ave
Melissa    | Williams       | Lettuce Development Corp     | 640 Nashua Court
Jake       | van de Kammps  | Braland                      | 1010 Main Street
Nathan     | Zuckerman      | Microshop                    | 43000 Rainbow Drive

Browse  |C:\dbase\CLIENTS          |Rec 1/15          |File  |
{F2}{Alt-f}{Enter}
  Enter the number of fields to remain stationary on the left when scrolling
```

Figure 8-13. Displaying the text of the macro on the message line with the **Talk** option

added an extra keystroke in the wrong place, it may cause your macro to perform in some unforseen way.

To see the keystrokes in your macro while dBASE IV is executing them, set the **Macro** menu's **Talk** option to On. To toggle the **Talk** option from Off to On, press ENTER while highlighting the option. With the **Talk** option set to On, dBASE displays your macro's text in the message line as it performs the keystrokes, as shown in Figure 8-13.

When you toggle **Talk** to On and start a macro, your macro executes one keystroke at a time at an even pace. To change the pace, you can use the < and > keys to slow down or speed up the macro's execution (you don't have to press SHIFT).

To try this option, toggle the **Talk** option to On and play back any macro you've created. As the macro is executing, try changing its speed with the < and > keys.

In this chapter, you learned how to automate a series of keystrokes by using macros. You created macros with the macro recorder, and you learned the three ways to play them back. You now know how dBASE stores your macro libraries and how to modify and troubleshoot a macro if it doesn't perform as expected.

Creating Input Forms

NINE

When you work in browse or edit mode, dBASE IV normally displays your data using a *default form*. In browse mode, the default form is a table that shows up to 17 records (on a standard 25-row screen), with one record per row. In edit mode, the default form shows only one record at a time, with the field names listed down the left side of the screen and data immediately to the right.

As you work with dBASE IV, you'll want to customize the screen display to suit your own needs. Unfortunately, you cannot modify the default browse form. In edit mode, however, you can use custom forms. By creating custom forms, you can, for example, add boxes and lines, move fields to different locations on the screen, control what data users can enter in a field, or add calculated fields to the display.

This chapter discusses how to create custom forms with the Forms Design screen. It shows you how to build a form and modify its layout. It also describes the tools you can use to enhance a form's appearance.

The Forms Design Screen

To create a custom form in dBASE IV, you use the *Forms Design screen*. By using this screen, you can access a special version of the word wrap text editor that allows you to change the layout of your forms. For example, you can completely rearrange the position of your database fields. You can also add (and remove) the following design elements:

- Fields from a database file or view
- Special calculated fields that you create for display purposes only
- Boxes and lines
- Your own text

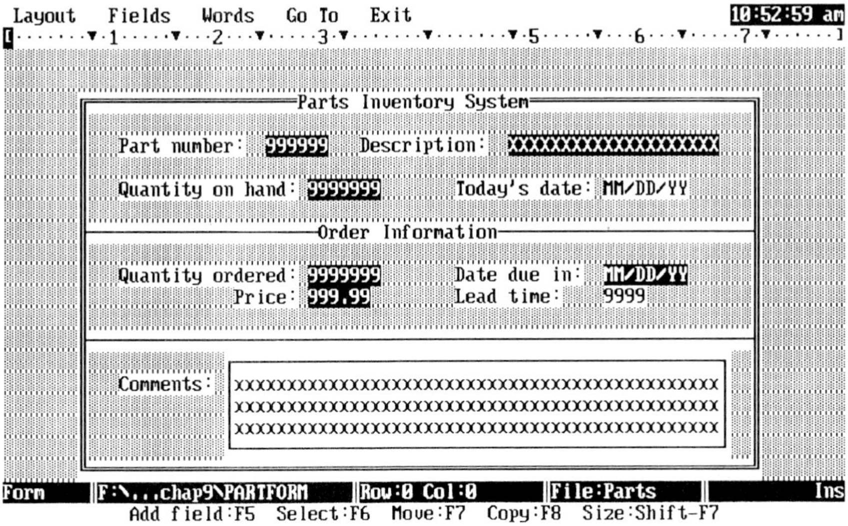

```
Layout   Fields   Words   Go To   Exit                                   10:52:59 am
[·······▼·1·····▼···2···▼·····3·▼·······▼·······▼·5·····▼···6···▼·····7·▼······]

          ═══════════════Parts Inventory System═══════════════
          Part number: 999999   Description: XXXXXXXXXXXXXXXXXXXX

          Quantity on hand: 9999999        Today's date: MM/DD/YY

          ──────────────────Order Information──────────────────

          Quantity ordered: 9999999        Date due in: MM/DD/YY
                     Price: 999.99         Lead time:   9999

          Comments:  XXXXXXXXXXXXXXXXXXXXXXXXXXXXXXXXXXXXXXXXXXXXXXX
                     XXXXXXXXXXXXXXXXXXXXXXXXXXXXXXXXXXXXXXXXXXXXXXX
                     XXXXXXXXXXXXXXXXXXXXXXXXXXXXXXXXXXXXXXXXXXXXXXX

Form    F:\...chap9\PARTFORM    Row:0 Col:0    File:Parts              Ins
        Add field:F5  Select:F6  Move:F7  Copy:F8  Size:Shift-F7
```

Figure 9-1. The Forms Design screen

Figure 9-1 shows an example form design in the Forms Design screen. Figure 9-2 shows the completed form it generates.

Tip: As you design a form in the Forms Design screen, you can press F2 to switch to edit mode and view the results. To get back to the Forms Design screen, press SHIFT-F2.

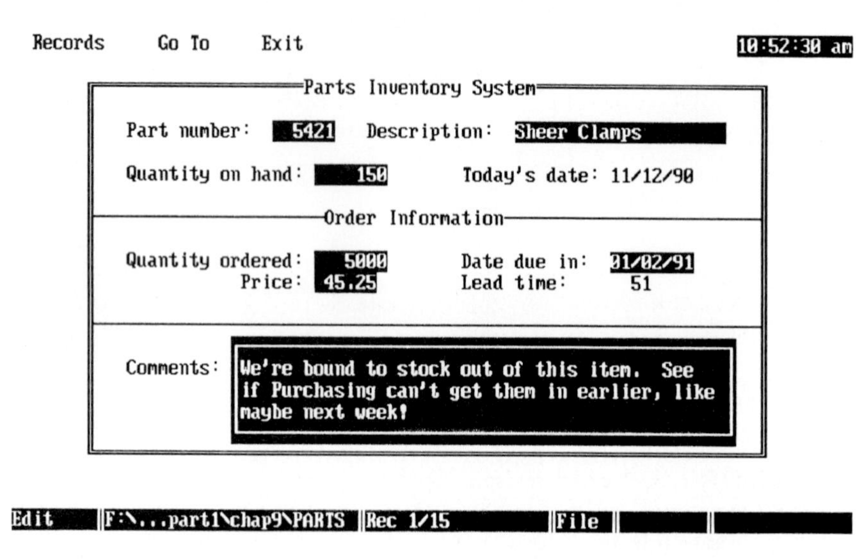

Figure 9-2. The finished form

The Different Types of Form Files

dBASE IV uses three different types of files to manage forms: .SCR, .FMT, and .FMO files.

- .SCR files contain the instructions dBASE IV needs to display a form in the Forms Design screen. These files are stored in a special non-ASCII format that is intelligible only to dBASE IV (and assembly language programmers). When you create or modify a form by using the Forms Design screen, you are actually working with an .SCR file.
- .FMT files contain the standard dBASE IV program code (for example, @...SAY...GETs, READ, and so on) that is

generated when you save a form in the Forms Design screen (see the section "Saving a Form").

- .FMO files are the compiled version of .FMT files. .FMO files are the actual object files dBASE IV reads when you use a form to display and edit data. (dBASE IV automatically generates an .FMO file from the .FMT when you save a form.)

These files are listed in the order in which you create them as you take a form through the design process. When you've completed a form, you should have one of each of the three file types.

Activating the Forms Design Screen

You access the Forms Design screen differently from the Control Center and the dot prompt. The way you access the Forms Design screen also depends on whether you want to open a database file first in order to use its fields within the form.

From the Control Center

To activate the Forms Design screen from the Control Center, highlight the name of a form in the Forms Panel and press SHIFT-F2. If you're creating a form from scratch, select the **<create>** option from the Forms Panel.

When you're creating a form from scratch, you should open a database before you activate the Forms Design screen from the Control Center. This way, you can easily use the database's fields within the form. To open a database from the Control Center, highlight in the Data Panel and press ENTER. Then select **Use file**.

From the Dot Prompt

To activate the Forms Design screen from the dot prompt, use the CREATE SCREEN or MODIFY SCREEN command. For example, to activate the Forms Design screen and create a form screen (.SCR) file called BUILD1, enter

```
. CREATE SCREEN Build1
```

The MODIFY and CREATE forms of the command are completely interchangeable. How dBASE IV responds to your command is determined by whether the .SCR file exists. If it exists, the command modifies it. If it does not exist, the command automatically creates one.

As in the Control Center, if you're building a form from scratch, you should open a database file before activating the Forms Design screen. This way, you can easily include the database's fields within the form. For example, to open a database called INVOICE and activate the Forms Design screen with a form called Payform, enter

```
. USE Invoice
. MODIFY SCREEN Payform
```

Entering a Quick Layout

When you first activate the Forms Design screen, its work surface is the equivalent of a blank edit screen. Rather than start with a blank slate, you can place some database fields on the work surface and then shape the fields and surrounding text to meet your needs.

The easiest way to place database fields on the screen is to start with a *quick layout.* Select **Quick layout** from the **Layout** menu. (If you've previously opened a database and you access the Forms Design screen from the Control Center, and you're automat-

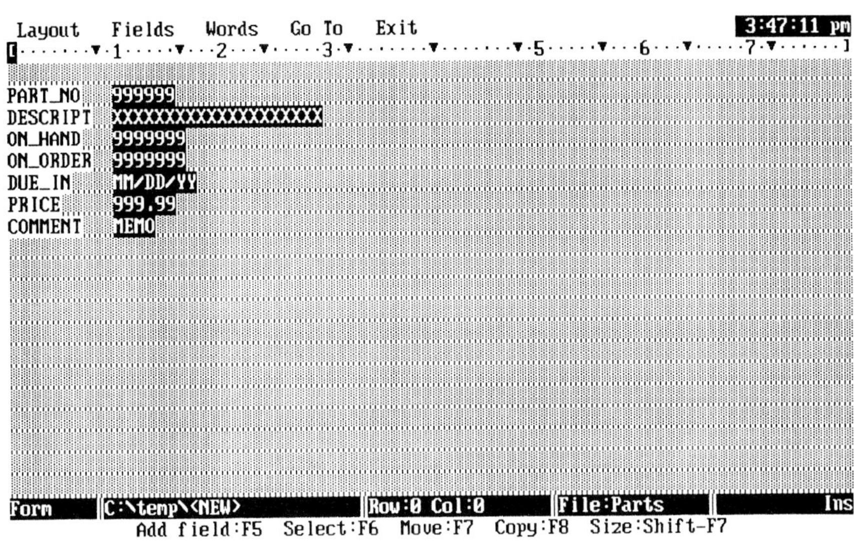

Figure 9-3. Using a quick layout

ically taken to this option.) dBASE IV will display the default edit form. Figure 9-3 shows an example for a PARTS database.

If you don't open a database before activating the Forms Design screen, you cannot access the **Quick layout** option from the **Layout** menu. To make the option available, open a file from within the Forms Design screen by selecting the **Use different database file or view** option in the **Layout** menu. (If you access the Forms Design screen from the Control Center without first opening a database, you're automatically taken to this option.) dBASE IV will open a database file you select from the list box. You can then use in your form the fields from the database.

Function Key	Action
F2 (Data)	Switches to edit mode (press SHIFT-F2 to return from edit mode to the Forms Design Screen)
F3 (Previous)	Moves to the previous field
F4 (Next)	Moves to the next field
F5 (Field)	Lets you add/modify a field in the layout surface
F6 (Extend Select)	Selects adjoining text and fields
F7 (Move)	Moves selected text and fields
F8 (Copy)	Copies selected text and fields
SHIFT-F1 (Pick)	Lets you pick from a list of existing database fields
SHIFT-F2 (Design)	Switches to the Queries Design screen
SHIFT-F5 (Find)	Finds a specified search string
SHIFT-F6 (Replace)	Replaces one string with another
SHIFT-F7 (Size)	Lets you change the size of design elements such as boxes and static memo windows

Table 9-1. Function Keys in the Forms Design Screen

Copying and Moving

To copy and move design elements on the work surface, use the F6 (Extend Select), F7 (Move), and F8 (Copy) function keys. You can use these keys to copy and move all of the different design elements: text, fields, boxes, lines, and so forth. Table 9-1 shows the function keys available in the Forms Design screen. Table 3-1 in Chapter 3 lists all of the navigation keys you can use in the Forms Design screen.

For example, suppose you want to move the field information in Figure 9-3 to a more central location on the screen. Press F6 to

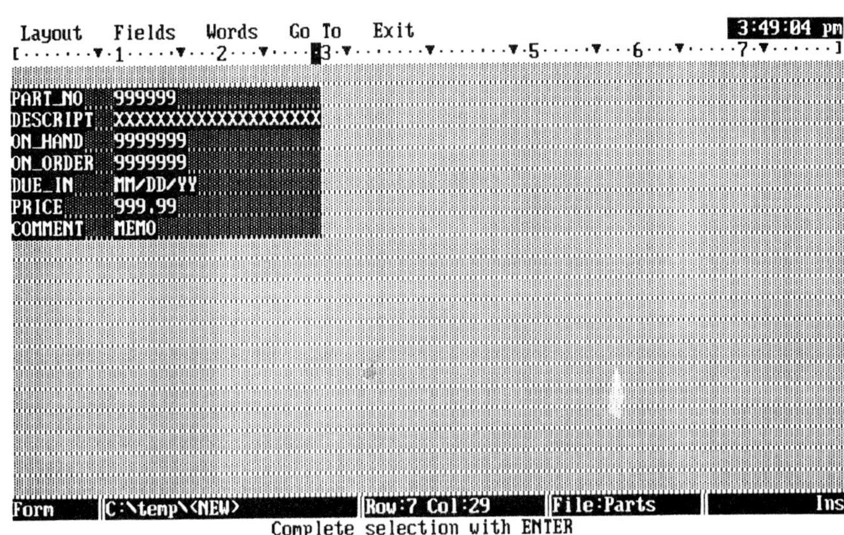

Figure 9-4. An extended selection

start the selection process, then use the arrow keys to extend the selection to include all the fields, as in Figure 9-4. Press ENTER to complete the selection. Next, move the cursor to the upper-left corner of where you want the information to be located, and press F7. dBASE IV moves the information to the new location. Use the arrow keys to adjust the positioning of the block, and press ENTER when you're ready to complete the move. Figure 9-5 shows the results (after you press ESC to remove the highlight from the selection).

If you try to copy or move text or fields to a location where it will overlap existing text or fields, dBASE IV prompts you "Delete covered text and fields? (Y/N):." If you press Y, dBASE eliminates the underlying elements as it completes the copy. Respond to this prompt with care. If you inadvertently eliminate needed items, you

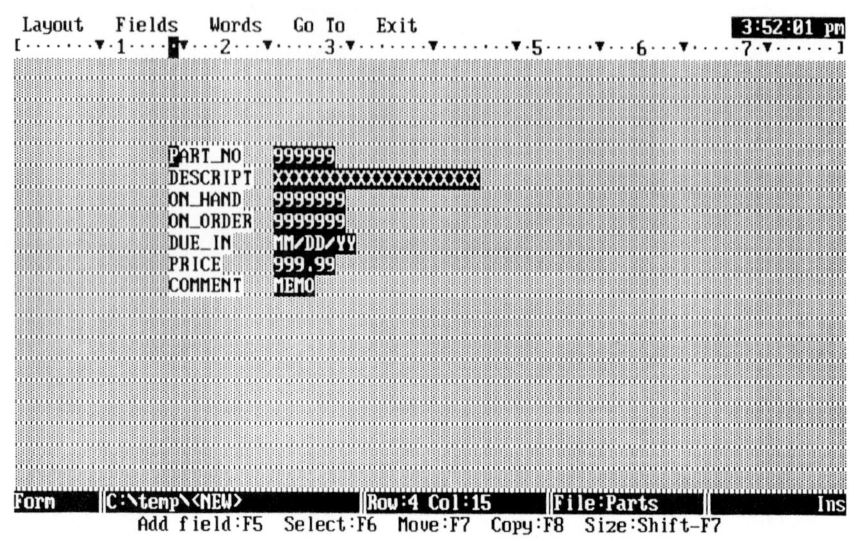

Figure 9-5. Results of the move

can always add them again, but you must do so manually. (See the section "Adding Fields.")

Tip: As you build a form in the Forms Design screen, you should periodically save your work. This way you recover at least some of your work if you make mistakes. To save your work, select the **Save this form** option from the **Layout** menu. (See the section "Saving a Form.")

Adding and Changing Text

It is very easy to add and modify design elements in the Forms Design screen. Adding and modifying text is particularly simple.

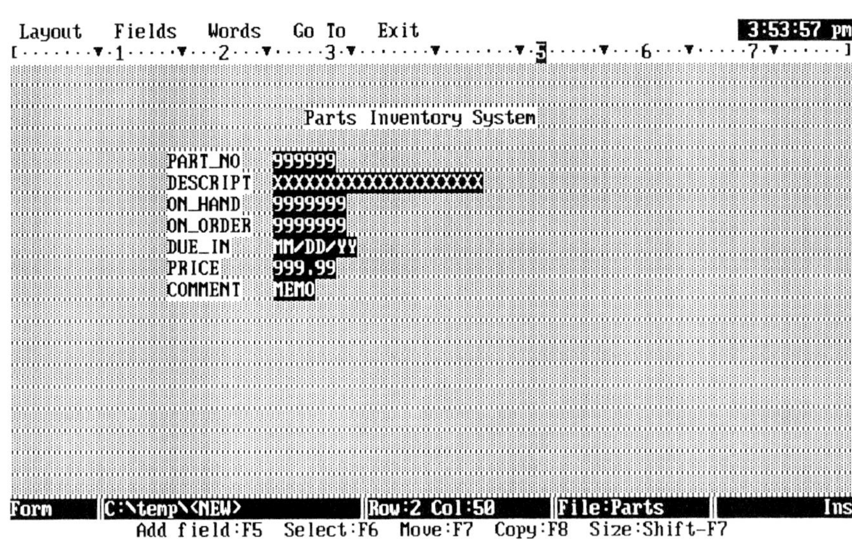

Figure 9-6. Adding text

You just move the cursor to the desired location and type the text from the keyboard.

For example, suppose you want to add the title Parts Inventory System to the form that appears in Figure 9-5. Move the cursor to the desired location and type the title, as in Figure 9-6.

There is nothing sacred about the field names that dBASE IV displays when you select the **Quick layout** option. You can change and rearrange the field names, as in Figure 9-7 for example. The prior example (Figures 9-4 and 9-5) rearranged an entire block. The same procedure applies when you move a single field.

Adding Boxes

dBASE IV makes it particularly easy to add boxes to your forms. With boxes, you can group related information and focus the user's

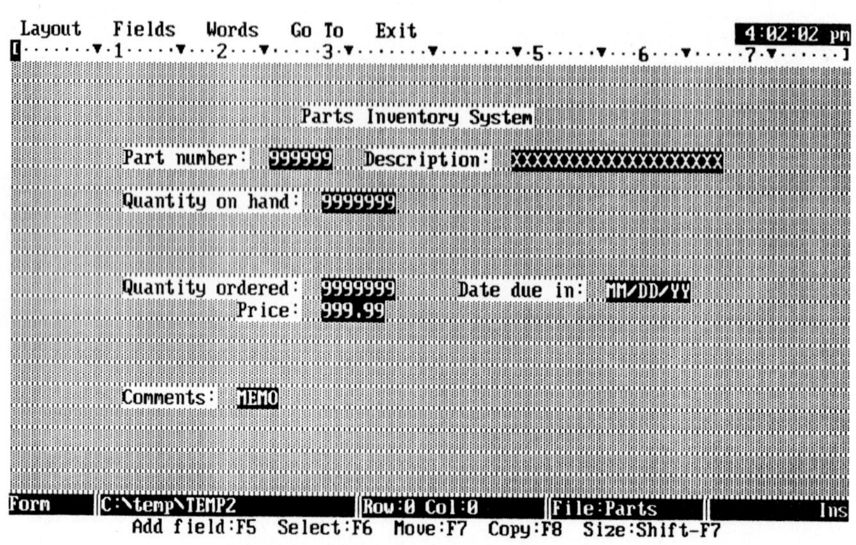

Figure 9-7. Modifying field names

attention to a particular area of the screen. You can create boxes with a single- or double-line border. You can also choose another ASCII character to be the border character (see the section "Using Specified Characters").

To create a box in the Forms Design screen, use the **Box** option from the **Layout** menu. When you select this option, your screen should look like Figure 9-8.

To put a double-line box around the fields in Figure 9-7, select the **Double line** option. Next, press ENTER to anchor one corner of the box. Then use the arrow keys to position the opposite corner of

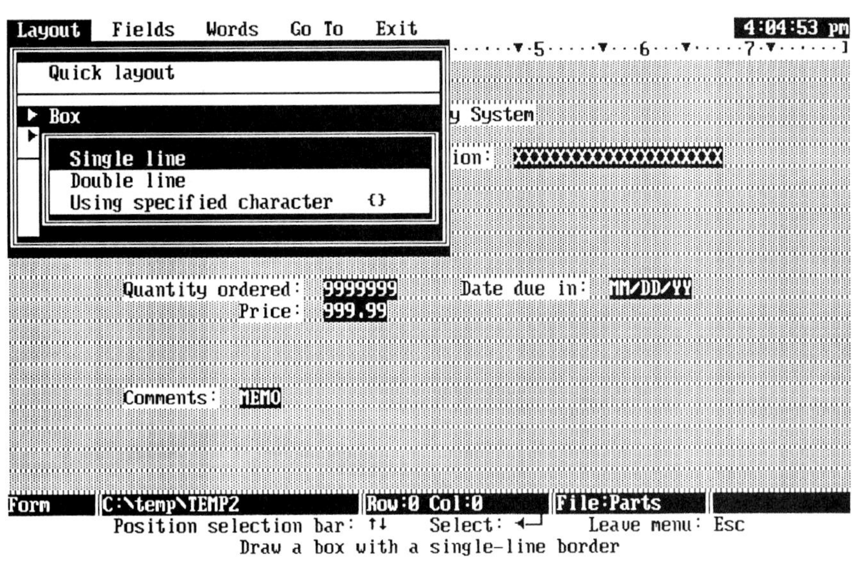

Figure 9-8. The **Box** option from the **Layout** menu

the box; dBASE IV expands and contracts the box as you go. Figure 9-9 shows the results after you press ENTER a second time to select the final location for the box. Notice that the box does not overwrite the existing title text. In fact, text and fields reside on a different plane than boxes and always appear in front of them.

You can change the appearance of the box by using the **Display** option from the **Words** menu. For example, if you have a monochrome screen, you can display the box highlighted or in reverse video (see the section "Changing the Display Appearance").

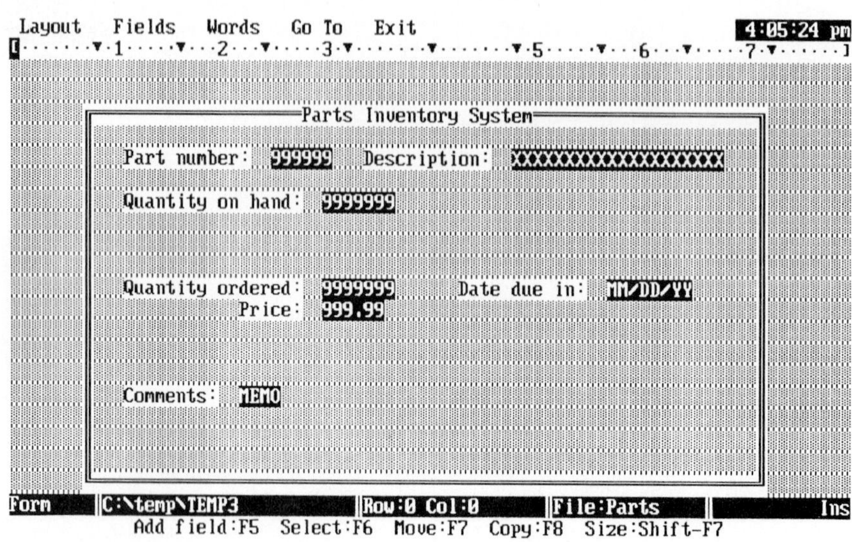

Figure 9-9. A double-line box

Tip: Once you've placed a box in a form, you can resize it by locating the cursor anywhere on the box and pressing SHIFT-F7. dBASE IV automatically moves the cursor to the lower-right corner of the box, and you can use the arrow keys to change the box size. Press ENTER to lock in the new size.

Adding Lines

Besides adding boxes, you can add lines to your forms. You can create a double line, a single line, or a line using a selected ASCII character.

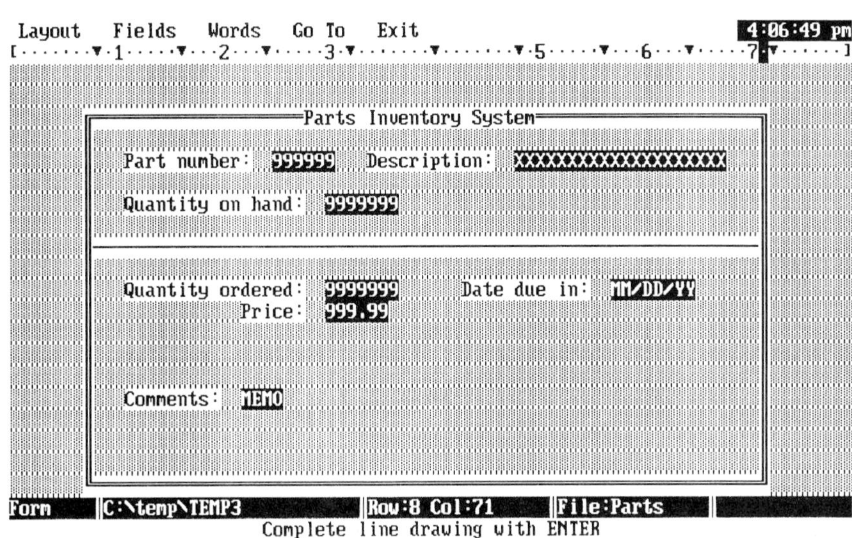

Figure 9-10. Form with a single line

To draw a line, position your cursor where you want to begin the line. Next, select **Line** from the **Layout** menu. You can then choose **Single line**, **Double line**, or **Using specified character**.

For example, suppose you want to create the single line that appears in Figure 9-10. After you select the **Single line** option from the **Line** menu, dBASE IV prompts you to press ENTER to lock down one end of the line. You can then move the cursor using the arrow keys; dBASE IV extends the line as you go.

If you change directions with the arrow keys, the line moves with you. This lets you build boxes by using lines. However, it is easier to build boxes with the **Box** option than with the **Line** option.

If you make a mistake while entering a line, you can press BACKSPACE to erase part of the line. Also, if you change directions while entering a line, and the line intersections do not work out as planned, you can retrace your steps and redraw the line. When all else fails, use the DEL key to erase an incorrect line, and start over.

Tip: You can type text while entering a line. The text you type appears in the same direction as the line. For example, if you're entering a line that heads upwards on the screen, the characters appear above one another as you type. To change the direction of the characters without entering line characters, press TAB and an arrow key for the desired direction.

While a box is treated as a distinct entity on the work surface, a line is not. The characters that make up a line are the same as characters you would type from the keyboard. If you want to change the line as a whole, say to modify the color, you must select all of the characters that make up the line.

Note: Unlike boxes, lines placed on the work surface overwrite any existing text or fields.

Using Specified Characters

In dBASE IV, you can build boxes and lines using your own specified ASCII character. When you select either **Box** or **Line** from the **Layout** menu, you can then choose **Using specified character**. dBASE IV will display a list of the available ASCII characters, from which you can choose the desired character, as in Figure 9-11.

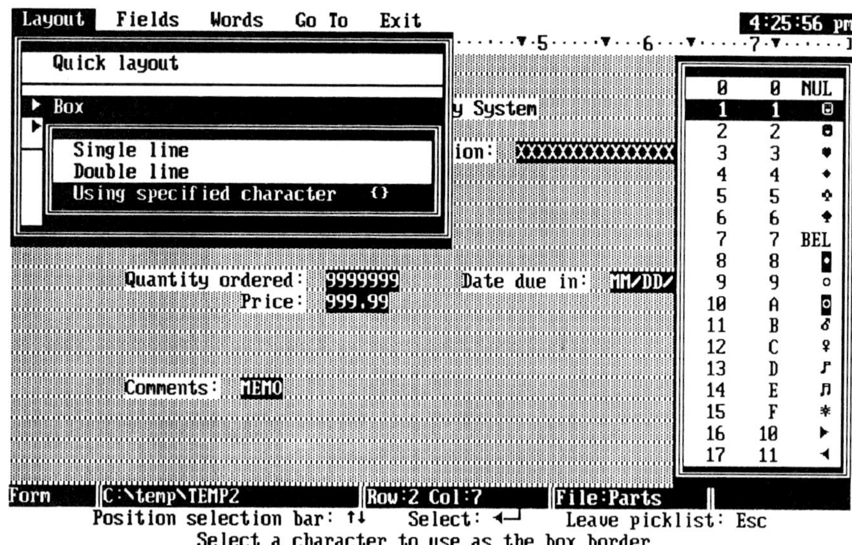

Figure 9-11. ASCII character list for **Using specified character**

Suppose you want to build a box using asterisks for the border. First select **Box** from the **Layout** menu; then select **Using specified character**. When dBASE IV displays the list of available ASCII characters, highlight the asterisk in the list and press ENTER. Figure 9-12 shows the results.

Adding Fields

When building a custom form, you can add three different types of fields to the work surface: existing fields, calculated fields, and

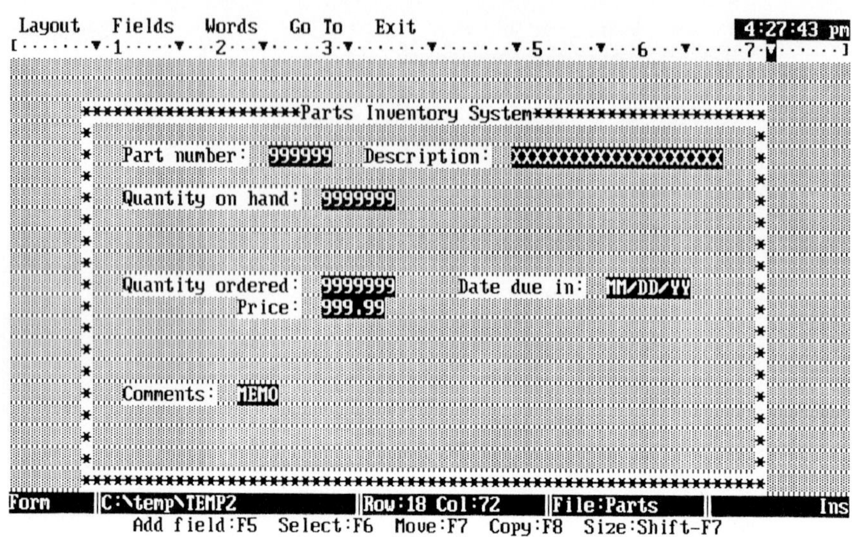

Figure 9-12. Using asterisks for the box border

memory variable fields. This section describes what these fields are and how you can add them to your form. It also describes how to customize a field's appearance and editing options.

Existing Fields

An *existing field* is a field from the open database file or view. (If you haven't yet opened a database file or view, you can do so from within the Forms Design screen by choosing **Use different database file or view** from the **Layout** menu.) To add an existing field to the work surface, locate the cursor where you want the field to begin and select **Add field** from the **Fields** menu. Your screen shows a two-column list, as in Figure 9-13.

The first column shows the existing field names from the current database file or view. (If the source of the fields is a view, this

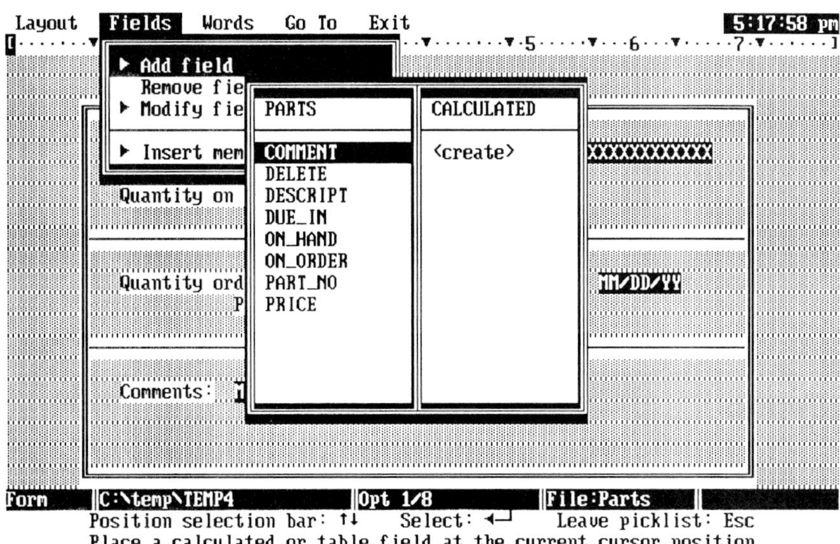

Figure 9-13. Adding a field

column shows the calculated fields from the view as well.) The second column shows the names of any calculated fields that have been defined thus far for the form.

Tip: The quickest way to add a field to a form is to put the cursor where you want the field to begin and press F5—the Field key.

After you select a field name from the first column in the list, a *field description menu* appears, as in Figure 9-14. As the name implies, you use this menu to describe the field being placed in the form. The information at the top of the menu is taken directly from the database file (or view definition), and you can't modify it in the Forms Design screen. The information below the separator line lets you control the appearance of the field on the screen by using templates and picture functions (see the sections "Field

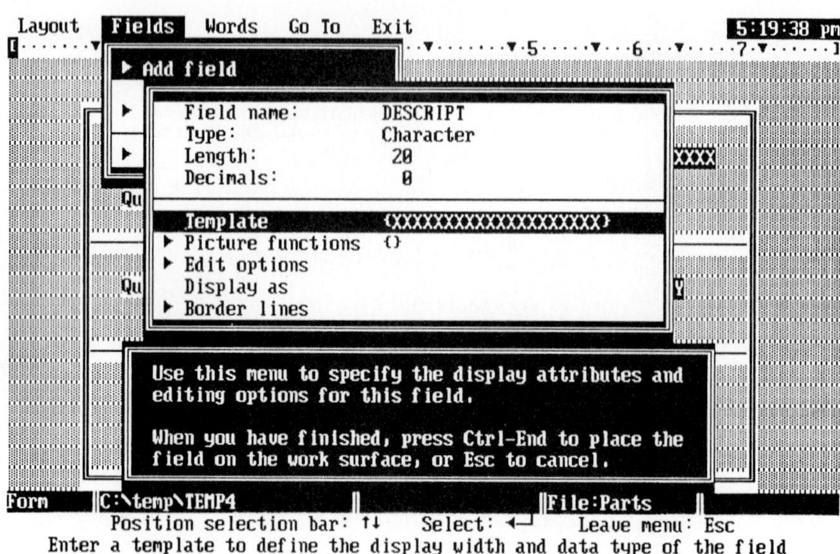

Figure 9-14. The field description menu

Templates" and "Picture Functions"). You can also define the editing options (see "Defining Edit Options").

Once you've established the settings you want for a field, press CTRL-END to save them. dBASE IV places the field in the form at the current cursor location. To cancel the operation and remove the field description menu from the screen, press ESC.

Calculated Fields

A *calculated field* is a field that you add to the form for display purposes only. A calculated field has no effect on the underlying database file or view, nor can users move to a calculated field and modify its contents.

To add a calculated field to the form, move the cursor to where you want the field to begin and select **Add field** from the **Fields**

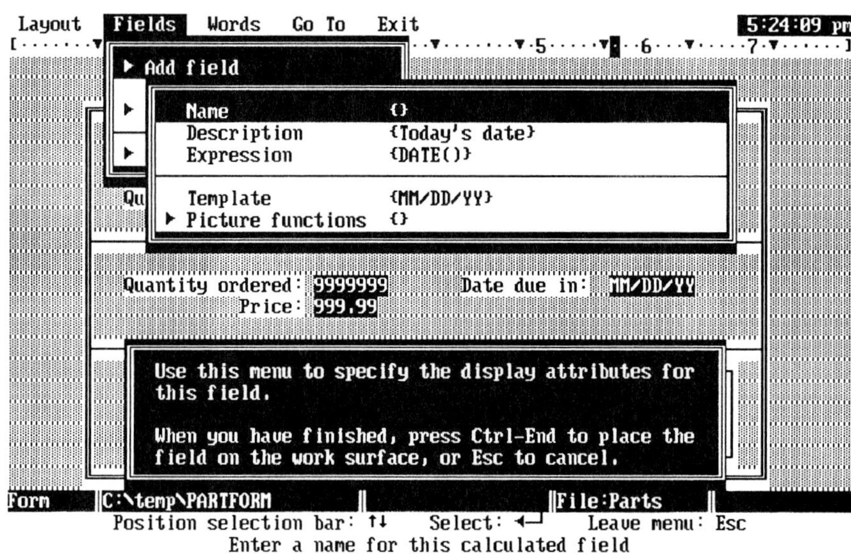

Figure 9-15. Field description menu for a calculated field date

menu. When dBASE IV displays the two-column list (see Figure 9-13), select the **<create>** option from the top of the right-hand column. dBASE IV then displays a field description menu for calculated fields, as in Figure 9-15.

The Field Description Menu for Calculated Fields

The field description menu has particular options for calculated fields. You can change any setting in this menu because calculated fields do not have any predefined settings. The options for calculated fields are as follows:

- **Name** Use this option to give the calculated field a unique name. A name is not required, but helps you identify the field in the submenu that appears when you select **Add field**, **Modify field**, or **Remove field** from the **Fields** menu. If you don't provide a name, dBASE IV identifies the field by its expression.

- **Description** This option lets you enter an 80-character description for the field, if you like.
- **Expression** This option defines the expression that dBASE IV uses to calculate the field. You cannot create a calculated field without an expression. You can use any valid dBASE IV expression, and you can even include memory variables. You cannot, however, include another calculated field from the current form in the expression. When you've entered the expression, press ENTER and dBASE IV immediately evaluates it. If you use memory variables in the expression, they must be previously defined or dBASE IV displays an error message.
- **Template** dBASE IV automatically fills in this option when it evaluates the expression. (dBASE IV uses the result of the expression to determine the proper field template.) You use the template setting to control how users can enter data in the field on a character-by-character basis. You can easily change the field template (see the section "Field Templates").
- **Picture functions** This option lets you control the overall template for the field (see "Picture Functions").

When you've entered the options for a calculated field, press CTRL-END. dBASE IV immediately places the calculated field in the form.

Tip: As you enter the expression in a calculated field, you can press SHIFT-F1 to access the Expression Builder. It shows you a complete list of the existing database field names, mathematical and logical operators, and functions from which to choose. (See Chapter 5 for more description of the Expression Builder.)

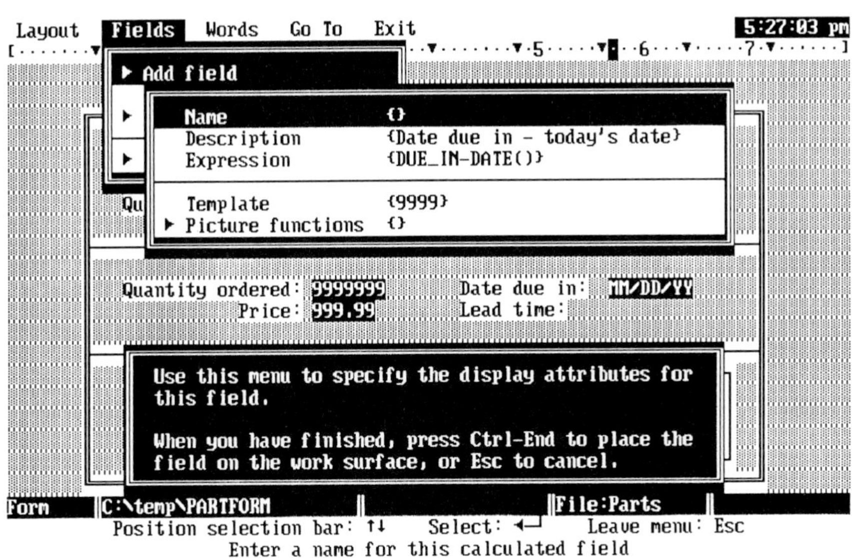

Figure 9-16. Information for a calculated field for lead time

An Example

Suppose you want to add two calculated fields to the form for the PARTS database. The first field shows today's date (using the DATE() function) and the second shows the lead time for a part (the value in the Due_in field minus the DATE() function).

To add a calculated field that displays today's date, locate the cursor where you want the field to appear and select **Add field** from the **Fields** menu. Next, select **<create>** from the CALCULATED column in the box that appears. You can then fill in the field description menu, as in Figure 9-15. As soon as you enter the expression **DATE()**, dBASE IV evaluates it and automatically inserts the template setting {MM/DD/YY}. Press CTRL-END to accept the settings, and dBASE IV places the field in the form.

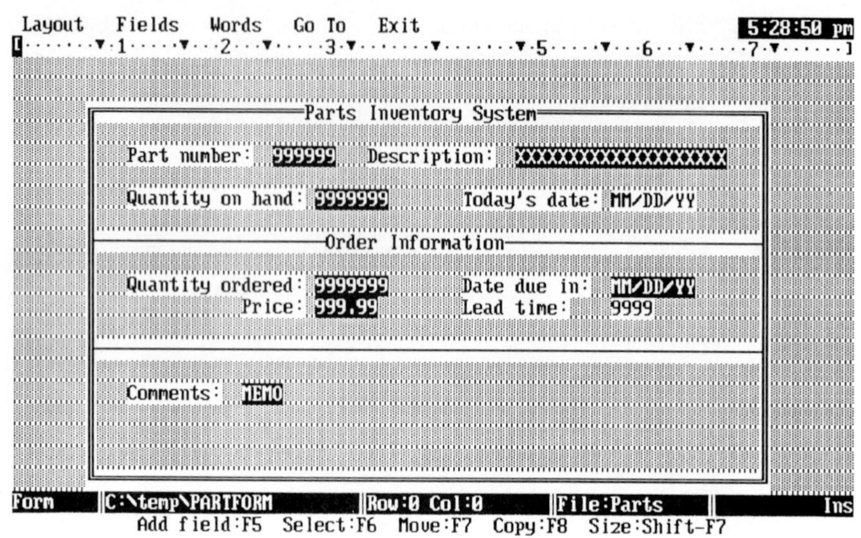
Layout Fields Words Go To Exit 5:28:50 pm
Parts Inventory System
Part number: 999999 Description: XXXXXXXXXXXXXXXXXXXX
Quantity on hand: 9999999 Today's date: MM/DD/YY
Order Information
Quantity ordered: 9999999 Date due in: MM/DD/YY
Price: 999.99 Lead time: 9999
Comments: MEMO
Form C:\temp\PARTFORM Row:0 Col:0 File:Parts Ins
Add field:F5 Select:F6 Move:F7 Copy:F8 Size:Shift-F7

Figure 9-17. Results of entering the calculated fields

To add a calculated field that computes lead time, follow the steps outlined for entering a calculated field. However, enter the values that appear in Figure 9-16 in the field description menu. Figure 9-17 shows the form for the PARTS database after you've entered both calculated fields.

Memory Variable Fields

Another type of field you can add to a form is a *memory variable field.* To add a memory variable field to a form, use the **Insert memory variable** option from the **Fields** menu. Then fill in the field description menu entries to match the memory variable you plan to use.

Before you edit your data using a form that contains a memory variable field, you must define the memory variable in a program or from the dot prompt. (You don't have to define the memory variable before adding it to the form in the Forms Design screen, however). When you enter the value for the **Name** option in the field description menu, make sure the name matches the memory variable you'll define before using the form to edit your data.

When choosing a value for the **Variable type** option in the field description menu, press the SPACEBAR to cycle through the available memory variable types.

For information on the proper entries for the **Template** and **Picture functions** options, see the sections "Field Templates" and "Picture Functions."

When you've entered the options for the field, press CTRL-END. dBASE IV immediately places the memory variable field in the form.

Note: If you attempt to activate a form that uses a memory variable field and you have not defined the memory variable, dBASE IV displays the error message "Variable not found," and you can't use the form.

Field Templates

The **Template** option in the field description menu lets you control how users can enter data in a field on a character-by-character basis. You enter a template by typing a string of symbols. The length of the string lets you specify the width of the field on the work surface. Each symbol within the string controls what users can enter in that column of the field. Table 9-2 shows the available template symbols. These are the same template symbols available for reports and labels.

For example, suppose you want to create a field for telephone numbers. If you specify (999)999-9999 for the template, the field appears with the parentheses and dashes already in place, and dBASE IV allows you to enter only numbers (due to the "9" templates). If the user types **6177958234**, dBASE IV automatically converts the input to (617)795-8234. Here are some other template examples.

Template Symbol	Effect on Entry or Display
!	Converts letters to uppercase; has no effect on other characters
#	Allows only digits, blanks, and signs
$	Displays the current SET CURRENCY string in place of leading zeros. The default SET CURRENCY string is $
*	Displays asterisks (*) in place of leading zeros
,	Displays commas in large numbers
.	Indicates the position of the decimal point
9	Allows digits only for character data. Allows digits and signs for numeric data
A	Data must be letters only
L	Data must be logical (T, F, Y, or N)
N	Allows letters and digits
X	Data can be any character
Y	For a character or logical field, data must be logical (Y, y, N, or n). Converts y and n to uppercase

Table 9-2. dBASE IV Template Symbols

- $9,999.99 allows you to enter numbers only, displays leading zeros as dollar signs ($), and shows a comma if the number is greater than 999.99. For example, if you type **1234.5,** dBASE IV converts the entry to $1,234.50.

- !AA lets you enter a three-character string. The first character can be a letter or number, and if it is a letter, it is automatically converted to uppercase. The next two characters must be letters and are not converted to uppercase. For example, if you type **cgs**, dBASE IV converts the entry to Cgs.

dBASE IV automatically assigns the **Template** option setting for date fields, and you can't change this setting. However, if you want to change the way dBASE IV displays dates, you can use the **Date order** and the **Date separator** options from the **Settings** submenu in the **Tools** menu of the Control Center (see Chapter 14). You can also change the way dBASE IV displays dates by using the SET DATE command from the dot prompt (see Chapter 32).

To change the appearance of the data within fields, you can use the display attributes available in the **Display** option of the **Words** menu. For example, if you have a monochrome screen, you can display fields in bold or reverse video. If you have a color monitor, you can assign different colors to a field. See the section "Changing the Display Appearance."

Tip: In the Forms Design screen, if you locate the cursor on a number or character field and press SHIFT-F7, you can resize the field with the arrow keys. When the field is the desired size, press ENTER. dBASE IV automatically changes the template setting for the field. Because date fields are a fixed size, you cannot resize them using SHIFT-F7. (For more information on resizing memo fields, see the section "Modifying a Memo Field.")

Picture Functions

Picture functions let you define the overall template for a field by using attributes. *Attributes* are special field format options that control how fields display on the screen as the user enters data. For example, you can have the values in a numeric field appear in exponential (scientific) format or have the values in a character field appear all in uppercase.

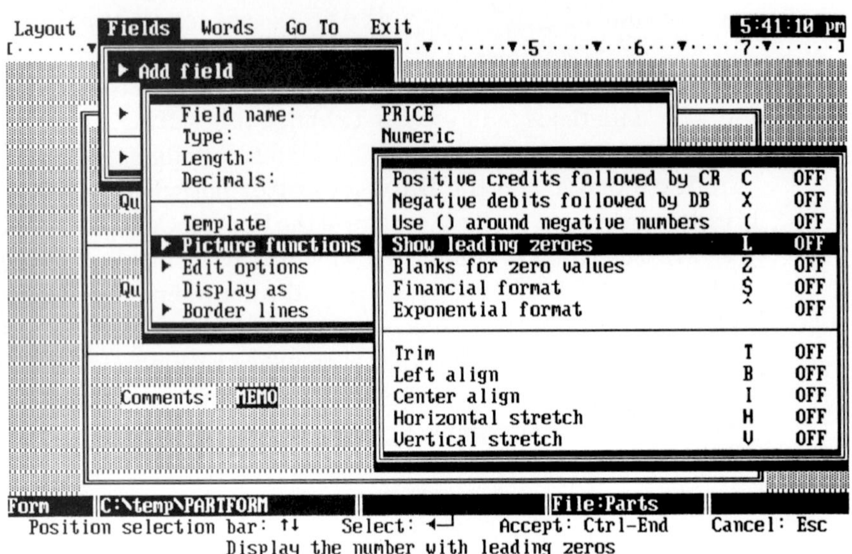

Figure 9-18. Numeric field picture functions

You choose the picture functions for a field by using the **Picture functions** option in the field description menu. The picture functions for numeric fields appear in Figure 9-18, and those for character fields appear in Figure 9-19. (Picture functions are not available for date, logical, and memo fields.) Table 9-3 lists and describes all of the available picture functions.

As the figures show, the attributes available for a field depend on the field's data type (whether numeric or character). They also depend on whether the selected field is an existing, calculated, or memory variable field. Unavailable attributes are not highlighted, and you can't select them from the menu.

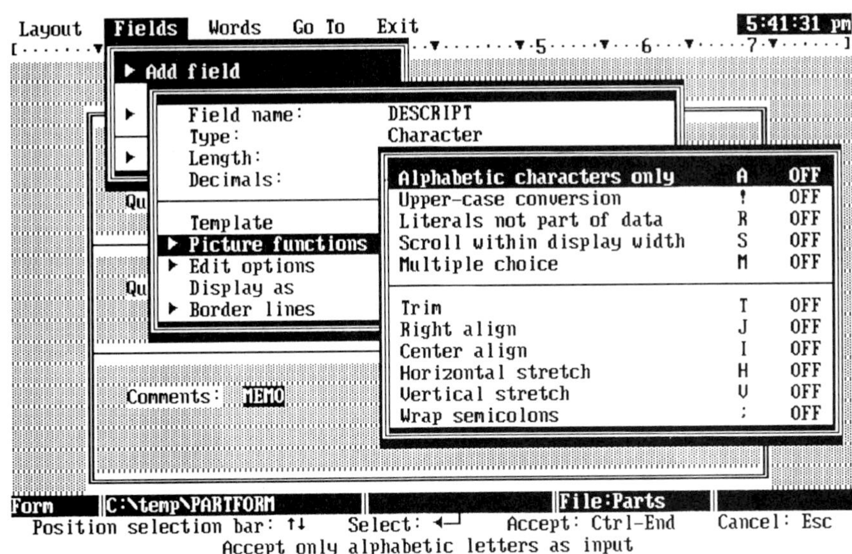

Figure 9-19. Character field picture functions

Note: Many of the listed but unavailable picture functions are used for reports and labels, not for forms. See Chapter 10, "Creating Reports," for more information.

To set a picture function for a field, move the highlight to the desired item and press ENTER to toggle the setting to ON.

Tip: You can set more than one picture function for a field. For example, to set a character field for alphabetic characters only *and* for uppercase conversion, toggle both the **A** and the **!** options to ON.

Picture Function	Effect on Display
!	Converts letters entered in a field to uppercase; does not affect other characters
^	Displays numbers in exponential format (scientific notation)
$	Displays data in financial (currency) format
(	Puts ( ) around negative numbers
A	Allows only letters to be entered in a field
B	Left-aligns a number
C	Displays CR (credit) after a positive number
I	Centers text and numbers within a field
J	Right-aligns text within a field
L	Displays leading zeros
M	Allows a multiple-choice list
R	Works in combination with a template to display literal characters in a field, but to remove those characters when the field is stored to disk. For example, a phone number is displayed as (415)325-1234, but is stored as 4153251234
S	Lets you scroll horizontally with long character fields. You must enter a number for the display width
T	Trims leading and trailing blanks from a field
X	Displays DB (debit) after a negative number
Z	Displays a blank string for a zero numeric value

Table 9-3. Picture Functions

When you've chosen the picture functions you want, press CTRL-END to lock them in and return to the field description menu.

The following three picture functions are particularly useful for creating forms because they affect how fields are displayed *and* how you can enter data:

- **A** Lets you enter only alphabetic characters in a character field. dBASE IV doesn't let you type numeric characters. What's more, if SET BELL is ON (the default), dBASE IV beeps each time you press a numeric key.

- **S** Allows horizontal scrolling on a wide character field. For example, suppose an existing character field is 20 characters wide and you use this attribute to set a width of 3. dBASE IV will display a field that is only 3 characters wide but will let you scroll within the field and enter a maximum of 20 characters.

- **M** Allows a multiple-choice list. The choices in the list can be numbers or strings and must be separated by commas. The first item in the list only appears when you move the cursor to that field. As you press the SPACEBAR, dBASE IV displays the additional items in the list. For example, if you enter **a,b,c** for the multiple choice list, dBASE IV displays "a" when you move the cursor to the field. If you press SPACEBAR, dBASE IV displays "b." Press SPACEBAR again and dBASE IV displays "c." Press ENTER to choose a value from the list.

Defining Edit Options

To set up specific limits for the values that a user can enter in a field, choose **Edit options** from the field description menu. Figure 9-20 shows the menu that appears. The options are as follows:

- **Editing allowed** If you want the user to be able to edit the values in field, leave this option set to YES. If you set this option to NO, the data in the field will display but the user can't modify it.

- **Permit edit if** Use this option to allow editing of the field only under certain conditions. When using this option, you must enter a dBASE IV expression. The expression is immediately evaluated when the user moves the cursor into the field. For example, Figure 9-20 uses the expression

  City="Santa Cruz" .OR. City="Soquel"

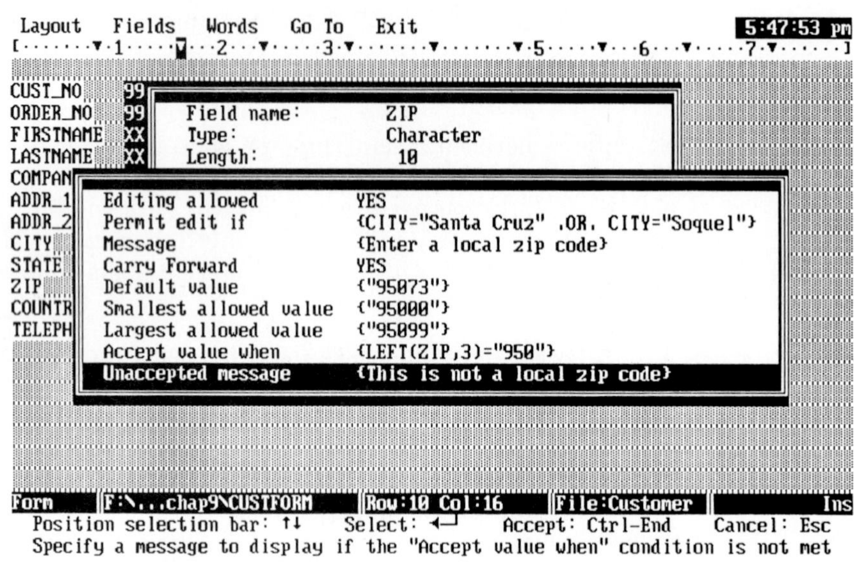

Figure 9-20. The **Edit options** menu

which permits editing of the Zip field only when the user enters **Santa Cruz** or **Soquel** for the City field.

- **Message** This option lets you place a message on the screen whenever the user moves the cursor into the field. For example, in Figure 9-20, the message "Enter a local zip code" appears when the user places the cursor in the Zip field.

- **Carry forward** If you want the value from the corresponding field in the previous record to appear in the current record, set this option to YES.

- **Default value** To have an initial value appear in the field when you add a new record, specify a value for this option. You can still modify the data if you want. For example, in Figure 9-20, the default value is 95073.

- **Smallest allowed value/Largest allowed value** Use these options to set a range for acceptable values. For example, Figure 9-20 allows entries from 95000 to 95099. If the user enters a value outside the range, dBASE IV displays the message "RANGE is 95000 to 95099 (press SPACE)."
- **Accept value when** Use this option to enter a dBASE IV expression that establishes the conditions under which data is accepted. For example, the expression in Figure 9-20 stipulates that the first three characters in the Zip field must be equal to 950. (For the example in Figure 9-20, the expression in this field is not really necessary because of the entries in the **Smallest allowed value** and **Largest allowed value** options.)
- **Unaccepted message** This option lets you specify the message that appears when the **Accept value when** conditions are not met.

When you've entered the editing options you want, press CTRL-END to save your changes and return to the field description menu.

Tip: The values you enter in the **Edit options** menu remain in effect when you switch from edit to browse mode.

Modifying Fields

To modify the characteristics of any field you've added to a form, locate the cursor anywhere within the field and select the **Modify field** option from the **Fields** menu. You can then change the field description menu. After you have made all the modifications you want, press CTRL-END to save your changes and return to the work surface.

Tip: Rather than using the menu system to add or modify a field, you can press F5 or CTRL-HOME. If you've located the cursor within a field, the field description screen for that field will appear. Otherwise, you get a menu that allows you to select an existing field or create a new calculated field.

Deleting Fields

To delete a field from a form, simply delete it from the work surface. Locate the cursor anywhere within the field and select the **Remove field** option from the **Fields** menu, or press DEL.

Memo Windows

When you use the default edit screen to modify your data, dBASE IV "zooms" the display to occupy the full screen if you press CTRL-HOME to add or modify text in a memo field. You then have plenty of room to enter and edit memo-field text, but you can't see the rest of your data.

When you design custom forms, you can expand memo fields to appear as *memo windows.* Memo windows usually occupy less space than a zoomed full-screen memo field, but still let you see the rest of your data.

There are two ways you can display a memo field in a form: as a memo marker or as a memo window. If you display the memo field as a memo marker and the memo field contains text, it appears as "MEMO" on the screen. It appears as "memo" when the memo field is empty. If you press CTRL-HOME, the memo field expands to fill the memo window you've defined (usually less than the full screen). You can also display a memo field as an open memo window (already expanded). In this case, the memo field is called a *static memo window*.

With static memo windows, you can have the text in the memo field appear in the form without having to expand the window, and the user can see the information immediately. However, static memo windows often require a substantial amount of space on the screen and can slow down scrolling between records.

Regardless of how you display a memo field, if you locate the cursor in the memo field while you're editing data and press CTRL-HOME to add or edit text in the memo, the memo field expands to fill the memo window. Then, when you press CTRL-END to save your memo text, the memo field contracts to its original size on the screen.

Adding a Memo Window to a Form

Adding a memo window to a form is like adding any other type of field, but the field description menu options are slightly different. Figure 9-21 shows the field description menu for a memo field, which lets you access two additional options: **Display as** and **Border lines**.

The **Display as** option lets you toggle between MARKER and WINDOW (press ENTER to toggle). Choosing MARKER (the default) lets you display the memo field as a standard four-character memo field marker. Choosing WINDOW, on the other hand, lets you display the memo as a static memo window.

Whichever setting you choose, when you press CTRL-END to save the field description settings, dBASE IV returns you to the work surface with the cursor located at its most recent position. You must then define the bounds of the memo window that opens when you use the memo field. Move the cursor to the location for

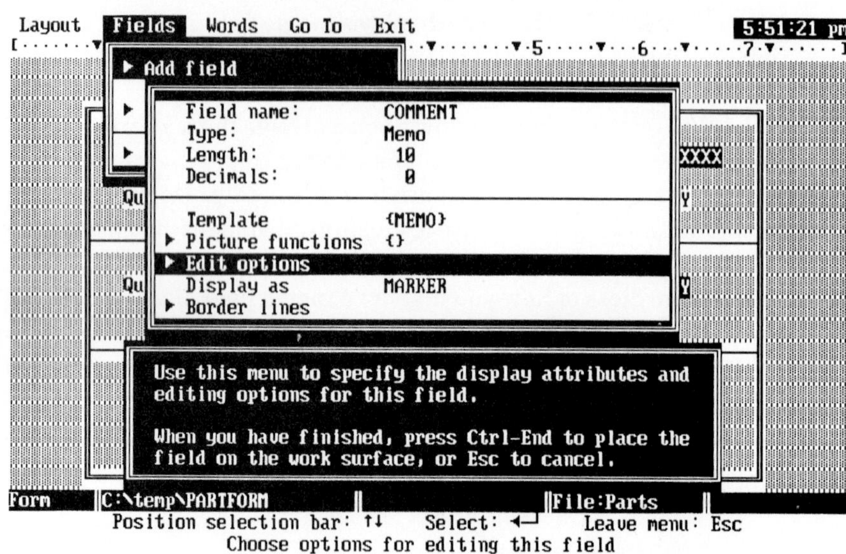

Figure 9-21. Field description menu for a memo field

the upper-left corner of the memo window and press ENTER. Next, position the cursor where you want the lower-right corner and press ENTER. dBASE IV creates a temporary window and expands its box as you move the cursor, as in Figure 9-22.

Tip: Always make your memo windows at least two lines deep. If you make them only one line deep, the ruler line fills the window when the user presses CTRL-HOME to enter memo text, and no editing is possible.

After you've pressed ENTER for the second time to define the bounds of the memo window, dBASE IV reacts in one of two ways, depending on whether you chose WINDOW or MARKER.

- If you chose the WINDOW setting, dBASE IV displays a finished memo window in place of the temporary memo window.

- If you chose the MARKER setting, dBASE IV keeps the temporary window on the screen and moves the cursor to the upper-left corner of the window. You must then position the cursor where you want the left side of the memo marker to appear (you can choose any location on the work surface). Press ENTER to lock in the position, and the temporary window disappears. The memo marker appears at the cursor position.

The **Border lines** option lets you define the border for a memo window. You can choose **Single line**, **Double line**, or **Using specified character**—the options that appear when you select

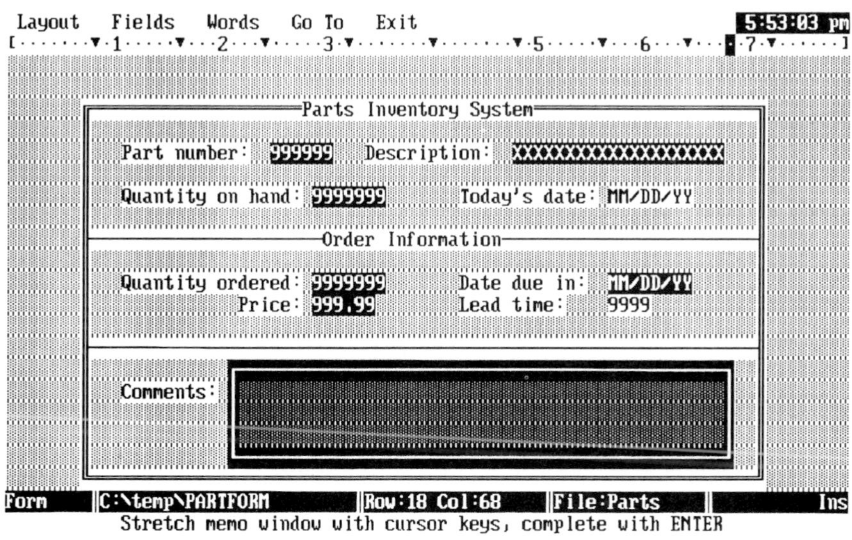

Figure 9-22. Defining the window bounds when adding a memo field

Line or **Box** from the **Layout** menu. (See the sections "Adding Boxes" and "Adding Lines.")

Modifying a Memo Field

You delete, copy, and move a static memory window or memo marker as you do any other type of field (see "Modifying Fields" and "Deleting Fields"). You cannot, however, resize a memo marker, because it has a fixed size on the screen (four characters).

To change the position or resize the memo window that appears when you use a memo field, follow these steps:

1. Position the cursor inside the memo marker or static memo window.

2. Press CTRL-HOME to display a temporary window that contains the current size and location of the memo field window.

3. Press F7 and use the arrow keys to move the window on the screen.

4. To resize the window, press SHIFT-F7. dBASE IV automatically relocates the cursor to the lower-right corner of the temporary window. Use the arrow keys to expand and contract the window from the right corner. (Repeat step 3 if you want to change the location of the upper-left corner of the window.)

5. Press CTRL-END to lock in the new size and return to the work surface.

Tip: When you're resizing the window that will be used for a memo field marker, don't move the cursor outside the bounds of the temporary window without first pressing F7 or SHIFT-F7. If you do, dBASE IV will beep and shrink the temporary window back down to the memo field marker.

Changing the Display Appearance

When you create a customized form, you can assign colors to text, fields, or boxes by using the **Display** option in the **Words** menu. The colors display when you use the form to modify your data. A color you assign to a field applies to all of the text that appears within the field.

Note: The **Display** option in the **Words** menu is like the **Display** option in the **Settings** submenu of the Control Center's **Tools** menu. For more information on this option, see Chapter 14, "Tools."

Before you can assign a color to an existing item on the screen, you must place the cursor anywhere within the item. For example, you can place the cursor on a field, box, or character. (You can also use F6 to select a group of characters to which you want to assign a color.) You can then use the **Display** option from the **Words** menu.

Besides assigning colors to existing material on the screen, you can assign colors to items that you will later place on the screen. Use the **Display** option from the **Words** menu to assign a color. When you add items later (such as boxes, lines, and text), dBASE IV will display them using the assigned color.

When you start up dBASE IV, it automatically senses your display type and sets the colors accordingly. It also uses this information to establish what colors you can assign to different objects on the screen, presenting a different **Display** menu for monochrome and color screens.

Note: If you're developing an application that will be used on a wide variety of machines, don't use the **Display** option in the **Words** menu to assign colors to your forms. You may create a form that cannot be displayed on both color and monochrome screens.

Monochrome Display

If your machine has a monochrome screen, dBASE IV shows four display attribute options when you select the **Display** option from the **Words** menu. You can use these options to change the display of the currently selected item.

- **Intensity** Lets you establish boldfaced, or highlighted, items.
- **Underline** Lets you underline text on the screen. (You can also underline other items, such as boxes, but the results are not very useful.)
- **Reverse video** Swaps the foreground and background colors. For example, on an amber monitor, you see black letters on a yellow background.
- **Blink** Lets you have an item flash on and off. Avoid this attribute unless you really want the user's attention.

Color Display

If you have a color monitor, dBASE IV lets you assign different colors to the foreground and background of a selected item. You can choose one of 16 different foreground colors and one of 8 different background colors. You can also have an item blink on the screen.

When you select the **Display** option from the **Words** menu, dBASE IV displays two columns of colors: a Foreground column and a Background column. In the Foreground column, each of the 16 available colors is displayed in its own color (for instance, **Red** is displayed as red and **Blue** as blue). dBASE IV displays these foreground colors against the currently selected background color (the color you've chosen from the Background column, which is black when you access the menu for the first time). In the Background column, dBASE IV lists the 8 available background colors. Each item in this column appears in the currently selected foreground color.

As you move around in the columns, dBASE IV changes the colors of the Foreground column, displaying the effect of your choice.

To navigate in the columns, use the UP and DOWN ARROW keys to move within a column and the LEFT and RIGHT ARROW keys to move between columns. To have an item blink, press B from anywhere in either column. Press CTRL-END to save your selection.

Suppose you want blue text to appear on a green background. From the **Display** menu, move the highlight to the **Blue** option in the Foreground column. Next, press the RIGHT ARROW key to move to the Background column. Use the DOWN ARROW key to select the **Green** option from this column. To save your choices and return to the work surface, press CTRL-END.

Changing the Position of Text and Fields

The **Position** option in the **Words** menu lets you realign your text and fields relative to the current margin settings for the word wrap ruler. The options are **Left**, **Centered**, and **Right**.

When you reposition material, dBASE IV behaves differently, depending on whether you've selected only one character or more than one character (you select material by pressing F6 and highlighting what you want).

- If you select only one character on the line, dBASE IV realigns all of the material on the line relative to the margin settings. The top half of Figure 9-23 shows some examples. Field1 is left-aligned, Field2 is centered, and Field3 is right-aligned within the margins. In all cases, you select only one character on the line before selecting the **Position** option from the **Words** menu and then the **Left**, **Centered**, or **Right** option.

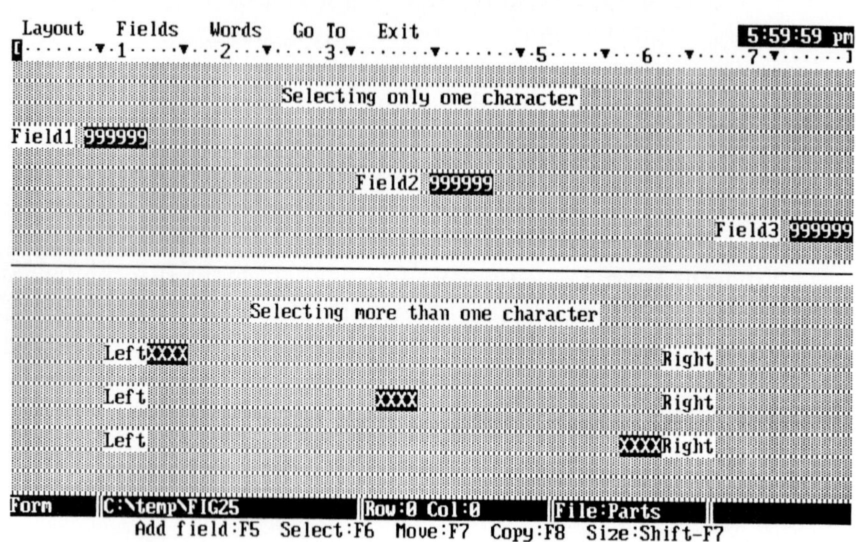

Figure 9-23. The effects of repositioning text

- If you select more than one character, dBASE IV finds the nearest text or field to the left and right and realigns the material between them. The bottom half of Figure 9-23 shows some examples. To create the first example, select the field template **XXXX** before choosing the **Position** option from the **Words** menu and then the **Left** option. Notice that dBASE IV aligns the XXXX between the text on the left (Left) and the text on the right (Right). To create the next two examples, perform the same steps, substituting the **Center** and **Right** options, respectively.

Modifying the Word Wrap Ruler

When you select the **Modify ruler** option in the **Words** menu, dBASE IV moves the cursor to the ruler line. You can then change the left and right margins, the paragraph indention, and the tab stops.

To navigate within the ruler, you can use any of the following keys:

- The cursor keys or the SPACEBAR.
- CTRL-← and CTRL-→ to move the cursor left and right eight spaces.
- TAB and SHIFT-TAB to move the cursor left and right one tab stop at a time.
- END and HOME to move the cursor to the right or left edge of that section of the ruler which appears on the screen. If you press END from the right edge of the screen, dBASE IV displays the next section of the ruler. Similarly, if you press HOME from the left edge of the screen, dBASE IV displays the previous section of the ruler.

To change the setting for the left margin, enter [where you want the left margin located. To change the setting for the right margin, enter] where you want the right margin. To reset the margins to their original settings, enter **0** anywhere on the line. Table 9-4 shows the widths for the word wrap editor in different settings.

Object	**Width (in characters)**
Forms Design screen	65
Reports and Labels Design screens	255 (variable)
Program editor (MODIFY COMMAND)	1,024
Text Editor (MODIFY FILE)	1,024
Zoom Editor (dot and SQL prompt)	80
Macro Editor	80

Table 9-4. Widths for the Word Wrap Editor

To set the paragraph indention for report bands (in the Reports Design screen) enter **#** where you want the indention. Keep in mind that you enter the **#** character relative to the left margin (the [character), and if you move the left margin, the indention character moves automatically.

To set a tab, type **!** where you want the tab. Tabs appear in the line as triangles. To set tabs at a specific interval, type **=**. Then, when prompted, enter the interval you want between tab stops. By entering **0** for the interval, you can create a ruler without any tab stops.

To remove margins, indentions, and tabs, use the DEL or BACKSPACE key.

To exit from the ruler, press CTRL-END or ENTER to accept the changes you've made. Press ESC to abandon the changes.

Tip: You can only change the ruler from the Forms, Reports, and Labels Design screens. You cannot change it when editing memo fields, programs, or text files. In these cases, dBASE IV uses the default settings for tab stops. You can change the default tab settings by changing the TABS setting in your CONFIG.DB file (see Chapter 35).

Saving a Form

To save the current form, use the **Save this form** option from the **Layout** menu. dBASE IV then prompts you for an eight-character file name for the form's files. dBASE actually creates three different files for the form: an .SCR, an .FMO, and an .FMT file (see "The Different Types of Form Files").

To save your form and return to the Control Center (or the dot prompt, depending on where you started from), perform any one of the following:

- Press CTRL-W
- Press CTRL-END
- Select **Save changes and exit** from the **Exit** menu

Tip: To see the code that dBASE IV generates when you save your form, you can SET INSTRUCT to OFF and SET TALK to ON.

Using a Form to Edit Data

After you've created a custom form in the Forms Design screen, you can easily use the form to modify your data. From the Control Center, highlight the name of the form in the Forms Panel and press ENTER. dBASE IV displays two menu options: **Display data** and **Modify form**. Select the **Display data** option to enter edit mode, where you can modify your database. (Use the **Modify form** option when you want to modify your form in the Forms Design screen.)

Note: If you used an existing database when you created your form, you don't have to open the database before selecting the form in the Forms Panel. dBASE IV automatically makes the connection between the form and the database.

To activate a custom form from the dot prompt, use the SET FORMAT command. For example, you can use the following commands to open the PARTS database and edit records in that database using a custom form named Partform:

```
. USE Parts
. SET FORMAT TO Partform
. EDIT
```

When you enter the **SET FORMAT** command to activate a custom form, dBASE IV uses that form to display database fields for all full-screen editing commands. These commands include READ, EDIT, APPEND, INSERT, and CHANGE. (See Chapter 19 on how to use a format file in a program.)

In this chapter, you have learned how to create custom forms using the Forms Design screen. You now know how to start with a quick layout and then use the various tools available for rearranging fields and other design elements. You now can also create boxes and lines to focus attention on a particular area of the screen. What's more, you can create calculated fields and memo windows to enhance the appearance of your form. You can also modify a field's display and set specific limits for the values that can be entered in a field. By applying the knowledge you've gained from this chapter, you can create a wide variety of custom forms.

Creating Reports

TEN

The Reports Design Screen
The Different Types of Report Files
Accessing the Reports Design Screen
The Two Editing Modes—Word Wrap and Layout
The Elements of Reports
Basic Bands
Entering a Quick Layout
Modifying the Contents of Basic Bands
Group Bands
Adding Fields
Field Templates
Picture Functions
Suppressing Repeated Values
Controlling the Style of Text
Creating Form Letters
Saving a Report
Printing Reports

In dBASE IV, there are many easy ways to enter information into a database (for example, EDIT, BROWSE, CHANGE, APPEND) but few easy ways to get information out in printed form. The reason, of course, is that nearly every printed report is unique. In fact, almost as soon as you start building a dBASE IV application, you'll need to create your own custom reports.

This chapter discusses the various aspects of creating reports from the Reports Design screen. First, it explains how to create a quick report layout. Next, it discusses the different elements of reports, including the various types of report bands. It then describes how to add fields to a report. Finally, it shows you how to create form letters.

To print reports and labels, you use the **Print** menu in the Reports Design and Labels Design screens. The **Print** menu is discussed in detail in the next chapter.

You can also use SHIFT-F9 (Quick Report) to print a simple report with the same format as the **Column layout** option in the **Layout** menu's **Quick layouts** option (discussed later). This "quick report" format shows field names for column headings, prints every record in the database, and shows a sum for every numeric field at the end of the report. You can use SHIFT-F9 to print a quick report from the edit and browse modes as well as the Queries Design screen. SHIFT-F9 is also discussed in detail in Chapter 12, "Printing."

Tip: To familiarize yourself with the quick report format, try using SHIFT-F9 with one of your databases (or one of dBASE IV's sample databases in the DBASE\SAMPLES directory).

The Reports Design Screen

Because of the new Reports Design screen, creating custom reports in dBASE IV is substantially easier than in earlier versions of dBASE. For example, in dBASE III PLUS, you could use the report generator to create custom reports, but it was difficult to print subtotals and to control headings and pagination. In the dBASE IV Reports Design screen, all of these options, and more, are built in.

Using the Reports Design screen, you can

- Control the layout and overall appearance of a report
- Split your data into related groups
- Limit a report to specific records and fields
- Control pagination automatically
- Merge field data and standard text
- Perform calculations on your data (for example, averages, counts, totals, and subtotals)

The Different Types of Report Files

dBASE IV uses three different types of report files: .FRM, .FRG, and .FRO files.

- **.FRM file** A *report form file* that contains the instructions dBASE IV needs to display a report design in the Reports Design screen. (.FRM files are stored in a special non-ASCII format.) When you create or modify a report by using the Reports Design screen, you're actually working with an .FRM file. If you delete the .FRM file, you will not be able to modify the report in the Reports Design screen.
- **.FRG file** A *generated report form file* that contains the standard dBASE IV program code (for example, ?, ??, PRINTJOB, and ENDPRINTJOB commands). This code is generated when you save a report in the Reports Design screen (see the section "Saving a Report").

- **.FRO file** A *report form object file* that is the compiled version of an .FRG file. This is the actual object file that dBASE IV creates and reads when you print output with a report. dBASE IV automatically generates an .FRO file from the .FRG file when you print the report (see the section "Printing Reports" later in this chapter).

Accessing the Reports Design Screen

You can access the Reports Design screen from the Control Center or the dot prompt. The procedures are slightly different depending on whether you want to create a new report or modify an existing one.

From the Control Center

To create a new report from the Control Center, first open a database file or view. (To open a database, highlight its file name in the Data Panel, press ENTER, and then select the **Use file** option.) Next, choose the **<create>** option from the Reports Panel.

To modify an existing report from the Control Center, select the report's name in the Reports Panel and press ENTER. Next, select the **Modify layout** option.

Tip: The quickest way to access the Reports Design screen from the Control Center is to highlight the report (or the **<create>** option) in the Reports Panel and press SHIFT-F2.

From the Dot Prompt

To access the Reports Design screen from the dot prompt, use the CREATE REPORT or MODIFY REPORT command. For example, to activate the Reports Design screen and create a report form (.FRM) file called LIST1, enter

```
. CREATE REPORT List1
```

The MODIFY and CREATE forms of the command verb are identical. If the .FRM file exists, the command modifies it. If it does not exist, the command automatically creates one.

As with the Control Center, if you're building a report from scratch, you should open a database file before activating the Reports Design screen. This way, you can easily reference the database's fields within the report. For example, to open a database called SALARY and activate the Reports Design screen with a report called PAYDAY, enter

```
. USE Salary
. MODIFY REPORT Payday
```

The Two Editing Modes—Word Wrap and Layout

The dBASE IV Text Editor has two different modes of operation in the Reports Design Screen: word wrap mode and layout mode.

Like a traditional word processor, *word wrap mode* wraps to a new line when you reach the right margin. You can use word wrap mode to place paragraphs of text in a report and to create form letters.

Layout mode is for entering nontextual elements such as fields, boxes, and lines. In layout mode, you can, for example, place fields on the work surface and then move them to different locations. Layout mode is the more common of the two modes.

Note: When you design a report, you can't place double quotes (") on the Reports Design screen because they interfere with the program code that dBASE IV generates when it creates the generated report form (.FRG) file. You can, however, place single quotes (') in a report.

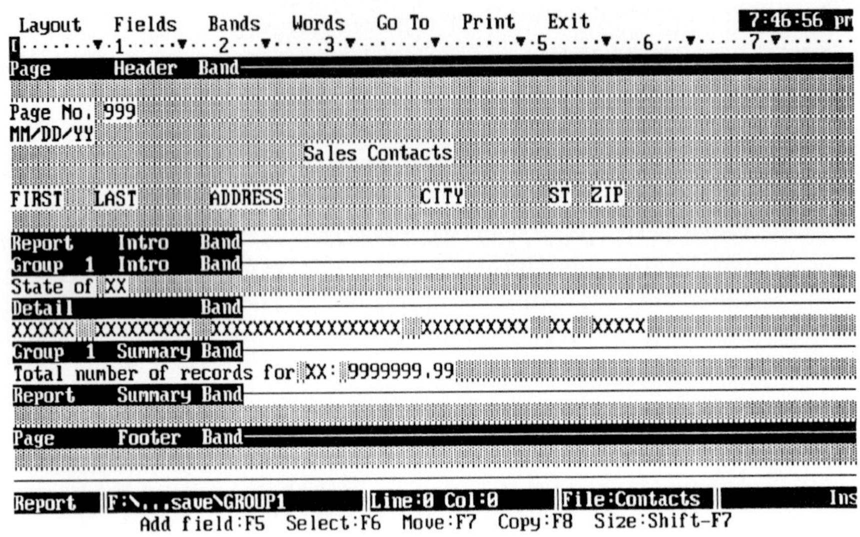

Figure 10-1. An example report in the Reports Design screen

The Elements of Reports

The work surface of the Reports Design screen uses a special formatting device called *report bands.* These bands separate a report into different parts and display those parts in a symbolic format. With report bands, you can see more of the report on the screen and how the different parts of a report relate to one another.

Besides report bands, other report design elements are

- Fields from a database file or view
- Special calculated fields that are not in the database but which you create for the report
- Lines and boxes
- Your own text

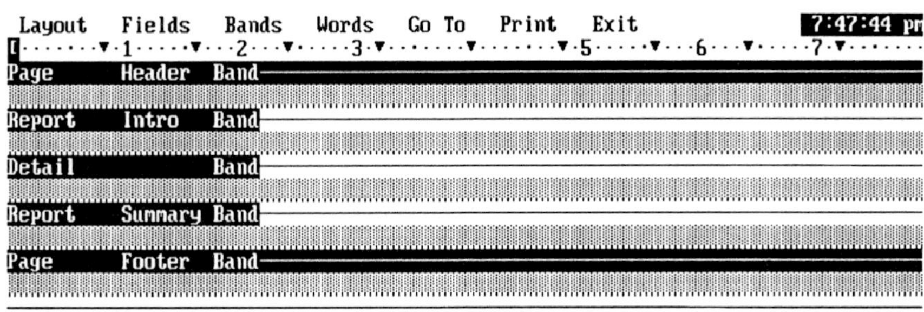

Figure 10-2. The initial Reports Design screen

Figure 10-1 shows an example report designed in the Reports Design screen.

Tip: As you design a report in the Reports Design screen, you can press F2 to switch to browse mode and view the data in the associated database. To get from browse mode back to the Reports Design screen, press SHIFT-F2.

Basic Bands

Figure 10-2 shows the screen that appears when you first access the Reports Design screen. (If you enter from the Control Center, press ESC to remove any automatically selected menus before you can see this screen.) The five report bands that appear in the Reports Design screen are found in all reports, and correspond to different sections of a report. The reports bands, and the sections to which they correspond, are as follows:

- **Page Header Band** The information between this band and the Report Intro Band makes up the page header. The *page header* is the area at the top of the page that contains information you want on each page of the report. For example, it may contain the page number, the date, column headings, and so on.

- **Report Intro Band** The material between this band and the next is the information that you want to appear at the beginning of the report. For example, it may contain the report title, an introductory paragraph (or group of paragraphs), or a cover letter.

- **Detail Band** The information below this band is the data from the records in the database file or view, the core of the report. For example, the Detail Band may contain customer numbers, company names, and shipping addresses. This band is different from the other bands because its components are repeated for every record in the database file or view.

- **Report Summary Band** The material below this band is information that you want to appear at the end of the report, such as totals and summary paragraphs.

- **Page Footer Band** This band functions like the Page Header Band, but the material below it appears at the bottom rather than the top of the page.

You can use a band in layout or word wrap mode. However, you can't set a band for both modes at once. For example, if you were entering a cover letter in the Report Intro Band, you would set that band for word wrap mode. Conversely, if you were entering the fields for a columnar report in the Detail Band, you would select layout mode.

When you're building reports in the Reports Design screen, you will most often use layout mode for your bands. Layout works well for entering fields in a band and rearranging the fields on the work surface. When you create form letters, however, dBASE IV automatically sets the Detail Band to word wrap mode. This mode is appropriate for form letters because you want your text to automatically reformat at print time. (You create form letters using the **Mailmerge layout** option in the **Quick layouts** menu. See the section "Creating Form Letters.")

Entering a Quick Layout

When you select the **<create>** option from the Reports Panel in the Control Center, dBASE IV takes you to the Reports Design screen and automatically highlights the **Quick layouts** option in the **Layout** menu. You can use this option to enter all of the fields from a database into a report quickly. You can then modify the quick layout as desired to produce a custom report.

The three types of quick layouts—column layout, form layout, and mailmerge layout—are described in the sections that follow.

Column Layout

If you select the **Column layout** option from the **Quick layouts** menu, dBASE IV creates a report layout identical to the "quick report" format. (As mentioned, you can get a quick report by pressing SHIFT-F9 from browse or edit mode.) The column layout format has the following characteristics:

- All of the field names in the current database (or view) are placed in a single row below the Page Header Band. The field names serve as column headers for the data below. In addition, a blank line appears below the field names to separate them from the data.

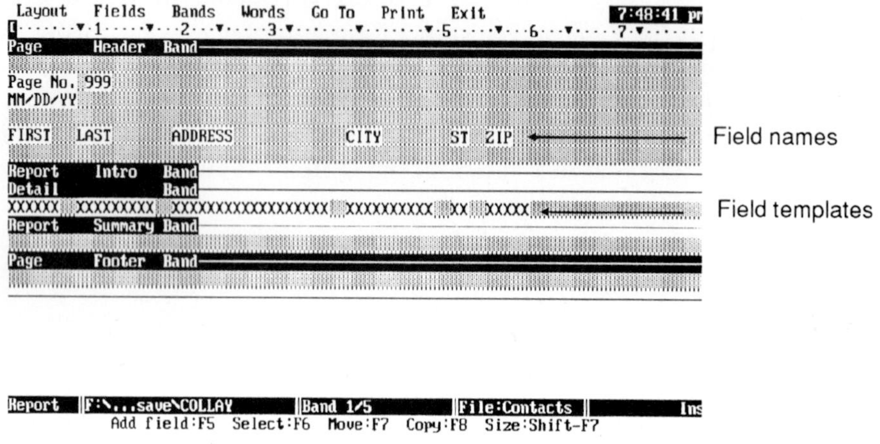

Figure 10-3. The **Column Layout** format

- The page number and date appear at the top of the Page Header Band.
- All of the field templates appear below the Detail Band. (For information on modifying field templates, see the section "Field Templates" later in this chapter.)
- dBASE IV places a template below the Report Summary Band for each numeric field in the current database. These templates produce and display a sum for every numeric field at the end of the report.

Figure 10-3 shows an example of the Reports Design screen when you select the **Column layout** option with the CONTACTS database active. Figure 10-4 shows some of the printed results.

Page No. 1
02/07/89

FIRST	LAST	ADDRESS	CITY	ST	ZIP
George	Mapels	221 Texasville Way	Dallas	TX	56902
Dick	Thoman	1234 Primrose Lane	Sunnyvale	CA	94086
Paul	Thomas	890 Circle Street	Fort Worth	TX	76129
Jerry	Gibson	876 Bradford Drive	Albany	NY	12237
Ron	Woods	6711 Waites Street	Vienna	VA	22180
David	Owen	9001 Frost Way	Providence	RI	02908
Keith	Davis	512 Blackhawk Avenue	San Jose	CA	95129
Kim	Tiernan	7950 Park Avenue	Soquel	CA	95073
Diana	Humphrey	1000 Frontage Road	Freedom	CA	95066
Steve	Zakon	36800 Luau Lane	Honolulu	HA	96815
Adene	Jones	2948 Drake Road	Felton	CA	95051
Mary	Powell	9743 Pine Avenue	Cambridge	MA	02142
Andrew	McCarthy	640 Nashua Court	Larkspur	CA	94964
Nathan	Bullock	43000 Rainbow Rd.	Redmond	WA	98052

Figure 10-4. Results of a column layout

Form Layout

If you select **Form layout** from the **Quick layouts** menu, you get a layout resembling dBASE IV's standard editing screen. A form layout has the following characteristics:

- Each field in the database appears on its own line in the Detail Band with the field name on the left-hand side of the screen and the field template immediately to the right.
- The Page Header Band contains only the page number and date, unlike column layout, where this band includes all the field names.

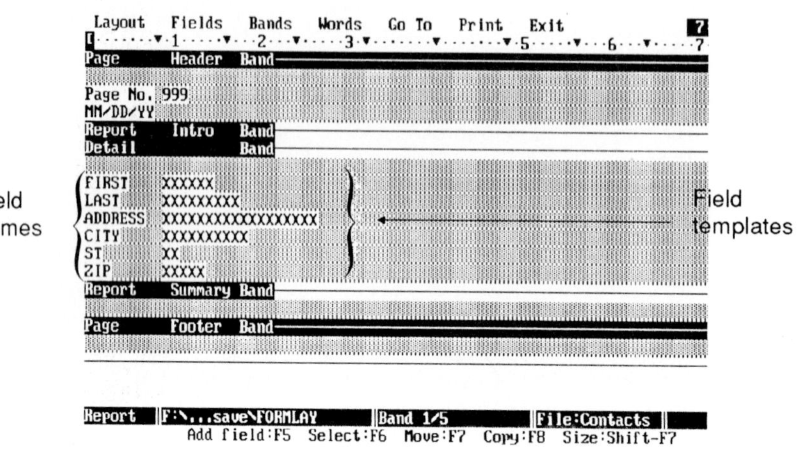

Figure 10-5. The **Form layout** format

Figure 10-5 shows an example of the form layout, and Figure 10-6 shows some results of printing with the report form.

Mailmerge Layout

If you select the **Mailmerge layout** option from the **Quick layouts** menu, dBASE IV enters a layout that is especially suited for printing form letters. For more on using this option, see the section "Creating Form Letters."

Modifying the Contents of Basic Bands

Once you've entered a quick layout in the Reports Design screen, you can easily modify the contents of the basic bands to suit your

```
Page No.   1
02/07/89

FIRST      George
LAST       Mapels
ADDRESS    221 Texasville Way
CITY       Dallas
ST         TX
ZIP        56902

FIRST      Dick
LAST       Thoman
ADDRESS    1234 Primrose Lane
CITY       Sunnyvale
ST         CA
ZIP        94086

FIRST      Paul
LAST       Thomas
ADDRESS    890  Circle Street
CITY       Fort Worth
ST         TX
ZIP        76129

FIRST      Jerry
LAST       Gibson
ADDRESS    876 Bradford Drive
CITY       Albany
ST         NY
ZIP        12237

FIRST      Ron
LAST       Woods
ADDRESS    6711 Waites Street
CITY       Vienna
ST         VA
ZIP        22180

FIRST      David
LAST       Owen
ADDRESS    9001 Frost Way
CITY       Providence
ST         RI
ZIP        02908

FIRST      Keith
LAST       Davis
ADDRESS    512 Blackhawk Ave.
CITY       San Jose
ST         CA
ZIP        95129

FIRST      Kim
LAST       Tiernan
ADDRESS    7950 Park Avenue
CITY       Soquel
ST         CA
ZIP        95073
```

Figure 10-6. The results of a form layout

needs. This section describes how you can modify the bands by adding and changing text, adding boxes and lines, and copying and moving design elements.

Adding and Changing Text

To add text to one of the basic bands, move the cursor to the desired location and type the text. For example, suppose you want to add the title "Customer Contacts List" to the quick report that appears in Figure 10-3. Move the cursor to the Page Header Band and type the title, as in Figure 10-7. Because the title is in the Page Header Band, it will appear on every page of the report.

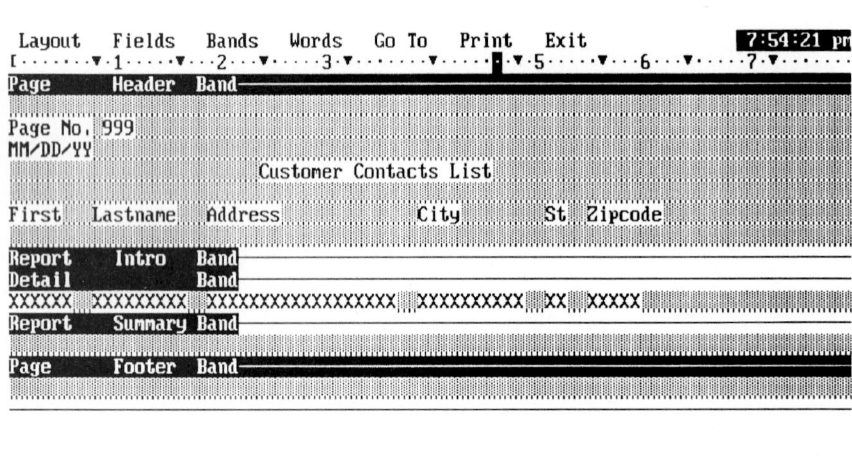

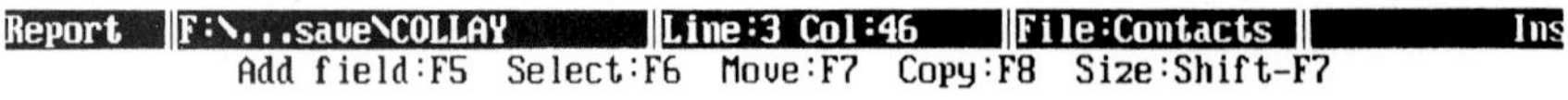

Figure 10-7. Adding text and modifying field names

Besides adding text, you can change text. For example, in Figure 10-7 the field names have been slightly changed from their original appearance in Figure 10-3.

Adding Boxes and Lines

To add boxes to a report, use the **Box** option from the **Layout** menu. To add lines, use the **Line** option from the same menu. (You can even add special characters using these options.) Placing boxes and lines in a report is like placing them in a form. See "Adding Lines" and "Adding Boxes" in Chapter 9, "Creating Input Forms."

Boxes and lines that you add to a report may appear quite smooth on the work surface but may appear rough when you print them, depending on your dBASE IV printer driver. For example, what looks like an uninterrupted line in the Reports Design screen may actually print as a series of dashes in your report.

Copying and Moving Design Elements

Table 10-1 shows the navigation and function keys you can use in the Reports Design screen. As indicated, to copy and move design elements on the work surface, you use F6 (Extend Select), F7 (Move), and F8 (Copy). You can use these keys to copy and move text, fields, boxes, lines, and so forth. Figure 10-8 shows the form layout from Figure 10-5 slightly rearranged.

Tip: As you're building a report in the Reports Design screen, you should periodically save your work, especially if you're new to the Reports Design screen. This way, you can always recover at least some of your work should you make a mistake that severely affects your report. To save your work, select **Save this report** from the **Layout** menu. (See the section "Saving a Report" that follows.)

Key	Effect
↓	Down one row
↑	Up one row
←	Left one character
→	Right one character
PGDN	Bottom of screen
PGUP	Top of screen
END	End of line
HOME	Beginning of line
BACKSPACE	Deletes character to the left
DEL	Deletes current character, or selected block or field
CTRL-N	Adds a line
CTRL-T	Deletes word to the right
CTRL-Y	Deletes current line
TAB	Moves to next tab stop
SHIFT-TAB	Moves to previous tab stop
F5	Adds a new field template or changes the one currently highlighted
F6	Selects blocks or fields
F7	Moves selected blocks or fields
F8	Copies selected blocks or fields
SHIFT-F7	Resizes the field template the cursor is in

Table 10-1. Keys for Designing Report and Label Forms

Group Bands

Besides the basic bands that appear in all reports, you can also use *group bands.* These are extra bands that you add to a report to organize records into groups.

You can group records in several ways. You can group them according to the value in a field (for example, all the records for a particular state), the value of an expression (for example, all the records for which the first three digits of the ZIP code are 900), or a record count (for example, every 20 records).

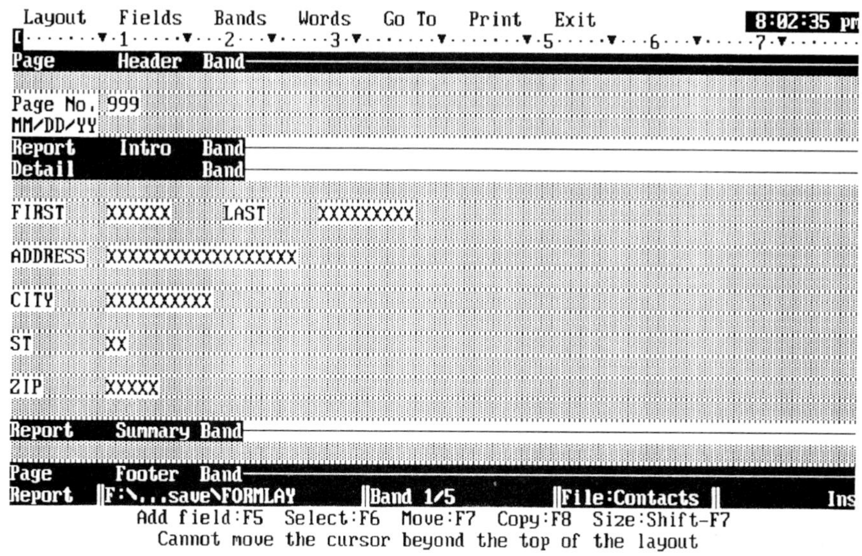

Figure 10-8. Results of moving fields

Organizing Your Database for Group Bands

To take advantage of group bands, you must first organize your database according to groups. That is, you must sort or index the database on the key field (or fields) on which the groups are based so that all the records belonging to a particular group are adjacent to one another.

For example, suppose you want to group your report according to the State field. To get the proper results, you need to first index (or sort) the database according to that field. Otherwise, the records will print randomly when you use the report.

Tip: A major reason to use group bands is to create subtotals. (See the section "An Example of Calculating Subtotals" later in this chapter.)

The Two Parts of Group Bands

There are actually two bands in a group band: a Group Intro Band and a Group Summary Band. The Group Intro Band usually contains two kinds of elements:

- Headings for the columns of information in the Detail Band
- Titles and other text that explain the contents of the group

A Group Summary Band, on the other hand, is most often used to show summary statistical information about a group. For example, you might show the total number of records in the group or the average, maximum, or minimum value for a field in the group. In fact, dBASE IV has seven special summary fields you can use in a Group Summary Band (or the Report Summary Band). They are

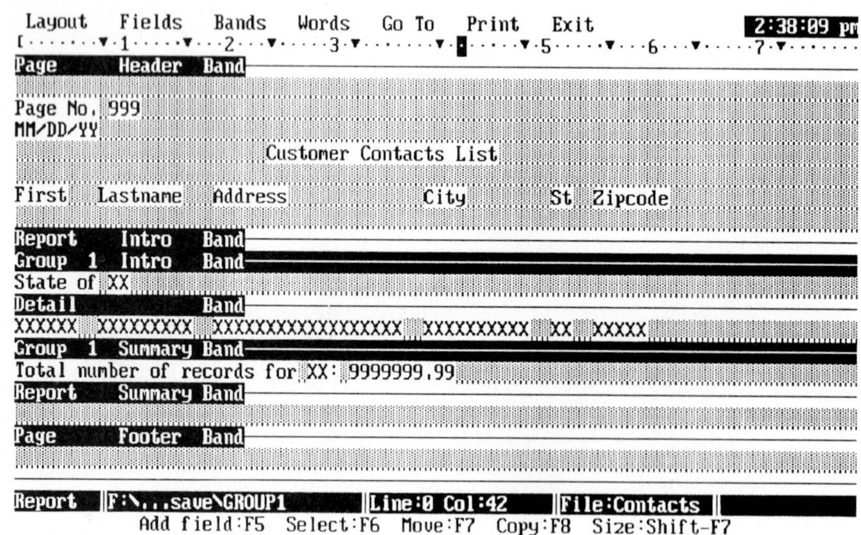

Figure 10-9. Group Intro and Group Summary Bands

Average

Count

Max (maximum)

Min (minimum)

Sum

Std (standard deviation)

Var (variance)

For more on using these special summary fields in a Group Summary Band, see the section "Adding a Summary Field" later in this chapter.

Figure 10-9 shows a group band for a report that prints records grouped by the State field. The title that appears in the Group Intro Band prints "State of" followed by the name of the state for each group in the report. (To create a Group Intro Band of this sort, you need to add the State field to the Group Intro Band. See the section "Adding Fields.") The Group Summary Band prints the string "Total number of records for" followed by the state and the number of records in that state. (To show the number of records in a group, you must add a special Count field.) Figure 10-10 shows some example results.

Adding a Group Band to a Report

To add a group band to a report, use the **Add a group band** option from the **Bands** menu. (Figure 10-11 shows the contents of the **Bands** menu.) When you select this option, dBASE IV displays three options: **Field value**, **Expression value**, and **Record count**. These options correspond to the three ways you can divide records into groups.

- **Field value** You can assign groups according to the value in a field. For example, when the information in the State field changes, you can assign the records that follow to a new group. In fact, you used this option to group records in Figure 10-9. When you select the **Field value** option,

```
Page No.  1
02/07/89
Customer Contacts List

First      Lastname    Address                        City        St      Zipcode

State of CA
Dick       Thoman      1234 Primrose Lane             Sunnyvale   CA      94086
Keith      Davis       512 Blackhawk Ave.             San Jose    CA      95129
Kim        Tiernan     7950 Park Avenue               Soquel      CA      95073
Diana      Humphrey    1000 Frontage Road             Freedom     CA      95066
Adene      Jones       2948 Drake Road                Felton      CA      95051
Andrew     McCarthy    640 Nashua Court               Larkspur    CA      94964
Total number of records for CA:           6.00
State of HA
Steve      Zakon       36800 Luau Lane                Honolulu    HA      96815
Total number of records for HA:           1.00
State of MA
Mary       Powell      9743 Pine Ave                  Cambridge   MA      02142
Total number of records for MA:           1.00
State of NY
Jerry      Gibson      876 Bradford Drive             Albany      NY      12237
Total number of records for NY:           1.00
State of RI
David      Owen        9001 Frost Way                 Providence  RI      02908
Total number of records for RI:           1.00
State of TX
George     Mapels      221 Texasville Way             Dallas      TX      56902
Paul       Thomas      890 Circle Street              Fort Worth  TX      76129
Total number of records for TX:           2.00
State of VA
Ron        Woods       6711 Waites Street             Vienna      VA      22180
Total number of records for VA:           1.00
State of WA
Nathan     Bullock     43000 Rainbow Rd.              Redmond     WA      98052
Total number of records for WA:           1.00
```

Figure 10-10. Results of the group band

dBASE IV always shows a list of the available fields from the active database file or view, as in Figure 10-12.

- **Expression value** You can assign records to a group based on the results of a dBASE IV expression. For example, you can extract the area code from a phone number field and assign records to a new group each time the area code changes. A typical expression you might enter to extract the area code is LEFT(PHONE,3).

Tip: You can press SHIFT-F1 to access the Expression Builder, which shows field names, logical and mathematical operators, and functions from which you can choose when building an expression.

- **Record Count** You can assign records to a group based on a record count. When you select this option, dBASE

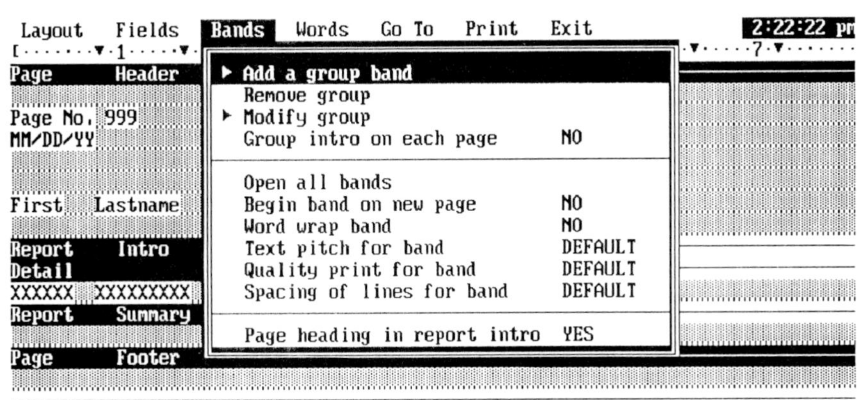

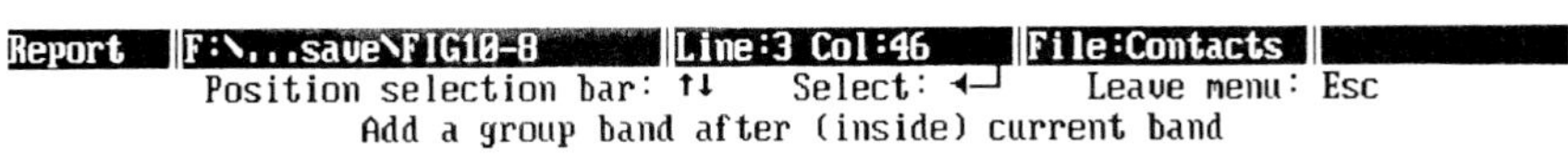

Figure 10-11. The **Bands** menu

prompts you to enter an integer. For example, to assign the first ten records to the first group, the next ten to the second group, and so on, you would enter ten in response to the prompt. If you like, you can combine the **Record count** option with the other two **Field value** options.

After you've entered a value for one of the options, press ENTER or CTRL-END to save the setting and return to the Reports Design screen.

Nesting Group Bands

Occasionally, you may want to nest one group band within another. Suppose you've created a group band based on the State field, and you want to group by city within each state.

To nest one group band within another, locate the cursor on the existing group's Group Intro Band and select **Add a group**

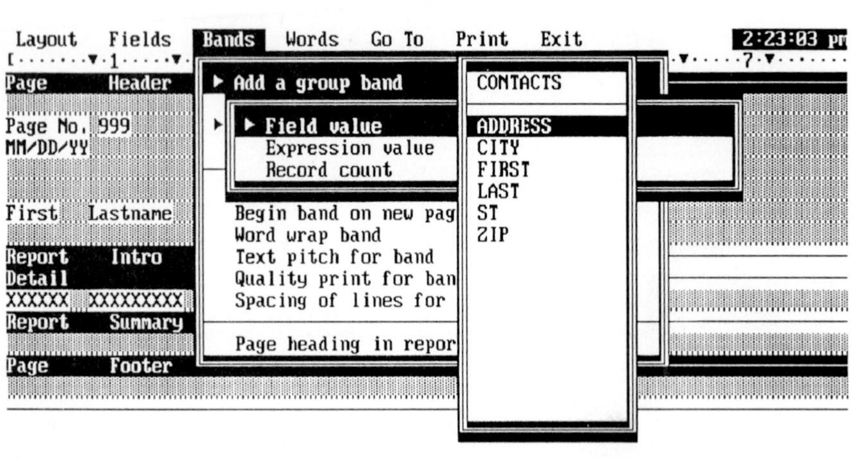

Figure 10-12. The **Field value** option in the **Bands** menu

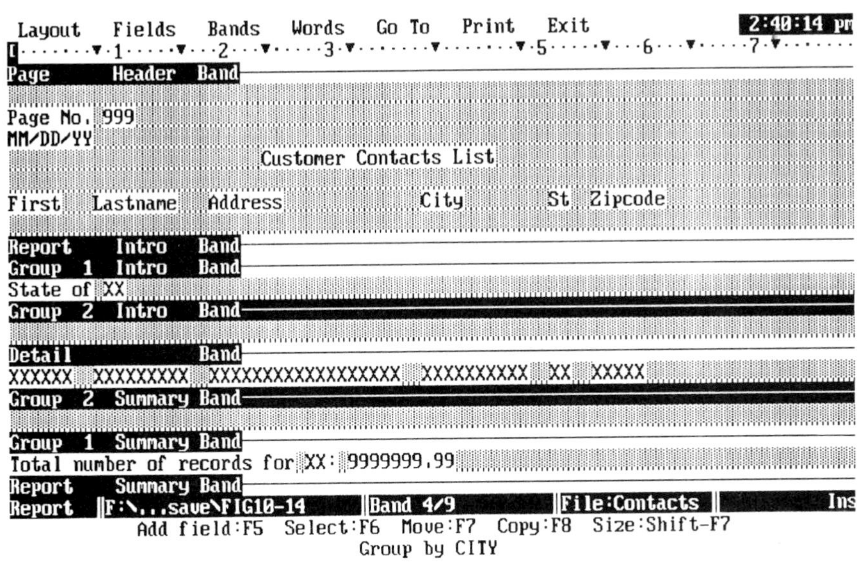

Figure 10-13. A City group band nested within a State group band

from the **Bands** menu. Next, select how you want to divide records into groups. For example, to group by city, select the **Field value** option and specify the City field. dBASE IV places a new group band within the existing group band, as in Figure 10-13.

To nest a group band outside another group band, locate the cursor above the existing group's Group Intro Band before selecting the **Add a group** option from the **Bands** menu. You might want to nest one band outside another, for example, when you want to group by Country and then by State.

In Figure 10-13, notice that dBASE IV has automatically labeled the outside band 1 and the inside band 2. If you nest another band within the level 2 band, say for a County field, it will be labeled 3. If, however, you place a group band outside of of the level 1 band, say for a Country field, all of the bands will be renumbered accordingly. That is, Country will be labeled 1, State 2, and City 3.

Note also that the Detail Band remains at the center of the report with all of the group bands placed around it. Therefore, dBASE IV won't let you add a group band with the cursor located in the Detail Band. You must locate the cursor outside of the Detail Band before adding a group band.

Note: If you nest group bands, you must index (or sort) your database to put it in the proper order for the grouping. For example, to group your data by city within each state, use a combination index expression such as State+City.

Removing a Group Band

To remove the current group, select the **Remove group** option from the **Bands** menu. dBASE IV asks you to confirm your choice and then removes the Group Intro and Group Summary Bands from the report.

A quicker way to remove a group is to locate the cursor on the Group Intro or Group Summary Band for a particular group and press DEL. After you confirm that you want the deletion, dBASE IV eliminates the band from the report and renumbers any remaining group bands accordingly.

Modifying a Group Band

Suppose you've added a group band to a report and you decide to change the field or expression on which the group is based. To modify a group band, select the **Modify group** option from the **Bands** menu. dBASE IV presents you with the same menu options as when you added the group band: **Field value**, **Expression value**, and **Record count**. To change the grouping method, select the appropriate option and enter a new value.

Repeating the Group Intro on Each Page

Normally, the material in the Group Intro Band appears only once in a report, that is, on the page where the group starts printing. However, if a group is rather large, you may want to repeat the Group Intro Band at the top of any succeeding pages. This would be convenient, for example, when the Group Intro Band contains column headings.

To repeat the Group Intro material, select the **Group intro on each page** option from the **Bands** menu and press ENTER to toggle the option from NO (the default) to YES.

Closing and Opening Bands

As mentioned, with report bands you can see more of the report on the screen. In fact, you can close or "collapse" a band so that text and other design elements within the band temporarily disappear from the screen. This way, you can focus on the contents of specific bands.

To close a band, place the cursor on the top border line of the band and press ENTER. To reopen the band, repeat the same steps.

To open all of the bands in a report (both report and group bands), select the **Open all bands** option from the **Bands** menu. dBASE IV does not have a counterpart to this command; you must close bands individually by using ENTER.

Note: If you close a band, it does not print because dBASE IV prints only open bands. You can, for example, design an intricate multilevel report and, by closing certain sections, print only those parts of the report that you need.

Beginning a Band on a New Page

Suppose you want to begin a group on a new page. Locate the cursor anywhere within the group's bands and select the **Begin band on new page** option from the **Bands** menu. When you select this option, dBASE IV places on a new page each set of records that constitutes a group.

Setting a Band for Word Wrap Mode

As mentioned, you can use either word wrap or layout mode in the Reports Design screen. Actually, most bands you enter in a report are automatically assigned layout mode. To change a band from layout mode to word wrap mode, select the **Word wrap band** option from the **Bands** menu and change the option from NO (layout) to YES (word wrap).

Note: When you select the **Mailmerge layout** option from the **Quick layouts** menu, dBASE IV automatically establishes the Detail Band as a word wrap band. (See the section "Creating Form Letters" later in this chapter.)

Controlling the Appearance of Text in a Band

The **Bands** menu has a few options for controlling the appearance and style of the text within a band. These options all work with options of similar names in the **Print** menu.

- **Text pitch for band** This option lets you control the text pitch for the current band (**Pica**, **Elite**, **Condensed**, or **Default**). It works with the **Text pitch** option in the **Control of printer** submenu of the **Print** menu. The **Print** menu controls the overall settings for a report, but you can set the text pitch for a particular band by using this option. If you choose the **Default** option, dBASE IV uses the **Print** menu settings.

- **Quality print for band** This option lets you control the quality of print for a band; choose **Yes** for near letter quality and **No** for draft. It works with the **Quality print** option in the **Control of printer** submenu of the **Print** menu. The **Print** menu controls the overall settings for a report, but you can set the quality of print for a particular band by using this option. If you choose the **Default** option, dBASE IV uses the **Print** menu settings.

- **Spacing of lines for band** This option lets you control the line spacing for a band (**Single**, **Double**, **Triple**, or **Default**). It works with the **Spacing of lines** option in the **Control of printer** submenu of the **Print** menu. The **Print** menu controls the overall settings for a report, but you can set the line spacing for a particular band by using this option. If you choose the **Default** option, dBASE IV uses the **Print** menu settings.

For more information on the **Print** menu options, see Chapter 12, "Printing."

Moving the Report Intro and Report Summary Bands

Suppose you're creating a report with a cover letter, but you don't want the information in the Page Header Band to appear at the top of the cover letter. Instead, you want the Page Header Band information to begin after the cover letter.

By selecting the **Page heading in report intro** option from the **Bands** menu and choosing **No**, you can have dBASE IV switch the position of the Report Intro Band and the Page Header Band. It also switches the position of the Report Summary Band and the Page Footer Band. Compare Figure 10-14 to Figure 10-13 to see how dBASE IV repositions the bands.

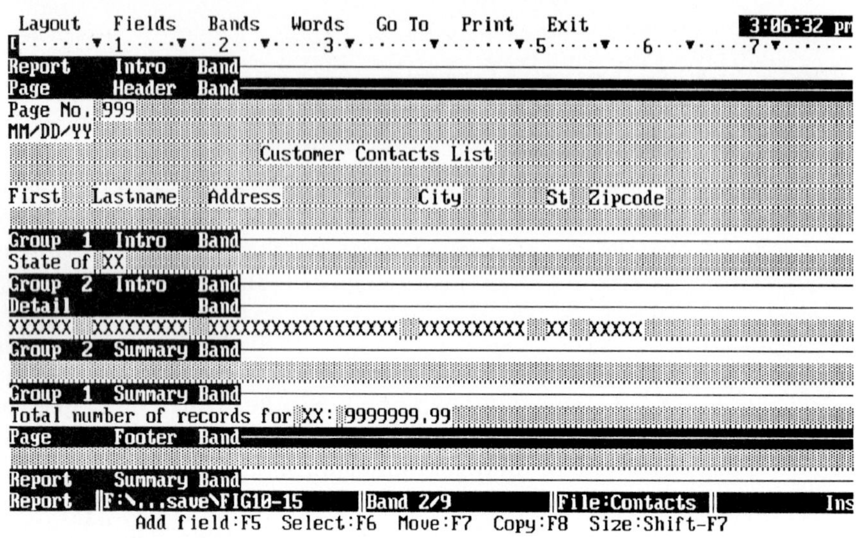

Figure 10-14. Effect of the **Page heading in report intro** option

Adding Fields

When building a custom report, you can add four different types of fields to the work surface: existing fields from the active database file or view, calculated fields that you create for the report, pre-defined fields, and summary fields. This section describes what these fields are and how you can add them to your report. It also describes how to customize a field's appearance.

Adding an Existing Field

An existing field is a field from the open database file or view. (If you haven't yet opened a database file or view, you can do so from within the Forms Design screen by choosing the **Use different**

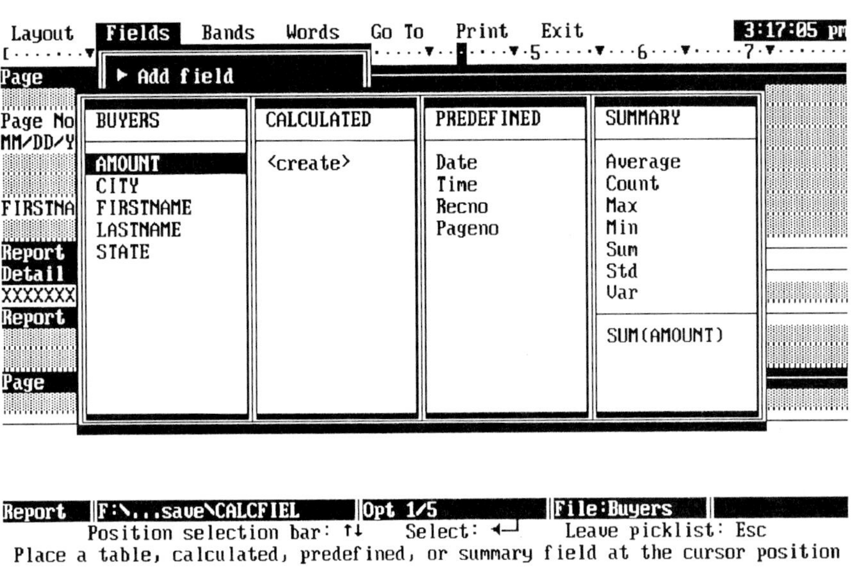

Figure 10-15. Adding a field

database file or view option from the **Layout** menu.) To add an existing field to the work surface, move the cursor to where you want the field to begin and select the **Add field** option from the **Fields** menu. Your screen should show a four-column list, as in Figure 10-15. The columns are as follows:

- The first column shows the existing field names from the current database file or view. (If the source of the fields is a view, this column shows the calculated fields from the view as well.)
- The second column shows the names of any calculated fields that you've defined for the form. To define a new calculated field, select the **<create>** option from this column (calculated fields are described later).

- The third column shows the names of four special *predefined fields* that dBASE IV creates automatically: Date, Time, Recno, and Pageno. The names of these fields are always the same. When you print a report, these fields show the current date, time, record number, and page number (predefined fields are described later).

- The fourth column has a list of generic *summary field* names: Average, Count, Max, Min, Sum, Std, and Var. Below this list of generic names is a list of specific summary field names already defined for the report (for example, SUM(AMOUNT)). (Summary fields are described later in this chapter.)

Tip: The quickest way to add a field to a report is to locate the cursor where you want the field to begin and press F5 (Field).

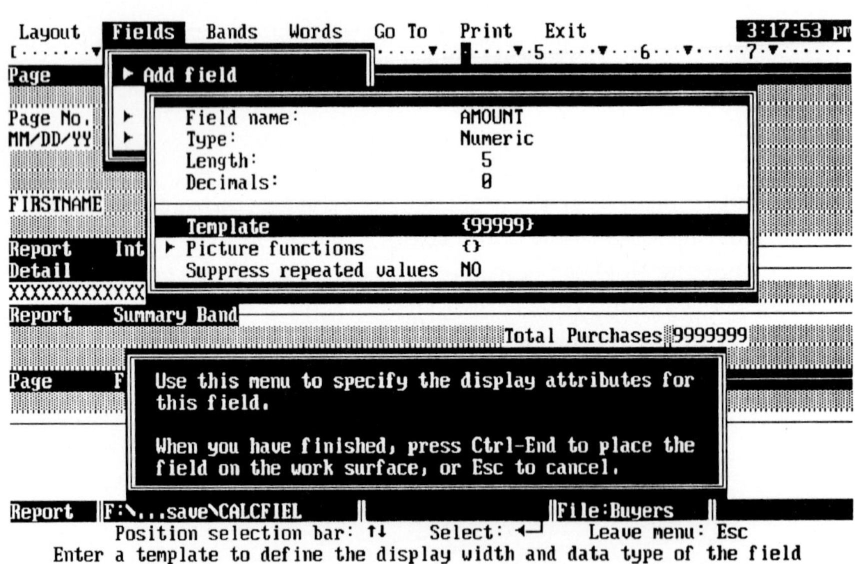

Figure 10-16. The field definition menu for an existing field

After you select a field name from the first column in the list, a *field definition menu* appears, as in Figure 10-16. You use this menu to describe the field that you are placing in the report. With existing fields, the information at the top of the menu is taken directly from the database file (or view definition), and you can't modify it in the Reports Design screen. The information below the separator line lets you control the appearance of the field on the screen by using templates and picture functions (see the sections "Field Templates" and "Picture Functions"). It also lets you suppress repeated values (see the section "Suppressing Repeated Values" later in this chapter).

Once you've established the desired settings for a field, press CTRL-END to save them. dBASE IV places the field in the report at the current cursor location. To cancel the operation, and remove the field definition menu from the screen, press ESC.

Adding a Calculated Field

A *calculated field* is a new field that you add to the report for printing purposes only. A calculated field has no effect on the underlying database file or view.

To add a calculated field to the report, start with the same steps as for an existing field. First, move the cursor to where you want the field to begin and select the **Add field** option from the **Fields** menu. When dBASE IV displays the four-column list (see Figure 10-15), select the **<create>** option from the top of the second column. dBASE IV then displays a field definition menu for calculated fields, as in Figure 10-17.

The Field Definition Menu for Calculated Fields

The field definition menu has particular options for calculated fields. You can change any setting in this menu because calculated fields do not have any predefined settings. The options are as follows:

- **Name** Use this option to give the calculated field a unique name. A name is not required but is helpful for identifying the field in the submenu that appears when you select **Add field**, **Modify field**, or **Remove field** from the **Fields** menu. If you don't provide a name, dBASE IV identifies the field by its expression.

- **Description** This option lets you enter an 80-character description for the field.

- **Expression** This option defines the expression that you want dBASE IV to use to calculate the field. You cannot create a calculated field without an expression. You can use any valid dBASE IV expression, and you can even include memory variables or user-defined functions. You cannot, however, include predefined fields (described later) from the current report. When you've entered the expression, press ENTER and dBASE IV immediately evaluates it. If you

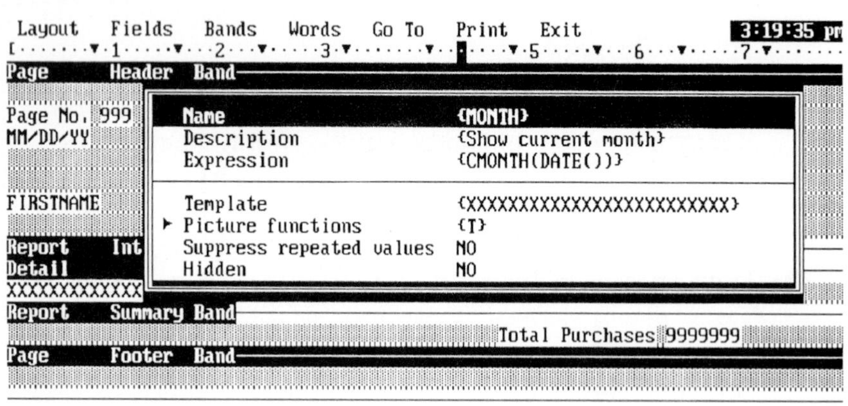

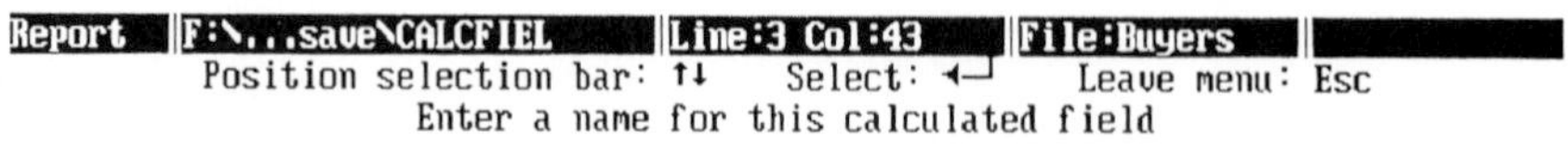

Figure 10-17. Field definition menu for a calculated field

use memory variables or user-defined functions in the expression, they must be previously defined or dBASE IV displays an error.

- **Template** The entry for this option is automatically filled in when dBASE IV evaluates the expression. (dBASE IV uses the result of the expression to determine the proper field template.) You use the template setting to control how data in the field is represented on the work surface. You can easily change the field template (see the section "Field Templates").
- **Picture functions** This option lets you control the overall template for the field (see the section "Picture Functions").
- **Suppress repeated values** This option lets you control whether you print the same value for a field more than once on a page (see the section "Suppressing Repeated Values").
- **Hidden** This option lets you hide a calculated field. If you make a field hidden, you can use it in a calculation but it does not appear on the Reports Design screen or in the final report.

When you've finished entering the options for a calculated field, press CTRL-END. dBASE IV immediately places the calculated field in the report.

Tip: As you enter the expression in a calculated field, you can press SHIFT-F1 to access the Expression Builder, which shows you a complete list of the existing database field names, mathematical and logical operators, and functions from which to choose. (See Chapter 5 for a more complete description of the Expression Builder.)

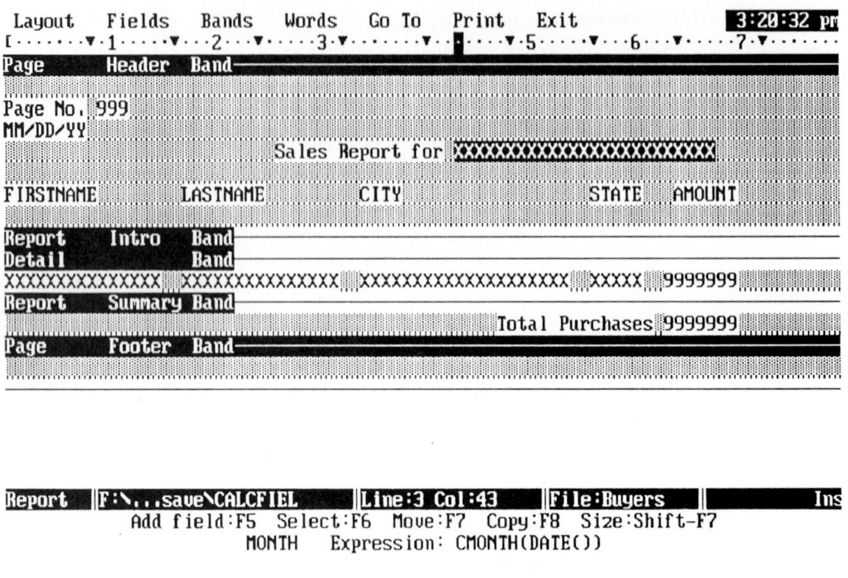

Figure 10-18. Results of entering the calculated field

An Example

Suppose you want to add a calculated field to the Page Header Band. The calculated field uses the expression CMONTH(DATE()) to determine the name of the current month, which it displays at the top of each page in the report.

To add a calculated field that displays the name of the current month, move the cursor to the location in the Page Header Band where you want the field to appear and select **Add field** from the **Fields** menu. Next, select **<create>** from the CALCULATED column in the box that appears. You can then fill in the field definition menu, as in Figure 10-17. Type **CMONTH(DATE())** and press ENTER, and dBASE IV immediately evaluates the expression and automatically inserts the template setting. Press CTRL-END to accept the field definition settings, and dBASE IV places the field in the report, as in Figure 10-18. If you then print the report, and the current month is January, dBASE IV prints "Sales Report for January" at the top of each page in the report.

Adding a Predefined Field

dBASE IV has four *predefined fields* that it creates automatically. They are

Date	Displays the current date
Time	Displays the current time
Recno	Displays the current record number
Pageno	Displays the current page number

When you create a column or a form layout, dBASE IV uses two of these fields, Pageno and Date, in the Page Header Band of the report.

To add a predefined field to a report, move the cursor to where you want the predefined field to appear and select **Add field** from the **Fields** menu. Next, select the field you want from the PREDEFINED column, and a field definition menu like the one in Figure 10-19 appears. After you fill in the field definition menu, press CTRL-END to place the field in the report.

Note: You can't use any of the predefined fields in the expression for a calculated field. You can, however, sometimes use functions such as DATE( ) and RECNO( ) to achieve similar results. See Chapter 33 for details on these functions.

Adding a Summary Field

dBASE IV has seven generic summary fields that you can add to a report. They are

Average	Computes the average value of a field in a group.
Count	Computes the number of records in a group

Max	Computes the maximum value for a field in a group
Min	Computes the minimum value for a field in a group
Sum	The sum of all the values for a field in a group
Std	Computes the standard deviation for a field in a group
Var	Computes the variance for a field in a group

Besides generic summary bands, you can add existing summary fields to a report. For example, when you use a column layout and you have numeric fields in the active database, dBASE IV

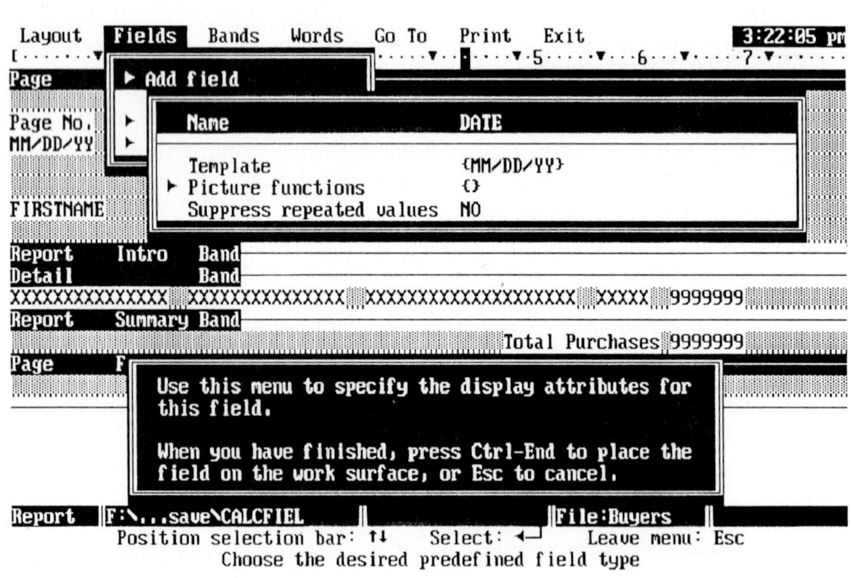

Figure 10-19. Field definition for a predefined field

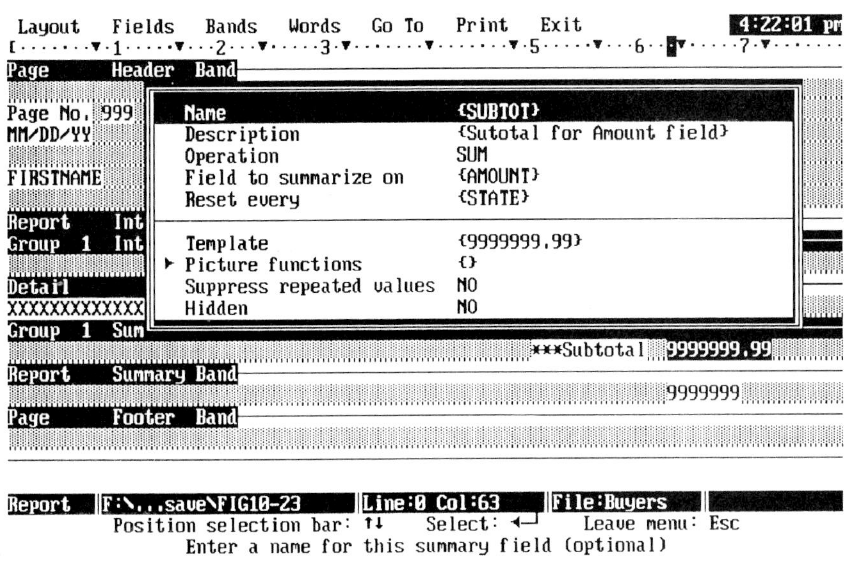

Figure 10-20. Field definition menu for a summary field

automatically creates summary fields for each numeric field and places them in the Report Summary Band. You can use any of these existing summary fields in your report.

Generally, you place summary fields in the Report Summary Band or in a Group Summary Band. Their effects are different depending on where you locate them and how you define them (see the section "Resetting by Group"). If you place them above the Detail Band, they always show 0 (or the field's first value). If you place them in the Detail Band, or below it, they show a cumulative result for the field.

To add a summary field to the report, move the cursor to where you want the field to begin and select **Add field** from the **Fields** menu. When dBASE IV displays the four-column list, select the name of a field from the SUMMARY column. To create a new summary field, select one of the seven generic summary field names. dBASE IV then displays a field definition menu for summary fields, as in Figure 10-20.

The Field Definition Menu for Summary Fields

The field definition menu has several unique options for summary fields. The options are as follows:

- **Name** Use this option to give the summary field a unique name. If you don't provide a name, dBASE IV identifies the field by the expression it creates for the field (for example, SUM(AMOUNT)).
- **Description** This option lets you enter an 80-character description for the field.
- **Operation** The entry for this option corresponds to the generic summary field name you chose from the four-column list (for instance, SUM). You can change this option if you like.
- **Field to summarize on** When you select this option, dBASE displays a list of fields. The list includes all the fields from the active database, and if you've defined any calculated fields, they appear in a second column.

Note: You cannot change the **Field to summarize on** option when you've chosen the Count generic summary field.

- **Reset every** This option lets you choose when the summary field is reset to zero. If you select **< PAGE >**, dBASE IV resets the summary field at the end of each page. If you select **< REPORT >**, dBASE IV does not reset the field until the end of the report (this is the default). When you place a summary field in one of the group bands, the choices are slightly different (see the next section).

The remaining options below the dividing line are identical to those for calculated fields (see the section "Adding a Calculated Field").

When you've finished entering the options for the summary field, press CTRL-END. dBASE IV immediately places the calculated field in the report.

Resetting by Group

When you include groups in your report, the options for resetting summary fields are more extensive. That is, when you select **Reset every**, dBASE displays not only the **< PAGE >** and **< REPORT >** options, but also the field names, expressions, or record counts you used to establish the groups in the report. To reset a summary variable for a group, select the item in the list that describes the grouping method. For example, if you've grouped according to the State field, select that field from the list.

Summary fields take on values as a report is printed. Do not place a summary field above the Detail Band because it won't have any data to summarize.

Summary fields are calculated starting from the Detail Band and working outward. If you have two groups surrounding the Detail Band, one for City (band 2) and one for State (band 1), a summary field is calculated according to the first surrounding band (band 2), and then the next surrounding band (band 1).

When you choose the reset value for a summary field, be careful to choose the grouping definition that corresponds to the group you want. Generally, you'll choose to reset every page or by the same field name or record count as the band containing the summary field.

An Example of Calculating Subtotals

As mentioned, group bands are most often used for creating subtotals. To create a subtotal, you need to use a summary field within a group band.

Suppose you're working with the BUYERS database, shown in Figure 10-21, and you want to group records according to the State field and create subtotals for each state using the Amount field. Because you're going to group according to the State field, you must first index the database according to that field (see Chapter 5, "Sorting and Indexing"). Then perform the following steps to create a calculated field.

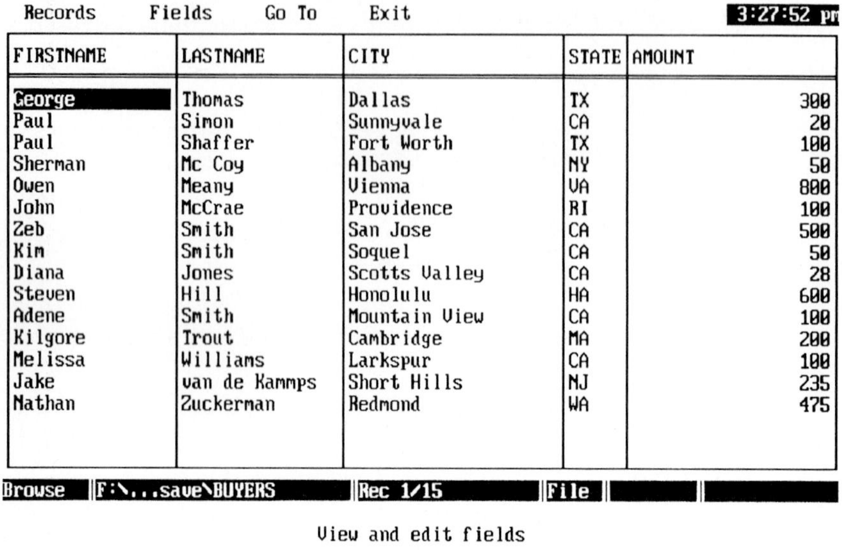

Records Fields Go To Exit 3:27:52 pm

FIRSTNAME	LASTNAME	CITY	STATE	AMOUNT
George	Thomas	Dallas	TX	300
Paul	Simon	Sunnyvale	CA	20
Paul	Shaffer	Fort Worth	TX	100
Sherman	Mc Coy	Albany	NY	50
Owen	Meany	Vienna	VA	800
John	McCrae	Providence	RI	100
Zeb	Smith	San Jose	CA	500
Kim	Smith	Soquel	CA	50
Diana	Jones	Scotts Valley	CA	28
Steven	Hill	Honolulu	HA	600
Adene	Smith	Mountain View	CA	100
Kilgore	Trout	Cambridge	MA	200
Melissa	Williams	Larkspur	CA	100
Jake	van de Kammps	Short Hills	NJ	235
Nathan	Zuckerman	Redmond	WA	475

Browse F:\...save\BUYERS Rec 1/15 File

View and edit fields

Figure 10-21. Buyers database for the subtotal example

1. Open the BUYERS database from the Control Center (highlight the database in the Data Panel, press ENTER, and select the **Use file** option).
2. Select **<create>** from the Reports Panel.
3. Select **Column layout** from the **Quick layouts** menu.
4. Select **Add a group band** from the **Bands** menu.
5. Enter **STATE** for the **Field value** option.
6. Move the cursor to the blank line in the Group 1 Summary Band and enter *****Subtotal** where it appears in Figure 10-22. Then use the RIGHT ARROW key to move the cursor directly below the Amount field.

7. Press F5, highlight Sum from the SUMMARY column, and press ENTER.

8. Select **Name** and enter a name for the field (such as **SUB-TOT**).

9. Select **Description** and enter a description (such as **Subtotal for Amount field**).

10. Select the **Field to summarize on** option and then select **AMOUNT**.

11. Press CTRL-END, and your screen should look like the one in Figure 10-22.

12. To print the report, select the **Print** menu and then the **Begin printing** option. Figure 10-23 shows the finished report.

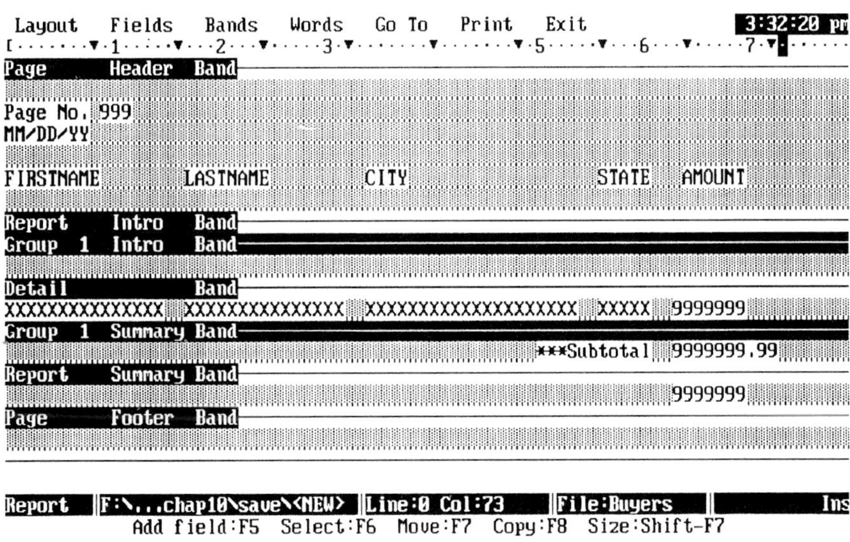

Figure 10-22. Creating a subtotal

```
Page No.  1
01/28/89

FIRSTNAME   LASTNAME        CITY            STATE        AMOUNT


Paul        Simon           Sunnyvale       CA           20
Zeb         Smith           San Jose        CA           500
Kim         Smith           Soquel          CA           50
Diana       Jones           Scotts Valley   CA           28
Adene       Smith           Mountain View   CA           100
Melissa     Williams        Larkspur        CA           100
                                        ***Subtotal      798.00

Steven      Hill            Honolulu        HA           600
                                        ***Subtotal      600.00

Kilgore     Trout           Cambridge       MA           200
                                        ***Subtotal      200.00

Jake        van de Kammps   Short Hills     NJ           235
                                        ***Subtotal      235.00

Sherman     Mc Coy          Albany          NY           50
                                        ***Subtotal      50.00

John        McCrae          Providence      RI           100
                                        ***Subtotal      100.00

George      Thomas          Dallas          TX           300
Paul        Shaffer         Fort Worth      TX           100
                                        ***Subtotal      400.00

Owen        Meany           Vienna          VA           800
                                        ***Subtotal      800.00

Nathan      Zuckerman       Redmond         WA           475
                                        ***Subtotal      475.00
                                                         3658
```

Figure 10-23. Results of the subtotal band

Field Templates

The **Template** option in the field definition menu lets you control on a character-by-character basis how data appears in a report. You enter a template by typing a string of symbols. The length of the string lets you specify the width of the field on the work surface. Each symbol within the string controls how the data appears in that column of the field.

For example, suppose you want to display a field that contains telephone numbers. If you specify (999)999-9999 for the template (9 meaning display a number), and the value in the field for the current record is 6177958234, dBASE IV automatically converts the value to (617)795-8234 when it prints the report. See "Field Templates" in Chapter 9 for a list of available template symbols (Table 9-2) and for more examples of field templates.

Note: You cannot change the template setting for a date field or for the predefined Time field.

Picture Functions

While field templates let you control field widths and how each character is displayed, picture functions let you define the overall template for a field. Choose **Picture functions** in the field definition menu. The picture functions for numeric fields appear in Figure 10-24; those for character fields appear in Figure 10-25. (Picture functions are not available for date, logical, and memo fields.) For a consolidated list of available picture functions, see Chapter 9 (Table 9-3).

As the figures show, the attributes available for a field depend on the field's data type (whether numeric or character). They also depend on whether the selected field is an existing, calculated, predefined, or summary field. Attributes not available for a par-

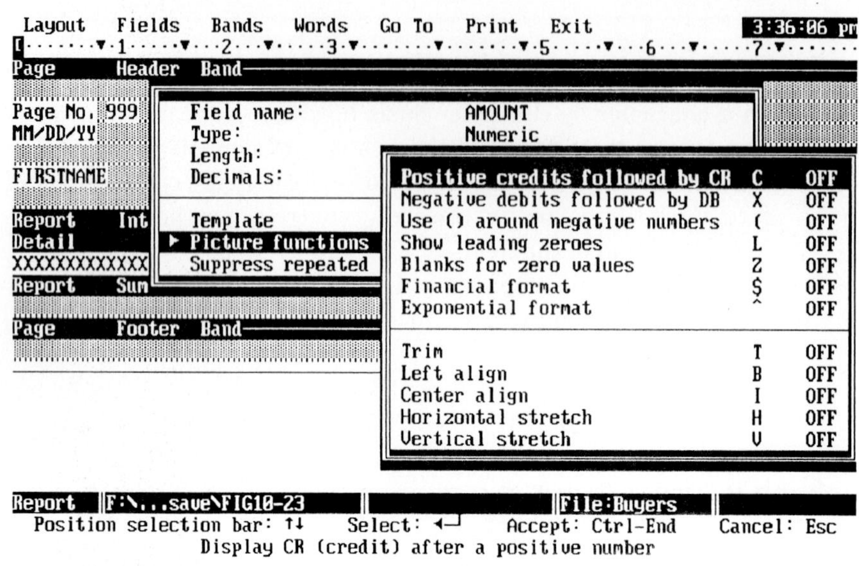

Figure 10-24. Numeric field picture functions

ticular field type are not highlighted, and you can't select them from the menu.

The Horizontal stretch and Vertical stretch Picture Functions

The **Horizontal stretch** and **Vertical stretch** picture functions control the appearance of long and short data values. They stretch and shrink the field to fit the data.

The **Horizontal stretch** picture function stretches or shrinks the field horizontally to fit the data. It either pushes to the right other material on the line, making room for long fields, or shrinks the field and pulls to the left any material to the right of short fields. You use this function in word wrap bands, especially for printing calculated fields or memo fields.

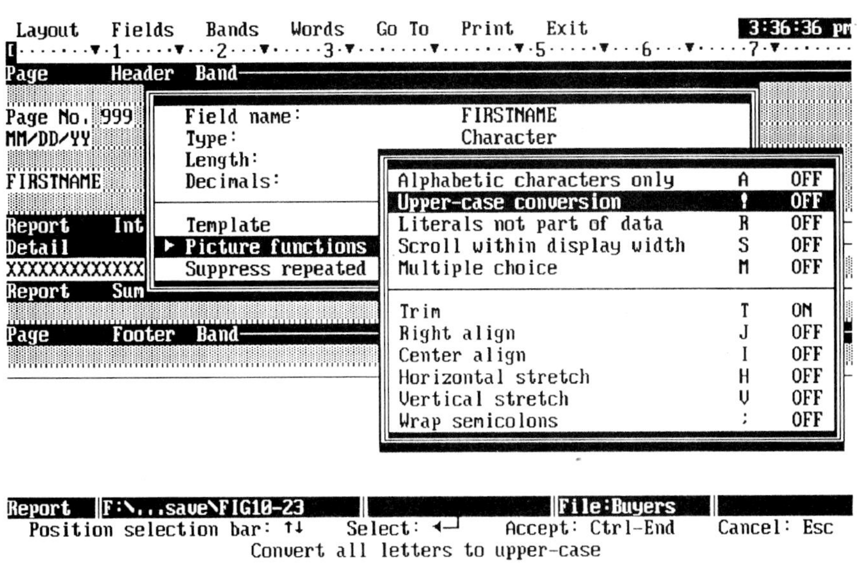

Figure 10-25. Character field picture functions

When you use a **Horizontal stretch** picture function, the data itself determines the width of the printed field. dBASE IV displays the template for this picture function as HHHHH, and you cannot modify the width. For an example, see the section "Creating Form Letters."

You can use the **Vertical stretch** picture function in both layout and word wrap bands. It stretches a field vertically (within a specified width) to fit the data. dBASE IV uses VVVV templates to represent fields that have this picture function. The number of Vs determines the width of the field. For example, a field with ten Vs wraps the text in the field to a column ten characters wide. When you specify **Vertical stretch**, the number of Vs is determined by the default field width.

With memo fields, the MEMOWIDTH setting controls the initial length of the **Vertical stretch** template (the default is 50).

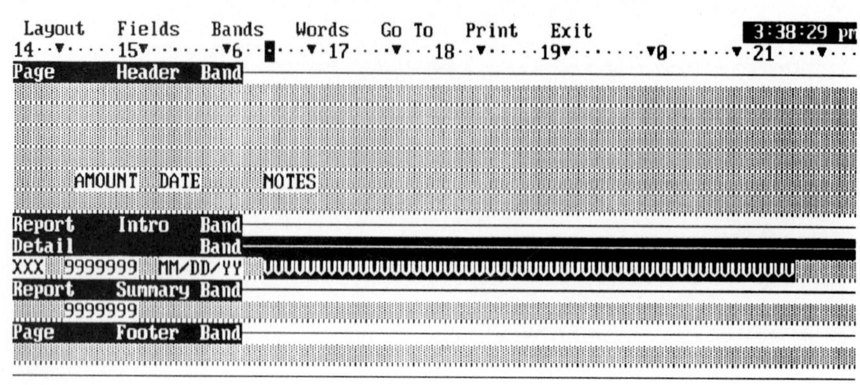

Figure 10-26. The **Vertical stretch** picture function for memo fields

To change the setting for the current session, select the **Settings** submenu from the Control Center's **Tools** menu. Then use the **Memo width** option in the **Options** menu.

As Figure 10-26 shows, dBASE IV automatically assigns the **Vertical stretch** picture function to memo fields when you place them in layout bands. In this example, if the memo field contains more than 50 characters, the text wraps to the next line in the report, creating, in effect, a column of text.

The **Vertical stretch** picture function is not available in the Forms Design Screen or with labels.

Tip: To adjust the length of a field's **Vertical stretch** template, place the cursor within the field on the work surface and press SHIFT-F7. You can then use the arrow keys to increase or decrease the size of the field. Press ENTER to lock in the new size.

The Trim Picture Function

The **Trim** picture function is another function that you can use with reports and labels. It removes all beginning and ending blanks from a field. In fact, whenever you place a character field in a report, dBASE IV automatically assigns a **Trim** picture function to the field. Also, in report word wrap bands and labels, dBASE IV automatically assigns the **Trim** function to all character, numeric, and memo fields.

When you use a word wrap band, to create a form letter for instance, you may want to combine the **Trim** and **Horizontal stretch** picture functions. The **Trim** function removes the beginning and ending blanks from the data in the field while the **Horizontal stretch** function expands and contracts the field to fit the data. The example in the section "Creating Form Letters" uses this technique.

Note: When you're connecting a trimmed field with material to the right, you must use a blank space (ASCII 32) between the two in order to hold them together. Otherwise, dBASE trims the field but leaves the material to the right in its original position. The result is that the two appear disconnected. For more information on using trimmed fields, see Chapter 11.

Suppressing Repeated Values

The **Suppress repeated values** option in the field definition menu lets you specify whether dBASE IV prints the same value for a field more than once on a page. For example, suppose you're creating a report for a parts database, and you have several adjacent records with "Widgets" in the Description field. Rather than repeat "Widgets" several times in a row, you can set the **Suppress repeated values** option to YES. In this case, only the first occurrence of "Widgets" appears on the page.

Controlling the Style of Text

When you create reports and labels, dBASE IV lets you control the style of text within fields via the **Style** option in the **Words** menu. There are six printing style options: **Normal**, **Bold**, **Underline**, **Italic**, **Superscript** (raised), and **Subscript** (lowered). You can also combine these different styles.

Some printers do not support all of the different printing styles, especially italics, superscript, and subscript. In these cases, dBASE IV directs the printer to print underlined.

When setting the print style for text, press F6 to select the block of text you want. Then use the **Style** option in the **Words** menu. When you're setting the style for a field, you can locate the cursor anywhere in the field before selecting the **Style** option.

When you've set the print style for an item, dBASE IV displays it in a special way on the screen. If you have a color screen, it displays bold items as bold and other print styles in colors. If you have a monochrome screen, dBASE IV displays underlined items as underlined, and other print styles as bold.

If you want text in a particular print style, select an option from the **Words** menu and then type in the text. The text and fields you enter from that point on will have your chosen style.

Tip: When creating forms and labels, you can use the **Position** option in the **Words** menu to realign your text and fields relative to the current margin settings for the word wrap ruler. See Chapter 9 for more on this option.

Creating Form Letters

Creating form letters is particularly easy in dBASE IV. The best way to start is to select the **Mailmerge layout** option from the **Quick layouts** menu. The mailmerge layout has the following characteristics:

- All the bands except the Detail Band are closed.
- The Detail Band appears blank, but it actually has two important settings assigned automatically by dBASE IV. First, if you select the **Word wrap** option from the **Words** menu, it is set to YES. (The Detail Band is set for word wrap mode. Any text you enter in this band is automatically wrapped when it exceeds the right margin.) Second, the **Begin band on new page** option in the **Words** menu is also set to YES. (Each new form letter will automatically begin on a new page.)
- If you add a field to the layout, when you enter the **Picture functions** option in the field definition menu, dBASE IV offers a **Horizontal stretch** picture function option. Selecting this function stretches or shrinks the field horizontally to fit the data. See the section "Picture Functions" for more information.

Figure 10-27 shows how the screen appears after you select **Mailmerge layout** from the **Quick layouts** menu.

Setting Margins for a Form Letter

When you use the **Mailmerge layout** option, dBASE IV automatically assigns a value of 1 to the left margin and 255 to the right margin. When creating a form letter, you should first enter the proper margin settings. Without a right margin setting, dBASE IV will not wrap your form letter text as you type.

To set the margins, use the **Modify ruler** option in the **Words** menu. See "Modifying the Word Wrap Ruler" in Chapter 9 for more information.

An Example

The following example shows you how to create a simple form letter using the CLIENTS database from previous chapters. It assumes you're working from the Control Center. Perform the following steps:

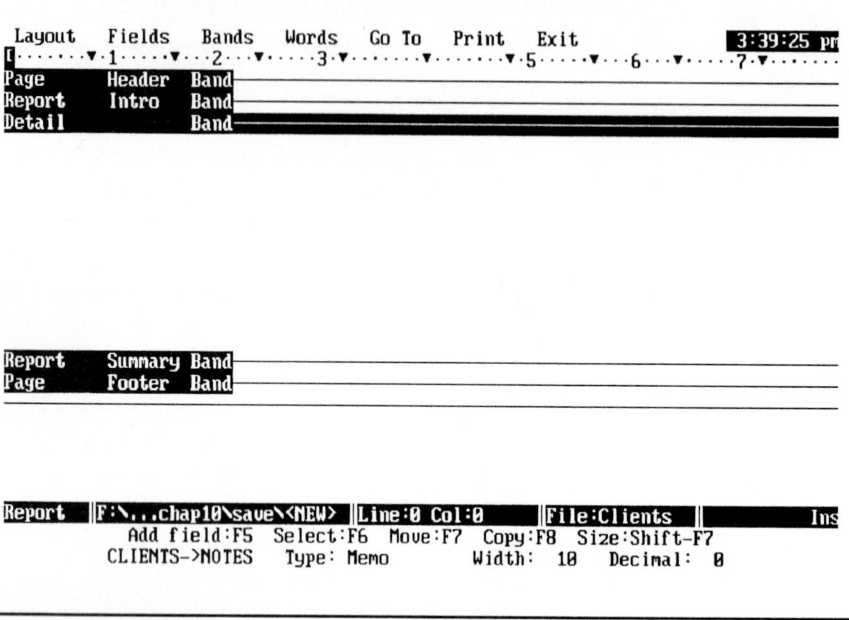

Figure 10-27. The **Mailmerge layout** format

1. Open the CLIENTS database and then select the **<create>** option from the Reports Panel.

2. Select the **Mailmerge layout** option from the **Quick layouts** menu. Your screen should look like the one in Figure 10-27.

3. Change the margin settings by selecting the **Modify ruler** option from the **Words** menu. Enter a left margin of 7 (type [at position 7) and a right margin of 72 (type] at position 72). Press ENTER to return to the work surface.

4. Press F5 and select the Firstname field from the first column in the four-column list. Press CTRL-END to accept

the field definition settings and place the field on the work surface.

5. Enter the field names (and text) shown in Table 10-2, using the method described in the previous step. Make sure to follow the directions in the Comments column immediately after entering each new field. Refer to Figure 10-28 for guidance.

6. Type the body of the letter up to Line 12, Col 21, as it appears in Figure 10-28. *Do not press* ENTER *at the end of a line*. Because you're in word wrap mode, dBASE IV wraps your text automatically when you reach the end of a line. In word wrap mode, press ENTER only when you reach the end of a paragraph.

7. Locate the cursor at Line 12, Col 23, and press F5. Select the Firstname field from the list, and press ENTER.

Position	**Field name**	**Comments**
Line 0, Col 23	Lastname	Move to end of line and press ENTER
Line 1, Col 7	Company	Move to end of line and press ENTER
Line 2, Col 7	Address	Move to end of line and press ENTER
Line 3, Col 7	City	Move to end of line, type , (comma), and press SPACEBAR
Line 3, Col 29	State	Move to end of line and press SPACEBAR
Line 3, Col 33	Zip	Move to end of line and press ENTER twice
Line 5, Col 7		Type **Dear** and press SPACEBAR
Line 5, Col 12	First	Move to end of line, type : (colon), and press ENTER twice

Table 10-2. Steps for Creating an Example Form Letter

8. Select the **Picture function** option from the field definition menu. Then set the **Horizontal stretch** option to ON. Press CTRL-END twice to return the work surface. (Notice that because of the horizontal stretch picture function, dBASE IV uses HHHHH for the field template.)

9. Enter the remainder of the letter, as in Figure 10-28, making sure to press ENTER at the end of each paragraph.

10. To print the form letter, select the **Begin printing** option from the **Print** menu. Your output should look like that shown in Figure 10-29.

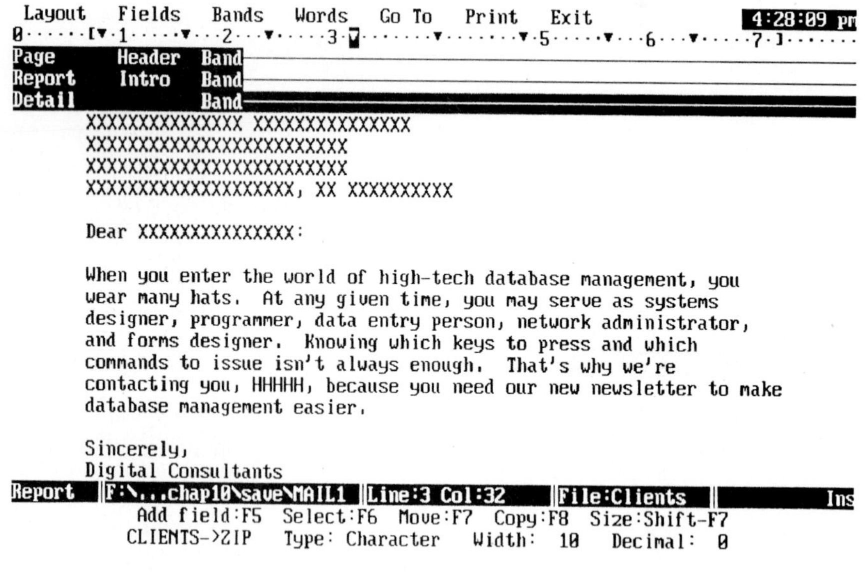

Figure 10-28. An example form letter

George Thomas
Texasville Pumps
221 Texasville Way
Dallas, TX 56902

Dear George:

When you enter the world of high-tech database management, you wear many hats. At any given time, you may serve as systems designer, programmer, data entry person, network administrator, and forms designer. Knowing which keys to press and which commands to issue isn't always enough. That's why we're contacting you, George, because you need our new newsletter to make database management easier.

Sincerely,
Digital Consultants

Figure 10-29. Sample form letter

Saving a Report

To save the current report, use the **Save this report** option from the **Layout** menu. dBASE IV then prompts you for an eight-character file name for the report's files. dBASE IV actually creates both an .FRM and an .FRG file for the report (see the section "The Different Types of Report Files").

To save your report and return to the Control Center (or the dot prompt, depending on where you started from), perform any one of the following:

- Press CTRL-W
- Press CTRL-END
- Select the **Save changes and exit** option from the **Exit** menu

Tip: To see the code that dBASE IV generates when you save your report, you can SET INSTRUCT to OFF and SET TALK to ON.

Printing Reports

To print a report from the Control Center, use the **Begin print** option from the **Print** menu.

To print a report from the dot prompt, you use the REPORT FORM command. For example, to print a report named Mailer using the CLIENTS database, enter

```
. USE Clients
. REPORT FORM Mailer TO PRINTER
```

For more detailed information on printing, see Chapter 12.

In this chapter, you learned how to start reports using a quick layout. You also learned about the different elements of reports, including basic report bands and group bands. You now know how to add four different types of fields to a report, including existing, calculated, predefined, and summary fields. You also learned how to create form letters.

Creating Labels

ELEVEN

Accessing the Labels Design Screen
The Different Types of Label Files
Adjusting the Size of the Work Surface
Adding Fields to the Work Surface
Saving a Label Design
Modifying the Label Design
Viewing Your Labels on the Screen
Selecting Labels to Print
Aligning and Printing Your Labels
Using a Different Database File or View
Using Labels from dBASE III PLUS
Other Menu Bar Options

dBASE IV's labels facility is extremely flexible. You can choose from a variety of popular label, envelope, and Rolodex card sizes. Moreover, you can create your own custom formats of up to 255 lines high and 255 characters wide. You can even create formats that print several labels across.

This chapter discusses how to create mailing labels using the various options in the Labels Design screen. First, you learn how to use dBASE IV's standard label formats. Then you learn how to create custom labels and how to add your own calculated fields.

Since many of the options in the Labels Design screen are identical to those in the Reports Design screen, this chapter only covers items that are unique to labels. Refer to the previous chapter if you have questions about options that are not covered in this chapter.

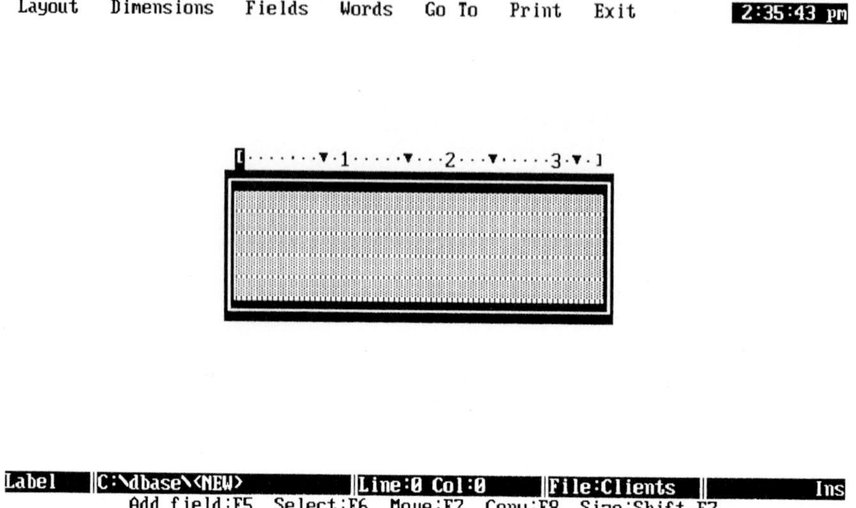

Figure 11-1. The Labels Design screen

Accessing the Labels Design Screen

Before you can access the Labels Design screen, you need to open a database file or view. You can then use the fields from the file or view in your label design.

From the Control Center, open a file by highlighting it in the Data Panel, pressing ENTER, and selecting **Use file**. Next, move to the Labels Panel and select the **<create>** option. dBASE IV takes you to the Labels Design screen, as shown in Figure 11-1. You design your labels in this screen by using the layout editing mode.

To access the Labels Design screen from the dot prompt, use the CREATE LABEL command. As in the Control Center, you should first open a database file or view. For example, to open a file named CLIENTS and create (or modify) a label form file named MAILER, use the following commands:

```
. USE Clients
. CREATE LABEL Mailer
```

The Different Types of Label Files

dBASE IV uses three different types of label files: .LBL, .LBG, and .LBO files.

- An .LBL file is a *label form file* that contains the instructions dBASE IV needs to display a label design in the Labels Design screen. (.LBL files are stored in a special non- ASCII format.) When you create or modify a label via the Labels Design screen, you're actually working with an .LBL file. If you delete the .LBL file, you will not be able to modify the label in the Labels Design screen.
- An .LBG file is a *generated label form file* that contains the standard dBASE IV program code (for example, ?, ??, PRINTJOB, and ENDPRINTJOB commands). This code is generated when you save a label in Labels Design screen (see the section "Saving a Label Design").
- An .LBO file is the compiled version of an .LBG file. This is the actual object file that dBASE IV creates and reads when you print labels. dBASE IV automatically generates an .LBO file from the .LBG file the first time you print with a new or modified label design (see the section "Aligning and Printing Your Labels").

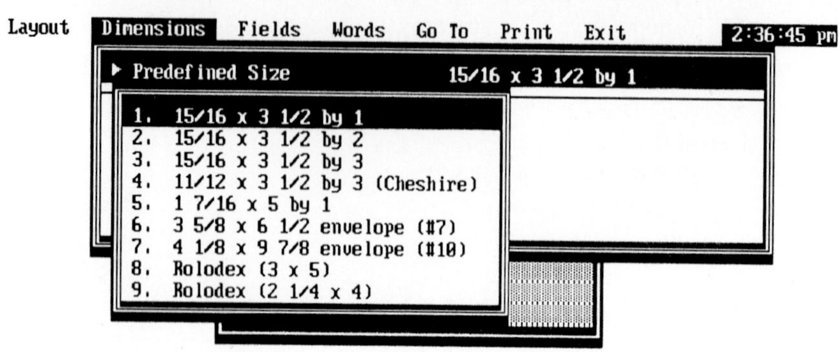

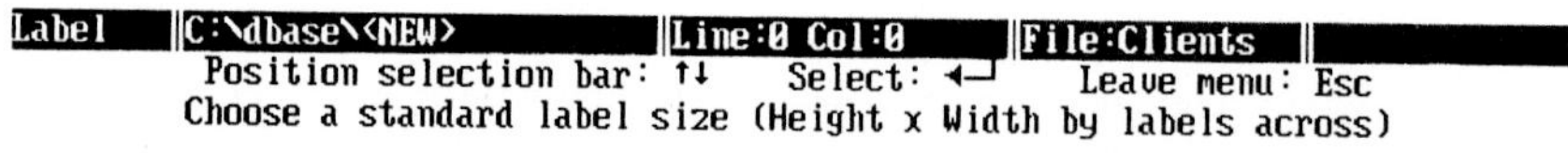

Figure 11-2. The predefined label sizes

Adjusting the Size of the Work Surface

Once you've accessed the Labels Design screen, you need to adjust the size of the work surface to match the size of the label you're using. You can choose from several predefined label sizes, or you can define your own label size. In either case, you use the **Dimensions** menu.

Selecting a Predefined Label Size

To select a predefined label size, use the **Predefined Size** option from the **Dimensions** menu. When you select this option, dBASE displays a submenu of nine standard label sizes, as shown in Figure 11-2.

The predefined label sizes can have up to three different dimensions—height, width, and columns. If only two dimensions appear, they refer to the height and width in inches of a single column of labels. The third dimension, columns, refers to the number of labels printed across the page. For example, if you select **15/16 x 3 1/2 by 2**, dBASE prints two columns of labels with a height of 15/16 inch and a width of 3 1/2 inches.

When you choose a predefined label size, dBASE automatically fills in the rest of the settings in the **Dimensions** menu, assuming the following:

- The **Width of label** setting is based on pica pitch (ten characters per inch).
- The **Height of label** setting is based on six lines per inch.

If your printer settings are not appropriate, you'll need to change these label-dimension settings (see the next section).

Even if you choose more than one column of labels, the Labels Design screen work surface is never larger than the size of a single label. When you print your labels, however, dBASE duplicates the label design in each column.

Tip: You can apply a label design to any database file or view that contains the same fields.

Defining Individual Label Dimensions

If you want to create a label that doesn't match any of the predefined label formats, you can use the remaining **Dimensions** menu options to define your label design. You should also use these options if your printer is set for a different pitch than pica or a different height than six lines per inch. Figure 11-3 illustrates how each of these options affects your label.

- The **Width of label** option refers to the total number of characters across that can appear on a single label. The maximum width is 255 characters. For example, if you're

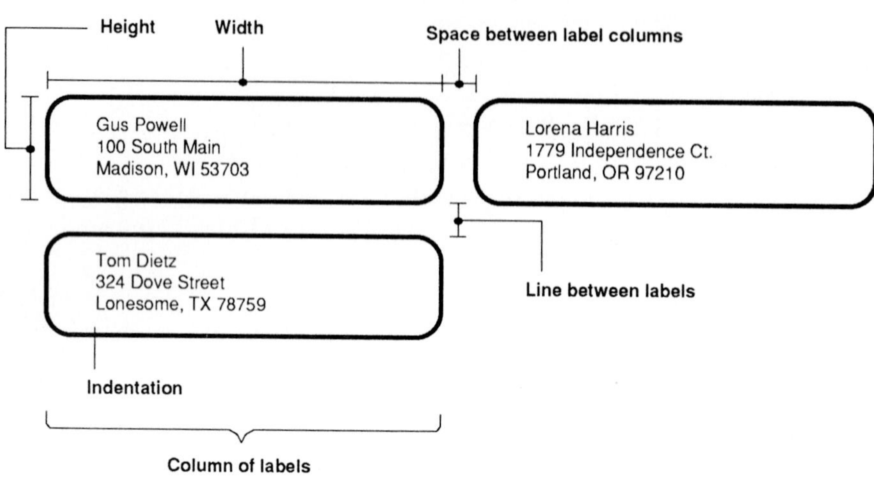

Figure 11-3. Label dimensions

using a label four inches wide and printing with a pica pitch (ten characters per inch), you can print up to 40 characters on your label. In this case, you might set the **Width of label** option to 35, leaving some room for error.

- The **Height of label** option refers to the number of printed lines that your label can contain. If your printer prints six lines to an inch and you have address labels 15/16 of an inch high, you can print five lines on each label. In this case, you would set this option to 5.

- The **Indentation** option refers to the amount of space you can add to the beginning print position set by the **Offset from left** option from the **Page dimensions** submenu of the **Print** menu. You can indent from 0 to 250 spaces. For example, if your **Offset from left** option is set to 0 (the default), and you enter 1 for the **Indentation** option, your label starts printing one character to the right of the first possible printing position.

- The **Lines between labels** option refers to the number of blank lines to leave between the bottom of one label and the top of the next. You can choose a setting from 0 to 16 lines. For example, enter **1** to leave one blank line between labels.
- The **Spaces between label columns** option refers to the number of spaces to leave between the end of one column of labels and the beginning of the next. You can choose a setting from 0 to 120 spaces. For example, enter **2** to leave two spaces between each column of labels.
- The **Columns of labels** option refers to the number of columns of labels to print. For example, enter **2** to create labels two columns across.

Once you've entered values for these options, press CTRL-END to save your new settings. dBASE displays the newly defined work surface at the center of the Labels Design screen. A ruler showing the width of your label appears above the work surface.

Adding Fields to the Work Surface

Once you've matched the dimensions of the Labels Design screen work surface to the dimensions of your label, you can begin adding fields to the work surface.

The **Fields** menu lets you add existing fields from a database file or view. Besides existing fields, you can add calculated fields and predefined fields, such as Date and Time. (See Chapter 10 for more information on calculated and predefined fields.)

To add a field to the work surface, position the cursor where you want the field to appear and select the **Add field** option from the **Fields** menu or simply press F5 (Add a Field). dBASE displays a list with three columns, as follows.

- The field names column contains the field names from the current database or view.
- CALCULATED shows the calculated fields that you have created.
- PREDEFINED shows the predefined fields Date, Time, Recno, and Pageno.

Adding fields in the Labels Design screen is like adding them in the Reports Design screen (see the section "Adding Fields" in Chapter 10).

The Labels Design screen's field definition menu does *not* support the following template and picture function options:

- **Suppress repeated values** option
- **Hidden field** option
- **Vertical stretch** picture function
- **Horizontal stretch** picture function
- **Wrap semicolons** picture function

For more on the template options and picture functions, see Chapter 10, "Creating Reports."

An Example

Suppose you want to create and print labels using a database named MAIL, which consists of the following six character fields and widths:

Firstname	12
Lastname	15
Address	30
City	18
State	2
Zipcode	9

To create standard mailing labels of 15/16 x 3 1/2 by 1 (the default), perform the following steps:

1. Open the MAIL database from the Control Center (highlight the database in the Data Panel, press ENTER, and select the **Use file** option).

2. Select **<create>** from the Labels Panel. dBASE takes you to the Labels Design screen.

3. With the cursor at Line 0, Column 0, press F5 and select the **Firstname** field from the first column in the three-column list. Press CTRL-END to accept the field definition settings and place the field on the work surface. Press SPACEBAR to insert a blank space after the Firstname field.

4. Enter the following field names (and text) as in the previous step, making sure to follow the directions in the Comments column immediately after entering each new field. See Figure 11-4 for guidance.

Position	Field name	Comments
Line 0, Col 13	Lastname	Press ENTER to move to the next line
Line 1, Col 0	Address	Press ENTER to move to the next line
Line 2, Col 0	City	Type , (comma) and press SPACEBAR
Line 2, Col 21	State	Press SPACEBAR
Line 2, Col 24	Zipcode	

5. To print the labels, select the **Begin printing** option from the **Print** menu. Your output should look like Figure 11-5.

The Trim Picture Function

When you add a field to the Labels Design screen work surface, dBASE IV automatically assigns the **Trim** picture function to it.

Layout Dimensions Fields Words Go To Print Exit 2:52:26 pm
XXXXXXXXXXXX XXXXXXXXXXXXXXX
XXXXXXXXXXXXXXXXXXXXXXXXXXXXXX
XXXXXXXXXXXXXXXXXX, XX XXXXXXXXX
Label C:\dbase\MAILER Line:0 Col:0 File:Mail Ins
Add field:F5 Select:F6 Move:F7 Copy:F8 Size:Shift-F7
MAIL->FIRSTNAME Type: Character Width: 12 Decimal: 0

Figure 11-4. An example label design

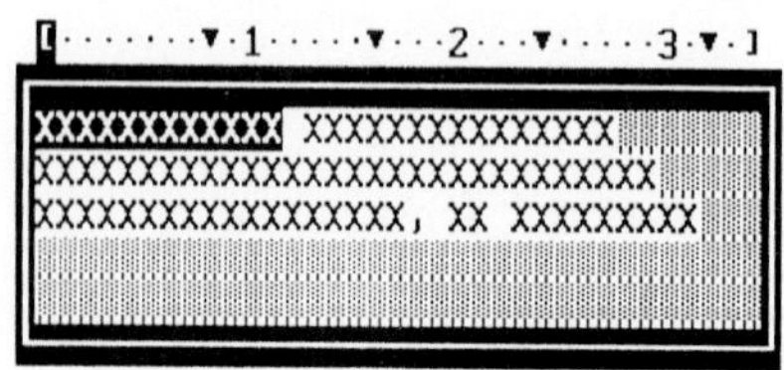

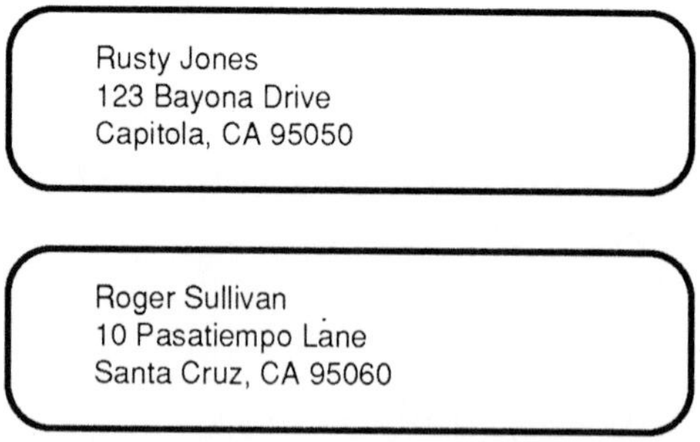

Rusty Jones
123 Bayona Drive
Capitola, CA 95050
Roger Sullivan
10 Pasatiempo Lane
Santa Cruz, CA 95060

Figure 11-5. Sample labels

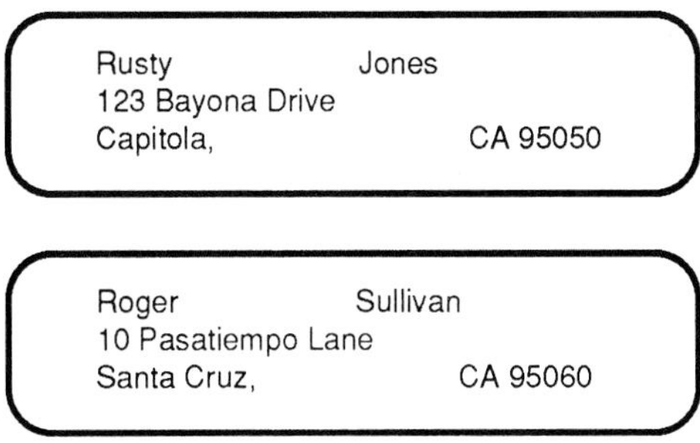

Figure 11-6. Labels printed without blank space connectors

The **Trim** function eliminates any blanks before and after a field's data.

When you're connecting a trimmed field with material to the right, you must use a blank space (a space created with the SPACEBAR) between the two in order to keep them together. Otherwise, dBASE trims the field but leaves the material to the right in its original position. The result is that the two fields appear disconnected.

For example, suppose you're using the MAIL database from the previous example, but instead of connecting the adjoining fields with spaces, you leave work surface space. Figure 11-6 illustrates what happens.

Saving a Label Design

You can save the current label design by selecting **Save this label design** from the **Layout** menu. When you select this option, dBASE prompts you for an eight-character file name for the label's files. (dBASE IV actually creates two files for a label: an .LBL and an .LBG file. See the section "The Different Types of Label Files.")

To save your label design and return to the Control Center (or the dot prompt, depending on where you started from), perform any one of the following:

- Press CTRL-W.
- Press CTRL-END.
- Select **Save changes and exit** from the **Exit** menu.

Modifying the Label Design

If you want to return to the Labels Design screen and modify the format of a label, highlight the label format (.LBL) file in the Labels Panel of the Control Center and press ENTER. Then select **Modify layout**. You can also select the label format file in the Labels Panel and press SHIFT-F2.

To see which field is associated with a field template, locate the cursor anywhere within the template. dBASE will display the associated field name and database in the message line, as well as the type of field, the width, and the number of decimal places. Figure 11-7 shows the cursor on the Lastname field of the MAIL database in the Labels Design screen.

As mentioned, you can add fields to the work surface by pressing F5 (Add a Field) or selecting the **Add field** option from the **Fields** menu.

To delete a field from the work surface, select the **Remove field** option from the **Fields** menu. You can also move the cursor to the field to be deleted and press DEL.

You can copy and move label text and fields, as in the Reports Design screen. See the section "Copying and Moving Design Elements" in Chapter 10.

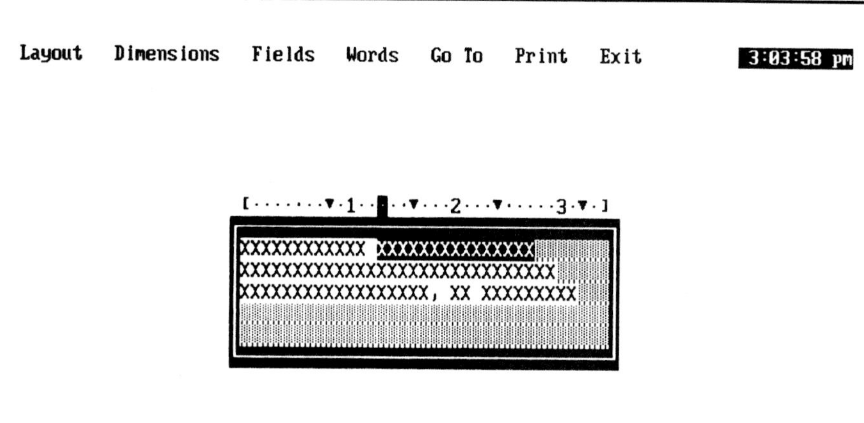

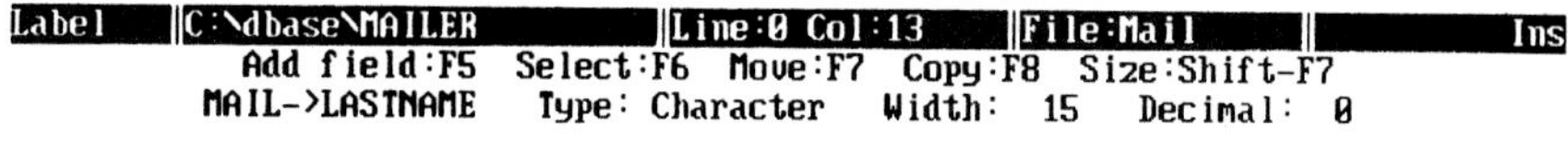

Figure 11-7. A field template's associated field

Viewing Your Labels on the Screen

Once you've created or modified a label design, you can select the **View labels on screen** option from the **Print** menu to see how your labels will appear without actually printing them. When you choose this option, dBASE directs the output to your screen rather than your printer. The output displays a screen at a time; press the SPACEBAR to see the next screen of output.

Selecting Labels to Print

You can use view queries to limit the records included when you print labels. By using view queries, you can select from a database certain records that meet a given condition. For more information on view queries, see Chapter 6, "Querying the Database."

If you're working from the dot prompt, you can also use a FOR or WHILE clause with the LABEL FORM command to print labels for only those records that meet a specified condition. For example, to print labels for everyone living outside of California, enter the following at the dot prompt:

```
. LABEL FORM TO PRINT FOR State <> "CA"
```

Tip: To print your labels in a particular order, you'll need to sort or index your database. For information on sorting and indexing, see Chapter 5.

Aligning and Printing Your Labels

Before you begin printing, you need to check that your labels are properly aligned with your printer. This can be an exacting task; fortunately, dBASE IV lets you print sample labels to test the alignment.

To print sample labels, select **Generate sample labels** from the **Print** menu. When you choose this option, dBASE prints a row of test labels using the letter "X." For example, Figure 11-8 shows sample labels generated using the labels form created for the MAIL database.

When you use the **Generate sample labels** option, you can generate sample labels as many times as you like. Just press Y or ENTER when dBASE prompts you "Do you want more samples? (Y/N)." When you've aligned the labels correctly, you can begin printing by pressing N at the prompt. dBASE beeps and immedi-

```
XXXXXXXXXXXXXXXXXXXXXXXXXXXX
XXXXXXXXXXXXXXXXXXXXXXXXXXXX
XXXXXXXXXXXXXXXXXXXXXXXXXXXX
XXXXXXXXXXXXXXXXXXXXXXXXXXXX
```

Figure 11-8. A test label

ately begins printing your labels. If at any time you want to quit the **Generate sample labels** option, press ESC.

Tip: You can print sample labels from the dot prompt by adding the SAMPLE clause to the LABEL FORM command. For example, the following command prints sample labels using a label form file named MAILING:

```
. LABEL FORM Mailing TO PRINT SAMPLE
```

If you've already aligned your labels and printer, you can select the **Begin printing** option from the **Print** menu to begin printing immediately. While dBASE is printing your labels, it prompts you to press ESC to cancel printing or CTRL-S to pause printing, as shown in Figure 11-9. Depending on your printer, printing may or may not stop immediately; the printer buffer may need to empty before printing pauses.

Using a Different Database File or View

If you have more than one database file or view with the same structure, you can select the **Use different database file or view** option to use a different database or view with a label design. This

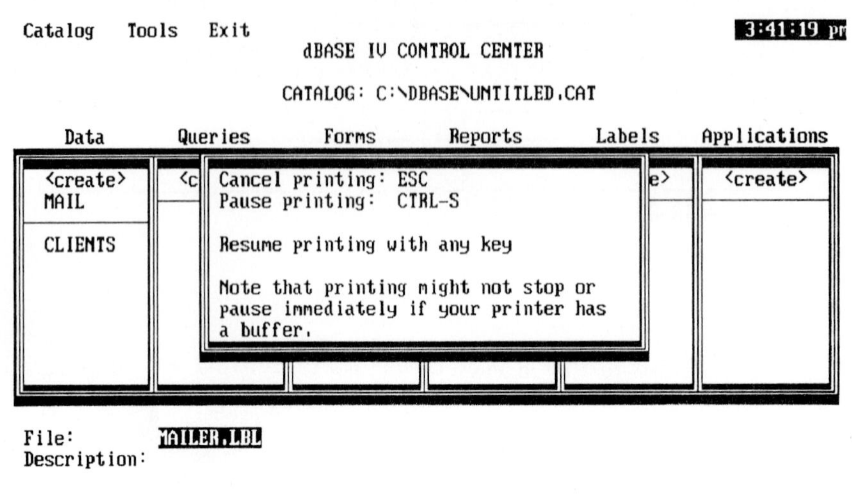

Figure 11-9. The printing message

option enables you to use a standard label format for more than one database.

If your label fields don't match your database or view when you select a new file or view, dBASE displays a message listing the field names not found in the selected database. You can then remove from the design screen any field templates that don't exist in the database file or view you've chosen.

Using Labels from dBASE III PLUS

You can use labels from dBASE III PLUS in dBASE IV without any modification. However, if you need to change the layout of the labels, you can import the label form (.LBL) file by choosing the **Add file to catalog** option from the Control Center's **Catalog** menu. Next, place the labels in the Labels Design screen.

When you place the dBASE III PLUS labels in the Labels Design screen, dBASE IV assigns them the appropriate field templates and gives each one the **Trim** picture function. If dBASE IV cannot create the proper field template, it converts the dBASE III PLUS expressions to calculated fields.

Other Menu Bar Options

The **Words, Go To,** and **Print** menus appear on the Labels Design screen but are described in detail in other chapters. Many of the **Words** menu options and all of the **Go To** options are described in Chapter 4, "Entering, Editing, and Displaying Data" and in Chapter 5, "Sorting and Indexing." For more on the **Print** menu, see the next chapter, "Printing."

You can use the **Style** option from the **Words** menu to change the type style of your data. There are six printing styles for labels: **Normal**, **Bold**, **Underline**, **Italic**, **Superscript** (raised), and **Subscript** (lowered). For more information on the **Style** option, see Chapter 10, "Creating Reports."

In this chapter, you learned how to use predefined label formats. You also learned how to create your own customized label formats. By now, you know how to create nearly any type of label design using existing fields, calculated fields, and predefined fields. You also know how to generate sample labels to help align your printer and to guarantee that your labels print exactly where you want them.

Printing

TWELVE

In dBASE IV, you can print from more than a dozen different locations. This chapter teaches you where those locations are. It also shows you how to use SHIFT-F9 (Quick Report) to print reports on the fly. In the process, you'll discover how to save the current print settings in a *print form file* and how to retrieve and activate those settings at a later time. You'll also learn how to use system memory variables to control your printer's output.

This chapter first explains how to access the dBASE IV **Print** menu. It then covers the **Print** menu options in the order in which they appear. Commands or system memory variables are mentioned when they can perform the equivalent of a **Print** menu option. Since some screens have print menus that include special options, the chapter discusses the differences between the various dBASE IV print menus.

The Print Menu

You can activate the **Print** menu from most of the Control Center panels, the various design screens, and the Browse and Edit screens. In the Reports, Labels, and Database Design screens and the dBASE IV Text Editor, the **Print** menu is part of the menu bar for the screen. When this is the case, the **Print** menu may show an additional option specific to that screen.

The **Print** menu presents options that control virtually every aspect of printing. Figure 12-1 shows the Print menu on the Control Center screen.

As you can see, the first five options of the **Print** menu are divided into two sets. The first set contains three options with which you can print labels and reports, eject a page, or view reports on your screen. The next set consists of two options for selecting and saving various printing formats.

The last third of the **Print** menu contains four submenus that allow you to

- Control the destination of reports and labels
- Control printing options such as pitch and print quality
- Manage output options, such as the number of pages and copies printed
- Determine page dimensions that define how your text is laid out on the page.

Accessing the Print Menu

You can display the Print menu by doing one of the following:

- Press SHIFT-F9 (Quick Report) while highlighting a file in any Control Center panel except the Applications Panel.
- Press SHIFT-F9 (Quick Report) in the Edit, Browse, or Queries Design screen.
- Select the **Print** menu from the menu bar when designing a report, label, or program.

You can also press ENTER with the highlight located on the file name of a report or label in either the Reports or Labels panel of the Control Center. dBASE IV presents an option box, as in Figure 12-2. Select the **Print report** (or **Print label**, depending upon the panel) option from the option box. dBASE IV displays the **Print** menu to print your report or label. Before you can use this

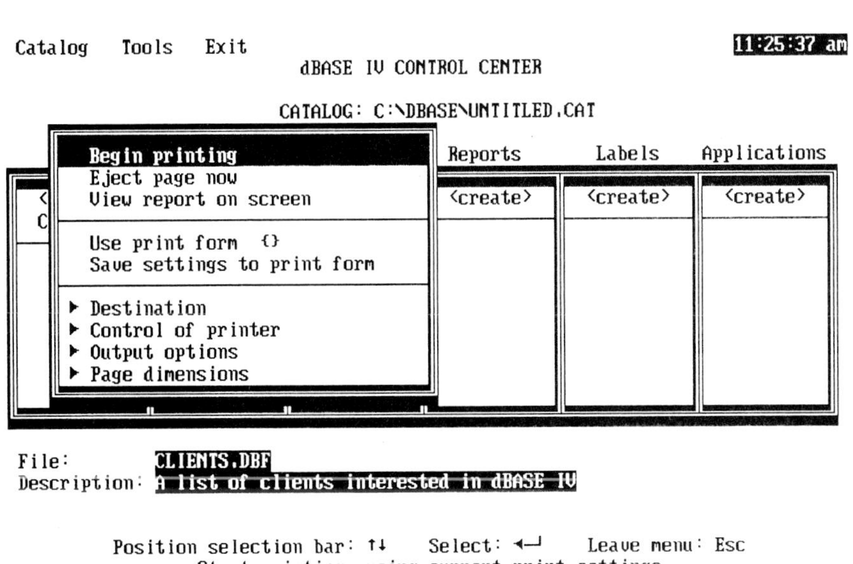

Figure 12-1. The **Print** menu

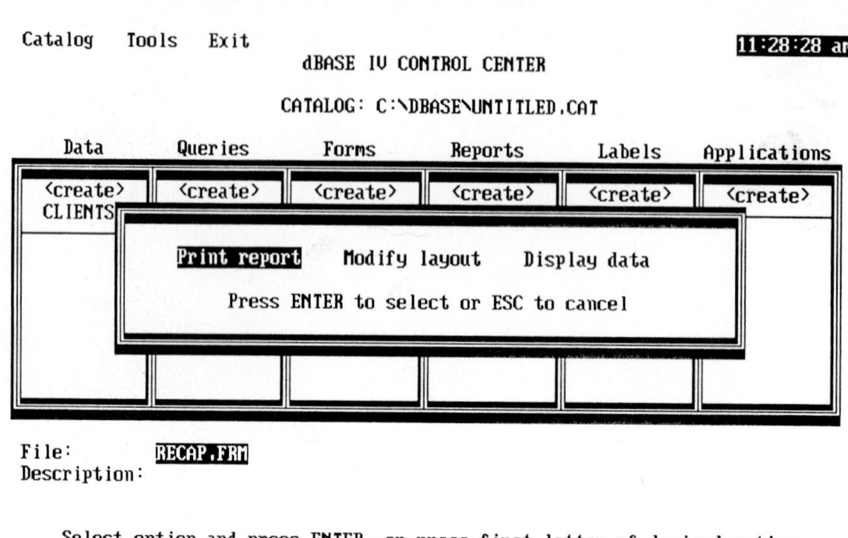

Figure 12-2. The Print option box

method of printing, you must open the database associated with the report or label.

Printing a Quick Report

You can print a "quick report" of the current database file or view by pressing SHIFT-F9 (Quick Report). You can use this key from the Edit, Browse, or Queries Design screens, or from any panel in the Control Center except the Applications Panel. Pressing SHIFT- F9 displays the **Print** menu. Once you've set the menu's options, you can print the quick report by selecting **Begin printing**. To cancel a quick report, press ESC.

You can use any database to print a quick report. Before you print a quick report, however, you must open the database. (To open a database, highlight its file name in the Data Panel and press

Page No. 1
01/26/89

FIRSTNAME	LASTNAME	COMPANY	ADDRESS
George	Thomas	Texasville Pumps	221 Texasville Way
Paul	Simon	dBASE Users Group	1234 Primrose Lane
Paul	Shaffer	Texas Connections	890 Circle Street
Sherman	Mc Coy	Mc Coy Instruments	876 Bradford Street
Owen	Meany	Meany Intl Parcel Service	6711 Waites Street
John	McCrae	Rhoad Island Research	9001 Frost Way
Zeb	Smith	Smith, Smith & Smith	512 Blackhawk Avenue
Kim	Smith	Smith, Smith & Smith	7950 Park Avenue
Diana	Jones	Rayman and Associates	1000 Frontage Road
Steven	Hill	Micro Processes Inc.	36800 Luau Lane
Adene	Smith	Smith, Smith & Smith	2948 El Camino Real
Kilgore	Trout	Ashton-Trout	9743 Pine Ave
Melissa	Williams	Lettuce Development Corp	640 Nashua Court
Jake	van de Kammps	Braland	1010 Main Street
Nathan	Zuckerman	Microshop	43000 Rainbow Drive

Figure 12-3. Results of a quick report

ENTER. Then select the **Use file** option.) Once you've opened a database in the Control Center, press SHIFT-F9, and the **Print** menu appears.

Figure 12-3 shows the results of a quick report. The report begins with the page number and current date followed by columns headed with the names of the fields in your database. If a field name is wider than the field's width, the field is widened to display the complete field name. dBASE prints only the fields that can fit on a single page. All numeric fields show totals in the last line of a quick report.

When you print a quick report from any panel other than Reports or Labels, (that is, Data, Queries, or Forms), dBASE IV prints the currently active database file or view. For example, if you move the highlight to the name of a form in the Forms Panel, dBASE IV composes a report using the active database or view. It does not print your form.

Printing Your Data

The **Begin printing** option starts printing the selected report, program, label, or database structure. You can pause printing by pressing CTRL-S. You can press ESC to stop printing altogether. If your printer contains a print buffer, it may continue to print even after you press CTRL-S or ESC.

For example, you can access this **Print** menu by moving the highlight to the name of the report in the Reports Panel and pressing SHIFT-F9. When you select the **Begin printing** option from this menu, dBASE IV begins printing the highlighted report.

Ejecting a Page

You can ensure that your reports and forms print starting at the top of a new page by using the **Eject page now** option from the **Print** menu. You can also eject a page by using the **New page** option from the **Control of printer** submenu. Both of these options eject a page and reset your printer to the top of a new page.

Tip: EJECT PAGE is the dot prompt equivalent of the **Eject page now** option.

Previewing a Report

Once you've created a report or label on the Reports or Labels Design screen, you can preview that report or label by using the **View report on screen** option in the **Print** menu. This option sends your report or label to the screen, one screen at a time. The report displays as it would on your printer. However, if your report is wider than 80 characters, dBASE wraps each line as it displays the report. After displaying a screenful of data, dBASE prompts you to press ESC to stop viewing your report or SPACEBAR to continue.

Printing with Predefined Forms

Print forms are binary files that contain print settings. Example settings include print pitch, print quality, line spacing, page layout, and more. dBASE saves these settings in print form files with a .PRF extension. Saving settings in print form files is covered in the next section, "Saving Settings to Print Forms."

To use a predefined print form to print the current label or report, select **Use print form** from the **Print** menu. dBASE IV displays a list of available print forms in the current directory in the upper-right corner of your screen. If no print forms are available in the current directory, dBASE uses the default print form file, REPORT.PRF, for reports, and the LABEL.PRF file for labels. These files reside in the directory where you installed dBASE IV.

Suppose you have just printed two copies of a report double spaced and in near letter quality print mode. You can save these settings to a print form and use them again on other reports. Figure 12-4 shows the results of selecting the **Use print form** option with three print forms listed. When you select a form by using the **Use print form** option, the settings defined in that form apply to the current print job.

As mentioned, a print form file saves the current print settings such as spacing, print pitch, and print quality. As you'll soon see, you can specify many of these options by using system memory variables. You can enter system memory variables at the dot prompt, or you can include them in a program file. When you enter system memory variables at the dot prompt, they apply to the entire document. However, when you use system memory variables in a program, you can have them apply to specific sections of a document. For a more complete description of system memory variables, see Chapter 34.

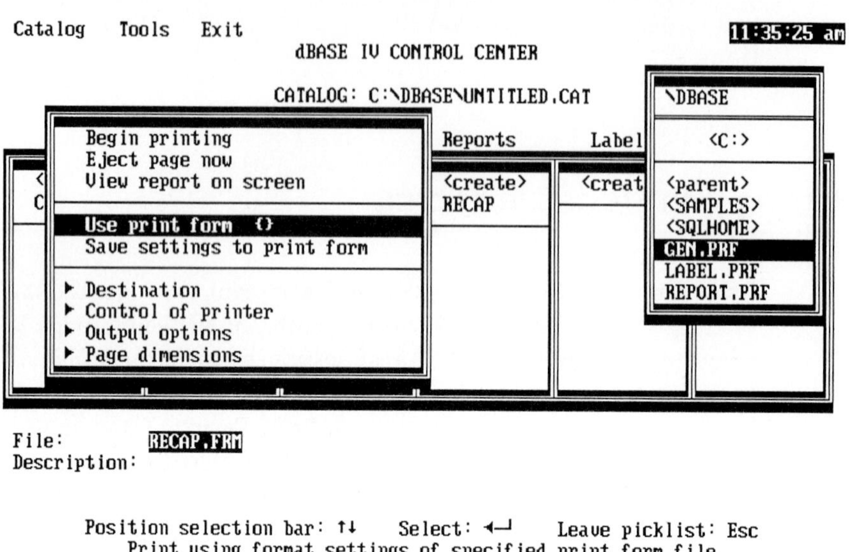

Figure 12-4. The **Use print form** submenu

Tip: You can activate a print form file from the dot prompt by using the system memory variable _pform. The syntax is

. _pform = "*<print form name>*"

For example, enter the following to print the INFO report from the dot prompt using a print form file named CLASSIC:

```
. _pform = "Classic"
. REPORT FORM Info TO PRINT
```

Saving Settings to Print Forms

The **Save settings to print form** option in the **Print** menu allows you to create or modify a print form that stores the currently selected print settings. When you select this option, dBASE prompts you to enter a file name. You can enter a name of up to eight characters, beginning with a letter. When you press ENTER, dBASE IV creates your print form, automatically adding the .PRF extension.

For example, to save a print form file with the name IMPRESS, select the **Save settings to print form** option from the **Print** menu and type **IMPRESS**. When you press ENTER, dBASE saves the file as IMPRESS.PRF. You can now use these printer settings again with another document by selecting the **Use print form** option from the **Print** menu and entering **IMPRESS** as the print form file.

Choosing a Destination for Your Output

By using the **Destination** submenu in the **Print** menu, you can determine where to send the output of a selected form, label, or report. You can send your output to either the screen, the printer, or a file. The **Destination** submenu lets you choose from the printer or a file. To send your output to the screen, use the **View report on screen** option from the **Print** menu.

Writing to a File

The **Write to** option in the **Destination** submenu determines whether your output is sent to a DOS file or to your printer when you select the **Begin Printing** option from the **Print** submenu. The **Write to** option gives you two choices.

- **PRINTER** Sends output directly to your printer
- **DOS FILE** Sends output to a DOS file

Press ENTER to toggle between the two options.

When you store your output to a DOS file, you can use that file to print your data at a later time or at another location. To save your output to a DOS file, select **DOS FILE** from the **Write to** submenu. Next, select a name for the DOS file by using the **Name of DOS file** option. dBASE IV gives your file a .PRT extension. If you don't provide a file name, dBASE IV provides one for you, based on the name of the report or label you're currently printing. For more on naming your DOS file, see the next section, "Naming Your DOS Files."

When dBASE IV creates a DOS file, the file meets the requirements of the printer shown in **the Printer model** option of the **Destination** menu. For example, the current printer model in Figure 12-5 is a Hewlett-Packard LaserJet. If you select **Begin printing** from the **Print** menu with this printer model active, dBASE adds the control characters specific to the Hewlett-Packard LaserJet directly to the DOS file.

After you've created a DOS file, you can print it out by entering the DOS command **COPY *<filename>*/B PRN**. DOS copies your file to the printer. The /B tells DOS to copy the entire file to the printer. The letters "PRN" refer to the DOS device name for your printer. For more information on saving and printing files, see the section "Choosing Your Printer Model."

To create a DOS file from the dot prompt, use the SET PRINTER TO FILE command. For example, to create a file named WORK.PRT, enter the following at the dot prompt:

```
. SET PRINTER TO FILE Work
```

dBASE adds the .PRT extension. When you send output to your printer, it is now sent to a file formatted for your printer with the name WORK.PRT.

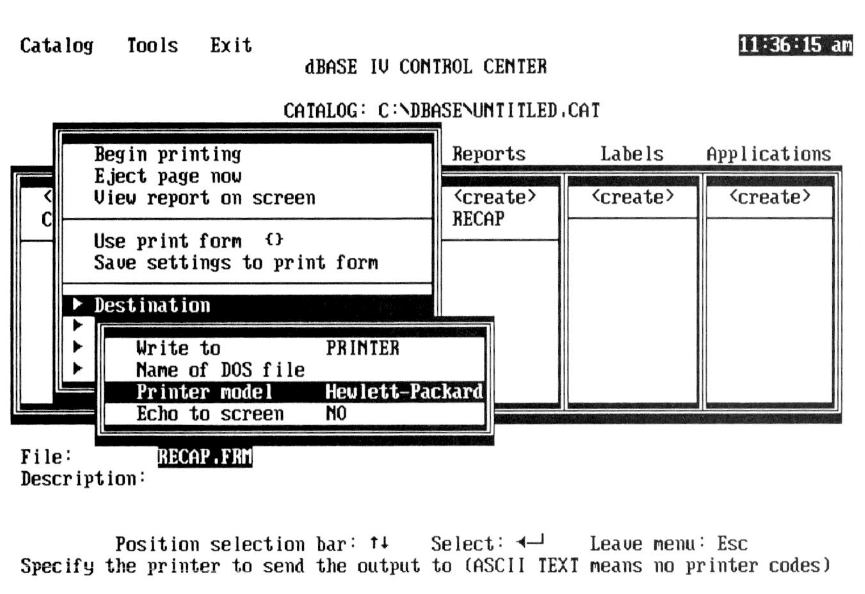

Figure 12-5. The **Destination** submenu

Naming Your DOS File

As mentioned, by selecting the **Name of DOS file** option from the **Destination** menu, you can name the DOS file that dBASE saves your text to when it prints to a DOS file. If you don't enter a name in this option, dBASE suggests a name based on the name of the report or label that you're writing to disk. For example, if you're printing a report named SALES.FRM, dBASE IV names your DOS file SALES.PRT.

dBASE usually saves a DOS file with the extension .PRT. However, if you have selected **ASCII Text** as your printer in the **Printer model** option, dBASE will store your file with the .TXT extension.

Choosing Your Printer Model

To use the **Print** menu, dBASE must have the name of a printer listed in the **Printer model** option of the **Destination** submenu. This way, when you print your output, dBASE embeds the correct printer control codes for the specified printer.

When you first install dBASE, you can install up to four printers. Even if you don't install a printer, dBASE allows you to use the **GENERIC** and **ASCII Text** printer choices. (For information on installing additional printers see Chapter 2, "Installing dBASE IV.") When you install a printer, you're actually giving dBASE access to a printer driver. dBASE allows you to choose from a list of available drivers when you select the **Printer model** option from the **Destination** submenu of the **Print** menu. Press SPACEBAR to have dBASE cycle through the available choices.

To create a report file without control characters, select the **ASCII Text** printer choice. When you create a file using this choice, you can modify its contents using any conventional word processor that works with ASCII files, including the Text Editor.

Tip: If you save your files with a printer model other than ASCII Text, use the DOS COPY command rather than the DOS TYPE or PRINT command to print your files. The DOS TYPE command stops if it reaches the ASCII character 26, since it interprets this character as an end-of-file marker. The DOS PRINT command embeds control characters of its own, making the file unusable.

If you're planning to use a modem to send your file, select the **ASCII Text** printer from the printer model list to strip any control characters from your file.

Tip: You can activate a printer driver by entering the driver name from the dot prompt using the system memory variable _pdriver. The syntax for changing the active printer driver is

. _pdriver = "*<printer driver filename>*"

For example, to activate the HPLAS100 driver for a Hewlett- Packard LaserJet printer, enter

```
. _pdriver = "HPLAS100.PR2"
```

Echoing Printed Output on Your Screen

You can choose whether to echo to your screen the text that is being sent to your printer or a file. You do this by using the **Echo to screen** option from the **Destination** submenu. If you select **YES**, dBASE IV prints the output to your screen as well as your printer. However, the text on your screen may appear slightly different than on your report because it is formatted for report output, not screen display. You can use this option to view the progress of your printed report.

Controlling the Printer— the Control of Printer Submenu

You can determine the quality and size of printed text and regulate form feed settings by using the **Control of printer** submenu from the **Print** menu. The options available from this submenu enable you to print in near letter quality or draft mode. You can also control the number of characters printed per inch. Moreover, you can use this option to control how your printer handles pages and to specify starting and ending control codes.

Specifying Text Pitch

The **Text pitch** option in the **Control of printer** submenu controls how many characters are printed per inch. dBASE supports four text pitches: pica, elite, condensed, and default.

- **PICA** is 10 characters per inch.
- **ELITE** is 12 characters per inch.
- **CONDENSED** depends on the individual printer but is approximately 17.16 characters per inch.
- **DEFAULT** is whatever pitch your printer is currently set up to print.

You can only use the pica, elite, and condensed pitch modes if your printer supports them (see your printer's manual to find this out).

Tip: You can set the printer pitch from the dot prompt by using the system memory variable _ppitch. The syntax for the _ppitch memory variable is

```
. _ppitch = "PICA"/"ELITE"/"CONDENSED"/"DEFAULT"
```

For example, enter the following at the dot prompt to set your printer to print condensed print:

```
. _ppitch = "CONDENSED"
```

Setting the Print Quality

You can use the **Quality print** option from the **Control of printer** submenu to set your printer to near letter quality printing mode. Press ENTER to toggle between **YES**, **NO**, and **DEFAULT**. **YES** means near letter quality. **NO** sets the printer to its fastest draft mode. **DEFAULT** sets the printer to the currently selected quality level. For example, if your printer is set to a standard mode between near letter quality and draft, choosing **DEFAULT** allows you to print in this standard mode.

Tip: You can select the quality of print from the dot prompt by using the _pquality system memory variable. This memory variable uses the logical values true (.T.) and false (.F.) to select either draft or near letter quality. Enter the following at the dot prompt to set the quality to near letter quality:

```
. _pquality = .T.
```

Ejecting Pages

You can control how dBASE IV ejects extra pages by using the **New page** option from the **Control of printer** submenu. It offers the following options:

- **BEFORE** Feeds a page before the report or labels are printed.
- **AFTER** Feeds a page after the report or labels are printed.
- **BOTH** Feeds a page both before and after printing a report or labels.
- **NONE** Ejects no new pages either before or after a report is printed.

To simply eject a page, you can select the **Eject page now** option from the **Print** menu.

Pausing Between Pages

If you want dBASE to pause between pages of reports or labels, select the **Wait between pages** option from the **Control of printer** submenu. Setting this option to **YES** makes dBASE wait until you press a key before continuing to the next page. You can use this method to print reports on different types of paper or to hand feed individual sheets of paper into a printer.

Tip: You can use the _pwait system memory variable at the dot prompt to determine whether the printer stops after printing each page. _pwait requires a true (.T.) or false (.F.) logical value. The syntax for this command is

```
. _pwait = .T.
```

Specifying Form and Line Feeds

You can use the **Advance page using** option from the **Control of printer** submenu to advance to the top of the next page using form feeds or line feeds. The **FORM FEED** choice instructs your printer to advance to the top of the next page using a form feed character (ASCII 12). The **LINE FEEDS** choice instructs dBASE to move to the top of the next page using the exact number of line feeds that will fill out the current page. (You specify the number of lines per page by using the **Length of page** option in the **Page dimensions** submenu.) These options are helpful if you're using an unusual paper size and you need to control the way dBASE IV advances to the top of the next page.

Specifying Starting Control Codes

Printer control codes are characters that you send to your printer with which it can perform certain actions besides those specified from the **Print** menu. You enter starting control codes by using the **Starting control codes** option from the **Control of printer** submenu. dBASE sends these control codes to the printer as it starts to print.

Most printer control codes begin with an *escape sequence.* An escape sequence starts with the ASCII equivalent for ESC and is delimited by curly braces. For example, the ASCII code for ESC is 27, so you enter it as {27}. Follow these escape sequences with a character string or ASCII code that is specific to your printer. Different character strings or ASCII codes perform different printer control functions. For the control codes specific to your printer, see your printer's manual.

You can use certain key names inside curly braces to specify escape sequences, instead of using the ASCII equivalent. For example, you can enter **{ESC}**, **{esc}**, or **{ESCAPE}** instead of **{27}**. You can also enter **{CTRL-[}** to indicate an escape sequence.

{ESC}15 is a typical escape sequence that tells an IBM graphics printer to print in condensed mode. Table 12-1 displays the con-

ASCII Code	Control Character
0	{NULL} or {CTRL-@}
1	{CTRL-A}
2	{CTRL-B}
3	{CTRL-C}
4	{CTRL-D}
5	{CTRL-E}
6	{CTRL-F}
7	{BELL} or {CTRL-G}
8	{BACKSPACE} or {CTRL-H}
9	{TAB} or {CTRL-I}
10	{LINEFEED} or {CTRL-J}
11	{CTRL-K}
12	{CTRL-L}
13	{RETURN} or {CTRL-M}
14	{CTRL-N}
15	{CTRL-O}
16	{CTRL-P}
17	{CTRL-Q}
18	{CTRL-R}
19	{CTRL-S}
20	{CTRL-T}
21	{CTRL-U}
22	{CTRL-V}
23	{CTRL-W}
24	{CTRL-X}
25	{CTRL-Y}
26	{CTRL-Z}
27	{ESC} or {ESCAPE} or {CTRL-[}
28	{CTRL-\}
29	{CTRL-]}
30	{CTRL-^}
31	{CTRL-_}
127	{DEL} or {DELETE}

Table 12-1. Control Code Equivalents

trol codes that you can use inside curly braces with dBASE IV. Check your printer manual for a list of control codes that your printer recognizes.

Tip: You can use control codes with the ?/?? and ??? commands to change your printer's output and bypass the installed printer driver. For example, you can use escape codes with the ?/?? command to change type styles for individual sections of text. On the other hand, you use escape codes with the ??? command to change the type style for an entire document.

For example, if you're using a Hewlett-Packard LaserJet, you can send a control code from the dot prompt that instructs the printer to underline the text throughout your document. To do this, enter the following at the dot prompt:

```
. ??? "{ESC}&dD"
```

To disable the underlining, enter

```
. ??? "{ESC}&d@"
```

Tip: You can also use the CHR() function to send an ASCII control code to your printer from the dot prompt. You can use this function to combine multiple ASCII control codes. For example, to print in italics using an IBM graphics printer, enter

```
. ??? CHR(27)+CHR(52)
```

to turn off the italics printing mode for an IBM graphics printer, enter

```
. ??? CHR(27)+CHR(53)
```

Specifying Ending Control Codes

Ending control codes are similar to starting control codes, but they are sent to the printer after reports or labels are printed. You use them to reverse the effects of starting control codes. You can add ending control codes by using the **Ending control codes** option

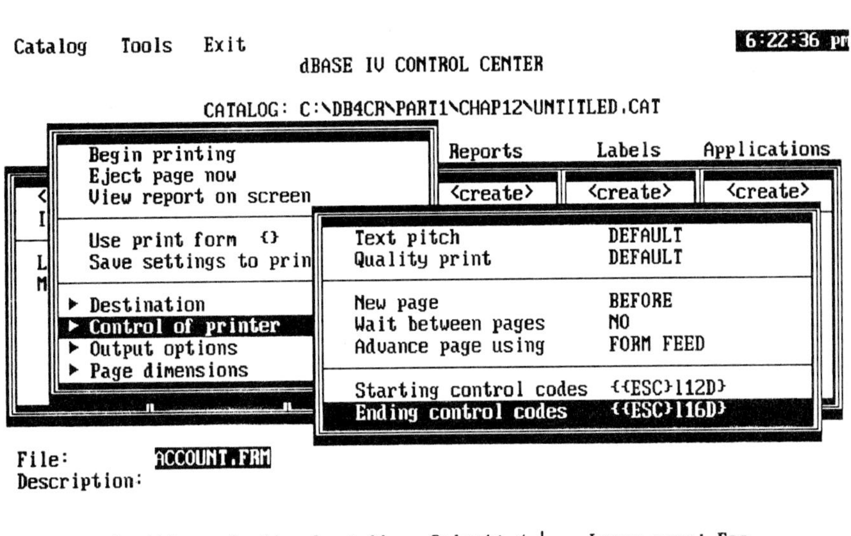

Figure 12-6. The **Control of Printer** submenu

from the **Control of printer** submenu. For example, {ESC}18 is a typical escape sequence you might enter to turn off printing in condensed mode with an IBM graphics printer.

If you use a starting control code, you should use an ending control code to reset your printer. For example, if you used the starting code "{ESC}&l12D" for a Hewlett-Packard LaserJet to print 12 lines per inch, you should also add an ending control code of "{ESC}&l6D" to set the line spacing back to 6 lines per inch. If you don't, dBASE prints any subsequent reports in the 12 lines per inch mode until you specify a new print form or enter another control code. Figure 12-6 shows both the starting and ending control codes for printing 12 lines per inch on a Hewlett-Packard LaserJet and resetting the line spacing to 6 lines per inch. These control codes appear next to the **Starting control code** and **Ending control code** options.

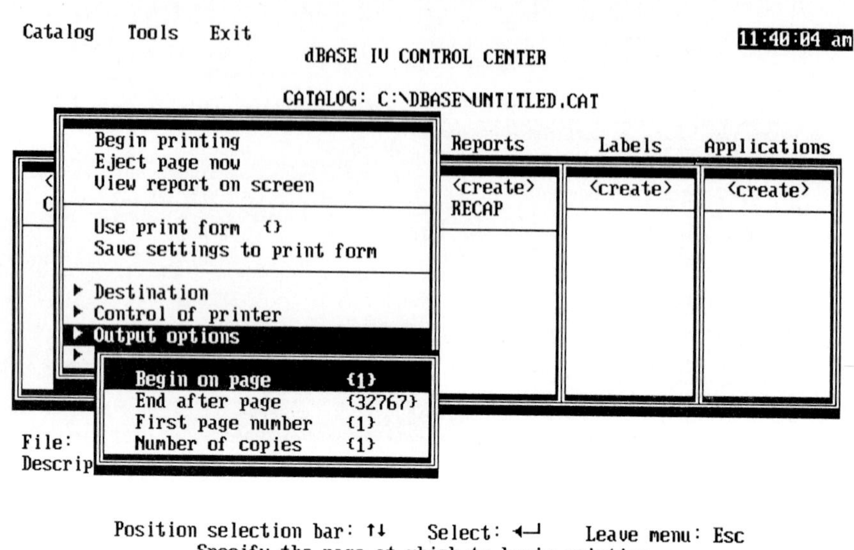

Figure 12-7. The **Output options** submenu

Controlling Output

By selecting the **Output options** submenu from the **Print** menu, you can select portions of text or specify the number of copies, to be sent to your printer. Figure 12-7 shows the **Output options** submenu.

Specifying the First Printed Page

You can start printing from any existing page by using the **Begin on page** option from the **Output options** submenu. dBASE accepts any page number from 1 to 32,767. Suppose that you want to print the middle section of a 30-page report. If you select the **Begin on page** option, you can enter **10** to begin printing on page

10, and then use the **End after page** option to specify the ending page number of your report.

Specifying the Last Printed Page

The number you enter for the **End after page** option is the last page that dBASE prints. For example, to print pages 10 through 20 of a 30-page report, select the **Begin on page** option and enter **10**. Then, select the **End after page** option and enter **20** as the last page for dBASE to print. When dBASE prints labels or a report, the number that automatically appears in this field will change to reflect the last page specified in the current print form or the last page of the last print form used. The default setting for the **End after page** option is 32,767.

Assigning a Number to the First Printed Page

You can assign a particular page number to the first page of a report by selecting the **First page number** option from the **Output options** submenu. This enables you to take pages from several different reports and number them consecutively.

For example, say you have two 20-page reports and you need to create a consecutively numbered report made up of the last five pages of both of these two reports. You can use the first report, select the **Begin on page** option, and enter the number **15.** Then, you can select the **First page number** option and enter **1** to begin consecutively numbering the first five pages of your new report. You can then use the second report and select the **Begin on page** option and again enter the number **15**. By selecting the **First page number** option again and entering **6**, you can continue the consecutive numbering of the last five pages for your new report. Your new report consists of the last five pages of the two 20-page reports and is consecutively numbered 1 through 10.

Tip: You can set the current page number from the dot prompt by using the _pageno system memory variable. To set the beginning page number, use the _pbpage system memory variable. See Chapter 34 for more information.

Specifying the Number of Copies

If you want to print more than one copy of a set of labels or a report, you can specify the number of printed copies with the **Number of copies** option. When dBASE IV finishes printing, it resets the **Number of copies** option to the specified number of copies in the current print form. You can print from 1 to 32,767 copies with this option.

Laying Out the Page

The **Page dimensions** submenu defines how dBASE places your text on a page. You can set the length of a page, line spacing, and print margins from this option. Figure 12-8 illustrates which section of the page each of these page dimension options affects.

Choosing the Length of a Page

dBASE IV defines the total page length as the number of printed lines from the top to the bottom of the page. You can use the **Length of page** option from the **Page dimension** submenu to define the length of a page from 1 to 32,767 lines. A sheet of 8 1/2- by 11-inch paper with a standard line spacing has room for 66 lines.

Tip: You can use the _plength system memory variable at the dot prompt to define the length of the page. The syntax for this memory variable is

```
. _plength = <type N expression>
```

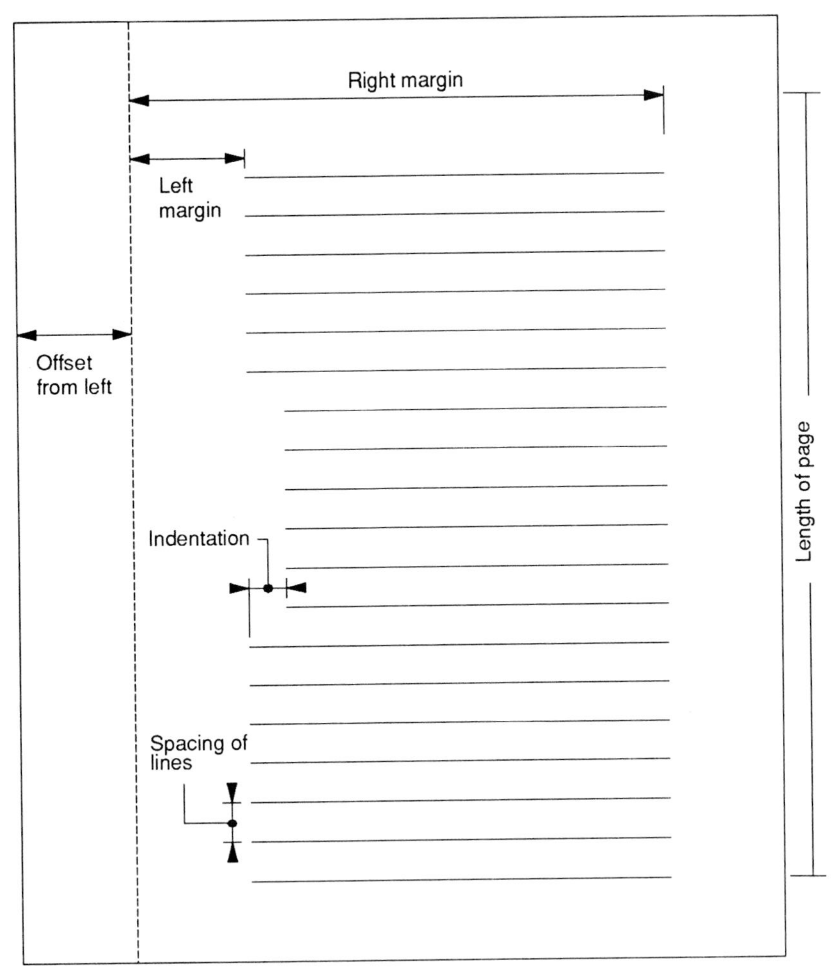

Figure 12-8. The basic page dimensions

For example, to assign at the dot prompt a page length of 50 lines to each page, enter

```
. _plength = 50
```

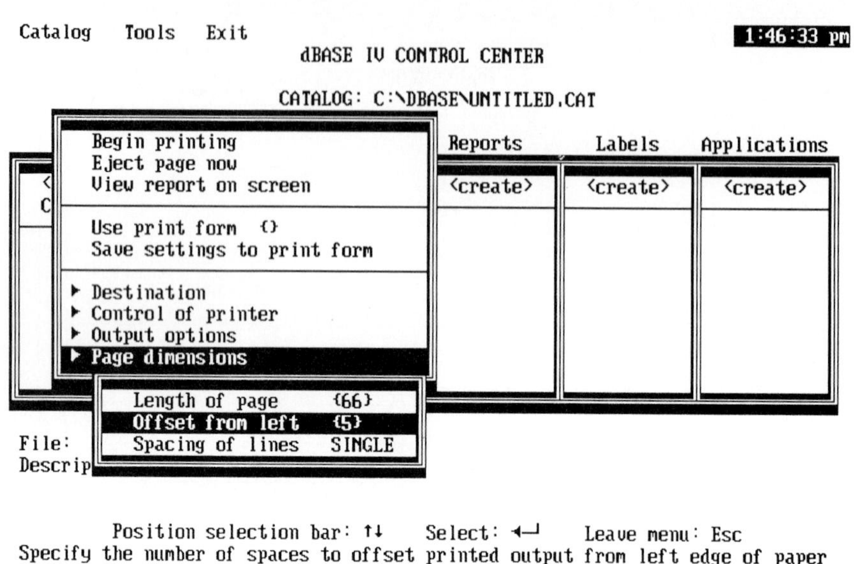
Catalog Tools Exit
1:46:33 pm
dBASE IV CONTROL CENTER
CATALOG: C:\DBASE\UNTITLED.CAT
Begin printing
Eject page now
View report on screen
Use print form {}
Save settings to print form
Destination
Control of printer
Output options
Page dimensions
Reports
Labels
Applications
<create>
<create>
<create>
Length of page {66}
Offset from left {5}
Spacing of lines SINGLE
File:
Descrip
Position selection bar: ↑↓ Select: ←┘ Leave menu: Esc
Specify the number of spaces to offset printed output from left edge of paper

Figure 12-9. The **Page dimensions** submenu

Offsetting Your Left Margin

You can set the number of spaces that dBASE includes before your margin by selecting the **Offset from left** option, as shown in Figure 12-8. dBASE allows you to change this setting from 0 to 32,767 columns. The position for the first printed column is the sum of the spaces that you enter in the **Offset from left** option and the left margin of the report.

For example, if you want your first character to appear 10 spaces from the left edge of your paper, you can offset the left by 5 spaces and use a left margin of 5 spaces. Figure 12-9 shows **Offset from left** with an entry of 5 spaces.

Choosing the Line Spacing

You can choose one of three line spacing options by using the **Spacing of Lines** option. Press ENTER to toggle between **SINGLE**, **DOUBLE**, or **TRIPLE** line spacing.

Tip: You can use the _pspacing system memory variable to establish the line spacing. The syntax is

. _pspacing = 1/2/3

For example, enter the following at the dot prompt to produce double spaced output:

```
. _pspacing = 2
```

Printing the Structure of a Database File

To print the structure of a database with the **Print** menu, highlight a database in the Data Panel of the Control Center and press SHIFT-F2 to enter the Database Design screen. Next, choose the **Print database structure** option from the **Layout** menu. When you select this option, the **Print** menu appears and you can print the database structure by selecting the **Begin printing** option.

Tip: You can print the structure of the current database from the dot prompt by using the LIST STRUCTURE TO PRINTER command.

Printing from the Dot Prompt

You can print reports and labels directly from the dot prompt to your screen, printer, or a file. Use the REPORT FORM command for reports and the LABEL FORM command for labels. These commands print reports and labels using the custom label and report forms that you've designed with the Reports and Labels Design screens. Before using these commands, you must activate a database with the USE command. You direct the output to a printer, to the screen, or to a file by adding the TO PRINTER, TO SCREEN, or TO FILE <*filename*> clauses. For example, to print a report with the name STATUS, enter

```
. USE Clients
. REPORT FORM Status TO PRINTER
```

You can also control page ejection, specify summary totals, print your reports without field headings, and more. In addition, you can specify conditions for the report. For example, the following command line gives the heading "Upper Management" to a report called SALARY.FRM, which uses the SALARY database. The TO PRINTER clause specifies the printer as the destination for this report. Finally, the FOR clause specifies that only records with a number in excess of 24,000 in the Gross field of the SALARY database are to be included in this report.

```
. USE Salary
. REPORT FORM Salary HEADING "Upper Management" TO PRINTER FOR Gross > 24000
```

For more about the many options available with the REPORT FORM command, see Chapter 31, "dBASE IV Commands." For control of special effects, you can open a print form file before using the REPORT FORM command; see the section "Printing with Predefined Forms" for more details.

As mentioned, you use the LABEL FORM command to print labels using a custom label form that you've defined via the Labels Design screen. Follow this command with the name of your label

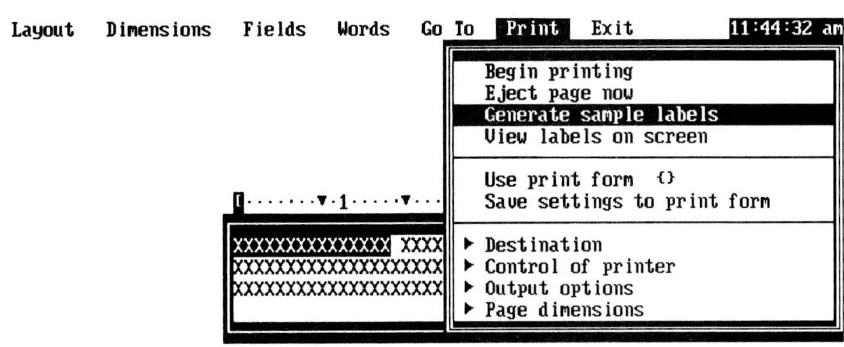

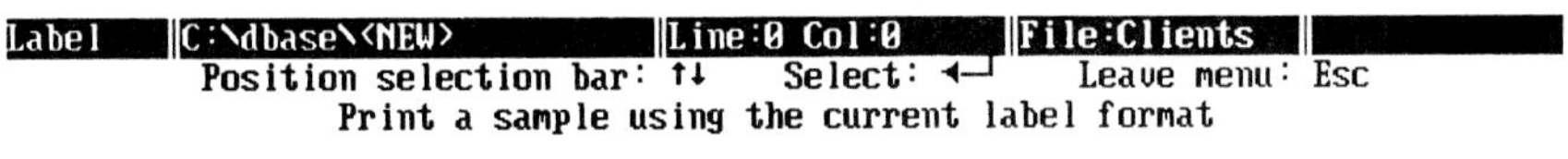

Figure 12-10. The **Generate sample labels** option box

form and then direct the output for the command by using the TO SCREEN, TO PRINTER, or the TO FILE <*filename*> clauses. For example, the following command line uses the label form FIRSTCL and directs its output to the printer:

```
. USE Clients
. LABEL FORM Firstcl TO PRINTER
```

Like the REPORT FORM command, the LABEL FORM command allows you to control how your labels are printed. For example, you can specify conditions for data drawn from an active database. You can also print sample labels to make sure your printer is aligned correctly. For more information, see Chapter 31.

```
*Program is MAILIT.PRG

SET TALK OFF
USE Mailist

*-----------------------Add a blank record to the database
APPEND BLANK
STORE " " TO Choice
DO WHILE Choice"Q"

    *------------------Activate custom format file
    SET FORMAT TO Mailer
    *------------------Use READ to activate GETs
    READ
    *------------------Close the format file
    CLOSE FORMAT

    STORE " " TO Choice

    @ 18,15 SAY "(A)dd Record, (E)dit Record, or (Q)uit :";
    GET Choice PICTURE "!"

    *------------------Use READ again to activate a GET
    READ
    *------------------Evaluate user input
    IF Choice="A"
       APPEND BLANK
    ENDIF

    LOOP

ENDDO
CLOSE DATABASES
RETURN

```

Figure 12-11. Results of selecting the **Line numbers** option

Differences in Print Menus

For the most part, the **Print** menu is the same no matter where you are in dBASE IV. However, two different **Print** menu options are available in the Labels Design screen and the dBASE IV Text Editor.

Labels and the Generate sample labels Option

When you use the **Print** menu in the Labels Design screen, there is an additional option, **Generate sample labels**, as shown in Figure 12-10. This option prints sample labels, allowing you to check your printer for proper alignment. For more on this option, see Chapter 11, "Creating Labels."

Printing Programs and the Line numbers Option

When you use the **Print** menu from the dBASE IV Text Editor or Debugger, there is an additional option, **Line numbers**, which enables you to print line numbers to the left of each line of code. To add line numbers to a program, select the **Line numbers** option and press ENTER and toggle the option to **YES**. Figure 12-11 shows some example results.

In this chapter you've learned various aspects of printing with the **Print** menu. You now know how to view or print a quick report, as well as how to use and save print forms. You can also change the destination of your output to a DOS file or to the screen. Furthermore, you can now change the model of your printer, change the text pitch and quality of print, and enter printer control codes. You can also specify page dimensions such as the length of a page and line spacing. Using the **Print** menu options, you can produce reports and labels to your own specifications.

Catalogs

THIRTEEN

When you first start using dBASE IV, it's not very difficult to keep track of your files. They are few in number and easy to find. The more applications you build, however, the more files you create. Before long, keeping track of your files can become quite an ordeal.

To help you manage your files in dBASE IV, you can use *catalogs*. Catalogs let you group your files according to applications. You can then load and use a catalog whenever you need to perform a particular task.

This chapter explains what dBASE IV catalogs are and how you can use them to help manage your files. It is easiest to work with catalogs from the Control Center. However, this chapter includes a few pointers on using catalogs from the dot prompt, should you decide to do so. (For more on using catalogs from the dot prompt, see the SET CATALOG command in Chapter 32.)

What Is a Catalog?

A catalog is a tool that you use to organize and list files. You can use a catalog to hold several associated files and assemble them for easy access. At first glance, a catalog may appear to be identical to a directory, but there is a clear distinction between the two.

A directory contains files on your disk. If you delete a file from a directory, the file is permanently erased from your disk.

A catalog, however, doesn't contain files but is a special type of database that contains a list of file names. (dBASE gives catalog files a .CAT extension.) Adding or deleting a file name from a catalog doesn't add or remove the file from your disk, it simply adds or removes it from the current list of file names stored in the catalog.

By using catalogs, you can group and display only the files needed for a particular task. For example, if you have several departments that use the same database, but each one requires unique forms or reports, you can tailor your catalogs to display the individual forms or reports for each department.

Creating a Catalog

You can create as many catalogs as you want in dBASE IV. You create a new catalog by selecting **Use a different catalog** from the **Catalog** menu and then selecting the **<create>** option. dBASE will prompt you to enter a file name of eight characters or less. The file name must begin with a letter, and you may use numbers and underscores, but no spaces. After you enter a file name, press ENTER, and dBASE IV creates the new catalog. The new catalog then becomes the *current catalog*, and its name appears between the menu bar and the top of the Control Center panels. (See Figure 13-1.) Any new files that you create are automatically added to the current catalog.

The first time you create a catalog, dBASE creates a *master catalog* named CATALOG.CAT in the directory from which you started dBASE. dBASE always checks to make sure that the master catalog exists and creates one if it doesn't. This master catalog keeps track of other catalogs. You may move the master catalog to another directory as long as that directory is in your path

```
Catalog   Tools   Exit                                          11:47:10 am
                       dBASE IV CONTROL CENTER

                    CATALOG: C:\DBASE\UNTITLED.CAT

    Data      Queries      Forms      Reports      Labels     Applications
  <create>   <create>    <create>    <create>    <create>     <create>

  CLIENTS

File:          New file
Description:   Press ENTER on <create> to create a new file

 Help:F1  Use:◄┘  Data:F2  Design:Shift-F2  Quick Report:Shift-F9  Menus:F10
```

Figure 13-1. The name of the current catalog

statement. (For additional help on setting your path statement, see the SET PATH command in Chapter 32.) If you delete the master catalog, dBASE creates another and stores it in your current directory.

Loading a Catalog

When you enter the Control Center, dBASE automatically loads the catalog previously in use. If you haven't created a catalog and you have at least one dBASE file in the current directory, dBASE creates a catalog for you. This initial catalog is named UNTITLED.CAT. If you don't have a dBASE file in the current directory, the catalog remains empty until you create or add a dBASE file to the current directory.

You can specify a catalog for dBASE to open automatically when you enter the Control Center. You do this by adding the name of the catalog to your CONFIG.DB file as follows:

CATALOG=<*catalog name*>

For more information on changing your CONFIG.DB file, see Chapter 35.

Tip: To change catalogs or turn a catalog on or off from the dot prompt, use the SET CATALOG TO command. If you follow the TO clause with the name of a catalog, dBASE loads that catalog. If you don't specify a catalog name, dBASE closes the current catalog. For more information on the SET CATALOG command, see Chapter 32.

The Catalog Menu

The **Catalog** menu is the first option in the Control Center menu bar. When you open this menu, by pressing ALT-C, your screen looks like Figure 13-2. The **Catalog** menu consists of two sets of options. The first set allows you to use a catalog or modify a catalog name or description. The second set allows you to alter a catalog by adding or removing a file or changing the description of a file in a catalog. The following sections discuss how to use the **Catalog** menu options.

Changing to a Different Catalog

Choosing the **Use a different catalog** option from the **Catalog** menu displays a list of available catalogs in the upper-right corner of your screen. If you've previously described a catalog, that description appears as you move the highlight up or down the list of

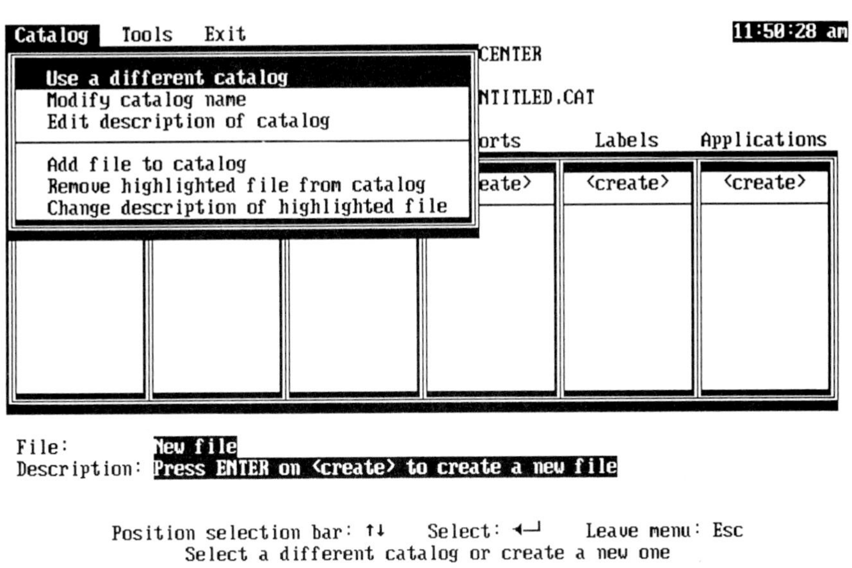

Figure 13-2. The **Catalog** menu

available catalogs. Figure 13-3 shows a list of three catalog names after the **Use a different catalog** option was selected from the **Catalog** menu. To select a different catalog, highlight the name of the desired catalog and press ENTER. dBASE then adds the files in the catalog to the Control Center panels.

If you're working with multiple catalogs, you can easily shift from one catalog to another by selecting this option and choosing the name of the desired catalog from the list of catalog names.

Changing the Name of the Current Catalog

You can change the name of the current catalog at any time by choosing the **Modify catalog name** option from the **Catalog** menu. When you select this option, dBASE prompts you to enter a path and file name for the current catalog. (When you choose a file

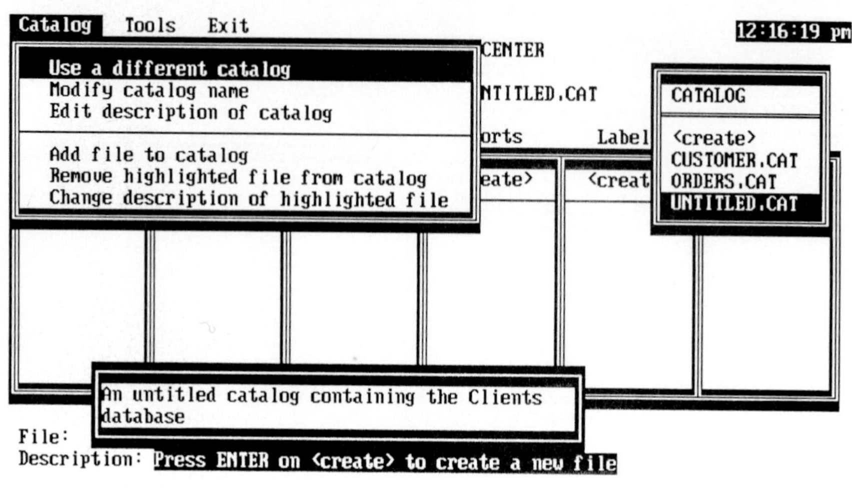

Figure 13-3. **Use a different catalog** displays three catalogs for your selection

name, remember that it should be eight characters or less and begin with a letter.) Change the current catalog name to any new name you desire and press ENTER. dBASE automatically adds the .CAT extension. After you press ENTER, dBASE IV displays the new name above the panels in the Control Center.

Changing a Catalog Description

You can add or edit a catalog description by selecting the **Edit description of catalog** option from the **Catalog** menu. dBASE prompts you for a description of the current catalog. You can enter a description of up to 80 characters.

Adding Files to a Catalog

You can use the current catalog to add up to 200 files to each panel of the Control Center. To add a file to the current catalog, use the **Add file to catalog** option from the **Catalog** menu. The panel your cursor is in when you choose this option is the panel that receives the file. However, each panel only permits you to add files that pertain to that panel. In other words, dBASE only allows you to add databases to the Data Panel, forms to the Forms panel, and so on.

You can only add databases and compiled query, form, report, label, or program files to the current catalog. For example, when you create a report using the Reports Design screen, dBASE IV actually creates three files. The first file is a *generated code* file with an .FRG extension. This file contains the dBASE IV command language commands that describe your report. The second file is a *binary* file with an .FRM extension. dBASE IV needs this file when you modify your report. The third file is a *compiled* file with an .FRO extension. It is this file that dBASE IV uses when it generates your report. You can include the compiled file in the current catalog. As a general rule, compiled files have an "O" as the last letter of their file extensions.

Table 13-1 lists the files (and their extensions) that dBASE allows in each Control Center panel. The file extensions for files that you can't use are also included, marked by an asterisk.

Using Files in Multiple Catalogs

You can use the same file in several different catalogs. This allows you, for example, to share a single database file across multiple catalogs, with each catalog containing different companion files (for example, reports and forms). Then, with a few keystrokes, you can load a whole new set of files designed to perform another task. The following tips about using multiple catalogs can save disk space and help increase your productivity.

Type of File	Panel	File Ext	Code Ext	Compiled Ext
Database	Data	.DBF	—	
View Query	Queries	.QBE*	—	.QBO
Update Query	Queries	.UPD*	—	.UPO
Form	Forms	.SCR*	.FMT*	.FMO
Report	Reports	.FRM*	.FRG*	.FRO
Labels	Labels	.LBL*	.LBG*	.LBO
Program	Applications	.APP*	.PRG*	.DBO

* The file extensions with an asterisk cannot be added to the Control Center panels.

Table 13-1. Files that Can Be Added to Catalogs

Most applications involve relatively few databases. However, there are often several different report, label, query, and program files that use those databases. Rather than keep all of your files in the Control Center panels at all times, you can group them in catalogs according to the tasks they perform. This way, you can load the catalog that contains the databases and companion files required to perform one task, and when you're finished with that job, you can load the next catalog.

You can create different catalogs tailored for different people with varying data needs. For example, someone in accounting might have an entirely different set of information needs than does another person in shipping. You can create different catalogs that list the same databases but contain different report, form, query, and program files suited to those two people's specific information requirements.

By using similar field names in your databases, you can create catalogs that pertain to different databases but use the same reports, labels, and forms. For example, you may have two separate databases that both contain the fields Name and Address. You can easily create a custom label file that uses those field names and then add that file to each of your catalogs. This allows you to use the same label file to perform a mailing for more than one database.

Removing File Names from a Catalog

To remove a file name from a catalog, select the **Remove highlighted file from Catalog** option from the **Catalog** menu. dBASE asks if you would like to delete the file from the catalog. If you press Y, dBASE asks if you would also like to remove the file from disk. Select N unless you want to permanently erase the file from your disk. When you remove a file from a catalog, you can easily add it back into the catalog. When you delete a file from your disk, however, you cannot recover it.

Changing a File Description

You can change the description of any file by highlighting the file name and selecting **Change description of highlighted file** from the **Catalog** menu. dBASE prompts you to enter the new description of the highlighted file. Use the BACKSPACE key to erase any previous file description and enter your new file's description. Press ENTER and the new file description appears below the file name and to the right of the word "Description" near the bottom left of your screen.

Viewing a Catalog from the Dot Prompt

dBASE actually stores catalog information in a special database file. Each record in a catalog database represents a file contained in that catalog. You can view this file just as you would view any dBASE IV database file.

For example, to view the contents of the UNTITLED.CAT catalog file, make sure you have at least one file showing in a Control Center Panel and enter the following commands at the dot prompt:

```
. CLOSE ALL
. USE UNTITLED.CAT
. EDIT
```

The first record of UNTITLED.CAT appears on your screen, as in Figure 13-4. This record contains seven fields of information that describe a given file included in the catalog. In this case, the file shown is the CLIENTS database. You can view the next record by pressing PGDN and the previous one by pressing PGUP. When you press PGDN past the last record in the catalog, dBASE IV displays the message "Add new records? (Y/N)". Press Y to have dBASE IV take you to a new blank record in the catalog. You can then add a file to the catalog by typing the information that describes that file. For more about how to fill in each of the fields in a catalog file record, see the SET CATALOG command in

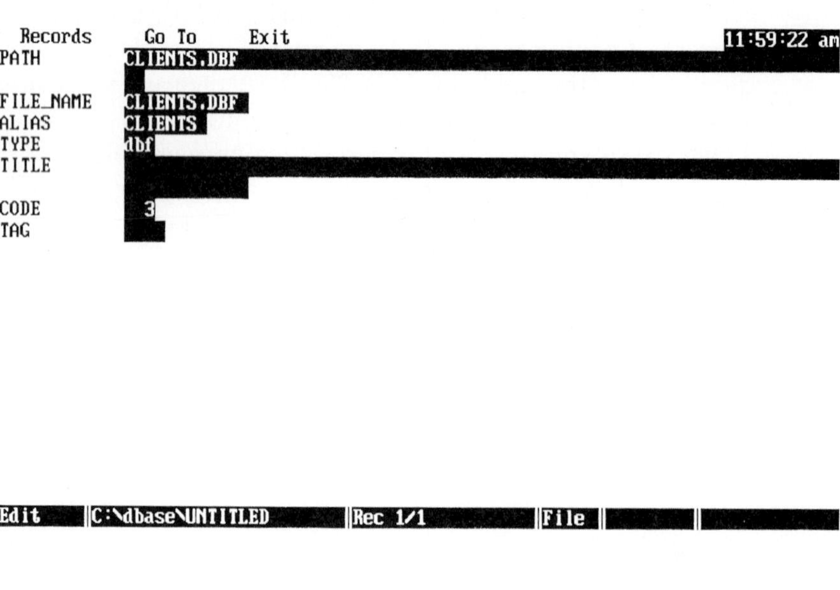

Figure 13-4. The first record of UNTITLED.CAT

Chapter 32. To avoid adding a new record to the catalog, press N. To save your changes, press CTRL-END. To abandon the UNTITLED catalog without making changes, press ESC. In either case, dBASE returns you to the dot prompt.

dBASE provides ten different work areas in which you can use databases. Whenever you activate a catalog, dBASE IV automatically reserves work area 10 for that catalog. If another database is open in work area 10 when you activate a catalog, that database is closed and the new catalog is opened in its place. For more information on work areas, see the SELECT command in Chapter 31.

Eliminating a Catalog

dBASE doesn't offer a menu choice for deleting a catalog from the Control Center. You can create a new catalog by renaming and modifying an existing catalog's contents, or you can delete the catalog file by using the **DOS utilities** option in the **Tools** menu. For more information on deleting files, see Chapter 14, "Tools."

In this chapter, you learned how to load, use, and change catalogs from the Control Center. You also learned how to add files to and remove files from a catalog. You now know the benefits of using catalogs to manage your files.

Tools

FOURTEEN

Importing Files
Exporting dBASE IV Files
DOS Utilities
File Protection
Changing dBASE IV Settings
Changing Display Screen Colors

dBASE IV has an impressive assortment of built-in utilities that were not available in earlier versions of the program. To access these utilities, you use the **Tools** menu from the Control Center (see Figure 14-1). With the options in this menu you can create and use macros, import and export data, invoke DOS utilities, set file protection, and customize several of dBASE IV's initial settings.

Except for the **Macros** option, covered in Chapter 8, this chapter covers the **Tools** menu options, in the order in which they appear on the menu. To open the **Tools** menu in the Control Center, press F10 and select **Tools** from the menu bar. You can also press ALT-T to go directly to the **Tools** menu.

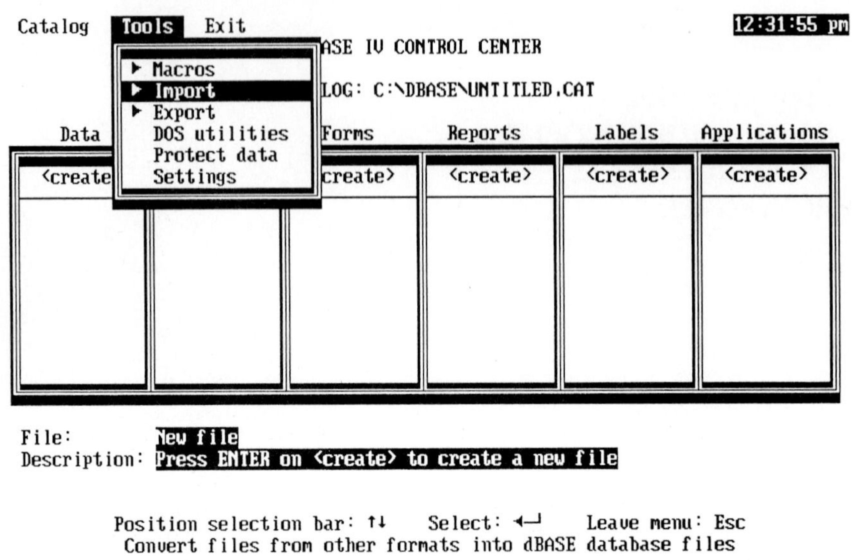

Figure 14-1. The **Tools** menu

Importing Files

To import files from other popular programs, select the **Import** option from the **Tools** menu. You will see a submenu of programs from which dBASE IV can import files, as in Figure 14-2. The **Import** option reads files from other software programs and creates dBASE IV database files from them. You can then use the data in those new files with dBASE IV.

To select a file to import, highlight the software program of your choice and press ENTER. dBASE displays a list of files available for that program, as in Figure 14-3. Move the highlight to the file name of your choice and press ENTER. dBASE then checks to see if that file name already exists in a dBASE IV format with a .DBF extension. If it does, you can overwrite the file or cancel the

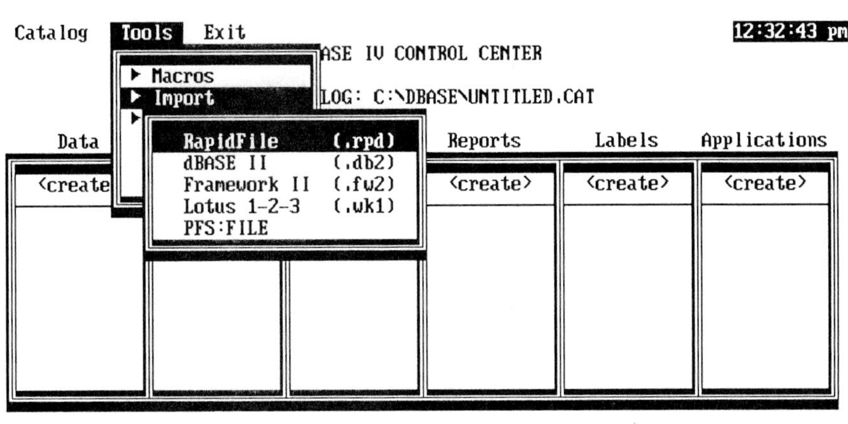

Figure 14-2. The **Import** submenu

current operation. If a .DBF file of the same name doesn't already exist, dBASE IV prompts you for a name for the new file. Enter a file name of eight characters or less and press ENTER. dBASE imports the new data and places it in a database file with the specified file name and a .DBF extension.

Table 14-1 lists the types of files that you can import with the **Import** menu. The table includes previous versions of dBASE, as well as other software products and file formats. It also lists the original file extensions associated with the type of file to be imported and comments about importing those files with dBASE IV.

The **Import** option on the **Tools** menu is analogous to the IMPORT command entered at the dot prompt. For more on the IMPORT command, see Chapter 31.

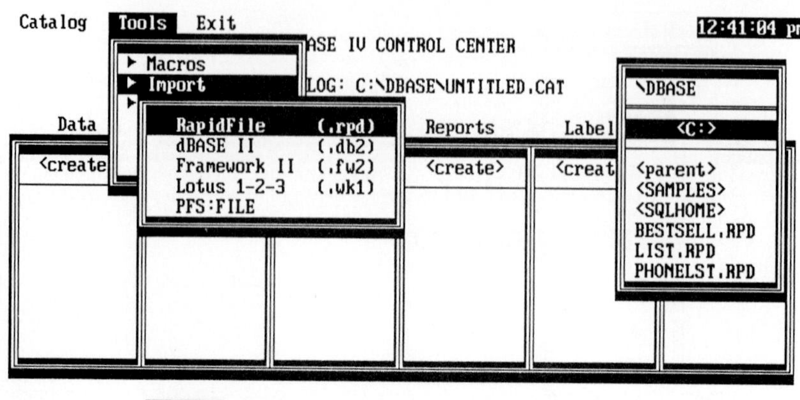

Figure 14-3. A list of files available to be imported

File Type	Extension	Comments
Rapid File	.RPD	dBASE displays only files with the extension .RPD.
dBASE II	.DB2	In order to import a dBASE II file you must first rename the file from .DBF to .DB2.
Framework II	.FW2	You can import both spreadsheet and database files by giving them an .FW2 extension.
Lotus 1-2-3	.WK1	Release 2 files only. To import older .WKS (Release 1A) files use the **Copy records from non-dBASE file** option from the Database Design screen's **Append** menu.
PFS:FILE	None	When you choose this option, you must choose a PFS file from a list of files with no extension. dBASE IV creates .DBF, .VUE, and .FMT files when importing a database with PFS:FILE.

Table 14-1. Files in the **Import** Menu

Tip: You can also transfer data between SQL databases and external non-SQL data files using SQL's LOAD and UNLOAD commands.

The APPEND FROM command, when entered at the dot prompt, offers the same file types as the **Import** menu option, plus some additional file types. For example, you can import ASCII files, SDF ASCII files, and Multiplan files.

Exporting dBASE IV Files

You can export your dBASE IV database data files to other software programs by using the **Export** option from the **Tools** menu.

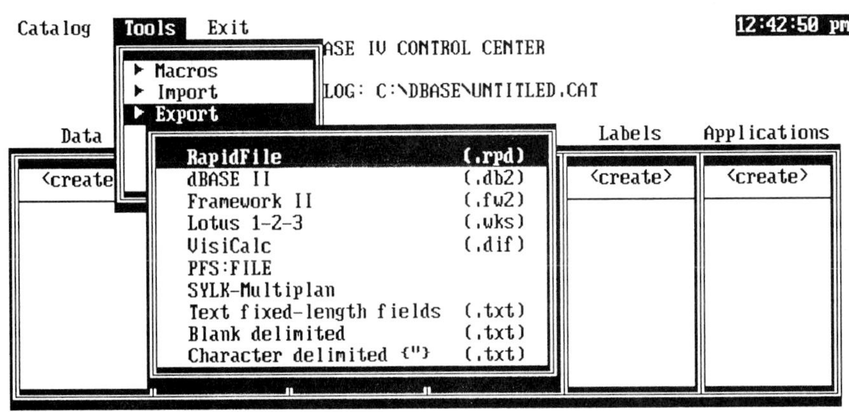

Figure 14-4. The **Export** submenu

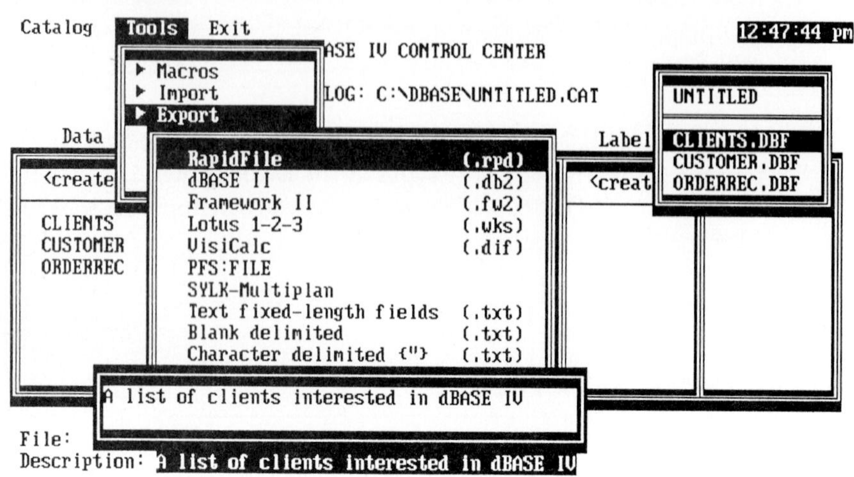

Figure 14-5. The **Export** option displays a list of Database files in the current directory

Like the **Import** option, the **Export** option prompts you with a submenu of file types from which to choose. Figure 14-4 shows the **Export** submenu, which lists the different program and file types for which dBASE can directly create compatible files.

When you select a file type from the **Export** menu, dBASE displays a list of database files in the current directory, as in Figure 14-5. Highlight the file name of your choice and press ENTER. dBASE IV creates a new file that is compatible with the file type you selected, automatically adding the appropriate file extension for the new file. If a file already exists with the new extension, dBASE allows you to either overwrite that file or cancel the export operation.

Always check the limitations of the program you're exporting to before you use the **Export** option. For example, when you export data, make sure that the field widths of your dBASE IV databases are no wider than the field width tolerance of the program that will ultimately use the data. dBASE IV supports field widths much wider than allowed by some other popular software programs. If one or more of your field widths is too wide, the data in those fields is truncated when you export.

There are other export considerations. For example, when you export dBASE IV format files as PFS:FILE compatible, make sure that your format file does not contain in excess of 200 @...SAY...GET file commands. Otherwise, PFS:FILE cannot read the file. There must also be a READ command every 21 rows to break that format file into 21 row pages. What's more, the row coordinates in the @...SAY...GET commands in each page cannot display data below line 20 on the screen. You can check a format file by selecting **View** from the **Operations** submenu of the **Tools** menu, as explained later in this chapter. Or, you can type **MODIFY COMMAND <*format filename*>.FMT** at the dot prompt to check a format file's contents.

Table 14-2 lists the types of files that dBASE can create using the **Export** option. This table includes the exported file's new extension and comments about exporting these files with dBASE IV. The **Export** option is a blend of the EXPORT and COPY TO dot prompt commands. For more on these commands, see Chapter 31.

Tip: If you want to export a memo field to a dBASE III PLUS format see the DBMEMO3 option of the COPY command in Chapter 31, "dBASE IV Commands."

DOS Utilities

When you select the **DOS utilities** option from the **Tools** menu, dBASE takes you to the DOS Utilities screen. This screen includes another menu bar with a collection of DOS utility options that rivals many of the DOS shells on the market. Using the menus from the Dos Utilities Screen, you can access DOS, sort, mark, rename, copy, move, view, and edit files.

File Type	Extension	Comments
Rapid File	.RPD	dBASE creates a data file with an .RPD extension.
dBASE II	.DBF	Copies a dBASE IV file to a dBASE II format. The file is given a .DB2 extension. So, you must rename the exported dBASE II file to .DBF from .DB2.
Framework II	.FW2	You can use this file as a Framework II spreadsheet.
Lotus 1-2-3	.WKS	Creates a Lotus 1-2-3 worksheet file usable by both Release 1A and Re-lease 2 users.
VisiCalc	.DIF	These files are exported in the standard Data Interchange Format structured in row and column form.
PFS:FILE	None	PFS:FILE formats don't require a file extension.
SYLK-Multiplan	None	dBASE records are converted to Multiplan rows and fields are converted to Multiplan columns. dBASE doesn't add an extension to the exported file.
Text fixed-length fields	.TXT	dBASE exports the file to a *system data format* .TXT file. These SDF files store data in records and fields of uniform length.
Blank delimited	.TXT	Creates a text file with a single space between each field. Every record ends with a carriage return line feed.
Character Delimited	.TXT	You may specify a character from a list of characters by pressing SHIFT-F1 after selecting this option. You can also specify a delimiting character that is not displayed on the menu. See the EXPORT and COPY commands for more on character delimited files.

Table 14-2. Files You Can Create with the **Export** Option

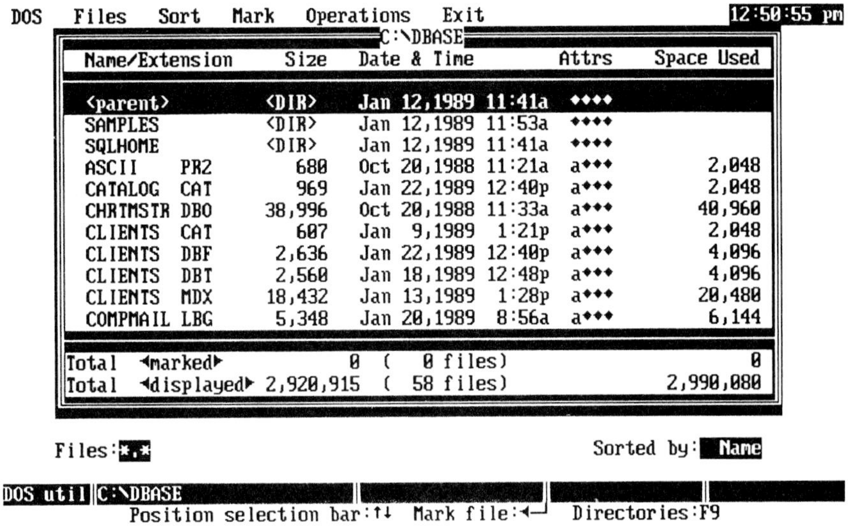

```
DOS   Files   Sort   Mark   Operations   Exit                              12:50:55 pm
                                   C:\DBASE
 Name/Extension        Size   Date & Time          Attrs     Space Used

 <parent>             <DIR>   Jan 12,1989 11:41a   ****
 SAMPLES              <DIR>   Jan 12,1989 11:53a   ****
 SQLHOME              <DIR>   Jan 12,1989 11:41a   ****
 ASCII     PR2          680   Oct 20,1988 11:21a   a***           2,048
 CATALOG   CAT          969   Jan 22,1989 12:40p   a***           2,048
 CHRTMSTR  DBO       38,996   Oct 20,1988 11:33a   a***          40,960
 CLIENTS   CAT          607   Jan  9,1989  1:21p   a***           2,048
 CLIENTS   DBF        2,636   Jan 22,1989 12:40p   a***           4,096
 CLIENTS   DBT        2,560   Jan 18,1989 12:48p   a***           4,096
 CLIENTS   MDX       18,432   Jan 13,1989  1:28p   a***          20,480
 COMPMAIL  LBG        5,348   Jan 20,1989  8:56a   a***           6,144

Total  ◄marked►             0  (   0 files)                           0
Total  ◄displayed► 2,920,915  (  58 files)                   2,990,080

 Files:*.*                                          Sorted by: Name

DOS util  C:\DBASE
        Position selection bar:↑↓  Mark file:◄┘  Directories:F9
```

Figure 14-6. The DOS Utilities screen

The Files List

Figure 14-6 shows the DOS Utilities screen, listing files from a dBASE directory. This display of files is referred to as a *files list,* and includes the name and extension of the files in the current directory, as well as their size, the date and time they were created, their attributes, and the space they use. The files list includes the categories that follow. For additional information, check your DOS manual.

- **Size** The number of characters in the file (the same as the amount of disk space taken up by a file). If <DIR> appears in the size column, the name refers to a directory rather than a file.

- **Date & Time** These columns show the date and time that the file was created or last changed.

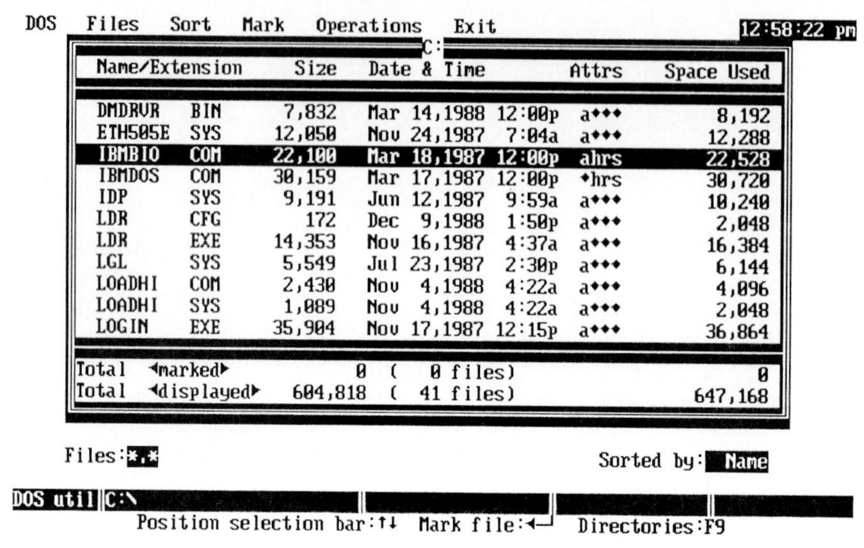

Figure 14-7. The DOS file IBMBIO.COM highlighted in the files list

- **Attrs** Refers to the attribute settings of each individual file. A file can have one or more of the following four attributes:

A read-only file (r)	A file that can't be changed or erased
A hidden file (h)	A file that doesn't appear in a normal DOS directory
An archive file (a)	A typical file that is marked to be backed up
A system file (s)	A file that is not displayed in a DOS directory and is used by DOS

If the file attribute has not been set, only diamonds appear in the Attrs column. Figure 14-7 shows the DOS file IBMBIO.COM, a hidden read-only system file, highlighted in the files list.

- **Space Used** Refers to the amount of space needed on the disk to store each file. This space differs from the Size column because the space used for each individual file depends on the cluster size that your disk uses to store a file. The values in this column are always equal to or greater than the size column. If your cluster size is 2048 bytes, the smallest file will take up at least 2048 bytes.
- **Total marked** Appears at the lower-left corner of the screen and shows the size and number of files marked for a particular operation. When you mark files, they are grouped for future file operations. Marking files is covered later in this chapter in the section "Marking Files."
- **Total displayed** Appears directly below Total marked and lists the size and number of the files displayed in the files list.
- **Files indicator** Appears below the Total markers and shows the expression used to select the files displayed in the files list.
- **Sorted by** Appears across from the Files indicator, on the lower-right corner of the screen. This feature shows the order in which the files in the files list are sorted. You can sort the files list by name, extension, date and time, or size, via the **Sort** submenu covered later in this chapter.

Navigating the Files List

You can move up or down the list of files by using the UP ARROW, DOWN ARROW, PGUP, PGDN, HOME, and END keys. If you highlight the name of a directory and press ENTER, dBASE takes you to the new directory. The files list then displays the files in that directory. To move up a directory from a subdirectory, place the highlight on the **<parent>** marker and press ENTER.

You can also move from one directory to another by pressing F9 (the Zoom key). dBASE replaces the files list screen with a directory tree, as shown in Figure 14-8. The subdirectories are shown indented under their parent directories.

You can use the UP ARROW, DOWN ARROW, PGUP, PGDN, HOME and END keys to move up and down the directory tree. If you press

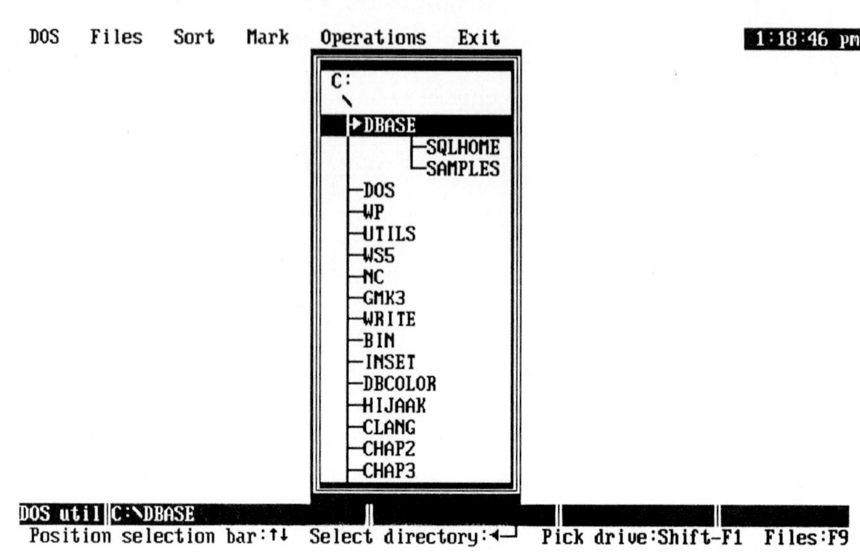

Figure 14-8. The dBASE IV directory tree

ENTER, dBASE takes you to that directory and displays the directory in the files list screen. To reaccess the directory tree, press F9 again.

To change to a new drive, go to the top of the directory tree, place the cursor on the current drive marker, and press ENTER. dBASE will display a list of available drives. The directory tree then displays the directories for the newly chosen drive.

You can easily select different drives and directories in the files list screen. However, when you select **Exit** to return to the Control Center, dBASE takes you back to the directory from which you entered the files list screen.

Using DOS Commands Within dBASE IV

You can use DOS commands without quitting dBASE by using the **Perform DOS command** option from the **DOS** submenu. This

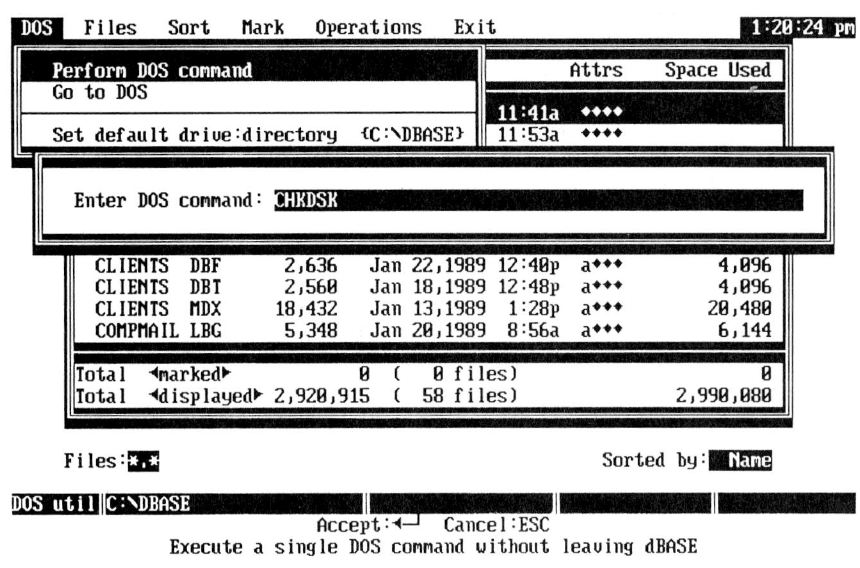

Figure 14-9. The DOS command CHKDSK entered using the **Perform DOS command** option

option allows you to enter a single DOS command. Figure 14-9 shows the DOS command CHKDSK entered after the **Perform DOS command** option has been selected. dBASE takes you to a screen consisting of the status bar only and returns the results of the DOS command. After completing the DOS command, dBASE displays a message prompting you to press any key to return to dBASE.

Exiting Temporarily to DOS

The **Go to DOS** option in the **DOS** submenu lets you exit temporarily to DOS. dBASE reminds you that any files you've marked will be unmarked if you temporarily exit to DOS. You can either proceed to DOS or cancel the **Go to DOS** selection. When you reach the DOS prompt, you can enter one or more DOS commands.

```
The IBM Personal Computer DOS
Version 3.30 (C)Copyright International Business Machines Corp 1981, 1987
         (C)Copyright Microsoft Corp 1981, 1986

dBASE DOS Window                               Type "EXIT←┘" to return to dBASE.

C:\DBASE>
```

Figure 14-10. The modified DOS prompt

Figure 14-10 shows the modified DOS prompt that appears after you select the **Go to DOS** option.

When you're finished using DOS, you can return to dBASE by typing **EXIT** and pressing ENTER. Between DOS commands, dBASE cues you to type **EXIT** to return to dBASE.

Tip: You can run any DOS command from the dot prompt by preceding a DOS command with the exclamation point. For example, entering **! CHKDSK** at the dot prompt performs the DOS CHKDSK command.

Setting the Default Drive and Directory

By selecting the **Set default drive:directory** option from the **DOS** submenu, you can change the default drive and directory. When you select this option, a dBASE prompt box requests that you enter your new drive or directory (see Figure 14-11). You can also use SHIFT-F1 to display the directory tree, from which you can select a drive or directory. To use the directory tree to specify a default directory, highlight the new directory and press ENTER. dBASE then stores your new files in the selected directory.

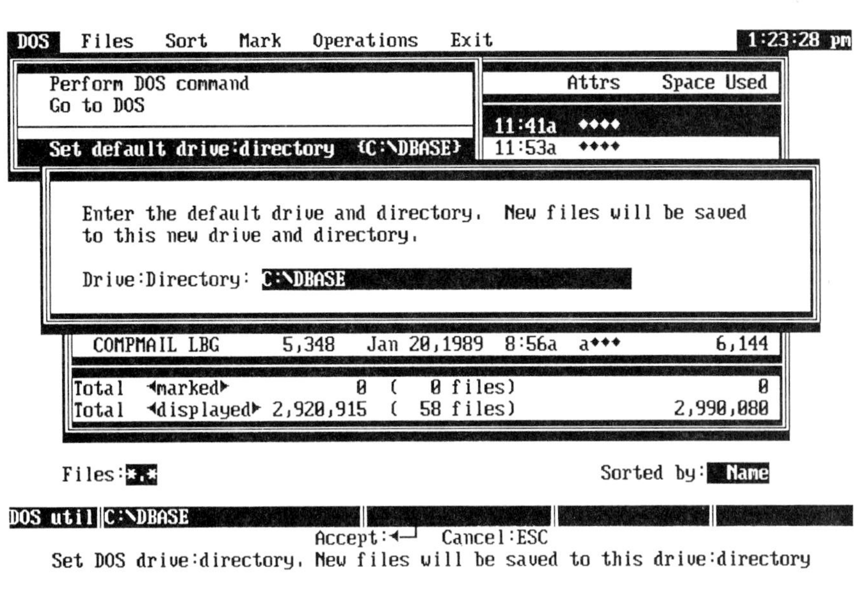

Figure 14-11. Prompt box requesting a new drive or directory

Selecting Files

The **Files** submenu enables you to temporarily change your drive and directory and to display and perform operations on selected files from the chosen drive or directory.

The **Change drive:directory** option of the **Files** submenu allows you to change to a different drive or directory. Using this option doesn't change your default drive or directory, but determines the files displayed in the files list. You can also use SHIFT-F1 to display the directory tree and use the navigation keys to select a different directory. dBASE displays the files from the selected directory.

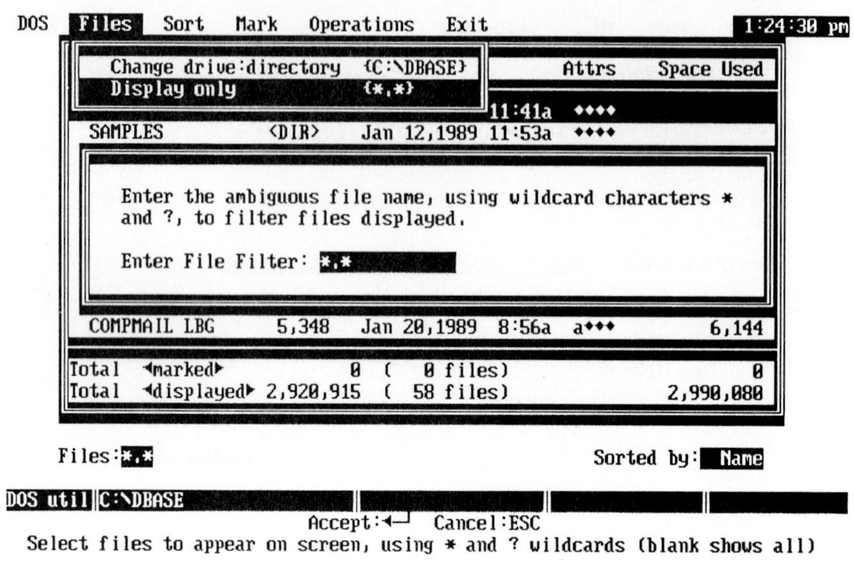

Figure 14-12. The **Display only** option from the **Files** submenu

By using the **Display only** option from the **Files** submenu, you can display only those files that meet a certain criteria. When you select this option, your screen should look like Figure 14-12. You can then enter the characters that describe the files you want to see on the files list screen. You can use either upper- or lowercase characters since the **Display only** option is not case sensitive. You can also use all standard wildcards such as * and ?. For example, by entering ***.DBF** in the **Display only** option box, you can display only database files in the files list. To display every file in the current directory, you can enter ***.*** or leave the option blank and press ENTER. Figure 14-13 shows the results of entering ***.DBF** in the **Display only** option from the **Files** submenu.

The current selection for the **Display only** option is located in the lower-left corner of your screen, preceded by the word "Files."

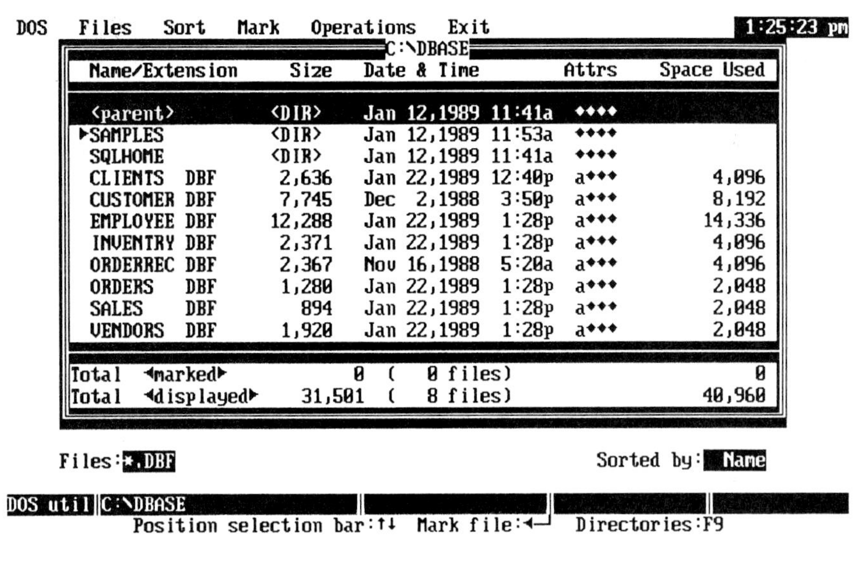

Figure 14-13. The results of entering ***.DBF** using **Display only**

Sorting Files

The **Sort** submenu doesn't actually sort your files on the disk, but it does allow you to view your files in one of the following orders:

- **Name** Lists the files alphabetically by their file names (the default).
- **Extension** Lists the files alphabetically by their extensions (for instance, .BAT, .DBF, .EXE).
- **Date and Time** Lists files in chronological order.
- **Size** Lists the files from the smallest to the largest.

```
DOS  Files   Sort   Mark   Operations   Exit                          4:55:04 pm
                                  C:\DBASE
  Name/Extension      Size   Date & Time          Attrs     Space Used

  <parent>           <DIR>   Jan 12,1989 11:41a   ****
  SAMPLES            <DIR>   Jan 12,1989 11:53a   ****
  SQLHOME            <DIR>   Jan 12,1989 11:41a   ****
  DBSETUP  RES      27,246   Oct 20,1988 11:14a   a***          28,672
  DBSETUP  PRD       5,893   Oct 20,1988 11:14a   a***           6,144
  DBSETUP  OVL     147,968   Oct 20,1988 11:14a   a***         149,504
  DBSETUP  EXE      80,784   Oct 20,1988 11:14a   a***          81,920
  ASCII    PR2         680   Oct 20,1988 11:21a   a***           2,048
  GENERIC  PR2         680   Oct 20,1988 11:21a   a***           2,048
  HPLAS100 PR2         808   Oct 20,1988 11:22a   a***           2,048
  IBMGP    PR2         808   Oct 20,1988 11:22a   a***           2,048

 Total ◄marked►            0  (   0 files)                           0
 Total ◄displayed► 2,979,097  (  74 files)                   3,067,904

 Files:*.*                                     Sorted by: Date & Time

DOS util ║C:\DBASE       ║              ║              ║
          Position selection bar:↑↓  Mark file:◄┘  Directories:F9
```

Figure 14-14. A directory sorted by date and time

To display your files sorted by their extensions, select the **Sort** submenu, move the highlight to the **Extension** option, and press ENTER. (The **Sort** submenu options are toggles.) You can return to the default sort by reselecting the **Extension** option and pressing ENTER. Figure 14-14 shows a directory in the files list sorted by date and time via the **Sort** submenu.

Marking Files

Using the **Mark** submenu, you can perform operations on several files at once. The **Mark** submenu gives you three options for marking your files in the files list. When you mark a file, dBASE places an arrow marker next to the marked file to the left of the Name/Extension column. Figure 14-15 shows the CUSTOMER.DBF and CLIENTS.DBF files marked in the files list. Once a file is marked,

```
DOS   Files   Sort   Mark   Operations   Exit                    1:25:23 pm
                          C:\DBASE
  Name/Extension      Size   Date & Time          Attrs    Space Used

  CHRTMSTR DBO      38,996   Oct 20,1988 11:33a   a***         40,960
  CLIENTS  CAT         607   Jan  9,1989  1:21p   a***          2,048
 ▸CLIENTS  DBF       2,636   Jan 22,1989 12:40p   a***          4,096
  CLIENTS  DBT       2,560   Jan 18,1989 12:48p   a***          4,096
  CLIENTS  MDX      18,432   Jan 13,1989  1:28p   a***         20,480
  COMPMAIL LBG       5,348   Jan 20,1989  8:56a   a***          6,144
  COMPMAIL LBL       1,665   Jan 20,1989  8:56a   a***          2,048
  COMPMAIL PRF         698   Jan 20,1989  7:34a   a***          2,048
  CONFIG   DB          642   Jan 22,1989 12:28p   a***          2,048
  CUSTOMER CAT         607   Jan 16,1989 11:55a   a***          2,048
 ▸CUSTOMER DBF       7,745   Dec  2,1988  3:50p   a***          8,192

Total  ◂marked▸        10,381  (  2 files)                     12,288
Total  ◂displayed▸  2,939,668  ( 63 files)                  3,014,656

Files:*.*                                         Sorted by: Name

DOS util ║C:\DBASE
           Position selection bar:↑↓  Mark file:◂┘  Directories:F9
```

Figure 14-15. The CUSTOMER.DBF and CLIENTS.DBF files marked in the files list

it remains marked until you return to the Control Center or choose the **Go to DOS** option from the **DOS** submenu.

The **Mark all** option marks all of the files displayed in the files list, even those that are scrolled out of view. For example, suppose you've set the **Display only** option to display only .DBF files in the files list. You can mark all of those .DBF files in the files list by selecting the **Mark all** option from the **Mark** submenu. If more .DBF files exist in the files list than can be seen on the display at one time, they are also marked.

The **Unmark all** option clears the files list of all file markers, even if a marked file is scrolled out of view.

The **Reverse marks** option lets you swap the file marks from the files that are marked to the ones that aren't. You can use this option to copy a certain group of files to floppy disk and then select the **Reverse marks** option to copy the remaining files to another floppy disk.

You can mark a file in the files list without using the **Mark** submenu by simply highlighting the file and pressing ENTER. dBASE places a marker next to the file name. You can unmark a marked file by highlighting the marked file and pressing ENTER again. Try marking and unmarking files in your files list. Before continuing, select the **Unmark all** option from the **Mark** submenu to ensure that no files are marked.

Performing Operations on Selected Files

Use the **Operations** submenu to perform operations on selected files. You can delete, copy, move, or rename one or more files by using this option.

Four of the six menu choices in the **Operations** submenu,— **Delete**, **Copy**, **Move**, and **Rename**—can apply to multiple files. The remaining two options—**View** and **Edit**—can only perform an operation on one file at a time. Using the **View** and **Edit** options, you can display files or edit the contents of a dBASE program file (.PRG), a dBASE SQL file (.PRS), or an ASCII-compatible file.

When you select the **Delete**, **Copy**, **Move**, or **Rename** options, dBASE asks which files you want to be affected by your selection. You can select

- The current file
- The marked files in the files list
- All of the files in the files list

Remember that you may not be able to see all of the marked files in the files list if they don't all fit on your screen at one time. You may want to double-check which files are marked before performing an operation on a group of marked files.

Deleting Files

If you select the **Delete** option from the **Operations** submenu, dBASE deletes all of the files that you've chosen from the **Opera-**

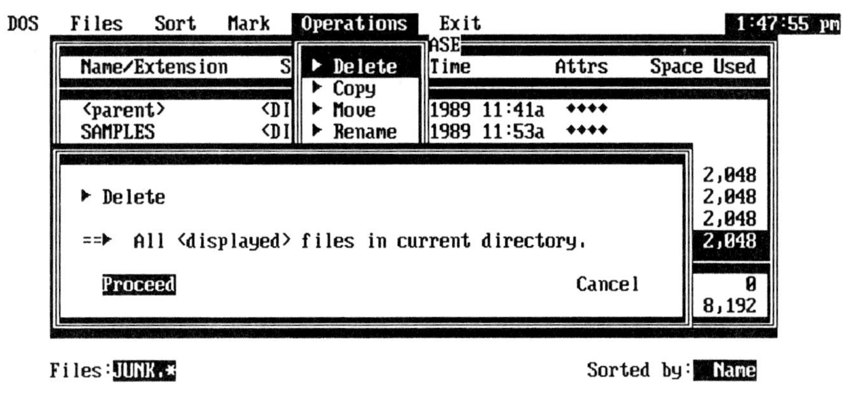

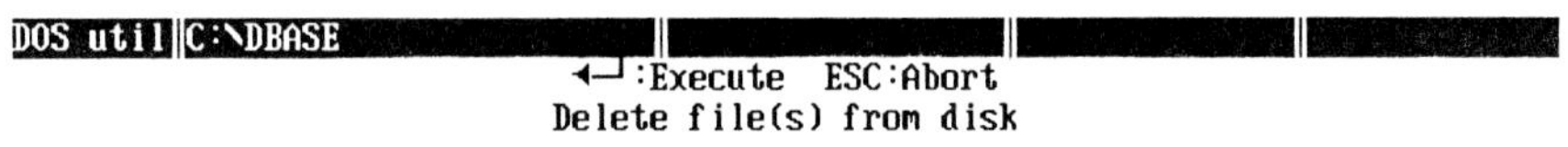

Figure 14-16. Prompt confirming the deletion of all currently displayed files beginning with the file name JUNK

tions submenu (the current file, marked files, or all files in the files list). dBASE displays a prompt box showing the files that are to be deleted, along with the options **Proceed** and **Cancel**. Figure 14-16 shows a dBASE prompt confirming the deletion of all the files currently displayed that begin with the file name JUNK. This filename was selected by using the **Display only** option in the **Files** submenu and typing **JUNK.***. Use the **Delete** option with caution. If you select **Proceed**, your files are erased and are not retrievable.

You can delete an individual file by highlighting that file in the files list and pressing DEL. dBASE allows you to cancel or proceed with the deletion.

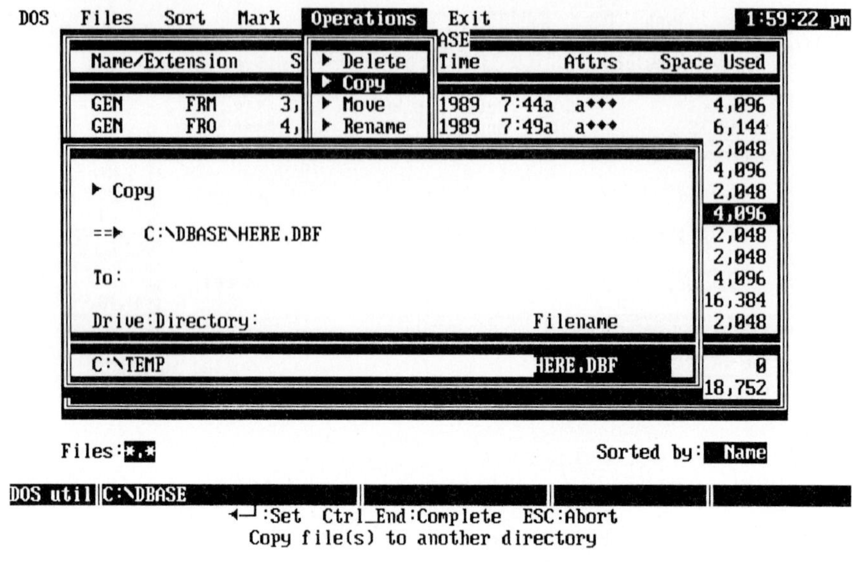

Figure 14-17. Prompt box to modify the default path for the file name to be copied

Copying Files

The **Copy** option from the **Operations** submenu lets you copy any of the files from the files list to a drive and directory of your choosing. When you select this option, dBASE displays a submenu for you to select a single file, marked files, or all displayed files to be copied. When you've made your selection, dBASE displays the current default directory and moves the cursor to the beginning of the "Drive:Directory" prompt to let you modify an existing destination drive and directory or enter a new one.

To copy one or more files from your dBASE directory to another directory, highlight or mark the files to be copied in the files list. Then, select the **Copy** option from the **Operations** submenu. dBASE will display a submenu listing three options: **Single File**, **Marked Files**, and **Displayed Files**. Choose one of these options for the file (or files) to be copied. dBASE then displays a

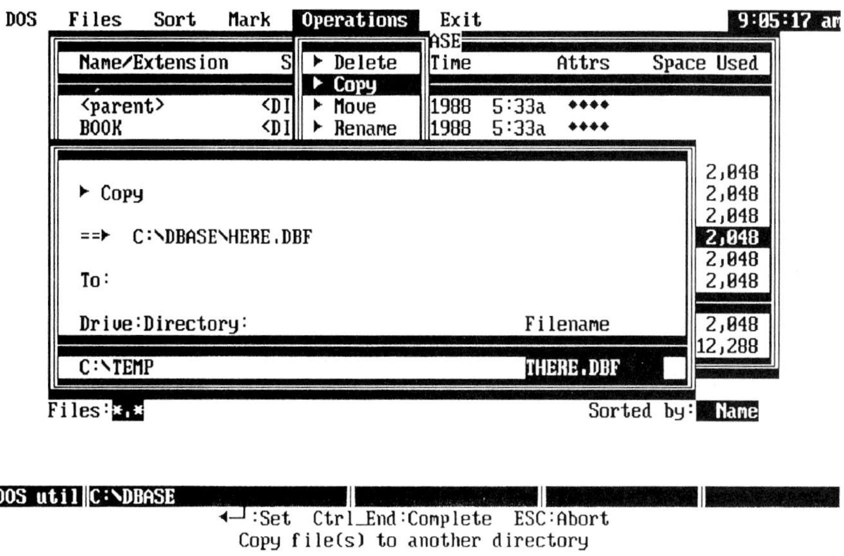

Figure 14-18. Prompt box to copy HERE.DBF to the TEMP directory on the C drive as THERE.DBF

prompt box that allows you to modify the default path for the file name to be copied, as shown in Figure 14-17. If you press ENTER, dBASE brings you to the right side of the prompt box to enter the file name for the copied file. Pressing CTRL-END completes the copy operation.

For example, suppose you want to copy a file named HERE.DBF to a directory named C:\TEMP. First, highlight the HERE.DBF file in the files list of the dBASE directory and select the **Copy** option. Then, choose the **Single File** option from the files prompt. Type **C:\TEMP** as the destination drive and directory. Press CTRL-END, and dBASE copies the HERE file to the C:\TEMP directory.

Using the **Copy** option from the **Operations** menu, you can also change the destination name of the file so that the file to be copied has a different name than the initial file. Figure 14-18 shows a file named HERE.DBF, which is to be copied to a directory named TEMP on the C drive and given a new destination file name of THERE.DBF.

You can also copy an individual file without using the **Copy** option by highlighting the file you want to copy and pressing F8 (the Copy key). dBASE presents the copy option box shown in Figure 14-17.

If you're copying a group of marked files, enter *.* as the destination name to ensure that the files retain their names when they are copied.

You can copy a group of files and change their file names or extensions by specifying a new file name or extension after selecting the **Copy** option. For example, suppose you want to back up a selection of marked files and store them in the same directory with a new name or extension. You can change the names of all the files

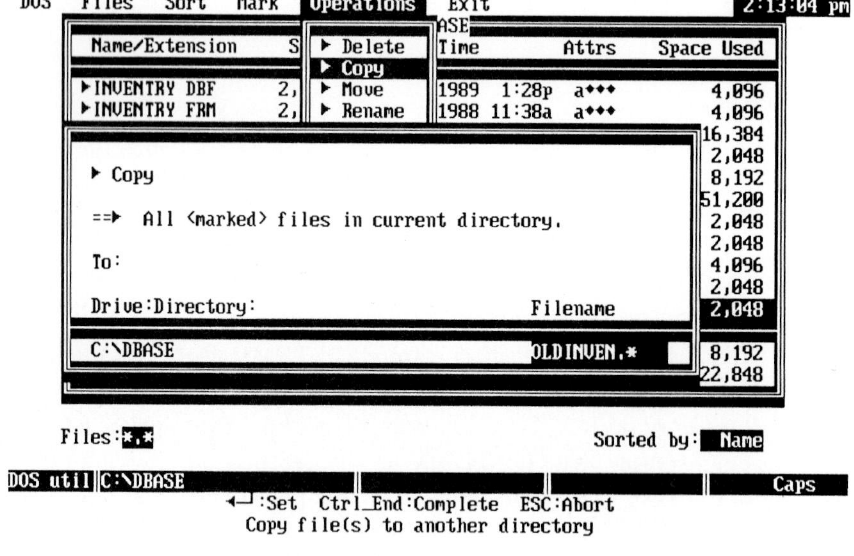

Figure 14-19. **OLDINVEN.*** entered as the destination file name for the copied files

```
DOS   Files   Sort   Mark   Operations   Exit                              2:16:34 pm
                                    C:\DBASE
  Name/Extension      Size   Date & Time          Attrs     Space Used

  <parent>           <DIR>   Jan 12,1989 11:41a   ****
  SAMPLES            <DIR>   Jan 12,1989 11:53a   ****
  SQLHOME            <DIR>   Jan 12,1989 11:41a   ****
  CLIENTS  DBF       2,636   Jan 22,1989 12:40p   a***           4,096
  CUSTOMER DBF       7,745   Dec  2,1988  3:50p   a***           8,192
  EMPLOYEE DBF      12,288   Jan 22,1989  1:28p   a***          14,336
  HERE     DBF       2,636   Jan 22,1989  1:52p   a***           4,096
  INVENTRY DBF       2,371   Jan 22,1989  1:28p   a***           4,096
  ORDERREC DBF       2,367   Nov 16,1988  5:20a   a***           4,096
  ORDERS   DBF       1,280   Jan 22,1989  1:28p   a***           2,048
  SALES    DBF         894   Jan 22,1989  1:28p   a***           2,048

Total ◄marked►              0  (   0 files)                          0
Total ◄displayed►      34,137  (   9 files)                     45,056

Files:*.DBF                                         Sorted by: Name

DOS util C:\DBASE                                                    Caps
         Position selection bar:↑↓  Mark file:◄┘  Directories:F9
```

Figure 14-20. A list of several database files in a files list

associated with a database named INVENTRY (for example, INVENTRY.DBF and INVENTRY.FRM) to OLDINVEN and keep the original extensions. First, mark the files beginning with the name INVENTRY. Then, select the **Copy** option from the **Operations** menu and select **Marked Files**. Press ENTER to accept the current drive and directory. dBASE takes you to the "Filename" prompt. You can now enter **OLDINVEN.*** as the destination file name for the copied files, as shown in Figure 14-19. After entering the new file name for your copied files, press CTRL-END to begin the copy operation.

As another example, Figure 14-20 displays a list of several database files in a files list. Figure 14-21 shows the effects of copying those database files by entering the extension *.BAK as their new destination extension.

```
DOS  Files  Sort  Mark  Operations  Exit                          2:17:43 pm
                              C:\DBASE
  Name/Extension      Size   Date & Time          Attrs    Space Used

  <parent>           <DIR>   Jan 12,1989 11:41a   ****
  SAMPLES            <DIR>   Jan 12,1989 11:53a   ****
  SQLHOME            <DIR>   Jan 12,1989 11:41a   ****
  CLIENTS  BAK       2,636   Jan 22,1989  2:16p   a***          4,096
  CUSTOMER BAK       7,745   Jan 22,1989  2:16p   a***          8,192
  EMPLOYEE BAK      12,288   Jan 22,1989  2:16p   a***         14,336
  HERE     BAK       2,636   Jan 22,1989  2:16p   a***          4,096
  INVENTRY BAK       2,371   Jan 22,1989  2:16p   a***          4,096
  ORDERREC BAK       2,367   Jan 22,1989  2:16p   a***          4,096
  ORDERS   BAK       1,280   Jan 22,1989  2:16p   a***          2,048
  SALES    BAK         894   Jan 22,1989  2:16p   a***          2,048

Total ◄marked►             0  (  0 files)                           0
Total ◄displayed►     34,137  (  9 files)                      45,056

   Files:*.BAK                                      Sorted by: Name

DOS util C:\DBASE                                                Caps
       Position selection bar:↑↓  Mark file:◄┘  Directories:F9
```

Figure 14-21. The effects of copying database files and entering ***.BAK** as their new destination extension

You cannot copy a file onto itself. Furthermore, if you try to copy a file into a directory that already contains a file with the same name, dBASE tells you that the existing file will be overwritten. You can overwrite the existing file or skip the copy operation.

Moving Files

The **Move** option is similar to the **Copy** option, but your original file is deleted from the original drive and directory after the file has been successfully copied to its new destination.

To move a file, first mark or highlight the file or files you want to move. Select the **Move** option from the **Operations Menu** and dBASE will display the **Single File**, **Marked Files**, or **Displayed Files** submenu. After you select one of these options, dBASE displays a prompt box in which to enter a destination drive and directory. If you change the drive and directory and press ENTER, dBASE

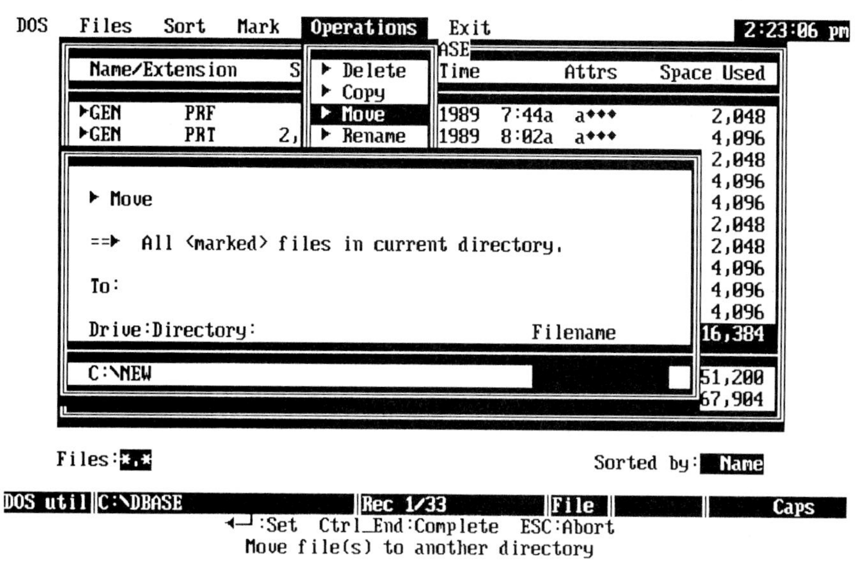

Figure 14-22. The move prompt box set up to move several marked files to C:\NEW directory

takes you to the right side of the prompt box to accept or modify the current file name. If you don't want to change the name of your file, just press CTRL-END to move the selected file or files to the new drive and directory.

The **Move** option consists of two DOS operations. First, dBASE copies the file (or files) to the new destination drive and directory. Then, it deletes the file (or files) from the current directory. Figure 14-22 shows the move prompt box set up to move several marked files to a directory named C:\NEW.

You can move a single file without the **Move** option by highlighting it in the files list and using F7 (the Move key) to move the file to a new destination.

If you try to move a file to a directory in which the file name already exists, dBASE prompts you with the message "Destination file already exists." You can either overwrite the existing file or skip the move operation.

Renaming Files

You can change the name of one or more of your files by using the **Rename** option from the **Operations** submenu.

To rename a single file, in the files list highlight the file to be renamed and select the **Rename** option from the **Operations** submenu. When you select this option, dBASE gives you the options **Single File**, **Marked Files**, and **Displayed Files**. Select the **Single File** option, and press ENTER. dBASE prompts you for a new name for the selected file. Enter a new name and press CTRL-END.

For example, suppose that you want to change the file name NEW.DBF to OLD.DBF. To do this, highlight the file NEW.DBF in the files list and select the **Rename** option from the **Operations** submenu. Enter **OLD.DBF** as the new name for the file and press CTRL-END to complete the operation.

If you want to rename a group of files, you'll need to use a wildcard in place of the file name or its extension. To rename a group of files with the name PRICE and any extension to OLDPRICE and the same extensions, begin by marking these files that begin with PRICE in the current directory. Next, select the **Rename** option in the **Operations** menu, followed by **Marked Files.** Then, enter **OLDPRICE.*** as the new name for that group. Press CTRL-END and dBASE renames any files beginning with the original name of PRICE to OLDPRICE. For example, PRICE.DBF is renamed OLDPRICE.DBF and PRICE.DBT is renamed OLDPRICE.DBT.

To change the extension of a group of file names to .BAK, mark the file names to change and enter the extension ***.BAK** as the new file extension. For example, suppose you've marked three files: ONE.DBF, TWO.TXT, and THREE.PRG. These three files are renamed ONE.BAK, TWO.BAK, and THREE.BAK.

If you try to name a file with a file name that already exists in the current directory, dBASE asks you if you want to overwrite the existing file or skip the renaming operation. If you're not sure, select **Skip**.

Viewing Files

The **View** option in the **Operations** submenu lets you display the contents of a highlighted file one screenful at a time. Before you select this option, however, you need to highlight your file in the files list. Then, when you select the **View** option, dBASE immediately displays the first screenful of text. You can move from one screen of text to the next by pressing SPACEBAR. On the other hand, you can press ENTER to view your file using a scrolling display, in which case the scrolling doesn't stop at every screenful. To pause the scrolling, press ENTER. You can also press the SPACEBAR at any point to begin displaying text one screenful at a time. When you reach the end of the file, dBASE displays the message "Press any key to continue." When you press a key, dBASE returns you to the DOS Utilities screen. To interrupt a file display at any point, press ESC and dBASE takes you back to the DOS Utilities screen.

The **View** option automatically filters out the nontextual characters that can make viewing a file difficult. Nontextual characters are control characters that may be embedded in the file. When you use the **View** option, you can see but cannot alter the file's contents.

Editing Files

To edit a file, highlight it in the files list and then select **Edit** from the **Operations** menu. When you select the **Edit** option, dBASE takes you to the dBASE IV Text Editor and displays the highlighted file you selected. You can then edit that file. The dBASE IV Text Editor is designed to work with files containing dBASE IV code or ASCII text files only (such as batch or text files). Therefore, you should only use the **Edit** option to edit dBASE files ending with the extensions .FRG, .FMT, .LBG, .PRG, and .PRS or files in ASCII format.

Note: *Don't use the **Edit** option to edit dBASE memo fields, executable, command, or overlay program files.* If you want to edit a memo field, use the edit screen from browse or edit mode. If you use the Text Editor to edit a memo field, dBASE IV may not be able to find and open that memo field again. If you try to edit program files ending with the extensions .EXE, .COM, or .OVL and save your changes, you can make these files and dBASE unusable!

The Exit Submenu

Use the **Exit** submenu to exit to the Control Center from the DOS Utilities screen.

File Protection

dBASE IV's file protection features are primarily designed for a networking environment. The **Protect** option in the **Tools** menu allows you to set up a security system that includes password protection and other file-access restrictions. You can also perform data encryption to limit access to your data. For more information on the **Protect** option, see Chapter 28.

Changing dBASE IV Settings

If you select the **Settings** option from the **Tools** menu, dBASE takes you to the **Options** submenu, which contains dBASE's most commonly used settings (see Figure 14-23). Using this submenu, you can temporarily change 16 dBASE settings. You can also change these settings by using the SET command at the dot prompt. For more information on SET commands, see Chapter 32.

Table 14-3 lists the selections available from the **Options** submenu, along with the effects of each setting.

Note: When you change the settings from the **Options** submenu, they are only temporarily changed. To change your settings permanently, you must use the DBSETUP program or modify your

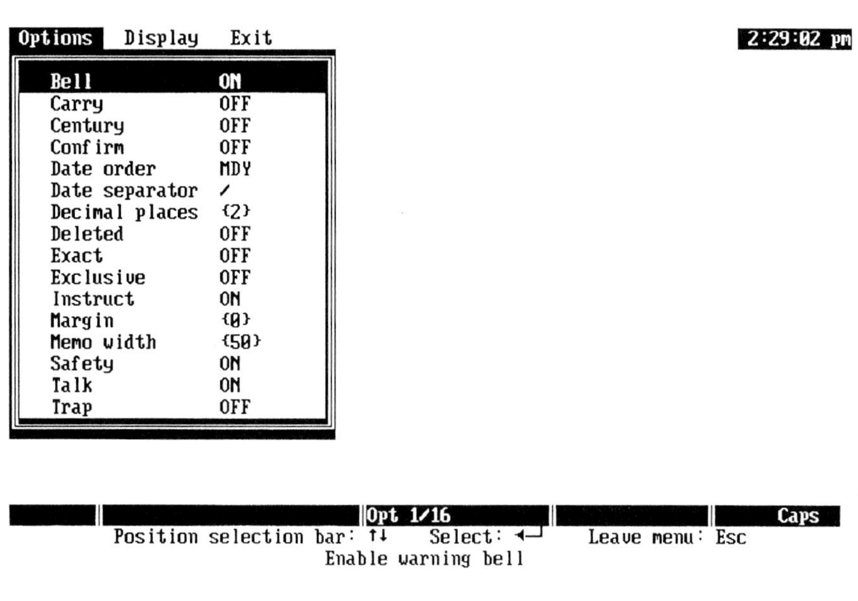

Figure 14-23. The **Options** submenu

CONFIG.DB file. For more information on DBSETUP, see Chapter 2. For more on modifying CONFIG.DB, see Chapter 35.

Changing Display Screen Colors

You can temporarily change your screen's display colors by selecting **Display** from the **Settings** submenu of the **Tools** menu. Figure 14-24 shows the results of selecting the **Display** option from the **Settings** submenu. There are two separate lists of available options, one for color and the other for monochrome monitors. dBASE IV automatically determines what type of monitor you have, displaying the appropriate **Display** menu.

Changing a Color Display

If you're using a color monitor, you can assign one of 16 colors to the foreground and one of 8 colors to the background. You can also display information in a blinking mode.

Option	Setting Results
Bell	
ON	Beeps when you reach the end of a field, edit screen, or custom form; also beeps when errors occur
OFF	Turns dBASE beep off
Carry	
ON	Carries information from the previous record to the next new record when you are entering data
OFF	Begins each new record with blank fields
Century	
ON	Displays the exact year in four digits (for example, 1990)
OFF	Displays the year in abbreviated form (for example, 90)
Confirm	
ON	When you are editing or entering data, waits for you to press ENTER before moving to the next field
OFF	Automatically moves the cursor to the next available field when the current field is full
Date Order	Allows you to choose from one of three order options for the order of the date: *month / day / year* (1/22/90), *day / month / year* (22/1/90), or *year / month / day* (90/1/22)
Date Separator	Allows you to choose from one of three characters to separate dates: 1-22-90, 1/22/90, or 1.22.90
Decimal Places	Allows you to set the number of decimal places displayed in calculation totals from none to 18; dBASE uses 2 as the default

Table 14-3. Settings Options

Deleted	
ON	Ignores records marked for deletion
OFF	Displays records marked for deletion
Exact	
ON	In a comparison, requires exact matches. For example, only strings that exactly match a search string's length are selected
OFF	Matches strings with differing lengths
Exclusive	
ON	Keeps other network users from sharing the currently active database
OFF	Allows users on a network to access the currently active database
Instruct	
ON	Enables instructional prompt boxes
OFF	Disables instructional prompt boxes
Margin	Adjusts the amount of space in the left margin. Same as choosing the **Offset from left** option from the **Print** menu
Memo Width	Adjusts the width of the memo field display from 5 to 250 characters
Safety	
ON	Warns you when dBASE is about to overwrite an existing file and prompts you to cancel or continue the operation
OFF	Immediately overwrites existing files without displaying a warning message
Talk	
ON	Displays on the screen the results of individual operations performed by dBASE
OFF	Does not show the results of individual operations on screen
Trap	
ON	Turns on the dBASE IV Debugger when an error occurs in a dBASE program
OFF	Leaves the dBASE IV Debugger off at all times; it is the default

Table 14-3. Settings Options (*continued*)

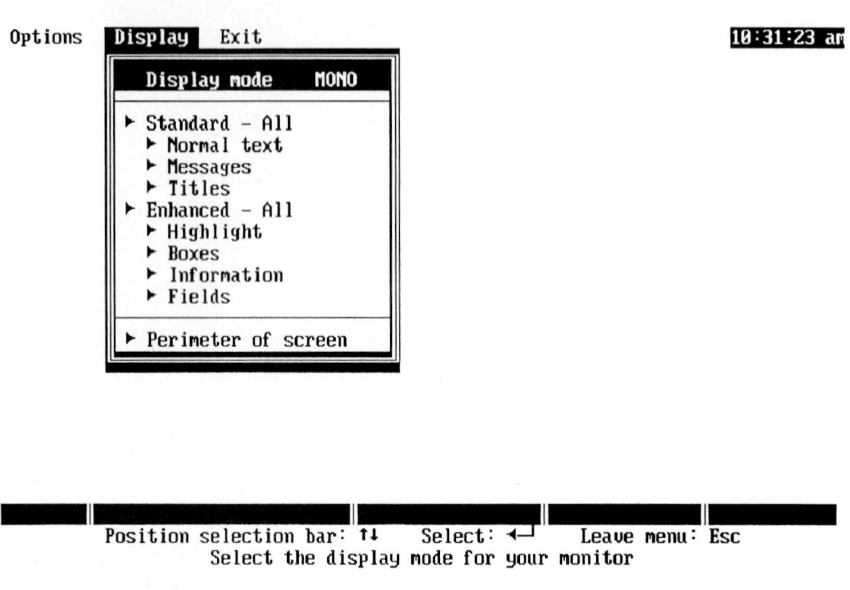

Figure 14-24. The **Display** option

The **Standard-All** option affects the color of text and the background on normal text or unhighlighted sections of the screen such as the work space, the navigation line, and the messages and titles. You can change these "standard" options collectively by selecting the **Standard-All** option or individually by selecting any of the three individual options following the **Standard-All** option: **Normal text**, **Messages**, or **Titles**.

The **Enhanced-All** option sets the color for highlighted text such as the status bar, text boxes, information and fields. You can change these "enhanced" options collectively by selecting the **Enhanced-All** option or individually by selecting any of the four individual options following the **Enhanced-All** option: **Highlight**, **Boxes**, **Information**, or **Fields**.

Figure 14-25 shows some of the **Display** options on the DOS Utilities Screen.

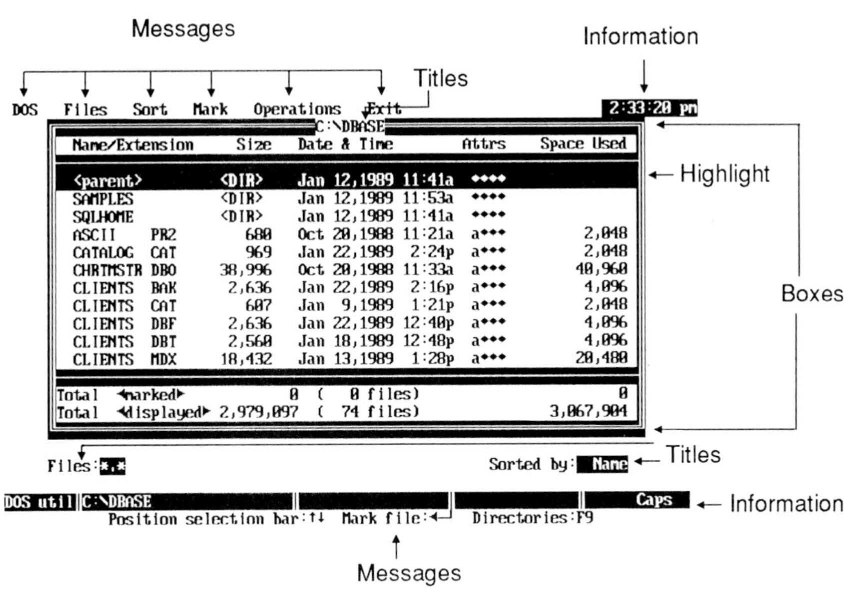

Figure 14-25. Some of the **Display** options on the DOS Utilities screen

After you select one of the area options from the **Display** menu, dBASE takes you to a menu of foreground and background colors. Two columns list your foreground and background color choices along with the **Blink** option.

You choose foreground and background colors by moving the marker up and down the columns with the arrow keys. You can use RIGHT ARROW, LEFT ARROW, or ENTER to move back and forth to the foreground and background columns. As you scroll through the colors, dBASE changes the screen to show you the results of the different color combinations.

Selecting one of the column's color choices shows its effect in the opposite column. When you choose a color from the background column, dBASE changes the background of the foreground menu to the particular color you've highlighted. The background color name disappears since it appears in the same background and foreground color. In other words, when you select blue as your background choice, the word "blue" disappears in the foreground column and the foreground column's background color turns blue.

When you choose a color for the foreground, the background color names change to the highlighted color in the foreground menu. Therefore, if you choose blue as your background color, move to the foreground column, and select the color red, the background choice of red seems to disappear since its red color is both the foreground and the background color. You can see what your red and blue color combination will look like on the screen by looking at the red highlight in the foreground column or the blue background block in the background column.

You can cause any of the display options to flash on and off by using the **Blink** option. You select **Blink** by pressing the letter B. This option is a toggle. You can turn the blink attribute off by pressing the letter B again.

When you select a color combinations, press CTRL-END to save your selection and use the **Exit** submenu to return to the Control Center.

Changing a Monochrome Display

If you're using a monochrome monitor, selecting the **Display** option from the **Settings** menu allows you to choose display attributes. You can change your monochrome screen to display standard or enhanced displays using any of these four options:

- **Intensity** Uses boldfaced characters to display data.
- **Underline** Displays your text underlined.
- **Reverse video** Switches foreground colors with your background color. For example, instead of amber letters and a black screen your text appears as black letters on an amber screen.
- **Blink** Causes text to be displayed as flashing on and off.

The **Tools** menu in the Control Center permits you to import and export files, perform file-management chores, and change your dBASE settings. It also let you perform DOS operations from within dBASE. It even adds some enhanced DOS utilities such as moving, viewing and editing files. If you wish, you can also use the **Tools** menu to temporarily change some of your dBASE settings and display colors to suit your needs.

The Applications Generator

PART TWO

Many users have trouble finding the time to learn dBASE programming. The Applications Generator is dBASE IV's answer to the nonprogrammer's dilemma. You can use the Applications Generator to create a reasonably sophisticated application without having to learn to write complicated programs. What's more, you can generate worthwhile applications that handle significant data management tasks in an efficient and professional manner.

If you're an experienced programmer, you can use the Applications Generator to call your own programs where appropriate. In addition, you can use it to write the code you'd ordinarily have to write yourself.

Two chapters make up this part of the book. Chapter 15 introduces the Applications Generator. This chapter defines an application and supplies some of the tools you will need to get started with the Applications Generator. Chapter 16 takes you through a sample application, giving you some hands-on experience with the Applications Generator.

Introduction to the Applications Generator

FIFTEEN

The Applications Generator is a design tool. You can use it to develop applications that perform significant data management tasks, without writing a single program.

The Applications Generator provides a bulletin-board-like design environment that allows you to create and position *objects*, such as menus, on the screen. Once you define and position these objects, you can define actions for them. When you're done with your design, dBASE IV generates the programs needed to run your application.

The chapter first defines what an application is and what the Applications Generator does. Next, you're given a brief tour of the Applications Generator menu system. You'll learn about the objects the Applications Generator allows you to create as well as the actions you can define for those objects. The chapter then shows you how to create a Quick Application and discusses some of the techniques you will be using to create the sample application in Chapter 16.

What's an Application?

An *application* is a menu-driven system that automates a data management task. For example, you might use an application to manage a mailing list database. However, instead of using a database, query, form, or report separately, you can combine these elements into a menu-driven system. For example, one menu selection might print a report, another might add records to the database using a custom form, and yet another might create a backup copy of the database.

When you create an application, it appears to run independently of dBASE IV. Anyone using the application only needs to know how to start dBASE IV and how to run the application. The menus that you use to drive your application take over from there. Furthermore, the dBASE IV menu system and status bar do not appear on the screen while your application is running.

However, your application still has all the power of the dBASE IV Control Center behind it. For example, you might specify **Browse** as an option in one of your application menus. When you select this option, you are taken to the dBASE IV Browse screen. All of the menus normally available for the Browse screen are also available for your application. When you press ESC or use the **Exit** menu, you are returned to your application.

An application is a collection of *programs*. The programs that make up an application are composed of the same written commands as in the dBASE IV command language. Each program in an application performs a specific computing task or operation for that application. For example, one program might present a menu system while the other programs carry out each of the actions specified by those menus. The purpose of the Applications Generator is to write these programs for you.

If you've used the Control Center's design screens to design a query, form, report, or label, you've already created some programs yourself. In fact, the purpose of each one of these facilities is to generate a program that describes a specific report, label, query, or form. The Applications Generator is a tool for creating a central system of menus that call those programs into use.

The Applications Generator

The Applications Generator is a menu-driven system for developing applications. It enables you to link the various components of dBASE IV (databases, queries, forms, reports, and so forth) by allowing you to define visual images of objects on the Applications Generator work surface. (An example of a visual object is a menu.) Once you define these objects, you can assign *actions* to them. An action is a procedure to be performed whenever that item is selected. For example, for a menu object, you would assign actions to each of the selections in that menu.

For example, in Figure 15-1, two types of objects appear on the screen. A *horizontal bar* menu runs across the top of the screen. In the upper-left corner of the screen, attached to the horizontal bar menu, is a *pop-up* menu. The horizontal bar menu contains five items—**Enter/Edit**, **Print**, **Maintain**, **Backup**, and **Quit**—each of which is assigned an action. That action is to open a pop-up menu, and whenever you select any of the items in the horizontal bar menu, the assigned pop-up menu appears. The overall effect is similar to that of dBASE IV's menu system. Furthermore, each of the items within the pop-up menus have an assigned action. For example, the **Add records** item in the pop-up menu shown in

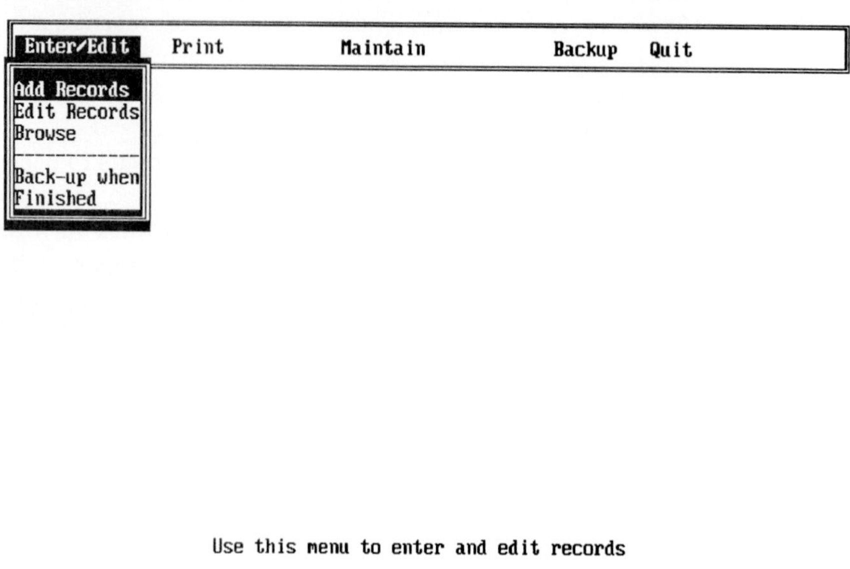

Figure 15-1. A horizontal bar menu with a pop-up menu

Figure 15-1 appends records to the database by using a custom form.

Getting to the Applications Generator

To access the Applications Generator, highlight the **<create>** option in the Applications Panel of the Control Center and press ENTER. dBASE IV displays a two-option submenu. Highlight **Applications Generator** and press ENTER. dBASE IV takes you to the Applications Generator and displays the Applications Definition form shown in Figure 15-2.

If you are working from the dot prompt, you can enter **CREATE APPLICATION *<application name>*** to access the Applications Generator.

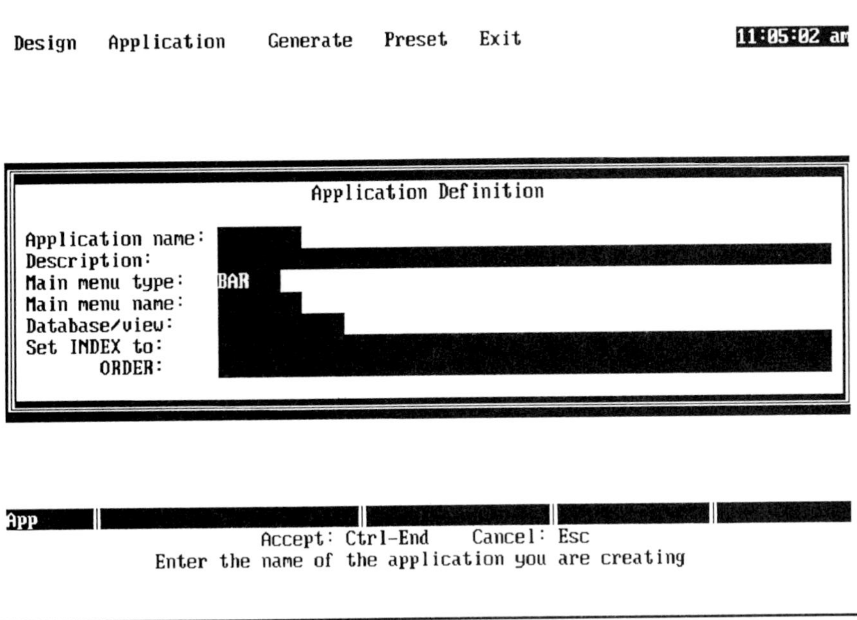

Figure 15-2. An Application Definition form

Defining the Default Environment

You use the Applications Definition form to define the default environment for your application. This is where you name your application, define its main menu, and specify a database or view that you want it to use. You can also use this form to specify a default index for your application. dBASE IV uses the information from this form to create two programs that define your application. One program describes the menu system and the other describes the actions you've assigned to those menus. The elements of the Applications Definition form follow.

- **Application name** Use this field to enter the name of your application. When the code for your application is generated, dBASE IV creates a program file with this name and a .PRG extension.

- **Description** Use this field to enter a description that is displayed whenever you highlight the name of an application in the Applications Panel of the Control Center.

- **Main menu type** Use this field to specify the opening menu type for your application. To see each type of menu, press SPACEBAR. dBASE IV allows you to enter one of three types of opening menus: **BAR**, **POPUP**, or **BATCH**. The first two options, **BAR** and **POPUP**, are two types of menus that you can create using the Applications Generator. The main menu type that you specify in this field is the one that will be displayed when you later run your application. The third option, **BATCH**, refers to a batch process, which performs a series of operations in a specified sequence. As one of the steps in that batch process, you can open a menu.

- **Main menu name** dBASE IV uses the contents of this field to name the program file for your main menu. If you specified a bar menu as your opening menu, dBASE IV uses the name you enter in this field with a .BAR extension. Pop-up menus receive a .POP extension, and batch processes are given a .BCH extension.

- **Database/view** This field allows you to designate a database or view you want the application to use. You can enter the name of a database, such as CLIENTS, or the name of a view you created by using the Queries Design screen.

- **Set INDEX to** and **ORDER** This is where you specify the name of a production index file associated with the database you entered in the Database/view field. For example, if the name of the database you entered is CLIENTS, you would enter **CLIENTS** here as well to specify the CLIENTS.MDX index file as the default index file. In the ORDER field, you enter one or more tag names from that production index file, separated by commas.

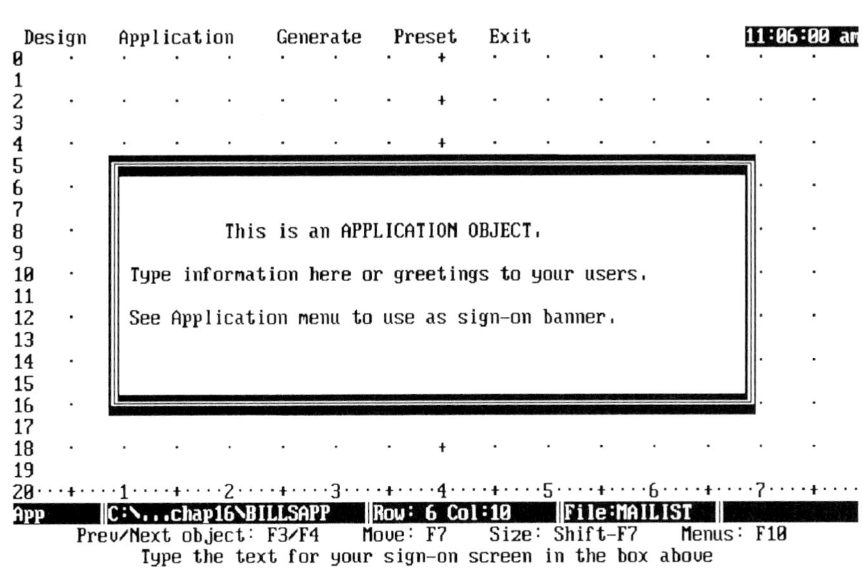

Figure 15-3. The Applications Generator work surface

You can also enter more than one index file name, separated by commas, in the Set INDEX to field. For example, you might enter the names of several single index (.NDX) files. In the ORDER field, you enter the file name of the controlling .NDX file.

Once you've entered the appropriate information in the Applications Definition form, press CTRL-END to save this definition in memory and move to the Applications Generator work surface.

The Application Object

Figure 15-3 shows what the Applications Generator work surface looks like when you first enter the Applications Generator. The large block in the middle of the work surface is called an *application object*. It stays on the screen throughout the applications development process.

You can use this application object as a sign-on banner that is displayed for about four seconds whenever you run your application. You can include the name of the application, your company name, and other appropriate information. To do this, press CTRL-Y to clear the default text and then type your own text.

To change the size of the application object, press SHIFT-F7. The border of the application object will start to blink. Use the DOWN ARROW, LEFT ARROW, and RIGHT ARROW keys to shrink or expand the application object border. When you achieve the desired size, press ENTER.

You can also move the application object. To do this, press F7, use the arrow keys to move the shadow of the application object to another area of the screen, and press ENTER. dBASE IV moves the application object to the new location.

To display the application object automatically as a sign-on banner at run time, press F10 and select the **Display sign-on banner** option from the **Application** menu. Choose **Yes** from the next prompt.

Defining Objects—the Design Menu

As mentioned, the Applications Generator is a design instrument. It generates programs that describe your application. The Applications Generator allows you to design objects of various types via a visual interface. Once you define these objects, you can assign actions to them. dBASE IV uses the objects you define and the actions you specify to generate the code for your application.

The Applications Generator allows you to define menus, lists, and batch processes. Each of these objects is available from the **Design** menu option in the Applications Generator menu bar.

Figure 15-4 shows the **Design** menu open on the Applications Generator screen. To select an object that you want to create, move

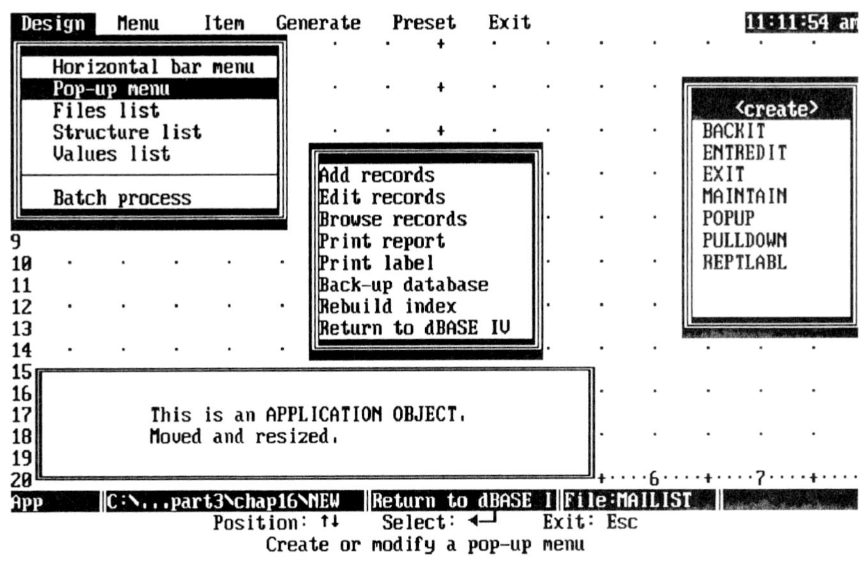

Figure 15-4. The Design menu used to create an object

the highlight to an object type and press ENTER. For example, to create a pop-up menu, select **Pop-up menu** and press ENTER. dBASE IV displays a files list box in the upper-right corner of the screen, as in Figure 15-4. Move the highlight to the **<create>** option and press ENTER. dBASE IV places that object on the Applications Generator work surface.

If the new object is a menu or a batch process, it arrives on the Applications Generator work surface as a blank box. You can then fill in the items for that menu. For example, Figure 15-4 shows a menu already on the screen with its items filled in. Each line in the menu represents an item, or menu selection. You can then assign an action to each item in the menu. If you do not assign an action to a menu item, dBASE IV still displays it as part of the menu, but you cannot select it. When the application is finished, press

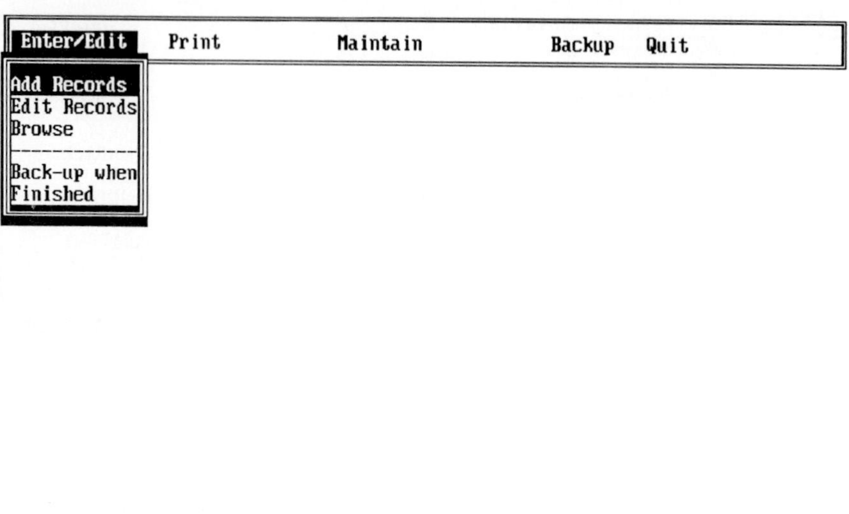

Figure 15-5. A horizontal bar menu with a pop-up menu

ENTER on an item in the menu and dBASE IV will initiate the action you've assigned to that item.

In Chapter 16, you'll create both menus and batch processes, and assign actions to the items within them. Also see Chapter 16 for a detailed description of how to use the **Design** menu option.

Menus

The Applications Generator allows you to specify three different types of menus.

- Horizontal bar menus
- Pull-down pop-up menus
- Stand-alone pop-up menus

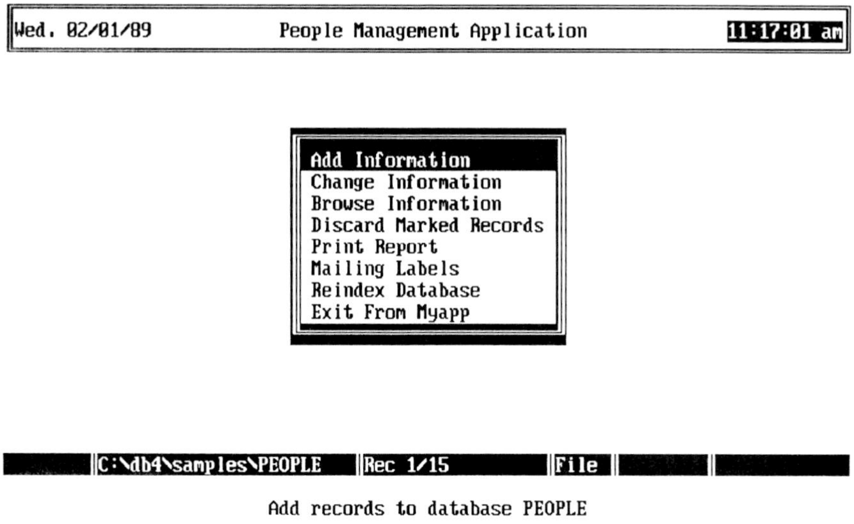

```
Wed. 02/01/89          People Management Application          11:17:01 am

                     Add Information
                     Change Information
                     Browse Information
                     Discard Marked Records
                     Print Report
                     Mailing Labels
                     Reindex Database
                     Exit From Myapp

     C:\db4\samples\PEOPLE  Rec 1/15        File
                     Add records to database PEOPLE
```

Figure 15-6. A stand-alone pop-up menu used as a main menu

Figure 15-5 shows a horizontal bar menu running across the top of the screen. Attached to it is a pop-up menu. You can use horizontal bar menus and pop-up menus together to simulate dBASE IV's menu system. Whenever you move to a menu choice in the horizontal bar menu, dBASE IV automatically displays the pop-up menu assigned to that menu choice.

You can also use a pop-up menu as a submenu for another pop-up menu. With this configuration, whenever you make a selection from one pop-up menu, another pop-up menu of subchoices appears.

Although pop-up menus work well with horizontal bar menus, you can also use them independently. For example, you can use a stand-alone pop-up menu as the main menu for an application, as in Figure 15-6.

Lists

List boxes contain the names of files, database field names, or the contents of specified fields in a database. List boxes work somewhat like menus in that they allow your user to make a selection from within them. There are three types of list boxes:

- Files list contain file names
- Structure list contain field names
- Values list contain the contents of database fields

A files list contains the names of files. Structure lists contain the names of the fields in the currently active database or view. Values lists show the contents of one or more fields in the currently active database or view. The information in each of these lists is available for selection.

For example, Figure 15-7 shows a sample values list containing the contents of the Lastname field of the MAILIST database. You can use a values list like this to give your user a list of last names from which to choose. You can then display the record corresponding to the selected last name.

Batch Processes

Batch processes allow you to specify a list of operations to be performed in sequence when a specific menu selection occurs. Unlike menus and list boxes, your user never sees batch processes, and doesn't need to. You might use a batch process to back up a database, also specifying the following operations:

- Mark records for deletion
- Delete those records
- Back up the database

Defining a batch process is similar to defining a menu. You type in plain English the descriptions for each step in the batch

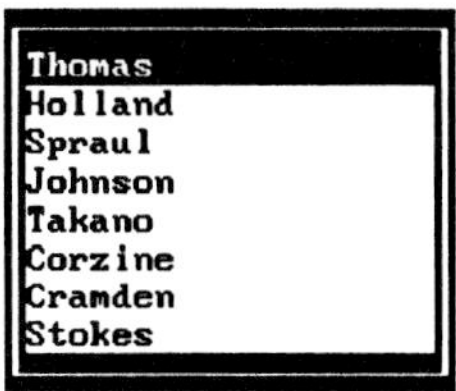

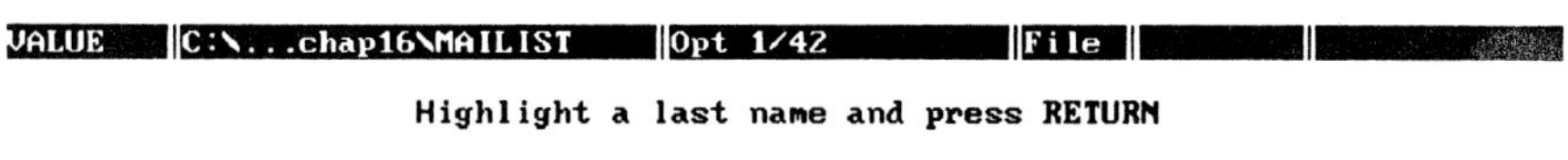

Figure 15-7. A sample values list

process frame. Next, you assign actions to each batch process item. Then you save the batch process, which can now be called from one of the menus you've defined. When a batch process is called into service, all of its items are automatically executed in sequence.

In Chapter 16, you'll learn how to create a Batch process, assign actions to it, and assign that batch process to a menu item.

The Application, Menu, and Batch Menu Options

Some of the choices in the Applications Generator menu bar change depending on the *current object*—the object that contains the cursor. For example, if an application object is the current object on the work surface, dBASE IV displays the **Application** menu option as the second choice in the Applications Generator menu bar.

However, if you move to another object, say a menu, that object becomes the current object. dBASE IV replaces the **Applica-**

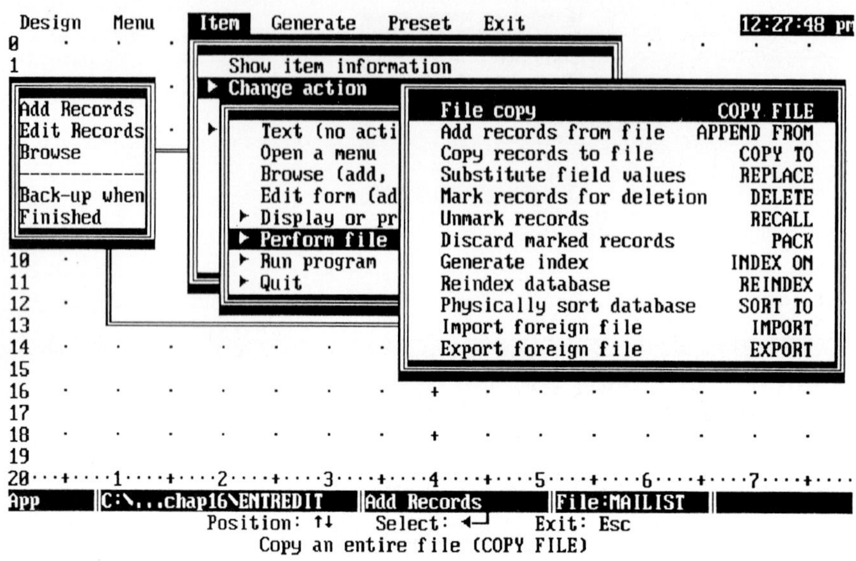

Figure 15-8. The **Item** menu assigns actions to object items

tions menu with the **Menu** and **Item** menus as the second and third choices in the Applications Generator menu bar. What's more, if you're working with a batch process, dBASE IV replaces **Menu** with **Batch**. The **Batch** menu contains options specifically for batch processes.

Assigning Actions—the Item Menu

Once you've defined your menus, and the items within them, you can assign actions to each menu item. Example actions are appending a record by using a custom form or printing a report.

```
Design   Menu   Item  Generate   Preset   Exit                    12:28:22 pm

                          Print a Report

 FORM name:
 HEADING:

 Report format:    FULL DETAIL
 Heading format:   PLAIN
 Before printing:  SKIP TO NEW PAGE
 Send output to:   PRINTER

 FILTER:
 SCOPE:
 FOR:
 WHILE:

18
19
20
App     C:\...chap16\ENTREDIT    Add Records     File:MAILIST
                      Accept: Ctrl-End     Cancel: Esc
                     Enter name of FORM file for report
```

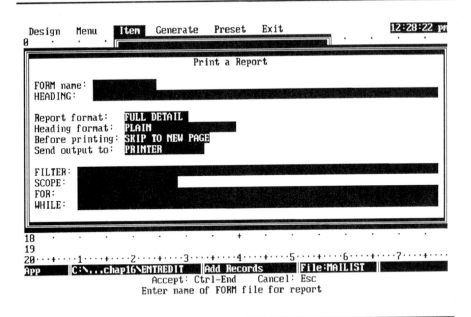

Figure 15-9. The **Print a Report** dialog box

You assign actions to menu items by using the **Item** option in the Applications Generator menu bar. To use the **Item** menu, first position the cursor on an item in a menu or a batch process. Then select **Item** from the Applications Generator menu bar. You can use each of the options in the **Item** menu tree to specify an action that applies to the current menu or batch process item.

From the **Item** menu, you can access a series of submenus. Immediately to the left of **Item** menu selections that have submenu choices, dBASE IV displays a small arrow. Figure 15-8 shows the **Item** menu with two of its submenus displayed. Note that many of the menu options in Figure 15-8 describe in plain English the action that they perform.

dBASE IV displays dialog boxes for many of the options in the **Item** submenu. For example, Figure 15-9 shows the **Print a Report** dialog box. This box allows you to specify the name of a report form created with the Reports Design screen and allows you to specify a heading for the report. You can also use this dialog box to state conditions for the data drawn from the default database or view that you specified in the Application Definition form.

You'll learn more about the options available in the **Item** menu in Chapter 16, "A Sample Application."

Generating the Code—the Generate Menu

When you're finished designing your menu system and assigning actions or batch processes to all menu items, you can generate the code for the application. Your application will not run unless you have dBASE IV generate the necessary program code.

To generate the required program code, use the **Generate** menu option in the Applications Generator menu bar. The **Generate** menu option has the following three submenu choices: **Begin generating**, **Select template**, and **Display during generation**.

Use the **Begin generating** menu option to generate both program code and program documentation. This documentation shows the objects you have defined and the actions you have specified for those objects.

Before you use the **Begin generating** option, you can use the **Select template** option to specify whether dBASE IV generates program code or program documentation. This option allows you to type one of three template file names.

MENU.GEN	Generates program code (the default)
DOCUMENT.GEN	Generates program documentation
QUICKAPP.GEN	Generates Quick Application program code

When you specify the MENU.GEN template file, dBASE IV generates the two program files needed to run your application, giving both files .PRG extensions.

You use the DOCUMENT.GEN template file to generate the documentation for your application. dBASE gives this file the name of your application and a .DOC extension. You can later view that documentation on the screen or print it out.

Use the QUICKAPP.GEN template file solely to generate the program code for a Quick Application. See the section "Creating a Quick Application" later in this chapter.

The **Display during generation** option in the **Generate** menu instructs dBASE IV to display the documentation for your application as it is being generated.

Presetting Application Settings—the Preset Menu

The **Preset** menu allows you to specify settings for future Applications Generator sessions. You can use this option to specify default path and drive settings, menu border options, color settings, and more. The attributes you specify with this menu are present whenever you enter the Applications Generator. You can change these settings for a given application by using the **Application** menu.

Returning to the Control Center—the Exit Menu

To return to the Control Center from the Applications Generator, select the **Exit** menu in the Applications Generator menu bar. You can then either save all changes and exit the Applications Generator or abandon all changes and exit.

You can use the **Exit** option while developing an application by selecting **Save all changes and exit**. This option saves all of your changes and returns you to the Control Center. You can later continue developing that application by pressing ENTER on its name in the Applications Panel of the Control Center and selecting **Modify application.** You can also highlight the application name in the Control Center Applications Panel and press SHIFT-F2.

The Applications Generator Function Keys

The following function keys play a major role when you design applications by using the Applications Generator:

- **F3 (Previous) and F4 (Next)** The F3 and F4 keys allow you to move back and forth between objects on the Applications Generator work surface. The object that contains the cursor is the current object. The **Applications**, **Menu**, **Batch**, and **Item** menus apply to the current object.
- **F5 (Field)** As you'll learn in Chapter 16, F5 marks the beginning and end of items in horizontal bar menus. To enter an item, press F5 to start, type the text, and press F5 to finish. You can also press ENTER to complete an item.
- **F7 (Move)** When you press F7, dBASE IV displays a menu with the two options **Entire frame** and **Item only**. **Entire frame** allows you to move an entire object. You can then use the arrow keys to position that object anywhere on the screen; the shadow of the object's frame will follow the cursor. To confirm the new position, press ENTER. dBASE IV moves the current object to the new location. Use **Item only** to move item choices within the current object or to another object. For example, you can press F7 on an item choice in one menu, press F4 to move to another menu, position the cursor, and press ENTER. dBASE IV will move the item to the new menu.

- **SHIFT-F7** When you press SHIFT-F7, the frame for the current object begins to blink. You can then use the arrow keys to expand or contract the frame for that object. When the frame is the desired size, press ENTER. dBASE IV adjusts the size of the item to suit your new specifications. Note that you cannot make a frame for an object smaller than the text already within that object's frame.

- **F8 (Copy)** You can use the F8 key to copy items within the current object or to another object of the same type. For example, suppose you want to include the same selection in two different pop-up menus. Both pop-up menus are currently on the Applications Generator work surface. You can press F8 on the item in one pop-up menu and press F3 or F4 to move to the other pop-up menu. Position the cursor where you want the item to appear and press ENTER. dBASE IV copies the item as well as any actions specified for the item.

- **F9 (Zoom)** The F9 key removes the Applications Generator menu bar and status bar. This gives you a full screen on which to lay out your objects and a rough preview of your application's on-screen appearance.

Creating a Quick Application

This section describes how to create a Quick Application. First, start your computer and change to the SAMPLES directory you created when you installed dBASE IV. This directory is a subdirectory of the directory in which you installed dBASE IV. The SAMPLES directory contains the files from Sample Program Disks 1, 2, and 3 that come with dBASE IV.

If you didn't create a SAMPLES directory when you installed dBASE IV, you can do so now by using the dBASE IV DBSETUP program. If you've already installed the SAMPLES directory, move on to the next paragraph. To use the DBSETUP program to create a SAMPLES directory, type **DBSETUP** at the DOS prompt. dBASE IV displays the Dbsetup menu. Then follow these steps.

1. Select **Transfer other files**.
2. Select **Sample files**.
3. Enter the name of the directory in which you installed dBASE IV.
4. Press ENTER to confirm the SQL home directory.
5. Press ENTER to create the SAMPLES subdirectory of the directory that contains your dBASE IV files.
6. dBASE IV prompts you to insert Sample Program Disk 1. Do so and press ENTER.
7. Repeat step 6 for Sample Program Disks 2 and 3.
8. When you're done, use the **Exit** menu to return to DOS.

Once you're in the SAMPLES directory, start dBASE IV and go to the Control Center. dBASE IV should display the files in the SAMPLES directory in the Control Center Panels. To create a Quick Application with some of these files, follow these steps:

1. Move the highlight to the **<create>** option in the Applications Panel and press ENTER. From the next menu, choose **Applications Generator**. dBASE IV displays the Application Definition form.
2. Fill in the Application Definition form, as shown in Figure 15-10.
3. Press CTRL-END. dBASE IV takes you to the Applications Generator.

```
Design   Application   Generate   Preset   Exit                    3:35:18 pm
```

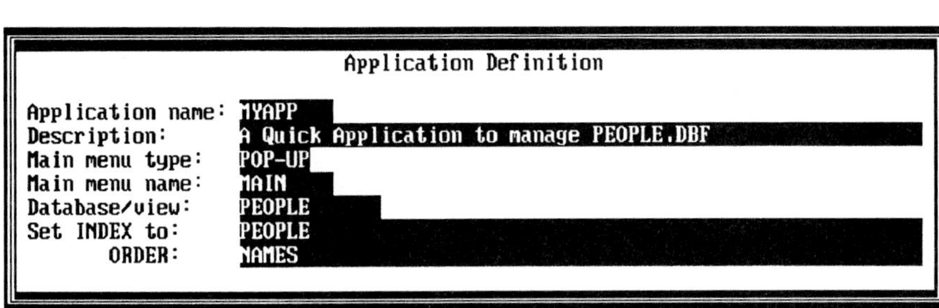

```
                        Application Definition

Application name:  MYAPP
Description:       A Quick Application to manage PEOPLE.DBF
Main menu type:    POP-UP
Main menu name:    MAIN
Database/view:     PEOPLE
Set INDEX to:      PEOPLE
      ORDER:       NAMES
```

```
App
                    Accept: Ctrl-End    Cancel: Esc
     Enter the name of the controlling index (to determine ORDER)
```

Figure 15-10. Application Definition form for a Quick Application

4. Press ALT-A to access the **Applications** menu. Your screen should look like Figure 15-11.

5. Select **Generate quick application** and press ENTER. dBASE IV displays the form you see in Figure 15-12.

6. Fill in the form, as in Figure 15-12. This provides a name for the application and indicates the components to be used from the Control Center panels.

7. Press CTRL-END.

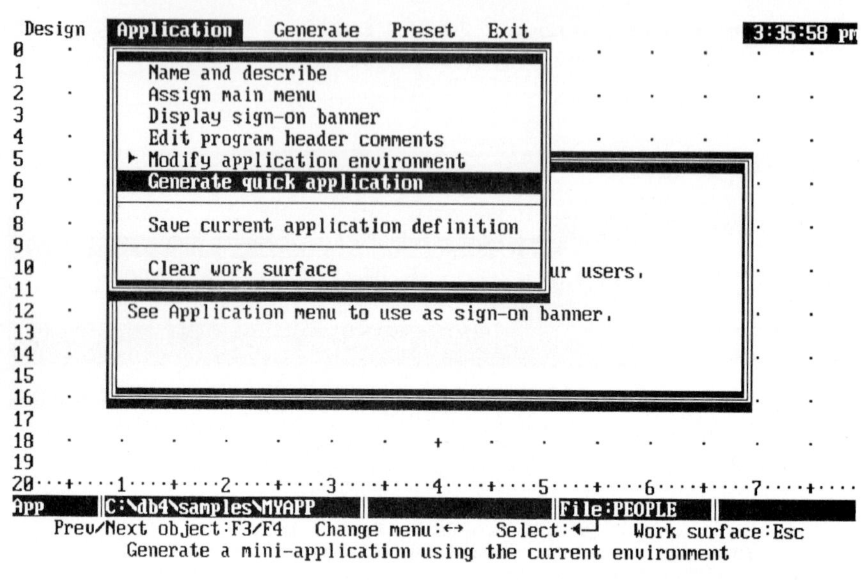

Figure 15-11. Press ALT-A to access the **Application** menu

8. Select **Yes** to begin generating the program code for the application. When dBASE IV finishes generating the code for the application, it displays the message "Generation complete. Press any key." Do so now.

   When you press any key, the **Application** menu is still open and waiting on the screen. If you press F10 again, the dialog box in Figure 15-12 reappears.

9. Press F10 and select **Save all changes and exit** from the **Exit** menu. dBASE IV returns you to the Control Center and displays the name of the Quick Application in the Control Center Applications Panel.

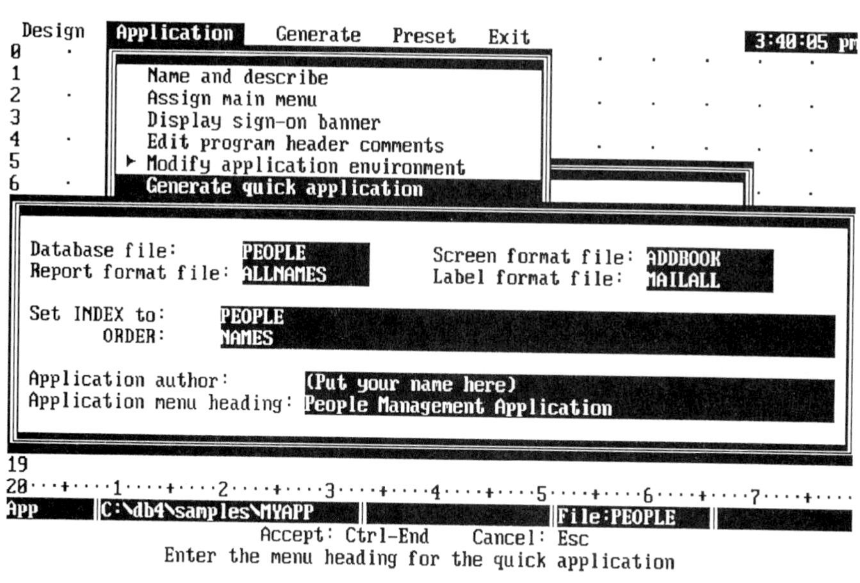

Figure 15-12. A Quick Application form

Running the Quick Application

To run a Quick Application, follow these steps:

1. Highlight the name of that application in the Control Center Applications Panel and press ENTER.

2. Accept the default, **Run application**, from the submenu that appears and press ENTER.

3. dBASE IV asks you to confirm your choice. Select **Yes** and press ENTER. dBASE IV starts your application.

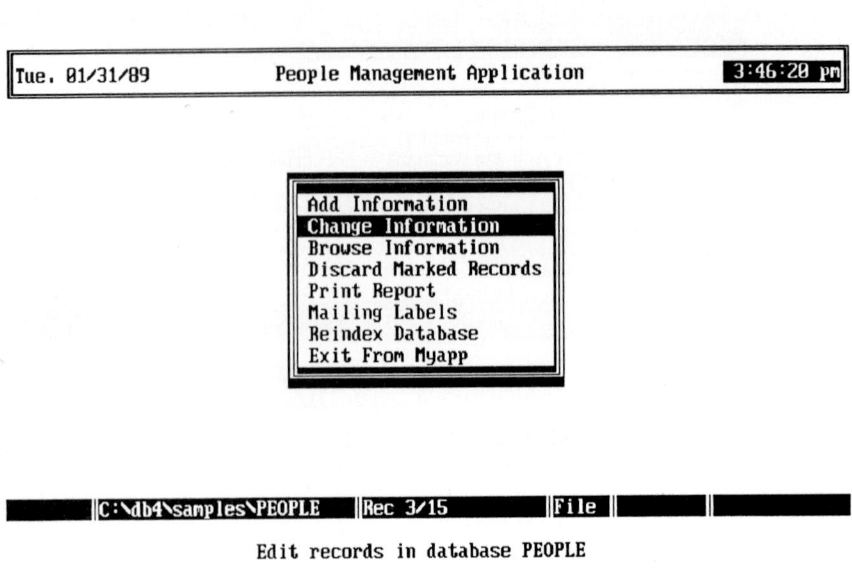

Figure 15-13. The finished Quick Application menu

When the Quick Application program begins running, dBASE IV displays a sign-on banner for about four seconds. If you entered the information from Figure 15-12, the banner displays your name and the application title. The next screen you see is shown in Figure 15-13.

When dBASE IV generates a Quick Application, it uses a stand-alone pop-up menu, as in Figure 15-13. This pop-up menu contains standard items that are provided for all Quick Applications. In Chapter 16, you'll learn how to create a pop-up menu like the one Figure 15-13. Take a moment to try out your new application.

The MYAPP application uses the PEOPLE database with a default-controlling production index tag called NAMES. When you select **Add Information** or **Change Information**, dBASE IV allows you to access the PEOPLE database using a custom form called ADDBOOK.FMT. When you select Browse Information, dBASE IV takes you to the dBASE IV Browse screen and displays the records in the PEOPLE database in order by last name. The **Discard Marked Records** option deletes all records marked for deletion. The **Print Report** option uses the ALLNAMES.FRM report form to print a report. The **Mailing Labels** option uses the label from MAILALL.LBL to print mailing labels for the records in the PEOPLE database. The **Reindex Database** option rebuilds the NAMES index tag, should a catastrophe such as a power failure occur. The **Exit From Myapp** option returns you to dBASE IV.

Creating Larger Applications

The MYAPP Quick Application you created in the previous section is a very simple application. You can also use the Applications Generator to create much larger and more complex applications.

Follow these steps when developing an application:

1. Write down your goals for the application.

   This is a paper and pencil step that involves making notes about what you want the application to do. Start with a broad statement of your goals and then work your way down to specifics. For example, you may want your application to manage a mailing list. However, you'll probably want to add records to the database and edit those records using a custom form. You'll also need several types of indexes for ordering your information by last name and by ZIP code. You'll also need several types of reports as well as label forms to print mailing labels. Tackling each smaller goal as an independent entity will make the job of development a great deal easier.

2. Design the database.

   Once you've defined your goals, you're ready to create the database. As you design database fields, keep your goals in mind. For a short discussion about database design, see Chapter 17.

3. Build the components.

   Next, design and build the components that your application will use, including views, forms, reports, and labels. Continue to keep your system goals in mind as you design these components. If you change your mind about the design of a component while developing your application, you can always go back and change it later.

4. Design the menu system.

   Take a moment to sketch the main menu and any pop-up menus or list boxes you may need. This sketch will be an invaluable tool once you enter the Applications Generator and begin developing your application.

5. Design the batch processes.

   Whenever you need a menu selection to perform more than one task, you'll need a batch process. Write down the steps for each batch process in simple English. You can assign actions for each of those steps when you get to the Applications Generator.

6. Develop the application.

   Now you're ready to enter the Applications Generator and develop your application. Keep your sketch of the menu system near at hand; you'll refer to it often. Follow the steps in Chapter 16, "A Sample Application," to experiment with the Applications Generator.

7. Test the application.

   Before you are finished developing an application, you must fully test every single menu in it using sample data. Only then is the application ready for use.

This chapter introduced the Applications Generator. You learned about the types of objects you can create by using the Applications

Generator and the actions you can assign to those objects. You also learned about the Applications Generator menu system.

Then you designed a Quick Application. You now know how to use the Applications Generator to link the various components of dBASE IV by using a menu-driven application. The chapter also outlined the steps required to design and build a larger, more complex application.

A Sample Application

SIXTEEN

In this chapter, you will build a sample application by using the Applications Generator. Follow the steps outlined in this chapter and you'll have a sample mailing list application called MAILAPP.

This chapter lays out some design objectives for the mailing list application before detailing the actual application development process. You will begin building an application by developing its components—forms, reports, labels, and so forth. Once the necessary components are in place, you will sketch a design for the menu system and other operations used in the application. Finally, you'll transfer to the Applications Generator and begin the process of developing an application.

This chapter assumes that you are familiar with the Database, Forms, Reports and Labels Design screens. If you aren't, refer to Part One of this book.

Laying Out Your Design Objectives

The sample application is primarily for maintaining a customer mailing list database. This involves adding records as well as editing and deleting records. In addition, the system must print a list of customers as well as form letters that refer to each customer by name. Finally, the system must produce mailing labels for those form letters. Additional system objectives for this sample application are as follows:

- Adding records
  - Use a custom form to add records to the database.
- Editing records
  - Edit records by using a custom form.
  - Find a specific record by using a name entered by the user. Display that record by using a custom form.
  - Present the user with a Browse screen that shows the database records in order by last name.
- Printing reports and labels
  - Print a report showing customers' names and addresses in order by last name.
  - Print form letters in ZIP code order for all customers.

- Print form letters in ZIP code order for those customers that have not received a mailing within the last six months.
- Print mailing labels in ZIP code order for all customers.
- Print mailing labels in ZIP code order for those customers that have not received a mailing within the last six months.

- Maintenance
  - Mark for deletion all records in the database for which the user has requested deletion.
  - Pack the database and permanently remove all records marked for deletion.
  - Update the mailing list database with today's date for all records recently mailed.
- Backup
  - Provide a back-up option to avoid possible loss of data.
- Exit System
  - Provide options to exit both to dBASE IV and to DOS.

The MAILIST Database

This application uses the MAILIST database, the structure of which appears in Figure 16-1. The Lastmail date field, the Oktomail logical field, and the Delete logical field will be used later to indicate the last time a customer received a mailing, whether it is okay to mail to a customer, and whether a record should be deleted.

Additionally, note that the Zip field has the letter "Y" in the Index column. This specifies an index tag called Zip in the production index (MAILIST.MDX) file for the MAILIST database. You'll need this index later to print reports and labels in ZIP code order.

```
Layout   Organize   Append   Go To   Exit                          4:30:34 pm
                                                          Bytes remaining:   3882
```

Num	Field Name	Field Type	Width	Dec	Index
1	FIRSTNAME	Character	8		N
2	LASTNAME	Character	12		N
3	COMPANY	Character	18		N
4	ADDRESS	Character	26		N
5	CITY	Character	18		N
6	STATE	Character	2		N
7	ZIP	Character	10		Y
8	TELEPHONE	Character	14		N
9	LASTMAIL	Date	8		N
10	OKTOMAIL	Logical	1		N
11	DELETE	Logical	1		N

```
Database C:\...chap16\MAILIST     Field 1/11
          Enter the field name. Insert/Delete field:Ctrl-N/Ctrl-U
Field names begin with a letter and may contain letters, digits and underscores
```

Figure 16-1. The MAILIST database

Create the database pictured in Figure 16-1 by using Database Design screen. This will allow you to follow along as the sample application is created.

To create the MAILIST database, press ENTER on the **<create>** option in the Data Panel of the Control Center. dBASE IV takes you to the Database Design screen. Enter the field definitions shown in Figure 16-1, and when you are done, use the **Save changes and exit** option in the **Exit** menu. dBASE IV will prompt you for a file name. Type **MAILIST** and press ENTER.

Tip: If you created the CLIENTS file used in earlier chapters, you can quickly create the MAILIST database by using the following dot prompt commands:

```
. USE Clients
. COPY STRUCTURE TO Mailist
. MODIFY STRUCTURE
```

Then, modify the data structure for each of the fields to match those shown in Figure 16-1.

Building a Complex Index

To display and print records that are in order by last name, you'll need to create a *complex index* (an index that involves more than one field). This index first orders the records in the database by last name, and then by first names within those last names.

To create this index, move to the Data Panel of the Control Center, highlight the MAILIST database, and press SHIFT-F2 to access the Database Design screen. Then perform the following steps:

1. From the **Organize** menu, select **Create new index**. dBASE displays the index prompt box.
2. In the Name of index field, type **BOTHNAME**.
3. In the Index expression field, type **TRIM(Lastname)+" "+TRIM(Firstname)**. This index expression trims trailing blanks from the Lastname and Firstname fields when the Bothname index is created. It also creates the index with a single space between last and first names.
4. Press CTRL-END to accept the rest of the defaults in the index prompt box.
5. Save the changes and return to the Control Center in the usual manner.

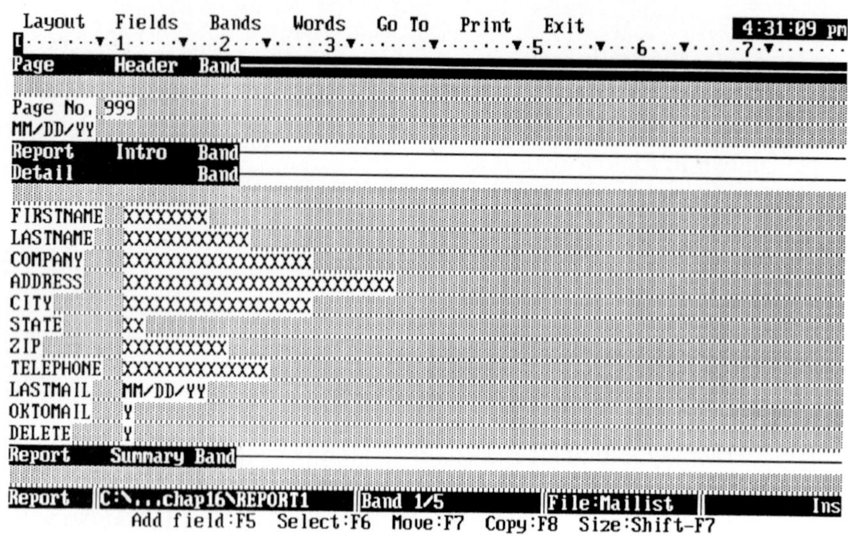

Figure 16-2. The REPORT1.FRM report

Building the Needed Reports

This application requires two reports, and you'll save the second report under two names. The first report, called REPORT1.FRM, is a simple form report that lists customer names and addresses in order by last name. The second report, called FRMLTTR.FRM, generates form letters that contain personalized information about the customers in the MAILIST database. The second report will be saved under FRMLTTR1.FRM, which will be sent to all customers in the MAILIST database, and under FRMLTTR2.FRM, which will be mailed to customers to whom letters have not been mailed in the last six months or have never been mailed.

The REPORT1.FRM report appears in Figure 16-2. You create this form by activating the MAILIST database, moving to the

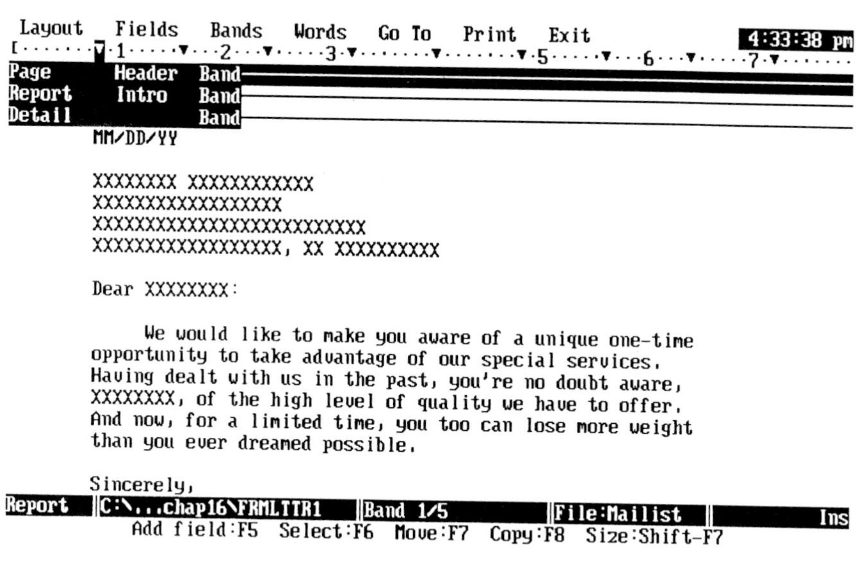

Figure 16-3. The FRMLTTR.FRM report

Reports panel in the Control Center, and pressing ENTER on the **<create>** option. When you reach the Reports Design screen, perform the following steps:

1. Select **Quick Layout** from the **Layout** menu. dBASE IV prompts you with an option box.

2. Select **Form Layout**. dBASE IV builds the report.

3. Press F10 and select **Save changes and exit** from the **Exit** menu. When dBASE IV prompts you for a file name, enter **REPORT1**.

Now you will create two versions of the form letter report displayed in Figure 16-3, one called FRMLTTR1.FRM and one called

FRMLTTR2.FRM. First, open MAILIST and highlight the **<create>** option in the Reports Panel of the Control Center. dBASE IV will take you to the Reports Design screen and display the **Layout** menu. Then perform the following steps:

1. Press ENTER on the **Quick layout** menu option. dBASE IV presents you with an option box.
2. Select **Mailmerge layout**. dBASE IV takes you to the forms letter design surface.
3. Press ALT-W and select **Modify ruler** from the **Words menu**. Use the [symbol to specify a left margin in the ruler and the] symbol to specify a right margin. Locate these symbols roughly where you see the margin markers in Figure 16-3. Press ENTER to finish setting the margins.
4. Press F5 to display the fields prompt box. Move the highlight to the PREDEFINED column and press ENTER on the **Date** option. Then press CTRL-END to place the system date template at the top of the form letter. This ensures that each letter is given today's date when it is printed.
5. Press F5 and CTRL-END again to place the Firstname, Lastname, Company, Address, City, State, and Zip fields on the work surface, positioning the cursor as you go. You are creating a name and address heading for this form letter, as follows:

Templates	**Fields**
XXXXXXXX XXXXXXXXXXXX	Firstname and Lastname
XXXXXXXXXXXXXXXXXX	Company
XXXXXXXXXXXXXXXXXXXXXXXXXX	Address
XXXXXXXXXXXXXXXXXX, XX XXXXXXXXXX	City, State, Zip

6. Finally, type some text of your choosing for the text of this form letter, pressing F5 and CTRL- END to place as many MAILIST database fields inside the letter as you want.

Remember to select the **Template** option and choose **Horizontal stretch** from the submenu for text fields that you place in the body of the letter.

7. Save the report using the **Save this report** option in the **Layout** menu. When prompted for a file name, enter **FRMLTTR1**, and press ENTER.
8. To save the form under a second name, repeat step 7 and enter a file name of **FRMLTTR2**.
9. Return to the Control Center by selecting the **Abandon changes and exit** option from the **Exit** menu.

Creating the Mailing Labels

This sample mailing list application requires a single label. However, you'll need to save that label form under two different names to match the two FRMLTTR files you created earlier. The first label file name you'll use is LABEL1.LBL, and the second file name is LABEL2.LBL. Figure 16-4 shows an example format for these labels on the Labels Design screen. Create the format for the label in Figure 16-4 by moving the highlight to the **<create>** option in the Labels Panel of the Control Center. dBASE IV will take you to the Labels Design screen. Use the F5 key and then CTRL-END to position the fields from the MAILIST database in the label box, as shown here:

Templates	**Fields**
XXXXXXXX XXXXXXXXXXXX	Firstname and Lastname
XXXXXXXXXXXXXXXXXXXX	Company
XXXXXXXXXXXXXXXXXXXXXXXXXXXXXX	Address
XXXXXXXXXXXXXXXXXXXX, XX XXXXXXXXXX	City, State, Zip

Then select **Save this label design** from the **Layout** menu and enter **LABEL1** for a file name. Repeat the procedure and enter

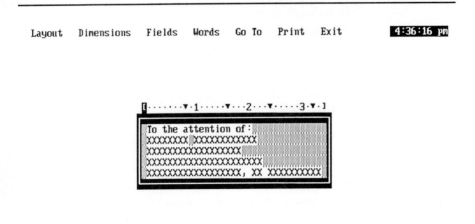

Layout Dimensions Fields Words Go To Print Exit 4:36:16 pm

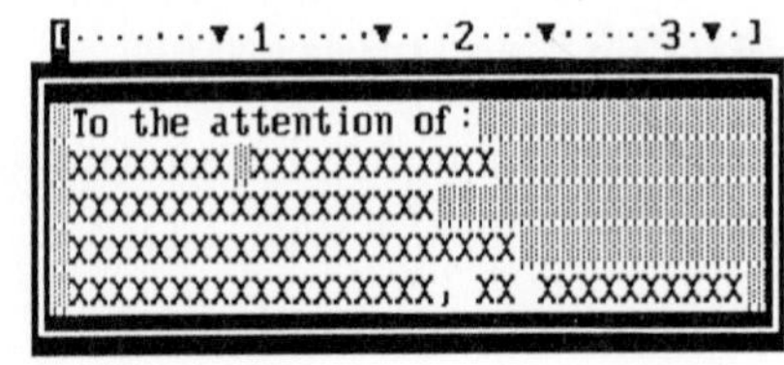

Figure 16-4. The LABEL.LBL label

a file name of **LABEL2**. Finally, return to the Control Center by selecting **Abandon changes and exit** from the **Exit** menu.

Designing the Form

The form in Figure 16-5 is used in this sample mailing list application (MAILAPP). To create this form, open the MAILIST database, move the highlight to the **<create>** option in the Forms Panel, and press ENTER. Then use the usual editing and design techniques to create a custom form of your choosing. However, be sure to include in the form all of the fields in the MAILIST database. Templates are recommended for the following fields:

Field	Template
State	!!
Zip	99999-9999
Telephone	(999)-999-9999
Oktomail	Y
Delete	N

Recall that you can specify a template for each field either as you add it to the form or after the fact by pressing F5. For example, suppose you have already created the form in Figure 16- 5. To specify a template for the State field such that all entries become uppercase, move the cursor to the State field and press F5. Select **Picture functions** from the prompt box and press ENTER. dBASE IV displays a submenu. Choose **Upper-case conversion** and press CTRL-END. dBASE IV returns to the Forms Design screen and places the template in the State field.

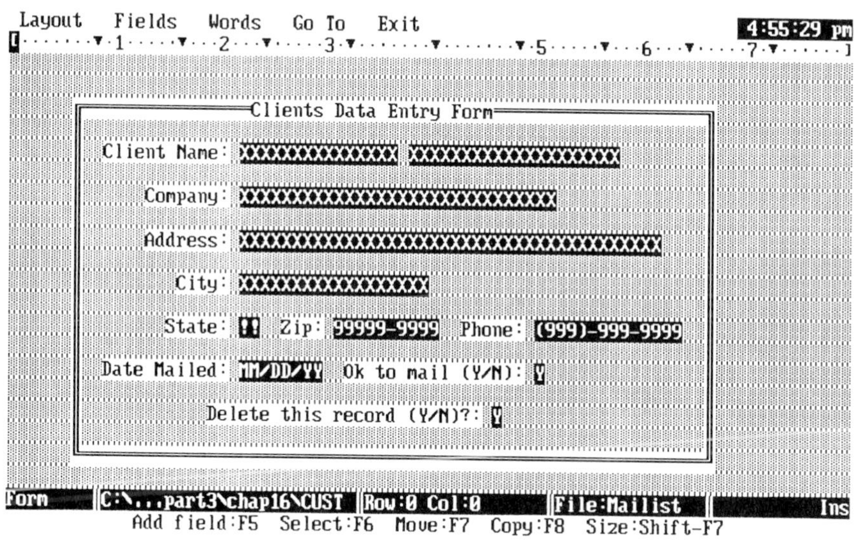

Figure 16-5. The CUST.FMT form

You'll also need to set templates and default values for both the Oktomail and Delete logical fields. Assuming that the form in Figure 16-5 is already created and on the Forms Design Screen, move to the Oktomail logical field and perform the following steps:

1. Press F5; dBASE IV displays a submenu
2. Select **Template** and press ENTER
3. Press Y
4. Select **Edit options** and press ENTER
5. Select **Default value**, press ENTER, and type **.Y.**
6. To save, press CTRL-END twice

To specify a default value for the Delete logical field, move the cursor to that field and repeat steps 1 through 6 above, except in step 5, after selecting **Default value** and pressing ENTER, type **.N.**.

When you have finished designing the form and specifying the appropriate templates, select **Save changes and exit** from the **Exit** menu to return to the Control Center. When prompted for a file name, enter **CUST**. dBASE automatically adds the .FMT extension for you.

Designing the Menu System

Now that the components are in place, you can begin building the application. However, before you begin, you should make a quick sketch of the menu system for the application. This sketch will help you keep your system objectives in mind as you navigate the extensive Applications Generator menu system. Figure 16-6 shows a menu system sketch for the MAILAPP application you're about to create.

The menu system sketch contains the two main Applications Generator menu types: horizontal bar menus and pop-up menus. The main menu for the system is a horizontal bar menu that runs across the top of the screen. This menu, **Mainmenu**, contains the five main menu selections for the system as a whole. When you're finished building the application, you can select items from this menu by highlighting the menu item and pressing ENTER, or by typing the first letter of a menu item's name.

Each item in the horizontal bar menu has a pop-up menu assigned to it. (Figure 16-6 shows the names for each of those pop-up menus.) Whenever you make a selection from the horizontal bar menu, the associated pop-up menu appears. Each pop-up menu works as a pull-down menu, presenting a submenu of choices for each item in the horizontal bar menu. The entire menu system works a great deal like the Control Center's menu system.

Designing the Application

Once you've defined your menus, you're ready to design the actions that each menu item will initiate. Again, it's a good idea to sketch your menu items, showing an action for each. For example, Figure 16-7 is a brief sketch for the MAILAPP application.

Next to each menu item in Figure 16-7, an action is described. Along with each action is the name of a custom form, report, or label that will be used to perform that action. Also, where appropriate, indexes describe the required order of information in the MAILIST database.

In Figure 16-7, the batch and file operations appear next to the submenu items in the pop-up menus under the **Maintain** and **Backup** horizontal bar menu selections. File operations perform a single operation on the currently active database file. *Batch operations* perform more than one operation.

For example, under the **Maintain** menu selection, the pop-up menu features three items, **Update all dates**, **Update old dates**, and **Pack old records**. The first and second options per-

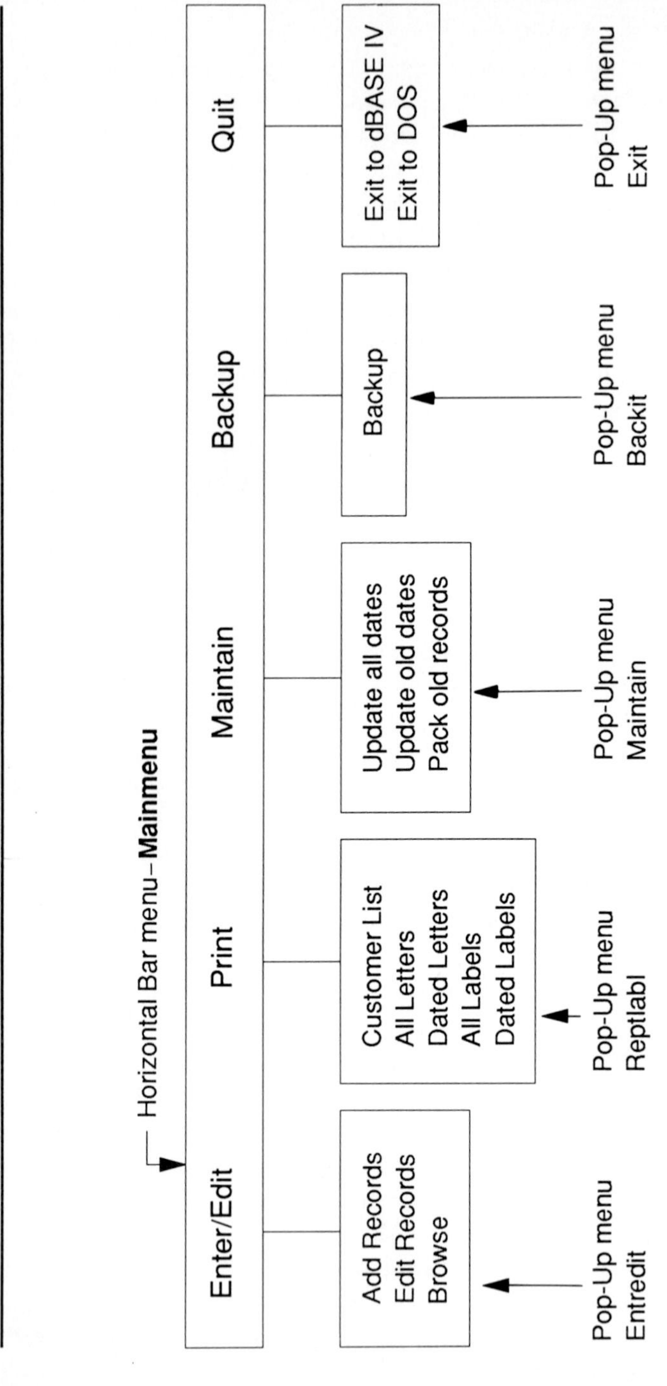

Figure 16-6. A sketch of the MAILAPP system menus

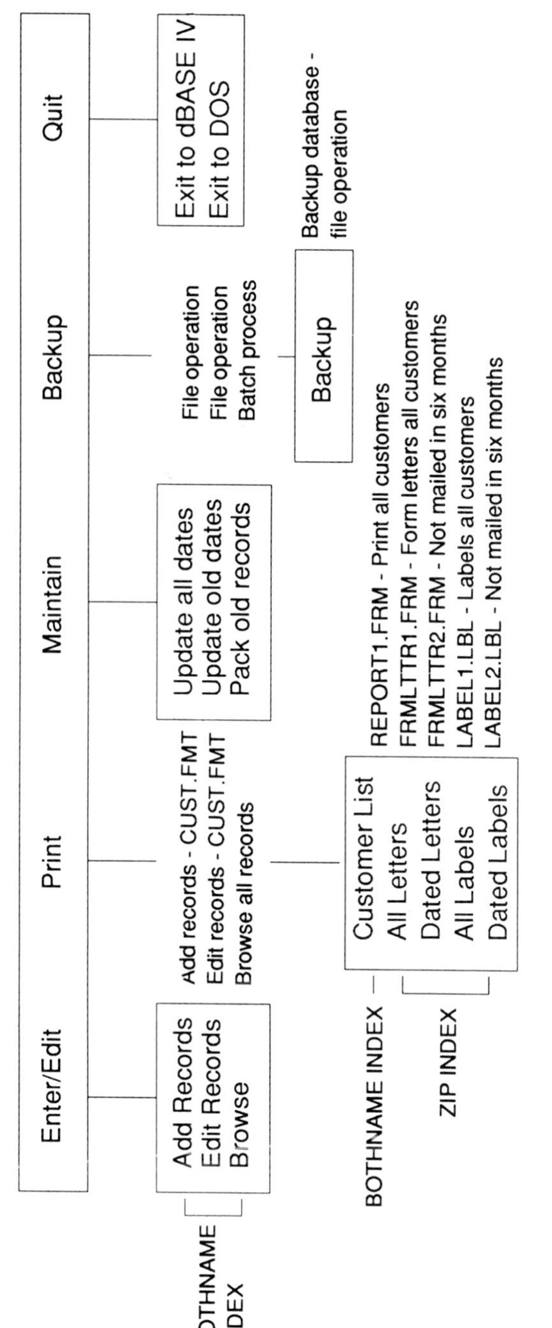

Figure 16-7. A sketch of the process design for the MAILAPP system

form single-step file operations that substitute new field values in the Lastmail date field of the MAILIST database. This field identifies the last time a customer received mail. The **Update all dates** option updates the Lastmail date field with today's date for every record in the database. You use this option after printing form letters for all customers by using the **All letters** option in the **Print** menu. On the other hand, you use the **Update old dates** option to update the mailing dates for only those customers who have not received a mailing in the last six months, or who have never received a mailing. The user can choose this option to update the Lastmail date field with today's date for those records printed with the **Dated letters** option in the **Print** menu.

The **Pack old records** submenu option calls for a batch process because packing the database is a two-step process. The first step is to define which records in the MAILIST database contain a logical true (.T.) in the Delete field and to mark those records for deletion. The second step is to pack the database, permanently removing those marked records.

Developing the MAILAPP Application

There are seven steps involved in creating an application with the Applications Generator.

1. Name the application and define its default environment.
2. Create the sign-on banner. This step is optional. However, it allows you to design a custom screen that appears each time the application is run.
3. Create the main horizontal bar menu and any pop-up menus.
4. Attach *actions* to each of the menu items. This involves defining an operation that will be performed when a menu item is selected.

5. Create batch processes. You use batch processes when more than one operation or action is required for a given menu item.

6. Generate the application. Once you've designed an application, dBASE IV takes that design and creates the files necessary to run your application. These files contain dBASE IV commands.

7. Save your design changes and exit the Applications Generator. You must follow this step to be able to modify your application later.

Getting to the Applications Generator

To access the Applications Generator from the Control Center, move the highlight to the Applications Panel and press ENTER on the **<create>** option. dBASE IV gives you a two-choice option box. Choose **Applications Generator** and press ENTER. dBASE IV takes you to the Applications Generator and presents the Application Definition screen displayed in Figure 16-8.

If you're working from the dot prompt, type the following command:

```
. CREATE APPLICATION Mailapp
```

Defining the Application

Once you enter the Applications Generator, you use the screen in Figure 16-8 to name your application and define its default environment. To do this for the MAILAPP application, perform the steps as follows:

1. For Application name, enter **MAILAPP**.
2. For Description, enter **Mailing list application**.
3. For Main menu type, accept the default, **BAR**, by pressing ENTER. (If you press the SPACEBAR, you can also select **POPUP** or **BATCH**.)
4. For Main menu name, enter **Mainmenu**.
5. For Database/view, enter **MAILIST**. (You can also use this field to enter the name of a view you've defined in the Queries Design screen.)
6. For Set INDEX to, enter **MAILIST**. This specifies the MAILIST production index file (MAILIST.MDX) as the default index.
7. For ORDER, enter **BOTHNAME**. This defines the BOTHNAME index tag you created earlier in this chapter as the default index.

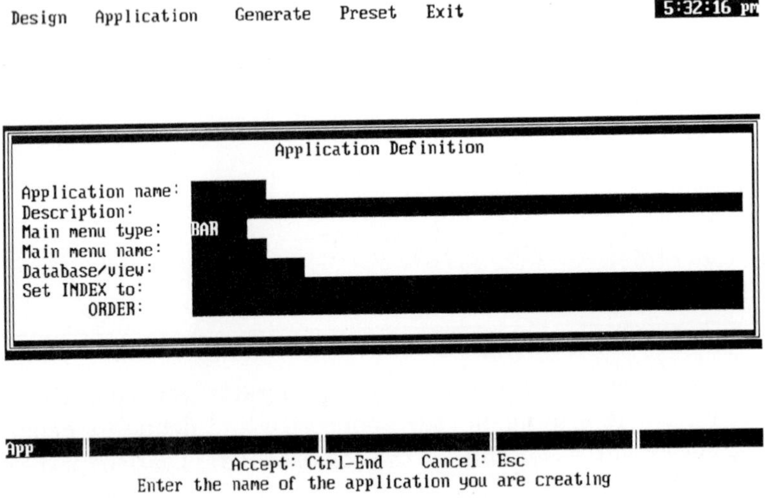

Figure 16-8. The application definition screen

8. Press CTRL-END to save this definition. dBASE IV saves the definition, takes you to the Applications Generator work surface, and displays an application object on the screen (Figure 16-9). You'll soon learn how to turn this application object into a sign-on banner.

Using the Applications Generator Menu System

You access the Applications Generator menu system as you access any other dBASE IV menu, by pressing F10 or by holding down ALT and pressing the first letter of the menu's name. However, the Applications Generator menu is slightly different than other dBASE IV system menus: its components change based on the type of ap-

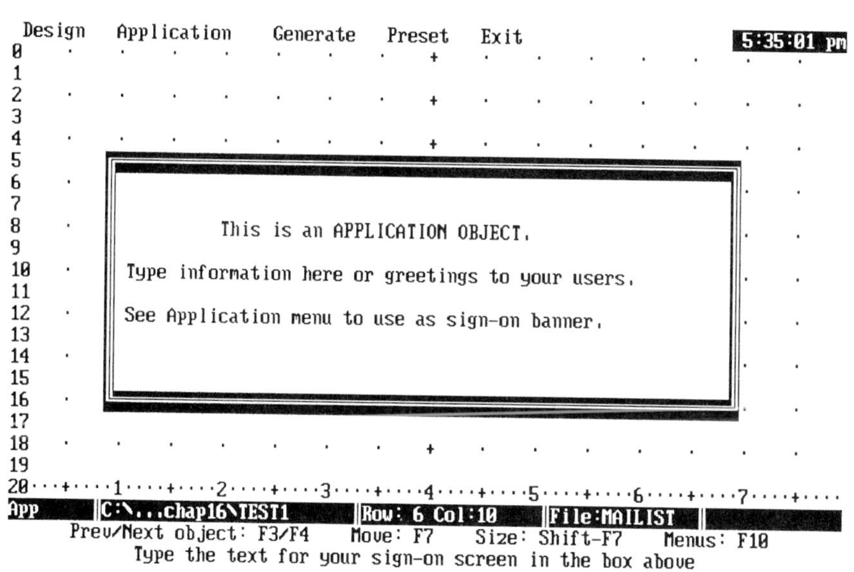

Figure 16-9. The default application object

plication object that is currently on the screen. For example, in Figure 16-9, since the application object is the current object, the **Application** option appears as the second choice in the main menu bar. However, if you place a menu object on the screen, it becomes the current object and two new menu options, **Menu** and **Item**, replace the **Application** menu option.

Creating a Sign-On Banner

The application object in Figure 16-9 remains on the screen throughout the applications development process. However, you can turn this application object into a sign-on banner that displays temporarily whenever your application is run. To create a sign-on banner from the application object, perform the following steps:

1. Press CTRL-Y until the default text is cleared from the application object.

2. Move the cursor down four lines, over ten spaces, and type **Welcome to the Mailing List System**.

3. Press SHIFT-F7. The outline of the application object will begin to blink.

4. Press UP ARROW three times and then press ENTER to confirm the new size of your completed sign-on banner.

5. To display this banner at run time, press F10 and select **Applications**. dBASE IV displays the **Applications** pull-down menu.

6. Select **Display sign-on banner** and press ENTER. dBASE IV displays an option box. Select **Yes** to complete the process.

Creating the Menus

The next phase of creating an application is to define its menus. You can create your application objects in any order. However, creating the main menu first establishes a foundation for the application. The main menu for the MAILAPP application is a horizontal bar menu. However, you could use a pop-up menu as your main menu.

Creating the Horizontal Bar Menu

Figure 16-10 shows the main horizontal bar menu for the MAILAPP application. To create this menu, perform the steps that follow.

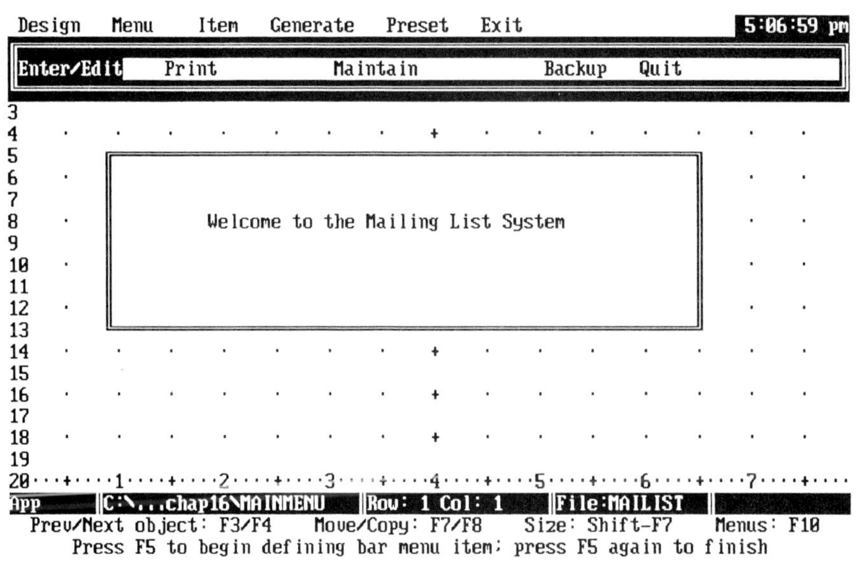

Figure 16-10. The **Mainmenu** horizontal bar menu

1. Select **Design** from the Applications Generator menu.

2. Select **Horizontal bar menu**. dBASE IV displays a files list selection box in the upper-right corner of your screen.

3. Press ENTER on the **<create>** option in the files list selection box. dBASE IV prompts you for a name, description, and message for the horizontal bar menu.

4. For Name, enter **Mainmenu**. (Note that this name matches the main menu name you defined when you first entered the Applications Generator). For Description, enter **Main mailing list horizontal bar menu**. Leave the Message line prompt blank. When you enter text in this area, that text is displayed in the message line whenever the horizontal bar menu is displayed. However, you'll define messages for each of your pop-up menus later, which make a message here unnecessary.

5. Press CTRL-END to confirm your entries and display a blank horizontal menu bar at the top of the Applications Generator work surface.

To fill in your new horizontal bar menu with menu choices, press F5, type the menu option name, and press F5 again. To enter choices for the **Mainmenu** horizontal bar menu, follow these steps:

1. Press F5, type **Enter/Edit**, and press F5 to complete the entry.

2. Press SPACEBAR four times and press F5. Type **Print** and press F5 to complete the entry.

3. Press the SPACEBAR 11 times, press F5, enter **Maintain**, and press F5 again.

4. Press the SPACEBAR 12 times, press F5, enter **Backup**, and press F5 again.

5. Press the SPACEBAR three times, press F5, enter **Quit**, and press F5 key to complete the menu.

   If you make a mistake on the spacing between menu choices, press DEL to remove excess spaces. To insert spaces, press INS and use SPACEBAR to insert the desired number of spaces.

   To get a preview of what your new menu bar looks like, without the Applications Generator menu or the status bar, press F9 (Zoom). dBASE IV displays your new menu and its choices, along with the sign-on banner that you created earlier. To redisplay the menus and status bar and get on with applications development, press F9 again.

6. When you finish step 5, press ALT-M to access the **Menu** option in the Applications Generator menu bar. (Note that this menu choice now appears, whereas before this position was occupied by the **Applications** menu).

7. To save your new horizontal menu bar, select **Save current menu** and press ENTER. To remove the **Menu** pull-down menu from the screen, press ESC.

Creating Pop-Up Menus

After completing the main horizontal bar menu for the MAILAPP application, you are ready to define its pop-up menus. Pop-up menus contain multiple choices stacked vertically. To define a pop-up menu, name the menu and then fill in its options in a blank pop-up box provided by dBASE IV. Then, press SHIFT-F7 to size that box to your liking. Next, press F7 to move that new pop-up menu to the desired location. See Figure 16-6 for the complete list of pop-up menus in the MAILAPP application. The sections that follow describe how to define each of those pop-up menus.

The Enter/Edit (Entredit) Pop-Up Menu

To create the **Entredit** pop-up menu, perform the following steps:

1. Press ALT-D to activate the **Design** menu. From that menu, select **Pop-up menu** and press ENTER. dBASE IV displays a files list selection box in the upper-right corner of your screen.
2. Highlight the **<create>** option in the files selection box and press ENTER. dBASE IV displays a blank menu description box.
3. Enter **Entredit** for a menu name.
4. Leave the Description blank and type **Use this menu to enter and edit records** for a Message line prompt. dBASE IV displays this message in the message line whenever you make a selection from this menu.
5. Press CTRL-END. dBASE IV displays a blank pop-up menu box in the middle of your screen.
6. Press SHIFT-F7, press LEFT ARROW eight times, and press ENTER.
7. Type **Add Records** and press ENTER.
8. Type **Edit Records** and press ENTER.
9. Type **Browse** and press ENTER.
10. Type ------------ (12 dashes) and press ENTER.
11. Type **Back-up when** and press ENTER.
12. Type **finished** and press ENTER.
13. Press SHIFT-F7, press UP ARROW twice, and press ENTER.
14. Press F7 (Move), select **Entire frame**, and press ENTER.

15. Use the Arrow keys to position the highlight of your new pop-up menu under **Enter/Edit** in the main horizontal menu bar. Press ENTER. Your screen should look like Figure 16-11.

16. Press ALT-M to display the **Menu** menu. Select **Put away current menu** and then **Save changes**. This saves your menu definition to a file with a .POP extension and clears the pop-up menu from the screen.

To create the remaining pop-up menus for the MAILAPP system, you'll use the same basic steps you just did to create the **Enter/Edit** pop-up menu. For each menu, repeat steps 1 and 2 of that process, that is, activate the **Design** menu, and select the **<create>** marker from the files list box that appears. Use the four sets of data that follow to create the four remaining pop-up menus, respectively, as shown in Figure 16-11. After you finish designing each menu, select **Put away current menu** from the **Menu** pull-down menu, followed by **Yes** to save the changes.

The Print (Reptlabl) Pop-Up Menu

- Menu name: **Reptlabl**.
- Message line prompt: **Use this menu to print reports and labels**.
- To size the blank box, press SHIFT-F7 and press LEFT ARROW seven times and UP ARROW three times.
- For the menu selections, enter

  Customer list

  All letters

  Dated letters

  All labels

  Dated labels

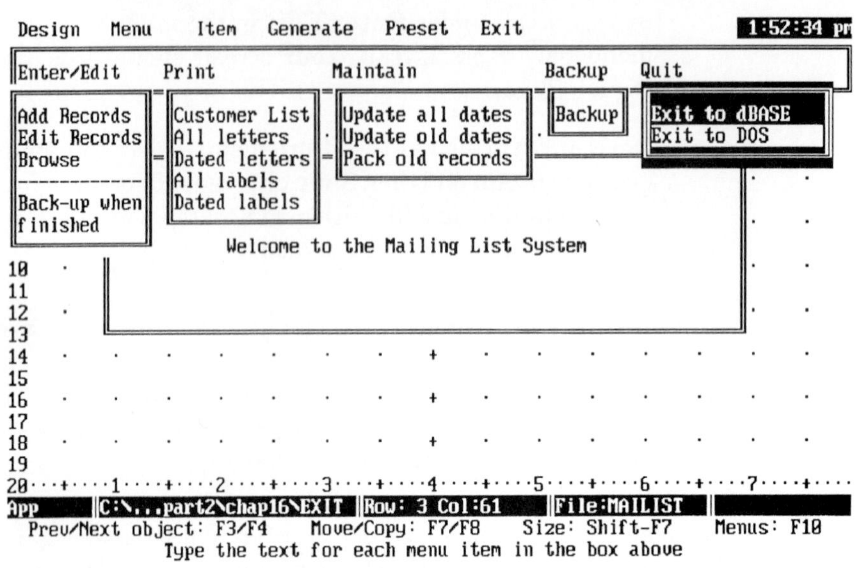

Figure 16-11. The five pop-up menus for the MAILAPP application

- Press F7 to position the **Reptlabl** menu under the main **Print** menu option as, shown in Figure 16-11.

The Maintain Pop-Up Menu

- Menu name: **Maintain**.
- Message line prompt: **Use this menu to update mailing dates and delete old records**.
- To size the blank box, press SHIFT-F7 and press LEFT ARROW three times and UP ARROW six times.
- For menu selections, enter

Update all dates

Update old dates

Pack old records

- Press F7 to position the Maintain menu under the main **Maintain** menu option, as shown in Figure 16-11.

The Backup (Backit) Pop-Up Menu

- Menu name: **Backit**.
- Message line prompt: **Use this menu to backup MAILIST.DBF to MAILBACK.DBF**.
- To size the blank box, press SHIFT-F7 and press LEFT ARROW 12 times and UP ARROW 7 times.
- Enter a single menu selection: **Backup**.
- Press F7 to position the **Backit** menu under the main **Backup** menu option, as shown in Figure 16-11.

The Quit (Exit) Pop-Up Menu

- Menu name: **Exit**.
- Message line prompt: None required.
- To size the blank box, press SHIFT-F7 and press LEFT ARROW three times and UP ARROW six times.
- For menu selections, enter

  Exit to dBASE

  Exit to DOS

- Press F7 to position the Exit menu under the main **Quit** menu option, as shown in Figure 16-11.

Specifying the Current Object

Before you assign actions to your menus, you may want to try moving around the work surface and specifying the current object. To move between objects on the work surface, use F3 (Previous) or F4 (Next).

The object that contains the cursor is the current object; the Applications Generator menus apply to that object. dBASE IV displays the border of the current object in reverse video. For example, press F4 to move the cursor from the **Mainmenu** horizontal bar pop-up menu to the application object. Note that its border lights up and that **Applications** now appears as the second choice in the menu bar. Press F4 again to move the cursor to the **Mainmenu** horizontal bar menu. Once again, its border is displayed in reverse video, and the menu bar now contains **Menu** and **Item**.

Clearing the Work Surface

To clear the work surface, use the **Clear work surface** option from the **Menu** menu. This option asks whether you want to **Save changes** for every displayed object on the work surface. Try this option now and select **Save changes** when you are prompted. The work surface will be cleared of all objects except the application object, which remains on the screen throughout the application development process.

Tip: You can save your changes and exit the Applications Generator at any time by selecting **Save all changes and exit** from the **Exit** menu. This option saves all of your work and returns you to the Control Center. You can modify the application later by pressing ENTER on the name of the application in the Applications Panel of the Control Center and selecting **Modify Application**.

Assigning Actions to Each Menu Item

The next step in developing an application is to assign actions to each of your menu items. dBASE provides a comprehensive menu-driven system for specifying menu selection actions.

Assigning Actions to the Horizontal Bar Menu

In this section, you'll assign actions to each of the items in the **Mainmenu** horizontal bar menu. You'll make each item activate a pop-up menu. First, assign an attribute to the menu that specifies that it will automatically display pop-up menus for each of the items in the horizontal bar menu. To do this, select **Attach pull-down menus** from the **Menu** pull-down menu, followed by **Yes**. Then perform the following steps:

1. Select **Horizontal bar menu** from the **Design** menu and press ENTER.
2. Select **Mainmenu** from the files list box displayed in the upper-right corner of your screen. Press ENTER.
3. Position the cursor on the **Enter/Edit** option in the horizontal bar menu and press ALT-I to access the **Item** menu.
4. Select **Change action**. dBASE IV displays a submenu, as in Figure 16-12.
5. Select **Open a menu**. dBASE displays a dialog box.
6. Press SPACEBAR to toggle the **Menu type** option in the dialog box to display **POPUP**. Press ENTER.
7. In the Menu name field, type **Entredit**. (Or, press SHIFT-F1 to display a list of pop-up menu names. Highlight **ENTREDIT** and press ENTER).

8. Press CTRL-END.

9. Press PGDN. dBASE IV moves to the next option, **Print**, in the **Mainmenu** horizontal bar menu. Note that its name now appears in the status bar (third block from the left). **Print** is now the current option.

10. Repeat steps 4 through 9 for the rest of the options in the **Mainmenu** horizontal bar menu, starting with **Print**, as follows:

Bar Option	**Pop-Up Menu (step 7)**
Print	Reptlabl
Maintain	Maintain
Backup	Backit
Quit	Exit

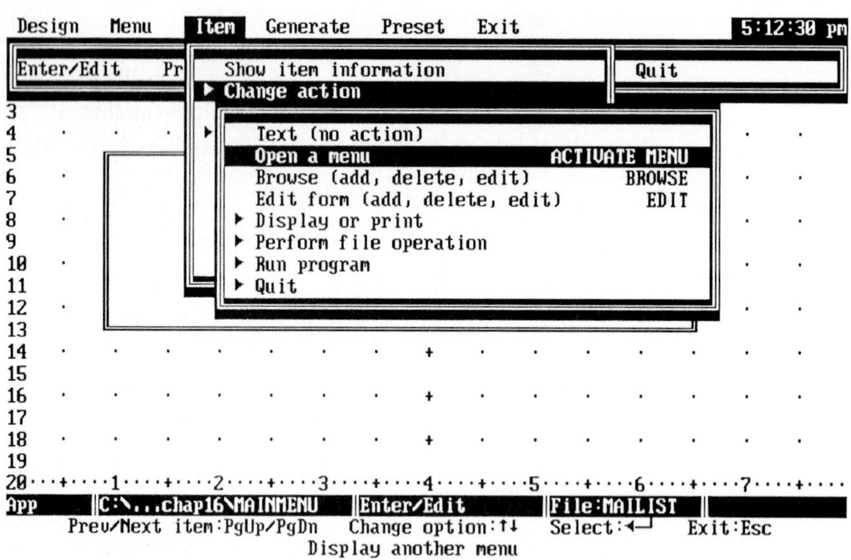

Figure 16-12. Open menu specifies activation of a pop-up menu

When you have assigned actions to each item in the horizontal bar menu, save it and remove it from the work surface using the **Put away current menu** option in the **Menu** pull-down menu.

Assigning Actions to the Pop-Up Menus

Assigning actions to each of the items in the pop-up menus is similar to assigning actions to the horizontal bar menu. The sections that follow show you how to assign actions to each of the items in the pop-up menus for the MAILAPP application.

Assigning Actions to the Entredit Menu

To assign actions to the **Entredit** pop-up menu, perform the following steps:

1. Select the **Pop-up menu** option from the **Design** menu and press ENTER. dBASE IV displays the files list box in the upper-right corner of your screen.

2. Select **Entredit** and press ENTER. dBASE IV places the **Entredit** pop-up menu on the work surface.

The Add Records Option The **Add Records** option appends records to the MAILIST database by using the custom form CUST.FMT defined earlier in this chapter. To assign an action to the **Add Records** option, follow these steps:

1. Press ALT-I to access the **Item** menu.

2. Select **Change action** and press ENTER.

3. Select **Edit form (add, delete, edit)** and press ENTER. dBASE IV displays the dialog box in Figure 16-13.

4. Type **CUST** (or press SHIFT-F1 to select **CUST**) for the FORMAT file: field and press ENTER.

5. Make sure the Mode field contains the word "APPEND." If it doesn't, press SPACEBAR until it does.

6. Accept the remainder of the defaults in the dialog box by pressing CTRL-END.

7. Press PGDN to get to the next option.

The Edit Records Option The **Edit Records** option displays the records of the MAILIST database using the custom form CUST.FMT. When you finish the application, you'll be able to use this option to view the records of the database. Furthermore, those records will be in order by last name because you specified BOTH-NAME as the default index when you first entered the Applica-

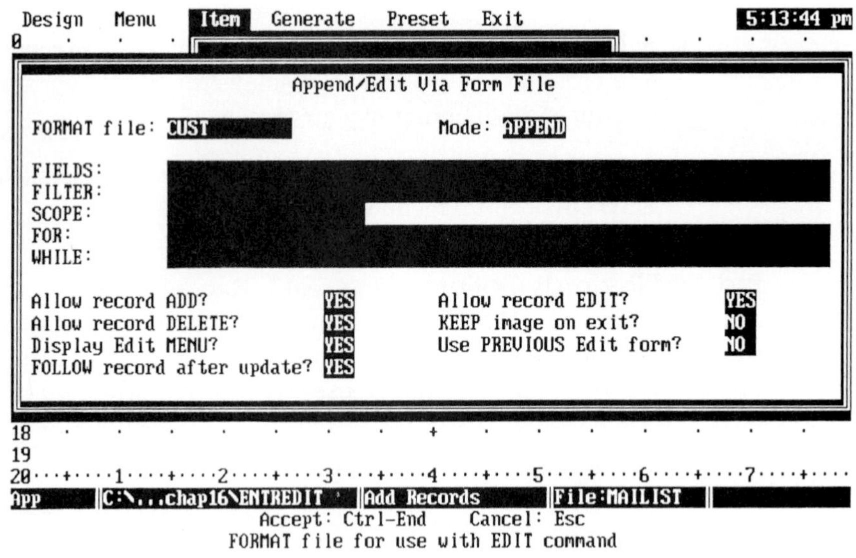

Figure 16-13. The Append/Edit dialog box set for append

tions Generator. To assign an action to the **Edit Records** option of the **Entredit** pop-up menu, perform the following steps:

1. Select **Change action** from the **Item** menu and press ENTER.
2. Select **Edit form (add, delete, edit)** and press ENTER. dBASE IV displays a dialog box.
3. Type **CUST** (or press SHIFT-F1 to select **CUST**) for the FORMAT file: field and press ENTER.
4. Make sure the **Mode** field contains the word "EDIT." If it doesn't, press the SPACEBAR until does.
5. Accept the remainder of the defaults in the dialog box by pressing CTRL-END.
6. Press PGDN to get to the next item.

The Browse Option The **Browse** option gives you a general-purpose view of the database in order by last name. To assign an action to the Browse option of the **Entredit** pop-up menu, perform the following steps:

1. Select **Change action** from the **Item** menu and press ENTER.
2. Select **Browse (add, delete, edit)** and press ENTER. dBASE IV displays a dialog box.
3. Press CTRL-END to accept the defaults in the dialog box.

You are done assigning actions for the **Entredit** pop-up menu. Don't worry about the **Back-up when finished** option below the dashes. If you do not assign actions to a row of text in a pop-up menu, dBASE IV ignores that text.

To save the assignments you've made, select **Put away current menu** from the **Menu** pull-down menu.

Assigning Actions to the Reptlabl Pop-Up Menu

Next you'll assign actions to each of the options in the **Reptlabl** pop-up menu. As mentioned, this menu stages various reports forms for printing data from the MAILIST database. To assign actions to the **Reptlabl** pop-up menu, perform the following steps:

1. Select the **Pop-up menu** option from the **Design** menu and press ENTER. dBASE IV displays the files list box in the upper-right corner of your screen.

2. Select **Reptlabl** and press ENTER. dBASE IV places the **Reptlabl** pop-up menu on the work surface.

The Customer List The **Customer list** option stages the REPORT1.FMT report to print the data in the MAILIST database. Recall that the REPORT1.FMT report is a form report that shows the contents of each record in the MAILIST database. As mentioned, since BOTHNAME is the default index for this application, the records printed by this item will appear in order by last name. To assign an action to this option, perform the following steps:

1. Select **Change action** from the **Item** menu and press ENTER.

2. Select **Display or print** and press ENTER. dBASE IV displays a submenu box.

3. Select **Report**. dBASE IV displays the dialog box shown in Figure 16-14.

4. Type **REPORT1** (or press SHIFT-F1 to select **REPORT1**) and press ENTER.

5. Press ENTER seven more times to get to the FOR field in the dialog box and type **.NOT. DELETE**.

   This expression provides a filter condition for the REPORT1.FMT report, excluding from printing those records in the MAILIST database that have a logical (.T.) in the Delete logical field. When you designed the CUST.FMT format file, you specified a default value of .N. or false for the Delete logical field. However, if, while adding or editing records, the user enters Y, the Delete logical field is given a true (.T.) value, and this filter condition excludes those records from printing.

6. Press CTRL-END to accept the defaults in the dialog box.
7. Press PGDN to get to the next option in the menu.

The All Letters Option The **All letters** option prints custom form letters for every customer in the MAILIST database. The report form used by this option is the FRMLTTR1.FRM designed

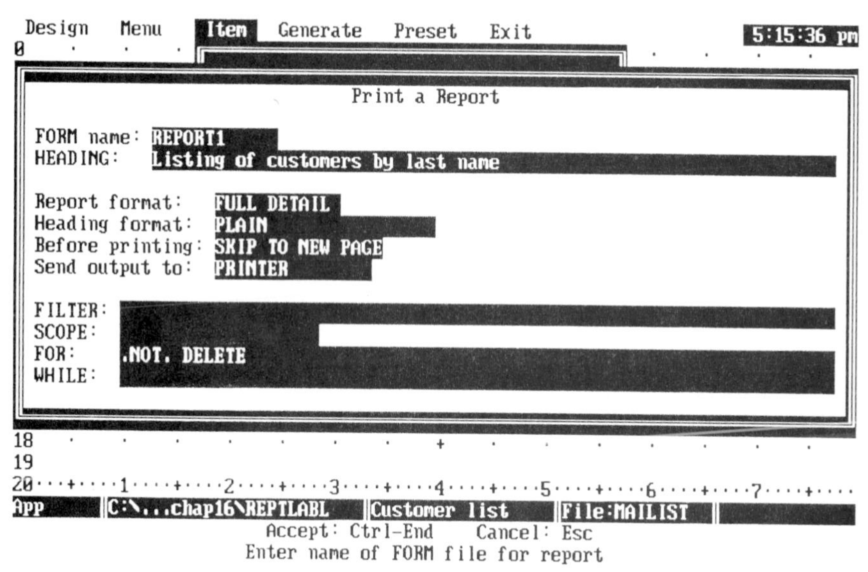

Figure 16-14. The Print a Report dialog box

earlier in this chapter. To assign an action to the **All letters** option, perform the following:

1. Select **Change action** from the **Item** menu and press ENTER.

2. Select **Display or print** and press ENTER. dBASE IV displays a submenu box.

3. Select **Report**.

4. Type **FRMLTTR1** (or press SHIFT-F1 to select **FRMLTTR1**) and press ENTER.

5. Press ENTER seven more times to get to the FOR field in the dialog box and type **Oktomail .AND. .NOT. Delete**.

   This expression defines a condition for the records to be included in the FRMLTTR1.FRM report. Only those records with a logical true (.T.) value in the Oktomail logical field and that do not contain a logical true (.T.) in the Delete logical field will be included in this report. While designing the CUST.FMT form, you defined a default value of .T. for the Oktomail logical field. Unless the user enters N in the Oktomail field, it will always have a value of logical true.

6. Press CTRL-END to accept the defaults in the dialog box.

7. Press PGDN to get to the next option in the **Reptlabl** menu.

The Dated Letters Option The **Dated letters** option prints form letters for customers who have not received a mailing in the last six months or have never received one. This option initiates the FRMLTTR2.FRM report. To assign an action to this option, perform the following:

1. Select **Change action** from the **Item** menu and press ENTER.

2. Select **Display or print** and press ENTER. dBASE IV displays a submenu box.

3. Select **Report**. dBASE IV displays a dialog box.

4. Type **FRMLTTR2** (or press SHIFT-F1 to select **FRMLTTR2**) and press ENTER.

5. Press ENTER five more times to get to the FILTER field and enter **Lastmail<=DATE( )-182 .OR. Lastmail={ }**.

   This expression specifies a filter condition for the FRMLTTR2.FRM report. In order for records in the MAILIST database to be included in this report, the date in the Lastmail date field must meet one of two conditions. The first condition, Lastmail<=DATE( )-182, uses the DATE( ) function to return today's date and subtracts 182 days (six months) from it. For a record to be printed, the date in the Lastmail field must be less than or equal to today's date, less 182 days. The second condition, Lastmail={}, selects records that do not have a date in the Lastmail date field, indicating that a customer has never received a mailing.

6. Press ENTER two more times to get to the FOR field in the dialog box and type **Oktomail .AND. .NOT. Delete**.

7. Press CTRL-END to accept the defaults in the dialog box.

8. Press PGDN to get to the next option in the **Reptlabl** menu.

The All Labels Option The **All labels** option prints mailing labels for each record in the database. This option compliments the **All letters** option defined earlier, because it prints a mailing label for each of the form letters printed by that option. To specify an action for this option, perform these steps.

1. Select **Change action** from the **Item** menu and press ENTER.

2. Select **Display or print** and press ENTER. dBASE IV displays a submenu box.

3. Select **Labels**. dBASE IV displays the dialog box in Figure 16-15.

4. Type **LABEL1** (or press SHIFT-F1 to select **LABEL1**) and press ENTER.

5. Press ENTER four more times to access the FOR field and enter **Oktomail .AND. .NOT. Delete**.

6. Press CTRL-END to accept the defaults in the dialog box.

7. Press PGDN to get to the next option in the menu.

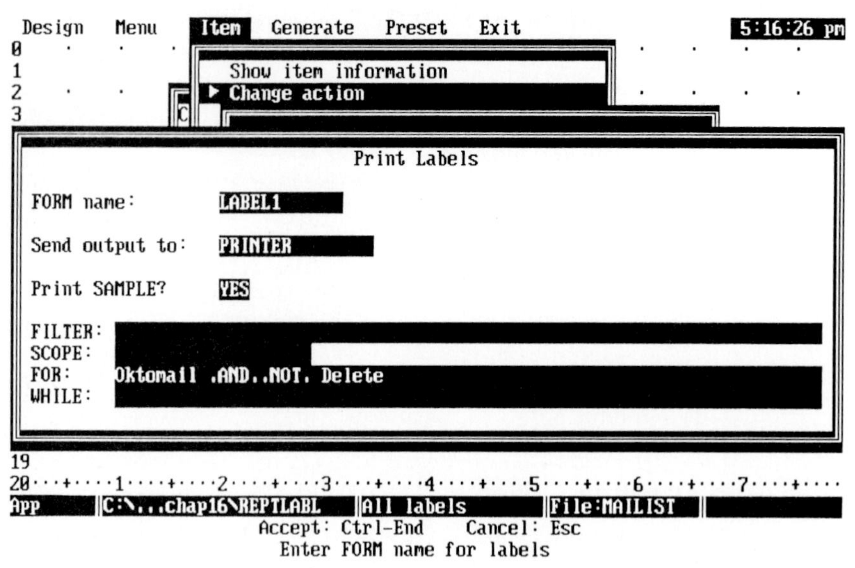

Figure 16-15. The Print Labels dialog box

The Dated Labels Option The **Dated labels** option prints the mailing labels for the form letters printed by the **Dated letters** option. To specify an action for this option, perform the following steps:

1. Select **Change action** from the **Item** menu and press ENTER.
2. Select **Display or print** and press ENTER. dBASE IV displays a submenu box.
3. Select **Labels**. dBASE IV displays a dialog box.
4. Type **LABEL2** (or press SHIFT-F1 to select **LABEL2**) and press ENTER.
5. Press ENTER two more times to get to the Filter field of the dialog box and type **Lastmail<=DATE( )-182 .OR. Lastmail={ }**.
6. Press ENTER two more times to get to the FOR field and enter **Oktomail .AND. .NOT. Delete**.
7. Press CTRL-END to accept the defaults in the dialog box.

You're done assigning actions to the **Reptlabl** pop-up menu. However, before you put this menu away and save the changes, you need to specify an index order for the **All letters**, **Dated letters**, **All labels**, and **Dated labels** menu selections. These letters and labels need to be printed in ZIP code order.

When you designed the MAILIST database on the Database Design screen, you created a Zip index tag for the MAILIST.MDX production index file by showing the letter "Y" in the Index column for the Zip field. You'll use that index now. Proceed as follows:

1. Press PGUP three times until the **All letters** menu item of the **Reptlabl** pop-up menu appears in the middle of the status bar at the bottom of your screen.

2. From the Applications Generator **Item** menu, select **Reassign index order** and press ENTER. dBASE IV presents a Set ORDER to: prompt box.

3. Type **Zip** and press ENTER.

4. Press PGDN to get to the next option in the menu.

5. Repeat steps 2 through 4 for the **Dated letters**, **All labels**, and **Dated labels** options.

When you've completed the preceding steps, save the **Reptlabl** pop-up menu and remove it from the work surface by using the **Put away current menu** option from the **Menu** pull-down menu.

Specifying Actions for the Maintain Pop-Up Menu

Next you'll assign actions to each of the options in the **Maintain** pop-up menu. As mentioned, this menu maintains mailing dates and deletes old records from the MAILIST database. Perform the following steps:

1. Select the **Pop-up menu** option from the **Design** menu and press ENTER. dBASE IV displays the files list box in the upper-right corner of your screen.

2. Select **Maintain** and press ENTER. dBASE IV places the **Maintain** pop-up menu on the work surface.

The Update All Dates Option The **Update all dates** option updates with today's date the Lastmail field for every record in the MAILIST database. Use this option after sending out form letters to all customers by using the **All letters** and **All labels** options in the **Reptlabl** menu. To assign an action to this option, follow these steps:

1. Select **Change action** from the **Item** menu and press ENTER.
2. Select **Perform file operation** and press ENTER.
3. Select **Substitute field values**. dBASE IV displays the dialog box in Figure 16-16.
4. Press ENTER three times to get to the field named column.
5. In row 1, enter **Lastmail** and press ENTER to get to the with this value column.
6. Type **DATE( )** and press ENTER.
7. Press CTRL-END.
8. Press PGDN to get to the **Update old dates** option.

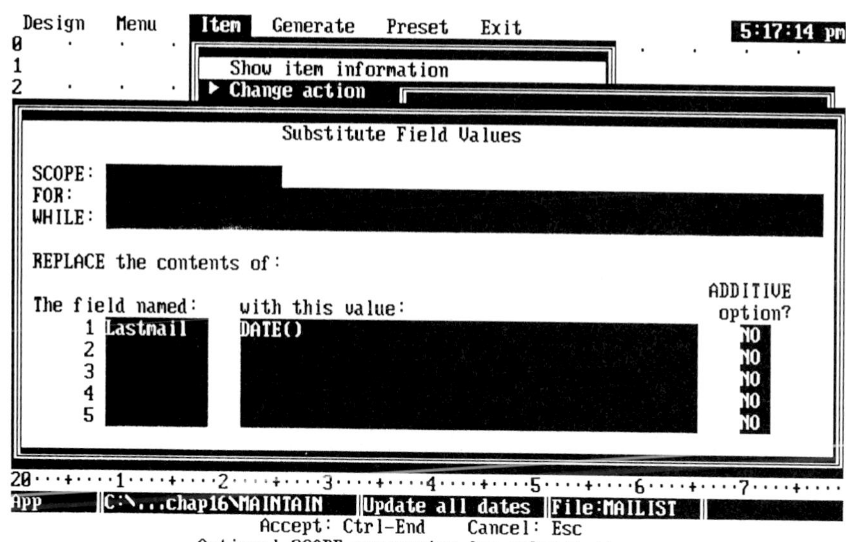

Figure 16-16. The Substitute Field Values dialog box

The Update Old Dates Option The **Update old dates** option updates the Lastmail date field after you use the **Dated letters** and **Dated labels** options in the **Reptlabl** pop-up menu. This option only updates the Lastmail date to today's date for records that have not received a mailing for six months, or that have never received a mailing. To assign an action for this option, follow these steps:

1. Select **Change action** from the **Item** menu and press ENTER.
2. Select **Perform file operation** and press ENTER.
3. Select **Substitute field values**.
4. Press ENTER so you can get to the FOR field, type **Lastmail<=Date( )-182 .OR. Lastmail={ }**, and then press ENTER.
5. Press ENTER again to get to the field named column.
6. In row 1, enter **Lastmail** and press ENTER to get to the **with this value:** column.
7. Type **DATE( )** and press ENTER.
8. Press CTRL-END.
9. Press PGDN to get to the **Pack old records** option.

The Pack Old Records Option You use the **Pack old records** option to remove records from the database for which the user has requested deletion. This option actually calls a batch process that you'll define later. To assign an action to this item, follow these steps:

1. Select **Change action** from the **Item** menu and press ENTER.

2. Select **Run program** and press ENTER.

3. Select **Execute batch process** and press ENTER. dBASE IV prompts you for a batch file name.

4. Type **PACK**. This has nothing to with the PACK command. It is simply a name for a batch process that you define later.

5. Press ENTER.

You are now done assigning actions to the options in the **Maintain** pop-up menu. However, before you put it away and save the changes, you should define a help message for the **Pack old records** option.

Displaying Help Messages

For any option in a pop-up menu, you can define a help message that displays whenever you move the cursor to that option. To define a help message for the **Pack old records** option of the **Maintain** pop-up menu, follow these steps:

1. Select the **Assign message prompt** option from the **Item** menu and press ENTER. dBASE IV displays a large dialog box at the bottom of your screen.

2. Type the sentence **This option permanently removes records marked for deletion**.

3. Press CTRL-END.

When you've assigned a help message for the **Pack old records** option, put away the **Maintain** pop-up menu by using the **Put away current menu** option in the **Menu** pull-down menu. Then select **Save changes**.

Assigning an Action to the Backit Pop-Up Menu

The **Backit** pop-up menu backs up the MAILIST database to another database called MAILBACK. It contains a single option, **Backup**, for this purpose. To assign an action to the **Backup** option, follow these steps:

1. Select the **Pop-up menu** option from the **Design** menu and press ENTER. dBASE IV displays the files list box in the upper-right corner of your screen.
2. Select **Backit** and press ENTER. dBASE IV places the **Backit** pop-up menu on the work surface.
3. Select **Change action** from the **Item** menu and press ENTER.
4. Select **Perform file operation** and press ENTER.
5. Select **Copy records to file** and press ENTER. dBASE IV displays a dialog box.
6. Type in **MAILBACK.DBF** and press ENTER four times to get to the FOR field.
7. Type **.NOT. Delete** and press CTRL-END.
8. Put away the **Backit** menu by selecting **Put away current menu** from the **Menu** pull-down menu. Then select **Save changes**.

Assigning Actions to the Exit Pop-Up Menu

You use the **Exit** menu to exit the MAILAPP system. This menu has one selection for returning to dBASE IV and one for exiting to DOS. To assign these actions to the **Exit** menu, follow these steps:

1. Select the **Pop-up menu** option from the **Design** menu and press ENTER. dBASE IV displays the files list box in the upper-right corner of your screen.

2. Select **Exit** and press ENTER. dBASE IV places the **Exit** pop-up menu on the work surface.

3. Select **Change action** from the **Item** menu and press ENTER.

4. Select **Quit** and press ENTER.

5. Select **Return to calling program** and press ENTER.

6. Press ENTER to confirm the OK box.

7. Press PGDN to move to the **Exit to DOS** option, and repeat steps 3 through 6, specifying **Quit to DOS** in step 5.

8. Put away the **Exit** menu by using the **Put away current menu** option in the **Menu** pull-down menu. Then select **Save changes**.

Defining a Batch Process

As mentioned, you'll need to define a batch process that performs a two-step operation called by the **Pack old records** option in the **Maintain** pop-up menu. To define this batch process, follow these steps:

1. Select **Batch process** from the **Design** menu and press ENTER. dBASE IV displays a files list box in the upper-right corner of your screen.

2. Press ENTER on the **<create>** option. dBASE IV prompts you for a name and description for the batch process.

3. Type **PACK**, press ENTER, and leave the Description field blank.

4. Press CTRL-END. dBASE IV displays a large box in the middle of the screen.

In the next two steps, you will enter brief descriptions of the two steps for the batch process. These are not commands, they are phrases that describe each step.

5. Type **Mark records with .T. in Delete** and press ENTER.
6. Type **Pack the marked records** and press ENTER.
7. Press UP ARROW twice to return the cursor to the **Mark records with .T. in Delete** bar.
8. Press ALT-I to access the **Item** menu.
9. Select **Change action** and press ENTER.
10. Select **Perform file operation** and press ENTER.
11. Select **Mark records for deletion** and press ENTER. dBASE IV displays a dialog box.
12. Press ENTER to get to the FOR field, type **DELETE**, and press CTRL-END.
13. Press PGDN to move to step two in the batch process.
14. Press ENTER on **Change action** in the **Item** menu.
15. Select **Perform file operation** and press ENTER.
16. Select **Discard marked records**, press ENTER, and press ENTER again to approve the OK box.
17. To save the batch process, select **Put away current batch process** from the **Batch** menu. Then select **Save changes**.

Note that defining actions for the each step of the batch process is remarkably similar to defining actions for options in pop-up menus. In effect, batch processes behave much like pop-up menus, except that each line in the batch process is processed one after the other by dBASE IV.

You have now finished defining the MAILAPP application.

Generating the Code

As mentioned, the Applications Generator is a design instrument that generates dBASE IV command language code. In order to run the MAILAPP application you've just created, you need to generate the code for it. To do so, follow these steps:

1. Press F10 and select **Select Template** from the **Generate** menu. dBASE prompts you for a template name.
2. Type **MENU.GEN**, if it's not there already, and press ENTER.
3. Select **Display during generation** and select **Yes** (this step is optional).
4. Select **Begin Generating**.

dBASE IV begins generating the code for your application. If you selected **Display during generation**, dBASE IV displays the documentation for the application as it generates the code. When the code is generated dBASE displays the message "Generation is complete. Press any key." If you press any key, dBASE IV returns you to the Applications Generator **Generate** menu.

In the next section, you'll generate the documentation for the MAILAPP application. If you do not want to generate documentation, select **Save all changes and exit** from the **Exit** menu. dBASE IV returns you to the Control Center and shows the name of the MAILAPP application in the Applications Panel.

Generating Documentation

You can also create written documentation for your applications with the Applications Generator. To do this, perform the following steps:

1. Choose **Select Template** from the **Generate** menu and press ENTER.
2. Type **DOCUMENT.GEN** and press ENTER.
3. Select **Begin Generating** and press ENTER. dBASE IV asks if you have an IBM graphics-compatible printer.
4. Press Y if you have an IBM graphics-compatible printer. Press N if you don't or are not sure. dBASE IV begins generating your documentation. When it's finished, you see the message "Generation is complete. Press any key."
5. Select **Save all changes and exit** from the **Exit** menu and press ENTER.

When dBASE IV creates documentation for your applications, it creates a file with the same name as your application and a .DOC extension. For example, for the MAILAPP application, dBASE IV creates a file called MAILAPP.DOC. You can view this file by selecting the **View** option from the **Operations** submenu of the **DOS Utilities** menu. Recall that you can access this menu by using the **Tools** menu in the Control Center. Alternately, you can enter **TYPE MAILAPP.DOC** at the dot prompt.

You can also print this documentation file by using the **Print** menu in the dBASE IV Text Editor. To access this menu, use the **DOS Utilities** option from the **Tools** menu in the Control Center. Highlight **MAILAPP.DOC**, select **Operations**, and select **Edit**. dBASE IV will take you to the dBASE IV Text Editor. Use the **Print** menu option in the menu bar in the usual way. Alternately, you can enter **TYPE MAILAPP.DOC TO PRINTER** at the dot prompt.

Running and Debugging the Application

Your MAILAPP application should now be ready to run. To run the application, highlight **MAILAPP** in the Applications Panel of the Control Center and press ENTER. dBASE IV displays the menu box in Figure 16-17 with the two choices **Run application** and **Modify application**.

Modify application returns you to the Applications Generator so that you can change or enhance your application. Use this option to fix any errors you may have made during the application development process.

When you select **Run application**, dBASE IV begins compiling your application (translating it into machine-readable code). As each line is compiled, dBASE IV checks it for acceptable command syntax. If no errors exist, dBASE IV presents you with a sign-

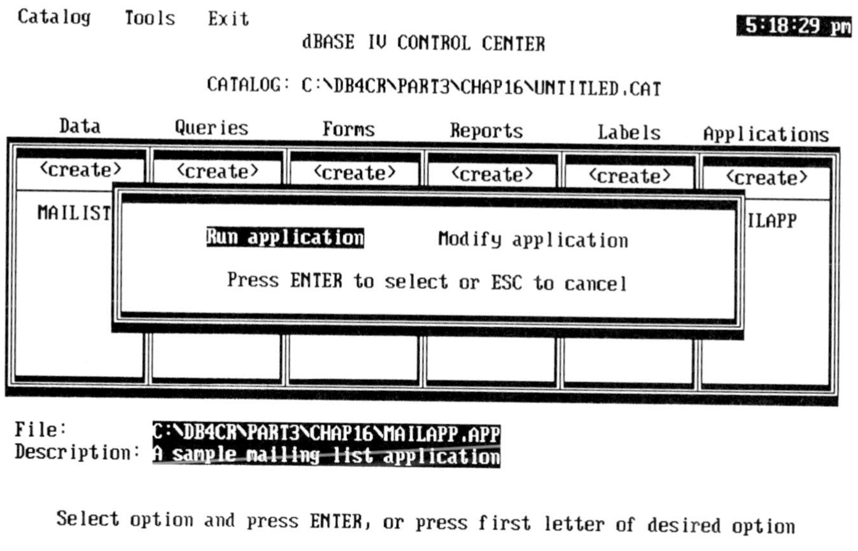

```
Catalog   Tools   Exit                                              5:18:29 pm
                          dBASE IV CONTROL CENTER

                 CATALOG: C:\DB4CR\PART3\CHAP16\UNTITLED.CAT

   Data        Queries       Forms       Reports       Labels     Applications
 <create>     <create>     <create>     <create>     <create>     <create>
 MAILIST                                                          ILAPP
              Run application         Modify application

                Press ENTER to select or ESC to cancel

File:         C:\DB4CR\PART3\CHAP16\MAILAPP.APP
Description:  A sample mailing list application

   Select option and press ENTER, or press first letter of desired option
```

Figure 16-17. Press ENTER on the name of your application to display this menu

on banner followed by the menus for your new application. At this point, you can begin testing each of the menus in the application.

If an error occurs while compiling or when you try a menu selection, dBASE IV displays a brief error message that describes the nature of the problem and the command line that caused the error. That command line should show one of the expressions that you entered during the applications development process. Next, dBASE IV displays an option box with **Cancel**, **Ignore**, or **Suspend**. Before you choose an option, read the error message and command line carefully. When you are ready, select **Cancel**. dBASE IV beeps and prompts you to press any key. Press any key and dBASE IV returns you to the Control Center.

To fix an error, return to the Applications Generator by pressing ENTER on the name of the application and selecting **Modify application**. dBASE IV returns you to the Applications Generator. Repeat the steps required to correct the error. When you're ready, generate new code for the application by using the **Generate** menu. Make sure to save all changes before you leave the Applications Generator by using the **Save changes and exit** option in the **Exit** menu.

Testing the Application

Before your application is complete, you must test every menu. Start with the **Append records** option from the **Enter/Edit** menu. This option displays the CUST.FMT form for data entry. Use this option to enter five or six example records, some with mailing dates and some without. (Normally, mailing dates are not input unless the user intends to mail to that customer on that very day). Also, make sure that at least one of the dates you enter is over six months old. Press F10 and select **Exit** from the **Exit** menu to return to MAILAPP application menus.

When you finish entering example records, try the **Edit records** option. This option displays the CUST.FMT form, which now contains information in the records you've just entered. You can press PGUP and PGDN to move through the records in the database. To select a specific record to edit, press F10 to access the menu system. Select **Go To** and then **Index key search**. Press ENTER to have dBASE IV prompt you for a last and first name search string. Enter the last and first name from one of your example records, press ENTER, and dBASE IV takes you to that record. To return to the menu system, use the **Exit** menu again.

Next, try the **Browse** option to see a general view of the records you've entered. Make a mental note of the data so that you can easily recall it when you test the **Print**, **Maintain**, and **Backup** menus. Return to the menu system by using the **Exit** menu.

When you've finished with the **Enter/Edit** menu, try all of the options in the **print** menu. However, before you try either **Dated letters** or **Dated labels**, make sure that at least one of the records in the database has a Lastmail date that is more than six months old.

Finally, try each of the options in the **Maintain** menu. After you try **Update all dates**, return to the **Browse** option in the **Enter/Edit** menu to observe the changes in the Lastmail date field. Set one of those dates to over six months ago and try the **Update all dates** option in the **Maintain** menu. This option should update to today's date the date that you set to over six months ago. Use the **Browse** option to check it. While you're on the Browse screen, enter **T** in the Delete field for one of your sample records. Next, use the **Pack old records** option in the **Maintain** menu to remove that record. Once again, use the **Browse or Edit records** option in the **Enter/Edit** menu to make sure that that record has been deleted.

When you've completed these tests, try the **Backup** menu of the MAILAPP application. This menu option saves the MAILIST database to a database called MAILBAK. Don't worry about saving the example data. When you try this option with "real" data, dBASE IV allows you to overwrite the MAILBAK backup database file with new data.

If all of the options in each of the menus are in working order, you have successfully completed the MAILAPP application.

In this chapter, you learned how to create an application by using the Applications Generator. First, you built the components to be used by the application. Next, you sketched a design for the application. Finally, you entered the Applications Generator and developed that application.

During the development process, you created both horizontal bar menus and pop-up menus and assigned actions to each of the options in those menus. For some of the menu selections, you assigned file operations and batch processes. Next, you learned how to generate the code for your application and to save your applications design. Finally, you tested each element of that application to check that all components were in proper working order.

Programming in dBASE IV

PART THREE

Programming in dBASE IV is relatively easy to learn. To program in dBASE IV, you use the dBASE IV command language. This language is composed of a series of English-like commands, each of which performs a specific task. You can group these commands in a program file and batch process them very rapidly. You can also combine program files to develop sophisticated applications handling virtually any data-management task.

Programming gives you a level of control over dBASE IV that is simply unavailable through the Control Center, the dot prompt, or even the Applications Generator. This is because programming gives you complete access to the dBASE IV command language. A number of the commands in this language can be accessed only through the use of a program.

Part Three of this book tells you how to go about programming in dBASE IV. It starts with an introduction to programming in general and to dBASE IV in particular. You'll learn the basics of programming, as well as a little about database design.

The chapters in this part will then take you through a series of basic programming topics, including how to use memory variables, how to program input and output operations, how to work with databases, and how to control the flow of your program. You can then delve into such topics as controlling user input, refining the user interface, event processing, and error trapping. You will also find a chapter on advanced topics, including user- defined functions, arrays, and creating your own pop-up menu system. Part Three concludes with a chapter on dBASE IV's new Program Debugger.

Setting Up a dBASE IV Program

SEVENTEEN

After a brief introduction to programming, this chapter will show you how to effectively use the dBASE IV Text Editor to write command-file programs. Command-file fundamentals, including program and database design, running a program, and modular programming are also covered. This chapter also discusses the dBASE IV automatic compiler as well as a host of other topics designed to get you programming in dBASE IV as quickly as possible.

If you're an experienced dBASE programmer, you probably will still want to scan this chapter since it describes a number of enhancements to common dBASE programming functions. For example, it describes dBASE IV's automatic program compiler, which makes your programs run faster than in prior versions of dBASE.

Tip: If you see a command in this chapter that you want to learn more about, refer to Part Five, "Command Reference." It lists all the dBASE IV commands in alphabetical order and gives examples of their use.

The dBASE IV programming language is made up of a series of commands, many of which you've encountered earlier in the book. Together, these commands form a powerful programming language with which you can develop highly sophisticated applications that can perform virtually any database management task.

To program in dBASE IV, you use dBASE IV *command files*—files that contain a series of dBASE IV commands. You can enter most of these same commands from the dot prompt or the Control Center menus and have dBASE IV perform them immediately. However, the command-file approach lets you save a series of commands in a file and then sequentially process those commands at a far greater rate of speed.

You can use command files to perform repetitive tasks for database management. For example, imagine that you are working with an inventory database and need to regularly check the quantities on hand for various items. You can write a program that requests a part number from the user, searches the database, and displays the status of an item on your screen.

You can also write a group of programs that work together to perform a specific task. Such a grouping of programs is called an *application*. In a multiple-program application, each program performs a specific segment of the overall job. For example, suppose you are writing an application that controls inventory for a retail store. One program might handle inquiries to an inventory database for quantities on hand and on order. Another program might handle shipments and receipts of goods, while yet another summarizes the value of the inventory.

A Sample Program

The program listing that follows is a dBASE IV command file. The purpose of the program is to display a customer name and address for a specific order number entered by the user.

The name of the program is FINDIT.PRG. The .PRG extension is the default for command files in dBASE IV. FINDIT.PRG uses the CUSTOMER.DBF database, the structure of which appears in Figure 17-1.

The first four lines in the program are comment lines. Note that each of them begins with an asterisk (*). This denotes a

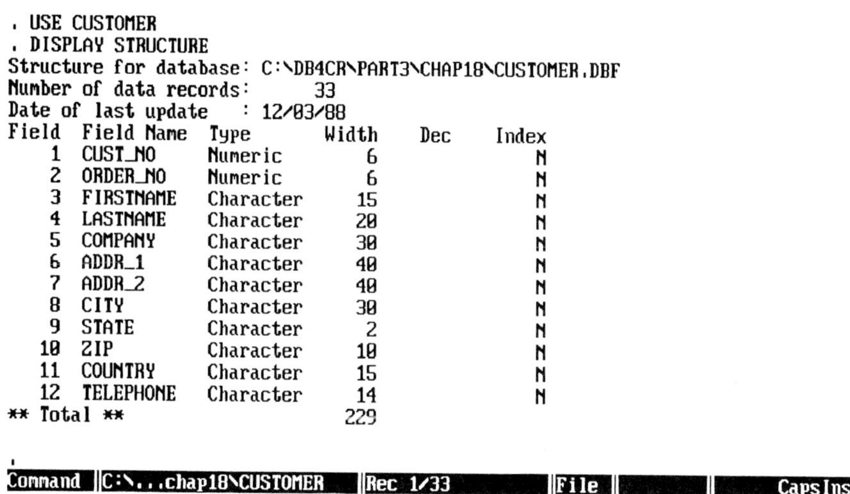

```
. USE CUSTOMER
. DISPLAY STRUCTURE
Structure for database: C:\DB4CR\PART3\CHAP18\CUSTOMER.DBF
Number of data records:       33
Date of last update   : 12/03/88
Field  Field Name  Type       Width    Dec    Index
    1  CUST_NO     Numeric        6               N
    2  ORDER_NO    Numeric        6               N
    3  FIRSTNAME   Character     15               N
    4  LASTNAME    Character     20               N
    5  COMPANY     Character     30               N
    6  ADDR_1      Character     40               N
    7  ADDR_2      Character     40               N
    8  CITY        Character     30               N
    9  STATE       Character      2               N
   10  ZIP         Character     10               N
   11  COUNTRY     Character     15               N
   12  TELEPHONE   Character     14               N
** Total **                     229

Command ||C:\...chap18\CUSTOMER ||Rec 1/33 ||File || || CapsIns
```

Figure 17-1. Structure for the CUSTOMER.DBF database

comment in dBASE IV. Also, note that some of the command lines have a double ampersand (&&) and some text following them. This is yet another way to add a comment to a command line.

The first command in the program, CLEAR, clears the screen. The second command, USE Customer, opens the CUSTOMER.DBF database. The third command, DO WHILE .T., is paired with the last command in the program, ENDDO. These two commands work together to place the program in a continuous *loop*. That is, when the program reaches the ENDDO statement, it jumps back to the DO WHILE statement to verify if the condition following the DO WHILE is true. In this case, it encounters the logical true (.T.)—which is, of course, always true—and tells dBASE IV to proceed.

```
* Program is Findit.prg
* Program uses Customer.dbf
* Program takes a user provided order number to search for a customer's
* name and address linked to that order number.
CLEAR                               && Clear the screen
USE Customer                        && Activate Customer.dbf database
DO WHILE .T.                        && Start a continuous loop
       ?
       ? "                      THE ACME SUPPLY COMPANY"
       ?
       INPUT "          Please Enter the Order Number: " TO Findit

       LOCATE FOR Order_no = Findit     && Search the database
       SET FORMAT TO Cust               && Use predesigned display form
       READ
       ?                                   && Skip down two lines
       ?
       WAIT "           Try Another (Y/N)?: " TO Decide
       IF UPPER(Decide)="Y"                && Evaluate user response
            LOOP
       ELSE
            EXIT                        && Exit loop, end program
       ENDIF
ENDDO
```

As the program progresses beyond the DO WHILE command, its next job is to put the company name on the screen. The ? command, followed by the name of the company in quotes, does this.

Next, the INPUT command places a message on the screen requesting the user to enter an order number. It stores that order number to a numeric *memory variable* called Findit; a memory variable is a small portion of memory used to store information.

The next command in the program, LOCATE, searches the CUSTOMER.DBF database. The LOCATE command searches the numeric field Order_no, included in the CUSTOMER.DBF database, to find a match for the order number information stored in the variable Findit.

Following LOCATE is the SET FORMAT TO Cust command, which calls a *display form* to the screen. This form displays the information in the database record found by the LOCATE command. The display form is actually generated on your screen using a file called CUST.FMT, which is created using the Forms Generator in the dBASE IV Control Center. An example of this form appears in Figure 17-2. The READ command, following the SET FORMAT command, displays the form and moves the cursor to the top of the form.

The next command, WAIT, places text on the screen that asks the user whether to search for another order number. The WAIT command then stores a single keystroke response from the user to another memory variable called Decide.

The next clause in the program evaluates the response to the WAIT command. It uses an IF...ENDIF command clause to evaluate the contents of the Decide memory variable. If Decide equals Y, the program executes the LOOP command following the IF. This causes the program to loop back to the DO WHILE and execute the loop again. On the other hand, if Decide equals N, the program jumps to the ELSE portion of the IF...ENDIF clause and uses the EXIT command to leave the DO WHILE...ENDDO loop, end the program, and return to the dot prompt.

If you are a beginning programmer, many of the concepts in this example program may seem a bit abstract. Keep in mind, however, that these areas are covered in detail both in this chapter and in the chapters that follow.

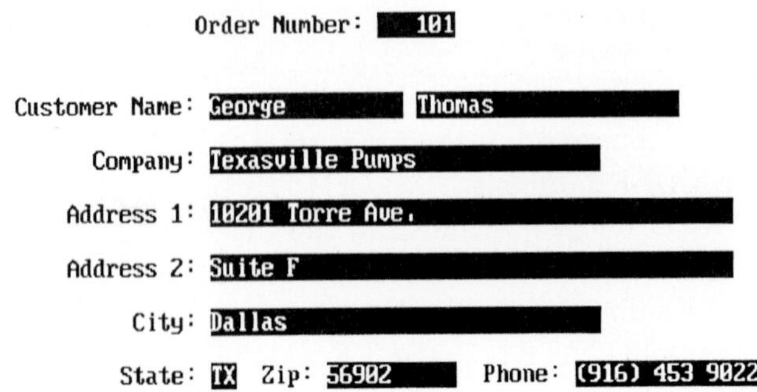

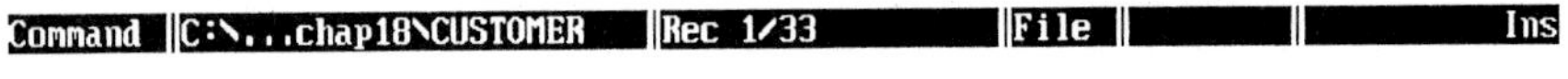

Figure 17-2. A custom form

Creating and Saving Programs

In dBASE IV, you use a special on-board word processor, called the Text Editor, to write programs. The Text Editor generates ASCII files. When you complete a program, you can save it to disk from within the Text Editor.

Tip: The dBASE IV Text Editor that you use to write command-file programs is the same word wrap text editor that you can access from the Control Center to edit memo fields, text files, and macros. You also see elements of this editor when you use the Control Center **Forms** and **Reports** options. However, when you create forms and reports from Control Center, the Text Editor is in layout mode.

Using the dBASE IV Text Editor

There are two ways you can invoke the dBASE IV Text Editor to begin writing programs. You can invoke it from the Control Center using the **Applications** menu or you can invoke it from the dot prompt using the MODIFY COMMAND *<filename>* command. Figure 17-3 shows what your screen looks like when you invoke the dBASE IV Text Editor.

Invoking from the Control Center

To invoke the dBASE IV Text Editor from the Control Center, you use the **Applications/Create** menu selection. When you select this option, dBASE IV displays a box with two options, **dBASE Program** and **Applications Generator**. If you choose **dBASE Program**, dBASE IV takes you directly to the Text Editor, and

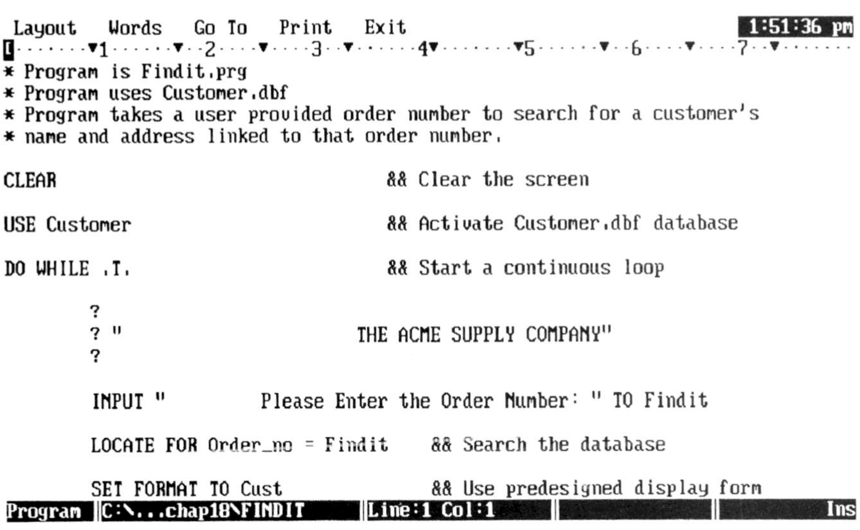

```
 Layout   Words   Go To   Print   Exit                                    1:51:36 pm
* Program is Findit.prg
* Program uses Customer.dbf
* Program takes a user provided order number to search for a customer's
* name and address linked to that order number.

CLEAR                                   && Clear the screen

USE Customer                            && Activate Customer.dbf database

DO WHILE .T.                            && Start a continuous loop

        ?
        ? "                          THE ACME SUPPLY COMPANY"
        ?

        INPUT "          Please Enter the Order Number: " TO Findit

        LOCATE FOR Order_no = Findit    && Search the database

        SET FORMAT TO Cust              && Use predesigned display form
Program  C:\...chap18\FINDIT    Line:1 Col:1                                   Ins
```

Figure 17-3. The dBASE IV Text Editor

you can begin entering your program.

To save your program, press F10 to activate the Text Editor menu and select either **Layout/Save this program** or **Exit/Save changes and exit**. The **Layout/Save this program** menu selection saves the current program to disk but leaves the Text Editor active. On the other hand, the **Exit/Save changes and exit** menu selection saves the current program and returns you to dBASE IV.

When you use the **Applications/Create** menu to invoke the dBASE IV Text Editor, the program file does not as yet have a file name. However, when you use either the **Layout** or **Exit** menu option, dBASE IV prompts you for a name for the new program file. Enter a file name of eight characters or less and press ENTER. dBASE IV automatically adds a .PRG file extension to the file name and saves the file.

Invoking from the Dot Prompt

To access the dBASE IV Text Editor from the dot prompt, type **MODIFY COMMAND <*filename*>** and press ENTER. The file name must be eight characters or less. dBASE IV takes you directly to the Text Editor and you can begin typing your program. For example, if you decide to name your file ACCOUNT, type

```
MODIFY COMMAND ACCOUNT
```

at the dot prompt. dBASE IV automatically assigns a .PRG extension to the file name.

If you use the MODIFY COMMAND command without entering a file name, dBASE IV prompts you for one. Enter a file name of eight characters or less and press ENTER. dBASE IV takes you directly to the Text Editor and you can begin typing your program.

When you complete your program, press F10 to invoke the **Text Editor** menu, and select **Layout/Save this program** or **Exit/Save changes and exit**. dBASE IV saves your file under the same name you assigned using MODIFY COMMAND.

Tip: Once your program file has a name, you can save it and exit the dBASE IV Text Editor by pressing either CTRL-END or CTRL-W.

You can also write a program, save it, and start a new program after using the MODIFY COMMAND <*filename*> command. To do this, use the the **Layout/Save this program** menu option to save your current program and press CTRL-Y to delete all the command lines on the screen. Then type your new program. When you are ready to save your new program, select the **Layout/Save this program** menu option. dBASE IV prompts you with the name of your old file. Use the BACKSPACE key to delete the name of the old file, enter a name for your new file, and press ENTER. dBASE IV saves the new file under the new name.

Using Another Word Processor

If you prefer, you can use a word processor other than the dBASE IV Text Editor to write your dBASE IV programs. You can invoke the word processor automatically from within dBASE IV, or you can use it independently of dBASE IV.

If you intend to use an alternative word processor, it must be able to read and save ASCII files. Furthermore, you must save your files using a .PRG extension. To determine if your word processor can read and save files in ASCII format, consult your word processor's user manual.

To have dBASE IV automatically invoke another word processor in place of the dBASE IV Text Editor, you need to add a line to dBASE IV's CONFIG.DB file. The CONFIG.DB file resides in the same directory in which you installed dBASE IV. dBASE IV reads the CONFIG.DB file to establish its operating parameters each time you start the program. To learn more about modifying your CONFIG.DB file so that dBASE IV will automatically invoke another word processor, see Chapter 35.

Modifying a Program

There are three ways to modify an existing program file in dBASE IV. They all involve the dBASE IV Text Editor.

- Using the MODIFY COMMAND *<filename>* command from the dot prompt invokes the dBASE IV Text Editor and retrieves an existing program file into active memory.
- Pressing ENTER on an existing file name in the Applications Panel of the Control Center and pressing **Modify Applications** causes dBASE IV to enter the Text Editor and display the program on screen.
- Using the **Modify a different program** option from the **Layout** menu from within the dBASE IV Text Editor retrieves another program file into the dBASE IV Text Editor.

Tip: You can also use the **Words/Read text file** menu selection from within the dBASE IV Text Editor to read existing program files into memory.

Using MODIFY COMMAND

Working from the dot prompt, use the MODIFY COMMAND *<filename>* command to activate the dBASE IV Text Editor and read an existing program file into memory. For example, if the name of the program file you need to modify is ENTRY.PRG, type

```
MODIFY COMMAND ENTRY
```

at the dot prompt. dBASE IV automatically adds a .PRG extension to the file name. When you enter this command, dBASE IV searches the current directory or the directory you specified in front of the file name. If dBASE IV finds the file, it invokes the dBASE IV Text Editor and reads the file into memory. If it cannot find the file, dBASE IV invokes the Text Editor and opens a new file using the file name you specified with the MODIFY COMMAND *<filename>* command. After you make your program modifications, save the file in the usual way.

From the Control Center

To modify an existing program from the Control Center, select **Applications**, move the cursor to highlight an existing program file name, and press ENTER. dBASE IV places an option box on your screen that contains two choices: **Run Application** and **Modify Application**. Select **Modify application** and press ENTER. dBASE IV invokes the Text Editor and retrieves your program file into memory. When you complete your modifications, save the program in the usual way.

To modify another program from within the dBASE IV Text Editor, use the **Layout/Modify a different program** menu selection and press ENTER. dBASE IV prompts you for a file name. Enter the file name of your choice and press ENTER. dBASE IV retrieves the file into memory. When you complete your modifications, save the program as you normally do.

Leaving the dBASE IV Text Editor

To leave the dBASE IV Text Editor and return to either the dot prompt or the Control Center, press F10 and select the **Exit** menu option. When you select **Exit**, dBASE IV gives you two choices: **Save changes and exit** and **Abandon changes and exit**. Depending on where you were when you first invoked the Text Editor, dBASE IV returns you to either the dot prompt or to the Control Center.

Command-File Fundamentals

dBASE IV programs are composed of *command lines.* Each command line contains a single dBASE IV command or expression. The following are examples of dBASE IV command lines:

```
USE Customer
LOCATE FOR Order_no = Findit
DISPLAY RECORD RECNO()
```

Unlike some programming languages, dBASE IV has relatively few restrictions on how you format your command lines. For example, you must separate words in a command line with at least one space, but you can also have more than one space between words. Furthermore, you can indent command lines to make your programs easier to read. Also, your command lines need not follow one another consecutively; you can have one or more blank lines in between command lines. Additionally, you can use upper- or lowercase letters. For example, the following command lines are acceptable:

```
USE       CUSTOMER
          LOCATE FOR ORDER_NO = FINDIT
DISPLAY RECORD recno()
```

You can also abbreviate commands. The syntax of dBASE IV commands requires that each command begin with a verb, and you can abbreviate these verbs to four letters. For example, LOCATE becomes LOCA, and DISPLAY becomes DISP. In addition, many dBASE IV command verbs are followed by nouns, such as GO BOTTOM or COPY STRUCTURE. You can also abbreviate nouns by entering only the first four letters.

Command lines can be up to 1024 characters in length, including spaces. However, to make your program more readable, you can interrupt a command line with a semicolon (;) and trail it onto the next line. For example, the following command line is acceptable:

```
REPLACE Order_no WITH Ordno, Firstname WITH First, Lastname ;
WITH Last, Company WITH Coname
```

Program Notation

Program notes, or comments, serve to remind you of the reasoning behind a section of code and are an invaluable tool when you later modify or enhance your program. Furthermore, program notes provide a guided tour to someone else working with your code. You should use program notes as much as possible. Also, try to add them as you go, not after the fact.

You can add program notes to programs with any of the following commands or symbols:

- **NOTE** Begins a program note
- **Asterisk** (*) Begins a program note and must be the first character in a line
- **Double Ampersand (&&)** Adds a note to the end of a command

Some examples of acceptable program notation follow:

```
* The name of this program is MAINMENU.PRG
NOTE This program uses CUSTOMER.DBF
SELECT 1        && Initialize CUSTOMER.DBF in work area one
```

Running a Program

After you've written your program and saved it to disk, you're ready to run it. There are three ways you can run your program in dBASE IV:

- Entering the DO <*filename*> command from the dot prompt
- Selecting **Exit/Run Program** from the dBASE IV **Text Editor** menu
- Pressing ENTER on a program name in the Applications Panel of the Control Center and selecting **Run Application**

From the Dot Prompt

You can run your programs in dBASE IV using the DO <*filename*> command from the dot prompt. As an example, to run the FINDIT.PRG program that appears at the beginning of this chapter, type

```
DO FINDIT
```

dBASE IV assumes a .PRG file extension and runs your program.

Tip: You can also include the DO command in a program. This command is often used to call another program. For more on this topic, see the section "Calling a Subprogram" later in this chapter.

From the Text Editor

You can also run your program from inside the dBASE IV Text Editor. If you've written or modified your program and want to run it, press F10 to invoke the Text Editor menu and select **Exit/Run program**. dBASE IV will exit the Text Editor and run the currently loaded program. Figure 17-4 shows an example of what the dBASE IV Text Editor screen looks like during this operation. If

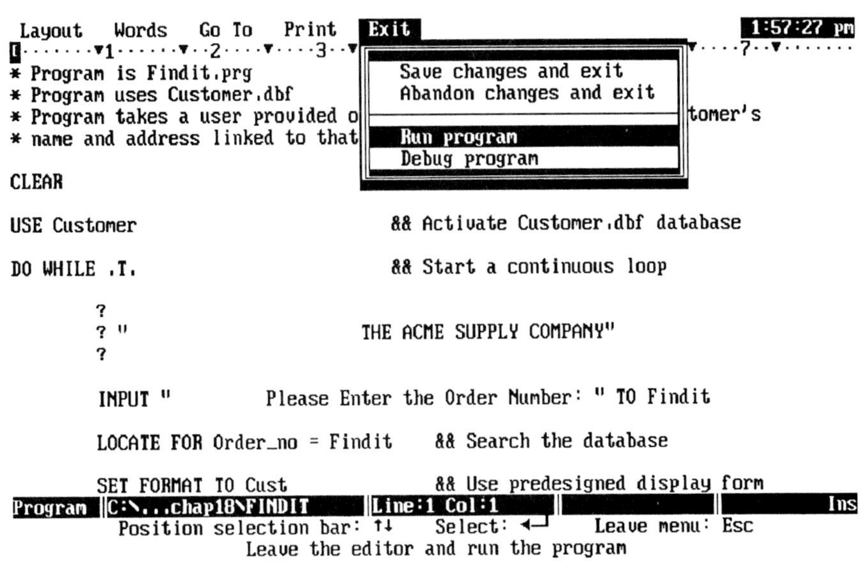

Figure 17-4. Running a program from the Text Editor

your program does not as yet have a file name, dBASE IV prompts you for a file name before exiting the Text Editor and running the program.

To run another program from inside the dBASE IV Text Editor, press F10 to invoke the **Text Editor** menu and select **Layout/Modify a different program**. dBASE IV prompts you for the name of the program to modify. Enter the file name and press ENTER. dBASE IV loads the new program file into memory. To run the program, select **Exit/Run program**. dBASE IV exits the Text Editor and runs the new program.

From the Control Center

To run a program from the Control Center, use the **Applications** menu selection. Move the cursor to highlight the name of an existing program file name and press ENTER. dBASE IV displays a box with two choices: **Run application** and **Modify application**. Select **Run application** and press ENTER. dBASE IV runs your program and, when it is finished, returns you to the Control Center.

For a given program name to appear in the Applications column of the Control Center, you must create that program by entering the dBASE IV Text Editor from the Control Center. In other words, if you write a program using the MODIFY COMMAND *<filename>* command from the dot prompt, dBASE IV does not show that program file name in the Applications column of the Control Center. This is because the program is not included in the current catalog.

There are two ways to include in the current catalog a program file created using MODIFY COMMAND. The first way is to move the cursor to the Applications Panel and press F10 to get the **Control Center** menu. Then select **Catalog/Add file to catalog**. dBASE IV prompts you with the names of the files in the current directory. Highlight the program file name of your choice and press ENTER. dBASE IV adds the file to the current catalog and it is thereafter displayed in the Applications Panel. The second way is to modify and save that same program by accessing the dBASE IV Text Editor from the Control Center.

The Automatic Compiler

Whenever you run a newly created or a recently modified program, dBASE IV automatically compiles it. If you're not familiar with what a compiler is or does, you're not the only one.

In prior versions of dBASE, such as dBASE III PLUS, your commands had to be filtered through an interpreter and translated one by one into machine-readable code. This slows down your programs and is one of the main reasons that a number of third-party compiler programs are so popular for prior versions of dBASE.

In dBASE IV, the automatic compiler translates the commands in your program into a machine-readable code that is much easier for your computer to interpret. As a result, your programs run faster.

dBASE IV compiles your programs immediately before it runs them. Once a program is compiled, it does not need to be compiled again unless you modify it.

The automatic compiler takes your .PRG program file and compiles it into a file of the same name with a .DBO extension. When you run a program using the DO command, dBASE IV first looks for a compiled .DBO file with the specified file name. If it finds the .DBO file, its runs it. Otherwise, it looks for a .PRG file with the same file name, compiles that file, and then runs the .DBO file that is produced.

When you modify an existing program with the dBASE IV Text Editor and save it to disk, dBASE IV automatically deletes the old outdated .DBO file. The next time you run the modified program, dBASE IV recompiles your .PRG file, creates a new .DBO file, and runs the new .DBO file.

When dBASE IV compiles a .PRG file into a .DBO file, it sends a message to the screen to let you know that your file is being compiled. The message simply says "Compile" and shows the line numbers of your program as the file is being compiled.

dBASE IV leaves your .PRG program files intact. Your .PRG program files serve simply as a source for the compiling operation to create a .DBO file, as shown in Figure 17-5.

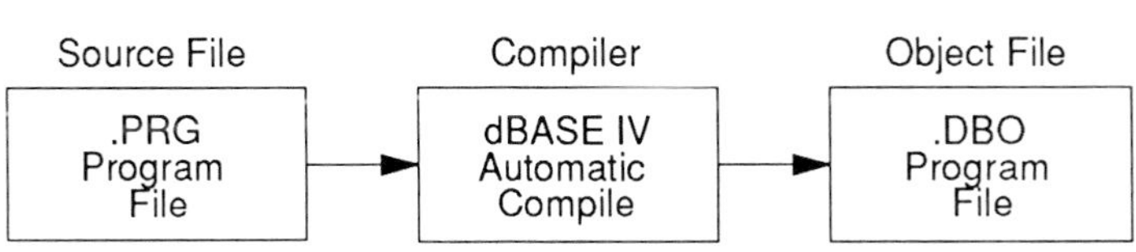

Figure 17-5. Compiling a .PRG file into a .DBO file

You can still load your original .PRG program file into the dBASE IV Text Editor at any time.

Using the COMPILE Command

Use the COMPILE <*filename*> command to compile any .PRG file into a .DBO file. For example, to compile and create a .DBO file for a file called MYFILE.PRG, enter the following command from the dot prompt:

```
COMPILE MYFILE
```

You can use the COMPILE command at any time to compile your command files. When you enter this command, dBASE IV compiles your .PRG source file and creates a compiled file with the same name and a .DBO extension. If a compiled .DBO file with the same name already exists, dBASE IV overwrites the old version with the new version.

You can also use the COMPILE command in conjunction with the SET DEVELOPMENT OFF/ON command. This applies primarily to programs you've modified using an external word processor. Recall from the previous section that when you modify a program using the dBASE IV Text Editor, dBASE IV automatically erases the old .DBO file and replaces it with a new .DBO file the next time you run the program. However, when you modify an existing program using an external editor, its sister .DBO file is not replaced. Thus, you risk using an outdated .DBO file when you return to dBASE IV and run the program. To get around this problem, use the SET DEVELOPMENT ON command.

When you enter the SET DEVELOPMENT ON command prior to running a program, dBASE IV compares the dates and times of a .PRG file with its companion .DBO file. dBASE IV runs the .DBO file if the date and time match that of your .PRG file. If the date and time do not match, dBASE IV replaces the outdated .DBO file with an updated version. With SET DEVELOPMENT

ON, you avoid the problem of accidentally using an outdated .DBO file.

You can enter the SET DEVELOPMENT ON command from the dot prompt or include it in a program. Once you enter this command, it remains in effect until you either enter the SET DEVELOPMENT OFF command or quit dBASE IV.

In version 1.0 of dBASE IV, the documentation indicates that the default for the SET DEVELOPMENT setting is OFF. However, if you modify a program externally, you'll soon find out that the default for the SET DEVELOPMENT setting is ON, not OFF, as documented. Version 1.0 of dBASE IV, as installed, compares the date and time of an externally modified .PRG file with those of the .DBO file and automatically creates an updated .DBO file. You can change this setting temporarily by using the SET DEVELOPMENT OFF command, or permanently by using the DBSETUP install program or by adding the line SET DEVELOPMENT=OFF to your CONFIG.DB file. For more on using the DBSETUP install program, see Chapter 2, "Getting Started." For more on modifying your CONFIG.DB file, see Chapter 35.

Tip: To check your dBASE IV version number, enter the VERSION( ) function at the dot prompt. dBASE IV returns the number of the version in use.

Designing an Application

System design is one of the most important things you can do before you write a multiple-program application. Simply stated, system design involves figuring out what you want to accomplish, and exactly how you're going to accomplish it, before you write your code.

The first step in system design is to define your objectives. For example, your initial objective may be as simple as "create an automated order entry system." However, as you delve further, you'll undoubtedly find there is more to system design than that.

Examine system requirements thoroughly. If you're automating an existing manual system, sit down with the people who are currently operating the system. Have them describe to you exactly what they do. Also, have them provide you with copies of reports sent to them (input) and copies of reports that they generate (output). If you're developing a new system, define exactly what you want out of the system, and exactly what the system needs in order to perform its job. Write your objectives down so that you can refer to them later. For example, suppose you want to create an order-entry system for a single product. A rudimentary list of system objectives might look like this:

1. Enter an order.
2. Find and edit an order.
3. Print invoices.
4. Print shipping labels.
5. Produce a monthly report.
6. Control the preceding operations using a main menu.

Database Design

Once you've defined your system objectives, the next step is to put some thought into the design and content of your database(s). Do this before you write your application. If you don't first lock in your database structure, you'll find yourself shooting at a moving target.

You'll need to answer a few key questions about database design. Should you use one database or more than one? What fields should be contained in each database? The next section contains some guidelines that should help you answer these questions.

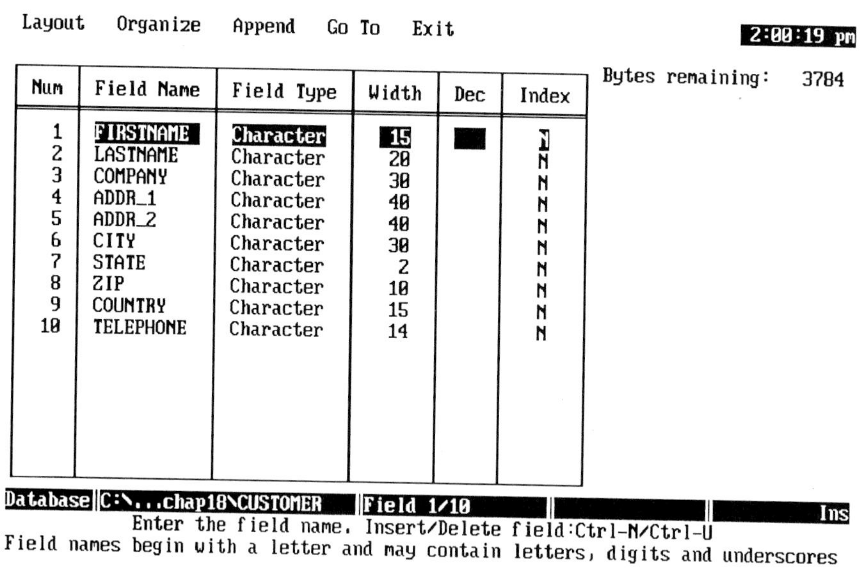

Layout Organize Append Go To Exit 2:00:19 pm

Num	Field Name	Field Type	Width	Dec	Index
1	FIRSTNAME	Character	15		N
2	LASTNAME	Character	20		N
3	COMPANY	Character	30		N
4	ADDR_1	Character	40		N
5	ADDR_2	Character	40		N
6	CITY	Character	30		N
7	STATE	Character	2		N
8	ZIP	Character	10		N
9	COUNTRY	Character	15		N
10	TELEPHONE	Character	14		N

Bytes remaining: 3784

Database C:\...chap18\CUSTOMER Field 1/10 Ins

Enter the field name. Insert/Delete field:Ctrl-N/Ctrl-U

Field names begin with a letter and may contain letters, digits and underscores

Figure 17-6. A sample mailing database

One Database or More?

The decision to use one database, or more than one, depends upon the type of application you're building. For example, if your application is a straightforward mailing list, you probably only need a single database. On the other hand, if you're creating a fairly extensive order-entry application, you'll probably need more than one database.

The One-to-One Relationship In general, you use a single database when you have a *one-to-one* relationship. The mailing list database in Figure 17-6 is a classic example of a one-to-one rela-

```
Layout   Organize   Append   Go To   Exit                          2:05:18 pm
                                                    Bytes remaining:   3778
 Num  Field Name   Field Type   Width  Dec  Index

  1   CUST_NO      Numeric         6    0     N
  2   FIRSTNAME    Character      15          N
  3   LASTNAME     Character      20          N
  4   COMPANY      Character      30          N
  5   ADDR_1       Character      40          N
  6   ADDR_2       Character      40          N
  7   CITY         Character      30          N
  8   STATE        Character       2          N
  9   ZIP          Character      10          N
 10   COUNTRY      Character      15          N
 11   TELEPHONE    Character      14          N

Database C:\...chap18\CUSTOMER  Field 1/11                              Ins
           Enter the field name.  Insert/Delete field:Ctrl-N/Ctrl-U
Field names begin with a letter and may contain letters, digits and underscores
```

Figure 17-7. CUSTOMER.DBF databases

tionship. That is, for each name in the database, you have one address, one company, one city, one state, and so on. In this type of application, the Firstname and Lastname fields are the controlling factor. Although two people may have the same name, the rest of the information in each record is different.

The One-to-Many Relationship You use more than one database when you have a *one-to-many* relationship. For example, imagine that you are creating an order-entry system and a number of your customers place more than one order in a given month. In other words, you have *one* customer placing *many* orders. The customer's name and address do not change each time he or she places an order. However, each order that the customer places has its own set of specific information that changes with each order.

This one-to-many relationship warrants at least two databases: one in which to store customer names and addresses and another in which to store information specific to each order placed

Layout Organize Append Go To Exit 2:08:47 pm

Bytes remaining: 3922

Num	Field Name	Field Type	Width	Dec	Index
1	CUST_NO	Numeric	6	0	N
2	ORDER_NO	Numeric	6	0	N
3	ORDER_DATE	Date	8		N
4	INV_NO	Character	9		N
5	UNITS	Numeric	4	0	N
6	PRICE	Numeric	6	2	N
7	TAX	Numeric	5	2	N
8	FOREIGN_SH	Numeric	5	2	N
9	TOTAL	Numeric	8	2	N
10	PART_NO	Numeric	3	0	N
11	ITEM	Character	7		N
12	DELETE	Logical	1		N
13	MSSG	Memo	10		N

Database C:\...chap18\ORDERREC Field 1/13 Ins

Enter the field name. Insert/Delete field:Ctrl-N/Ctrl-U

Field names begin with a letter and may contain letters, digits and underscores

Figure 17-8. ORDERREC.DBF database structure

by a customer. Figures 17-7 and 17-8 show sample structures for the two databases. CUSTOMER.DBF is the first database and the second is ORDERREC.DBF.

You relate, or *link,* the two databases in Figures 17-7 and 17-8 using a common or *key* field. In this case, the key field that appears in both databases is Cust_no. (Note that the key field is a numeric field with the same number of digits in both databases.) Using this field, each customer in the CUSTOMER.DBF database is given a unique customer number. In the second database, ORDERREC.DBF, the customer number appears with each order. Thus, Cust_no provides a bridge between a customer's unique order number in CUSTOMER.DBF and the various orders placed by that customer in ORDERREC.DBF. Figure 17-9 shows some example records from both databases.

This multiple-database approach will help you in a number of ways. First, you avoid entering redundant data and wasting valuable disk space. Second, you avoid spending the time and

CUSTOMER.DBF

Cust_no	Firstname	Lastname	Company	Addr_1
1001	George	Thomas	Texasville Pumps	10210 Torre Ave.
1002	Earl	Holland	Holland Industries	5806 Columbia Ave.
1003	Jack	Spraul		3490 Sevilla Dr.

ORDERREC.DBF

Cust_no	Order_no	Order_date	Inv_no	Units	Price	Tax
1001	101	11/14/88	LEB123557	1	24.95	0.00
1002	102	11/15/88	LEB123558	1	27.95	0.00
1001	134	12/22/88	LEB123589	1	24.95	0.00
1001	135	12/30/88	LEB123597	1	24.95	0.00

Figure 17-9. Two databases linked on a key field

money required to repeatedly enter the customer names and addresses. Third, the overall size of each database is smaller, and this tends to increase the speed of your application by reducing the amount of time spent searching for data in the databases.

Another way to handle the one-to-many relationship is to use a master database that is periodically updated by one or more transaction databases. This approach is commonly used for inventory and accounting applications. For example, in an accounting application, the master database often contains the balances for each account. The transaction databases are used to capture receipts and disbursements, adjusting entries, and so forth. The transaction databases are then used to periodically update the master database. In this case, the key field linking the master and transaction databases is the account number field. In an inventory application, the key field would be the part number field.

The Many-to-Many Relationship You use more than one database when you have a *many-to-many* relationship. For example, suppose you are running a warehouse. In the warehouse, you have *many* rack locations in which you store *many* different part numbers with different quantities in each location. Furthermore,

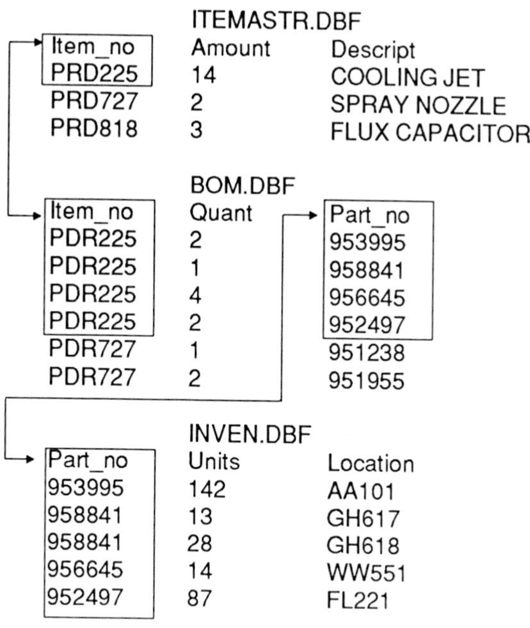

Figure 17-10. The many-to-many relationship

each of these parts is used in varying quantities in different items produced by your company. You are given a list of finished products that will be produced that day. You must pull the parts required to assemble each finished product and get them to the manufacturing floor.

With a many-to-many relationship of this type, you definitely need more than one database. For example, to solve the warehouse problem, you need three databases, as shown in Figure 17-10.

The first database, ITEMASTR.DBF, has three fields: (1) item number, (2) amount to produce, and (3) description. The item number field in this database is the item number for the finished product.

The second database, BOM.DBF, also has three fields: (1) item number, (2) quantity required, and (3) part number. This database identifies what part numbers go into each finished product.

The third database, INVEN.DBF, has three fields: (1) part number, (2) units available, and (3) location. This database shows what parts are available and where they are located.

Ultimately, your program relates ITEMASTR.DBF to BOM.DBF in order to determine what parts are needed, and then uses INVEN.DBF to find out where those parts are located. The final result is a "pick-list" that you can hand to a warehouse employee.

The fields that link the databases in Figure 17-10 are the numeric fields Item_no, which appears in both ITEMASTR.DBF and BOM.DBF, and Part_no, which appears in both BOM.DBF and LOCATE.DBF. The record content of the first two databases, ITEMASTR.DBF and BOM.DBF, changes only rarely. However, the LOCATE.DBF database is in a constant state of change as parts are added to and removed from rack locations.

Chapter 21 provides a detailed discussion of commands and programming techniques you can use to link key fields and access information across databases.

Some Common-Sense Database Design Rules

As you make the decision to use a single database or more than one database, keep in mind the three common-sense rules of database design:

- **Don't capture redundant data.** If you find yourself entering the same information twice or repeating a field title in a database, you probably need another database.
- **Make all fields relevant to the key fields.** When you have two or more key fields in a database, make sure the other fields in the database are directly related to those key fields. For example, the BOM.DBF database in the previous many-to-many example has two key fields, Item_no and

Part_no. The only other field in the database, Quant, is directly related to both Item_no and Part_no. If another field, such as vendor number, were to appear in the database, it would only be related to the Part_no field and not the Item_no field.

- **Don't mix temporarily related groups of data.** Make sure that fields within your database are permanently related to your key fields. For example, it doesn't make much sense to put your customers' names and addresses in a database where the key field is a product number. Because some customers buy more than one product, you would wind up repeating customer information more than once. Also, if you stopped using a product number, you might not be able to access the customer information.

Designing Database Fields

After you have decided how many databases you need, you're ready to design the fields within the databases. As you design the fields, distinguish between the information you need to capture and use later and the information you need to control your system.

System-Control Fields Table 17-1 shows the same two databases used earlier in the chapter, CUSTOMER.DBF and ORDERREC.DBF. Both of these databases contain fields that address system-control objectives. An asterisk appears next to fields involved in system control.

As mentioned, both databases contain a customer number field. This is a key field that provides a link between the customer names and addresses in CUSTOMER.DBF and the customer orders in ORDERREC.DBF.

Note also that ORDERREC.DBF contains an order number field. This field allows a single unique customer from CUSTOMER.DBF to place multiple orders in ORDERREC.DBF without losing track of those individual orders.

ORDERREC.DBF also contains another important system-control field—the Delete field. This logical field lets you mark a record for deletion. False (.F.) is the default. If you enter a .T. in

CUSTOMER.DBF

Database Field	**Needed For**
Customer Number	* Link ORDERREC.DBF, ACCTSREC.DBF
First Name	Mailing
Last Name	Mailing
Company Name	Identification, searching, shipping
Address, City, State, Zip	Shipping
Phone Number	Telephone calls

ORDERREC.DBF

Database Field	**Needed For**
Customer Number	* Link to CUSTOMER.DBF, ACCTSREC.DBF
Order Number	* Single customer, multiple orders
Invoice Number	Accounting, increase by one each time
Purchase Order No.	Customers P.O.#, used on packing list
Units	Invoice, used for Total field
Price	Invoice, used for Total field
Tax	Total field, invoice, tax returns
Foreign Shipment	Invoice, used for Total field
Total	Total charge, used on invoice
Delete	* Mark an order for deletion
Part Number	Invoice, linked to INVENTRY.DBF
Item	Description, supplied by system

Table 17-1. System Control Fields Marked with an Asterisk

this field, you can then have your program delete that record from the database. For more information on deleting records from a database, see Chapter 21.

Information-Capture Fields Both databases in Table 17-1 contain fields that address information-capture objectives. Information-capture fields should contain the raw materials you'll need to produce system output and calculations. For example, the CUSTOMER.DBF database fields contain the components required for both order entry and shipping. The ORDERREC.DBF

```
 Layout   Words   Go To   Print   Exit                                    2:29:42 pm
[·······▼1······▼··2····▼····3··▼·······4▼·······▼5······▼··6····▼····7··▼·······
*File is DESGNMEN.WS
Design for the program MAINMENU.PRG

SET TALK, ECHO, SAFETY, SCOREBOARD, ESCAPE to OFF
Start a DO WHILE .T. continous loop
CLEAR the screen.
? " Build the screen"
WAIT "the user's respose" TO a variable
DO CASE the user's response
    CASE A - DO order entry
    CASE B - DO order edit
    CASE C - DO label print
    CASE D - DO invoice print
    CASE E - DO monthly report
    CASE Q - EXIT the loop
ENDCASE the DO CASE
ENDDO the DO WHILE
SET TALK, ECHO, SAFETY, SCOREBOARD, ESCAPE to ON

Program ||C:\...chap18\DESGNMEN ||Line:1 Col:1 ||                ||            Ins
```

Figure 17-11. Program design notes

database contains fields that address components needed for invoicing, accounting, inventory control, and tax returns.

Program Design

Whenever you create a dBASE IV program, you should take some time to design it before you write it. Figuring out ahead of time exactly what you want to accomplish and how you're going to accomplish it can save a great deal of coding time.

Once you've decided what you want to accomplish with your program, try to break it down into a list of tasks. Each task then becomes a program module.

Once you've defined the tasks that each module is to perform, you're ready to begin designing your program in detail. One common way to design a program is to make a series of notes that include dBASE IV commands. Often, dBASE IV commands read much like the English language and you can fit them into regular sentences. For example, Figure 17-11 shows a list of design notes for the MAINMENU.PRG program.

Modular Programming

Once you've defined your objectives and built your databases, you're ready to design and program your application. For ease of development as well as speed of operation, most experienced programmers break down their systems into modules and program each module separately. This concept is called *modular programming* and allows you to concentrate on the code for each module as a separate issue, instead of trying to design your application all in one large program.

Figure 17-12 shows a diagram of a simple modular order-entry system. Each of the boxes represents a program. This diagram shows five subprograms under the control of one main menu program. Controlling subprograms with a main menu is a common technique used in dBASE IV programming. In this case, the MAINMENU.PRG program calls the following programs:

ORDFORM.PRG	Adds an order to the database
ORDEREDI.PRG	Finds an order for viewing and editing
INVPRIN.PRG	Prints invoices for orders
LABPRIN.PRG	Prints mailing labels for orders
MR.PRG	Summarizes the database and prints reports

Note that INVPRIN.PRG calls several other subprograms—LASTINV.PRG, SPECINV.PRG, and SERINV.PRG. These subprograms provide invoice printing for the system. LASTINV.PRG prints the invoice for the last order entered. SPECINV.PRG prints a specific invoice entered by the user. The last subprogram,

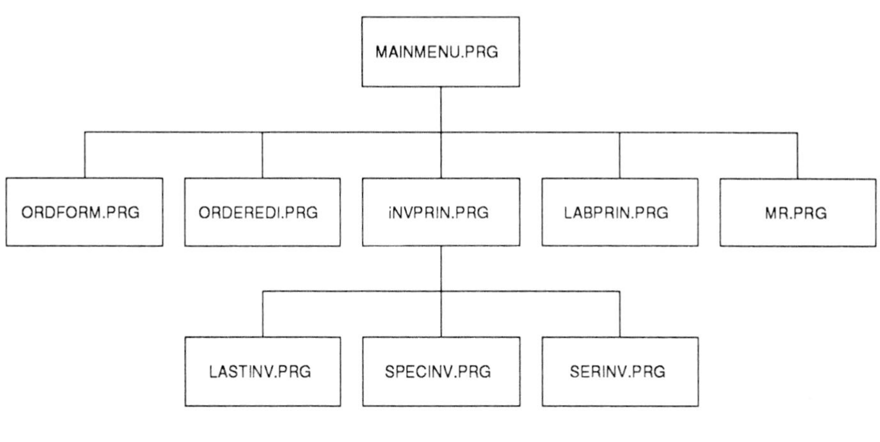

Figure 17-12. A modular order-entry system

SERINV.PRG, prints a series of invoices based upon starting and ending order numbers entered by the user.

Calling a Subprogram

When you break your system down into program modules, one program must activate, or "call," another subprogram. One program activating another subprogram is referred to as *calling,* which is a very important concept in dBASE IV programming.

You call a subprogram in dBASE IV using the DO <*program name*> and RETURN commands, as shown in Figure 17-13. When you place the DO command in a higher level program, it activates a subprogram. If you place the RETURN command within, or at the end of, the subprogram, it returns control to the higher level program, starting at the line following the DO command. For

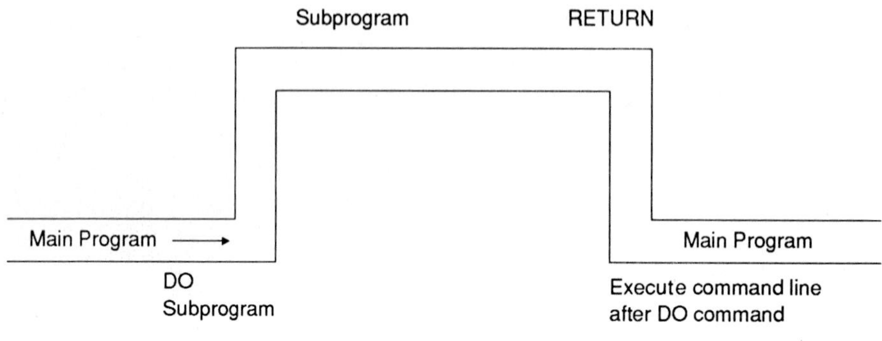

Figure 17-13. Calling or activating a subprogram

example, in the following program listings, the program MAINPROG.PRG calls the subprogram SUBPROG.PRG.

```
***Program is MAINPROG.PRG***
*Program calls the subprogram SUBPROG.PRG
? " This is the main program "    && Place a message on the screen
WAIT                              && Press any key to continue
DO SUBPROG                        && Starts the subprogram SUBPROG.PRG
? " We're back "                  && Place a message on the screen
WAIT                              && Press any key to continue
RETURN                            && Return from MAINPROG to dBASE IV
```

The program SUBPROG.PRG then returns control to the calling program, MAINPROG.PRG.

```
***Program is SUBPROG.PRG***
*Program is called by MAINPROG.PRG
? " You made it to the subprogram "      && Place a message on the screen
WAIT                                     && Press any key to continue
RETURN                                   && Return to calling program
```

There is virtually no limit on the number of levels of subprograms you can have. From a practical standpoint, however, most systems don't get beyond seven or eight levels of subprograms.

Tip: Use dBASE IV's calling capabilities to work with programs you've generated using the Control Center Applications Generator. For example, use the Applications Generator to produce a menu system that contains options that call your program.

Procedure Files

dBASE IV has another modular programming convention—*procedure files*. Procedure files work much like subprograms. However, unlike standard command files, procedure files usually contain only a few command lines and perform routine operations that are repeated often in a given application. The advantage of procedure files is that you can quickly call and execute them using a single command line.

You can often use procedures across applications because they perform routine tasks and allow *parameter passing*. Parameter passing refers to sending information to and from a procedure. After a while, you can develop a library of procedures that you can use again and again in different applications.

In dBASE IV, you can include procedures in the current program or in a separate file. You can also place multiple procedures in a file to create a procedure library.

You activate an independent procedure file and load it into memory using the SET PROCEDURE TO <*procedure filename*> command. Once loaded, you can execute the procedures in that file usinng the DO <*procedure filename*> command.

If the procedure is located within the current command file, you just need the DO *<procedure filename>* command to activate and run the procedure. The SET PROCEDURE TO command is not required because the procedure is, in effect, already loaded into memory.

Whether a procedure is in the current file or a separate file, you must begin the procedure with the PROCEDURE *<procedure name>* command and end it with the RETURN command. The RETURN passes control back to the calling command file and starts with the line following the DO command.

For more information on creating and using procedure files, see Chapter 20.

User-Defined Functions

Modular programming is further enhanced in dBASE IV with the advent of the *user-defined function.* User-defined functions work a great deal like procedure files. However, instead of using the PROCEDURE *<procedure name>* command, you use the FUNCTION command followed by the name of the user-defined function. You can create user-defined functions to perform operations on data that go beyond the scope of the normal dBASE IV functions listed in Chapter 33.

All functions accept input and return a result. For example, the CTOD( ) (character to date) function takes character text, such as "11/31/91," and turns it into a date format that is recognizable to dBASE IV. The data can then be entered into a date field in a database or used in a mathematical expression.

Occasionally, you may need to use repeatedly a function that dBASE IV does not support. If so, you can construct your own function with the FUNCTION command.

The FUNCTION command allows you to pass data, using the PARAMETERS command, from your main program to a user-defined function. The user-defined function then takes the data passed to it by your program, performs a calculation, and returns the result to your program.

```
================================
=== ORDER ENTRY SYSTEM MENU ===
================================

    TASK CODE     TASK DESCRIPTION

    [A]...........ENTER an ORDER
    [B]...........EDIT an ORDER
    [C]...........PRINT LABLES
    [D]...........PRINT INVOICES
    [E]...........PRINT MONTHLY SALES REPORT
    [Q]...........QUIT

Enter your choice (type in task code):



MAINMENU
```

Figure 17-14. A sample main menu

For more information on creating user-defined functions, see Chapters 24 and 31.

Menus

Menus are a common way to communicate with and get input from the user. They are also useful for controlling a large program or a multiple-program application. dBASE IV offers two types of menus: displayed menus and *pop-up menus*. You can create both types of menus using command files. Displayed menus are discussed in Chapter 22, pop-up menus are described in Chapter 24.

Figure 17-14 shows an example menu for a multiple-program order-entry application. The following listing is the command file that generates the menu. Note that the menu in Figure 17-14 enables the user to execute various programs within the application. It also gives the user a way to quit the application and return to dBASE IV.

There is another special feature of the menu in Figure 17-14: it is the only means to enter the application and leave it. All subprograms within the application eventually return to this menu. In short, there is only one way into the system, and one way out.

```
* The program is MAINMENU.PRG
* This program puts up the main menu for the order entry system
* ———————Set Environmental Parameters
SET TALK OFF
SET ECHO OFF
SET SAFETY OFF
SET SCOREBOARD OFF
SET ESCAPE OFF
* ————————Store memory variables - none required
 *————————-Start program body
DO WHILE .T.                         && Start a loop
     CLEAR                           && Clear the screen
     * ————————Build the Screen
     ?"                   ================================"
     ?"                   === ORDER ENTRY SYSTEM MENU ==="
     ?"                   ================================"
     ?
     ?"                     TASK CODE     TASK DESCRIPTION"
     ?
     ?"                     [A]...........ENTER an ORDER"
     ?"                     [B]...........EDIT an ORDER"
     ?"                     [C]...........PRINT LABELS"
     ?"                     [D]...........PRINT INVOICES"
     ?"                     [E]...........PRINT MONTHLY SALES REPORT"
     ?"                     [Q]...........QUIT"
     ?
     ?
     * ———————Get input from the user
     WAIT  "        Enter your choice (type in task code): " TO CHOICE
     * ———————Evaluate the user's response
     DO CASE
          CASE UPPER(Choice)="A"
              DO ORDFORM
          CASE UPPER(Choice)="B"
              DO ORDEREDI
          CASE UPPER(Choice)="C"
              DO LABPRIN
          CASE UPPER(Choice)="D"
              DO INVPRIN
          CASE UPPER(Choice)="E"
              DO MR
          CASE UPPER(Choice)="Q"
```

```
            EXIT
        OTHERWISE
            LOOP
   ENDCASE
ENDDO                           && End the loop
 *---------Program Closing
SET SAFETY ON
SET SCOREBOARD ON
SET ESCAPE ON
SET TALK ON
SET ECHO ON
```

Debugging Your Programs

If you're having a problem with one of your programs, use the dBASE IV Debugger. This is one of the most valuable components of dBASE IV. Chapter 25 includes a detailed explanation of the dBASE IV Debugger. To use the Debugger, enter **DEBUG** ***<filename>*** from the dot prompt. For example, to debug the program MYFILE.PRG, type

```
DEBUG MYFILE
```

This chapter has given an introduction to programming in dBASE IV, including how to use the dBASE IV Text Editor to write and modify programs. Several command-file fundamentals, including how to build command lines and run a program, were covered. An introduction to both program and database design, including controlling a program and modular program design, completed this chapter's discussion.

Memory Variables

EIGHTEEN

This chapter discusses commands and techniques you can use to enter data in memory variables. Memory variables are an important part of dBASE IV programming because they play a key role in controlling programs, capturing user input, and working with databases.

First you will see how to create and name memory variables, then how to use memory variable files and relate memory variables across programs. A discussion of macro substitution of memory variables in command lines completes this chapter.

Introduction

In dBASE IV, you can assign a name to a small section of your computer's RAM and temporarily store data in it. The dBASE IV term for a small section of named memory is a memory variable. Sometimes you'll see this term abbreviated to memvar.

Memory variables are often used in a dBASE IV program to capture input from a user so that a program can react to that input. For example, the following section of code uses a memory variable called Choice to capture user input. It then evaluates that input using an IF...ENDIF condition.

```
WAIT "Do you wish to continue the search (Y/N)? " TO Choice
IF Choice="Y"
     CONTINUE
ELSE
     RETURN
ENDIF
```

When you use a program to capture information in a memory variable, the information stays there until your program either changes the information, gets rid of the memory variable, or returns control to dBASE IV. In other words, once you create a memory variable in one section of your program, you can then reuse the information in that memory variable in a later section of your program.

In dBASE IV, the default for the number of active memory variables is 500. However, you can increase this limit to as much as 15,000 active variables using the commands MVMAXBLKS and MVBLKSIZE in your CONFIG.DB file. From a practical standpoint, however, the number of active memory variables you can have is a function of your computer's available memory.

Creating and Naming Memory Variables

There are two ways to create and name memory variables: the STORE command and the equal sign (=). For example, the following two command lines both create a memory variable named Option and store the number 0 in it.

```
STORE 0 to Option
Choice=0
```

Memory variable names can be up to ten characters long. They must start with a letter and cannot contain blank spaces, but they can contain numbers and underscores. When choosing names for memory variables, stay away from dBASE IV commands and functions, which might cause dBASE IV to confuse one of your variable names with a command. For example, if you use the expression Cancel = 10 to create a memory variable, dBASE IV will read the line as the CANCEL command and immediately halt your program.

Tip: You can also use the ACCEPT, INPUT, WAIT, and READ commands to create memory variables. For more on using these commands with memory variables, see Chapter 19.

Memory Variable Types

As with database fields, you assign memory variables a character, numeric, date, or logical data type. However, there is no memory variable equivalent for a memo field. If you don't assign a data type to a memory variable, dBASE IV does it for you. It does this using its best logical guess, taken from the context of your program.

You designate a memory variable's data type when you create the memory variable. For example, Table 18-1 includes some

Type	Store	=
Character	STORE "hello" TO Greet	Greet="hello"
Numeric	STORE 0 TO Findit	Findit=0
Date	STORE {12/31/89} TO Today	Today={12/31/89}
Logical	STORE .T. TO Verify	Verify=.T.

Table 18-1. Assigning Data Types to Memory Variables

expressions you might use to designate memory variable data types.

Character Variables

To store character data in a memory variable, you must enclose the information in quotes, as in Table 18-1. However, you can also create blank character variables (and store information in them at a later time) using either quotes (" ") or the SPACE( ) function.

Use quotes (" " or ' ') when you're not sure of the length of the character string to be stored in the memory variable. Names are a good example here. The first line of the following section of code uses double quotes to create a blank character variable.

```
STORE " " TO Mlname
@ 14,21 SAY "Please enter your last name: " GET Mlname
READ
```

Tip: The @...SAY command followed by the READ command is one way you can display a memory variable for user input. For more on the @...SAY command, see the section "Getting User Input" in Chapter 19.

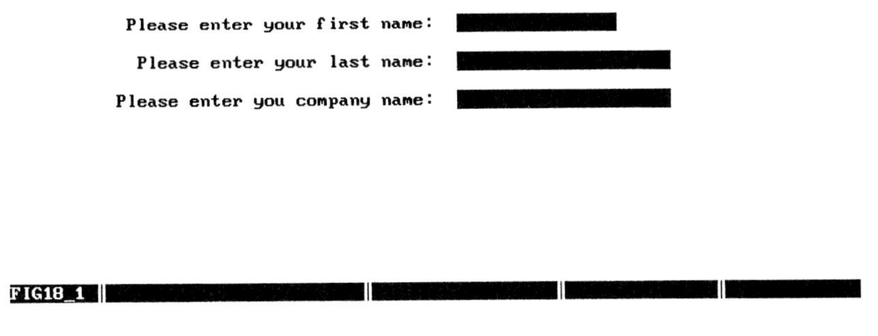

Figure 18-1. Displayed variable created using the SPACE( ) function

Use the SPACE( ) function when you want to control the number of characters entered into a blank character variable. The SPACE( ) function designates a specific number of blank spaces, up to 254. When you use the SPACE( ) function to create a character variable, the variable can only accept input up to the assigned number of characters.

When you use the SPACE( ) function to create a character memory variable, the variable is displayed in reverse video when it is called to the screen. Figure 18-1 shows some example character variables displayed on a screen. This screen is generated by using the SPACE( ) function in the following section of code.

```
STORE SPACE(15) TO Mfname
STORE SPACE(20) TO Mlname
STORE SPACE(20) TO Mconame
@ 8,10 SAY " Please enter your first name: " GET Mfname
@ 10,10 SAY "   Please enter your last name: " GET Mlname
@ 12,10 SAY "Please enter your company name: " GET Mconame
READ
```

```
. STORE 1 TO FIRST
        1
. STORE 2 TO SECOND
        2
. STORE 3 TO THIRD
        3
. FOURTH=FIRST+SECOND+THIRD
        6
.
Command ||                    ||              ||              ||       Caps
```

Figure 18-2. Numeric variables used in an equation

Numeric Variables

To create a numeric memory variable, you must assign a number to it. For example, the commands STORE 113.56 TO Price and Price=113.56 both store the value 113.56 to the variable named Price.

Once you assign a number to a numeric memory variable, you can use that numeric memory variable name in an equation. For example, you can use three numeric memory variables to get some numbers from the user, and a fourth variable to hold the answer for the equation. Figure 18-2 shows some dot prompt commands that demonstrate numeric variables at work in dBASE IV.

You cannot mix numeric variables and character variables in an equation. If you do, dBASE IV issues the "Data type mismatch" error message. For instance, if a numeric variable named Cost contains the value 24.95 and a character variable named Units contains the character string "5", you cannot multiply Units by Cost. If you do, you are in effect multiplying a number by a letter. To get around this problem, use the VAL( ) function. For example, you can convert the character variable named Units to a number, as in the expression Cost * VAL(Units).

Date Variables

To create a date memory variable, you can use a date function or date delimiters ({ }) or take a date from a database field. For example, the command STORE CTOD("12/31/89") TO Today uses the CTOD( ) (character to date) function to convert the string 12/31/89 to a date format recognizable by dBASE IV. Another function example, Today=DATE( ), uses the DATE( ) function to return the system date from your computer. An example of the use of date delimiters would be STORE {12/31/89} TO Today. Using a database field example, the expression Shipdate=Ship_date gets a date from the field Ship_date, located in the current record of an active database, and stores that date to the variable named Shipdate.

Once a date type memory variable is properly created, you can use it in a mathematical expression. For example, Nextmonth=Today+30 adds 30 days to a date variable called Today, and that value is stored to a variable called Nextmonth.

Logical Variables

Logical variables must contain a single character, indicating a true (.T.) or false (.F.) value. For example, Pass=.T. stores the value true to the variable Pass. You can also use .t., .y., or .Y. in place of .T.; dBASE IV replaces these synonyms with .T.. Conversely, the statement Pass=.F. stores the value false to the memory variable Pass. You can substitute .n., .N., or .f., all of which are converted to .F..

Summarizing a Database Field in a Memory Variable

You can also summarize data in a database to a numeric variable using the COUNT, SUM, and AVERAGE commands. These commands create their own numeric memory variables. Therefore, you do not have to create memory variables for use with these commands.

Use the COUNT command to count the number of records in a database. For example, the following section of code counts the number of records in the CUSTOMER.DBF database and then stores that count to a newly created numeric variable called Add_m_up.

```
Use Customer
COUNT TO Add_m_up
```

Similarly, the next section of code uses the SUM command to sum the numeric content of the database field Total, located in each record of the database INVENTRY.DBF. The total for all records is then stored in a numeric variable called Totl. The program section also takes an average of another numeric database field called Item_cost and stores that average to a memory variable called Mean.

```
USE INVENTRY
SUM Total TO Totl
AVERAGE Item_cost to Mean
```

Getting Rid of Memory Variables

The RELEASE command erases memory variables for memory. You can use it with a single variable name or multiple variable names separated by commas (for instance, RELEASE Opinput, Cost). The RELEASE command also has an ALL option (for example, RELEASE ALL) that you can use to erase all active variables from memory. Furthermore, you can qualify the RELEASE command using the LIKE or EXCEPT option. For example, RELEASE ALL LIKE s* gets rid of all active variables that begin with the letter "s." Conversely, the command: RELEASE ALL EXCEPT Cost, Units, Total erases all active variables except the variables named Cost, Units, and Total.

When used in a program, the RELEASE ALL command erases all memory variables in the current program and in any subprograms. However, the RELEASE ALL command does not erase any memory variables in higher level programs. When you use the RELEASE ALL command from the dot prompt, all memory variable at all levels are erased. For more on how memory variables are used in higher versus lower level programs, see the section "Relating Memory Variables Across Program Files" later in this chapter.

You can also use the CLEAR command to eliminate variables from memory. The CLEAR ALL and CLEAR MEMORY commands erase *all* active variables from memory, regardless of where they are used.

Tip: When dBASE IV encounters an error in a program, it halts execution of the program and issues an error message. At this point you are given the choices **Cancel, Suspend,** and **Ignore.** Choose **Suspend** instead of **Cancel. Cancel** clears all memory variables, whereas **Suspend** does not. **Suspend** lets you check the contents of your memory variables up to the point of error.

Memory Variable Files

In dBASE IV, you can save memory variables in a disk-based memory variable file and retrieve them later for use in your program. The .MEM file extension denotes memory variable files.

Memory variable files are a good way to permanently store the contents of memory variables on disk. For example, imagine you're working with a system that requires sequential order numbers. You can store the last order number used in a memory variable and save that variable to a memory variable file. The next time you run the system, you can restore that memory variable file and use the order number variable to update your system.

Creating a Memory Variable File

To create a memory variable file, use the SAVE TO command. The syntax for the command is SAVE TO <*memvar filename*>. You can use this command to create a memory variable file either from the dot prompt or from within a program.

When you use the SAVE TO command without a qualifier, dBASE IV saves all active memory variables to a file. For example, the following section of code creates two memory variables and then saves them to a file called MEMVAR.MEM.

```
STORE 12345 TO Mcustno
STORE 45678 TO Morderno
SAVE TO Memvar
```

You can also use the ALL LIKE and EXCEPT options to qualify the SAVE TO command. For example, the command SAVE TO <*memvar filename*> ALL LIKE m* saves all active memory variables that begin with the letter "m." The command SAVE TO <*memvar filename*> ALL LIKE ????d saves all memory variables with the letter d as the fourth letter in the memory variable name. Furthermore, the command SAVE TO <*memvar filename*> ALL EXCEPT m* saves all active memory variables to a file except those that begin with the letter "m."

When you use the SAVE TO command to save active memory variables to a .MEM file that already exists, dBASE IV overwrites the file. For example, suppose the file MEMVAR.MEM contained the two variables Mordno and Mcustno. These two variables are also active in memory, plus one more, Minvno. When you enter the command SAVE TO memvar, dBASE IV writes all three memory variables and their new contents to the memory variable file MEMVAR.MEM.

Tip: Use the SET SAFETY OFF command at the start of your programs that contain the SAVE TO command. This allows dBASE IV to overwrite existing files without your manual approval. Otherwise, dBASE IV stops and requires a confirmation.

Activating Memory Variables Files

Use the RESTORE FROM command to activate an existing memory variable file. The format of this command is RESTORE FROM <*memvar filename*>. This command deletes all current memory variables and activates the memory variables stored in the memory variable file. The newly activated variables from the memory variable file are only available for use in the current program, unless you first use the PUBLIC command. For more on using public memory variables, see the next section, "Relating Memory Variables Across Program Files."

You can also use the ADDITIVE option with the RESTORE FROM command to activate a memory variable file without deleting any current memory variables. For example, the command RESTORE FROM Memvar ADDITIVE activates the memory variables in the file MEMVAR.MEM, without deleting any other active memory variables.

Tip: To display all active memory variables names and their contents, use the DISPLAY MEMORY command, either from the dot prompt or from within your program.

Relating Memory Variables Across Program Files

Any program that activates another subprogram (contains the DO command) is a higher level program. This higher versus lower level program relationship has a great deal to do with how memory variables relate to one another across programs in dBASE IV.

When you create a memory variable in a higher level program, that memory variable is also available for use in lower level programs. For example, the following illustration shows a series of subprograms controlled by a main menu. Beneath the first tier of subprograms lies yet another tier of subprograms. If you create a memory variable in the highest level program (MAIN-

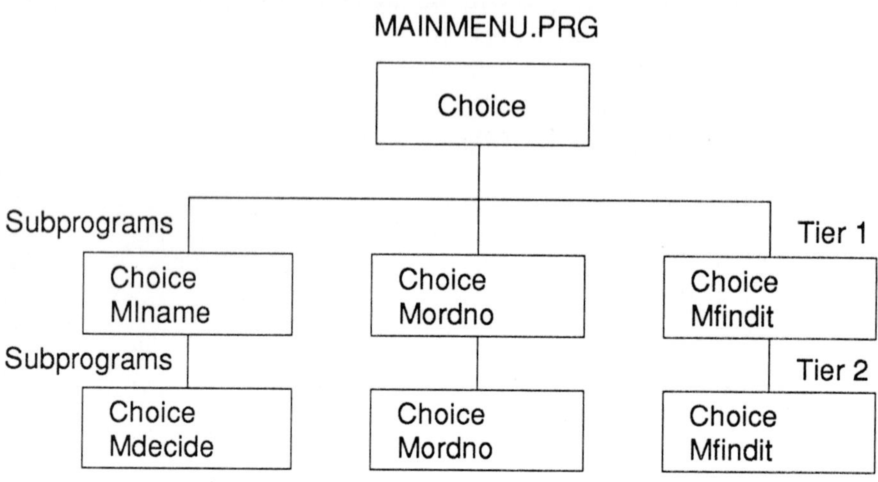

Figure 18-3. Memory variables created in lower level programs are not available in higher level programs

MENU.PRG), you can call on that variable name, and its contents, in both the first and second tier of subprograms.

Thus, memory variables created in a program are available for use in all subprograms and procedures called by that program. However, if you create a memory variable in a subprogram, that memory variable is not available for use in a higher level, or calling, program. For example, in Figure 18-3 the variable Mdecide is not available for use in the calling program MAINMENU.PRG.

Private Memory Variables

When you create a memory variable in a dBASE IV program, it is a *private* memory variable. That is, it is only available for use in the current program and any programs called by the current program. When dBASE IV encounters a RETURN (end program) command in the current program, it erases the memory variables created by that program. In addition, all memory variables created in programs are erased when the last program ends and dBASE IV returns to the dot prompt.

Public Memory Variables

Public memory variables are variables that can be used by all programs. Unlike private memory variables, public memory variables are not erased when a RETURN (end program) command is encountered.

To create a public memory variable, use the PUBLIC command before you create a memory variable. The format of this command is PUBLIC <*memvar name*>. For example, in the following section of code, the command PUBLIC Ordno makes the memory variable Ordno available for use in all programs.

```
PUBLIC Ordno
STORE 0 TO Ordno
```

If you need to restore memory variables as public from a memory variable file, you must first use the PUBLIC command to do so. For example, the following section of code restores as public the memory variables Custno, Ordno, and Invno from the file MEMVAR.MEM.

```
PUBLIC Custno, Invno, Ordno
RESTORE FROM Memvar ADDITIVE
```

You can use the PUBLIC command at any time prior to creating a memory variable. dBASE IV uses the PUBLIC command to store a variable as a logical value until you later initialize it, using the STORE or = command.

Tip: All memory variables restored with the RESTORE FROM command at the dot prompt are restored as public.

Hiding Memory Variables

In dBASE IV, you can use the PRIVATE command to hide a memory variable in a higher level program while you change the contents of that variable in a lower level program. The format of this command is PRIVATE <*memvar name*>. For example, the command PRIVATE Custno in the current program temporarily hides the variable Custno in any higher level programs. While in the current program, you can change the contents of the Custno variable without affecting its value in higher level programs. When control is returned to a higher level program, the variable Custno comes out of hiding with its original contents intact.

Macro Substitution

You can substitute the contents of character memory variables in command lines using the & macro substitution symbol. For example, the following section of code creates a character variable and then uses the & macro symbol to substitute the contents of the variable in an @...SAY...GET command line. After the variable is substituted, the command line appears to dBASE IV as @ 10,10 SAY "Please enter your company name: " GET Company.

```
STORE "Please enter your company name: " TO Mcompname
@ 10,10 SAY &Mcompname GET Company
```

You can also place conditional statements in a memory variable and use the & macro symbol to substitute them in commands. For instance, the following section of code places a condition in the character variable Condit and then substitutes that condition after a DO WHILE loop command. The condition in this case is the logical .NOT. operator followed by the EOF( ) (end of file) function. When the end of file marker is reached, the condition becomes true and dBASE IV exits the DO WHILE...ENDDO loop.

```
USE Customer
STORE ".NOT. EOF()" to Condit
DO WHILE &Condit
      * More commands lines
ENDDO
```

This chapter has shown how to create, name, and erase memory variables, how to use memory variable files and relate memory variables across program files. Additionally, this chapter has presented ways to use the macro symbol to substitute the contents of memory variables in command lines.

Programming Input and Output

Getting User Input
Displaying Data

NINETEEN

This chapter introduces the commands and techniques you can use to program input and output operations in dBASE IV. It shows you how to get input from the user, explaining the use of input commands and custom forms. It then shows you different ways to send data to the screen or to the printer.

Getting User Input

The two most common methods for getting user input are through user-input commands and custom forms. User-input commands let you get specific instructions or data from a user so that your program can react accordingly. Custom forms, on the other hand, provide an attractive on-screen input form for data entry.

The User-Input Commands

The ACCEPT, INPUT, WAIT, and @...SAY...GET...READ commands temporarily halt your program to allow user input. The input is then stored to memory variables and your program can react to the contents of those variables. Some situations where you might use these commands include

- Getting a selection from a multiple-choice menu
- Getting a number or text string to search for in the database
- Getting a number or text string to place in a database field

The ACCEPT Command

You use the ACCEPT command to halt program execution and prompt the user for text input. Once the user types the text string and presses ENTER, the information is entered into a character variable for later use. For example, the following command line halts program execution, places a message on the screen, and stores the response in a variable called Lname.

```
ACCEPT "Type in your last name and press ENTER: " TO Lname
```

If you type either a number or a date in response to the ACCEPT command, dBASE IV accepts the entry but stores it to the variable as text. Therefore, numbers are not immediately useful in a numeric calculation unless you use the VAL( ) (value) function to convert them to a numeric form. Similarly, dates are not immediately useful unless you convert them to the date form using the CTOD( ) (character to date) function.

An added advantage to the ACCEPT command is that it creates its own memory variable. Thus, when you use this command, you need not use the STORE or = command to create the memory variable beforehand.

Tip: Unless the SET ESCAPE OFF command is in force, pressing ESC in response to the ACCEPT command ends a program.

The INPUT Command

Unlike the ACCEPT command, you can use the INPUT command to prompt the user for either numeric, character, or date input. Like the ACCEPT command, this command creates its own memory variable in which to store the input. However, the type of memory variable created depends upon the type of data entered.

Just like the ACCEPT command, the INPUT command halts a program, places a message on the screen, and stores the user's response in a memory variable. Again, the user must complete the entry by pressing ENTER. For example, the following command line stores a numeric response to a numeric variable called Ordno.

```
INPUT "Please enter an order number and press ENTER: " TO Ordno
```

If you enter text in response to the INPUT command, it must be delimited (enclosed) in quotes (" " or ' ') or square brackets ([ ]). If the text is not properly delimited, dBASE IV issues the error message "Variable not found" and repeats the INPUT command. Similarly, if you enter a date, it must be enclosed in curly braces, (for example, {12/31/90}). If you enter a date in date format (such as 12/31/90) without enclosing it in curly braces, dBASE IV accepts the entry. However, because it performs division using the three numbers you provided, dBASE IV stores an obscure numeric result to the variable.

If you just press ENTER in response to the INPUT prompt, dBASE IV displays the INPUT prompt again. However, if you enter a number, dBASE IV accepts it and stores it to a numeric variable. This is why you'll often see the ACCEPT command used to capture character data and the INPUT command used to capture numbers.

The WAIT Command

The WAIT command creates a character variable and captures a single keystroke in it. This command is often used with multiple-choice menus because, unlike other user-input commands, the

WAIT command doesn't require you to press ENTER to complete data entry.

The following command line shows an example of the WAIT command. This command line halts the program, places a message on the screen, and stores a single keystroke response to a variable called Decide.

```
WAIT "Do you wish to continue the search (Y/N)?" TO Decide
```

You can also use the WAIT command all by itself to put the message "Press any key to continue" on the screen. When you use it in this context, the WAIT command halts program execution until any key is pressed.

The @...SAY...GET...READ Commands

The @...SAY...GET...READ commands allow you to choose a screen location for a user-input prompt. Furthermore, these commands let you enter data into either a memory variable or a database field. The syntax for @...SAY...GET...READ is

@ *<row>*,*<column>* SAY *<character expression>* GET *<variable><field>*

READ

The @...SAY...GET...READ command sequence is broken down as follows:

- The *<row>*,*<column>* part of the command refers to rows and columns on your screen, working from the upper left-hand corner. For example, most conventional screens display 24 rows (0 to 23) and 80 columns (0 to 79). When you enter the coordinates 2,10 for *<row>* and *<column>*, respectively, this refers to the second row down and the tenth column over, starting from the upper left-hand corner of your screen.

- The <*character expression*> part of the command can contain a text message enclosed in quotes (" " or ' '). For example, you might enter the phrase "Please enter your name".
- The GET part of the command calls either an active variable, previously created with the STORE or = command, or a database field from the currently active database record.
- The READ command, on the next line, activates the GET part of the @...SAY...GET command and displays the memory variable or database field for data entry.

Putting it all together, the following command lines tell dBASE IV to display the various messages that appear with each command. Immediately following each message, the GETs call the various database fields in the database file CUSTOMER. The READ command following the @...SAY...GET commands activates the GETs in each command and displays the database fields for editing. Figure 19-1 shows the results.

```
CLEAR
USE Customer
@ 1,8 SAY "  First Name: " GET Firstname
@ 3,8 SAY "   Last Name: " GET Lastname
@ 5,8 SAY "    Company : " GET Company
@ 7,8 SAY "   Address 1: " GET Addr_1
@ 8,8 SAY "   Address 2: " GET Addr_2
@ 10,8 SAY "        City : " GET City
@ 12,8 SAY "        State: " GET State
@ 12,25 SAY      "    Zip: " GET Zip
@ 14,8 SAY "      Country: " GET Country
@ 14,37 SAY    "     Phone: " GET Telephone
READ
```

When specifying row and column coordinates with @...SAY...GET commands, keep in mind that rows 0 and 22 are used by dBASE IV. These rows contain the scoreboard and status bar. Although an @...SAY...GET command that uses one of these rows will not interfere with dBASE IV, it will make your screen appear to be in conflict. If you need to display data in rows 0 and

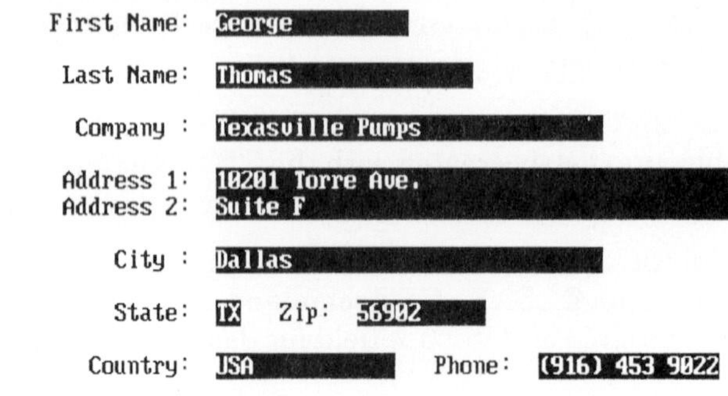

Figure 19-1. @...SAY...GET commands displayed

22, use the SET SCOREBOARD OFF and SET STATUS OFF commands to hide the scoreboard and status bar.

You can also use memory variables with the @...SAY...GET commands. Actually, it is common practice to store user input in variables before loading a database. This enables you to place a confirmation step in your program that asks the user to review the information prior to proceeding. Once the memory variables are loaded and the input reviewed, you can use the REPLACE command to replace the fields in the current database record with the information in the memory variables. For example, the following section of code uses memory variables to gather information, an IF...ENDIF command sequence to confirm the input, and the REPLACE command to load the database.

```
STORE SPACE(15) TO Fname
```

```
STORE SPACE(20) TO Lname
CLEAR
@ 10,10 SAY " Enter your first name :" TO Fname
@ 12,10 SAY "  Enter your last name :" TO Lname
READ
?
WAIT "Is this input correct (Y/N)? " TO Decide
IF UPPER(Decide)="Y"
     REPLACE Firstname with Fname, Lastname with Lname
ELSE
     RETURN
ENDIF
```

Custom Forms

Custom forms are most often used to provide an attractive on-screen form for displaying and entering data. You can build custom forms yourself by creating a format (.FMT) file with the dBASE IV Text Editor, or you can have dBASE IV help you to create a custom form using either the CREATE SCREEN command at the dot prompt or the Forms Panel in the Control Center to access the Forms Design screen.

Whichever method you use, the result is a format file that builds a custom screen form. You can then call that format file from your program to display, edit, and add database records. Figure 19-2 shows a sample custom form.

Creating Format Files

As mentioned, you can create your own custom forms manually, or you can have dBASE IV help you to create custom forms. Either way, the result is a *format file.* A format file works like a program to build a custom screen. It contains a series of @...SAY...GET commands that display text and graphics on your screen, along with the fields for the currently active database. As you might expect, the field names used in the @...SAY...GET commands in the format file must match the field descriptions of the currently active

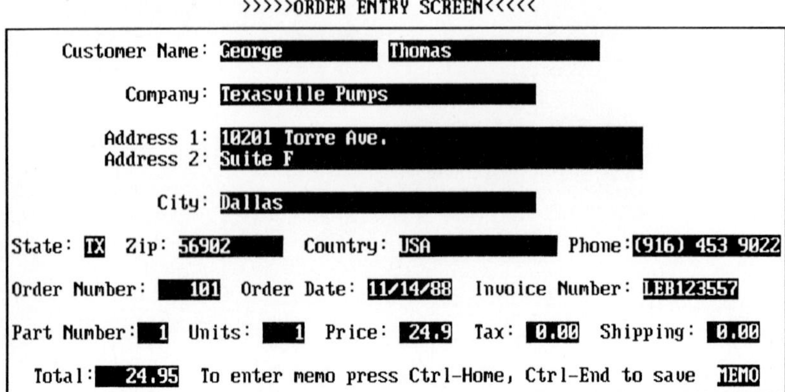

>>>>>ORDER ENTRY SCREEN<<<<<

Customer Name: George Thomas

Company: Texasville Pumps

Address 1: 10201 Torre Ave.
Address 2: Suite F

City: Dallas

State: TX Zip: 56902 Country: USA Phone: (916) 453 9022

Order Number: 101 Order Date: 11/14/88 Invoice Number: LEB123557

Part Number: 1 Units: 1 Price: 24.9 Tax: 0.00 Shipping: 0.00

Total: 24.95 To enter memo press Ctrl-Home, Ctrl-End to save MEMO

C:\...chap20\CUSTOMER | Rec 1/33 | File | Ins

Figure 19-2. An example custom form

database. The listing that follows is the format file that was used to create the form in Figure 19-2.

```
********************************************************************************
*-- Name....: SCREEN1.FMT
*-- Date....: 11-15-88
*-- Version.: dBASE IV, Format 1.0
********************************************************************************

SET SCOREBOARD OFF

*--Define memo window.----------------------------------------

DEFINE WINDOW Wndw1 FROM 12,4 TO 18,73
SET WINDOW OF MEMO TO Wndw1

*--Draw a box around the screen.--------------------------------------

@ 1,1 TO 18,75

*-- @@ SAY GETS Processing. -----------------------------------------

@ 0,15 SAY "          >>>>>ORDER ENTRY SCREEN<<<<<"
```

```
@ 2,2 SAY "     Customer Name: "
@ 2,22 GET Customer->Firstname PICTURE "XXXXXXXXXXXXXXX"
@ 2,37 SAY " "
@ 2,38 GET Customer->Lastname PICTURE "XXXXXXXXXXXXXXXXXXXX"
@ 4,2 SAY "           Company: "
@ 4,22 GET Customer->Company PICTURE "XXXXXXXXXXXXXXXXXXXXXXXXXXXXXX"
@ 6,2 SAY "         Address 1: "
@ 6,22 GET Customer->Addr_1 PICTURE "XXXXXXXXXXXXXXXXXXXXXXXXXXXXXXXXXXXXXXXX"
@ 7,2 SAY "         Address 2: "
@ 7,22 GET Customer->Addr_2 PICTURE "XXXXXXXXXXXXXXXXXXXXXXXXXXXXXXXXXXXXXXXX"
@ 9,2 SAY "              City: "
@ 9,22 GET Customer->City PICTURE "XXXXXXXXXXXXXXXXXXXXXXXXXXXXXX"
@ 11,2 SAY "State: "
@ 11,9 GET Customer->State PICTURE "XX"
@ 11,11 SAY "  Zip: "
@ 11,18 GET Customer->Zip PICTURE "XXXXXXXXXX"
@ 11,28 SAY "  Country: "
@ 11,39 GET Customer->Country PICTURE "XXXXXXXXXXXXXXX"
@ 11,54 SAY " Phone:"
@ 11,61 GET Customer->Telephone PICTURE "XXXXXXXXXXXXXX"
@ 13,2 SAY "Order Number: "
@ 13,16 GET Order_no PICTURE "999999"
@ 13,22 SAY "  Order Date: "
@ 13,36 GET Order_date
@ 13,44 SAY "  Invoice Number: "
@ 13,62 GET Inv_no PICTURE "XXXXXXXXX"
@ 15,2 SAY "Part Number: "
@ 15,14 GET Part_no PICTURE "999"
@ 15,17 SAY "  Units: "
@ 15,26 GET Units PICTURE "9999"
@ 15,30 SAY "  Price: "
@ 15,39 GET Price PICTURE "999.99"
@ 15,44 SAY "  Tax: "
@ 15,51 GET Tax PICTURE "99.99"
@ 15,56 SAY "  Shipping: "
@ 15,68 GET Foreign_sh PICTURE "99.99"
@ 17,2 SAY "  Total: "
@ 17,10 GET Total
*--Memo Window: Wndow1

@ 17,20 SAY "To enter memo press Ctrl-Home, Ctrl-End to save "
@ 17,69 GET Memo WINDOW Wndow1

*-- Format file exit code -----------------------------------------------------

RELEASE WINDOWS Wndow1
SET SCOREBOARD ON
```

Tip: The PICTURE commands that appear after the commands @...SAY...GET in the preceding format file allow you to control the data type that is entered into the blanks in a custom form. The PICTURE command is discussed in Chapter 22.

To create an .FMT file yourself, enter the MODIFY COMMAND command at the dot prompt. For example, to create the format file named SCREEN1, type

```
MODIFY COMMAND SCREEN1.FMT
```

at the dot prompt. (Don't forget to include the .FMT extension.) dBASE IV takes you directly to the Text Editor and you can begin typing the @...SAY...GET commands that make up your format file. When you are finished, press CTRL-END, or press F10 followed by **Exit/Save changes and exit**, to save the format file.

When you complete your format file, you can try it out using the SET FORMAT TO command followed by the READ command. However, don't forget to activate the appropriate database first. Otherwise, dBASE IV will issue a number of "Variable not found" error messages. You can enter these commands either from the dot prompt or from within a program. For example, if the name of your format file is SCREEN1.FMT and the name of the database used with the form is CUSTOMER.DBF, enter the following:

```
USE Customer
SET FORMAT TO Screen1
READ
```

dBASE IV will run the format file. However, immediately before it runs your format file, dBASE IV compiles it. When an .FMT file is compiled, an .FMO file is created. dBASE IV actually uses the .FMO file to create the custom form on your screen.

You can also use the CREATE SCREEN command to create a format file. The syntax for this command is CREATE SCREEN *<format filename>*. For example, to create a format file called SCREEN1.FMT, type

```
CREATE SCREEN SCREEN1
```

at the dot prompt. When you enter this command, dBASE IV takes you directly to the Forms Design screen that you learned about in Chapter 9. Recall that you can access this same screen using the Forms Panel in the Control Center. For a complete description of how to use the Forms Design screen to create a custom form, see Chapter 9. When you complete the design of your custom form, save it in the usual way.

To modify an existing form created with the CREATE SCREEN command, use the MODIFY SCREEN command followed by the name of the form. For example, to modify a form called SCREEN1, type

```
MODIFY SCREEN SCREEN1
```

dBASE IV will take you directly to the Forms Design screen and place the form SCREEN1 on the screen. Make your modifications and save the form in the usual way.

When you use the Forms Design screen to create a custom form, dBASE IV actually creates three files. The first file, which dBASE IV uses to display a custom form, has a default .SCR (screen) file extension. You can only alter this file through the Control Center. The second file that dBASE IV creates has an .FMT (format) file extension. This file contains a series of @...SAY...GET commands similar to those which appear in the format file just discussed. If you want, you can alter this file with the MODIFY COMMAND *<format filename>*.FMT command also just discussed. The third file is an .FMO compiled file that is a compiled version of the .FMT format file. dBASE IV uses this compiled .FMO version when you use the SET FORMAT TO command to call the format file into use from your program.

Although this section shows you how to create custom forms manually, you should use the power of dBASE IV to help you create them. There are two reasons for this. First of all, it is usually faster to create a custom form from the Control Center Forms Panel, or by using the CREATE SCREEN command, than it is to type @...SAY...GET commands in the dBASE IV Text Editor. Second, it is often quicker and more efficient to modify a format file using the Control Center or the MODIFY SCREEN command than it is to do it yourself, by hand, in the dBASE IV Text Editor. Once the format file is created, you can insert your own custom command lines to mold it to your precise needs.

Tips for Creating Format Files

You may find the following tips helpful when you create a format file using the dBASE IV Text Editor. These tips should help the process to go a little faster and should give you a certain measure of control over how the form is used.

- Keep a copy of the database structure(s) handy. That way, you won't forget a database field, misspell a field header, or forget the size or data type of a field.
- You can use the @...SAY command without GET to display text on the screen or to display a database field. For example, @ 14,10 SAY "First Name" displays the text string "First Name" starting at row 14, column 10 of your screen. Similarly, if a name of the field in the database is Order_no, you can use the command @ 14,10 SAY Order_no. This command simply displays the contents of the field. When the READ command in your program activates the other GETs in the format file, the results of this command are displayed. However, you cannot edit the field.
- You can use memory variables in @...SAY...GET commands in a format file, as long as you have created those memory variables sometime prior to activating the format file with the SET FORMAT TO command. dBASE IV accepts the memory variables in your format file with no problem.
- You don't have to use all of the fields in the database in your form. You can show only the fields you need for data entry or display, and leave other fields out of the picture altogether. To leave out selected fields, simply don't call for them with an @...SAY...GET command.

```
Layout   Words   Go To   Print   Exit                                    11:21:43 am
[·······▼1······▼··2····▼····3··▼······4▼·······▼5······▼··6····▼····7··▼·······

@ 3,10 SAY " ASCII Characters common in format files "

@ 5,10 SAY "Character 27"
@ 5,25 SAY CHR(27)
@ 7,10 SAY "Character 26"
@ 7,25 SAY CHR(26)
@ 9,10 SAY "Character 25"
@ 9,25 SAY CHR(25)
@ 11,10 SAY "Character 24"
@ 11,25 SAY CHR(24)
@ 13,10 SAY "ENTER Symbol"
@ 13,25 SAY CHR(17)+CHR(196)+CHR(217)




Program ||C:\...chap20\FIG20_3   ||Line:1 Col:1   ||          ||          Ins
```

Figure 19-3. The CHR( ) function generates ASCII characters

Adding Graphics to Format Files

You can also add boxes, lines, and special ASCII characters to your format files. These additions tend to make your display appear more attractive and professional. You can also use them to draw attention to a specific section of your form.

To draw a box around a section of your screen, use the @...TO command. The format of this command is @ *<row>*,*<column>* TO *<row>*,*<column>*. The first set of screen coordinates designates the top-left corner of the box. The second set designates the bottom-right corner. For example, the command @ 0,0 TO 23,79 draws a single-line box around the entire perimeter of the screen. Similarly, the command @ 14,10 TO 16,20 draws a single-line box around columns 10 to 20 of rows 14 to 16 of your screen. However, the command @ 14,10 TO 14,20 draws a straight line from column 10 to column 20 of row 14.

```
ASCII Characters common in format files

Character 27  ←

Character 26  →

Character 25  ↓

Character 24  ↑

ENTER Symbol  ↵
```

Figure 19-4. The results of the program in Figure 19-3

You can also use the DOUBLE option with the @...TO command to draw double-line boxes around objects on your form. The syntax for this form of the command is @ *<row>*,*<column>* TO *<row>*,*<column>* DOUBLE. For example, the command @ 14,10 TO 16,20 DOUBLE draws a double-line box that encloses columns 10 to 20 of rows 14 to 16 of your screen. Similarly, the command @ 14,10 TO 14,20 DOUBLE draws a straight double line from column 10 to column 20 of row 14.

You can also place special ASCII characters in your forms using the CHR( ) function. For example, CHR(24) returns ↑. As another example, the command

```
@ 10,10 SAY "Type your name and press"+CHR(17)+CHR(196)+CHR(217)  GET Firstname
```

produces the message "Type your name and press ↵." Figures 19-3 and 19-4 show some more examples and the code used to generate them. For a complete listing of ASCII characters and their numbers, refer to Appendix A, "ASCII Character Codes."

Using Format Files

As mentioned, once you've created a custom form, you can activate it using the SET FORMAT command followed by the name of the format file. Once you enter the SET FORMAT command, you can display the form using any of the full-screen commands, including EDIT, APPEND, READ, INSERT, and CHANGE. For example, the following section of code initializes the database file CUSTOMER, calls the format file SCREEN1 to the screen, and uses it to add a record to the database.

```
USE Customer
SET FORMAT TO Screen1.fmt
APPEND
```

Once a database record is displayed in your custom form, you can move to other records in the database and your custom form will remain on the screen. For example, to get to the previous record, press PGUP. To move to the next record, press PGDN. However, if you press PGDN from the last record in the database, dBASE IV issues the message "Add new records? (Y/N)." If you press Y, a record is added to the database, using your custom form. You can then enter data into the record. If you press N, dBASE IV remains on the last record in the database.

There are a number of command sequences for controlling how your forms are used and what kind of data goes into them. For a complete discussion of these commands and techniques, see Chapter 22, "The User Interface."

Closing Format Files

Use the CLOSE FORMAT or SET FORMAT command to close your open format files. When you use the SET FORMAT command to open a format file, it stays open. Thus, the next time dBASE IV encounters a full-screen command such as EDIT or READ, your custom form is called to the screen, perhaps in an inappropriate place. CLOSE FORMAT closes any open format files in the currently selected work area. The command SET FORMAT TO, when not followed by a format file name, does the same thing.

Modifying Format Files

To modify a format file, you can use the MODIFY COMMAND command. The syntax for this command is

MODIFY COMMAND <*format filename*>.FMT

You can also use the Control Center Forms Panel to modify a format file. However, if you've made any modifications of your own, such as including ASCII characters in some of your @...SAY commands, dBASE IV completely overwrites them when it creates the new format file.

When you enter the MODIFY COMMAND command followed by the name of a format file, dBASE IV loads your format file and takes you directly to the dBASE IV Text Editor. You can then modify your format file. When you're finished, press CTRL-END, or press F10 **Exit/Save changes and exit**, to save the format file.

Multiple-Screen Forms

You can also create *multiple-page* (screen) forms. Multiple-page forms are useful when you're working with large databases that have more fields than will fit on a single screen.

When you use the Control Center Forms Panel to create a form that extends beyond a single screen, dBASE IV automatically uses the READ command to create a second page for the form. If you're creating a custom form on your own, independent of the Control Center or the CREATE SCREEN command, you can create a second page by inserting a READ command in your format file. That way, when the user fills in the last field in the first page, dBASE IV jumps to the next page. The user can move back and forth between pages by pressing PGUP and PGDN. When the user reaches the last page and presses PGDN, dBASE IV moves to the next record.

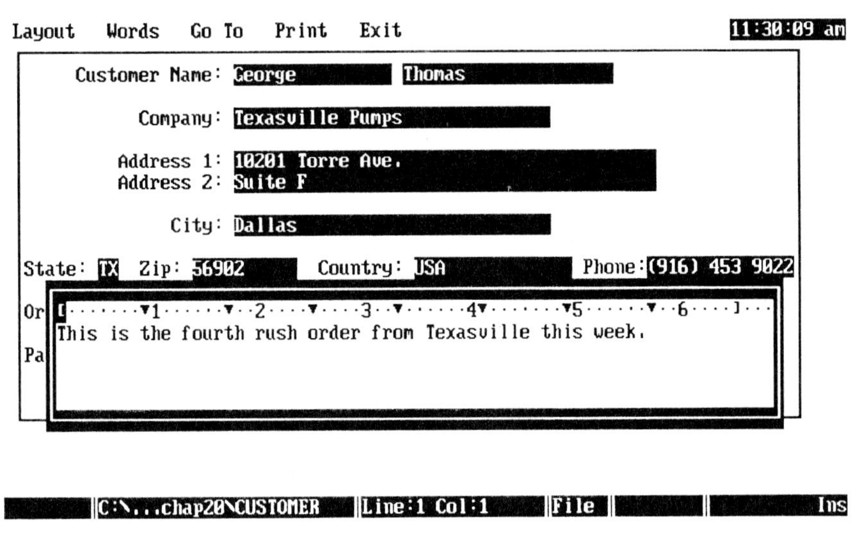

Figure 19-5. An input window displayed on a custom form

Setting Up an Input Window

You can also include in your format file an input window for editing memo fields. Figure 19-5 shows an example.

Input windows are linked to memo fields. Normally, when you move the cursor to a memo field and press CTRL-HOME, the dBASE IV Text Editor is activated and appears as a full screen. However, you can use an input window to place the dBASE IV Text Editor inside a window that is less than full-screen size. That way, when you press CTRL-HOME, the dBASE IV Text Editor comes up inside a predefined window, while everything else on the screen remains the same.

You can program an input window into a format file yourself, or you can have the Control Center do it. Either way, the same commands are used to define, activate, and display an input window. For example, the following section of code creates a window called Wndow1 and calls it to the screen.

```
DEFINE WINDOW Wndow1 FROM 12,4 TO 18,73
SET WINDOW OF MEMO TO Wndow1
@17,6 GET Mssg WINDOW Wndow1
READ
```

The command DEFINE WINDOW Wndow1 FROM 12,4 TO 18,73 defines the window called Wndow1. The screen coordinates of the top-left corner of the window are row 12, column 4. Likewise, the window's bottom-right corner screen coordinates are row 18, column 73.

The command SET WINDOW OF MEMO TO Wndow1 activates the Wndow1 window and readies it for use.

Tip: Be sure to place the two preceding commands at the top of your format file, before any @...SAY...GET commands. Otherwise, dBASE IV issues a format file termination error message.

The command @17,6 GET Mssg WINDOW Wndow1 places the actual database memo field called Mssg on the screen. The second part of the command, WINDOW Wndow1, tells dBASE IV to use a predefined window, called Wndow1, to display the Text Editor when the user presses CTRL-HOME.

For more about commands that generate input windows, see DEFINE WINDOW in Chapter 31 and SET WINDOW in Chapter 32. These commands are also discussed in more detail in Chapter 22.

Using More Than One Database with a Format File

As mentioned, you can use more than one database with a format file. However, you must first activate the databases and place them in separate work areas. Then you must relate the databases to one another using one of the three methods listed next. You must set up a relationship between the databases in order to ensure that the record pointer is on the correct record in each database. If it is not, your format file might return inaccurate results.

Recall from Chapter 7 that dBASE IV allows you to have up to ten active databases. You set up each database in its own separate work area, using either the SELECT or USE commands. In the following program section, the SELECT command is used to place two databases in separate work areas.

After you have activated your databases, you must relate them to one another in one of the following three ways:

- Use the SET RELATION TO command to establish a relationship between databases indexed on a common field. This command is discussed further in the context of programming in Chapter 21.
- Use the SET VIEW TO command to activate a query (.QBE) file created using the Queries Design screen. You access the Queries Design screen by using either the **Query/<create>** menu selection in the Control Center or the CREATE QUERY command at the dot prompt. Creating .QBE (query by example) files is discussed in Chapter 6. The SET VIEW TO command is covered in Chapter 21.
- Use a .VUE (view) file. This topic is also discussed in Chapter 21.

The following section from a program uses the SELECT command in conjunction with the SET RELATION TO command to activate and relate the CUSTOMER.DBF and ORDERREC.DBF databases.

```
SET TALK OFF
SET BELL OFF
SELECT 1
USE Customer Order Cust_no
SELECT 2
USE Orderrec
SET RELATION TO Cust_no INTO Customer
INPUT "Please enter a customer number: " TO Findit
```

```
LOCATE FOR Cust_no=Findit
IF FOUND()
     SET FORMAT TO SCREEN1
     READ
ELSE
     ? "Customer number not found"
ENDIF
```

CUSTOMER.DBF contains the name and address of each customer. ORDERREC.DBF contains the order information for those customers. Both databases contain a numeric field called Cust_no. This field is used in CUSTOMER.DBF to hold each customer's unique customer number. The same unique number appears in the Cust_no field in ORDERREC.DBF to identify that customer's order.

The SELECT and SET RELATION TO commands work together to activate the two databases, place them in separate work areas, and relate them on the common Cust_no field. The CUSTOMER.DBF database is placed in work area 1 and ORDERREC.DBF is placed in work area 2. Since work area 2 is selected last, it remains the currently active work area. Since ORDERREC.DBF is in the currrently active work area, the SET RELATION TO command establishes ORDERREC.DBF as the parent file and CUSTOMER.DBF as the child file in this relationship. Furthermore, note that the Cust_no field for CUSTOMER.DBF is indexed. The child file must always be indexed with the SET RELATION TO command. dBASE IV uses this index to find the record number in CUSTOMER.DBF for which the Cust_no field contains the same unique customer number as in ORDERREC.DBF. Matching customer numbers in this manner ensures that the format file activated in the preceding program uses the correct records from each database.

Once you have activated the databases and related them, you can use your format file to *point* to specific fields in a database. You point to a database from your format file using the —> symbol in an @...SAY...GET command. The —> symbol is preceded by the name of the database and followed by a field name within that database. For example, imagine you are working with the same two databases, CUSTOMER.DBF and ORDERREC.DBF. The currently active work area is work area 2, which contains ORDER-REC. The CUSTOMER database resides in work area 1 and contains the field Company. The following format file command line points to the field Company in CUSTOMER.DBF.

```
@ 10,21 SAY " Company: " GET Customer->Company
```

You must use pointers in your format file because dBASE IV can only have one currently active work area. In the previous example, the currently active work area is work area 2, which contains the ORDERREC database. You don't need to point to field names in OREDERREC. However, you *do* need to point to field names in CUSTOMER in work area 1, the noncurrent work area. The pointer (—>) in this case tells dBASE IV to look in other work areas for the CUSTOMER.DBF database and to get the field Company from within that database.

Displaying Data

This section covers some commands and techniques you can use to have your program send data to your screen or your printer. You learned about many of these commands in Chapter 7, "The Dot Prompt." However, the commands appear here in the context of a program.

The ? Command

The ? command is one of the most useful output commands in dBASE IV. This command sends output directly to your screen. If SET PRINT ON is active, the ? command sends its output to your printer.

When you use the ? command in a program, it issues a carriage return line feed, causing dBASE IV to jump to the next line on your screen or printer. Therefore, when you follow the ? command with text in quotes or a variable name, the data is displayed (or printed) on the line following the ? command.

You can build complex display expressions, containing up to 1024 characters, using the ? command. These expressions can include variable names, character strings, and mathematical equations. Some examples of the ? command appear in the following program. Note that the ? command is used throughout the program to skip lines on the screen. Also note the use of plus signs (+) with the ? command toward the end of the program. You can use the plus sign to combine expressions for display. For example, the line

? "Your name is: "+fname+" "+name

combines the string "Your name is: " with the variable Fname, followed by a space (" ") and the variable Lname. The output from the program appears in Figure 19-6.

```
* Program to demostrate the ? command
SET TALK OFF
SET ECHO OFF
CLEAR
?
?
ACCEPT "        Please enter your first name: " TO Fname
?
ACCEPT "         Please enter your last name: " TO Lname
?
INPUT "Please enter today's date {##/##/##}: " TO Today
?
WAIT "           dBASE is fun (.T. or .F.): " TO New
?
?
? "    Your name is: "+TRIM(Fname)+" "+TRIM(Lname)
? " Today's date is: "+DTOC(Today)
? "    dBASE is fun: "+New
RETURN
```

The ? command is further enhanced by the AT *<expression>* clause. This clause allows you to pinpoint the position of your output on a given line. The format of this command is ? *<expression>*

```
        Please enter your first name: Harry H.

         Please enter your last name: Harrigan

Please enter today's date {##/##/##}: {11/27/90}

           dBASE is fun (.T. or .F.): T


   Your name is: Harry H. Harrigan
Today's date is: 11/27/90
   dBASE is fun: T




Command ||                                                        Ins
```

Figure 19-6. The ? command used to display output

AT *<numeric expression>*. For example, to print the string "Welcome to the new system" 20 spaces from from the left side of the screen, use the following command:

```
? "Welcome to the new system" AT 20
```

The ?? Command

The ?? command works like the ? command, except that it does not issue a carriage return line feed before displaying the data. That is, it does not cause dBASE IV to skip to the next line. Instead, this command prints on the same line, or it picks up where the previous display command left off. For example, the following program includes the ?? command. Figure 19-7 shows the output from the program.

```
This is a string of text.
This is anotherandThis is another





Command ║C:\...chap20\CUSTOMER   ║Rec 1/33        ║File ║     ║        Ins
```

Figure 19-7. The ?? command displays output on the same line

```
* Program to demonstrate the ?? command
SET TALK OFF
SET ECHO OFF
CLEAR
STORE "This is a string of text." TO Text1
STORE "This is another" TO Text2
? Text1
? Text2
?? "and"+Text2
RETURN
```

The ??? Command

The ??? command sends output to your printer. Like the ?? command, the ??? command does not issue a carriage return line feed. This command also bypasses your installed printer driver and can help you to perform tasks not supported by your printer driver. For example, the following program sends out a printer control code that causes an HP LaserJet printer to switch from portrait (up and down) to landscape (sideways) printing.

```
*Program to send a printer control code to a printer

SET TALK OFF
SET ECHO OFF

Wait "Change Laser Jet to landscape mode (Y/N): " TO Myes

IF UPPER(myes)="Y"
     ??? {27}&l1O
ENDIF
RETURN
```

Note the line ??? {027}&l1O in the preceding program. This is the line that does the work. The {27} is an ASCII equivalent of the ESC key. (See the ??? command in "Command Reference," Part Six, for more information on other ASCII codes you can use.) The &l1O that follows the {27} comes straight from the HP printer manual. Consult your own printer's manual for printer control codes that apply to your specific printer.

You can also use the ??? command to send dBASE IV system memory variables to your printer. dBASE IV system memory variables let you change type styles for printed output. However, when you use the ??? command to send system memory variables to your printer, the changes you make apply to the entire document. For more about dBASE IV system memory variables, see Chapter 34. For the ??? command, see Chapter 31.

The DISPLAY Command

As you recall from Chapter 7, you can use the DISPLAY command at the dot prompt to display data in a database. You can also use this command in a program. However, when you use DISPLAY in a program, you have more control over the the appearance of the screen. For example, the following program uses the LOCATE com-

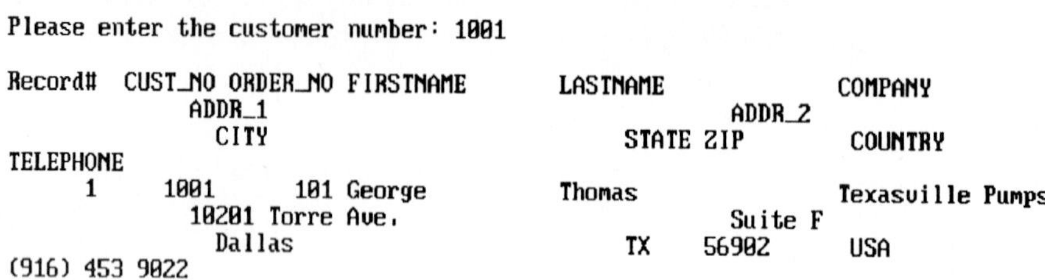

Please enter the customer number: 1001
Record# CUST_NO ORDER_NO FIRSTNAME LASTNAME COMPANY
ADDR_1 ADDR_2
CITY STATE ZIP COUNTRY
TELEPHONE
1 1001 101 George Thomas Texasville Pumps
10201 Torre Ave. Suite F
Dallas TX 56902 USA
(916) 453 9022

Figure 19-8. The DISPLAY command poorly executed

mand to search a database record in the database CUSTOMER.DBF. The DISPLAY command is then used just as you would use it from the dot prompt. Figure 19-8 shows the results. Note the disorganized appearance of the data.

```
SET ECHO OFF
SET TALK OFF
CLEAR
USE Customer
?
INPUT "Please enter the customer number: " TO Custno
LOCATE FOR Cust_no=Custno
IF FOUND()
     DISPLAY
ENDIF
RETURN
```

```
Please enter the account number: 101

RECORD  ACCOUNT CHECK NO.   DISBURSED     RECEIVED      DEBIT      CREDIT
======  ======= ========    =========     ========      =====      ======

     2  101       1217        2725.00         0.00       0.00        0.00
    80  101                      0.00         0.00    7678.20        0.00
    86  101       1218         500.00         0.00       0.00        0.00
    90  101                      0.00      5000.00       0.00        0.00
   107  101       1219         300.00         0.00       0.00        0.00
   116  101                      0.00      4500.00       0.00        0.00
   129  101                      0.00         0.00       0.00    13347.01
   130  101       1220        3500.00         0.00       0.00        0.00

Command ||C:\...chap20\ACCOUNT   ||Rec EOF/130   ||File ||   ||   Ins
```

Figure 19-9. The DISPLAY command under the control of a program

The following program, ACCTSRCH.PRG, cleans up the mess. This program uses an accounting database called ACCOUNT.DBF. It searches and displays all records that have a specific account number. The program uses a variable called Macct to store input from the user. Next, it uses the ? command to display its own set of underlined column titles. The DISPLAY command, with a qualifier, is then used to display the data.

The qualifier used in the DISPLAY command is FOR Acct_no=Macct, followed by the FIELDS command. This command tells dBASE IV to display only selected fields from records that have the appropriate account number in the Acct_no field of the ACCOUNT.DBF database. The order of the fields displayed is determined by the order in which they are listed after the FIELDS command. Figure 19-9 shows the results.

```
SET TALK OFF
SET ECHO OFF
CLEAR
USE Account
```

```
SET HEADING OFF
?
ACCEPT "Please enter the account number: " TO Macct
?
? "RECORD  ACCOUNT CHECK NO.    DISBURSED       RECEIVED       DEBIT        CREDIT"
? "======  ======= ========     =========       ========       =====        ======"
DISPLAY ALL FOR Acct_no=macct FIELDS Acct_no,Check_no,Disburse,Receipt,;
Debit,Credit
RETURN
```

If you want, you can qualify the DISPLAY command in the preceding program even further. For example, you could include another user-input command in the program to create a variable called Endacct for use in the DISPLAY ALL command. The variable would contain another account number entered by the user. Your program could then display all records that have an account number between Macct and Endacct. For example, the DISPLAY command line might read

```
DISPLAY ALL FOR Acct_no>=Macct .AND. Check_no<=endacct FIELDS;
Acct_no,Checkno,Disburse,Receipt,Debit,Credit
```

You can also have your program send data directly to your printer with the DISPLAY command, using the TO PRINT option. For example, you could use the command

```
DISPLAY ALL FOR Lastname = "Smith" TO PRINT.
```

with a mailing list database to display all records that have the name Smith in the Lastname field and send the output to your printer.

The TEXT...ENDTEXT Commands

The TEXT...ENDTEXT commands are a simple way to have your program display text on the screen. For example, the following program section uses these commands to place a mock license agreement on the screen before continuing with the rest of the program. Figure 19-10 shows the results.

```
This exclusive license agreement is granted to you under the authority of
Jack Spratt's Software, Inc. Failure to observe all the tenants of this
agreement may result in your license being revoked.

Press any key to continue...




FIG20_10 C:\...chap20\CUSTOMER  Rec 1/33  File
```

Figure 19-10. The TEXT...ENDTEXT command displays text

```
SET ECHO OFF
SET TALK OFF
CLEAR
?
TEXT
This exclusive license agreement is granted to you under the authority of
Jack Spratt's Software, Inc.  Failure to observe all the tenants of this
agreement may result in your license being revoked.
ENDTEXT
?
WAIT
RETURN
```

The @...SAY...GET and CLEAR GETS Commands

The @...SAY...GET command was introduced earlier in the chapter as a way to get user input. You can also use it to display output with the aid of the CLEAR GETS command. The CLEAR GETS command tells dBASE IV to release the GET part of an

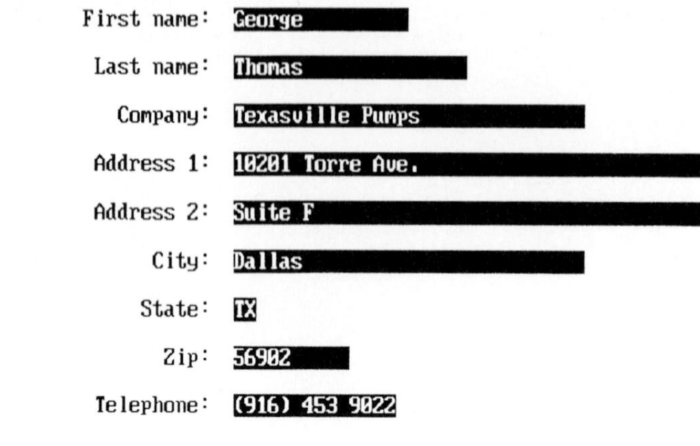

First name: George
Last name: Thomas
Company: Texasville Pumps
Address 1: 10201 Torre Ave.
Address 2: Suite F
City: Dallas
State: TX
Zip: 56902
Telephone: (916) 453 9022
FIG20_11 C:\...chap20\CUSTOMER Rec 1/33 File

Figure 19-11. The CLEAR GETS command allows display but does not allow editing

@...SAY...GET command. That way, the information in a database is displayed, but the user cannot edit the information. You must place the CLEAR GETS command immediately in front of a READ command that is used to display @...SAY...GET commands.

The following program demonstrates the CLEAR GETS command. The program locates a record in a database called CUSTOMER.DBF and uses a series of @...SAY...GET commands to place the information in the record on the screen. The READ command following the @...SAY...GET commands activates the @...SAY...GET commands. However, immediately prior to the READ command, the CLEAR GETS command makes this output display only. Figure 19-11 shows the results.

Tip: You can also use a CLEAR GETS command in a format file to declare @...SAY...GET commands above the CLEAR GETS command "off limits" for editing.

```
SET ECHO OFF
SET TALK OFF
CLEAR
USE Customer
STORE 0 TO Choice
@ 10,10 SAY "Please enter the customer number" GET Choice
READ
LOCATE FOR Cust_no=Choice
CLEAR
@ 2,5 SAY "  First name: " GET Firstname
@ 4,5 SAY "   Last name: " GET Lastname
@ 6,5 SAY "     Company: " GET Company
@ 8,5 SAY "   Address 1: " GET Addr_1
@ 10,5 SAY "   Address 2: " GET Addr_2
@ 12,5 SAY "        City: " GET City
@ 14,5 SAY "       State: " GET State
@ 16,5 SAY "         :Zip: " GET Zip
@ 18,5 SAY "   Telephone: " GET Telephone
CLEAR GETS
READ
RETURN
```

The @...SAY Command

You can use the @...SAY command, without a GET, to display data. If you precede this command with SET DEVICE TO PRINT, dBASE IV sends the output of the command to your printer. To revert back to screen display, enter SET DEVICE TO SCREEN.

The syntax for the @...SAY command is @ *<row>*,*<column>* SAY *<any acceptable dBASE expression>*. You can use memory variables, strings in quotes, and mathematical equations with the @...SAY command.

The advantage to the @...SAY command is its "point-and-shoot" capability. That is, you can specify screen coordinates and display data on the screen with a high degree of control. For example, the following program shows some ways that you can

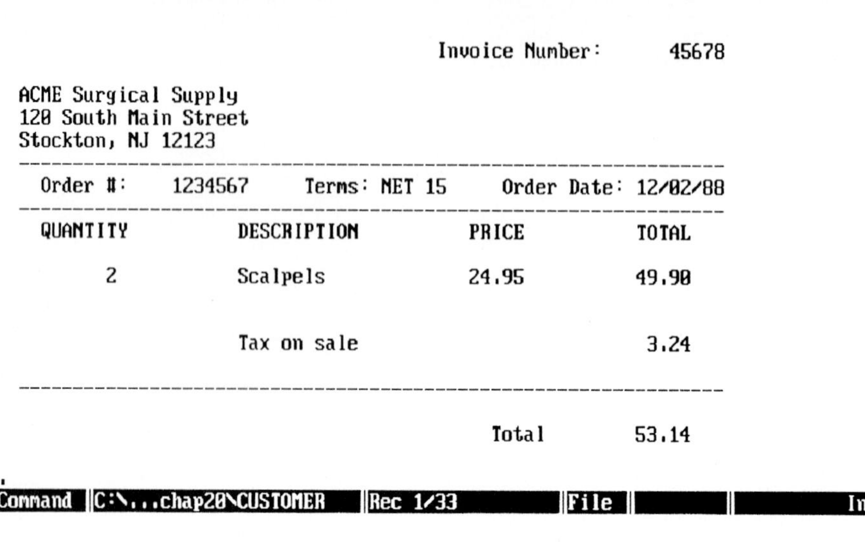

Invoice Number: 45678
ACME Surgical Supply
120 South Main Street
Stockton, NJ 12123
Order #: 1234567 Terms: NET 15 Order Date: 12/02/88
QUANTITY DESCRIPTION PRICE TOTAL
2 Scalpels 24.95 49.90
Tax on sale 3.24
Total 53.14
Command C:\...chap20\CUSTOMER Rec 1/33 File In

Figure 19-12. A mock invoice generated using @...SAY commands

manipulate text strings and memory variables with the @...SAY command. The result is the mock invoice in Figure 19-12.

```
*Program that shows the point and shoot capabilties of @@...SAY

SET TALK OFF
SET ECHO OFF
CLEAR

*---------Store some variables for use in @@...SAY commands

STORE 1234567 TO Ord
STORE 45678 TO Invno
STORE 2 to Units
STORE 24.95 TO Price
STORE .065 TO Tax
STORE DATE() to Today
STORE "NET 15" TO Terms
STORE "ACME Surgical Supply" TO Name
STORE "120 South Main Street" TO Addrl
```

```
STORE "Stockton, NJ 12123" TO Addr2
STORE "--------------------------------------------------------;
--------" TO line

*---------Build and on-screen invoice using @...SAY commands

@ 2,40  SAY "Invoice Number: "+TRIM(STR(Invno))
@ 4,2   SAY Name
@ 5,2   SAY Addr1
@ 6,2   SAY Addr2
@ 7,2   SAY Line
@ 8,4   SAY "Order #: "+STR(Ord)+SPACE(5)+"Terms: "+Terms+SPACE(5)+;
"Order Date: "+DTOC(Today)
@ 9,2   SAY Line
@ 10,4  SAY "QUANTITY"+SPACE(10)+"DESCRIPTION"+SPACE(10)+"PRICE";
+SPACE(10)+"TOTAL"
@ 12,1  SAY Units
@ 12,22 SAY "Scalpels"
@ 12,35 SAY Price
@ 12,50 SAY Units*Price
@ 15,22 SAY "Tax on sale"
@ 15,50 SAY (Units*Price)*Tax
@ 17,2  SAY Line
@ 19,45 SAY "Total: "
@ 19,50 SAY (Units*Price)*Tax+(Units*Price)
```

In this chapter, you've learned the basics of getting user input both through the user-input commands and through custom forms. You've also learned how to display data on both your screen and your printer.

Program Control

Decision-making Commands
Looping
Nesting
Macro Substitution
Subprograms and Procedures

TWENTY

This chapter shows you some commands and techniques for controlling your dBASE IV programs. As you might expect, you control a program by placing special command lines at key points within the program. These command lines determine whether and how often a section of code is processed.

The chapter begins with a discussion of conditional statements, commands that allow your programs to make decisions. It then discusses looping, a commonly used technique for repeating selected program sections. This chapter also shows you how to pass information to subprograms and procedures.

Decision-making Commands

You can get a dBASE IV program to make a decision by using a conditional statement. A conditional statement evaluates a condition and then acts upon it. If the condition is true, one course of action is taken. If the condition is not true, another course of action is taken.

You can also make your program deal with multiple conditions. dBASE IV itself provides examples of multiple conditions. For instance, most of the Control Center pull-down menus involve multiple choices. Depending upon which menu option you select (which condition you specify), dBASE IV must take a given course of action.

The IF...ELSE...ENDIF Command

The IF...ELSE...ENDIF command is one of the most frequently used conditional statements in dBASE IV. It is primarily used to evaluate a single condition. The syntax for this command is

```
IF <condition>
      *Execute these command lines
ELSE
      *Execute these command lines
ENDIF
```

When the condition following the IF command is true, dBASE IV executes the commands immediately following IF. When the condition following the IF statement is false, dBASE IV jumps directly to the ELSE command and executes the lines following it. After dBASE IV finishes processing the commands between the IF...ENDIF commands, it passes control to the command line immediately following the ENDIF. The ELSE command is optional in the IF...ENDIF statement. If an ELSE command is not included, and the condition following IF evaluates as false, dBASE IV jumps directly to the command line following ENDIF.

There is virtually no limit to the number of IF...ENDIF statements you can include in a program. However, every IF command must be followed by an ENDIF command.

Tip: dBASE IV ignores any text immediately to the right of an ENDIF command. If you leave at least one space after the ENDIF, you can include a program note there without using &&.

The ELSE part of the statement is optional, but, if used, it must appear between the IF and the ENDIF commands to which it corresponds. For example, if several IF...ENDIF commands are nested together (as explained in the following section, "Nesting IF...ENDIF commands"), an ELSE command applies to the immediately preceding IF command.

The following program includes an IF...ELSE...ENDIF statement. It first prompts the user for a response and stores that response to a memory variable called Answr. Then an IF...ELSE...ENDIF statement evaluates the contents of the variable. If Answr contains a "Y", dBASE IV appends a blank record to the database and displays a custom form. If Answr contains an "N" or is blank, the program resets TALK to ON and clears the screen.

```
Program is IF1.prg
The program's purpose is to demonstrate an IF..ENDIF statement
SET TALK OFF
CLEAR
?
Accept " Do you want to continue data entry (Y/N)?: " to Answr

IF UPPER(Answr)="Y"
     APPEND BLANK
     SET FORMAT TO Screen 1
     READ
ELSE
     SET TALK ON
     CLEAR
ENDIF

RETURN
```

You can also use the IF...ENDIF statement to determine if a program section should be processed at all. For example, the following section of code asks the user to respond to a question. If the proper response is given, the section of code between IF and ENDIF is processed. Otherwise, the program section is skipped.

```
Accept " Do you want a printed report on this (Y/N)? " TO Decide
IF UPPER(Decide) = "Y"
     USE Sales INDEX Sales
     REPORT FORM Sales TO PRINT
ENDIF
```

Using Multiple IF...ENDIF Commands

You can follow one IF...ENDIF statement in your program with another. This allows you to evaluate several independent conditions within a program section. For example, the following section of code captures user input regarding bell and color settings. It then uses two different IF...ENDIF statements to evaluate the input.

```
WAIT " Turn the system bell off (Y/N)? " TO belloff
?
WAIT " Display database fields in color (Y/N)? " TO Coloron

IF Belloff="Y"
     SET BELL OFF
ENDIF

IF ISCOLOR( ) .AND. Coloron="Y"
     SET COLOR TO B/W             && Blue on white background
ENDIF
```

Note that in order for the second IF...ENDIF to be processed, two conditions must be met. First, the ISCOLOR( ) function must be true. That is, there must be a color monitor in use. Second, the memory variable Coloron must contain "Y". If either one of these conditions is not met, the line SET COLOR TO B/W is skipped and dBASE IV passes control to the command line following the ENDIF.

Nesting IF...ENDIF Commands

You can also nest IF...ENDIF statements. *Nesting* refers to placing one IF...ENDIF statement within another. For an internal IF...ENDIF statement to be processed, the condition for the IF...ENDIF statement that surrounds it must first be true. For example, the following section of code shows two nested IF...ENDIF statements that accomplish the same task as the previous example accomplished.

```
WAIT " Display database fields in color (Y/N)? " TO Coloron

IF Coloron="Y"
     IF ISCOLOR( )
          SET COLOR TO B/W       && Blue on white background
     ENDIF
ENDIF
```

In this example, the outer IF...ENDIF statement controls the IF...ENDIF statement contained within it. If the condition Coloron="Y" in the first IF command is not true, the internal IF...ENDIF statement is not processed at all. dBASE IV skips directly to the last ENDIF. On the other hand, if the first condition, Coloron="Y", is true, the internal IF...ENDIF statement is processed. Thus, in order for the command line SET COLOR TO B/W to be processed, the conditions in both the first and second IF...ENDIF statements must evaluate to true.

IIF( )—the Abbreviated IF...ENDIF

The IIF( ) function is an abbreviated form of the IF...ENDIF command. The syntax for the IIF( ) function is

IIF(*<condition>*,*<expression 1>*,*<expression 2>*)

If the condition is true, dBASE IV performs the first expression. If not, it performs the second one. For example, the following program line includes an IIF( ) function:

```
Totl=(Units*Price)*IIF(Tax=.T.,1.065,1)
```

where Totl and is a memory variable, Units and Price are numeric database fields, and Tax is a logical database field. The program line uses the IIF( ) function to determine whether to add tax to the memory variable Totl. If Tax contains .T., the expression (Units*Price) is multiplied by 1.065. However, if Tax contains .F., the expression (Units*Price) is multiplied by 1.

The DO CASE...CASE...OTHERWISE...ENDCASE Commands

The DO CASE....ENDCASE conditional statement is used to respond to a single event from among multiple possibilities. This statement works like a multiple-choice menu in which multiple courses of action are available yet only one is selected. The format of the DO CASE...ENDCASE statement is as follows:

DO CASE

CASE *<condition 1>*

    * Execute these commands

CASE *<condition 2>*

    * Execute these commands

OTHERWISE

    * Execute these commands

ENDCASE

When dBASE IV enters the DO CASE...ENDCASE statement, it evaluates the CASE *<condition>* statements in the sequence in which they appear. (You can include as many CASE *<condition>* statements as you want.) When it finds a CASE *<condition>* statement that is true, it executes the command lines immediately following it. When execution of these command lines is complete, dBASE IV jumps directly to the command line following the ENDCASE.

If none of the CASE <*condition*> statements are true, dBASE IV goes directly to the OTHERWISE statement and executes the command lines immediately following it. If an OTHERWISE statement is not included in the DO CASE...ENDCASE statement and none of the CASE conditions are true, dBASE IV jumps directly to the command line following ENDCASE.

You can include a virtually unlimited number of DO CASE...ENDCASE statements in a program. However, you must follow each DO CASE command with an ENDCASE. Furthermore, if you use an OTHERWISE statement, it must appear between the DO CASE and ENDCASE commands to which it corresponds. If you nest multiple DO CASE...ENDCASE statements within a program, an OTHERWISE command applies to the immediately preceding DO CASE.

The following program, MAINMENU.PRG, includes a DO CASE...ENDCASE statement. The program drives a multiple-choice menu. It begins by building a four-option menu on the screen and storing the user's response to a memory variable called Choice. The following DO CASE...ENDCASE statement includes a CASE <*condition*> statement for each of the four menu options. After each of the first three CASE <*condition*> statements, a DO command activates a different subprogram. When a subprogram finishes running, it returns control to this program and executes the line following the DO command. In this case, that command line is ENDCASE.

```
* The program is MAINMENU.PRG
* This program puts up a main menu for an order entry system

* --------------Set Environmental Parameters

SET TALK OFF
CLEAR

*----------------Start program body

* ----------------Build the Screen

?"                  ================================"
?"                  === ORDER ENTRY SYSTEM MENU ==="
```

```
?"                        ================================"
?
?"                         TASK CODE     TASK DESCRIPTION"
?
?"                         [A]...........ENTER an ORDER"
?"                         [B]...........EDIT an ORDER"
?"                         [C]...........PRINT INVOICES"
?"                         [Q]...........QUIT"
?
?

* --------------Get input from the user

WAIT  "         Enter your choice (type in task code): " TO Choice

* --------------Evaluate the user's response

DO CASE

     CASE UPPER(Choice)="A"
          DO ORDFORM
     CASE UPPER(Choice)="B"
          DO ORDEREDI
     CASE UPPER(Choice)="C"
          DO INVPRIN
     OTHERWISE
          RETURN
ENDCASE
```

The DO CASE...ENDCASE statement also includes an OTHERWISE statement. This statement handles situations where you press a key not included in any of the CASE <*condition*> statements. The RETURN command immediately following the OTHERWISE statement returns control to dBASE IV.

You can also nest one DO CASE...ENDCASE statement within another. For example, the following syntax for the DO CASE...ENDCASE command is acceptable in dBASE IV:

DO CASE

CASE <*condition 1*>

CASE <*condition 2*>

DO CASE

CASE <*condition A*>

```
            CASE <condition B>
        ENDCASE
    OTHERWISE
ENDCASE
```

Looping

Looping is a technique you can use to have dBASE IV repeat a program section. As with the decision-making commands just explained, you control looping with a conditional statement. As long as the condition remains true, dBASE IV repeats the program section. When the condition becomes false, dBASE IV exits the loop and continues with the rest of your program.

The DO WHILE...LOOP...EXIT...ENDDO Commands

The DO WHILE...LOOP...EXIT...ENDDO commands are the most common looping commands in dBASE IV. The syntax for the DO WHILE...ENDDO statement is as follows:

```
DO WHILE <condition>
    * Series of dBASE IV commands
    [LOOP]
    [EXIT]
ENDDO
```

For the commands within the DO WHILE and ENDDO commands to be processed, the condition following the DO WHILE command must be true. If not, the program section is skipped and dBASE IV picks up processing with the command line following ENDDO.

The DO WHILE and ENDDO commands form the boundaries of the loop. The DO WHILE command starts the loop and the ENDDO command reevaluates the condition following the DO WHILE command each time through the loop. If the condition remains true, the program section is repeated. If not, the program section is skipped and dBASE IV passes control to the command line following ENDDO.

The LOOP command within a DO WHILE...ENDDO loop is optional. However, if a LOOP command is encountered prior to the ENDDO command, dBASE IV loops back to the DO WHILE statement. The commands between the LOOP and the ENDDO commands are not processed. If, upon looping back to the DO WHILE statement, the condition is still true, the program section is repeated.

The EXIT command is also an option you can use within a DO WHILE...ENDDO loop. However, if an EXIT command is encountered within a DO WHILE...ENDDO loop, dBASE IV exits the loop and passes control to the command line following ENDDO. This is one of the more common techniques for exiting a program loop in dBASE IV.

The following program includes a DO WHILE...ENDDO loop. The menu program used in the previous section has been enhanced to include a DO WHILE...ENDDO loop. In this case, the loop continuously repeats the body of the program.

```
* The program is MAINMEN.PRG
* This program controlls a menu using a DO WHILE...ENDDO loop

* --------------Set Environmental Parameters
SET TALK OFF
CLEAR
*-----------------Start program body

DO WHILE .T.

* ----------------Build the Screen

     ?"                    ================================"
     ?"                    === ORDER ENTRY SYSTEM MENU ==="
     ?"                    ================================"
     ?
```

```
    ?"                        TASK CODE     TASK DESCRIPTION"
    ?
    ?"                        [A]...........ENTER an ORDER"
    ?"                        [B]...........EDIT an ORDER"
    ?"                        [C]...........PRINT INVOICES"
    ?"                        [Q]...........QUIT"
    ?
    ?

    * --------------Get input from the user

    WAIT  "         Enter your choice (type in task code): " TO Choice

    * --------------Evaluate the user's response

    DO CASE

         CASE UPPER(Choice)="A"
              DO ORDFORM
         CASE UPPER(Choice)="B"
              DO ORDEREDI
         CASE UPPER(Choice)="C"
              DO INVPRIN
         CASE UPPER(Choice)="Q"
              EXIT
         OTHERWISE
              LOOP
    ENDCASE

ENDDO

RETURN
```

Note that the DO WHILE command itself reads

DO WHILE .T.

This places a condition that is always true after the DO WHILE command. Thus, the loop is processed repeatedly until either an EXIT command is encountered, which exits the loop, or a RETURN command is encountered, which returns control to dBASE IV.

An EXIT command is used to exit the loop in the previous program. Note its location after the

CASE UPPER(Choice)="Q"

command that appears within the DO CASE...ENDCASE statement. Thus, if the "Q" option is selected and stored to the variable

Choice, dBASE IV exits the loop and passes control to the command line immediately following ENDDO. In this case, it is the RETURN command, which returns control to dBASE IV.

A LOOP command appears in the program as well. This command is located after the OTHERWISE command within the DO CASE...ENDCASE statement. That way, if you press a key other than those included in the previous CASE statements, the program loops back to the DO WHILE .T. command, displays the menu again, and waits for another user response.

An alternative to the DO WHILE .T. command in the previous program is

```
DO WHILE Choice<>Q
```

In order to use this command, however, you should remove the EXIT command which appears after the command line

```
CASE UPPER(Choice)="Q"
```

Thus, when this CASE statement is reached, its condition is found to be true. However, there are no command lines to process so dBASE IV skips immediately to the ENDDO command. The ENDDO command then reevaluates the DO WHILE condition

```
DO WHILE Choice<>Q
```

Now the Choice variable does equal "Q" and the condition is no longer valid. Therefore, the program section within the DO WHILE...ENDDO loop is not repeated and dBASE IV passes control to the command line following ENDDO. In this case, that command line is RETURN, and control is returned to dBASE IV.

You can also use the DO WHILE...ENDDO construction to control user input. For example, the following program section uses a DO WHILE...ENDDO loop to control an @...SAY...GET command. The program won't let you out of the loop until you enter the proper response.

```
STORE " " TO Choice
DO WHILE .NOT. UPPER(Choice) $"ABCQ"
     @ 19,5 SAY " Please enter your choice (A,B,C, or Q): "  GET Choice
     READ
     IF .NOT. Upper(Choice) $"ABCQ"
          @ 21,5 SAY "Improper Key Selected"
     ENDIF
ENDDO
```

The program first creates a variable called Choice and stores a blank in it. It then uses

```
.NOT. UPPER(Choice) $"ABCQ"
```

as a condition for a DO WHILE...ENDDO loop. (The $ relational operator performs a substring comparison. That is, the value of UPPER(Choice) must be contained within "ABCQ" to generate a logical true.) Once inside the loop, your input is stored in the Choice variable. If you enter the correct response (A, B, C, or Q), the condition following DO WHILE becomes true, and dBASE IV exits the loop and continues with your program. Otherwise, the command @...SAY...GET is redisplayed for the proper response.

There are an infinite number of ways to use program loops in dBASE IV. This section only covers a few of them. However, other examples of loops appear throughout Part Three and Part Five of this book.

The SCAN...LOOP...EXIT...ENDSCAN Commands

The SCAN...LOOP...EXIT...ENDSCAN commands are an alternative to the DO WHILE...ENDDO commands. However, you use the SCAN...ENDSCAN commands exclusively to scan and act on information in database records. Thus, you must activate a database before using the SCAN...ENDSCAN command structure. The syntax for the SCAN...ENDSCAN commands is

```
SCAN [<scope>] FOR [<condition>] WHILE [<condition>]

    * Series of dBASE IV commands

    [LOOP]

    [EXIT]

ENDSCAN
```

The SCAN...ENDSCAN commands make dBASE IV loop through each record in the database, one by one, until it finds a record that matches the scope or conditions following the SCAN command. When it finds such a record, dBASE IV executes all the commands between the SCAN and ENDSCAN commands, jumps to the next record, and starts the scanning process over again. When dBASE IV has reviewed all the records in the database and determined that no more records meet the criteria following the SCAN command, it exits the SCAN...ENDSCAN loop and continues with the command line following ENDSCAN.

Normally, the SCAN command starts scanning at the first record in the database. However, the *scope* qualifier following the SCAN command lets you select a group of records within the database. If you don't use a *scope* qualifier, dBASE IV uses *all* the records in the active database. The following are some sample *scope* qualifiers to scan for specific records whose fields contain data that meet a given condition:

- **SCAN RECORD 5** Start scan at record number 5.
- **SCAN NEXT 20** Starting at current record, scan next 20 records.

You can use the FOR [*condition*] following the SCAN command to specify records whose fields contain data that meets a given condition. For example, imagine you're working with a mailing list database. Each record in the database contains an alphanumeric field called Zip. You're interested in all records that have a ZIP code of 95073. The following section of code activates the MAILIST.DBF database, scans all its records, and displays those records whose Zip field contains 95073.

```
USE Mailist
SCAN FOR Zip="95073"
     ? Firstname,Lastname,Address,City,State,Zip
ENDSCAN
```

The SCAN command also supports a WHILE *condition* that allows you to further limit the SCAN...ENDSCAN looping operation. The WHILE *condition* after the SCAN...ENDSCAN command performs the same function as the WHILE *condition* part of the DO WHILE *condition*...ENDDO loop. As long as the condition remains true, the loop is performed. For example, imagine you are working with a mailing list database that is indexed on last name. In addition, you only want to print those records A through Smith. The command

```
SCAN WHILE Lastname < "Smith"
```

scans the database for records until the name Smith is encountered in the Lastname field.

The SCAN...ENDSCAN commands are a replacement for the DO WHILE .NOT. EOF( )...ENDDO construction. For example, the following program uses a DO WHILE .NOT. EOF( )...ENDDO construction to loop through the records in a mailing list database. This time, the MAILIST.DBF database is indexed on the Zip field. Furthermore, it contains a logical field called Oktomail, indicating those clients to whom it is OK to mail.

The loop in the following program is started by the command line

```
DO WHILE .NOT. EOF( ) .AND. Zip=<60000
```

The EOF( ) function identifies an end-of-file marker. When the end-of-file marker is reached, the EOF( ) function becomes true and dBASE IV exits the loop. The second condition in the command line,

```
.AND. Zip=<60000
```

tells dBASE IV to exit the loop when it reaches a number less than or equal to 60,000 in the indexed Zip field. The IF...ENDIF conditional statement nested within the DO WHILE...ENDDO loop evaluates the Oktomail logical field for each record each time through the loop.

Note the use of the SKIP command in the following program. You need this with DO WHILE...ENDDO in order to get dBASE IV to skip to the next record each time through the loop. Recall that the SCAN...ENDSCAN commands automatically skip to the next record for you.

```
SET TALK OFF
SET ECHO OFF
USE Mailist ORDER Zip
GO TOP
DO WHILE .NOT. EOF( ) .AND. Zip<="60000"
     IF Oktomail
          ?
          ? TRIM(Firstname)+" "+TRIM(Lastname)
          ? Addr_1
          ? Addr_2
          ? TRIM(City)+", "+State+" "+Zip
          ?
          ?
     ENDIF
     SKIP
ENDDO
WAIT
RETURN
```

The following program performs the operation performed in the previous example. However, it uses the SCAN...ENDSCAN commands rather than DO WHILE .NOT. EOF( )...ENDDO construction to display records. Note that there is less code involved. The command

```
SCAN FOR Oktomail WHILE Zip=<"60000"
```

evaluates both the Oktomail logical field and the indexed Zip field in a single command line. Since the SCAN...ENDSCAN loop automatically advances by one record each time through the loop, a SKIP command is not required. As soon as dBASE IV reaches a record that has a number less than or equal to 60,000 in the Zip field, it exits the SCAN...ENDSCAN loop.

```
USE Mailist ORDER ZIP
SCAN FOR Oktomail WHILE Zip<="60000"
     ?
     ? TRIM(Firstname)+" "+TRIM(Lastname)
     ? Addr_1
     ? Addr_2
     ? TRIM(City)+", "+State+" "+Zip
     ?
     ?
ENDSCAN
WAIT
RETURN
```

Nesting

The term nesting refers to placing one command structure inside another. However, you must make sure to open and close each command structure. That is, each DO CASE must have an ENDCASE, each DO WHILE must have an ENDDO, and so forth.

There are virtually an infinite number of ways that you can nest together the decision-making commands and looping commands. What follows is just one example.

```
DO WHILE
     SCAN
          DO CASE
               IF
               ENDIF
```

```
            ENDCASE
        ENDSCAN
    ENDDO
```

When nesting commands, you can avoid some common pitfalls by keeping a few simple tips in mind.

- When you are nesting multiple IF...ELSE...ENDIF statements, each ELSE applies to the immediately preceding IF.
- When you are nesting multiple DO CASE...OTHERWISE...ENDCASE statements, each OTHERWISE applies to the immediately preceding DO CASE.
- When you are nesting the DO WHILE...ENDDO and SCAN...ENDSCAN statements, both command structures allow LOOP and EXIT commands. These commands apply to the most recently activated loop.
- Use indentation to help you keep track of nested loops and conditional statements. With indentation, you can determine at a glance where conditional statements and loops both begin and end.

Macro Substitution

You can use *macro substitution* with the decision-making and looping commands to help control your program. You accomplish macro substitution by using the & function followed by a variable name. For example, the following program uses the & function to substitute the contents of a memory variable named Insert for the condition in a SCAN...ENDSCAN command sequence. It also uses the contents of a memory variable called Pchange within the body of the SCAN...ENDSCAN. After macro substitution, the SCAN command line reads

```
SCAN FOR Part_no=Findit
```

Similarly, the REPLACE command line reads

```
REPLACE Price WITH Increase
```

```
STORE "Part_no=Findit" TO Insert
STORE "Price WITH Increase" TO Pchange
INPUT "Please enter the part number: " TO Findit
INPUT "Please enter the new price:  " TO Increase
SCAN FOR &Insert
     REPLACE &Pchange
ENDSCAN
```

When you use macro substitution to specify a condition for a DO WHILE...ENDDO loop, make sure that you don't change the macro's contents from inside the loop. dBASE IV performs the macro substitution only once at the beginning the loop. Therefore, once the loop is in progress, it won't recognize any changes you make to the variables or field names that affect the DO WHILE *condition*.

Subprograms and Procedures

As your programs grow in size and complexity, they can become difficult to manage. An easy way to limit the size and complexity of a program is to break it down into subprograms and procedures. You can then call the subprograms and procedures from higher level programs as you need them. By parceling out the work to subprograms and procedures, you limit the size and complexity of any one module. Your programs will become much easier to code and maintain.

The Difference Between Subprograms and Procedures

In dBASE IV, you can call one program from another with the DO *<filename>* command. dBASE IV locates the subprogram in the current directory and begins executing it. When dBASE IV completes the called program, it returns to the line following the DO command in the calling program.

Procedures are just like subprograms, except that they begin with a PROCEDURE command and end with a RETURN. What's more, procedures can reside in the current file or in other separate command files. In this way, you can place multiple procedures in a single file and call each of them by their individual names.

Actually, dBASE IV makes very little distinction between subprograms and procedures. When you compile a command file into an object code file (.DBO file), dBASE IV creates a *procedure list* from the contents of the file. The procedure list contains the name of the command file along with the names and locations of all the procedures within the file. Any procedure in the procedure list can be called by any other subsequently activated command file (or procedure), and vice versa. Therefore, program files are, for all practical purposes, identical to procedures.

Calling a Procedure

As mentioned, all procedures, whether they appear in the current command file or in an independent file, must begin with the PROCEDURE command and end with the RETURN command. (The RETURN command returns control to the calling program.) If you place more than one procedure in a file, each procedure must still begin with the PROCEDURE command and end with RETURN. The syntax for the PROCEDURE command is

PROCEDURE *<procedure name>*

For example, to assign the name Cleanup to a procedure, enter **PROCEDURE Cleanup** as the first line of the procedure.

Procedure names follow the same conventions as file names, but without the .PRG extension. That is, they can be up to eight characters long, must start with a letter, and may include numbers and underscores. The maximum number of procedures you can include in a file is 963.

Tip: Be careful not to give a procedure the same name as the program that calls it.

How dBASE IV Locates Procedures

When your program calls a procedure, dBASE IV looks in the following places to find it:

1. The current command file
2. A command file activated with the SET PROCEDURE command
3. Other active .DBO compiled files, in the order in which they were activated
4. Inactive .DBO files with the same name, which are then activated
5. An uncompiled (.PRG) file with the same name, which is then automatically compiled

If a procedure is contained in a separate command file but it does not bear the same name as that command file, you must use the SET PROCEDURE command to activate it. For example, to activate a procedure called Cleanup in a command file called CLOSEOUT.PRG, include the command line

```
SET PROCEDURE TO Closeout
```

in your program. dBASE IV searches for and opens the command file that contains the procedure. You can then call the Cleanup procedure from your program at any time by using the DO command.

Examples of Using Procedures

The following example shows the structure of a command file called ORDFORM.PRG, which contains two procedures, Proc1 and Proc2. Both procedures are called from within the main program.

```
*
* ORDFORM.PRG-order entry program
*


*
* Commands for the Ordform program
*
DO Proc1
DO Proc2
*
*
RETURN

PROCEDURE Proc1
* Commands for Proc1
RETURN

PROCEDURE Proc2
* Commands for Proc2
RETURN
```

Suppose you want to create a separate procedure library file containing Proc1 and Proc2. You would need the following structure:

```
*
* ORDFORM.PRG—order-entry program
*

SET PROCEDURE TO PROCLIB
*
* Other commands for the Ordform program
*
DO Proc1
DO Proc2
*
*
RETURN
```

The file PROCLIB.PRG would contain Proc1 and Proc2.

```
PROCEDURE Proc1
* Commands for Proc1
RETURN

PROCEDURE Proc2
* Commands for Proc2
RETURN
```

Passing Information to Subprograms and Procedures

In dBASE IV, you can pass information to subprograms and procedures from higher level programs. This lets you control the information a subprogram or procedure uses when it is executed.

The vehicle for passing information to subprograms or procedures is the DO...WITH command. This command activates a subprogram or procedure and is always located in the calling program. It is paired with the PARAMETERS command, which is always located in the subprogram or procedure being called. The DO...WITH command sends the information from the calling program; the PARAMETERS command receives that information in the subprogram or procedure.

The syntax for the DO...WITH command is

DO <*program name*> WITH <*parameter list*>

where *program name* is the name of a dBASE IV program or procedure file and *parameter list* is a list of memory variables, values, dates, calculations, or character strings, separated by commas.

You can send virtually any type of data from a calling program to a subprogram or procedure using the DO...WITH command. However, the parameter list in the calling program must match the parameter list in the subprogram or procedure, both in terms of the number of items and the data types. Furthermore, the PARAMETERS command should appear at the top of the receiving subprogram or procedure to immediately accept the incoming data. The syntax for the PARAMETERS command is

PARAMETERS <*parameter list*>

The following two programs demonstrate the DO...WITH and PARAMETERS commands. The first program, CALLER.PRG, is an excerpt from an order entry program. When you press Q to quit order entry, the program stores the contents of selected database fields to memory variables. The first two fields, Cust_no and Order_no, are numeric. The third field, Inv_no, is a character field. The fourth field, Order_date, is a date field. The fifth field, Total, is another numeric field. When the contents of these fields are stored to memory variables, those memory variables automatically take on the same data type as the database fields that were assigned to them.

The command line

```
DO Receive WITH Custno,Orderno,Invno,Orderdate, Total
```

tells dBASE IV to start the subprogram called RECEIVE.PRG. It also tells dBASE IV to pass to that subprogram the contents of the variables following the DO...WITH command.

```
* Program is Caller
* Exerpt from order entry program
* Program sends data as parameters to a subprogram that updates Acctsrec

SET TALK OFF
SET BELL OFF
USE Orderrec

STORE " " TO Choice
DO WHILE .NOT. UPPER(Choice) $"ABCQ"
     @@ 19,5 SAY " Please enter your choice (A,B,C, or Q): "  GET Choice
     READ
ENDDO

IF UPPER(Choice)="Q"
     STORE Cust_no TO Custno
     STORE Order_no TO Orderno
     STORE Inv_no TO Invno
     STORE Order_date TO Orderdate
     STORE Total TO Totl

     DO Receive WITH Custno,Orderno,Invno,Orderdate,Totl

ENDIF
RETURN
```

The second program, RECEIVE.PRG, is the receiving subprogram. Note that the PARAMETERS command begins the program. Also note that the *parameters list* following the PARAMETERS command matches the number of items and data types of the *parameters list* following the DO...WITH command in the first program. RECEIVE.PRG then appends a record to the ACCTSREC.DBF database. It uses the REPLACE command to replace the empty record in the ACCTSREC with the parameters passed to it by CALLER.PRG.

```
* Program is RECEIVE.PRG
* Program called by CALLER.PRG
* Program uses Acctsrec.dbf
* Program appends a record for later use
* Program accepts parameters from CALLER.PRG

PARAMETERS Cust,Order,Inv,Date,Totl

USE Acctsrec
APPEND BLANK
REPLACE Cust_no WITH Cust, Order_no with Order,Inv_no WITH ;
Inv,Order_date WITH Date,Total WITH Totl
RETURN
```

The next program, called TERM.PRG, demonstrates the DO...WITH and PARAMETERS commands used to call a procedure named Cterm contained in the same command file. The procedure calculates the number of periods it will take for an investment to reach a specified future value at a fixed rate of interest. Note that the techniques just described are used to activate the procedure and pass parameters to it. However, in this case the procedure uses the Answer memory variable to pass information back to the calling program so that it can be displayed on the screen. The Answer variable is given a zero value at the beginning of the main program and is then assigned a new value using the calculation in the Cterm procedure. If the same procedure were located in a separate file of procedures called PROC.PRG, you would also need to include the command

```
SET PROCEDURE TO Proc
```

to activate the file that contained the Cterm procedure. However, upon completion of the Cterm procedure, the information is still passed back to the calling program for display.

```
* Program uses a procedure to calculate the number of periods required;
* for an investment to reach a specific future value at a fixed rate;
* of interest.

SET TALK OFF
SET ECHO OFF
CLEAR
STORE 0 TO Answer

INPUT " Please enter the initial investment: " TO Pv
?
INPUT " Please enter the desired future value: " TO Fv
?
INPUT " Please enter the interest rate: " TO Int

DO Cterm WITH Pv,Fv,Int
?
? " The term for this investment is "+LTRIM(STR(Answer))+" "+"periods"

PROCEDURE Cterm
PARAMETERS Pv,Fv,Int
Answer=LOG(Fv/Pv)/LOG(1+Int)
RETURN
```

In this chapter, you've learned some commands and techniques for controlling your programs. You now know how to let your programs make decisions by using conditional statements. You also know how to use loops to repeat sections of a program and scan for records in a database. Furthermore, you've learned about subprograms and procedures and how to pass parameters to them.

Working with Databases

TWENTY ONE

This chapter addresses issues of interest to programmers working with databases. In particular, it covers entering data in a database and using multiple databases.

Entering data into a database, from a programmer's viewpoint, is different than simply entering data from the dot prompt. Often your program needs to control which record is being edited as well as what data is being placed in that record.

Some sophisticated applications require more than one database. This chapter shows you how to have more than one database active at any one time as well as how to relate one database to another.

Adding Data

From the dot prompt, you can use the APPEND command to add records to a database. You can also use APPEND in your programs, but it does not provide the level of control you need to properly manage data entry in important databases. The APPEND command allows users to page up and down through the records in the database and alter records as they please. In this context, the user rather than your program, controls which records in the database are altered.

There is another disadvantage to the APPEND command. With APPEND, your program cannot perform any calculations using data in the current or another database until the APPEND command is finished. This true for both background and on-screen calculations.

The APPEND BLANK Command

You can use the APPEND BLANK command to restrict data entry to a single record. This command appends a single blank record to the end of a database. Once the record is appended, dBASE IV moves the record pointer to the new record, which becomes the active record. Your program can then fill in the fields for the record as appropriate.

In order to use the APPEND BLANK command, your program must first activate a database. The following section of code illustrates the syntax of the APPEND BLANK command:

```
USE Customer
APPEND BLANK
```

Your user cannot see the effects of the APPEND BLANK command, other than as an increased number of records in the database. Furthermore, programs that issue an APPEND BLANK command retain control of dBASE IV, keeping the user from altering another record in the database.

The READ Command

The READ command only reads one database record at a time. This enables you to control which data record is being read. You can prevent users from modifying other records in the database, unless they do it through your program.

In addition, since only one record is in use at any one time with the READ command, your program can perform calculations using data from within that record. For example, your program can evaluate the information in the record. It can also use data from various fields within the record to calculate the values for other fields in the record.

The function of the READ command is to activate the GETs in @...SAY...GET commands. To use the READ command to read the contents of a single record, first position the record pointer on a single record. Then, use @...SAY...GET commands in your program, or in a format file, that call for the individual field names within that record. Finally, you can use the READ command to access and display the contents of the GETs in the @...SAY...GET commands.

The following simple mailing list data entry program demonstrates the READ command.

```
*Program is MAILIT.PRG
*Program demonstrates the READ command.

SET TALK OFF
SET ECHO OFF

USE Mailist

*-------------------------Add a blank record to the database
APPEND BLANK

STORE " " TO Choice

DO WHILE Choice<>"Q"

     *-------------------Activate custom format file
     SET FORMAT TO Mailer
```

```
    *-------------------Use READ to activate GETs
    READ
    *-------------------Close the format file
    CLOSE FORMAT

    STORE " " TO Choice

    @ 18,15 SAY "(A)dd Record, (E)dit Record, or (Q)uit:";
    GET Choice PICTURE "!"

    *-------------------Use READ again to activate a GET
    READ
    *-------------------Evaluate user input
    IF Choice="A"
         APPEND BLANK
    ENDIF

    LOOP

ENDDO
CLOSE DATABASES
RETURN
```

Figure 21-1 shows the screen that the program displays. The READ command is used in two instances. First, it activates the @...SAY...GET commands in a format file called MAILER.FMT, a listing for which appears in Figure 21-2. Second, the READ command displays a menu that stores a letter in a variable called Choice. The Choice variable is included in the command

```
@ 18,15 SAY "(A)dd Record, (E)dit Record, or (Q)uit: ";
GET Choice PICTURE "!"
```

The PICTURE "!" clause after the @...SAY...GET command assures that all user input to the Choice variable occurs in uppercase. The Choice memory variable also appears later in an IF...ENDIF conditional statement.

The command that positions the record pointer in the mailing list program is the APPEND BLANK command. This command

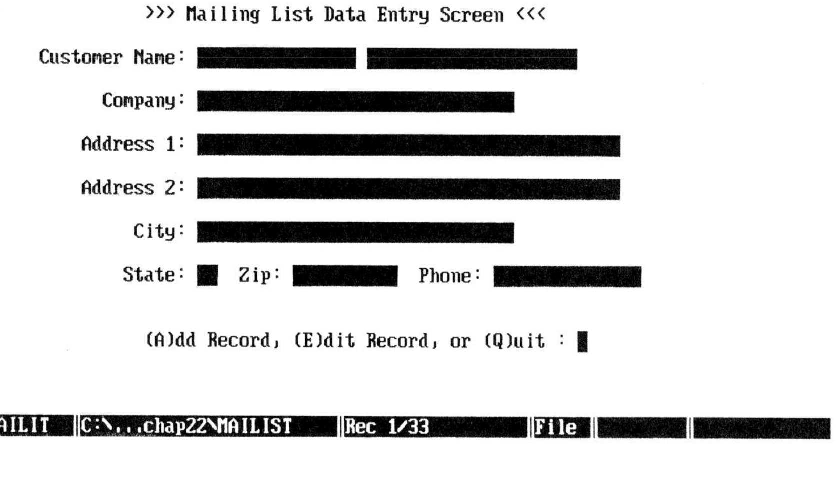

Figure 21-1. On-screen appearance of the mailing list program

appends a blank record to the MAILIST database. This newly appended record then becomes the active record.

The program then goes into a DO WHILE...ENDDO loop. The loop repeats until the Choice variable contains a value of "Q". The command SET FORMAT TO Mailer at the top of the loop calls the MAILER.FMT format file. The READ command then activates the @...SAY...GET commands in the format file. Finally, if you enter A in the Choice variable in response to the @...SAY...GET command, the APPEND BLANK command within the IF...ENDIF conditional statement appends yet another blank record to the MAILIST database. That record then becomes the active record, and the loop is repeated.

Tip: The CLOSE FORMAT command is very important to the previous program. Without it, the second READ command in the program reads the @...SAY...GET commands in the MAILER.FMT

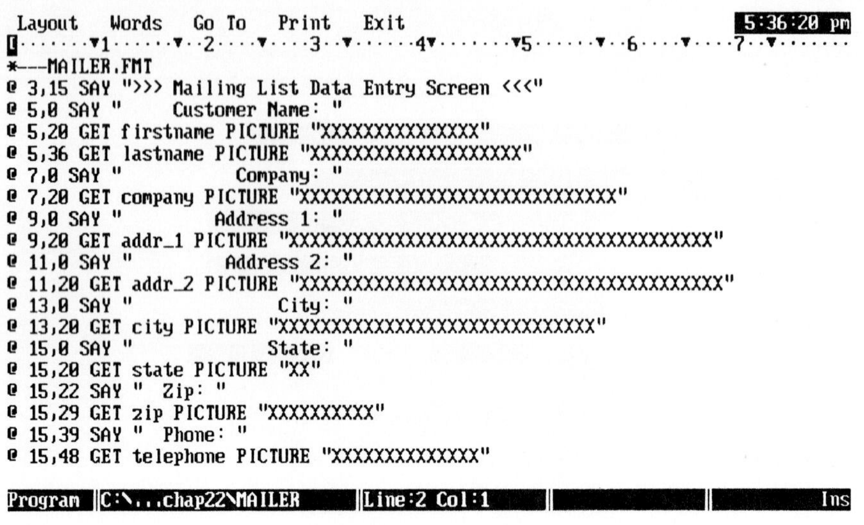

```
 Layout   Words   Go To   Print   Exit                                   5:36:20 pm
*---MAILER.FMT
@ 3,15 SAY ">>> Mailing List Data Entry Screen <<<"
@ 5,0 SAY "      Customer Name: "
@ 5,20 GET firstname PICTURE "XXXXXXXXXXXXXX"
@ 5,36 GET lastname PICTURE "XXXXXXXXXXXXXXXXXXX"
@ 7,0 SAY "            Company: "
@ 7,20 GET company PICTURE "XXXXXXXXXXXXXXXXXXXXXXXXXXXXXX"
@ 9,0 SAY "          Address 1: "
@ 9,20 GET addr_1 PICTURE "XXXXXXXXXXXXXXXXXXXXXXXXXXXXXXXXXXXXXXXX"
@ 11,0 SAY "          Address 2: "
@ 11,20 GET addr_2 PICTURE "XXXXXXXXXXXXXXXXXXXXXXXXXXXXXXXXXXXXXXXX"
@ 13,0 SAY "               City: "
@ 13,20 GET city PICTURE "XXXXXXXXXXXXXXXXXXXXXXXXXXXXXX"
@ 15,0 SAY "              State: "
@ 15,20 GET state PICTURE "XX"
@ 15,22 SAY "  Zip: "
@ 15,29 GET zip PICTURE "XXXXXXXXXX"
@ 15,39 SAY "  Phone: "
@ 15,48 GET telephone PICTURE "XXXXXXXXXXXXXX"

Program  C:\...chap22\MAILER   Line:2 Col:1                          Ins
```

Figure 21-2. MAILER.FMT format file

format file instead of the @...SAY...GET command in the program. The Choice variable would then remain a blank space (" "), and the program would get stuck in a continuous loop.

Avoiding Blank Records

The following program is a modified version of MAILER.PRG that does not allow the user to append blank records.

```
*Program is MAILER.PRG
*Program doesn't allow appending of blank records.
SET TALK OFF
SET ECHO OFF
USE Mailist
APPEND BLANK
STORE .T. TO Entry
DO WHILE Entry
     SET FORMAT TO Mailer
```

```
        *-----------Use READ to activate GETs in MAILER.FMT
        READ
        *-----------If Company field is blank, DELETE the record, exit loop
        IF Company=" "
             DELETE
             Entry=.F.
             CLOSE FORMAT
             LOOP
        ENDIF
        CLOSE FORMAT
        STORE " " TO Choice
        @ 18,15 SAY "(A)dd Record, (E)dit Record, or (Q)uit: " ;
        GET Choice PICTURE "!"
        READ
        *-------------------Evaluate user input
        DO CASE
             CASE Choice="A"
                  APPEND BLANK
             CASE Choice="Q"
                  Entry=.F.
        ENDCASE
ENDDO
CLOSE DATABASES
RETURN
```

Once again, the APPEND BLANK and READ commands limit editing to a single record. The record is again displayed using the MAILER.FMT format file.

Immediately following the READ command, which displays the newly appended record, is an IF...ENDIF conditional statement. This statement evaluates the data entered into the record. If the Company field is blank, the DELETE command marks the newly appended record for deletion. Furthermore, the condition for the DO WHILE...ENDDO loop in the program, ENTRY=.T., is set to false (.F.). The LOOP command then sends the program back to the beginning of the loop. (The rest of the code in the program is never processed.) Upon returning to the beginning of the loop, the condition following the DO WHILE command is found to be false, dBASE IV exits the loop, and the program ends.

On-Screen and Background Calculations

When dBASE IV is under the control of your program, your program can perform both on-screen and background calculations. For example, the following program performs an on-screen calculation using a memory variable called Totl. It also performs a background

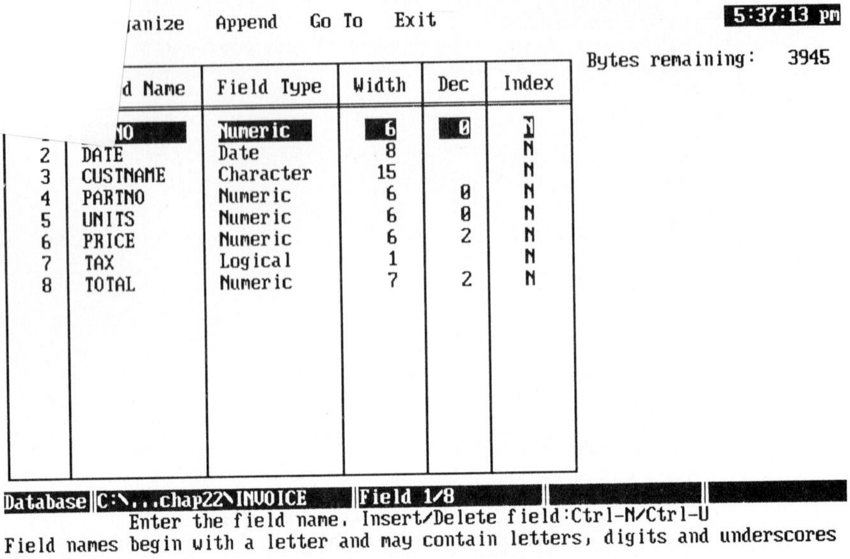

```
,anize   Append   Go To   Exit                          5:37:13 pm
                                                   Bytes remaining:   3945
     d Name       Field Type   Width   Dec   Index
       NO         Numeric        6      0      N
  2  DATE         Date           8             N
  3  CUSTNAME     Character     15             N
  4  PARTNO       Numeric        6      0      N
  5  UNITS        Numeric        6      0      N
  6  PRICE        Numeric        6      2      N
  7  TAX          Logical        1             N
  8  TOTAL        Numeric        7      2      N

Database C:\...chap22\INVOICE   Field 1/8
        Enter the field name, Insert/Delete field:Ctrl-N/Ctrl-U
Field names begin with a letter and may contain letters, digits and underscores
```

Figure 21-3. Structure of the INVOICE database

calculation by replacing the Total field in a database called INVOICE with the contents of the Totl memory variable. Figure 21-3 shows the structure of the INVOICE database. Figure 21-4 shows the screen the following program displays.

```
* Program is ONSCREEN.PRG
* Program demonstrates on-screen calculations
SET TALK OFF
SET ECHO OFF
CLEAR
STORE SPACE(8) TO Totl
STORE " " To Choice
USE Invoice
APPEND BLANK
DO WHILE UPPER(Choice)<>"Q"
     @ 3,15 SAY ">>>> ORDER ENTRY SCREEN <<<<"
     @ 5,15 SAY "       Invoice: " GET Invno
     @ 7,15 SAY "    Order date: " GET Date
     @ 9,15 SAY "Customer name: " GET Custname
     @ 11,15 SAY "  Part number: " GET Partno
     @ 13,15 SAY "        Units: " GET Units
     @ 15,15 SAY "        Price: " GET Price
```

```
     @ 17,15 SAY "      Tax: " GET Tax PICTURE "Y"
     READ
     @ 18,15 say "               =========="

     *--------Use the Totl Variable for an on-screen display

     Totl=(Units*Price)*IIF(Tax,1.065,1)
     @ 19,15 SAY "       Total: " GET Totl PICTURE "99999.99"
     READ
     @ 21,10 SAY "(A)dd record (E)dit record (Q)uit: " Get Choice
     READ

     *--------Evaluate input, if Choice variable is A or Q
     *--------Replace the Total field with the Totl variable.
     DO CASE
          CASE UPPER(Choice)="A"
               REPLACE Total WITH Totl
               APPEND BLANK
          CASE UPPER(Choice)="Q"
               REPLACE Total WITH Totl
               LOOP
     ENDCASE
ENDDO
CLOSE DATABASES
RETURN
```

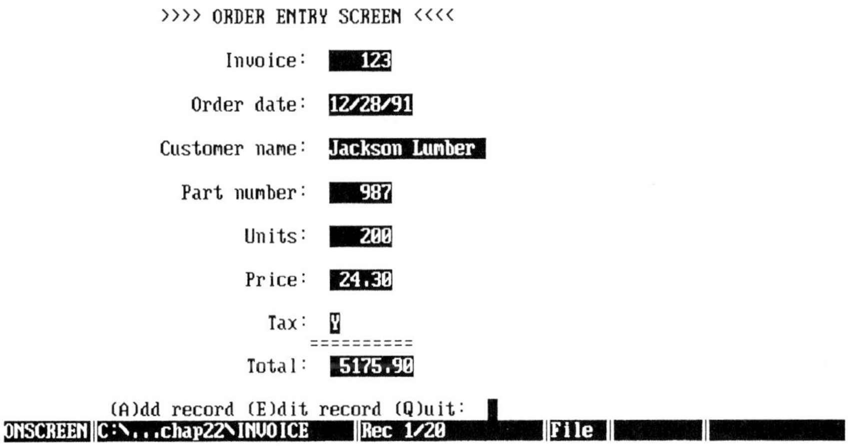

```
                >>>> ORDER ENTRY SCREEN <<<<

                         Invoice:    123

                      Order date:  12/28/91

                   Customer name:  Jackson Lumber

                     Part number:    987

                           Units:    200

                           Price:  24.30

                             Tax:  Y
                                 ==========
                           Total:  5175.90

           (A)dd record (E)dit record (Q)uit:
ONSCREEN  C:\...chap22\INVOICE   Rec 1/20        File
```

Figure 21-4. ONSCREEN.PRG performs an on-screen calculation

In brief, the program uses the APPEND BLANK and READ commands to append a record to the end of the database and display it on the screen. Next, after data is entered into the displayed database fields, a total for the order is calculated. The command line that performs the calculation is

```
Totl=(Units*Price)*IIF(Tax,1.065,1)
```

This command uses the data entered into the Units, Price, and Tax fields of the newly appended record to perform a calculation. The IIF( ) function in the command line evaluates the contents of the Tax logical field. If the Tax logical field has a true (.T.) value, the (Units*Price) expression is multiplied by 1.065. If not, it is multiplied by 1. Once the value of the Totl variable is calculated, it is displayed on the screen.

The next key point in the program occurs where user input is evaluated. If you enter A to add another record or Q to quit the program, the value for the Totl memory variable replaces the value of the Total field in the newly appended record in the INVOICE database. Note that the replacement does not occur until after you have had a chance to edit the record. If you enter any letter other than A or Q in response to the prompt, the program loops back and redisplays the current record. That way, if changes are made, the Totl memory variable is recalculated. Not until you are ready to add another record or quit the program is the value of the Totl memory variable substituted for the Total field in the INVOICE database.

Using Memory Variables

You can also use memory variables to store your data before adding it to the database. If you do this, the quality and content of the data can be verified before it is placed in the database. You can then add the contents of the memory variables to the data record with the REPLACE command. Since this method is somewhat slower than adding data directly to a database, you should only use it with smaller databases or when data verification is critical.

The following program is a modified version of the order entry program used in the previous section. However, instead of using database fields for data entry, the program uses memory variables to capture entered data. The program also uses an IF...ENDIF statement that asks the user to verify the information entered. In the menu section of the program, the DO Replacit command calls the Replacit procedure, which uses the REPLACE command to replace the fields in the current data record with the contents of the memory variables.

```
* Program is VERIFY.PRG
* Program uses memory variables to add data to a database
SET TALK OFF
SET ECHO OFF
CLEAR
*---------------------Create necessary variables
STORE SPACE(8) TO Totl
STORE 0 TO minvno
STORE {11/11/11} TO mdate
STORE SPACE(15) TO mcustname
STORE 0 TO mpartno
STORE 0 TO munits
STORE 0 TO mprice
STORE .F. TO mtax
STORE " " TO Choice
STORE " " TO Decide
USE Invoice

DO WHILE UPPER(Choice)<>"Q"
     @ 3,15 SAY ">>>> ORDER ENTRY SCREEN <<<<"
     @ 5,15 SAY "      Invoice: " GET minvno PICTURE "999999"
     @ 7,15 SAY "   Order date: " GET mdate PICTURE "99/99/99"
     @ 9,15 SAY "Customer name: " GET mcustname
     @ 11,15 SAY "  Part number: " GET mpartno PICTURE "999999"
     @ 13,15 SAY "        Units: " GET munits PICTURE "99999"
     @ 15,15 SAY "        Price: " GET mprice PICTURE "9999.99"
     @ 17,15 SAY "          Tax: " GET mtax PICTURE "Y"
     READ
     @ 18,15 say "                ========="

     Totl=(munits*mprice)*IIF(mtax,1.065,1)
     @ 19,15 SAY "        Total: " GET Totl PICTURE "99999.99"
     READ

     *--------Have the user evaluate the information.

     @ 20,15 SAY "Is this information correct (Y/N)? " GET Decide
     READ
     IF UPPER(Decide)="Y"
```

```
     @@ 20,1
     ELSE
          LOOP
     ENDIF

     @ 21,15 SAY "(A)dd record (Q)uit: " Get Choice
     READ

     *--------Evaluate menu response, if Choice variable is A or Q,
     *--------append a blank record and perform the Replacit procedure
     *--------replace fields with variables. If Choice contains Q
     *--------the DO WHILE condition becomes false.
     DO CASE
          CASE UPPER(Choice)="A"
               APPEND BLANK
               DO Replacit
               CLEAR
          CASE UPPER(Choice)="Q"
               APPEND BLANK
               DO Replacit
     ENDCASE
ENDDO

*------------------Procedure to replace fields and blank variables
PROCEDURE Replacit
REPLACE Total WITH Totl,Invno WITH Minvno,Date WITH Mdate,;
Custname WITH Mcustname,Partno WITH Mpartno,Units WITH Munits,;
Price WITH Mprice,Tax WITH Mtax
STORE 0 TO Minvno
STORE {11/11/11} TO Mdate
STORE SPACE(15) TO Mcustname
STORE 0 TO Mpartno
STORE 0 TO Munits
STORE 0 TO Mprice
STORE .F. TO Mtax
RETURN

CLOSE DATABASES
RETURN
```

Note the many lines of code at the start of the program, and in the Replacit procedure, that you need to control the memory variables. In the beginning of the program, the memory variables are created with the STORE command. In the Replacit procedure, the same memory variables are returned to their original values with the STORE command. Because of the extra work required, you should only use memory variables in this way when verification is important.

Using a Second Database

Some of your applications may require a second database to temporarily hold data. For example, you may want to add records to a temporary database before appending them to the main database. Or, you may want to create another database composed of only selected records from the main database.

Temporary Databases

Many applications use a temporary database to store data before appending it to the main database. In this way, the data can be checked manually by the data entry person before it is added to the database. In addition, you can check it with your program by establishing certain conditions that must be met before a record is appended to the main database.

The following program uses a temporary database that is called INVTEMP.

```
* Program is DTEMP.PRG
* Program uses a temporary database called Invtemp to hold records
* prior to their being appended to Invoice. Records are not appended
* if the Total field is equal to zero.

SET TALK OFF
SET BELL OFF
SET SAFETY OFF
CLEAR
STORE SPACE(8) TO Totl
STORE " " To Choice

*------------------Create a temporary database
USE Invoice
COPY STRUCTURE TO Invtemp
USE Invtemp
APPEND BLANK

DO WHILE UPPER(Choice)<>"Q"

     SET FORMAT TO Onscreen
     READ
```

```
          CLOSE FORMAT
          Totl=(Units*Price)*IIF(Tax,1.065,1)
          @ 19,15 SAY "         Total: " GET Totl PICTURE "99999.99"
          READ
          @ 21,10 SAY "(A)dd record (E)dit record (Q)uit: " Get Choice
          READ

          *---------Evaluate input. If Choice variable equals "A"
          *---------append a blank record to Invtemp. If the Choice
          *---------variable equals "Q", append the records in the
          *---------Invtemp database to Invoice, for records that
          *---------do not have a Total field equal to zero.
          DO CASE
          CASE UPPER(Choice)="A"
               REPLACE Total WITH Totl
               APPEND BLANK
          CASE UPPER (Choice)="Q"
               REPLACE Total WITH Totl
               USE Invoice
               APPEND FROM Invtemp FOR Total<>0
               Use Invtemp
               ZAP
          ENDCASE
     ENDDO
     CLOSE DATABASES
     RETURN
```

The program is a revision of the order entry program featured earlier in this chapter. In the opening of the program, the COPY STRUCTURE command copies the structure of the INVOICE database to a new database called INVTEMP. Then, the INVTEMP database is opened and a blank record is appended to it with the APPEND BLANK command. Next, a format file displays the new record for data entry. The format file, called ONSCREEN.FMT, appears in Figure 21-5. Once the data is entered, a total for the order is calculated and stored in a variable called Totl.

The next key point in the program occurs where user input is evaluated in response to a menu selection. The user's response is stored in a memory variable called Choice. Then a DO CASE...ENDCASE statement evaluates the content of the Choice variable. If the variable contains the letter "A," the INVTEMP database remains in use. A blank record is appended to the database, and the program loops for another data entry cycle. However, if the Choice variable contains the letter "Q," the main INVOICE database is opened and those records in INVTEMP that do not

```
Layout   Words   Go To   Print   Exit                                    5:40:33 pm
[·······▼1······▼··2····▼····3··▼·······4▼·······▼5······▼··6····▼····7··▼·······
*---Format file ONSCREEN.FMT

@ 3,15 SAY ">>>> ORDER ENTRY SCREEN <<<<"
@ 5,15 SAY "      Invoice: " GET Invno
@ 7,15 SAY "   Order date: " GET Date
@ 9,15 SAY "Customer name: " GET Custname
@ 11,15 SAY "  Part number: " GET Partno
@ 13,15 SAY "        Units: " GET Units
@ 15,15 SAY "        Price: " GET Price
@ 17,15 SAY "          Tax: " GET Tax PICTURE "Y"









Program ||C:\...chap22\ONSCREEN  ||Line:1 Col:1  ||        ||        Ins
```

Figure 21-5. ONSCREEN.FMT format file

have a 0 value in the Total field are appended to the INVOICE database. (It is assumed that those records with a zero value in the Total field are blank.) The APPEND FROM command with a FOR clause performs this function. Finally, since the INVTEMP database is no longer required, it is opened and totally erased with the ZAP command.

The COPY TO Command

You can use the COPY TO command to create a database that only contains selected data. The COPY TO command creates a new database using either all or part of the records in the currently active database. For example, the following program creates a new database called MAIL2 by using records from the MAILIST database.

The program first opens the MAILIST database and activates the Lastname index tag with the ORDER clause. Activating the Lastname index tag arranges the records in the database in order by last name. Next, the TEXT...ENDTEXT commands place some text on the screen that tells the user how the program works. Then, the program prompts the user for two last names. These are stored in two variables called First and Second. Some more text is then placed on the screen to let the user know the program is working. The next line in the program

```
COPY TO Mail2 FOR Lastname>=First .AND. Lastname<=Second
```

does all the work.

This command selects all names in the Lastname field of the MAILIST database that are greater than or equal to the character string in the First variable and less than or equal to the character string in the Second variable. A new database called MAIL2 is then created, and all records in MAILIST that meet the condition are copied into MAIL2.

```
* Program is PARTIAL.PRG
* Program copies selected data to a second database
SET TALK OFF
SET ECHO OFF
CLEAR
USE Mailist Order Lastname
TEXT
This program extracts records from the mailing list database
and places them in a new database called MAIL2.DBF. Please
provide two last names.  The progam then writes all records
between those last names to the new file.
ENDTEXT
WAIT
?
ACCEPT "Please enter the first last name: " TO First
?
ACCEPT "Please enter the second last name: " TO Second
?
? "Working"
COPY TO MAIL2 FOR Lastname>=First .AND. Lastname<=Second
```

```
? "Done"
RETURN
```

Using Multiple Databases

As mentioned, in dBASE IV you can have up to ten databases active at any one time. You do this by placing those databases in separate *work areas.*

You can only have one database active in each work area. If a database is already open in a given work area and you specify that another database is to be opened in that work area, dBASE IV automatically closes the first database before opening the second.

Each of the ten possible work areas is assigned a number or a letter, 1 through 10 or A through J. When you first start dBASE IV, work area 1 is the default. You can then place a database in each of the ten available work areas.

When you place a database in a work area, dBASE IV uses that space to open other files associated with that database, such as index files, format files, or query files.

dBASE IV reserves work area 10 for open catalogs. If you have a database open in work area 10 and then open a catalog, dBASE IV closes your database and opens that catalog in work area 10.

Setting Up Databases in Work Areas

You can use two commands, USE and SELECT, to place a database in a work area. The USE command opens a database in a specified work area and closes any database currently open in that work area. On the other hand, the SELECT command does not open a database; however, it allows you to choose a work area in which to open a database or to point to a work area in which a database is already open.

Opening Multiple Databases with the USE Command

The syntax for the USE command for activating multiple databases in different work areas is

> USE <*database filename*> [IN <*work area*>] [ALIAS <*alias name*>]

The IN <*work area*> clause with the USE command allows you to stipulate the work area in which to open a database. For example, the following section of code opens the CUSTOMER database in work area 1 and the ORDERREC database in work area 2:

```
USE Customer IN 1
USE Orderrec IN 2
```

The ALIAS <*alias name*> clause with the USE command allows you to temporarily assign an alternate name to a database in a given work area. You can then refer to that database by its alias name later in your program. For example, the following section of code opens the CUSTOMER database in work area 1 and gives it an alias name of Cus12_90. The ORDERREC database is opened in work area 2 and is given an alias of Ord12_90.

```
USE Customer IN 1 ALIAS Cus12_90
USE Orderrec IN 2 ALIAS Ord12_90
```

If you don't assign an alias to a database by using the ALIAS clause, dBASE IV assigns an alias for you. dBASE IV uses the name of the database, without the .DBF file extension, as a default alias. Unlike database file names, aliases must begin with a letter, and can be up to ten characters in length, including letters, numbers, and underscores. When a database file name does not conform to this format (for example, if it begins with a number), dBASE IV uses the current work area letter (A through J) as a default alias.

The SELECT Command

As mentioned, you use the SELECT command to choose a work area in which to open a database as well as to specify a work area in which a database is already open. When you use the SELECT command to specify a work area in which a database is already open, the database in that work area becomes the currently active database. The syntax for the SELECT command is

SELECT <*work area / alias*>

To use the SELECT command, you must first assign your databases to their respective work areas. You can then use the SELECT command to specify the currently active database by selecting its work area. For example, the following section of code opens the CUSTOMER database in work area 1. It then opens the ORDERREC database in work area 2. Since ORDERREC was assigned to its work area last, it remains the currently active database and a blank record is appended to it. Next, the command SELECT 1 tells dBASE IV to refer to work area 1, where the CUSTOMER database resides. Now that work area 1 has been selected, CUSTOMER becomes the currently active database and a blank record is appended to it as well.

```
SELECT 1
USE Customer ORDER Cust_no
SELECT 2
USE Orderrec ORDER Order_no
APPEND BLANK
SELECT 1
APPEND BLANK
```

Pointing to Fields Across Databases

Once you have opened your databases in different work areas, you can point to the fields in an inactive database by using the —> pointer. You do not need to use the —> pointer to point to field names in the currently active database. The —> pointer is preceded by the name or alias of an open, but inactive, database in another work area and is followed by the name of a field from that database. For example, the following section of code opens the CUSTOMER database in work area 1 and the ORDERREC database in work area 2. Since the ORDERREC database was opened last, it remains the currently active database. Next, the —> pointer is used in an @...SAY...GET command line to point to a field called Company in the CUSTOMER database. Finally, another @...SAY...GET command displays a database field from the currently active ORDERREC database. Note that since ORDERREC is the currently active database, the —> pointer is not required.

```
SELECT 1
USE Customer ORDER Cust_no
SELECT 2
USE Orderrec
@ 10,10 SAY "Enter the company name:" GET Customer->Company
@ 10,12 SAY "Enter the total due: " GET Total
```

If a database field and a memory variable have the same name, the -> always points to the database field name first. If you want a memory variable to take precedence over a database field of the same name, you can use the special M—> pointer (which is strictly for memory variables). For example, imagine that the currently active database has a field named Cust_no. Furthermore, the current program creates a memory variable named Cust_no. To point to the Cust_no memory variable in an expression, you would use the following command line:

```
@ 10,10 SAY "Enter the customer number: " GET M->Cust_no
```

When you use a function with a field pointer, make sure to include the database name, field pointer, and the field name inside of the function parentheses ( ). For example, imagine you are using the STR() function to convert a numeric entry in a field called Invno to character status. You might use the following expression:

```
STR(Orderrec->Invno)
```

Setting up a Relationship Between Databases

You need to establish a relationship between databases when you are adding or editing related data to two or more databases at the same time. For example, imagine you are entering an order. Part of the information you are entering is stored in one database and the balance of that information is stored in yet another database. You must establish a relationship between the two databases so that you can later find the information from both parts of the same order.

You can establish a relationship on the basis of record numbers or on the basis of fields that are common to both databases. You establish a relationship between databases with the SET RELATION command. The syntax for the SET RELATION command is

SET RELATION TO <*common field*/RECNO()> INTO <*filename/alias*>

The SET RELATION command links the currently active database to an open database in another work area. The currently active database is the one that controls the relationship and is referred to as the *parent* file. The other open database in the noncurrent work area is referred to as the *child* file. You link the databases with either an expression, such as RECNO( ), or any combination of field names that are common to both databases. Use the INTO <*filename/alias*> clause after the SET RELATION command to specify the file name of the child file that is being linked. Instead of the file name of the child file, you can use the number or letter of the work area that contains that file, or an alias name for the child file.

To use the SET RELATION command, you must use the SELECT command to open and place in their respective work areas the databases you intend to link. Then use the SET RELATION command to link them.

Linking on Record Numbers

You can use the RECNO( ) function with the SET RELATION command to link two database on the basis of record number. When you use the RECNO( ) function to link databases, any command line that moves the record pointer in the first database also moves the record pointer to the same record in the second database. In the following section of code, the SELECT command opens the MAIL2 database in work area 1 and the MAILIST database in work area 2. The MAILIST database remains the active or parent file. The RECNO( ) function is then used with the SET RELATION command to link two databases on the basis of record number.

```
Select 1
USE Mail2
SELECT 2
USE Mailist
SET RELATION TO RECNO() INTO Mail2
```

A problem can occur when both databases do not receive equal treatment. For example, if a record in the first database is deleted and packed, but the second database is not given the same treatment, the two databases have an unequal number of records. When this is true, the SET RELATION command does not return accurate results.

Linking on Common Fields

You can also use the SET RELATION command to establish a relationship between databases by using one or more common fields from both databases. The common field must have the same name, width, and data type. You achieve the best results when the common field is a numeric field that contains unique values.

Linking databases by using a common numeric field that contains unique values gives you a reliable method of matching records between two databases. Often, character fields do not afford the same level of accuracy.

For example, consider the case of using last names to link the employee ADDRESS and SALARY databases. Both databases have the last name Smith in five different records. dBASE IV has no way of knowing which record in the SALARY database belongs to which record in the address database. You may end up sending the wrong check to the wrong employee. Although you can further refine the relationship by linking the databases with both first and last names, if you have two employees with the same name, your problem is not solved. However, if you use unique employee numbers to link the databases, all ambiguities are eliminated.

Another advantage of using numeric fields to link databases is that you can have your program create the next unique number. That way the numbering scheme is controlled by your program and the integrity of your database link is preserved.

For you to use a common field to establish a relationship between databases, the file being linked (the child file) *must* be indexed on the common field. This is because dBASE IV uses that index to link the two databases. It takes the contents of the common field in the current record of the active or parent database file and refers to the child file index to find a matching record in the child database. What's more, the common field expression in the SET RELATION command must exactly match the index key expression.

Before you link databases using a common field, you must structure your databases properly. For example, imagine you are working with an order entry system that uses two databases called CUSTOMER and ORDERREC. The CUSTOMER database holds customer names and addresses. The ORDERREC database holds all of the orders placed by those customers. As each order is entered, information is added to both the CUSTOMER and ORDERREC databases. The field name that both databases have in common is Cust_no. In the CUSTOMER database, this field holds a unique customer number that identifies each customer's name and address. In the ORDERREC database, the Cust_no field contains that same unique customer number and is used to identify all of the orders placed by a given customer. In this way, you can use the Cust_no field to establish a relationship between a customer's name and address in CUSTOMER and all of the orders placed by that customer in ORDERREC.

The following section of code sets up a relationship between the CUSTOMER and ORDERREC databases. The code is entered from the dot prompt so that you can see dBASE IV's reaction to the command lines. The relationship between the ORDERREC and CUSTOMER databases is established by using the Cust_no field, which is common to both databases. In this relationship, the CUSTOMER database is the currently active database, and is the parent file. The child database is ORDERREC. Note that the ORDERREC database is indexed on the Cust_no field.

```
. SELECT 1
. USE Orderrec ORDER Cust_no
Master index: CUST_NO
. SELECT 2
. USE Customer
. SET RELATION TO Cust_no INTO Orderrec
. LIST Cust_no,Lastname,Orderrec->Total
Record#  Cust_no          Lastname  Orderrec->Total
1        1001             Thomas    24.95
2        1002             Holland   27.95
3        1003             Spraul    26.57
4        1004             Johnson   53.14
5        1005             Takano    34.95
6        1006             Corzine   26.57
7        1007             Cramden   49.90
8        1008             Stokes    24.95
9        1009             Harding   59.53
10       1010             Hinckley  24.95
11       1011             Manley    24.95
12       1012             Schumann  27.95
```

In dBASE IV, you can set up multiple child relationships for a single parent database. The child files must still be indexed on the common field, but you can follow the SET RELATION command with multiple INTO clauses. For example, the following section of code sets up a relationship between three databases: CUSTOMER, ACCTSREC and ORDERREC. The code is initiated from the dot prompt so that you can immediately see its effects. Note that the CUSTOMER database is not indexed. This is because CUSTOMER is the parent file in this relationship.

```
. SELECT 1
. USE Orderrec ORDER Cust_no
Master index: CUST_NO
. SELECT 2
. USE Acctsrec ORDER Cust_no
Master index: CUST_NO
. SELECT 3
. USE Customer
. SET RELATION TO Cust_no INTO Orderrec, Cust_no INTO Acctsrec
. DISPLAY Cust_no,Orderrec->Cust_no,Acctsrec->Cust_no
Record#  Cust_no Orderrec->Cust_no Acctsrec->Cust_no
     1    1001              1001              1001
. GOTO 5
CUSTOMER: Record No       5
. DISPLAY Cust_no,Orderrec->Cust_no,Acctsrec->Cust_no
Record#  Cust_no Orderrec->Cust_no Acctsrec->Cust_no
     5    1005              1005              1005
```

Accessing Multiple Child Records

Often a child database contains more than one record that matches the currently active relationship to the parent database. When this is the case, dBASE IV only accesses the first record in the child database that matches the relationship. However, you can use the SET SKIP command to access all the matching records in the child file. The syntax for the SET SKIP command is

SET SKIP TO [<*alias 1*>[,<*alias 2*>]...]

The SET SKIP command tells dBASE IV to access all records in the child file that match the relationship before moving on to the next record in the parent database. For example, using the CUSTOMER and ORDERREC relationship just described, the ORDERREC database could contain more than one record that has a matching unique customer number in the Cust_no field. If this is the case, you can have dBASE IV use all the matching records in the ORDERREC database by including the following command line in your program:

```
SET SKIP TO Orderrec
```

To turn off the SET SKIP command, enter it with no file name. dBASE IV accesses only the first matching record in the child file. For more about the SET SKIP command, see Chapter 32.

Specifying Selected Fields for a Relationship

You can specify a fields list for the currently active relationship by using the SET FIELDS command. This command limits the available fields to those you specify in one or more open databases. For example, the following command line limits the fields used in the current relationship to the Cust_no field in the currently active or parent file and the Lastname and Total fields in the CUSTOMER database.

```
SET FIELDS TO Cust_no,Lastname,Orderrec->Total
```

The SET FIELDS command by itself does not establish a relationship. It only specifies the fields that are used in the relationship. Therefore, before using the SET FIELDS command to specify a fields list for the currently active relationship, you must set up the relationship with the SET RELATION command.

Relating Databases Using Query and View Files

You can save active relationships between databases with either a query (.QBE) file or a view (.VUE) file. You can later restore those relationships by calling either .QBE or .VUE files from your program.

Query (.QBE) Files

You create a query (.QBE) file using the CREATE VIEW *<filename>* command. This command gives you access to the menu-assisted Queries Design screen. (This special screen is described in detail in Chapter 6). The Queries Design screen lets you open database files and specify relationships between them. You can also specify filter conditions and field lists for the relationship. When you finish designing the query file, dBASE IV saves it under the file name you specified with the CREATE VIEW command. You can then reinstate that relationship at any time by activating the query file from your program.

To activate a query file from your program, use the SET VIEW TO *<filename>* command. This command activates a query (.QBE) file and immediately establishes the relationships, fields list, and filter conditions referenced in the file. For example, to activate the query file ORDERS.QBE, include the following command line in your program:

```
SET VIEW TO Orders
```

To deactivate the current view established by a query file, use the SET VIEW TO command without an argument. You can also use the CLOSE ALL or CLEAR ALL commands to deactivate the current query file.

View (.VUE) Files

You can create a view file that saves the currently active relationships in the dBASE IV environment. To do this, use the CREATE VIEW *<filename>* FROM ENVIRONMENT command. This command saves all parameters from the current environment and places them in a view (.VUE) file. The parameters saved include

- Currently open files, including databases and indexes
- Active relationships among databases
- Filter conditions
- Field lists
- The current work area number
- The names of any active format files

To activate a .VUE file and immediately restore the environment saved in it, use the SET VIEW TO command followed by the name of the .VUE file. For example, the following command line activates the .VUE file called VIEW1.VUE:

```
SET VIEW TO View1
```

To deactivate the current .VUE file and return dBASE IV to its default environment, use the SET VIEW TO command without a .VUE file name.

Transaction Databases

You can use one database to update another. When one database updates another, the database doing the updating is referred to as a *transaction database*. The update operation is usually performed with the UPDATE command, which has the following syntax:

> UPDATE ON <*key field*> FROM <*alias*> REPLACE <*field name 1*> WITH <*expression 1*> [,<*field name 2*> WITH <*expression 2*>]...]

The UPDATE command uses specified fields from a transaction database to update or replace the fields in the currently active database. dBASE IV manages the update by matching records in the two databases using the contents of a single field common to both files. For the UPDATE command to work, both databases must be opened and placed in their respective work areas. Furthermore, the database being updated must be the active database. Beyond that, both databases must be indexed or sorted on the common field.

The following section of code uses the UPDATE command to update an accounting database. The update uses the Acct_no field that is common to both the ACCTG and TRANSACT databases. The code first uses the TOTAL ON command to total the numeric fields of the DAILY database by account number to the TRANSACT database. Next, the TRANSACT database is activated and indexed on the Acct_no field. Then, the master accounting database ACCTG is opened in work area 2 and indexed on the Acct_no field. The ACCTG data-base then becomes the active database. Finally, the UPDATE command replaces the Debit and Credit fields in the ACCTG database with their current values plus the values from the Receipt and Disburse fields in the TRANSACT database. Note that you need pointers to point to the Receipt and Disburse fields in the TRANSACT database.

```
USE Daily ORDER Acct_no
TOTAL ON Acct_no TO Transact
USE Transact
INDEX ON Acct_no TAG Acct_no
USE Acctg ORDER Acct_no IN 2
UPDATE ON Acct_no FROM Transact REPLACE Debit WITH Debit;
+Transact->Receipt,Credit WITH Credit+Transact->Disburse
```

Tip: The LUPDATE() function returns the date the database was last updated. For example, if the ACCTG database is active, the command ? LUPDATE() returns the last update date for the ACCTG database.

Joining Two Databases

You can join two databases using the JOIN command. This command creates a third joined file using two currently open databases. However, the JOIN command does not work with memo fields. The syntax for the JOIN command is

> JOIN WITH <*alias*> TO <*filename*> FOR <*condition*> [FIELDS <*fields list*>]

As mentioned, before you use the JOIN command, two databases must be opened and placed in their respective work areas. The *alias* refers to the nonselected database and can be the name of the database, its alias, or the number of the work area in which the database resides. The TO <*filename*> clause specifies the name of the new file that is to be created. The FOR <*condition*> clause specifies a condition that a record must meet before it is added to the new file. The optional FIELDS <*fields list*> clause specifies certain fields within the two databases that are to be included in the new file. If you do not specify a fields list, all the fields in both databases are used.

The following command lines join the Company field in the CUSTOMER database with the Cust_no and Total fields from the ORDERREC database to create a new database called COMBINE.

```
SELECT A
USE Customer
SELECT B
USE Orderrec
JOIN WITH Customer TO Combine FIELDS Cust_no,Total;
A->Company
```

In this chapter, you learned about entering data in a database and using multiple databases. You now know how to use a program to control the entry of data to a database. Furthermore, you can use a temporary database to hold data before appending it to the main database. Additionally, you know how to use multiple databases simultaneously and how to relate them to one another.

The User Interface

TWENTY TWO

Controlling User Input
Checking Input After the Fact
An Example Program
Controlling the Screen
Placing Messages on the Screen
Clearing the Screen
Drawing Lines and Boxes
Setting Colors
Setting Intensity and Delimiters
Using Windows

The user interface is one of the most important aspects of applications programming. An effective user interface lets you control the actions of your user while providing a friendly and informative screen display. To help you to accomplish both of these objectives, this chapter discusses both controlling user input and controlling the screen.

This chapter first shows you how to control user input either by filtering input as it occurs or by checking the input after it occurs. You can use the techniques provided to have your program control the data entry process.

This chapter next explains how to control the screen. You'll learn how to display lines and boxes as well as how to use windows to display output. You will also learn how to place messages on the screen, clear portions of the screen, and make portions of the screen appear in different colors.

Controlling User Input

You can have your program check user input both at the point of entry and after the fact. Both ways are equally valid.

To check data at the point of entry, you specify filter conditions that the data must meet before being placed in a database field or memory variable. This method tends to require less code and to stop problems before they start.

To check data after the fact, you must permit data entry to occur and then evaluate the data with a conditional statement. If the data does not meet the specified condition, you can then redisplay the data for correction.

Filtering Data at the Point of Entry

Some of the more common ways to filter user input at the point of data entry are as follows:

- Provide a *template* or model for data entry that prescribes the format and data type of the input.
- Allow the entry to occur, but immediately convert it to the proper format in the same command line.
- Do not allow entry to a field unless a specific condition is met.
- Specify upper and lower limits for the input.

Filtering Input with @...SAY...GET

The @...SAY...GET command allows you to position the cursor on the screen, prompt the user with a message, and display a database field or a memory variable for data entry. In addition to the @...SAY...GET command, you can include various clauses that filter input at the point of data entry. The PICTURE, RANGE, and WHEN clauses are most commonly used in this situation.

Symbol	Description
!	Converts letter to uppercase
#	Permits only numbers, blanks, and signs
$	Displays the $ sign in place of leading zeros
*	Displays asterisks in place of leading zeros
,	Displays "," for numbers in the thousands
.	Positions the decimal point
9	Permits only numbers for character data and numbers and signs for numeric data
A	Letters only
L	Logical data only
N	Letters and numbers
X	Any character
Y	Logical data only. Accepts Y, y, N, or n. All lowercase letters are converted to uppercase

Table 22-1. Template Symbols Used in PICTURE Clauses

The PICTURE clause of the @...SAY...GET command allows you to specify a template for data entry. You can use a template to specify both the type and format of the data being entered. You build a template by using the PICTURE clause followed by various symbols enclosed in quotes. Table 22-1 lists these symbols and what they represent. The number of symbols you include in a template specifies the width of the data entry field. For example, the following command line restricts data entry in the Lastname field to letters only by using the A symbol. Furthermore, although the Lastname field in the current database may be 15 characters wide, only 10 of its spaces are displayed for data entry.

```
@ 10,10 SAY "Enter last name: " GET Lastname PICTURE "AAAAAAAAAA"
```

You can also use the PICTURE clause to specify a more exacting template. For example, imagine you are working with a payroll application that requires social security numbers displayed with dashes (for example, 272-55-8921). The following command line use the 9 symbol to enter a social security number to a variable called Ss. The 9 symbol allows only numbers to be entered for character data. When the Ss field is displayed for data entry, it appears as three blank spaces, a dash, two more blank spaces, another dash, and four blank spaces.

```
@10,5 SAY "Social security number: " GET Ss PICTURE "999-99-9999"
```

You can also use a template to convert the format of the data as it is being entered. For example, when you use the ! symbol with the PICTURE clause, it creates a template that converts all letters to uppercase, regardless of how they are entered. This PICTURE symbol is particularly useful with multiple-choice menu options.

Because dBASE IV is case sensitive, it considers the letter "X" to be different from the letter "x." When you use the ! symbol to convert all input to a memory variable to uppercase, your program need only evaluate a single condition as opposed to two conditions. For example, the following command line presents the user with a multiple-choice menu. The user's input is stored in a memory variable called Choice. The ! symbol is used with the PICTURE clause to create a template that permits only a single uppercase letter to be entered in response to the prompt. When the input is later evaluated in a DO CASE...ENDCASE conditional statement, only single-character uppercase letters need to be evaluated.

```
@ 20,10 SAY "(A)dd record, (E)dit record, or (Q)uit: " GET Choice;
PICTURE "!"
DO CASE
     CASE Choice="A"
          APPEND BLANK
     CASE Choice="Q"
          Enter=.F.
ENDCASE
```

Table 22-1 shows other symbols you can use to build PICTURE clause templates for the @...SAY...GET command. These symbols provide a template for data display as well as data entry.

Use the WHEN clause with the @...SAY...GET command to restrict data at the point of entry, based on a given condition. Data can only be entered when the condition is true. If the condition is not true, the database field or memory variable is skipped.

For example, the following section of code includes two @...SAY...GET commands. The first command stores a response to a database field called On_order. This field identifies the amount of a particular item that is on order. The second @...SAY...GET command includes a WHEN clause and stores user input to a database field called Due_in. This field identifies the due date for materials on order. The Due_in field does not need a date unless material is on order. Consequently, the information in the Due_in field is dependent upon the information in the On_order field. The condition following the WHEN clause in the second @...SAY...GET statement only allows you to enter data into the Due_in field when the On_order field contains a number greater than 0.

```
@  8,10 SAY " On Order: " GET On_Order
@ 10,10 SAY " Due Date: " Get Due_in WHEN On_order>0
```

You can also use the RANGE option with the @...SAY...GET command to specify both upper and lower limits for the data entered into a memory variable or database field. For example, the following command line uses a RANGE clause to restrict data entered into the Part_no field to a number between 1000 and 9000.

```
@ 2,10 SAY "Enter part number" GET Mpart_no RANGE 1000,9000
```

Checking Input After the Fact

As mentioned, to check input after the fact, you let data entry occur and then evaluate the data with a conditional statement. If the data does not meet the specified condition, you can redisplay the database field or memory variable for correction.

For example, the following section of code uses an IF...ENDIF conditional statement to evaluate the contents of a database field called Descript. The process begins with a DO WHILE...ENDDO loop. The Descript database field is then displayed for data entry with the command line

```
@ 4,10 SAY " Description: " GET Descript
```

After the user has been given a chance to enter data into the Descript field, the field is evaluated in the IF...ENDIF conditional statement. If the Descript field is blank, the message "A description must be entered!" appears below the status bar. The program then loops back to the DO WHILE statement and redisplays the data field for correction.

```
STORE .T. TO Enter
DO WHILE Enter
     *-----More @...SAY...GET commands
     @ 4,10 SAY " Description: " GET Descript
     *-----More @...SAY...GET commands
     READ
     If Descript = " "
          SET MESSAGE TO "A description must be entered! "
          WAIT
          CLEAR
          SET MESSAGE TO
          LOOP
     ENDIF
     *------More commands
ENDDO
```

Catching Duplicate Entries

Sometimes your applications require that an entry not be duplicated. For example, imagine you are maintaining a customer database, and that each customer in that database has a unique customer number that cannot be repeated in another customer's record. You can have your program allow the entry of a customer number and then check to see if a duplication has occurred.

The following section of code opens the CUSTOMER database and sets the index tag to the Cust_no field, which holds the unique customer numbers in the CUSTOMER database. Next, the program goes into a DO WHILE...ENDDO loop. The user is then asked to enter a customer number, which is stored to a memory variable called Mcust_no. Next, the SEEK command quickly searches the Cust_no field in the CUSTOMER database for the value stored in the Mcust_no variable. If the value is found, the program places a message on the screen informing the user that the customer number is already in use. It then loops back to the DO WHILE statement and the user is requested to enter another customer number. If the customer number is not found, a new record is appended to the CUSTOMER database and the Mcust_no variable replaces the value of the Cust_no field in the newly appended record.

```
USE Customer ORDER Cust_no
STORE .T. TO Enter
DO WHILE Enter
     @ 2,10 SAY "Enter the customer number: " Get Mcust_no
     READ
     SEEK Mcust_no
     IF FOUND()
          CLEAR
          @10,20 SAY "Customer number already in use."
          @11,20 SAY "Please enter a new customer number"
          WAIT
          CLEAR
          LOOP
     ENDIF
ENDDO
APPEND BLANK
REPLACE Cust_no WITH Mcust_no
*---More commands to display the new record and enter data into it.
```

Evaluating Menu Responses

Since you cannot control which keys your user presses in response to a multiple-choice menu, you must structure your program accordingly. If the response is an appropriate one, your program can continue. If it is not, the user should be given a chance to correct the error.

There are several techniques that you can use to trap and evaluate users' errant menu responses. They all involve a DO WHILE...ENDDO loop that repeats the program section containing the menu.

The following program section assumes that an incorrect key might be pressed in response to a menu selection. The program begins with a DO WHILE...ENDDO loop. As explained later, this loop causes both the current record and a multiple-choice menu to be redisplayed. The user is then prompted with @...SAY...GET commands to enter data in the current record. Finally, a multiple-choice menu is presented that allows the user to press A to add another record, E to edit the current record, or Q to quit the program.

The menu selection is then evaluated using a DO CASE...ENDCASE conditional statement. If either the Q or A key is pressed, the CASE statements that follow capture those keystrokes and the program reacts accordingly. However, if any other key is pressed, dBASE IV jumps to ENDDO. This causes the DO WHILE statement to be reevaluated, and the current record is then redisplayed. After the user moves the cursor past the last field in the current data record, the multiple-choice menu is displayed again for a correct entry.

```
STORE .T. To Enter
DO WHILE Enter
*---A series of @...SAY...GET commands are placed here to
*---prompt the user to add data to the current record.
*---A multiple choice menu is then displayed.
@ 18,10 SAY "(A)dd record, (E)dit record, or (Q)uit: " GET Choice;
PICTURE "!"
     DO CASE
          CASE Choice="A"
               APPEND BLANK
          CASE Choice="Q"
               Enter=.F.
     ENDCASE
ENDDO
```

You can also allow a menu selection to occur, then transforming the entry to meet the needs of your program. For example, the following program section presents the same multiple-choice menu as before, but this time the UPPER( ) function converts any lowercase letters to uppercase. This way, evaluation of the Choice variable is confined to uppercase letters.

```
STORE " " TO Choice
@ 18,10 SAY "(A)dd record, (E)dit record, or (Q)uit: " GET Choice
DO CASE
     CASE UPPER(Choice)="A"
          APPEND BLANK
     CASE UPPER(Choice)="Q"
          Enter=.F.
ENDCASE
```

You can also place the multiple-choice menu itself inside a DO WHILE...ENDDO loop. Once inside the loop, your user cannot escape until an acceptable response is given. For example, the following section of code uses the $ substring comparison operator to specify a condition for a DO WHILE command. The condition becomes false when the Choice variable becomes equal to A, E, or Q. Unless the user responds with one of these letters, the DO WHILE condition remains true, and the menu is redisplayed.

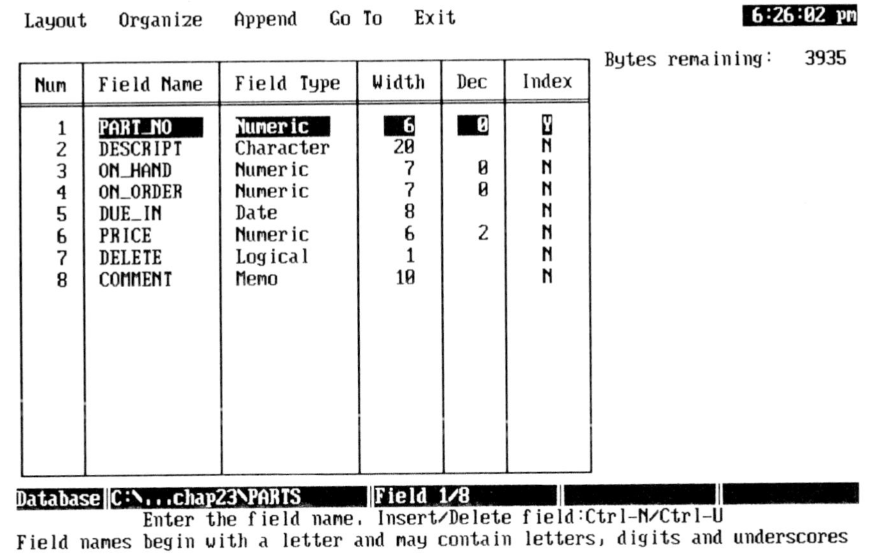

```
Layout   Organize   Append   Go To   Exit                         6:26:02 pm
                                                       Bytes remaining:   3935
```

Num	Field Name	Field Type	Width	Dec	Index
1	PART_NO	Numeric	6	0	Y
2	DESCRIPT	Character	20		N
3	ON_HAND	Numeric	7	0	N
4	ON_ORDER	Numeric	7	0	N
5	DUE_IN	Date	8		N
6	PRICE	Numeric	6	2	N
7	DELETE	Logical	1		N
8	COMMENT	Memo	10		N

```
Database ‖C:\...chap23\PARTS        ‖Field 1/8
            Enter the field name. Insert/Delete field:Ctrl-N/Ctrl-U
Field names begin with a letter and may contain letters, digits and underscores
```

Figure 22-1. Structure for the PARTS database

```
STORE " " TO Choice
DO WHILE .NOT. Choice$"AEQ"
@ 18,10 SAY "(A)dd record, (E)dit record, or (Q)uit: " GET Choice;
PICTURE "!"
READ
ENDDO
```

An Example Program

The following program demonstrates most of the techniques mentioned for controlling user input. The program, named PARTMSTR.PRG, is used to enter data in the PARTS database. Each part listed in the database must have a unique part number. The structure of the PARTS database appears in Figure 22-1.

```
* Program is PARTMSTR.PRG
* Program demonstrates some user input control techniques

SET TALK OFF
SET ECHO OFF
SET ESCAPE OFF
CLEAR

USE Parts ORDER Part_no
APPEND BLANK
STORE RECNO() TO Mrec
STORE .T. TO Enter
STORE 0 To Mpart_no

DO WHILE Enter
     *---------Restrict entry to a given range
     @ 2,10 SAY "Enter Part number: " GET MPart_no PICTURE "9999";
     RANGE 1000,9000
     READ
     *---------Check to see if the part number is used
     SEEK Mpart_no
     IF FOUND()
          CLEAR
          @ 10,10 SAY "Part number already in use."
          @ 11,10 SAY "Please Select Another."
          WAIT
          CLEAR
          LOOP
     ENDIF
     *---------Position record pointer after SEEK
     GO Mrec
```

```
     *--------Loop to check for a blank Descript field
DO WHILE Descript=" "

     *--------------Part number available. Fill in rest of record
     *--------------using PICTURE, RANGE, and WHEN Clauses.
     @ 4,10 SAY "      Description: " GET Descript
     @ 6,10 SAY "          On hand: " GET On_hand PICTURE "9999"
     @ 8,10 SAY "         On Order: " GET On_order RANGE 0,1000
     @ 10,10 SAY "         Due Date: " GET Due_in WHEN On_order<>0
     @ 12,10 SAY "            Price: " GET Price PICTURE "999.99"
     @ 14,10 SAY "     Delete (Y/N): " GET Delete PICTURE "Y"
     @ 16,10 SAY "          Comment: " GET Comment MESSAGE "Press;
      CTRL-HOME to enter CTRL-END to save"

     READ
     *---------If the Descript field is blank, redisplay
     IF Descript=" "
          SET MESSAGE TO "No description entered"
          WAIT
          SET MESSAGE TO
          CLEAR
          LOOP
     ENDIF

ENDDO (Descript=" ")

     STORE " " TO Choice

     *--------Place menu in a loop
DO WHILE .NOT. Choice$"AEQ"

     *---------Get a response from the user in uppercase
     STORE " " TO Choice
     @ 18,10 SAY "(A)dd record, (E)dit record, or (Q)uit: " GET;
     Choice PICTURE "!"
     READ
     *---------Evaluate user input, and add a record, loop, or
     *---------quit.
     DO CASE
         CASE Choice="A"
              REPLACE Part_no WITH Mpart_no
              STORE 0 TO Mpart_no
              APPEND BLANK
              STORE RECNO() TO Mrec
              CLEAR
         CASE CHOICE="Q"
              REPLACE Part_no WITH Mpart_no
              Enter=.F.
     ENDCASE
ENDDO (Choice<>$ "AEQ")

ENDDO (Enter)
RETURN
```

The program first opens the PARTS database and sets the index to the Part_no field. The Part_no field contains the unique part numbers for each item listed in the PARTS database. Next, the APPEND BLANK command adds a blank record to the PARTS database. The record number of the newly appended record is then stored to a memory variable called Mrec for later use. Then two more memory variables, Enter and Mpart_no, are created. The Enter variable is a logical variable that contains the value .T. (logical true). This variable states the condition for the upcoming DO WHILE command, and is later made false (.F.) to end the loop. The Mpart_no variable is given a value of 0 and is used later to get a part number from the user.

The Mpart_no variable is displayed for data entry by the first @...SAY...GET command in the program. The @...SAY...GET command is followed by both a PICTURE and a RANGE clause. The PICTURE clause creates a template that allows only four characters to be input to the Mpart_no variable. What's more, those characters must be numbers, as specified by the 9 symbol. The RANGE clause requires that only numbers between 1000 and 9000 be entered into the Mpart_no variable.

The SEEK command then quickly searches the Mpart_no field of the PARTS database to determine if the part number entered has already been used. The FOUND( ) function then states a condition for an IF...ENDIF statement that evaluates the value of the Mpart_no variable. If the number in the Mpart_no variable is found, the FOUND( ) function returns true (.T.) and a screen message informs the user that the part number is already in use. The program then loops back to request another part number. If the part number is not found, the program jumps to the command following ENDIF. In this case, the command is GO Mrec. This command positions the record pointer to the newly appended record. You need this command because the SEEK command trips the end-of-file marker—that is, EOF( ) returns .T.—when a search is not successful.

The program then goes into another DO WHILE...ENDDO loop. From inside the loop, a series of @...SAY...GET commands with various PICTURE, RANGE, and WHEN clauses are used to filter data as it is entered into the newly appended record. After this stage is completed, an IF...ENDIF statement evaluates the contents of the Descript field. If the user failed to enter data into the Descript field, the program loops back to the

```
DO WHILE Descript= " "
```

statement, and the database fields are redisplayed for data entry.

Finally, another loop begins with the

```
DO WHILE .NOT. Choice$"AEQ"
```

command line. Inside this loop is a multiple-choice menu, which stores a user response to a variable called Choice. Unless the user enters either an A, E, or Q, the program remains inside the loop. Once an appropriate response is entered, the loop is exited and either a new record is appended, the current record is edited, or the program ends.

Controlling the Screen

dBASE IV offers a number of commands for controlling the screen. In dBASE IV, controlling the screen means more than simply displaying text and database fields. For example, you can clear the screen, draw lines and boxes, use a variety of colors, define data entry windows, and program messages that automatically appear when your user makes a certain entry.

Placing Messages on the Screen

dBASE IV provides several commands that allow you to place messages on the screen. You already know how to use @...SAY...GET to place a message on the screen that prompts the user to enter data in a database field or memory variable. However, you can also display messages by using the MESSAGE clause with an @...SAY...GET command, the SET MESSAGE command, the WAIT command, and the TEXT...ENDTEXT commands.

The MESSAGE Clause

You can use the MESSAGE clause with the @...SAY...GET command to display a message beneath the status bar. The @...SAY....GET command containing the MESSAGE clause is activated by the READ command. However, its message is not displayed until the cursor enters the database field or memory variable referenced in the @...SAY...GET command. (For the MESSAGE clause to work, SET STATUS must be set to ON).

For example, the following command line displays a memo field called Comment for data entry. Two messages are displayed. The message " Comments: " appears next to the Comment memo field and the message "Press CTRL-HOME to enter a memo, and CTRL-END to save it." appears at the bottom of the screen, below the status bar.

```
@ 16,10 SAY " Comments: " GET Comment MESSAGE "Press CTRL-HOME;
to enter a memo, and CTRL-END to save it."
```

The @...SAY Command

You can also use the @...SAY...GET command minus the GET clause to display messages on the screen. For example, the following section of code includes two @...SAY command lines. The first one displays the message "Deleted" starting on row 18, column 10. Next, the DELETED( ) function is used in an @...SAY command with a PICTURE clause to display the deletion status for the current record, starting at row 18, column 18. If the record is marked for deletion, the display appears as "Delete Y." If the record is not marked for deletion, the display appears as "Delete N."

```
@ 18,10 SAY "Deleted"
@ 18,18 SAY DELETED() PICTURE "Y"
```

The SET MESSAGE Command

You can also use the SET MESSAGE command to display a message at the bottom of the screen. For this command to work, SET STATUS must be set to ON. SET MESSAGE TO without a character string following it erases the current message. Furthermore, any MESSAGE option used with an @...SAY...GET command temporarily overrides a message displayed by the SET MESSAGE command.

The SET MESSAGE command is often included in a conditional statement to display a message when a given condition is present. For example, the following section of code displays a message when the Descript field is empty. It then pauses for the user to press any key, and erases the message.

```
IF Descript=" "
     SET MESSAGE TO "No description entered"
     WAIT
     SET MESSAGE TO
ENDIF
```

The TEXT...ENDTEXT Commands

The TEXT...ENDTEXT commands provide a convenient way to place messages on the screen from your program. The TEXT command begins the message and the ENDTEXT command marks the end of the message. For example, the following section of code uses the TEXT...ENDTEXT commands to place instructions on the screen that tell the user about the current program.

```
TEXT
You have accessed the master parts list database program. You will
be requested to enter a part number. If the part number is unique,
you will then be asked to fill in the balance of the record.
ENDTEXT
```

The WAIT Command

The WAIT command places a message on the screen and stops the program for the user to press any key. If you do not specify a message for the WAIT command, it displays the message "Press any key to continue." To specify your own message, enclose the desired text in quotes immediately after the WAIT command. You can use the WAIT command to pause program execution while the user reads a message. For example, the following program section uses the WAIT command to halt program execution while the user reads text displayed on the screen by the TEXT...ENDTEXT commands.

```
TEXT
You have accessed the master parts list database program. You will
be requested to enter a part number. If the part number is unique,
you will then be asked to fill in the balance of the record.
ENDTEXT

WAIT
```

Clearing the Screen

In dBASE IV programming, you frequently need to clear the screen. You can clear the entire screen with the CLEAR command or clear the screen on a row-by-row basis with the @ command.

The CLEAR command erases the screen, moves the cursor to its lower-left corner, and releases any pending GETs created with the @ command. You will often use the CLEAR command at the beginning of a program to clear the screen in readiness for the new program. Furthermore, you can use the CLEAR command at various points within a program to blank the screen between displays. The syntax for the CLEAR command is

CLEAR

You can also use the @ command followed only by row and column coordinates to clear the screen. The row you specify is cleared starting at the column you specify. You use this technique to clear a single line message after the user has had a chance to read it. For example, the following section of code displays a message starting at row 10, column 10, pauses to let the user read the message, and then erases the message:

```
@ 10,2 SAY "You have entered an invalid date"
WAIT
@ 10,2
```

To clear rectangular portions of the screen or an active window, use the @...CLEAR command. The @...CLEAR command supports two sets of screen coordinates. The first set specifies the upper-left corner of a rectangular portion of the screen you want to clear. The second set of screen coordinates specifies the lower-right corner of the rectangle. For example, to clear the screen from row 2, column 5 to row 10, column 60, use the following command line in your program:

```
@ 2,5 CLEAR TO 10,60
```

Drawing Lines and Boxes

dBASE IV offers several commands that allow you to draw lines and boxes on the screen. Lines and boxes are useful when you want to separate or highlight information on the screen.

Drawing Lines

You can create broken lines and solid lines on the screen. Create broken lines with the REPLICATE function. Create solid lines with the @...TO command.

The REPLICATE Command

The syntax for the REPLICATE function is

REPLICATE(<*character expression*>,<*numeric expression*>)

Character expression is any character string enclosed in quotes and *numeric expression* is the number of times you want the character expression replicated. For example, the following command line replicates the - character 80 times to make a broken line that spans the screen, as shown in Figure 22-2.

```
? REPLICATE("-",80)
```

Tip: You can also draw a double broken line with the REPLICATE function using the equal sign (=) as a character string, as shown in Figure 22-2.

The @...TO Command

You can draw a solid line on the screen by using the @...TO command. The syntax for the @...TO command is

@<*row 1*>,<*column 1*> TO <*row 2*>,<*column 2*>

where the first set of row and column coordinates are the start of the line and the second set are the end of the line. For example, the following command line fashions a solid line starting at row 10, column 1 and extending to row 10, column 79. In other words, it draws a solid line across the screen at row 10. Figure 22-2 shows a solid line drawn with the @...TO command.

```
@ 10,1 TO 10,79
```

You can also draw double lines by following the @...TO command with the DOUBLE clause. For example, this command line

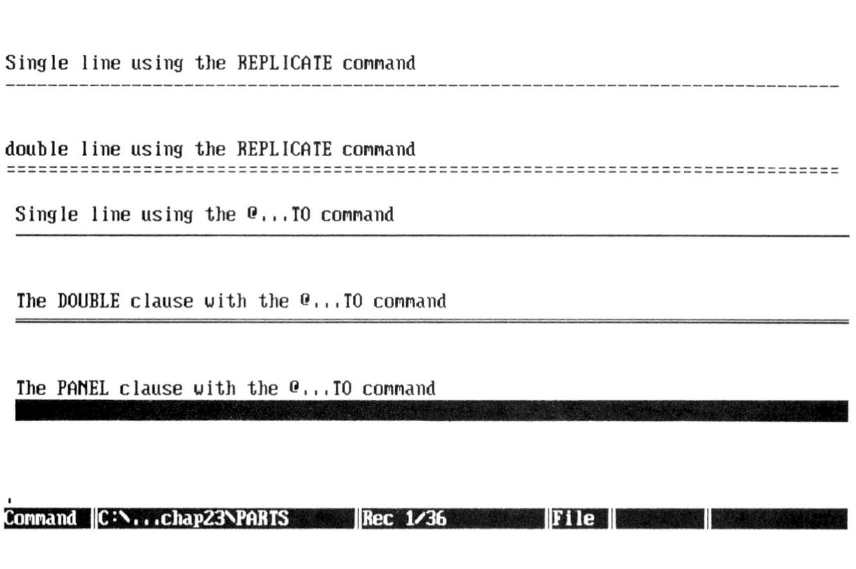

Figure 22-2. Lines drawn with REPLICATE( ) and @...TO

draws a solid double line extending from row 10, column 1 to row 10, column 79:

```
@ 10,1 TO 10,79 DOUBLE
```

The PANEL option for the @...TO command draws a line that appears on your screen as a reverse video bar, as shown in Figure 22-2. To draw a line like the one in Figure 22-2, use a command like this:

```
@ 10,1 TO 10,79 PANEL
```

You can also make your lines appear in different colors by using the COLOR clause with the @...TO command. The COLOR clause uses the same color codes for foreground and background display as the SET COLOR command explained later in this chapter. Color codes specify the colors you want for both foreground and background display. You need two color codes separated by a slash (/) for the COLOR clause of the @...TO command. The color code to the left of the slash specifies the foreground color and the color code to the right of the slash specifies the background color. For example, the following command line specifies a double black line on a cyan (light blue) background.

```
@ 10,1 TO 10,79 DOUBLE COLOR N/BG
```

Tip: For a complete list of available color codes, see the SET COLOR command later in this chapter.

Drawing Boxes

You can use the @...TO command to draw boxes. To do this, specify the coordinates of the upper-left and lower-right corners of the box by using the @...TO command. For example, the following command line draws a single-line box starting at row 10, column 1 and extending to row 15, column 50. That is, this command line constructs a box that is six rows deep and 50 columns wide.

```
@ 10,1 TO 15,50
```

The @...TO command, when used for boxes, still supports the DOUBLE, PANEL, and COLOR clauses. Thus, you can draw double-line boxes, boxes that appear in reverse video, and boxes that appear in different colors. Figure 22-3 shows some sample single-line, double-line, and reverse-video boxes.

Once your boxes are drawn on the screen, you can use @...SAY...GET commands to place user input prompts and database fields inside them. However, be careful not to let your prompts or database fields extend beyond the limits of the box. If they do, the box is overwritten and the display appears sloppy. To deal with this problem, you can use the S<*number*> formatting option with

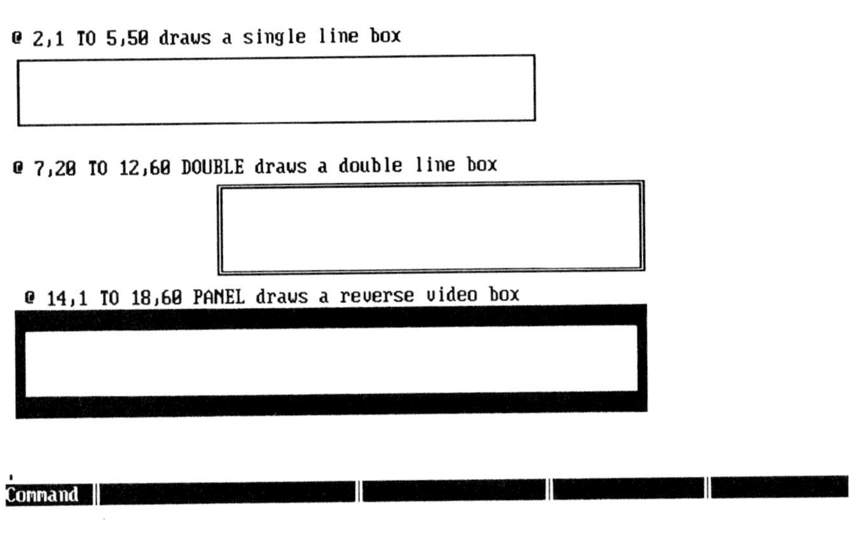
@ 2,1 TO 5,50 draws a single line box
@ 7,20 TO 12,60 DOUBLE draws a double line box
@ 14,1 TO 18,60 PANEL draws a reverse video box
Command

Figure 22-3. Various boxes drawn with @...TO

the PICTURE or FUNCTION clause of the @...SAY...GET command to scroll a database field.

The S<*number*> formatting option stipulates a numeric column width for a database field on the screen. When your data entry exceeds the width of the displayed field, dBASE IV scrolls the entry from right to left as more characters are added. For example, both of the following command lines display the Lastname field in the CUSTOMER database. The Lastname field is normally 20 characters wide. However, the following command lines only allow a display of ten characters and scroll the Lastname field when additional characters are entered. The first command line displays the S<*number*> format function with the PICTURE clause. When you use the S<*number*> formatting option with the PICTURE clause, the @ symbol must be the first character in the clause. The second command line uses the FUNCTION clause. Note that the @ symbol is not required.

```
@ 10,20 SAY "Lastname" GET Lastname PICTURE "@S10"
@ 10,20 SAY "Lastname" GET Lastname FUNCTION "S10"
```

Setting Colors

In dBASE IV, you can use various commands to display different parts of the screen in different colors. You can control the colors that appear on the screen with the commands SET COLOR, @...FILL...COLOR, @..SAY...GET...COLOR, and @...TO...COLOR.

The SET COLOR Command

The SET COLOR command sets colors for different parts of the screen. For example, you can use it to set colors for displayed database fields, boxes, text, and messages. There are two versions of the SET COLOR command. You use the first version to set colors globally for different types of displayed data. You use the second version when you want to set colors not only for displayed data but for dBASE IV. The syntax for the first SET COLOR command is as follows:

SET COLOR TO [<*standard*>][,<*enhanced*>][,<*perimeter*>]
[,<*background*>]
SET COLOR ON/OFF

Standard refers to normal dBASE IV screen text, such as what is displayed by the LIST, DISPLAY, ?, and SAY commands. The *enhanced* part of the command refers to highlighted or reverse-video areas of the screen, such as database fields displayed in reverse-video by the READ command. *Perimeter* refers to the screen bor-

Color	Color Code
Black(natural)	N
Gray	N+
Blue	B
Green	G
Cyan	BG
Red	R
Magenta	RB
Brown	GR
Yellow	GR+
White	W
Blank	X
Blinking	*
High intensity	+
Inverse video	I
Underline	U

Table 22-2. dBASE IV Color Codes

der (if your monitor has one), and *background* is the background setting for some, but not all, color monitors.

SET COLOR ON/OFF switches back and forth between color and monochrome screens for those computers that have both.

You specify colors for displayed data using color codes. A list of available dBASE IV color codes is provided in Table 22-2. When you specify colors, you must specify both a background color code and a foreground color code, separating the two with a slash (/). The foreground color code appears on the left side and the background color code appears on the right side of the slash. For example, the following command line specifies that all standard screen text appear as white on a green background.

```
SET COLOR TO W/G
```

Tip: If you have a monochrome monitor, you can use only N for black, U for underlining, I for inverse video, and * for blinking.

The following command line specifies colors for both standard screen text and enhanced displays, such as database fields displayed by the @...SAY...GET...READ commands and the status bar. Note that two distinct sets of color codes, separated by commas, are included in the command. The first set applies to standard screen text and the second set applies to enhanced or reverse-video displays. Standard screen text is displayed as blue on a magenta background and enhanced displays appear as red on a white background.

```
SET COLOR TO B/RB,R/W
```

With the second version of the SET COLOR command, you can be a great deal more specific about setting colors both for displayed data and for dBASE IV itself. The syntax for the second SET COLOR command is

> SET COLOR OF NORMAL/MESSAGES/TITLES/BOX/
> HIGHLIGHT/INFORMATION/FIELDS TO
> [*<color attribute>*]

NORMAL refers to normal screen output initiated by your program. MESSAGES refers to messages such as those generated using the SET MESSAGE TO command. TITLES refers to headings such as those present with the LIST or DISPLAY command. BOX refers to error or message boxes displayed by dBASE IV. HIGHLIGHT refers to dBASE IV menu and list choices. FIELDS refers to editable fields in @...SAY...GET commands generated by your program. The *color attribute* portion of the command allows color codes separated by a slash.

For example, the following three command lines set various colors for the display of data. The first command line sets normal screen output, such as that displayed by the LIST or DISPLAY command, to blue on a white background. Thus, the entire dBASE IV screen is displayed as white, except for the status bar and screen output, which are blue. The second command line stipulates that all column heads generated by the LIST or DISPLAY command appear as green on a red background. The third command line specifies that all editable database fields or memory variables displayed by @...SAY...GET commands are displayed as red on a cyan background.

```
SET COLOR OF NORMAL TO B/W
SET COLOR OF TITLES TO G/R
SET COLOR OF FIELDS TO R/BG
```

Tip: The SET COLOR command is oriented toward color monitors. You can use the ISCOLOR( ) function to determine if your user has a color monitor. This function returns true if a color monitor is present, and false if not.

The @...FILL Command

The @...FILL command changes the colors of a rectangular region of the screen or active window. The syntax for this command is

> @ *<row 1>*,*<column 1>* FILL TO *<row 2>*,*<column 2>*
> COLOR *<color attribute>*

The @...FILL command applies to data that is already on the screen. It specifies the color for a rectangular block on the screen by specifying the coordinates of the block's upper-left corner (row 1 and column 1) and its lower-right corner (row 2 and column 2). The COLOR *<color attribute>* clause specifies colors for the region, using color codes to specify a foreground and a background color. The color codes are the same as the codes used with the SET COLOR command.

For example, the following command line paints a rectangular region of the screen extending from row 10, column 1 to row 20, column 50 as a white foreground on a red background. As mentioned, this command only applies to data already on the screen. Therefore, if you subsequently change or add any data to this portion of the screen, it is displayed in the current default color or in a color you have specified as the default using the SET COLOR command.

```
@ 10,1 FILL TO 20,50 COLOR W/R
```

The @...SAY...GET...COLOR Command

The COLOR clause of the @...SAY...GET command specifies the colors for both memory variables or text following SAY, and database fields or memory variables following GET. The syntax for this command is

> @ *<row>*,*<column>* [SAY *<expression>*] [GET *<variable>*] [COLOR [*<standard>*][,*<enhanced>*]]

The *standard* after the COLOR clause applies to the *expression* after SAY, and *enhanced* applies to the *variable* after GET. The colors you specify override those colors set with the SET COLOR command, but only for the current @ command. You specify the colors for both the standard and enhanced display with the same color codes you use with the SET COLOR command. For example, the following command line displays the expression "Enter last name:" as white on a red background, and the database field Lastname as green on a brown background:

```
@ 10,10 SAY "Enter last name: " GET Lastname COLOR W/R,G/GR
```

The @...TO...COLOR Command

As mentioned, you can use the @...TO...COLOR command to specify colors for lines and boxes. The syntax for this command is

> @ *<row 1>*,*<column 1>* TO *<row 2>*,*<column 2>* COLOR *<color attribute>*

The COLOR <*color attribute*> portion of the command allows you to specify colors for the line or box using the same color codes you use with SET COLOR. For example, the following command line draws a box that appears as a double black line on a red background extending from row 10, column 1 to row 20, column 50.

```
@ 10,1 TO 20,50 DOUBLE COLOR N/R
```

Setting Intensity and Delimiters

You can modify enhanced (reverse video) database fields to appear in standard format (non-reverse video) by using the SET INTENSITY OFF command. Normally, SET INTENSITY is set to ON. With this command enhanced displays, such as database fields displayed with @...SAY...GET...READ, appear in standard format.

In dBASE IV, you can use the SET DELIMITER command to specify various delimiters for the display of database fields and memory variables. This command determines the characters used to delimit fields when they are displayed on the screen. Normally, fields are displayed in reverse video. However, you can also display them delimited with [ ], ( ), or { } by using the SET DELIMITER command. The syntax for the SET DELIMITER command is

SET DELIMITER TO <*delimiter symbols*>
SET DELIMITER ON/OFF

Using the SET DELIMITER command is a two-step process. You must first specify a delimiter with SET DELIMITER TO and then activate the specified delimiter with SET DELIMITER ON. For example, the following command lines specify [ ] as the currently active field delimiter symbols. Note that the SET INTENSITY OFF command is also used so that fields are not displayed in reverse video. Figure 22-4 shows the effects of these command lines.

```
            >>> Mailing List Data Entry Screen <<<

    Customer Name: [George     ]   [Thomas          ]

          Company: [Texasville Pumps    ]

        Address 1: [10201 Torre Ave.              ]

        Address 2: [Suite F                       ]

             City: [Dallas              ]

            State: [TX]  Zip: [56902     ]  Phone: [(916) 453 9022]
```

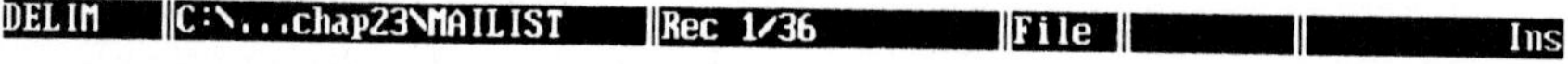

Figure 22-4. The SET DELIMITERS command specifies [ ]

```
SET DELIMITER TO "[]"
SET DELIMITER ON
SET INTENSITY OFF
SET FORMAT TO Mailer
READ
```

Using Windows

In dBASE IV, you can use windows to display program output. You can also use a window to contain the dBASE IV Text Editor while your user is editing memo fields.

Displaying Output in Windows

You define windows with the DEFINE WINDOW command. The syntax for this command is

> DEFINE WINDOW <*window name*> FROM
> <*row 1*>,<*column 1*> TO <*row 2*>,<*column 2*>
> [DOUBLE/PANEL] [COLOR [<*standard*>][,<*enhanced*>]]

Window name is the name of the window. *Row 1* and *column 1* are the screen coordinates of the window's upper-left corner, and *row 2* and *column 2* are the coordinates of the window's lower-right corner. [DOUBLE/PANEL] refers to either a double-line or paneled (reverse-video) window border. (Single-line windows are the default.) [COLOR [<*standard*>][,<*enhanced*>]] specifies colors for the window using the same color codes as the SET COLOR command. *Standard* specifies foreground and background colors for the data inside the window, and *enhanced* specifies foreground and background colors for the window border.

For example, the following command line defines a double-line window called Help extending from row 6, column 1 to row 10, column 60. Additionally, the text inside the window is displayed as white on a red background.

```
DEFINE WINDOW Help FROM 6,1 TO 10,60 DOUBLE COLOR W/R
```

To use a defined window, you must activate it with the ACTIVATE WINDOW command. This command makes the window appear on the screen in the region you specified with the DEFINE WINDOW command. From then on, all output is directed to the window until you deactivate it with the DEACTIVATE WINDOW command.

The following program uses the DEFINE WINDOW, ACTIVATE WINDOW, and DEACTIVATE WINDOW commands. The program provides its own on-line help facility by causing help messages to appear in the Help window, which is activated whenever the user presses F1.

```
SET TALK OFF
*------Trap the F1 key when pressed
ON KEY LABEL F1 DO Help_me

*------Define a window
DEFINE WINDOW Help FROM 6,1 TO 10,60

CLEAR
USE Mailist
*------Tell the user how to get help
@ 2,10 SAY "Press F1 for HELP"
*------Display a field for editing
@ 4,10 SAY "Enter last name: " GET Lastname
*------More @...SAY...GET commands
READ

*-----Procedure to activate and display the Help window
PROCEDURE Help_me
CLRBUFF = INKEY()           && Clear typeahead buffer

ACTIVATE WINDOW Help        && Activate the Help window

*-----Display the following message in the Help window
? "Please enter the customer's last name"
? "The correct spelling is important"
WAIT

DEACTIVATE WINDOW Help      && Deactivate the Help window

RETURN
```

The program first specifies a trap for the F1 key by using the ON KEY LABEL command. If F1 is pressed, the program performs a procedure called Help_me, also listed in the program. (The ON KEY LABEL command is explained in Chapter 23.)

Next, a window called Help is defined using the DEFINE WINDOW command. (The on-screen appearance of the Help window is displayed in Figure 22-5.) After that, the MAILIST database is opened and a message is displayed on the screen that tells the user to press F1 for help.

```
Press F1 for HELP

Enter last name: Thomas

Please enter the customer's last name
The correct spelling is important
Press any key to continue...

WNDW  C:\...chap23\MAILIST  Rec 1/36  File
```

Figure 22-5. Program output displayed in a window

Then the program uses an @...SAY...GET command to display a database field called Lastname from the MAILIST database. If the user presses F1 at this time, the Help_me procedure is started.

The Help_me procedure is identified by the command line PROCEDURE Help_me. The Help_me procedure first activates the Help window with the command ACTIVATE WINDOW Help. Text is then placed inside the window with the ? command. The WAIT command in the Help_me procedure pauses the program so that the user can read the text in the Help window. When the user presses any key, the Help window is deactivated with the DEACTIVATE WINDOW Help command. The window disappears from the screen and the user is returned to the Lastname database field in the @...SAY...GET command.

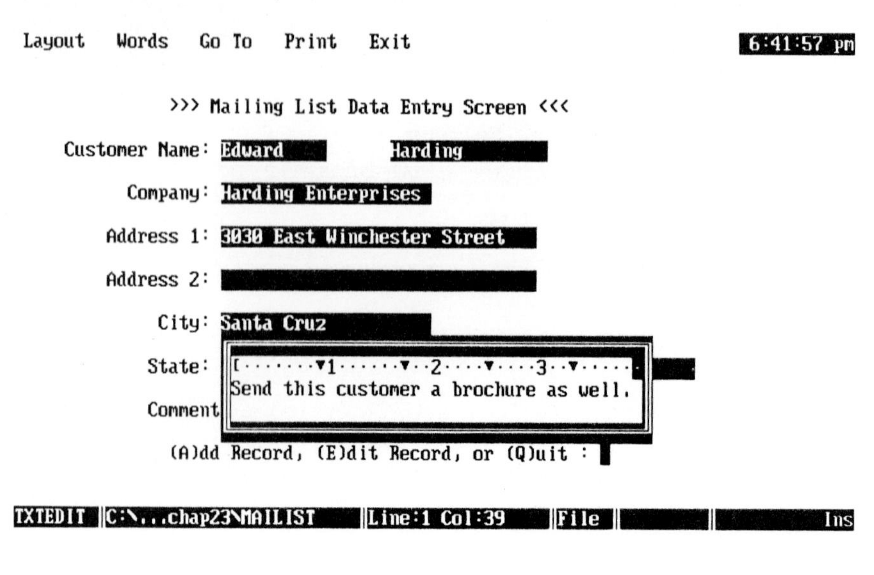

Figure 22-6. The Text Editor displayed in a window

Windowing the Text Editor

You can also define a window for the dBASE IV Text Editor. You can then use that window to display the Text Editor for editing memo fields. Placing the Text Editor inside a window and displaying it for editing memo fields is a three-step process.

1. Define the window with the DEFINE WINDOW command.

2. Establish the window as the default window with the SET WINDOW OF MEMO command followed by the name of the defined window.

3. Call the window to the screen for editing a memo field using the WINDOW <*window name*> clause with the @...SAY...GET command.

The following program uses these three steps to display the Text Editor in a window. First, a window called Wndw1 is defined with the command DEFINE WINDOW Wndw1 FROM 14,20 TO 18,60 DOUBLE. Next, the Wndw1 window is established as the default window with the command SET WINDOW OF MEMO TO Wndw1. Finally, the window is activated with the following command:

```
@17, 13 SAY "Comments: " GET Mssg WINDOW Wndwl
```

When the cursor is in the Mssg memo field and the user presses CTRL-HOME to edit it, the Wndw1 window is displayed on the screen with the dBASE IV Text Editor inside it. Figure 22-6 shows the results. When the user presses CTRL-END to save the memo, the window disappears from the screen and dBASE IV continues with the rest of the program.

```
*Program is TXTEDIT.PRG
SET TALK OFF
USE Mailist
*-----------Define a window and set it as the default
DEFINE WINDOW Wndwl FROM 14,20 TO 18,60 DOUBLE
SET WINDOW OF MEMO TO Wndwl

SET FORMAT TO Mailer
APPEND BLANK
STORE .T. TO Entry

DO WHILE Entry
     READ
     CLOSE FORMAT

     *----------Open Wdwl to edit a memo field
     @ 17,13 SAY "Comments: " GET Mssg WINDOW Wndwl;
     MESSAGE "Press CTRL-HOME to enter a memo, CTRL-END to save it."

     STORE " " TO Choice
     @ 19,15 SAY "(A)dd Record, (E)dit Record, or (Q)uit :";
     GET Choice PICTURE "!"
     READ
     DO CASE
       CASE Choice="A"
            APPEND BLANK
       CASE Choice="Q"
            Entry=.F.
     ENDCASE
ENDDO
*----------Release Wdnwl as the default window.
```

```
RELEASE WINDOW Wndw1

CLOSE DATABASES
RETURN
```

In this chapter, you learned some techniques for controlling user input. You now know how to use RANGE, PICTURE, and WHEN clauses with @...SAY...GET commands to filter user input at the point of data entry. You are also familiar with techniques for evaluating user input after the fact and redisplaying data entry fields for correction.

You also learned some commands and techniques for controlling the screen. You now know how to draw lines and boxes on the screen and how to change colors on the screen. Furthermore, you've learned how to use windows to display data and edit memo fields.

Event Processing and Error Trapping

The ON Command
Event Processing
Error Trapping with ON ERROR

TWENTY THREE

This chapter covers commands and techniques that you can use to have your program perform event processing and error trapping.

Event processing involves trapping user keystrokes and having your program respond to those keystrokes by performing a routine. The routine can begin when the user presses any key on the keyboard. You can also link the routine to a specific key.

Error trapping refers to trapping dBASE IV system errors. When a system error occurs, you can have your program perform a given operation. This prevents dBASE IV from displaying an unfriendly error message or ending your program and returning to the dot prompt.

The ON Command

You use the ON command for both event processing and error trapping. The ON command supports three clauses: KEY, ESCAPE, and ERROR. Use KEY and ESCAPE for event processing. Use the ERROR clause for error trapping.

You use the ON command to check for a specific event (a user keystroke) or an error (a dBASE IV system error) and take action when that event or error occurs. When you use the ON command early in a program to specify either a keystroke or an error, dBASE IV watches for the rest of the program for that keystroke or error to occur. When the keystroke or error does occur, you can have your program branch to a subprogram or procedure designed to handle the situation.

The ESCAPE, KEY, and ERROR clauses of the ON command are referred to as *program interrupts.* They interrupt the current program temporarily so that another subprogram or procedure can be performed.

Event Processing

As mentioned, event processing involves capturing a user keystroke and then branching to a subprogram or procedure. Use the KEY and ESCAPE clauses of the ON command for this purpose. The ESCAPE clause captures only the ESC key; the KEY clause captures any key on the keyboard.

The ON KEY Command

The ON KEY command performs a subprogram or procedure when a specified keystroke occurs. The syntax for this command is

ON KEY [LABEL <*key name*>] [<*command*>]

Keyname can be any of the printable characters you see on your keyboard as well as keys and key sequences that are not printable. For example, the letter "A" is a printable character. However, the F1 key is not printable, nor is the key sequence CTRL-HOME, yet you can specify either of these with the ON KEY command. For a complete list of nonprintable characters that you can use with the ON KEY command, see the ON KEY command in Chapter 31. If a key label name specified using the LABEL clause does not appear after the ON KEY command, dBASE IV executes the command following ON KEY when any key is pressed. The command that follows ON KEY is usually the DO command followed by the name of a subprogram or procedure.

The ON KEY command is not case sensitive. Thus, whenever a key you specify is pressed, dBASE IV captures it whether it is entered in upper- or lowercase.

To deactivate the current ON KEY command, use ON KEY again but do not follow it with either a key label name or a command. This disables the previous ON KEY command, returning all the keys on the keyboard to their normal behavior.

In the following program, PARTMSTR.PRG, the ON KEY command provides an on-line help facility. Whenever the user presses F1, a window provides instructions for filling in the current database field for the PARTS database. The program uses DEFINE WINDOW to define a window called Help_me in which to display the help instructions. Next, the command

```
ON KEY LABEL F1 DO Help
```

instructs dBASE IV to perform the Help procedure whenever the F1 key is pressed.

```
= * Program is PARTMSTR
SET TALK OFF
SET ECHO OFF
CLEAR
USE Parts ORDER Part_no
*-----Define a window for help messages
DEFINE WINDOW Help_me FROM 10,10 TO 15,60 DOUBLE
*-----Do the Help procedure when F1 is pressed.
ON KEY LABEL F1 DO Help

STORE .T. TO Enter
DO WHILE Enter
     @ 0,10 SAY "    >>>Master Parts List Data Entry<<<"
     @ 1,10 SAY "           (Press F1 for Help)"
     @ 3,10 SAY "  Enter Part number: " GET Part_no
     @ 5,10 SAY "        Description: " GET Descript
     @ 7,10 SAY "            On hand: " GET On_hand
     @ 9,10 SAY "           On Order: " GET On_order
     @ 11,10 SAY "           Due Date: " GET Due_in WHEN On_order<>0
     @ 13,10 SAY "              Price: " GET Price
```

```
     @ 15,10 SAY "Delete Record(Y/N)?: " GET Delete PICTURE "Y"
     @ 17,10 SAY "            Comment: " GET Comment MESSAGE "Press;
CTRL-HOME to enter CTRL-END to save"
     STORE " " TO Choice
     DO WHILE .NOT. Choice$"AEQ"
           *-----Get a response from the user in uppercase
           STORE " " TO Choice
           @ 19,10 SAY "(A)dd record, (E)dit record, or (Q)uit: " GET Choice;
            PICTURE "!"
           READ
           *-----Evaluate user input, and add a record, loop, or quit.
           DO CASE
               CASE Choice="A"
                      APPEND BLANK
                      CLEAR
               CASE CHOICE="Q"
                      Enter=.F.
           ENDCASE
     ENDDO (.NOT. Choice$ "AEQ")
ENDDO (Enter)
*-----Procedure for On-line Help
PROCEDURE Help
ACTIVATE WINDOW Help_me
DO CASE
     CASE VARREAD() = "PART_NO"
           ? "Enter unique part numbers only"
     CASE VARREAD() = "DESCRIPT"
           ? "Enter the vendor description"
     CASE VARREAD() = "ON_HAND"
           ? "Enter the total in stock for this part."
     *
     *--More CASE statements go here...
     *
ENDCASE
WAIT
DEACTIVATE WINDOW Help_me
RETURN

RETURN
```

The Help procedure provides the on-line help facility for the PARTMSTR.PRG program. The procedure appears toward the end of the program and begins with the command PROCEDURE Help. The next command,

```
ACTIVATE WINDOW Help_me
```

activates the Help_me window and directs dBASE IV output to that window. Next, a DO CASE...ENDCASE statement presents a series of CASEs for dBASE IV to evaluate. In each CASE, the

VARREAD( ) function is used in a comparison to return the name of the database field or memory variable being edited. Note that the database field names opposite each VARREAD( ) function appear both in quotes and uppercase; otherwise, the VARREAD( ) function will not perform properly. Once the CASE statements identify which field contains the cursor, a message for that database field is displayed in the Help_me window. For example, assuming that the cursor is presently located in the Part_no field of the PARTS database, dBASE IV sends the message "Enter unique part numbers only" to the Help_me window.

Next, the WAIT command pauses program execution and displays the message "Press any key to continue..." in the Help_me window. Without the WAIT command here to pause program execution, the Help_me window would be just a momentary flash on your screen. When the user presses any key in response to the WAIT command, the command

```
DEACTIVATE WINDOW Help_me
```

removes the Help_me window from the screen. The cursor then reappears in the Part_no database field and the user can edit the remaining fields in the current record.

Tip: You can use the INKEY( ) function with a 0 argument in place of the WAIT command in the PARTMSTR.PRG program. This function pauses program execution for a specified number of seconds or until the user presses any key. For example, INKEY(0) specifies an indefinite waiting period for the INKEY( ) function, INKEY(5) specifies a five-second waiting period, and so on. When you use this function, place a message of your own on the screen that tells your user what to do next.

The ON ESCAPE Command

Pressing the ESC key in the middle of a program can often bring your program to an abrupt end. When this happens, dBASE IV returns to the dot prompt and displays a box with the message "***INTERRUPTED***" followed by the options **Cancel**, **Ignore**, and **Suspend**. To avoid this message box, use the ON ESCAPE command.

The ON ESCAPE command allows you to tailor dBASE IV's response to the ESC key. Instead of having the ESC key end your program, you can use the ON ESCAPE command to trigger the start of another subprogram or procedure. The syntax for the ON ESCAPE command is

ON ESCAPE *<command>*

The command following ON ESCAPE is most often the DO command followed by the name of a subprogram or procedure. dBASE IV performs the command following ON ESCAPE whenever the ESC key is pressed. To disable the previous ON ESCAPE command, use the ON ESCAPE command without an argument.

The ON ESCAPE command takes precedence over the ON KEY command when they appear in the same program. That is, if your user presses ESC, the ON ESCAPE routine executes, not the ON KEY routine.

The following program, ESCMESSG.PRG, uses the ON ESCAPE command to interrupt an update of the accounts receivable database from the orders database. The command

```
ON ESCAPE DO Former
```

starts the Former procedure whenever the ESC key is pressed. The Former procedure rolls back any transactions to a database called ACCTSREC and reverts it to its former state.

```
* Program is ESCMSSG.PRG
* Program uses ON ESCAPE to interrupt an UPDATE and roll it back
SET TALK OFF
SET SAFETY OFF
CLOSE ALL
*----Use the ESC key to roll back a transaction
ON ESCAPE DO Former
*----Press ESC to stop the update
? "                    Press ESC to stop the update"
WAIT
USE Orderrec ORDER Cust_no
TOTAL ON Cust_no TO Temp FOR .NOT. Paid
USE Temp in 2
```

```
USE Acctsrec ORDER Cust_no
?
BEGIN TRANSACTION
? "                     Updating..."
UPDATE ON Cust_no FROM Temp REPLACE Total WITH ;
Total+Temp->Total
END TRANSACTION
?
CLOSE ALL
USE Temp
ZAP
ON ESCAPE
RETURN
PROCEDURE Former
IF ISMARKED()
     ? "                     The update has been cancelled..."
     ROLLBACK
     USE TEMP
     ZAP
     ON ESCAPE
ENDIF
RETURN
```

The ESCMSSG.PRG program begins with the

```
ON ESCAPE DO Former
```

command. Next, a message informs the user that pressing ESC will stop the updating process. Then, the database containing customer orders, ORDERREC, is opened and the Cust_no (customer number) index tag is selected. This indexes the ORDERREC database by customer number. Then, the TOTAL ON command sums the numeric fields of the ORDERREC database by customer number for those records that do not have an entry in the Paid logical field (which indicates whether or not customers have paid their bills). That data is then used to create a new database called TEMP.

The TEMP database is the database that is used later in an UPDATE command to update the accounts receivable database, ACCTSREC. Once the TEMP database is created, it is opened in work area 2. You need to do this in order to later use the UPDATE command. Finally, the ACCTSREC database is opened in work area 1 and its Cust_no index tag is activated. The program is then ready to begin the updating process.

The updating process is controlled by the BEGIN TRANSACTION, END TRANSACTION, and ROLLBACK commands. Although these commands are most often used in a network environment, you can also use them with the single-user version of dBASE IV. The BEGIN TRANSACTION command marks the beginning of a transaction. In this case, the transaction is the UPDATE command that updates the ACCTSREC database. The END TRANSACTION command marks the end of a transaction. These two commands work together to record a transaction as a distinct entity.

The ROLLBACK command reverses a transaction recorded by the BEGIN TRANSACTION and END TRANSACTION commands. The ROLLBACK command for the program is located in the Former procedure, which is started anytime the user presses ESC. The ROLLBACK command here reverses any changes made to ACCTSREC by the command

```
UPDATE ON Cust_no FROM Temp REPLACE Total WITH
Total+Temp->Total
```

ROLLBACK appears within an IF...ENDIF conditional statement. The condition used for the statement is the ISMARKED( ) function, which returns true (.T.) if the currently active database is in a state of change and false (.F.) if it is not. You need this statement to prevent ROLLBACK from crashing the program if the user presses ESC before the program processes the BEGIN TRANSACTION command.

The Former procedure also performs some other functions. For example, since TEMP is no longer required, it is opened and its records are erased with the ZAP command. Also, the ON ESCAPE command is used without an argument to return the ESC key to its normal behavior. Note that a similar train of events takes place at the close of the ESCMESSG.PRG program.

Tip: Note the use of the SET SAFETY OFF command at the beginning of the ESCMSSG.PRG program. This command permits dBASE IV to overwrite existing files without getting an on-screen confirmation from your user.

Event Processing Functions

Three functions—INKEY( ), LASTKEY( ), and READKEY( )—are often used in event processing. INKEY( ) returns an integer corresponding to the ASCII code for the key most recently pressed by the user. Similarly, the LASTKEY( ) function returns the ASCII decimal number for the last key pressed. The READKEY( ) command returns an integer value for the keystroke used to terminate data entry during a full-screen editing command such as APPEND or READ. You can use all three functions in your program to branch to a procedure or to perform a routine. For more on these functions, see Chapter 33.

Error Trapping with ON ERROR

As mentioned, error trapping refers to trapping dBASE IV system errors. The ON ERROR command is used to perform this function. The ON ERROR command executes a subprogram or procedure when a dBASE IV system error occurs. The syntax for the ON ERROR command is

ON ERROR *<command>*

The command most often used after the ON ERROR command is the DO command followed by the name of a subprogram or procedure. The subprogram or procedure contains code that evaluates the error and either rectifies the problem or informs the user how to correct it.

To cancel the previous ON ERROR command, use the ON ERROR command again, without an argument. Unless you use this command, the ON ERROR interrupt remains active after your program is completed. Any errors subsequently made at the dot prompt result in an error box calling for the command or procedure you specified with the ON ERROR command.

In practice, the ON ERROR command is used to correct problems that are easily rectified, such as too many open databases or a full disk.

Note that the ON ERROR command traps dBASE IV system errors only. It cannot trap operating system (DOS) errors. When DOS errors occur, dBASE IV displays a message that is not under the control of the ON ERROR command.

Two functions, ERROR( ) and MESSAGE( ), complement the ON ERROR command. Whenever a dBASE IV system error takes place, the ERROR( ) function is given a number that represents the specific error. In addition, the MESSAGE( ) function is given a character string that briefly describes the nature of the error. Both of these functions are quite useful as you program your error trapping routines. A complete list of dBASE IV system error messages and their numbers is in the back of your dBASE IV *Language Reference* manual.

Another command useful for error trapping is RETRY. This command reexecutes the code that caused the error. Once your error correction routine has had a chance to correct the error, you can use RETRY to repeat the code that originally caused the problem.

The following program, BACKUP.PRG, backs up the specified database to drive A. The program asks the user to enter a database file name and to place a disk in drive A.

```
* Program is BACKUP.PRG
* Program backs-up the specified database to drive A.
SET TALK OFF
CLEAR
*-------Perform the Err_hand procedure when error occurs
ON ERROR DO Err_hand
Accept "Enter name of database to copy to drive A: " To Filename
COPY FILE &Filename TO A:&filename
ON ERROR
RETURN
*-------Procedure to handle common system errors
PROCEDURE Err_hand
DO CASE
     *--Filename does not exist
     CASE ERROR() = 1
          ? MESSAGE()
          ACCEPT "Check filename and enter again:" TO Filename
          RETRY
     *--Error reading on drive, gate left open
```

```
     CASE ERROR() = 29
            ? MESSAGE()
            WAIT "Check the drive gate, and press a key to try again"
            RETRY
     *--Disk full
     CASE ERROR() = 56
            ? MESSAGE()
            WAIT "Disk full. Insert new disk, and press any key"
            RETRY
     *--Catch all
     OTHERWISE
            ? "Error number is "+STR(ERROR(),3)+" "
            ?? MESSAGE()
           WAIT
ENDCASE
RETURN
```

The program begins with the command

```
ON ERROR DO Err_hand
```

It executes the Err_hand procedure whenever a fatal system error occurs. Next, the ACCEPT command prompts the user to enter a database file name, which is stored in a memory variable called Filename. This memory variable is used later with macro substitution (&) in the command

```
COPY FILE &Filename TO A:&Filename
```

which tells dBASE IV to copy the file to the disk in drive A.

While dBASE IV copies the specified database to drive A, a number of fatal system errors can occur. For example, if the user places a disk in drive A that is already full, dBASE IV issues error number 56 and assigns that value to the ERROR( ) function. In addition, the character string "Disk full when writing file: *<filename>*" is assigned to the MESSAGE() function.

The Err_hand procedure uses ERROR( ) and MESSAGE( ) functions as well as the RETRY command. The ERROR( ) function is used in CASE comparisons in a DO CASE...ENDCASE construction to identify the current error. Then, the MESSAGE( ) function displays a brief message that describes the error. Next, the program provides its own code to allow the user to correct the error.

Finally, the RETRY command reruns the code that originally caused the error.

Note that the last statement in the DO CASE...ENDCASE construction is an OTHERWISE statement. This statement is a catchall for the Err_hand error trapping procedure—a good idea because it is next to impossible to anticipate every possible user error. The commands following the OTHERWISE statement in the Err_hand procedure,

```
? "Error number is "+STR(ERROR(),3)+" "
```

and

```
?? MESSAGE( )
```

display both the error number and its message. For example, if your user simply presses ENTER in response to the request to enter a database file name, dBASE IV displays the message "The error number is 36 Unrecognized phrase/Keyword in command."

In this chapter, you learned some event processing and error trapping commands and techniques. Under event processing, you learned how to use the ON KEY and ON ESCAPE commands to have your program branch to a procedure whenever the ESC key or another key is pressed.

Under error trapping, you learned about the ON ERROR and RETRY commands as well as the ERROR( ) and MESSAGE( ) functions. You now know how to use the ON ERROR command to activate an error-handling procedure. You also learned how to use the ERROR( ) and MESSAGE( ) functions to identify errors and display messages for them. Finally, you now know how to use the RETRY command to rerun the code that caused the error.

Advanced Topics

User-Defined Functions
Using Arrays
Using Pop-Up Menus
STEP IVWARD

TWENTY FOUR

The chapter addresses issues of interest to the advanced programmer. The main topics—user-defined functions, arrays, and pop-up menus—are all features new to dBASE IV. Also discussed is the new STEP IVWARD product from Ashton-Tate, which allows you to upgrade applications you've developed for dBASE III PLUS with the Clipper, FoxBASE+, and Quicksilver compilers to run under dBASE IV.

At times, you may need a function that dBASE IV does not offer. If so, you can develop your own user-defined functions. User-defined functions work much like standard dBASE IV functions in that they return a single result to the expression from which they are called.

dBASE IV treats arrays as do a number of higher level programming languages. However, dBASE IV allows you to place more than one data type in an array.

dBASE IV's pop-up menus offer the advanced programmer a new level of sophistication in presenting menus. In many ways, pop-up menus emulate the user interface offered through dBASE IV's Control Center.

User-Defined Functions

In dBASE IV, you can use the FUNCTION command to create user-defined functions (UDFs). You use UDFs to perform tasks not addressed by any of the other dBASE IV functions listed in Chapter 33. Once you create a user-defined function, you can use that function in a dBASE IV expression.

Like other dBASE IV functions, you use UDFs to return a single value to the function reference in an expression. Therefore, you should only use user-defined functions when you need to calculate a single value. Conversely, use subprograms and procedures to return none, one, or many different values.

User-defined functions, like procedures, are called from the main program as a subroutine. However, UDF procedures receive values from the main program, use those values to calculate a single result, and return that result to the command line that contains the UDF name.

You use the FUNCTION command to identify the location of a UDF, as you use the PROCEDURE command to identify the location of a procedure. The FUNCTION command is followed by the name of the user-defined function and marks the beginning of a UDF subroutine. Furthermore, much like procedures, UDF subroutines must end with a RETURN command. However, the RETURN command that ends a UDF is always followed by an expression, as in RETURN(M_tax). The expression following the RETURN command contains the value generated by the UDF; this is the value passed back to the calling command line.

Rather than being called by the DO command, as with procedures, user-defined functions are referenced by their name in an expression. For example, you might give a UDF the name of ADD_TAX( ). When dBASE IV encounters this function name, it searches for a FUNCTION subroutine with the same name. Values passed to the function subroutine are used to calculate a result, and that result is returned to the command line that contains the ADD_TAX( ) function.

UDF names can be up to eight characters long, must begin with a letter, and may contain numbers and underscores. The name for the UDF in a command line must match the name following the FUNCTION command in the UDF procedure; this enables dBASE IV to find the code for the UDF. The UDF name cannot match the name of a dBASE IV command.

To pass values to a UDF procedure from a command line, you include those values, separated by commas, inside the parentheses following the UDF name. The values passed can be numbers, as in ADD_TAX(.065,100), or a combination of values and variables, as in ADD_TAX(M_tax,100). In order to receive the values passed to it, each user-defined function must contain a PARAMETERS command as the first line in the function procedure. The PARAMETERS command is followed by memory variable names separated by commas. These variables receive data passed to the UDF in the same order in which it is sent.

The following example shows two sections of code. The first section contains a single command line that includes a user-defined function reference called ADD_TAX( ). The parentheses following the ADD_TAX name contain three values (51, 100, and .065). These values represent units, price, and tax, respectively.

The second section of code is a UDF procedure. Note that the UDF procedure begins with the FUNCTION command and is followed by the name for the UDF, ADD_TAX. The second command in the UDF is the PARAMETERS command, followed by variable names separated by commas. These variables receive information passed from the UDF in the calling command line in the same order in which it is sent. For example, the first memory variable, M_units, receives the value 50. The second variable, M_price, receives the value 100, and so on. These variables are then used to perform a calculation, the result of which is stored in the variable M_total. The UDF concludes with the RETURN(M_total) command. This command returns the value of the M_total variable from the ADD_TAX UDF procedure to the calling command line in the first section of code. The value of the M_total variable is then substituted in the command line for the ADD_TAX( ) function.

```
* Section 1: command line in calling program
* Units=50, Price=100, Tax=.065
Invtotal=Add_tax(50,100,.065)

* Section2: UDF command lines
FUNCTION Add_tax
PARAMETERS M_units,M_price,M_tax
M_total=(M_units*M_price)+M_tax*(M_units*M_price)
RETURN(M_total)
```

When you compile a file that contains a UDF, the name of the UDF is listed in the header for the file, along with other procedure and program names. Theoretically, user-defined functions can be located anywhere that a procedure can be located. For example, you can include a UDF in the current program file, in another procedure file (provided SET PROCEDURE is used), or in another active program file.

When you include a UDF in another file, make sure that the file is compiled before the UDF procedure is called. dBASE IV does not compile another file solely to use a UDF procedure from within that file.

dBASE IV does not allow certain commands in UDF procedures (over 80 of them, as a matter of fact). These commands are listed in Chapter 31, along with additional information about the FUNCTION command.

Using Arrays

dBASE IV supports the use of *arrays,* which allow you to store memory variable values in tabular form. Arrays are composed of rows and columns that form an imaginary grid in your computer's memory. You can create a one-dimensional array that contains a single row and multiple columns, or a two-dimensional array that contains more than one row and more than one column. Although you cannot actually see an array, Figure 24-1 shows what one-dimensional and two-dimensional arrays might look like.

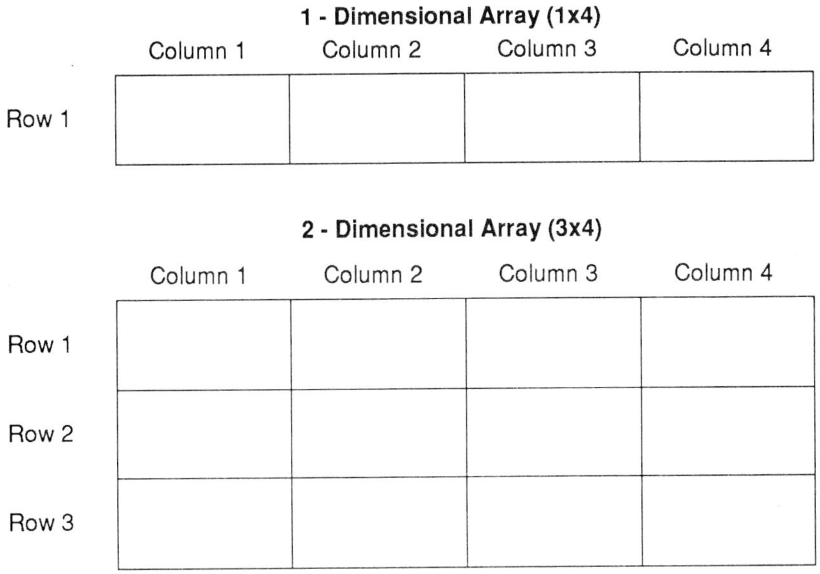

1 - Dimensional Array (1x4)

	Column 1	Column 2	Column 3	Column 4
Row 1				

2 - Dimensional Array (3x4)

	Column 1	Column 2	Column 3	Column 4
Row 1				
Row 2				
Row 3				

Figure 24-1. dBASE IV arrays

Each cell of an array grid is referred to as an *element.* You can use each element in an array as a memory variable. You can also copy data from either memory variables or database records into those array elements. In addition, you can use the data in array elements in your program to perform calculations. Furthermore, you can copy information from array elements into memory variables or database fields.

Like memory variables, arrays are stored in your computer's memory. Therefore, getting information to and from an array is much faster than getting that same information from disk.

Creating and Naming Arrays

As with memory variables, you must give each array a name. However, unlike memory variables, you must specify the size of an array in terms of columns and rows. To create and name an array, you use the DECLARE command, whose syntax is

> DECLARE *<array name>* [{*<number of rows>*,}
> {*<number of columns>*}]{,*<array name 2>*
> [{*<number of rows>*,}{*<number of columns>*}]..}

Curly braces ({ }) are used to specify optional clauses, because square brackets ([ ]) are used as part of the DECLARE command statement.

The DECLARE command provides both a name and dimensions for an array. Before you can use an array, you must declare it with the DECLARE command. If you try to use an array without first declaring it, dBASE IV issues the error message "Not an array." Array names can be up to ten characters, must begin with a letter, and can contain numbers and underscores. The array name you choose cannot match the name of a dBASE IV command.

You specify the dimensions for an array by using one or two numbers, separated by commas, and enclosed in square brackets ([ ]). If you use a single number, the array created is one-dimensional. That is, it contains a single row, and the number provided specifies the number of columns only. If you use two numbers, the array created is two-dimensional. The first number specifies the number of rows and the second number specifies the number of columns. You cannot create a three-dimensional array.

The following command line , when entered at the dot prompt or in a program, creates and names a one-dimensional array called Data. Since the number 2 is enclosed in square brackets following the name for the array, this array has one row and two columns.

```
DECLARE Data[2]
```

You may use two numbers to create a one-dimensional array. However, the first number must be a 1. For example, the following command line creates a one-dimensional array called Oneten that has one row and ten columns.

```
DECLARE Oneten[1,10]
```

To create a two-dimensional array, you use two numbers enclosed in square brackets. For example, the following command line creates an array called Grid that is three rows deep and four columns wide.

```
DECLARE Grid[3,4]
```

You can also use the DECLARE command to create and name more than one array. For example, the following command line creates two two-dimensional arrays and stores them in memory. The first array is called Grid_one and the second array is called Grid_two.

```
DECLARE Grid_one[3,5],Grid_two[4,6]
```

When you use the DECLARE command to declare an array at the dot prompt, that array, and the information in it, is public to all commands and programs. However, when you create an array in a program, the information in that array is private to that specific program. That is, the array is not available for use by other programs, and ceases to exist when the program ends. However, you can declare an array as public from a program by using the PUBLIC ARRAY command to create the array. For example, the following command creates an array called Data that is public to all active programs:

```
PUBLIC ARRAY Data[4,6]
```

Storing and Using Data in Arrays

dBASE IV handles arrays as memory variables, no matter how big or how complex they are. Furthermore, you can use all of the standard commands you use to store and use data in memory variables to store and use data in arrays.

When you use the DECLARE command to create an array, dBASE IV actually creates a set of memory variables, one for each element in the array. Initially, each element within an array contains a logical false (.F.) value. This value does not change until data is stored in the element. When you store data in an array element, that element takes on the data type of the information stored there.

You store and refer to information in an array by using the row and column coordinates of a specific element in that array. The coordinate numbers are enclosed in square brackets ([ ]). For example, the coordinates [1,1] refer to row 1, column 1, the coordinates [2,2] refer to row 2, column 2, and so on. If you refer to an array coordinate that does not exist, dBASE IV gives you the error message "Bad array dimension(s)."

The following command lines use the STORE command to place values in array elements. The STORE command is followed by the name of the array as well as the coordinates of an element within the array in which to store the data.

```
STORE 42 TO Taxtab[3,4]
STORE "Stockout" TO Invntry[11,21]
STORE {12/19/92} TO Sched[2,4]
STORE .T. TO Salry[1,6]
```

dBASE IV treats array elements as if they are memory variables, so all of the commands you use with memory variables you can also use with arrays. Here is a list of those commands:

- ?
- AVERAGE
- CALCULATE
- CLEAR ALL
- CLEAR MEMORY
- LIST/DISPLAY MEMORY
- RELEASE

- RESTORE
- SAVE
- STORE
- SUM

The program that follows, SUMARRAY.PRG, shows how you might use an array to summarize the data in a database. The program opens the SALARY database and declares a two-element one-dimensional array called Data. The array contains a single row and has two columns. Next, the command

CALCULATE CNT( ), AVG(Gross) TO ARRAY Data

counts the records in the SALARY database and takes an average of the Gross salary field. That data is then stored in the first and second elements of the Data array. Finally, the ? command and the LTRIM( ) and STR( ) functions display the information stored in the array elements.

```
* Program is SUMARRAY.PRG
* Program uses an array to summarize the SALARY.DBF database
USE SALARY
DECLARE Data[2]
CALCULATE CNT(), AVG(GROSS) TO ARRAY Data
? LTRIM(STR(Data[1])),"Employees"
? "Earn an average salary of $ "+LTRIM(STR(Data[2]))
RETURN
```

The SUMARRAY.PRG program brings up an important point about how dBASE IV loads one-dimensional arrays. Note that the result of the first function, CNT( ), is stored to the first element in the Data array. Furthermore, the result of the second function in the expression list, AVG( ), is stored in the second element. As individual bits of information are provided to a one-dimensional array, dBASE IV places the first piece of data in the first column, the second in the second column, and so forth.

In addition, you cannot use commands like CALCULATE and AVERAGE to store information to a two-dimensional array. If you try to do so, dBASE IV issues the message "Bad array dimension(s)."

The COPY TO ARRAY Command

You can use the COPY TO ARRAY command to copy records from an existing database into an existing array. The syntax for the COPY TO ARRAY command is

COPY TO ARRAY *<array name>* [FIELDS *<fields list>*] [*<scope>*] [FOR *<condition>*] [WHILE *<condition>*]

When you enter this command, dBASE IV copies the first record in the database to the first row in the array, repeating this process until there are no more records in the database or no more rows in the array. The contents of the first database field are placed in the first column of the array, the second database field in the second column of the array, and so forth. If there are more fields in the database than there are columns in the array, the remaining database fields are ignored. If there are more records in the database than rows in the array, the excess records in the database are not used. If there are more columns in the array than there are fields in the database, the unused columns in the array retain their original value. When the copying process is complete, the elements in the array take on the same data type as the fields copied in from the database.

If you use the COPY TO ARRAY command without first declaring an array, dBASE IV issues an error message. Normally, you declare a two-dimensional array before using this command. This is because a one-dimensional array limits the copy to a single data record.

You can be selective about the COPY TO ARRAY command. For example, the FIELDS clause allows you specify selected fields to be copied to the array. You can use the FOR clause to specify a condition that must be met by one or more of the fields in a record before that record can be copied. The *scope* clause lets you specify limits for the copy with clauses such as NEXT 10, meaning the next ten records, or REST, meaning the rest of the records in the database, starting with the current record. The WHILE clause further limits the copy based on a condition. The copying continues while the condition remains true, and stops when it becomes false. For example, the following listing limits the copy to three specified fields. Only those records with a .T. in the Bonus logical field are used, and the scope of the copy is limited to the next ten records, starting with the current one.

```
DECLARE Data[10,3]
COPY TO ARRAY Data FIELDS Firstname,Lastname,Gross FOR Bonus;
NEXT 10
```

The following program section uses the COUNT command to declare an array of the appropriate size for the COPY TO ARRAY command. It begins counting the records in the PARTS database, and storing that information in a variable called M_rec. The value of M_rec is then used as the first numeric argument in the DECLARE command to state the number of rows for the Part array. The fields in the PARTS database are then counted with the COUNT command. However, the records counted are in a database called TEMP, created with the COPY STRUCTURE EXTENDED command. This command creates a new database whose records are limited to the field names of the PARTS database. The record count from this database is stored in a variable called M_cols. This variable is used as the second numeric argument for the DECLARE command to state the number of columns to be included in the Part array.

```
USE Parts
COUNT TO M_rows
COPY TO Temp STRUCTURE EXTENDED
SELECT 2
USE TEMP
COUNT TO M_cols
SELECT 1
DECLARE Part[M_rows,M_cols]
COPY TO ARRAY Part FIELDS Part_no,On_hand,On_order;
FOR .NOT. DELETED()
```

The APPEND FROM ARRAY Command

The APPEND FROM ARRAY command appends records from a declared array to the currently active database. The rows in the array are appended to the database as records. If an array is not declared before the APPEND FROM ARRAY command, dBASE IV issues an error message. The syntax for the APPEND FROM ARRAY command is

APPEND FROM ARRAY <*array name*> [FOR <*condition*>]

The appending process occurs row by row from the array and continues until there are no more rows in the array. The data types of the columns in the array must match the data types of the fields in the database. The first column in the array becomes the first field in the new records added to the database. The second column in the array becomes the second database field in the new records, and so forth. If there are more columns in the array than there are fields in the database, the excess columns are ignored. If the database has more fields than the array has columns, the excess fields are left empty.

The FOR clause allows you to state a condition that must be met before a row from the array is appended to the database as a record. However, the condition following the FOR clause must use the name of one or more fields in the database. Because array columns do not have field names, the database, not the array, must serve as the frame of reference for the condition. If the condition is logical true (.T.), the current row in the array is appended as a record to the database. If not, the row is skipped and the next row is evaluated.

The following command lines declare an array called Temp, store data in it, and use the APPEND FROM ARRAY command to append data in the array to the SALARY database. The commands are entered at the dot prompt so you can see their immediate effect. First the DECLARE command is entered to create a one-dimensional 11-column array called Temp. Next, 11 STORE commands are used to store data in the Temp array that matches the number of fields, and their data type, from the SALARY database. Finally, the APPEND FROM ARRAY command is used to append the data in the Temp array to the SALARY database.

```
. DECLARE Temp[11]
. STORE "John" TO Temp[1]
John
. STORE "McMillan" TO Temp[2]
McMillan
. STORE .T. TO Temp[3]
.T.
. STORE 27500 TO Temp[4]
     27500
. STORE 6875 TO Temp[5]
      6875
. STORE 2065.25 TO Temp[6]
      2065.25
. STORE 962.5 TO Temp[7]
      962.50
. STORE 17597.25 TO Temp[8]
    17597.25
. STORE "B" TO Temp[9]
B
. STORE .F. TO Temp[10]
.F.
. STORE 1 TO Temp[11]
     1
. USE Salary
. APPEND FROM ARRAY Temp
     1 record added
```

Using an Array as a Table

You can also use an array as a permanent reference table. For example, the following program, called TAXCALC.PRG, uses an array called Tax to calculate tax to be withheld from employee's paychecks. Figure 24-2 shows the values for the elements in the Tax array. This array contains the IRS tax rates for single tax payers who are paid every two weeks.

The Tax array in Figure 24-2 was created by using the STORE command to store values to each of the elements in the

	Paycheck over Column 1	Paycheck not over Column 2	Carry forward Column 3	Tax % Column 4	Excess over Column 5
Row 1	42	756	0	0.15	42
Row 2	756	1769	107.10	0.28	756
Row 3	1769	4055	390.70	0.33	1769
Row 4	4055	100,000	1,145.12	0.28	4055

Figure 24-2. The Tax array for single biweekly employees

array. In order to save the array for later use, the SAVE command was used to save the array to a .MEM memory variable file. The titles that appear at the head of some of the columns are strictly for reference purposes; arrays do not have column or row titles.

In the Tax array table in Figure 24-2, rows 1 through 4 represent graduated tax rates. Columns 1 and 2 represent the minimum and maximum paychecks that fall into each tax rate category. The amount of money an employee makes determines which row is used to calculate his or her tax. For example, if an employee makes $1000 every two weeks, he or she falls into row 2, because the number 1000 is between the numbers 756 and 1769 in columns 1 and 2.

The virtue of the TAXCALC.PRG program is not that it calculates taxes, but that it uses a counter to advance row by row through the Tax array, until the proper tax category for a given employee is found. The program uses the RESTORE command to restore the Tax array table from a memory variable file called SNGLBI.MEM. Next, a SCAN...ENDSCAN loop loops through the records in the database, selecting those records with a B (for biweekly) in the Status field of the SALARY database. Then, the employee's annual salary is divided by 26 to get the biweekly rate of pay. That value is stored in a memory variable called Calcval, which is used to find the appropriate tax rate in the Tax array.

The counter used to advance through the Tax array is started with the command X=1. The command appears immediately before a DO WHILE...ENDDO loop. Once inside loop, the X counter is advanced by one each time. The loop is repeated until X becomes equal to 4, once for each possible row in the Tax array. The command

```
IF Calcval>=Tax[X,1] .AND. Calcval<=Tax[X,2]
```

compares the contents of columns 1 and 2 of the Tax array to the Calcval variable. If the value of Calcval is between the values in columns 1 and 2 of row 1 of the Tax array, the values in that row are used to calculate the employee's tax. If not, the counter is advanced by one, and columns 1 and 2 of row 2 are evaluated the next time through the loop. The process continues until the proper tax category is found. Figure 24-3 shows the output from the program.

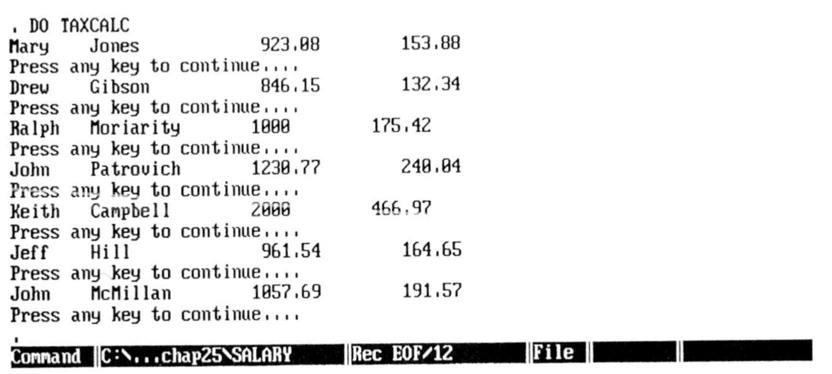

```
. DO TAXCALC
Mary     Jones            923.08          153.08
Press any key to continue....
Drew     Gibson           846.15          132.34
Press any key to continue....
Ralph    Moriarity        1000         175.42
Press any key to continue....
John     Patrovich        1230.77         240.04
Press any key to continue....
Keith    Campbell         2000         466.97
Press any key to continue....
Jeff     Hill             961.54          164.65
Press any key to continue....
John     McMillan         1057.69         191.57
Press any key to continue....
.
Command  C:\...chap25\SALARY   Rec EOF/12   File
```

Figure 24-3. The output from the TAXCALC.PRG program

```
* Program is TAXCALC.PRG
* Program uses an array to calculate federal withholding
* on employee paychecks.
SET TALK OFF
USE Salary
*-------- Restore an array called Tax from a memory variable file
*-------- called SNGLBI.MEM. This array contains a tax table for
*-------- single employees that are paid every two weeks. This array
*-------- is 4 rows deep and 5 columns wide.

RESTORE FROM Snglbi

SCAN FOR Status = "B"

*--------Calculate the employee's bi-weekly salary
     Calcval=Gross/26         && Annual salary/26 paychecks

*-------- Use a loop with a counter to check the Calcval variable
*-------- versus the values in columns 1 and 2 of each row of the
*-------- Tax array. When the right row is found, calculate the tax
*-------- to withhold and place that value in a variable.

     X=1                     && Begin counter
     DO WHILE X<=4
       IF Calcval>=Tax[X,1] .AND. Calcval<=Tax[X,2]
          Wthhld=Tax[X,3]+Tax[X,4]*(Calcval-Tax[X,5])
       ENDIF
       X=X+1                && Advance counter by 1
     ENDDO
     *-------- Display for each record that applies
     ? Firstname,Lastname,Calcval,Wthhld
     WAIT

ENDSCAN
RETURN
```

Memory Considerations

When you create a memory variable, dBASE IV uses one slot in the memory variable pool. When you create an array name, dBASE IV also uses one slot in the same memory variable pool. However, dBASE IV uses a separate block of memory to store the elements for that array. When you create an array that is too large to fit in available memory, dBASE IV issues the error message "Insufficient memory." Once you declare an array, you treat its elements as you would any other memory variable, regardless of how dBASE IV stores those elements.

You can create an array containing up to 1023 elements. However, the maximum size of the array you can create is a function your computer's RAM memory. In dBASE IV, arrays tend to require a great deal of memory. Keep this in mind as you develop applications that use arrays. Use the DISPLAY MEMORY command both before and after you create an array to determine the amount of memory it consumes. Perform the same test after you fill the array with data. You may be surprised at the amount of memory consumed.

Using Pop-Up Menus

Pop-up menus are new to dBASE IV. You can use them to make your applications look highly professional. You can structure pop-up menus to resemble the pull-down menus in the dBASE IV Control Center.

Three Types of Pop-Ups

There are three types of pop-up menus: horizontal bar menus, pull-down menus, and list menus. *Horizontal bar menus* appear in a horizontal line across your screen. This type of menu usually contains the selections for the main menu. You can place *pull-down menus* anywhere you want on the screen. However, pull-down menus are often attached to a horizontal bar menu and are used to provide submenu level choices. These pull-down menus pop up as your user moves the highlight to the various options in the horizontal bar menu. *List menus* provide your user with a list of files, database fields, or records from which to choose.

All three menu types are shown in Figure 24-4. The horizontal bar menu appears as a line of menu options spanning the upper portion of the screen. The pull-down menu appears below the first horizontal bar menu selection. It is composed of two menu bars stacked vertically. This menu appears whenever you move the cursor to the first horizontal bar menu selection. The list menu in Figure 24-4 appears in the upper-right portion of the screen and contains a list of database files.

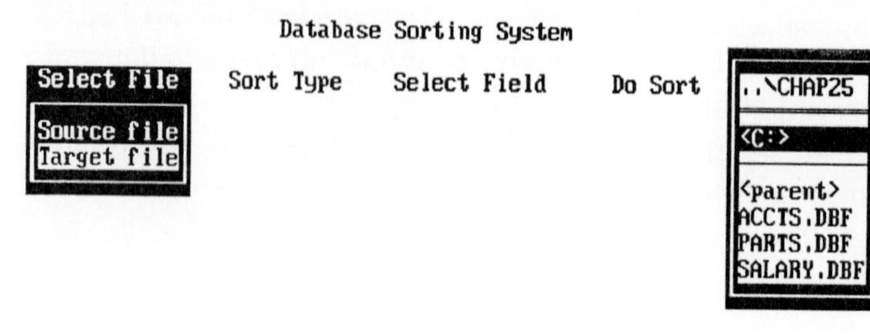

Figure 24-4. Horizontal bar and pop-up menus displayed

Designing a Menu System

There are four basic steps to designing and coding a menu system. The commands used in each step are shown in Table 24-1. Keep these steps in mind as you program your pop-up menus.

1. Define each menu and the items within it. This includes the main menu as well as submenus.

2. Specify the actions to be taken when the items in each menu are selected. You also activate submenus in this step.

3. Activate the main menu last.

4. Deactivate or release menus when they are no longer needed. When you deactivate a menu, it is cleared from the screen, but not from memory. When you release a menu, it is cleared both the screen and from memory.

Tip: You can also design pop-up menus using the dBASE IV Applications Generator. The Applications Generator generates a program file containing the same commands explained in this section. You can use the Applications Generator to generate the initial code for your pop-up menus and embed your own custom requirements at a later time.

Step	Description	Horizontal Bar	Pop-Up Menu
1	Naming menus	DEFINE MENU	DEFINE POPUP
1	Naming menu items	DEFINE PAD	DEFINE BAR
2	Specifying action	ON PAD or ON SELECTION-PAD	ON SELECTION-POPUP
3	Open menus	ACTIVATE MENU	ACTIVATE POPUP
4	Close menus	DEACTIVATE-MENU	DEACTIVATE-POPUP
4	Release menus	RELEASE MENUS or CLEAR MENUS	RELEASE POPUPS or CLEAR POPUPS
Other	Show static menu	SHOW MENU	SHOW POPUP
	Return menu name	MENU( )	POPUP( )
	Return choice name	PAD( )	BAR( )
	Return field, file, or record in list box	PROMPT( )	PROMPT( )

Table 24-1. Commands Used with Pop-Up Menus

Defining Horizontal Menu Bars

As mentioned, horizontal bar menus usually run across the top of the screen. These menus contain a list of choices, which are referred to as *pads*.

The DEFINE MENU Command

To define a horizontal bar menu, you must first use the DEFINE MENU command. This command does not in itself define the menu. It lets you name the menu and provide an optional message, which can be up to 79 characters long and which appears centered at the bottom of the screen in the message line. The syntax for DEFINE MENU is

DEFINE MENU <*menu name*> [MESSAGE <*character expression*>]

For example, the following command line names a menu **Sort_men** and displays the message "Main menu" in the message line.

```
DEFINE MENU Sort_men MESSAGE "Main menu"
```

The DEFINE PAD Command

The next step in creating a horizontal bar menu is to use the DEFINE PAD command to define the pads that make up that menu. To define more that one pad, repeat the DEFINE PAD command. The syntax for DEFINE PAD is

DEFINE PAD <*pad name*> OF <*menu name*> PROMPT <*character expression*> [AT <*row*>,<*column*>] [MESSAGE <*character expression*>]

where *pad name* is the name of the pad and *menu name* is the name of a menu that you have previously defined with the DEFINE MENU command. Pad names can be ten characters in length, must begin with a letter, and may contain numbers and underscores.

The PROMPT clause specifies the character string to be used as a title for the pad. This title appears in the menu bar on your screen. A blank space is added to each side of the prompt before it is displayed.

You use the AT clause to position the pad on your screen. *Row* and *column* refer to screen coordinates that mark the starting position of the pad prompt. This clause allows you to place a pad anywhere on the screen. Thus, although the title for this section is "Defining Horizontal Menu Bars," you can just as easily define vertical menu bars. If you do not specify coordinates, dBASE IV places the first pad at coordinates 0,0 (the upper-left corner of your screen). Each subsequent pad you define without coordinates is placed on the same line, one space to the right of the previous pad. If you do not specify coordinates, make sure to use the SET SCOREBOARD OFF command so that dBASE IV does not overwrite your pads with normal system messages during program execution.

The MESSAGE clause allows you to specify a message of up to 79 characters. This message appears centered at the bottom of the screen whenever you move the cursor onto the pad.

To move back and forth between pads, use the RIGHT ARROW and LEFT ARROW keys. As you move the cursor to each pad, dBASE IV displays a reverse-video box around the pad prompt. You can also move back and forth between pads by selecting the first letter of a pad name. When you assign prompt names to your pads, be sure to give them names that start with different first letters. If two pads begin with the same first letter, pressing that letter selects the first pad.

For example, the following command lines create five pads for a horizontal bar menu called **Sort_men**. Each pad is given a name, a prompt, a location, and a message that appears in the message line whenever the cursor is located on the pad.

```
*-------- Name the main bar menu and display a message
DEFINE MENU Sort_men MESSAGE "Main menu"

*-------- Define pad locations for main bar menu
DEFINE PAD File_nm OF Sort_men PROMPT "Select File" AT 4,5;
     MESSAGE "Select a source and target file"
DEFINE PAD Srt_type OF Sort_men PROMPT "Sort Type" AT 4,20;
     MESSAGE "Select a sort type"
DEFINE PAD Key_nm OF Sort_men PROMPT "Select Field" AT 4,37;
     MESSAGE "Press ENTER to select sort field"
DEFINE PAD Prfrm OF Sort_men PROMPT "Do Sort" AT 4,50;
     MESSAGE "Press ENTER to start sorting"
DEFINE PAD Endit OF Sort_men PROMPT "Quit" AT 4,65;
     MESSAGE "Press ENTER to return to the dot prompt"
```

The ON SELECTION PAD Command

The ON SELECTION PAD command specifies an action that takes place when you select a specific pad in a horizontal bar menu. You can use this command to execute a command, a procedure, another program, or to activate a pop-up menu. To select a pad, move the cursor to the pad and press ENTER. The syntax for the ON SELECTION PAD command is

> ON SELECTION PAD <*pad name*> OF <*menu name*>
> [<*command*>]

Pad name is the name of the selected pad, *menu name* is the name of a previously defined menu that contains that pad, and *command* is an acceptable dBASE IV command that performs an operation or calls a subprogram or procedure. After the command, procedure, or program following the ON SELECTION PAD command is finished running, the cursor returns to that pad. You use ON SELECTION PAD to specify an action for each pad in a horizontal bar menu. For example, the following command line executes a procedure called Getfile when a pad called File_name in the Sort_men menu is selected.

```
ON SELECTION PAD File_name OF Sort_men DO Getfile
```

You can use two functions in a procedure to determine the currently active menu and the pad that has been selected. The MENU( ) function returns the name of the active menu. The PAD() function returns the name of the current pad. You can use these functions to evaluate menu selections.

For example, the following section of code uses two ON SELECTION commands, one for the File_name pad and one for the Fld_name pad. Both commands activate a procedure called Getfile, which contains both the MENU( ) and PAD( ) functions. The MENU( ) function is used in an IF...ENDIF conditional statement to return the name of the currently active menu. If the currently active menu is Sort_men, the code inside the IF...ENDIF statement is executed. Inside the IF...ENDIF procedure, the PAD() function is used in a DO CASE...ENDCASE construction to evaluate which pad in the Sort_men menu has been selected.

```
*--------Assign actions to pad selections
ON SELECTION PAD File_name OF Sort_men DO Getfile
ON SELECTION PAD Fld_name OF Sort_men DO Getfile

PROCEDURE Getfile

IF MENU() = Sort_men
     DO CASE
          CASE PAD() = File_name
               DO Fileget
          CASE PAD() = Fld_name
               ACTIVATE POPUP Fld_pop
     ENDCASE
ENDIF
RETURN
```

You can also display a pad and have it immediately selected when the cursor is moved onto it. To do this, exclude the SELECTION part from the ON SELECTION PAD command. For example, the following command line activates a pop-up submenu called S_T_pop immediately after you move the cursor into the File_name pad of the Sort_men menu.

```
ON PAD File_name OF Sort_men ACTIVATE POPUP S_T_pop
```

The ACTIVATE MENU Command

You activate a horizontal bar menu with the ACTIVATE MENU command. This command activates and displays for use an existing bar menu. For the menu to work properly, you must locate this command after the DEFINE MENU, DEFINE PAD, and ON SELECTION PAD commands. The syntax for the ACTIVATE MENU command is

ACTIVATE MENU <*menu name*> [<PAD <*pad name*>]

Menu name is the name of a menu you defined previously with the DEFINE MENU command, and *pad name* is a pad you defined previously with the DEFINE PAD command.

When you use the ACTIVATE MENU command, the menu you specify becomes the active menu and is displayed over any existing display. The PAD clause allows you to specify the pad position of the highlight when the menu appears. If you do not use a PAD clause with this command, dBASE IV displays the highlight on the first pad you defined with the DEFINE PAD command.

dBASE IV only supports one active menu at a time. The menu that is activated last is the current menu. If you use an ON PAD or ON SELECTION PAD command to activate another menu from the current menu, the new menu becomes the current menu. The first menu does not disappear but remains inactive until the current menu is deactivated.

You deactivate the current menu by activating another menu, using the DEACTIVATE MENU command, or pressing ESC. When a menu is deactivated it remains in memory and can be activated at a later time with the ACTIVATE MENU command. To counteract deactivation of the current menu by pressing ESC, you can use the SET ESCAPE or ON ESCAPE command.

The following command line activates the Sort_men horizontal bar menu and places the highlight on the Srt_type pad.

```
ACTIVATE MENU Sort_man PAD Srt_type
```

The DEACTIVATE MENU Command

As mentioned, you use the DEACTIVATE MENU command to deactivate the currently active horizontal bar menu. When you use this command, the currently active menu disappears, and any text underneath the menu reappears. However, this command simply deactivates a menu; it does not delete it from memory. You can easily reactivate the menu at any time by using the ACTIVATE MENU command. The syntax for DEACTIVATE MENU is

DEACTIVATE MENU

Note that a menu name does not follow the DEACTIVATE MENU command. Since only one menu can be active, this command deactivates that menu. When you use this command, dBASE IV resumes processing with the command line immediately after the command that activated the menu.

You use the DEACTIVATE menu command in either an ON SELECTION PAD or ON SELECTION POPUP statement or in a procedure called by one of these commands. For example, the following command line uses the DEACTIVATE MENU command in an ON SELECTION PAD statement:

```
ON SELECTION PAD Exit OF Sort_men DEACTIVATE MENU
```

Pop-Up Pull-Down Menus

Pop-up pull-down menus are windows that contain a vertical list of selectable items. You can select an item from this type of menu by typing the first letter of its name, or by moving the highlight to the desired item and pressing ENTER.

As mentioned, you can attach pop-up pull-down menus to pads in horizontal bar menus. This way, as you move the highlight across the horizontal bar menu pads, the pop-up menus assigned to each pad appear automatically. However, this is just one option. You can place pop-up pull-down menus anywhere on the screen.

To create pop-up menus, you use the same four steps used to create horizontal bar menus.

1. Define each pop-up menu and the items within it.
2. Specify the actions to be taken when the items in each pop-up menu are selected.
3. Activate the pop-up menu last.
4. Deactivate or release pop-ups when they are no longer needed. When you deactivate a pop-up, it is cleared from the screen, not from memory. When you release a menu, it is cleared both from the screen and from memory.

The DEFINE POPUP Command

You use the DEFINE POPUP command to define a pop-up menu. This command defines a pop-up menu's name, location, and prompts. It also allows you display a message in the message line at the bottom of the screen. The syntax for DEFINE POPUP is

DEFINE POPUP <*pop-up name*> FROM <*row1*>,<*column1*>
TO <*row2*>,<*column2*>
[PROMPT FIELDS<*field name*>/PROMPT FILES
[LIKE <*skeleton*>]/PROMPT STRUCTURE]
[MESSAGE <*character expression*>]

Pop-up menu names can be up to ten characters long, must start with a letter, and can include letters, numbers, and underscores. You use the name assigned to a pop-up when you later activate it with the ACTIVATE POPUP command.

Each menu item or selection within a pop-up menu window is called a *bar*. You define the text for a bar by using the DEFINE BAR command discussed in the following section.

You use the FROM and TO clauses of the DEFINE POPUP command to define the location and size of your pop-up menu window. The coordinates after the FROM clause specify the screen location for the upper-left corner of the pop-up menu window, and the coordinates after the TO clause specify its lower-right corner. When the pop-up menu window is displayed, it covers any data already on the screen. When you deactivate a pop-up menu with the DEACTIVATE POPUP command, the pop-up menu disappears, revealing any data displayed underneath it. Since dBASE IV only allows one active pop-up menu, you can use the same screen coordinates for several different pop-up menu windows.

The TO clause of the DEFINE pop-up command is optional. When you omit this clause, dBASE IV expands the pop-up menu window to include all of the bars you later define with the DEFINE BAR command. It also expands the width of the pop-up menu window to include the longest text prompt specified with the DEFINE BAR command.

When you use the TO clause to limit the size of a pop-up menu window, any bar text that is too long for the width of the window is truncated. If you specify too many bars to fit in the pop-up menu window, dBASE IV scrolls the bars as you move the cursor. For these two reasons, avoid using the TO clause unless you have to. First, it is time-consuming to adjust the window coordinates until you get the right width to include all of the text strings in your bars. Second, it is not good practice to place menu selections where your users cannot see them.

The PROMPT clause of the DEFINE MENU command is for creating list pop-up menus. For an explanation of the PROMPT clause of the DEFINE pop-up command, see the "List Menus" section later in this chapter.

The MESSAGE clause of the DEFINE pop-up command allows you to specify messages of up to 79 characters. When the pop-up menu window is activated, this message appears centered at the bottom of the screen in the message line.

The following command lines create five different pop-up menus. All five menus start in row 5. The TO clause is omitted from each command line in order to allow for the full length and width of any bars defined later with the DEFINE BAR command.

```
*-------- Define popup menu names and locations
DEFINE POPUP S_T_pop FROM 5,5 MESSAGE "Select an option"
DEFINE POPUP A_D_pop FROM 5,20 MESSAGE "Select an option"
DEFINE POPUP Pkfld_pop FROM 5,35
DEFINE POPUP Sortmn FROM 5,50
DEFINE POPUP Exitmn FROM 5,65
```

The DEFINE BAR Command

As mentioned, the individual menu choices that appear in pop-up menus windows are called bars. You define each individual bar in your pop-up menus by using the DEFINE BAR command, whose syntax is

> DEFINE BAR <*line number*> OF <*pop-up name*> PROMPT <*character expression*> [MESSAGE <*character expression*> [SKIP [FOR <*condition*>]]

Each bar in a pop-up menu is given a line number. To specify more than one bar in a pop-up menu, you repeat the DEFINE BAR command and advance the line number by one for each bar. You can specify as many bars as you want in a pop-up menu. However, you must specify at least one bar; otherwise, the pop-up menu is empty and cannot be activated with ACTIVATE POPUP.

You use the OF clause to specify the name of a previously defined pop-up menu in which to include the bar.

You use the PROMPT clause to specify the text string that you want to appear inside a bar. If you've specified a width for the pop-up menu window by using the TO clause of the DEFINE POPUP command, keep this width in mind as you compose your bar prompts. If you make them too long, they appear cut off when the pop-up menu is later displayed.

The MESSAGE clause allows you to specify a message that will be displayed whenever the cursor is moved into the bar. The message can be up to 79 characters and appears centered in the message line at the bottom of the screen.

The following section of code defines a pop-up menu and then defines two bars for that menu. Note that the first bar is given the line number 1 and the second bar is given line number 2.

```
*-------- Define popup menu names and locations
DEFINE POPUP S_T_pop FROM 5,5;
     MESSAGE "Select an option and press ENTER"
*--------Define menu bars for popup menus
DEFINE BAR 1 OF S_T_pop PROMPT "Source file";
     MESSAGE "Press ENTER to select a source file"
DEFINE BAR 2 OF S_T_pop PROMPT "Target file";
     MESSAGE "Press ENTER to type in a target file";
```

You also use the SKIP clause with the DEFINE BAR command to skip bars in a pop-up menu. The SKIP clause without an argument specifies an item as unselectable and causes the highlight to skip over it. For example, the following section of code uses the SKIP clause to give a pop-up menu a title and to make dotted lines appear between menu choices.

```
DEFINE BAR 1 OF S_T_pop PROMPT "**Option Menu**" SKIP
DEFINE BAR 2 OF S_T_pop PROMPT "--------------- " SKIP
DEFINE BAR 3 OF S_T_pop PROMPT "Source File"
DEFINE BAR 4 OF S_T_pop PROMPT "Target File"
DEFINE BAR 5 OF S_T_pop PROMPT "--------------- " SKIP
DEFINE BAR 6 OF S_T_pop PROMPT "Quit           "
```

You can also skip for a condition by using the SKIP clause. For example, the following command line skips bar 1 of the **S_T_pop** pop-up menu while the Text memory variable is blank. When a character expression is finally stored in the Text variable, dBASE IV opens access to this bar 1 option.

```
DEFINE BAR 1 OF S_T_pop PROMPT "Target file";
     SKIP FOR Text = " "
```

You can also leave blank spaces between menu choices using the DEFINE BAR command. To do this, skip a bar number. For example, define bar 7 immediately after bar 5. Bar 6 will appear as a blank space. Your user cannot select the blank space. Instead, the cursor skips over it.

The ON SELECTION POPUP Command

You use the ON SELECTION POPUP command to specify a command or procedure to run when a pop-up menu bar is selected. You can use this command to have dBASE IV execute a command, perform a subprogram or procedure, or activate another pop-up menu. The syntax for this command is

ON SELECTION POPUP <*pop-up name*>/ALL
[<*command*>]

where *pop-up name* is the name of a previously defined pop-up menu and *command* is an acceptable dBASE IV command. Whenever you make a selection from one of the menu bars in the named pop-up, dBASE IV executes the specified command. If you use the ALL clause in place of a pop-up name, the command applies to all pop-up menus.

Often the command following the ON SELECTION POPUP command is the DO command followed by the name of a procedure. That procedure is performed whenever a selection is made from the named menu.

You use the BAR( ) function to evaluate which selection has been made from a pop-up menu. This function returns the prompt from the most recently selected bar. You can then use this function in a DO CASE...ENDCASE construction in order to specify different courses of action for each item selected. For example, the following section of code uses the BAR( ) function to evaluate menu selections from the **A_D_pop** pop-up menu.

```
*--------Define popup menu name and location
DEFINE POPUP A_D_pop FROM 5,5
*--------Define menu bars for popup menus
DEFINE BAR 1 OF A_D_pop PROMPT "Source file"
DEFINE BAR 2 OF A_D_pop PROMPT "Target file"

*--------Set reactions for popup menus
ON SELECTION POPUP A_D_pop DO Sort_ord

*-------- Procedure to store sort order to a variable
PROCEDURE Sort_ord
IF POPUP() = A_D_pop
     DO CASE
          CASE BAR() = 1
               STORE "ASCENDING" TO Ordr
          CASE BAR() = 2
              STORE "DESCENDING" TO Ordr
     ENDCASE
ENDIF
DEACTIVATE POPUP
RETURN
```

This procedure also uses the POPUP( ) function, which returns the name of the currently active pop-up menu.

The ACTIVATE POPUP Command

To activate pop-up menus, you use the ACTIVATE POPUP command. Make sure to use this command after you have defined your pop-up menus and specified actions for them. The syntax for ACTIVATE POPUP is

ACTIVATE POPUP *<pop-up name>*

Only one pop-up menu can be active at any one time. When you activate a pop-up menu while another pop-up is active, the original pop-up menu is deactivated but remains in memory. You can then reactivate that pop-up later by using the ACTIVATE POPUP command. When you use one pop-up menu to activate another pop-up menu, the first pop-up menu continues to appear on the screen. However, it is inactive until the second pop-up is deactivated.

You can also use ACTIVATE POPUP with the ON PAD and ON SELECTION POPUP commands. This automatically activates a pop-up menu when you select a pad from a horizontal bar menu or a bar from a pop-up menu. The following command lines show an example of each:

```
ON PAD File_nm OF Sort_men ACTIVATE POPUP S_T_pop
ON SELECTION POPUP Key_nm OF Sort_men ACTIVATE POPUP Pkfld_pop
```

The DEACTIVATE POPUP Command

To deactivate a pop-up menu and erase it from the screen, use the DEACTIVATE POPUP command. Any text beneath the pop-up menu is redisplayed. Since only one pop-up menu can be active, you do not have to specify a pop-up name for this command. DEACTIVATE POPUP does not remove the pop-up from memory; it deactivates it and erases it from the screen. You can reactivate that same menu at any time by using the ACTIVATE POPUP command.

The DEACTIVATE POPUP command appears most often in a procedure called by the ON SELECTION POPUP command. The DEACTIVATE POPUP command usually appears at the end of the procedure after a menu selection from that pop-up has already been evaluated and the pop-up menu is no longer required. In this way, a pop-up menu is immediately cleared from the screen after it is used. For example, in the following section of code, the ON SELECTION command calls a procedure named Fl_list to evaluate a menu choice from a pop-up called S_T_pop. At the end of the Fl_list procedure, the DEACTIVATE POPUP command clears the S_T_pop menu from the screen.

```
ON SELECTION POPUP S_T_pop DO Fl_list

*-------- Procedure to store source and target file
PROCEDURE Fl_list
DO CASE
     CASE BAR() = 1
       STORE " " TO Data
       ACTIVATE POPUP Fl_pop
     CASE BAR() = 2
       @ 15,15 SAY "Enter target filename: " GET Target
       READ
ENDCASE
DEACTIVATE POPUP
RETURN
```

List Menus

As mentioned, list pop-up menus contain lists of files, database records, or database field names. You can present such a list to your user for selection. You define list pop-up menus by using the PROMPT clause of the DEFINE POPUP command. Remember, the syntax for DEFINE POPUP is

> DEFINE POPUP *<pop-up name>* FROM *<row1>*,*<column1>* TO *<row2>*,*<column2>* [PROMPT FIELDS*<field name>* /PROMPT FILES [LIKE *<skeleton>*]/ PROMPT STRUCTURE] [MESSAGE *<character expression>*]

The PROMPT clause has three forms: PROMPT FIELDS, PROMPT FILES, and PROMPT STRUCTURE. Using any of these three clauses defines a list pop-up menu. Therefore, you cannot use the DEFINE BAR command to specify bars for this menu, because its selection contents have already been defined as either files, database records, or field names.

The PROMPT FIELDS clause allows you to display the contents of specified fields in the currently active database. You cannot specify a memo field by using the PROMPT FIELDS clause. However, you can precede the field name with a database alias name and a —> pointer to point to a database in another work area, as in the following.

```
DEFINE POPUP Pop_men FROM 1,60 TO 10,75 PROMPT FIELDS;
Mailist->Lastname
```

The PROMPT FILES clause allows you to list all of the files in the current catalog in a list pop-up menu. However, you can specify a file skeleton by using the LIKE operator to specify different types of files to be displayed inside the list pop-up menu. For example, the following command line specifies a database file extension by using an asterisk (*) followed by .DBF.

```
DEFINE POPUP Fl_pop FROM 3,60 PROMPT FILES LIKE *.dbf
```

The PROMPT STRUCTURE clause displays the field names of the currently active database in a list pop-up menu. If the SET FIELDS <*field list*> command is active, this clause honors that command. The following command line shows the PROMPT STRUCTURE clause used with the DEFINE POPUP command:

```
DEFINE POPUP Fld_pop FROM 3,60 PROMPT STRUCTURE
```

The PROMPT( ) function is important for use with list pop-up menus. This function returns the prompt selected from a list pop- up menu. The following section of code sets up two list pop-up menus. The first one, called Fld_pop, uses the PROMPT STRUCTURE command to list the field names in the currently active database. The second list pop-up menu, called Fl_pop, uses the PROMPT FILES LIKE clause with a file skeleton that specifies database files. The PROMPT( ) function is used in the two following procedures to capture file and field selections from the Fld_pop and Fl_pop menus and store them in memory variables for later use.

```
*-------- Define list popup menus to display files and fields
DEFINE POPUP Fld_pop FROM 3,60 PROMPT STRUCTURE
DEFINE POPUP Fl_pop FROM 3,60 PROMPT FILES LIKE *.dbf
ON SELECTION POPUP Fl_pop DO Setfile
ON SELECTION POPUP Fld_pop DO Setfld

PROCEDURE Setfile
STORE PROMPT() TO Data
DEACTIVATE POPUP
RETURN

PROCEDURE Setfld
STORE PROMPT() TO Fldname
DEACTIVATE POPUP
RETURN
```

An Example Program

The following program, SHOWPOP.PRG, uses many of the techniques for pop-up menus discussed in this section. It builds the pop-up menus shown in Figure 24-4.

The SHOWPOP.PRG program provides a menu-driven interface for sorting databases. You are prompted through a series of five pop-up pull-down menus attached to a horizontal bar menu called Sort_men. Through these pop-ups, you are asked to choose a source file, type a target file, specify a sort order, specify a sort field, perform the sort, and quit the program. The choices for the Sort_men bar menu are shown in Figure 24-5. The image of the first pop-up menu, S_T_pop, appears as well.

Each of the five pop-up menus appears when you move the cursor onto a different pad in the Sort_men horizontal bar menu. The five pop-ups are linked to the five pads of the Sort_men menu with the following code.

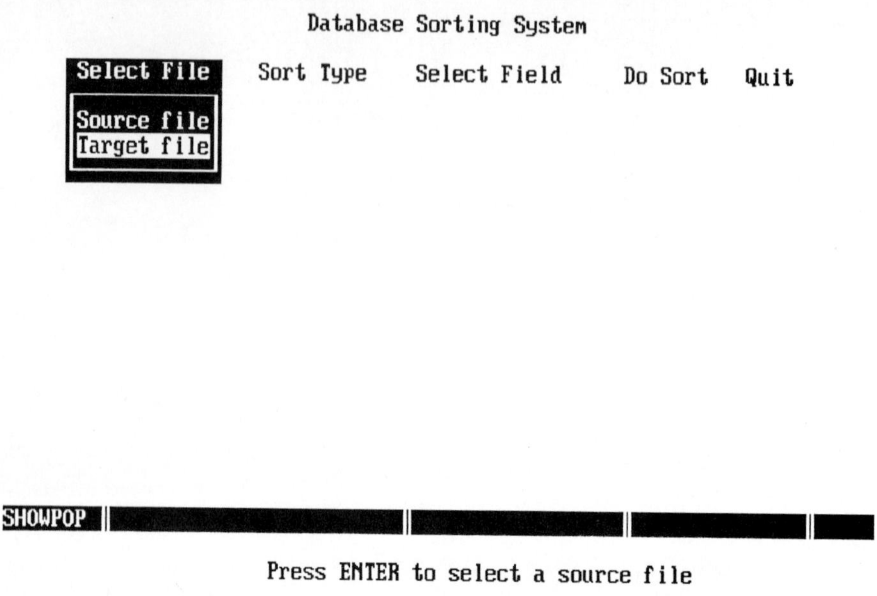

```
                    Database Sorting System
 Select File   Sort Type    Select Field     Do Sort   Quit
 Source file
 Target file

SHOWPOP
                  Press ENTER to select a source file
```

Figure 24-5. The S_T_pop pop-up menu with the Sort_men bar menu

```
*--------Assign pop menus to pad selections
ON PAD File_nm OF Sort_men ACTIVATE POPUP S_T_pop
ON PAD Srt_type OF Sort_men ACTIVATE POPUP A_D_pop
ON PAD Key_nm OF Sort_men ACTIVATE POPUP Pkfld_pop
ON PAD Prfrm OF Sort_men ACTIVATE POPUP Sortmn
ON PAD Endit OF Sort_men ACTIVATE POPUP Exitmn
```

In addition, two list pop-up menus are included in the program. The first list pop-up is defined with the command

```
DEFINE POPUP Fl_pop FROM 3,60 PROMPT FILES LIKE *.dbf
```

and the second with the command

```
DEFINE POPUP Fld_pop FROM 3,60 PROMPT STRUCTURE
```

These list pop-up menus allow you to select from database files in the current catalog and choose a field on which to sort from the specified database. Both list pop-ups occupy the same space in order to give a consistent feel to the program. However, they are activated by different pop-up menus using the commands

```
ON SELECTION POPUP S_T_pop DO Fl_list
```

and

```
ON SELECTION POPUP Pkfld_pop DO Pck_it
```

The Fl_list and Pck_it procedures contain ACTIVATE POPUP commands that activate these two list menus at different times. In that way, they can occupy the same space.

The program contains no error-handling code in order to make it more readable; however, there is one conditional statement in the program. The command

```
DEFINE BAR 2 OF S_T_pop PROMPT "Target file";
MESSAGE "Press ENTER to type in a target file" SKIP FOR Data = " "
```

causes dBASE IV to skip the Target file bar (bar 2) of the S_T_pop pop-up menu unless the Data memory variable contains a character string. That character string is a database name selected from the Fl_pop list menu. You define the Data variable in the Set file procedure by using the command **STORE PROMPT( ) TO Data.** This procedure is called by the command

```
ON SELECTION POPUP Fl_pop DO Setfile
```

In this way, you cannot enter a target file to which to sort the selected database until you have selected a database from the Fl_pop menu.

Note the location of the ACTIVATE MENU command in the POPSHOW.PRG program. The command **ACTIVATE MENU Sort_men** appears after the main horizontal bar menu and all of its pop-ups have been defined. Note that it also appears after all of the pads, bars, and actions for all pop-ups have been assigned. This command activates the main Sort_men horizontal bar menu. Since all other pop-ups are called from this menu, the entire menu system is activated with a single command.

Moreover, virtually every operation in the POPSHOW.PRG program is handled through procedures. At the end of almost every procedure, the DEACTIVATE POPUP command deactivates each pop-up and removes it from the screen after it is used.

```
* Program is SHOWPOP.PRG
* Program uses popup menus
SET TALK OFF
CLEAR
STORE " " TO Data
STORE " " TO Fldname
STORE SPACE(8) TO Target
STORE " " TO Ordr

*-------- Place a header message on the screen
@ 2,25 SAY "Database Sorting System"

*-------- Name the main bar menu and display a message
DEFINE MENU Sort_men MESSAGE "Main menu"

*--------Define pads for main menu bar menu
DEFINE PAD File_nm OF Sort_men PROMPT "Select File" AT 4,5;
     MESSAGE "Press ENTER to select source and target file"
DEFINE PAD Srt_type OF Sort_men PROMPT "Sort Type" AT 4,20;
     MESSAGE "Press ENTER to select the sort type"
DEFINE PAD Key_nm OF Sort_men PROMPT "Select Field" AT 4,33;
     MESSAGE "Press ENTER to select sort field"
DEFINE PAD Prfrm OF Sort_men PROMPT "Do Sort" AT 4,50;
     MESSAGE "Press ENTER to start sorting"
DEFINE PAD Endit OF Sort_men PROMPT "Quit" AT 4,60;
     MESSAGE "Press ENTER to return to the dot prompt"

*--------Assign pop menus to pad selections
ON PAD File_nm OF Sort_men ACTIVATE POPUP S_T_pop
ON PAD Srt_type OF Sort_men ACTIVATE POPUP A_D_pop
ON PAD Key_nm OF Sort_men ACTIVATE POPUP Pkfld_pop
```

```
ON PAD Prfrm OF Sort_men ACTIVATE POPUP Sortmn
ON PAD Endit OF Sort_men ACTIVATE POPUP Exitmn

*-------- Define popup menu names and locations
DEFINE POPUP S_T_pop FROM 5,5 MESSAGE "Select an option"
DEFINE POPUP A_D_pop FROM 5,20 MESSAGE "Select an option"
DEFINE POPUP Pkfld_pop FROM 5,33
DEFINE POPUP Sortmn FROM 5,50
DEFINE POPUP Exitmn FROM 5,65

*--------Define menu bars for popup menus
DEFINE BAR 1 OF S_T_pop PROMPT "Source file";
     MESSAGE "Press ENTER to select a source file"

*-------- Skip this field if no source file is defined
DEFINE BAR 2 OF S_T_pop PROMPT "Target file";
     MESSAGE "Press ENTER to type in a target file";
     SKIP FOR Data = " "

DEFINE BAR 1 OF A_D_pop PROMPT "Ascend";
     MESSAGE "Press ENTER to select an ascending sort"
DEFINE BAR 2 OF A_D_pop PROMPT "Descend";
     MESSAGE "Press ENTER to select a descending sort"
DEFINE BAR 1 OF Pkfld_pop PROMPT "Select field";
     MESSAGE "Press ENTER for a list of fields"
DEFINE BAR 1 OF Sortmn PROMPT "Sort to new database";
     MESSAGE "Press ENTER to perform the sort"
DEFINE BAR 1 OF Exitmn PROMPT "Return to dot prompt"

*--------Set reactions for popup menus
ON SELECTION POPUP S_T_pop DO Fl_list
ON SELECTION POPUP A_D_pop DO Sort_ord
ON SELECTION POPUP Pkfld_pop DO Pck_it
ON SELECTION POPUP Sortmn DO Sort_it
ON SELECTION POPUP Exitmn DO Exit

*-------- Define list menus to display files and fields
DEFINE POPUP Fld_pop FROM 3,60 PROMPT STRUCTURE
DEFINE POPUP Fl_pop FROM 3,60 PROMPT FILES LIKE *.dbf
ON SELECTION POPUP Fl_pop DO Setfile
ON SELECTION POPUP Fld_pop DO Setfld

*--------Activate the menu system
```

```
ACTIVATE MENU Sort_men

RETURN                              && End the program

*-------- Evaluate Popup menu bar selections using procedures

*-------- Procedure to get source and target filenames
PROCEDURE Fl_list
DO CASE
     CASE BAR() = 1
       STORE " " TO Data
       ACTIVATE POPUP Fl_pop
     CASE BAR() = 2
       @ 15,15 SAY "Enter target filename: " GET Target
       READ
ENDCASE
DEACTIVATE POPUP
RETURN

*-------- Procedure to get field name selection
PROCEDURE Pck_it
STORE " " TO Fldname
USE &Data
ACTIVATE POPUP Fld_pop
RETURN

*-------- Procedures to store selections from list menus
*--------to memory variables

PROCEDURE Setfile
STORE PROMPT() TO Data
DEACTIVATE POPUP
RETURN

PROCEDURE Setfld
STORE PROMPT() TO Fldname
DEACTIVATE POPUP
RETURN

*-------- Procedure to store sort order to a variable
PROCEDURE Sort_ord
DO CASE
```

```
     CASE BAR() = 1
       STORE "ASCENDING" TO Ordr
     CASE BAR() = 2
       STORE "DESCENDING" TO Ordr
ENDCASE
DEACTIVATE POPUP
RETURN

*-------- Procedure to sort to a new database
PROCEDURE Sort_it
@ 17,15 SAY "Sorting...."
USE &Data
SORT ON &Fldname TO TRIM(Target)+".dbf"+" "+Ordr
RETURN

*--------Procedure to exit menu
PROCEDURE Exit
CLEAR
CLOSE ALL
RELEASE MENUS
RETURN
```

STEP IVWARD

You can update your Clipper, FoxBASE+, and Quicksilver applications to run under dBASE IV by using a new product from Ashton-Tate called STEP IVWARD. This product does not come with dBASE IV; you must purchase it separately.

Earlier versions of dBASE did not support certain advanced commands and functions offered by various compiler products. For example, the Clipper compiler offered user-defined functions and arrays while earlier versions of dBASE did not. However, dBASE IV now supports many of these advanced features with its own standardized command set.

The STEP IVWARD product can convert Clipper, FoxBASE+, and Quicksilver commands to match the dBASE IV command set. Therefore, the STEP IVWARD product converts your source code, not your object code. When you apply the STEP IVWARD product to one of your external compiler applications, dBASE IV actually creates a new source-code program that matches the dBASE IV command set. When you run the converted program under dBASE IV, it is compiled and executed as a .DBO file, just like any other dBASE IV program.

STEP IVWARD won't handle every conceivable conversion. However, it does the lion's share of the work. For items it can't handle, STEP IVWARD prints out a series of comment lines. You can look for those comment lines and make manual conversions as necessary.

In this chapter, you learned about user-defined functions, arrays, and pop-up menus. You now know how to create a user-defined function by using the FUNCTION command to return a single value to an expression in a command line.

You're also familiar with how to create and name an array. Furthermore, you can now store information in arrays and use them as reference tables. In addition, you can copy information into arrays from a database, and can use arrays to append information to a database.

Finally, you now know how to program your own pop-up menus. You can create horizontal bar menus and link pull-down pop-up menus to them. You can also create list pop-up menus that allow you to choose from data in fields in your databases, files in the current catalog, and field names in the currently active database.

Debugging Your Program

What Does the Debugger Do?
Accessing the Debugger
Using the Debugger Windows
Using Debugger Commands

TWENTY FIVE

One of dBASE IV's most powerful programming tools is its new Program Debugger. If you've ever used DOS's Debug program, you'll find it extremely easy to use the dBASE IV Program Debugger. But even if you're new to debuggers, it is easy to understand and use the dBASE IV Debugger to troubleshoot your programs.

This chapter shows you how to use all of the features of the Debugger. When you are done, you should have a good handle on how to debug any dBASE IV program.

What Does the Debugger Do?

The final step in developing any program or application is to test it completely. The dBASE IV Program Debugger helps you do just that. What's more, if you're having trouble with a particular program, the Debugger can usually lead you directly to the source of the problem.

The dBASE IV Debugger provides a visual environment in which to debug your programs. It allows you to display your program on the screen and trace its actions line by line while it's executing. Although dBASE IV is actually running the compiled

```
C:\DB4CR\APPENDIX\ORDFORM.PRG
35 SELECT 1
36 USE Customer ORDER Custno
37 APPEND BLANK
38 STORE RECNO() TO Crec
39
40 REPLACE Order_no WITH Mordno,Country WITH Mcountry,;
41 Cust_no WITH Mcust
42
43 SELECT 2
44 USE Orderrec
45 SET RELATION TO Cust_no INTO Customer

DISPLAY                                      BREAKPOINTS
Mcust            :        1046               1: LINENO() = 45
                 :                           2:
                 :                           3:
                 :                           4:

DEBUGGER
Work Area: 1     Database file: CUSTOMER.DBF    Program file: ordform.prg
Record:  42      Master Index: CUST_NO          Procedure:    ORDFORM
ACTION:                                         Current line: 43

Stopped for step.
```

Figure 25-1. The dBASE IV Program Debugger

version of your program (the .DBO file), the Debugger displays your source program text (the .PRG file), highlighting each line as it is executed. You can switch between the Program Debugger window and the dBASE IV display screen by pressing F9. Figure 25-1 shows what the dBASE IV Program Debugger might look like on your screen.

If dBASE IV encounters an error during the debugging process, it halts your program and displays an error message. The command line that caused the error message remains highlighted. This allows you to pinpoint the precise command line that caused the error and to see the sequence of events leading up to the error.

You can use the Program Debugger to trace the execution path of your program. You can also use it to

- Determine the values of memory variables at different points in your program.
- Run a section of code, starting at a specific line number.
- Establish *breakpoints*—logical expressions that halt your program when the expression becomes true.

Accessing the Debugger

You can access the dBASE IV Program Debugger by using one of two commands at the dot prompt.

- SET TRAP ON
- DEBUG *<program filename>*

If SET TRAP is ON, dBASE IV displays the Program Debugger whenever an error occurs in a program, or whenever you press ESC while a program is running (if SET ESCAPE is ON).

The second way to activate the Program Debugger is to enter the DEBUG command, followed by the name of your program, at the dot prompt. For example, if the name of your program is MYPROG.PRG, enter **DEBUG MYPROG** at the dot prompt. dBASE IV will take you to the Debugger and display your program in the Debugger window. You can then step through the program by pressing ENTER to execute each line of code.

Using the Debugger Windows

The dBASE IV Program Debugger is composed of four windows, three of which are displayed in the Debugger screen.

- The Debugger window
- The Display window
- The Breakpoint window

The fourth window is an edit window that displays the dBASE IV Text Editor. You can use this window to edit your program.

The Debugger Window

The Debugger window appears at the bottom of the Debugger screen. As shown in Figure 25-1, this window contains information about the current work area, record number, database in use, master index, program name, procedure name, and line number.

The Debugger window is also the window from which you specify actions or commands for the Debugger. To specify an action, type a letter at the "ACTION:" prompt. Table 25-1 lists the letters you can enter and the actions those letters represent. This list appears on your screen when you first access the Debugger or when you press F1 for help.

Accessing the Display Window—D

The Display window lets you view the status of any key expression you enter. To access the Display window, press D at the Debugger window "ACTION:" prompt. dBASE IV moves the cursor into the Display window, where you can enter one or more dBASE IV expressions. To return to the "ACTION:" prompt, press ESC or press CTRL-END.

As shown in Figure 25-1, the Display window has two sides. The left side is where you enter an expression. The right side is where dBASE IV displays the result of that expression. You cannot access or edit the right side. There are ten lines in the Display window, and you can only enter one distinct expression per line.

Letter/ Key	Description
B	Moves cursor to Breakpoint window
D	Moves cursor to Display window
E	Displays or edits program in Text Editor
R	Runs program until breakpoint or error occurs
L	Starts executing at a specific line number
[<*n*>]S	Moves through program *n* lines at a time. Default is one line at a time
[<*n*>]N	Moves through current program or higher level program *n* lines at a time. Use [<*n*>]S for lower level programs. Default is one line at a time
P	Shows programs names and line numbers that called the current program
X	Suspends program and returns to dot prompt. Memory variables retain current values. Enter **RESUME** at the dot prompt to reenter the Debugger and continue
Q	Cancels current program, releases all memory variables, and returns to dot prompt
ENTER	Executes program lines using the values for 1S or 1N, whichever you used most recently
[<*n*>] ENTER	Repeats last *n* steps, or next *n* steps
[<*n*>] UP ARROW	Moves *n* lines up in the source listing
[<*n*>] DOWN ARROW	Moves *n* lines down in the source window
F1	Displays help
F9	Toggles user display on and off

Table 25-1. The Debugger "ACTION:" Prompt Letters and Keys

You can, for example, use the Display window to determine the current value of one or more memory variables. For example, imagine that the current program defines a variable named Choice. You can type **CHOICE** in one of the lines on the left side of the Display window (you do not have to precede your entries with ?). You can then press ENTER to have dBASE IV display the value of the Choice variable in the right side of the Display window. Press ESC or CTRL-END to return to the "ACTION:" prompt. As you step through each line of the current program (by pressing ENTER), you can check to see if the value of the Choice variable changes.

Tip: When you enter a variable name in the Display window, dBASE IV frequently issues the error message "Variable not found." If you've spelled the variable name properly, you can usually ignore this message; it simply means that dBASE hasn't yet encountered the variable in your program. However, you can also get this error message if you never define the variable, or release the variable (with RELEASE) too soon.

Accessing the Breakpoint Window—B

You can use the Breakpoint window to halt your program when an expression evaluates to true. To access the Breakpoint window, press B at the "ACTION:" prompt. dBASE IV moves the cursor to the first line in the Breakpoint window. You can then type up to ten dBASE IV expressions, one per line. Each expression must be a logical expression (returns .T. or .F.). dBASE IV assigns a number to each expression. To return to the "ACTION:" prompt, press ESC or CTRL-END.

dBASE IV evalutes all of your breakpoint expressions as each line of code is processed. When a breakpoint expression evaluates to true (.T.), dBASE IV halts your program and activates the Debugger window. It also displays the message "Breakpoint" in the message line at the bottom of your screen, followed by the line number of the breakpoint expression that halted the program. You can then enter a letter at the "ACTION:" prompt.

For example, suppose you want the current program to halt when the Choice variable becomes equal to "Q". To specify this breakpoint, press B at the action prompt, and enter **Choice = "Q"** in the Breakpoint window. Press ESC to return to the Debugger window. Press R to have dBASE IV run your program. When dBASE IV reaches a point where the Choice variable equals "Q", it halts the program and displays the message "Breakpoint 1" in the message line ("1" is the line number of the breakpoint expression).

You can also use the LINENO( ) function to establish a breakpoint. This function returns the line number that is about to be processed from the currently active program. When you use LINENO( ) as a breakpoint expression, dBASE IV stops program execution when it reaches that line, transferring control to the Debugger window. You can then type an action letter at the "ACTION:" prompt.

For example, if you want program execution to stop at line 34, press B to access the Breakpoint window. Then type the expression **LINENO( ) = 34**. Next, press ESC to leave the Breakpoint window and press R to run your program. When line 34 is about to be processed, dBASE IV suspends program execution and places the cursor at the "ACTION:" prompt.

You can also use the LINENO( ) function with the PROGRAM( ) function to specify a breakpoint in a specific program. The PROGRAM( ) function returns the name of the currently active program or procedure. You combine the two functions with the .AND. operator. For example, to suspend program execution just before line 34 in a program called MYPROG.PRG, type the following in the Breakpoint window:

```
LINENO( ) = 34 .AND. PROGRAM( ) = MYPROG
```

Accessing the Edit Window—E

To access the Edit window, press E at the "ACTION:" prompt. dBASE IV transfers you to the dBASE IV Text Editor and displays the current program on the work surface. You can then edit the program. To save the changes you make, press CTRL-END. Press ESC to return to the "ACTION:" prompt without saving changes.

Recall that dBASE IV is actually running the compiled version of your program (the .DBO file) and displaying the noncompiled version (the .PRG file). Therefore, any changes that you make to your program in the Edit window are not reflected in the current Debugger session. To make your changes effective, exit the Debugger by pressing Q and recompile the program. To compile the program, use the COMPILE *<program filename>* command or return to the Debugger by using the DEBUG *<program filename>* command (dBASE IV compiles your program automatically before displaying it in the Debugger screen).

Using Debugger Commands

As mentioned, to enter a Debugger command you press an action letter at the "ACTION:" prompt. You've already used D, B, and E to access the Display, Breakpoint, and Edit windows. However, the dBASE IV Debugger offers a host of other action letters, as shown in Table 25-1. dBASE IV displays a list of these letters when you first enter the Debugger, as in Figure 25-2.

Processing Multiple Command Lines—S and N

As mentioned, you can step through your programs one command line at a time by pressing ENTER. However, you can also process more than one command line at a time when you press ENTER. To do this, you use the S command letter at the "ACTION:" prompt. To specify the number of command lines to process, precede the S action letter with a number. For example, to process five command lines when you press ENTER, type **5S** at the "ACTION:" prompt. The Debugger still stops at command lines that cause errors, or at specified breakpoints.

The S action letter only works once. Thereafter, dBASE IV reverts to processing a single command line each time you press ENTER. To have dBASE IV process more than a single command line again, you must use the S action letter again.

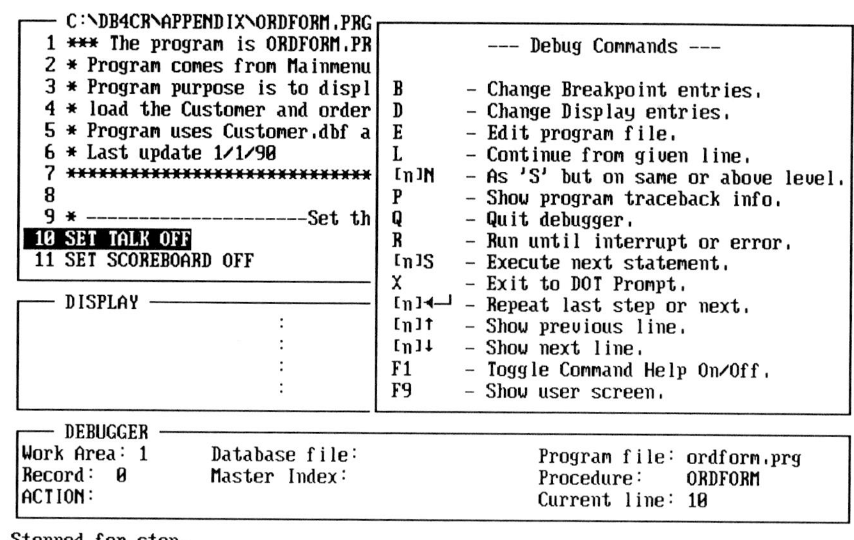

Figure 25-2. The Debugger displays a list of action letters

To have dBASE IV count only command lines at the current program level or higher when you press ENTER, use the N action letter. When you use this action letter, dBASE IV does not count command lines it processes in lower level programs or procedures. For example, to have dBASE IV process five command lines at a time in the current or higher level program, type **5N** at the "ACTION:" prompt.

Running a Program—R

To run the program currently on the Debugger screen, press R at the "ACTION:" prompt. This is an alternative to pressing ENTER to process a limited number of command lines. When you use this command, the entire program executes until dBASE IV encounters an error or a breakpoint.

Running Part of a Program—L

To begin debugging your program at a specific line number, press L at the "ACTION:" prompt. When you press this letter, dBASE IV prompts you for a line number at which to begin running your program. Enter the line number of your choice and press ENTER. dBASE IV begins debugging you program starting at the specified line number. At an error or breakpoint, dBASE IV halts program execution and awaits the next action letter.

Showing Procedure Calls—P

To display a list of all programs and procedures that were used to get to the current program, type P at the "ACTION:" prompt. dBASE IV displays a list of calling programs and procedures below the Debugger window. The lineage of the program is traced all the way back to the dot prompt. Use this command to trace the programs that called the current program when you're debugging a multiple program application.

Quitting or Suspending the Debugger—Q or X

To quit the Debugger, enter Q at the "ACTION:" prompt. This cancels program execution, releases all variables, and returns you to the dot prompt.

On the other hand, press X to temporarily suspend program execution, leave the Debugger, and return to the dot prompt. All memory variables remain in memory. You can enter dot prompt commands to perform other tasks. At any time, however, you can type **RESUME** at the dot prompt to return to the Debugger and continue debugging your program.

In this chapter, you learned how to activate the dBASE IV Program Debugger. You also learned about its features and how to use them. By now, you should know how to use the Debugger to troubleshoot any dBASE IV program that you write.

Networking dBASE IV

PART FOUR

dBASE IV has several new automated networking features that make it easy to share files among multiple users on a local area network (LAN). For example, in dBASE III PLUS, you must lock the entire shared file before performing an operation on a record. In dBASE IV, however, when you perform an operation on a record, dBASE automatically locks that record and leaves the rest of the file accessible to other users.

This part of the book covers all aspects of using dBASE IV on a network. Chapter 26, "Installing dBASE IV on a Network," begins with some general networking concepts, including hardware requirements and how to configure your network. It then gives step-by-step instructions for installing dBASE IV on a network.

Chapter 27, "Using dBASE IV on a Network," is written for network users. It describes how to start dBASE IV on a network and how to use its built-in security features. It also familiarizes you with dBASE IV's file- and record-sharing commands.

Chapter 28, "Network Administration," shows you how to establish security procedures for controlling access to files, how to institute a back-up system, and how to perform housekeeping chores to ensure the smooth running of your network.

Earlier versions of dBASE require you to do a great deal of hand coding to create a program that operates in a multi-user environment. In dBASE IV, however, network programming is a great deal easier. It frees you to concentrate on the peculiar problems that can arise when users share files. Chapter 29, "dBASE IV Network Programming," describes these problems and shows you how to write network programs that get around them.

Chapter 30 provides a comprehensive list of network-related commands and functions.

Installing dBASE IV on a Network

TWENTY SIX

One of dBASE IV's more powerful features is its networking capability. On a local area network (LAN), multiple users can edit, view, print, and query a single database file at the same time. The multi-user version of dBASE IV has file- and record-locking features that work with your networking software to allow file sharing among network users.

This chapter covers a broad range of network-related issues. First it discusses the software you'll need to run dBASE IV on a network. Then it deals with some general networking concepts, including hardware requirements, network configuration, and network administration. Finally, the chapter describes how to install dBASE IV on a network, including how to add and remove users from the network through the dBASE IV Access Control program.

dBASE IV Software Requirements

You can install the single-user version of dBASE IV to run on a LAN, but it doesn't permit you to share files. The multi-user version of dBASE IV, however, is designed for file sharing.

The multi-user version of dBASE IV is available in the standard dBASE IV package. (In fact, you may have noticed the **Multi-user installation** option when you first installed dBASE.) However, if you install a standard copy of dBASE IV for multi-user mode, only one user can log on to dBASE IV, and you won't really get the benefits of networking.

If you have additional copies of dBASE IV, you can install additional network users. To do so, install one copy of dBASE IV in multi-user mode. Then add one network user for each additional copy of dBASE IV you have. (See the section "Adding and Deleting Users Through the Access Control Program" near the end of this chapter.)

A better alternative is to install the multi-user version of dBASE IV and add additional network users with the dBASE IV LAN-Pack. This setup allows up to six users to work with files simultaneously. You can purchase additional LAN-Pack Access disks to increase the number of users to more than six.

The dBASE IV Developer's Edition enables up to three users to share the dBASE IV environment and files.

The Advantages of Networking

There are many advantages to networking. For example, in the single-user version of dBASE IV, a database file has to be copied onto to each user's PC for editing or viewing. In the multi-user version, a file can reside on one hard disk and be accessed by several users at once. This also eliminates the risk of data loss through trading disks and updating fields. What's more, records can be modified by one user and immediately viewed by another without "disk-swapping."

Planning a Network

There are some important items to consider when planning a network:

- You can run the single-user version of dBASE IV on a network, but only one person at a time can work with a file.
- If you run the multi-user version of a single copy of dBASE IV on a network, files are shareable in theory, but only one user may log on to dBASE at a time.
- You must purchase a dBASE IV LAN-Pack, multiple copies of dBASE IV, or the dBASE IV Developer's Edition to allow multiple users to take advantage of networked databases.
- Hardware requirements are different for networks.
- Printer setups and handling may be different on networks.
- Certain commands will execute differently when run on a network.
- You may need to use security procedures to control access to database files.

The Concept of a Local Area Network

A *local area network* (LAN) enables multiple users to share application software and data files. The LAN system consists of a *file server* and one or more *workstations,* or *network nodes,* as they are sometimes called. The file server may be a PC with a hard disk, or it may be a stand-alone central processing unit with a large hard disk but no floppy drive, keyboard, or monitor. Workstations are individual PCs which may have floppy drives or even a hard disk. The file server and PCs are connected to each other by a network cable that carries instructions and data between the workstations and file server.

You can compare an LAN to the main office of a bank and its smaller branch offices. Transactions are generated and processed at the local branches, but, when completed, they are stored at the main branch. Information flows between the main office of the bank and the branches by couriers. A file server is like the main office of the bank and the workstations are like branch offices. The network cables are similar to bank couriers, carrying information back and forth between the file server and the workstations. Software and data files are stored on the file server and are accessed by a workstation when needed. You run application programs and information processing at the workstation level. When you finish your work, data is sent to the file server for storage.

The LAN software, such as 3COM 3+ Share or Novell SFT NetWare, is the network administrator that routes "packets" of information to their correct destinations, which can be workstations, a file server, or a printer. This software controls the sharing of directories, applications software, data files, and devices such as printers or modems.

Multi-user dBASE IV controls the use of shared dBASE files, protecting the integrity of the data as multiple users simultaneously update, view, organize, or print the information in the files.

General Considerations for Network Installation

dBASE IV Multi-user officially supports the following networks:

- IBM PC LAN Program—version 1.2 or later—and Token-Ring
- Novell SFT Netware 286 with TTS—version 2.1
- Ungerman-Bass Net/One PC System—version 15.2
- 3Com 3+ Share Software—version 1.2

You may install multi-user dBASE IV on networks other than the four just mentioned, but Ashton-Tate promises only limited technical support and warns that performance may be unpredictable.

This chapter assumes that you are familiar with the network software installed on your LAN system, have system administrator or supervisor status, and are capable of creating shared directories and modifying user log-in routines to access the new dBASE directories and files. If not, consult your networking software manual and set aside some time to learn about sharing and linking directories and printers.

As the network administrator, you must make certain decisions before installing dBASE IV. Which directory should be shared for the dBASE IV multi-user program files? Which data files should go into a user's home directory and which should be in a directory shared by all users? Should all data directories have read/write/create attributes? Should local workstation printers or network printers be used for printing dBASE IV reports? Should your users be assigned security codes in order to limit access to data files? Planning ahead will make the installation of dBASE IV easier and will result in a network better suited to the requirements of your office.

You must install and configure the networking software on your file server before installing the dBASE IV software.

Hardware Requirements and Setup

This section describes hardware and setup considerations for a LAN. It discusses the unique requirements of the file server and workstations.

File Server and Workstations

Both file server and workstations must be 100% IBM PC-compatible computers. If you are using microcomputers as part of the network system, they must be running DOS 3.1 or higher. To access files on the file server, the workstations must also be running the network program shell.

You can use one of two types of file server configurations as the core of a network system: a dedicated file server or a concurrent file server.

A *dedicated* file server is a computer that has no function other than network file storage and network management. It is the unit in which the network software programs, applications programs (such as dBASE IV), and data files are stored. The networking functions are handled by the processor in this computer. As a dedicated file server, it is never used as a workstation and may or may not have a monitor, keyboard, or floppy drives.

A *concurrent* file server doubles as a workstation. It has a monitor and keyboard, and you can run applications on this computer while it is acting as a file server to other workstations. The processor has to handle two functions at once, however, and this affects the performance of both the file server and workstation functions. In other words, you need a dedicated file server for maximum network performance.

Some networking software allows you to use a concurrent file server, while others require a dedicated server as the core of the network. If your network software allows either a concurrent or a dedicated server, you should understand which operations are run by the file server and which are run by a workstation.

File Server Operations

The file server provides shared device support (drives, printers, and modems) and shared file support (both applications and data). It also handles general utility functions such as archiving, directory management, user management, print spooling, and performance monitoring. The file server file also does reads and writes, in shared or exclusive mode. Print jobs are "queued" and sent sequentially to the printer. Communication with remote workstations or other computers is handled at this level.

Workstation Operations

A workstation relies on the file server to read and write files and handle all network print jobs. The data and instructions from files opened by the file server are transferred into the workstation memory. All software execution, whether a word processor, spreadsheet, or database program, is done by the workstation processor, and workstation RAM is used to run the application.

Choosing a Network Configuration

Understanding the division of work between the file server and workstations makes it easier to choose your network configuration. Disk-intensive programs, such as dBASE IV, require maximum performance at the file server level because of the constant read and write operations that must be performed during indexing, sorting, record searching, and listing. If these operations must share the file server processor with a concurrent workstation, the amount of processor time available for both may be cut dramatically.

When choosing a file server for disk-intensive applications, consider carefully the access time of the disk and disk- or RAM-caching capability.

For less disk-intensive programs, such as spreadsheets, word processors, communications programs, or any other application where files are not constantly being read or written, the speed of the file server operations becomes less important to overall performance. In this type of system, a concurrent file server is more acceptable.

Tip: Ashton-Tate recommends that you use a dedicated file server to run multi-user dBASE IV. They promise only limited technical support if you run multi-user dBASE IV on a concurrent file server.

RAM Requirements

The file server and each workstation must have a minimum of 640K of RAM.

Note: You need 512K of free RAM to run dBASE IV, and this affects the use of multi-user dBASE IV on a network. Some network software may occupy as much as 100K of RAM on each workstation in addition to the amount of RAM used by DOS. This brings available RAM below the required 512K, and you cannot run dBASE IV. At this time, both multi- and single-user versions of dBASE IV version 1.0 do not support expanded or extended memory. You can work around this limitation by using an extended memory card in the server and each workstation to store the network program shell. Multi-user dBASE IV supports the memory extension cards and/or software listed in Table 26-1.

Disk Storage

The file server you choose for your network must have at least one hard disk. Some network systems require that the server also have a 3.5-inch or 5.25-inch floppy drive. Your server hard disk must have a minimum of 3.77MB available to install multi-user dBASE IV or 5MB available to install the dBASE IV Developer's Edition. You must also consider the amount of space needed for the database files created and used by each workstation.

Tip: Remember that certain operations in dBASE create additional files, and you must allow room for those as well. For example, if you create an index for a large database, the index file may also be quite large. Also, the SORT command creates a new file as large as the original database. Furthermore, when you modify the structure of a file, you need twice the space for the file being modified. Not allowing enough space on the disk for these functions may crash an application, or cause a loss of data.

	IBM PC LAN	IBM PC LAN with Token Ring	Novell	3Com
8086/ 8088	HICard	HIcard	No additional requirements with RX-Net or Ethernet	HIcard with Etherlink or Etherlink II; or Etherlink Plus
80286	HICard	HIcard	No additional requirements with RX-Net or Ethernet	HIcard with Etherlink or Etherlink II; or Etherlink Plus
PS2/ Systems	Model 80 with 386MAX	Model 80 with 386MAX	No additional requirements with RX-Net or Ethernet	Model 80 with 386MAX
80386	386MAX or HIcard	386MAX or HIcard	No additional requirements with RX-Net or Ethernet	Etherlink or Etherlink II, plus 386MAX or HIcard
Diskless work-station	Not supported	Not supported	Supported	Supported

Table 26-1. Memory Extension Cards and Software Supported by Multi-User dBASE IV

Workstations do not need a hard disk, but you need at least one workstation with a floppy drive to install dBASE IV. Make sure that your workstation floppy drive is the same size as the program disks you order from Ashton-Tate. You may order your new dBASE IV system on either 5.25-inch 360K or 3.5-inch 720K disks.

Be sure to read your networking manual thoroughly to see if there are additional requirements for your system.

Preliminary Steps

This section describes the steps you need to take before installing dBASE IV on a network. These steps include assessing your needs, defining access privileges, and preparing the network.

Assessing Your Needs

As the network administrator, you should take the following steps prior to actually installing dBASE IV LAN-Pack:

- Determine what type of dBASE IV applications will be run on your network, which users will need to access them, and where the program and data files should be kept.
- Have a planning session with your users. Ask them what programs and files they want to have on the network. Have them estimate the size of the files they may be using. Find out which files and applications would be for individual use and which should be available to multiple users.
- Decide whether users will have a "home" directory on the file server or will use a local drive to store their non- shared files.
- Consider using dBASE IV's PROTECT command to control your users' access to the data files. Chapter 28 discusses the PROTECT command in detail.
- Plan for the use of network or local workstation printers. Determine which reports should go to the network printer and which could be run on a local printer.
- Create your directory system for dBASE IV. Use directory names that indicate the purpose of the files stored there. Use your network software commands to assign the sharenames and the correct read/write/create status for each directory.
- For future reference, write down and/or diagram the directory names, sharenames, status, and purpose of each of the directories.

- Plan the dBASE IV "environment" for each user, to be set through individual CONFIG.DB files and batch files on the workstations. (See the section "Setting the Environment for Each User with CONFIG.DB" that follows.)

Defining Access Privileges

Each type of networking software has its own conventions for creating directories on the file server hard disk, but all share certain common features. Directories that you want to make available to multiple users must be "shared" through a process explained in the section "Preparing the Network." In addition, you must assign the type of user access—read, write, create, or any combination of the three.

- A directory with *read* privileges contains files that you may read into workstation memory and view, print, or send through a communications program.
- A directory with *write* status has files that you can modify and write back to the disk.
- A directory with *create* status allows you to create and add new files to the directory.

A directory that has only read privileges does not allow you to make any changes to files. For example, an archive directory may contain files that no longer need changing but may need to be reviewed from time to time. A directory with write-only status allows you to write to the directory but not read files or create new files. This type of directory might be for temporary files used while running an application program. If a directory has read and write privileges and has not been assigned a create status, you may read or modify files, but may not add new files to that directory. By omitting the create status, you can control the types of files stored in a certain directory and prevent random file creation by users.

Most directories that contain shared user files have at least read/write status. You should give a user's home directory a read/write/create status.

To create directories on the file server hard disk, you need to have *administrative* status. As a network administrator, you must log in with an administrator password in order to make changes to the print and file services on the network. To create a new directory, begin with the DOS MKDIR or MD command. After creating the directory, you must assign a *sharename*. The sharename allows users logged in at their workstations to *link*, or assign the shared directory to a logical drive letter. This process shares among network users the files in a directory.

Each networking system has different commands for file services. Before continuing, you should read the section in your networking manual that discusses assigning sharenames and read, write, or create status to a directory.

Preparing the Network

To prepare your network for the dBASE IV installation, perform the following steps:

1. At any workstation, log on to the file server hard disk drive.

2. Use the DOS editor EDLIN, or another text editor, to modify the CONFIG.SYS file in each workstation's root directory. Include the following settings:

   FILES = 99
   BUFFERS = 15
   LASTDRIVE = *x*

   (*x* can be A - Z and should be the highest-lettered logical drive you plan to use.)

Tip: Some networking programs occupy a large amount of RAM and require that the system configuration be set to utilize the minimum amount of RAM possible. You may change your FILES setting to as low as 40, which will result in a slight increase in available RAM.

3. Create a directory named DBASE on your network. Suggested procedures for the four networks supported by multi-user dBASE IV are described in the sections that follow. Skip to the section that is appropriate for your network.

IBM PC Network, IBM PC Token-Ring Network, and Ungerman-Bass Net/One Network

The procedure that follows assumes that your file server hard disk is drive C.

1. To create a directory named DBASE on the network, type

```
C> MD DBASE ↵
```

2. To create dBASE directory with read, write, and create privileges and assign a network name, DBASE, to the directory, type

```
C> NET SHARE DBASE = C:\DBASE /RWC ↵
```

3. To link a workstation to dBASE IV, enter the following NET USE command at the workstation:

```
A> NET USE D: \\servername\DBASE ↵
```

4. You are now ready to install multi-user dBASE IV using the instructions in the section "Installing Multi-User dBASE IV on the Network" that follows.

5. After installation, change to the drive and directory in which you've installed dBASE IV, and make the files read-only.

```
C> ATTRIB +R *.* ↵
```

Note: The file ATTRIB.EXE must be present in the DBASE directory, or the DOS PATH command must be set to the directory in which the ATTRIB.EXE file resides.

6. Start multi-user dBASE IV.

```
C> PATH = D:\ ↵
C> DBASE ↵
```

3COM 3+ Network

The procedure that follows assumes that your file server hard disk is drive C.

1. Create a shared directory on the network called C:\APPS and, using the 3Com 3+ Share 3F program, create the sharename APPSADMN with read, write, and create privileges. The programs 3F.EXE and LOGIN.EXE should be available from the \APPS directory.

2. Log in as the server/user at a workstation, and create a DBASE directory.

   ```
   C> 3F LOGIN [server]; LINK D: APPS ↵
   C> D: ↵
   D> MD DBASE ↵
   D> 3F ↵
   3F> SHARE ? ↵
   Sharename? DBASE ↵
   Path? C:\DBASE ↵
   Password? [optional password or leave blank] ↵
   Access (R/W/C)? (press ↵ here to accept default)
   ```

   The following message should appear, indicating that you have successfully shared the DBASE directory:

   ```
   \\Server:Domain:Org\DBASE shared
   ```

   This directory will receive the installed dBASE IV program files and the dBASE IV LAN-Pack files.

3. You may create any other shared or private directories for data files at this time. Here is an example that creates a data directory called DBDATA:

```
D> MD DBASE\DBDATA ↵
D> 3F ↵
3F> SHARE ? ↵
Sharename? DBDATA ↵
Path? C:\DBASE\DBDATA ↵
Password? [optional password or leave blank]  ↵
Access (R/W/C)? (press ↵ here to accept default)
```

4. You are now ready to install multi-user dBASE IV using the instructions in the section "Installing Multi-User dBASE IV on the Network" that follows.

5. After installation, change to the drive and directory in which you've installed dBASE IV, and make the files read-only by using the DOS ATTRIB command.

```
D> ATTRIB +R *.*  ↵
```

Note: The file ATTRIB.EXE must be present in the DBASE directory, or the DOS PATH command must be set to the directory in which the ATTRIB.EXE file resides.

6. Start multi-user dBASE IV.

```
C> 3F LOGIN [user-name] ↵
C> D: ↵
D> 3F LINK E: \\[server]\DBASE ↵
D> 3F LINK F: \\[server]\DBDATA ↵
```

If you plan to use a network printer, link the printer sharename to a logical printer port (LPT1, LPT2, or LPT3) using the 3P program. Consult your 3Com manual for instructions on configuring, sharing, and linking printers.

```
D> 3P LINK LPT2: = LASER ↵
```

Start dBASE IV.

```
D> E: ↵
E> PATH = F:\ ↵
```

```
E> DBASE ↵
```

Novell Network

The procedure that follows assumes that the default network drive is logical drive F. Create a multi-user dBASE IV directory mapped to a logical drive letter not already in use.

1. Log in as **SUPERVISOR** at a workstation and create the DBASE directory from the file server's root directory.

   ```
   F> MD DBASE ↵
   ```

2. Using the Novell MAP SEARCH command, make the SYS:DBASE directory accessible through search drives.

   ```
   F> MAP SEARCH3: = SYS:DBASE ↵
   ```

3. Assign a drive letter to the DBASE directory.

   ```
   F> MAP F: = SYS:DBASE ↵
   ```

4. Create any other shared or private data directories at this time. Use the MAP command to assign a drive letter to each directory. Use the SYSCON command for storing the mapping of the directories to logical drives to a log-in script for each user. See your Novell documentation for details.

5. Use the SYSCON command to make trustee assignments for each directory, as shown in Table 26-2.

6. Install multi-user dBASE IV and, if you have one, the LAN-Pack from a workstation.

7. Use the SPOOL or CAPTURE command to direct print jobs from this workstation to a network printer. Here is an example:

   ```
   F> SPOOL L = 2 TI = 5 ↵
   ```

8. To start multi-user dBASE IV, type

```
F> DBASE ↵
```

Tip: To make it easier for users to log in and start up dBASE IV, create a batch file and/or log-in script (Novell) containing the pathing (IBM PC Network), linking (3Com), or mapping (Novell) steps. You can include this batch file in the log-in process for each user. It will ensure that correct logical drives have been assigned to all shared directories and that print services are redirected to the correct service.

Installing Multi-User dBASE IV on the Network

When you have prepared your network for multi-user dBASE IV, you're ready to install your new software. The dBASE IV Install program is completely menu-driven and very easy to follow. This section describes how to install dBASE IV and, if you have one, the dBASE IV LAN-Pack.

1. Make sure that you are logged in to your network at a workstation and have assigned a logical drive letter to the shared DBASE directory. Place the Installation Disk

Directory	Read	Write	Create	Open	Search	Delete	Parental
SYS:DBNETCTL.300	YES	YES	NO	YES	YES	NO	NO
SYS:DBASE	YES	YES*	YES	YES	YES	YES*	YES
SYS:DBASE/SQLHOME	YES	YES	YES	YES	YES	YES	YES
SYS:DBASE/SAMPLES	YES	YES*	YES	YES	YES	YES*	

* Indicates additional rights that may be assigned to each directory to give the user full access to the dBASE IV environment.

Table 26-2. Novell Trustee Assignments

from your copy of dBASE IV in drive A, and log on to that drive by typing **A:** and pressing ENTER. Type **INSTALL** and press ENTER. Once you start the dBASE IV Install program, you will be prompted for each response from an easy-to-follow menu.

The Ashton-Tate logo appears, followed by the copyright screen. Press ENTER to continue to the software registration screen. The information you enter here will appear on the registration screen every time you run dBASE IV. Once you've saved it you cannot change it.

2. Enter your name, or company name, and the serial number on the label of System Disk #1. Press CTRL-END to save the information you have entered. Press ESC to abandon the information you have typed into the registration screen.

3. Next you tell dBASE IV what kind of equipment you are using. The Hardware Setup screen appears with four options to be filled in. The arrow keys allow you to move up or down through these options. A highlighted bar indicates the current option.

4. The first option is **Multi-user installation**. Pressing SPACEBAR or ENTER toggles the option from Yes to No. Press the SPACEBAR to make the Yes appear.

5. Use the DOWN ARROW key to move to the **Display mode** option. Again, pressing SPACEBAR or ENTER toggles you through a series of choices. Toggle through all of the choices at least once to make sure you find the correct one for your system. Press the DOWN ARROW key when your display type appears.

   If you have a color monitor, use the DOWN ARROW key to move to the **Optimize color display** option and press ENTER. You are prompted to correct a "snow" effect on your monitor or to skip to the printer setup. If you select **Proceed**, you are asked if you see a snow effect on your monitor. If you do, press Y. Otherwise, answer No by pressing N. Pressing any key will return you to the hardware menu.

6. Press DOWN ARROW to move to the **Printers** option and press ENTER. A printer definition table appears below the setup menu. dBASE IV allows you to install four printer drivers. From this menu, you can indicate your printer name, driver, and the printer port to which it is attached. Highlight line 1 and press SHIFT-F1 to display a list of printer names. Scroll through this list and press ENTER when you have highlighted the correct name. A list of models and their associated printer drivers appears next. Highlight your printer model and press ENTER. The printer name, model, and driver name appear on line 1

   If the name of your printer is not listed, you can consult your printer manual to see if the printer can emulate a printer on the list. If it can, follow the instructions in your printer manual to set the printer emulation to one available in dBASE IV. As an alternative, you can choose the **Generic Driver** option from the printer list on the screen.

7. Next, choose the DOS or network device to which this printer is attached. Pressing SHIFT-F1 again displays a list of devices. Understanding your network print services will help you make the correct choice of a device.

   Some networks, such as 3Com, assign logical devices to network printers. A laser printer, for instance, might be connected to and configured for your file server serial port COM1. When you've configured the printer for the network, a sharename of Laser, for example, and the serial port COM1 is assigned. However, when a user logs in to the network, the log-in sequence links the printer sharename Laser to the logical port, LPT2.

   With the Novell network, network printers are assigned at log-in to \\SPOOLER or \\CAPTURE, rather than a physical printer port.

The device you choose during printer installation should be the logical device assigned to the network printer in the user log-in sequence for multi-user dBASE IV.

If a workstation has a local printer (a printer physically attached to the PC workstation rather than the file server), install that printer for dBASE IV and use the physical workstation port to which it is attached as the device.

Repeat this sequence to install additional printers.

8. After choosing your printer(s), review the list to make sure that your printer names and devices are correct. If you need to change any of the information, simply move to that line, place your cursor in the field you wish to change, and press SHIFT-F1 to redisplay your choices.

9. To save your printer definitions, press CTRL-END. A list of your printer drivers appears and you are prompted to choose your default printer driver. dBASE IV will automatically use for all print jobs the driver you choose here. Highlight your choice and press ENTER. If you wish to cancel the settings you have chosen, press ESC and verify with Y or N that you wish to abandon the printer definitions.

Tip: When working with multi-user dBASE IV, directing output to a printer may require additional commands. Review the SET PRINTER TO command in Chapter 30 for information on network printing. If you don't use SET PRINTER correctly, some networks may not send dBASE IV data to the printer until you exit to DOS.

10. To save your hardware settings, press CTRL-END. To abandon the hardware setup, press ESC.

11. Next, you are prompted to **Proceed**, **Modify hardware setup**, or **Exit** to leave the multi-user dBASE IV installation. If you need to make changes to the hardware

settings you just entered, choose the **Modify** option. If you wish to abandon the installation, choose **Exit**.

If you choose to proceed with the installation, you must tell dBASE IV in which drive and directory the dBASE system files are to be installed. Enter the logical drive letter you assigned to your DBASE directory, followed by a colon and a backslash, and press ENTER. If your logical drive is D, type

```
D:\ ↵
```

12. Next, verify the drive and directory for the SQL system files. The logical drive used for the dBASE IV system files appears as a default. Press ENTER to accept this drive or type the letter of the drive you wish to use. The drive letter, if different from the drive suggested, must represent a logical drive that you assigned to a shared directory before starting the installation.
    If you use the default drive letter for the SQL files, they are installed in a subdirectory to the DBASE directory. The new directory is called SQLHOME and is created during installation.

    After your drives and directories are verified, the dBASE IV Install program will verify that the installation can proceed by checking the following:

- If there is not enough disk space for the dBASE IV files, you are prompted to enter another drive or to exit the program.
- If no target directory exists, you may enter a new drive and directory or let the Install program create the directory for you.
- If multi-user dBASE IV has already been installed in that directory, you can overwrite it or abandon the installation.
- If multi-user dBASE III PLUS has been installed on your network, it will not run after you've installed multi-user dBASE IV. At this point, you may exit the Install program or proceed with the installation.

- If a copy-protected version of dBASE exists in the target directory, you must choose a different drive for multi-user dBASE IV or exit the installation. Use the Uninstall program provided with the previous version of dBASE to uninstall it from the network. Run the multi-user dBASE IV Install program after uninstalling the copy-protected version.

13. Once you have taken the preceding steps, the Install program is ready to begin copying your system files into the target directories. You are prompted to place the Installation Disk in drive A and press ENTER. Your hardware setup is recorded on that disk and you are then asked to place System Disk #1 in drive A and press ENTER. The System Disk number is located next to the words "System Disk"; it is not the number in the red box in the upper-right corner of the disk label. If you insert the System Disks in the wrong sequence, the Install program prompts you to insert the correct disk. The system files from each disk are copied into the target directory on the file server.

14. When all system files and SQL files are installed, you can invoke the Access Control program. Installing multi-user dBASE IV automatically enables one user to run dBASE IV on the network. The Access Control program allows you to add an additional five users to your dBASE IV system. You can add users now, or proceed with the installation and add users at another time.

15. See the section "Adding or Deleting Users through the Access Control Program" if you wish to add users at this time.

    When all System files have been installed, a screen appears stating that multi-user dBASE IV has been installed successfully.

16. If you proceed with the installation, you may modify your AUTOEXEC.BAT and CONFIG.SYS files through the Install program or skip those modifications. You must modify the CONFIG.SYS file to include the following lines:

    FILES = 99
    BUFFERS = 15

    If you have not already modified the CONFIG.SYS file, as discussed in the section "Preparing the Network," choose **Proceed** to allow the Install program to add the new settings for you.

17. The next step in the Install program is to copy the sample files. You may skip this step if you wish. If you choose **Proceed**, Install asks you to verify a drive letter and directory for these files. Type a new logical drive letter or press ENTER to use the default directory. The drive letter, if different from the drive suggested, must represent a logical drive that you assigned to a shared directory before starting the installation. (If there is not enough space on the drive for the sample files, you are asked for another drive.) Insert the Sample Program Disks as prompted and press ENTER.

18. Follow the same procedure if you wish to copy the tutorial files onto the network.

    At this point, all files have been installed. An additional directory called DBNETCTL.300 has been created as a subdirectory to the DBASE directory. Control files that record the number of installed users are kept in this directory.

19. The screen offers two choices at the end of the Install program. You can leave Install and exit to DOS, or you can return to the DBSETUP menu to modify your hardware settings or edit the CONFIG.DB file.

Setting the Environment for Each User with CONFIG.DB

The CONFIG.DB file, created during installation, provides initial settings for the dBASE IV environment. These settings include screen color, paths to SQL and data directories, the word processor used to edit memo fields, the number of open files allowed, and the first command to be executed when you start up dBASE IV. The many other settings available are listed in Chapter 35.

Various network users may use different directories for data files. One user may need to start dBASE IV and go directly into a dBASE application. Other users may wish to use the dBASE IV Control Center. When users need different dBASE IV environments, you use the CONFIG.DB file to customize multi-user dBASE IV for each workstation.

As suggested earlier, you should do some initial planning with each user before modifying the CONFIG.DB file. After determining what dBASE IV should look like to each user, you can create a special CONFIG.DB file, which you place on each user's start-up disk or home directory. Each CONFIG.DB file should include the following commands:

SQLHOME = *<pathname>*	This command establishes the drive and directory where the SQL sample files reside.
SQLDATABASE = *<database name>*	This command establishes the name of the SQL sample database.
FDRIVER = *<printer driver filename>*	Supply the printer driver that indicates the workstation. This must be a valid printer driver installed through the hardware setup menu in DBSETUP.

You can create and modify CONFIG.DB files with the DBSETUP program, the dBASE IV Text Editor (see MODIFY COMMAND in Chapter 7), or any ASCII text editor, including the DOS editor EDLIN.

Starting Multi-User DBASE IV

You can start multi-user dBASE IV on the network from a workstation menu or user log-in script. If menus or log-in scripts are not available, you must assign logical drive letters to the DBASE and data directories, log on to the DBASE drive, assign a path to the data directory, type **DBASE**, and press ENTER. The last method is tedious and involves a number of network commands. A batch file or log-in script simplifies start-up and ensures that the right settings and commands are employed.

You use the DBASE command to start multi-user dBASE IV. If you are working with an application program written in dBASE IV, you can include the name of the program as part of the start-up command. For example, if the application is an accounts payable program called ACCTSPAY, the command to load dBASE IV and begin running the payable program is **DBASE ACCTSPAY**.

This start-up command can be part of a batch file, log-in script, or the user's CONFIG.DB file. Be sure to include a path statement to the directory in which the ACCTSPAY program resides.

Adding and Deleting Users Through the Access Control Program

When you install multi-user dBASE IV, one user is automatically set up and added to the user count. You may add up to five additional users with the dBASE IV LAN-Pack. If you own additional packages of standard dBASE IV, you may add one additional user from each copy of System Disk #1.

You can add new users to your multi-user dBASE IV system in two ways:

- During installation of multi-user dBASE IV
- By invoking the ADDUSER4.COM program from DOS

To add users during installation, use the Access Control program after the system files are installed. This process requires that you use the Access Disk provided with the dBASE IV LAN-Pack or System Disk #1 provided with dBASE IV, Standard Edition. The Access Disk records the number of users added to the system and allows you to install a maximum of five additional users. You can purchase additional LAN-packs or copies of dBASE IV, standard version, if you wish to increase your user base to more than the maximum allowed by your current installation. Each System Disk #1 from a standard edition of dBASE IV will allow one additional user.

To call the Access Control Program menu from DOS, log on to the drive and directory containing the dBASE IV program files, type **ADDUSER4** at the system prompt, and press ENTER. The Access Control Program screen will appear (see Figure 26-1). Place the Access Disk in your workstation's floppy drive. You are asked to type the letter of the drive in which the DBNETCTL.300 directory is located.

To add a user, type **1** to choose the **Add users** option from the menu, and enter the letter of the drive containing the Access Disk or System Disk #1. The user count is increased on the Access Disk, and the control files in the DBNETCTL.300 directory are updated to the new user count.

Repeat this process for each user you wish to add. When you are through, press 3 to display the user count and verify the number of users added.

To remove users, place in your workstation floppy drive the Access Disk that you used to add users. Choose option 2, **Subtract users**, and follow the prompts on the screen. Repeat this process

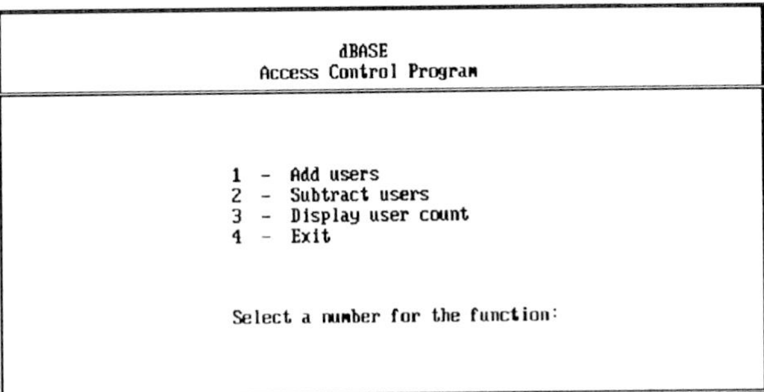

Figure 26-1. The Access Control program screen

for each user you wish to subtract. When you are finished, press 3 to verify the current user count.

To exit the Access Control program, press 4. You are returned to DOS or to the Install program, depending on which method you used to enter the Access Control program.

Uninstalling Multi-User dBASE IV

You may uninstall dBASE IV from your network hard disk by using the DBSETUP program. From DOS, log on to the logical drive containing the dBASE IV system files, type **DBSETUP**, and press ENTER. Choose the **Uninstall dBASE IV** option from the Install menu. Press ENTER to accept the suggested drive and directory in which the program files are located, or type the correct information if your system drive and directory are different than the default. If the Uninstall program locates the drive and directory and finds dBASE IV installed there, the dBASE IV program files are deleted. Any data files in the DBASE directory are left undisturbed.

Uninstalling multi-user dBASE IV returns the installed user count to 0.

In this chapter, you've learned how to set up your network environment for multi-user dBASE IV and how to install your software in the configuration that fits your system. You've also discovered that single-user dBASE IV differs from multi-user dBASE IV on a network, and that certain commands and functions may perform differently in each environment.

Using dBASE IV on a Network

File-Sharing Basics
Starting dBASE IV on a Network
Logging In as a dBASE IV User
Network File-Sharing Conventions
Sharing a Network Printer

TWENTY SEVEN

In multi-user mode, dBASE IV looks and feels identical to the standard version of dBASE IV, with only a few exceptions. These exceptions are the file- and printer-sharing services provided by multi-user dBASE IV for use on a network.

When you don't have a networked system, you enter information on one computer, print it out or copy it to a disk, and transfer it to another department at the end of the day, or, worse, at the end of the week or month. Decision making is delayed until updated data is received.

When you use dBASE IV on a network, decisions can be more immediate. Sharing database files among multiple users allows an instantaneous flow of information from workstation to workstation and department to department. For example, one user can update a customer's account balance field, and, seconds later, a user at another workstation can view the same record with its new account balance and make a decision regarding the customer's credit.

The subjects discussed in this chapter require a basic knowledge of dBASE IV. Before you continue you should familiarize yourself with the dBASE IV menus and data entry methods presented in Chapters 3 and 4 of this book.

File-Sharing Basics

For various users to work compatibly on a network, they need a basic understanding of the way dBASE IV shares files. Network users need to know about commands and functions that lock files and records.

For example, you can accidentally start a command that locks a file during the network's heaviest usage, preventing all others from accessing the file. If you don't know how file and record locks are created, you can become confused or frustrated when a message informs you that a file is already in use. After all, doesn't networking mean that all files are shareable at all times?

When you understand dBASE IV's file-sharing conventions, you can perform file and record operations that create locks—such as sorting, indexing, updates, and deletions—when other users do not need unlimited access to a database file.

Note: The delay caused by a file lock is minimal on small database files, but may be significantly longer on large databases. The network administrator can determine which database files may have housekeeping routines run at any time and which need to be run during times of least usage.

Starting dBASE IV on a Network

After logging on to your network from a workstation, you can start dBASE IV in one of three ways:

- Log on to the logical drive in which the dBASE IV program files are located and type **DBASE**. The dBASE IV logo and registration screens appear, followed by the **Control Center** menu (see Figure 27-1). You can begin your dBASE IV work session from the Control Center.

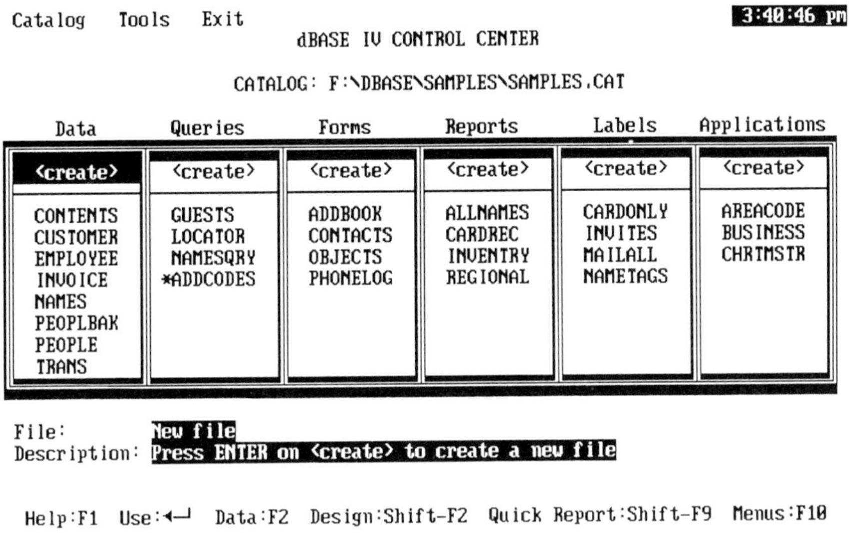

```
Catalog   Tools   Exit                                                    3:40:46 pm
                        dBASE IV CONTROL CENTER

                 CATALOG: F:\DBASE\SAMPLES\SAMPLES.CAT

   Data       Queries      Forms       Reports      Labels     Applications
 <create>    <create>    <create>    <create>     <create>     <create>

 CONTENTS    GUESTS      ADDBOOK     ALLNAMES     CARDONLY     AREACODE
 CUSTOMER    LOCATOR     CONTACTS    CARDREC      INVITES      BUSINESS
 EMPLOYEE    NAMESQRY    OBJECTS     INVENTRY     MAILALL      CHRTMSTR
 INVOICE     *ADDCODES   PHONELOG    REGIONAL     NAMETAGS
 NAMES
 PEOPLBAK
 PEOPLE
 TRANS

File:         New file
Description:  Press ENTER on <create> to create a new file

 Help:F1  Use:◄┘  Data:F2  Design:Shift-F2  Quick Report:Shift-F9  Menus:F10
```

Figure 27-1. The **Control Center** menu

- Log on to the logical drive in which the dBASE IV program files are located and type **DBASE** and a dBASE IV program name, as in the following example:

  ```
  DBASE INVOICE
  ```

  This command starts dBASE IV and also starts a dBASE application program called INVOICE, bypassing the **Control Center** menu and immediately invoking a program.

Note: Take care when running on your network an application written for single-user dBASE IV. Certain functions and commands perform differently when run in a network environment. In addition, you will need to make some program code adjustments if the application uses shared files. See Chapters 29 and 30 for more information on network programming and network commands and functions.

- Use a predefined network menu that loads dBASE IV when you press a single keystroke. The network administrator or programmer can set up this menu after installing dBASE IV. You can include the steps mentioned in the first two items in a batch file. This saves the user all the keystrokes required to start multi-user dBASE IV on a network. Refer to the section in your networking manual for more information on creating batch files.

If you are the network administrator, refer to Chapter 28 for additional information on dBASE IV network administration.

Logging In as a dBASE IV User

If dBASE IV is in protect mode, a log-in screen appears after you've started dBASE, as in Figure 27-2. Before you respond to the log-in screen, ask your network administrator for your assigned group name, log-in name, and password. (For more information on the PROTECT command, see Chapter 28.)

Enter your group name at the prompt. This name, assigned through the PROTECT command, determines file access rights for a group of users. Next, enter your log-in name and password. Your password will not appear on the screen as you type it. If you have

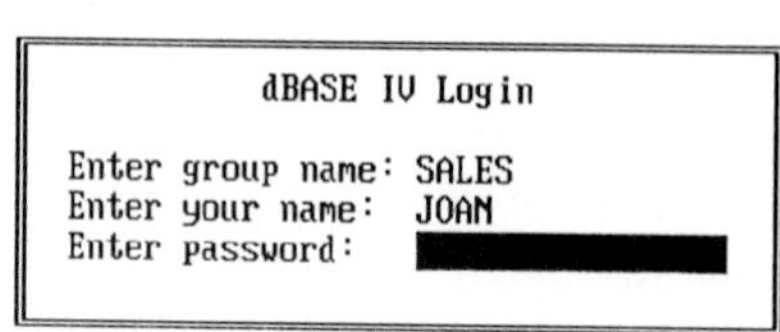

Figure 27-2. The log-in screen

entered your log-in information correctly, the dBASE IV logo and copyright screens appear, followed by the **Control Center** menu.

You are now ready to start working in dBASE IV. Before you begin, however, you should know a few things about sharing files with other users on a network.

Network File-Sharing Conventions

Since dBASE IV automatically controls the file and record locking necessary for shared file operations on a network, you don't need to worry about conflicts during record or file updates. Should you need them, there are also optional commands for locking records and files manually.

File Locking

Certain dBASE IV commands could damage a database if attempted by more than one user at the same time. In multi-user mode, dBASE IV automatically locks database files to prevent such "data collisions" when these commands are in use. Only one user at a time can change or update a file. All actively related files are locked as well.

Table 27-1 lists the dBASE IV commands that cause automatic file locks.

File locks can be automatic or manual. *Automatic file locks* are created by one of the commands shown in Table 27-1. They allow you to open or continue to use a file locked by another user, but not to modify the data in the file in any way. An automatic lock allows limited access to a shared file and prevents more than one user from simultaneously running any of the commands in Table 27-1. dBASE IV's automatic file locks are removed only when the command that created them is completed or aborted.

The FLOCK( ) function creates a *manual file lock* that is similar to an automatic file lock. A file lock created by FLOCK( ) also allows other users limited file access for viewing but not

APPEND FROM	AVERAGE
CALCULATE	COPY TAG/INDEX
COPY [STRUCTURE]	COUNT
DELETE/RECALL	INDEX
JOIN	LABEL
REPLACE [*scope*]	REPORT
SET CATALOG ON	SORT
SUM	TOTAL
UPDATE	

Table 27-1. Commands That Cause Automatic File Locks

modifying until the lock is removed. Typing **? FLOCK( )** at the dot prompt locks the file in the currently selected work area. You can also lock open files in other work areas by using FLOCK( ). If work area 2 has an open file called Clients, typing the command

```
? FLOCK("CLIENTS")
```

from work area 1 will lock Clients. Typing **UNLOCK** at the dot prompt manually unlocks a file locked with this function. Any related files are unlocked at the same time.

Note: Only the user who created a file lock can remove it. You cannot remove it by typing **UNLOCK** from another workstation.

You can also manually lock a file with the EXCLUSIVE keyword. When combined with the USE command, this keyword creates a lock that denies access to *all* other users and makes the file unshareable as long as it is open in exclusive mode. Typing **USE INVOICE EXCLUSIVE** at the dot prompt opens the database file Invoice in exclusive (unshared) mode. The message "Excl-Lock" appears at the right end of the status bar. Other users who

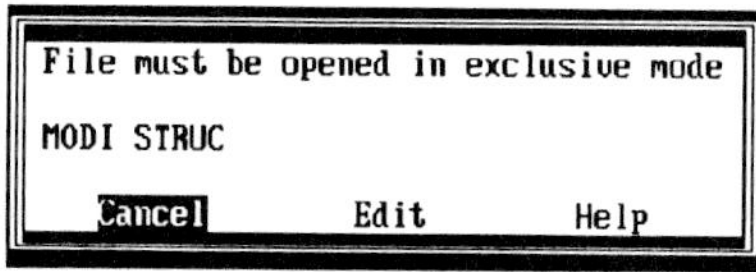

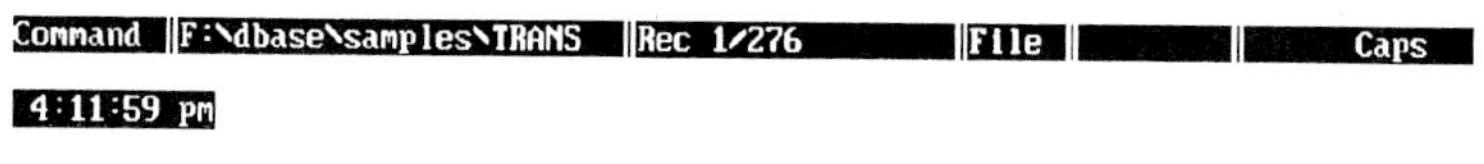

Figure 27-3. Error from a MODIFY STRUCTURE command

attempt to open Invoice will get an error message. When the file is closed, it becomes shareable again.

You can also use the EXCLUSIVE keyword as part of a SET command. Typing **SET EXCLUSIVE ON** at the beginning of a work session opens all databases in locked mode. If you attempt this when the file has already been opened at another workstation, you get an error message stating that the file is already in use.

Tip: Commands that physically change a database require that you open the file in exclusive mode. For example, you can only use MODIFY STRUCTURE, PACK, and ZAP if you have opened your database file using the EXCLUSIVE keyword. You can imagine the results of trying to delete or rename a field in a database with MODIFY STRUCTURE while another user is editing or viewing the same file. If you do not open your file in exclusive mode, you see the error message pictured in Figure 27-3.

See Chapter 30 for more information on SET EXCLUSIVE and FLOCK( ).

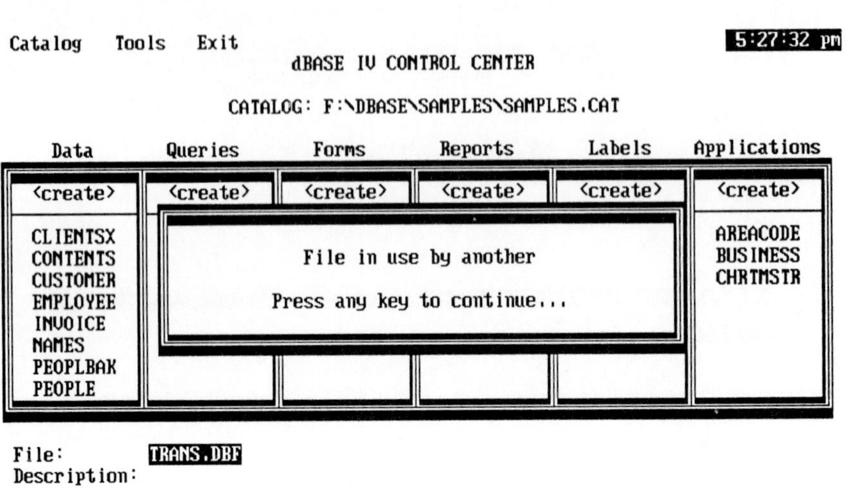

Figure 27-4. File-lock message from the Control Center

dBASE IV displays a file-lock error message when you attempt to do any of the following:

- Open a database that has already been opened for exclusive use by another user
- Use the exclusive mode or FLOCK( ) to lock a database that has already been locked by another user
- Use one of the commands shown in Table 27-1 on a database that has been locked by another user

Figure 27-4 shows a file-lock message from the Control Center and Figure 27-5 shows a file-lock message from the dot prompt.

Suppose you log in to dBASE IV, open a file, and lock it. If other users attempt to use that file, the file-lock message that they

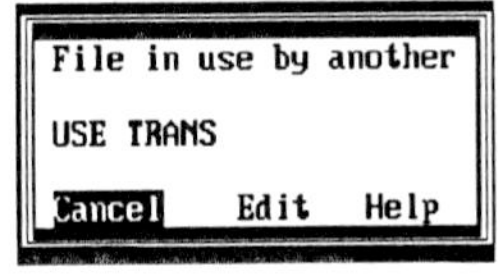

Figure 27-5. File-lock message from the dot prompt

receive may give your name and workstation number. If your network software does not supply your name and workstation number to dBASE IV, the message simply states that the file is in use by "another."

When a file-lock error message appears, you can wait until the file is unlocked, at which time the error message disappears and you have access to the file. As an alternative, you can press ESC to cancel your attempt to use the file.

Choosing to wait for the file to be unlocked by another user may tie up your workstation indefinitely. Users often open a file in exclusive mode and get sidetracked by a phone call or other interruption. The file remains open at that workstation and locked to all other users.

If the error message on the screen gives the culprit's name, you may want to call them and negotiate use of the file for your workstation. Perhaps they can delay their exclusive use of the file while you use it for a short time. If the other user must keep the file in exclusive mode, you can press ESC to clear the error message and continue with other work.

If the error message states only that the file is in use by another, you can either try to track down the workstation using the file or press ESC to cancel your attempt to open the file.

Note: Typing **DISPLAY USERS** at the dot prompt may also list the workstation numbers and names of any other users, depending on the network software you are using. See Chapter 30 for more information on the DISPLAY USERS command.

Record Locking

Multi-user dBASE IV provides automatic record locking to prevent damage caused by more than one user attempting to change a record at the same time. If you're editing an existing record or adding a new record, other users will be "locked out" of that record until you're finished. You can view a record that's been locked from another workstation, but you cannot make any changes until the other user has finished the command or function that caused the record lock.

For example, suppose you have begun to edit record number 3 in a file called Invoice using BROWSE, EDIT, or CHANGE. All other users will be prevented from editing that record, or from indexing, counting, or using other commands that may depend on or change the information in record 3. As soon as the edit is finished, dBASE IV unlocks record number 3 and makes it available again.

Table 27-2 lists the dBASE IV commands that cause a record lock. During EDIT, CHANGE, or BROWSE, the automatic record lock occurs when you press a key other than a direction key. If you enter a number or character from the keyboard, the message "Press space to continue" appears at the bottom of your screen. Pressing SPACEBAR allows you to make changes to the field in

@ GET/READ	APPEND [BLANK]
BROWSE	CHANGE
DELETE/RECALL	EDIT
REPLACE	

Table 27-2. Commands That Cause a Record Lock

which your cursor appears. While you are editing your record, the message "RecLock" appears at the right end of the status bar. Automatic record locks are released when the command that sets them finishes execution.

Tip: If you've created an automatic record lock by using the EDIT, CHANGE, or BROWSE command, you must move the record pointer to another record or press CTRL-END to release the lock.

Tip: If another user is editing records in the database you are using, the changes to each record will not be visible to you until you position your record pointer on the modified record. Using the SET REFRESH option (see Chapter 30) allows you to see changes made at other workstations without repositioning the record pointer.

If you attempt to modify a locked record, you get the error message shown in Figure 27-6.

Records in another work area that are actively related to a locked record or file are also automatically locked.

You can lock records manually from the keyboard in three ways:

- From the BROWSE command, using the **Records menu**. Press F10 to access the **Records** menu and then select the **Lock record** option. The message "RecLock" appears on the right side of the status bar. You can unlock the record from the **Record** menu as well.

- By pressing CTRL-O while in edit or browse mode. Position your record pointer on the record you wish to lock and press CTRL-O. The message "RecLock" appears on the right side of the status bar. Use CTRL-O again to unlock the record.

- With the functions RLOCK( ) and LOCK( ), which are interchangeable. If you type **? RLOCK( )** at the dot prompt, the current record is locked. Typing **? RLOCK("1,4,7","INVOICE")** locks records 1, 4, and 7 in the open file, Invoice.

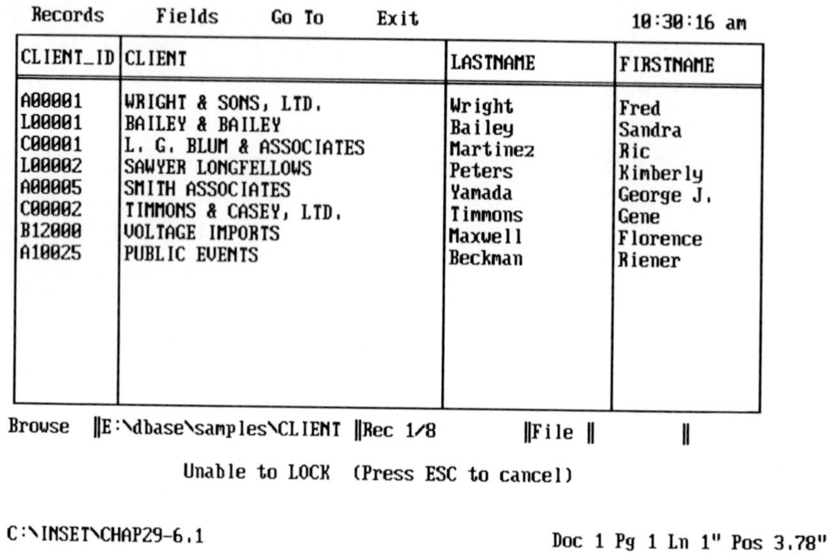

```
Records      Fields      Go To      Exit                          10:30:16 am

CLIENT_ID  CLIENT                          LASTNAME       FIRSTNAME

A00001     WRIGHT & SONS, LTD.             Wright         Fred
L00001     BAILEY & BAILEY                 Bailey         Sandra
C00001     L. G. BLUM & ASSOCIATES         Martinez       Ric
L00002     SAWYER LONGFELLOWS              Peters         Kimberly
A00005     SMITH ASSOCIATES                Yamada         George J.
C00002     TIMMONS & CASEY, LTD.           Timmons        Gene
B12000     VOLTAGE IMPORTS                 Maxwell        Florence
A10025     PUBLIC EVENTS                   Beckman        Riener

Browse  ||E:\dbase\samples\CLIENT ||Rec 1/8        ||File ||        ||

              Unable to LOCK  (Press ESC to cancel)

C:\INSET\CHAP29-6.1                          Doc 1 Pg 1 Ln 1" Pos 3.78"
```

Figure 27-6. Locked record error message

You can also use RLOCK( ) to lock records of a file open in another work area. Positioning your record pointer on one of these three records while in browse or edit mode displays the message "RecLock" on the right side of the status bar, as shown in Figure 27-7.

Typing **UNLOCK** at the dot prompt unlocks records that have been locked manually.

Note: You can only release a record lock from the workstation at which it was created. You cannot remove it by typing **UNLOCK** from another workstation.

```
Records    Fields    Go To    Exit                                   1:31:34 pm

CLIENT_ID  CLIENT                        LASTNAME     FIRSTNAME     ADDRE
A00001     WRIGHT & SONS, LTD.           Wright       Fred          3232
L00001     BAILEY & BAILEY               Bailey       Sandra        5132
C00001     L. G. BLUM & ASSOCIATES       Martinez     Ric           4818
L00002     SAWYER LONGFELLOWS            Peters       Kimberly      12300
A00005     SMITH ASSOCIATES              Yamada       George J.     7500
C00002     TIMMONS & CASEY, LTD.         Timmons      Gene          310-2
B12000     VOLTAGE IMPORTS               Maxwell      Florence      8506
A10025     PUBLIC EVENTS                 Beckman      Riener        332 S

Browse  |G:\dbase\samples\CLIENT |Rec 4/8          |File |RecLock |
                          View and edit fields
```

Figure 27-7. "RecLock" message on the status bar

The syntax for the commands in Table 27-2, the UNLOCK command, and the RLOCK( ) and LOCK( ) functions is discussed in detail in Chapter 30.

Modifying the Effects of File and Record Sharing

dBASE IV provides some commands with which you can modify the effects of sharing files on a network.

SET REFRESH TO sets a time interval between screen updates that show changes made to a file through browse and edit modes. The default on this SET command is 0, which means that no screen updates occur until the record pointer has been positioned on a record changed from another workstation. If you are browsing or editing a file that is being updated by another user, you will not see the changes made by the other users without scrolling through all the updated records. Setting REFRESH to a value other than 0 will display changes at the periodic intervals you specify, no matter where your record pointer is located.

SET REPROCESS TO allows you to determine how many retries dBASE IV will attempt when trying to lock a file or record that has already been locked by another user. The default number of retries is 0, which causes dBASE IV to retry the lock indefinitely. The error message caused by a failed lock attempt states that "File is in use by another, Retrying lock, Press ESC to cancel." You can wait until the lock is removed by the other user or press ESC to stop trying. To limit the number of lock attempts dBASE IV will make, set REPROCESS to try only a few times before giving up. Setting REPROCESS to a value greater than 0 makes dBASE IV retry the command for the specified number of times, with no error message during the retries. If the file is still locked after the specified number of retries, an error message appears, allowing you to cancel or edit the command.

Chapter 30 discusses the syntax and uses of the preceding commands.

Sharing a Network Printer

Some networks use a shared printer (referred to as a *network* printer) while other networks have a printer connected to a local workstation (a *local* printer). Some networks may have both types of printers. To send dBASE IV output to a printer, you need to take several steps. Check with your network administrator to find out if you are using a local or network printer and which printer port you are using.

When you are sending a report to the printer, make sure that dBASE IV knows which printer port you are using. There are

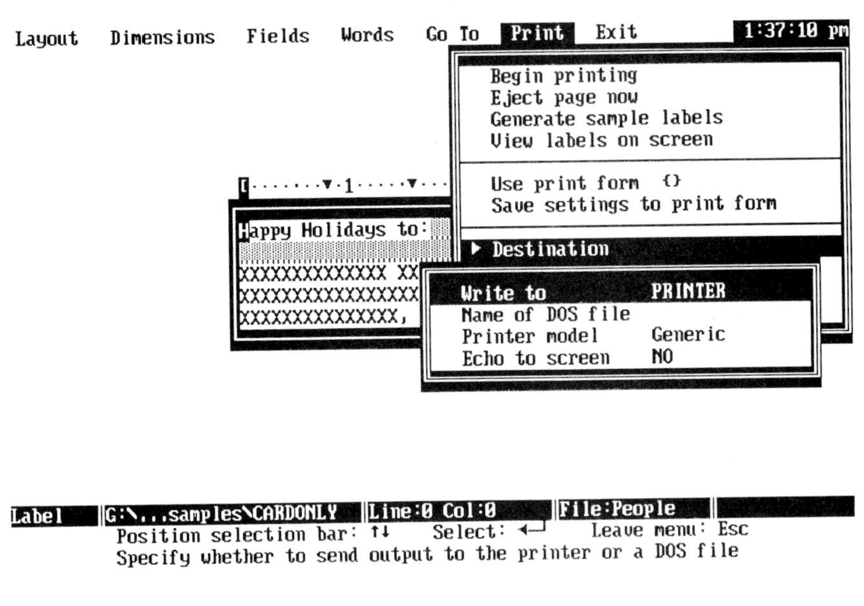

Figure 27-8. The **Print/Destination** menu

several ways to check this. If you have created a report or label form, select the **Print** menu from the Forms or Labels Design screen and choose **Destination**. This submenu allows you to view and select the desired printer driver. To choose one of several network or local printers, press ENTER to toggle a display of printer driver names installed for dBASE IV. Figure 27-8 shows the **Print/Destination** menu from the Labels Design screen.

If you select a network printer, the port specified for the driver you choose must be the port to which the network printer is linked. Refer to the SET PRINTER TO command in Chapter 30 for more information on redirecting a printer to the correct print queue or port.

Network printers collect print jobs in a print *queue* or *spooler*. Each print job, whether sent by your word processor, spreadsheet, or dBASE IV, is stacked in a print queue. The print jobs are then passed to the printer in the order in which they entered the network print queue. If many jobs are stacked in the queue, your report or labels may take a while to print. Your network administrator can use commands that are provided with your network software to change the order of the print jobs in the queue if necessary.

Tip: When you issue a print command from the dot prompt in dBASE IV and you're using a network printer, your print job will not actually become part of the print queue until you type **SET PRINTER TO** after your print command has executed. Using the **Print** menu from the Control Center eliminates this step. See the SET PRINTER TO command in Chapter 30 for more information.

In this chapter, you learned about dBASE IV's file-sharing conventions, and that users must be "network aware" to peacefully coexist in a network environment. You learned how to start dBASE IV on a network and how to log in when dBASE IV is set for protect mode. At this point, you should be familiar with dBASE IV's file- and record-sharing commands. You should also know how to use a network printer.

With a basic understanding of the concepts presented in this chapter, network users can maximize the powerful file-sharing capacity of dBASE IV and speed the flow of information throughout the system.

Network Administration

Security Issues
Security Levels
Using the PROTECT Security Command
Using Protected Files

TWENTY EIGHT

In most cases, the responsibility of data management and security falls to the network administrator. Managing files in shared directories and controlling access to those files becomes a major issue on a networked system. As the network administrator, you need to define security procedures to control access to files.

You can administer database file management and security at the operating system level or from within dBASE IV. In the dBASE IV environment, the PROTECT command provides log-in security, file and field access security, and encryption of database files. You can also do file backups from within dBASE IV, through the use of batch files or established procedures that you set for each user.

Through prudent planning, supervision, and user training, you as the network administrator can effect a security system well-suited to your particular networking environment.

Security Issues

When multiple users share files, several security problems arise. The first, of course, is the problem of too many cooks spoiling the broth. The potential for data damage is increased with each new user who has access to the file. A user looking at the file out of simple curiosity may inadvertently change a record or the file as a whole. Or, someone may open the file and begin to edit or browse a record, leave the workstation, and accidentally lock the record and file to other users indefinitely.

Another security problem arises with files that contain certain information necessary to a user along with other data that should not be seen by that user. Take the case of a payroll file, for instance. A clerical person may be responsible for updating the personnel file of a company with 1000 employees. New employees need to be added to the file, other employees removed, and changes to addresses, phone numbers, and positions must be kept current. However, the salary and wage fields in the personnel file are considered confidential, and the data in those fields is maintained by a member of the personnel staff with higher clearance. The company would prefer that the clerical staff not have access to the wage and salary information.

A third security problem is that of sensitive files trading hands. Often, files contain information that is the lifeblood of a company. A client list carefully compiled over the years, company financial status, or product or pricing information, among other things, could mean disaster to an organization if placed in the wrong hands.

Security Levels

dBASE IV provides a security system through the PROTECT menu. You can invoke this menu by typing **PROTECT** at the dot prompt in either the single-user environment on a stand-alone PC or the multi-user environment on a network. The security scheme that the PROTECT command lets you create can be as simple as establishing a user log-in sequence that grants access to dBASE IV, or as complex as setting multiple access levels for database files and fields. You can also *encrypt* files with PROTECT, making them unreadable to all but authorized users. The network administrator or system administrator (in the case of a single-user system) plans and implements the security scheme with the PROTECT menu.

You can set two levels of security through the PROTECT menu. The one you select is determined by your system needs.

- **Level 1: Access to dBASE IV** Presents users with a log-in screen that requires them to enter a user name, group name, and password to enter dBASE IV. You establish this security level by creating *user profiles* with the PROTECT menu. A user profile consists of a user log-in name, password, group name, full name, and access level, which control the degree of freedom the user has with database file operations.

- **Level 2: Access to files, fields, and data encryption** Sets access levels for each user to files and fields within those files. It also encrypts files, making them unreadable to all but authorized users.

You need not use both security levels. Often, the only security a system requires is to control access to dBASE IV. If this is the case, the network or system administrator can set up user profiles that determine which users are authorized to enter dBASE IV.

Before entering the PROTECT menu for the first time, you should take time to plan the security scheme that best fits your system. However, the access levels you set may be modified later as your security requirements change.

File Access Levels

dBASE IV lets the system administrator assign up to eight different access levels to both file privileges and field privileges. Access levels are given values 1 through 8, with 1 having the least restricted access and 8 having the most restricted access.

There are four file privileges:

READ	View the file contents
EXTEND	Add records to the file
UPDATE	Edit existing records
DELETE	Delete records from the file

The default access level for each file privilege is 8, the most restricted access. Users assigned the least restricted access, 1, are allowed all of these privileges. A sample file-privilege scheme is shown in Figure 28-1.

Field Access Levels

Field privileges within a file are also given values 1 through 8. Each field may be designated FULL, NONE, or R/O as follows:

FULL	Allows the field to be viewed or changed. The field contents appear in enhanced (highlighted) mode.
NONE	The user cannot see or change the field. If this privilege is assigned, the field appears to be missing from the database.
R/O	Users can view but not edit the field. The field contents appear in regular display mode rather than the enhanced (highlighted) mode of fields assigned the FULL privilege. If you attempt to edit a field with R/O privileges, the computer bell sounds and no change is made to the data.

File Privilege scheme: Clients.dbf

PRIVIELGE	ACCESS LEVEL
READ	8
UPDATE	6
EXTEND	6
DELETE	2

Figure 28-1. A sample file-privilege scheme

Figure 28-2 shows a sample field-privilege scheme for a file.

How File and Field Access Levels Are Used

The administrator also assigns an access level to each user through PROTECT's **Users** menu (see the section "Adding a User Profile"). When someone attempts to open a protected database file, dBASE IV compares the access level of the user with that assigned to the

FILE: Personne.dbf FIELD ACCESS PRIVILEGES

FIELDS	1	2	3	4	5	6	7	8
Lastname	FULL	FULL	FULL	FULL	R/O	NONE	NONE	NONE
Firstname	FULL	FULL	FULL	FULL	R/O	NONE	NONE	NONE
Department	FULL	FULL	R/O	R/O	R/O	NONE	NONE	NONE
Pay_type	FULL	FULL	R/O	NONE	NONE	NONE	NONE	NONE
Wage	FULL	R/O	NONE	NONE	NONE	NONE	NONE	NONE
Supervisor	FULL	FULL	R/O	R/O	NONE	NONE	NONE	NONE
Address	FULL	FULL	FULL	FULL	NONE	NONE	NONE	NONE
City	FULL	FULL	FULL	FULL	NONE	NONE	NONE	NONE
St	FULL	FULL	FULL	FULL	NONE	NONE	NONE	NONE
Phone	FULL	FULL	FULL	FULL	NONE	NONE	NONE	NONE

Figure 28-2. A sample field-privilege scheme

file privileges. The file can be opened and data added, updated, or deleted if the file and field privilege access levels match that of the user.

You do not need to use all eight access levels when defining file and field privileges. You may only wish to use the first two access levels if your system has one or two users. The number of levels you'll want to use depends on the number of users in the system, the sensitivity or confidentiality of the data, and the efficiency you desire for your system.

It is possible to clog up a system by using more security measures than are really warranted. If files are segregated into too many small groups, users are forced to quit dBASE IV and then reenter, logging in under a new group name, each time they wish to use a file in another group. This is tedious and time-consuming and creates a cumbersome system. In an overly complex security system, users often become careless because they have to remember and protect too many passwords or group names, and the hoped-for security evaporates.

Note: The protection provided by the access levels you've assigned to users and files does not take effect until the encrypted files are converted to database files. This conversion process is discussed in this chapter's section, "Using Protected Files."

Planning Your Security System

This section suggests how to plan a security scheme to fit your system. Once you have completed the outlined steps, you'll find it easy to set up your security system through the PROTECT menu.

- Decide which network users should have access to dBASE IV. In the case of a single-user environment on one PC, determine who of those sharing the PC need access to dBASE IV.

- Decide whether the administrator or user will create the log-in name and password for each user profile.

- If the users select their own passwords and log-in names, distribute a form similar to the one in Figure 28-3 to collect the information from each person. Emphasize that the passwords should use all 16 characters allowed by PROTECT for maximum security. It is much harder for someone to guess all 16 characters of a password than two or three characters. Make sure these forms are kept confidential.
- Choose a 16-character (alphanumeric) administrator password. This password allows access to the PROTECT menu, and is necessary to create or modify user profiles and file access and to print the security reports. Once you have chosen your administrator password, write it down and file it in a secure place. If you lose or forget it, you'll be denied admittance to the PROTECT security system.
- Use a matrix similar to the one in Figure 28-4 to group database files according to their function or use. A file may not be in more than one group. List all user names across the top of the matrix. Check off the files to be made accessible to each user. Remember to keep your scheme simple if you have only a few users and files.

USER PROFILE INFORMATION

Log-in name [ ][ ][ ][ ][ ][ ][ ][ ] Group name [ ][ ][ ][ ][ ][ ][ ][ ]

Password [ ][ ][ ][ ][ ][ ][ ][ ][ ][ ][ ][ ][ ][ ][ ][ ]

Full name [ ]

USER REFERENCE SHEET - FILE COPY

Log-in name [ ][ ][ ][ ][ ][ ][ ][ ] Group name [ ][ ][ ][ ][ ][ ][ ][ ]

Password [ ][ ][ ][ ][ ][ ][ ][ ][ ][ ][ ][ ][ ][ ][ ][ ]

Full name [ ]

Figure 28-3. A sample form for collecting log-in names and passwords

- Assign a name to each group of files. You'll also need to assign this group name to a user's profile to control which group of files the user can access. A user can access more than one group of files if you create two or more user profiles for the user, each with a different group name.
- Decide how many access levels you need in your security scheme. Use the form in Figure 28-2 to record the access level for each user.
- Decide which access levels should be assigned to each of the file privileges, READ, EXTEND, UPDATE, and DELETE. You can use the form in Figure 28-4 to help you determine the desired access levels.
- If you wish to control user access to individual fields in a protected file, choose a set of privileges for each of your access levels. A sample field-privilege scheme is shown in Figure 28-5. Use a matrix format to record these on paper, as you did with the file and user groups.

	USERS/ACCESS LEVELS						PRIVILEGES				
	LANA	JANE	LARR	SUSA			READ	UPDATE	EXTEND	DELETE	
FILES	4	7	2	1		GROUPS					COMMENTS
Payroll	Y	Y	Y			Accounts	7	4	4	2	
Personne	Y		Y			Accounts	4	2	2	1	
Sales	Y	Y				Accounts	8	8	8	4	
Acct_Pay	Y	Y				Accounts	8	8	8	2	
Clients			Y	Y		Admin	3	2	2	1	
Contacts			Y	Y		Admin	2	2	2	1	

Figure 28-4. A sample form for assigning file and user groups

```
Users   Files   Reports   Exit                                     11:11:49 am

Filename     E:\DBASE\SAMPLES\PERSONNE.CRP
Group Name   PAYROLL

 Read privilege   4
 Update privilege 2
 Extend privilege 2
 Delete privilege 1

                                   Access Levels
Fieldname        1     2     3     4     5     6     7     8
==========     ===== ===== ===== ===== ===== ===== ===== =====
IDNUM          FULL  R/O   R/O   R/O   FULL  FULL  FULL  FULL
LASTNAME       FULL  FULL  FULL  FULL  FULL  FULL  FULL  FULL
FIRSTNAME      FULL  FULL  FULL  FULL  FULL  FULL  FULL  FULL
MIDDLE         FULL  FULL  FULL  FULL  FULL  FULL  FULL  FULL
DEPARTMENT     FULL  FULL  FULL  R/O   FULL  FULL  FULL  FULL
BUILDING       FULL  FULL  FULL  R/O   FULL  FULL  FULL  FULL
PAY_TYPE       FULL  FULL  R/O   NONE  FULL  FULL  FULL  FULL
WAGE           FULL  R/O   NONE  NONE  FULL  FULL  FULL  FULL

Protect
                      Press any key to continue...
                     Display information about file
```

Figure 28-5. A sample field-privilege scheme

Using the PROTECT Security Command

To start PROTECT from the Control Center, choose the **Tools** menu and select the **Protect data** option. To start from the dot prompt, type **PROTECT** and press ENTER. Have your administrator password ready.

The dBASE IV Password Security System screen appears, as shown in Figure 28-6. Type your administrator password as prompted and press ENTER. If this is the first time you've used PROTECT, you'll be prompted to confirm the password by typing it a second time.

The PROTECT menu appears next. You may create or modify user profiles, protect files, or print user and file information from this menu.

```
dBASE IV Password Security System

Enter password
```

Figure 28-6. The dBASE IV Password Security System log-in screen

Use your LEFT ARROW and RIGHT ARROW keys to highlight the menu option you want and press ENTER to open its menu. Once a menu is open, you can access its options by highlighting them with the UP ARROW and DOWN ARROW keys and pressing ENTER. A small triangle appears next to the option, pointing to the area where you can type your data.

The Users Menu

You can use the **Users** menu to add, change, or delete user profiles. This menu also allows you to create or change user access levels. Figure 28-7 shows the Users Profile screen.

Adding a User Profile

To add a new user profile, supply the following information at the **Users** menu prompts:

- **Login name** This name can be from one through eight alphanumeric characters and is requested when the user logs in to dBASE IV. This entry is converted to uppercase after you press ENTER.
- **Password** You can enter up to 16 alphanumeric characters for the user password.
- **Group name** Enter the name of the file group to which the user is assigned. A group name can be from one through eight alphanumeric characters and is converted to uppercase by dBASE IV when you press ENTER.
- **Full name** You can enter up to 24 characters for the user's full name. This item is optional but if used provides a more complete user profile.

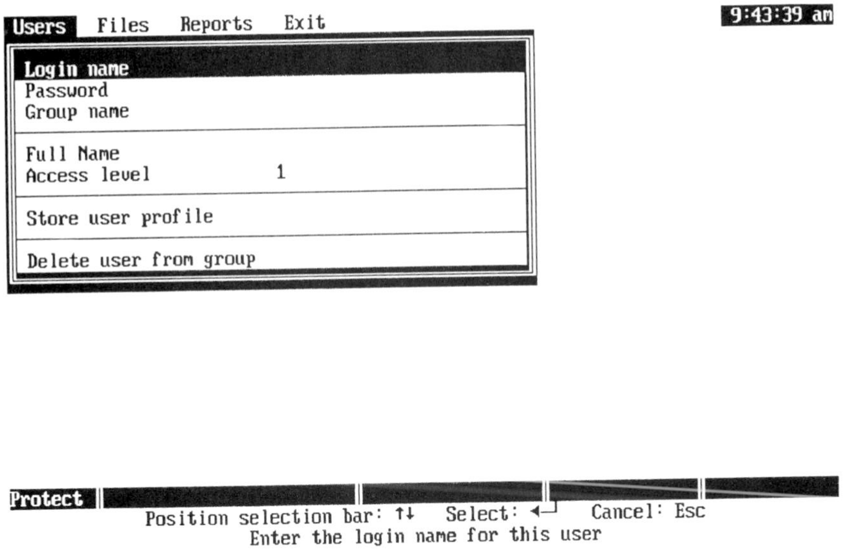

```
Users  Files  Reports  Exit                                    9:43:39 am

Login name
Password
Group name

Full Name
Access level            1

Store user profile

Delete user from group

Protect
       Position selection bar: ↑↓   Select: ←┘   Cancel: Esc
               Enter the login name for this user
```

Figure 28-7. The Users Profile screen

- **Access level** Enter the user's access level as a value from 1 through 8. The default is 1. This value should, but does not have to, correspond to one of the access levels chosen for the file- and field-protection scheme in that group. The value chosen as the access level will be matched with a file group name to determine which files, fields, and commands are available to the user.

After entering the information for the new user, you can store it with the **Store user profile** option. When you select this option, the **Users** menu is cleared and you can enter another profile.

Note: A user can have more than one profile. If the user needs access to several groups of files, enter a new profile for each group, using the same data and changing only the group name.

Note: If the user intends to use SQL, you must use the "super user" log-in name SQLDBA as the log-in name. This name gives access to all operations in SQL mode. File and field access are then controlled by the SQL GRANT and REVOKE commands.

Changing a User Profile

If you need to modify an existing user profile, open the **Users** menu and enter the log-in name, password, and group name of the profile. dBASE IV checks to see if the profile has already been defined. If it has, the rest of the menu items are filled in with their current values.

A window opens and the message "User already exists, do you want to edit? (Y/N)" appears. Press Y and you may highlight and change any of the values on the screen. Store the changes by highlighting the **Store user profile** option and pressing ENTER.

Note: You should use special caution when changing group names. If you eliminate all user profiles with a certain group name, the files in that group cannot be accessed.

When exiting from PROTECT, choose the **Exit** menu. Your changes are automatically saved when you highlight and press ENTER on the **Exit** option. You are returned to the dot prompt or Control Center.

Deleting a User Profile from a Group

When a user no longer needs access to a group of files or has terminated a relationship with an organization, you should remove the user profile from its group. To maintain the integrity of your security system, do this without delay.

Open the **Users** menu and enter the appropriate log-in name, password, and group name. If dBASE IV locates and displays the rest of the profile information, highlight the **Delete user from group** option and press ENTER.

The File Menu

You use the **File** menu to create, modify, or cancel file- and field-privilege schemes. You must assign access levels to files and fields to match user access levels and save them in the database file structure.

From the **File** menu, you can

- Assign a file to a group of files
- Create or change access levels for each of the four file privileges
- Assign or change access levels to each of the fields within the file

Use your LEFT and RIGHT ARROW keys to highlight the **Files** option and press ENTER to open the menu. Choose the menu options by highlighting them with the UP and DOWN ARROW keys and pressing ENTER. A small triangle will appear next to the option, pointing to the area where you enter your data.

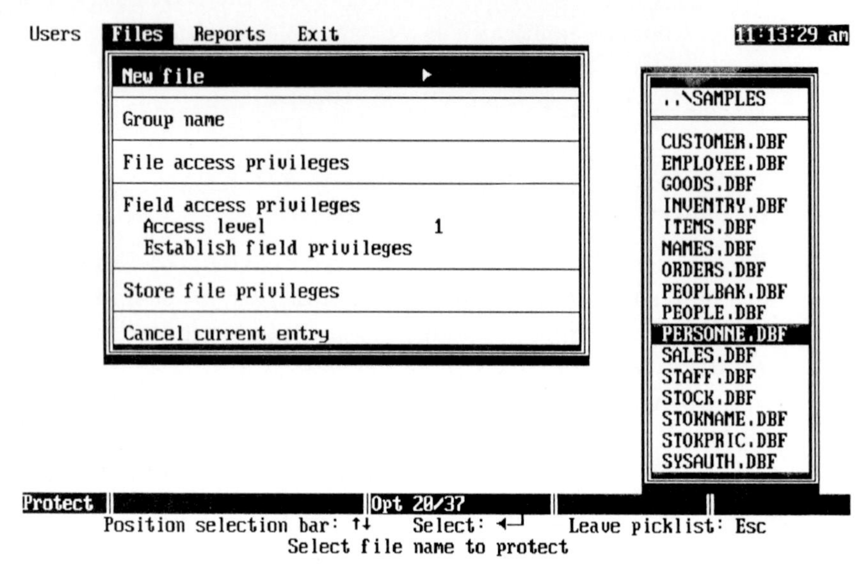

Figure 28-8. The **New File** option of the **Files** menu

Creating a File-Privilege Scheme

To create a file-privilege scheme for your system, perform the following steps:

- Enter the **Files** menu and press ENTER to choose the **New file** option, as illustrated in Figure 28-8.
- Select a file from the list presented (the files listed are from the current directory rather than from the selected catalog). If the current drive or directory is not correct, choose the drive letter or directory name you want by highlighting it and pressing ENTER.
- Enter the name of the group to which this file belongs. A file can only belong to one group. If you attempt to enter a file-privilege scheme for a file under a second group, the file

is cancelled from its previous group and is no longer accessible to the users in that group.

- Assign the access level for each file privilege. All levels with values lower than the one you enter (less security restrictions) will be allowed access to that privilege as well. The default access level for all file privileges is 8. Press the LEFT ARROW key to close the window and continue with the file access definition.

- Each field within a protected database may have a set of privileges assigned to any or all of the eight access levels. A sample field-privilege scheme is shown in Figure 28-9. Enter an access level and then choose **Establish field privileges** to complete the access definition for that level.

- Highlight a field name with the UP ARROW or DOWN ARROW key, and press ENTER to toggle among the privileges avail-

```
Users  Files  Reports  Exit                                  11:14:33 am

 New file                      PERSONNE.DBF     ADDRESS      FULL
                                                BUILDING     R/O
 Group name                    PAYROLL          CITY         FULL
                                                DEPARTMENT   R/O
 File access privileges                         FIRSTNAME    FULL
                                                FULL_PART    R/O
 Field access privileges                        IDNUM        R/O
   Access level                7                LASTNAME     FULL
   Establish field privileges ▸                 MIDDLE       FULL
                                                PAY_TYPE     R/O
 Store file privileges                          PHONE        FULL
                                                ST           FULL
 Cancel current entry                           SUPERVISOR   R/O
                                                WAGE         NONE

Protect  E:\...samples\PERSONNE  Opt 14/15          ReadOnly
   Position selection bar: ↑↓   Select: ◄┘   Leave picklist: Esc
 Define individual field privileges for the access level displayed above
```

Figure 28-9. A sample field-privilege scheme

able: FULL, NONE, and R/O. Use the LEFT ARROW key to return to the **Files** menu when you have defined all field privileges.

Field access privileges are optional and need not be defined. The default privilege for all fields at each access level is FULL.

You can continue defining field privileges for each access level in a file until all levels are completed. You need not define all eight levels. Remember, however, that the access levels you choose for both file and field privileges should be consistent with those you have assigned to the user profiles.

- Store the access information for the file by highlighting **Store file privileges** and pressing ENTER. Enter a new file name, or use the RIGHT ARROW or LEFT ARROW key to choose another option from the PROTECT menu.

You may create up to nine file-privilege schemes at a time. If you attempt to set up a tenth in the same session, you get the error message "Too many files are open." After setting up the ninth scheme, select the **Exit** option from the PROTECT menu, and choose **Save** or **Exit** before defining any more file schemes.

Tips on Creating a File-Privilege Scheme

If you have set a file privilege to NONE, it is irrelevant to assign field privileges for that access level. What's more, file privileges override field privileges. For example, imagine that the file privileges for a file named PAYROLL are all set to an access level of 6. If the field privileges for access level 7 are set to FULL in the same file, a user with an access level of 7 cannot open the file, much less view, change, or delete records. Users with access levels of 7 or 8 have more security restrictions placed on them, and cannot access security schemes with lower levels.

Setting field access levels to R/O or NONE does not prevent data destruction with ZAP or DELETE. To guard against data loss from the improper use of these commands, you must set the file privileges to READ rather than UPDATE.

Be careful not to set R/O or NONE privileges on fields that are key fields in the production .MDX file associated with the protected database. If you attempt to open the file, you will get the error message "Illegal key expression" and you will not be able to open the file. For example, access level 7 in the CLIENT file has the Lastname field set to R/O, and Lastname is also a key field for the .MDX file, CLIENT. A user with an access level of 7 cannot open CLIENT because the key field, Lastname, is not available to the .MDX file which is opened automatically at the same time. You can remedy this situation by setting the Lastname field to FULL access for level 7 field privileges.

Cancelling File Privileges

You can only cancel a file-privilege scheme while you're setting the file and/or field privileges for the current file. Highlight the **Cancel current entry** option from the **Files** menu and press ENTER. The file name will disappear from the screen and you may start over or return to the PROTECT menu.

Changing a File-Privilege Scheme

To change an existing file-privilege scheme, open the **Files** menu and enter the name of the file. PROTECT checks to see if the file-privilege scheme has already been defined for this file. If a definition is found, the message "File already exists, overwrite it? (Y/N)" appears on the screen. If you choose to overwrite the file, all existing file and field privileges will be cancelled and you'll need to assign new access levels to file privileges and all levels of field privilege. Remember to store your changes with the **Store file privileges** option in the **Files** menu. Exiting from the PROTECT menu saves and encrypts the file-protection schemes.

Note: If the file has already been encrypted and converted to a .DBF file, you must create an unencrypted version of the file to change the privilege scheme. Refer to the section "Using Protected Files" to learn more about working with encrypted files.

Printing Security Reports

The user profiles and file-privilege schemes you have created through the PROTECT menu are stored in the encrypted file DBSYSTEM.DB. Once created, this file cannot be read or viewed in the normal way, and you can only view the information stored in DBSYSTEM.DB through the **Reports** menu. You can view user or file information on the screen or print hard-copy records to keep in your files.

Use your RIGHT ARROW and LEFT ARROW keys to highlight the **Report** option in the PROTECT menu and press ENTER. You may choose to print or view user information or file information.

If you choose **User information**, you can send to the printer or the screen a list of the names of all dBASE IV users along with their passwords, groups, full names, and access levels, as shown in Figure 28-10.

The **File information** option prompts you to choose from a list of encrypted files. The report lists the file name, group to which it is assigned, file privileges, and the field privileges assigned for each of the eight access levels. Figure 28-5 shows a sample File information report. You cannot run this report if you have not already saved the file-privilege scheme using one the **Exit** menu options, **Save** or **Exit**.

When you choose either the **User information** or **File information** report, the message "Send report to the printer, Yes or No" prompts you for a decision. Press Y to print a hard copy of the report or N to see the report on the screen.

Note: The one piece of security information not available through the **Reports** menu is the administrative password that allows access to the PROTECT menu system. You must write down this password and file it in a safe place because it is not accessible anywhere in dBASE IV.

Users Files **Reports** Exit 11:15:46 am

User name	Password	Group	Fullname	Level
SUSAN	SUSANJONES090945	PAYROLL	SUSAN JONES	4
JANE	C020145MARYJOEL	PAYROLL	JANE BYERS	2
LARRY	XXXXXXXLARRYXXXX	PAYROLL	LARRY MANDRAKE	2

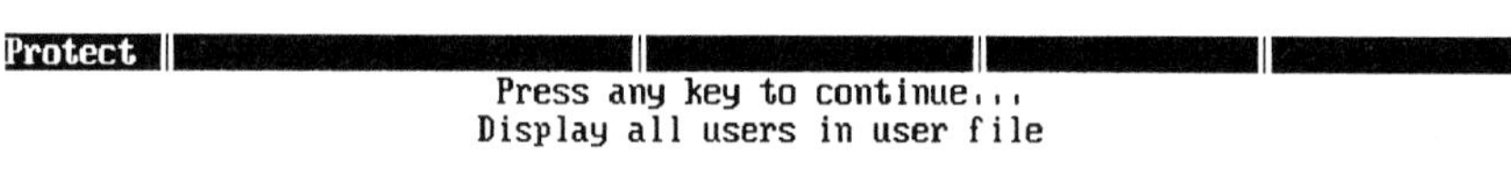

Figure 28-10. A User information security report

Leaving the Protect Menu

The following three options are available from the **Exit** menu:

- **Save** Records all new or modified user profiles and file-privilege schemes stored during the current session. User profiles are written to a file named DBSYSTEM.DB, and file-privilege schemes are saved in the database file header. Database files are also encrypted at this time. You may save user profiles at any time during their definition. You must save file-privilege schemes after nine schemes have been defined (see the earlier section "Creating a File-Privilege Scheme").

- **Abandon** Cancels all new or updated user profiles and file-privilege schemes. If you used the **Save** option during the PROTECT session, only the changes made after you saved will be cancelled.
- **Exit** Ends the PROTECT session and returns control to the dot prompt or Control Center. All changes stored during the session will be saved.

Using Protected Files

Before the careful planning and implementation of your security scheme will pay off, you must take one more step. You must convert back to database files the encrypted files that you created with PROTECT.

When a file-privilege scheme is saved during a PROTECT session, an encrypted version of the database file is created. This new file has the same file name as the original database file but with a .CRP extension. Any memo files belonging to that file are also saved in encrypted versions, with file extensions of .CPT. The original database and memo field files are left unchanged.

You must follow these two steps for your file-protection scheme to take effect:

1. Create working copies of the encrypted files.
2. SET ENCRYPTION to ON to maintain security.

Creating Working Copies of Encrypted Files

In order to use your encrypted files, you must copy or rename them. The encrypted file in the following example is called CLIENT.CRP. It has an associated memo file called CLIENT.CPT. The original files, CLIENT.DBF and CLIENT.DBT, still exist in their un-encrypted form. To save these unencrypted versions, you can

- Copy them to another directory and delete them from the current directory
- Rename them and leave them in the current directory

To create usable working files from the files you encrypted with PROTECT, you can

- Copy the encrypted files to new files with the correct file extensions. If you plan to use the same file name for the new files, make sure you have renamed or moved the unencrypted versions of the files. Type the following commands at the dot prompt:

```
. COPY FILE CLIENT.CRP TO CLIENT.DBF
. COPY FILE CLIENT.CPT TO CLIENT.DBT
```

- If you forgot to rename or move the unencrypted versions of your files prior to this step, dBASE IV displays the message "File already exists, overwrite? (Y/N)." You must decide whether to overwrite (and lose) the original, unprotected version of your file or cancel the command.
- Rename the encrypted files with new file extensions of .DBF (database file) and .DBT (memo field file). If you plan to keep the same file name, make sure you have renamed or moved the unencrypted versions before beginning this step. Type the following commands at the dot prompt:

```
. RENAME CLIENT.CRP TO CLIENT.DBF
. RENAME CLIENT.CPT TO CLIENT.DBT
```

Tip: It's a good idea to keep the unencrypted versions of your database and memo field files by renaming or copying them. If anything goes wrong while you are converting your newly encrypted files to working files, you'll have the original files on hand and can run the protection process over again.

Versions of encrypted files cannot be read by unauthorized users. The data is scrambled to all users but those with access levels matching the file-privilege scheme for the encrypted file.

Using the SET ENCRYPTION Command

Once your databases have been encrypted, you can use the SET ENCRYPTION command to ensure that no unencrypted versions of the files will be created with the COPY, TOTAL, and JOIN commands.

As network administrator, you must make sure that SET ENCRYPTION is ON in any workstation environment that uses protected files. You can do this in one of three ways:

- Include the statement ENCRYPTION = ON in the CONFIG.DB file.
- Type the command **SET ENCRYPTION ON** at the dot prompt and press ENTER before any encrypted files are opened.
- Use the SET ENCRYPTION ON command in a dBASE IV application that uses encrypted files.

With encryption set ON, any new file created with the COPY TO, JOIN, or TOTAL commands will be encrypted. If encryption is set OFF during the use of these commands, an unencrypted version of the file is created and is readable by unauthorized users. For more information on SET ENCRYPTION, see Chapter 30, "Networking Commands and Functions."

Note: The COPY FILE command is insensitive to SET ENCRYPTION. When used to copy an encrypted file, COPY FILE *always* creates an encrypted file.

Note: SET ENCRYPTION has no effect on files that have not been protected through the PROTECT menu.

Unencrypting Files

When you need to change a file-privilege scheme or modify the structure of an encrypted database, you must first create an unencrypted version of the file.

To unencrypt a file, perform the following steps:

1. Set encryption OFF by typing **SET ENCRYPTION OFF** at the dot prompt and pressing ENTER.
2. Open the encrypted file.
3. Use the COPY TO command to copy the open database to a new file with a different file name.

The new file will be unencrypted. You can then modify the structure or change the file-privilege scheme of the new file.

Remember that you must create a new file-privilege scheme through the PROTECT menu and make a working copy of the encrypted file if you wish to include the file in your security system. (See the previous sections "Creating Protected Files" and "Using Protected Files.")

A good security system requires a balance of planning, user training, and regular supervision. To be effective, the system should be as simple as possible so that it does not intrude into the work patterns of system users. Careful planning and organization can create a system that is unobtrusive to the user and yet maintains tight control over the database files and the information they contain.

The PROTECT command provides an easy but sophisticated way to set up your security scheme. If you understand how the PROTECT and SET ENCRYPTION commands interact, you can create a security system that is well-suited to your users and your organization.

dBASE IV Network Programming

Security
Data Protection
Transaction Processing
Converting Single-User Programs for Multi-User Mode

TWENTY NINE

dBASE IV's automatic file- and record-locking features make it easier to adapt new and existing programs to a multi-user environment. File and record locks are handled automatically by dBASE IV and are invisible to the user. Thus the work related to coding network programs consists of anticipating and circumventing the problems that can arise when users share resources. This is a welcome change from the locking and unlocking instructions required to modify records or files in dBASE III PLUS programs.

When writing applications for a network or converting existing single-user programs to network versions, you must plan for

- Security
- Data protection
- Transaction processing
- The conversion of single-user programs to a multi-user environment

If you are familiar with dBASE IV commands and functions and have a basic understanding of dBASE IV programming concepts, this chapter provides information you need to write a reliable network application. If you are not conversant with dBASE IV programming, read Part Three, "Programming dBASE IV," before continuing.

Security

When multiple users can access dBASE IV, security becomes an issue. Should all users be allowed to use all files? Is there a danger of file damage caused by inexperienced users? Are some files, or the information in certain fields in a file, confidential? Who will be allowed to run the housekeeping tasks such as packing or erasing files, modifying file structures, and copying or backing-up files?

You can design a dBASE IV security system by using one, or a combination, of the following methods:

- Instituting a log-in procedure and assigning a unique password to each user. You can do this at the operating system level or through dBASE IV. If you wish to assign user names and passwords through dBASE IV, refer to the section on the PROTECT command in Chapter 28.

- Limiting access to files by assigning read/write privileges to shared network directories. See your network software manual for information on shared directories. Remember, the privilege level you assign to a directory affects *all* of the files in that directory.

- Assigning read/write file attributes to individual files through the DOS operating system. Use the DOS ATTRIB command to selectively set read-only or read/write attributes to individual files. Your DOS manual describes the correct syntax and usage for the ATTRIB command.

- "Protecting" files with file and field access privilege schemes you set up via the dBASE IV PROTECT command. Encrypted database files you create with PROTECT may be read or modified only by users with access levels corresponding to those defined in the file-privilege scheme. See Chapter 28 for a detailed discussion of the PROTECT command.

When you set up a security system with PROTECT, the log-in procedures take place when the user enters dBASE IV, before your program is started. If file-privilege schemes are used, your program should check the user's access level and store it as a memory variable. Once the access level is determined, your application can use the variable to determine whether the user can run routines that use protected files.

Use the ACCESS( ) function to learn the access level of the current user, and then screen this variable when branching to routines using protected files.

In the following example, the user's access level is checked before the program branches to the New_acct routine. The ACCESS( ) function returns the access level of the user at the current workstation. This value must equal, or be lower than, the UPDATE and EXTEND file privileges of 5 that were assigned to the database ACCOUNTS with the PROTECT command. If it is, the program branches to New_acct. An access level higher than 5 (meaning a more restricted user) causes a beep, and a message box on the screen states that access is denied. The program waits for a user keypress before continuing.

```
User_lev = ACCESS( )
IF User_lev <= 5
   USE Accounts
   DO New_acct
ELSE
   ?? CHR(7)
   @ 10,15 TO 13,65 DOUBLE
   @ 11,17 SAY 'Sorry...access to Account Update is denied.'
   @ 12,17 SAY '  Press any key to return to the menu...'
   SET CONSOLE OFF
   WAIT ''
   SET CONSOLE ON
   CLEAR
ENDIF
```

File protection adds a new element to program planning. When you use protected files, you must incorporate the file-privilege schemes into the program. User access levels should be checked with ACCESS( ) and matched against file-privilege levels before the program branches to routines that open or modify database files. Otherwise, dBASE IV error messages appear during program execution and the user may not be able to exit without crashing the program.

Using LOGOUT to Screen User Access

On some network systems, several users may share a workstation. This adds a new twist to your security problems. Each of the users may have a different access level. If so, each user needs to log in before starting a program in order for the dBASE IV log-in system to verify and store their access level. Once a user has entered dBASE IV, no more verifications occur. If the first user leaves the workstation without exiting dBASE IV, another person can use the program under the first person's access level.

You can avoid this problem by using the LOGOUT command in your programs. When using routines requiring an access level, include the LOGOUT command at the end of the program to clear the screen and close database and program files. The dBASE IV log-in screen will appear, requiring a user to log in before the program can be accessed again. This procedure places the responsibility for logging out under the control of your program. LOGOUT does not require an exit from dBASE IV to the operating system.

Note: You must use the PROTECT command to add user names, passwords, and access levels before LOGOUT will work with your system. (See Chapter 30, "Networking Commands and Functions," for more information.)

Data Protection

Fortunately, dBASE IV has made record and file locking automatic for commands that modify records or files, preventing data collisions when files are shared. However, allowing multiple users to access files simultaneously can create a unique set of problems. Several problems related to network programming are caused by data collisions and deadlocks.

Data Collisions

Data collisions, or *lost-updates*, may be *hard* or *soft*. Hard collisions occur when two or more users attempt to edit a record at the same time, or attempt to modify a whole database simultaneously. The result can be lost or damaged records or files.

Soft collisions, on the other hand, are usually the result of poor programming, when two sections of the same program attempt to enter or edit data simultaneously. Soft collisions do no physical damage to files or records. However, the data entered simultaneously through the program does not get saved to the file.

Deadlocks

Deadlocks occur when two or more users try to open and lock two files simultaneously from the dBASE IV dot prompt. Suppose John and Marcia are working from the dot prompt at their own workstations. They each plan to run some commands that require exclusive (nonshared) use of two files. Watch what happens:

JOHN	MARCIA
. SET EXCLUSIVE ON	. SET EXCLUSIVE ON
. SELECT 1	. SELECT 1
. USE Accounts	. USE Credit
. SELECT 2	. SELECT 2
. USE Credit	. USE Accounts

Each user has opened a file in the exclusive mode, chosen a different work area, and tried to open the file made exclusive by the other user. The second file cannot be opened because it was opened in unshared mode by the other user. This creates a standoff between the two users, referred to as a *deadlock* or *deadly embrace*. You can cause deadlocks by placing manual locks on files or records with the FLOCK( ) and RLOCK( ) functions. Deadlocks can occur in interactive mode or during a program, as in the following example:

JOHN

```
SELECT 1
USE Accounts
* test for & place a lock
DO WHILE .NOT. FLOCK()
ENDDO
SELECT 2
USE Credit
* test for & place a lock
DO WHILE .NOT. FLOCK()
ENDDO
*
* process file in area 2
*
UNLOCK
```

MARCIA

```
 SELECT 1
 USE Credit
 * test for and place a lock
DO WHILE .NOT. FLOCK()
 ENDDO
 SELECT 2
 USE Accounts
 * test for and place a lock
DO WHILE .NOT. FLOCK()
 ENDDO
 *
 * process file in area 2
 *
 UNLOCK
```

John and Marcia are using different programs, but both routines require that the files CREDIT and ACCOUNTS be opened in different work areas. The files opened in work area 1 are manually locked with the FLOCK( ) function. John's program is attempting to lock the CREDIT file, which is open and already locked in Marcia's work area 1. This results in an endless loop. Marcia is attempting to lock the ACCOUNTS file, which is open and already locked in John's work area 1. This triggers the same endless loop.

The only way out of this deadlock is to select one user as the *victim*. To release the deadlock, the victim's program must be aborted and their transaction sacrificed.

When opening the same files in different programs, you can use the following procedures to avoid deadlocks:

- Limit the number of attempts your program makes to set file or record locks. If the routine is not successful after a specified number of attempts, branch to an error-handling routine that allows the user to retry or exit that routine.
- Consider whether a manual file or record lock is really necessary. Perhaps the dBASE IV automatic locks will suffice, or perhaps you can make the locking process more efficient with networking functions such as CHANGE( ) and LKSYS( ), discussed later in this chapter.
- When the same two databases are opened concurrently in several of your routines, as in the previous example, always select work areas and open files in the same sequence. John and Marcia's deadlock could have been prevented simply by opening ACCOUNTS first in work area 1 in both routines, and then opening CREDIT in work area 2 in each routine.

File Open Modes

In dBASE IV, you can open files in either *exclusive* or *shared* modes.

The Exclusive Mode

When you open a file in the exclusive mode, certain principles apply.

- Only one user at a time may open the file. A file opened in exclusive mode may not be read, processed, or modified by another user until the first user closes the file.
- File or record locks are not necessary because the file cannot be shared by another user.
- The following dBASE IV commands require that the database file be opened in exclusive mode:

CONVERT	PACK
INDEX ON *<key expression>* TAG	REINDEX
INSERT [BLANK]	RESET
MODIFY *<any option>*	ZAP

The Shared Mode

Database files that you open in shared mode follow these principles:

- Multiple users can simultaneously access the files.
- Files and records should be locked before modifying or updating.

File Open Modes Set by dBASE IV

dBASE IV commands open files in either exclusive or shared mode. These defaults, preset by dBASE IV, are defined to prevent file-sharing conflicts in a multi-user environment. Table 29-1 lists commands that open files, their file types, and their default open modes.

Command	File Type	How Opened
APPEND FROM	Database (.DBF)	Shared
COPY STRUCTURE TO	Database (.DBF)	Exclusive
COPY TO	Database (.DBF)	Exclusive
CREATE	Database (.DBF)	Exclusive
CREATE <*file 1*>	Database (.DBF)	Exclusive
FROM <*file 2*>	Database (.DBF)	Shared
CREATE LABEL	Label (.LBL)	Exclusive
CREATE QUERY	Query (.QRY)	Exclusive
CREATE REPORT	Report (.FRM)	Exclusive
CREATE VIEW	View (.VUE)	Exclusive
DO <*filename*>	Command (.PRG)	Shared
INDEX ON	Index (.NDX)	Exclusive
	Index (.MDX)	Exclusive
JOIN	Database (.DBF)	Exclusive
MODIFY COMMAND <*filename*>	Command (.PRG)	Exclusive
MODIFY COMMAND <*filename*>	Format (.FMT)	Exclusive
MODIFY COMMAND <*filename*>	Procedure (.PRG)	Exclusive
MODIFY LABEL	Label (.LBL)	Exclusive
MODIFY QUERY	Query (.QRY)	Exclusive
MODIFY REPORT	Report (.FRM)	Exclusive
MODIFY VIEW	View (.VUE)	Shared
REPORT FORM	Report (.FRM)	Shared
RESTORE	Memory (.MEM)	Shared
SAVE	Memory (.MEM)	Exclusive
SET ALTERNATE TO	Alternate (.TXT)	Exclusive
SET CATALOG TO	Catalog (.CAT)	Shared
SET FILTER TO FILE	Query (.QRY)	Shared
SET FORMAT TO	Format (.FMT)	Shared
SET INDEX TO	Index (.NDX)	Exclusive*
SET PROCEDURE TO	Procedure (.PRG)	Shared
SET VIEW TO	View (.VUE)	Shared
SORT	Database (.DBF)	Exclusive
TOTAL	Database (.DBF)	Exclusive
UPDATE FROM	Database (.DBF)	Shared
USE	Database (.DBF)	Exclusive*
USE <*file*> INDEX	Index (.NDX)	Exclusive*
	Memo (.DBT)	Exclusive*

*Opened in exclusive mode only if SET EXCLUSIVE is ON

Table 29-1. Default File Open Modes Set by dBASE IV

Using EXCLUSIVE to Control File Access

You must open some files in exclusive mode, either to meet the requirements of certain dBASE IV commands or to prevent other users from accessing the file during a critical routine in a program.

You can use two commands to open database files in exclusive mode:

- **SET EXCLUSIVE ON** Type this command from the dot prompt, or choose it from the **Settings** submenu in the **Tools** menu of the Control Center. This sets the default file open mode to exclusive for all files you open after you issue the command.
- **USE *<filename>* EXCLUSIVE** Issue this command from the dot prompt to open just one database in exclusive mode. This command does not set the default file open mode, as did the previous command.

Once you have opened a database file in exclusive mode, other users attempting to open the file see the message "File has been opened by another" and must retry or cancel their command.

Note: When you open a database file in the exclusive mode, all associated memo files and index files are also opened exclusively.

Tip: If you've opened a database file in the exclusive mode, typing **SET EXCLUSIVE OFF** while the file is open does *not* remove the exclusive setting. Similarly, typing **SET EXCLUSIVE ON** after you have opened a file in shared mode does not change that file open mode to exclusive. You must issue the EXCLUSIVE command either before or while you are opening the file.

For more information on the EXCLUSIVE command, see Chapter 30, "Networking Commands and Functions."

File and Record Locks Within an Application

To avoid conflicts caused by shared files within an application, you must understand the two types of locks available in dBASE IV:

- Automatic (implicit) file locks are file and record locks that are set automatically by commands that update or modify files and records, such as EDIT, REPLACE, or COUNT. See Chapter 30, "Networking Commands and Functions," for a list of commands that cause file or record locks.
- Explicit file locks are locks that you place "manually" with the FLOCK( ), RLOCK( ), and LOCK( ) dBASE IV functions, and with the SET EXCLUSIVE command. These functions and commands are covered later in this section.

To determine the appropriate locking method, you must carefully analyze which files are to be shared, how data is to be collected and processed, and which subroutines will be run concurrently with the shared files. Do not become complacent about shared file operations, in spite of dBASE IV's automatic locking features. You need to be on the lookout for situations that may cause a conflict during file sharing.

Within a program, file modifications, such as adding or editing records, are handled differently than at the dot prompt or Control Center. For example, from the dot prompt, you might enter the EDIT or APPEND command to enter new information in a database; dBASE IV handles file and record locking with little risk of one user's work overwriting another's. A program, on the other hand, may use a variety of other commands and command sequences to display and accept data from the user and unwittingly set up a situation in which data can get "misplaced."

For instance, suppose John and Marcia are both updating records in the file ACCOUNTS. They are using a program called EDITACCT, which locates the account, stores the data in the fields to memory variables, allows changes to the memory variables, and replaces the record with the modified variables, as follows.

```
USE Accounts ORDER Acct_no
Macct_no = SPACE(5)
@ 1,1 SAY 'Enter an account number: ' GET Macct_no
READ
SEEK Macct_no
IF FOUND()
   Mname = Name
   Maddress = Address
   Mphone = Phone
   Mcredit = Credit
   @ 2,1 SAY 'Name           :' GET Mname
   @ 3,1 SAY 'Address        :' GET Maddress
   @ 4,1 SAY 'Telephone      :' GET Mphone
   @ 5,1 SAY 'Credit Limit :' GET Mcredit PICTURE '99999.99'
   READ
   REPLACE Name WITH Mname,Address WITH Maddress,;
   Phone WITH Mphone,Credit WITH Mcredit
ENDIF
```

The ACCOUNTS file is opened in *shared* mode, so other users can also open the file. Both John and Marcia use EDITACCT to open the file, seek a record, and store the contents to memory variables. The problem arises when the field contents in the record are replaced by the memory variables. Both John and Marcia can replace their fields almost simultaneously, unaware of each other's access to the same record. A file lock occurs with the REPLACE command, but the operation is so fast that the delay to another user is negligible.

However, a problem can occur. John and Marcia had the same data on their screens when they began editing. Marcia changed the credit limit. John changed the phone number and address. If John saves his changes first, the fields in the record are replaced with the unchanged name and credit limit, and a new address and phone number. These changes are not reflected in the memory variables shown on Marcia's screen. Seconds later, the fields in that record are replaced once more as Marcia saves her adjusted credit limit, and old names, address, and phone number. John's changes to the phone number and address are overwritten by Marcia's memory variables. John's loss of data probably won't be discovered until billing time, when the statement goes to the old address and is returned.

This is a soft data collision. The program didn't crash, no damage was done to the data files, and John probably got blamed for not entering the data. Soft data collisions like this are difficult to identify because their occurrence is so random. You must use foresight and planning to circumvent such file-sharing conflicts.

You can avoid such problems by placing a manual lock on the record with the dBASE IV RLOCK( ) or LOCK( ) function (see Chapter 27 for more information on file and record locks). You can also include the SET REPROCESS command to control the number of locking attempts dBASE IV makes before displaying an error message. A simplified revision of the previous program segment is shown here:

```
USE Accounts ORDER Acct_no
SET REPROCESS TO 10
Macct_no = SPACE(5)
@ 1,1 SAY 'Enter an account number: ' GET Macct_no
READ
SEEK Macct_no
IF FOUND()
  IF RLOCK()
     Mname = Name
     Maddress = Address
     Mphone = Phone
     Mcredit = Credit
     @ 2,1 SAY 'Name          :' GET Mname
     @ 3,1 SAY 'Address       :' GET Maddress
     @ 4,1 SAY 'Telephone     :' GET Mphone
     @ 5,1 SAY 'Credit Limit :' GET Mcredit PICTURE '99999.99
     READ
     REPLACE Name WITH Mname,Address WITH Maddress,;
     Phone WITH Mphone,Credit WITH Mcredit
     UNLOCK
  ENDIF
ENDIF
```

This example tests RLOCK( ) before storing the fields in memory variables. If the record has not been locked by another user, the program locks the record and stores the field data to memory variables. The program waits for the user to edit the variables, and replaces the field contents. Then the record lock is removed. If the program cannot lock the record, the dBASE IV error message that appears on the screen depends on the value of the SET REPROCESS command.

If you include the statement SET REPROCESS TO 10 in the program before the RLOCK( ) function, as shown, dBASE IV makes ten attempts to lock the record before displaying an error message. This error message allows the user to cancel or retry the record lock attempt.

If the value of SET REPROCESS is 0 (the default value), the error message states that the record has been locked by another user, and that pressing ESC will cancel the retry. dBASE IV will continue trying until the record lock is removed by the other user or the current user presses ESC.

To determine the value to use with SET REPROCESS, you should calculate the average length of time needed to edit a record. You can test SET REPROCESS from the dot prompt while a user at another workstation edits a record. The number of retries should be high enough to prevent error messages from appearing too frequently, but not so high that users have a long wait before accessing each record. (For more information on the SET REPROCESS command, see Chapter 30, "Networking Commands and Functions.")

Using a manual record lock prevents more than one user from editing the record and ensures that the current edits are not lost. However, if the user causing the lock pauses to answer a phone call or go to lunch, the record remains locked to other users.

The CONVERT Command

A more sophisticated method of preventing a soft collision involves testing for record changes before replacing the field contents. The CONVERT command and its associated function, CHANGE( ), let you avoid the manual record-locking method and test for changes to the record since it was first read, as in the following example:

```
USE Accounts ORDER Acct_no
Macct_no = SPACE(5)
@ 1,1 SAY 'Enter an account number: ' GET Macct_no
READ
SEEK Macct_no
IF FOUND( )
   Mname = Name
   Maddress = Address
   Mphone = Phone
   Mcredit = Credit
   @ 2,1 SAY 'Name         :' GET Mname
   @ 3,1 SAY 'Address      :' GET Maddress
   @ 4,1 SAY 'Telephone    :' GET Mphone
   @ 5,1 SAY 'Credit Limit :' GET Mcredit PICTURE '99999.99'
   READ
   IF CHANGE()
      Oth_user = LKSYS(2)
      Choice = ' '
      @ 7,1 TO 10,55 DOUBLE
      @ 8,1 SAY 'This record has been updated by user '+ Oth_user
      @ 9,1 SAY 'Press 1 to Overwrite, or 2 to Abort' GET Choice
      READ
   ENDIF
   IF .NOT. CHANGE() .OR. Choice = '1'
      REPLACE Name WITH Mname,Address WITH Maddress,;
      Phone WITH Mphone,Credit WITH Mcredit
   ENDIF
ENDIF
```

In the preceding program segment, the user is informed of the change to the record by another user, and can choose whether to overwrite the record or abort the changes. If the edit is aborted, the user may call up the record again to see the data entered by the other user.

Converting a File with the CONVERT Command

To take advantage of the CHANGE( ) and LKSYS( ) functions, you must first use the CONVERT command to add the field _dbaselock to a database file. The _dbaselock field, once added to the file, is not accessible or even visible through the EDIT or BROWSE commands. The contents of this field can consist of up to four pieces of information about the lock status of a record in the multi-user environment. The amount of information is determined by the length of the field, which can be from 8 to 24 characters. The default length is 16 characters.

The four lock status conditions that you can store in the _dbaselock field are

- **Count** A 2-byte hexadecimal number used by the CHANGE( ) function to determine whether a record has been changed since it was last read. A true or false value is returned with CHANGE( ).
- **Time** A 3-byte hexadecimal number that records the time a lock was placed.
- **Date** A 3-byte hexadecimal number that records the date a lock was placed.
- **Name** A 0- to 16-character representation of the last workstation that placed a lock.

The syntax for the CONVERT command is

CONVERT [TO <*type N expression*>]

where *type N expression* is the optional field length, which can be from 8 to 24 characters. If you use CONVERT without the field length option, the length will default to 16. The sequence of information in _dbaselock is always the same—count, time, date, name. If you choose a field length of 8, only the count, time, and date values will be included in the field. A length of 16 characters will include the first 8 characters of the log-in name. Choosing 24 as the field length will allow a full 16 characters for the log-in name.

When you convert a file with CONVERT, a backup file is created with a .CVT extension. This file contains the original file structure and data. A new file is created with the modified structure, bearing the same name as the original file. The other fields in the file are undisturbed by this process.

Tip: If you decide to change the field length of the _dbaselock field, you do not need to convert the file again. You can change the field length to a value from 8 to 24 with the MODIFY STRUCTURE command.

Once your file is converted, you can ask questions by using the CHANGE( ) function. If your converted file is open in multiuser mode, and other users are accessing the file, you can ask if the current record has been updated since you first positioned your record pointer on it. Typing **? CHANGE( )** at the dot prompt will return logical true (.T.) if another user has changed the record, or false (.F.) if no changes are recorded in the _dbaselock field.

Use the LKSYS( ) function to find the date, time, and log-in name of the last user to lock the current record. The value, from 0 to 2, that you enter between the parentheses determines the type of information returned.

- LKSYS(0) returns the time of the last lock
- LKSYS(1) returns the date of the last lock
- LKSYS(2) returns the network log-in name of the user (Novell network) or workstation name (all other networks). The length of the _dbaselock field determines how the log-in name is stored.

Length	**Returns**
8	No log-in name
16	First 8 characters of log-in name
24	16-character log-in name

To test the LKSYS( ) function, type **? LKSYS(0)** at the dot prompt. dBASE IV displays the time of the last lock on the current record. Use the function again, substituting the values 1 and 2, to display the date and log-in name (depending on the field length).

Tip: For you to use the LKSYS( ) function to determine the lock status of a record, another person using the file must first open the file in exclusive mode and use the CONVERT command to add the _dbaselock field. The user who has converted the file cannot use the LKSYS( ) function to get information about another user's record locks. This conversion process must take place each time the file is used, serving as a rather clumsy programming tool (see Chapter 30, "Networking Commands and Functions," for more information).

Transaction Processing

Traditionally, minicomputer and mainframe database management systems have offered transaction control services. This group of commands and functions allows you to verify transactions and "undo" them if they are interrupted by system failures or some other source.

dBASE IV now offers transaction processing for personal computers. Although it is designed to provide a data recovery solution for network system interruptions to dBASE IV programs, you can use transaction processing in single-user dBASE IV as well—in programming or from the dot prompt.

A *transaction* is a unit of work, consisting of one or more operations performed on single or multiple databases. It can be as simple as an edit to a record or an update to a field, as in the following example. It can also be a complex series of operations in which multiple related databases are modified.

```
USE Credit
REPLACE ALL Cred_lim WITH Cred_lim * .25;
FOR Cred_rat = "A"
```

Interruptions to database operations can come from many sources—hardware failures, power fluctuations, programming errors, or user intervention. Consider what might happen if a power failure occurs during the previous transaction. The transaction is incomplete. The CREDIT file has over 5000 records with customer names, credit ratings, and credit limits. When you restart the network, how will you know where the replace process was interrupted? Which of the credit limits were changed and which remain the same?

In the past, the only way to recover from an interrupted transaction was to restore the file from a backup copy. However, the ideal recovery from an interrupted transaction would be to undo the changes, reset the file to its original state, and retry the transaction.

The Transaction Log File

The commands BEGIN TRANSACTION and END TRANSACTION allow you to recover from interrupted file operations. dBASE IV creates a transaction log file when it encounters a BEGIN TRANSACTION command, recording all subsequent file operations. A log file is created for each workstation that initiates a transaction, and is stored in the current directory unless you include a different path in the BEGIN TRANSACTION command (see Chapter 30). The END TRANSACTION command signals that the transaction is completed.

```
USE Credit
BEGIN TRANSACTION
REPLACE ALL Cred_lim WITH Cred_lim * .25;
FOR Cred_rat = "A"
END TRANSACTION
```

In this example, the BEGIN TRANSACTION statement is used before any operation on the CREDIT database is performed. If the program executes the REPLACE command successfully, the program terminates with the END TRANSACTION command.

dBASE IV also tracks the status of a transaction by setting an integrity flag in the database file header. A database is in a *consistent* state before a transaction begins and after a transaction has been successfully completed. The integrity flag is set to OFF in the consistent state. During a transaction, a database is in an *inconsistent* state, a state of change, and the integrity flag is set to ON.

If the transaction concludes successfully and an END TRANSACTION command is encountered, the log file is deleted and the integrity flag is once again set to OFF.

You can name multi-user transaction log files in one of two ways:

- On a Novell network, the name is *username*.LOG, where *username* is the first eight characters of the user's network log-in name.

- On all other networks, the log file is named *workstation name*.LOG, where *workstation name* is the name (or number, in some cases) assigned to each computer during the network software installation.

Single-user transaction log files are always named TRANSLOG.LOG.

Note: For transaction processing to work successfully in multiuser mode, the first eight characters of each workstation name must be unique. If two workstations have the same name, the transaction log file for one workstation will overwrite the log file of the other workstation with the same name.

Tip: The names used for the transaction log file are displayed when you use the LIST/DISPLAY USERS command.

Reversing Transactions

If a transaction is interrupted, you use the transaction log file to restore any affected database files to their original state. All of the changes to the files, including deletions and appended records, are reversed.

The ROLLBACK Command

The process of recovering from an interrupted transaction is called a *rollback*. To roll back a transaction, you must have used the BEGIN TRANSACTION command before the group of commands that make up the transaction. The ROLLBACK command restores files to their pretransaction state, sets the integrity flags to OFF, and deletes the transaction log file. All files are closed after a rollback.

To roll back a transaction, you must issue the ROLLBACK command before the END TRANSACTION command. You can include the ROLLBACK command in an error-handling routine to ensure that an incomplete transaction is reversed if interrupted during an application.

```
PROCEDURE Credit
ON ERROR DO Err_hand
BEGIN TRANSACTION
   USE Credit
   REPLACE ALL Cred_lim WITH Cred_lim * .25;
   FOR Cred_rat = "A"
END TRANSACTION

PROCEDURE Err_hand
@ 21,20 TO 24,60 DOUBLE                    && Draw message box
DO CASE
   CASE ERROR() = 108 .OR. ERROR() = 372   && File in use errors
      Choice = "Y"
      Oth_user = LKSYS(2)                  && Who placed lock
      @ 22,23 SAY 'The file is being used by ' + Oth_user
      @ 23,23 SAY 'Would you like to try again? (Y/N) ';
      GET Choice PICTURE '!'
      READ
      IF Choice = 'Y'
         RETRY
         @ 22,23 CLEAR TO 23,60
         RETURN
      ELSE
         @ 22,23 SAY 'Reversing your transaction...'
         @ 23,23 SAY '     Please start over.       '
         ROLLBACK                          && Reverse transaction
      ENDIF
      @ 22,23 CLEAR TO 23,60
      RETURN
   CASE ERROR() = 109 .OR. ERROR() = 373   && Record in use errors
      * Similar treatment as above
ENDCASE
RETURN
```

Note: The LKSYS( ) function, which determines the name of the user or workstation placing the lock, is only effective when you have used the CONVERT command to include the _dbaselock field in a database. See the section "Data Protection" for more information on LKSYS( ) and CONVERT.

In a system failure, a transaction is interrupted, but so is the program. The error routine just shown could not recover the aborted transaction because the whole system would be down. The files are left in a state of partial change; the network administrator

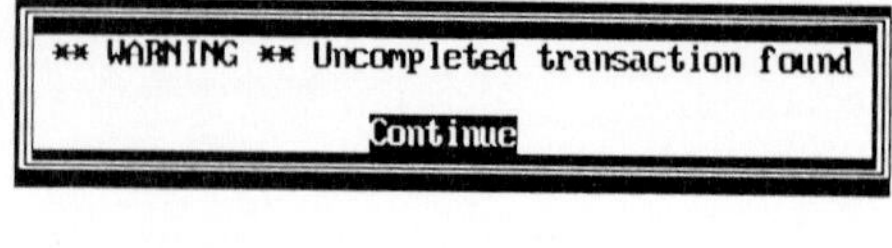

Figure 29-1. Uncompleted transaction error message at log in

must log in to dBASE IV and issue a manual ROLLBACK command.

Tip: If you press the ESC key during a transaction and choose **Cancel**, a rollback is automatically executed. The transaction log file is deleted, integrity flags set to Off, and all database files closed.

Recovering Database Files from the Dot Prompt

When a transaction is incomplete and you have not used ROLLBACK before exiting dBASE IV, you get an error message when you start dBASE IV again (see Figure 29-1). If you open one of the files from the uncompleted transaction, a similar message appears on the message line at the bottom of the screen.

You can use the COMPLETED( ) function to test whether a transaction or a rollback has completed. COMPLETED( ) returns logical true (.T.) if a transaction has been completed and the END TRANSACTION has been executed, or if a ROLLBACK command has been successfully executed. If a transaction is interrupted and ROLLBACK has not been used, COMPLETED( ) returns logical false (.F.).

Follow these procedures to reverse transactions after system or program failures:

- Log in as network administrator and check the dBASE IV directories for transaction log files.
- For each transaction log file found on Novell networks, you must log in to the network as that user, start dBASE IV, and enter the ROLLBACK command at the dot prompt.
- For each transaction log file found on networks other than Novell, you must log in to the network from that workstation, start dBASE IV, and enter the ROLLBACK command at the dot prompt.
- On a single-user system, start dBASE IV and use the ROLLBACK command at the dot prompt.

The ROLLBACK( ) Function

To find out if the last ROLLBACK command worked, you can type **? ROLLBACK( )** at the dot prompt. This function returns a logical true (.T.) if ROLLBACK was successful and false (.F.) if not.

If transaction log files cannot be found or have accidentally been deleted, you cannot complete a successful rollback. The database files involved in the transaction still have the integrity flag set On. You can test and reset these flags when rollbacks have not been successful, or if you wish to exempt a certain file from the reversal process.

Using ISMARKED( ) and RESET

To test a database file's integrity flag setting, use the function ISMARKED( ). Open the database and type **? ISMARKED( )** at the dot prompt. If the function returns a logical true (.T.), the file open in the current work area is in a state of change due to an incomplete transaction. A logical false (.F.) indicates that the database is in a consistent state, and that transactions or rollbacks were completed successfully.

A file that returns true in response to the ISMARKED( ) function has been changed. You should use ROLLBACK to restore the file to its original, unchanged state. If you cannot use ROLLBACK, you can only recover the original data by restoring the file from a backup copy.

If the ISMARKED( ) function returns true but a rollback is not possible, you can reset the flag with the RESET command. Type **RESET** at the dot prompt and press ENTER. The integrity flag for the database open in the current work area will be reset to Off. If you use the ISMARKED( ) function after the RESET command, the result will be a logical false (.F.).

Error-Trapping Routines

When you use error-trapping routines to correct interrupted transactions, keep the user informed of the transaction status. The next example uses the COMPLETED( ) and ROLLBACK( ) functions to determine whether a rollback is appropriate. The user is advised whether or not the rollback was successful.

```
PROCEDURE Err_hand
@ 21,15 TO 24,65 DOUBLE
DO CASE
  CASE ERROR() = 108 .OR. ERROR() = 372     && File in use errors
     Choice = "Y"
     Oth_user = LKSYS(2)                    && Who set lock
     @ 22,28 SAY "The file is being used by " + Oth_user
     @ 23,28 SAY "Would you like to try again? (Y/N) ";
     GET Choice PICTURE "!"
     READ
     IF Choice $ "Y"
        RETRY
     ELSE
        IF .NOT. COMPLETED()
           @ 22,20 SAY  "Attempting to reverse your transaction..."
           ROLLBACK
           IF .NOT. ROLLBACK()               && Test for rollback
              @ 22,24 SAY "Your transaction could not be reversed."
              @ 23,24 SAY "  Notify your network administrator.   "
              RESET
           ELSE
              @ 22,28 SAY "Transaction successfully reversed."
              @ 23,28 SAY "       Please reenter data.       "
```

```
            ENDIF
         ENDIF
      ENDIF
      @ 22,16 CLEAR TO 23,65              && clear message box
      RETURN
   CASE ERROR() = 109 .OR. ERROR() = 373  && Record in use errors
        * Similar treatment as above
ENDCASE
RETURN
```

For more information on BEGIN TRANSACTION, END TRANSACTION, ROLLBACK, COMPLETED( ), ROLLBACK( ), ISMARKED( ), and RESET, see Chapter 30, "Networking Commands and Functions."

When you use dBASE IV's transaction-processing capabilities, remember to nest all commands related to the transaction between the BEGIN TRANSACTION and END TRANSACTION commands. This ensures that you can use the ROLLBACK command to completely reverse the transaction if necessary.

Converting Single-User Programs for Multi-User Mode

You can fairly easily convert most programs written for single-user dBASE IV to multi-user mode. Consider the following steps when converting an application for network use:

- Check all routines that allow changes to files and consider whether the automatic file locking provided by dBASE IV will be sufficient to prevent data collisions (see the section "Data Protection" in this chapter). Include the FLOCK( ) or RLOCK( ) command prior to commands that may create a conflict during file sharing.
- Review the list of commands that require exclusive use of database files (see the section "File Open Modes Set by dBASE IV") and include either the SET EXCLUSIVE ON

or USE <*filename*> EXCLUSIVE commands where necessary.

- Evaluate your housekeeping routines to determine whether you should limit access to these routines to certain users and processing times.
- Check for routines that open several databases concurrently in different work areas. Be sure to open the files in the same sequence in each routine to prevent deadlocks.
- Review the dBASE IV error messages related to record and file locks and transaction processing. Include routines to trap these errors and provide the user with alternative courses of action.
- Consider securing your program and the files it uses with the dBASE IV PROTECT command. If you define file-privilege schemes with PROTECT, you must coordinate user access levels with the access levels assigned to files in each routine.
- If you plan to write a program for use in both single- and multi-user environments, place the NETWORK( ) function at the beginning of the program to determine if the network version of dBASE IV is running. This function returns a logical true (.T.) if the current version of dBASE IV is installed in multi-user mode. You can store this value to a memory variable and use it to branch to network-related commands in multi-user mode, or to non-network commands if single-user mode is detected. (See Chapter 30, "Networking Commands and Functions," for more information.)
- Test your application on the network with *at least* two concurrent users before installing it for general use.

With a little planning, you should be able to use most of your existing code, with a few modifications, when converting programs to multi-user mode.

When you are programming for a network environment, always remember to perform the following actions.

- **Anticipate** Try to envision problems that may occur when two or more users want to use the same files. You should understand dBASE IV record- and file-locking conventions, as well as your organization and its systems.
- **Plan** Design your program to work around the potential conflicts that may occur when users share files.
- **Test** Verify that the program works with *more than one user* before installing it for general use.

Because dBASE IV makes most file- and record-locking operations automatic, programmers can focus on writing comprehensive multi-user applications, without worrying so much about the details of file and record locks. By anticipating and planning for problems that may arise when users share resources, you can develop a smooth and dependable program that serves all users well.

Networking Commands and Functions

THIRTY

This chapter lists the commands and functions you can use in dBASE IV multi-user mode. Many of the commands also work in a single-user environment. Those that apply only to a network environment are labeled "Multi-user mode only."

The first section of this chapter lists commands and the second section lists functions. The syntax for each command is also described in Chapter 31.

COMMANDS

The following commands are covered in the command section and are presented in a multi-user format:

BEGIN TRANSACTION	SET
CHANGE/EDIT	SET AUTOSAVE
CONVERT	SET ENCRYPTION
DISPLAY/LIST STATUS	SET EXCLUSIVE
DISPLAY/LIST USERS	SET LOCK
END TRANSACTION	SET PRINTER
LOGOUT	SET REFRESH
RESET	SET REPROCESS
RETRY	UNLOCK
ROLLBACK	USE EXCLUSIVE

BEGIN TRANSACTION

BEGIN TRANSACTION marks the beginning of a transaction and must be used with the associated command, END TRANSACTION. You can use this set of commands in programming, or interactively from the dot prompt.

Syntax

BEGIN TRANSACTION [<*pathname*>]

*

* dBASE IV commands making up the transaction

*

END TRANSACTION

Notes

Transaction processing, developed with mainframe and minicomputer database management systems, is a method of recovering from transactions aborted by system or program failures.

A transaction occurs when you change a database by modifying, deleting, or adding records. It may be as simple as an update to a single field, or may involve a series of changes to related fields in multiple databases. If a transaction is interrupted, you can reverse changes and input the transaction again.

In dBASE IV, transactions can take place during a program or from the dot prompt. Whichever method you use, you can only achieve full recovery from an aborted transaction if all changes related to a transaction are nested within the BEGIN TRANSACTION and END TRANSACTION commands.

The Transaction Log File

The BEGIN TRANSACTION command causes two "invisible" events during the ensuing transaction:

- An *integrity flag,* located in the file header of the database files opened, is set to ON, indicating that the file is in a state of change.
- A *transaction log* is created, either in the current directory or in the directory specified in the *pathname* option. The transaction log contains a log of each record that is changed, recording its pre- and post-transaction contents. This file is used to reverse a transaction, if necessary, restoring all records to their pre-transaction state.

  The name of the transaction log file is determined by the network mode and the log-in name of each workstation:

- In multi-user mode, the transaction log file name is the first eight characters of the workstation log-in name (all networks excepting Novell), or the first eight characters of a user log-in name (Novell networks), followed by a .LOG extension.

  For example, if your network software is 3COM, the transaction log file name may be 02698C75.LOG, representing the NetBIOS address that is your workstation name. On a Novell network, the transaction log file name might be MARYJ.LOG, which is the log-in name of the current user.

- In single-user mode, your transaction log file is always named TRANSLOG.LOG.

Note: You should never erase the transaction log file. The information it contains is essential for transaction reversal.

Note: The commands BEGIN TRANSACTION and END TRANSACTION affect only transactions that are started at the current workstation.

Example

```
. USE Client
. USE Invoice IN 2 ORDER Client_id
. BEGIN TRANSACTION
. UPDATE ON Client_id FROM Invoice ;
   REPLACE Balance WITH Balance + Client->Amount
. END TRANSACTION
. CLOSE ALL
```

The UPDATE command, placed between the BEGIN TRANSACTION and END TRANSACTION statements, is the actual transaction. If the transaction is interrupted while UPDATE executes, you can use the ROLLBACK command to reverse the changes made to the CLIENT file, restoring it to it pre-transaction state.

Options

You can specify an optional *pathname* when using the BEGIN TRANSACTION command. This path name determines the directory in which the transaction log file is written. Make sure that the directory you specify has read/write privileges.

If you enter **BEGIN TRANSACTION \Payroll** at the dot prompt or in a program, the transaction log file will be written to the PAYROLL directory on the current drive.

BEGIN and END TRANSACTION are discussed in detail in Chapter 29.

See also: RESET, ROLLBACK, ISMARKED( ), ROLLBACK( )

CHANGE/EDIT

CHANGE and EDIT, which are interchangeable, allow you to view and modify existing records in full-screen mode.

Syntax

CHANGE [<*scope*>] [FIELDS <*field list*>] [FOR <*condition*>] [WHILE <*condition*>] [NOFOLLOW] [NOMENU] [NOCLEAR] [<*record number*>] [NOINIT] [NOAPPEND] [NOEDIT] [NODELETE]

or

EDIT [<*scope*>] [FIELDS <*field list*>] [FOR <*condition*>] [WHILE <*condition*>] [NOFOLLOW] [NOMENU] [NOCLEAR] [<*record number*>] [NOINIT] [NOAPPEND] [NOEDIT] [NODELETE]

Notes

CHANGE and EDIT are presented in detail in Chapter 31. These commands are discussed here only as applies to multi-user mode.

CHANGE and EDIT attempt to place an automatic record lock on a record when you press any key other than a direction key. Once the record lock is successful, dBASE IV checks the record to see if any changes have been made by other users since you accessed it. If changes are detected, you see the message "Data in record has changed. Press ESC to abandon and any other key to continue." You can continue, overwriting the changes, or you can press ESC to leave the edit.

In multi-user mode, the status bar displays messages relevant to multi-user operations. On the right end of the status bar, the messages "FileLock" and "RecLock" are displayed as record and file locks are set. If you open a file in exclusive mode, "ExclLock" appears on the status bar.

You can use SET REFRESH and SET REPROCESS to control the multi-user environment when you edit records.

- SET REFRESH allows you to control the frequency of screen updates when you are in edit or browse mode. When the value of SET REFRESH is 0 (the default), the screen is not updated with changes made by another user. With SET REFRESH set to a value (time in seconds) other than 0, the records on your screen are updated at regular intervals and any changes to field contents are displayed.

Note: Database files must be modified with the CONVERT command in order for you to use SET REFRESH.

- SET REPROCESS determines the number of attempts dBASE IV makes to lock a record or file before displaying an error message. If SET REPROCESS is set to 0 (the default), dBASE will continue trying to place a lock indefinitely. A message to that effect appears on the screen and you can abort the attempt by pressing ESC. With SET REPROCESS set to a value greater than 0, 10 for instance, 10 lock attempts are made before you see an error message.

See also: CONVERT, SET REFRESH, and SET REPROCESS

CONVERT

The CONVERT command creates a special field in a database file that stores information about changes to shared files and records (multi-user mode only).

Syntax

CONVERT [TO <*type N expression*>]

Notes

The CONVERT command modifies the structure of a database file, adding a field called _dbaselock. This field, intended for the multi-user environment, records information about changes to shared files and returns this information by means of the functions CHANGE( ) and LKSYS(). CONVERT also enables an automatic screen refresh feature for the BROWSE and EDIT commands.

Your file must be opened in exclusive mode (see USE EXCLUSIVE in this chapter) before you can modify it with CONVERT. If you don't include an optional type N expression with the CONVERT command, the new field, _dbaselock, defaults to a length of 16 characters.

Once you convert your file, other users sharing the file can use the CHANGE( ) and LKSYS( ) functions to find out

- If you have changed a record since their record pointer was first positioned on it
- The time you last placed a lock on the file
- The date you last placed a lock on the file
- Your log-in name or workstation name (if the _dbaselock field is longer than eight characters

When you have modified a file with CONVERT, you can use the SET REFRESH command to update other user's Browse and Edit screens. See SET REFRESH in this chapter.

Tip: After CONVERT has executed, remember to close the file and open it again in shared mode.

Note: The _dbaselock field created with the CONVERT command will not yield any valid information when used in single-user mode. The CHANGE( ) function will always return a logical false (.F.) and the LKSYS( ) function returns a null string (blank) for any of its three options.

Options

You can specify a numeric value from 8 to 24 for the type N expression. This value will set the length of the _dbaselock field from 8 to 24 characters.

For more information on this command, see Chapter 29.

DISPLAY/LIST STATUS

These two commands both provide a screen display of information about the current dBASE IV work session and environment.

Syntax

LIST STATUS [TO PRINTER/FILE <*filename*>]

DISPLAY STATUS [TO PRINTER/FILE <*filename*>]

Notes

Use DISPLAY/LIST STATUS to see a list of the following information:

- Currently selected database
- Open database files and their
  - Work area number
  - Alias
  - Open index filenames with Master index and keys
  - Memo file name (if any)

  In multi-user mode, you will also see

  - A list of locked records (if any) for each file
  - The file lock status of each open file
- Relations between databases, if any
- File search path
- Default disk drive
- Print job destination
- Margin setting
- Refresh count
- Reprocess count
- A list of environment settings and their On/Off status
- Number of open files
- Programmable function keys and their current assignments

DISPLAY/LIST STATUS gives a complete picture of the dBASE IV environment for each workstation. When working from the Control Center or dot prompt (interactive mode), you should use this command to orient yourself when working with multiple open files. Otherwise, it is easy to get lost when several database files are open and related in different work areas, with index orders set for each file.

In multi-user mode, DISPLAY/LIST STATUS provides additional information about file and record locks, REFRESH and REPROCESS settings, and the On/Off status of certain network-related environment settings, such as ENCRYPTION, EXCLUSIVE, and LOCK.

The information displayed fills more than one screen. When you choose the DISPLAY STATUS command, the display will pause as each screen is filled, allowing you to view the information before continuing to the next screen. The LIST STATUS command, on the other hand, displays all data without pausing. LIST STATUS makes a more presentable printout, eliminating the "Press any key to continue...," prompt included with DISPLAY STATUS.

If you use the TO PRINTER option with LIST/DISPLAY STATUS, the display is sent to the default printer, unless you have selected another printer with the SET PRINTER command.

The TO FILE option writes the screen display to the file name you specify when issuing the command.

DISPLAY/LIST USERS

When used in multi-user mode, DISPLAY/LIST USERS displays the workstation or log-in name of each user currently working with dBASE IV (multi-user mode only).

Syntax

DISPLAY USERS

LIST USERS

Notes

Both versions of this command list the workstation names of those currently using dBASE IV. For most networks, those names were assigned to each workstation when the network software was installed. The name assigned to the workstation may be that of the workstation department, such as "Payroll," or the name of the user, "Jim," for instance. In the example, it is the NetBIOS address of the workstation.

On a Novell network, DISPLAY/LIST USERS displays the network log-in names assigned to Novell users. This command is invaluable when a file or record lock prevents access to a file. The list of active users lets you see the workstation locking the file, track down the lock, and negotiate a release.

Example

On a Novell network, the output from the DISPLAY/LIST USERS command may look like this:

```
. LIST USERS
Computer name
-------------
> GEORGIAMACK
> BRIANC
> LUCYANNJONES
```

A 3Com network, on the other hand, will probably display numbers rather than names:

```
. LIST USERS
Computer name
-------------
> 02608C752709
> 02670F608901
> 02607A800950
```

Tip: In network programming, you can include the DISPLAY/LIST USERS command under a menu option, allowing users to see a list of other workstations sharing dBASE IV files.

END TRANSACTION

With BEGIN TRANSACTION, END TRANSACTION delineates a command or group of commands that constitute a transaction.

Syntax

BEGIN TRANSACTION [<*pathname*>]

*

* dBASE IV commands making up the transaction

*

END TRANSACTION

Notes

You must precede this command with the BEGIN TRANSACTION command. See BEGIN TRANSACTION in this chapter.

LOGOUT

The LOGOUT command logs out the current dBASE IV user and prompts a new user to log in.

Syntax

LOGOUT

Notes

LOGOUT closes all database files, their associated files, and program files. It also clears the current screen and displays the dBASE IV log-in screen. After LOGOUT, no more work can be done in dBASE IV until a new user logs in. You cannot use the LOGOUT command until user names and passwords have been set up through the PROTECT menu.

You can enter **LOGOUT** at the dot prompt, or include it in a dBASE IV program, to control user access to database files and applications within dBASE IV.

When you use the PROTECT menu to add users and passwords, assign them to groups, and assign optional access levels, a log-in screen controls entry to dBASE IV. Only authorized users will be allowed to use dBASE IV. Once in the system, however, the user can access all unencrypted files, and any protected files that have file-privilege access levels matching or higher than theirs. (See the section "Security" in Chapter 28 for more information on the PROTECT command.)

RESET

The RESET command resets the integrity flag in a database file header after the file has been changed by an uncompleted transaction.

Syntax

RESET [IN <*alias*>]

Notes

During transaction processing, dBASE IV uses an integrity flag to indicate whether a file is in a consistent (transaction complete) or inconsistent (transaction incomplete) state. The integrity flag is set On at the beginning of a transaction. If the transaction is closed with the execution of an END TRANSACTION or ROLLBACK command, the integrity flag is set to Off.

When a transaction is interrupted and a ROLLBACK is not successful, the integrity flag remains set to On and you cannot initiate another transaction using that database file. The RESET command sets the integrity flag to Off, making the file available for a new transaction.

Only the network administrator should be able to use RESET. Moreover, its use is limited to the dot prompt. You should first test the setting of integrity flags with the ISMARKED( ) function to see if the database is still in an inconsistent state.

Example

```
USE Client
? ISMARKED( )
* If a logical true (.T.) is returned
RESET
```

Options

The IN <*alias*> option allows you to reset a file in another work area by supplying the number or letter of the work area, the file name, or the alias. In the following example, the CLIENT file was opened in work area 3 with an alias of CLI. You can reset the integrity flag for CLIENT with any of the following commands.

```
. RESET IN 3        && supplies the work area number as the option
. RESET IN C        && supplies the work area letter as the option
. RESET IN Client   && supplies the filename as the option
. RESET IN Cli      && supplies the alias as the option
```

ROLLBACK

ROLLBACK reverses changes in files caused by an uncompleted transaction, restoring the files to their pre- transaction state.

Syntax

ROLLBACK [<*database filename*>]

Notes

When a transaction has been interrupted, the ROLLBACK command restores to their original state database and index files changed during the transaction. An interrupted transaction, caused by a power fluctuation or system failure, may leave database and index files in a state of partial change, or an inconsistent state. In most cases, manually scanning each database, record by record, to reverse the changes and start over, would be an exorbitant effort. The ROLLBACK command, using the transaction log file as a guide, automatically performs this reversal of changes, returning to their original state all database and index files altered by the transaction.

You can use ROLLBACK from the dot prompt, or from within a program as part of an error routine. If a transaction is interrupted by a program error, such as a failed attempt at a record lock, the ROLLBACK command, with no file name specified, reverses all changes and closes the transaction.

If a transaction is interrupted by a system failure of some kind, you can use the ROLLBACK command after restarting the system and entering dBASE IV. If the transaction log file is still available, you can use the ROLLBACK command with no file name to roll back the entire transaction, or with a file name to reverse the changes to that database file only.

Once the entire transaction has been successfully reversed, ROLLBACK erases the transaction log file, resets the integrity flag in each affected database, and closes the transaction. All associated databases are returned to their pre-transaction state.

The ROLLBACK command cannot work in two situations:

- Inconsistencies between a records pre- and post-transaction contents prevents transaction reversal.

- A damaged or nonexistent transaction log file.

Note: ROLLBACK must be used at the workstation where the interrupted transaction occurred. You cannot use another workstation to roll back a transaction from the current workstation.

Example

```
. BEGIN TRANSACTION                    && Initiate transaction
. USE Customer
. REPLACE ALL Discount WITH ;          && transaction command
```

```
   Balance * .15  FOR Avg_purc > 2500
* During the REPLACE command the power goes out.
* Start the system and log in to dBASE IV
* dBASE IV displays interrupted transaction message at startup
. ROLLBACK                            && Reverse changes to Customer
```

For additional information about transaction processing, see Chapter 29.

See also: BEGIN TRANSACTION, END TRANSACTION, RESET, ROLLBACK( ), and ISMARKED( ).

SET

The SET command calls a full-screen menu system, which allows you to modify a group of settings that control the dBASE IV environment.

Syntax

SET

SET *<command>* ON/OFF/TO *<type N expression>*

Notes

When used without a command option, the SET command displays a menu that allows you to view, select, and change the settings that control screen attributes, default drive and path, left margin, and the many ON/OFF SET commands used in programming. Because this group of commands is discussed in detail in Chapter 35, only those relevant to multi-user mode are discussed in this section.

SET AUTOSAVE	SET PRINTER
SET ENCRYPTION	SET REFRESH
SET EXCLUSIVE	SET REPROCESS
SET LOCK	

Tip: The settings established with any of the following commands are in effect only for the current dBASE IV session. To make the settings permanent, include them in your CONFIG.DB file by using the DBSETUP program or the dBASE Text Editor.

SET AUTOSAVE

With the SET AUTOSAVE command, you can set On or Off automatic updating of disk files and directories.

Syntax

SET AUTOSAVE on/OFF

The default setting for this command is OFF.

Notes

Saving data is a common frustration of database management system (DBMS) users. Unlike other applications programs, which allow you to determine when a file is saved to disk, dBASE IV saves to disk on an internal schedule controlled by available RAM, operating system buffers, record and file size, and the particular file operation in progress. You rarely know when a file is being saved other than when it is closed, when, of course, it is always saved.

Actually, dBASE IV is constantly reading and writing groups of records in an open file to and from the disk during commands such as DELETE, APPEND, EDIT, or UPDATE. This continual read/write process makes database files vulnerable when system interruptions occur due to power failures, brown-outs (diminished power), or equipment failures. A brownout during a disk-write operation can corrupt the section of the file being recorded on the disk. This requires an elaborate set of procedures to recover the lost or "scrambled" data. Sometimes, the whole file is so badly corrupted that recovery is impossible.

When AUTOSAVE is set ON, records are saved to the disk immediately after modification. Upon completion of any command that updates a record, dBASE IV immediately updates the disk directory and file allocation table. Commands that affect a file as a whole, such as REPLACE, SORT, and TOTAL, save after the complete operation is finished. Commands that update individual records, such as EDIT, APPEND, or BROWSE, save each record as it is changed.

Tip: As always, there is a trade-off for increased security—performance is slowed by the more frequent disk access caused by SET AUTOSAVE ON. On a network, this increased access multiplies geometrically as each new user logs in to the system and opens shared files. The overall performance of your network system will generally dictate which method is best for your dBASE IV environment.

SET ENCRYPTION

SET ENCRYPTION determines whether encrypted files that you copy with the COPY, JOIN, or TOTAL commands are created in encrypted or nonencrypted format.

Syntax

SET ENCRYPTION on/OFF

Notes

You can encrypt dBASE IV database files by creating file- privilege schemes with the PROTECT menu. Then you can use the SET ENCRYPTION command to

- Ensure encryption of any new files created from an encrypted file

- Create nonencrypted copies of encrypted files

Encrypted files can only be opened by users logged into dBASE IV and with access levels that match, or are lower than, the access levels assigned to the protected files. They cannot be opened by another dBASE IV system, or by dBASE III PLUS, unless the user is logged in through the dBASE security system and has access levels compatible with the file-privilege scheme.

Once a database file is encrypted, you may copy it to a new file with the COPY, COPY TO, JOIN, and TOTAL commands. If ENCRYPTION is set to ON, the new file created by one of these commands will also be encrypted. If SET ENCRYPTION is OFF, the new file will be unencrypted and will be accessible to anyone.

If you use the JOIN command to create a new file from two existing files, *both* files must be of the same type—encrypted or unencrypted. you cannot join an encrypted file with an unencrypted file.

The default setting for SET ENCRYPTION is OFF.

The following three commands that create new files require that the original file be unencrypted:

- The COPY TO options—EXPORT, FIELDS, FOR, WHILE, TYPE DELIMITED, WITH BLANK, DIF, SDF, SYLK, and WKS

- COPY STRUCTURE EXTENDED
- MODIFY STRUCTURE

Example

Modifying the structure of an encrypted file involves four steps:

1. Make an unencrypted copy of the file.
2. Open the new file and modify the structure.
3. Use the PROTECT menu to set the file-privilege schemes and encryption.
4. Copy the encrypted file and memo file to files with .DBF and .DBT file extensions. Reindex to encrypt any existing index files.

```
. SET ENCRYPTION OFF
. USE <filename>
. COPY TO <new file>
. USE <new file>
. MODIFY STRUCTURE
. PROTECT
. USE
. COPY FILE <new file>.CRP TO <new file>.DBF
. COPY FILE <new file>.CRT TO <new file>.DBT
. USE <new file>
. REINDEX
```

Note: Memo (.DBT) files belonging to an encrypted database file are also encrypted. However, associated index files are only encrypted *after* encryption of a database file, if you reindex existing files or create new index files.

Tip: You cannot create encrypted files from unencrypted files through any command other than PROTECT.

For more information on SET ENCRYPTION and PROTECT, see Chapter 28.

SET EXCLUSIVE

SET EXCLUSIVE is a network-related command that sets the default file open mode to exclusive or shared for all databases (multi-user mode only).

Syntax

SET EXCLUSIVE on/OFF

Notes

You can open database files in shared mode, which permits other users to open and modify the file. You can also open files in exclusive mode, which prevents other users from opening the file.

In single-user dBASE IV, all files are opened in exclusive mode. In multi-user dBASE IV, database files are opened as shared files unless SET EXCLUSIVE is ON.

On a network, you must open dBASE IV database files in exclusive mode in order to execute the following commands:

CONVERT	PACK
INDEX ON <*key expression*> TAG	REINDEX
INSERT [BLANK]	RESET
MODIFY <*any option*>	ZAP

For information on the exclusive use of files, see the section "Data Protection" in Chapter 29.

Example

In order to reindex the files ACCOUNTS and SALES, set EXCLUSIVE to ON, open each file, and execute the REINDEX command. Remember to set EXCLUSIVE to OFF when you are done to allow other users access to the files.

```
. SET EXCLUSIVE ON
. USE Accounts
. REINDEX
. USE Sales
. REINDEX
. USE
. SET EXCLUSIVE OFF
```

Tip: Routines that require exclusive use of files should take place when network use is at its lowest. For instance, you can time file packing and reindexing to occur during the evening, when users are gone.

SET LOCK

The SET LOCK command determines whether a lock occurs during certain dBASE IV commands that cause automatic record and file locks (multi-user mode only).

Syntax

SET LOCK ON/off

Notes

You can use SET LOCK to disable locking for a subset of the 24 commands that set automatic file or records locks during execution. The disabling feature works on commands that are read-only or read/write, as listed in Table 30-1.

If a command is read-only, such as COUNT, SET LOCK OFF disables the normal file lock placed when you issue the command. On the other hand, if the command involves a read/write combination, such as JOIN, SET LOCK OFF does not lock the file while the data is being read into memory (RAM), but places a lock as soon as dBASE IV begins writing the file to the disk.

Automatic locks on read-only commands ensure the integrity of the data analyzed by the command. With SET LOCK OFF, another user may change the file while your command executes. Suppose you've entered **SET LOCK OFF** at the dot prompt and plan to use the SUM command to find the total amount of accounts receivable in a file. While the SUM command executes, another user may have updated a customer's balance. You see an amount returned on the screen, but is it valid?

With small files, automatic locking is barely noticeable because most commands are executed so quickly. SET LOCK can be set to ON, with little or no impact to users. On very large files, in contrast, the automatic locking features may become intrusive to users sharing files, and you may want to disable locks on read-only operations. Remember, however, when SET LOCK is OFF data integrity may be in question.

The default setting for the SET LOCK command is OFF.

Note: SET LOCK OFF does not release explicit (manual) record or file locks placed with FLOCK( ) or RLOCK( ). You must use the UNLOCK command to release explicit locks.

SET PRINTER

You use the SET PRINTER command in networking to direct printed output to a specific printer. The syntax for this command depends on your network software.

Command	Operation	Lock	Set Lock Disable
@ GET/READ	Edit	Record	No
APPEND FROM	Update	File	No
APPEND [*blank*]	Update	Record	No
AVERAGE	Read-only	File	Yes
BROWSE	Edit	Record	No
CALCULATE	Read-only	File	Yes
CHANGE/EDIT	Edit	Record	No
COPY TAG/INDEX	Read/Write	File	Read Yes Write No
COPY [STRUCTURE]	Read/Write	File	Read Yes Write No
COUNT	Read-only	File	Yes
DELETE/RECALL	Update	File/Record	No
EDIT	Edit	Record	No
INDEX	Read/Write	File	Read Yes Write No
JOIN	Read/Write	File	Read Yes Write No
LABEL	Read-only	File	Yes
REPLACE [*scope*]	Update	File/Record	No
REPORT	Read-only	File	No
SET CATALOG ON	Catalog	File	No
SORT	Read/Write	File	Read Yes Write No
SUM	Read-only	File	Yes
TOTAL	Read/Write	File	Read Yes Write No
UPDATE	Update	File	No

Table 30-1. Commands That Place Automatic Locks

Syntax

SET PRINTER on/OFF

SET PRINTER TO *<DOS device>*

SET PRINTER TO *<server name>**<printer name>* = *<destination>*

SET PRINTER TO \\SPOOLER

SET PRINTER TO \\CAPTURE

SET PRINTER TO FILE *<filename>*

Directing Screen Output to a Printer

SET PRINTER ON redirects all screen output to the default printer. This command is often used to produce hard copy of a dBASE IV session and is a good teaching tool for new users. With a printout of commands and their results, a dBASE IV novice can look back over a work session and see what did and didn't work (error messages are also sent to the printer). The default for SET PRINTER is OFF.

The next four commands are discussed in relation to their network applications only. (For more information about SET PRINTER in single-user mode, see Chapter 32.)

Printing on a Local Printer

SET PRINTER TO *<DOS device>* directs the printed output from reports, labels, or the screen to a specific DOS device. The DOS device in this case is a printer port and can be one of three parallel ports—LPT1, LPT2, LPT3—or one of two serial ports—COM1, COM2. The default DOS device is PRN, which you can assign to any one of the parallel or serial ports. If no assignment is made in DOS, PRN defaults to LPT1. (For more information on DOS device assignments, consult your DOS manual.) On a network, the print job goes to a local printer attached to the specified DOS device on your workstation.

The default device for SET PRINTER TO is determined when dBASE IV is installed and can be changed through the DBSETUP program.

Sending Print Jobs to a Network Printer

Several steps are necessary before you can print dBASE IV reports on a network. These steps involve your network software and are generally handled by the network administrator. (See your network manual for specific guidelines on setting up your printers.)

- You must configure your network printers for the network by using your network software.

- At the beginning of each work session, the network printers must be assigned to a logical port or a spooler at each workstation. You do this with network software commands, usually executed by a batch file or log-in script. (For sample start up routines, see Chapter 26.)

To handle print jobs, network systems use a file or buffer that collects print jobs from all workstations. This file is usually called a print *queue* or *spooler,* depending on the network you are using. For each network printer, a queue, or spooler, serves as a holding file for all print jobs directed to that printer. The jobs are released to the printer in the order in which they are received and stored in the queue (you can change this order or cancel print jobs from a queue by using your network software commands).

You must use three commands to send a print job to a network printer:

- When you are ready to print from dBASE IV, use the SET PRINTER TO command appropriate for your network (see the section "Example" that follows) to direct the output to the correct printer.

- A print command such as REPORT FORM or LIST TO PRINT sends the data to the queue or spooler.

- SET PRINTER TO <*optional device*> signals the queue that the end of a print job has been reached, and the report is released to the printer.

Example

The following examples illustrate the commands appropriate for IBM PC, Token Ring, 3Com, Ungerman-Bass, and Novell networks.

IBM PC, Token Ring, 3COM, or Ungerman-Bass Networks

When printers are configured for these networks, sharenames are assigned to each printer. For example, a laser printer may have the sharename Laser, and a dot matrix printer the sharename Dotmatrix. These printer sharenames are used as part of the SET PRINTER TO command, along with the name assigned to the network server. In this example, the name assigned to the network server is Server1.

At the startup of each workstation, printer sharenames are assigned, or "linked," to logical devices. This process is similar to assigning logical drives to shared directories.

On a 3Com network, a workstation log-in batch file might include the 3Com command

```
3P LINK \\SERVER1\LASER LPT1:
```

which assigns the print queue for the laser printer to the logical port LPT1. (The print jobs are actually released to the physical port to which the laser printer is connected.) Run this batch file before starting of dBASE IV.

The SET PRINT TO command directs the dBASE IV print job to the correct queue:

```
. SET PRINTER TO \\Server1\Laser = LPT1    && Directs print jobs to LPT1 queue
. REPORT FORM Sales TO PRINT               && Sends report to the print queue
. SET PRINTER TO                           && Closes queue & resets to default
```

Novell Networks

On a Novell network, include an instruction in the user log-in script directing printer output to a spooler or capture file. The instruction

SPOOL L = 2 TI = 5

directs the spooler to logical device LPT2 and sets the timeout option to 5. You run this log-in script before starting dBASE IV.

To send a report to the spooler, enter

```
. SET PRINTER TO LPT2            && Directs reports to spooler device LPT2
. REPORT FORM Sales TO PRINT     && Sends the report Sales to the spooler
. SET PRINTER TO                 && Closes spool file & resets to default
```

Tip: You can send a number of print jobs to a queue or spooler by omitting the instruction SET PRINTER TO after each print command. When all reports have been sent to the queue, the command SET PRINTER TO closes the queue and releases all jobs to the printer.

Tip: When writing print commands into your network routines, make sure to coordinate the device names with those set up for each workstation during network log-in. When a list of client names and phone numbers suddenly starts printing on the network printer loaded with checks for cash disbursements, you may get angry phone calls from your users. Test all reporting routines carefully on the network printers.

SET REFRESH

When used with the CONVERT command, SET REFRESH updates at regular intervals records displayed in the edit and browse modes (multi-user mode only).

Syntax

SET REFRESH TO *<type N expression>*

Notes

The N expression for SET REFRESH ranges from 0 to 3600 and represents how many times an hour the screen is updated during a multi-user BROWSE or EDIT session. If 0 is the value, no screen updates occur. If 10 is the value, the screen will be updated every 10 seconds, and changes to the records made by other users will appear on your screen. A value of 3600 refreshes the screen once an hour. The default for this setting is 0.

Before you use SET REFRESH, you must use the CONVERT command to add the _dbaselock field to a database file. Once a file has been converted, you can set REFRESH to the value that best suits your editing procedures.

Example

You can allow users to set screen updates by including a routine in a program, as shown here.

```
PROCEDURE Set_scr
Screen = 0
@ 22,7 SAY 'How many times a minute would you ';
+ 'like your screen updated? ' ;
GET Screen PICTURE '99' RANGE 0,60     && get value from user/limit range
READ
SET REFRESH TO INT(60/Screen)          && compute seconds/convert to integer
RETURN
```

SET REPROCESS

The SET REPROCESS command determines how many attempts dBASE IV makes to lock a record or file before displaying an error message (multi-user mode only).

Syntax

SET REPROCESS TO [*type N expression*]

Notes

When a lock attempt on a file or record fails, an error message is displayed. You can abort the lock attempt or allow dBASE IV to continue trying to lock the record. With the SET REPROCESS command, you can specify the number of lock attempts to be made on a file already in use before dBASE IV displays an error message.

You can set REPROCESS to a numeric value from -1 to 32,000. It affects any commands that place locks on records or files. If you enter **SET REPROCESS TO 10** at the dot prompt and then use a command that places a lock, such as EDIT or REPLACE, dBASE makes a maximum of 10 lock attempts before an error occurs. If the file is not already locked by another user, the value you assign to SET REPROCESS has no effect.

The default value of SET REPROCESS is 0. If a file is already locked, a setting of 0 causes an infinite number of lock attempts. You can press ESC to abort the command.

If you choose a setting of -1, dBASE IV attempts an infinite number of retries, as with 0, but no error message is displayed. The ESC key will not abort the command attempting the lock. The only way out of this one is to find the user that placed the lock and have it released.

Tip: When setting the environment for your application, choose a value for SET REPROCESS that will make a reasonable number of attempts at a lock before producing an error message.

See also: SET LOCK, UNLOCK, FLOCK( ), and RLOCK( ).

UNLOCK

You use the UNLOCK command to remove record and file locks, enabling other users to update or process shared files (multi-user mode only).

Syntax

UNLOCK [ALL/IN <*alias*>]

Notes

When you place a lock on a record or file, another user cannot update it until the lock is removed. Automatic locks are set by commands such as EDIT, REPLACE, or UPDATE are removed as soon as the command executes. Manual locks set with FLOCK( ) or RLOCK( ), however, can only be removed with the UNLOCK command. You can use the UNLOCK command in three ways:

- UNLOCK releases locks to the file or records placed by the current user in the selected work area.
- UNLOCK ALL releases all locks placed by the current user in all work areas.
- UNLOCK IN <*alias*> releases locks to the file or records placed by the current user in the designated work area.

If a record lock was the last type of lock placed, UNLOCK releases record locks. If a file lock was last placed, UNLOCK releases file locks.

Any related files or records are unlocked with UNLOCK.

Tip: You don't need to use UNLOCK with commands that set automatic locks, unless the command was interrupted and could not execute.

USE EXCLUSIVE

The USE EXCLUSIVE command opens a database with its index and memo files in exclusive, or nonshared, mode. USE EXCLUSIVE is intended for multi-user mode and has no effect on files opened in single-user mode.

Syntax

USE [<*filename*>] [INDEX <*.NDX or .MDX file list*>]
EXCLUSIVE [ALIAS <*alias*>]

Notes

USE EXCLUSIVE opens a file in exclusive mode, setting the file open attribute to exclusive and the file access to read/write. The file cannot be accessed by another user once it has been opened in this mode. To make the file available to other users on the network, you must close it with USE, CLOSE, or CLEAR ALL.

The following commands require that a file be opened in exclusive mode:

CONVERT	PACK
INDEX ON <*key expression*> TAG	REINDEX
INSERT [BLANK]	RESET
MODIFY <*any option*>	ZAP

The USE EXCLUSIVE command behaves like the USE command, except that it opens files in exclusive mode. The [INDEX] and *<alias>* options are discussed fully under the USE command in Chapter 31.

Example

In the following example, the ACCOUNTS file is opened in exclusive mode, the structure is modified, and the file is opened once more in shared mode, allowing other users to access the modified file.

```
. USE Accounts EXCLUSIVE
. MODIFY STRUCTURE
. USE Accounts
```

FUNCTIONS

The following functions are described in a multi-user format. Many of the functions listed below can also be found in Chapter 33.

ACCESS( )	NETWORK( )
CHANGE( )	RLOCK( )/LOCK( )
FLOCK( )	ROLLBACK( )
ISMARKED( )	USER( )
LKSYS( )	

ACCESS( )

The ACCESS( ) function returns the access level of the last user logged in to the current workstation.

Syntax

```
ACCESS( )
```

Notes

The ACCESS( ) function works in conjunction with the file- and field-privilege schemes defined through the PROTECT menu. The numeric value returned by the function, ranging from 1 to 8, indicates the privilege level assigned to the user. If ACCESS( ) returns a value of 1, the least restrictive security level, the user has unlimited access to protected files. An access level of 8, on the other hand, is the most restrictive level, carrying the fewest file and field access privileges to protected files.

If you enter dBASE IV without logging in, the value returned by ACCESS( ) will be 0.

ACCESS( ) is generally used in programming rather than at the dot prompt level. It acts as a screening device in allowing users access to routines and file operations. When screening the user access level and incorporating that value into a program, check all routines that use protected files and coordinate the file privilege levels with the access level your program requires for entrance to a routine. If you allow a user with an access level of 7 to start a routine that uses a file with a privilege level of 4, an attempt to open the file will produce an error.

Tip: Make sure that the DBSYSTEM.DB file is stored in the same directory as dBASE IV. If it cannot be located at startup, the dBASE IV log-in screen is not used and all access levels are set to 0.

Note: Access levels have no impact with unencrypted files.

Example

The following example lists two procedures. The first allows an authorized user to restore memory variables containing the file-privilege levels required for each routine, change them, and save them back to the .MEM file.

The second routine restores the memory variables and uses the ACCESS( ) function to check the user's access level against the file-privilege level (Rout2) required for PAYROLL.

```
PROCEDURE Secure
RESTORE FROM Acc_lev ADDITIVE        && read memory variables from file
Ch_lev = .T.
CLEAR
@ 7,15 TO 15,65 DOUBLE               && Draw screen box
@ 8,17 SAY  'Enter changes to required security levels'
DO WHILE Ch_lev
   @ 10,17 SAY 'Personnel Update............' ;
   GET Rout1 PICTURE '99' RANGE 1,8
   @ 11,17 SAY 'Payroll Update..............' ;
   GET Rout2 PICTURE '99' RANGE 1,8
   @ 12,17 SAY 'Insurance/Benefits Update....' ;
   GET Rout3 PICTURE '99' RANGE 1,8
   READ
   Mfix = 'S'
   @ 15,17 SAY '(S) Save changes  (E) Edit changes:';
   GET Msave PICTURE '!'
   IF Msave = 'S'
      SAVE ALL LIKE Rout* TO Acc_lev  && Save variables to a .MEM file
      Ch_lev = .F.
   ENDIF
ENDDO
CLEAR
RETURN

PROCEDURE Payroll
RESTORE FROM Acc_lev ADDITIVE             && restore from .MEM file
```

```
IF ACCESS() > Rout2                       && Check current user access
   ?? CHR(7)                              && sound bell
   @ 22,15 SAY 'SORRY...ACCESS IS DENIED"
   WAIT
   RETURN
ENDIF
*
* Execute payroll program
*
RETURN
```

CHANGE( )

The CHANGE( ) function detects a change made to a record by other users since it was read by the current user (multi-user mode only).

Syntax

CHANGE([<*alias*>])

Notes

You use the CHANGE( ) function with its associated command, CONVERT, to test for changes made to the current record by other users. The _dbaselock field, added to a database with the CONVERT command, stores the byte count of the current record. The CHANGE( ) function queries this count to see if it differs from the count when the record was first read. If the record has been updated, a logical true (.T.) is returned. If no change has been detected, a logical false (.F.) is the result. If a database has not been modified to include the _dbaselock field, CHANGE( ) returns a false.

You can use CHANGE( ) in programming to test a record before replacing the field contents with memory variables. If multiple users are updating records in a file, two users might edit the same record simultaneously, one overwriting the other's update.

You can test the record with CHANGE( ) before using the REPLACE command, thus allowing the user to abort the edit if the CHANGE( ) function returns a true.

Example

In the next example, field contents are stored to memory variables and edited by the user. Before replacing the fields with the updated variables, the CHANGE( ) command tests the record, replacing the fields if CHANGE( ) returns a false. If the result of CHANGE( ) is true, the program displays a message about an update by another user, waits for a keypress, and loops back to the edit routine with updated variables.

```
USE Payroll ORDER Emp_acct
Macct_no = SPACE(5)
@ 1,1 SAY 'Enter the Employee Account Number: ' GET Macct_no
READ
SEEK Macct_no
IF FOUND()
   DO WHILE .NOT. CHANGE()
      Mhours = Hours
      Movertime = Overtime
      Mbonus = Bonus
      @ 2,1 SAY 'Regular Hours:' GET Mhours PICTURE '999.99
      @ 3,1 SAY 'Overtime      :' GET Movertime PICTURE '999.99'
      @ 4,1 SAY 'Bonus         :' GET Mbonus PICTURE '9999.99'
      READ
      IF .NOT. CHANGE()
         REPLACE Hours WITH Mhours, Overtime WITH Movertime,;
         Bonus WITH Mbonus
     ELSE
         @ 6,1 SAY 'This record has been updated by another user'
     WAIT
     ENDIF
  ENDDO
ENDIF
```

Options

You can specify an optional alias when using the CHANGE( ) function. The alias may be a work area letter or number, a file name, or assigned alias. The CHANGE( ) status of the current record in the specified work area will be returned.

FLOCK( )

The FLOCK( ) function tests for a file lock and, if none exists, places a lock on the file and returns a logical true (.T.) (multi-user mode only).

Syntax

FLOCK([<*alias*>]

The optional argument *alias* lets you specify a file name, work area number or letter, or an alias assigned when the file was opened. (See the USE command in Chapter 31 for information about aliases.)

Notes

The FLOCK( ) function places an explicit (manual) lock on a file, after testing to see if a lock is already present. Once the lock is placed, the file is available to other users in read-only mode. If other users attempt to execute commands that set locks, they get an error message at their workstations. If FLOCK( ) detects an existing lock, it cannot successfully lock the file and returns a logical false (.F.).

You use FLOCK( ) from the dot prompt or, more typically in programming, to place a lock on a file before an update operation. The file lock prevents other users from updating the file at the same time, avoiding a data collision. The data in the file can be viewed by other users, but not changed in any way.

Use the FLOCK( ) function when you are planning update operations involving the whole database. If only a few records are to be changed, use the RLOCK( ) function instead (see RLOCK( ) in this chapter).

Locking a file with FLOCK( ) also locks all actively related files.

You can remove an explicit file lock placed by FLOCK( ) by

- Using the UNLOCK command (see UNLOCK in this chapter)
- Closing the file with USE, CLOSE, or CLEAR ALL
- Quitting from dBASE IV

When you remove a file lock, any actively related files are also unlocked.

Example

Often, a report or batch operation requires that a file remain unchanged during the operation. You can use FLOCK( ) to prevent updates to the file while a program is running, allowing other users to access the file for viewing. FLOCK( ) is less restrictive than EXCLUSIVE (see USE EXCLUSIVE in this chapter) but ensures that no changes will be made until the operation is completed.

In the routine that follows, FLOCK( ) tests for a file lock. If the lock is successful, the PAYROLL file is locked, preventing changes by other users while the PAYROLL report is run. If a lock cannot be placed, the routine is exited.

```
USE Payroll ORDER Emp_name
IF FLOCK()
   DO Pyrl_rep
ELSE
     @ 22,15 SAY 'Sorry, can't run report...the Payroll file is in use'
   WAIT
ENDIF
USE
RETURN
```

Tip: You should not use FLOCK( ) in programs where user intervention occurs, (@ *<row>*,*<column>* GET/READ routines, for instance). If the user leaves the computer in the middle of one of these sequences, the file will remain locked for an indefinite length of time. Try placing a record lock with RLOCK( ) instead. This ties up only one record, rather than the whole file.

ISMARKED( )

The ISMARKED( ) function checks an integrity flag in the file header of the current database to see if the file is in a state of change caused by an uncompleted transaction.

Syntax

ISMARKED( )[<*alias*>]

The <*alias*> option can be a work area number or letter, file name, or alias specified when a file is opened. (See the USE command in Chapter 31 for information about aliases.) If you don't specify an *alias*, the file in the current work area is tested. If you use an *alias*, the file in the alias work area is tested.

Notes

When you start a transaction with BEGIN TRANSACTION, any database files changed during the transaction are marked, indicating that they are in an inconsistent state, or state of change. Each database has a file header—a block of data at the beginning of each database file containing information about the structure, size, and state of the file. A 1-byte section of the file header is reserved as an integrity flag, which is set to On at the start of a transaction and reset to Off when a transaction has been completed.

ISMARKED( ) tests the setting of the integrity flag. If the flag is on, ISMARKED( ) returns a logical true (.T.), indicating that the file is part of a transaction in process. A logical false (.F.) signifies a closed transaction, effected with the END TRANSACTION or ROLLBACK command.

If ISMARKED( ) returns .F., the file is available for another transaction. A file testing to .T. with the ISMARKED( ) function cannot be used in another transaction until one of two things has happened.

- The original transaction has been closed with the END TRANSACTION or ROLLBACK command, resetting the integrity flag.

- If you cannot complete a transaction, you must reset the integrity flag to Off with the RESET command (see RESET in this chapter).

See also: BEGIN TRANSACTION, END TRANSACTION, ROLLBACK, RESET, ISMARKED( ), and ROLLBACK( ) in this chapter and in Chapter 29.

Example

ISMARKED( ) is useful in network programming, since it enables you to test for an active transaction before allowing another user to access a file. In the following example, a file is tested with ISMARKED( ) before an update is attempted. If a transaction is in process, the user is directed to another operation. Otherwise, the update proceeds.

```
USE Stock
IF ISMARKED()
   @ 22,15 SAY 'Sorry...this file has a transaction in process'
   @ 23,15 SAY '      Please try another menu option...'
   WAIT ''
   RETURN
ELSE
   DELETE ALL FOR On_hand = 0
ENDIF
```

LKSYS( )

You use the LKSYS( ) function to find the date, time, and log-in name of the last user to place a lock on the current record. You can only use this function on a file modified by CONVERT (multi-user mode only).

Syntax

LKSYS(<*type N expression*>)

The N expression must be a value from 0 to 2.

Notes

You must use the CONVERT command to modify a database file at another workstation before you use the LKSYS( ) function. If the file you open has been converted by another user to add the _dbaselock field (see CONVERT in this chapter), you can use the LKSYS( ) function to obtain three pieces of information about file locks placed by that user:

- LKSYS(0) returns the time of the last lock.
- LKSYS(1) returns the date of the last lock.
- LKSYS(2) returns the network log-in name of the user (Novell network) or workstation name (all other networks). The length of the _dbaselock field determines how the log-in name is stored:

Length	Returns
8	No log-in name
16	First 8 characters of log-in name
24	16-character log-in name

You can use LKSYS( ) from the dot prompt or in programming. For it to work successfully, you must take the following steps in each work session.

- Each user must open the file in exclusive mode and use the CONVERT command to add the _dbaselock field. This must be done at the start of *each* work session, even if the file was converted during a previous session.
- The file must be reopened in the shared mode to allow other users to access the data.
- A user at another workstation can type **? LKSYS(0)** to inquire about the time a lock was placed. Type **? LKSYS(2)** to return the name or workstation ID of the user placing the lock. If no lock is detected, a null string (blank) is returned.

Example

If the current record is locked by another user, you can find the time that the lock was placed and the name or ID of the workstation.

```
 . ? LKSYS(0)
10:31:42

 . ? LKSYS(2)
CHARLIESM
```

Tip: A file must be opened in exclusive mode and the CONVERT command must be used before LKSYS( ) will return a value. On a network system with more than two users, this can inhibit file sharing and be a rather cumbersome programming tool. As an alternative, you might include the DISPLAY/LIST USERS command as part of an error routine. If a prolonged file or record lock denies a user access to a file, the error routine displays a list of dBASE IV users, one of which is bound to be the guilty party.

See also: CONVERT, SET LOCK, UNLOCK, CHANGE( ), FLOCK( ), RLOCK( ),

NETWORK( )

The NETWORK( ) function indicates whether the multi- or single-user version of dBASE IV is running, and returns a logical true (.T.) or false (.F.).

Syntax

NETWORK( )

Notes

You can place the NETWORK( ) function at the beginning of routines to determine if the network version of dBASE IV is running. The value returned, true or false, can be used to branch to network- related commands for multi-user mode, or to non-network commands if single-user mode is detected. (See Chapter 29 for more information.)

Example

In the following routine, the PAYROLL file has records marked for deletion that are ready for removal with the PACK command. In network mode, you cannot execute PACK unless a file has been opened in exclusive mode. The file open mode is determined by the (.T.) or (.F.) returned by the NETWORK( ) function.

```
IF NETWORK()
   USE Payroll EXCLUSIVE
ELSE
   USE Payroll
ENDIF
PACK
RETURN
```

RLOCK( )/LOCK( )

You use RLOCK( ) and LOCK( ) to lock one or more records; the two functions may be used interchangeably (multi-user mode only).

Syntax

RLOCK([<*type C expression list*>,<*alias*>]/[<*alias*>]

or

LOCK([<*type C expression list*>,<*alias*>]/[<*alias*>]

The optional expression list is a character list of record numbers. You can also specify a list of optional aliases, work area numbers or letters, or file names. (See USE in Chapter 31 for more information on aliases.)

Notes

RLOCK( ) tests for an existing lock on the current record. If none is detected, it locks the record and returns a logical true (.T.). If another lock is detected, the lock attempt is unsuccessful and RLOCK( ) returns a logical false (.F.). Any records actively related to the current record with the SET RELATION command are also locked with RLOCK( ).

The record lock placed by RLOCK( ) is explicit (manual) and can only be removed by the UNLOCK command or by closing the file. The lock is also a *shared* lock, which means that other users can view, but not update, the record.

RLOCK( ), without a record list or alias specified, attempts to lock the current record in the current work area.

You can lock more than one record with the RLOCK( ) function. Suppose you have opened the STOCK file and want to lock records 5, 12, and 25. Enter **? RLOCK("5","12","25")** at the dot prompt. When you position your record pointer on one of these records, the right end of the status bar displays the message "RecLock."

You can also lock records in files open in other work areas. Perhaps you need records 20 and 21 locked in the STOCK file, which is open in work area 2. You can do this from the dot prompt in several ways:

```
. ? RLOCK("20,21","Stock")      && Uses the filename as alias
.T.

. ? RLOCK("20,21","2")          && Uses the work area number as alias
.T.

. ? RLOCK("20,21","B")          && Uses the work area letter as alias
.T.
```

You can check the status of these record locks with the DISPLAY STATUS command. All open files and record locks are listed on the screen.

The maximum number of records that you can lock at any one time is 50. Attempts to lock more than 50 result in the error message "Lock table full." If you need to lock 50 records at once, you should probably use the FLOCK( ) command to lock the whole file.

RLOCK( ) is an additive function. Locking a new record does not unlock previously locked records. Both the UNLOCK command and the FLOCK( ) function will unlock all records in the current work area, and any actively related records.

Tip: When using RLOCK( ) in a program, remember to include the UNLOCK command in the routine to free the record for another user to update.

For more information on the RLOCK( ) command, see Chapter 27.

See also: FLOCK( ), DISPLAY/LIST STATUS, SET LOCK, SET RELATION, UNLOCK.

ROLLBACK( )

You use the ROLLBACK( ) function to test for a successful execution of the ROLLBACK command.

Syntax

ROLLBACK( )

Notes

If a transaction has been interrupted and cannot complete successfully, you use the ROLLBACK command to reverse the transaction and restore files to their pre-transaction state. The ROLLBACK( ) function tests for successful execution of ROLLBACK, and returns a logical true (.T.) if that is the case. If ROLLBACK was unable to reverse the transaction, a logical false (.F.) is returned. You can use ROLLBACK( ) from the dot prompt or in a program.

This function is usually employed by programmers and network administrators to determine whether a RESET command is needed to reset the integrity flag in the database file headers and to free files for the next transaction.

Example

For an example and more information on transaction processing, see Chapter 29.

See also: BEGIN/END TRANSACTION, RESET, ROLLBACK, ISMARKED( ).

USER( )

USER( ) returns the dBASE IV log-in name of the current user, if the PROTECT system has been used.

Syntax

USER( )

Notes

When the PROTECT command is used to set up a security system—requiring that each user log in to dBASE IV using a log-in name, password, and group name—the USER( ) function provides the name of the user. If the PROTECT system has not been set up, USER( ) returns a null string (blank).

Example

If a user logs in to dBASE IV, performs a few operations, and then leaves the workstation unattended, you can query dBASE IV to find the name of the culprit.

```
 . ? USER( )
MARCIA
```

Some programmers like to personalize their programs, making them more user-friendly. The USER( ) function allows you to incorporate the user's name into the program and include it in screen messages, as in the following example:

```
@ 22,15 SAY 'Hello ' + USER() + '... please select a menu option'
```

Command Reference

PART FIVE

This part of the book is a comprehensive listing of dBASE IV commands, SET commands, functions, system memory variables, and CONFIG.DB parameters. Although many of the items discussed here are mentioned elsewhere in the book, these chapters contain the most in-depth information on syntax, available options, and rules for using an item. They also include many examples to help you understand how an item actually works.

If you're entering commands from the dot prompt or writing programs, you'll find the material presented in this part quite beneficial. For more in-depth descriptions of commands and functions specific to networking, see Chapter 30, "Networking Commands and Functions."

dBASE IV Commands

This chapter lists all of the dBASE IV commands that you can include in a command line. You can enter a command line from the dot prompt or place it in a program. Each command description has at least one example, when appropriate, and frequently mentions other related commands and functions.

The General Syntax of dBASE IV Commands

This is the general syntax of dBASE IV commands:

> <*command verb*> [<*expression list*>] [<*scope*>] [FOR <*condition*>] [WHILE <*condition*>] [TO FILE <*filename*> / TO PRINTER / TO ARRAY <*array list*> / TO <*memory variable*>] [ALL [LIKE / EXCEPT <*skeleton*>]] [IN <*alias*>]

Command verb is the name of the dBASE IV command. Brackets ([]) indicate an optional item. Angle brackets (<>) indicate that you must include a specific value for the item type within the brackets. Slash (/) indicates a choice. Ellipsis (...) indicates you can repeat a series of options more than once.

The *scope* lets you set the number of records a command affects. The keywords for the *scope* are

- RECORD <*n*> lets you specify a single record by its number.
- NEXT <*n*> lets you set the number of records (<*n*>) the command affects, beginning with the current record.
- ALL specifies all the records in the database.
- REST specifies all the remaining records in the database, starting with the current record-pointer position.

Although you can apply the general syntax to nearly all dBASE IV commands, you'll find many exceptions. See the "Syntax" section for each command to see its unique syntax rules. Also, be aware that you can vary the order of the options when you build a command line. You'll also find that many of the commands do not require any options.

?/??

The ?/?? command displays information on the screen. It is especially convenient for determining the value of fields and memory variables.

Syntax

?/?? [<*expression1*> [PICTURE <*string expression*>]
[FUNCTION <*function list*>] [AT <*type N expression*>]
[STYLE <*font number*>]]
[,<*expression2*> ...] [,]

Notes

? issues a carriage return and line feed before displaying the results of the expressions and clauses.

?? displays the results of the expressions and clauses beginning at the current cursor position. It does not issue a carriage return line feed.

If SET PRINTER is ON, ?/?? sends its output to the printer.

Tip: A single ? command, without any options, displays a blank line. You can use this command when you want your output to skip a line. To control the line spacing of your output (for example, single and double spacing), see the _pspacing system memory variable in Chapter 34.

Options

With the PICTURE or FUNCTION, AT, and STYLE options, you can customize printed reports.

PICTURE and FUNCTION

PICTURE templates and functions format the output of the ?/?? command. See the @ command in this chapter for a complete list of templates. All of them work with ?/??.

Six PICTURE functions are especially useful when you work with the ?/?? command. These functions work with *long fields* and *short fields*. Long fields are fields whose contents are longer than the PICTURE template. Short fields are fields whose contents don't fill the PICTURE template.

The Stretch Functions—H and V The H and V PICTURE functions control the appearance of long and short fields, enabling you to modify the height and width of the display. They cause the fields to stretch and shrink to fit the contents of the field. H and V work only with the ?/?? command (not with the @ command). You must precede H and V with the FUNCTION or PICTURE keyword.

H stretches or shrinks the field horizontally to fit the data. For long fields, it pushes to the right other material on the line. For short fields, it shrinks the field accordingly and pulls to the left any material to the right. However, if you use an AT option to control the exact column on the line where other fields begin, the H function will not pull the fields to the right. To use word wrapping with the H function, you must set the _wrap system memory variable to logical true (.T.).

V<*n*> stretches the field vertically to fit the data. The *n* parameter represents the maximum number of columns or rows in the field display. The V function elongates fields vertically down the page. It treats output in columnar fashion. You can use the *n* parameter to limit the number of columns a field can stretch to. Characters beyond the *n* bound are dropped. If you do not include the *n* parameter, the field will stretch to accommodate all the data.

If you do not use either the H or V function, the width of the template controls the number of characters that are output. Long fields are truncated to fit within the bounds of the template, and a field is limited to one line.

Short Field Functions—B, I, J, and T As mentioned, short fields contain data that doesn't entirely fill the PICTURE template. The ?/?? command has four functions for aligning short fields. These functions also work with the @ command:

@B	Aligns text to the left within a field
@I	Centers text within a field
@J	Aligns text to the right within a field
@T	Removes all beginning and ending blanks from a field

You can combine the T function with one of the other functions. For example, you can use the T and J functions together to trim a field's data and align it to the right within the template.

Note: If you don't use an alignment function, dBASE aligns strings to the left and numbers to the right within a template.

The Floating Currency Symbol Function—$ The ?/?? command lets you use the $ function to display a currency symbol within a numeric field. The currency symbol appears before or after the amount, depending on the SET CURRENCY setting. If SET CURRENCY is LEFT, the symbol appears before the amount. If SET CURRENCY is RIGHT, the symbol appears after the amount.

The Leading Zeros Function—L The ?/?? command also lets you use the L function to display leading zeros. When the data does not fill a numeric field's template, you can use the L function to display zeros in front of the number.

AT and STYLE

The AT clause lets you control the exact column in which a field begins. You can use the AT clause to control the alignment of columns of text.

The STYLE clause lets you control the style of text. For example, you can make text appear in bold or italics. When you use the STYLE option, dBASE may not change the appearance of text on your monitor. However, it does change the appearance of printed output.

You can combine numbers and letters in the STYLE clause. You can use the numbers 1 through 5, which correspond to the fonts you've defined in your CONFIG.DB file (see Chapter 35, "Customizing dBASE IV"). You can use the letters

B	Bold
I	Italic
U	Underline
R	Superscript (raised)
L	Subscript (lowered)

Whereas the ?/?? command lets you change type styles for individual fields within your output, the ??? command and the _pscode and _pecode system memory variables let you change type styles for an entire document. See the ??? command in this chapter for more information. See Chapter 34 for more detailed information on the _pscode and _pecode system memory variables.

Examples

The following example activates the CLIENTS database and then uses the SET PRINTER ON command to direct the output to the printer. Next, the first ? command shows what happens when you display the Firstname and Lastname fields without using any ? command options. The second ? command trims the Firstname field and aligns it to the right. It also boldfaces the Firstname and Lastname fields.

```
. USE Clients
. SET PRINTER ON
. ? Firstname, Lastname
George          Thomas
. ? Firstname PICTURE "@TJ" STYLE "B", Lastname STYLE "B"
         George Thomas
```

The printed output from this example is

```
George          Thomas
         George Thomas
```

The next example program shows that while the ? command issues a carriage return line feed, the ?? command does not.

```
USE Clients
SET TALK OFF
? Firstname
?? Lastname
```

The output is

```
George          Thomas
```

See also: ???, @, and SET PRINTER.

???

??? lets you send printer control codes directly to your printer.

Syntax

??? <*string expression*>

Notes

When your printer driver doesn't support a particular printing function, you can use the ??? command to send printer control codes. Printer control codes are unique for each printer. Consult your printer manual for the required codes.

Since ??? bypasses the printer driver, be careful when you use codes that modify the current column or row for the printer. Otherwise, dBASE IV and your printer may become out of synch.

The ?/?? command and the _pscode and _pecode system memory variables send printer control codes of their own to the printer. Therefore, use the following guidelines to control your output:

- Use the ?/?? STYLE clause when you want to control the type style for a particular text item within a document.
- Use ??? when you want to control the type style or orientation for several items at once within a document.
- Use _pscode and _pecode when you want to set the overall type style or orientation for the document.

You can use any character, except the double quote mark ("), for a printer control code. Several characters are *nonprintable*; Table 31-1 shows how you can represent those characters in ???. You must include the nonprintable character in curly braces ({ }). For example, to represent the ESC character, you can use {ESC}, {ESCAPE}, or {CTRL-[}.

Examples

The following example enables automatic underlining on an HP LaserJet printer.

```
. ??? "{ESCAPE}&dD"
```

ASCII Code	Control Character Specifier
0	{NULL} or {CTRL-@}
1	{CTRL-A}
2	{CTRL-B}
3	{CTRL-C}
4	{CTRL-D}
5	{CTRL-E}
6	{CTRL-F}
7	{BELL} or {CTRL-G}
8	{BACKSPACE} or {CTRL-H}
9	{TAB} or {CTRL-I}
10	{LINEFEED} or {CTRL-J}
11	{CTRL-K}
12	{CTRL-L}
13	{RETURN} or {CTRL-M}
14	{CTRL-N}
15	{CTRL-O}
16	{CTRL-P}
17	{CTRL-Q}
18	{CTRL-R}
19	{CTRL-S}
20	{CTRL-T}
21	{CTRL-U}
22	{CTRL-V}
23	{CTRL-W}
24	{CTRL-X}
25	{CTRL-Y}
26	{CTRL-Z}
27	{ESC} or {ESCAPE} or {CTRL-[}
28	{CTRL-\}
29	{CTRL-]}
30	{CTRL-^}
31	{CTRL-_}
127	{DEL} or {DELETE}

Table 31-1. Control Character Specifiers

You can accomplish the same effect with

```
. ??? CHR(27)+"&dD"
```

The @ command lets you create custom forms for data input and output. It lets you display and accept data in a given format at a given set of screen coordinates.

Syntax

@ <*row*>, <*col*>
[SAY <*expression*>
[PICTURE <*string expression*>][FUNCTION <*function list*>]]
[GET <*variable*>
[[OPEN] WINDOW <*window name*>]
[PICTURE <*string expression*>]
[FUNCTION <*function list*>]
[RANGE [<*low*>][,<*high*>]]
[VALID <*condition*> [ERROR <*string expression*>]]
[WHEN <*condition*>]
[DEFAULT <*expression*>]
[COLOR [<*standard*>][,<*enhanced*>]]

Notes

Row and *column* are numeric expressions that represent zero-based screen coordinates. *Row* can be from 0 to the number of lines on the display. *Column* can be from 0 to 79 columns. If you use the SET DEVICE TO PRINTER command to route @ commands to the printer, you can set *row* from 0 to 32,767 and *column* from 0 to 255.

Tip: When you assign the values for *row* and *column*, keep in mind that 0,0 is the upper-left corner of the active window. The active window may encompass the entire screen, or it may be a window you've defined.

Line 22 of the screen is reserved for the status bar when SET STATUS is ON (the default). If SET STATUS is OFF, dBASE IV uses line 0 for status information, provided SET SCOREBOARD is OFF (the default). If you want to use the entire display screen, SET STATUS to OFF and SET SCOREBOARD to OFF.

The SAY option lets you display information using any valid dBASE IV expression. You can, for example, use a character string to prompt the user for input.

The GET option displays data values from fields, memory variables, or arrays. It also allows editing of those data values. The READ command launches full-screen editing mode and activates the GETs. You can then change the values in the GET fields.

You can create a format file that contains @ commands. A format file is a text file that you can build using the MODIFY COMMAND editor. You can also use the CREATE/MODIFY SCREEN command to help you build format files. (Chapter 9, "Creating Input Forms," describes in detail how to build format files.) Once you've created a format file, you can use it with the READ, APPEND, EDIT, CHANGE, and INSERT commands.

You can use the SET DEVICE TO PRINTER command to direct @ commands to the printer.

Options

The @ command options are described in alphabetical order.

If you use the @ <*row*>, <*column*> command without any options, you clear the given row beginning at the given column position.

COLOR lets you control the colors that appear for the SAY and GET variables. The *standard* option controls the color for the SAY variables, and the *enhanced* option controls the color for GET variables. To set colors for these options, follow the same rules as for the SET COLOR command (see Chapter 32). You can set both a foreground and background color for each variable. The colors you provide override the colors you've defined with the SET COLOR command. However, they only apply to the output from the current @ command.

DEFAULT lets you assign a value to the GET variable, provided you match the GET variable's data type. Any value that is passed from the previous record to the current record overrides the DEFAULT value.

ERROR lets you display an error message when the VALID <*condition*> is not met. The message you provide appears in place of dBASE IV's default error message, "Editing condition not satisfied."

FUNCTION lets you format the displayed data. See the PICTURE option for more details.

MESSAGE lets you display a message when a READ command is executed. The message appears when you locate the cursor on the GET field.

PICTURE *<string expression>* lets you format the data that is displayed or restrict the data that the user can enter in a variable. The *string expression* can include a function with an @ symbol at the start, which affects the input or output of the variable as a whole, and/or a template, which affects the input or output of the variable on a character-by-character basis.

You can include any string expression for the PICTURE clause. However, you typically use a string of characters between quotes (see the following examples). PICTURE functions and templates are described in more detail later.

RANGE [*<low>*][,*<high>*] lets you specify boundaries for data input. You can use the RANGE option with character, numeric, and date variables. To specify a range, provide upper and lower boundaries of the same data type. If you specify only one boundary, precede or follow it with a comma. For example, enter **RANGE ,100** to include an upper boundary of 100. To include a lower boundary of 50, enter **RANGE 50,**. If you enter a value outside the specified range, dBASE IV prompts you for another entry and shows the upper and/or lower boundaries.

VALID *<condition>* lets you specify a condition that must be met in order for dBASE to accept data into the GET variable. If the condition is not met, dBASE IV displays the error message "Editing condition not satisfied."

Tip: You can enter a user-defined function as the *condition* for the VALID clause, provided that the function returns a logical value. You can use this technique to perform extensive data checking on values. For more information on user-defined functions, see the FUNCTION command in this chapter and the section "User-Defined Functions" in Chapter 25.

WHEN lets you set a condition that must be met before the cursor will move into a GET field. If the condition is true, you can move the cursor into the GET field. If the condition is false, the cursor skips to the next field.

WINDOW lets you open a separate editing window when you use a memo field for the GET variable. To open the memo window, place the cursor on the memo marker and press CTRL-HOME. To close the memo window, press CTRL-END. The *window name* that you provide for the WINDOW option must be previously defined with DEFINE WINDOW. If you don't use the WINDOW option to define a separate editing window, dBASE uses the full screen for editing memo fields.

OPEN WINDOW lets you display the memo field as already opened. In other words, you don't need to press CTRL-HOME to open the window, or CTRL-END to close it.

Format Functions

Table 31-2 lists the format functions you can use with PICTURE and FORMAT clauses. Functions control the overall appearance or acceptable entries of a variable or field. If you use a format function in a PICTURE clause, you must precede the clause with an @ symbol. If, on the other hand, you use a format function with a FUNCTION clause, you don't need

Picture Function	Effect on Display
!	Converts to uppercase letters entered in a field; has no effect on other characters
^	Displays numbers in exponential format (scientific notation)
$	Displays data in financial (currency) format
(	Puts () around negative numbers
A	Allows only letters to be entered in a field
B	Left-aligns a number
C	Displays CR (credit) after a positive number
I	Centers text and numbers within a field
J	Right-aligns text within a field
L	Displays leading zeros
M	Allows a multiple-choice list
R	Works with a template to display literal characters in a field, but to remove those characters when the field is stored to disk. For example, a phone number is displayed as (415)325-1234, but is stored as 4153251234
S<*n*>	Lets you scroll horizontally with long character fields. *N* is a number for the display width of the field and must be a literal positive integer
T	Trims leading and trailing blanks from a field
X	Displays DB (debit) after a negative number
Z	Displays a blank string for a zero numeric value

Table 31-2. Picture Functions

to include the @ symbol. If you include both a format function and a template in a PICTURE clause, you must separate them by a space.

Many format functions work only with specific data types:

- The ^, $, (, C, L, X, and Z functions work only with numeric data. What's more, you can only use (, C, and X to display data (in the SAY clause).
- The D and E functions work only with date data.
- The A, M, R, and S<*n*> functions work only with character data.

You can combine certain format functions. For example, you can use AI to accept only alphabetic characters and center text within a field.

The S<*n*> function lets you display and edit long character variables by scrolling horizontally within a specified number of columns (*n*). The value you supply for *n* must be a literal integer and be less than the total width of the character field or memory variable.

Note: When you use the S<*n*> function, do not put any spaces between the S and the integer. Also, do not include the angle brackets (<>).

The M function lets you create a multiple-choice list for the GET variable. Use the following syntax for the M function:

FUNCTION "M <*list of choices*>"

The *list of choices* can include only literal strings or numbers, which must be separated by commas. The first choice in the list only appears when you move the cursor to the GET variable position. To cycle through the available choices, press SPACEBAR. Press ENTER to select a choice and move to the next variable or field. You can also press the first character of a choice to select it.

Templates

Table 31-3 shows the templates you can use in a PICTURE clause. Templates let you control what the user can enter in a field or variable or how a field or variable is displayed on a character-by-character basis.

You can use the !, #, 9, A, N, and X template symbols for both input and output (SAYs and GETs). The 9, #, A, N, and X symbols prevent you from entering any undefined characters, but they have no effect on the characters you display.

Template Symbol	Effect on Entry or Display
!	Converts letters to uppercase; has no effect on other characters
#	Allows only digits, blanks, and signs
$	Displays the current SET CURRENCY string in place of leading zeros. The default SET CURRENCY string is $
*	Displays asterisks (*) in place of leading zeros
,	Displays commas in large numbers
.	Indicates the position of the decimal point
9	Allows digits only for character data. Allows digits and signs for numeric data
A	Data must be letters only
L	Data must be logical (for example, T, F, Y, or N)
N	Allows letters and digits
X	Data can be any character
Y	For a character or logical field, data must be logical Y, y, N, or n. Converts y and n to uppercase

Table 31-3. dBASE IV Template Symbols

You can use the R function with a template to have characters appear in a template but not be stored as part of the GET variable. If you don't use the R function, however, the characters are stored as part of the GET variable. (You can only use the R function with character type variables.) If you use non-template symbols with numeric fields, they are never stored as part of the field template. Do not use non-template symbols for date or logical variables or fields.

Suppose you want to use a PICTURE template to get a decimal number. In this case, you must include the decimal point as part of the template. The template must also have at least one position to the left of the decimal point and enough room for a sign (if you want the user to be able to enter a sign).

Tip: If you want to create a multi-screen format (.FMT) file, place a READ statement in the file wherever you want a new screen to appear. When you use the file, press PGUP and PGDN to navigate between the screens. Note that a multi-screen format file only works when you open the file using the SET FORMAT command.

To create a custom format file complete with all of the necessary @ commands, use the CREATE/MODIFY SCREEN command to access the Forms Design screen. To activate a format file, use the SET FORMAT TO command. You can then use any of the full-screen editing commands (for example, APPEND or EDIT) to add or edit records.

Examples

The following example uses an @ command to display values in the first record of the CUSTOMER database:

```
. USE Customer
. @ 1,10 SAY TRIM(Firstname)+" "+Lastname
```

The displayed output is

```
George Thomas
```

The next example shows how you can use the @ command to get user input via a multiple-choice list. You display a list of area codes from which to choose.

```
SET TALK OFF
CLEAR
Marea = "408"
Mphone = ""
@ 1,8 SAY "Enter area code: " GET Marea;
     PICTURE "@M 408,415,912,960"
@ 3,8 SAY "Enter phone number: " GET Mphone;
     PICTURE "999-9999"
READ
```

The next example uses a user-defined function as part of the VALID clause to perform data checking. It also uses a RANGE clause to verify that the entry you make is from 110 to 140.

```
CLEAR
SET TALK OFF
How_2_ship = 0
@ 10,10 SAY "Enter a shipping code: " GET How_2_ship PICTURE "999";
     VALID Chekship();
     RANGE 110,140
READ
RETURN

FUNCTION Chekship
DO CASE
     CASE How_2_ship = 110   && Ship prepaid
          RETURN .T.
     CASE How_2_ship = 120   && Ship FOB
          RETURN .T.
     CASE How_2_ship = 130   && Ship COD
          RETURN .T.
     CASE How_2_ship = 140   && Ship special handling
          RETURN .T.
ENDCASE
RETURN (.F.)
```

See also: ?/??, ACTIVATE WINDOW, APPEND, CHANGE, CREATE/MODIFY SCREEN, EDIT, INSERT, MODIFY COMMAND, SET COLOR, SET CONFIRM, SET CURRENCY, SET DELIMITERS, SET DEVICE, SET FIELDS, SET FORMAT, SET INTENSITY, SET POINT, SET SEPARATOR, SET WINDOW or MEMO, COL(), PCOL(), PROW(), READ, ROW(), and TRANSFORM().

@...CLEAR

@...CLEAR clears the screen or active window within a specified area.

Syntax

@ *<row1>*, *<col1>* [CLEAR [TO *<row2>*,*<col2>*]]

The *row1* and *col1* parameters are the coordinates of the upper-left corner of the area of the screen to be erased. The *row2* and *col2* parameters represent the coordinates of the lower-right corner.

Tip: When you specify coordinates with @...CLEAR (and other commands that require screen coordinates like @ and @...FILE), be aware that the coordinate system is *zero-based.* That is, the coordinates 0,0 represent the upper-left corner of the screen, and the coordinates 24,79 represent the lower-right corner on a standard 25-line by 80-column screen.

Notes

The @...CLEAR command erases the screen beginning at *row1, col1* and extending to *row2, col2.* If you do not include the phrase CLEAR TO <*row2*>, <*col2*>, dBASE IV begins at *row1, col1* and erases to the end of the line. If you do not include the TO <*row2*>, <*col2*> phrase, but do include the CLEAR keyword, dBASE IV begins at *row1, col1* and erases to the lower-right corner of the screen.

Example

The following example erases the area of the screen beginning at coordinates 3,5 column and extending to coordinates 15,70.

```
. @ 3,5 CLEAR TO 15,70
```

See also: CLEAR and @...FILL.

@...FILL

@...FILL lets you change the colors within a specified area of the screen or active window.

Syntax

@ <*row1*>, <*col1*> FILL TO <*row2*>,<*col2*> [COLOR <*color attribute*>]

The *row1* and *col1* parameters are the coordinates of the upper-left corner of the area of the screen whose color is to be changed. The *row2* and *col2* parameters represent the coordinates of the lower-right corner.

The *color attribute* is any one, or a combination, of the color codes you can use with SET COLOR. (See SET COLOR in Chapter 32.)

Notes

The @...FILL command lets you change only the standard foreground and background colors within the specified screen area. You can, for example, change the color of the text in the specified area.

@...FILL applies only to the material that is already on the screen. If you use an @...FILL command to change the color within a specified area, and then use another command to write the area, the new material appears in the default screen colors, not the colors you set with @...FILL.

If you do not include the COLOR *<color attribute>* phrase, @...FILL works just like @...CLEAR. That is, it clears the specified area of the screen.

Example

The following example places some arbitrary text on the screen by issuing the LIST STATUS command. It then uses the @...FILL command to change the screen colors to white text on a green background. The @...FILL command affects the area of the screen beginning at coordinates 0,0 (the upper-left corner) and extending to coordinates 20,20.

```
. LIST STATUS
. @ 0,0 TO 20,20 COLOR W/G
```

To change dBASE IV's colors for the duration of the current session, see the SET COLOR command. To change dBASE IV's default colors on a more permanent basis, see Chapter 35.

@...TO

@...TO draws a box (or line) on the screen or active window. You can specify a single-line (the default) or double-line border, or you can define your own border.

Syntax

@ *<row1>*, *<col1>* TO *<row2>*, *<col2>*
[DOUBLE/PANEL/*<border definition string>*]
[COLOR *<color attribute>*]

The *row1* and *col1* parameters are the coordinates of the upper-left corner of the box. The *row2* and *col2* parameters represent the coordinates of the lower-right corner.

If the row coordinates are the same, @...TO draws a horizontal line. If the column coordinates are the same, it draws a vertical line.

Notes

The default setting for the border is a single line. You can change the default setting with the SET BORDER command.

The default setting for the color is NORMAL. You can change the color setting with the SET COLOR command followed by the NORMAL keyword (for example, SET COLOR OF NORMAL TO W+/R).

By using the @...TO command options to define a border, you can override the SET BORDER default setting.

Options

The DOUBLE option lets you specify a double-line border.

The PANEL option lets you specify a solid reverse-video border.

By providing a *border definition string,* you can use a list of character strings (or numbers) to define a border. The character strings are referred to as *attributes,* and must have the following characteristics:

- They must be delimited (enclosed in quotes, for example).
- They must be separated by commas.
- They must be in the following order: top, bottom, left, right, top-left corner, top-right corner, bottom-left corner, bottom-right corner.

If you include the first attribute (top) in the border definition string but omit the others, the rest default to the same value.

If you omit an attribute from the list, it retains its previous value. To omit an attribute at the beginning of the list, use a comma for its place in the list. If the attribute falls at the end of the list, omit it by not including it in the list.

If you prefer to use numbers instead of character strings, use the decimal numbers from the IBM Extended Character Set. This is a superset (0 to 255) of the ASCII character set (0 to 127). You can also enter numbers with the CHR() function; enter a number as the argument to the function and do not enclose it in quotes (for example, CHR(189)).

When you use the COLOR option, you must include color codes for the *color attribute* parameter. You must provide color codes for the foreground, background, or both. See the SET COLOR command for a complete list of color codes. If you include the PANEL option, the box is drawn in the foreground color only. If you do not include color codes, the box is drawn with the NORMAL colors from the SET COLOR command.

Programming Considerations

As you might expect, you can use @...TO from the dot prompt, in a program, or in a format file.

To place a field wider than a box within that box, use the @ command with the S<*n*> function. This combination limits the size of the input field but allows horizontal scrolling within the input area for the field.

Example

The following example draws a magenta double-line box on the screen. The interior of the box appears in the default screen color.

```
. @ 2,15 TO 10,65 DOUBLE COLOR N/RB
```

See also: @, @...CLEAR, @...FILL, SET BORDER, SET COLOR, and CHR().

ACCEPT

Use ACCEPT to prompt a user for keyboard input. It creates a character memory variable in which to store the input. The user must press ENTER to complete the entry.

Syntax

ACCEPT [<*prompt string*>] TO <*character memory variable*>

The *prompt string* can be any valid character string—a character memory variable, a literal character string, or a valid character expression. Literal character strings must be delimited. That is, they must be enclosed in single quotes (' '), double quotes (" "), or square brackets ([ ]).

Notes

You use ACCEPT for character-type input. If you want to get numeric-type input from the user, use the INPUT command.

Since ACCEPT treats all user input as character-type input, the user does not need to enclose the input in quotes. (For the INPUT command to accept character-type data, it must be enclosed in quotes.) If the user enters numbers in response to the prompt, ACCEPT treats those numbers as characters.

If the user presses just ENTER in response to the prompt, dBASE IV stores a null string (" ") in the character memory variable.

The user can enter up to 254 characters in response to the ACCEPT prompt.

Tip: If the user presses ESC in response to the ACCEPT command, the program terminates unless SET ESCAPE is OFF. Because SET ESCAPE is normally ON, you must set it OFF if you do not want the user to terminate the program in this way.

Example

The following example prompts the user to enter a telephone number:

```
. ACCEPT "Enter your telephone number: " TO Mphone
Enter your telephone number:
```

ACCEPT stores the telephone number as character type data in the memory variable Mphone.

See also: @, INPUT, READ, SET ESCAPE, and WAIT.

ACTIVATE MENU

ACTIVATE MENU activates and displays an existing bar menu. The bar menu must have been previously defined with DEFINE MENU.

Syntax

ACTIVATE MENU <*menu name*> [PAD <*pad number*>]

Notes

ACTIVATE MENU displays a previously defined menu over existing material on the screen. By using the PAD *<pad number>* option with the ACTIVATE MENU command, you can specify which pad the highlight bar appears in when the menu is activated. If you do not include this option, the highlight bar automatically appears in the first pad.

When you use ACTIVATE MENU, the menu that you activate becomes the only active menu. You can use the LEFT and RIGHT ARROW keys to move back and forth between the menu pads. The menu pads appear in the menu in the order in which they were defined. You can deactivate a menu by activating another menu, pressing ESC, or using the DEACTIVATE MENU command.

When you activate a menu from another menu, the first menu is suspended until the second menu is deactivated. When a menu is deactivated, it is automatically removed from the screen.

Example

The following example activates a previously defined menu called **Main** and places the highlight bar in the pad called Sort. (The Sort pad must also have been previously defined using DEFINE PAD.)

```
. ACTIVATE MENU Main PAD Sort
```

For other examples of ACTIVATE MENU, see the DEACTIVATE MENU command in this chapter and the PAD() function in Chapter 33.

See also: DEACTIVATE MENU, DEFINE MENU, ON PAD, SHOW MENU, MENU(), and PAD().

ACTIVATE POPUP

ACTIVATE POPUP activates and displays an existing pop-up. The pop-up must have been previously defined with DEFINE POPUP.

Syntax

ACTIVATE POPUP *<pop-up name>*

Notes

ACTIVATE POPUP activates and displays a previously defined pop-up menu over existing material on the screen. Only one pop-up can be active at a time. You can deactivate a pop-up by activating another pop-up with ACTIVATE POPUP, pressing ESC, or using the DEACTIVATE POPUP command.

When you activate a pop-up menu from another pop-up menu, the first pop-up menu is suspended until the second pop-up menu is deactivated. When a pop-up menu is deactivated, it is automatically removed from the screen.

Example

The following command activates a previously defined pop-up called Pop_sort, which displays a pop-up menu of sort options:

```
. ACTIVATE POPUP Pop_sort
```

For an example of how to use ACTIVATE POPUP within some program code, see the BAR() function in Chapter 33.

ACTIVATE SCREEN

When you define a window and then activate it, dBASE IV directs all screen output to that window. To restore screen output to the entire display screen rather than the recently activated window, use the ACTIVATE SCREEN command.

Syntax

ACTIVATE SCREEN

Notes

ACTIVATE SCREEN sends output to the entire display screen rather than to a recently active screen. When you issue **ACTIVATE SCREEN**, you do not lose the previously active window's image or definition in memory.

You can use ACTIVATE SCREEN to restore output to the entire display screen while keeping the recently active window's image available in memory to reference or redisplay later. The window does not get updated, however. Also, as output appears in the full screen, it may overwrite any vestiges of the window or cause the window to scroll off the screen. To restore the window's image from memory to the screen, use the ACTIVATE WINDOW command.

You can use the ACTIVATE SCREEN command to temporarily leave an active window and place messages outside of it. Such a message might signal an error or provide some extra information to the user. After placing the text outside of the window, you can redirect screen output to the window with the ACTIVATE WINDOW command.

A window you activate with ACTIVATE WINDOW remains on the screen until you deactivate it. If you later reactivate the window, it will overwrite any material from the full screen that's in its way.

Example

The following example defines and activates a window called Small_win. It then uses MODIFY COMMAND to activate the dBASE IV full-screen Text Editor, which appears within the confines of the Small_win window. The ACTIVATE SCREEN command then restores the entire screen for output, rather than the previously active Small_win window.

```
. DEFINE WINDOW Small_win FROM 1,1 TO 10,79
. ACTIVATE WINDOW Small_win
. MODIFY COMMAND       && Start the text editor
. ACTIVATE SCREEN
```

To redirect screen output to Small_win, use the ACTIVATE WINDOW command a second time.

ACTIVATE WINDOW

ACTIVATE WINDOW activates and displays a predefined window, to which it directs all screen output.

Syntax

ACTIVATE WINDOW *<window name list>* / ALL

If you include more that one window name in the *window name list*, ACTIVATE WINDOW places each window on the screen, beginning with the first one in the list. Because only one window can be active at a time, the window that is active when the command finishes executing is the last window in the list.

Notes

ACTIVATE WINDOW displays a defined window's image on the screen. To use this command, you must have defined at least one window with the DEFINE WINDOW command.

If you use the ALL option, all windows in memory are displayed on the screen in the order in which they were defined.

Example

See the previous command, ACTIVATE SCREEN, for an example.

See also: CLEAR WINDOW, DEACTIVATE WINDOW, DEFINE WINDOW, MOVE WINDOW, RESTORE WINDOW, SAVE WINDOW, and SET BORDER.

APPEND

The APPEND command lets you add a new record to the end of the active database.

Syntax

```
APPEND [BLANK]
```

Notes

APPEND is a full-screen command. That is, it uses a display form that occupies the entire screen.

If you've previously specified a display form, APPEND uses that form. Otherwise, it uses a default display form. In either case, APPEND shows only one record at a time.

You can exit the APPEND command by pressing ENTER or ESC immediately after a new blank record is displayed in the form. You can also press CTRL-END. However, if you press CTRL-END after a new record is displayed, a blank record is added to the end of the file.

The PGUP and PGDN keys move you backwards and forwards through the records in the database, letting you edit the records as you go. The records appear in natural order, not in indexed order.

To access the APPEND screen's menu bar, press F10.

If you've located the cursor on a memo field and you want to add some text to the memo, press CTRL-HOME. dBASE IV displays the text for the memo field in the Text Editor. (If you prefer to use your own text editor, you must modify the CONFIG.DB file. See Chapter 35.) To leave the Text Editor, press CTRL-END.

APPEND adds records to the end of a single database file only. To add records to the end of more than one database at a time, follow these steps:

1. Create a format file that uses @...GET commands that reference fields from several related database files.
2. Use APPEND BLANK with each of the related files to add a blank record to the end of each file.
3. Use a READ command with the format file you've created to add information to the records at the end of each file.

APPEND BLANK adds a blank record to the end of a database file, but it does not use the display form to enter full-screen mode. The newly appended record becomes the current record.

As you append records to a file, all active indexes (.MDX tags) are updated.

Tip: If SET AUTOSAVE is OFF (the default), the database file on disk may not reflect all the newly appended records until you close the file. If SET AUTOSAVE is ON, each newly appended record is immediately saved to disk.

Example

The following example opens the CUSTOMER database file and enters full-screen mode, enabling you to add records to the end of the file:

```
. USE Customer
. APPEND
```

The next example appends one blank record to the end of the CUSTOMER database file but does not enter full-screen mode.

```
. USE Customer
. APPEND BLANK
```

See also: BROWSE, EDIT, SET AUTOSAVE, and SET CARRY.

APPEND FROM

APPEND FROM lets you copy records from a source file to the end of the active database file. The source file can be a dBASE IV file or any one of a number of other file types.

Syntax

APPEND FROM *<filename>* / ? [[TYPE] *<file type>*]
[FOR *<condition>*]

If the source file your are appending from does not reside on the default drive, *filename* must include a drive designator. Likewise, if the source file does not reside on any directory in the search path, *filename* must include a directory designator. (You can set the default drive with SET DEFAULT and the search path with SET PATH.)

If you do not include a file extension for *filename,* dBASE IV assumes a .DBF extension.

Table 31-4 shows the different options available for *file type.*

If you include a TYPE *<file type>* phrase but omit the file extension, dBASE IV assumes that the file has the default file extension supplied by the software package. For example, if you use TYPE WKS, dBASE IV assumes a .WKS extension.

If you specify SDF or DELIMITED as the *file type* but omit the file extension, dBASE IV assumes a .TXT extension.

If the source file you're appending from does not have an extension, you should include a period after the file name to prevent dBASE IV from assuming a particular extension.

<file type> **Options**	**Description**
DBASEII	A dBASE II database file.
DELIMITED	An ASCII text file in a delimited format. Data is appended character-by-character starting on the left. A carriage return line feed (CR/LF) must end each record. Commas separate each field. Double quotation marks (") surround character data
DELIMITED WITH BLANK	ASCII text file containing fields separated by one space. Commas are not used to separate the fields. Records end with CR/LF
DELIMITED WITH *<delimiter>*	ASCII text file containing fields separated by commas with character data surrounded by the specified delimiter
DIF	The VisiCalc file format. Rows convert to records and columns convert to fields
FW2	Framework II database or spreadsheet frame
RPD	RapidFile file
SDF	System Data Format ASCII file. A fixed-length file for which data gets appended character-by-character starting from the left. Each record in the source file is the same length. A carriage return line feed (CR/LF) ends each record. Individual fields are not delimited
SYLK	MultiPlan spreadsheet format in row major order. Rows convert to records and columns convert to fields. A SYLK file saved in column major order will not work with dBASE IV
WKS	Lotus 1-2-3 version 1A file format. Rows convert to records and columns convert to fields. The data in the file must begin in cell A1

Table 31-4. APPEND FROM Foreign File Types

Notes

If the source file you are appending from is a dBASE IV file, you should be aware of the following rules:

- If SET DELETED is OFF, records marked for deletion are appended and are not marked for deletion in the active database file. If SET DELETED is ON, only those records not marked for deletion are appended.
- Only those fields with matching field names are appended. The fields do not have to be in any special order.
- You should not specify a file type in the case of dBASE IV files.

If a field in the source file you are appending from is longer than the same field in the active database file, dBASE IV truncates the values to fit. Likewise, if numeric data is larger than the receiving field, the numeric values are replaced by asterisks.

If the active database file has an open index file, the index is automatically updated for the appended data.

If the source file you're appending from is a spreadsheet file, blank rows in the spreadsheet get converted to blank records in the database file. Make sure that the columns in the spreadsheet file match the order and data type of the active database's file structure. What's more, you should remove all column headings from the spreadsheet file.

If the source file you're appending is a Lotus 1-2-3 worksheet file, start your data in cell A1 of the worksheet. Otherwise, blank rows will result in blank database records, and blank columns may mean that the data is appended to the wrong database fields.

Tip: If you want to use a PFS:FILE file or a Lotus 1-2-3 Release 2 or 2.01 file, you should use the IMPORT command rather than APPEND FROM. The IMPORT command specifically handles these file formats, while the APPEND FROM command does not.

If the source file you're appending from is an ASCII text file, date fields must be in the form *yyyymmdd,* not delimited (where *yyyy* is the year, *mm* is the month, and *dd* is the day). Otherwise, dBASE IV will not recognize them.

Example

The following example appends a Lotus 1-2-3 Release 1A file named SALES.WKS to the CUSTOMER database:

```
. USE Customer
. APPEND FROM Sales TYPE WKS
```

See also: COPY, IMPORT, and SET DELETED.

APPEND FROM ARRAY

APPEND FROM ARRAY adds records to a database file from the contents of an array.

Syntax

APPEND FROM ARRAY *<array name>* [FOR *<condition>*]

The optional FOR *<condition>* gets evaluated *before* each row is added to the database. Note that the *condition* must include a database field name. If the *condition* evaluates to true (.T.), a row is appended to the database. If the *condition* evaluates to false (.F.), the row is skipped.

Notes

In dBASE IV, arrays are defined in *row, column* format. You must declare the array (with DECLARE) and store information to the array (with STORE) before you can append from it.

One row in the array corresponds to one record in the database. The contents of an array are added to the active database as follows:

- For each row in the array, the data in the first column is appended to the first field, the data in the second column is appended to the second field, and so on.
- Appending takes place until there are no more rows in the array or no more columns in the database.
- If the database has more fields than the array has columns, the excess fields are left empty. If the array has more columns than the database has fields, the excess columns are disregarded.

The data type for each column in the array must match the data type for its target field in the database.

Example

The following example declares and then stores information in a simple two-dimensional array called Sal_array. (Sal_array has one row and eight columns.) After a row's worth of data is stored to the array, the APPEND FROM command adds the contents of the array to the end of the SALARY database.

```
. DECLARE Sal_array[1,8]
. Sal_array[1,1] = "Jeremy"          &&Firstname
Jeremy
. Sal_array[1,2] = "Gibson"          &&Lastname
Gibson
. Sal_array[1,3] = .T.               &&Bonus
.T.
. Sal_array[1,4] = 25000             &&Gross
     25000
. Sal_array[1,5] = 25000 * .25       &&Fed
      6250
. Sal_array[1,6] = 25000 * .0751     &&Fica
      1877.50
. Sal_array[1,7] = 25000 * .035      &&State
       875
. Sal_array[1,8] = 25000 * (1 -  .25 - .0751 - .035)   &&Net
     15997.50
. USE Salary
. APPEND FROM ARRAY Sal_array
      1 record added
```

See also: APPEND, COPY TO ARRAY, DECLARE, and STORE.

APPEND MEMO

APPEND MEMO copies a specified text file to the end of a named memo field.

Syntax

APPEND MEMO <*memo field name*> FROM <*filename*>
[OVERWRITE]

If you do not include a file extension for *filename,* dBASE IV assumes a file extension of .TXT.

If you use the optional OVERWRITE keyword, APPEND MEMO erases the contents of the memo field before copying the contents of the text file to it.

Notes

APPEND MEMO reads the contents of an ASCII text file and adds those contents to the end of a specified memo field. In the case of an error, dBASE IV returns one of the following messages:

"Field not found"	If dBASE IV cannot find the named field
"Field must be a memo field"	If you try to copy the contents of the named file to a non-memo field
"File does not exist"	If dBASE IV cannot find the named file

Examples

The following example uses the dBASE IV Text Editor to build a text file on disk.

```
. MODIFY FILE Appendit.txt
```

Suppose you enter the string "Make sure to send 3 new brochures in our next mailing." to the APPENDIT.TXT file. You get the following results when you activate the ORDERREC database and add the contents of the text file to the Mssg memo field in the first record of the database:

```
. USE Orderrec
. ? Mssg
This is the fifth rush order from Texasville Pumps
this month!
. APPEND MEMO Mssg FROM Appendit
. ? Mssg
This is the fifth rush order from Texasville Pumps
this month!
Make sure to send 3 new brochures in our next
mailing.
```

ASSIST

ASSIST activates the dBASE IV Control Center.

Syntax

ASSIST

Notes

If you use the ASSIST command to activate the Control Center, you can access the extensive menu system in dBASE IV.

Whenever you activate the Control Center, it opens a catalog. The catalog it chooses is the one you most recently opened. If it cannot find a catalog, it creates a new one called UNTITLED.CAT. See Chapter 13 for a complete discussion of catalogs.

You can leave the Control Center and return to the dBASE dot prompt by

- Pressing ESC.
- Selecting the **Exit to dot prompt** option from the **Exit** menu. (To access the **Exit** menu, press ALT-E.)

See Part One of this book for a complete description of all of the different aspects of the Control Center.

AVERAGE

AVERAGE lets you determine the arithmetic mean for a list of numeric expressions.

Syntax

AVERAGE [<*type N expression list*>] [<*scope*>] [FOR <*condition*>] [WHILE <*condition*>] [TO <*memory variable list*> / TO ARRAY <*array name*>]

Notes

If you use the AVERAGE command without any options, it averages all of the numeric fields in the active database. If you include a *type N expression* list, it averages only those numeric fields in the expression list. You can further limit the fields that are averaged by including a FOR or WHILE clause.

If you use the TO ARRAY phrase, dBASE IV stores the results of the AVERAGE command in an array. The array you provide must be one-dimensional. dBASE averages the first field in the numeric expression list and places the result in the first column of the array. It places the second result in the second column, and so on. If there are more results than there are columns in the array, the extra results are lost. If there are fewer results than columns in the array, the extra columns are ignored.

Example

The following example computes the averages of all numeric fields in the SALARY database:

```
. USE Salary
. AVERAGE
       GROSS            FED           FICA          STATE          NET
    27454.55        6863.64        2061.84         823.64     17705.44
```

BEGIN/END TRANSACTION

You use the BEGIN and END TRANSACTION commands in transaction processing. A *transaction* is an application-specific sequence of commands that change records in a database file. It is bounded by a BEGIN TRANSACTION command and an END TRANSACTION or ROLLBACK command. END TRANSACTION is used for successful termination and ROLLBACK is used in the case of unsuccessful termination.

Syntax

BEGIN TRANSACTION [<*path name*>]
*
<*transaction commands*>
*
END TRANSACTION

Notes

See "Transaction Processing" in Chapter 29 for more information.

See the COMPLETED() function in Chapter 33 for a transaction processing example. Also, Chapter 30, "Networking Commands and Functions," gives an example of the BEGIN and END TRANSACTION commands in a network environment.

For other commands and functions related to transaction processing, see RESET, ROLLBACK, CHANGE(), ISMARKED(), LKSYS(), and ROLLBACK().

BROWSE

BROWSE is a menu-driven command for editing and appending records to database files and views.

Syntax

BROWSE [NOINIT] [NOFOLLOW] [NOAPPEND] [NOMENU]
[NOEDIT] [NODELETE] [NOCLEAR] [COMPRESS]
[FORMAT] [LOCK <*type N expression*>]
[WIDTH <*type N expression*>] [FREEZE <*field name*>]
[WINDOW <*window name*>]
[FIELDS <*field name 1*> [/R] [/<*column width*>]
/ <*calculated field name 1*> = <*expression 1*>
[, <*field name 2*> [/R] [/<*column width*>]
/ <*calculated field name 2*> = <*expression 2*>..]

If you enter BROWSE without any options and a database file is not in use (that is, you didn't enter a USE command), dBASE IV prompts you for a database file name.

Notes

BROWSE is a full-screen command. That is, it uses a display form that occupies the entire screen. If you activate the BROWSE command from the dot prompt, you return to the dot prompt when you exit BROWSE. If you activate BROWSE from a program, you return to the statement immediately following the BROWSE command.

BROWSE displays records from a database file or view in a tabular format. All of the fields are listed in the order that appears in the database structure. (You can change the order that appears in the table by using the FIELD option discussed later.)

Tip: You can change from BROWSE to EDIT by pressing F2.

While in browse mode, you can edit all of the fields in the database except calculated fields and read-only fields. (You can have BROWSE display calculated fields and read-only fields by using the FIELDS option discussed later.) All editable fields appear in reverse video. If you make changes to a field that affects a calculated field, BROWSE redisplays the calculated field immediately.

If an index file is active and you edit a value in the index field, the record is immediately repositioned in the database according to the new value of the index field. The record you edit remains the current record. (Use the NOFOLLOW keyword, discussed later, if you don't want the edited record to remain the current record.)

While in browse mode, you can add records to a file or view. To do so, move the cursor to the last field in the last record and press DOWN ARROW. When dBASE IV asks you whether you want to add records, press Y for yes. dBASE IV immediately shifts to append mode, and you can add a record to the file.

To activate the menu bar in browse mode, press F10. Chapter 4, "Entering, Editing, and Displaying Data," describes the various BROWSE menu options and the special keys available in browse mode.

Tip: If SET AUTOSAVE is OFF (the default), the database file on disk may not reflect all the newly added records until you close the file. If SET AUTOSAVE is ON, each newly appended record is immediately saved to disk.

Options

NOINIT lets you use the same command line options you used from a previous BROWSE command. It tells the BROWSE command to use the table from the previous BROWSE without starting anew.

NOFOLLOW is for indexed files only. Normally, when you edit the value in a key field, dBASE IV repositions the record according to the index value and still keeps it the current record. If you use the NOFOLLOW keyword and you change the index field contents, the record is repositioned. The new record that occupies the original record's position in the index becomes the current record.

NOAPPEND prevents you from entering new records to the end of the database file while in browse mode.

NOMENU prevents the BROWSE menu from appearing.

NOEDIT makes all fields in the database read-only. You can display the records in the database, but you cannot edit them. You can, however, add records to the end of the database file. You can also mark records for deletion by pressing CTRL-U.

NODELETE prevents you from marking records for deletion by pressing CTRL-U while in browse mode.

NOCLEAR keeps the BROWSE table on the screen after you exit browse mode.

COMPRESS reduces the size of the BROWSE table, allowing you to see more records on the screen. BROWSE normally displays 17 records on a standard 25-line screen. If you use the COMPRESS option, BROWSE displays 19 records on standard screen.

FORMAT tells BROWSE to use all of the @...GET commands in the active format (.FMT) file. However, because BROWSE always displays records in a tabular format, all the @ row and column options in the format file are ignored.

LOCK *<type N expression>* lets you control the number of adjacent fields that remain together in the same position on the screen when you scroll the BROWSE table to the left or right. (You scroll the BROWSE table to the left by using F3 and to the right by using F4.) To reset locked fields and allow normal scrolling, enter **LOCK 0**.

WIDTH *<type N expression>* lets you set an upper limit for the column widths that are displayed in the BROWSE table. Normally, the widths conform to the database file structure. WIDTH lets you override the file structure width. If you provide both a WIDTH and a *column width*, the smallest one is used.

Because logical and memo fields have a fixed width, WIDTH has no effect on these field types. Numeric and date fields do not display if the WIDTH you provide for them is narrower than the width you define in the database file structure.

FREEZE *<field name>* lets you confine editing to one field (column) in the database. Other fields are displayed on the screen if they fit, but you cannot edit them. If you use FREEZE without a *field name*, you can reset a previous FREEZE command.

WINDOW *<window name>* lets you use a predefined window to display the BROWSE table in. The BROWSE table appears within the border of the window, and the rest of the screen remains untouched. When you leave browse mode, the window is automatically deactivated and removed from the screen. (You can have the window remain on the screen by using the NOCLEAR keyword discussed previously.) If a window is already active when you enter the BROWSE command, BROWSE uses that window.

FIELDS lets you control which fields appear in the BROWSE table and the order in which they appear. By using the different options available with FIELDS, you can create calculated fields and have fields display as read-only.

To create a calculated field, you assign a field name to an expression. The result of the expression becomes the value for the calculated field. For example, you can create a calculated field for the SALARY database with

Netpay = Gross - Fed - Fica - State

The field name you assign becomes the column header in the BROWSE table. By evaluating the expression in the first record, dBASE IV automatically determines the column width for the calculated field in the BROWSE table.

With the /R option, you can make a field read-only. The field appears in the BROWSE table, but you cannot edit it. Calculated fields do not need the /R option because they are read-only by default.

The optional /<*column width*> lets you define the column width for a field in the BROWSE table. The *column width* is a literal numeric value (for example, 4, 10), and you can use a *column width* value for each field in the FIELDS list. Note that the slash (/) is mandatory.

The *column width* can be between 4 and 100 for character fields and between 8 and 100 for numeric and date fields. Because logical and memo fields have a fixed width, the *column width* option has no effect on these field types. If you provide both a WIDTH and a *column width* option, dBASE IV takes the smaller value of the two. It also ignores the <column width> option for date and numeric fields when the width you provide is less than the width in the database file structure.

Example

The following example filters the ORDERREC database for only those orders that occurred in November. Next, it uses BROWSE to display certain fields in the ORDERREC database. The last field in the list, Gross, is a calculated field. It calculates the gross revenue from a sale with the equation Gross = Units * Price.

```
USE Orderrec
SET FILTER TO MONTH(Order_date) = 11  && Look at November only
BROWSE FIELDS Order_no, Order_date, Units, Price, Gross = Units *  Price
```

See also: APPEND and EDIT.

For more information on using BROWSE with PROTECT, see Chapter 30, "Networking Commands and Functions."

CALCULATE

CALCULATE lets you use certain financial and statistical functions to compute results for the current database.

Syntax

CALCULATE [*scope*] <*option list*>
[FOR <*condition*>] [WHILE <*condition*>]
[TO <*memory variable list*> / TO ARRAY <*array name*>]

The *option list* can include any one of the following *aggregate* functions:

AVG(<*type N expression*>)

CNT()

MAX(<*expression*>)

MIN(<*expression*>)

NPV(<*discount rate*>, <*cash flows*> [,<*initial investment*>])

STD(<*type N expression*>)

SUM(<*type N expression*>)

VAR(<*type N expression*>)

Notes

CALCULATE uses the specified function to return results for the current database. You can limit the records that are involved in the calculation by including a *scope*. You can further limit the records involved by using the optional FOR and WHILE clauses. CALCULATE returns one or more type N numbers.

If you include the optional FOR clause, dBASE IV evaluates the *condition* for each record. If the *condition* is true (.T.), the specified functions are carried out.

If you include the optional TO *<memory variable list>* clause, you can store the results of the CALCULATE command to memory variables. Alternately, if you include the optional TO ARRAY clause, you can store the results of the CALCULATE command in a predefined array. The array must be one-dimensional. The array elements are assigned results beginning with the first element and continuing in order.

If SET HEADING is ON (the default), the results are displayed on the sceen and show the function and field name. Of course, SET TALK must be ON in order for the results to appear on the screen.

Options

AVG(*<type N expression>*) returns the arithmetic mean of the values in a specified database field. For example, to compute the mean for a numeric field called Sales, you would use AVG(Sales).

CNT() lets you determine the number of records in the database file. The FOR condition lets you restrict the records involved in the count. If the *condition* is true (.T.), the record is included in the count.

MAX(*<expression>*) determines the largest number value in a specified database field. The *expression* you provide can be a numeric, date, or character expression and normally returns the name of a field.

MIN(*<expression>*) determines the smallest number value in a specified database field. As with MAX(), the *expression* you provide can be a numeric, date, or character expression and normally returns the name of a field.

NPV(*<discount rate>*, *<cash flows>* [,*<initial investment>*]) lets you calculate the *net present value* of a series of cash flows. The *cash flows* are the values in a specified database field. The NPV() function evaluates the flows by adjusting them back to their present value equivalents. This process is referred to as "discounting to the present value."

The *discount rate* is a decimal number representing the interest rate used to discount the flows back to the present. When you use the NPV() function, the period of the *discount rate* (usually annual) must agree with those of the *cash flows*.

Cash flows is a series of periodic cash flows that are equally spaced in time. *Cash flows* can be any valid numeric, date, or character expression, but is normally the name of a field.

The optional *initial investment* is a numeric expression that represents the initial outlay to produce the cash flows. For example, it may be the cost of a piece of capital equipment. Because the initial investment is a cash outlay, it should be a negative number.

STD(<*type N expression*>) calculates the *standard deviation* of the values contained in a database field. Standard deviation measures the degree to which each individual score in a sample varies from the mean of the scores in the sample.

SUM(<*type N expression*>) calculates the sum of the values in a given database field. The *type N expression* is a numeric expression that is normally the name of a field or an expression involving the name of a field. dBASE IV evaluates the FOR <*condition*> for each record, and if the *condition* is true (.T.), it adds the value of the given field to the accumulated total.

VAR(<*type N expression*>) determines the population variance in the given database field. The *type N expression* is a numeric expression that is normally the name of a field or an expression involving the name of a field.

Example

The following example calculates the total bonus amount for employees in the SALARY database:

```
. USE Salary
. CALCULATE FOR Bonus SUM(Gross*.10) CNT() TO Mbonus, Memploys
SUM(Gross*.10)       CNT()
        20500            7
. ? "The total bonus amount is $"+LTRIM(STR(Mbonus,8,2))+ " for  "
        +LTRIM(STR(Memploys,2))+" employees."
The total bonus amount is $20500.00 for 7 employees.
```

CALL

You use the CALL command in conjunction with the LOAD command to execute binary (.BIN) program files that have been loaded into memory.

Syntax

CALL <*module name*> [WITH <*expression list*>]

The *expression list* is list of up to seven expressions. These can be character expressions, field names, memory variables, or array elements of any data type.

Notes

Binary program modules are programs written in assembly or C language and compiled to form executable subroutines. Files that contain binary program modules almost always have a .BIN extension.

Before you can execute a binary program module by using CALL, you must first load it into memory with the LOAD command. Once a module is loaded, you can execute it from memory without reloading it from disk. You can have up to 16 binary program modules loaded at once. Each module can be up to 32K.

The binary program module takes the list you pass to it with the WITH *<expression list>* clause and then modifies the contents of the list if it needs to return something to dBASE IV.

Before you can pass a memory variable to a binary program module, you must first define it. Likewise, if you want to pass an array element, you must first declare the array (see the DECLARE command).

Example

See the LOAD command for an example.

See also: CALL(), LOAD, and RUN/!.

CANCEL

CANCEL stops a command file program from executing, closes all open command files, and returns to the dot prompt. It does not close procedure files.

Syntax

```
CANCEL
```

Notes

For more information on procedure files, see SET PROCEDURE in the next chapter.

Example

When an error occurs in a program and you want to stop the program, you can place the CANCEL command in a strategic location within the program. This command is most often placed in an IF...ENDIF or DO CASE...ENDCASE statement. For example, the following program segment cancels program execution when an error occurs. The Errflag memory variable must be set elsewhere in the program before the following segment is executed.

```
IF Errflag
     CANCEL
ENDIF
```

See also: CLOSE, RETURN, RETRY, RESUME, SET REPROCESS, and SUSPEND.

CHANGE

CHANGE is exactly like the EDIT command. It is a full-screen command that you can use to display and edit records in the active database file (or view).

Syntax

CHANGE [NOINIT] [NOFOLLOW] [NOAPPEND] [NOMENU]
[NOEDIT] [NODELETE] [NOCLEAR]
[<*record number*>] [FIELDS <*field list*>]
[<*scope*>] [FOR <*condition*>] [WHILE <*condition*>]

Notes

See the EDIT command for more on the CHANGE command.

CLEAR

CLEAR erases the screen and places the cursor at the lower-left corner of the screen. It also clears all pending GETs that you've created with the @ command. You can also use CLEAR to

- Close databases
- Release memory variables, menus, pop-ups, windows, and field lists
- Clear the type-ahead buffer of any characters

Syntax

CLEAR [ALL/FIELDS/GETS/MEMORY/MENUS/POPUPS/TYPEAHEAD/WINDOWS]

Notes

You can use the CLEAR command alone or with *one* option only.

Options

ALL closes almost everything in dBASE IV memory (except system memory variables) and selects work area 1. It closes all open database files, including their associated index files (.MDX and .NDX), format files (.FMT), and memo files (.DBT). It also releases all memory variables, array elements, and menu and pop-up definitions. What's more, if a catalog file (.CAT) is active, ALL closes it too.

FIELDS releases the field list that you've created with a SET FIELDS command.

GETS releases all GETs that you've created with the @ command. It releases only those GETs issued since the last READ, CLEAR GETS, or CLEAR ALL command. CLEAR GETS does not release memory variables or array elements.

MEMORY releases all memory variables, except system memory variables. It also releases all array elements. From the dot prompt, the CLEAR MEMORY command is identical to the RELEASE ALL command. However, these commands are different in programs. In programs, CLEAR MEMORY releases all PUBLIC and PRIVATE memory variables and array elements. RELEASE ALL, on the other hand, releases only PRIVATE memory variables and array elements. (PRIVATE memory variables and array elements are those established in the currently executing program.)

MENUS clears all menus from the screen. It also clears all menu definitions from memory.

POPUPS clears all pop-up menus from the screen. It also clears from memory and deactivates all pop-up menu definitions.

TYPEAHEAD erases the contents (keystrokes) of the type-ahead buffer. Use CLEAR TYPEAHEAD to clear the type-ahead buffer before you use an EDIT, READ, or WAIT command. This command checks that the type-ahead buffer does not contain any previously entered, unwanted characters.

WINDOWS clears all windows from the screen. It also clears all window definitions from memory. By saving your windows to disk before issuing a CLEAR WINDOWS command, you can restore them to memory with the RESTORE WINDOWS command when you need them. (See the SAVE WINDOW command for more on saving window definitions to disk.)

Examples

The following command clears the screen and places the cursor at the lower-left corner. It also clears all pending GETs.

```
. CLEAR
```

The next example releases all memory variables (except system memory variables) and array elements.

```
. CLEAR MEMORY
```

See also: @, @...FILL, @...TO, CLOSE, READ, RELEASE, SET FIELDS, SET FORMAT, and SET TYPEAHEAD.

CLOSE

CLOSE lets you close database files, format files, index files (both .MDX and .NDX), procedure files, and alternate files (text files you've created with SET ALTERNATE TO).

Syntax

CLOSE ALL/ALTERNATE/DATABASES/FORMAT/INDEX
/PROCEDURE

Notes

The CLOSE ALL command is the most comprehensive form of the CLOSE command. It closes *all* files of *all* types and selects work area 1.

CLOSE DATABASES closes all databases and associated index files (both .MDX and .NDX), memo files (.DBT), and format files (.FMT).

Tip: To close only the current database, use the USE command (without any options) instead of the CLOSE command.

Examples

The following command closes all open files:

```
. CLOSE ALL
```

To close all databases and associated index and format files, type

```
. CLOSE DATABASES
```

COMPILE

COMPILE takes a dBASE IV source-code file and creates an executable (object-code) file from it.

Syntax

COMPILE <*filename*> [RUNTIME]

If you include the optional RUNTIME, you can have dBASE IV print errors that arise from commands that aren't allowed during RunTime. (*RunTime* is a special version of dBASE IV that comes with the Developer's Edition. It is functionally equivalent to dBASE IV, but you can distribute it freely with your programs. RunTime is not offered in the Standard Edition of dBASE IV.)

Defaults

COMPILE reads a file with a .PRG extension, unless you specify some other extension in the command line. It always writes a file with a .DBO extension.

COMPILE reads source-code files only. dBASE IV source-code files have one of the following extensions: .PRG (program), .PRS (SQL), .FMT (format), .FRG (generated report), .LBG (generated label), .QBE (query), and .UPD (update query).

When you issue the COMPILE command, dBASE IV looks for the source file in the current drive and directory. If it cannot find it, dBASE looks for the file in the path you set using the SET PATH command. If the file is not located in either of these places, you need to include a drive designator and/or a path name as part of the file name.

Notes

COMPILE reads a source-code file and creates an executable program file in object-code form. Earlier versions of dBASE do not create object-code files, nor do they read them. Because dBASE IV compiles programs, it runs much faster than earlier versions.

Normally, you create a source-code file and then use the DO command to execute it. dBASE IV automatically compiles the program into object-code form and executes it (if no errors occurred). If you want to make a change to the program, rather than modifying the object code file, you change and reexecute the source-code file.

When you compile your programs, dBASE IV checks the syntax and order of commands. It issues error messages when you've made mistakes.

Use the COMPILE command when you want to compile a program but do not want to immediately execute it. For example, the file may contain a group of procedures that are called by other programs. It doesn't make sense to compile the file and immediately execute it with the DO command. Because the file is only executed when called from another program, you want to use the COMPILE command to compile it first.

IF SET DEVELOPMENT is ON (the default), and you issue a DO command, dBASE IV compares the time and date of the .PRG file with the time and date of its associated .DBO file. If the .PRG file is newer than the .DBO file, dBASE IV deletes the old .DBO file, compiles the .PRG file, and executes the new .DBO file.

If you use MODIFY COMMAND to access the dBASE IV Text Editor, it deletes the old .DBO file when you modify the associated .PRG file. If you use an external editor in place of MODIFY COMMAND, dBASE

IV automatically deletes the old .DBO file when you modify a .PRG file, as long as you place the name of the external editor in the CONFIG.DB file.

If you use an external editor to modify your programs, and SET DEVELOPMENT is OFF, you must either erase the old .DBO files manually or use the COMPILE command to compile your source-code files. Otherwise, if you try to use the DO command, dBASE IV will simply run your old .DBO file.

See also: DEBUG, DO, MODIFY COMMAND, SET DEBUG, SET DEVELOPMENT, SET PATH, and SET TRAP.

CONTINUE

CONTINUE picks up where the last LOCATE command left off. That is, it locates the next record in the active database file that meets the condition defined in the last LOCATE command.

Syntax

```
CONTINUE
```

Notes

When you issue a LOCATE command to find a record in the active database file that meets a specific condition, dBASE IV positions the record pointer at any such records. To continue the search, use the CONTINUE command. CONTINUE stops searching when it finds a record that meets the LOCATE condition, reaches the end of the LOCATE <*scope*>, or reaches the end of the file.

The LOCATE and CONTINUE commands operate in the current work area.

Example

As the following example indicates, dBASE IV displays the record number when CONTINUE successfully locates a record. dBASE IV returns the message "End of LOCATE scope" when CONTINUE cannot find a record that meets the LOCATE condition.

```
. USE Customer
. LOCATE FOR LASTNAME = "Borros"
Record =        14
. CONTINUE
Record =        31
. CONTINUE
End of LOCATE scope
. ? EOF()
.T.
```

See also: FIND, LOCATE, SEEK, EOF(), FOUND(), and SEEK().

CONVERT

CONVERT adds a field called _dbaselock to the structure of the currently selected database file. This field is required for multi-user lock detection. For more information on CONVERT, see Chapter 30, "Networking Commands and Functions."

COPY

COPY copies all or part of the current database file to a new database file. You can also use COPY to export data to non-dBASE programs.

Syntax

COPY TO <*filename*>
[[TYPE] <*file type*>] [FIELDS <*field list*>]
[<*scope*>] [FOR <*condition*>] [WHILE <*condition*>]

Notes

When you use COPY TO <*filename*> without any options, dBASE IV duplicates *all* records, even those marked for deletion, unless SET DELETED is ON. You can further limit the records that are copied by using a FOR or WHILE clause.

COPY duplicates all fields in the new file, unless you use a FIELDS clause to limit the fields. (You can also limit the fields with a SET FIELDS command.) Memo fields are copied only when the new file is a dBASE IV file.

You can specify the optional TYPE <*file type*> clause to export dBASE IV data to another software program's file format. Table 31-5 shows the different options available for the file type. When you use COPY to create a spreadsheet file in one of the three supported formats (WKS, SLYK, and DIF), dBASE IV places the database field names at the top of the columns that contain the data for those fields. With MultiPlan files, the spreadsheet file is created in row major order.

If you do not specify a file type, the file is copied to a dBASE IV database (.DBF) file. The COPY command also automatically copies memo (.DBT) files when the new file is a dBASE IV database file.

Tips

When dBASE IV files contain memo fields, they are not compatible with dBASE III PLUS unless you use the COPY command with the TYPE DBMEMO3 option.

Use the EXPORT command, instead of the COPY command, to convert files to PFS:FILE format.

dBASE IV reserves the letters "A" through "J" and "M" for default alias names. Do not use these letters as database file names when you us the COPY TO command.

Example

The following example copies to a new file all records in the ORDERREC database with an order date of November 15, 1988. The new dBASE IV file that is created is NOV_15.DBF.

```
. USE Orderrec
. COPY TO Nov_15 FOR Order_date = {11/15/88}
     2 records copied
. USE Nov_15
. LIST Cust_no, Order_no, Order_date, Total
Record#  Cust_no Order_no Order_date     Total
      1     1002      102 11/15/88       27.95
      2     1003      103 11/15/88       26.57
```

See also: APPEND FROM, COPY FILE, COPY STRUCTURE, EXPORT, IMPORT, SET DELETED, and SET FIELDS.

***<file type>* Options**	**Description**
DBASEII	A dBASE II database (.DB2) file. This file type is given a .DB2 extension to differentiate it from a dBASE IV file. Rename the file with a .DBF extension to use it with dBASE II
DBMEMO3	dBASE III PLUS format for database (.DBF) and memo (.DBT) files. When dBASE IV database files contain memo fields, they are not compatible with dBASE III PLUS unless you copy them with this option
DELIMITED	An ASCII text file (.TXT) in a delimited format. Data gets appended character-by-character starting on the left. A carriage return line feed (CR/LF) ends each record. Commas separate each field. Double quotation marks (") surround character data
DELIMITED WITH BLANK	ASCII text file (.TXT) containing fields separated by one space. Commas are not used to separate the fields. Records end with CR/LF
DELIMITED WITH *<delimiter>*	ASCII text file (.TXT) containing fields separated by commas with character data surrounded by specified delimiter. Records area variable length and ends with CR/LF
DIF	The VisiCalc file (.DIF) format. Database records convert to VisiCalc rows, and fields convert to columns
FW2	Framework II (.FW2) database
RPD	RapidFile (.RPD) data file

Table 31-5. COPY TO File Type Options

<file type> **Options**	**Description**
SDF	System Data Format ASCII (.TXT) file. A fixed-length file for which data gets appended character-by-character starting from the left. Each record in the target file is the same length, that is, the length of the database record. A carriage return line feed (CR/LF) ends each record. Individual fields are not delimited
SYLK	MultiPlan spreadsheet format. Database records convert to MultiPlan rows and fields convert to columns. No file extension is included
WKS	Lotus 1-2-3 Version 1A file (.WKS) format. Database records convert to 1-2-3 rows and fields convert to columns

Table 31-5. COPY TO File Type Options (*continued*)

COPY FILE

COPY FILE lets you create a copy of a file and give it a new name.

Syntax

COPY FILE *<source filename>* TO *<target filename>*

Notes

COPY FILE creates a duplicate file from a file on disk. You cannot use COPY FILE to copy an open file. To copy records from an open file, use the COPY TO command.

When you use the COPY FILE command, dBASE IV looks for the source file in the current drive and directory. If dBASE cannot find it there, it looks for the source file in the path you set with the SET PATH command (or the path setting in the CONFIG.DB file). If the source file is not in either of these places, you need to include a drive designator and/or a path name as part of the file name. You also need to include a drive designator and/or a path name as part of the target file name if you want to copy the target file to another drive or directory.

When you use the COPY FILE command to copy a database (.DBF) file, it copies only that file. If you want to copy the associated memo (.DBT) file and index (.MDX and .NDX) files, you must do so separately.

dBASE IV reserves the letters "A" through "J" and "M" for default alias names. Do not use these letters as database file names when you use the COPY FILE command.

Example

The following example copies the PRDERREC database file to a new database file, SAVEORD. Include the .DBF extensions so that the copied file will have the proper extension.

```
. COPY FILE Orderrec.dbf TO Saveord.dbf
   2891 bytes copied
```

COPY INDEXES

COPY INDEXES converts a list of .NDX files into tags in a single .MDX (multiple index) file.

Syntax

COPY INDEXES <*.NDX file list*> [TO < *.MDX filename*>]

Notes

When you use COPY INDEXES without the optional TO clause, dBASE IV copies the tag to the production .MDX file. If the production .MDX file doesn't exist, dBASE IV creates one.

If you use the optional TO clause, dBASE IV writes the tag to the given .MDX file name. If the given .MDX file doesn't exist, dBASE IV creates it and then adds the tag to it.

You can include up to 47 .NDX files in the *.NDX file list*. That is the maximum number of tags an .MDX file can contain.

Example

The following example converts a preestablished .NDX file, ZIPCODE.NDX, to a tag in the production .MDX file. (To see how the ZIPCODE.NDX file was created, see the example for the NDX() function in Chapter 33.)

```
. USE Customer INDEX Zipcode
Master index: ZIPCODE
. COPY INDEX Zipcode
  100% indexed          33 Records indexed
. DISPLAY STATUS
Currently Selected Database:
Select area:  1, Database in Use: C:\DBASE\CUSTOMER.DBF    Alias: CUSTOMER
    Master Index file:  C:\DBASE\ZIPCODE.NDX  Key: Zip
Production   MDX file:  C:\DBASE\CUSTOMER.MDX
           Index TAG:     CUST_NO  Key: Cust_no
           Index TAG:     CUST_NAME  Key: Lastname+Firstname
           Index TAG:     ZIPCODE  Key: Zip
```

See also: COPY TAG, INDEX, SET INDEX, SET ORDER, USE, KEY(), MDX(), and NDX().

COPY MEMO

COPY MEMO copies the text in a single memo field to a text file on disk.

Syntax

COPY MEMO <*memo field name*> TO <*filename*> [ADDITIVE]

If you do not include a file name extension, dBASE IV uses .TXT.

Notes

COPY MEMO copies the contents of a memo field to a text file on disk. To copy the file to another drive or directory, include that drive or directory in the file name.

By using the ADDITIVE option, you can append text to the end of a text file.

If you do not use the ADDITIVE option and the file already exists, dBASE IV overwrites the file. Whether it overwrites the file immediately or prompts you first depends on the status of SET SAFETY. If SET SAFETY is ON (the default), dBASE IV prompts you before overwriting. If SET SAFETY is OFF, dBASE overwrites the file immediately.

Example

The following example copies the text in the Mssg memo field for the current record to the SAVEMSSG.TXT file. It then displays the contents of the file by using the TYPE command.

```
. COPY MEMO Mssg TO Savemssg
. TYPE Savemssg.txt
Savemssg.txt 01/04/89                                                    1
This is the fifth rush order from Texasville Pumps this month!
Make sure to send 3 new brochures in our next mailing.
```

See also: APPEND MEMO and COPY FILE.

COPY STRUCTURE

COPY STRUCTURE lets you copy the structure of the active database file to a new file. No records are copied in the process.

Syntax

COPY STRUCTURE TO <*filename*> [FIELDS <*field list*>]

Notes

COPY STRUCTURE copies the entire database structure to a new file. You can, however, limit the fields that are copied by using the FIELDS <*field list*> clause. The *field list* should include the names of only those fields you want to include in the new structure.

If SET SAFETY is ON (the default), dBASE IV prompts you before overwriting an existing file. If SET SAFETY is OFF, dBASE IV immediately overwrites the file.

To copy the file to another drive or directory, include that drive or directory in the file name. If you don't include an extension, the file name is automatically given the .DBF extension.

Example

You can use the COPY STRUCTURE command to create a temporary, or *transaction,* file for storing records from the current database. For example, the following block of code creates a temporary file, TEMP, with the same structure as the ORDERREC database. It then appends all of the records for the current day's transactions to the temporary file.

```
USE Orderrec
SET SAFETY OFF
COPY STRUCTURE TO Temp
USE Temp
APPEND FROM Orderrec FOR Order_date = DATE()
SET SAFETY ON
```

See also: APPEND, APPEND BLANK, APPEND FROM, and SET SAFETY.

COPY STRUCTURE EXTENDED

COPY STRUCTURE EXTENDED creates a special database file that contains records detailing the structure of the current database file.

Syntax

COPY TO <*filename*> STRUCTURE EXTENDED

Notes

The database that COPY STRUCTURE EXTENDED creates is called an *extended structure* database. It contains five fields.

Field_name	Field name
Field_type	Field type
Field_len	Length of field
Field_dec	Number of decimal places
Field_idx	Index flag

dBASE IV creates one record in the *extended structure* database for each field in the active database.

You generally use the COPY STRUCTURE EXTENDED command with the CREATE FROM command. CREATE FROM creates a database from the information in the extended structure database.

You may wonder why you would use COPY STRUCTURE EXTENDED and CREATE FROM when you could use the COPY STRUCTURE command. However, suppose you want to modify a copied structure without doing it interactively with the CREATE or MODIFY STRUCTURE commands. You can modify the extended structure database created with the COPY STRUCTURE EXTENDED command by using any of the standard dBASE IV commands. The following example shows how.

Example

The following block of code copies the structure of the SALARY database to an extended structure file called NEWSTRUC. It then uses the NEWSTRUC file to change the width of the Gross field from eight to ten characters. Finally, it uses the CREATE FROM command to create a new database, NEWSAL, from the information in the NEWSTRUC extended structure file.

```
USE Salary
COPY TO Newstruc STRUCTURE EXTENDED
USE Newstruc
REPLACE FOR Field_name = "GROSS" Field_len WITH 10
CREATE NewSal FROM Newstruc
```

See also: APPEND FROM, CREATE FROM, and CREATE STRUCTURE.

COPY TAG

COPY TAG converts an .MDX (multiple index) tag to an .NDX file.

Syntax

COPY TAG <*tag name*> [OF <*.MDX filename*>] TO <*.NDX filename*>

By using the OF clause, you can indicate an open .MDX file that contains the *tag name*. If you do not include the OF clause, dBASE IV uses the production .MDX file.

Notes

Before you can use the COPY TAG command, you must have a database in use. If you use the optional OF clause, the named .MDX file must be in use. dBASE IV creates the .NDX file from the key expression in the .MDX tag. COPY TAG can convert only one .MDX tag at a time.

As COPY TAG creates .NDX files, it leaves them open. You can reach the maximum of ten open .NDX files for the current database file if you use the COPY TAG command several times in a row.

If you are using dBASE IV in a network environment, the database file must be in exclusive mode before you can use the COPY TAG command to copy an .MDX tag to an .MDX file.

Example

The following example copies the Cust_name tag from the production .MDX file for the CUSTOMER database to an .NDX file called CUST_NAM.NDX. The DISPLAY STATUS command shows the open index files (both .NDX and .MDX) before and after the COPY TAG command.

```
. USE Customer
. DISPLAY STATUS
Currently Selected Database:
Select area:  1, Database in Use: C:\DBASE\CUSTOMER.DBF   Alias: CUSTOMER
Production   MDX file:  C:\DBASE\CUSTOMER.MDX
           Index TAG:      CUST_NAME  Key: Lastname+Firstname
           Index TAG:      CUST_NO  Key: Cust_no

. COPY TAG Cust_name TO Cust_nam
  100% indexed          33 Records indexed
. SET INDEX TO Cust_nam
Master index: CUST_NAM
. DISPLAY STATUS
Currently Selected Database:
Select area:  1, Database in Use: C:\DBASE\CUSTOMER.DBF   Alias: CUSTOMER
    Master Index file:  C:\DBASE\CUST_NAM.NDX  Key: Lastname+Firstname
Production   MDX file:  C:\DBASE\CUSTOMER.MDX
           Index TAG:      CUST_NAME  Key: Lastname+Firstname
           Index TAG:      CUST_NO  Key: Cust_no
```

See also: COPY INDEX, INDEX, SET INDEX, SET ORDER, MDX(), NDX(), and TAG().

COPY TO ARRAY

COPY TO ARRAY copies the data from one or more records in the active database file to an existing array.

Syntax

COPY TO ARRAY <*array name*> [FIELDS <*fields list*>] [<*scope*>] [FOR <*condition*>] [WHILE <*condition*>]

Notes

The COPY TO ARRAY command fills an existing array with the contents of one or more database records.

In dBASE IV, arrays are defined in *row, column* format. You must declare the array with the DECLARE command.

COPY TO ARRAY fills the contents of an array as follows:

- For each record in the database file, the first field is stored in the first column of the array, the second field in the second column of the array, and so on.
- Each record becomes a row in the array.
- Copying takes place until there are no more fields in the database or no more columns in the array.
- If the database has more fields than the array has columns, the excess fields are not included in the array. If the array has more columns than the database has fields, the excess columns are ignored.
- You cannot copy memo fields to an array.

Unless you include a SCOPE clause, dBASE IV copies all of the records in the database, beginning with the first record and continuing to the end of the file or until the array is full. The data types in the array match the data types in the database fields.

You can limit the fields that are copied to the array by using the FIELDS <*field list*> clause. The *field list* should include the names of only those fields you want to include in the array. You can also use the SET FIELDS command to limit the fields that are copied.

If you include a FOR clause, dBASE IV evaluates the condition before it copies the data in each record to the array. dBASE IV copies the data in the record if the condition evaluates to logical true (.T.). If you include a WHILE clause, dBASE IV copies data from records until the condition evaluates to logical false (.F.).

When fields are copied to an array, the items are read in one column at a time. For example, suppose you have an array called Amt declared as follows:

```
. DECLARE ARRAY Amt[5,4]
```

Data items are read into the array elements in the following order:

Amt[1,1]

Amt[1,2]

Amt[1,3]

Amt[1,4]

Amt[2,1]

Amt[2,2]

Amt[2,3]

Amt[2,4]

Amt[3,1]

.

.

.

Amt[5,3]

Amt[5,4]

Example

The following example determines the number of records in the SALARY database for which the Bonus field has a value of true (.T.). It then declares an array of sufficient size to copy the appropriate records into. Next, it copies the records to the array using COPY TO ARRAY. Finally, it shows a small portion of the first row in the array.

```
. USE Salary
. COUNT FOR Bonus TO Mcols
      7 records
```

```
. DECLARE Bon_array[Mcols,8]
. COPY TO ARRAY Bon_array FOR Bonus
     7 records copied
. ? Bon_array[1,1],Bon_array[1,2],Bon_array[1,3]
Drew    Gibson    .T.
```

See also: APPEND FROM ARRAY, COPY FILE, COPY STRUCTURE, and EXPORT.

COUNT

COUNT returns the number of records in the active database that match a given set of conditions.

Syntax

COUNT [TO <*memvar*>] [<*scope*>] [FOR <*condition*>]
[WHILE <*condition*>]

Notes

COUNT determines the number of records and, if SET TALK is ON, displays that number on the screen. You can limit the records that are counted by defining a scope. You can further limit the records by using a FOR or WHILE clause.

If you use a TO clause, you can have COUNT save its results to a memory variable.

Tip: If you're using dBASE IV on a network and SET LOCK is ON (the default), COUNT locks the file while it totals the number of records. If SET LOCK is OFF, COUNT still determines a total, but the results may be suspect if a user is changing the database.

Example

The following example determines the number of employees in the SALARY database who will receive bonuses for the year:

```
. USE Salary
. COUNT FOR Bonus TO Bon_no
    7 records
. ? "There are "+LTRIM(STR(Bon_no,2))+" employees who will get bonuses"
There are 7 employees who will get bonuses
```

See also: AVERAGE, CALCULATE, RECCOUNT(), and SUM.

CREATE or MODIFY STRUCTURE

CREATE or MODIFY STRUCTURE let you access the Database Design screen. If you use CREATE, you can build a new structure for a new database. If you use MODIFY STRUCTURE, you can modify an existing structure for a previously created database.

Syntax

CREATE <*filename*> / MODIFY STRUCTURE

Defaults

If you do not want the file to reside on the current drive and directory, you must provide another file and/or directory as part of the file name. Also, when you do not include an extension for the database file name, dBASE IV automatically assigns the .DBF extension.

Since MODIFY STRUCTURE can only work with the current database, you need not include a file name with this command. If no file is in use, dBASE IV prompts you for a file name.

If a catalog is active when you create a database file, dBASE IV automatically adds the file to the catalog.

Notes

You define the structure of a database by establishing the field names, field types, field lengths, number of decimal places (in the case of numeric fields), and a field index flag for each field (indicating whether an .MDX tag exists for that field). Both the CREATE and MODIFY STRUCTURE commands provide the Database Design screen, in which you can design the file structure.

For a complete description of the Database Design screen, see Chapter 4.

When you issue the MODIFY STRUCTURE command, dBASE IV immediately makes a backup copy of the database file and assigns it a .BAK extension. It also copies the memo field (.DBT) file and gives it a .TBK extension. When you've completed the modifications to the database structure, dBASE IV reads the contents of the backup file and appends them to the modified database file. If the current disk is full, dBASE IV cannot make backup copies. For this reason, make sure that there is sufficient disk space before you modify the structure of a database file.

If you're using dBASE IV in a network environment, you must use the database in exclusive (unshared) mode before you can modify its structure. See Chapter 29 for more details.

Tip: If you use CREATE to create a new database file or MODIFY STRUCTURE to modify an existing database file that you want to use in SQL mode, you must first issue SQL's **DBDEFINE** command. This command updates SQL's system catalogs to include the file. If you do not use the DBDEFINE command, SQL will not be able to find your file. In fact, you should always use SQL's DBDEFINE command whenever you want to use a *foreign* file (one not created in SQL) with dBASE IV's SQL.

Data Type Conversions

If you change a database field from one data type to another, dBASE IV converts the data automatically, provided the conversion makes sense. If the conversion does not make sense, dBASE IV does not perform the conversion and you lose the data in that field.

Tip: To be on the safe side, you should always save a backup copy of the database before you change a field's data type. Also, you should check the results of the conversion to make sure that dBASE IV handled the conversion properly.

Here are the results for some of the more common conversions:

- **Numeric fields to character fields** dBASE IV converts the numbers in the numeric fields to character strings.
- **Character fields to numeric fields** dBASE IV converts each numeric character in the character field to digits in the numeric field. It stops when it finds a nonnumeric character. If the first character in the character field is nonnumeric, dBASE IV enters 0 in the numeric field.
- **Logical fields to character fields** dBASE IV converts logical true (.T.) to T and logical false (.F.) to F.
- **Character fields to logical fields** dBASE IV converts T to logical true (.T.) and F to logical false (.F.).
- **Logical fields to numeric fields** dBASE IV cannot convert logical fields to numeric fields.

- **Character fields to date fields** If character strings are formatted as dates (for example, *mm-dd-yy* or *mm/dd/yy*), dBASE IV converts them properly.
- **Date fields to character fields** dBASE IV makes this conversion without any problems.

Tip: dBASE IV does not convert memo fields to other data types, nor does it convert other data types to memo fields.

If you modify the field name, length, or type of a field that has an index tag in the production .MDX file, dBASE IV automatically updates the tag.

See also: APPEND FROM, APPEND MEMO, COPY STRUCTURE, COPY STRUCTURE EXTENDED, CREATE FROM, SET BLOCKSIZE, and SET SAFETY.

CREATE FROM

CREATE FROM builds a new database file from the extended structure file created with the COPY STRUCTURE EXTENDED command.

Syntax

CREATE <*filename*> FROM <*extended structure file*>

Notes

You generally use the CREATE FROM command with the COPY STRUCTURE EXTENDED command. CREATE FROM creates a database from the information in the extended structure database provided by the COPY STRUCTURE EXTENDED command.

See the COPY STRUCTURE EXTENDED command in this chapter for more information.

Example

For an example of CREATE FROM, see the COPY STRUCTURE EXTENDED command.

See also: COPY, COPY STRUCTURE, COPY STRUCTURE EXTENDED, and LIST/DISPLAY STRUCTURE.

CREATE VIEW FROM ENVIRONMENT

CREATE VIEW FROM ENVIRONMENT lets you create a view (.VUE) file and is included in dBASE IV only to maintain compatibility with dBASE III PLUS.

Syntax

CREATE VIEW <.*VUE filename*> FROM ENVIRONMENT

Unless you provide another extension, this command automatically attaches a .VUE extension to the .VUE *filename*.

Notes

CREATE VIEW FROM ENVIRONMENT is a dBASE III PLUS command for creating view (.VUE) files that save the following information:

- Open database files
- Open format files
- Open index files
- The current work area for each file
- The currently selected work area number
- File relations
- Active field lists (from SET FIELDS)
- Filter conditions (from SET FILTER)

The SET VIEW command in dBASE III PLUS activates a .VUE file and reinstitutes the environment saved in the file.

CREATE VIEW FROM ENVIRONMENT is obsolete in dBASE IV because the query (.QBE) files and update query (.UPD) files you can create with the dBASE IV Queries Design screen are more powerful than view (.VUE) files. (You access the Queries Design screen with the CREATE/MODIFY QUERY and CREATE/MODIFY VIEW commands.) dBASE IV lets you create .VUE files from the current environment to maintain compatibility with dBASE III PLUS.

To deactivate a view (.VUE) file, you can select another view file or use the CLOSE DATABASES command.

See also: SELECT, SET FORMAT, SET FIELDS, SET INDEX, SET RELATION, and SET VIEW.

CREATE/MODIFY APPLICATION

CREATE/MODIFY APPLICATION lets you access the dBASE IV Applications Generator. You can use the Applications Generator to automatically generate program code for linking database files, index files, reports, queries, forms, menus, and more.

Syntax

CREATE/MODIFY APPLICATION <*filename*> / ?

If you use the ? symbol, you can enter the file name later in the Application Definition dialog box. If you include a *filename,* you can change the name later in the Application Definition dialog box.

Notes

The CREATE APPLICATION and MODIFY APPLICATION commands are equivalent.

Part Two of this book discusses the Applications Generator.

CREATE/MODIFY LABEL

CREATE/MODIFY LABEL lets you access the Labels Design screen, which you can use to design label form (.LBL) files.

Syntax

CREATE/MODIFY LABEL <*filename*> / ?

Unless you provide another extension, this command automatically attaches an .LBL extension to the file it creates and an .LBG file extension to the file it generates.

The ? symbol looks in the current catalog (if one is open) for all available .LBL files identified with the active database file or view. If a catalog is not open, the ? symbol presents all of the .LBL files in the current directory. You can then choose the label form file you want.

Notes

The CREATE LABEL and MODIFY LABEL commands are equivalent. You use them to create and modify label form (.LBL) files.

Chapter 10, "Creating Reports and Labels," discusses in detail how to use the CREATE LABEL and MODIFY LABEL commands.

See also: LABEL FORM and SET CATALOG.

CREATE/MODIFY QUERY/VIEW

CREATE/MODIFY QUERY and CREATE/MODIFY VIEW let you access the Queries Design screen, which you can use to create query (.QBE) files. Query files let you set up conditions for extracting records from a database. They also let you build update query (.UPD) files, which can modify records in a database.

Syntax

CREATE/MODIFY QUERY <*filename*>/?

or

CREATE/MODIFY VIEW <*filename*>/?

If you use the ? symbol, dBASE IV looks in the current catalog (if one is open) for the .QBE and .UPD files identified with the active database file. If a catalog is not open, the ? symbol presents all of the .QBE and .UPD files in the current directory. Then, you can choose the query (or query update) file you want.

Notes

When you use the Queries Design screen to create a .QBE file, you define a set of conditions that determine what records are displayed when you issue commands. A .UPD file, on the other hand, contains actual instructions that update records in a database file. dBASE IV produces a .UPD file only when you place an *update operator* under the name of the file in the Queries Design screen.

The CREATE/MODIFY QUERY and CREATE/MODIFY VIEW commands both let you access the Queries Design Screen. The CREATE and MODIFY forms of the commands are equivalent. How dBASE IV responds to your command is determined by whether a query file (either .QBE or .UPD) exists. If it exists, dBASE IV asks you whether you want to modify it. If it does not exist, dBASE IV automatically creates one.

The view (.VUE) files that dBASE III PLUS creates (with CREATE VIEW FROM ENVIRONMENT) are a subset of the query files (both .QBE and .UPD) that dBASE IV creates. dBASE IV can read .VUE files, but creates .QBE files from them. As you might expect, the .QBE files that dBASE IV produces cannot be read by dBASE III PLUS.

If you do not include a file name extension, dBASE IV looks in the current directory for a .QBE or .UPD file. If it finds one, it uses that file. Otherwise, it looks for a .VUE file from an earlier version of dBASE. If dBASE IV cannot find any of these files, it automatically creates a .QBE or .UPD file, depending on the situation.

The SET VIEW command activates a .QBE file. When you first use this command with a .QBE file, dBASE IV creates a .QBO (object) file and writes it to disk. From then on, dBASE IV uses the .QBO file when you use the SET VIEW command to activate the query.

You use the DO command to activate a .UPD file. When you first activate a .UPD file, dBASE IV creates a .DBO (object) file and writes it to disk. If you like, you can rename the .DBO file to a .QBO file to keep your update query files distinct from your program files. In fact, if you want your update query files to appear in the Queries Panel of the Control Center, you must rename them with a .QBO extension.

You can activate the Queries Design screen from the Control Center. Chapter 6, "Querying the Database," discusses this topic in detail.

Tip: If you use the MODIFY command or your own text editor to modify a .QBE or .UPD file, you'll need to erase the old .DBO or .QBO file yourself. You can then use the SET VIEW or DO commands to create new object files.

See also: SET CATALOG, SET SAFETY, and SET VIEW.

CREATE/MODIFY REPORT

CREATE/MODIFY REPORT lets you access the Reports Design screen, from which you can create your own customized reports. The Reports Design screen builds report form (.FRM) files that use certain fields in the current database file or other related database files.

Syntax

CREATE/MODIFY REPORT *<filename>/?*

If you do not provide another extension, this command automatically attaches an .FRM extension to the report form file it creates. CREATE REPORT always generates a file with an .FRG extension, which you cannot override. If SET CATALOG is ON (the default is OFF), and you've opened a catalog, dBASE IV places the report form file in the open catalog.

The ? symbol looks in the current catalog (if one is open) for all available .FRM files identified with the active database file or view. If a catalog is not open, the ? symbol presents all of the .FRM files in the current directory. Then you can choose the one you want to alter.

Notes

CREATE/MODIFY REPORT lets you build a report form (.FRM) file that has all the necessary information for a report design. You use the report design to print reports from a database file or view.

The CREATE REPORT and MODIFY REPORT commands are interchangeable. How dBASE IV responds to your command is determined by whether a report form (.FRM) file exists. If it exists, the command modifies it. If it does not exist, the command automatically creates one.

Chapter 10, "Creating Reports," discusses in detail how to use CREATE/MODIFY REPORT and the Reports Design screen.

See also: REPORT FORM, SET CATALOG, SET DESIGN, and SET VIEW.

CREATE/MODIFY SCREEN

CREATE/MODIFY SCREEN lets you access the Forms Design screen, which lets you design custom forms. By using custom forms, you can control how fields appear on the screen when you use a full- screen command such as EDIT or BROWSE to have the user edit data.

Syntax

CREATE/MODIFY SCREEN *<filename>/?*

Unless you provide another extension, this command automatically attaches an .SCR extension to the screen file it creates. CREATE REPORT also generates a format file with an .FMT extension. If SET CATALOG is ON (the default is OFF), and a catalog is open, dBASE IV places the format files in the open catalog.

The ? symbol looks in the current catalog (if one is open) for all available .SCR files identified with the active database file or view. If a catalog is not open, the ? symbol presents all the .SCR files in the current directory. You can than choose the one you want to alter.

Notes

A screen (.SCR) file contains all of the information (in non-ASCII form) dBASE IV needs to display your form in the Forms Design screen. A format (.FMT) file contains the actual dBASE IV commands required (for example, @SAY...GETs) to display the form on the screen.

CREATE/MODIFY SCREEN lets you build a screen (.SCR) file and have dBASE IV generate a format (.FMT) file. When you create or modify a screen, you are actually working with the screen (.SCR) file.

The CREATE SCREEN and MODIFY SCREEN commands are interchangeable. How dBASE IV responds to your command is determined by whether a screen form (.SCR) file exists. If it exists, the command modifies it. If it does not exist, the command automatically creates one.

You can use the SET FORMAT command to open (or close) a format file you've created.

Chapter 9, "Creating Input Forms," discusses in detail how to use CREATE/MODIFY SCREEN and the Forms Design screen.

See also: @, APPEND, BROWSE, EDIT, INSERT, SET CATALOG, SET FORMAT, and SET VIEW.

DEACTIVATE MENU

DEACTIVATE MENU deactivates an active menu bar and removes it from the screen. However, the menu bar still remains in memory. You use DEACTIVATE MENU as part of an ON SELECTION statement. You can also place it in a procedure called by an ON SELECTION statement.

Tip: When a menu is active, it retains control of dBASE IV until you leave the menu. The DEACTIVATE MENU command does nothing when you enter it from the dot prompt because a menu cannot be active at that time.

Syntax

DEACTIVATE MENU

Notes

DEACTIVATE MENU deactivates the currently active menu and removes it from the screen. Because only one menu can be active at a time, you do not need to include a menu name with the command. When dBASE IV removes the menu from the screen, it exposes any material that may be underneath it.

Tip: DEACTIVATE MENU does not remove a menu from memory, so you can reactivate the menu at any time with ACTIVATE MENU.

The ON PAD command lets you set up a pop-up menu for a given bar menu. If an ON PAD command is in effect, the DEACTIVATE MENU command deactivates the pop-up menu that ON PAD produces.

Example

The following program displays a menu with three options: **Display memory**, **Display status**, and **Quit**. If you choose **Display memory**, the program issues a DISPLAY MEMORY command. If you select **Display status**, the program issues a DISPLAY STATUS command. Finally, if you select **Quit**, the program deactivates the menu with a DEACTIVATE MENU command.

```
DEFINE MENU Menu_mem MESSAGE "Display memory or status"
DEFINE PAD Pad_mem OF Menu_mem PROMPT "Display memory" AT 0,1
DEFINE PAD Pad_stat OF Menu_mem PROMPT "Display status" AT 0,2
DEFINE PAD Pad_quit OF Menu_mem PROMPT "Quit" AT 0,40
ON SELECTION PAD Pad_mem OF Menu_mem DISPLAY MEMORY
ON SELECTION PAD Pad_stat OF Menu_mem DISPLAY STATUS
ON SELECTION PAD Pad_quit OF Menu_mem DEACTIVATE MENU
ACTIVATE MENU Menu_mem
```

See also: ACTIVATE MENU, DEFINE MENU, ON SELECTION, and RELEASE MENUS.

DEACTIVATE POPUP

DEACTIVATE POPUP deactivates the active pop-up menu, erasing it from the screen yet leaving it available in memory.

Syntax

DEACTIVATE POPUP

Notes

When you use DEACTIVATE POPUP, dBASE IV removes the pop-up menu from the screen, exposing whatever was underneath it.

Tip: When a pop-up is active, it controls dBASE IV until you leave the pop-up. The DEACTIVATE POPUP command does nothing when you enter it from the dot prompt because a pop-up cannot be active at that time.

You use DEACTIVATE POPUP as part of an ON SELECTION statement. You can also place it in a procedure called by an ON SELECTION statement.

If you press ESC while in a pop-up, dBASE IV automatically deactivates the pop-up and transfers control to the statement following the command that activated the pop-up. This command is either ACTIVATE POPUP or ACTIVATE MENU (when a pop-up is part of a menu).

Example

The following program uses a pop-up called Sort_pop with three menu options. The first two options sort the CUSTOMER database in ascending or descending order. The third option deactivates the pop-up and terminates the program.

```
* Define the popup's three bars
DEFINE POPUP Sort_pop FROM 3,6 MESSAGE "Select sort order"
DEFINE BAR 1 OF Sort_pop PROMPT "Ascending";
     MESSAGE "Sort the Customer database in ascending order"
DEFINE BAR 2 OF Sort_pop PROMPT "Descending";
     MESSAGE "Sort the Customer database in descending order"
DEFINE BAR 3 OF Sort_pop PROMPT "Exit to dot prompt";
     MESSAGE "Leave the program"
```

```
* Setup procedure for popup
ON SELECTION POPUP Sort_pop DO Sort_proc

* Use CUSTOMER.DBF and activate popup
SET TALK OFF
USE Customer
ACTIVATE POPUP Sort_pop
SET MESSAGE TO      && Clear the message line
SET TALK ON
RETURN

PROCEDURE Sort_proc
DO CASE
     CASE BAR() = 1
          SET MESSAGE TO "Sorting..."
          SORT TO Temp ON Lastname
     CASE BAR() = 2
          SET MESSAGE TO "Sorting..."
          SORT TO Temp ON Lastname DESCENDING
     CASE BAR() = 3
          DEACTIVATE POPUP
ENDCASE
RETURN
```

See also: ACTIVATE POPUP, CLEAR POPUPS, DEFINE POPUP, ON SELECTION, RELEASE POPUP, BAR(), and POPUP().

DEACTIVATE WINDOW

DEACTIVATE WINDOW deactivates a given window (or set of windows) and removes it from the screen. However, the window remains active in memory.

Syntax

DEACTIVATE WINDOW *<window name list>*/[ALL]

Notes

DEACTIVATE WINDOW deactivates windows in the *window name list.* It removes them from the screen but does not remove them from memory. You can reactivate a window with the ACTIVATE WINDOW command.

When you deactivate a window, any other active window becomes the current window. The ALL option deactivates all windows and returns dBASE IV to full screen.

Example

See the VARREAD() function in Chapter 33 for an example of DEACTIVATE WINDOW.

See also: ACTIVATE WINDOW, DEFINE WINDOW, MOVE WINDOW, RESTORE WINDOW, and SAVE WINDOW.

DEBUG

DEBUG lets you access the dBASE IV Program Debugger.

Syntax

DEBUG <*filename*>/<*procedure name*> [WITH <*parameter list*>]

The WITH clause lets you pass parameters to a program or procedure, as does the DO command. The *parameter list* can accept a maximum of eight constants, including a file name. However, you can include an unlimited number of variables in the *parameter list*.

Notes

DEBUG is similar to the DO command in that it executes a program or procedure. However, it also activates the dBASE IV Program Debugger.

Chapter 25, "Debugging Your Program," discusses the dBASE IV Program Debugger in detail.

See also: COMPILE, DO, MODIFY COMMAND, SET DEBUG, SET ECHO, SET STEP, SET TALK, and SET TRAP.

DECLARE

DECLARE lets you create one- and two-dimensional arrays. The arrays that you create are arrays of memory variables.

Syntax

DECLARE *<array name 1>* [{*<number of rows>*,} {*<number of columns>*}] {,*<array name 2>* [{*<number of rows>*,} {*<number of columns>*}]...}

Note: In this format, the square brackets ([ ]) are a required part of the command, so the curly braces ({ }) indicate optional items.

Public Versus Private

When you use the DECLARE command from the dot prompt, the array you create is automatically made public. To make an array public from within a program, you must use the PUBLIC command. For example, the following command line, when used in a program file, creates a public array called Save_array:

```
PUBLIC ARRAY Save_array[10,10]
```

To declare a private version of Save_array from within a program, use the following:

```
DECLARE ARRAY Save_array[10,10]
```

For a description of the difference between public and private memory variables, see Chapter 18, "Memory Variables."

Notes

Use the following conventions when naming an array:

- Can be ten characters or less
- Can use letters, numbers, or underscores
- Must begin with a letter and cannot include blank spaces
- Avoid dBASE IV command names

When you declare an array, besides giving it a name you also establish its dimensions by using numbers in square brackets. The first number represents the number of rows in the array. The second number is the number of columns. If you use only one number, the array is said to be *one-dimensional*. If you use two numbers, separated by commas, the array is *two- dimensional*. The maximum number of dimensions for a dBASE IV array is two.

For example, when you enter the following command from the dot prompt, you declare a one-dimensional array called Sale_items containing 20 elements:

```
. DECLARE Sale_items[20]
```

The elements in the Sale_items array are numbered from 1 to 20.

To declare a two-dimensional array called Parts, you could enter the following command:

```
. DECLARE Parts[10,5]
```

The parts array is 10 rows by 5 columns. There are a total of 50 elements in the Parts array.

Note: Creating a single-row array (for example, Sale_items[1,20]) is the same as creating a one-dimensional array (for example, Sale_items[20]).

You refer to an element within an array by using the array name and specifying the position using row and column numbers. For example, Amount[6] and Rates[7,4] are typical elements.

Defaults

When you create an array, dBASE IV *initializes* (automatically assigns values to) the array elements to logical false (.F.) values. However, the array elements do not actually have a data type until you assign values to them by using STORE. For example, the following command stores the string "Varnish" to the array element Sale_items[3,5]:

```
. STORE "Varnish" TO Sale_items[3,5]
```

Note: dBASE IV lets you assign different data types to the elements within an array. For example, you can assign one element a date type value and another element a character type value.

Memory Considerations

When you create a memory variable, dBASE IV uses one slot in the memory variable pool. When you create an array name, dBASE IV also uses one slot in the same memory pool. When you assign elements, however, dBASE IV stores them in a block of memory allocated specifically for elements. If you declare an array and dBASE IV doesn't have sufficient memory, it displays the error message "Insufficient memory." After you declare an array, you treat its elements like other memory variables, regardless of how dBASE IV actually stores them.

Tip: In dBASE IV, arrays consume a great deal of memory. If you're developing an application that may use arrays, test their memory consumption first. For example, declare a large array (for instance, 5 columns by 100 rows) and use the DISPLAY MEMORY command both before and after to determine the memory consumed.

Commands That Work with Arrays

All of the standard dBASE IV commands that work with memory variables also work with array elements. However, before you can use the commands with array elements, you must first declare the array. You must also properly refer to the elements within an array. If you try to use row and/or column coordinates that are outside of the dimensions of the array, dBASE IV returns the error message "Bad array dimension(s)." Similarly, if you try to refer to an array name that is not declared, dBASE IV issues the error message "Not an array."

dBASE IV has two special commands for working with arrays. COPY TO ARRAY copies the data in one or more records in the active database file to an existing array. APPEND FROM ARRAY adds records to a database file from the contents of an array.

The following commands that operate with memory variables also work with arrays:

- AVERAGE
- CALCULATE
- CLEAR ALL
- CLEAR MEMORY
- LIST/DISPLAY MEMORY
- RELEASE
- RESTORE

- SAVE
- SUM

Example

The following example computes the averages of all numeric fields in the SALARY database and stores the results to the Avgs array:

```
. USE Salary
. DECLARE Avgs[5]
. AVERAGE TO ARRAY Avgs
     12 records averaged
        GROSS           FED          FICA         STATE          NET
     27250.00       6812.50       2046.48        827.92     17563.11
.  ? "The average gross pay is $"+LTRIM(STR(Avgs[1]))+"."
The average gross pay is $27250.
```

For other examples that use the DECLARE command, see the APPEND FROM ARRAY and COPY TO ARRAY commands in this chapter.

See also: APPEND FROM ARRAY, AVERAGE, CALCULATE, CLEAR ALL, CLEAR MEMORY, COPY TO ARRAY, COUNT, LIST/DISPLAY MEMORY, PUBLIC, RELEASE, RESTORE, SAVE, and SUM.

DEFINE BAR

The DEFINE BAR command lets you establish a bar in a pop-up menu.

Syntax

DEFINE BAR *<line number>* OF *<pop-up name>*
PROMPT *<character expression>*
[MESSAGE *<character expression>*] [SKIP [FOR *<condition>*]]
[NOSPACE]

Background

In dBASE IV, you can create custom pop-up menus. A pop-up menu is made up of of one or more vertically stacked prompts, or bars. You can have a pop-up menu appear as part of a menu (see the DEFINE PAD and ON PAD commands), or you can have it appear by itself.

There are two main types of pop-ups: You can fill pop-ups with information from the active database or with file names from the current catalog. In addition, you can fill pop-ups with your own menu bars.

To create a pop-up that you fill with information from the active database or file names from the current catalog, use the DEFINE POPUP command and one of these three forms of the PROMPT option:

- **PROMPT FIELD** Fills a pop-up with the contents of a named field in the active database file.
- **PROMPT FILES** Fills a pop-up with the file names in the current catalog.
- **PROMPT STRUCTURE** Fills a pop-up with the defined field names (that is, the fields in the structure) for the active database file.

To create a pop-up consisting of your own menu bars, first use the DEFINE POPUP command to name the pop-up and set up its coordinates on the screen. Then use the DEFINE BAR command to establish bars within the pop-up.

Notes

If you want to use the DEFINE BAR command to set up your own pop-up menu bars, you cannot use the PROMPT FIELD, PROMPT FILES, or PROMPT STRUCTURE option of the DEFINE POPUP command. These options are not acceptable because the items they place within a pop-up appear in place of menu bars.

To establish a menu bar for a pop-up, you must give it a line number. The *line number* represents the line number position within the pop-up menu. Use only positive whole numbers; dBASE IV truncates fractional numbers.

If you assign the same line number to more than one bar, only the last bar to which you assigned the number will appear within the pop-up window.

If you assign more line numbers than there are lines in the pop-up window, the prompts scroll vertically as you move the highlight inside the pop-up window.

If you skip a line number when you define the menu bars, a blank row appears in the pop-up window. As you move the selection bar within the pop-up window, it skips the blank row.

You define the text for a menu bar by using the PROMPT *<character expression>* option. How much of the text appears in the pop-up window is determined by the width of the pop-up window itself. (You set the width of the pop-up window by defining its screen coordinates in the DEFINE POPUP command.) If the length of the text exceeds the width of the window, the prompt is truncated. You cannot scroll horizontally in a pop-up window.

Since you cannot activate a pop-up window unless it contains at least one bar, you must define at least one bar.

The MESSAGE *<character expression>* option lets you display a message of up to 79 characters on the screen. Extra characters are truncated. The message appears centered on the last line of the screen, outside of the pop-up. You can define a message for each bar within a pop-up; the message will appear when you highlight the bar within the pop-up window.

The SKIP option lets you display in the pop-up window a bar that the user cannot select. The SKIP FOR option lets you set up a menu bar that can only be selected when the FOR condition is true.

The NOSPACE option causes text within a pop-up menu to appear flush left against the pop-up menu border. Normally, there is a space between the border of the pop-up menu and bar text.

Example

The following program displays a pop-up window with five menu bars. The third menu bar—Delete an order—appears only when the No_delete flag is false (.F.). The fourth menu bar is a line of dashes that separates the **Exit** option from the other options.

```
* Set the flag for whether a menu bar appears
No_delete = .T.
* Define the pop-up window itself
DEFINE POPUP Ord_pop FROM 3,6 MESSAGE "Order entry menu"
* Define the bars within the pop-up window
DEFINE BAR 1 OF Ord_pop PROMPT " Add an order"
DEFINE BAR 2 OF Ord_pop PROMPT " Change an order"
DEFINE BAR 3 OF Ord_pop PROMPT " Delete an order" SKIP FOR No_delete
DEFINE BAR 4 OF Ord_pop PROMPT REPLICATE("-",17) SKIP
DEFINE BAR 5 OF Ord_pop PROMPT " Exit"
* Activate the pop-up
ACTIVATE POPUP Ord_pop
```

See also: ACTIVATE POPUP, DEACTIVATE POPUP, DEFINE POPUP, ON SELECTION POPUP, SHOW POPUP, BAR(), and POPUP().

DEFINE BOX

DEFINE BOX lets you print a box around lines of text.

Syntax

DEFINE BOX FROM *<print column>* TO *<print column>*
HEIGHT *<type N expression>* [AT LINE *<print line>*]
[SINGLE/DOUBLE/*<border definition string>*]

Notes

To have a box appear around your printed text, you can use the DEFINE BOX command. You use the FROM clause to set the left and right columns for the box, the AT LINE clause to set the beginning line for the top of the box, and the HEIGHT clause to set the height of the box. If any of the beginning values for these clauses are less than the current coordinates, dBASE IV ignores them and begins the box at the current line.

If you don't include an AT LINE clause, dBASE IV begins the box at the current line.

See the SET BORDER command in Chapter 32 for more about the *border definition string*. The default border is a single line.

The _box system memory variable must be set to true (.T., the default) for you to be able to print boxes.

DEFINE MENU

The DEFINE MENU command lets you define a bar menu. You can use it with the DEFINE PAD command to build menus.

Syntax

DEFINE MENU *<menu name>* [MESSAGE
<character expression>]

Notes

The DEFINE MENU command is the preliminary step in creating a bar menu. You must then use other commands, such as DEFINE PAD and DEFINE POPUP, to finish the menu.

The DEFINE MENU command assigns a name to a bar menu and lets you attach a message of up to 79 characters to the menu by using the MESSAGE clause. The message appears at the bottom of the screen when you issue the ACTIVATE MENU command.

You use the DEFINE PAD command to define the pads to be attached to a menu. You can attach a message to each of the pads within a menu bar. If you assign messages to the pads, they overwrite the message from the DEFINE MENU command.

Examples

The following command defines a menu called **Start**:

```
. DEFINE MENU Start
```

See the next command, DEFINE PAD, for a more complete example. For other examples, see the DEACTIVATE MENU command in this chapter and the PAD() function in Chapter 33. Chapter 24, "Advanced Topics," gives an in-depth explanation of how to build menus.

See also: DEFINE PAD, ON PAD, ON SELECTION PAD, MENU(), and PAD().

DEFINE PAD

The DEFINE PAD command lets you define a pad on a bar menu. You must use DEFINE PAD once for each pad on the menu.

Syntax

DEFINE PAD *<pad name>* OF *<menu name>*
PROMPT *<string expression>* [AT *<row>*,*<column>*]
[MESSAGE *<string expression>*]

Notes

Use DEFINE PAD to define the pads for a bar menu. *Pad name* follows the same naming conventions as aliases (see the USE command in this chapter).

The *menu name* must be the name of a previously defined menu. (You define a menu with DEFINE MENU.)

You use the PROMPT clause to define the text that is displayed inside the menu option. dBASE IV adds a blank space to both ends of the prompt before placing it on the screen.

You can place menu prompts anywhere on the screen by using the optional AT clause. The coordinates for the AT clause determine the beginning point for the text. If you do not include coordinates, dBASE IV places the first menu prompt in the upper-left corner of the display and the next prompt just to the right of it, separating the two by a blank space. It repeats this process for each DEFINE PAD command.

Tip: If you place a lengthy menu on line 1 of the display, SET SCOREBOARD to OFF to prevent the scoreboard information from interfering with the menu.

To navigate through the prompts, use the LEFT ARROW and RIGHT ARROW keys.

The optional MESSAGE clause establishes a message of up to 79 characters for a pad. dBASE IV places the message at the bottom of the screen (centered) when the user locates the cursor on the pad.

Tip: Use the message text with a pad to display an explanation of the menu item.

Example

The following example creates a simple menu (called Main) with three pads: Copy, Sort, and Exit. The Copy pad's pop-up has two bars: Database file and Text file. The Sort and Exit pads each have pop-ups with only one bar. The ACTIVATE MENU command places the menu on the display.

```
* Define Main menu and define the pads to hang from it

DEFINE MENU Main
DEFINE PAD Copy OF Main PROMPT "Copy" AT 2,2
DEFINE PAD Sort OF Main PROMPT "Sort" AT 2,10
DEFINE PAD Exit OF Main PROMPT "Exit" AT 2,20
```

```
* Tell each pad which pop-up to activate

ON PAD Copy OF Main ACTIVATE POPUP Pop_copy
ON PAD Sort OF Main ACTIVATE POPUP Pop_sort
ON PAD Exit OF Main ACTIVATE POPUP Pop_exit

* Define the Copy pad's pop-up with its two bars

DEFINE POPUP Pop_copy FROM 3,2 MESSAGE "Copy a file"
DEFINE BAR 1 OF Pop_copy PROMPT "Database file"
DEFINE BAR 2 OF Pop_copy PROMPT "Text file"

* Define the Sort pad's pop-up with its single bar

DEFINE POPUP Pop_sort FROM 3,10 MESSAGE "Sort a file"
DEFINE BAR 1 OF Pop_sort PROMPT "Database file"

* Define the Exit pad's pop-up with its single bar

DEFINE POPUP Pop_exit FROM 3,20 MESSAGE "Exit application"
DEFINE BAR 1 OF Pop_exit PROMPT "Exit to DOS"

* Put up the menu

ACTIVATE MENU Main
```

For other examples, see the DEACTIVATE MENU command in this chapter and the PAD() function in Chapter 33. Also, Chapter 24, "Advanced Topics," gives an in-depth explanation of how to build menus.

See also: DEFINE MENU, ON PAD, ON SELECTION PAD, SET SCOREBOARD, and PAD().

DEFINE POPUP

The DEFINE POPUP command lets you define a pop-up menu. There are two types of pop-up menus. One type is similar to the pull-down menus that appear in dBASE IV's Control Center. The other type is like the list boxes that appear in the Control Center (for example, when you press SHIFT-F1 to get a list of options).

Syntax

DEFINE POPUP *<pop-up name>* FROM *<row1>*,*<column1>* [TO *<row2>*,*<column2>*] [PROMPT FIELD *<field name>*/
PROMPT FILES [LIKE *<skeleton>*]/
PROMPT STRUCTURE] [MESSAGE *<string expression>*]

Notes

Pop-up name follows the same naming conventions as aliases and field names (see the USE command for information on aliases). You must name a pop-up to be able to display it with the ACTIVATE POPUP command.

The FROM and optional TO coordinates define the upper-left and lower-right corners of the pop-up window. When you activate a pop-up, it overwrites any existing material on the screen. When you deactivate it, the underlying material reappears.

If you do not include the TO coordinates, dBASE IV automatically sets the window's width to fit the longest bar prompt or field. It also sets the window's length to fit all of the pop-up's bars.

If you provide TO coordinates, dBASE IV truncates prompts that are too long to fit within the pop-up window. If there are too many prompts to fit within the window's length, dBASE IV lets you scroll the prompts vertically within the window when you move the cursor.

The three PROMPT options let you create different types of list boxes. If you use any of the three, you cannot use the DEFINE BAR command later to define pull-down menu items for the pop-up. In other words, you will have committed the pop-up to being a list box rather than a pull-down menu.

The PROMPT FIELD option places the values from a named field inside the pop-up. For example, to put a series of last names within the pop-up window, you can use

```
PROMPT FIELD Lastname
```

if the active database has a field named Lastname.

Note: You cannot use a memo field with the PROMPT FIELD option.

If you use the PROMPT FILES option, all of the files from the current catalog are placed within the pop-up window. You can use the optional LIKE clause to limit the files to those that match a skeleton (for instance, *.DBF).

If you use the PROMPT STRUCTURE option, dBASE IV lists all of the fields from the file structure of the currently active database.

The optional MESSAGE clause establishes a message of up to 79 characters for the pop-up window. dBASE IV displays the message at the bottom of the screen when the pop-up window is active.

Examples

For an example of the DEFINE POPUP command, see the DEFINE PAD command. For other examples, see the BAR(), PAD(), and PROMPT() functions in Chapter 33. (The BAR() function shows you how to use the PROMPT FIELDS option.)

DEFINE WINDOW

The DEFINE WINDOW command lets you define a window and its associated border and screen colors.

Syntax

DEFINE WINDOW *<window name>* FROM *<row1>*,*<column1>*
TO *<row2>*,*<column2>*
[DOUBLE/PANEL/NONE/*<border definition string>*]
[COLOR [*<standard>*] [,*<enhanced>*] [,*<frame>*]

Notes

This command lets you place a window on the screen by using specified coordinates. The FROM coordinates define the upper-left corner of the window and the TO coordinates define the lower-right corner.

The default border for the window is a single line. You can use the DOUBLE option to create a double-line border. The PANEL option defines a reverse-video panel. You can also use the *border definition string* to define your own border characters. (See the SET BORDER command for more information on how to do this.)

The COLOR option lets you set the foreground and background colors for the window. See the SET COLOR command in Chapter 32 for more information on setting colors.

Example

The following example creates a window at the center of the screen. The window uses a border definition string to display a window with double lines on the top and bottom and single lines on the sides.

```
. DEFINE WINDOW Boxer FROM 8,20 TO 14,60 CHR(205),CHR(205),
    CHR(179),CHR(179),CHR(213),CHR(184),CHR(212),CHR(190)
. ACTIVATE WINDOW Boxer
```

See also: ACTIVATE WINDOW, DEACTIVATE WINDOW, RESTORE WINDOW, SAVE WINDOW, SET BORDER TO, and SET COLOR.

DELETE

The DELETE command marks records for deletion.

Syntax

DELETE [<*scope*>] [FOR <*condition*>] [WHILE <*condition*>]

The optional *scope,* FOR, and WHILE clauses let you set conditions for records marked for deletion. Using DELETE without any options marks only the current record for deletion.

Notes

The DELETE command marks records in the active database file for deletion. It does not, however, remove them from the database. You must use the PACK command to remove records that are marked for deletion.

You can use the RECALL command to unmark records that are marked for deletion.

When you use EDIT or BROWSE (as well as other full-screen commands), records marked for deletion show "Del" on the status bar. To mark a record for deletion while in a full-screen command, press CTRL-U. (To unmark a record, press CTRL-U again.)

When you use the LIST or DISPLAY command to show a list of records, records marked for deletion appear with an asterisk (*) by them.

Note: DELETE does not affect the position of the record pointer, provided you haven't used a *scope,* FOR, or WHILE clause.

Example

The following example activates the CUSTOMER database and marks the first seven records for deletion. It then uses the RECALL command to unmark the records.

```
. USE Customer
. DELETE NEXT 7
    7 records deleted
. RECALL ALL
    7 records recalled
```

See also: PACK, SET DELETED, RECALL, ZAP, and DELETED(), .

DELETE TAG

The DELETE TAG command deletes the specified tags from a multiple index (.MDX) file or closes an index (.NDX) file.

Syntax

DELETE TAG <*tag name 1*> [OF <*.MDX filename*>] /< *.NDX filename 1*>
[,<*tag name 2*> [OF <*.MDX filename*>] /< *.NDX filename 2*> ...]

Notes

You can use the DELETE TAG command to remove an index tag from any active multiple index file. When you use this command to delete an index tag, dBASE IV removes the tag permanently. The file must be active before you can delete a tag from a multiple index file.

If you delete all of the tags from a multiple index file, dBASE IV deletes the multiple index file as well.

You can use the OF clause to control which .MDX file the tag is deleted from.

When you use DELETE TAG with .NDX files, it closes rather than deletes the .NDX file.

See Chapter 5, "Sorting and Indexing," for a complete explanation of multiple index (.MDX) and single index (.NDX) files.

Example

The following example deletes the Cust_name tag from the CUSTOMER database's production .MDX file:

```
. DELETE TAG Cust_name OF Customer
```

See also: INDEX, SET INDEX, SET ORDER, USE, MDX(), NDX(), ORDER(), and TAG().

DIR

The DIR command displays a list of files from a specified directory. It resembles the DIR command in DOS.

Syntax

DIRECTORY/DIR [[ON] <*drive*>:] [[LIKE] [<*path*>] <*skeleton*>]

If you use the DIR command without any options, it lists only the names of the database files in the current directory.

Notes

The DIR command displays the database file names, number of records, date of last update, file size in bytes, total number of bytes for the displayed files, and total number of bytes remaining on disk.

Note: The DIR command may not show the most recent activity in a file if you haven't yet closed the file.

Examples

The following command displays all databases in the current directory:

```
. DIR
```

The next command shows all of the compiled program files in the current directory:

```
. DIR *.DBO
```

To display all of the files in the current directory, use the following command:

```
. DIR *.*
```

To show all of the program source files in the \PROGRAMS subdirectory, use the next command:

```
. DIR \PROGRAMS\*.PRG
```

See also: LIST/DISPLAY FILES.

DISPLAY Commands

The following DISPLAY commands are similar to the analogous LIST commands, but they display only one screenful of information at a time. (Press a key to see the next screenful of information.) For more information on these commands, see the analogous LIST commands.

LIST/DISPLAY
LIST/DISPLAY FILES
LIST/DISPLAY HISTORY
LIST/DISPLAY MEMORY
LIST/DISPLAY STATUS
LIST/DISPLAY STRUCTURE
LIST/DISPLAY USERS

DO

Use the DO command to execute a dBASE IV command file or procedure. If the command file or procedure has not been compiled, DO compiles it to an object (.DBO) file and then runs the object file. You can also pass parameters to a program when using DO.

Syntax

DO <*program filename*>/<*procedure name*>
[WITH <*parameter list*>]

Notes

When you issue the DO command, dBASE IV looks for the program file name in the current drive and directory. If dBASE cannot find the program name, it looks for the file in the path you set with the SET PATH command. If the file is not in either of these places, you need to include a drive designator and/or a path name as part of the file name.

When you use a DO command, dBASE IV uses the following search order:

1. It searches the current .DBO file for a procedure, if a .DBO file is being executed.
2. If a SET PROCEDURE command has activated a procedure file, dBASE IV searches for a procedure within that file.
3. dBASE IV searches for a procedure in other open .DBO files.
4. dBASE IV searches for a .DBO file with the associated file name (that is, the same name as the *program filename* or *procedure name*).
5. dBASE IV searches for a .PRG file with the associated name. If it finds one, it compiles the file and executes the resulting .DBO file.
6. dBASE IV searches for a .PRS file with the associated name. If it finds one, it compiles the file and then executes the resulting .DBO file. (A .PRS file is a SQL command or program file.)

Procedure Names

dBASE IV maintains a procedure list in every object (.DBO) file. If a source file does not start with a PROCEDURE or FUNCTION command, dBASE IV compiles the contents of the file as a procedure. It then uses the name from the source file as the name for the procedure and places that name in the procedure list of the object file. For example, if you create the following .PRG file

```
* Filename is WHEN.PRG
? DATE()
RETURN
```

and use the DO command to execute it, dBASE IV compiles the file into a .DBO file and assigns the procedure name WHEN.

You can place more than one procedure in a source file. For example, the following source file has two procedures, WHEN and Get_time:

```
* Filename is WHEN.PRG
? DATE()
? TIME()
DO Get_time
RETURN

PROCEDURE Get_time
? TIME()
RETURN
```

You can use the DO command to execute any procedure in any active .DBO file. For example, if FILE1.DBO calls FILE2.DBO and FILE2.DBO calls FILE3.DBO, all of the procedures in FILE1, FILE2, and FILE3 are available to the procedures in FILE3. You can have up to 32 active .DBO files.

When the program called with DO is finished executing, control returns to the calling program. If you execute a DO from the dot prompt or Control Center, however, control returns to that point.

Memory variables and arrays that you create within a program normally have a limited life span. When the program terminates, dBASE IV releases the program's memory variables and arrays. You can, however, designate them as PUBLIC, in which case you can use them after the program terminates.

If SET DEVELOPMENT is ON (the default), dBASE IV checks the date and time stamp of the source file against those of the associated object file. If the source file is newer than the object file, dBASE IV deletes the old object file, compiles a new one, and executes it.

When you access the dBASE IV Program Editor using MODIFY COMMAND, dBASE IV deletes the old .DBO file when you modify the associated .PRG file.

The WITH clause lets you pass up to 64 parameters to a procedure. The list you provide with WITH can contain any valid dBASE expression.

Tip: When you pass parameters with WITH, field names take precedence over memory variables. Therefore, if you have a memory variable and a field with the same name, you can distinguish between the two by placing M-> in front of the memory variable name.

When a procedure calls itself with a DO, it is said to be *recursive*. In dBASE IV, you can call a command file recursively. That is, a procedure can execute itself over again with DO, or a subroutine can call the original command file with DO. However, in both cases, dBASE IV opens two files. Because dBASE IV by default allows up to 20 DOs, you may run into difficulty if you call a file recursively too many times. Note that you can change the value of DO = in the CONFIG.DB file to increase the default number of DOs.

Examples

The following command file, named CIRC.PRG, computes the circumference of a circle using the formula circumference = π * diameter:

```
* CIRC.PRG
PARAMETERS M_diam, M_circ
M_circ = M_diam * PI()
RETURN
```

When you execute the CIRC program file with DO, you must pass it a value for the diameter. You must also include a memory variable so that CIRC can pass back the circumference.

```
. M_return = 0
        0
. DO Circ WITH 5, M_return
        15.71
. ? M_return
        15.71
```

See also: CANCEL, COMPILE, DEBUG, FUNCTION, MODIFY COMMAND, PARAMETERS, PRIVATE, PROCEDURE, PUBLIC, RESUME, RETURN, SET DEBUG, SET DEVELOPMENT, SET ECHO, SET PROCEDURE, SET TRAP, and SUSPEND.

DO CASE

The DO CASE command selects a single course of action from a set of alternatives.

Syntax

```
DO CASE
CASE <condition>
<commands>
[CASE <condition>
<commands>]
.
.
.
[OTHERWISE
<commands>]
ENDCASE
```

You can place any number of CASE statements between DO CASE and ENDCASE. The OTHERWISE statement is executed if none of the preceding conditions are met. The ENDCASE command is required to terminate a DO CASE structure.

Notes

Unlike the IF command, you can list many mutually exclusive alternatives between the DO CASE and ENDCASE commands.

You can nest DO CASE...ENDCASE, IF...ENDIF, and DO WHILE...ENDDO command pairs within a DO CASE...ENDCASE structure.

Each CASE statement is followed by a *condition* that includes a logical expression, such as ERROR() = 108 or M_var = 7. When the logical expression evaluates to logical true (.T.), dBASE IV executes the commands immediately following the CASE statement until it encounters another CASE, OTHERWISE, or ENDCASE statement.

After dBASE has found a CASE statement to be true and executed the subsequent commands, it transfers control to the statement immediately following ENDCASE. If dBASE does not find any of the CASE statements to be true, it executes the OTHERWISE statement. If there is no OTHERWISE statement, dBASE skips to the command following the ENDCASE statement.

Example

This example uses the value of the How_2_ship variable to display a message indicating how to ship an order. See the IF command for an example of how to accomplish the same programming task using IF.

```
DO CASE
     CASE How_2_ship = 110
          ? "Ship prepaid"
     CASE How_2_ship = 120
          ? "Ship FOB"
     CASE How_2_ship = 130
          ? "Ship COD"
     CASE How_2_ship = 140
          ? "Ship special handling"
     OTHERWISE
          ? "Ship by slow boat"
ENDCASE
```

See also: DO, DO WHILE, IF, and IIF().

DO WHILE

The DO WHILE command lets you build *iterative* (repetitive) loops in a program. dBASE repeats the command statements between the DO WHILE and associated ENDDO while the specified condition is true.

Syntax

DO WHILE *<condition>*
<commands>
[LOOP]
[EXIT]
ENDDO

Notes

The DO WHILE command executes subsequent commands while the logical expression specified for *condition* evaluates to true (.T.). One of the most common logical expressions is .NOT. EOF(). Other typical expressions are M_var = 7, Workarea <= 10, and COL() < R_margin.

If the condition evaluates to true (.T.), dBASE executes all of the commands until it encounters an ENDDO, LOOP, or EXIT command. If dBASE finds an ENDDO or a LOOP, it moves back up to the DO WHILE command and reevaluates the DO WHILE condition. If, on the other hand, it finds an EXIT, dBASE transfers control to the command immediately following the ENDDO.

By including a LOOP statement, you can have dBASE move back up to the DO WHILE command. In this case, it does not execute any of the commands following the LOOP statement in the DO WHILE...ENDDO block.

You must always include an ENDDO statement to terminate a DO WHILE structure.

Tip: You can place comments on an ENDDO command line in the space following the ENDDO statement without using &&. dBASE ignores any text on the line following the ENDDO.

You can nest DO WHILE...ENDDO, DO CASE...ENDCASE, and IF...ENDIF command pairs within a DO WHILE...ENDDO structure.

Occasionally, the statements within the DO WHILE never get executed. This occurs when the condition initially evaluates to false (.F.). In this case, dBASE skips to the statement following the ENDDO.

The SCAN command is a simplified version of the DO WHILE command, tailored specifically for selecting records from a database file.

Programming Notes

dBASE IV evaluates the DO WHILE statement the first time through the loop. From then on, it executes the DO WHILE statement from memory. Therefore, you can use macro substitution in the conditional part of a DO WHILE command, provided that your program does not attempt to change the value of the variable involved in the substitution. dBASE will simply disregard the change.

Example

The following example shows how you can use DO WHILE to read through a database. The program lets you view records in the CUSTOMER database with a ZIP code that is less than 60000. See the SCAN command in this chapter for another program that accomplishes the same effect.

```
USE Customer ORDER Zip
GO TOP
DO WHILE .NOT. EOF() .AND. Zip <= "60000"
     ?
     ? TRIM(Firstname)+" "+Lastname
     ? Addr_1
     ? Addr_2
     ? TRIM(City)+", "+State+" "+Zip
     ?
     WAIT
     SKIP
ENDDO
RETURN
```

See also: DO, DO CASE, IF, RETURN, and SCAN.

EDIT

EDIT is a full-screen command that you can use to display and edit records in the active database file (or view). EDIT and CHANGE are identical.

Syntax

EDIT [NOINIT] [NOFOLLOW] [NOAPPEND] [NOMENU]
[NOEDIT] [NODELETE] [NOCLEAR]
[<*record number*>] [FIELDS <*field list*>]
[<*scope*>] [FOR <*condition*>] [WHILE <*condition*>]

The optional *scope*, FOR, and WHILE clauses let you set conditions for records that EDIT will display. Use EDIT without any options to navigate through all of the records in the database.

Note: If you use a *scope,* FOR, or WHILE clause, dBASE doesn't let you use EDIT's **Go To** menu, nor does it let you switch to browse mode by pressing F2.

Notes

EDIT is a full-screen command (it uses a display form that occupies the entire screen). If you activate the EDIT command from the dot prompt, you return to the dot prompt when you exit EDIT. If you activate EDIT from a program, you return to the statement immediately following the EDIT command.

EDIT uses a default display format that shows only one record at a time with the field names listed down the left side of the screen and data immediately to the right. However, if a format (.FMT) file is active, EDIT displays records according to its display format. BROWSE, on the other hand, shows records in a tabular format with one record per row.

Tip: You can change from EDIT to BROWSE by pressing F2.

To activate the menu bar in edit mode, press F10. Chapter 4, "Entering, Editing, and Displaying Data," describes the various menu options and the special keys available in edit mode.

While in edit mode, you can add records to a file or view. To do so, move the cursor to the last field in the last record and press DOWN ARROW. When dBASE IV asks you whether you want to add records, press Y for YES. dBASE IV immediately shifts to append mode, and you can add a record to the file.

Tip: If SET AUTOSAVE is OFF (the default), the database file on disk may not reflect all of the newly added records until you close the file. If SET AUTOSAVE is ON, each newly appended record is immediately saved to disk.

Options

NOINIT lets you use the same command line options you used from a previous EDIT command. It tells the EDIT command to use the table from the previous EDIT.

NOFOLLOW is for indexed files only. Normally, when you edit the value in a key field, dBASE IV repositions the record according to the index value and still keeps it the current record. If you use the NOFOLLOW keyword and you change the index field contents, the record is repositioned, and the new record that occupies the original record's position becomes the current record.

NOAPPEND prevents you from entering new records at the end of the database file while in edit mode.

NOMENU prevents the EDIT menu from appearing.

NOEDIT makes all fields in the database read-only (you can display but cannot edit the records in the database). You can, however, add records to the end of the database file. You can also mark records for deletion by pressing CTRL-U.

NODELETE prevents you from marking records for deletion by pressing CTRL-U while in edit mode.

NOCLEAR keeps EDIT's display form on the screen after you exit edit mode.

Record number lets you start editing at a given record. You can then move to other records in the file. You can limit editing to a single record by using the RECORD keyword with the *scope* option. (See the introduction of this reference section for other *scope* options.) If you use this combination, you cannot access other records in the file.

FIELDS lets you control which fields appear in the EDIT form and the order in which they appear.

For information on using EDIT in a network environment, see Chapter 30, "Networking Commands and Functions."

See also: BROWSE, CHANGE, CREATE/MODIFY QUERY/VIEW, MODIFY COMMAND, SET AUTOSAVE, SET DESIGN, SET FIELDS, SET FORMAT, SET LOCK, SET REFRESH, and SET WINDOW OF MEMO.

EJECT

EJECT causes your printer to skip to the top of the next page. EJECT affects only the printer. (See the PAGE EJECT command for controlling streaming output.)

Syntax

```
EJECT
```

Notes

EJECT issues a form feed (ASCII code 12) to the printer. However, if you set the _padvance variable to "LINEFEEDS", EJECT issues line feeds (ASCII code 10) instead.

EJECT reinitializes PROW() and PCOL() to 0.

Tip: If you plan to use EJECT in a program, consider using PRINTSTATUS() beforehand. PRINTSTATUS() verifies whether the printer is ready for output.

See also: ???, EJECT PAGE, ON PAGE, PRINT, SET PRINTER, PCOL(), PRINTSTATUS(), PROW(), _padvance, _pageno, _pcolno, and _plineno.

EJECT PAGE

EJECT PAGE advances the streaming output to the start of the next page, or triggers a previously defined ON PAGE page-handling routine.

Syntax

```
EJECT PAGE
```

Notes

If you've previously defined an ON PAGE page-handling routine (see the ON PAGE command), dBASE IV checks to see whether the current line number (_plineno) is greater than the ON PAGE line number. (You set up a line number for ON PAGE by using the AT LINE clause.) If _plineno is less than the ON PAGE line, EJECT PAGE sends sufficient line feeds to trigger the ON PAGE page-handling routine. If _plineno is greater than the ON PAGE line (or if you don't have an ON PAGE page-handling routine), EJECT PAGE advances the streaming output as follows:

- If _padvance is set to "FORMFEED" and SET PRINTER is ON, dBASE issues a form feed (ASCII code 12) to the printer.
- If _padvance is set to "LINEFEED" and SET PRINTER is ON, dBASE issues sufficient line feeds (ASCII code 10) to the printer

to eject the current page. It uses the formula _plength - _plineno to calculate the number of line feeds to issue to the printer.

- If you've redirected streaming output to a destination other than the printer (for example, you've used SET ALTERNATE or SET CONSOLE), dBASE IV uses the formula (_plenth - _plineno) to calculate the number of line feeds to send.

dBASE IV then increments _pageno and resets _plineno to 0.

Tip: To eject a page without affecting the _pageno and _plineno settings, use an EJECT command.

See also: ?/??, EJECT, ON PAGE, SET ALTERNATE, SET CONSOLE, SET PRINTER, _padvance, _pageno, _plength, and _plineno.

ERASE

ERASE deletes a file from disk.

Syntax

ERASE <*filename*>/?

or

DELETE FILE <*filename*>/?

If you use the ? symbol, dBASE IV displays a menu of files. You must include an extension for the *filename*. Also, if the file is not on the current drive and directory, you must include a drive and directory as part of *filename*.

Notes

If a file is open, you must close it before you can delete it.

When you erase a database (.DBF) file, dBASE IV does not automatically erase the associated memo (.DBT) file and production (.MDX) file. You must delete these files yourself.

Note: The DELETE command does allow wildcard characters.

See also: CLOSE, DELETE, DELETE TAG, USE, and FILE().

EXPORT

EXPORT lets you copy an open database file to another file in PFS:FILE, dBASE II, Framework II, or RapidFile file format.

Syntax

EXPORT TO <*filename*> [TYPE] PFS/DBASEII/FW2/RPD
[FIELD <*field list*>] [<*scope*>]
[FOR <*condition*>] [WHILE <*condition*>]

Notes

EXPORT lets you create files that you can use in PFS:FILE, dBASE II, Framework II, or RapidFile. If you want to create files for other file formats, see the COPY command.

If you're using an index when you export the file, dBASE IV uses that index to order the records it outputs.

If you're exporting a file in PFS:FILE format, you can use a format (.FMT) file to set the screen format for the exported file. If you do not activate a screen format (using SET FORMAT), dBASE IV uses the default EDIT format for the PFS:FILE screen format.

SET SAFETY to OFF if you do not want to be prompted when dBASE IV is about to overwrite an existing file.

See also: COPY IMPORT, SET FORMAT, and SET SAFETY.

FIND

The FIND command conducts a very rapid search of an indexed database for a specified character string or number. If the search is successful, FIND positions the record pointer at the first record that matches the search value.

Syntax

FIND *<literal key>*

Before you can use the FIND command to search a database, that database must be indexed on the fields that you intend to search. Furthermore, since the FIND command only searches for literal values, you do not have to enclose character strings in quotes (for example, FIND Smith).

Notes

Unlike the SEEK and LOCATE commands, the FIND command does not support the use of expressions. Therefore, you cannot use FIND to locate values that match a given expression. This limits the use of the FIND command in programming applications. The SEEK command does support the use of expressions, and is used most often in a program to search an indexed database.

Because FIND does not support expressions, you must use the & macro substitution symbol to search for the contents of a memory variable with the FIND command. For example, to search for the contents of the memory variable named Findit, use the command line

```
FIND &Findit
```

You can use the FIND command to search a partial character string if SET EXACT is set to OFF. For example, to find the character string "Johnson" in an indexed database, you could use the command

```
FIND John
```

If SET EXACT is set to ON, the FIND command requires an exact match for the character string.

As mentioned, if the search is successful, the FIND command positions the record pointer at the record that matches the specified search value. FOUND() returns a logical true (.T.). However, if the search is not successful, dBASE IV positions the record pointer at the end of the database file. EOF() returns a logical true (.T.), and FOUND() returns a logical false (.F.).

The FIND command honors the SET NEAR, SET DELETED, and SET FILTER settings. When SET NEAR is ON, and a matching record is not found, the FIND command positions the record pointer immediately after the closest matching record in the database. When SET DELETED is ON, the FIND command does not position the record pointer on a record that is marked for deletion. When a SET FILTER condition is present, the FIND command ignores records specified by the filter condition.

Example

The following dot prompt commands demonstrate the FIND command.

```
. USE Customer ORDER Cust_no
Master index: CUST_NO
. FIND 1032
. ? Firstname,Lastname
Richard          Winnebego
. FIND 1055
Find not successful
. ? FOUND()
.F.
. ? EOF()
.T.
. GO TOP
CUSTOMER: Record No       1
. SET ORDER TO Lastname
. FIND Win
. ? Firstname,Lastname
Richard          Winnebego
```

FUNCTION

FUNCTION establishes a user-defined function (UDF).

Syntax

FUNCTION <*procedure name*>

Notes

You can create your own functions to perform tasks that dBASE IV's functions cannot accomplish. When dBASE IV encounters a user-defined function, it moves to the FUNCTION procedure of the same name. It then executes the code in the FUNCTION procedure and returns a value to the line that contains the user-defined function.

APPEND
APPEND FROM
APPEND FROM ARRAY
ASSIST
BEGIN TRANSACTION/
END TRANSACTION
BROWSE
CANCEL
CHANGE
CLEAR ALL/FIELDS
CLOSE
CLOSE ALTERNATE
CLOSE FORMAT
CLOSE PROCEDURE
COMPILE
CONVERT
COPY
COPY FILE
COPY INDEXES
COPY MEMO
COPY STRUCTURE
COPY STRUCTURE EXTENDED
COPY TAG
COPY TO ARRAY
CREATE or MODIFY
STRUCTURE
CREATE FROM
CREATE VIEW FROM
ENVIRONMENT
CREATE/MODIFY LABEL
CREATE/MODIFY QUERY/VIEW
CREATE/MODIFY REPORT
CREATE/MODIFY SCREEN
DEBUG
DEFINE BAR
DEFINE BOX
DEFINE MENU
DEFINE PAD
DEFINE POPUP
DEFINE WINDOW
DELETE TAG
DIR
DISPLAY
EDIT

ERASE or DELETE FILE
EXPORT
HELP
IMPORT
INDEX
INSERT
JOIN
LABEL FORM
LIST
LOAD
LOGOUT
MODIFY COMMAND/FILE
MOVE WINDOW
ON ERROR/ESCAPE/KEY
ON PAD
ON PAGE
ON READERROR
ON SELECTION PAD
ON SELECTION POPUP
PACK
PRINTJOB/ENDPRINTJOB
PROTECT
QUIT
REINDEX
REPORT FORM
RESTORE
RESTORE MACROS
RESTORE WINDOW
RESUME
ROLLBACK
SAVE
SAVE MACROS
SAVE WINDOW
SET
SORT
SUSPEND
TOTAL
TYPE
UPDATE
ZAP

Table 31-6. Commands Not Available in a User-Defined Function

You can place a FUNCTION procedure in the current program file, in a procedure file, or in its own file.

FUNCTION procedures are like other procedures. However, they begin with a FUNCTION command (rather than a PROCEDURE command), and they *must* end with a RETURN *<expression>* command. When you call a user-defined function, you must pass it parameters. The FUNCTION procedure operates on these parameters. It then returns a value through the RETURN command.

When you create a user-defined function, you should always match the name of the function with the associated FUNCTION *<procedure name>*. However, you should never use the same name as a dBASE IV command or function. Function names can be up to eight characters long and must begin with a letter.

If you place a user-defined function in a separate file, you must compile the function before you call it from a program or the dot prompt.

You cannot use all dBASE IV commands in a user-defined function. Table 31-6 lists the commands that you cannot use. Table 31-7 shows the SET commands that you cannot use in user-defined functions.

Note: You cannot use the macro substitution function (&) in user-defined functions. You can, however, use indirect file and alias references.

Example

The following function, CTERM, calculates the number of periods required to achieve a specific future value when you make a single initial deposit or investment. To reproduce the example, place CTERM in its own file (CTERM.PRG) and compile it with the COMPILE command.

```
* File is CTERM.PRG
FUNCTION Cterm
PARAMETERS M_fv, M_pv, M_int
M_cterm = LOG(M_fv / M_pv) / LOG(1 + M_int)
RETURN(M_cterm)
```

You can then call Cterm in the following manner:

```
. SET TALK OFF
. Fv = 24000
. Pv = 12000
. Int = .105/12
. ? Cterm(Fv, Pv, Int)
        79.56
```

CATALOG	FORMAT	SKIP	TRAP
DEBUG	PROCEDURE	SQL	VIEW
DEVICE	RELATION	STEP	WINDOW
FIELDS			

Table 31-7. SET Commands Not Available in a User-Defined Function

See also: DO, PARAMETERS, PROCEDURE, RETURN, and SET PROCEDURE.

GO/GOTO

The GO/GOTO command lets you position the record pointer at a specific record in the active database.

Syntax

GO/GOTO BOTTOM/TOP [IN *<alias>*]

or

GO/GOTO [RECORD] *<record number>* [IN *<alias>*]

or

<record number>

Notes

If you're not using an index and you use GO TOP or GO BOTTOM, dBASE IV moves the record pointer to the first and last record in the database. If you're using an index, dBASE IV locates the record pointer at the first or last record in the index file.

GO *<record number>* moves the record pointer to a specific record in the database, not to a relative position in the index file. You can also use a record number alone, without GO or GOTO, to position the record pointer at a specific record.

If you set a relation between two or more files and you use GOTO to reposition the record pointer in the parent file, dBASE IV also repositions the record pointer in the child database files. If a child database file does not have a corresponding record, dBASE IV positions the record pointer at the end of the child file. Repositioning the record pointer in a child file does not reposition the pointer in the parent file.

The IN clause lets you reposition the record pointer in another work area. If you use IN with GOTO, you do not have to use the SELECT command to activate the database in the other work area. You can designate the *alias* as

- A number from 1 to 10
- A letter from "A" to "J"
- The alias you established through the ALIAS option in the USE command

Examples

The following example shows some ways to navigate through a database with GOTO:

```
. USE Customer
. 13
CUSTOMER: Record No      13
. Mrecno = RECNO()
        13
. GO TOP
CUSTOMER: Record No       1
. GO BOTTOM
CUSTOMER: Record No      33
. GO Mrecno
CUSTOMER: Record No      13
```

See also: ON ERROR, SET DELIMITED, SET FILTER, SET RELATION, SKIP, and RECNO().

HELP

The HELP command lets you access dBASE IV's Help system.

Syntax

HELP [<*dBASE IV keyword*>]

Notes

To display the Help screen for a particular command, you can include the *dBASE IV keyword*. If you do not include this option, dBASE IV displays the Help Table of Contents.

Tip: When you press ESC to leave the Help system, the help text remains on the screen until you press ENTER. This enables you to use the information in the help text while you are working from the dot prompt.

Example

The following example gives you help on the PV() function.

```
. HELP PV()
```

See also: SET HELP and SET INSTRUCT.

IF

IF lets you make a decision when there are two alternative outcomes.

Syntax

IF *<condition>*
<commands>
[ELSE
<commands>]
ENDIF

Notes

You can only use the IF command in a program, you cannot use it at the dot prompt.

For a complete discussion of IF, see the IF...ELSE...ENDIF command in Chapter 20, "Program Control."

Example

This example yields the same result as the example for the DO CASE command. The nested IFs determine the value of the How_2_ship variable and print a message stating how to ship an order.

```
IF How_2_ship = 110
   ? "Ship prepaid"
ELSE
   IF How_2_ship = 120
      ? "Ship FOB"
   ELSE
      IF How_2_ship = 130
         ? "Ship COD"
      ELSE
         IF How_2_ship = 140
            ? "Ship special handling"
         ELSE
            ? "Ship by slow boat"
         ENDIF
      ENDIF
   ENDIF
ENDIF
```

See also: DO CASE, DO WHILE, SCAN, and IIF().

IMPORT

You use the IMPORT command to create a dBASE IV database from files created by other software programs. The supported software programs include PFS:FILE forms, dBASE II database files, Framework II database and spreadsheet frames, RapidFile data files, and Lotus 1-2-3 .WK1 (Release 2.0 or 2.01) worksheet files.

Syntax

IMPORT FROM <*filename*> [TYPE]
PFS/DBASEII/FW2/RPD/WK1

Filename is the non-dBASE file you're importing. The TYPE clause tells dBASE IV the name of the software program whose file is being imported.

Notes

The file name you specify must include the full file extension, if one exists, of the file you're importing. For example, dBASE II files have a .DBF extension that you must rename .DB2, RapidFile files have an .RPD extension, Framework II files have an .FW2 extension, and Lotus 1-2-3 files have a .WK1 extension. PFS:FILE files do not have file extensions.

The database dBASE IV creates has the same name as the original file and is given a .DBF extension. When importing dBASE II files, the dBASE II file must first be renamed with a .DB2 extension.

See also: APPEND FROM, COPY, and EXPORT.

INDEX

You use the INDEX command to create an index that specifies the order of information in a database. You can use this command to create both single index (.NDX) and multiple index (.MDX) files.

Syntax

INDEX ON <*key expression*> TO < *.NDX filename*>
/TAG <*tag name*> [OF <*.MDX filename*>]
[UNIQUE] [DESCENDING]

Key expression refers to an expression involving one or more database fields, as in

```
UPPER(Lastname)+" "+UPPER(Firstname)
```

Use the TO <*.NDX filename*> clause to create single index (.NDX) files.

TAG <*tag name*> specifies the tag name for an index in a multiple index (.MDX) file. If you do not include an OF clause, the specified tag is included in the production index (.MDX) file associated with the currently active database.

Use the OF clause to specify an independent multiple index (.MDX) file.

The UNIQUE clause specifies that only one unique value in the fields is included in the index. For example, if your database contains three John Smiths, only the first one is included in the index.

Normally, indexes order the records in ascending alphabetical, chronological, or numeric order. However, you can use the DESCENDING clause to specify descending order.

Notes

The index file you create with the INDEX command is written to disk. It contains the values from the fields specified in the key expression along with the record numbers from which those values are drawn. Once you activate an index with either the USE, SET INDEX, or SET ORDER commands, it specifies the order in which records from the database are displayed. It also controls the movement of the record pointer within the database. However, the original database used to create the index is not affected in any way.

Indexes are always associated with the database that was used to create them. Before you can use an index or the INDEX command, the database associated with that index must be open.

Indexes specify the order of information in a database and speed up processing. For example, once a database is indexed you can use the FIND and SEEK commands as well as the LOOKUP() or SEEK() functions to quickly locate data in a database. These commands are much faster than the LOCATE command that you use for non-indexed databases.

There are two types of index files: single index files and multiple index files. Single index files are compatible with dBASE III PLUS and have an .NDX file extension. On the other hand, multiple index files have an .MDX file extension and can contain up to 47 indexes, each identified by a tag name. Tag names can be up to ten characters, must begin with a letter, and can contain numbers and underscores.

There are two types of .MDX files, production index files and independent .MDX files. A production index file is created automatically when you create a database and is given the same name as the database and an .MDX extension. Each database can have only one production index. Furthermore, the database file header is flagged to indicate that a production index file exists for that database. On the other hand, you create independent multiple index files with the INDEX command and the TAG and OF clauses.

The naming conventions for both single and multiple index files follow those of DOS files. An index file name can be up to eight characters and can only contain characters allowed by DOS. To create a single index file, follow the INDEX command with the TO clause. To create a tag in a production index, follow the INDEX command with the TAG clause. To create a tag in an independent multiple index file, follow the INDEX command with the TAG *and* OF clauses.

Indexes take on the data type (numeric, character, or date) of the data used to create them. You cannot index a logical field unless you first convert it to a character string by using the IIF() function. For example, if you have a logical field called Bonus, the expression

```
IIF(Bonus, "T","F")
```

returns a "T" character string for those records where Bonus is true and an "F" character string for those records where Bonus is false.

When you create an index, it is opened and becomes the controlling or master index. The master index controls the order of information in the database. dBASE IV only allows one master index at a time. To specify another index as the master index, use the SET ORDER command followed by the name of an .NDX file or an .MDX tag name. Before you can use the SET ORDER command, you must activate the index file.

To activate an index file, you must open it. Production index files are opened automatically when the database associated with them is opened. Consequently, all tags within that production index are automatically updated for any changes to the database. On the other hand, you must open single index files and independent multiple index files by using the SET INDEX command. If either of these index file types are not open, the indexes or tags within them are not updated for changes to the database. To update these indexes or tags, you must use the REINDEX command. If the index is no longer required but you still want the indexes or tags updated, you can use the SET ORDER TO 0 command.

Index Expressions

You can combine fields from the current database in an index expression. To combine fields, use the plus sign (+). You can also use functions to format the information stored in an index. For example, the following expression combines two fields called Lastname and Firstname. Note that both of these fields have a character data type. It also uses the UPPER() function to generate the index in uppercase letters.

```
INDEX ON UPPER(Lastname)+" "+UPPER(Firstname) TAG Allnames
```

To combine fields of differing data types, you must use functions to covert them to the same data type. For example, the following command line uses the DTOS() function to convert a date field called Maildate to a character expression to match the Lastname character field.

```
INDEX ON DTOS(Maildate)+Lastname TO Datename
```

Examples

The following dot prompt commands demonstrate the INDEX command:

```
. USE Salary
. LIST
Record#  FIRSTNAME LASTNAME     GROSS
      1  Mary      Jones     24000.00
      2  Drew      Gibson    22000.00
      3  Ralph     Moriarity 26000.00
      4  Clive     Bunker    23000.00
      5  John      Patrovich 32000.03
      6  Suzanne   Chambers  17000.00
      7  Keith     Campbell  52000.00
      8  George    Haenszel  22000.00
      9  Jeff      Hill      25000.00
     10  Sam       Hammons   31000.00
     11  Kevin     Anderson  28000.00

. INDEX ON TRIM(Lastname)+Trim(Firstname) TAG Allnames
  100% indexed          11 Records indexed
. LIST
Record#  FIRSTNAME LASTNAME     GROSS
     11  Kevin     Anderson  28000.00
      4  Clive     Bunker    23000.00
      7  Keith     Campbell  52000.00
      6  Suzanne   Chambers  17000.00
      2  Drew      Gibson    22000.00
      8  George    Haenszel  22000.00
     10  Sam       Hammons   31000.00
      9  Jeff      Hill      25000.00
      1  Mary      Jones     24000.00
      3  Ralph     Moriarity 26000.00
      5  John      Patrovich 32000.03

. SET ORDER TO
Database is in natural order
```

See also: CLOSE, COPY INDEX, COPY TAG, DELETE TAG, FIND, REINDEX, SET DELETED, SET FILTER, SET INDEX, SET NEAR, SET ORDER, SET UNIQUE, SORT, USE, KEY(), MDX(), NDX(), ORDER(), SEEK(), and TAG().

INPUT

INPUT lets you get input from the user in a dBASE IV program.

Syntax

INPUT [<*prompt*>] TO <*memory variable*>

The *prompt* can be a character expression. If you use a literal string, you must enclose it within single quotes (' '), double quotes (" "), or square brackets ([ ]).

Notes

Although you can use INPUT to get any type of data from the user, it is used mostly for numeric-type input. To get character-type input from the user, use the ACCEPT command.

Tip: The user must delimit character-type input for the INPUT command. If you want to get only character input, use the ACCEPT command, which doesn't require delimiters.

dBASE IV creates a memory variable to contain the expression that you enter at the prompt, if you haven't created one already. The type of expression that you enter determines the type of memory variable that dBASE IV creates. If you enter a number, dBASE IV creates a type N numeric memory variable.

You must press ENTER to complete your response to the INPUT command. If you don't enter any data before pressing ENTER, dBASE IV redisplays the prompt.

You can use the INPUT command to get complex expressions from the user. You can also use it to get date input. However, if you do get date input, make sure to remind the user to enter the data between curly braces ({ }). You can have the user enter the date in character format and convert the input to date format with the CTOD() function.

See also: @, ACCEPT, PRIVATE, PUBLIC, READ, STORE, and WAIT.

INSERT

INSERT lets you add a new record to a database at the current record pointer location.

Syntax

INSERT [BEFORE] [BLANK]

Notes

INSERT is a full-screen command (its display form occupies the entire screen). When you use INSERT to add a record to the database, dBASE IV displays a data-entry screen in which you can type the data for the record.

When you use INSERT without any options, dBASE IV places the new record immediately after the current record.

INSERT lets you add multiple records to the end of the file either when the record pointer is located at the end of the file or when the file is indexed.

Chapter 4, "Entering, Editing, and Displaying Data," describes the various menu options and the special keys available for INSERT.

You can use the BEFORE clause to insert a new record *before* the current record.

If you include the BLANK clause, dBASE IV inserts a new empty record but does not enter full-screen mode. You can then add data using BROWSE, EDIT, CHANGE, or REPLACE.

Example

The following example inserts a new record after record 6 in the SALARY database:

```
. USE Salary
. GO 6
SALARY: Record No      6
. INSERT
```

See also: @, APPEND, CHANGE, EDIT, MODIFY COMMAND, READ, SET AUTOSAVE, SET CARRY, and SET FORMAT.

JOIN

JOIN lets you merge the records from two open database files into a third database file.

Syntax

JOIN WITH <*alias*> TO <*filename*> FOR <*condition*>
[FIELDS <*field list*>]

A FOR <*condition*> clause is mandatory for the JOIN command.

If you do not include a drive and directory for the TO <*filename*> clause, dBASE IV assumes the current drive and directory. Also, if you do not include a file extension, dBASE IV assumes a .DBF extension.

Notes

To join two database files, you must open them in separate work areas. You can then use an alias to address the file in the unselected work area. (See the example that follows.)

When joining two databases, you can use FIELDS <*field list*> to limit the fields that are included. You can use any field type from both files. However, you cannot use memo fields.

When dBASE IV joins two files, it places the record pointer on the first record of the active file. It then scans the second file to find records that match the FOR condition. If it finds the FOR condition to be true, it adds a record to the new file. After dBASE IV has scanned all of the records in the second file, it returns to the first file and advances the record pointer to the second record in the file. It then repeats the process for the second record, continuing in this way until it has processed all records in the active file. As you can imagine, the process can take quite a long time with lengthy files.

If you do not include a FIELDS <*field list*>, dBASE IV assigns all of the fields from the active file to the new file. It then assigns the fields from the second file, until it reaches the limit of 255 fields. As dBASE IV assigns fields, it eliminates any duplicate field names.

If a catalog is open and SET CATALOG is ON, JOIN updates the catalog with the name of the new file.

Tip: When joining files, avoid using the single letters "A" through "J" and "M" for file names. dBASE IV uses these letters for aliases.

Because of the way that JOIN merges files, be careful when you use it with large files. For example, suppose you have two files with 500 records each. If, when you join the files, the condition in the FOR clause is always true, your new file will have 250,000 records (500 * 500).

If both files have a common field name but you want to include the field from the file in the unselected work area, precede the field name with an alias.

Example

Suppose you want to create a new database file, named SALES_12, that combines fields from the CUSTOMER database and fields from the ORDERREC database. The fields you want to include in the new database file are Client_no (contained in both databases), Lastname (from CUSTOMER), Order_date (from ORDERREC), Total (from ORDERREC), and Orderno (from ORDERREC). Furthermore, you want the SALES_12 database to include only information since December 1, 1988. Here's how to create the new database, identifying the fields in work area 2 by the alias B (for ORDERREC):

```
. USE Customer
. USE Orderrec IN 2
. JOIN WITH Orderrec TO Sales_12 FOR Cust_no = B->Cust_no .AND.
    B->Order_date >= {12/01/88} FIELDS Cust_no, Lastname,
    B->Order_date, B->Total, B->Order_no
    18 records joined
. USE Sales_12
. DISPLAY STRUCTURE
Structure for database: F:\DB4CR\PROGRAMS\SALES_12.DBF
Number of data records:      18
```

```
Date of last update   : 02/01/89
Field  Field Name  Type       Width    Dec    Index
    1  CUST_NO     Numeric        6              N
    2  LASTNAME    Character     20              N
    3  ORDER_DATE  Date           8              N
    4  TOTAL       Numeric        8      2       N
    5  ORDER_NO    Numeric        6              N
** Total **                      49

. LIST NEXT 6
Record#  CUST_NO LASTNAME                     ORDER_DATE     TOTAL  ORDER_NO
      1     1016 Michaelman                   12/02/88       53.14       116
      2     1017 Jones                        12/02/88       26.57       117
      3     1018 Smith                        12/03/88       29.77       118
      4     1019 Antonio                      12/05/88       59.53       119
      5     1020 Smythe                       12/06/88       31.95       120
      6     1021 Shields                      12/07/88       27.95       121
```

See also: SET FIELDS and SET RELATION.

LABEL FORM

The LABEL FORM command lets you use a given label format file to print, display, or output labels to a file.

Syntax

LABEL FORM <*label filename*>/?
[<*scope*>] [FOR <*condition*>] [WHILE <*condition*>]
[SAMPLE] [TO PRINTER/TO FILE <*filename*>]

Without a FOR or WHILE clause (or a filter), dBASE IV prints labels for all records in the active database.

If you do not include a drive or path as part of the file name, dBASE IV assumes that the file is located on the current drive and path.

You can use the ? symbol to display a menu of label files from which to choose.

Notes

To create a label design, you use the CREATE/MODIFY LABEL command. dBASE IV gives the resulting label form file an .LBL extension. Besides an .LBL file, dBASE IV creates an .LBG file that contains the program code (for example, ?, ??, PRINTJOB, and ENDPRINTJOB commands) needed to print your labels.

When you use the LABEL FORM command to print labels, dBASE IV compiles the .LBG file to an .LBO file. It then uses the .LBO file to print your labels.

You can use dBASE III PLUS label files in dBASE IV without any modification. When dBASE IV reads the label file, it determines the file's origin from the file header. If the file is from dBASE III PLUS, dBASE IV uses the dBASE III PLUS label engine to print the labels.

You can print sample labels by adding the SAMPLE option to the LABEL FORM command. This allows you to check that your labels are properly aligned. When you use the SAMPLE option, dBASE IV prints a single row of test labels using the letter "X" rather than data from the database. You can generate sample labels as many times as you like. Just press Y or ENTER when dBASE displays the prompt "Do you want more samples? (Y/N)." When the labels are correctly aligned, press N at the prompt. dBASE beeps and immediately begins printing your labels using data from the database.

To send the labels to a disk file rather than the screen or printer, use the TO FILE option. The type of file that dBASE IV creates depends on the printer driver that you have installed. For example, if you have installed the ASCII text printer driver (ASCII.PR2), dBASE IV creates a file that does not contain any escape sequences and gives the file a .TXT extension. However, if you've installed dBASE IV for a particular printer, it creates a file with the .PRT extension that may contain escape sequences for your printer.

For a complete discussion of creating labels using the Labels Design screen, see Chapter 11, "Creating Labels."

See also: CREATE/MODIFY LABEL and SET PRINTER.

LIST/DISPLAY

The LIST/DISPLAY command shows the contents of a database file in a columnar list.

Syntax

LIST/DISPLAY [[FIELDS] <*expression list*>] [OFF]
[<*scope*>] [FOR <*condition*>] [WHILE <*condition*>]
[TO PRINTER/TO FILE <*filename*>]

Without a FOR or WHILE clause, LIST shows the records in the current database. DISPLAY shows only the current record, unless you include a FOR or WHILE clause, in which case it displays all records that match the conditions. You can further limit both LIST and DISPLAY by using SET FILTER or SET DELETED.

Notes

The DISPLAY command displays only one screenful of information at a time. (Press a key to see the next screenful of information.) The LIST command displays the information in a continuous stream.

Press CTRL-S to halt the display or records. Press any key to resume the display. To interrupt the display and return to the dot prompt, press ESC.

LIST/DISPLAY does not show the contents of a memo field unless you specifically include the memo field name in the FIELDS list. If you do, its contents are displayed in a 50-character wide column. (You can use the SET MEMOWIDTH command to change the display width of memo fields.)

If you use the LIST/DISPLAY command to display a record that is wider than 80 characters, dBASE IV wraps the remaining characters to the next line.

The TO PRINTER clause lets you direct output to the printer. The TO FILE clause lets you direct output to a file on disk.

Normally, the LIST/DISPLAY command shows a record number column (see the following example). You can eliminate the record number column with the OFF option.

If SET HEADING is ON (the default), dBASE IV gives a heading to each column of LIST/DISPLAY output. The headings appear as you type them. For example, if you type **LIST FIRSTNAME**, dBASE IV displays the heading as "FIRSTNAME." On the other hand, if you type **LIST Firstname**, dBASE IV displays the heading as "Firstname."

If you use an expression in the FIELDS list (for example, TRIM(Lastname)), dBASE IV uses that expression for the heading.

Example

The following example activates the CUSTOMER database and lists the Lastname and City fields when the Cust_no field is less than or equal to 1010:

```
. USE Customer
. LIST Lastname, City FOR Cust_no <= 1010
Record#  Lastname            City
      1  Thomas              Dallas
      2  Holland             Louisville
      3  Spraul              Soquel
      4  Johnson             Santa Monica
      5  Takano              Chiyoda-ku, Tokyo 101
      6  Corzine             Capitola
      7  Cramden             Indianapolis
      8  Stokes              Evanston
      9  Harding             Santa Cruz
     10  Hinckley            Cincinnati
```

See also: SET HEADING, SET MARGIN, and SET MEMOWIDTH.

LIST/DISPLAY FILES

The LIST/DISPLAY FILES command lists directory information, like the DIR command in DOS.

Syntax

LIST/DISPLAY FILES [LIKE <*skeleton*>]
[TO PRINTER/TO FILE <*filename*>]

If you use the command without any options, it lists only the names of the database files in the current directory.

Notes

The LIST/DISPLAY FILES command displays the database file names, number of records, date of last update, file size in bytes, total number of bytes for the displayed files, and total number of bytes remaining on disk.

LIST/DISPLAY FILES and DIR are equivalent, except that DIR does not provide the TO PRINTER option for sending the results to the printer or the TO FILE option for sending the results to a file.

Note: The LIST/DISPLAY FILES command may not show the most recent changes to a file if you haven't yet closed the file.

Example

The following example shows that there are 9 database files in the current directory:

```
. LIST FILES
Database Files      # Records      Last Update       Size
ACCTSREC.DBF               29      05/12/88         11877
CUST2.DBF                  33      12/13/88          7975
ORDERREC.DBF               33      01/31/89          2891
CUSTOMER.DBF               33      01/29/89          7975
MEMO.DBF                    1      12/18/88            77
SALARY.DBF                 12      01/02/89           950
SAVEORD.DBF                33      01/04/89          2891
NEWSTRUC.DBF                8      01/04/89           346
CLIENTS.DBF                15      01/31/89          2636

  37618 bytes in      9 files
3237888 bytes remaining on drive
```

See also: DIR, SET AUTOSAVE, and FILE().

LIST/DISPLAY HISTORY

LIST/DISPLAY HISTORY displays the contents of the history buffer.

Syntax

LIST/DISPLAY HISTORY [LAST <*type N expression*>]
[TO PRINTER/TO FILE <*filename*>]

The default setting for the number of commands stored in the history buffer is 20. You can change this number with the SET HISTORY command (see Chapter 32).

Notes

dBASE IV stores your last 20 commands in a section of memory called the history buffer. You can use the LIST/DISPLAY HISTORY command to see the contents of the history buffer.

The DISPLAY HISTORY command displays only one screenful of information at a time. (Press a key to see the next screenful of information.) The LIST HISTORY command displays the information in a continuous stream.

LIST/DISPLAY HISTORY shows the entire contents of the history buffer, unless you limit the display by using the LAST clause. For example, if you enter **DISPLAY HISTORY LAST 10**, dBASE IV displays the last ten commands.

The TO PRINTER clause lets you direct output to the printer. The TO FILE clause lets you direct output to a file on disk.

See also: SET HISTORY.

LIST/DISPLAY MEMORY

LIST/DISPLAY MEMORY displays various information about your PC's memory.

Syntax

LIST/DISPLAY MEMORY [TO PRINTER/TO FILE <*filename*>]

Notes

The DISPLAY MEMORY command displays only one screenful of information at a time. (Press a key to see the next screenful of information.) The LIST MEMORY command displays the information in a continuous stream.

The LIST/DISPLAY MEMORY command displays

- The names of all active memory variables and array elements
- Whether the memory variables and array elements are public or private, along with their current values

- The amount of memory consumed by active windows, menus, pads, and pop-ups
- The settings for all system memory variables
- The amount of memory still available

The number of memory variables you can have is determined by your current MVBLKSIZE and MVMAXBLKS settings. These settings are in your CONFIG.DB file.

The TO PRINTER clause lets you direct output to the printer. The TO FILE clause lets you direct output to a file on disk.

Example

The following example stores values to four different memory variables:

- Mlastname, a character variable
- Mcount, a type N (binary coded decimal) number
- Mtest, a logical variable
- Mpi, a type F (floating point binary) number

It then uses DISPLAY MEMORY to show how dBASE IV allocated memory for the variables.

```
. Mlastname = "Weston"
. Mcount = 1
. Mtest = .F.
. Mpi = PI()
. DISPLAY MEMORY
          User Memory Variables

MPI          pub   F          3.14  (3.1415926535897931l6)
MTEST        pub   L   .F.
MCOUNT       pub   N            1  (1.000000000000000000)
MLASTNAME    pub   C   "Weston"

     4 out of 500 memvars defined (and 0 array elements)
      .
      .
      .
```

See also: DECLARE, DEFINE, DEFINE MENU, DEFINE PAD, DEFINE POPUP, DEFINE WINDOW, PRIVATE, PUBLIC, RELEASE, RESTORE, SAVE, and STORE.

LIST/DISPLAY STATUS

LIST/DISPLAY STATUS displays information about the current dBASE IV work session and environment.

Syntax

LIST/DISPLAY STATUS [TO PRINTER/TO FILE <*filename*>]

Notes

The DISPLAY STATUS command displays only one screenful of information at a time. (Press a key to see the next screenful of information.) The LIST STRUCTURE command displays the information in a continuous stream.

LIST/DISPLAY STATUS displays for each open database the following information:

- Current work area number
- Database name, including the driver, path, alias name
- Read-only status, if the file is write-protected
- Open .NDX and .MDX index file names
- Index key expressions for each index file and tag
- Whether an index is unique or descending
- Open memo file names
- Filter formulas

It also displays information regarding the current environment.

- File search path
- Default disk drive
- Print destination
- Loaded modules
- Currently selected work area
- Left margin setting
- Currently open procedure file
- Reprocess count
- Refresh count
- The setting for DEVICE (whether SCREEN, PRINT, or FILE)
- Currency symbol
- Delimiter symbols
- Number of files open
- ON command settings
- Most of current settings for ON/OFF SET commands
- Function key assignments

The TO PRINTER clause lets you direct output to the printer. The TO FILE clause lets you direct output to a file on disk.

The LIST/DISPLAY STATUS command displays extra information in a network environment. See Chapter 30, "Network Commands and Functions."

See also: DIR, INDEX, ALIAS(), DISKSPACE(), FILE(), KEY(), MDX(), MEMORY(), NDX(), ORDER(), OS(), PROGRAM(), SET TAG(), and VERSION().

LIST/DISPLAY STRUCTURE

LIST/DISPLAY STRUCTURE displays the structure and associated field definitions of a database file.

Syntax

LIST/DISPLAY STRUCTURE [IN <*alias*>]
[TO PRINTER/TO FILE <*filename*>]

The IN <*alias*> clause lets you display the structure for a file in another work area. You do not have to leave the current work area to see the structure of another one.

The TO PRINTER clause lets you direct output to the printer. The TO FILE clause lets you direct output to a file on disk.

Notes

The LIST/DISPLAY STRUCTURE command displays a database's file name, number of records, the date the file was last updated, the entire field structure (including whether a field has an .MDX tag in the production .MDX file), and the total length of a record.

Tip: The total length of the record includes all of the field widths plus one extra byte (for the deleted record marker).

The DISPLAY STRUCTURE command displays only one screenful of information at a time. (Press a key to see the next screenful of information.) The LIST STRUCTURE command displays the information in a continuous stream.

If SET FIELDS is ON, a > symbol appears next to fields that you specified with the SET FIELDS TO command.

Example

The following example displays the structure of the Orderrec database. Notice that two of the fields, Cust_no and Order_no, have .MDX tags in the production .MDX file.

```
. USE Orderrec
. LIST STRUCTURE
Structure for database:F:\DB4CR\PROGRAMS\ORDERREC.DBF
Number of data records:       33
Date of last update    : 01/31/89
Field  Field Name  Type        Width    Dec     Index
```

```
     1  CUST_NO      Numeric       6          Y
     2  ORDER_NO     Numeric       6          Y
     3  ORDER_DATE   Date          8          N
     4  INV_NO       Numeric       6          N
     5  UNITS        Numeric       4          N
     6  PRICE        Numeric       6     2    N
     7  TAX          Logical       1          N
     8  FOREIGN_SH   Numeric       5     2    N
     9  TOTAL        Numeric       8     2    N
    10  PART_NO      Numeric       3          N
    11  ITEM         Character     7          N
    12  DELETE       Logical       1          N
    13  MSSG         Memo         10          N
    14  INVOICED     Logical       1          N
** Total **                       73
```

See also: COPY STRUCTURE, COPY STRUCTURE EXTENDED, CREATE or MODIFY STRUCTURE, CREATE FROM, and SET FIELDS.

LIST/DISPLAY USERS

In a networking environment, LIST/DISPLAY USERS displays the workstation or log-in name of each user currently working with dBASE IV. See Chapter 30, "Networking Commands and Functions," for a complete description of this command.

LOAD

The LOAD command lets you load a binary program (.BIN) file into memory. You can then execute the file by using the CALL command or the CALL() function.

Syntax

LOAD <*binary filename*>

Notes

When you load a binary program file with CALL, you can use the program as a subroutine. You can load up to 16 files into memory at any one time. The maximum size for a binary file is 32,000 bytes.

Each binary file you load must have a unique name. dBASE IV uses a default extension of .BIN. To see a list of the loaded files, use the LIST/DISPLAY STATUS command.

Example

The dBASE IV sample programs contain a sample binary program module—GETDRIVE.BIN. If you copied the sample programs to your hard disk during the installation process, GETDRIVE.BIN is on your SAMPLES subdirectory.

```
. LOAD C:\DBASE\SAMPLES\GETDRIVE
. Drive = " "

. CALL Getdrive WITH Drive
. ? "Current drive = ",Drive
Current drive =  C
```

See also: CALL, LIST/DISPLAY STATUS, RELEASE, RUN/!, and CALL().

LOCATE

LOCATE lets you search the active database file for a record that meets a given condition.

Syntax

LOCATE [FOR] *<condition>* [*<scope>*] [WHILE *<condition>*]

Notes

You use the LOCATE command to perform a sequential search through a database file. LOCATE reads each record and tests whether it meets a specified condition, usually a FOR condition. When dBASE evaluates the condition for a record, it leaves the record pointer at the record if the result is true. Also, dBASE IV displays the record number screen and FOUND() returns true (.T.).

If LOCATE can't find a match, dBASE IV leaves the record pointer at the end of the file, or the end of the scope, if you define one. In this case, dBASE IV displays the message "End of LOCATE scope," and FOUND() returns false (.F.).

You don't need to use an indexed file with LOCATE, but if you've activated an index, LOCATE will follow the index order. However, because LOCATE reads a file sequentially, it can be quite slow with large files. FIND and SEEK, which both work with indexed files, are faster methods of locating records.

You must place a logical condition in the FOR clause. For example, you might enter

```
LOCATE FOR Bonus
```

(where Bonus is a logical field) or

```
LOCATE FOR Lastname = "Sullivan"
```

Once you've issued a LOCATE command, you can use CONTINUE to locate the next record in the database that meets the specified condition.

LOCATE always repositions the record pointer at the start of the file when it starts its search, unless you specify otherwise with a *scope* or WHILE clause.

You can use NEXT <*n*> with the *scope* to limit the number of records (*n*) that the LOCATE command searches through. In this case, LOCATE does not reposition the record pointer to the start of the database but begins at the current record.

Example

The following example shows the results of searching the CLIENTS database for records with a value in the Lastname field equal to "McCrae."

```
. Mlast = "McCrae"
McCrae
. USE Clients
. LOCATE FOR Lastname = Mlast
Record =       6
```

```
. ? Lastname, Firstname
McCrae          John
. CONTINUE
End of LOCATE scope
. ? FOUND()
.F.
. ? EOF()
.T.
```

See also: CONTINUE, FIND, SEEK, and FOUND().

LOGOUT

The LOGOUT command logs out the current dBASE IV user and prompts a new user to log in. This command is covered in detail in Chapter 30, "Networking Commands and Functions."

MODIFY COMMAND

Use MODIFY COMMAND to access the dBASE IV Text Editor. You can use this editor to create and change dBASE program and format files and to work with standard ASCII files.

Syntax

MODIFY COMMAND/FILE <*filename*> [WINDOW <*window name*>]

Notes

If you do not include a drive or directory as part of the file name, dBASE IV uses the current drive and directory. dBASE also assumes a .PRG extension if you do not include an extension.

You can use MODIFY FILE to access the Text Editor. When you use the command, dBASE IV does not assume a default extension. If you create a file and save it without an extension, dBASE IV does not provide an extension.

You can use your own external word processor in place of the dBASE IV Text Editor by modifying your CONFIG.DB file. See Chapter 35, "Customizing dBASE IV," for more details.

When you issue a MODIFY COMMAND command, dBASE IV first searches for the specified file. If it finds the file, it uses the file's contents. Otherwise, it creates a new file with the name you've specified.

Tip: Whenever you edit a file, dBASE IV saves the previous version of the file with .BAK extension.

See also: COMPILE, CREATE, DO, NOTE/*/&&, RENAME, SET DEVELOPMENT, and TYPE.

MODIFY Commands

The following MODIFY commands are similar to the analogous CREATE commands. For more information on these commands, see the CREATE commands.

MODIFY APPLICATION

MODIFY LABEL

MODIFY QUERY/VIEW

MODIFY REPORT

MODIFY SCREEN

MODIFY STRUCTURE

MOVE WINDOW

You can use the MOVE WINDOW command to move a previously defined window to another location on the screen.

Syntax

MOVE WINDOW <*window name*> TO <*row*>,<*column*>/
BY <*delta row*>,<*delta column*>

Notes

You can use the TO clause to move a window to a new location on the screen using absolute screen coordinates (that is, relative to the upper-left corner of the screen). You can use the BY clause to move a window to a new location relative to its current position.

Examples

The following example defines and activates a window called Small_win:

```
. DEFINE WINDOW Small_win FROM 1,1 TO 10,70
. ACTIVATE WINDOW Small_win
```

To move the Small_win window to new coordinates, you could enter

```
. MOVE WINDOW Small_win TO 5,1
```

To move the window down ten rows and over five columns, you would enter

```
. MOVE WINDOW Small_win BY 10,5
```

See also: ACTIVATE SCREEN, ACTIVATE WINDOW, DEACTIVATE WINDOW, DEFINE WINDOW, RESTORE WINDOW, SAVE WINDOW, and SET WINDOW OF MEMO.

NOTE/*/&&

You can use a NOTE, asterisk (*), or double ampersand (&&) to place comments lines in a program file.

Syntax

NOTE/* *<text>*

and

[*<command>*] && *<text>*

Notes

You can use any one of these commands to tell dBASE IV that you are placing a comment in a program file. The comment text documents your code.

You must place NOTE or * at the start of a line (but not necessarily in column 1).

You can use && on the same line as program commands to enter comments after the commands. You can also place && at the start of a line.

If you place a semicolon after a NOTE or &&, dBASE IV reads the next line as part of the comment.

Examples

The following example shows how you might use * to comment on some text:

```
* Loop until current time = Timeout or key is pressed
Key_in = 0
DO WHILE VAL(SUBSTR(TIME(),7,2)) <> Timeout .AND. Key_in = 0
     Key_in = INKEY()
ENDDO
```

The next example uses && to place a comment on a program line:

```
? CHR(7)+"Database not loaded"     && Sound the bell
```

See also: MODIFY COMMAND and PROCEDURE.

ON ERROR/ESCAPE/KEY

The ON ERROR/ESCAPE/KEY command executes a command or program when a dBASE IV system error occurs, the ESC key is pressed, or a specified key is pressed. When you use the ON ERROR/ESCAPE/KEY command early in a program to specify either a keystroke or an error, dBASE IV watches for that keystroke or error to occur for the rest of the program. You can have your program branch to a subprogram or procedure when the keystroke or error takes place.

Syntax

ON ERROR <*command*>
/ESCAPE <*command*>
/KEY [LABEL <*key label name*>][<*command*>]

ON ERROR <*command*> executes *command* when a dBASE IV system error occurs. Syntax or evaluation errors are examples of this type of error. ON ERROR is primarily used to perform a subprogram or procedure when a dBASE IV system error occurs. The called procedure identifies the type of error and corrects it if possible. Use this command early in your program to prevent dBASE IV from displaying an error message or causing your program to crash back to the dot prompt.

ON ESCAPE executes *command* when you press the ESC key. The ON ESCAPE command allows you to tailor dBASE IV's response to the ESC key. Instead of having the ESC key end your program, you can use ON ESCAPE to trigger the start of another subprogram or procedure.

ON KEY LABEL with *key label name* executes *command* when you press *key label name* (dBASE IV only). *Key label name* is the name of a key on your keyboard and is restricted to the key label name description provided in Table 31-8 in the Notes section.

ON KEY LABEL without *key label name* executes *command* when you press any key (same as in dBASE III PLUS).

ON KEY by itself resets the key trap and turns it off.

Command is the name of a dBASE IV command. Most often, this command is the DO command followed by the name of a subprogram or procedure. You can also use the name of a user-defined function.

Notes

If you issue more than one ON ERROR/ESCAPE/KEY <*command*>, dBASE IV processes ON ERROR first, ON ESCAPE next, and ON KEY last. To stop the effect of an ON ERROR/ESCAPE/KEY <*command*>, issue either ON ERROR, ON ESCAPE, or ON KEY without *command.*

When you issue ON ERROR <*command*> and *command* in a program or procedure, the error-handling program disables the ON ERROR <*command*> in the calling program. If you want the called program to also use the ON ERROR command, issue another ON ERROR <*command*>

Key Label Names		
BACKSPACE	ALT-0...ALT-9	TAB
BACKTAB	F1...F9	INS
DEL	CTRL-F1...CTRL-F10	ALT-A...ALT-Z
DNARROW	CTRL-A...CTRL-Z	
END	CTRL-LEFTARROW	
HOME	CTRL-RIGHTARROW	
LEFTARROW	CTRL-HOME	
PGUP	CTRL-END	
PGDN	CTRL-PGUP	
RIGHTARROW	CTRL-PGDN	
UPARROW	SHIFT-F1...SHIFT-F9	

Table 31-8. *<Key label name>* Descriptions for Non-printing Keys

from within the error-handling program. When the error-handling program returns to the original program, it releases the nested ON ERROR condition. ON ERROR doesn't handle hardware errors, such as when you try to send input to a printer that's turned off.

ON KEY without a label executes *command* after the current command completes. For example, if you press a key while using the SORT command to sequence records, the key is ignored until the SORT command completes (as in dBASE III PLUS).

ON KEY with a label interrupts most commands, but it doesn't interrupt commands that rely on uninterrupted processing to ensure data accuracy, such as INDEX, PACK, and SORT. You can use a memory variable for *key label name* as long as you include the ampersand (&), signaling a macro substitution.

When you press the key represented by *key label name, command* executes. Table 31-8 lists the valid descriptions for *key label name.*

However, you should note these special conditions:

- ON ESCAPE doesn't work if you issue SET ESCAPE OFF.
- ON KEY takes priority when SET FUNCTION and SET KEY define the same *key label name.*
- The WAIT command takes priority over the ON KEY option.

Note: User-defined functions and the ON KEY <*command*> can't include particular dBASE functions. See the FUNCTION command for a list.

You should compile programs or user-defined functions (.UDF) before using them in *command.*

Tip: For a complete explanation and more examples of the ON ERROR/ESCAPE/KEY commands, see Chapter 23, "Event Processing and Error Trapping."

Example

The following program shows a typical use of the ON ERROR command. The program backs up a file to a disk in drive A. The command **ON ERROR DO Err_hand** tells dBASE IV to branch to the Err_hand procedure whenever a system error occurs.

```
* Program is BACKUP.PRG
* Program backs-up the specified database to drive A.
SET TALK OFF
CLEAR
*----------- Perform the Err_hand procedure when error occurs
ON ERROR DO Err_hand
Accept "Enter name of database to copy to drive A: " To Filename
COPY FILE &Filename TO A:&filename
ON ERROR
RETURN

*----------- Procedure to handle common system errors
PROCEDURE Err_hand
DO CASE
     *---- Filename does not exist
     CASE ERROR() = 1
       ? MESSAGE()
       ACCEPT "Check filename and enter again:" TO Filename
       RETRY
     *---- Error reading on drive, gate left open
     CASE ERROR() = 29
       ? MESSAGE()
       WAIT "Check the drive gate, and press a key to try again"
       RETRY
     *----Disk full
     CASE ERROR() = 56
       ? MESSAGE()
       WAIT "Disk full. Insert new disk, and press any key"
       RETRY
     *----Catch all
     OTHERWISE
```

```
        ? "Error number is "+STR(ERROR(),3)+" "
        ?? MESSAGE()
           WAIT
ENDCASE
RETURN
```

See also: ON READERROR, PROCEDURE, READKEY(), RETRY, RETURN, SET ESCAPE, SET PROCEDURE, WAIT, ERROR(), INKEY(), LASTKEY(), READKEY(), AND UPPER().

ON PAD

The ON PAD command allows you to display bar and pop-up menus simultaneously.

Pad refers to a menu choice in a horizontal bar menu. Often, a pad activates a specific pop-up menu that contains a submenu of choices related to the pad.

Syntax

ON PAD <*pad name*> OF <*menu name*>
[ACTIVATE POPUP <*pop-up name*>]

Pad name is the name of the menu pad the cursor must be on for the pop-up menu to appear.

OF <*menu name*> is the name of the horizontal bar menu the pad is connected with.

ACTIVATE POPUP connects a pop-up menu to <*pad name*> OF <*menu name*>.

Pop-up name is the name of a pop-up menu you've previously created with DEFINE POPUP.

ON PAD <*pad name*> without ACTIVATE POPUP removes the connection between a horizontal bar menu pad and its assigned pop-up menu.

Notes

With both pop-up and bar menus active, use the RIGHT ARROW and LEFT ARROW keys to move between menu bars and the UP ARROW and DOWN ARROW keys to move between pop-up menus.

You can't use ON PAD with ON SELECTION PAD.

See also: DEFINE MENU, DEFINE PAD, DEFINE POPUP, ON SELECTION PAD

Example

See the example for the DEFINE PAD command.

ON PAGE

The ON PAGE command lets you define a command or program that is executed when printed output reaches a specific line on the current page. For example, you can use ON PAGE during a ?/?? or PAGE EJECT command to print headers and footers at each page break.

Syntax

ON PAGE [AT LINE <*number*> <*command*>]

ON PAGE allows you to specify a command or procedure to be performed whenever your printed output reaches a specific line number.

AT LINE <*number*> is the line number at which you want to call a special page formatting routine. dBASE IV counts the number of lines printed on the current page by keeping track of the value returned by the _plineno system memory variable (see Chapter 34). As soon as the value of AT LINE <*number*> is exceeded, dBASE IV executes the *command* following ON PAGE.

Command is the name of a dBASE IV command, program, or procedure. Usually the *command* is a DO command followed by the name of a procedure.

ON PAGE by itself disables the previous ON PAGE command.

Notes

When you print headers and footers, the ON PAGE command calls a procedure when the _plineno system memory variable reaches the line number that signifies the end of a page. That procedure may, for example, call two other procedures before returning to the main program. The first procedure prints the footer on the current page. The second procedure prints the header on the following page.

Header routines begin with EJECT PAGE in order to assure that the printed matter occurs at the top of the following page. The EJECT PAGE command also sets the _plineno system memory variable back to 0. The ? command is often used at the beginning of a header procedure to skip several lines before printing the header information. The ? command is also used at the end of the procedure to skip several lines before printing the text for the page.

Footer routines usually begin with the ? command to move several lines below the last line of text. Furthermore, the ?? command is often used with the _pageno system memory variable to print a page number for each page on the same line as the footer information.

To calculate the appropriate footer position, add the number of lines for the bottom margin and the number of lines for the footer text to get the total for the bottom of the page. Then subtract this total from the total number of lines per page. Use this result to specify a number for the AT LINE clause of the ON PAGE command. If you exceed the number of lines allowed per page with the footer, the remainder prints on the next page.

Note: Much like user-defined functions, the ON PAGE *command* cannot support certain dBASE IV commands and functions. (See the list under FUNCTION command.)

Example

This example program prints the contents of the CUSTOMER database with headers and footers. The command

```
ON PAGE AT LINE 55 DO Headfoot
```

executes the Headfoot procedure when the value of the _plineno function reaches 55. The Headfoot procedure in turn calls two other procedures named Head and Foot. The Foot procedure is called first to print the footer for the current page. The Head procedure is called next to print the header for the next page. Note that the EJECT PAGE command is used at the beginning of the Head procedure to move to the next page and reset the _plineno system memory variable to 0.

```
* Program is Custprnt.prg
* Program prints customer names and addresses by customer number.
* Program provides printed output with headers and footers.
ON PAGE AT LINE 55 DO Headfoot
CLEAR
SET TALK OFF
USE Customer ORDER Cust_no
SET PRINTER ON
```

```
DO Head                        && Print first page header
SCAN FOR .NOT. DELETED()
     ? Cust_no,Firstname,Lastname,Addr_1,City,State,Zip
ENDSCAN
EJECT PAGE                     && Eject last page
DO Foot                        && Print last footer
SET PRINT OFF
ON PAGE                        && Disable previous ON PAGE
RETURN

*------------------ Procedure to start Head and Foot procedures
PROCEDURE Headfoot
DO Foot                        && Print current page first
DO Head                        && Print new page next

*------------------ Procedure to print page header
PROCEDURE Head
EJECT PAGE                     && Always printed on next page
?
?                              && Skip 2 lines
? "Current Customer Listing",DATE() AT 65
?
?                              && Skip 2 more lines
RETURN

*------------------Procedure to print footer
PROCEDURE Foot
?
?                              && Skip 2 lines from text
? "Customer listing by customer number"
?? "Page " AT 65, LTRIM(STR(_pageno,4,0))
RETURN
```

See also: PRINTJOB, PROCEDURE, REPORT FORM, SET PRINTER, _plength, and _plineno.

ON READERROR

The ON READERROR command executes a dBASE command or program during full-screen operations.

Syntax

ON READERROR [<*command*>]

ON READERROR releases the routine associated with a particular kind of error.

ON READERROR <*command*> executes *command* when a dBASE IV error occurs. Syntax or evaluation errors are examples of this type of error.

The *command* is the name of a dBASE IV command, program, user-defined function, or procedure.

Notes

ON READERROR traps the following kinds of input errors:

- Invalid dates
- Input that is outside the boundaries specified by a RANGE option (see the @ command for a description of the RANGE option)
- Input that does not meet the condition specified in a VALID option (see the @ command for a description of the VALID option)

Use ON READERROR to recover from these errors or send a helpful message to the screen.

Note: User-defined functions and the ON READERROR <*command*> can't include particular dBASE functions. See the FUNCTION command for a list.

You should compile any program or user-defined function (.UDF) before using it in *command.*

Example

The following example prompts the user to enter an order date. If the date entered is not between 1/1/89 and 12/31/89 (inclusive), dBASE executes the READERR procedure, as specified by the ON READERROR command.

```
SET TALK OFF
CLEAR
ON READERROR DO Readerr
Mdate = DATE()
@ 10,10 SAY "Enter the order date: " GET Mdate;
     RANGE {01/01/89},{12/31/89}
READ
RETURN

PROCEDURE Readerr
```

```
@ 12,10 SAY "You've entered an invalid date..."
@ 13,10 SAY "Please enter a date between 1/1/89 and 12/31/89"
RETURN
```

See also: @, APPEND, CHANGE, EDIT, INSERT, ON ERROR, and READ.

ON SELECTION PAD

The ON SELECTION PAD command connects a particular menu bar pad with a dBASE command, procedure, or program.

Syntax

ON SELECTION PAD *<pad name>* OF *<menu name>* [*<command>*]

ON SELECTION PAD without *command* breaks the connection between the menu bar pad and *command.*

The *pad name* is the name of the menu pad the cursor must be on for *command* to execute.

OF *<menu name>* is the name of the menu to which *command* is connected.

The *command* is the name of a dBASE IV command, program, user-defined function, or procedure.

Notes

When you've used an ON SELECTION PAD command and you select a pad from an active menu, dBASE IV executes what you've specified in the *command* clause. You can place a dBASE IV command or DO *program name/procedure name* in the clause.

A procedure you've associated with an ON SELECTION PAD command can use such functions as MENU() and PAD() to determine what action to perform. (The MENU() function returns the active menu name; the PAD() function returns the last pad used.)

The ON SELECTION PAD command can execute other commands, as long as it doesn't originate with a user-defined function or an ON KEY, ON READERROR, or ON PAGE command.

Example

The following example executes a pop-up called Bye_pop when you press ENTER on the Bye pad of the main menu:

```
ON SELECTION PAD Bye OF Main ACTIVATE POPUP Bye_pop
```

For another example, see DEACTIVATE MENU in this chapter.

See also: DEFINE MENU, DEFINE PAD, ON PAD, MENU(), PAD(), and PROMPT().

ON SELECTION POPUP

The ON SELECTION POPUP command connects a pop-up menu selection with a dBASE command or procedure.

Syntax

ON SELECTION POPUP <*pop-up menu name*>/ALL [<*command*>]

The *pop-up menu name* is the name of the pop-up menu you created with DEFINE POPUP.

ALL connects *command* with all pop-up menus.

The *command* is the name of a dBASE IV command, program, user-defined function, or procedure.

Use ON SELECTION POPUP without a pop-up menu name to disable the active pop-up.

Notes

When defining pop-up menus, issue the DEFINE POPUP command first, the ON SELECTION POPUP command next, and the ACTIVATE POPUP command last. When you select a prompt from the pop-up menu, and *command* executes, the pop-up menu is inactivated. It is reactivated when *command* is completed.

The ON SELECTION POPUP command can execute other commands, as long as it doesn't originate with a user-defined function or an ON KEY, ON READERROR, or ON PAGE command.

Example

See the example for DEACTIVATE POPUP in this chapter.

See also: DEFINE BAR, DEFINE POPUP, BAR(), POPUP(), and PROMPT().

PACK

The PACK command removes records marked for deletion from the active database.

Syntax

```
PACK
```

Notes

When you use the DELETE command, it marks records for deletion but doesn't actually remove the records from the database. When you issue the PACK command, all records marked for deletion are permanently removed and can't be reinstated with the RECALL command.

If you issue SET AUTOSAVE OFF before using PACK, the DIR and LIST command don't reflect the decrease in records until you close the database.

See also: COPY, DELETE, DIR, RECALL, REINDEX, SET AUTOSAVE, ZAP, and DELETED().

PARAMETERS

The PARAMETERS command establishes local variables to receive items passed from a calling program.

The DO <*program name*> WITH <*parameter list*> command lets you call another program or procedure and pass parameters to it. That program or procedure must contain a PARAMETERS command in order to receive the parameters you pass with DO.

Syntax

PARAMETERS *<parameter list>*

Parameter list is a list of up to 50 variables that will receive the values from a calling program. You must separate the variable names with commas.

Notes

To call another program and pass information to it, make the PARAMETERS statement the first statement in the receiving program file. Pass exactly the same number of values you defined in the PARAMETERS statement. You can then call the program using this syntax:

DO *<program name>* WITH *<value1, value2,...,value50>*

If the number of values you pass in the calling program doesn't match the number of values specified in the PARAMETERS command in the receiving program, you get the message "Wrong number of parameters."

You can also pass information to a procedure. If the procedure is contained within a program, the PARAMETERS statement must appear after the PROCEDURE *<filename>* statement.

The parameters you pass to a program can be literal values or any dBASE IV expression. The parameter list in the receiving program contains local variables that receive parameters from the calling program. dBASE discards the local variables in the receiving program when it returns control to the calling program.

When you pass a memory variable in the parameter list, the receiving program may change the value of the memory variable. It then transfers the changed value back to the calling program. When you pass an expression, a local memory variable receives the value of the expression and is released when the program completes.

Example

This example uses a simple area calculation program. Here's the contents of the AREACALC command file:

```
PARAMETERS L, W, Area
? L, W, Area
Area = L * W
? L, W, Area, "SQ. FT."
```

The following dot prompt commands show what happens when you call the AREACALC command file and pass parameters to it. Notice that the Marea memory variable was initialized with 0 and then updated with the result of the calculation.

```
. Marea = 0
         0
. DO Areacalc WITH 23, 57, Marea
        23      57    0
        23      57    1311 SQ. FT.
```

See also: @, DO, PRIVATE, PROCEDURE, PUBLIC, SET PROCEDURE, and STORE.

PLAY MACRO

The PLAY MACRO command executes a macro contained in the active macro library.

Syntax

PLAY MACRO *<macro name>*

The *macro name* can be up to ten characters and cannot contain any spaces.

Notes

See Chapter 8 for complete instructions on how to create and execute macros.

When you issue **PLAY MACRO** at the dot prompt, the macro executes immediately. When you issue the PLAY MACRO command from within a program, the macro doesn't execute until the program reaches a point that allows input. If you issue another PLAY MACRO command before the original PLAY MACRO can be executed, dBASE stacks the new PLAY MACRO command on top of the original PLAY MACRO. Macros play in last-in-first-out order (LIFO).

Examples

To play back from the dot prompt a macro that is assigned to F2, enter

```
. PLAY MACRO F2
```

Similarly, to play back a macro that is assigned to the letter key L, enter

```
. PLAY MACRO L
```

To play back a macro that has been assigned the name Salemac, enter

```
. PLAY MACRO Salemac
```

Notice that you do not enclose the macro name in quotes.

See also: RESTORE MACROS and SAVE MACROS.

PRINTJOB

The PRINTJOB command initiates a set of structured programming commands that control a printer task.

Syntax

PRINTJOB
<commands>
ENDPRINTJOB

Notes

When the PRINTJOB command executes, dBASE IV

- Sends to the printer print codes contained in the system memory variable _pscodes
- Ejects paper when the system memory variable _peject is set to either "BEFORE" or "BOTH"
- Sets the system memory variable _pcolno to 0

When the ENDPRINTJOB command executes, dBASE IV

- Sends to the printer codes contained in the system memory variable _pecodes
- Ejects paper when the system memory variable _peject is set to either "AFTER" or "BOTH"
- Loops back to PRINTJOB to produce another copy until the number of copies produced equals the system memory variable and _pcopies

Before using the PRINTJOB command, you must set the relevant system memory variables. For more on system memory variables, see Chapter 34.

There are two limitations to this command:

- PRINTJOB can only execute from within a program.
- You can't nest PRINTJOB commands (you can't execute a PRINTJOB command from within another PRINTJOB command).

See also: ON PAGE, PROCEDURE, REPORT FORM, RETURN, SET PRINTER, SET TALK, _pcopies, _pecodes, _peject, _plineno, _pscodes.

PRIVATE

The PRIVATE command declares a memory variable as private (or local) to the program in which you declare it.

Syntax

PRIVATE ALL [LIKE/EXCEPT *<skeleton>*]

or

PRIVATE *<memory variable list>*

PRIVATE ALL declares all memory variables as private to the current program.

LIKE declares as private memory variables with names similar to *skeleton*.

EXCEPT declares local memory variables as private unless they met the conditions of *skeleton.*

Memory variable list is a list of created memory variables separated by commas.

Notes

When a memory variable is private, only the program in which you declared the variable as private can display or update it. You can give memory variables in the current program the same names as memory variables in other programs. dBASE keeps them separate as long as at least one of the variables is private.

Private memory variables can have the same name as other public memory variables. When you assign the same name, the private memory variable masks or covers the public memory variable for the life of the program. When the program completes, the private variable is released and the public memory variable reappears unchanged. Private memory variables can use the same name as system memory variables. dBASE creates the private variable from the system memory variable and initializes it with the value stored in the system memory variable.

Tip: If you're having problems with a program and you don't want it to release its own memory variables, change them to public until you finish debugging and then change them back to private for the final program.

See also: DECLARE, DO PARAMETERS, PUBLIC, and STORE.

PROCEDURE

The PROCEDURE command identifies the beginning of a subroutine.

Syntax

PROCEDURE <*procedure name*>

The *procedure name* has an eight-character maximum, cannot contain spaces, and must start with a letter. Don't create procedures with the same name as calling programs or other procedures.

Notes

Subroutines are procedures that you call with the DO command; they must end with RETURN. You can place procedures at the bottom of a program file, or you can place them in a separate procedure file.

When you tell dBASE IV to execute a procedure, it looks for the procedure in the following sequence:

1. The current object (.DBO) file
2. File specified in SET PROCEDURE command
3. Other open object (.DBO) files in most recently opened to first opened order
4. An object file with <*procedure name*>.DBO
5. A dBASE program file with <*procedure name*>.PRG; if found, dBASE compiles the program file and executes the object file
6. A SQL program file with <*procedure name*>.PRS; if found, dBASE compiles the program file and executes the object file

Although dBASE IV allows up to 1170 procedures per program or procedure file, you are limited by your system's available memory.

The RETURN command line you use in a procedure cannot include an expression.

See Chapter 20, "Program Control," for more on procedures.

See also: COMPILE, DEBUG, DO, FUNCTION, PARAMETERS, RETRY, RETURN, and SET PROCEDURE.

PROTECT

The PROTECT command turns on the dBASE IV security system and includes security maintenance facilities. See Chapter 28, "Network Administration."

Syntax

```
PROTECT
```

PUBLIC

The PUBLIC command makes memory variables and array elements accessible by any dBASE program or procedure.

Syntax

PUBLIC <*memory variable list*>/[ARRAY <*array element list*>]

Notes

Any program can access a public memory variable or array element. Be careful to assign unique names to public memory variables or array elements. You must declare the variable or array type as public before you assign it a value.

When you create a memory variable from the dot prompt, it is created as a public variable (global). System memory variables are also created as public when dBASE starts up. When you create a memory variable in a program, it is created as a private variable.

When you save memory variables in a memory variable file (with the SAVE command), and restore them (with RESTORE), they are restored as public variables if you restore them from the dot prompt. If you restore them in a program, however, they are restored as private.

Public memory variables aren't released when the program ends unless you explicitly issue the RELEASE command.

Note: When you first declare a public memory variable, dBASE IV stores it as a logical type variable until you give it a value.

For a complete discussion of public versus private memory variables, see Chapter 18, "Memory Variables."

See also: DECLARE, DO PARAMETERS, PRIVATE, RELEASE, RESTORE, SAVE, and STORE.

QUIT

The QUIT command terminates the dBASE IV session and returns you to the operating system prompt.

Syntax

QUIT

Notes

The QUIT command automatically closes any open files, releases memory variables, and does other cleanup before exiting. Don't use your computer reset button or other methods to exit dBASE IV as this can damage open files and make you lose information.

READ

The READ command stores input to @...GET commands in memory variables or fields.

Syntax

READ [SAVE]

READ puts input into memory variables or fields and clears the GETs.

READ SAVE does not clear the GETs. It saves the input for the most recent GETs and displays that input the next time you use the READ command.

Notes

The READ command works with the @...GET command. You can use these two commands together to get user input and save it into memory variables or fields. You can use a single READ command to activate several @...GET commands at once.

The READ command is usually found in dBASE programs designed for full-screen entry or editing data. By combining the @...GET and READ commands, you can create application programs that allow users to enter and edit data.

Example

This example shows how you can store the user's menu selection into a memory variable (Pick) by using the @...GET and READ commands. In an application program, you might follow this statement with CASE or IF statements to call different menus or routines based on the input.

```
. Pick = 0
         0
. @10,5 SAY "Enter selection" GET Pick
. READ
. ? Pick
         5
```

The @ command example also shows the READ command.

See also: @, CLEAR, CLEAR GETS, CLEAR MEMORY, CREATE/MEMORY, CREATE/MODIFY SCREEN, REPLACE, SET DEVICE, SET FORMAT, and STORE.

RECALL

The RECALL command removes the deletion mark from records in the active database.

Syntax

RECALL [<*scope*>] [FOR <*condition*>] [WHILE <*condition*>]

RECALL without any FOR or WHILE clause removes the deletion flag from the current record.

Notes

If you have issued the PACK or ZAP command, you can't use RECALL to bring back the records that were removed.

If you issue SET DELETED ON, you can only RECALL records by entering **RECALL RECORD <*number*>**.

Example

This example uses the PEOPLE database in the \DBASE\SAMPLES directory. First, it attempts to recall the first record even though it isn't marked for deletion. Then it deletes the first record. Notice that when you display the record, there is an asterisk following the record number, signifying that the record is ready to be removed from the system. Then the example recalls the record. Notice that the asterisk (*) disappears.

```
. USE SAMPLES\People
. RECALL
No records recalled
. DELETE RECORD 1
1 record deleted
. DISPLAY
Record#  LASTNAME            FIRSTNAME           ADDRESS
       CITY            STATE ZIP        PHONE       CARDSENT
      1 *Berrigan            Michael             1550 Keystone St.
       Burlington      VT    05401      (802)555-0778 .T.
. RECALL
1 record recalled
. DISPLAY
Record#  LASTNAME            FIRSTNAME           ADDRESS
        CITY           STATE ZIP        PHONE       CARDSENT
      1  Berrigan            Michael             1550 Keystone St.
       Burlington      VT    05401      (802)555-0778 .T.
```

See also: DELETE, PACK, SET DELETED, ZAP, and DELETED().

REINDEX

The REINDEX command rebuilds active single (.NDX) and multiple (.MDX) index files in the active work area. It also rebuilds the production index file (.MDX).

Syntax

REINDEX

Notes

The REINDEX command rebuilds all active index files, including .MDX file tags. If you reindex a database that you created with SET UNIQUE ON (or with the UNIQUE keyword in the INDEX command), dBASE IV rebuilds the index and keeps the unique status regardless of whether SET UNIQUE is ON or OFF.

See also: INDEX, PAC, SET INDEX, SET ORDER, SET UNIQUE, USE, ZAP, KEY(), MDX(), and NDX().

RELEASE

The RELEASE command lets you remove memory variables, menus, pop-ups, and windows from memory. It also lets you remove assembly language programs that you've loaded into memory with the LOAD command.

Syntax

RELEASE <*memory variable list*>

or

RELEASE ALL [LIKE/EXCEPT <*skeleton*>]

or

RELEASE MODULE [<*module name list*>]
/MENUS [<*menu name list*>]
/POPUPS [<*pop-up name list*>]
/WINDOWS [<*window name list*>]

Memory variable list is a list of existing memory variables separated by commas.

Entering **RELEASE ALL** from the dot prompt removes all memory variables except system memory variables.

When used within a program, RELEASE ALL removes the program's private variables only. One program can't remove another program's private variables.

RELEASE MODULE without a list removes all binary program modules (assembly language programs) that you've loaded into memory with the LOAD command. By including *module name list*, you can remove selected assembly language modules placed in memory by the LOAD command.

RELEASE MENUS without a list removes all menus. By including *menu name list,* you can release selected menus from the screen and memory.

RELEASE POPUPS without a list removes all pop-up menus. By including *pop-up name list,* you can erase selected pop-up menus from the screen and memory.

RELEASE WINDOWS without a list removes all windows. By including *window name list,* you can erase selected windows from the screen and memory.

Notes

The RELEASE command doesn't remove system memory variables.

The RELEASE MENUS command clears all ON SELECTION and ON PAD commands associated with the menus. You can't release a menu that is currently in use; you must deactivate it before you release it.

The RELEASE POPUPS command clears all ON SELECTION POPUP commands associated with pop-up menus.

The RELEASE WINDOWS command restores any text masked by the window after the window is removed from the screen.

Example

This example creates and displays three memory variables, issues the RELEASE command to release variable X, and releases the rest of the variables with the ALL option.

```
. X = 1
        1
. Y = 2
        2
. Z = 3
        3
. RELEASE X
. RELEASE ALL
```

See also: CALL, CLEAR ALL, CLEAR MEMORY, LOAD, RESTORE, RETURN, SAVE, STORE, and CALL().

RENAME

The RENAME command changes the name of an existing file.

Syntax

RENAME *<old filename.ext>* TO *<new filename.ext>*

Notes

The RENAME...TO command allows you to rename files without exiting dBASE IV and returning to the operating system level.

If you change the name of a database file that has an associated memo file (.DBT), change the memo file name so that it matches the database's new file name.

Example

This example displays directory information for the STAFF database, changes its extension from .DBF to .SAV by using the RENAME command, and then makes the same request for directory information. The STAFF file's information isn't displayed because dBASE's DIR command displays only files with the .DBF extension unless you request otherwise. Then the example restores the STAFF database to its original database extension (.DBF). It appears in the directory listing again.

```
. DIR SAMPLES\Staff
Database Files     # Records     Last Update      Size
STAFF.DBF                 12     12/27/88         1702
. RENAME SAMPLES\Staff.dbf TO SAMPLES\Staff.sav
. DIR SAMPLES\Staff
Database Files     # Records     Last Update      Size
None
. DIR SAMPLES\Staff.sav
STAFF.SAV
. RENAME SAMPLES\Staff.sav TO SAMPLES\Staff.dbf
. DIR SAMPLES\Staff
Database Files     # Records     Last Update      Size
STAFF.DBF                 12     12/27/88         1702
```

See also: CLOSE, COPY, COPY FILE, and USE.

REPLACE

The REPLACE command changes the contents of a specified field in the active database.

Syntax

REPLACE ALL/<*field*> WITH <*expression*> [ADDITIVE]
[,<*field*> WITH <*expression*> [ADDITIVE]]
[<*scope*>] [FOR <*condition*>]
[WHILE <*condition*>]

Field is any field in the active database, including a memo field.

The data type of *expression* must match the data type of *field*.

Use ADDITIVE to build a single memo field from multiple character strings.

FOR <*condition*> and WHILE <*condition*> determine which records the REPLACE command updates. If they are not included, the REPLACE command updates all records.

Notes

When *expression* exceeds *field*, dBASE IV makes some adjustments:

- If *expression* is a number and is wider than the field width, it is saved in scientific notation.
- If *expression* is a memo field and is wider than the character field, the memo field is truncated.

When an index is on and you use *scope* or the FOR or WHILE clause, the record pointer moves to the updated record. This may cause undesirable results, such as moving the first record and the record pointer to the end of the database and then exiting without processing any more records. To control this, turn off the index or issue **SET ORDER TO 0** while using the REPLACE command. Then use the REINDEX command to rebuild the index files.

If you use the REPLACE command while an index is in use, the index is updated when an index key is changed.

Example

This example goes to a record (4) in the PEOPLE database and displays the City field. Then it replaces the original value ("Los Angeles") with another new value ("L.A."), and displays the result. Because the example uses the ALL form of the RELEASE command, any other records with the City field equal to "Los Angeles" are also changed.

```
. USE SAMPLES\People
. GOTO 4
PEOPLE: Record No      4
. DISPLAY City
Record#  City
      4  Los Angeles
. REPLACE ALL City WITH "L.A." FOR City = "Los Angeles"
1 record replaced
. GOTO 4
PEOPLE: Record No      4
. DISPLAY City
      4  L.A.
```

See also: ORDER, REINDEX, SET INDEX, SET ORDER, and STORE.

REPORT FORM

The REPORT FORM command lets you use a given report form file to print, display, or output a report to a file.

Syntax

REPORT FORM <*report form filename*> /? [PLAIN] [HEADING <*character string*>] [NOEJECT] [SUMMARY] [<*scope*>] [FOR <*condition*>] [WHILE <*condition*>] [TO PRINTER/TO FILE <*filename*>]

Without a FOR or WHILE clause (or a filter), dBASE IV produces a report that includes all records in the active database.

If you do not include a drive or path as part of the file name, dBASE IV assumes that the file is located on the current drive and path.

You can use the ? symbol to display a menu of report form files from which to choose.

Notes

To create a report design, you use the CREATE/MODIFY REPORT command. This command takes you to the Reports Design screen, from where you can design your report and save it to a file. dBASE IV gives the resulting report form file an .FRM extension. Besides an .FRM file, dBASE IV also creates an .FRG file which contains the program code (for example, ?, ??, PRINTJOB, and ENDPRINTJOB commands) needed to print your report.

When you use the REPORT FORM command to print your reports, dBASE IV compiles the .FRG to an .FRO file. It then uses the .FRO file to print your report.

To send the report to a disk file rather than the screen or printer, use the TO FILE option. The type of file that dBASE IV creates depends on the printer driver that you have installed. For example, if you have installed the ASCII text printer driver (ASCII.PR2), dBASE IV creates a file that does not contain any escape sequences and gives the file a .TXT extension. If, however, you have installed dBASE IV for a particular printer, it creates a file that may contain escape sequences for your printer, and gives the file a .PRT extension.

For a complete discussion of creating reports using the Reports Design screen, see Chapter 10, "Creating Reports."

See also: CREATE/MODIFY REPORT and SET PRINTER.

RESET

The RESET command removes a data integrity flag from a database file.

Syntax

RESET [IN <*alias*>]

IN allows you to work with a database file in another work area without using the SELECT command to change active work areas.

Alias is the name of a database file open in another work area.

Notes

The RESET command works in conjunction with the BEGIN TRANSACTION/END TRANSACTION command loop. The BEGIN TRANSACTION command sets a data integrity flag in the file header for the database in which the transaction occurs. The flag remains in that file until the transaction is completed, or until a successful ROLLBACK takes place. If the transaction or rollback is not successful, you can use the RESET command to remove the data integrity flag from the file. This prepares the file for the next transaction. See the BEGIN TRANSACTION command for more on the RESET command.

Tip: Don't use the RESET command in a program. Use it only from the dot prompt as needed.

See also: BEGIN TRANSACTION, END TRANSACTION, ROLLBACK, ISMARKED(), and ROLLBACK().

RESTORE

The RESTORE command finds a memory file (.MEM) created with the SAVE command and restores to active memory the memory variables or arrays it contains. You can then use those memory variables or arrays as you normally would.

Syntax

RESTORE FROM <*filename*> [ADDITIVE]

RESTORE FROM <*filename*> removes existing memory variables from memory and replaces them with ones contained in *filename*.MEM.

ADDITIVE adds memory variables contained in *filename*.MEM to already existing memory variables.

Notes

Variables restored from within a program are private unless you declare otherwise and use the ADDITIVE option. Variables restored from the dot prompt are public.

The CONFIG.DB file controls the number of memory variables allowed. The default installation value is 500. You can have as many as 25,000 memory variables, if your system has enough available memory.

Use the SAVE command to save memory variables in a file.

See also: PRIVATE, PUBLIC, RELEASE, SAVE, and STORE.

RESTORE MACROS

The RESTORE MACROS command finds a macro library file (.KEY) and restores to active memory the macros that it contains.

Syntax

RESTORE MACROS FROM <*filename*>

Notes

The RESTORE MACROS command overwrites existing macros that are assigned to the same keys as the macros being restored. When you restore macros from a file that has an extension other than .KEY, include the extension with the *filename*.

Use the SAVE MACROS command to save macros in a file.

See also: PLAY MACRO and SAVE MACROS.

Example

This example loads macros from a macro library file in the SAMPLES directory.

```
RESTORE MACROS FROM SAMPLES\Invoice2
```

RESTORE WINDOW

The RESTORE WINDOW command finds on disk a window file (.WIN) that you created using the SAVE WINDOW command and restores to memory the windows that it contains. You can then call that window to the screen by using the ACTIVATE WINDOW command.

Syntax

RESTORE WINDOW <*window name list*>/ALL FROM <*filename*>.WIN

Window name list is one or more window names, separated by commas, defined in *filename*.WIN. Use it to restore to active memory only selected windows saved in the .WIN file on disk.

ALL FROM restores to memory all windows in *filename*.WIN.

Notes

The RESTORE WINDOW command overwrites existing windows in memory when the existing window name is the same as the restored window name. When restoring windows from a file that has an extension other than .WIN, you must include the extension with the *filename*.

Use the SAVE WINDOW command to save a window in a file.

See also: ACTIVATE WINDOW, DEFINE WINDOW, and SAVE WINDOW.

RESUME

The RESUME command continues the execution of a program paused by the SUSPEND command.

Syntax

RESUME

Notes

The RESUME command restarts program execution immediately following the line on which the file stopped. The RESUME command also restarts a suspended DEBUG command. dBASE IV returns you to the Debugger and resumes with the command line following the one on which you suspended debugging.

You should use the CLEAR command and then the RESUME command to clear the screen of data. This removes from the screen data placed there by commands you may have entered while the program was suspended.

See also: BEGIN TRANSACTION, CANCEL, CLEAR, DEBUG, RETURN, ROLLBACK, and SUSPEND.

RETRY

The RETRY command reruns a command sequence after a dBASE IV system error occurs.

Syntax

RETRY

Notes

You use the RETRY command primarily to help your program recover from dBASE IV system errors that occur during program execution. It retries the command that caused the error. Use it with ON ERROR DO *<program>* to find errors in your application program. This command usually appears in an error-handling procedure called from a program by the ON ERROR command. The called procedure identifies and corrects the system error by using the ERROR() function. RETRY clears the error returned by the ERROR() function. Once the error is corrected, the RETRY command retries the command line that caused the error.

Note: RETRY doesn't evaluate an IF or DO WHILE condition.

See also: ON ERROR, RETURN, and ERROR().

Example

For an example of how to use RETRY, see the ON ERROR command. For a complete discussion of error handling in a programming environment, see Chapter 23, "Event Processing and Error Trapping."

RETURN

The RETURN command returns control from the current procedure or program to a calling program or procedure. Upon return to the calling program, dBASE IV executes the command line that follows the calling command line. When you use the RETURN command to end a user-defined function, it returns the result of that function to the calling command line.

Syntax

RETURN [<*expression*> /TO MASTER/TO <*procedure name*>]

Include *expression* when returning from user-defined functions. TO MASTER returns control to the highest level calling program. TO <*procedure name*> gives control to the named procedure.

Notes

You use the RETURN command at the end of a program, procedure, or user-defined function to end that operation, close the file, and return control to the calling program or to dBASE IV.

The RETURN command releases private memory variables. When used in a user-defined function, the RETURN command returns a result. When you use it in this context, follow the RETURN command with an expression enclosed in parentheses that contains the result of the function. This expression is usually a memory variable. If the function doesn't have a result, it returns logical false (.F.). When used with the ERROR() function, the RETURN command clears out its value.

See also: COMPILE, DO, ERROR, FUNCTIONS, PARAMETERS, PRIVATE, PROCEDURE, PUBLIC, RESUME, and SUSPEND.

ROLLBACK

The ROLLBACK command restores databases and index files to their original state.

Syntax

ROLLBACK

Notes

You use the ROLLBACK command in programs. Issue it after the BEGIN TRANSACTION command and before the END TRANSACTION command. See "Transaction Processing" in Chapter 27 for an explanation.

See also: BEGIN TRANSACTION, RESET, COMPLETED(), ISMARKED(), and ROLLBACK().

RUN/!

The RUN/! command allows you to execute an operating system level command or program from within dBASE IV.

Syntax

RUN/! *<DOS command>*

Notes

For the RUN command to work, your system must have enough available memory to load the operating system's COMMAND.COM file and then the program. If your system doesn't have enough memory, it displays the message "Insufficient memory."

When *DOS command* finishes executing, the operating system returns control to dBASE IV.

The operating system's COMMAND.COM file must be in the current directory or there must be a path into a directory containing COMMAND.COM (you can use the SET PATH or the SET COMSPEC command at the operating system level).

Some operating system commands, such as ASSIGN and PRINT, remain in memory. If you plan to use these commands from within dBASE IV, load them and then load dBASE IV to ensure that you have enough memory to run both.

Example

This example uses the dBASE time function and then the DOS TIME command to display the system time.

```
. ? TIME()
17:00:58
```

```
. RUN TIME
Current time is 17:00:42.56
Enter new time:
```

SAVE

The SAVE command puts all or some active memory variables in a memory variable (.MEM) file on disk. You can later reuse the values stored in those memory variables by restoring them to memory with the RESTORE command.

Syntax

SAVE TO <*filename*> [ALL LIKE/EXCEPT <*skeleton*>]

ALL LIKE uses *skeleton* to determine which memory variables to save in the file.

EXCEPT uses *skeleton* to determine which memory variables to exclude from the file.

Notes

Use the RESTORE command to restore memory variables saved in a file.

Example

The first command in this example saves all memory variables that start with the letter "C" in a file called CVAR.MEM. The second command saves all memory variables that start with any letter but the letter "C" in a file called NOTCVAR.MEM.

```
. SAVE TO Cvar ALL LIKE C*
. SAVE TO Notcvar ALL EXCEPT C*
```

See also: PARAMETERS, PRIVATE, PUBLIC, RESTORE, SET SAFETY, and STORE.

SAVE MACROS

The SAVE MACROS command puts all existing macros in a macro file (.KEY).

Syntax

SAVE MACROS TO *<macro filename>*

Notes

Macro keys are ALT-F1 through ALT-F9 or ALT- F10 followed by any letter in the alphabet. These key combinations allow you to specify up to 35 macros to save on a macro (.KEY) file.

Use the RESTORE MACROS command to restore macros saved in a file and place them in memory for your use.

See also: PLAY MACRO and RESTORE MACROS.

Example

This command saves all defined macros to a file (TESTMAC.KEY):

```
SAVE MACROS TO Testmac
```

SAVE WINDOW

The SAVE WINDOW command puts all existing window definitions in a window (.WIN) file.

Syntax

SAVE WINDOW *<window name list>*/ALL TO *<filename>*

SAVE WINDOW with *window name list* saves selected windows in *filename*.WIN.

SAVE WINDOW without *window name list* saves all windows in *filename*.WIN.

Window name list is one or more window names to save in <*filename*>.WIN. You must separate each window name with a comma.

ALL TO saves all of the defined windows in *filename*.WIN.

Notes

Use the RESTORE WINDOW command to restore windows saved in a file.

See also: DEFINE WINDOW and RESTORE WINDOW.

Example

This command saves all defined windows to a file (TESTWIND.WIN):

```
. SAVE ALL TO Testwind
```

SCAN

The SCAN command is a simplified version of the DO WHILE command, tailored specifically for selecting records from a database file.

Syntax

SCAN [<*scope*>] [FOR <*condition*>] [WHILE <*condition*>]
[<*commands*>]
[LOOP]
[EXIT]
ENDSCAN

SCAN without a *scope* or FOR or WHILE conditions operates on all records.

Scope defaults to all records. However, you can use NEXT for the *scope* clause to specify a limited number of records, as in NEXT 10. This specifies the next ten records, starting with the current record. You can also use REST to specify the rest of the records in the database, starting with the current one.

LOOP sends the program back to the SCAN command.

EXIT ends a scan procedure.

FOR <*condition*> and WHILE <*condition*> limit the records within the *scope* that dBASE acts on. If you do not include them, the SCAN command works on all records in the *scope*.

Notes

The SCAN command begins a scan procedure or routine that ends with the ENDSCAN command. Usually, you want to take some action when SCAN finds a record matching its scope and conditions. Use the SCAN command in a program or a procedure.

The SCAN command goes through the active database, finds each record that matches its scope and conditions, and performs the commands within the SCAN...ENDSCAN block. It begins at the beginning of a database file (or first index record), unless the FOR clause, WHILE clause, or *scope* moves the record pointer. The ENDSCAN command doesn't move the record pointer. Usually the SCAN command leaves the record pointer at the end of the database file, unless an EXIT command interrupts the SCAN.

Example

The following example shows how you can use SCAN to read through a database. It lets you view records in the CUSTOMER database with a ZIP code less than 60000. See the DO WHILE command in this chapter for a program that accomplishes the same effect.

```
USE Customer ORDER Zip
SCAN FOR Zip <= "60000"
     ?
     ? TRIM(Firstname)+" "+Lastname
     ? Addr_1
     ? Addr_2
     ? TRIM(City)+", "+State+" "+Zip
     ?
     WAIT
ENDSCAN
```

See also: CONTINUE, DO WHILE, and LOCATE.

SEEK

The SEEK command looks for a record in an indexed database file that meets an expression.

Syntax

SEEK *<expression>*

Expression is any valid expression with the same data type as the indexed field. Often, the expression is a memory variable created in a program.

Notes

Use the SEEK command with an indexed database. SEEK honors restrictions set with the SET EXACT, SET DELETED, and SET FILTER commands. If the SEEK command finds a record, it positions the record pointer at the record and sets the FOUND() function to logical true (.T.).

If no record that matches *expression* is found, the record pointer is left at the end of the database file and dBASE IV displays the message "Find not successful." If you've issued SET NEAR ON and no record matching *expression* is found, the record pointer is left at the closest match.

See also: CONTINUE, FIND, INDEX, LOCATE, SET DELETED, SET EXACT, SET FILTER, SET INDEX, SET NEAR, SET ORDER, USE, EOF(), FOUND(), KEY(), MDX(), NDX(), and TAG().

Example

This example indexes the PEOPLE database and displays the results of an exact match and a near match. The second SEEK command uses the SET NEAR ON command to find the first last name that begins with the letter "T." If you SET NEAR to OFF, the second SEEK command will position the record pointer at the end of the database.

```
. SET EXACT ON
. SET NEAR ON
. USE SAMPLES\People
. INDEX ON Lastname TO SAMPLES\Lname
  100% indexed          15 Records indexed
. SEEK "King"
. DISPLAY
```

```
Record#  LASTNAME            FIRSTNAME           ADDRESS
       CITY            STATE ZIP        PHONE          CARDSENT

      2  King                Matt                520 S. 8th St. #22
       Baltimore       MD    21202      (301)555-3193 .T.

. SEEK "T"
Find not successful
. DISPLAY
Record#  LASTNAME            FIRSTNAME           ADDRESS
       CITY            STATE ZIP        PHONE          CARDSENT
     12  Tobias              Susan               7010 Balcom Ave., Apt. A
       Durham          NC    27701      (919)555-2459 .T.
```

SELECT

The SELECT command defines the active work area. You can use it to define a work area in which to open a database. You can also use it to change to a work area in which a database is already open.

Syntax

SELECT *<work area name/alias>*

Work area name is a number from 1 through 10. The default is work area 1.

Alias is the letter "A" through "J" or another alias for a database.

Notes

dBASE IV supports ten different work areas in which you can open a database. You cannot have the same database open in two different work areas at the same time. Each work area is designated by a number (1-10) or a letter (A-J). Follow the SELECT command with either a number or letter to have dBASE IV select that work area. You can then open a database in that work area or use information from a database already open in that work area.

When you open a database in a work area you opened with the SELECT command, you associate that database with that work area. When you open a database in a given work area, its companion files are also opened in the same work space. The SELECT command allows you to move between the different work areas. When you change work areas with the SELECT command, dBASE IV activates the database in the selected work area and deactivates the database in the original work area.

Each work area has a separate record pointer. Moving between work areas doesn't affect the record pointer's position.

Work area 10 is reserved for an open catalog. If you have a database open in work area 10 and you open a catalog file, the open database is automatically closed. If you have a catalog open, you can't open a database in work area 10.

See also: CLOSE, CONTINUE, LOCATE, SET CATALOG, SET FIELDS, SET VIEW, USE, and ALIAS().

Example

The following example uses the SELECT command to select work area 1 and open the CUSTOMER database in that work area. Next, it selects work area 2 and opens ORDERS in that work area. At this point, the ORDERS database is the active database. Next, the example establishes a relationship between the two databases with the SET RELATION command. Finally, it selects work area 1, making CUSTOMER the active database.

```
. SELECT 1
. USE Customer ORDER Cust_no
. SELECT 2
. USE Orders
. SET RELATION TO Cust_no INTO Customer
. SELECT 1
```

SET

If you enter the SET command at the dot prompt, it displays a full-screen menu for modifying many of dBASE IV's most commonly used default settings. See Chapter 35 for a detailed description of how to use this command.

See also the SET commands in Chapter 32.

SHOW MENU

The SHOW MENU command displays but does not activate a horizontal bar menu.

Syntax

SHOW MENU <*menu name*> [PAD <*pad name*>]

Notes

The SHOW MENU command displays *menu name* and highlights *pad name*, but doesn't allow you to position the cursor on it or use its options. The menu is displayed over any existing display. Use the SHOW MENU command to check how a horizontal bar menu appears on your screen.

See also: ACTIVATE MENU, CLEAR, CLEAR MENU, DEFINE MENU, and DEFINE PAD.

SHOW POPUP

The SHOW POPUP command displays but does not activate a pop-up menu.

Syntax

SHOW POPUP <*pop-up name*>

Pop-up name is the name of a pop-up menu previously defined with DEFINE POPUP.

Notes

The SHOW POPUP command displays a pop-up menu but doesn't allow you to position the cursor on it or use its options. Messages associated with the menu are not displayed. Use the SHOW POPUP command to check how a menu appears on the screen.

See also: ACTIVATE POPUP, CLEAR, DEFINE BAR, DEFINE POPUP, and POPUP().

SKIP

The SKIP command moves the record pointer.

Syntax

SKIP <*number*>] [IN <*alias*>]

Number is a positive or negative number or expression that is only restricted by the number of records in the database.

IN <*alias*> moves the record pointer in an open database existing in a different work area.

Notes

If the accessed database is indexed, the SKIP command advances in indexed order. If the database is not indexed, SKIP advances in record number order. When *number* is positive, the record pointer advances. When *number* is negative, the record pointer moves backward.

The IN option allows you to move a record pointer in another work area without using the SELECT command to activate the database in the work area.

If the record pointer is at the end of the database and you issue the SKIP command, the value of RECNO() is one greater than the number of records in the database and EOF() is set to logical true (.T.). If the record pointer is at the top of the database and you issue **SKIP -1**, the pointer is moved to the beginning of the database file, and the BOF() function returns a logical true (.T.).

See also: GO/GOTO, BOF(), EOF(), and RECNO().

Example

This example shows several ways to use the SKIP command. The first SKIP command moves the record pointer using the default, that is, one record. The second SKIP command moves the record pointer up two records. The third SKIP command uses a memory variable to determine the number of records to skip and skips two records (the value of the variable). The third SKIP command adds three to the variable's value, causing it to skip five records.

```
. USE SAMPLES\People
. SKIP
PEOPLE: Record No       2
. SKIP 2
PEOPLE: Record No       4
. Mnum = 2
. SKIP Mnum
```

```
PEOPLE: Record No       6
. SKIP Mnum+3
PEOPLE: Record No      11
```

SORT

The SORT command creates from an existing database a new database with the records in the requested order. Unlike the INDEX command, the SORT command changes record numbers for the information stored in the new database.

Syntax

SORT TO <*filename*> ON <*field1*> [/A] [/C] [/D]
[,<*field2*> [/A] [/C] [/D]...]
[<*scope*>] [FOR <*condition*>] [WHILE <*condition*>]

/A sorts in ascending order. This is the default.
/C disregards case.
/D sorts in descending order (same as DESCENDING).
Field has a ten-field maximum (field1-field10). Separate each field name option combination with commas.

Notes

The SORT command arranges records in ascending ASCII order unless you use /D or DESCENDING for descending ASCII order or /C for a non-case-sensitive sort. The SORT command creates a new physical database that is stored on disk. The new database name cannot be the same as the one used for the sort.

When you use more than one option, use only one slash. For example, enter **/AC**, not **/A /C**. Options A and D work on only one field and can't be used together.

You can't use the SORT command with logical or memo fields.

Tip: When using the SORT command with multiple fields, put the most important field first and separate the field names with commas.

There are no advantages to using the SORT command rather than the INDEX command to specify the order of records in a database.

However, the SORT command may be appropriate when you want to create a "snapshot" view of a database at a specific point in time.

See also: COPY and INDEX.

Example

The following command line creates a new database called INORDER from the CLIENTS database. The records for the INORDER database are in order by last name.

```
. USE Clients
. SORT ON Lastname,Firstname TO Inorder
  100% Sorted          33 Records sorted
```

STORE

The STORE command creates and initializes memory variables. It can also assign values to elements in an array previously created with the DECLARE command.

Syntax

STORE *<expression>* TO *<memory variable list>/<array element list>*

or

<memory variable>/<array element> = *<expression>*

Notes

The first form of the STORE command allows you to define one or more memory variables and array elements. You can mix variables and array elements freely. The second form of the STORE command (=) only allows you to define one memory variable or array element at a time. The name of the memory variable or array element must appear on the left side of the equal sign (=) and the expression defining that variable or element must appear on the right. Each variable's data type is determined by the data type of the first value you store in it.

Assign names to memory variables with care. If a memory variable of the same name already exists, the STORE command overwrites it, unless one variable is private and the other is public.

Also, if you attempt to assign or use a memory variable with the same name as a database field, the database field takes priority. You can avoid this problem by always starting your variable names with the same letter. You can also use the M-> pointer in front of the name of the memory variable in a command line to specify a memory variable over a database field of the same name.

Memory variable names can be up to ten characters, must begin with a letter, and may contain numbers and underscores. Do not use the single letters "A" through "J" for memory variable names. These may conflict with aliases for databases.

The maximum number of memory variables and array elements allowed depends on the values for MVBLKSIZE and MVMAXBLKS, set in the CONFIG.DB file. If you didn't change the default values, use the following chart to calculate how many memory variables you can have active at once:

MVBLKSIZE = 50

MVMAXBLKS = 10

TOTAL VARIABLES = MVBLKSIZE * MVMAXBLKS

TOTAL VARIABLES = 500

Each array takes up one memory variable slot, no matter how many elements it contains. Elements for the array are stored in a separate section of memory allocated just for that purpose.

Tip: See the DECLARE command for more information on how to create arrays and assign values to their elements. Also, Chapter 18 contains a detailed discussion of how you might use memory variables in a program.

Note: Numeric variables are binary coded decimal (BCD) unless converted to floating-point values with the FLOAT() function.

See also: &, CLEAR ALL, CLEAR MEMORY, DECLARE, LIST/DISPLAY MEMORY, PARAMETERS, PRIVATE, PUBLIC, RELEASE, RESTORE, and SAVE.

Examples

The following example uses the STORE command to store ten blank spaces to a list of memory variables:

```
. STORE SPACE(10) TO M_first, M_second, M_third
```

The next example creates a name from two fields in the PEOPLE database and stores it in a memory variable:

```
. USE SAMPLES\People
. DISPLAY Firstname, Lastname
Record #   Firstname    Lastname
1          Michael      Berrigan
. STORE TRIM(Firstname)+" "+TRIM(Lastname) TO Name
Michael Berrigan
. ? Name
Michael Berrigan
```

SUM

The SUM command adds numeric expressions and saves the results in memory variables or an array.

Syntax

SUM [<*expression list*>] TO [*memory variable list*] /TO ARRAY <*array name*>] [<*scope*>] [FOR <*condition*>] [WHILE <*condition*>]

TO puts totals in either *memory variable list* or *array name.* If you don't include TO, totals are displayed on the screen only.

Expression list is usually a list of valid numeric database fields. If you do not include *expression list*, all numeric fields in the database are added together.

Array name is the name of a one-dimensional array. The SUM command does not sum values to a two-dimensional array.

FOR <*condition*> and WHILE <*condition*> determine which records the SUM command adds together. If you do not include them, the SUM command totals all records.

Notes

The SUM command stores fixed numeric values in memory variables or array elements. When you list more than one memory variable, the first total is placed in the first variable, the second total in the second variable, and so on, until all variables have been used or all totals have been stored. The same is true for array elements. If you run out of variables or array elements, the remaining totals aren't stored. If you run out of totals, the remaining variables or array elements retain their original value.

Example

This example totals all of the fields in the GOODS database to the screen and then totals just one field (Cost) and stores it in a memory variable (Mcost). It displays the total stored in the memory variable.

```
. USE SAMPLES\Goods
. SUM
LEAD_TIME       PRICE QTY_2ORDER QTY_ONHAND        COST
      1710      30775          111          164       20565
. SUM Cost TO Mcost
      Cost
. ? Mcost
     20565
```

See also: AVERAGE, CALCULATE, DECLARE, STORE, TOTAL, FIXED(), and FLOAT().

SUSPEND

The SUSPEND command halts program execution. It helps you debug your application programs.

Syntax

SUSPEND

Notes

To access the SUSPEND command, you can

- Put a SUSPEND statement in your application program
- Enter X at the debugger's action prompt
- Select **Suspend** from the error prompt "Cancel Ignore Suspend"

After the SUSPEND command halts the program, you can enter commands at the dot prompt. Use the RESUME command to continue program execution. Don't use the DO command to restart the program; this stores an additional copy of the program in memory.

You can use the CANCEL or CLOSE PROCEDURE command to end the program prematurely. The CANCEL command closes suspended programs. The CLOSE PROCEDURE command closes suspended procedure files.

The memory variables created by a suspended program retain their assigned values. While a program is suspended, you can enter commands at the dot prompt that use those memory variables.

You can only use the Debugger's editor to access suspended programs. If you try to edit the program with the program editor, you see the message "File already open." Any memory variables that you create during suspension are private to the suspended program.

See also: CANCEL, COMPILE, DEBUG, DO, RESUME, SET ECHO, SET PROCEDURE, SET STEP, SET TALK, and SET TRAP.

TEXT

The TEXT command sends text blocks to the screen or printer. You can use this command in your programs to communicate with your user.

Syntax

TEXT
<text characters>
ENDTEXT

Notes

You use the TEXT command in programs to create and output text blocks. The text is displayed as it appears in the program. Special characters, such as the macro substitution symbol (&), print as regular characters and don't cause some action to occur as long as they are included within the text block.

Use the SET PRINTER ON command to send the text to the printer.

See also: @, ?/??, ???, LIST/DISPLAY, and SET PRINTER.

Example

The following command lines send a short message to the screen and then prompt the user to press Y to continue.

```
CLEAR
DO WHILE .T.
     TEXT
     Use this program to back up the database of your choosing to
     a disk in drive A. If you've changed your mind about
     performing this operation, type N at the prompt. If you wish
     to continue, type Y at the prompt.
     END TEXT
     WAIT "Continue operation (Y/N))? " TO Choice
     IF UPPER(Choice) = "Y"
          EXIT
     ENDIF
     IF UPPER(Choice)= "N"
          RETURN
     ENDIF
ENDDO
```

TOTAL

The TOTAL command sums numeric fields using an index field and creates a new database containing the results of the calculations.

Syntax

TOTAL ON <*key field*> TO <*filename*> [FIELDS <*fields list*>] [<*scope*>] [FOR <*condition*>] [WHILE <*condition*>]

Notes

The TOTAL command consolidates all records with the same key field into a single record and creates a new database. It consolidates all the same-key information in numeric fields. It extracts only the first same-key information in the character fields. TOTAL doesn't copy memo fields to the new database.

If the total is larger than the target field, dBASE puts asterisks in the field, signifying that an overflow has occurred and that the data can't accurately be saved in the new database. To correct this problem, expand the size of the field in the source database to the largest total it will hold in the target database and rerun the TOTAL command.

FOR <*condition*>, WHILE <*condition*>, and *scope* limit which records the TOTAL command accesses. Without them, all records are used. If you SET CATALOG to ON, the new database is added to the catalog.

See also: AVERAGE, CALCULATE, INDEX, MODIFY STRUCTURE, SET SAFETY, SORT, and SUM.

Example

This example shows how to create a new database containing the quantities that each customer ordered. First it indexes the ORDERS database. (Remember, you can't use the TOTAL command unless the database is indexed.) Then it uses the TOTAL command to create a new database. The new database, CUSTTOTS, is then opened and its contents are displayed.

```
. USE SAMPLES\Orders
. INDEX ON Cust_id TO Cidndx
. LIST Cust_id, Part_qty
Record#  Cust_id Part_qty
     15  A00001         5
     16  A00001         3
     12  A10025         1
     13  A10025         5
     14  A10025        15
      2  C00001         1
      3  C00001         5
      4  C00001         1
      5  C00001         1
      6  C00001         1
      7  C00001         7
      8  C00001         2
      9  C00001         4
     10  C00001         5
     11  C00001        10
      1  C00002         1
. TOTAL ON Cust_id TO Custtots
. USE Custtots
```

```
. DISPLAY ALL Cust_id, Part_qty
Record#  Cust_id Part_qty
      1  A00001          8
      2  A10025         21
      3  C00001         37
      4  C00002          1
```

TYPE

The TYPE command displays the contents of a file on your screen. This command is like the DOS TYPE command; it scrolls the contents of the file across your screen. To stop the display from scrolling, press ALT-S.

Syntax

TYPE <*filename*> [TO PRINTER/TO FILE <*filename*>]
[NUMBER]

Filename is the name of a file containing ASCII text, including the extension.

TO PRINTER sends the output to the printer.

TO FILE sends the output to *filename*.

NUMBER includes line numbers when the text displays.

Notes

The TYPE command's display includes a heading with the file name, date, and page number. If you don't want this information, issue **SET HEADING OFF**.

See also: SET DATE, SET HEADING, SET PATH, and SET PRINTER.

UNLOCK

The UNLOCK command releases record and file locks used to preserve data integrity in a multi-user environment.

Syntax

UNLOCK [ALL/IN <*alias*>]

Notes

Chapter 30 discusses networking and the UNLOCK command.

See also: SET RELATION, FLOCK(), and RLOCK().

UPDATE

The UPDATE command uses data from a different database to replace fields in the current indexed or sorted database. It matches records based on a key field.

Syntax

UPDATE ON <*key field*> FROM <*alias*>
REPLACE <*field name 1*> WITH <*expression 1*>
[, <*field name 2*> WITH <*expression 2*>...]
[RANDOM]

Notes

The UPDATE command is similar to the REPLACE command in that it changes the information contained in multiple records. However the REPLACE command uses a value supplied by an expression, while the UPDATE command uses information from another database. The update is accomplished by matching the values in the *key field* for the database being updated to the values in the *key field* from the database supplying the data.

The active database is the one you update to. Its name doesn't appear in the UPDATE command. The FROM database is inactive but open in a different work area. For the UPDATE command to be successful, the key field names in the two databases must be the same.

If you use the RANDOM option, only the active database's key field needs to be indexed or sorted. If you don't use the RANDOM option, both databases' key fields must be indexed.

See also: INDEX, JOIN, REPLACE, SORT, and TOTAL.

Example

The following example updates a database called ACCTS from a database called TRANSACT. Note that TRANSACT is opened in work area 2 and then ACCTS is opened in the current work area. Both databases are indexed on account number. However, ACCTS remains the active database. Next, the UPDATE command updates all of the affected records in ACCTS from TRANSACT. The name of the matching field in each database is Acct_no. The values for this field in the ACCTS database are matched with those in the same field of the TRANSACT database. Note the use of the pointers (->) in the expressions following the UPDATE command. These point to the fields in the noncurrent work area.

```
USE Transact IN 2 ORDER Acct
USE Accts ORDER Acct
UPDATE ON Acct_no FROM Transact REPLACE ;
  Debit WITH Debit+Transact->Debit,Credit WITH ;
  Credit+Transact->Credit
```

USE

The USE command opens a database and its associated memo (.DBT) file, if one exists. If the database you specify has a production index (.MDX) file, that file is opened automatically as well. You can also use this command to simultaneously open any associated single index (.NDX) files or independent multiple index (.MDX) files.

Syntax

USE [?/[<*database filename*>][IN <*work area number*>]
[[INDEX <*index file list*>]
[[ORDER [TAG] <*index filename*>/< *.MDX tag*>
[OF <*.MDX filename*>]] [ALIAS <*alias*]
[EXCLUSIVE] [NOUPDATE]]]]

USE opens a *database filename* you specify in the current work area. If a database is currently active in that work area, dBASE IV closes that database, and any associated index files, before opening the specified database. When you open a database file with the USE command, dBASE IV assumes a .DBF extension.

USE ? displays a menu of database files from the current catalog, if one is open, or from the current directory, if a catalog is not in use.

Database filename is the name of an existing database.

You use the IN <*work area number*> clause to specify a number from 1 to 10 or a letter from "A" to "J" representing one of ten possible work areas in which to open the database. You can also substitute an expression that yields a value in these ranges. Use the IN clause to open a database in a work area other than the current one.

You use the INDEX clause to specify the names of one or more index files separated by commas. These index files are opened simultaneously with the database. You do not need to specify the production index file name here, because that index file is opened automatically with the database. However, you can use this clause to specify the names of single index (.NDX) files or independent multiple index files (.MDX) files. If you specify an index file name without an extension, dBASE IV first tries to open an .MDX file. If it cannot find one, it tries to open an .NDX file.

The ORDER clause sets the controlling index to either *index filename* or *.MDX tag*. *Index filename* is the name of a single index (.NDX) file, and *.MDX tag* is a valid tag in the production index (.MDX) file for the specified database.

You use the OF <*.MDX filename*> clause to qualify the ORDER clause and refer to an independent (non-production) multiple index (.MDX) file.

ALIAS <*alias*> is an alternate name of your choosing for the specified database.

EXCLUSIVE opens a private database in a network environment. The file cannot be shared by, or accessed by, others until you close the database using CLOSE ALL, CLEAR ALL, or USE.

NOUPDATE means that you can read but cannot change information in the opened database.

The USE command by itself closes any open database in the current work area. If you include the optional IN <*work area number*> clause, dBASE IV closes the open database and any associated index files in the work area you specify.

Notes

When you open a database, the USE command positions the record pointer at the beginning of the database. However, if you specify an index, the record pointer goes to the first record pointed to by the controlling index file.

The ORDER clause determines the controlling or master index. The index name can be that of a tag in a multiple index (.MDX) file or the name of a single index (.NDX) file. Use the ORDER clause when more than one index tag name is present in a multiple index file or when more than one .NDX index file is specified after the INDEX clause. The controlling index determines which key fields commands the SEEK and FIND commands use in their searches. If you specify only one index, it is the controlling index by default and you don't need to use the ORDER clause.

When you use the ALIAS clause, you can assign an alias to the database you are activating with the USE command. You can use the alias in place of the database name in other commands. If you don't use the ALIAS option, the default alias is the same as the database name.

Note: As an alternative, you can assign as an alias one of the dBASE reserved characters (A- J) or reserved numbers (1-10, corresponding to the ten work areas).

See also: CLEAR ALL, CLOSE, COPY INDEX, COPY TAG, DELETE TAG, INDEX, SELECT, SET CATALOG, SET EXCLUSIVE, SET INDEX, SET ORDER, SET REPROCESS, and DBF().

Examples

What follows are two examples of the USE command. The first example opens the CUSTOMER database in the current work area and establishes the Cust_no tag of the production index file as the controlling index.

```
. USE Customer ORDER Cust_no
```

The next command opens the CUSTOMER database in work area 2 and specifies the Cust_no tag.

```
. USE Customer IN 2 ORDER Cust_no
```

WAIT

The WAIT command halts activity and waits for you to press any key.

Syntax

WAIT [<*prompt*>] TO [<*memory variable*>]

Prompt is a character expression that appears in place of the dBASE message "Press any key to continue."

The TO <*memory variable*> clause creates a character type memory variable that you can use to get user input from a program. The memory variable stores a single character. If you press ENTER in response to the prompt, the memory variable is given a null value. If you enter a nonprinting character, the memory variable will yield the graphic character of the same ASCII value.

Notes

The WAIT command is frequently used to halt program execution while an instructional message is displayed. You can use the WAIT command by itself to display the message "Press any key to continue."

You can also use the WAIT command to get single keystroke responses to simple Yes/No menus during program execution. (See the example for this command.)

See also: ACCEPT, INPUT, ON KEY, and STORE.

Example

This example shows how to use the simplest form of the WAIT command. Then it shows how to change the default message and store the input in a memory variable named Ans.

```
. WAIT
Press any key to continue...
. WAIT "Is the printer ready (Y/N) " TO Ans
Is the printer ready (Y/N) Y
. ? Ans
Y
```

ZAP

ZAP erases all of the records from an active database file.

Syntax

ZAP

Notes

ZAP eliminates the entire contents of the database file. If SET SAFETY is ON, dBASE IV issues a "ZAP <*filename*> ? (Y/N)" prompt.

If there are any open index files in the current work area, dBASE IV automatically updates them to reflect the empty database file.

See also: DELETE, PACK, and SET SAFETY.

SET Commands

THIRTY TWO

You can use SET commands to control various dBASE IV settings. They all begin with the keyword SET. There are two kinds of SET commands: commands that simply turn something on and off and commands that set an option to a value. For example, the SET PRINTER command is the first kind of SET command. It sends screen output to the printer when you set it to ON. When you set it to OFF, the screen output routes to the screen only. The SET DATE command is the second kind of SET command. It instructs dBASE IV to display all dates in a specified format. For example, use it to display dates as *mm/dd/yy*, *yy/mm/dd*, or *mm-dd-yy*.

This chapter lists the dBASE IV SET commands alphabetically. Each section contains the command's name and a brief command description. Then, the command's default format is given in uppercase in the syntax statement. There are also notes about the command, and an example.

dBASE IV has two modes: dBASE and SQL. You can't use certain dBASE SET commands in SQL mode. These SET commands are noted as "dBASE mode only" in the command summary. When the mode is not listed, you can use the SET command in either mode.

Any changes you make with SET commands remain in effect for the length of your dBASE IV session. Changes to your CONFIG.DB file take effect when you start up dBASE IV. The Notes section lets you know if you can add a particular command to your CONFIG.DB file, and also lists any related commands. Some Note sections include information meant for application programmers and advanced dBASE users.

Examples are included as needed. Many SET commands just turn something on or off, so examples are not really necessary. However, examples are included when turning the command on causes a major visible effect. There are examples for SET commands that set a value which produces a visible result. NO examples are included that would require you to reconfigure your system, such as commands that work in the multi-user, network environment. Some examples use the databases in the SAMPLES directory. To work these examples, you'll need to install the demonstration disks included in your dBASE IV release package.

Note: When a SET command has an ON/OFF option, the "Syntax" section shows the default in uppercase. For example, in

SET ALTERNATE on/OFF

the default setting for the command is OFF.

SET

The SET command allows you to access SET commands and change their defaults in a menu-driven environment (dBASE mode only).

Syntax

SET

Notes

When you enter **SET** at the dot prompt, dBASE displays a full screen menu for modifying many of dBASE IV's more common settings. You can use this menu as an alternative to entering SET commands at the dot prompt. For a complete description of how to use the SET full-screen menu, see Chapter 35. A trimmed-down version of this menu appears when you select the **Settings** option in the **Tools** menu of the Control Center (see Chapter 14, "Tools").

SET ALTERNATE

The SET ALTERNATE command records in a text file the commands you issue and their results. It does not record the output of full-screen or @...SAY commands.

Syntax

SET ALTERNATE TO [<*filename*> [ADDITIVE]]

SET ALTERNATE on/OFF

SET ALTERNATE TO <*filename*> opens a file. If *filename* doesn't exist, it creates <*filename*>.TXT.

SET ALTERNATE ON sends output to the file.

SET ALTERNATE OFF stops sending output to the file but doesn't close the file. This is the default.

The ADDITIVE option records output at the end of <*filename*>.TXT. If you do not use the ADDITIVE option and <*filename*>.TXT already exists, you receive the message "File already exists." You can either overwrite or cancel the command.

Notes

For the correct results, you must use the SET ALTERNATE commands in the sequence shown in the "Syntax" and "Example" sections. For example, if you issue **SET ALTERNATE ON** and you haven't routed the output to a file with the SET ALTERNATE TO command, output is not recorded.

<*filename*>.TXT is a text file in standard ASCII format. You can edit it with the MODIFY COMMAND command, a word processor, or a text editor. The output recorded in <*filename*>.TXT consists of keyboard entries and screen displays. It does not include full-screen command output, such as output from @...SAY, EDIT, BROWSE, and APPEND commands.

After you open the file, you can send and suspend output to *<filename>*.TXT, as long as you don't issue the **CLOSE ALTERNATE** command. SET ALTERNATE TO automatically issues a CLOSE ALTERNATE command before it opens another *<filename>*.TXT.

Related command: CLOSE ALTERNATE

Example

This example creates a text file called ALTFILE.TXT, prepares the file to record commands, records a directory listing, suspends recording, and closes the file.

```
. SET ALTERNATE TO Altfile
. SET ALTERNATE ON
. DIR
. SET ALTERNATE OFF
. CLOSE ALTERNATE
```

SET AUTOSAVE

The SET AUTOSAVE command either saves a record to disk immediately after you access it or waits for you to write your changes.

Syntax

SET AUTOSAVE on/OFF

SET AUTOSAVE ON saves information to disk each time you change or add a record.

SET AUTOSAVE OFF keeps information in memory until the buffer is full or you tell the system to save it to disk. This is the default.

Notes

SET AUTOSAVE ON reduces chances of data loss but takes more time. SET AUTOSAVE OFF is faster because it writes your changes to disk less often. It also allows you to abandon changes or additions to databases.

You can make the change permanent by putting the command in your CONFIG.DB file.

SET BELL

The SET BELL command determines whether you hear a tone when you make an error or reach the end of a field. You can use this command to change the tone's duration and frequency.

Syntax

SET BELL ON/off

SET BELL TO [<*frequency*>,<*duration*>]

SET BELL ON makes the tone sound at the default frequency and duration (512,2). This is the default.

SET BELL OFF disables the tone.

SET BELL TO restores the default.

frequency is a number between 19 and 10,000 representing cycles per second. The default is 512 hertz.

duration is a number between 2 and 19 ticks. (A tick is about 0.0549 seconds.) The default is 2 ticks.

Notes

If you want a low tone, use a value between 20 and 549. For a high tone, use a value between 550 and 5500.

You can make the change permanent by putting the command in your CONFIG.DB file.

Example

This example enables the tone, plays the default, sets and plays a low tone for a relatively long period, sets and plays a high tone for a relatively short period, and resets and plays the default.

```
SET BELL ON
? CHR(7)
SET BELL TO 20,10
? CHR(7)
SET BELL TO 5000,1
? CHR(7)
SET BELL TO 512,2
? CHR(7)
```

SET BLOCKSIZE

The SET BLOCKSIZE command changes the block size for memo fields and multiple index files (.MDX) (dBASE mode only).

Syntax

SET BLOCKSIZE TO <*multiplier*>

multiplier is a number from 1 to 32. Actual block size is *multiplier* * 512 bytes of active memory. The default is 1.

Notes

For dBASE III PLUS compatibility, *multiplier* must equal 1, which is why 1 is the default value.

You can make the change permanent by putting the command in your CONFIG.DB file.

Related commands: COPY, CREATE/MODIFY STRUCTURE

Example

This example changes the block size to 1024 bytes and is not compatible with dBASE III PLUS.

```
SET BLOCKSIZE TO 2
```

SET BORDER

The SET BORDER command sets the border for menus, windows, and @ commands.

Syntax

SET BORDER TO [SINGLE/DOUBLE/PANEL/NONE/
<*border string*>]

SET BORDER command options are

SINGLE	Creates a single-line box; this is the default
DOUBLE	Creates a double-line box
PANEL	Create a reverse-video box (ASCII 219)
NONE	Removes the border

Here's the format for the *border string*:

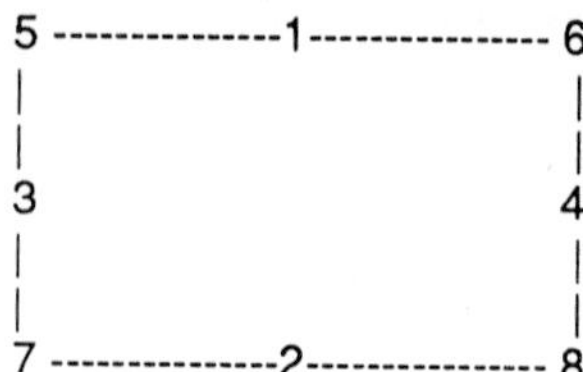

Figure 32-1. Screen areas

[<1>][,[<2>][,[<3>][,[<4>][,[<5>][,[<6>][,[<7>][,[<8>]]]]]]]

Notes

The *border string* option allows you to draw lines by using the decimal value for any IBM extended ASCII character. It uses numbers that represent screen areas. Each number represents an area on the screen that can have a character assigned. The numbers 1 through 4 represent the sides; the numbers 5 through 8 represent the corners.

Figure 32-1 shows the screen areas that SET BORDER accesses.

Screen area numbers are shown between substitution brackets (<>). To use the option, substitute the ASCII code for the area number and remove the angle brackets. You must separate each screen area with a comma. To use the current setting for an area, enter a comma without an ASCII code (see the "Example" section).

The border setting influences @...SAY and @...TO commands and window borders. Lines drawn with @ commands use the SET BORDER default.

Related commands: @...SAY, @...TO

Example

This example sets the borders to hearts (3) and diamonds (4), and the corners to clubs (5) and spades (6).

```
SET BORDER TO 3,3,4,4,5,5,6,6
```

SET CARRY

The SET CARRY command passes values to some or all fields (dBASE mode only).

Syntax

SET CARRY on/OFF

SET CARRY TO [<*field list*> [ADDITIVE]]

SET CARRY ON passes field values from the current record to the next record.

SET CARRY OFF stops passing field values from the current record to the next record. This is the default.

SET CARRY TO <*field list*> allows you to select the fields whose values you want passed.

field list is a list of the dBASE fields.

ADDITIVE adds *field list* to any existing carry fields.

SET CARRY TO without *field list* sets carry fields back to all (same as SET CARRY ON when first issued).

Notes

After dBASE applies the current record's values to the new record, the new record appears on the screen with the values. At this time, you can change any values, whether they were passed or not.

You can use the SET CARRY TO command to speed data entry. For example, if you have a database that has an Invoiced field, all new records are set to no (or false) until invoicing occurs.

CARRY affects the APPEND, BROWSE, and INSERT commands. It does not affect the INSERT BLANK or APPEND BLANK commands.

Related commands: APPEND, BROWSE, EDIT, INSERT, READ, SET FIELDS, SET FORMAT

Example

This example activates the PEOPLE database in the SAMPLES directory, activates CARRY, sets the field to carry to Cardsent, and starts the input process. After you issue the **APPEND** command, enter a record and go to the next record. Notice how the Cardsent field is already filled in.

```
. USE People
. SET CARRY ON
. SET CARRY TO Cardsent
. APPEND
```

SET CATALOG

The SET CATALOG command creates a new or opens an existing catalog file (.CAT) and maintains a list of the database and its associated files (dBASE mode only).

Syntax

SET CATALOG on/OFF

SET CATALOG TO [<*filename*> /?]

COPY STRUCTURE	IMPORT FROM
COPY STRUCTURE EXTENDED	INDEX
CREATE	JOIN
CREATE FROM	SET FILTER TO FILE
CREATE/MODIFY LABEL	SET FORMAT
CREATE/MODIFY QUERY	SET VIEW
CREATE/MODIFY REPORT	SORT
CREATE/MODIFY SCREEN	TOTAL
CREATE/MODIFY VIEW	USE

Table 32-1. The Catalog File Update Commands

SET CATALOG TO <*filename*> creates and opens a new catalog file or opens an existing catalog file named *filename*.CAT. It activates the catalog automatically by issuing the **SET CATALOG ON** command.

SET CATALOG ON activates the catalog file associated with the database in use. This command works with an open catalog file.

SET CATALOG OFF deactivates the catalog file associated with the database in use. You can still use the query option (?) to list entries in the catalog file. This is the default.

SET CATALOG TO closes an open or active catalog file.

SET CATALOG TO ? lists available catalogs, which you can highlight and select.

filename follows dBASE naming conventions and has a maximum of eight characters.

Notes

A catalog file records information about the database and its associated index, query, format, report, and label files. Table 32-1 shows commands that automatically update the catalog file.

If you issue the **SET TITLE ON** command and then create a catalog file, you are asked to provide a one-line description. SET CATALOG TO ? displays the description as part of the list. To change the title in a catalog, issue **USE *<catalog name>*.CAT** and **EDIT**. If the catalog is already in use, issue **SELECT 10** and **EDIT**.

When you open an existing catalog file, dBASE checks the catalog's contents against the files on the disk. If files are missing from the catalog, dBASE deletes them from the catalog list. You may change the catalog file entries and the catalog when the catalog file is inactive. If so, you receive the message "SET CATALOG was OFF when the active database file was USEd" when you activate the catalog file.

When you first issue **SET CATALOG TO *<filename>***, dBASE sets up a master catalog file in which it records the catalog you are creating. Subsequently, new catalogs you create are added to the master catalog file list. The master catalog file exists in the dBASE IV home directory. If you move it to a different directory or delete it, dBASE creates the master catalog in the current directory the next time you issue the command SET CATALOG TO *<filename>*.

The catalog file stores information in a database structure that you can access like any other database. Here's the structure of the catalog file.

Field	Field Name	Type	Width	Dec
1	Path	Character	70	
2	File_name	Character	12	
3	Alias	Character	8	
4	Type	Character	3	
5	Title	Character	80	
6	Code	Character	3	
7	Tag	Character	4	
Total		181		

The fields in the catalog file are described as follows:

Path	Path where the catalog is located; used when catalog is not on default drive and path
File_name	File name and extension, default or specified
Alias	Used when database is given a name other than the database file name
Type	File extension, default only
Title	Description entered when catalog created with SET TITLE ON
Code	Program files = 0, database files = sequential number, associated files = same as number assigned to database they reference
Tag	Not used

Note: Catalog files are automatically opened in work area 10. When a catalog is open, you can't select and use work area 10 for another database file.

Related command: SET TITLE

Example

This example turns on the catalog description prompt, displays a list of catalog files (if any exist), creates and opens a new catalog file called NEWCAT, and activates the catalog. Any objects you create will now be listed in the NEWCAT.CAT file.

```
. SET TITLE ON
. SET CATALOG TO ?
. SET CATALOG TO Newcat
. SET CATALOG ON
```

SET CENTURY

The SET CENTURY command determines whether a century is added to the year display.

Syntax

SET CENTURY on/OFF

SET CENTURY OFF assumes a 20th century date. It doesn't ask for or display a century, only the year (*mm/dd/yy*). This is the default.

SET CENTURY ON turns on the century capability for dates. You can enter and display non-20th century dates with this option (*mm/dd/yyyy*).

Notes

This command affects all full-screen editing commands and date displays. Its significance increases as the 21st century approaches.

Note: Because of the way dBASE stores numbers internally, the date field is eight characters although the date with the century added appears to use ten characters.

Related functions: CTOD(), DATE(), DTOC(), DTOS(), SET DATE(), YEAR()

Example

This example turns on the century option, displays today's date by using the DATE() function, and turns the century option off.

```
. SET CENTURY ON
. ? DATE()
04/06/89
. SET CENTURY OFF
```

SET CLOCK

The SET CLOCK command allows you to display a clock and change its position.

Syntax

SET CLOCK on/OFF

SET CLOCK TO [<*row*>,<*column*>]

SET CLOCK OFF is the default.

SET CLOCK ON displays a clock in the upper-right corner of your screen. The default coordinates are 0,69.

SET CLOCK TO [<*row*>,<*column*>] changes the position of the clock on your screen when you enter new *row* and *column* coordinates.

SET CLOCK TO restores the default.

Notes

The maximum value for *row* equals the number of lines your particular monitor can display. The maximum value for *column* is 69.

Example

This example displays the clock in the upper-right corner of your screen, moves the clock to the lower-right corner, puts it in the upper-left corner, and removes it from the screen.

```
. SET CLOCK ON
. SET CLOCK TO 20,69
. SET CLOCK TO 1,1
. SET CLOCK OFF
```

SET COLOR

The SET COLOR command displays and changes colors and attributes for color and monochrome monitors.

Syntax

SET COLOR ON/OFF

SET COLOR TO [[<*standard*>][,[<*enhanced*>]
[,[<*perimeter*>] [,[<*background*>]]]]]

SET COLOR OF <*area*> TO [<*color attribute*>]

SET COLOR ON switches to the color monitor.

SET COLOR OFF switches to the monochrome monitor.

SET COLOR TO restores dBASE default colors set when you start dBASE IV.

SET COLOR TO <*area*> sets colors for the following:

standard or text

enhanced or highlighted areas

perimeter or boundary

background or background

SET COLOR OF <*area*> selects colors for particular groups of dBASE activities. The *area* groups are

NORMAL

MESSAGES

TITLES

BOX

HIGHLIGHT

INFORMATION

FIELDS

TO *<color attribute>* is a one- or two-character color letter. Table 32-2 lists the color letters. Table 32-3 lists the areas covered by each group.

Notes

The SET COLOR command is hardware-dependent. If you have a monochrome monitor, skip any information about color settings. You can, however, use U for underline and I for reverse video to emphasize certain screen areas.

To change the color settings, specify letter codes for *standard, enhanced, perimeter,* or *background.* Use the appropriate color letter from Table 32-2.

To make a particular type blink on and off, put an asterisk after the color letter. For example, B* blinks in blue. Select high intensity by putting a plus symbol (+) after the color letter. For example, B+ gives high intensity blue. You can't use the plus symbol (+) with brown (GR), yellow (GR+), or gray (N+). (Yellow already uses the plus symbol (+) to change brown to yellow.) To mask a particular area of the screen with blanks, enter X.

If your display adapter allows different colors for standard and enhanced text, enter the colors as pairs, separated with a slash

Color	Letters	Color	Letters
black	N or blank	red	R
blue	B	magenta	RB
green	G	brown	GR
cyan	BG	yellow	GR+
blank	X	white	W
gray	N+		

Table 32-2. Color Letters

(/). When you don't specify colors for both letters in a pair, black is selected.

If you have an enhanced graphics adapter card, you cannot use high intensity colors for background. If you attempt to do so, the attributes for the background are applied to the foreground.

If you have either an EGA, VGA, or other enhanced graphics adapter card, you can select colors from a menu using the **Display** option of the main **Set** menu.

When you use the SET COLOR OF...TO command to change the *color attribute* of screen areas, you change the color for the entire group. Table 32-3 describes what areas are changed when you change *color attribute* for one of the screen groups.

You can make the change permanent by putting the command in your CONFIG.DB file. When you start dBASE IV, the colors set in the CONFIG.DB file override dBASE color settings. When SET COLOR TO restores the default colors, it doesn't access CONFIG.DB.

Related commands: SET, SET DISPLAY

Example

This example sets prompt to yellow and status bar to blue. Then it restores the default settings.

```
. SET COLOR TO GR+,B
. SET COLOR TO
```

SET CONFIRM

The SET CONFIRM command determines whether the cursor goes to the next field automatically when it reaches the end of the current field.

NORMAL

Uncontrolled @...SAY output
Unselected fields in BROWSE
Layout editor design surface (dim)
Unselected text on design surface
Unselected uncolored display-only field templates
Static memo, window borders
Conditions in QBE file skeleton
Conditions in QBE condition box
Calculated filed expressions
Unselected, uncolored box borders in Layout editor
Uncolored box borders drawn with @...TO command
User-entered text in the applications generator

MESSAGES

Message line bright
Navigation line
Available, unselected menu and list choices (bright)
Error box interiors
File window contents
Help box interiors
File window contents
Help box interiors
Bold help box text (bright)
Prompt box interiors
Unselected prompt box buttons (bright)
Unselected error box buttons (bright)
Unselected help box buttons (bright)

TITLES

List headings
Help box headings
Control Center banner
Control Center catalog name heading and file name
Control Center filename and file description headings
BROWSE field name headings
BROWSE table grids (dim)
Database design column labels
Database design field numbers
Directory name at top of file window
Files: heading

Table 32-3. Screen Area Color Control

TITLES (*continued*)

Sorted by: heading
Unselected report design band lines
QBE file skeleton field names and file name
QBE view skeleton field names and view name
QBE view skeleton grid (dim)
QBE file skeleton grids (dim)
QBE calculated field skeleton grids (dim)
QBE condition box border (dim)
QBE condition box heading
Ruler line
Text styles defined with the Style menu (bright)
Text that is underlines in help screens (bright)
Static text in applications generator forms
Underlined help box text (bright)
Database design grid

BOX

Menu borders
File and sorted by information
File window border
List borders
Prompt box borders
Label design layout box border
Unselected applications generator object border

HIGHLIGHT

Highlighted menu and list choices
Highlighted prompt box buttons
Selected static text on design surface
Selected box
Control Center filename and file description
Flying cursor in ruler line
Report design band line labels
Report design selected band lines
Information box borders
Information box interiors
Current field in the applications generator
Static text under the cursor on design surface
Box under the cursor on design surface
Field under the cursor on design surface

Table 32-3. Screen Area Color Control (*continued*)

INFORMATION

Clock
Error box borders
Help box borders
Status line
Selected button in error box
Selected button in help box

FIELDS

Database design in select field
Fields you can edit in @...GET
Field design surface field templates you can edit
Prompt box data entry areas
Selected field in BROWSE
Unselected fields in the application generator

Table 32-3. Screen Area Color Control (*continued*)

Syntax

SET CONFIRM on/OFF

SET CONFIRM OFF advances the cursor to the next field when it reaches the end of the current field. This is the default.

SET CONFIRM ON doesn't advance the cursor to the next field unless you press ENTER.

Notes

With SET CONFIRM ON, if you overtype a field and keep typing, the extra characters are typed over the last character in the field. They don't spill into the next field. This prevents you from accidentally typing over other fields.

With SET CONFIRM OFF, extra characters spill into the next fields. This way, you don't have to press ENTER every time you enter a field.

SET CONSOLE

The SET CONSOLE command determines whether to send output from an application program to the screen.

Syntax

SET CONSOLE ON/off

SET CONSOLE ON routes output to the screen. This is the default.

SET CONSOLE OFF suppresses output to the screen.

Notes

Use the SET CONSOLE OFF option when you don't want output going to the printer to appear on the screen also. You can still input information at the keyboard, but the screen remains blank.

@...SAY...GET command output, error messages, and safety prompts are not suppressed.

SET CURRENCY

The SET CURRENCY command changes the character used for the currency sign in @...PICTURE clauses.

Syntax

SET CURRENCY TO [<*character string*>]

SET CURRENCY TO restores the default, the dollar sign. *character string* is a character string of up to nine characters.

Notes

Related commands: SET POINT, SET SEPARATOR, SET CURRENCY LEFT/RIGHT

Example

This example program shows the results of the SET CURRENCY RIGHT/LEFT, SET CURRENCY TO, SET POINT TO, and SET DECIMAL commands as it displays currency with @...SAY commands.

```
Money = 1234.567
@1,10 SAY Money FUNCTION "$"     && Result: $1234.57
*
SET CURRENCY RIGHT
@3,10 SAY Money FUNCTION "$"     && Result: 1234.57$
*
SET CURRENCY TO "&"
@5,10 SAY Money FUNCTION "$"     && Result: 1234.57&
*
SET POINT TO "%"
@7,10 SAY Money FUNCTION "$"     && Result: 1234%57&
*
SET CURRENCY TO
SET CURRENCY LEFT
@9,10 SAY Money FUNCTION "$"     && Result: $1234%57
*
SET DECIMAL TO 5
@11,10 SAY Money FUNCTION "$"    && Result: $1234%56700
*
SET POINT TO
@13,10 SAY Money FUNCTION "$"    && Result: $1234.56700
*
SET DECIMAL TO 2
@15,10 SAY Money FUNCTION "$"    && Result: $1234.57
```

SET CURRENCY LEFT/RIGHT

The SET CURRENCY LEFT/RIGHT command positions the currency symbol to the left or right of the currency value.

Syntax

SET CURRENCY LEFT/RIGHT

SET CURRENCY LEFT moves the symbol to the left of the amount. This is the default.

SET CURRENCY RIGHT moves the symbol to the right of the amount.

Notes

Some countries place the currency symbol to the right of the amount. When this is the case, you can use this command to move the symbol.

You can make the change permanent by putting the command in your CONFIG.DB file.

Example

See the SET CURRENCY TO example.

SET DATE

The SET DATE command changes the format used to display dates.

Syntax

SET DATE <*date type*>

Use SET DATE <*date type*> to change the default date format. Date types are

AMERICAN	*mm/dd/yy*
ANSI	*yy.mm.dd*
BRITISH/FRENCH	*dd/mm/yy*
GERMAN	*dd.mm.yy*
ITALIAN	*dd-mm-yy*
JAPAN	*yy/mm/dd*
USA	*mm-dd-yy*
MDY	*mm/dd/yy*
DMY	*dd/mm/yy*
YMD	*yy/mm/dd*

Notes

You can make the change permanent by putting the command in your CONFIG.DB file.

Related functions and commands: DATE(), DMY(), MDY(), SET CENTURY

Example

This example shows the default date format, changes the format to Japanese and displays the result, and changes the format back to American and displays the result.

```
. ? DATE()
01/08/89
. SET DATE JAPAN
. ? DATE()
```

```
89/01/08
. SET DATE AMERICAN
. ? date()
01/08/89
```

SET DEBUG

The SET DEBUG command allows you to send output from the SET ECHO command to the printer. Use this command to debug application programs.

Syntax

SET DEBUG on/OFF

SET DEBUG ON sends output from SET ECHO commands to the printer instead of the screen.

SET DEBUG OFF sends output from SET ECHO commands to the screen. This is the default.

Notes

The SET DEBUG ON option prevents interference between the application program's screen operations and the screen display generated by the debugging process. In other words, when you route SET ECHO commands to the printer, you can view the screen output as if you were actually using the application program.

When SET DEBUG and SET ECHO are ON, SET TALK, LIST, and DISPLAY commands and error messages are sent to the printer only if you have issued the **SET PRINTER ON** command.

Related commands: SET DEBUG, SET ECHO, SET TALK

SET DECIMALS

The SET DECIMALS command changes the number of decimal places dBASE IV displays in results of numeric functions and calculations.

Syntax

SET DECIMALS TO *<number>*

number is a number from 0 to 18. The default is two decimal places.

Notes

The value for *number* applies to division, multiplication, and mathematical, trigonometric, and financial calculations. The maximum *number* value, 18, shows 20 numbers, including the decimal point.

SET DEFAULT

The SET DEFAULT command selects the drive in which operations take place and files are stored.

Syntax

SET DEFAULT TO [*<drive letter>*:]

SET DEFAULT TO restores the default. The default is the drive on which you started dBASE IV.

drive letter is a letter between A and Z representing the drive you want to work on.

Notes

The SET DEFAULT command doesn't check to see if the drive is valid. It also doesn't affect the drive you end up on when you exit dBASE IV (the drive from which you started dBASE IV).

When you change the default drive to a new drive, you end up in the directory last changed into.

You can make the change permanent by putting the command in your CONFIG.DB file.

Related command: SET PATH

Example

This example changes the default drive to D:

```
SET DEFAULT TO D:
```

SET DELETED

The SET DELETED command determines whether other commands include records marked for deletion.

Syntax

SET DELETED on/OFF

SET DELETED OFF treats deleted records as any other. This is the default.

SET DELETED ON ignores deleted records for most dBASE commands.

Notes

The SET DELETED command doesn't affect the INDEX and REINDEX commands. If you SET DELETED ON, the RECALL ALL command won't recall any deleted records.

Related function and command: DELETED(), SET FILTER

SET DELIMITERS

The SET DELIMITERS command determines whether to enclose full-screen mode fields with a character. You can use this command to change the default delimiters to some other character.

Syntax

SET DELIMITERS on/OFF

SET DELIMITERS TO <*character string*> /DEFAULT

SET DELIMITERS OFF means entry fields are not enclosed in delimiters. This is the default.

SET DELIMITERS ON encloses fields with colons (:), the default character.

SET DELIMITERS TO <*character string*> allows you to specify what delimiters are used when you SET DELIMITERS ON.

character string has a two-character maximum.

SET DELIMITERS TO DEFAULT restores the colon default.

Notes

character string can be one or two characters. If you use one character, it appears at the beginning and end of the field. If you use two characters, the first defines the beginning of the field and the second defines the end of the field. If you enter more than two characters, the extra characters are ignored.

Issue **SET DELIMITERS ON** before **SET DELIMITERS TO** ***<character string>*.**

Related commands: @, APPEND, CHANGE, EDIT, INSERT, READ, SET INTENSITY

SET DESIGN

The SET DESIGN command controls whether you can access design facilities from the Control Center.

Syntax

SET DESIGN ON/off

SET DESIGN ON permits you to access the design mode. This is the default.

SET DESIGN OFF prevents design mode access.

Notes

Design facilities include the Data, Queries, Forms, Reports, Labels, and Applications Design screens in the Control Center. SET DESIGN OFF denies access to these design facilities and turns off SHIFT-F2. However, the user can still access the Control Center's menu bar options.

SET DEVELOPMENT

SET DEVELOPMENT controls whether you use the most current version of a program's object code (.DBO) file (dBASE mode only).

Syntax

SET DEVELOPMENT ON/off

Notes

SET DEVELOPMENT ON activates an archive program that checks the date and time of compiled object-code (.DBO) files and source-code (.PRG) files when you use MODIFY COMMAND. If the source-code file is more current than the object-code file, the object-code file is removed, and the .PRG file is recompiled the next time you run the program. SET DEVELOPMENT OFF inactivates the archive program, and dBASE IV doesn't check dates.

Related commands: COMPILE, MODIFY COMMAND

SET DEVICE

The SET DEVICE command selects a screen, printer, or file for output routing of @...SAY commands.

Syntax

SET DEVICE TO SCREEN/PRINTER/FILE <*filename*>

SCREEN routes output to the screen. This is the default.
PRINTER routes output to the printer.
FILE <*filename*> routes output to <*filename*>.TXT.

Notes

SET DEVICE controls output from @...SAY commands. When you set it to PRINTER, it ignores @...GET commands. Use the EJECT command or send the printer a blank line to clear the printer buffer.

Related commands: @, EJECT, SET FORMAT

Example

This example routes the text between quotes to a file called TEXT. The last command routes the output back to the screen. The output routed to TEXT.TXT is shown at the end.

```
. SET DEVICE TO FILE TEXT.TXT
. @1,1 SAY "THIS IS SIMILAR TO SET ALTERNATE"
. @2,1 SAY "BUT IT ONLY WORKS FOR"
. @3,1 SAY "@...SAY COMMANDS"
. SET DEVICE TO SCREEN
```

SET DISPLAY

Use the SET DISPLAY command to select the type of monitor you have.

Syntax

SET DISPLAY TO MONO/COLOR/EGA25/EGA43/MONO43

MONO	Selects the 25-line monochrome display
COLOR	Selects the 25-line color monitor (not enhanced)
EGA25	Selects the 25-line enhanced color monitor
EGA43	Selects the 43-line enhanced color monitor
MONO43	Selects the 43-line enhanced monochrome monitor

Notes

To use the SET DISPLAY command, you should have two monitors or the ability to handle more than one mode. If you don't have the appropriate hardware, you receive the error message "Display mode not available."

Related commands: SET, SET COLOR OF, SET COLOR TO

Example

If you use this example with a high-resolution color monitor and an EGA or VGA graphics adapter, the first command changes the display from 23 to 43 lines. If you don't have this capability, you receive an error message. If you have no monochrome monitor attached, the error message "Display mode not available" appears in the dBASE IV error box when you execute the second line. When you exit dBASE, the monitor does not return to its original state.

```
. SET DISPLAY TO EGA43
. SET DISPLAY TO MONO
```

SET DOHISTORY

The SET DOHISTORY command is included in dBASE IV only for compatibility with dBASE III PLUS. It has no effect in dBASE IV.

Syntax

SET DOHISTORY on/OFF

SET ECHO

The SET ECHO command determines whether commands in an application program are output to your screen or printer as the application program executes. This command aids debugging.

Syntax

SET ECHO on/OFF

SET ECHO OFF doesn't display commands. This is the default.

SET ECHO ON displays commands.

Notes

Use SET ECHO ON to watch commands execute in a program. When SET ECHO and SET DEBUG are ON at the same time, commands are printed instead of displayed.

Related commands: DEBUG, SET DEBUG, SET PRINT, SET STEP, SET TALK

SET ENCRYPTION

SET ENCRYPTION establishes whether files are written in encrypted format. See Chapter 30 for a complete description of this command.

Syntax

SET ENCRYPTION on/OFF

SET ESCAPE

The SET ESCAPE command determines whether dBASE IV acknowledges or ignores ESC.

Syntax

SET ESCAPE ON/off

SET ESCAPE ON allows you to use ESC to stop programs, displays, and control output. This is the default.

SET ESCAPE OFF deactivates ESC. The only way to stop a program or command is to restart the system. Also, you can no longer control scrolling with CTRL-S.

Notes

If you interrupt a command or program when ESC is allowed, you may receive the message "*** INTERRUPTED *** Cancel, Ignore, Suspend? (C,I, or S)."

Related commands and functions: ON KEY, ON ERROR, INKEY(), READKEY()

SET EXACT

Use the SET EXACT command in character string comparisons. It determines if the strings have to be the same length to meet the comparison conditions.

Syntax

SET EXACT on/OFF

SET EXACT OFF finds a character string match to be logical true even when the string lengths don't match. This is the default.

SET EXACT ON doesn't find a character string match to be logical true when string lengths don't match.

Notes

Blank spaces are often accidentally added to character strings. Also, when you import or append a database into dBASE IV, blank spaces are sometimes added to fill character fields. The SET EXACT OFF command ignores blank spaces at the end of a field. Use SET EXACT ON when the blank spaces should be considered as a valid part of the comparison.

When the comparison occurs, dBASE compares the first string's first character to the second string's first character. It performs the same kind of comparison at the second character, and so on, advancing until it reaches the end of the character string. If the strings match, the comparison returns logical true (.T.). If they don't match, the comparison returns logical false (.F.).

SET EXCLUSIVE

SET EXCLUSIVE is a network-related command that sets the default file open mode for all databases to exclusive or shared. For more information on the command, see the section entitled "Data Protection" in Chapter 29.

Syntax

```
SET EXCLUSIVE on/OFF
```

SET EXCLUSIVE ON sets the file for private access (local).

SET EXCLUSIVE OFF is the default. It allows access to the database by all users.

Notes

When you create or save a file with SET EXCLUSIVE ON, no one else in your network can access the file.

Related commands: COPY INDEXES/TAG, INDEX ON, PROTECT, SET ENCRYPTION

SET FIELDS

The SET FIELDS command lists database fields that you can access from the current work area.

Syntax

SET FIELDS on/OFF

SET FIELDS [<*field name*>[/R] / <*calculated field identifier*>...] [,<*field name*>[/R] / <*calculated field identifier*>...]

SET FIELDS TO ALL [LIKE/EXCEPT <*skeleton*>]

With SET FIELDS OFF, you can access all fields in the active database. This is the default.

SET FIELDS ON limits access to the specified fields. Issue this command after you've defined a *field list*.

SET FIELDS TO lists fields or expressions that define one or more database files. You can also use it to set some fields as read-only.

field name is a list of field names.

R sets the read-only flag on the field just named.

calculated field identifier is the result of a dBASE expression.

SET FIELDS TO removes from the field list any fields associated with the active database.

SET FIELDS TO ALL includes in the field list all of the active database's fields.

SET FIELDS TO ALL LIKE selects fields that will match *skeleton*.

SET FIELDS TO ALL EXCEPT selects fields that don't match *skeleton*.

skeleton defines a string that can be compared to field names for inclusion in the field list. It can include the multiple wildcard character (*) and the single wildcard character (?).

Notes

The SET FIELDS command defines a list of default fields for commands that support a fields list. Table 32-4 shows a list of these commands. When you SET FIELD TO a field list, the list can span more than one database. To establish a link between two databases, you must use the SET RELATION command.

To include fields in other work areas, select the file's work area and use SET FIELD TO or use the database file's alias with a field name. If you access fields in different databases that have the same name, you must alias one of the databases. If you don't use an alias, dBASE searches only until it finds the first match.

The SET FIELDS command is more advanced than most. You usually use it in conjunction with two databases that have been linked with the SET RELATION command. Don't use it when you are adding records to a database.

Related commands: CLEAR FIELDS, CREATE/MODIFY VIEW, CREATE VIEW FROM ENVIRONMENT, SET RELATION, SET SKIP, SET VIEW

Example

This example uses the ITEMS database. It selects fields with any first four characters (????) and the last three characters "_no". Then it displays a record. Notice that the only selected field is PART_NO.

Next, it selects fields with any first five characters and the last three characters "_no". It displays the same record. Notice that the Order_no field meets the criteria and is added to the PART_NO field. The example then restores the default to all fields and displays the same record.

```
. USE Samples\Items
. SET FIELDS TO ALL LIKE ????_no
. DISPLAY
Record#  PART_NO
     1  001032
. SET FIELDS TO ALL LIKE ?????_no
. DISPLAY
Record#  PART_NO ORDER_NO
     1  001032  020002
. SET FIELDS TO
. DISPLAY
Record#  ORDER_NO PART_NO QTY SHIPPED
     1  020002   001032    2 .F.
```

SET FILTER

The SET FILTER command selects records for display based on conditions (dBASE mode only).

Syntax

SET FILTER TO [FILE <*filename*> /?] [<*condition*>]

SET FILTER TO turns off the filter for the active database.

FILE <*filename*> uses conditions from a query file and adds it to a catalog if one is open and you have issued the **SET CATALOG ON** command.

? displays query file names in a catalog file.

condition is a dBASE expression that sets up a filter (for example, Zipcode = 95073 or Lastname = "Borros").

Notes

SET FILTER TO <*condition*> applies only to the database file open in the work area in which you issue the command. You can have a different filter for each work area. Commands that work with an

APPEND	DISPLAY
AVERAGE	EDIT
BROWSE	EXPORT
CALCULATE	JOIN
CHANGE	LIST
CREATE/MODIFY VIEW	SUM
FROM ENVIRONMENT	TOTAL
COPY TO	
COPY STRUCTURE	

Table 32-4. Field List Commands

active database (one activated with the USE command), such as EDIT and BROWSE, can use *condition*.

FILE <*filename*> reads the *condition* from a query file you created using the CREATE QUERY or MODIFY QUERY command. If an open catalog exists, SET FILE TO ? displays a list of query files.

After you have set up a filter, it becomes active when the record pointer moves. You should follow SET FILTER <*condition*> with a GO TOP or SKIP command, which will move the record pointer and activate the filter.

You can use but not modify dBASE III PLUS query files in dBASE IV.

Related commands: CREATE/MODIFY QUERY, SET DELETED

Example

This example uses the PEOPLE database and shows how to use the SET FILTER command to output only those records whose State field contains the character string "CA".

```
. USE SAMPLES\PEOPLE
. SET FILTER TO State = "CA"
. GO TOP
. LIST
Record#  LASTNAME             FIRSTNAME              ADDRESS
CITY          STATE ZIP PHONE CARDSENT
```

```
        4  Day                Diane              14234
Riverside Dr. Los Angeles CA 90044 (213)555-9875 .F.
        6  Robeson            Peter              10564
Ballot St. Orange         CA 92666 (714)555-2711 .F
        9  Clements           Curt               5934 Ocean
  Blvd. Laguna Hills        CA 92301 (714)555-3928 .F.
       13  Caldicott          Howard             854
Rushmore Ave. Hollywood   CA 90028 (213)555-0292 .F.
       15  Rao                Kim                2015
Edmonton Ave. Long Beach  CA 90804 (213)555-7891 .F.
```

SET FIXED

The SET FIXED command is included in dBASE IV only for compatibility with dBASE III PLUS. It has no effect in dBASE IV.

Syntax

SET FIXED on/OFF

Notes

The dBASE IV SET DECIMALS command replaces this dBASE III PLUS command.

SET FORMAT

The SET FORMAT command lets you use a custom form with full-screen editing commands such as READ, EDIT, CHANGE, APPEND, and INSERT. The form is stored in a format file (.FMT or .FMO).

Syntax

SET FORMAT TO [<*filename*> /?]

SET FORMAT TO (without a file name) closes an open format file. It is the same as the CLOSE FORMAT command.

filename is the name of the file containing the format. It is saved as *filename*.FMT.

? displays a list of format files from a catalog file.

Notes

dBASE provides default formats for data entry. You use them when you add or change a record. You can create your own forms in a format file. The SET FORMAT command accesses any format file you've created.

To create a format (.FMT) file, use the CREATE SCREEN command. dBASE takes you to the Forms Design screen. (The use of this screen is described in Chapter 9.) Alternatively, you can enter @...SAY...GET commands in a command file with an .FMT extension.

When you use the Forms Design screen to create a format file, dBASE creates two files. The first file is a binary file with an .SCR extension. The second file contains dBASE commands and has an .FMT extension. When you use the SET FORMAT command to activate a format file, dBASE compiles your .FMT file into an .FMO file. It uses the .FMO file to display your form.

To change a format file, use MODIFY SCREEN. Using MODIFY COMMAND can introduce an undesirable discrepancy between the .FMT and .SCR files.

When you request a format file, dBASE IV

1. Looks for a compiled format file, <*filename*>.FMO.

2. If it finds the compiled format file, dBASE executes it.

3. If dBASE can't find the compiled format file, it looks for a source format file, <*filename*>.FMT.

4. If dBASE finds a source format file, it compiles it to create the compiled format file <*filename*>.FMT and executes it.

5. If dBASE can't find the format file, you get the error message "File does not exist."

Note: Don't include a READ command at the end of the .FMT file. dBASE IV interprets this as a page break, and the cursor stops in the corner of the screen waiting for input. Each work area can have an open format file. SET FORMAT TO closes the format file in the active work area.

Related commands: APPEND, CHANGE, CLOSE, EDIT, INSERT, READ, SET DEVICE

SET FULLPATH

The SET FULLPATH command aids dBASE III PLUS and dBASE IV compatibility. In dBASE IV, the NDX() and DBF() functions return the full path and file name. However, in dBASE III PLUS, only the drive letter and file name are returned. SET FULLPATH makes dBASE III PLUS programs compatible with dBASE IV by suppressing the return of full path names.

Syntax

SET FULLPATH on/OFF

dBASE IV users should set their systems to SET FULLPATH OFF. This is the default.

Use SET FULLPATH ON to suppress full file specification returns of dBASE III PLUS programs that use the functions NDX() and DBF().

Notes

You can make the change permanent by putting the command in your CONFIG.DB file.

SET FUNCTION

The SET FUNCTION command assigns characters, usually representing some dBASE IV command, to a function key.

Syntax

SET FUNCTION *<number>*/*<character string>*/*<key label>* TO *<character string>*

number is a number between 2 and 29 that represents a function key.

character string is a character string that represents some command or group of commands separated with semicolons.

key label is used for SHIFT- and CTRL-key combinations.

Notes

You can change function key assignments in three ways:

- Use the SET command at the dot prompt to access the SET menu. Then, use the **Keys** menu option to assign new functions.
- Use the SET FUNCTION command from an application program or at the dot prompt.
- Make your changes permanent by entering new function key assignments in your CONFIG.DB file.

Here are the default function key assignments:

Key	**Value**	**Key**	**Value**
F1	HELP;	F6	DISPLAY STATUS;
F2	ASSIST;	F7	DISPLAY MEMORY;
F3	LIST;	F8	DISPLAY;
F4	DIR;	F9	APPEND;
F5	DISPLAY STRUCTURE;	F10	EDIT;

You can program the following function keys:

Keys	Key Numbers
F2 - F10	2 through 10
SHIFT-F1 - SHIFT-F9	21 through 29
CTRL-F1 - CTRL-F10	11 through 20

However, there are the following restrictions:

- You can't program F1; it is assigned to the HELP command.
- You can't program F11 and F12, even if your keyboard has them.
- You can't program SHIFT-F10 and ALT keys; they are used for macros.

Use the semicolon at the end of command if you want it to execute when you press the appropriate function key. Don't use the semicolon if you want the command to pause so you can enter more information at the prompt.

Note: If SET FUNCTION and ON KEY assign different character strings to the same key, ON KEY takes precedence over SET FUNCTION.

Example

This example shows how to change the functions keys assignments from dBASE commands to SQL commands. You can use the LIST STATUS or DISPLAY STATUS command to view function key assignments. Only this part of the STATUS report is shown.

```
. LIST STATUS
Programmable function keys:
F2        - assist;
F3        - list;
F4        - dir;
F5        - display structure;
F6        - display status;
```

```
F7       - display memory;
F8       - display;
F9       - append;
F10      - edit;

. SET FUNCTION F2 TO "SELECT"
. SET FUNCTION F3 TO "INSERT"
. SET FUNCTION F4 TO "DROP"
. SET FUNCTION F8 TO "CREATE"
. SET FUNCTION F9 TO "ALTER TABLE"
. SET FUNCTION F10 TO "SELECT * FROM"
. LIST STATUS

Programmable function keys:
F2       - SELECT
F3       - INSERT
F4       - DROP
F5       - display structure;
F6       - display status;
F7       - display memory;
F8       - CREATE
F9       - ALTER TABLE
F10      - SELECT * FROM
```

SET HEADING

The SET HEADING command allows you turn off field column headings when using DISPLAY, LIST, SUM, and AVERAGE.

Syntax

SET HEADING ON/off

SET HEADING ON turns on the column headings some commands include as part of their output. This is the default.

SET HEADING OFF turns off the column headings some commands include as part of their output.

Related commands: DISPLAY, LIST, SUM, AVERAGE

Example

This example uses the PEOPLE database, turns off the headings, displays a record, turns on the headings, and displays the same record.

```
. USE People
. SET HEADING OFF
. DISPLAY
     1  Berrigan         Michael            1550
Keystone St.
   Burlington       VT 05401     (802)555-0778 .T.
. SET HEADING ON
. DISPLAY
Record#  LASTNAME           FIRSTNAME           ADDRESS
   CITY            STATE ZIP         PHONE      CARDSENT
  1       Berrigan           Michael             1550
Keystone St.
   Burlington     VT     05401      (802)555-0778 .T.
```

SET HELP

The SET HELP command affects the Help window that pops up when you enter a command incorrectly at the dot prompt.

Syntax

SET HELP ON/off

SET HELP ON allows you to access the help menus from the error box. This is the default.

SET HELP OFF doesn't allow you to access help menus from the error box.

Notes

The error box that pops up when you make an error allows you to **Cancel**, **Edit**, or get **Help** with the incorrectly entered command. When you SET HELP OFF, you no longer see the **Help** option in the error box.

Related commands: HELP, SET INSTRUCT

SET HISTORY

The SET HISTORY command saves commands in a buffer and controls the buffer size.

Syntax

SET HISTORY ON/off

SET HISTORY TO <*number*>

SET HISTORY ON saves commands in the buffer. This is the default.

SET HISTORY OFF clears the history buffer and doesn't save commands.

SET HISTORY TO <*number*> controls the number of commands saved in the history buffer.

number is any number from 0 to 16,000. Its default value is 20. *number* is limited by the memory available in your system.

Notes

A buffer is a place to store information, like a memory variable. However, buffers are managed differently from an internal standpoint.

Commands you issue at the dot prompt are placed in the buffer when you press ENTER. Commands in application programs aren't placed in the history buffer. From the dot prompt, use the UP and DOWN ARROW keys to access commands in the history buffer. Use the DISPLAY or LIST HISTORY commands to see what is in the buffer.

Note: To calculate the amount of memory the history buffer uses, add nine bytes to the number of bytes in each command.

Related commands: DISPLAY HISTORY, LIST HISTORY

Example

This example shows what's in the history buffer when you first start dBASE IV (nothing), turns on the history buffer (if it isn't on already), issues some commands, and displays the history buffer again.

```
. DISPLAY HISTORY
. SET HISTORY ON
. DIR
. HELP
. DISPLAY HISTORY
DISPLAY HISTORY
SET HISTORY ON
DIR
HELP
DISPLAY HISTORY
```

SET HOURS

The SET HOURS command toggles the clock display between a 12-hour and a 24-hour clock.

Syntax

SET HOURS TO [12/24]

[12/24] changes the clock shown in full-screen mode to military time (24-hour) or civilian time (12-hour). The default is 12.

SET HOURS TO restores the default.

Notes

You can make the change permanent by putting the command in your CONFIG.DB file.

Related command: SET CLOCK

SET INDEX

The SET INDEX command selects an index file (.NDX or .MDX) (dBASE mode only).

Syntax

SET INDEX TO [?/<*filename*> [ORDER [TAG] <*filename*.NDX> / <*tagname*> [OF <*filename*>.MDX]]]

SET INDEX TO closes all open index files in the current work area, as does CLOSE INDEX. The current production index (.MDX) file remains open.

filename is the name of a single (.NDX) or multiple index (.MDX) file that controls the database's record pointer.

ORDER names the master index file (.NDX or .MDX) that controls the database's record pointer. If you only name one .NDX file name, it automatically becomes the master index file. When you open a database, and thus its associated production (.MDX) index file, the index tags for that production index are also automatically opened.

TAG <*tagname*> is a tag in the multiple index file (.MDX). You can have up to 47 tag names.

OF <*filename*>.MDX determines which multiple index file (.MDX) from which to use the tag when more than one multiple index file exists in a directory or when the tag isn't in the production index file.

Notes

An index file doesn't change the physical order of the records in the database file. Rather, it maintains a series of keys in a particular sequence you specify in the INDEX ON command. A key points at a record in the database in which the physical data is kept. INDEX ON, when followed by an .NDX file name, automatically issues SET INDEX TO <*filename*>.NDX.

You activate existing indexes with the SET INDEX TO command. You can list more than one index file. The first one you list becomes the master index file, which controls the record pointer in the database file. The other indexes are updated when you change information affecting their keys, but they don't influence the record pointer.

SET INDEX TO <*filename*> closes open indexes other than the production index file (.MDX). Then it opens the index requested in *filename* and puts the record pointer at the first key. Use the SET ORDER command to change the controlling or master index file without closing any of the other index files listed in SET INDEX TO.

You can have up to ten index files open at any one time. This can be any combination of single index files (.NDX) and/or multiple index files (.MDX), including production multiple index files and independent multiple index files.

Index File Extensions

.NDX	Single index file
.MDX	Production index file
.MDX	Independent multiple index file

Related commands and functions: CLOSE, DELETE TAG, DISPLAY INDEXES, INDEX, REINDEX, SET ORDER, USE, KEY(), MDX(), NDX(), ORDER(), TAG()

SET INSTRUCT

The SET INSTRUCT command enables dBASE to display prompts (dBASE mode only).

Syntax

SET INSTRUCT ON/off

SET INSTRUCT ON enables the dBASE menu prompts that work with full-screen operations, such as APPEND, BROWSE, and EDIT. This is the default.

SET INSTRUCT OFF disables the dBASE menu prompts.

SET INTENSITY

The SET INTENSITY command controls screen enhancements in full-screen mode.

Syntax

SET INTENSITY ON/off

SET INTENSITY ON highlights fields. This is the default.
SET INTENSITY OFF causes fields to not be highlighted.

Notes

SET INTENSITY ON causes @...SAY commands to display with the standard screen attribute and @GET...commands to display with the enhanced screen attribute.

With SET INTENSITY OFF, the enhanced attribute is not used. @...SAY and @...GET commands use the standard screen attribute.

SET COLOR allows you to assign attributes to standard and enhanced display.

Related commands: SET, SET COLOR, SET DISPLAY

SET LOCK

The SET LOCK command applies to multi-user environments. It prevents more than one user from accessing the same record at the same time. See Chapter 30, "Networking Commands and Functions," for a detailed explanation.

Syntax

SET LOCK ON/off

SET MARGIN

The SET MARGIN command sets the printer's left margin.

Syntax

SET MARGIN TO <*number*>

number is the offset (indent) for the left margin. The maximum is printer-dependent. The default for the left margin is 0.

Notes

The SET MARGIN command changes the value stored in a system memory variable called _ploffset. You check its value with the LIST STATUS command.

This command does not affect screen display. The setting for the left margin remains in effect as long as you are in dBASE.

Note: When the system memory variable _wrap is false, SET MARGIN and _lmargin aren't added. When the _wrap system memory variable is true, the _lmargin value is added to the SET MARGIN value.

SET MARK

The SET MARK command changes the character used to separate the month, day, and year.

Syntax

SET MARK TO [<*character string*>]

SET MARK TO restores the default character.
character string is a single character.

Notes

The default character used depends on the country or type you select in SET DATE. For example, the default for American is a slash (/). SET DATE lists the default dates with their respective date delimiters.

Related functions and commands: DATE(), DMY(), MDY(), SET CENTURY, SET DATE

Example

This example changes the symbol used to separate month, day, and year to the pound (#). It displays today's date with the new format.

Then it restores the default and displays today's date with the default format.

```
. SET MARK TO "#"
. ? DATE()
01#09#89
. SET MARK TO
. ? DATE()
01/09/89
```

SET MEMOWIDTH

The SET MEMOWIDTH command adjusts the width for memo field output (dBASE mode only).

Syntax

SET MEMOWIDTH TO [<*number*>]

SET MEMOWIDTH TO restores the maximum memo field width to the 50- character default.

number is a number from 8 to 32,000 that defines the maximum width for memo fields.

Notes

SET MEMOWIDTH alters the width of the memo field for output only. It doesn't affect data entry.

You can make the change permanent by putting the command in your CONFIG.DB file.

Related functions and commands: MEMLINES(), MLINE(), SET (), @PICTURE clauses

SET MENU

The SET MENU command provides compatibility with dBASE III PLUS. This command does not affect dBASE IV.

Syntax

SET MENU ON/off

SET MESSAGE

The SET MESSAGE command places a message you define underneath the status line.

Syntax

SET MESSAGE TO [<*character string*>]

SET MESSAGE TO restores the default, which is to display dBASE messages.

SET MESSAGE TO [<*character string*>] displays a message you define.

character string has a 79-character maximum.

Notes

The SET MESSAGE command doesn't show a message unless you SET STATUS ON. In full-screen mode, user-defined messages are overridden by messages from application programs, @...GET commands, pop-ups, and menus. The message displays below the status bar, usually at line 23.

For *character string,* you can use a character string, a memory variable (character data type), or a field that contains a literal text string.

Related command: SET STATUS

SET NEAR

The SET NEAR command controls the record pointer location after an unsuccessful search takes place (dBASE mode only).

Syntax

SET NEAR on/OFF

SET NEAR OFF moves the pointer to the end of the database when the search is unsuccessful. This is the default.

SET NEAR ON puts the record pointer on a record immediately following the record that nearly matched the search conditions in an unsuccessful search.

Notes

When it is turned on, the SET NEAR command positions the pointer on the record immediately following the likely location of the requested record. Otherwise the pointer goes to the end of the database.

When you use SET NEAR with SET DELETED or SET FILTER, it uses the conditions defined. If the two commands are in effect, it uses both conditions.

Related functions and commands: EOF(), FOUND(), SEEK(), FIND, LOCATE, SEEK, SET FILTER, SET DELETED

Example

This example uses the PEOPLE database, creates an index on Lastname, and deliberately uses the FIND command to look for an incorrect name. Since SET NEAR is OFF, it positions the record pointer at the end of the file, which is verified with the DISPLAY command. Then it turns on SET NEAR, tries the same search, and shows where the record pointer is positioned.

```
. USE People
. INDEX ON Lastname
Enter destination index file: LASTNAME.
   100% indexed    17 Records indexed
. SET NEAR OFF
. FIND Michel
Find not successful
. DISPLAY
. SET NEAR ON
. FIND Michel
Find not successful
. DISPLAY
Record#  LASTNAME          FIRSTNAME            ADDRESS
  CITY          STATE ZIP PHONE CARDSENT
      8  McDaniel          Janice               203 E. 3rd
St., #505 Eugene OR 97401 (503)555-2134 .T.
```

SET ODOMETER

The SET ODOMETER command sets the record update interval for commands that show a record count.

Syntax

SET ODOMETER TO <*number*>

number is a number from 1 to 200. The default is 1.

Notes

The SET ODOMETER command sets the interval at which commands such as COPY and RECALL update the record counter displayed on your screen.

The record counter only appears if you SET TALK ON.

Related command: SET TALK

SET ORDER

The SET ORDER command assigns master index control to, or takes it away from, an index file or tag name (dBASE mode only).

Syntax

SET ORDER TO

SET ORDER TO <*number*>

SET ORDER [TAG] <*filename*>/<*tagname*> [OF <*filename*>.MDX]

SET ORDER TO restores the database's natural order.

number is included for dBASE III PLUS compatibility. It is a number from 1 to 10 and refers to the order in which files are listed in the SET INDEX command.

filename is the name of a single index (.NDX) or multiple index (.MDX) file that controls the database's record pointer.

TAG <*tagname*> is a tag in the multiple index file (.MDX). You can have up to 47 tag names.

OF <*filename*>.MDX determines the multiple index file (.MDX) from which to use the tag when more than one multiple index file in a directory contains the same tag name.

Notes

Although dBASE IV allows up to ten open indexes at a time, only one of them can be the master index that controls the order of records in the database. You can use the SET ORDER command to change that master index. To do so, first use the INDEX or USE command to open the index. If the index is a tag in the current production index (.MDX) file, that file is automatically opened when you activate its associated database.

The SET ORDER command does not close other open index files (.NDX or .MDX), or move the record pointer, when it switches control to a new index file. Therefore, those open but inactive index files continue to be updated for changes to the database. However, the more index files you have open, the slower dBASE IV runs. For this reason, it's a good idea to keep an index file open only if you need to.

Related commands and functions: DISPLAY, INDEX, KEY(), MDX(), ORDER(), REINDEX, SET INDEX, TAG(), USE

SET PATH

The SET PATH command defines directories that dBASE IV can search when it can't find an application program in the current directory.

Syntax

SET PATH TO [<*path list*>]

SET PATH TO restores the path to the default.

path list lists one or more path names separated by commas or semicolons; it has a 60-character maximum. The default is the current directory.

Notes

The current directory is the one you are working in. Usually you start at the root or top-level directory, and then change to another directory. Each time you change, the directory you move into becomes your current directory.

The default directory is the one from which you started dBASE, unless you changed directories with the DOS CHDIR command or changed drives with the dBASE SET DEFAULT command. The SET PATH command doesn't affect dBASE's DIR command. If you want to use a directory other than the one you are in, you must list the path as part of the database name.

dBASE IV and DOS don't know about each other's paths.

Related commands: DIR, SET DEFAULT

Example

This example calls a program in the SAMPLES directory with dBASE IV starting from \DBASE. The first time you call the application program, the error box alerts you that the application program doesn't exist. Then the SET PATH command tells dBASE to look in the SAMPLES directory. The second time you call the application program, it executes successfully.

```
. DO Orders
. SET PATH TO \DBASE\SAMPLES\
. DO Orders
```

SET PAUSE

The SET PAUSE command controls the display of SQL data.

Syntax

SET PAUSE on/OFF

SET PAUSE OFF doesn't pause and ask you to continue when the screen fills. This is the default.

SET PAUSE ON stops and prompts you for continuation when the screen fills.

Notes

You can issue SET PAUSE ON in dBASE mode, but it doesn't affect dBASE's display.

Related command: SET SQL

SET POINT

The SET POINT command changes the character used for the decimal point.

Syntax

SET POINT TO [<*character string*>]

SET POINT TO restores the default.

character string is any single character that is not a digit or space. The default is the period.

Notes

The SET POINT command is most commonly used to change the period to a comma for countries that use a comma as the decimal point.

Example

See the SET CURRENCY TO example.

SET PRECISION

The SET PRECISION command sets the number of digits used to calculate type N numbers in dBASE IV internal math calculations.

Syntax

SET PRECISION TO [<*number*>]

SET PRECISION TO restores the default.
number is a number from 10 to 20. The default value is 16.

Notes

Using large numbers increases accuracy. Using small numbers increases calculation speed.

You can make the change permanent by putting the command in your CONFIG.DB file.

Related command: SET DECIMALS

SET PRINTER

The SET PRINTER command sends output to different printers or to a printer-readable file. The printer can be private (local) or part of a network (LAN).

Syntax

SET PRINTER on/OFF

SET PRINTER TO *<DOS device>*

SET PRINTER TO FILE *<filename>*

SET PRINTER OFF sends screen output to the screen only. This is the default.

SET PRINTER ON sends screen output to both the screen and the printer, including output from the TALK, LIST, and ? commands.

SET PRINTER TO *<DOS device>* sends screen output to a particular printer port, a network printer, or a printer-readable file.

DOS device is the device name of a local printer you want to send the output to. It defaults to DOS's print utility, PRN. You can substitute any one of three parallel ports (LPT1, LPT2, or LPT3) or two serial ports (Com1 or Com2).

SET PRINTER TO FILE *<filename>* creates a file containing the output and the appropriate printer codes.

For ways to use SET PRINTER with a network, see Chapter 30.

Notes

SET PRINTER ON doesn't send the output from @...SAY commands to the printer. If you need to do this, use the SET DEVICE TO PRINTER command.

SET PRINTER TO FILE *<filename>* creates a file that contains printer-control codes for printing on your specific printer and gives the file a .PRT extension. If you want to print an ASCII file, you must set the _pdriver system memory variable to the ASCII.PRG printer driver, as in the following:

```
. _pdriver = "ASCII.PRG"
```

If you then use SET PRINTER TO *<filename>*, dBASE prints an ASCII file with a .TXT extension.

Related commands: ?/??, ???, LABEL FORM, LIST/DISPLAY, REPORT FORM, SET DEBUG, SET DEVICE

SET PROCEDURE

The SET PROCEDURE command opens a procedure file.

Syntax

SET PROCEDURE TO [*<procedure filename>*]

SET PROCEDURE TO closes the current procedure file, as does the CLOSE PROCEDURE command.

procedure filename is the name of a procedure file with a .DBO, .PRG, or .PRT extension. You can have only one procedure active at a time.

Notes

You can put procedures in either a procedure file or an application program. (dBASE III PLUS doesn't support procedures in application programs.) The word "PROCEDURE" marks the beginning of each routine. Although a procedure can contain 1170 routines, it's limited by available memory.

When you use *procedure filename* without specifying an extension, dBASE IV looks for an executable procedure file (*<procedure filename>*.DBO). If it doesn't find one, it looks for the dBASE procedure source file (*<procedure name>*.PRG) or the SQL procedure source file (*<procedure name>*.PRS). If it finds a match, it uses the source file to create an executable procedure file (*procedure filename*.DBO) and executes it.

Related commands: COMPILE, DO PARAMETERS

SET REFRESH

The SET REFRESH command defines a time interval used for file change checks on a network during a BROWSE or EDIT command. It only works with files created with the CONVERT command. See Chapter 30 for a complete discussion.

Syntax

SET REFRESH TO <*number*>

SET REFRESH TO restores the default.

number is a number from 1 to 3600 that expresses time in seconds (3600 is one hour). The default is 0, which means that REFRESH doesn't take place.

SET RELATION

The SET RELATION command links two open databases in different work areas according to a key expression common to both files (dBASE mode only).

Syntax

SET RELATION TO

SET RELATION TO <*number*>

SET RELATION TO <*number*> INTO <*alias*> [,<*number*> INTO <*alias*>]...

SET RELATION TO breaks the link between the two databases.

number is a record number through which databases are synchronized. It is usually returned through the RECNO() function.

INTO <*alias*> specifies the file containing the key expression that controls the relationship between the two database files.

Notes

For a complete discussion of this command, see Chapter 21.

The SET NEAR command only affects the controlling file.

Related commands: CREATE/MODIFY VIEW, SET FIELDS, SET SKIP, SET VIEW

SET REPROCESS

The SET REPROCESS command defines the number of times dBASE tries a network file or issues a record lock command before you get an error message. See Chapter 30, "Networking Commands and Functions," for a complete description.

Syntax

SET REPROCESS TO <*number*>

number is a number from -1 to 32,000 that defines the number of retries. The default is 0.

SET SAFETY

The SET SAFETY command protects you from accidentally overwriting an existing file.

Syntax

SET SAFETY ON/off

SET SAFETY ON gives you a warning when you attempt to overwrite an existing file. This is the default.

SET SAFETY OFF allows you to overwrite files without receiving a message.

Notes

SET SAFETY ON alerts you to the existence of a file with the message "File already exists. **Overwrite Cancel**." Choose **Cancel** to abort the operation or **Overwrite** to proceed.

Related commands: COPY, COPY FILE, INDEX, JOIN, SAVE, SORT, TOTAL, UPDATE, ZAP

SET SCOREBOARD

The SET SCOREBOARD command shows the status of certain critical keyboard keys, such as NUM LOCK and CAPS LOCK, on line 0 of the screen.

Syntax

SET SCOREBOARD ON/off

SET SCOREBOARD ON displays the status of special keys on the screen even when SET STATUS is off. This is the default.

SET SCOREBOARD OFF doesn't display the status of special keys on the screen.

Notes

With SET STATUS ON, the status of special keys appears in the right box of the status bar. With SET STATUS OFF, the status of special keys appears in the top right corner (line 0), the "scoreboard." When this is the case, use SET SCOREBOARD OFF in your program if you need to display data on line 0 of the screen.

Related commands: SET MESSAGE, SET STATUS

SET SEPARATOR

The SET SEPARATOR command changes the place separator from the comma to some other character.

Syntax

SET SEPARATOR TO [<*character string*>]

SET SEPARATOR TO restores the comma default.

character string is a single character to use as the placeholder in numbers.

Notes

You can make the change permanent by putting the command in your CONFIG.DB file.

Related command: SET POINT

SET SKIP

The SET SKIP command allows access to records in linked files matching a key (dBASE mode only).

Syntax

SET SKIP TO <*database aliases*>

SET SKIP TO restores the default.

database aliases consists of aliases separated by commas; the database aliases must match those used in SET RELATION.

Notes

The SET SKIP command only works with files that have been linked with the SET RELATION command. Used together, the SET RELATION and SET SKIP commands determine the order in which the database files are updated. The SET SKIP command works with any commands that have FOR and WHILE clauses.

Update commands begin with the first database listed in *database aliases*. The record pointer in each related database moves up the relationship chain toward the active database (parent file). You don't have to specify the active database in *database aliases*; it is always updated. When you don't include it in the list, it is updated last.

Related command: SET RELATION, FOR clauses, WHILE clauses

SET SPACE

The SET SPACE command puts extra space between fields you display by using ? or ??.

Syntax

SET SPACE ON/off

SET SPACE ON puts in an extra space. This is the default.
SET SPACE OFF runs the fields together.

Example

This example uses the PEOPLE database, turns off the extra space, and displays the Firstname and Lastname fields. Then it turns on the extra space and displays the same fields. The TRIM() function removes the extra space from Firstname.

```
. USE People
. SET SPACE OFF
. ? Firstname, Lastname
MichaelBerrigan
. SET SPACE ON
. ? TRIM(Firstname),Lastname
Michael Berrigan
```

SET SQL

The SET SQL command gives you access to SQL commands in SQL mode. dBASE commands are restricted in this mode.

Syntax

SET SQL on/OFF

SET SQL OFF puts you in dBASE mode. This is the default.
SET SQL ON puts you in SQL mode.

Notes

SQL is a relational database query language. Some dBASE commands can't be used in SQL mode. You can make the change permanent by putting the command in your CONFIG.DB file. You can't issue this command from within an application program.

SET STATUS

The SET STATUS command determines whether the status bar appears at the bottom of your screen.

Syntax

SET STATUS ON/off

SET STATUS ON displays the status bar at the bottom of your screen. This is the default.

SET STATUS OFF removes the status bar.

Notes

The status bar shows the command name, file in use, and record number/total records. If SET SCOREBOARD is ON, the status bar also includes the status of special keys. When you do something, such as use a new database or do an application program, the status bar is updated.

Note: When you use STATUS ON with SET FORMAT and READ commands, be careful not to output information below line 21 (41 in EGA mode) unless you want to overwrite the status bar.

You can make the change permanent by putting the command in your CONFIG.DB file.

Related commands: SET MESSAGE, SET SCOREBOARD

Example

See the SET SCOREBOARD example.

SET STEP

The SET STEP command determines whether application programs execute one line at a time. This command aids debugging.

Syntax

SET STEP on/OFF

SET STEP OFF executes the application program without stopping. This is the default.

SET STEP ON stops the application program and outputs a message each time it executes a line.

Notes

With SET STEP ON, you receive the message "Press SPACE to Step, S to Suspend, or ESC to Cancel..." after an instruction executes. It waits for you to enter your choice.

Related commands: COMPILE, DEBUG, DO SET DEBUG, SET DEVELOPMENT, SET ECHO, SET TALK

SET TALK

The SET TALK command affects how some dBASE commands display.

Syntax

SET TALK ON/off

SET TALK ON displays messages. This is the default.

SET TALK OFF suppresses messages, including compiler warning messages.

Notes

SET TALK messages are about record numbers, memory variables, results from APPEND FROM, COPY, PACK, STORE, and SUM commands, and other record-related commands, as well as compiler warning messages.

Related commands: SET DEBUG, SET ECHO, SET STEP

SET TITLE

The SET TITLE command allows you to add a title to catalog names and file names (dBASE mode only).

Syntax

SET TITLE ON/off

SET TITLE ON prompts you for catalog file descriptions. This is the default.

SET TITLE OFF doesn't prompt you for a description.

Notes

The SET TITLE command is related to the SET CATALOG command. If you issue **SET TITLE ON** and then **SET CATALOG ON**, dBASE prompts you for a one-line file name or catalog description, which is added to the catalog file along with the name.

Related commands: EDIT, REPLACE, SET CATALOG

SET TRAP

The SET TRAP command calls the dBASE IV Debugger, an error routine, or an error screen when an application program error occurs or you press ESC while an application program is executing.

Syntax

```
SET TRAP on/OFF
```

SET TRAP OFF displays an error screen with options when an application program error occurs. This is the default.

SET TRAP ON calls the dBASE IV Debugger when an application program error occurs.

Notes

If SET TRAP is ON when an error occurs, or you press ESC, dBASE checks for an ON ERROR routine. If none exists, dBASE calls the dBASE IV Debugger. When an error occurs and SET TRAP is OFF and ON ERROR is not present, dBASE displays an error screen with the following:

- **Cancel** the application program
- **Ignore** the error

- **Suspend** the program

ON ERROR overrides SET TRAP options.

Related commands: DEBUG, ON ERROR, SET DEBUG, SET DEVELOPMENT

SET TYPEAHEAD

The SET TYPEAHEAD command controls how many characters you can enter ahead of dBASE processing.

Syntax

SET TYPEAHEAD TO <*number*>

number is from 0 to 32,000 and sets the size of the typeahead buffer. 0 prevents you from typing ahead of processing. 20 is the default.

Notes

The typeahead buffer saves characters dBASE can't process because it's busy. If you type faster than dBASE can process your input, increase the size of the typeahead buffer. If you are making mistakes because you get too far ahead of dBASE, decrease the size of the buffer. When you set *number* to 0, you can't type ahead and the ON KEY command and INKEY() function are deactivated.

Full-screen EDIT and APPEND commands use a 20-character buffer, no matter how you set the buffer size with SET TYPEAHEAD.

Related function and commands: INKEY(), ON, SET BELL, SET ESCAPE

SET UNIQUE

The SET UNIQUE command designates whether records with the same information in the indexed field are also entered in the index file (dBASE mode only).

Syntax

SET UNIQUE on/OFF

SET UNIQUE OFF adds a key to the index file for every database record. This is the default.

SET UNIQUE ON adds a key only for unique records.

Notes

An index file contains keys that point to the database in which the record information is kept. The index file can contain a key for every record in the database or just one key for each unique record in the database.

When you create an index with SET UNIQUE ON and later reindex the index file with SET UNIQUE OFF, the reindexed file retains a unique record index.

Note: To get rid of unique indexes, rebuild the index with the INDEX ON command and with SET UNIQUE OFF.

Related commands and function: FIND, INDEX, REINDEX, SEEK, SET INDEX, SET ORDER, USE, SEEK()

Example

This example uses the Goods database and indexes on the Part_name field because it contains duplicate part names (keys). The first INDEX ON command indexes 33 records (the total size of the database). Then the UNIQUE option is turned on. The same index command is issued and the index file is overwritten. With

UNIQUE ON, the identical INDEX ON command indexes only 14 records.

```
. USE Samples\Goods
. INDEX ON Part_name TO Pname
  100% indexed           33 Records indexed
. SET UNIQUE ON
. INDEX ON Part_name TO Pname
  100% indexed           14 Records indexed
```

SET VIEW

The SET VIEW command executes a query file or updates a view file (dBASE mode only).

Syntax

SET VIEW TO <*query name*> /?

query name is the name of a file containing a query, with a .QBO or .QBE extension.

? displays a list of queries if a catalog is active.

Notes

To create a query, you can use the Control Center's Query Design feature, the CREATE/MODIFY QUERY command, or the CREATE MODIFY VIEW command.

When you use *query name* and don't specify an extension, dBASE IV looks for an executable query file (<*query name*>.QBO). If it doesn't find one, it looks for the query source file *query name*. If it finds one, it uses it to create an executable query file (<*query name*>.QBO) and executes it.

If you request a dBASE III PLUS .VUE query file, dBASE IV creates a .QBE file, which it then compiles into a .QBO file and executes.

Related commands: CREATE/MODIFY VIEW/QUERY, SET CATALOG, SET FIELDS, SET FILTER, SET FORMAT, SET INDEX, SET ORDER, SET RELATION, SET TITLE

SET WINDOW

The SET WINDOW command opens a window used to edit a memo field (dBASE mode only).

Syntax

SET WINDOW OF MEMO TO <*window name*>

window name is the name of a window you created with the DEFINE WINDOW command.

Notes

If *window name* doesn't exist, you see the message "Window has not been defined." Use the DEFINE WINDOW command to create and name a window.

The APPEND, BROWSE, CHANGE, EDIT, and READ commands access memo fields using a window if one is active. The @...GET command's WINDOW clause overrides the SET WINDOW command.

Related commands: ACTIVATE SCREEN, ACTIVATE WINDOW, CLEAR WINDOW, DEFINE WINDOW, MOVE WINDOW

Functions

This chapter includes a complete listing of dBASE IV functions in alphabetical order.

Functions perform operations in dBASE IV that would otherwise take several dBASE command lines to produce, or that you could not perform at all using standard dBASE commands. Functions perform calculations, evaluations, and conversions. A function always returns a result.

In dBASE IV, you can create your own user-defined functions (UDFs). See the FUNCTION command in Chapter 31, "dBASE IV Commands."

Conventions

This chapter uses certain conventions to describe function syntax:

- All functions (and dBASE IV commands) appear in uppercase letters. You can enter the functions in either upper- or lowercase.
- Square brackets ([]) indicate an optional argument. For example, in the following function, the *type N expression* argument is optional:

  ALIAS([<*type N expression*>])

- Angle brackets (<>) indicate that you *must* enter the enclosed item. For example, in the following function, you must enter the type N expression:

  ACOS(*<type N expression>*)

- When two options are separated by a slash (/), they are interchangeable. For example, you can use either a character string or a memo field for the first argument in the following function:

  LEFT(*<character string>*/*<memo field>*,*<type N expression>*)

&

& is used for macro substitution. That is, dBASE IV takes the contents of the character memory variable that follows the & function, not the name of the variable itself. You use the macro substitution function in cases where dBASE IV expects a literal value; for example, with FIND, USE, and any other commands where dBASE IV requires a file name.

Syntax

& *<character memory variable>* [.]

The period (.) is an optional terminator. If you are using the macro as a prefix to a literal string, you can use the period to signal the end of the macro. (See the second example.)

Examples

The following example uses FIND with a memory variable:

```
. Mlastname = "Manley"
Manley
. USE Customer ORDER Cust_name
Master index: CUST_NAME
. FIND &Mlastname
. ? Firstname, Lastname
Thomas          Manley
```

This next example illustrates the use of the optional period:

```
. ACCEPT "Enter the directory for the database: " TO Mdirect
Enter the directory for the database: db4cr
. ACCEPT "Enter the database filename: " TO Mfile
Enter the database filename: Customer
. USE C:\&Mdirect.\&Mfile
. ? DBF()
C:\CUSTOMER.DBF
```

Unfortunately, dBASE IV does not show the full directory after the DBF() function, the second-to-last line of the example. The last line of the example should more appropriately read C: \DB4CR \CUSTOMER.DBF

ABS()

The ABS() function returns the absolute value of a numeric expression. As you would expect, ABS() always returns a positive value.

Syntax

ABS(*<type N expression>*)

The argument for ABS() can be any valid numeric expression of type N. (Numbers that you input into dBASE IV are type N by default.)

Example

The following example determines the difference between the current column and the right margin system memory variable called _rmargin:

```
. curr_col = COL()
                  42
. ? _rmargin
                  80
. ? ABS(curr_col - _rmargin)
                  38
. ? ABS(_rmargin - curr_col)
                  38
```

For more on the _rmargin system memory variable, see the next chapter.

ACCESS()

Use the ACCESS() function in networking environments to return the access level of the current user. It allows you to build security into a network application. You use the ACCESS() function to verify the privilege level that has been assigned to a user with PROTECT.

See Part Four, "Networking dBASE IV," for a complete description of the ACCESS() function.

ACOS()

ACOS() returns the arc cosine, an angle measured in radians, of the cosine value. The value returned is always between 0 and π.

Syntax

ACOS(<*type N expression*>)

The type N numeric expression is the cosine of an angle and must be between -1 and +1. To convert radians to degrees, use the RTOD() function.

Example

The ACOS function is often useful when you are solving right triangles. Suppose the length of the hypotenuse is 13, the length of the adjacent side is 5, and you need to solve for the associated angle. The following example shows one way to solve for the angle:

```
. SET DECIMALS TO 5
. Side = 12
                    12
. Hypotenuse = 13
                    13
. Angle = ACOS(Side/Hypotenuse)
             0.39479
. Degrees = RTOD(Angle)
             22.61986
```

The angle is approximately 22.62 degrees.

ALIAS()

You use the ALIAS function to return the alias name for a given work area. If you do not specify a work area for the function argument, ALIAS returns the name of the current work area.

Syntax

ALIAS([<*type N expression*>])

The optional numeric expression is between 1 and 10 and indicates which work area to check.

Example

The following example opens two database files: CUSTOMER in work area 1 and ACCTREC in work area 2. It then shows some results of the ALIAS function.

```
. USE CUSTOMER IN 1
. USE ACCTSREC IN 2 ALIAS AR
. ? ALIAS(1)
CUSTOMER
. ? ALIAS(2)
AR
. ? ALIAS(3) = ""
.T.
```

As the example shows, when you load a database with the USE command, dBASE IV automatically uses the database name for the alias name, unless you use the ALIAS parameter to assign your own unique alias. (See the USE command in Chapter 31 for more on setting an alias name when you load a database file.) Also, if you have not assigned a database to a given work area, dBASE IV returns a null string (" ").

ASC()

The ASC() function returns the ASCII decimal code for the first character in a string. Appendix A includes a complete listing of ASCII codes.

Syntax

ASC(<*string expression*>)

String expression can be a literal string, field, variable, or any other valid character string expression.

Examples

Compare the following results to the ASCII chart in Appendix A.

```
. ? ASC("Test")
                      84
. String = "saywhat?"
saywhat?
. ? ASC(String)
                     115
. ? ASC("")
                       0
```

Notice in the final example that the null string (" ") is equal to 0.

ASIN()

ASIN() returns the arc sine, an angle measured in radians, of the sine value. The value returned is always between -π/2 and +π/2.

Syntax

ASIN(<*type N expression*>)

The type N numeric expression is the sine of an angle and must be between -1 and +1. To convert radians to degrees, multiply the value by 180/PI().

Example

The ASIN function is often useful when you know the length of two of the sides of a right triangle and you want to determine the angle. For example, suppose you know that the opposite side of the right triangle is 5 and the hypotenuse is 13. You can determine the angle as follows:

```
. SET DECIMALS TO 5
. Side = 5
                   5
. Hypotenuse = 13
                  13
. Angle = ASIN(Side/Hypotenuse)
              0.39479
. Degrees = RTOD(Angle)
             22.61986
```

The angle is approximately 22.62 degrees.

AT()

The AT() function lets you determine the starting location of one string within another string. The string for which you are searching is the *substring*. If dBASE IV cannot find the substring within the string to be searched, it returns 0.

Syntax

AT(<*substring*>,<*string to search*>/<*memory variable*>)

Substring and *string to search* can be any valid character string expression. *String to search* can also be a memory variable.

Example

The following example tests the first and second records in the CUSTOMER database to see whether their telephone numbers contain the 916 area code.

```
. USE Customer
. ? AT("(916)",TELEPHONE) <> 0
.T.
. SKIP
CUSTOMER: Record No       2
. ? AT("(916)",TELEPHONE) <> 0
.F.
```

See the related string functions SUBSTR(), RIGHT(), LEFT(), and LIKE().

ATAN()

The ATAN() function returns the arc tangent, an angle measured in radians, of the tangent value. The value returned is always between $+\pi/2$ and $-\pi/2$.

Syntax

ATAN(*<type N expression>*)

The numeric expression specified as the argument is the tangent of the angle to be solved for. To convert radians to degrees, use the RTOD() function.

Example

The ATAN() function is useful for solving right triangles when you know the length of some of the sides and want to solve for the angle. For example, suppose you know that the side opposite the angle is 5 and the adjacent side is 12. You can solve for the angle as follows:

```
. SET DECIMALS TO 5
. Opp_side = 5
                    5
. Adj_side = 12
                   12
. Angle = ATAN(Opp_side/Adj_side)
              0.39479
. Degrees = RTOD(Angle)
             22.61986
```

The angle is approximately 22.62 degrees.

ATN2()

The ATN2() function returns the four-quadrant arc tangent, an angle measured in radians, from the sine and cosine of a given point.

Syntax

ATN2(<*type N expression1*>, <*type N expression2*>)

Type N expression1 is the sine and *type N expression2* the cosine of a particular angle. The result of *type N expression1/type N expression2* must be between +π and -π.

Notes

The ATN2() function lets you calculate the value of the arc tangent (that is, the angle in radians) by specifying the x and y coordinates in a four-quadrant system instead of using the value of the tangent, as with ATAN(). The ATN2() function also eliminates the zero-divide errors that might occur with ATAN().

Example

The following example has two parts. The first part shows how to derive the arc tangent of a 45-degree angle. The second part shows how to derive the arc tangent of a -135-degree angle.

```
. x = SIN(DTOR(45))
                    0.71
. y = COS(DTOR(45))
                    0.71
. ? RTOD(ATN2(x,y))
                      45
. x = SIN(DTOR(-135))
                   -0.71
. y = COS(DTOR(-135))
                   -0.71
. ? RTOD(ATN2(x,y))
                    -135
```

See the DTOR() and RTOD() functions for converting degrees to radians and vice versa.

BAR()

The BAR() function lets you monitor which bar is selected from a pop-up menu. The BAR() function returns a number corresponding to the line number within the pop-up menu area.

Syntax

BAR()

Notes

The BAR() function returns the BAR number—an integer corresponding to the menu bar's position within a pop-up menu. dBASE IV assigns the first line of the pop-up menu as 1, the second line as 2, and so on. For example, if you select the fourth menu option within the pop-up menu, BAR() returns the number 4.

The BAR() function returns 0 under the following conditions:

- There is no pop-up menu defined. (You did not use the DEFINE POPUP or DEFINE BAR command to define a pop-up menu.)
- A pop-up menu is not active.
- You pressed ESC to deactivate the pop-up menu.

Example

The following program sets up a simple pop-up menu using DEFINE POPUP. It displays the Lastname field from the CUSTOMER database within the pop-up screen area. After you've selected a last name from the pop-up menu, the program displays the results of the BAR() function.

```
*
* This program displays a pop-up menu of last names. After a menu
*      selection is made, the user can edit the corresponding
*      record.
*
USE Customer
DEFINE POPUP Pop_last FROM 1,50 TO 15,70 PROMPT FIELD Lastname;
     MESSAGE "Highlight a last name and press RETURN"
ON SELECTION POPUP Pop_last DO Pop_proc
ACTIVATE POPUP Pop_last
RETURN

PROCEDURE Pop_proc
```

```
    GOTO BAR()              && Go to record corresponding to selection
    EDIT                    && Edit the record
    DEACTIVATE POPUP        && Remove the pop-up menu
RETURN
```

Other commands related to pop-up menus are DEFINE BAR, DEFINE POPUP, ACTIVATE POPUP, SHOW POPUP, and DEACTIVATE POPUP.

BOF()

The BOF() function lets you test whether the record pointer is at the beginning of a file. You use the BOF() function when you are reading backwards through a database and want to know whether you've reached the beginning of the file. BOF() returns logical true (.T.) when the record pointer is at the beginning of the file.

Syntax

BOF([<*alias*>])

The optional *alias* argument lets you use a database's alias name. (See the USE command for setting up an alias.)

Notes

You can use the BOF() function to determine whether a database is in use. If a database is not in use, BOF() returns logical false (.F.).

Example

When you first open a database, the record pointer is positioned on the first record. As the following example shows, this is not actually the beginning of the file. You must place the record pointer before the first record to be actually at the beginning of the file.

```
. USE Customer
. ? RECNO()
                    1
. ? BOF()
.F.
. SKIP -1
CUSTOMER: Record No       1
. ? BOF()
.T.
```

See EOF() for testing the end-of-file condition.

CALL()

Use the CALL() function in conjunction with the LOAD command to execute binary (.BIN) program files within dBASE IV programs. The CALL() function is the equivalent of the CALL WITH command.

Syntax

CALL(*<filename>*,*<string expression>*/*<memory variable>*)

Notes

Binary program modules are programs written in assembly or C language and compiled to form executable subroutines. Files that contain binary program modules almost always have a .BIN extension.

Before you can execute a binary program module with CALL(), you must load it into memory with the LOAD command. The binary program module takes the memory variable or array element you pass it and then modifies that memory variable or array element if it needs to return something to dBASE IV.

You can pass memory variables or array elements to binary program modules. Of course, before you can pass a memory variable to a binary program module, you must first define it. Likewise, if you want to pass an array element, you must first declare the array (see the DECLARE command) and then reference the element's coordinate (for example, Sales[1]).

You can pass up to seven parameters to the module you execute with Call().

Example

The dBASE IV sample programs contain a sample binary program module—GETDRIVE.BIN. If you copied the sample programs to your hard disk during the installation process, you'll find GETDRIVE.BIN on your SAMPLES subdirectory.

```
. LOAD C:\DBASE\SAMPLES\GETDRIVE
. Drive = " "

. ? "Current drive = ",CALL("GETDRIVE",Drive)
Current drive =  C
. ? Drive
C
```

Notice that the binary program module has modified the contents of the string variable that was passed to it.

For other commands related to loading and executing external programs, see CALL, DECLARE, LOAD, RUN/!, and STORE.

CDOW()

You use the CDOW() function to get the name of the day of the week from a date expression.

Syntax

CDOW(<*date expression*>)

Date expression can be a literal date value ({*mm/dd/yy*}), a memory variable, or a field. It can also be the results of a function that returns a data type of date.

Examples

This example returns the name of the day of the week for the literal date value {1/22/89}.

```
. ? "January 22, 1989 is a "+CDOW({1/22/89})
January 22, 1989 is a Sunday
```

The next example returns the day of the week for the current system date.

```
. ? CDOW(DATE())
Monday
```

See the DOW() function if you want to get a number that represents the day of the week.

CEILING()

The CEILING() function returns the smallest integer that is greater than or equal to a given numeric expression.

Syntax

CEILING(<*type N expression*>)

Example

```
. Testvar = 234.56789
        234.56789
. ? CEILING(TESTVAR)
        235
```

See also the FLOOR() function, which returns an integer less than or equal to the result of a numeric expression.

CHANGE()

Use the CHANGE() function in the multi-user version of dBASE IV to ascertain whether a record has been changed since it was opened. In the single-user version of dBASE IV, CHANGE() always returns logical false (.F.). See Chapter 30, "Networking Commands and Functions," for a complete description.

CHR()

The CHR() function converts a number from the ASCII code table to a character. You can use CHR() to display special characters on your screen or send control codes to your printer.

Syntax

CHAR(<*type N expression*>)

Type N expression must result in an integer from 1 to 255.

Notes

The CHR() function is useful for accessing special characters (for instance, box characters, and the pound sign) from the ASCII character set. Using CHAR(), you can send special characters to the screen or printer. However, even though you may be able to display special characters on your screen, your printer may not be able to print them.

Examples

The following example shows how to display a capital Z (ASCII code 90):

```
. ? CHR(90)
Z
```

To sound the bell in dBASE IV, use ASCII decimal code 7.

```
. ? CHR(7)+"This shows how to sound the bell"
```

See ASC() if you want to determine the ASCII decimal code for the first character in a string.

CMONTH()

The CMONTH() function returns the month, in character format, for a given date expression.

Syntax

CMONTH(<*date expression*>)

Date expression can be a literal value ({*mm/dd/yy*}), memory variable, field, or any other expression that returns a date type.

Example

The following example returns the name of the month from the current system date, 01/23/89:

```
. ? "This is "+CMONTH(DATE())
This is January
```

COL()

The COL() function returns the column in which the cursor is currently positioned.

Syntax

COL()

Notes

You can use the COL() function as you use the special operator $ with @...SAY and @...GET commands. That is, both COL() and $ return the current column position on the screen or the page. Both of the following commands print the current column position and "Hello" at row 5:

```
@ 5, COL() SAY "Hello"

@ 5, $ SAY "Hello"
```

Example

The following example prints the title "Monthly Report for LeBlond Group" starting at row 2, column 10 on the screen or printed page:

```
@ 2,10 SAY "Monthly Report for "
@ 2,COL() SAY "LeBlond Group"
```

The next example executes a loop while the current column is less than a given value.

COMPLETED()

The COMPLETED() function determines whether a transaction has been successfully carried out. A *transaction* consists of an application-specific sequence of commands, beginning with a BEGIN TRANSACTION command and ending with either an END TRANSACTION or a ROLLBACK command. END TRANSACTION is used for successful termination, and ROLLBACK is used in the case of unsuccessful termination.

Syntax

COMPLETED()

Notes

In classic database design, transactions are explicitly bounded by BEGIN TRANSACTION and END TRANSACTION or ROLLBACK commands. The COMPLETED() function lets you determine whether a transaction failed, that is, whether neither an END TRANSACTION nor a ROLLBACK was executed. With the COMPLETED() function, you can determine whether to issue an END TRANSACTION or ROLLBACK command to complete the transaction.

In its default state, COMPLETED() is set to logical true (.T.). When you issue a BEGIN TRANSACTION command, it is automatically set to logical false (.F.). Either an END TRANSACTION or a ROLLBACK command resets COMPLETED() to true (.T.).

The COMPLETED() function is most often used with the multi-user version of dBASE IV, but it also works with the single-user version. You can use the COMPLETED() function from within a program or from the dot prompt.

Example

In general, when a transaction is interrupted by an error, you should roll back the entire transaction. This prevents the error from causing unwanted changes in your data and returns your database to its status at the time of the last successful transaction. In this way, you can protect the integrity of your database.

You'll most often use the COMPLETED() function in error-handling routines to determine whether to roll back an unsuccessful transaction.

```
ON ERROR DO Err_hand
USE Customer
BEGIN TRANSACTION
     REPLACE ALL Order_no WITH Order_no + 100
END TRANSACTION

PROCEDURE Err_hand
IF .NOT. COMPLETED()
     ROLLBACK                && Roll it back
     IF .NOT. ROLLBACK()          && Rollback didn't worked
          IF ISMARKED()           && Is header marker there?
               RESET              && Rollback impossible: reset marker.
          ENDIF
          ? "The transaction could not be completed."
          ? "Unable to reverse the transaction."
     ENDIF
ENDIF
RETURN
```

For other commands and functions related to transaction processing, see BEGIN TRANSACTION/END TRANSACTION, ROLLBACK, CONVERT, ISMARKED(), ROLLBACK(), CHANGE(), and LKSYS().

COS()

The COS() function returns the cosine for an angle given in radians.

Syntax

COS(<*type N expression*>)

The *type N expression* is the size of an angle in radians. To convert an angle in degrees to radians for use with the COS() function, use the DTOR() function. The values returned by COS() vary between -1 and 1.

Example

The following example determines the cosine for an angle of 30 degrees. It also determines the secant, which you can produce by dividing 1 by the value of the cosine.

```
. SET DECIMALS TO 5
. ? COS(DTOR(30))
          0.86603
. Secant = 1/COS(DTOR(30))
          1.15470
```

CTOD()

The CTOD() function converts a character string expression to a date data type.

Syntax

CTOD(<*string expression*>)

String expression must be in the American format (*mm/dd/yy*). However, you can change this default format setting by using SET DATE and SET CENTURY. You can enter a string between the values of "01/01/0100" and "12/31/9999".

Notes

Rather than use the CTOD() function, it is much easier to use curly braces to create a date variable from a literal value. You can enter the date in the form {*mm/dd/yy*}.

Example

The following example converts the literal string "12/30/89" to a date value in a memory variable:

```
. Mdate = CTOD("12/30/89")
12/30/89
. ? TYPE("Mdate")              && Notice the quotes!
D
. SET CENTURY ON
. ? Mdate
12/30/1989
```

DATE()

The DATE() function returns the system date.

Syntax

DATE()

Notes

The system date is the date returned from DOS. To get the correct date with dBASE IV, you must have properly set the system date at the DOS level.

The DATE() function returns a date in the American format (*mm/dd/yy*), unless you change the default format with SET DATE or SET CENTURY.

Example

The following example displays the system date and then stores it to the variable Today:

```
. ? DATE()
12/30/89
. Today = DATE()
12/30/89
```

DAY()

The DAY() function returns the day of the month, in numeric format, for a given date expression.

Syntax

DAY(<*date expression*>)

Date expression can be a literal date value ({*mm/dd/yy*}), a memory variable, or a field. It can also be the results of a function that returns a date data type.

Example

This example returns the day of the month for the current system date.

```
. ? DAY(DATE())
        12
. STORE DAY(DATE()) TO Day_of_mth
        12
. ? TYPE("Day_of_mth")       && Notice the quotes!
N
```

DBF()

The DBF() function returns the name of the active database file in the current work area. If no database is in use in the current work area, DBF() returns a null string.

Syntax

DBF([<*alias*>])

The optional *alias* argument lets you use a database's alias name. (Refer to the USE command in Chapter 31 to see how to set up an alias.)

Notes

When you've set up an alias name for a database and are using more than one database at a time in a program, the DBF() function is particularly useful for determining what work area a given database is located in.

Example

The following example prompts the user for a directory and a database file name. After activating the database, it uses the DBF() function to return the name of the currently active database.

```
. ACCEPT "Enter the directory for the database: " To Mdirect
Enter the database file directory: db4cr
. ACCEPT "Enter a database filename: " To Mfile
Enter a database filename: customer
. USE "C:\"+Mdirect+"\"+Mfile
. ? DBF()
C:CUSTOMER.DBF
```

See the ALIAS() function to learn how to determine the alias name for a given work area.

DELETED()

The DELETED() function indicates whether the current record in a specified work area is marked for deletion. It returns logical true (.T.) if the record is so marked, and logical false (.F.) if it is not. If no database file is currently in use, DELETED() returns false (.F.).

Syntax

DELETED([<*alias*>])

The optional *alias* argument lets you use a database's alias name. (Refer to the USE command to see how to set up an alias.)

Example

This example activates the CUSTOMER database and positions the record pointer at the fifth record. It then shows the results of the DELETED() function before and after the record is marked for deletion. Notice that the RECALL command "un-marks" the record for deletion.

```
. USE Customer
. GOTO 5
CUSTOMER: Record No       5
. ? DELETED()
.F.
. DELETE
     1 record deleted
. ? DELETED()
.T.
. RECALL
     1 record recalled
. ? DELETED()
.F.
```

DIFFERENCE()

The DIFFERENCE() function returns a number that expresses the difference between two *sound-alike* codes. In dBASE IV, you use sound-alike codes to phonetically search a database when you don't know the exact spelling for an entry.

Syntax

DIFFERENCE(*<string expression1>*, *<string expression2>*)

The two expressions you evaluate can be literal strings, fields, variables, or any other valid character string expressions.

Notes

The DIFFERENCE() function evaluates the difference between sound-alike codes and returns an integer between 0 and 4. As the example indicates, two sound-alike codes that are quite similar cause DIFFERENCE() to return a value of 4. On the other hand, if two codes have no matching letters, DIFFERENCE() returns a value of 0.

Example

```
. USE Customer
. ACCEPT "Enter lastname to compare: " TO Mname
Enter lastname to compare: Borrowes
. DISPLAY ALL Lastname FOR DIFFERENCE(Lastname, Mname) > 1
Record#  Lastname
      1  Thomas
      5  Takano
      6  Corzine
     13  Bachtel
     14  Borros
     17  Jones
     22  Bergstrom
     23  Wainwright
     26  Woods
     29  Finke
     30  Parish
     31  Borros
. DISPLAY ALL Lastname FOR DIFFERENCE(Lastname, Mname) > 2
Record#  Lastname
     14  Borros
     22  Bergstrom
     30  Parish
     31  Borros
. DISPLAY ALL Lastname FOR DIFFERENCE(Lastname, Mname) > 3
Record#  Lastname
     14  Borros
     31  Borros
```

For more on sound-alike codes, see the SOUNDEX() function.

DISKSPACE()

The DISKSPACE() function returns the number of bytes available on the default drive. The number returned is an integer.

Syntax

DISKSPACE()

Notes

Use the DISKSPACE() function when you want to determine whether you have sufficient space available before writing information to disk. For example, suppose you want to back up an entire database to a floppy disk in drive A. You can use the DISKSPACE() function to determine the amount of room available on your disk.

Examples

The following example shows the results both of running the external DOS program CHKDSK and of using the DISKSPACE() function. As you might expect, both produce identical results for the amount of disk space available on drive A. (For this example to work, CHKDSK must be available on your dBASE IV default directory.)

```
. SET DEFAULT TO A
. !CHKDSK A:
1457664 bytes disk space
    512 bytes in 1 user files
1457152 bytes available on disk
 654336 bytes total memory
 143856 bytes free

. ? DISKSPACE()
1457152
```

The ! and RUN commands are equivalent. See the RUN/! command for information on running external programs from within dBASE IV.

DMY()

The DMY() function converts a date from any valid date expression to a string of the form *dd month yy* (for example, 14 November 89).

Syntax

DMY(<*date expression*>)

Date expression can be a literal value in curly braces (as in {11/14/89}), a memory variable, a field, or any other expression that evaluates to a date.

Notes

The date that DMY() returns is in the format *dd month yy*. That is, the day is shown without a leading 0 and is either one or two digits. The month is fully spelled out. The year is always two digits long.

If SET CENTURY is ON, the DMY() function returns a date in the format *dd month yyyy*.

Example

```
. Datevar = {11/14/89}
11/14/89
. ? DMY(Datevar)
14 November 89
. SET CENTURY ON
. ? DMY(Datevar)
14 November 1989
. SET CENTURY OFF
```

DOW()

The DOW() function takes any valid date expression and returns a number representing the day of the week. Sunday is considered the first day of the week.

Syntax

DOW(*<date expression>*)

The *date expression* can be a literal value in curly braces (for example, {11/14/88}), a memory variable, a field, or any other expression that evaluates to a date.

Example

The following example shows the day of the week for the current system date. It then stores that value to the variable Day_no.

```
. ? DOW(DATE())
        2
. Day_no = DOW(DATE())
        2
. ? Day_no
        2
```

See CDOW() if you want to get the name of the day of the week from a date expression.

DTOC()

The DTOC() function converts a date from any valid date expression to a character string. Use the DTOC() function when you want to compare a date to a character string representing a date.

Syntax

DTOC(<*date expression*>)

Date expression can be a literal value in curly braces (for example, {11/14/88}), a memory variable, a field, or any other expression that evaluates to a date.

Example

```
. Ddate = DATE()
11/14/88
. Cdate = "11/14/88"
11/14/88
. ? TYPE("Ddate")             && Notice the quotes!
D
. ? TYPE("Cdate")             && Notice the quotes!
C
. ? Cdate = DTOC(Ddate)
.T.
. ? "The current system date is "+DTOC(Ddate)
The current system date is 11/14/88
```

DTOR()

The DTOR() function takes the size of an angle measured in degrees and converts it to radians.

Syntax

DTOR(<*type N expression*>)

The *type N expression* is the size of an angle in degrees. If the angle has minutes or seconds, you should convert them to decimal form before using the DTOR() function.

Example

The following example converts a 45-degree angle to radians:

```
. SET DECIMALS TO 5
. ? DTOR(45)
        0.78540
```

To convert radians to degrees, see the RTOD() function.

DTOS()

The DTOS() function converts a date to a character string and is used specifically for indexing databases.

Syntax

DTOS(<*date expression*>)

The *date expression* can be a literal value in curly braces (as in, {11/14/89}), a memory variable, a field, or any other expression that evaluates to a date.

Notes

The DTOS() function is designed for combining date and character strings together to create a single index expression. The DTOS() function takes a date expression and returns a character string of the form *ccyymmdd*. For example, given the literal date {11/15/88}, DTOS() returns the string "19881115". It returns the character string in this form regardless of the SET CENTURY and SET DATE settings.

Example

The following example indexes the ORDERREC database using a string expression that concatenates the Inv_no character field to the Order_date date field. Prior to concatenation, the Order_date date field is converted to a string with the DTOS() function.

```
. USE Orderrec
. INDEX ON DTOS(Order_date) + Inv_no TO Ord_inv
  100% indexed           33 Records indexed
. LIST NEXT 10 Order_date, Inv_no
Record#  Order_date Inv_no
      1  11/14/88   LEB123557
      2  11/15/88   LEB123558
      3  11/15/88   LEB123559
      4  11/16/88   LEB123560
      5  11/17/88   LEB123561
      6  11/18/88   LEB123562
      7  11/21/88   LEB123563
      8  11/21/88   LEB123564
      9  11/22/88   LEB123565
     10  11/23/88   LEB123566
```

EOF()

The EOF() function lets you test whether the record pointer is at the end of a file. Use EOF() when you are reading through a database and want to know when you've passed the last record in the file. EOF() returns logical true (.T.) when the record pointer is at the end of the file.

Syntax

EOF([<*alias*>])

The optional *alias* argument lets you use a database's alias name. (See the USE command to learn how to set up an alias.)

Notes

When you've reached the end of a file (that is, when EOF() is true), RECNO() is actually greater than RECCOUNT(). If you try to move beyond the end of the file, by using SKIP for example, dBASE IV returns an error.

You can also use the EOF() function to determine whether a database is in use. If a database is not in use, EOF() returns logical false (.F.).

Example

The following example shows the value returned by EOF() when you use the GO BOTTOM command to position the record pointer at the last record in a file. As the example shows, you must move beyond the last record in the database to reach the end of a file. When you do so, the value returned by RECNO() is greater than the value returned by RECCOUNT().

```
. USE Orderrec
. GO BOTTOM
ORDERREC: Record No      33
. ? EOF()
.F.
. SKIP
ORDERREC: Record No      34
. ? EOF()
.T.
. ? RECCOUNT()
        33
. ? RECNO()
        34
```

See the BOF() function for another example of the EOF() function.

ERROR()

The ERROR() function lets you determine the error number that caused an ON ERROR condition.

Syntax

ERROR()

Notes

The ERROR() function returns a number corresponding to the error that caused an ON ERROR condition. For dBASE IV to return a number, you must have an ON ERROR statement in your program.

The following commands have a special purpose when an ON ERROR condition arises:

- **CANCEL** Terminates unrecoverable errors
- **RETURN** Clears the error number (and the message) trapped by the ON ERROR condition and terminates the program
- **RETRY** Clears the error number (and the message) trapped by the ON ERROR condition and retries the command that caused the error

Tip: DOS-level failures (for example, disk full, sector error, and read error) cannot be trapped with the ON ERROR command. In fact, the ON ERROR command only traps dBASE IV-level errors.

Example

The following program prompts for a file name to copy from the current drive and directory to drive A. If an error arises during the copying process, the error-handling procedure Err_hand is called to process the error. It explicitly handles ERROR() equals 1 (the file does not exist) and ERROR() equals 29 (dBASE IV is unable to write to drive A—for instance, the disk may be write-protected.)

```
* Main program
ON ERROR DO Err_hand
ACCEPT "Enter name of file to copy to drive A:\ " TO Filename
COPY FILE &Filename TO "A:\"
RETURN

* Error handling procedure
PROCEDURE Err_hand
ON ERROR
DO CASE
     CASE ERROR() = 1
          ? "***File does not exist***"
     CASE ERROR() = 29
          ? "***Write error on drive A:\***"
     *
     *
     *
     OTHERWISE        && Display dBASE error number and message
          ? "***Error number is "+STR(ERROR(),3)
          ? MESSAGE()
ENDCASE
RETURN
```

For another example of ERROR(), see the PROGRAM() function.

For other commands and functions related to error trapping, see MESSAGE() and ON ERROR.

EXP()

The EXP() function returns the value of the constant e raised to the power specified by the argument for the function. It represents the inverse of the LOG() function.

Syntax

EXP(<*type N expression*>)

Notes

The EXP() function uses the constant e, which is approximately equal to 2.7182818. This represents the constant of base e used in natural logarithms. The *type N expression* that you supply in the function represents the exponent, or power, by which the constant e is raised in calculation. The number that EXP() returns is a real number.

Examples

The following example shows raising e to 1 returns a value of e.

```
. SET DECIMALS TO 7
. ? EXP(1)
        2.7182818
```

The next example shows how to calculate 3 * 4 using natural logs.

```
. y = 3
         3
. z = 4
         4
. Log_save = LOG(y * z)
         2.4849066
. ? EXP(Log_save)
        12
```

FIELD()

The FIELD() function returns a field name when given a number corresponding to a field's position within the structure of the selected database file.

Syntax

FIELD(<*type N expression*> [,<*alias*>])

Include the *alias* argument to have dBASE IV return field names from databases in different work areas.

Notes

The numeric expression you enter for FIELD() can be between 1 and 255. However, if the database has only ten fields, for example, the function will return a null string for a numeric expression greater than 10.

The FIELD() function returns field names in all uppercase letters.

Example

The following example activates two databases: CUSTOMER in work area 1 and ORDERREC in work area 2. Because work area 1 is the active work area, the FIELD() function returns field names from CUSTOMER. When you include an alias of ORDERREC, FIELD() returns field names from that database.

```
. USE Customer IN 1
. USE Orderrec IN 2
. ? FIELD(2)    && With no alias, FIELD() uses current work area
FIRSTNAME
. Field_no = 5
         5
. ? FIELD(Field_no)
ADDR_1
. ? FIELD(Field_no,"Orderrec")
PRICE
```

See the DISKSPACE() function for another example of the FIELD() function.

FILE()

The FILE() function lets you determine whether a file exists. FILE() returns logical true (.T.) if the file exists and logical false (.F.) if it does not.

Syntax

FILE(<*string expression*>)

You *must* include both the file name and its extension in the *string expression*.

Notes

If the file name is not on the default drive and directory, you must supply the proper drive and directory as part of the *string expression*.

Examples

As the following example illustrates, the FILE() function is not case sensitive. Also, you must be careful to include the file extension.

```
. ? FILE("Customer.dbf")
.T.
. ? FILE("Customer")
.F.
. ? FILE("C:\LEBLOND\INVEN.DBF")
.T.
```

See the SET DEFAULT command to learn about setting the default drive and the SET PATH command to learn about setting the directory search path.

FIXED()

The FIXED() function converts type F (IEEE long, real floating point) numbers to type N (binary coded decimal) numbers. The range for type F numbers is 10^{308} to 10^{-308}.

Syntax

FIXED(<*type F expression*>)

If the expression you provide includes both type N and type F numbers, all numbers are converted to type F.

Notes

You may lose some precision when FIXED() converts your numbers. See the FLOAT() function to learn about converting type N numbers to type F numbers.

FKLABEL()

The FKLABEL() function returns the name assigned to a function key.

Syntax

FKLABEL(*<type N expression>*)

Notes

In dBASE IV, there are 28 programmable function keys assigned as follows:

Number	Function Keys
1 - 9	F2 - F10
10 - 19	CTRL-F1 - CTRL-F10
20 - 28	SHIFT-F1 - SHIFT-F9

The F1 function key is reserved for Help and cannot be programmed. Likewise, SHIFT-F10 is reserved for the macro recorder. Notice also that F11 and F12 function keys (as well as their SHIFT and CTRL combinations) are not available in dBASE IV even though they may be available on your computer's keyboard.

There are three basic ways to assign commands to the programmable function keys:

- You can use the full-screen SET command, which shows a complete list of the programmable keys. You assign commands to individual keys using the **Keys** option from the main SET menu.

- You can program keys from the dot prompt using the SET FUNCTION command. See the SET FUNCTION command in Chapter 31.
- You can modify the CONFIG.DB file. See Chapter 35, "Customizing dBASE IV."

Example

The following example shows how you can get the FKLABEL() name for a function key:

```
. ? FKLABEL(1)
F2
. ? FKLABEL(10)
CTRL-F1
. ? FKLABEL(20)
SHIFT-F1
```

FKMAX()

The FKMAX() function returns an integer corresponding to the number of programmable function keys in dBASE IV. Because this function always returns a value of 28, it has very little practical use.

Syntax

FKMAX()

Notes

In dBASE IV, there are 28 programmable function keys assigned as follows.

Number	Function Keys
1 - 9	F2 - F10
10 - 19	CTRL-F1 - CTRL-F10
20 - 28	SHIFT-F1 - SHIFT-F9

The F1 function key is reserved for Help and cannot be programmed. Likewise, SHIFT-F10 is reserved for the macro recorder. Notice also that F11 and F12 function keys (as well as their SHIFT and CTRL combinations) are not available in dBASE IV even though they may be available on your computer's keyboard.

Example

```
. ? FKMAX()
        28
```

See the FKLABEL() function and the SET and SET FUNCTION commands for more on programmable function keys.

FLOAT()

The FLOAT() function converts type N (binary coded decimal) numbers to type F (IEEE long, real floating point) numbers.

Syntax

FLOAT(<*type N expression*>)

Notes

See the FIXED() function for converting type F numbers to type N numbers.

FLOCK()

Use the FLOCK() function in the multi-user version of dBASE IV to lock a database file. If the database is successfully locked, FLOCK() returns logical true (.T.). See Chapter 30, "Networking Commands and Functions," for a complete description.

FLOOR()

The FLOOR() function returns the largest integer that is less than or equal to a given numeric expression.

Syntax

FLOOR(<*type N expression*>)

Example

```
. Testvar = 234.56789
        234.56789
. ? FLOOR(Testvar)
        234
```

See also the CEILING() function, which returns the smallest integer greater than or equal to the result of a numeric expression.

FOUND()

The FOUND() function lets you verify the results of the last FIND, LOCATE, SEEK, or CONTINUE command. FOUND() returns logical true (.T.) if the operation was successful and logical false

(.F.) if it was not. If you move the record pointer with a command other than FIND, LOCATE, SEEK, or CONTINUE, FOUND() returns logical false (.F.).

Syntax

FOUND([<*alias*>])

The optional *alias* argument lets you use a database's alias name to determine the value of FOUND() for a noncurrent work area. (See the USE command for setting up an alias.) If you do not include an alias name, FOUND() operates in the current work area.

Notes

You use the FOUND() function mostly to determine whether certain entries are present in a file. Each work area returns its own value for FOUND(). To get the value of FOUND() for a particular work area, you must include an alias.

When you link databases with the SET RELATION TO command, dBASE IV keeps the related databases in synch as you search through the active file. It also updates the value of FOUND() in each work area.

See the SET RELATION TO command in Chapter 33 for more on related databases.

Example

The following example performs a sequential search through the CUSTOMER database with the LOCATE command (CUSTOMER is not indexed). The FOUND() function establishes whether a particular record was located.

```
. Mlastname = "Borros"
Borros
. USE Customer
. LOCATE FOR Lastname = Mlastname
Record =       14
. ? FOUND()
.T.
. ? Lastname, Firstname
Borros                  Brian
. CONTINUE
Record =       31
. ? FOUND()
.T.
. ? Lastname, Firstname
Borros                  David
. CONTINUE
End of LOCATE scope
. ? FOUND()
.F.
```

FV()

The FV() function returns the future value of an annuity, given the payment per period, the discount rate, and the number of periods.

Syntax

FV(<*payment*>, <*discount rate*>, <*periods*>)

The *payment* is a type N numeric expression that can be positive or negative.

The *discount rate* is the interest rate and must be positive. The FV() function assumes that interest is compounded each period. If you are using a yearly interest rate but the payments occur monthly, you should divide the rate by 12.

The *periods* is a type N numeric expression representing the term of the annuity.

Notes

The FV() function assumes that the payments are made at the end of each period. To determine an *annuity due*, in which payments are made at the beginning of the period, multiply the results of the FV() function by 1 plus the discount rate (1 + *<discount rate>*).

Example

The following example shows an annuity with a payment of $785, a yearly discount rate of 12%, and 36 monthly payments:

```
. INPUT "Enter payment: " TO Payment
Enter payment: 785.00
. INPUT "Enter discount rate: " TO Discount
Enter discount rate: .12
. INPUT "Enter number of payment periods: " TO Periods
Enter number of payment periods: 36
. ? FV(Payment, Discount/12, Periods)
     33815.35
```

You might add the following line to compute an annuity due:

```
. ? FV(Payment, Discount/12, Periods) * (1 + Discount/12)
    34153.50
```

GETENV()

The GETENV() function returns the DOS environment settings, for example, the COMSPEC, PATH, and PROMPT settings. To determine an environment setting, enter one of the DOS system variables as a character string or character variable.

Syntax

GETENV(*<string expression>*)

If GETENV() cannot find the system variable you've entered, it returns a null string.

Notes

The GETENV() function lets you check the settings for the DOS environment. If you are not familiar with DOS environment settings, you can read about them in your DOS manual under the PATH, PROMPT, and COMSPEC commands. Unless you are a system programmer, however, you probably will not use the GETENV() function in dBASE IV.

Example

The following example shows the results of the GETENV() function for a system with (1) a default drive of C, with COMMAND.COM loaded from the root directory; (2) a PATH setting with several directories, including a DB4 directory for dBASE IV; and (3) a DOS prompt setting made in AUTOEXEC.BAT that shows the current drive and directory (for example, C:\DB4>).

```
. ? GETENV("comspec")
C:\COMMAND.COM
. ? GETENV("path")
C:\BIN;C:\DB4;C:\WP50;C:\DV
. ? GETENV("prompt")
$P$G
```

IIF()

The IIF() function is sometimes called the *immediate IF* function. It is similar to the IF...ENDIF command sequence but is in dBASE IV function format.

Syntax

IIF(<*conditional expression*>,<*expression1*>,<*expression2*>)

If *conditional expression* is true, IIF() returns the result of *expression1*. Otherwise, it returns the result of *expression2*.

Expression1 and *expression2* can be logical, character, numeric, or date expressions. They must both be of the same type.

Notes

A big disadvantage of the IF...ENDIF command sequence is that you cannot use it from the dot prompt. (You can only use it from within programs.) However, you can use the IIF() function from the dot prompt, from within commands (for example, CREATE/MODIFY LABEL), or from within programs. You can even use it within DEBUG to set conditional break points (see Chapter 25, "Debugging Your Program").

Example

Consider the following IF...ENDIF command sequence for setting a logical variable:

```
IF Sales >= 50000
     Quota_met = .T.
ELSE
     Quota = .F.
ENDIF
```

To accomplish the same thing with IIF(), you can use the following:

```
Quota_met = IIF(Sales >= 50000, .T., .F.)
```

INKEY()

The INKEY() function returns the decimal ASCII value corresponding to the last key you pressed. It is often used in programming for branching.

Syntax

INKEY([*n*])

The optional *n* argument represents the number of seconds you want INKEY() to wait for a key press before returning control to your program.

Notes

You can use the INKEY() function to check the value of the first character in the type-ahead buffer. It returns a value between 0 and 255, corresponding to a character's ASCII code (see Appendix A for a complete list of ASCII codes). INKEY() returns negative values for the following:

- Function keys (for example, F10) with the exception of F1

- Function keys in combination with CTRL and SHIFT (for instance, CTRL-F2 and SHIFT-F7)

After reading the key from the buffer, INKEY() removes that key from the buffer.

You can use INKEY() to read many different kinds of key presses. For example, besides reading standard keys (such as "y" or "N"), you can also read arrow keys, function keys, CTRL keys, and ALT keys. You can even read function keys in combination with SHIFT and CTRL.

You cannot, however, use INKEY() to read function keys in combination with ALT (such as ALT-F2); these keys are trapped by the macro facility and are therefore not available to INKEY(). Two other keys you cannot read with INKEY() are ESC (or CTRL-[) and CTRL-S.

If no key has been pressed, INKEY() returns 0.

By using a value of 0 for the optional *n* argument, as in INKEY(0), you can have INKEY() pause indefinitely for a key press. See the example for the VARREAD() function.

Table 33-1 shows the key names and the companion values that INKEY() returns. Table 33-2 shows the values INKEY() returns for ALT-key combinations, such as ALT-G and ALT-4.

Example

The following example program displays for 4 seconds a simple banner screen for an application, unless you press a key.

```
SET TALK OFF
* Get current time plus 4 seconds
Timeout = VAL(SUBSTR(TIME(),7,2))+4

* Put up banner screen
CLEAR
@ 10,15 SAY "ABC Company Inventory Control Program"
@ 12,11 SAY "Developed by Softree, Inc.  Copyright 1989."

* Loop until current time = Timeout or key mashed
Key_in = 0
DO WHILE VAL(SUBSTR(TIME(),7,2)) <> Timeout .AND. Key_in = 0
     Key_in = INKEY()
ENDDO

CLEAR
```

Key Names		Decimal Value
CTRL-A	HOME	1
CTRL-B	CTRL-RIGHT ARROW	2
CTRL-C	PGDN	3
CTRL-D	RIGHT ARROW	4
CTRL-E	UP ARROW	5
CTRL-F	CTRL-END	6
CTRL-G	DEL	7
CTRL-H		8
CTRL-I	TAB	9
CTRL-J		10
CTRL-K		11
CTRL-L		12
CTRL-M	ENTER	13
CTRL-N		14
CTRL-O		15
CTRL-P		16
CTRL-Q		17
CTRL-R	PGUP	18
CTRL-S	LEFT ARROW	19
CTRL-T		20
CTRL-U		21
CTRL-V	INS	22
CTRL-W	CTRL-END	23
CTRL-X	DOWN ARROW	24
CTRL-Y		25
CTRL-Z		26
ESC	CTRL-[	27
F1	CTRL-\	28
F1	CTRL-HOME	29
CTRL-]	CTRL-PGDN	30
CTRL-^	CTRL-PGUP	31
SPACEBAR		32
BACKTAB		-400
CTRL-BACKSPACE		-401
CTRL-ENTER		-402
F2		-1
F3		-2
F4		-3
F5		-4
F6		-5
F7		-6
F8		-7

Table 33-1. INKEY( ) Return Values

Key Names	Decimal Value
F9	-8
F10	-9
CTRL-F1	-10
CTRL-F2	-11
CTRL-F3	-12
CTRL-F4	-13
CTRL-F5	-14
CTRL-F6	-15
CTRL-F7	-16
CTRL-F8	-17
CTRL-F9	-18
CTRL-F10	-19
SHIFT-F1	-20
SHIFT-F2	-21
SHIFT-F3	-22
SHIFT-F4	-23
SHIFT-F5	-24
SHIFT-F6	-25
SHIFT-F7	-26
SHIFT-F8	-27
SHIFT-F9	-28
SHIFT-F10	-29

Table 39-1. INKEY( ) Return Value *(continued)*

For other commands and functions related to getting keys, see LASTKEY(), ON KEY, READ, READKEY(), SET TYPEAHEAD.

INT()

The INT() function converts a numeric expression to an integer by truncating the digits to the right of the decimal.

With Letters				With Numbers	
A	-435	N	-422	0	-452
B	-434	O	-421	1	-451
C	-433	P	-420	2	-450
D	-432	Q	-419	3	-449
E	-431	R	-418	4	-448
F	-430	S	-417	5	-447
G	-429	T	-416	6	-446
H	-428	U	-415	7	-445
I	-427	V	-414	8	-444
J	-426	W	-413	9	-443
K	-425	X	-412		
L	-424	Y	-411		
M	-423	Z	-410		

Table 33-2. ALT-key Combination Values Returned by INKEY( )

Syntax

INT(<*type N expression*>)

Example

```
. ? INT(9.001)
        9
. ? INT(9.999)
        9
```

For functions that do not truncate numbers, see CEILING(), FLOOR(), or ROUND().

ISALPHA()

The ISALPHA() function reads the first character in a character string and returns logical true (.T.) if it is alphabetical.

Syntax

ISALPHA(<*string expression*>)

String expression can be a literal string, field, variable, or any other valid character string expression.

Notes

An alphabetical character is any letter between a and z, either upper- or lowercase.

Examples

```
. ? ISALPHA("4word")
.F.
. ? ISALPHA("word4")
.T.
. ? ISALPHA("Word4")
.T.
```

For other functions related to alphabetic characters, see ISLOWER(), ISUPPER(), LOWER(), and UPPER().

ISCOLOR()

The ISCOLOR() function lets you determine whether a computer can display color. It returns logical true (.T.) for a color screen and logical false (.F.) for monochrome.

Syntax

ISCOLOR()

Notes

The ISCOLOR() function reads the actual hardware installed, not the dBASE IV screen driver. Therefore, the ISCOLOR() command may be inaccurate with certain hardware configurations. For example, if you have a color graphics card with a single-color monitor, ISCOLOR() returns true (.T.), even though the correct answer should be false.

Example

The following example uses the ISCOLOR() function to read the screen type and sets dBASE IV's color patterns accordingly. For a color screen, dBASE IV shows blue text on a white background, and for a monochrome screen, it shows white characters on a black background (the default for monochrome).

```
IF ISCOLOR()
     SET COLOR TO B/W     && Blue on white background
ELSE
     SET COLOR TO W       && White
ENDIF
```

ISLOWER()

The ISLOWER() function enables you to determine whether the first character in a character string is a lowercase alphabetical character.

Syntax

ISLOWER(<*string expression*>)

String expression can be a literal string, field, variable, or any other valid character string expression.

Notes

The ISLOWER() function returns logical false (.F.) if the first character in the specified string is an uppercase alphabetical character or a nonalphabetical character.

Examples

```
. ? ISLOWER("1234")
.F.
. ? ISLOWER("pass")
.T.
. ? ISLOWER("Pass")
.F.
. ? ISLOWER("@Pass")
.F.
```

For other functions related to alphabetic characters, see ISALPHA(), ISUPPER(), LOWER(), and UPPER().

ISMARKED()

The ISMARKED() function reads the file header of the database file in the current work area to see if the file is in a state of change.

Syntax

ISMARKED([<*alias*>])

With the optional *alias* argument, you can use a database's alias name to determine the value of ISMARKED() for a database in a noncurrent work area. (See the USE command for setting up an alias.) If you do not include an alias name, ISMARKED() operates in the current work area.

Notes

In dBASE IV, every database file has a variable-length block of code at the start of the file—the file header—which contains information about the file structure. Within the file header is a 1-byte flag that indicates whether the database is in a state of change. The BEGIN TRANSACTION, END TRANSACTION, and ROLLBACK commands affect the state of this flag as follows:

- BEGIN TRANSACTION sets the flag to 1.
- END TRANSACTION and ROLLBACK set the flag to 0.

The ISMARKED() function checks the value of the 1-byte flag. It returns true (.T.) when the flag is set to 1; the file is in a state of change, that is, a transaction is in progress. It returns logical false (.F.) when the flag is 0; the file is not in a state of change, that is, a transaction is not in progress.

Example

See the example for the COMPLETED() function in this chapter. Also, Chapter 30, "Networking Commands and Functions," shows how to use ISMARKED() in a network environment.

For other commands and functions related to transaction processing, see BEGIN TRANSACTION/END TRANSACTION, ROLLBACK, CONVERT, COMPLETED(), ROLLBACK(), CHANGE(), and LKSYS().

ISUPPER()

The ISUPPER() function lets you determine whether the first character in a character string is an uppercase alphabetical character.

Syntax

ISUPPER(<*string expression*>)

The *string expression* can be a literal string, field, variable, or any other valid character string expression.

Notes

The ISUPPER() function returns logical false (.F.) if the first character in the specified string is a lowercase alphabetical character or a nonalphabetical character.

Examples

```
. ? ISUPPER("1234")
.F.
. ? ISUPPER("Pass")
.T.
. ? ISUPPER("pass")
.F.
. ? ISUPPER("@pass")
.F.
```

For other functions related to alphabetic characters, see ISALPHA(), ISLOWER(), LOWER(), and UPPER().

KEY()

The KEY() function returns the key expression corresponding to an index file. KEY() lets you determine the key expressions for both .MDX and .NDX index files.

Syntax

KEY([<*.MDX filename*>,] <*type N expression*> [,<*alias*>])

Notes

If you do not include an optional *.MDX filename*, dBASE IV uses the open index files in the current work area, including .NDX files.

Type N expression is the key (or tag) to interpret.

If you do not include the optional *alias* argument, KEY() operates in the current work area.

Example

The following example uses the CUSTOMER database and shows the expressions defined for the tags (keys) in the production .MDX file for that database, CUSTOMER.MDX.

```
. USE Customer
. ? KEY(1)
Lastname+Firstname
. ? KEY(2)
Cust_no
```

LASTKEY()

The LASTKEY() function returns the decimal ASCII value corresponding to the last key you pressed.

Syntax

LASTKEY()

Notes

LASTKEY() returns the same values as INKEY(). See INKEY() for a table of return values.

You can use LASTKEY() in a program to get a user's response and act upon it. For example, you can have your program branch, display a menu or message, or execute a procedure.

Example

The following example puts up a screen using @...SAY...GET commands. If you press F10, the program displays a list of options. LASTKEY() is how the program determines whether you have pressed F10.

```
* Set F10 equal to CTRL-END. This lets the user leave the
*   screen at any time.
SET FUNCTION F10 TO CHR(23)

DO WHILE .T.
     *
     * Get variables here with @...SAY...GET commands
     *
     @ 20,25 SAY "Press F10 for a list of options"
     READ
     IF LASTKEY() = -9          && F10 was mashed
          DO Put_list
          LOOP
     ELSE
          EXIT
```

```
    ENDIF
ENDDO

PROCEDURE Put_list
*
* Code for putting up list goes here
*
WAIT
RETURN
```

For other functions related to determining the last key pressed, see INKEY() and READKEY().

LEFT()

The LEFT() function returns a specified number of characters from a character string or memo field, beginning at the left-most character in the string or field.

Syntax

LEFT(*<character string>*/*<memo field>*,*<type N expression>*)

Type N expression is the number of characters to extract. If it is greater than the length of *character string*, LEFT() returns the entire string.

Notes

LEFT() is the equivalent of the SUBSTR() function with a starting position of 1.

Examples

The following example extracts the three left-most characters from a string.

```
. ? LEFT("123 Soquel Dr.",3)
123
```

The next example combines LEFT() with AT() to extract all the characters within a string up to the first blank.

```
. Street = "59 Temple St."
59 Temple St.
. ? LEFT(Street,AT(" ",Street))
59
```

For other functions related to manipulating strings, see AT(), LTRIM(), RIGHT(), RTRIM(), STUFF(), SUBSTR(), and TRIM().

LEN()

The LEN() function returns the length of a character string or memo field.

Syntax

LEN(<*character string*>/<*memo field*>)

Notes

The LEN() function lets you determine the length of a memory variable, database field, or memo field. It returns 0 in the case of a null string (" ").

Example

The following example uses the LEN() function to determine the length of the Company field in the CUSTOMER database.

```
. USE Customer
. ? Company
Texasville Pumps
. ? LEN(Company)
        30
. ? LEN(RTRIM(Company))
        16
```

LIKE()

The LIKE() function lets you compare two character strings. With LIKE(), you can use wildcards in your comparison.

Syntax

LIKE(*<pattern>*,*<string expression>*)

Notes

The LIKE() function lets you determine if the string pattern on the left appears within the character string on the right. The function returns logical true (.T.) if it does and logical false (.F.) if it does not.

LIKE() lets you use the DOS wildcard conventions: the asterisk (*) stands for any number of consecutive characters, and the question mark (?) stands for a single character. Both wildcard characters can appear within the string pattern, and both can appear more than once (see the next examples).

LIKE() is case sensitive. For example, LIKE("xyz", "uvwxyz") returns true (.T.), but LIKE("xyz", "UVWXYZ") returns false (.F.). Wildcard characters can stand for upper- or lowercase letters.

Examples

The following examples show that you can use wildcard characters anywhere within the string pattern, and that you can use them more than once.

```
. ? LIKE("cap*", "capacity")
.T.
. ? LIKE("*cap*", "hub caps")
.T.
. ? LIKE("?ub*cap*", "hub caps")
.T.
. ? LIKE("?ub*cap*", "Hub Caps")
.F.
```

LINENO()

The LINENO() function returns the relative line number of the next line to be executed within a command or procedure file.

Syntax

LINENO()

Notes

LINENO() is useful for debugging your programs because it lets you set a breakpoint within the dBASE IV Debugger. To set a breakpoint with LINENO(), follow these steps:

1. Start the Debugger by entering **DEBUG *filename*** at the dot prompt. For example, type **DEBUG MYPROG**. dBASE IV loads your program into the Debugger and locates the cursor at the "Action" prompt.

2. Enter B at the "Action" prompt to access the Breakpoint window of the Debugger.

3. Enter an expression using LINENO(). For example, type **20 = LINENO()** and press ENTER to set a breakpoint at line 20 of the program.

4. Press ESC to return to the "Action" prompt.

5. Enter R to execute the program up to the breakpoint.

When you set breakpoints using LINENO(), you can execute a program up to a specific point and then have the Debugger window reappear. You can then perform other actions with the Debugger, such as stepping through the program one step at a time, setting other breakpoints, and so on.

For more on the Debugger, see the DEBUG command in Chapter 31, "dBASE IV Commands." Also, Chapter 25, "Debugging Your Program," covers the Debugger in detail.

Example

For a programming example using LINENO(), see the PROGRAM() function.

Other useful commands and functions related to program development are DEBUG, SET DEVELOPMENT, RESUME, SUSPEND, and PROGRAM().

LKSYS()

Use the LKSYS() function in the multi-user version of dBASE IV to determine the log-in name of the user who has locked a record or file. See Chapter 30, "Networking Commands and Functions," for a complete description.

LOG()

The LOG() function returns the natural logarithm of a number.

Syntax

LOG(<*type N expression*>)

Notes

The LOG() function solves for the logarithm of a number using base e (the mathematical constant approximately equal to 2.7182818). Given the value of x as its argument, LOG() returns the value of y from the following equation:

$$y = e^x$$

LOG() returns a type F (long real) number.

Example

The following example shows one way to compute 12 * 12 using natural logs. It also shows how to get the value at the end of the logarithmic calculation.

```
. x = LOG(12) + LOG(12)
         4.97
. ? EXP(x)
      144
```

For another example of LOG(), see the EXP() function.

LOG10()

The LOG10() function returns the logarithm of a number. It solves for the logarithm to base 10.

Syntax

LOG10(<*type N expression*>)

Notes

The LOG10() function is the reciprocal of base 10 exponentiation, or scientific notation. When you use it in dBASE IV, the number you supply as the argument must not be 0 or negative.

Example

The following example computes the base 10 log of 5. It then shows that the base 10 log of 5 * 5 is the same as adding the base 10 log of 5 to itself.

```
. ? LOG10(5)
        0.70
. ? LOG10(5 * 5)
        1.40
. ? LOG10(5) + LOG10(5)
        1.40
```

LOOKUP()

The LOOKUP() function searches for a record within a given database file and returns the value from a specified field.

Syntax

LOOKUP(<*return field*>, <*look-for expression*>, <*look-in field*>)

Both *return field* and *look-for expression* are any valid dBASE IV expressions. To have dBASE IV look outside the current work area, you must specify an alias.

Look-in field is a field name in the database file that you are searching. Again, to have dBASE IV look outside the current work area, you must specify an alias.

Notes

dBASE IV performs a sequential search, unless you've previously created an index which matches *look-in field*. As always, you can minimize the search time by opening an .MDX tag or .NDX file.

The LOOKUP() function has dBASE IV locate the record pointer in the first record of the database file where *look-for expression* matches the value in *look-in field*. If it cannot find a match, it locates the record pointer at the end of the file.

Example

The following example demonstrates how you can use the LOOKUP() function with two databases. It first loads the CUSTOMER database indexed according to Cust_name (Lastname+Firstname). Next, it loads the ORDERREC database in work area 2 indexed according to Cust_no. (Cust_no is the key field that links CUSTOMER and ORDERREC.) The next step performs a SEEK on CUSTOMER to locate the record corresponding to "Finke". The next two print statements (?) show you that the two databases are out of synch.

```
. USE Customer ORDER Cust_name
Master index: CUST_NAME
. USE Orderrec ORDER Cust_no IN 2
Master index: CUST_NO
. SEEK "Finke"
. ? Cust_no
1029
```

```
. ? Orderrec->Cust_no
1001
. ? LOOKUP(Orderrec->Order_date, Cust_no, Orderrec->Cust_no)
12/15/88
. SELECT 2
. DISPLAY Cust_no, Order_date
Record#  Cust_no Order_date
     29     1029 12/15/88
```

Notice that the LOOKUP() statement causes dBASE IV to move the record pointer in the ORDERREC database—the database being searched. It locates the record pointer at the record that corresponds to CUSTOMER's Cust_no (1029) and returns ORDERREC's Order_date (the date the order was placed, which is 12/15/88).

LOWER()

The LOWER() function converts all the characters in a string to lowercase.

Syntax

LOWER(*<string expression>*)

Example

```
. ? LOWER("dBASE IV: The Complete Reference")
dbase iv: the complete reference
```

See also ISLOWER(), ISUPPER(), ISALPHA(), UPPER().

LTRIM()

The LTRIM() function eliminates leading blanks from a character string.

Syntax

LTRIM(<*string expression*>)

Example

The following example creates a string with 15 blank spaces followed by "Orsen". It then trims the leading spaces with LTRIM().

```
. Temp_str = SPACE(15)+"Orsen"
                  Orsen
. ? LTRIM(Temp_str)
Orsen
```

LUPDATE()

The LUPDATE() function reads the file header of a database file and returns the date of the last update.

Syntax

LUPDATE([<*alias*>])

The optional *alias* argument lets you determine the value of LUPDATE() for a database in a noncurrent work area. (See the USE command for setting up an alias.) If you do not include an alias name, LUPDATE() operates in the current work area.

Notes

In dBASE IV, every database file has a variable-length block of code at the start of the file—the file header—which contains information about the file structure. Within the file header is a 3-byte field which indicates the date the database was last updated. LUPDATE() returns the date in that field.

If no database is in use, LUPDATE() returns a blank date.

Example

Use the LUPDATE() to determine whether a database reflects the current day's transactions. As the following example indicates, you must close and then reopen a database before LUPDATE() reflects the current day's activity.

```
. USE Customer
. ? LUPDATE()
12/02/88
. ? DATE()
12/03/88
. EDIT          && Update the database
. ? LUPDATE()
12/02/88
. CLOSE DATABASES
. USE Customer
. ? LUPDATE()
12/03/88
```

MAX()

The MAX() function returns the larger value of two character, numeric, or date expressions.

Syntax

MAX(<*expression1*>, <*expression2*>)

The two expressions can be character, numeric, or date expressions.

Notes

The MAX() function is different from the aggregate MAX() function used as part of the CALCULATE command. See the CALCULATE command in Chapter 31 for more information.

Examples

The following example shows the results of the MAX() function with character strings and numbers:

```
. Str_1 = "abc"
abc
. Str_2 = "def"
def
. ? MAX(Str_1, Str_2)
def
. Price_1 = 14.95
        14.95
. Price_2 = 15.95
        15.95
. ? MAX(Price_1, Price_2)
        15.95
```

With dates, MAX() returns the later of the two.

```
. ? DATE()
12/03/88
. ? MAX(DATE(), {12/04/88})
12/04/88
```

MDX()

The MDX() function returns the .MDX file name associated with a given index order number.

Syntax

MDX(<*type N expression*> [,<*alias*>])

Type N expression specifies the file position in the .MDX file list that dBASE IV maintains for the current work area. You set up the .MDX file list with the SET INDEX TO <*index filename list*> command. If you do not include the optional *alias* argument, MDX() operates in the current work area.

Notes

The MDX() function is useful when you have more than one index file active for a database. It lets you determine the index file name from dBASE IV's directory of indexes.

Example

The following example shows the results of MDX() when you've set up the CUSTOMER database in work area 1 and the ORDERREC database in work area 2. The production .MDX files for these databases are automatically opened when you open the database files.

```
. USE Customer
. USE Orderrec IN 2
. ? MDX(1)
C:CUSTOMER.MDX
. ? MDX(1, "Orderrec")
C:ORDERREC.MDX
```

For related functions and commands, see KEY(), NDX(), ORDER(), TAG(), and SET INDEX.

MDY()

The MDY() function takes a date expression and returns the date in *month day, year* format. If SET CENTURY is ON, you can have MDY() return the date in full correspondence form (for example, December 12, 1989).

Syntax

MDY(<*date expression*>)

Notes

The MDY() function returns a string with the following form:

Month	Fully spelled out
Day	Two digits
Year	Two digits. If SET CENTURY is ON, MDY() returns four digits

Example

The following example converts the date 12/12/89 to MDY() format:

```
. Date = {12/12/89}
12/12/89
. ? MDY(Date)
December 12, 89
. SET CENTURY ON
. ? MDY(Date)
December 12, 1989
```

MEMLINES()

The MEMLINES() function returns the number of lines needed to display a memo field at the current MEMOWIDTH setting.

Syntax

MEMLINES(<*memo field name*>)

Notes

The MEMLINES() function uses the current SET MEMOWIDTH setting to determine the number of lines.

Example

The following example shows the results of MEMLINES() for a memo field called Dcl_ind. Notice that the SET MEMOWIDTH setting controls the width of the lines.

```
. SET MEMOWIDTH TO 30
. ? Dcl_ind
When in the course of human
events it becomes necessary
. ? MEMLINES(Dcl_ind)
         2
. SET MEMOWIDTH TO 10
. ? Dcl_ind
When in
the course
of human
events it
becomes
necessary
. ? MEMLINES(Dcl_ind)
         6
```

For other functions related to memo fields, see MLINE() and LEN().

MEMORY()

The MEMORY() function returns the amount of available RAM in kilobytes.

Syntax

MEMORY()

Notes

Because the MEMORY() function lets you check the amount of available memory in kilobytes (1024-byte units), you can use it before running applications that use menus, windows, and arrays, which require additional memory. You can also use it before the RUN/! command, which lets you execute external DOS programs and commands.

Example

In the following example, the MEMORY() function determines whether there is sufficient memory available before declaring a large array.

```
IF MEMORY() < 58
     ? "Not enough memory"+CHR(07) && Display error and sound bell
ELSE
     DECLARE Accts[99,10]
ENDIF
```

MENU()

The MENU() function lets you determine the name of the active menu.

Syntax

MENU()

Notes

The MENU() function returns the name of the most recently activated menu in character string format. (To activate a menu, use the ACTIVATE MENU command.) If a menu is not currently active, it returns a null string (" ").

Use the MENU() function when you've branched to Help by pressing F1 (see the VARREAD() function) and want to return to the active menu from which you called Help.

Example

The following example shows that the active menu is the main menu.

```
. ? MENU()
MAIN
```

For another example of MENU(), see the PAD() function.

For other menu-related commands and functions, see ACTIVATE MENU, DEFINE MENU, and PAD().

MESSAGE()

The MESSAGE() function lets you determine the message that corresponds to the error that produced an ON ERROR condition.

Syntax

MESSAGE()

Notes

An error, which causes an ON ERROR condition, produces both a number and a message. To determine the number, use the ERROR() function. To determine the message, use the MESSAGE() function.

Example

For an example, see the ERROR() function.

MIN()

The MIN() function returns the smaller value of two character, numeric, or date expressions.

Syntax

MIN(<*expression1*>, <*expression2*>)

The two expressions can be character, numeric, or date expressions.

Notes

The MIN() function is different from the aggregate MIN() function that you use as part of the CALCULATE command. See the CALCULATE command in Chapter 31 for more information.

Examples

The following example shows the results of the MIN() function with character strings and numbers:

```
. Str_1 = "abc"
abc
. Str_2 = "def"
def
. ? MIN(Str_1, Str_2)
abc
. Price_1 = 14.95
        14.95
. Price_2 = 15.95
        15.95
. ? MIN(Price_1, Price_2)
        14.95
```

With dates, MIN() returns the earlier of the two.

```
. ? DATE()
12/03/88
. ? MIN(DATE(), {12/04/88})
12/03/88
```

MLINE()

The MLINE() function extracts a specified numbered line of text from a memo field in the current record.

Syntax

MLINE(<*memo field name*>, <*type N expression*>)

Notes

The MLINE() function extracts a line of text specified in *type N expression* from a memo field. It uses the current memo width setting, which you set with the SET MEMOWIDTH command.

Example

The following example shows how the SET MEMOWIDTH setting controls the width of memo lines and how it affects the results of the MLINE() function.

```
. SET MEMOWIDTH TO 30
. ? Dcl_ind
When in the course of human
events it becomes necessary
. ? MLINE(Dcl_ind, 2)
events it becomes necessary
. SET MEMOWIDTH TO 10
. ? Dcl_ind
When in
the course
of human
events it
becomes
necessary
. ? MLINE(Dcl_ind, 2)
the course
```

For other functions related to memory variables, see MEMLINES() and LEN().

MOD()

The MOD() function returns the remainder after division of two numbers. In mathematics, this remainder is referred to as the *modulus,* thus the name MOD().

Syntax

MOD(<*type N expression1*>, <*type N expression2*>)

Type N expression1 is the dividend and *type N expression2* is the divisor.

Notes

The MOD() function is useful for converting units of measure, such as ounces to pounds or meters to yards, where you need to use the remainder.

Examples

The following example shows a simple use of MOD():

```
. ? MOD(48,36)
          12
```

By combining the IIF() function with the MOD() function, you can easily test whether a value is odd or even and print a message to that effect.

```
. Test = 33
          33
. ? IIF(MOD(Test, 2) = 0, "Test is even", "Test is odd")
Test is odd
. Test = 66
          66
. ? IIF(MOD(Test, 2) = 0, "Test is even", "Test is odd")
Test is even
```

MONTH()

The MONTH() function returns the month, in numeric format, for a given date expression.

Syntax

MONTH(<*date expression*>)

Date expression can be a literal date value ({*mm/dd/yy*}), a memory variable, or a field. It can also be the results of a function that returns a data type of date.

Example

This example returns the month for the current system date.

```
. ? MONTH(DATE())
        12
. STORE MONTH(DATE()) TO Month_no
        12
. ? TYPE("Month_no")       && Notice the quotes!
N
```

NDX()

The NDX() function returns the name of an open .NDX file.

Syntax

NDX(<*type N expression*> [,<*alias*>])

The *type N expression* represents the position of an open .NDX index file in the index file list that dBASE IV maintains for the current work area. If you do not include the optional *alias* argument, NDX() operates in the current work area.

Notes

When you open one or more .NDX index files with the SET INDEX TO *<index file list>* or the USE INDEX *<index file list>* command, dBASE IV creates an entry for each .NDX file in the index file list for the current work area. The *type N expression* is the position of an open .NDX file within that index file list. The NDX() function returns the name of the open .NDX file in uppercase letters.

If the *type N expression* is greater than the number of open .NDX files in the current work area, dBASE IV returns a null string (" ").

The NDX() function is especially useful for managing more than one open index file when you don't know the underlying .NDX file names.

Example

The following example sets up two .NDX index files for the CUSTOMER database. The first, ORDNO.NDX, indexes CUSTOMER by the Order_no field. The second, ZIPCODE.NDX, indexes CUSTOMER by the Zip field.

```
. USE Customer
. INDEX ON Order_no TO Ordno
  100% indexed          33 Records indexed
. INDEX ON Zip TO Zipcode
  100% indexed          33 Records indexed
```

The next series of commands opens the two index files, ORDNO.NDX and ZIPCODE.NDX, and orders the CUSTOMER database by ORDNO.NDX. The DISPLAY STATUS command shows the open .NDX files, as well as the contents of the production .MDX file. Finally, the NDX() function confirms the order of the .NDX index files.

```
. SET INDEX TO Ordno, Zipcode ORDER Ordno
Master index: ORDNO
. DISPLAY STATUS

Currently Selected Database:
Select area:  1, Database in Use: C:\DB4CR\PART6\CUSTOMER.DBF   Alias: CUSTOMER
Master Index file:  C:\DB4CR\PART6\ORDNO.NDX  Key: Order_no
           Index file:  C:\DB4CR\PART6\ZIPCODE.NDX  Key: Zip
Production   MDX file:  C:\DB4CR\PART6\CUSTOMER.MDX
           Index TAG:     CUST_NAME  Key: Lastname+Firstname
           Index TAG:     CUST_NO  Key: Cust_no

. ? NDX(1)
C:ORDNO.NDX
. ? NDX(2)
C:ZIPCODE.NDX
```

NETWORK()

The NETWORK() function lets you determine whether dBASE IV is running on a network. It returns logical true (.T.) or logical false (.F.).

Syntax

NETWORK()

Notes

Use the NETWORK() function to determine whether a network is present. If so, your program could, for example, execute some network-specific code.

Example

The following example indicates that a network is not present:

```
. ? NETWORK()
.F.
```

For other environment-related functions, see OS() and GETENV().

ORDER()

The ORDER() function returns the name of the controlling index, or .MDX tag, for a database.

Syntax

ORDER([<*alias*>])

The optional *alias* argument lets you use a database's alias to determine the value of ORDER() for a database in a noncurrent work area. (See the USE command for setting up an alias.) If you do not include an alias name, ORDER() operates in the current work area.

Notes

If an .NDX file is the active index file, ORDER() returns the root portion of the file name (without the .NDX extension) in uppercase letters. If there is no active .NDX file, ORDER() returns the name of the .MDX tag name.

Example

```
. USE Customer ORDER Cust_no
Master index: CUST_NO
. ? ORDER("Customer")
CUST_NO
. SET ORDER TO TAG Cust_name
Master index: CUST_NAME
. ? ORDER()
CUST_NAME
```

OS()

The OS() function returns the name of the operating system in which dBASE IV is running.

Syntax

OS()

Example

```
. ? OS()
DOS 3.30
```

PAD()

The PAD() function lets you monitor activity within the active bar menu. It returns a string corresponding to the most recently selected PAD within the menu.

Syntax

PAD()

Notes

The PAD() function returns the active PAD name. A PAD becomes the most recently selected option PAD when you highlight a menu option and press ENTER. If you press ESC, PAD() returns a null string.

Example

The following program sets up a simple menu bar with two pop-ups, **Sort** and **Exit**. When you highlight an option from within one of the pop-ups and press ENTER, the program displays the results of the PAD() function. For example, if the cursor is located on the Sort/Ascending menu option and you press ENTER, the program displays "SORT" at row 12, column 1, on the screen.

```
*
* This program creates a simple menu with two pop-ups, then
*     shows the results of the MENU(), POPUP(), and PAD()
*     functions.
*

* Create Main menu and define its two pads

DEFINE MENU Main
DEFINE PAD Sort OF Main PROMPT "Sort Database" AT 2,6
DEFINE PAD Exit OF Main PROMPT "Exit" AT 2,20

* Assign pop-ups to pads

ON PAD Sort OF Main ACTIVATE POPUP Sort_pop
ON PAD Exit OF Main ACTIVATE POPUP Exit_pop

* Define Sort pad's pop-up and two bars

DEFINE POPUP Sort_pop FROM 3,6 MESSAGE "Select sort order"
DEFINE BAR 1 OF Sort_pop PROMPT "Ascending"
DEFINE BAR 2 OF Sort_pop PROMPT "Descending"

* Define Exit pad's pop-up and bar

DEFINE POPUP Exit_pop FROM 3,20 MESSAGE "Exit program"
DEFINE BAR 1 OF Exit_pop PROMPT "Exit to dot prompt"

* Setup procedures for pop-ups

ON SELECTION POPUP Sort_pop DO Sort_proc
ON SELECTION POPUP Exit_pop DO Exit_proc

* Activate Main menu

ACTIVATE MENU Main
```

```
RETURN

* These procedures do nothing except return the value of MENU(),
*    POPUP(), and PAD().

PROCEDURE Sort_proc
@ 10,1 SAY MENU()
@ 11,1 SAY POPUP()
@ 12,1 SAY PAD()
RETURN

PROCEDURE Exit_proc
@ 10,1 SAY MENU()
@ 11,1 SAY POPUP()
@ 12,1 SAY PAD()
RETURN
```

Some other commands and functions related to menus are DEFINE BAR, DEFINE MENU, DEFINE PAD, DEFINE POPUP, ON PAD, MENU(), and POPUP().

PAYMENT()

The PAYMENT() function calculates the payment required to amortize a loan, given the beginning amount of the principal, the interest rate, and the number of payments.

Syntax

PAYMENT(<*principal*>, <*interest rate*>, <*periods*>)

Principal is a type N numeric expression representing the beginning amount of the principal on the loan.

Interest rate is the interest rate and must be positive. The PAYMENT() function assumes a constant interest rate over the life of the loan. If you are using a yearly interest rate but the payments occur monthly, you should divide the rate by 12.

Periods is a type N numeric expression representing the number of payment periods. dBASE IV rounds off any fractional amounts.

Notes

The PAYMENT() function is an easy method to determine the loan payment required to borrow a specific amount at a fixed rate of interest.

Example

The following example determines the payment required for a $100,000 15-year loan at 9.88%.

```
. INPUT "Enter the principal amount of the loan: " TO Principal
Enter the principal amount of the loan: 100000
. INPUT "Enter the interest rate: " TO Int_rate
Enter the interest rate: .0988
. INPUT "Enter the term in years: " TO Years
Enter the term in years: 15
. ? PAYMENT(Principal, Int_rate/12, Years*12)
      1067.28
```

PCOL()

The PCOL() function lets you track the current printer column position from within a program. It returns the current column position of the printer relative to _ploffset (a system memory variable for the page left offset).

Syntax

PCOL()

Notes

Use the PCOL() function for relative addressing during printing. The value returned by PCOL() is relative to the current _ploffset. That is, you must add the PCOL() value to the _ploffset value to determine the exact column position on the page.

PCOL() and the special operator $ have the same effect when you use them with @...SAY and @...GET commands to indicate the column position on the printed page. For example, the following two commands are synonymous:

```
@ 1, PCOL() + 20 SAY "Total"

@ 1, $ + 20 SAY "Total"
```

They both print "Total" 20 character positions to the right of the current print-head position.

While PCOL() works only with the printer, you can use the $ special operator to control both the printer and the display.

Example

The following example shows the column position of the printer before and after you print the message "Hello world".

```
. SET DEVICE TO PRINTER
. ? PCOL()
        0
. @ 1, PCOL() SAY "Hello world"
. ? PCOL()
       11
. SET DEVICE TO SCREEN
```

PI()

The PI() function returns the value of the constant π, approximately 3.14159.

Syntax

PI()

Notes

The SET DECIMALS and SET PRECISION commands affect the accuracy of the displayed value of PI().

Example

The following example shows a way to calculate the circumference of a circle with a radius of 3:

```
. ? PI()
          3.14
. r = 3
          3
. Circumf = PI() * r^2
         28.27
```

POPUP()

Use the POPUP() function to determine the name of the active pop-up menu.

Syntax

POPUP()

Notes

The POPUP() function returns the name of the active pop-up menu in uppercase character string format.

Example

The following example shows that the active pop-up is Exit_pop.

```
. ? POPUP()
EXIT_POP
```

For another POPUP() example, see the PAD() function.

For other commands and functions related to pop-up menus, see DEFINE POPUP, ACTIVATE POPUP, BAR(), PAD(), and MENU().

PRINTSTATUS()

The PRINTSTATUS() function lets you determine whether the printer is ready for output. It returns true (.T.) if the printer is ready and false (.F.) if it is not.

Syntax

```
PRINTSTATUS()
```

Notes

Before you print a report, you can check the status of the print device with PRINTSTATUS(). It checks the status of the most recently selected printer. You can select the printer with any one of the following methods:

- SET PRINTER ON
- SET DEVICE TO PRINTER
- CTRL-P
- Any command that allows a TO PRINTER clause

Example

The following example checks the printer with PRINTSTATUS() before sending output the printer.

```
DO WHILE .T.
     CLEAR
     @ 5,15 SAY 'Please be sure printer is ready'
     WAIT
     IF .NOT. PRINTSTATUS()          && Printer not ready?
          LOOP                       &&   then loop again
     ENDIF
ENDDO
USE Account ORDER Checkno
REPORT FORM Acct5 TO PRINT
RETURN
```

PROGRAM()

The PROGRAM() function lets you determine what program or procedure was executing when an error occurred.

Syntax

PROGRAM()

Notes

The PROGRAM() function returns, in character string form, the name of the program or procedure that was executing. For programs, PROGRAM() does not include the file extension. For procedures, PROGRAM() returns the actual procedure name, not the name of the file containing the procedure.

You can use PROGRAM() as a debugging tool in any of the following ways:

- If an error occurs when you're executing a program from the dot prompt, select **Suspend** and PROGRAM() determines the errant program or procedure.

- You can place PROGRAM() within a program file (see the example that follows).
- You can also use PROGRAM() in the Breakpoint and Display windows of the dBASE IV Debugger. (For information on the Debugger, see the DEBUG command in Chapter 31, "dBASE IV Commands." Chapter 25, "Debugging Your Program," also covers the Debugger in detail.)

Example

When placed in a program, the following statement uses the PROGRAM(), LINENO(), and ERROR() functions to return a detailed error message to the screen.

```
ON ERROR ? "***Error in " + PROGRAM() + " line " +;
     LTRIM(STR(LINENO())) + ".  Error number is " +;
     LTRIM(STR(ERROR())) + "."
```

A sample error message produced by this statement is "***Error in ACCOUNT line 5. Error number is 29."

For other functions and commands related to debugging, see DEBUG, SUSPEND, RESUME, SET DEVELOPMENT, and LINENO().

PROMPT()

The PROMPT() function returns the prompt of the most recently selected pop-up menu option.

Syntax

PROMPT()

Notes

PROMPT() returns a text string that mimics the prompt of the most recently selected option from a menu or pop-up. If you press ESC to exit the menu or pop-up, or no menu or pop-up is active, PROMPT() returns a null string (" ").

When you define a pop-up using the DEFINE POPUP command, you can include any of three different prompt options—FIELD, FILES, and STRUCTURE—to control the contents of the pop-up's window. If you use any of these options, the PROMPT() function returns varying results, as follows:

FIELD	Returns the contents of the chosen field
FILES	Returns the path, file name, and file extension
STRUCTURE	Returns the field name

Example

The following program creates a simple pop-up menu and then displays the prompt from the chosen option using the PROMPT() function. For example, if you select the **Ascending** pop-up menu option, the program displays the message "You selected Ascending" on line 10 of the screen.

```
* Define a popup with two bars

DEFINE POPUP Sort_pop FROM 3,6 MESSAGE "Select sort order"
DEFINE BAR 1 OF Sort_pop PROMPT "Ascending"
DEFINE BAR 2 OF Sort_pop PROMPT "Descending"

* Setup procedure for popup

ON SELECTION POPUP Sort_pop DO Sort_proc

* Activate popup
```

```
ACTIVATE POPUP Sort_pop

RETURN

* This procedure displays the prompt on the screen

PROCEDURE Sort_proc
@ 10,1 SAY "You selected " + PROMPT()
DEACTIVATE POPUP
RETURN
```

For other commands and functions related to pop-ups and menus, see BAR(), POPUP(), DEFINE POPUP, ON SELECTION POPUP, and ON SELECTION PAD.

PROW()

The PROW() function returns the current row position of the printer.

Syntax

PROW()

Notes

Use the PROW() function for relative addressing during printing. After a page eject, PROW() is set to 0. As the print head moves down the page, PROW() is incremented accordingly.

Example

The following example shows the printer row position before and after printing a message.

```
. SET DEVICE TO PRINTER
. ? PROW()
        0
. @ PROW()+10,1 SAY "Now printing on line " + LTRIM(STR(PROW()))
. ? PROW()
       10
. SET DEVICE TO SCREEN
```

For other printer-related functions and commands, see PCOL(), ROW(), COL(), @, EJECT, SET DEVICE, and SET PRINTER.

PV()

The PV() function returns the present value of an annuity, given the payment per period, the discount rate, and the number of payment periods.

Syntax

PV(<*payment*>, <*discount rate*>, <*periods*>)

Payment is a type N numeric expression which can be positive or negative.

Discount rate is the interest rate and must be positive. The PV() function assumes that interest is compounded each period. Therefore, if you are using a yearly interest rate but interest is compounded monthly, you should divide the rate by 12.

Periods is a type N numeric expression representing the number of periodic payments.

Notes

The PV() function assumes that payments are made at the end of each period.

Example

The following example uses the PV() function to determine the present value of an annuity in which $225 is invested monthly at a rate of 10% for a period of 36 months:

```
. INPUT "Enter periodic payment: " TO Payment
Enter periodic payment: 225.00
. INPUT "Enter discount rate: " TO Discount
Enter discount rate: .10
. INPUT "Enter number of payment periods: " TO Periods
Enter number of payment periods: 36
. ? PV(Payment, Discount/12, Periods)
      6973.03
```

For other financial functions, see @FV and @PAYMENT.

RAND()

The RAND() function returns a random number between 0 and 0.999999, inclusive.

Syntax

RAND([<*type N expression*>])

By using the optional *type N expression*, you can seed the random number generator. If you enter a negative number, dBASE IV uses the system clock to generate the seed.

Notes

The RAND() function generates a random number, whether you include an argument or not. When you use RAND() without an argument, it starts with 100001 as the default number for the seed and then generates numbers in sequence.

By starting with the same seed value each time, you can reconstruct the exact number sequence. For example, if you start with 56 as the seed number and use RAND() without an argument, dBASE IV generates the following sequence of numbers:

```
. ? RAND(56)
        0.31
. ? RAND()
        0.12
. ? RAND()
        0.44
```

To reproduce the same sequence of numbers, start with the same seed value.

Example

The following example generates a sequence of random numbers after seeding the random number generator from the system clock.

```
. ? RAND(-1)
        0.51
. ? RAND()
        0.92
. ? RAND()
        0.52
```

READKEY()

The READKEY() function returns an integer corresponding to the key you press when exiting from a full-screen command. This function also indicates whether changes where made to the data during the full-screen command.

Syntax

READKEY()

Notes

Use READKEY() in programming to determine which key the user pressed to exit any of the full-screen commands (APPEND, BROWSE, CHANGE, CREATE, EDIT, INSERT, MODIFY, and READ). Your program can then branch based on the return value. If the user changes any of the data during one of these commands, the integer returned by READKEY() also changes.

Table 33-3 shows the values for READKEY(). The first column lists the integers returned by READKEY() when the user exits a full-screen command and does not change any data; the code numbers returned are between 1 and 36. If the user changes any field on the screen, however, READKEY() returns the values in column 2. Notice that the code numbers are increased by 256 when data is changed.

Example

The following program segment uses the values returned by READKEY() to determine how you exited a screen. If you type past the end of the screen without making any changes, READKEY() returns a value of 15 and the program skips to the next record. However, if you modify the contents of any of the memory variables on the screen and press CTRL-END, READKEY() returns a value of 270. In this case, the program saves the memory variables to a record in the database.

```
SET FORMAT TO Somescrn
READ
IF READKEY() = 15              && If no change in data,
     SKIP                      &&   show the next record
ENDIF
IF READKEY() = 270             && If change in data, update record
     REPLACE Field1 WITH MField1, Field2 WITH MField2
ENDIF
```

Non-Updated Code Number	Updated Code Number	Key Pressed	Meaning
0	256	CTRL-S, LEFT ARROW, CTRL-H	Backward one character
---	256	BACKSPACE	Backward one character
1	257	CTRL-D, CTRL-L, RIGHT ARROW	Forward one character
4	260	CTRL-E, CTRL-K, UP ARROW	Backward one field
5	261	CTRL-J, CTRL-X, DOWN ARROW	Forward one field
6	262	CTRL-R, PGUP	Backward one screen
7	263	CTRL-C, PGDN	Forward one screen
12	---	CTRL-Q, \ ESC	Terminate without save
---	270	CTRL-W, CTRL-END	Terminate with save
15	271	ENTER, CTRL-M	ENTER pressed or last record filled
16	---	ENTER, CTRL-M	At beginning of record in APPEND
33	289	CTRL-HOME	Menu display toggle
34	290	CTRL-PGUP	Zoom out
35	291	CTRL-PGDN	Zoom in
36	292	F1	Help function key

Table 33-3. READKEY( ) Values

See Chapter 22, "The User Interface," for another example of READKEY().

For other commands and functions related to getting input, see INKEY(), LASTKEY(), ON KEY, and READ.

RECCOUNT()

The RECCOUNT() function returns the number of records in an active database file.

Syntax

RECCOUNT([<*alias*>])

The optional *alias* argument lets you use RECCOUNT() with a database in a non-current work area. (See the USE command for setting up an alias.) If you do not include an alias name, RECCOUNT() operates in the current work area.

Notes

With the RECCOUNT() function, you can determine the total number of records in a database without moving the record pointer. RECCOUNT() returns a value that includes all records, regardless of whether certain records are marked for deletion or you've set up a filter (SET FILTER is ON). If there are no records in the database, RECCOUNT() returns a value of 0.

Example

The following example determines the number of records in the CUSTOMER database:

```
. USE Customer
. ? RECCOUNT()
        33
```

RECNO()

The RECNO() function returns the current record number in an active database file.

Syntax

RECNO([<*alias*>])

The optional *alias* argument lets you use RECNO() with a database in a noncurrent work area. (See the USE command for setting up an alias.) If you do not include an alias name, RECNO() operates in the current work area.

Notes

The RECNO() function returns 0 when there are no records in the database (EOF() is logical true). It returns 1 in the following cases:

- There is no database file in use.
- The record pointer is located before the first record in the database (BOF() is logical true).

If the record pointer is located past the last record in the file (EOF() is logical true), RECNO() returns the number of records in the database plus 1.

Example

```
. USE Customer
. ? RECNO()
         1
```

```
. ? BOF()
.F.
. SKIP -1
CUSTOMER: Record No       1
. ? RECNO()
          1
. ? BOF()
.T.
. GO BOTTOM
CUSTOMER: Record No      33
. ? RECNO()
         33
. SKIP
CUSTOMER: Record No      34
. ? RECNO()
         34
```

RECSIZE()

The RECSIZE() function returns the size of a record in an active database file.

Syntax

RECSIZE([<*alias*>])

The optional *alias* argument lets you use RECSIZE() with a database in a noncurrent work area. (See the USE command for setting up an alias.) If you do not include an alias name, RECSIZE() operates in the current work area.

Notes

If your program backs up database files, you can use the RECSIZE(), RECCOUNT(), and DISKSPACE() functions to determine the amount of disk space required. The first part of the program should include a code segment that determines whether there is sufficient space for the file header. You can determine the header size using the equation

$$32 * \textit{<number of fields>} + 35$$

Examples

The following example determines the size of a record in the CUSTOMER database file.

```
. USE Customer
. ? RECSIZE()
       229
```

The next example determines if there is sufficient space before copying an entire database file to a floppy disk in drive A.

```
*
* Program to backup an entire database to a floppy in drive A.
*
SET TALK OFF
ACCEPT "Enter a file to backup: " TO Mfilename
USE &Mfilename
Field_no = 0
DO WHILE "" <> FIELD(Field_no + 1)   && Find number of fields
     Field_no = Field_no + 1
ENDDO
Mheader = 32 * Field_no + 35         && Determine file header size
Mfilesize = RECCOUNT() * RECSIZE() + Mheader     && and file size
SET DEFAULT TO A
WAIT "Place a disk in drive A.  Press any key to continue..."
IF DISKSPACE() < Mfilesize
     ? "Not enough room on this disk"
ELSE
     COPY TO A:\<backup name>
ENDIF
CLOSE DATABASE
SET DEFAULT TO C
SET TALK ON
```

See the DISKSPACE() function for another variation of the database backup program.

REPLICATE()

The REPLICATE() function repeats a character string a given number of times.

Syntax

REPLICATE(*<string expression>*, *<type N expression>*)

Notes

REPLICATE() returns a character string that repeats *string expression* the number of times specified in *type N expression*. The total length of the returned string cannot exceed 254.

Examples

This example uses the REPLICATE() function to repeat the pattern "* " 20 times.

```
. ? REPLICATE("* ",20)
* * * * * * * * * * * * * * * * * * * *
```

The next block of code repeats the same pattern across the width of a report.

```
INPUT "Enter the left margin: " TO L_margin
INPUT "Enter the right margin: " TO R_margin
SET DEVICE TO PRINTER
@ PROW(), L_margin SAY REPLICATE("* ",(R_margin - L_margin) / 2)
SET DEVICE TO SCREEN
```

RIGHT()

The RIGHT() function returns a specified number of characters from a character string or memory variable, beginning from the right-most character.

Syntax

RIGHT(*<character string>*/*<variable>*, *<type N expression>*)

Type N expression is the number of characters to extract. If it is greater than the length of *character string*, RIGHT() returns the entire string.

Examples

The following example extracts the three right-most characters from a string:

```
. ? RIGHT("123 Soquel Dr.",3)
Dr.
```

The next example combines RIGHT(), LEN(), and AT() to extract all the characters from a string starting after the first blank.

```
. Street = "59 Temple St."
59 Temple St.
. ? RIGHT(Street,LEN(Street) - AT(" ",Street))
Temple St.
```

For other functions related to manipulating strings, see AT(), LTRIM(), LEFT(), RTRIM(), STUFF(), SUBSTR(), and TRIM().

RLOCK()/LOCK()

Use the RLOCK() function in the multi-user version of dBASE IV to lock multiple records. (RLOCK() and LOCK() are equivalent.) See Chapter 33, "Networking Commands and Functions," for a complete description of RLOCK().

ROLLBACK()

The ROLLBACK() function lets you determine whether the last ROLLBACK command was successful.

Syntax

ROLLBACK()

Notes

In dBASE IV transaction processing, transactions must be explicitly bounded by a BEGIN TRANSACTION and an END TRANSACTION or ROLLBACK command. The ROLLBACK() function lets you determine whether a ROLLBACK command was successfully executed.

By default, the ROLLBACK() function returns true (.T.). However, if you execute a ROLLBACK command and it is not successful, ROLLBACK() returns false (.F.).

Example

See the example for the COMPLETED() function in this chapter. Also, Chapter 30, "Networking Commands and Functions," shows how to use COMPLETED() in a network environment.

For other commands and functions related to transaction processing, see BEGIN TRANSACTION/END TRANSACTION, ROLLBACK, CONVERT, COMPLETED(), ISMARKED(), CHANGE(), and LKSYS().

ROUND()

The ROUND() function rounds a number to a given number of decimal places.

Syntax

ROUND(*<type N expression1>*, *<type N expression2>*)

Type N expression1 is the number to be rounded, and *type N expression2* is the number of decimals places to round to.

Notes

If you include a negative number for the *type N expression2*, ROUND() rounds to the left of the decimal. For example, ROUND(1292,-2) returns 1300.

Examples

```
. ? ROUND(34.5678,2)
        34.570
. ? ROUND(128.1219,3)
       128.122
. ? ROUND(44.3,0)
        44
. ? ROUND(10.78,-1)
        10
```

Related functions are CEILING(), FLOOR(), and INT().

ROW()

The ROW() function returns the row in which the cursor is currently positioned.

Syntax

ROW()

Notes

You can use the ROW() function for relative addressing when writing information to the screen. ROW() is always equal to 21 when running commands at the dot prompt, unless SET STATUS is OFF, in which case ROW() equals 24.

Example

The following example displays the title "Sales Analysis" starting at row 4, column 14 on the screen. It then uses relative addressing to display "ABC Corporation" two lines below.

```
@ 4,14 SAY "Sales Analysis"
@ ROW()+2,10 SAY "ABC Corporation"
```

See also COL(), PCOL(), and PROW().

RTOD()

The RTOD() function converts radians to degrees.

Syntax

RTOD(*<type N expression>*)

Type N expression represents an angle in degrees.

Example

The following example shows how to use RTOD() with one of dBASE IV'S trigonometric functions, ACOS().

```
. SET DECIMALS TO 5
. Side = 4
         4
. Hypotenuse = 5
         5
. Angle = ACOS(Side/Hypotenuse)
         0.64350
. Degrees = RTOD(Angle)
        36.86990
```

The angle is approximately 36.87 degrees.

For other trigonometric functions, see SIN(), COS(), TAN(), ASIN(), ACOS(), ATAN(), ATN2(), and DTOR().

RTRIM()

The RTRIM() function trims the trailing blanks from a character string. RTRIM() and TRIM() are equivalent.

Syntax

RTRIM(<*string expression*>)

Notes

When you enter a character string into a database field and the string is less than the total width of the field, dBASE IV pads the string with blanks. You can remove the padded blanks with the RTRIM() function.

Example

```
. USE Customer
. ? Firstname + Lastname
George          Thomas
. ? TRIM(Firstname) + " " + Lastname
George Thomas
```

For other string-manipulation functions, see LEFT(), TRIM(), RIGHT(), LEFT(), and SUBSTR().

SEEK()

The SEEK() function lets you look up records in an indexed database. It returns logical true (.T.) if an index key is found and logical false (.F.) if the key is not found.

Syntax

SEEK(<*expression*> [,<*alias*>])

The optional *alias* argument lets you use SEEK() with a database in a noncurrent work area. (See the USE command for setting up an alias.) If you do not include an alias name, SEEK() operates in the current work area.

Notes

To locate a record in an indexed database, you can use SEEK with FOUND(), as follows:

```
SEEK Lastname
IF FOUND()
     ? "Current record is "+Lastname
ENDIF
```

To accomplish the same task with SEEK(), you can enter

```
IF SEEK(Lastname)
     ? "Current record is "+Lastname
ENDIF
```

SEEK() produces the same effect as the SEEK and FOUND() combination because it moves the record pointer and produces a logical result.

Example

The following program activates the CUSTOMER database in work area 1. It then moves to work area 2 and activates the ORDERREC database. Next, it uses the SEEK() function to move the record pointer in the noncurrent work area—work area 1.

```
. USE Customer ORDER Cust_no
Master index: CUST_NO
. SELECT 2
. USE Orderrec
. GO 10
ORDERREC: Record No      10
. ? Cust_no
1010
. ? Customer->Cust_no
1001
. ? SEEK(Cust_no, "Customer")
.T.
. ? Customer->Cust_no
1010
```

For other index-related commands and functions, see FIND, SEEK, LOOKUP(), and FOUND().

SELECT()

The SELECT() function allows you to determine the number of the highest unused work area. It returns a number from 1 to 10, inclusive.

Syntax

SELECT()

Example

SELECT() returns the number of the highest unused work area, not the next highest unused work area. Suppose, for example, you have databases active in work areas 1 and 2. If you enter SELECT(), you get the following results:

```
. ? SELECT()
        10
```

SET()

The SET() function returns the status of the SET commands. It returns ON, OFF, or an integer.

Syntax

SET(<*string expression*>)

String expression is the keyword following SET for any SET command that accepts an integer or an ON/OFF value.

Notes

Some SET commands can accept both an integer and an ON/OFF value. With these commands, SET() returns only ON or OFF.

Example

The following example determines the status of the SET COLOR command:

```
. ? SET("COLOR")
ON
```

SIGN()

The SIGN() function lets you determine the sign of a numeric expression. It returns one of the following values.

Number Type	Return Value
Positive	1
Negative	-1
Zero	0

Syntax

SIGN(<*type N expression*>)

Example

```
. ? SIGN(123)
         -1
. ? SIGN(-123)
        -1
. ? SIGN(0)
         -0
```

SIN()

The SIN() function returns the sine of an angle given in radians.

Syntax

SIN(<*type N expression*>)

The type N numeric expression is the size of an angle in radians. To convert an angle in degrees to radians for use with the SIN() function, use the DTOR() function. The values returned by SIN() vary between -1 and 1. The SIN() function returns a type F number.

Example

The following example determines the sine for an angle of 60 degrees.

```
. SET DECIMALS TO 5
. ? SIN(DTOR(60))
        0.86603
```

SOUNDEX()

The SOUNDEX() command creates a sound-alike code. This code performs a phonetic search on a database when you don't know the exact spelling of an entry.

Syntax

SOUNDEX(<*string expression*>)

Notes

The SOUNDEX() function lets you look up a record in a database when you don't know the exact spelling.

The SOUNDEX() function creates a four-character code of the form "letter digit digit digit" to perform the sound-alike search. It uses the following rules to create the code:

- It skips any initial blank spaces and uses the first letter of the character string for the first character in the sound-alike code. For example, if you enter **"Borrowes"** for the character string, dBASE IV retains the initial B for the first character in the code.

- It eliminates all cases of the letters a, e, i, o, u, h, w, y, except when one of these letters is the first character in the character string. For example, "Borrowes" becomes "Brrs" for purposes of determining the sound-alike code.

- It assigns numbers to the remaining values, using the following table:

Letter	Number
b f p	1
c g j k q s x z	2
d t	3
l	4
m n	5
r	6

  For example, "Brrs" becomes "B662".

- If adjacent letters have the same code, SOUNDEX() drops all but the first letter. For example, "B662" becomes "B62".

- To produce a full 4-character code of the form "letter digit digit digit," SOUNDEX() adds trailing zeros when there are less than three digits after the initial alpha. If there are more than three digits, it drops all the excess digits. In the current example, it produces the code "B620".

- If you include nonalphabetical characters in the character string you pass to SOUNDEX(), it stops at the first nonalphabetical character. For example, if the first character in the string is nonalphabetical, it creates the code "0000".

Example

The following example indexes the CUSTOMER database according to sound-alike codes. Next, it prompts for a last name to search for within the indexed database. It then seeks a record with a similar name based on the sound-alike code. Finally, it displays a record with a similar last name.

```
. USE Customer
. INDEX ON SOUNDEX(Lastname) TO Phonetic
  100% indexed          33 Records indexed
. ACCEPT "Enter a lastname to search for: " TO Mlast
Enter a lastname to search for: Borrowes
. Phon_code = SOUNDEX(Mlast)
B620
. SEEK Phon_code
. DISPLAY Firstname, Lastname
Record#  Firstname         Lastname
     14  Brian             Borros
```

The function DIFFERENCE() determines the difference between two sound-alike codes.

SPACE()

The SPACE() function generates a blank character string of a given length.

Syntax

SPACE(<*type N expression*>)

Notes

The maximum number of spaces you can generate with the SPACE() function is 254.

Example

The following example creates a memory variable of ten blank spaces.

```
. STORE SPACE(10) TO Ten_blanks
. ? "Sherman"+Ten_blanks+"Peabody"
Sherman          Peabody
```

SQRT()

The SQRT() function returns the square root of a given positive number.

Syntax

SQRT(<*type N expression*>/<*type F expression*>)

You can specify a type N or a type F number for SQRT(). However, SQRT() always returns a type F number.

Examples

```
. ? SQRT(144)
        12
. ? SQRT(13*13)
        13
```

STR()

The STR() function converts a number to a character string.

Syntax

STR(<*type N expression*> [,<*length*>] [,<*decimal*>])

The optional *length* option lets you stipulate the overall length of the string that STR() creates. STR() returns asterisks if you enter a number less than the total number of digits to the left of the decimal in *type N expression*. When determining a value for *length*, keep in mind that each decimal place takes one character, as do the decimal point and minus sign, if present.

The *decimal* option represents the total number of decimal places to be included in the string.

Notes

If you do not include a *length* or *decimal* option, STR() creates a string with the following attributes:

- An overall length of ten characters
- The number is rounded to an integer

Examples

```
. Num = 1234.6789
      1234.68
. ? STR(Num, 6)
1235
. ? STR(Num, 6, 1)
1234.7
. ? STR(Num, 7, 2)
1234.68
. ? STR(Num, 8, 2)
1234.68
```

STUFF()

The STUFF() function lets you replace one part of a character string with another given character string.

Syntax

STUFF(<*string expression1*>, <*type N expression1*>, <*type N expression2*>, <*string expression2*>)

String expression1 can be a string expression or variable name. It represents the original string in which you want to do the replacing.

Type N expression1 and *type N expression2* are numeric expressions. *Type N expression1* indicates the position at which the substitution is to start. *Type N expression2* represents the number of characters to be removed from the original string.

String expression2 is a string expression or variable name representing the string to be inserted within the original string.

Notes

The STUFF() function lets you substitute one string within another (*string expression2* within *string expression1*), without having to build a complex string expression. Assigning values to the different options actually removes a part of the original string (beginning at *type N expression1* and extending for a length of *type N expression2*) before inserting the new string.

If you set *type N expression2* to 0, no characters are removed from the original string and *string expression2* is inserted.

If *type N expression1* is 0, STUFF() actually uses 1, which may cause some unexpected results. For example, suppose you use AT("*", Field1) for *type N expression1*. If Field1 does not contain an asterisk and the function resolves to 0, STUFF() performs the substitution anyway beginning at position 1.

If *type N expression1* is greater than the length of the original string, STUFF() concatenates *string expression2* to the end of the original string.

If *type N expression2* is greater than the length of *string expression2*, the original string will grow in length. Likewise, if *type N expression2* is less than *string expression2*, the original string will shrink.

Example

The following example shows how you can use the STUFF() and AT() functions together to replace part of one string with another.

```
. STORE "Venix 100X Processor" TO Item
Venix 100X Processor
. ? STUFF(Item, AT("10", Item), 2, "5")
Venix 50X Processor
```

SUBSTR()

The SUBSTR() function lets you extract one string from another, beginning at a given starting position and extending for a given length.

Syntax

SUBSTR(*<string expression>/<memo field name>*, *<start po-sition>* [,*<number of characters>*])

If you do not include the optional *number of characters* argument, SUBSTR() returns a substring that begins at *start position* and extends to the end of the original character string.

Notes

If you include a *number of characters* that, when added to *start position*, is greater than the length of the original string, SUBSTR() returns a string beginning at *start position* and extending to the end of the original string.

Example

The following example extracts the substring "14" from the string "12 13 14 15 16".

```
. Master = "12 13 14 15 16"
12 13 14 15 16
. ? SUBSTR(Master,7,2)
14
```

For other string-related functions, see AT(), LEFT(), RIGHT(), STUFF(), LTRIM(), and STR().

TAG()

The TAG() function returns the name of an index in a given .MDX file.

Syntax

TAG([<*.MDX filename*>,] <*type N expression*> [,<*alias*>])

The optional *.MDX filename* lets you reference a specific .MDX file. If you do not include this option, TAG() uses all the open indexes.

Type N expression specifies the .MDX file position in the index file name list. You set up the index file name list using the SET INDEX TO <*index filename list*> command. dBASE IV maintains a directory of open index files.

The optional *alias* argument lets you use TAG() in a noncurrent work area. (See the USE command for setting up an alias.) If you do not include an alias name, TAG() operates in the current work area.

Notes

Use the SET INDEX TO command to open index files. These files can include both index (.NDX) and multiple index (.MDX) files.

The TAG() function lets you determine exactly what index files are open and, in the case of .MDX files, the tags within those files. It returns the name of an index file (.NDX) or an .MDX tag.

Example

The following example uses the TAG() function to return the names of the first two tags in the production .MDX file for the CUSTOMER database:

```
. USE Customer
. ? TAG(1)
CUST_NAME
. ? TAG(2)
CUST_NO
```

For other functions and command related to indexes, see KEY(), MDX(), NDX(), ORDER(), and SET INDEX.

TAN()

The TAN() function returns the tangent of an angle specified in radians.

Syntax

TAN(<*type N expression*>)

The *type N expression* is the size of an angle in radians. To convert an angle in degrees to radians for use with the TAN() function, use the DTOR() function.

Notes

The values returned by TAN() increase from 0 to infinity when *type N expression* is between 0 and $\pi/2$ radians. The TAN() function returns a type F number.

Example

The following example computes the tangent of 45 degrees:

```
. ? RTOD(PI()/4)
        45
. ? TAN(PI()/4)
         1
```

For other trigonometric functions, see SIN(), COS(), ASIN(), ACOS(), ATAN(), and ATN2().

TIME()

The TIME() function returns the system time as a character string. The format of the string is *hh:mm:ss.*

Syntax

TIME()

Notes

Because TIME() returns the system time as a character string, you need to convert it to numbers using SUBSTR() and VAL() if you want to use it in a calculation.

Examples

The following example returns the current system time:

```
. ? TIME()
16:27:03
```

For another example that uses TIME(), see the INKEY() function. The DATE() function returns the current system date.

TRANSFORM()

The TRANSFORM() function lets you format character, logical, date, and numeric data using PICTURE formatting. TRANSFORM() gives you the benefit of PICTURE formatting without your having to use the @...SAY command.

Syntax

TRANSFORM(<*expression*>, <*string expression*>)

String expression is the PICTURE format for *expression*. *Expression* may be a number or a character string.

Notes

The TRANSFORM() function lets you apply PICTURE formatting without using the @...SAY command. It always returns character type data, whether *expression* is character or not.

For a complete list of PICTURE formatting functions and template symbols, see the @ command.

Example

The following example activates the ORDERREC database and formats the Total field for the first record.

```
. USE Orderrec
. ? Total
24.95
. ? TRANSFORM(Total, "@T$##,###.##")
$24.95
```

TYPE()

The TYPE() function returns the data type for a character expression representing the name of a field or memory variable. The data type is returned as a single uppercase letter.

Syntax

TYPE(<*string expression*>)

Notes

The TYPE() function returns one of the following uppercase letters:

Character	Data Type
C	Character
N	Numeric
L	Logical
M	Memo
D	Date
F	Float
U	Undefined

Examples

The following example shows the results of using TYPE() with a numeric and a character string memory variable. In the last TYPE() example, Test_str references the Cust_no field in the CUSTOMER database.

```
. Test_no = 123
       123
. ? TYPE("Test_no")
N
. Test_str = "Cust_no"
Cust_no
. ? TYPE(Test_str)
U
. ? TYPE("Test_str")
C
. USE Customer    && Cust_no is a numeric field in CUSTOMER.DBF
. ? TYPE(Test_str)
N
```

UPPER()

The UPPER() function converts all the characters in a string to uppercase.

Syntax

UPPER(<*string expression*>)

Example

```
. ? UPPER("dBASE IV: The Complete Reference")
DBASE IV: THE COMPLETE REFERENCE
```

See also the functions ISALPHA(), ISLOWER(), ISUPPER(), and LOWER().

USER()

In the multi-user version of dBASE IV, the USER() function returns the log-in name of a user on a system that uses protected files. See Chapter 30, "Networking Commands and Functions," for a complete description.

VAL()

The VAL() function converts character strings that contain numbers into numeric expressions.

Syntax

VAL(<*string expression*>)

Notes

The VAL() function reads the *string expression* starting at the leftmost character in the string. It then converts the numeric characters it encounters into numeric values. It ignores leading spaces, but it stops if it finds a nonnumeric character (such as a trailing blank).

Character strings that represent numbers in scientific notation (for example, 123e2) are converted properly by VAL(). If the character string you supply for VAL() contains a leading nonnumeric character, VAL() returns 0.

Examples

```
. ? VAL("123")
       123
. ? VAL("123ABC")
       123
. ? VAL("123e10")
1230000000000
. ? VAL("ABC")
         0
```

The STR() function converts numbers into character strings.

VARREAD()

The VARREAD() function returns the name of the field or memory variable currently being edited. Use VARREAD() to create context-sensitive help screens.

Syntax

VARREAD()

Notes

When you use @ or any of the full-screen editing commands to get input from the user, dBASE IV keeps track of the name of the field or memory variable currently being modified. To get that field or memory variable name from dBASE IV, use the VARREAD() function.

With VARREAD(), you can create your own context-sensitive help for the value that VARREAD() returns. For example, if, during a full-screen command, the user presses F1 while editing the Address field, you can have your program display a special help window related to entering that field.

Example

The following example shows how to use the VARREAD() function and WINDOW commands to create context-sensitive help. When the user presses F1, the program activates the Help_me procedure.

When coding context-sensitive help, you should know about a special technique used in Help_me. It involves the INKEY() function. Notice that the first INKEY() function clears the F1 key press from the type-ahead buffer. Otherwise, the second INKEY() function would automatically read the F1 key press and would not wait for a key press. Also, by using INKEY(0), you can have a help window display indefinitely, waiting for a key press.

```
*
* Program shows how to use VARRREAD() to create context-sensitive help.
*
SET TALK OFF
ON KEY LABEL F1 DO Help_me
DEFINE WINDOW Help_me FROM 1,15 TO 6,60 DOUBLE
CLEAR
USE Customer
@ 1,8 SAY "  First Name: " GET Firstname
```

```
@ 3,8 SAY "   Last Name: " GET Lastname
@ 5,8 SAY "    Company : " GET Company
@ 7,8 SAY "   Address 1: " GET Addr_1
@ 8,8 SAY "   Address 2: " GET Addr_2
@ 10,8 SAY "       City : " GET City
@ 12,8 SAY "       State: " GET State
@ 12,25 SAY      "   Zip: " GET Zip
@ 14,8 SAY "     Country: " GET Country
@ 14,37 SAY    "   Phone: " GET Telephone
READ

PROCEDURE Help_me
Whatever = INKEY()    && Clear the key buffer of the last key press
ACTIVATE WINDOW Help_me
DO CASE
     CASE VARREAD() = "FIRSTNAME"
          ? "Please enter the customer's first name."
          ? "Make sure you've got the proper spelling."
     CASE VARREAD() = "LASTNAME"
          ? "Please enter the customer's last name."
          ? "Make sure you've got the proper spelling."
     *
     * More CASE commands go here...
     *
ENDCASE
? INKEY(0)     && Pause display indefinitely waiting for key press
DEACTIVATE WINDOW Help_me
RETURN
```

For window and full-screen commands, see DEFINE WINDOW, ACTIVATE WINDOW, READ, EDIT, and APPEND.

VERSION()

The VERSION() function returns the number of the currently running dBASE IV version.

Syntax

VERSION()

Notes

Use the VERSION() function to determine what version of dBASE IV is currently running and to decide whether to use features specific to that version. This function returns the version number that appears on the dBASE IV banner screen.

Example

```
. ? VERSION()
dBASE IV  1.0
```

YEAR()

The YEAR() function takes a date expression and returns the year in 4-digit numeric format.

Syntax

YEAR(<*date expression*>)

Examples

```
. ? YEAR(DATE())
     1988
. Save_year = YEAR({12/30/89})
     1989
. ? TYPE("Save_year")     && YEAR() returns a number, not a string
N
```

dBASE IV System Memory Variables

THIRTY FOUR

dBASE IV system memory variables control aspects of the information flow between dBASE IV and the various output devices attached to the system. An output device is usually a screen, a printer, or a file. There are four variable types: streaming output variables, printer variables, printer task (printjob) variables, and text block variables. The system memory variable groups are shown in Table 34-1. In this chapter, the variables are presented in alphabetical order, and the variable type is indicated in parentheses following each description.

Each time you want something printed, you give the printer a *task* to perform. Whether one page or 200 pages, each request is considered a separate task. (Some people use the word "job" instead of task.) Printer task variables work with the task as a whole and usually are part of an application program.

When the printer ejects a page or prints type in a particular size, it performs functions that are part of its hardware capability. Printer variables control printer-related functions. They don't apply to screen or file output. For example, _wait controls whether the printer stops after it ejects a page.

Certain commands output information as part of their function. With the exception of the @, @...TO, and EJECT commands, commands capable of producing output produce *streaming output*. You control streaming output destinations with the SET CONSOLE, SET PRINTER, and SET ALTERNATE commands and the TO PRINTER/TO FILE options of the LIST and DISPLAY commands.

A block of text is created every time you type a paragraph into a file or enter a line at the dot prompt. Text block variables control

Printer Variables
_padvance
_pdriver
_ploffset
_ppitch
_pquality
_pwait

Printjob Variables
_pbpage
_pcopies
_pecode
_ppeject
_pepage
_pscode

Streaming Output Variables
_box
_pageno
_pcolno
_pform
_plength
_plineno
_pspacing
_tabs

Text Block Variables
_alignment
_indent
_lmargin
_rmargin
_wrap

Table 34-1. System Memory Variable Groups

how text is positioned on the page. For example, you can use the _alignment variable to display right- or left-justified text.

dBASE IV initializes each system memory variable with a default value. You can change these values from the dot prompt, from within an application program, or when you design reports or labels through the Control Center's design screens.

A dBASE IV system memory variable begins with the underscore character (_), which you can't use as the first character in memory variables you create yourself. The CLEAR MEMORY and RELEASE commands don't remove system memory variables from memory.

_alignment

The _alignment variable controls which margin to align text with for ?/?? command output, when _wrap is logical true (.T.) (text block).

Syntax

_alignment = "LEFT"/"CENTER"/"RIGHT"

"LEFT" aligns text with the left margin (left-justified). This is the default.

"CENTER" centers text between left and right margins.

"RIGHT" aligns text with the right margin (right-justified).

Notes

The _alignment variable aligns text between the margins. It only works when _wrap is logical true (.T.).

Related variables and functions: _lmargin, _rmargin, _wrap, @ (PICTURE functions B, I, and J), STR()

Example

This example sets _wrap to logical true so you can view how changing the _alignment variable affects the display. Then it shows the default value for _alignment (left-justified) and displays today's date. Next, it sets the alignment to "CENTER" and displays today's date. Finally, it sets the alignment to "RIGHT" and displays today's date.

```
. _wrap =.T.
.T.
. ? _alignment
LEFT
. ? DATE()
01/17/89
. _alignment = "CENTER"
CENTER
. ? DATE()
                                    01/17/89
. _alignment = "RIGHT"
RIGHT
. ? DATE()
                                                                       01/17/89
```

_box

The _box variable determines when to display boxes defined with the DEFINE BOX command (streaming output).

Syntax

_box = <*condition*>

condition is a logical value, either true (.T.) or false (.F.). Logical true (.T.) is the default.

Notes

For you to show a box created with the DEFINE BOX command, _box must be set to logical true (.T.). Since this is the default, change it only if you don't want the box to show. You can use the _box variable to draw partial boxes by setting _box to false (.F.) in the middle of printing. Then you can set it to true (.T.) later and print the rest of the box.

You can also create boxes with the @...TO command, no matter what _box's value is.

Related command and function: DEFINE BOX, SPACE()

_indent

The _indent variable determines first line indentation for paragraphs output with the ? command. This variable works only when _wrap is logical true (.T.) (text block).

Syntax

_indent = <*number*>

number is limited by the values of _lmargin and _rmargin. Its default is 0.

Notes

The ? command defines where a new paragraph indentation occurs. The ?? command defines where normal indentation is used.

The sum of _indent and _lmargin must be less than the value of _rmargin. _wrap must be logical true (.T.) for indentation to occur.

Related variables and commands: _lmargin, _ploffset, _rmargin, _wrap, ?/??

Example

This example sets _wrap to logical true (.T.), shows the default for _indent, and displays some text. Then it sets _indent to 10 and displays some more text. Next, it sets _indent to 90, intentionally going beyond the right margin, and shows the resulting error message.

```
. _wrap = .T.
.T.
. ? _indent
        0
. ? "No indentation here"
No indentation here
. _indent = 10
       10
. ? "10 spaces indentation here"
          10 spaces indentation here
. _indent = 90
Left margin plus indentation must be less than right margin
```

_lmargin

The _lmargin variable determines the position of the left margin for ? command output when _wrap is logical true (.T.) (text block).

Syntax

_lmargin = <*number*>

number is an integer from 0 to 254, but it is restricted by _rmargin's value. The default is 0.

Notes

The _lmargin variable determines how many spaces to insert before printing text. The sum of _indent and _lmargin must be less than the value of _rmargin. _wrap must be logical true (.T.) for left margin spacing to occur.

_lmargin is not the same as the SET MARGIN command.

Related variables and commands: _indent, _ploffset, _rmargin, _wrap, ?/??

Example

This example sets _wrap to logical true (.T.) and displays memory values using _lmargin's default. Then it sets _lmargin to 10 and displays the same memory variables. Notice the indentation in the second display. Also see the example for the _wrap variable.

```
. _wrap = .T.
.T.
. ? _wrap,_lmargin
.T.          0
. _lmargin = 10
         10
. ? _wrap,_lmargin
          .T.          10
```

_padvance

The _padvance variable controls how the printer advances the paper (printer).

Syntax

_padvance = "FORMFEED"/ "LINEFEEDS"

"FORMFEED" advances the paper one sheet at a time. This is the default.

"LINEFEEDS" advances the paper one line at a time.

Notes

When _padvance is set to "FORMFEED", dBASE IV uses the printer's internal form length setting. When _padvance is set to "LINEFEEDS", dBASE IV calculates the number of line feeds after checking the eject mode.

A page eject is issued from streaming output in the following situations:

- When the EJECT command doesn't have an ON PAGE handler
- When the EJECT command has an ON PAGE handler, but the current line position is beyond the ON PAGE line
- When _peject causes a page eject from within a PRINTJOB/ENDPRINTJOB construct in an application program

When the mode is streaming output, dBASE subtracts the value for _plength from _plineno to calculate the number of line feeds it needs to issue to reach the end of the page.

An eject is issued from any mode other than streaming output in the following situations:

- When you issue an EJECT command
- When SET DEVICE TO PRINTER forces a page eject using an @ command

When the mode is any mode other than streaming output, dBASE subtracts MOD(PROW(),_plength) from _plength.

CHR(12) issues a form feed no matter how you set _padvance.

Sometimes you want to sidestep the printer form feed. Say you want to print mailing labels and the labels are on a strip of paper 30 lines long. By setting the page length variable, _plength, to 30 and the page advance variable, _peject, to "LINEFEEDS", you sidestep the printer's form advance. dBASE IV determines when the labels are at the top of the form.

Make the three system variables—_pageno, _pbpage, and _pepage—consistent and logical. _pageno should be less than or equal to _pepage and greater than or equal to _pbpage for any pages to print. For example, if _pageno = 5 and _pbpage = 7, no pages will print because the starting page is after the page to print. Also, if _pageno = 25 and _pepage = 13, no pages will print because the ending page is before the page to print.

Related variables, command, and function: _peject, _plength, _plineno, EJECT, PROW()

_pageno

The _pageno variable determines or sets the current page number (streaming output).

Syntax

_pageno = <*number*>

number is an integer from 1 to 32,767. The default is 1.

Notes

_pageno starts with an initial value, either 1 (the default) or some other value you assign. The value you assign to _pageno affects the page numbering system. As each page of output is produced, _pageno is incremented.

Before producing output, you can set _pageno to some page other than 1, if you are beginning in the middle of some output. To actually begin in the middle of some output, you need to set the _pbpage variable. You can also use _pageno to print the current page number on your output, since it is incremented each time the command produces a page of output.

The allowed value for _pageno depends on the value of _plineno and _plength.

Related variables and command: _pbpage, _pepage, _plength, _plineno, ON PAGE

_pbpage

The _pbpage variable determines the page output starts on (print-job).

Syntax

_pbpage = <*number*>

number is an integer from 1 to 32,767, representing the starting page number. The default is 1.

Notes

Use _pbpage to recover from paper jams or printer interruptions. When you have a long report, you can start from where the paper jammed instead of reprinting the entire report.

Make the three system variables—_pageno, _pbpage, and _pepage—consistent and logical. _pbpage can't be greater than _pageno (see _pageno).

Related variables and commands: _pageno, _pepage, PRINTJOB/ENDPRINTJOB

_pcolno

The _pcolno variable positions output at the beginning of a particular column in the current line (streaming output).

Syntax

_pcolno = <*number*>

number is an integer from 0 to 255. The default is 0.

Notes

_pcolno keeps track of what column the output is currently in. You can change the column by assigning it a different value. Since _pcolno is incremented for the current column, you can use it to find out the current column position at any given time.

You can use this option to overstrike parts of your text. To do this, set _wrap equal to false (.F.) and set _pcolno to the starting column for the word or words you want to overstrike. Set _pcolno to a value less than its current value. If you set _pcolno to a value less than its current value and _wrap is .T., text in the internal buffer is overwritten but not displayed.

Related variables, functions, and command: _plineno, _rmargin, LEN(), PCOL(), REPLICATE(), TRIM(), SET PRINTER

_pcopies

The _pcopies variable determines how many copies of a particular job to print (printjob, program only).

Syntax

_pcopies = <*number*>

number is an integer from 1 to 32,767. The default is 1.

Notes

This variable requires the PRINTJOB/ENDPRINTJOB command. Set the _pcopies variable before issuing the PRINTJOB command.

Related Commands: @, PRINTJOB/ENDPRINTJOB

_pdriver

The _pdriver variable selects a printer driver (printer).

Syntax

_pdriver = "<*print driver filename*>"

printer driver filename is a normal DOS file name that represents a file containing a particular printer driver. Printer driver files have a .PR2 extension.

Notes

Printer drivers translate dBASE output into code a printer understands. Some printer drivers help a partially compatible printer map the IBM extended character set. When the printer's character set doesn't include IBM extended characters, the printer driver substitutes other characters. For example, it might replace a double-line border symbol with an equal sign (=).

The default driver is whatever you installed during the installation process. dBASE IV put it in your CONFIG.DB file during installation. Thus, when you start dBASE, if *<printer driver filename>*.PR2 exists, the driver is installed and you receive the message "Print driver installed." If *<printer driver filename>*.PR2 doesn't exists, you receive the message "File does not exist."

Available printer drivers are listed when you install dBASE IV. If your printer isn't listed by name, check your printer manual to see if your printer emulates a popular standard, such as Epson or Hewlett-Packard. If it does, use that driver. If not, try using the GENERIC.PR2 printer driver file. If you set _pdriver to "ASCII", dBASE IV generates ASCII text files in place of printer output. Printer codes are not placed in the ASCII text file.

Related variables and commands: _ppitch, _pquality, ?/??, SET PRINTER

_pecode

The _pecode variable provides ending printer control codes (print-job, program only).

Syntax

_pecode = <*character string*>

character string is a range of codes from 0 to 255. Its length can't exceed 255 characters. The default is a null string.

Notes

Use _pecode to restore the original type style settings changed in _pscode.

This variable requires the PRINTJOB/ENDPRINTJOB command. Set the _pecode variable before issuing the ENDPRINTJOB command. Control codes are sent to the printer when the application program issues the ENDPRINTJOB command. To change the type style without using an application program, use the **Style** option of the ?/?? command.

Related variable and commands: _pscode, ?/??, ???, PRINTJOB/ENDPRINTJOB

_peject

The _peject variable controls when a sheet of paper ejects (printjob, program only).

Syntax

_peject = "BEFORE"/ "AFTER"/ "BOTH"/ "NONE"

"BEFORE" ejects the page before the job begins. This is the default.

"AFTER" ejects the page after the job ends.

"BOTH" ejects a page before the job begins and after the job ends.

"NONE" doesn't eject a page.

Notes

This variable requires the PRINTJOB/ENDPRINTJOB command. Set the _peject variable before issuing the PRINTJOB command in an application program.

Related variable and commands: _padvance, EJECT, EJECT PAGE, PRINTJOB/ENDPRINTJOB

_pepage

The _pepage variable determines the ending page for a print job (printjob).

Syntax

_pepage = <*number*>

number is an integer from 1 to 32,767. The default is 32,767, which always prints to the end of any job.

Notes

This variable sets an ending page boundary for printouts.

The value for _pepage can't be less than the value for _pbpage. Make the three system variables—_pageno, _pbpage, and _pepage—consistent and logical (see _pageno).

Related variables and commands: _pageno, _pbpage, PRINT-JOB/ENDPRINTJOB

_pform

The _pform variable specifies a print job file that contains print settings (streaming output).

Syntax

_pform = "<*print form filename*>"

print form filename is a file that contains settings for system memory variables that relate to printers. The default is a null string (" ").

Notes

System memory variables that you can set from within a print form file are _padvance, _pageno, _pbpage, _pcopies, _pecode, _peject, _pepage, _plength _ploffset, _ppitch, _pquality, _pscode, _pspacing, and _pwait. When you save a report or label, the values for these system memory variables are also saved. They are loaded automatically when you issue the REPORT FORM or LABEL FORM commands. To use settings from a file other than the one saved with a report or label, set _pform to the name of the file.

To create a print form file that contains the current print settings, use the **Save settings to print form** option from the **Print** menu.

Related Commands: CREATE/MODIFY LABEL, CREATE/MODIFY REPORT, LABEL FORM, REPORT FORM

_plength

The _plength variable sets the length of the output page (streaming output).

Syntax

_plength = <*number*>

number is an integer from 1 to 32,767. The default is 66 lines.

Notes

Total page length is calculated by counting the number of lines between the top and bottom of a page. You can use ON PAGE to control where headers, footers, and text are printed on a page.

Related variable and commands: _padvance, EJECT, EJECT PAGE, ON PAGE

_plineno

The _plineno variable sets the starting line number for a page (streaming output).

Syntax

_plineno = <*number*>

number is an integer from 0 to _plength - 1. The default line number is 0.

Notes

dBASE IV uses _plineno to keep track of what line number your printout is on.

The _plineno variable is similar to the PROW() function. However, _plineno can't exceed _plength and PROW() can. Also, unlike PROW(), _plength works even if you turn off the printer and use the screen for output.

Related variable, commands, and functions: _plength, EJECT PAGE, ON PAGE, PCOL(), PROW()

_ploffset

The _ploffset variable determines the left side offset for printed pages (printer).

Syntax

_ploffset = <*number*>

number is an integer from 0 to 254. The default for the left side page offset is 0.

Notes

The left offset is calculated by measuring in from the left side of the paper. _lmargin begins at _ploffset. For example, if you set _ploffset to 5 and _lmargin to 10, the left margin indents to 15. Since the default for _ploffset is 0, you don't usually have to add _ploffset to _lmargin to calculate the new margin.

_ploffset shifts the text on the page the requested number of characters. You can use _ploffset to make overall page layout adjustments. Assigning values to _ploffset is equivalent to using the SET MARGIN command.

Related variable and command: _lmargin, SET MARGIN

_ppitch

The _ppitch variable sets how many characters print per inch (printer).

Syntax

_ppitch = "PICA"/ "ELITE"/ "CONDENSED"/ "DEFAULT"

"PICA" is 10 characters per inch.
"ELITE" is 12 characters per inch.
"CONDENSED" is approximately 17.16 characters per inch.
"DEFAULT" is the normal pitch setting for your particular printer.

Notes

Pitch is the horizontal density of letters. _ppitch sets the number of characters you can print per inch based on letter size In order to use an option with this command, it must be supported by the currently active printer driver.

Related variables: _pdriver, _pquality

_pquality

The _pquality variable determines whether to use quality or draft mode for your printout (printer).

Syntax

_pquality = <*condition*>

condition is logical true (.T.) for quality mode or logical false (.F.) for draft mode. The default is .F. for draft mode.

Notes

Quality mode stands for letter-quality output. Because this mode produces letters of a higher resolution than draft output, it takes longer to print. Generally, you use draft mode for output you don't plan to show to others.

Related variables: _pdriver, _ppitch

_pscode

The _pscode variable provides starting printer control codes (print-job, program only).

Syntax

_pscode = <*character string*>

character string is a range of codes from 0 to 255. It cannot exceed 255 characters. The default is a null string.

Notes

Sometimes you want to print a report in a different way. For example, suppose you want to print a condensed report in normal size or a letter-quality report in draft quality for speed. Use _pscode to change the print style. Then use _pecode to restore the original type style. Printer codes for your particular printer are listed in your printer manual.

This variable requires the PRINTJOB/ENDPRINTJOB command. Set the _pscode variable before issuing the PRINTJOB command. To change the type style without using an application program, use the **Style** option of the ?/?? command.

Related variable and commands: _pecode, ?/??, ???, PRINTJOB/ENDPRINTJOB

_pspacing

The _pspacing variable sets the spaces between lines (streaming output).

Syntax

_pspacing = 1/2/3

1 puts no blank lines between each line of text. This is the default.

2 puts one blank line between each line of text.

3 puts two blank lines between each line of text.

Notes

The _pspacing variable sets the number of spaces between each line of text.

It also affects the height of boxes created with the DEFINE BOX command. To calculate the height of a box, multiply the box's height by the value for _pspacing. Since the default value of _pspacing is 1, the box's output height usually equals the box's requested height.

Related commands: ?/???, LIST, DISPLAY

Example

This example shows how to use the _pspacing variable to change the amount of space shown by the ? and LIST commands. Notice how changing _pspacing's value also affects the confirmation display shown when you assign a value to a variable.

```
. ? _pspacing
         1
. USE SAMPLES\PEOPLE
. LIST Firstname, Lastname FOR Lastname < "C"
Record#  Firstname            Lastname
      1  Michael              Berrigan
     14  Malcolm              Ali

. SET _pspacing = 2
. _pspacing = 2

         2

. LIST Firstname, Lastname FOR Lastname < "C"

Record#  Firstname               Lastname

      1  Michael                 Berrigan

     14  Malcolm                 Ali
```

_pwait

The _pwait variable determines whether the printer pauses after producing a page (printer).

Syntax

_pwait = <*condition*>

condition is logical true (.T.) for pause or logical false (.F.) for no pause. The default is .F. for no pause.

Notes

Use this variable when you want to print using cut sheets—single noncontinuous sheets of paper. dBASE IV stops after issuing a page eject or when the number of lines exceeds the value for _plength. You can then insert more paper and resume printing.

When you set this variable in an application program, set the _pwait variable before issuing the PRINTJOB command.

Related variable and commands: _plength, EJECT, EJECT PAGE

_rmargin

The _rmargin variable determines the position of the right margin for ?/?? command output, when _wrap is logical true (.T.) (text block).

Syntax

_rmargin = <*number*>

number is a number from 0 to 255. The default is 80.

Notes

To get the minimum value for _rmargin, add the values for _lmargin and _indent and add 1 to the total. The _rmargin variable only has an effect when _wrap is logical true (.T.).

Related variables: _indent, _lmargin, _ploffset, _wrap

Example

See the _wrap variable.

_tabs

The _tabs variable sets one or more tab stops for ?/?? command output and the dBASE IV Text Editor (streaming output).

Syntax

_tabs = <*character string*>

character string defines a list of tab stops. The default is a null string.

Notes

Tabs are an abbreviated form of blank space (also called white space). Tabs are commonly found in tables and other special formats that use columnar output. A tab stop defines how much white space the output device inserts in place of the tab symbol. For example, suppose you have some text and a tab symbol, CHR(9). dBASE IV puts space between the column the text ended in and the column the next tab is set for.

The dBASE IV Text Editor tabs start at eight spaces and are eight spaces each. These settings remain in effect until you change them by setting _tabs.

Related variable: _indent

Example

This example sets five tabs ten spaces apart.

```
. _tabs = "10, 20, 30, 40, 50"
```

_wrap

The _wrap variable controls whether words wrap between margins (text block).

Syntax

_wrap = <*condition*>

condition is logical true (.T.) for wrapping or logical false (.F.) for no wrapping. The default is .F. for no wrapping.

Notes

When you set the _wrap variable to logical true (.T.), you activate the streaming output variables _alignment, _indent, _lmargin, and _rmargin.

The _lmargin and _rmargin variables define the margin used to wrap the output of ? and ?? commands. When the output is wrapped, dBASE IV checks the value of _rmargin. When a word's position exceeds the value, dBASE IV goes to the next line and displays the next word or number.

Related variables: _alignment, _indent, _lmargin, _rmargin

Example

This example shows how text appears with the defaults and how you can change it by changing the values for the _wrap, _lmargin, and _rmargin variables. Extra lines have been added to make this example easier to read.

```
. ? "Here is some text using the defaults"
Here is some text using the defaults

. _wrap = .T.
.T.
. ? "Here is some text with wrap set to logical true"
Here is some text with wrap set to logical true

. _lmargin = 20
        20
. ? "Here is some text with left margin at 20"
                    Here is some text with left margin at 20

. _rmargin = 40
        40
. ? "Here is some text with right margin at 40"
                    Here is some text
                    with right margin at
                    40

. ? _wrap, _lmargin, _rmargin
                    .T.         20
                    40
```

Customizing dBASE IV

THIRTY FIVE

This chapter shows you how to change dBASE IV's default settings to meet your specific needs. Among other things, you can change the colors used for display, the default printer, and whether dBASE IV starts in the Control Center, at the dot prompt, or in your custom application menu.

You can customize dBASE IV's configuration settings either temporarily or permanently. This chapter first shows you different methods for temporarily changing dBASE IV's default settings from either the Control Center or the dot prompt. It then explains how to permanently change dBASE IV's configuration settings by modifying your CONFIG.DB file. As you'll soon see, dBASE IV uses the CONFIG.DB file to establish default settings when you start up your computer.

Customizing dBASE IV Temporarily

You can temporarily change your dBASE settings in any of the following three ways:

- Select the **Settings** submenu from the **Tools** menu on the Control Center menu bar.
- Activate the SET full-screen menu by entering **SET** at the dot prompt.
- Enter SET commands from the dot prompt or from a program.

From the Control Center

When you select the **Settings** submenu from the **Tools** menu in the Control Center, dBASE IV presents the three-option submenu shown in Figure 35-1. You can use these options to temporarily alter many of dBASE IV's default settings.

By using the **Options** submenu, you can modify any of 16 commonly used SET command settings. Changing any of these options is equivalent to entering the corresponding SET command at the dot prompt. To modify a given setting, highlight it and press ENTER. Pressing ENTER on some options, such as **Bell** or **Carry**, toggles those options on and off. When you press ENTER on other options, such as **Date order**, dBASE IV presents alternative formats for your selection. Finally, when you press ENTER on other options, such as **Decimal places** or **Memo width**, dBASE IV prompts you for a default value. For more about each of the settings in the **Options** menu, refer to the SET commands in Chapter 32.

You can temporarily change your display colors by using the **Display** submenu. This option allows you to specify colors for various components of dBASE IV's display. The **Display** option of the **Settings** submenu is explained in detail in Chapter 14, "Tools."

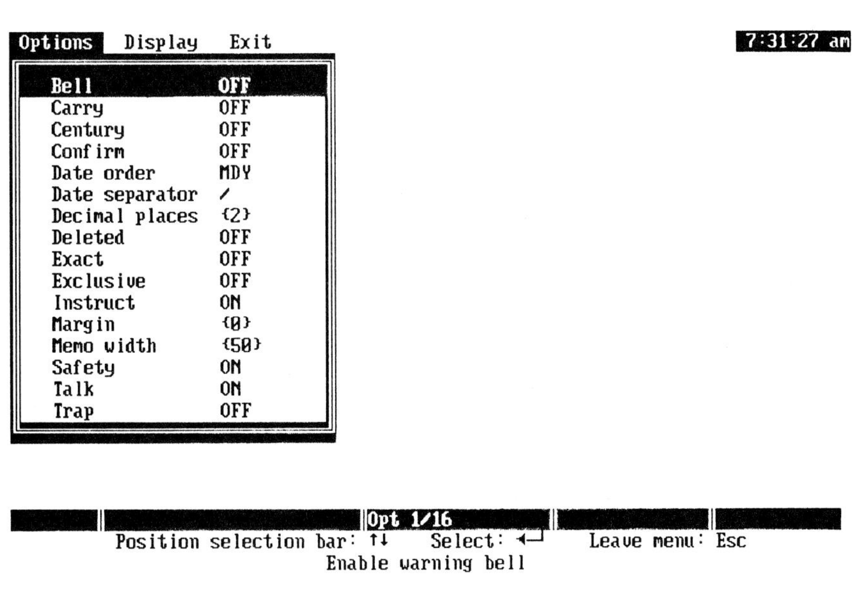

Figure 35-1. **Settings** submenu (**Options** selection)

From the Dot Prompt

By entering **SET** at the dot prompt, you can activate the SET full-screen menu to temporarily customize dBASE IV (see Figure 35-2). By using the **Options** submenu, you can modify over 40 different SET commands settings. To modify a setting, highlight it and press ENTER. dBASE IV then toggles the option on or off, presents alternate choices, or prompts you to enter a value. The SET full-screen menu also includes a **Display** submenu, which also appears in the **Settings** submenu from the **Tools** menu. As mentioned, this menu is covered in detail in Chapter 14.

Pressing ENTER to modify any of the choices in the **Options** submenu is equivalent to entering one of the many dBASE IV SET

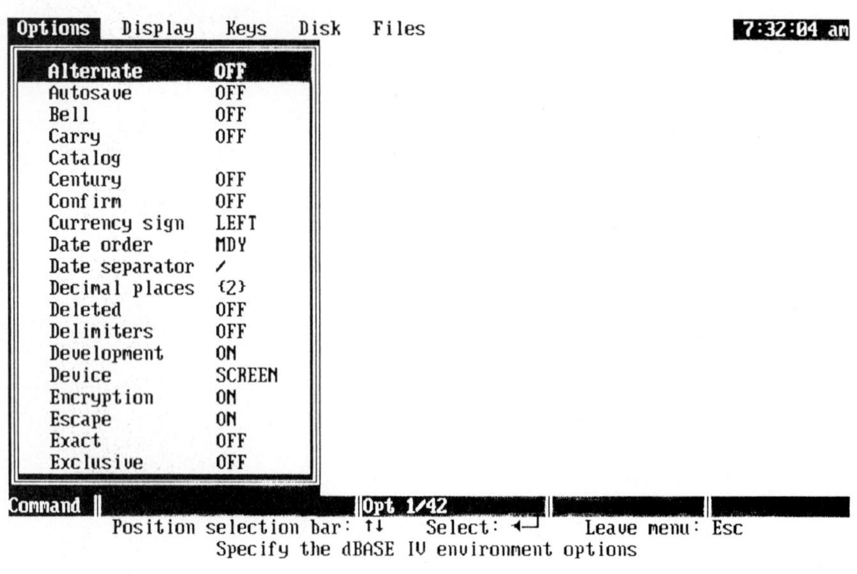

Figure 35-2. SET full-screen menu (**Options** submenu)

commands at the dot prompt. As mentioned, Chapter 32 provides an alphabetical list of the SET commands, along with explanations.

In addition to the **Options** submenu and the **Display** submenu, the following three submenus are available from the SET full-screen menu:

- The **Keys** submenu allows you to program function keys and key combinations. If you press ENTER on any of the key names in this menu, you can enter a dBASE IV command that will be executed whenever that key is pressed.

- The **Disk** submenu allows you to change the default disk drive and the drive search path for the current dBASE IV session.
- The **Files** submenu allows you to specify alternate, format, device, or index file names.

The **Files** submenu, available from the SET full-screen menu, has four options. The **Alternate** option of the **Files** submenu allows you to enter the name of a default alternate file. Alternate files are used to record commands and output from the current dBASE IV session. This option is equivalent to using the SET ALTERNATE dot prompt command. Data is stored in the form of ASCII text that you can view and edit by using a conventional word processor that edits ASCII files, such as the dBASE IV Text Editor.

To open an alternate file and begin recording, press ENTER on the **Alternate** option in the **Options** menu or use the SET ALTERNATE ON command at the dot prompt. To stop recording, set ALTERNATE to OFF. To view and edit the file, first close the file by using the CLOSE ALTERNATE command at the dot prompt, and then load the file into the dBASE IV Text Editor by using the MODIFY COMMAND <*filename*>.TXT command.

The **Device** option of the **Files** submenu allows you to enter a default file name for dBASE IV output. Once again, output to this file is stored in the form of ASCII text. However, unlike the **Alternate** option, the **Device** option captures output from @...SAY commands. Using this option is equivalent to using the SET DEVICE TO FILE <*filename*> command at the dot prompt.

The **Format** option of the **Files** submenu allows you to specify a format (.FMT) file that is displayed after full-screen commands such as APPEND, EDIT, CHANGE, or INSERT. The file name you enter must be an existing format file created with the Forms Design screen or the dBASE IV Text Editor.

The **Index** option of the **Files** submenu allows you to enter the name of an index file. This option is equivalent to the SET INDEX TO command at the dot prompt.

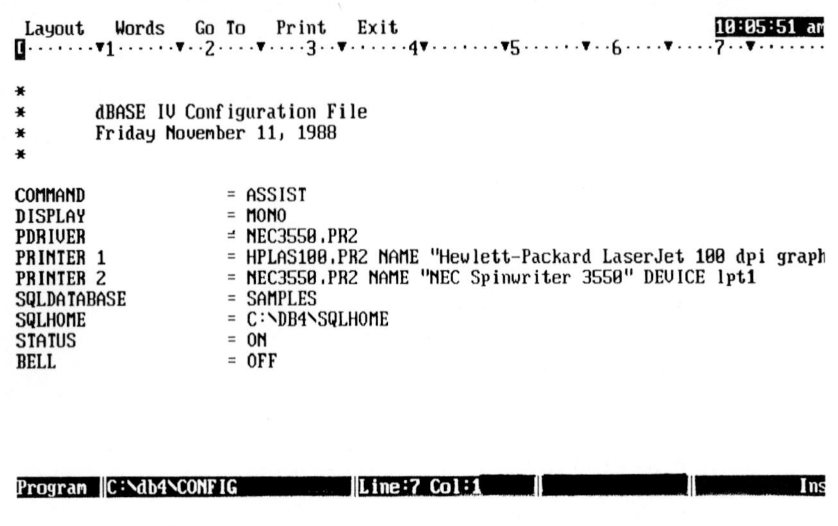

Layout Words Go To Print Exit
10:05:51 am
*
* dBASE IV Configuration File
* Friday November 11, 1988
*
COMMAND = ASSIST
DISPLAY = MONO
PDRIVER = NEC3550.PR2
PRINTER 1 = HPLAS100.PR2 NAME "Hewlett-Packard LaserJet 100 dpi graph
PRINTER 2 = NEC3550.PR2 NAME "NEC Spinwriter 3550" DEVICE lpt1
SQLDATABASE = SAMPLES
SQLHOME = C:\DB4\SQLHOME
STATUS = ON
BELL = OFF
Program C:\db4\CONFIG Line:7 Col:1 Ins

Figure 35-3. CONFIG.DB file displayed in the Text Editor

Customizing dBASE IV Permanently

To customize dBASE IV on a permanent basis, you must change your CONFIG.DB file. This file loads dBASE IV program parameters on startup. Each parameter has a value that you can change to suit your needs. When you install dBASE IV, a CONFIG.DB file containing certain default parameters is copied to your dBASE directory. You can modify the contents of this file using any ASCII text editor, including the dBASE IV Text Editor, or you can create a new CONFIG.DB using the DBSETUP program explained in Chapter 2. Figure 35-3 shows an example CONFIG.DB file displayed in the dBASE IV Text Editor.

Each time you start dBASE IV, it reads the CONFIG.DB file from the current directory and loads that file's specified program parameters. dBASE IV allows you to have several CONFIG.DB files with different parameters in different directories. However, if you do this, the directory that contains your dBASE IV system files must be in your path statement. Otherwise, the CONFIG.DB file must reside in the same directory as your dBASE IV system files.

You can change five types of parameters in a CONFIG.DB file:

- Configuration commands
- Memory allocation
- Function key definitions
- Most of the SET command values
- The colors for the dBASE IV display

Configuration Commands

The configuration commands that follow can only be executed from a CONFIG.DB file. They have no effect when you enter them at the dot prompt. You use these commands to establish the default environment in which dBASE IV operates. For example, you can specify a default printer and specify an alternate word processor for editing programs or memo fields.

Tip: If you modify your CONFIG.DB file, you must restart dBASE IV to have it recognize the changes.

BUCKET

You use the BUCKET command in your CONFIG.DB file to specify the size of memory blocks in kilobytes. You can specify a setting from 1K to 31K. The default is 2. Changing the value for the BUCKET command is appropriate if you're using very large format files with multiple screens and templates. Such format files require large amounts of memory in their compiled form. To specify larger memory blocks, increase the value of BUCKET.

Default: BUCKET = 2; Range: 1K to 31K

COMMAND

You can use any valid dBASE IV command with the COMMAND setting. dBASE IV automatically executes the command at startup. You can use this command to specify whether dBASE IV starts in the Control Center or at the dot prompt. You can also use it to have dBASE IV execute an application you've written using the dBASE IV Text Editor or the Applications Generator.

When you install dBASE IV, the default for COMMAND is

```
COMMAND = ASSIST
```

This specifies the Control Center as the default first screen. You can change this setting to display the dot prompt on startup by eliminating COMMAND from you CONFIG.DB file, or by preceding it with an asterisk (*).

You can also use COMMAND in conjunction with the DO command to have dBASE IV automatically execute one of your applications at startup. For example, to have an application named SALESYST.PRG execute immediately upon startup, include the following statement in your CONFIG.DB file:

```
COMMAND = DO Salesyst
```

You can have dBASE IV override the COMMAND setting on startup by specifying a program file name when you start dBASE IV. For example, to have dBASE IV immediately run a program called STARTUP.PRG, enter **DBASE STARTUP** at the DOS prompt.

DO

dBASE IV limits the number of DO commands that you can nest in a program file. The DO configuration command specifies the number of nested DO calls allowed in a program. The default is 20. If you get the error message "DOs nested too deep," try raising the value of the DO parameter above 20. You may need to do this when you're using a program file to call many different procedures.

Default: DO = 20; Range: 1 to 256

EEMS

The EEMS command is not available in version 1.0 of dBASE IV but will be available in future versions of dBASE. This command allows you to access extended versus expanded memory.

EXPSIZE

As dBASE IV compiles your programs, it temporarily stores the expressions from each command line in a memory buffer called the EVAL work area. dBASE IV uses this work area to evaluate your expressions for syntax errors.

You use the EXPSIZE command to change the amount of memory allocated to the EVAL work area. The default of 100 refers to 100 bytes. If you're using several large expressions in one or more command lines, you may get the error message "EVAL work area overflow." Try increasing the expression size buffer to a value greater than 100 bytes.

Default: EXPSIZE = 100; Range: 100 to 2000

FASTCRT

If your screen has flickering white specks, FASTCRT allows you to eliminate this "snow" effect. The default for this command is ON.

However, if you're using an IBM PC Color Graphics Adapter (CGA) or a compatible adapter, the setting for this command should be OFF. With the DBSETUP program, you can determine the optimal setting for your equipment. Type **DBSETUP** at the DOS prompt. When dBASE IV presents a menu, choose **Optimize color display** from **Modify hardware setup** in the **Install** menu.

Default: FASTCRT = ON

FILES

dBASE IV limits the number of files that you can have open at any one time. You can use the FILES command in your CONFIG.DB file to adjust the maximum number of open files allowed by dBASE IV. The setting that you use for this command cannot exceed the number of files specified in your CONFIG.SYS file. For every file you specify using the FILES command in your CONFIG.DB file, dBASE IV reserves 20 bytes of RAM. (This is in addition to 48 bytes reserved by DOS.)

From a practical standpoint, the number of files you can have open in dBASE IV is a function of your computer's available memory. You can specify as many as 99 open files.

Default: FILES = 40; Range: 15 to 99

GETS

The GET command limits the number of @...GET statements that you can have active at any one time. The default is 128. If you are using a large format file that contains in excess of 128 @...GET commands, you can use the GETS command in your CONFIG.DB file to increase the number of allowed GETs to as many as 300.

Default: GETS = 128; Range: 128 to 300

INDEXBYTES

Within an index file, each record in a database file is represented by an item of data called a *node*. Each node in an index file holds the key expression value for a record in the database and a reference to the next node in the index file. When an index file is in use, dBASE IV loads groups of these nodes into memory as they are needed to access records in the associated database. The more nodes that you have in memory from a given index file, the faster the index runs.

dBASE IV loads nodes from disk into memory in 512K blocks. The more blocks you have in memory, the more nodes are present and the faster the index runs. You use the INDEXBYTES command to specify the number of allowed 512K memory blocks occupied by index nodes. The default is 2.

You may profit by increasing the INDEXBYTES setting if you are using large and complicated index key expressions. If you set INDEXBYTES to a high value, you can load more nodes into memory at one time. However, if you have large database files with short index key expressions, increasing the INDEXBYTES value will just reserve precious RAM for unneeded index file nodes. If you get the error message "Insufficient memory," try lowering the value of the INDEXBYTES setting.

Default: INDEXBYTES = 2

PDRIVER

Use PDRIVER in your CONFIG.DB file to specify the default printer driver. Printer drivers are files containing the print codes specific to a given printer. The syntax for this command is

PDRIVER = *<printer driver filename>*

The *printer driver filename* must be a valid printer driver file supported by dBASE IV. It must also reside in the same directory as dBASE IV, or in directory that is included in your path statement.

When you install dBASE IV, you can specify up to four different printers from a list of printer drivers provided with dBASE IV. PDRIVER allows you to specify the default printer driver from among these. If you do not use the PDRIVER command in your CONFIG.DB file, dBASE IV defaults to GENERIC.PR2, a rudimentary printer driver that does not support control codes and whose styles are limited to standard text, underline, and bold.

For example, to specify a printer driver for an IBM graphics printer, enter the following in your CONFIG.DB file:

```
PDRIVER = "IBMGP"
```

Default: PDRIVER = GENERIC.PR2 (default device is LPT1)

PRINTER

You can configure dBASE IV to recognize up to four different printer drivers at once. You can also designate from one to five different fonts for each printer. The files containing the drivers and their fonts must be in your dBASE IV directory or in a directory that is included in your path statement. You can specify one of your installed printer drivers by using the **Destination** submenu in the **Print** menu. You can also specify a printer driver by changing the value of the system variable _pdriver. For more about the **Print** menu, see Chapter 12. For more about the _pdriver system memory variable, see Chapter 34.

The syntax for the PRINTER command is

PRINTER <*printer int*> = <*filename*> [NAME <*name string*>] [Device <*device string*>]

Here is a description of each of these parameters:

- *Printer int* is the number of the printer to use (1-4).
- *Filename* is the name of the printer driver to use.
- NAME <*name string*> is the character string that will appear in the **Destination** submenu of the **Print** menu when you select your printer model.
- DEVICE is the output port your printer uses (LPT1, COM1).

Example: To install the printer driver for the Hewlett-Packard LaserJet, use the command

```
PRINTER 1 = HPLAS100.PR2 NAME "Hp Laser Jet" DEVICE COM1
```

You can install or change the printer fonts for a printer by using the following command:

> PRINTER <*printer int*> FONT <*font int*> = <*begin code*>,<*end code*> [NAME <*font name string*>]

- *Printer int* is the number of the previously installed printer (1-4).
- *Font int* is the font number. You can indicate up to 5 fonts (1-5).
- *Begin code* is the starting code that turns the font on. Consult your printer's manual for this code.
- *End code* is the ending code that turns the font off. Consult your printer's manual for this code.
- NAME <*font name string*> is displayed in the **Destination** submenu of the **Print** menu when you start a print job.

Example: To use an ASCII font rather than the default Roman 8 font on an HP LaserJet, enter the following:

```
PRINTER 1 FONT1 = {ESC}(0U,{ESC}(#@, Name = "USA ASCII Symbol Set"
```

To install more than one font for a given printer, you must enter one PRINTER command in your CONFIG.DB file for each font you want to use, up to a total of 5.

PROMPT

You can change the dBASE IV dot prompt (.) to display a text string of up to 19 displayable ASCII characters. Avoid using ASCII decimal values (7-14 and 23-27). You use these characters to send commands to your printer. The default for this command is

PROMPT = .

Example: If you include the statement

```
PROMPT = ENTER A COMMAND
```

in your CONFIG.DB file, the dot prompt then appears as "ENTER A COMMAND:".

RESETCRT

When you exit from dBASE to an external program, the display mode of your screen may be changed. For example, you might temporarily exit to an external editor to edit a program file or a memo field. When RESETCRT is set to ON (the default), dBASE IV resets the display mode back to the way it was before you ran the external program.

Default: RESETCRT = ON

SQL

There are three commands you can include in your CONFIG.DB file that take dBASE IV directly into SQL mode immediately upon startup. These commands are

SQL = ON

SQLHOME = <*path name*>

SQLDATABASE = <*SQL database name*>

You can have dBASE IV to go directly into SQL mode on startup by adding the following command to your CONFIG.DB file:

```
SQL = ON
```

To specify the home directory that contains your SQL system files, use the SQLHOME command. For example, if you installed SQL when you installed dBASE IV, the following command line was placed in your CONFIG.DB file:

```
SQLHOME = C:\DBASE\SQLHOME
```

If you want dBASE IV to automatically activate an SQL database on startup, designate the database name in the CONFIG.DB file by using the SQLDATABASE command. For example, if you installed SQL when you installed dBASE IV, the following command line was placed in your CONFIG.DB file:

```
SQLDATABASE = SQLSAMPLES
```

TEDIT and WP

You can use the TEDIT and WP commands to specify an external word processor for editing programs and memo fields. The word processor you specify using TEDIT is activated by MODIFY COMMAND. dBASE IV uses the word processor you specify with WP to edit memo fields. In both cases, your computer must have enough memory to load the word processor you specify and the DOS COMMAND.COM file. For example, to have dBASE IV use WordStar as an external editor whose files are located in a directory called WS5, enter the following in your CONFIG.DB file.

```
TEDIT = C:\WS5\WS
```

When you use the dBASE IV Text Editor to edit your programs, it automatically deletes outdated .DBO files when you edit the matching .PRG file. You can have dBASE IV perform this operation for your external editor by adding to your CONFIG.DB file the following command:

```
DEVELOPMENT = ON
```

As mentioned, the word processor you specify with WP is used to edit memo fields. If you use an external editor to edit your memo fields, be sure to save your memo fields in an ASCII text format. Otherwise, control codes may be embedded in your text, making it unreadable in dBASE IV. For example, to specify WordStar, whose files are located in a directory called WS5, as your default editor for editing memo fields, enter the following in your CONFIG.DB file:

```
WP = C:\WS5\WS
```

Function Key Definitions

You can program the following function keys:

F2 through F10

SHIFT-F1 through SHIFT-F9

CTRL-F1 through CTRL-F10

You cannot program function keys F1 and SHIFT-F10. They are used to access the Help screens (F1) and the **Macro** menu (SHIFT-F10). You use this syntax to define a function key in CONFIG.DB:

<key label> = *<expC>*

For example, to program the F2 function key to execute the SET PRINT ON command, include the following line in your CONFIG.DB file:

```
F2 = "SET PRINT ON"
```

If you want dBASE to execute your expression or command immediately after you press the function key, finish your expression or command with a semicolon (;).

Table 35-1 shows the default settings for the function keys. You can use any of the following three methods to change the function key settings.

Function Key	**Original Setting**
F1 *	HELP;
F2	ASSIST;
F3	LIST;
F4	DIR;
F5	DISPLAY STRUCTURE;
F6	DISPLAY STATUS;
F7	DISPLAY MEMORY;
F8	DISPLAY;
F9	APPEND;
F10	EDIT;
SHIFT-F10 *	MACRO MENU

* Not programmable

Table 35-1. CONFIG.DB Function Key Settings

- The SET full-screen menu command
- The SET FUNCTION TO command at the dot prompt
- The CONFIG.DB function key settings

You can enter the LIST or DISPLAY STATUS command at the dot prompt to see the current setting of the function keys. For more information on programming function keys, see SET FUNCTION in Chapter 32, "SET Commands."

The CONFIG.DB SET Commands

You can add to your CONFIG.DB file almost all of the SET command program parameters. However, the CONFIG.DB file uses an equal sign between the keyword of the SET command and the chosen setting. For example, the dot prompt command SET INSTRUCT ON becomes

```
INSTRUCT = ON
```

The SET commands contained in your CONFIG.DB file are set permanently. To change these settings temporarily, you can enter the corresponding SET commands at the dot prompt. You can also use the **Settings** submenu of the **Tools** menu in the Control Center, or the SET full-screen menu, accessed by using the SET command at the dot prompt. However, remember that these are temporary changes that remain in effect only until another SET command changes them or until you quit dBASE IV. When you restart dBASE IV, the SET commands in your CONFIG.DB file once again become the default settings.

Table 35-2 lists the SET commands that you can use within your CONFIG.DB file. The default values established when you first install dBASE IV are shown in uppercase. An asterisk indicates that you *cannot* access the command from the SET full-screen menu that you access by typing **SET** at the dot prompt. Refer to Chapter 32, "SET Commands," for more information on the SET commands.

SET Command	Argument	Action/Default/Ranges
ALTERNATE =	on/OFF	Set ON starts sending output of commands and results to a text file. Set OFF stops sending output to a file but doesn't close the file
ALTERNATE =	*<filename>*	Opens a file. If the file doesn't exist, dBASE creates *filename*.TXT
AUTOSAVE =	on/OFF	Automatically saves information each time you change or add a record
BELL =	ON/off	Determines whether you hear a tone when you make an error or reach the end of a field
* BELL =	frequency, duration	Frequency range is 19-10,000 cycles per second. Duration: 2-19. Default is 512,2

Table 35-2. SET Commands Accessible Using the CONFIG.DB file (* means not accessible from the SET full-screen menu)

SET Command	Argument	Action/Default/Ranges
* BLOCKSIZE =	<*expN*>	Changes the block size for memo fields and .MDX files
* BORDER =	SINGLE/ double/panel/ none/<*border definition string*>	Changes the border of menus, windows, and @ commands from a single-line box to a different border character.
CARRY =	on/OFF	Passes field values from the current record to the next record
CATALOG =	on/OFF	Activates the catalog file with the associated database
* CATALOG =	<*filename*>	Opens an existing catalog or creates and opens a new catalog file if catalog *filename* doesn't exist
CENTURY =	on/OFF	Set OFF assumes a 20th century date
* CLOCK =	on/OFF	Set ON puts a clock in upper-right corner of screen. Set OFF, no clock appears
* CLOCK =	<*row*>, <*column*>	Changes the position of the clock. Default is 0, 69
COLOR =		See SET COLOR command in Chapter 32

Table 35-2. SET Commands Accessible Using the CONFIG.DB file (*continued*)

SET Command	Argument	Action/Default/Ranges
CONFIRM =	on/OFF	Set OFF advances the cursor to the next field when it reaches the end of the current field. Set ON waits until you press ENTER to advance to next field
* CONSOLE =	ON/off	Set ON sends output to the screen. Set OFF suppresses output to the screen
* CURRENCY =	<*expC*>	Changes $ character to a character string of up to nine characters. Default is $
CURRENCY =	LEFT/right	Positions currency symbol to the left or right of currency value
DATE =	AMERICAN/ansi/british/french/german/italian/japan/usa/mdy/dmy/ymd	Changes default date format. Default is *mm/dd/yy*
* DEBUG =	on/OFF	Set OFF sends output from SET ECHO commands to the screen. Set ON sends output from SET ECHO commands to printer

Table 35-2. SET Commands Accessible Using the CONFIG.DB file (*continued*)

SET Command	Argument	Action/Default/Ranges
DECIMALS =	*<expN>*	Changes the number of decimal places. Default is 2; range 0-18
DEFAULT =	*<expC>*	Sets the default drive name
DELETED =	on/OFF	Set OFF treats deleted records as any other. Set ON ignores deleted records for most dBASE commands
DELIMITERS	on/OFF	Determines whether to surround full-screen mode fields with a character
* DELIMITERS	*<expC>*	Default is a colon (:)
DESIGN	ON/off	Controls access to the design facilities from the dot prompt
DEVELOPMENT =	ON/off	Set ON recompiles source-code files with different date and times than object-code files. Set OFF doesn't check dates or recompile
DEVICE =	SCREEN/ printer/file *<filename>*	Selects output device for output
DISPLAY =	MONO /COLOR /EGA25/ EGA43 /MONO43	Selects type of monitor in use. Default is set during installation

Table 35-2. SET Commands Accessible Using the CONFIG.DB file (*continued*)

SET Command	Argument	Action/Default/Ranges
* ECHO =	on/OFF	Set ON displays commands. Set OFF doesn't display commands
ESCAPE =	ON/off	Set ON allows ESC to stop programs. Set OFF turns off ESC and CTRL-S functions
EXACT =	on/OFF	Set OFF finds character strings even when lengths don't match. Set ON checks for lengths to match character strings
EXCLUSIVE =	on/OFF	Set OFF sets the file for group access. Set ON sets the file for private access
FULLPATH =	on/OFF	Set ON when using dBASE III PLUS programs that use the functions NDX() and DBF() to suppress full file specification returns
FUNCTION =	*<expN>*, *<expC>*	Function key label, assigns characters or dBASE IV command to a function key. See Table 35-1 for defaults
HEADING =	ON/off	Set ON displays column headings. Set OFF suppresses column headings
HELP =	ON/off	Set ON allows access to Help menus. Set OFF doesn't allow access to Help menus from error boxes

Table 35-2. SET Commands Accessible Using the CONFIG.DB file (*continued*)

SET Command	Argument	Action/Default/Ranges
* HISTORY	ON/off	Set ON dBASE saves previous commands in a buffer. Set OFF, clears the buffer
* HISTORY =	<*expN*>	Controls the number of commands saved in the history buffer. Default is 20; range 0-16,000
HOURS =	12/24	Toggles between a 12- and 24-hour clock. Default is 12
INSTRUCT =	ON/off	Set ON enables dBASE menu interface. Set OFF disables dBASE menu interface
INTENSITY =	ON/off	Set ON highlights fields. Set OFF doesn't highlight fields
LOCK =	ON/off	Set ON protects record access. Set OFF disables automatic locking for a read-only subset of commands
MARGIN =	<*expN*>	Sets left printer margin. Default is 0; range 0 to 254
MEMOWIDTH =	<*expN*>	Changes width of the memo field for output only. Default is 50; minimum 8, maximum 32,000
* MENUS =	ON/off	This command is for dBASE III PLUS compatibility only and doesn't affect dBASE IV

Table 35-2. SET Commands Accessible Using the CONFIG.DB file (*continued*)

SET Command	Argument	Action/Default/Ranges
NEAR =	on/OFF	Set OFF moves the record pointer to the end of the database when a search is unsuccessful. Set ON puts the record pointer near a record that was close to the search conditions
* ODOMETER =	*<expN>*	Sets the record update interval for commands that show a record count. Default is 1; range is 1 to 200
PATH =	*<path list>*	Lists one or more path names of directories to search for application program in the current directory. Path list can be up to 60 characters
PAUSE =	on/OFF	Set OFF doesn't pause and ask to continue when screen fills. Set ON stops display and prompts for continuation when screen fills
* POINT =	*<expC>*	Changes the character used for a decimal point. Default is period; one character allowed, space and numbers not allowed

Table 35-2. SET Commands Accessible Using the CONFIG.DB file (*continued*)

SET Command	Argument	Action/Default/Ranges
PRECISION =	*<expN>*	Sets the number of digits used to calculate type N numbers in dBASE IV internal math calculations. Default is 16; range 10 to 20
PRINTER	OFF/on	Set OFF sends output to screen only. Set ON sends output to both the screen and the printer. Appears as Print on the SET full-screen menu
* PRINTER =	PRN/lpt1/lpt /lpt3/com1/ com2	Sends the output to the selected printer. Printer is first set during installation
REFRESH	*<expN>*	Defines a time interval for file change checks on a network during BROWSE and EDIT command. REFRESH only works with files created with the CONVERT command. Default is 0; range 0 to 3,600
* REPROCESS =	*<expN>*	Defines the number of times dBASE tries a network file or issues a record lock command before you get an error message. Default is 0; range -1 to 32,000

Table 35-2. SET Commands Accessible Using the CONFIG.DB file (*continued*)

SET Command	Argument	Action/Default/Ranges
SAFETY =	ON/off	Set ON gives you a warning when you attempt to overwrite an existing file. Set OFF allows you to overwrite existing files without a warning message
SCOREBOARD =	*<expC>*	Set ON puts status of special keys on screen even when SET STATUS is OFF. Set OFF doesn't display special keys on screen
SEPARATOR =	*<expC>*	Changes the place separator to any single character. Default is a comma (,)
SPACE =	ON/off	Set ON puts an extra space between fields when you display them using the ? or ?? command
* SQL =	on/OFF	Set OFF puts you in dBASE mode. Set ON puts you in SQL mode after the COMMAND = option terminates
STATUS =	on/OFF	Set OFF no status bar appears. Set ON the status bar appears at the bottom of the screen
* STEP =	on/OFF	Set OFF executes programs without stop

Table 35-2. SET Commands Accessible Using the CONFIG.DB file (*continued*)

SET Command	Argument	Action/Default/Ranges
		ping. Set ON stops program each time a line executes and outputs a message
* TABS =	*<expC>*	Sets the initial value of the _tabs system memory variable. Default is an empty string (" ")
TALK =	ON/off	Set ON displays messages. Set OFF suppresses messages
TRAP =	on/OFF	Set OFF displays an error screen with options when an application error occurs. Set ON takes you to the Debugger when an application program error occurs
* TYPEAHEAD =	*<expN>*	The number of characters you can enter ahead of dBASE processing. Default is 20; range 0 to 32,000
UNIQUE =	on/OFF	Set OFF adds a key to the index file for every database record. Set ON adds a key only for unique records
* VIEW =	*<query filename>* /*<view filename>*	Executes a query file or updates a view file

Table 35-2. SET Commands Accessible Using the CONFIG.DB file *(continued)*

The Color Settings

You can use several options to change the colors for all parts of the display screen via your CONFIG.DB file. You can set the default colors for text and background from your CONFIG.DB file by using the following command syntax:

COLOR = [<*standard*>]
[,[<*enhanced*>][,[<*perimeter*>][,[<*background*>]]]]

Standard refers to standard screen text, *enhanced* refers to reverse-video portions of the screen, *perimeter* refers to the border setting for some, but not all, monitors, and *background* refers to the background color.

For a detailed list of the COLOR parameter selections, see the SET COLOR command in Chapter 32, "SET Commands."

In addition to the COLOR command, you can include the following commands in your CONFIG.DB file to change display colors:

COLOR OF NORMAL =

COLOR OF HIGHLIGHT =

COLOR OF MESSAGES =

COLOR OF TITLES =

COLOR OF BOX =

COLOR OF INFORMATION =

COLOR OF FIELDS =

Here is an example of default color settings in a CONFIG.DB file.

COLOR OF NORMAL = W+/B

COLOR OF HIGHLIGHT = GR+/BG

COLOR OF MESSAGES = W/N

COLOR OF TITLES = W/B

COLOR OF BOX = GR+/BG

COLOR OF INFORMATION = B/W

COLOR OF FIELDS = N/BG

Table 35-3 lists the attribute letters assigned to the colors you can use to change your color settings in dBASE IV. For more information on changing your display colors, see the SET COLOR command in Chapter 32, "SET Commands." If you want to temporarily set your display colors, use the **Settings** submenu from the **Tools** menu (see Chapter 14, "Tools").

If your computer has a color and a monochrome monitor, specify which monitor dBASE IV is to use with the command COLOR = ON/OFF.

Color	**Letter**
Black	N or blank
Blue	B
Green	G
Cyan	BG
Blank	X
Gray	N+
Red	R
Magenta	RB
Brown	GR
Yellow	GR+
White	W

Table 35-3. Color Attributes Table

Note: If you include a color setting that does not match the monitor you are using, dBASE will produce a blank screen.

In this chapter, you learned about four of the five types of configuration commands you can use in your CONFIG.DB file to control dBASE IV default settings. You now know how to change the configuration commands by using your CONFIG.DB file. You also learned how to change function key definitions using your CONFIG.DB file. You can refer to the table of SET commands to change the default settings in your CONFIG.DB file. In addition, you learned how to use your CONFIG.DB file to customize dBASE IV's color settings.

APPENDIX A

ASCII Characters

Reprinted by permission of Ashton-Tate.

Binary	Hex	Decimal	Character	Code	Symbol	Description
00000000	00	0		^@	NUL	Null
00000001	01	1	☺	^A	SOH	Start of Heading
00000010	02	2	☻	^B	STX	Start of Text
00000011	03	3	♥	^C	ETX	End of Text
00000100	04	4	♦	^D	EOT	End of Transmission
00000101	05	5	♣	^E	ENQ	Enquiry
00000110	06	6	♠	^F	ACK	Acknowledge
00000111	07	7	•	^G	BEL	Bell
00001000	08	8	◘	^H	BS	Backspace
00001001	09	9	○	^I	SH	Horizontal Tabulation
00001010	0A	10	◙	^J	LF	Line Feed
00001011	0B	11	♂	^K	VT	Vertical Tabulation
00001100	0C	12	♀	^L	FF	Form Feed
00001101	0D	13	♪	^M	CR	Carriage Return
00001110	0E	14	♫	^N	SO	Shift Out
00001111	0F	15	☼	^O	SI	Shift In
00010000	10	16	►	^P	DLE	Data Link Escape
00010001	11	17	◄	^Q	DC1	Device Control 1
00010010	12	18	↕	^R	DC2	Device Control 2
00010011	13	19	‼	^S	DC3	Device Control 3
00010100	14	20	¶	^T	DC4	Device Control 4
00010101	15	21	§	^U	NAK	Negative Acknowledge
00010110	16	22	▬	^V	SYN	Synchronous Idle
00010111	17	23	↨	^W	ETB	End of Transmission Block
00011000	18	24	↑	^X	CAN	Cancel
00011001	19	25	↓	^Y	EM	End of Medium

Binary	Hex	Decimal	Character	Code	Symbol	Description
00011010	1A	26	→	^Z	SUB	Substitute
00011011	1B	27	←	^[	ESC	Escape *
00011100	1C	28	∟	^\	FS	File Separator
00011101	1D	29	↔	^]	GS	Group Separator
00011110	1E	30	▲	^^	RS	Record Separator
00011111	1F	31	▼	^-	US	Unit Separator
00100000	20	32				
00100001	21	33	!			
00100010	22	34	"			
00100011	23	35	#			
00100100	24	36	$			
00100101	25	37	%			
00100110	26	38	&			
00100111	27	39	'			

* Escape cannot be trapped

Binary	Hex	Decimal	Character	Binary	Hex	Decimal	Character
00101000	28	40	(	00110111	37	55	7
00101001	29	41	)	00111000	38	56	8
00101010	2A	42	*	00111001	39	57	9
00101011	2B	43	+	00111010	3A	58	:
00101100	2C	44	,	00111011	3B	59	;
00101101	2D	45	-	00111100	3C	60	<
00101110	2E	46	.	00111101	3D	61	=
00101111	2F	47	/	00111110	3E	62	>
00110000	30	48	0	00111111	3F	63	?
00110001	31	49	1	01000000	40	64	@
00110010	32	50	2	01000001	41	65	A
00110011	33	51	3	01000010	42	66	B
00110100	34	52	4	01000011	43	67	C
00110101	35	53	5	01000100	44	68	D
00110110	36	54	6	01000101	45	69	E

Binary	Hex	Decimal	Character
01000110	46	70	F
01000111	47	71	G
01001000	48	72	H
01001001	49	73	I
01001010	4A	74	J
01001011	4B	75	K
01001100	4C	76	L
01001101	4D	77	M
01001110	4E	78	N
01001111	4F	79	O
01010000	50	80	P
01010001	51	81	Q
01010010	52	82	R
01010011	53	83	S
01010100	54	84	T
01010101	55	85	U
01010110	56	86	V
01010111	57	87	W
01011000	58	88	X
01011001	59	89	Y
01011010	5A	90	Z
01011011	5B	91	[
01011100	5C	92	\
01011101	5D	93	]
01011110	5E	94	^
01011111	5F	95	_
01100000	60	96	\'
01100001	61	97	a
01100010	62	98	b
01100011	63	99	c
01100100	64	100	d
01100101	65	101	e

Binary	Hex	Decimal	Character
01100110	66	102	f
01100111	67	103	g
01101000	68	104	h
01101001	69	105	i
01101010	6A	106	j
01101011	6B	107	k
01101100	6C	108	l
01101101	6D	109	m
01101110	6E	110	n
01101111	6F	111	o
01110000	70	112	p
01110001	71	113	q
01110010	72	114	r
01110011	73	115	s
01110100	74	116	t
01110101	75	117	u
01110110	76	118	v
01110111	77	119	w
01111000	78	120	x
01111001	79	121	y
01111010	7A	122	z
01111011	7B	123	{
01111100	7C	124	|
01111101	7D	125	}
01111110	7E	126	˜
01111111	7F	127	⌂
10000000	80	128	Ç
10000001	81	129	ü
10000010	82	130	é
10000011	83	131	â
10000100	84	132	ä
10000101	85	133	à

Binary	Hex	Decimal	Character
10000110	86	134	å
10000111	87	135	ç
10001000	88	136	ê
10001001	89	137	ë
10001010	8A	138	è
10001011	8B	139	ï
10001100	8C	140	î
10001101	8D	141	ì
10001110	8E	142	Ä
10001111	8F	143	Å
10010000	90	144	É
10010001	91	145	æ
10010010	92	146	Æ
10010011	93	147	ô
10010100	94	148	ö
10010101	95	149	ò
10010110	96	150	û
10010111	97	151	ù
10011000	98	152	ÿ
10011001	99	153	Ö
10011010	9A	154	Ü
10011011	9B	155	¢
10011100	9C	156	£
10011101	9D	157	¥
10011110	9E	158	₧
10011111	9F	159	ƒ
10100000	A0	160	á
10100001	A1	161	í
10100010	A2	162	ó
10100011	A3	163	ú
10100100	A4	164	ñ
10100101	A5	165	Ñ
10100110	A6	166	ª
10100111	A7	167	º
10101000	A8	168	¿
10101001	A9	169	⌐
10101010	AA	170	¬
10101011	AB	171	½
10101100	AC	172	¼
10101101	AD	173	¡
10101110	AE	174	«
10101111	AF	175	»
10110000	B0	176	░
10110001	B1	177	▒
10110010	B2	178	▓
10110011	B3	179	│
10110100	B4	180	┤
10110101	B5	181	╡
10110110	B6	182	╢
10110111	B7	183	╖
10111000	B8	184	╕
10111001	B9	185	╣
10111010	BA	186	║
10111011	BB	187	╗
10111100	BC	188	╝
10111101	BD	189	╜
10111110	BE	190	╛
10111111	BF	191	┐
11000000	C0	192	└
11000001	C1	193	┴
11000010	C2	194	┬
11000011	C3	195	├
11000100	C4	196	─
11000101	C5	197	┼

Binary	Hex	Decimal	Character	Binary	Hex	Decimal	Character
11000110	C6	198	╞	11100011	E3	227	π
11000111	C7	199	╟	11100100	E4	228	Σ
11001000	C8	200	╚	11100101	E5	229	σ
11001001	C9	201	╔	11100110	E6	230	µ
11001010	CA	202	╩	11100111	E7	231	τ
11001011	CB	203	╦	11101000	E8	232	Φ
11001100	CC	204	╠	11101001	E9	233	Θ
11001101	CD	205	═	11101010	EA	234	Ω
11001110	CE	206	╬	11101011	EB	235	δ
11001111	CF	207	╧	11101100	EC	236	∞
11010000	D0	208	╨	11101101	ED	237	φ
11010001	D1	209	╤	11101110	EE	238	ε
11010010	D2	210	╥	11101111	EF	239	∩
11010011	D3	211	╙	11110000	F0	240	≡
11010100	D4	212	╘	11110001	F1	241	±
11010101	D5	213	╒	11110010	F2	242	≥
11010110	D6	214	╓	11110011	F3	243	≤
11010111	D7	215	╫	11110100	F4	244	⌠
11011000	D8	216	╪	11110101	F5	245	⌡
11011001	D9	217	┘	11110110	F6	246	÷
11011010	DA	218	┌	11110111	F7	247	≈
11011011	DB	219	█	11111000	F8	248	°
11011100	DC	220	▄	11111001	F9	249	∙
11011101	DD	221	▌	11111010	FA	250	·
11011110	DE	222	▐	11111011	FB	251	√
11011111	DF	223	▀	11111100	FC	252	^{n}
11100000	E0	224	α	11111101	FD	253	^{2}
11100001	E1	225	ß	11111110	FE	254	■
11100010	E2	226	Γ	11111111	FF	255	

AT®	International Business Machines Corporation
Clipper™	SPSS, Inc.
COMPAQ®	COMPAQ Computer
dBASE II®	Ashton-Tate
dBASE III®	Ashton-Tate
dBASE III PLUS®	Ashton-Tate
dBASE IV™	Ashton-Tate
Disk Optimizer™	Softlogic Solutions
EtherLink™	3Com Corporation
EtherLink Plus™	3Com Corporation
Etherlink II™	3Com Corporation
FoxBASE+™	Fox Software, Inc.
Framework II™	Ashton-Tate
HiCard™	RYBS Electronics
HiJaak™	Inset Systems, Inc.
IBM®	International Business Machines Corporation
IBM PC™	International Business Machines Corporation
IBM® PC Token-Ring®	International Business Machines Corporation
InSet™	Inset Systems, Inc.
Intel®	Intel Corporation
LaserJet®	Hewlett-Packard Company
Lotus®	Lotus Development Corporation
Multiplan®	Microsoft Corporation
Net/One®	Ungerman-Bass, Inc.
Netware®	Novell Corporation
Novell®	Novell Corporation
1-2-3®	Lotus Development Corporation
OS/2®	International Business Machines Corporation
Norton Utilities Advanced Edition®	Peter Norton, Inc.
PFS:FILE®	Software Publishing Corporation
PS/2®	International Business Machines Corporation

Quicksilver™	WordTech Systems
RapidFile™	Ashton-Tate
Runtime™	Ashton-Tate
SFT™	Novell Corporation
SideKick®	Borland International, Inc.
Step IVward™	Ashton-Tate
SuperKey®	Borland International, Inc.
3 Plus®	3Com Corporation
3Com®	3Com Corporation
386MAX™	Qualitas, Inc.
VisiCalc®	Lotus Development Corporation
WordStar®	MicroPro International Corporation
XT®	International Business Machines Corporation

INDEX